The World Since 1914

THE MACMILLAN COMPANY
NEW YORK · BOSTON · CHICAGO · DALLAS
ATLANTA · SAN FRANCISCO

MACMILLAN AND CO., LIMITED
LONDON · BOMBAY · CALCUTTA · MADRAS
MELBOURNE

THE MACMILLAN COMPANY
OF CANADA, LIMITED
TORONTO

The World Since 1914

BY

WALTER CONSUELO LANGSAM, PH. D.

UNION COLLEGE

FIFTH EDITION

NEW YORK

THE MACMILLAN COMPANY

1943

Fifth Edition Copyrighted, 1943,
BY WALTER C. LANGSAM

PUBLISHED JUNE, 1943

REPRINTED NOVEMBER, 1943

TO JULIE
*whose help makes every
task a pleasure*

FOREWORD TO THE FIRST EDITION

Today more than at any previous time it is essential for the preservation of civilization that citizens everywhere be familiar with the outstanding issues that confront the nations. The period since 1914 has been crowded with events of world importance, with complex questions of war guilt, reparation, war debts, disarmament, reconstruction, national minorities, territorial readjustments, economic upheaval, and dictatorships. The mind is easily confused by the magnitude of some of the problems and by the technical aspects of others. Yet, only in the widespread knowledge of the origins and history of these factors can there be any real hope of future international harmony.

It is the aim of this volume to contribute to a clarification of the issues and to provide a readable, organized, and compact exposition of the world developments which, at the time of writing, appeared to be the most promising—or the most portentous.

February 1933   **W. C. L.**

FOREWORD TO THE THIRD EDITION

The organization adopted in this edition is, in general, the same as that of the original issue. Every chapter, however, has been entirely rewritten and one new chapter—on Latin America—has been added. The map equipment has, it is hoped, been greatly improved. The spellings of place names vary somewhat from the forms used in the earlier editions because it has seemed advisable, for the sake of uniformity, to employ in every case the orthography of the *Sixth Report of the United States Geographic Board 1890–1932,* 1933. Names of governing bodies are capitalized only when given in exact or full and literally-translated form. For the convenience of the reader, the dates of treaties and of the births and deaths of important individuals have been included in the index. The bibliography has been brought up to date, annotated, and extended so as to include references to each subject from differing view-points.

December 1935   **W. C. L.**

vii

FOREWORD TO THE FOURTH EDITION

The chief innovation of this edition is the inclusion of a Part IV, entitled "The Road to Another War." This part covers the major European and Asiatic developments since 1935 and carries the story of international relations down to the outbreak of the new European war in September 1939. The organization of this part parallels that in the main body of the text and, wherever necessary, cross-references have been provided to tie up all portions of the book. The bibliography has been enlarged, brought up to date, and subdivided for the longer chapters. The index is unusually full. The whole story is related in such a way that the teacher or reader who feels that the account is somewhat lengthy may, by beginning with either Chapter IV or Chapter V, start his study with the year 1918 rather than go back to 1914.

January 1940   W. C. L.

FOREWORD TO THE FIFTH EDITION

Every chapter in this edition has been rewritten, so that not one page has remained without some change, large or small. The changes generally were made for one or more of three reasons: either because new material had come to light, or because recent events dictated a shift in emphasis, or to conserve space. All material formerly printed in supplements has been rewritten and woven into the body of the text. The volume fortunately reverses an earlier trend by being somewhat shorter than its predecessor. But the lengthy bibliography has been retained and brought up to date. Throughout I have tried—how successfully remains for the reader to judge—to keep the narrative balanced, though it was written in a time, not merely of national, but of world crisis.

June 1943   W. C. L.

TABLE OF CONTENTS

Part I: War and Peace, 1914–1919

Chapter I. THE COMING OF WAR 3
The Background of Conflict 3
The Immediate Cause of War 13
The Last Days of Peace 15

Chapter II. A WORLD WAR 20
The Spread of the Conflagration, 1914–1917 20
The Entry of the United States 26
   a. Neutrality in Thought and Deed 26
   b. Problems of International Law 28
   c. From Peace to War 32
   d. Twenty-three to Four 39

Chapter III. THE ALTAR OF MARS 40
Advantages of the Belligerents 40
Military Operations, 1914–1915 42
Military Operations, 1916 48
Military Operations, 1917 54
Colonial, Naval, and Aerial Operations 60
Poison Gas and Propaganda 64
Peace Moves and War Aims 67
The End of Military Operations, 1918 70
The Price of War 77

Chapter IV. THE PEACE CONFERENCE OF PARIS 79
The Conference Leaders 79
The Organization of the Conference 84
The Problems Facing the Delegates 87
Drafting the Versailles Treaty 90
The Signing of the Treaty 98

Chapter V. THE TREATIES OF PEACE 101
Versailles, with Germany 101
Saint Germain-en-Laye, with Austria 110

Neuilly, with Bulgaria   112
Trianon, with Hungary   113
Sèvres, with Turkey   114
The Protection of Minorities   115
The New World: Future Imperfect   116

Part II: Twenty Years' Armistice, 1919–1939

Chapter VI. THE LEAGUE OF NATIONS   123
Origin, Membership, and Organization   123
The Permanent Court and the I.L.O.   128
The Pacific Settlement of Disputes   132
League Administration of Territory: The Saar   140
The Protection of Mandates and Minorities   144
The Worth of the League   146

Chapter VII. REPARATION, DEBTS, DEPRESSION   148
The First Four Years, 1919–1923   148
The Dawes and Young Plans, 1924–1931   153
Depression and Moratorium, 1931–1932   159
The Inter-Allied War Debts   165
Since 1933: The Economic Conference and After   169

Chapter VIII. THE SEARCH FOR SECURITY   173
The Revival of Alliances, 1920–1927   173
The Era of Pacts, 1923–1933   178
Disarmament and Rearmament   185
From Revisionist Bloc to Axis   193

Chapter IX. UNREST IN AFRICA AND ASIA   200
Black and White in Africa   200
The "Westernization" of Asia   205

Chapter X. CHANGING LATIN AMERICA   211
Participation in the First World War   211
General Economic Development to 1940   211
Rise of the Middle and Laboring Classes   215
Education, Students, Politics   221
Brazil   223
Recent Mexican Developments   227
The Church in Latin America   228

Part III: National Developments, 1919–1939

Chapter XI. GREAT BRITAIN 235

Six Difficult Years, 1918–1924 235

Five Years of Conservative Rule, 1924–1929 242

The Second Labor Government, 1929–1931 247

The National Coalition to 1939 252

Great Britain and the Dominions 258

Chapter XII. SOME BRITISH PROBLEMS OF EMPIRE 261

Ireland 261

 a. "England's Necessity Is Ireland's Opportunity" 261

 b. Free Staters versus Republicans 264

 c. The Cosgrave Administration, 1922–1932 266

 d. The Rule of de Valera 270

Egypt 275

India 282

 a. India and the War of 1914–1918 282

 b. The "Great Soul" 285

 c. The Continuance of Strife 287

Palestine 294

Chapter XIII. UNHAPPY FRANCE 302

Politics in the Third French Republic 302

The Franc and Its Savior 304

Seven Trying Years, 1929–1936 307

The Popular Front 315

The Last Years of Peace, 1937–1939 317

France and the Papacy 322

The Problem of Alsace-Lorraine 323

The Syrian Mandate 326

France and the French 329

Chapter XIV. FASCIST ITALY 332

The Reward of Victory 332

Mussolini: From Private to Premier 335

Making Italy Fascist 339

The First Corporate State 343

Fascist Domestic Policies 348

Alto-Adige, the Former South Tirol 352

The Lateran Accord 354

Nationalism and Population Pressure ... 359
Italian Foreign and African Relations ... 360
Italy and Albania ... 369

Chapter XV. SPAIN ... 372
Historical Factors ... 372
Domestic Unrest and Colonial Defeat, 1917–1923 ... 375
Dictatorship, 1923–1930 ... 377
Birth and Problems of the Republic ... 382
Civil War, 1936–1939 ... 391
The "Little World War" ... 396

Chapter XVI. GERMANY ... 399
From Empire to Republic ... 399
The Weimar Assembly ... 404
The Defense of the Republic, 1919–1923 ... 409
Finances, Low and High ... 411
Disappointment and Hope ... 415
Parties and Politics, 1924–1932 ... 418
Economic Recovery and Decline, 1924–1932 ... 427
Foreign Relations, 1919–1932 ... 433
Der Führer ... 437
Anti-Semitism ... 441
Political Totalitarianism ... 445
Economic Coördination ... 447
Culture, Education, Law ... 453
Attempted Religious Coördination ... 454
Politics, 1933–1939 ... 459
The Problem of Refugees ... 462

Chapter XVII. TWO HEIRS OF THE HABSBURGS ... 465
Austria ... 465
a. From Monarchy to Republic, 1918–1920 ... 465
b. Storm and Stress, 1921–1932 ... 469
c. The Anschluss Question and Foreign Relations to 1932 ... 473
d. The Five-Year Fight against Nazism, 1933–1938 ... 476
The Kingdom of Hungary ... 485
a. The Failure of Liberalism, 1918–1919 ... 485
b. "Red" versus "White" ... 487
c. Finances and Economics ... 490
d. Restoration and Revision ... 492

Chapter XVIII. TWO SLAVIC REPUBLICS 500
Czechoslovakia 500
  a. The Winning of Independence 500
  b. Constitution and Land Reform 503
  c. Economics and Foreign Affairs 506
  d. The Problem of Minorities 508
  e. The Sudeten-German Crisis and Munich 510
  f. The Collapse of "Czecho-Slovakia" 514
Poland 518
  a. Pilsudski and Paderewski 518
  b. Internal Political Affairs, 1919–1939 521
  c. Financial and Economic Affairs 525
  d. The Minorities 528
  e. Danzig and the Polish Corridor 532
  f. Vilnius: Another Boundary Dispute 535
  g. Foreign Affairs 536

Chapter XIX. THE SOVIET UNION 539
The Old Regime 539
The Two Revolutions of 1917 544
Lenin and Trotsky 549
The End of Foreign and Civil War 551
Government in the Soviet Union 555
The Communist Party 561
An Attempt at Pure Communism, 1917–1921 564
The New Economic Policy, 1921–1928 568
Party Conflicts and the Supremacy of Stalin 571
The Five-Year Plans 577
Education and Religion 585
The U.S.S.R. in International Affairs 588
  a. The Comintern 588
  b. Conflict and Truce, 1918–1924 590
  c. Fifteen Difficult Years, 1924–1939 592

Chapter XX. SOUTHEASTERN EUROPE 598
Europe's "Witches' Cauldron" 598
Romania 598
Bulgaria and Macedonia 607
Greece 614
Yugoslavia 620

Chapter XXI. TURKEY FOR THE TURKS 630
From Sèvres to Lausanne 630

The Turks, the Greeks, and the Kurds   636
Kemal, the Dictator   637
Religious and Social Changes   639
Legal and Educational Reform   641
"Efficient Turks for Turkey"   643
Turkey's International Relations   645

Chapter XXII. THE FAR EAST   648
The Course of Revolution in China   648
The Twenty-one Demands   651
China and the First World War   653
The Washington Conference   654
Education and Nationalism in China, 1919–1931   658
Economics in Manchuria and in Japan   662
China, "Manchoukuo," Japan   665
Toward a "New Order" in Eastern Asia   673

Chapter XXIII. THE UNITED STATES   681
Troublous Times, 1918–1921   681
Harding and the "Return to Normalcy"   684
Coolidge and "Safe and Sane" Politics   689
Hoover: "The Engineer in Politics"   693
Broadening Public Interests   698
Foreign Investments and Affairs, 1923–1933   700
Roosevelt and "Nira"   705
A Second Term, and a Third   714
Foreign Relations under Roosevelt   720

Part IV: The Second World War

Chapter XXIV. THE RETURN TO WAR   727
Twenty Years' Armistice, 1919–1939   727
Renewed Resort to Force, 1939   733
The Fifth Partition of Poland   737
Precautions of the Soviet Union, 1939–1940   742

Chapter XXV. SITZKRIEG AND BLITZKRIEG
IN THE WEST   751
The War in the West, September 1939–March 1940   751
Three Months of Blitzkrieg, April–June 1940   756
From Third Republic to Vichy France   773
Dauntless Britain, 1940   782
Air Power and the War   787

Chapter XXVI. A SECOND WORLD WAR   791

    War in Africa, the Balkans, and the Near East   791

    The War and the Far East to 1941   804

    The Invasion of the Soviet Union   808

    Entry of the United States   814

    Global Warfare   825

BIBLIOGRAPHY

INDEX

MAPS

Europe 1914—Europe 1937 (*colored*)   *Frontispiece*
War Area of Western Europe (*colored*)   *following* 42
Farthest German Advance in France   45
War Area of Eastern Europe (*colored*)   *facing* 46
The Austro-Italian War Area   51
The Eastern Front, 1914–1917   53
After Brest-Litovsk, 1918   59
The Western Front, 1914 and 1918   74
Europe 1914   102
Postwar Europe   103
The Rhineland to 1934   181
Africa 1935 (*colored*)   *following* 200
Asia 1935 (*colored*)   *following* 206
South America 1935 (*colored*)   *facing* 212
The Eleven Provinces of British India   291
Ethiopia, 1935   363
Germany before and after the War   427
A Hungarian Revisionist Map (*colored*)   *facing* 494
Central and Southeastern Europe, 1934   501
Republics of the Soviet Union, 1940   *following* 554
The Near East to 1938   630
The Far East 1935   669
Europe, Autumn 1939 (*colored*)   *following* 732
Poland: Recreated and Repartitioned   740
The Finnish-Soviet War, 1939–1940   747
Russia's Western Border, 1914–1941   749
The Scandinavian Region, 1940   759
The Invasion of France, 1940   771
Great Britain versus Germany, Winter 1940–1941   783
The East-Central Mediterranean Area, Winter 1940–1941   793
The Partition of Romania, 1940   798
The Burma Road   805

The Far East, 1937 and 1940   807
The Pacific Area 1941   *following* 830
The Solomon Islands, February 1943   832
Europe and North Africa, January 24, 1943   *following* 834

CHARTS AND TABLES

United States War Loans   166
The Inter-Allied War Debts   167
Price Indices of World Trade, 1913–1938   172
World Armament Expenditures, 1913–1938   193
The Futile Search for Security, 1920–1935   197
Latin-American Foreign Commerce, 1910–1940   212
The German Elections, 1919–1933   440
The Soviet Political Structure until 1936   559

ILLUSTRATIONS

J. Ramsay MacDonald and Edouard Herriot at Lausanne,
    1932   *facing* 164
Eamon de Valera   *facing* 264
Benito Mussolini   *facing* 336
Paul von Hindenburg   *facing* 420
Adolf Hitler   *facing* 424
Nicolas Horthy   *facing* 490
Thomas Garrigue Masaryk   *facing* 502
Joseph V. Stalin   *facing* 572
Alexander of Yugoslavia and Carol II of Romania   *facing* 604
Mustapha Kemal Átatürk   *facing* 638
Chiang Kai-shek   *facing* 660
Washington, D. C.   *facing* 698
Henri H. Giraud, Franklin D. Roosevelt, Charles J. de Gaulle,
    and Winston S. Churchill at Casablanca, 1943   *facing* 836

PART I

War and Peace, 1914–1919

CHAPTER I

The Coming of War

THE BACKGROUND OF CONFLICT

Shortly before noon on Sunday, June 28, 1914, Archduke Francis Ferdinand, heir-presumptive to the thrones of Austria and Hungary, and his wife, Sophie, were assassinated by Gavrilo Princip in the Bosnian city of Sarajevo. Six weeks later Austria-Hungary and Germany were involved in an armed struggle with Serbia, Russia, France, Belgium, and Great Britain. Two pistol shots, some weeks of mingled fear and hope, and a great war! The morbid action of a psychopathic Bosnian student, however, only precipitated hostilities. The basic origins of the conflict dated back for more than a century.

First among the fundamental causes of the war was the force of nationalism, heritage of the French revolutionary epoch and the era of Metternich. The political history of Europe from 1815 to 1914 was shaped largely by the actions of the Congress of Vienna in repudiating the principles of nationality and democracy. The congress failed to organize a united German state; it tolerated a heterogeneous central-European federation of Germans, Poles, Magyars, Italians, Czechs, Slovaks, and Southslavs; and it repartitioned Poland. It also assigned Belgium to the Netherlands, allowed the continued subjection of the Balkans to Turkey, and placed Italy under the divided control of Austria, the pope, and the king of Naples. By the end of the nineteenth century the forces of nationalism had rectified some of these territorial maladjustments, but in the process there were created several other nationalist sore spots.

Thus, in 1871, the new German Empire took from France, chiefly for strategic reasons, most of Alsace and eastern Lorraine. Other claims of Germany to the provinces were that various rulers of France had taken them from the Holy Roman Empire in the first place and that a majority of the inhabitants were racially and linguistically German. Language and history, however, were of minor consequence in this instance, since the inhabitants, at the time of transfer in 1871, generally preferred to consider themselves French rather than German nationals. Accordingly the government of the Third Republic spared no pains to keep alive among its subjects the spirit of revenge and the hope for a restoration of the provinces. The black-draped statue of Strasbourg in the *Place de la Concorde* in Paris continued to remind Frenchmen of the lost territories, while Daudet's *La dernière classe* drew tears and juvenile threats of vengeance from French school children, and the songs of Paul Déroulède imbued the young men with a desire for *revanche*.

In addition to sentiment and the wish for revenge, France had an economic motive for desiring the return of Alsace-Lorraine. It was general knowledge that the remarkable industrial progress of Germany was based in large degree upon the iron mines of Lorraine. Hence French iron and steel magnates must have found it difficult to repress sighs when they thought of all the wealth that was accruing to Germany from land which rightfully belonged to their country.

East of the Adriatic Sea, behind the mountains of Dalmatia, was another "Alsace-Lorraine"—the provinces of Bosnia and Hercegovina. In 1878 these Southslavic areas had been occupied by Austria-Hungary. Thirty years later, over the bitter protests of Serbia, they had been annexed outright by the Dual Monarchy. A lively agitation was thereupon set afoot in Serbia with the object of forcing Austria to give up these regions and permit their union with the realm of King Peter. Actually, the Bosnians seem to have been less anxious for union with Serbia than for independence from Austria-Hungary, but Serbian aid was none the less welcome.

Italy, too, desired territory controlled by the Habsburgs, for Italian unification had not been completed when the troops of Victor Emmanuel II entered Rome in 1870. The Trentino and the area around the port of Trieste, which were inhabited by large Italian populations, still remained "unredeemed." The oft-heard cry of *Italia Irredenta* ("Unredeemed Italy"), therefore, was one of war. Besides, coupled with this desire to complete national unification, was Italy's competition with Austria for control of the Adriatic Sea. Only when they worked together to keep Serbia from getting an Adriatic port did the two rivals have compatible maritime and naval policies.

Further, the Austro-Hungarian state itself was a challenge to nationalism. The polyglot character of the Dual Monarchy, in which Austrians and Magyars ruled over Poles, Czechs, Slovaks, Southslavs, Italians, Ruthenians, and Romanians, made dissolution inevitable. The popularity of Francis Joseph and the veneration for his age alone seemed to make continued coöperation possible. It became almost a commonplace that the Dual Monarchy would break up with the death of the old emperor.

Finally, trouble was latent in the "Near-Eastern Problem." Turkish misrule, Greco-Serbo-Bulgarian rivalry for the control of fertile Macedonia with its racially mixed population, the mutual jealousies of all Christian Balkan states, Russia's persistent attempts at interference and control, the ardor of Pan-Slavism, the Austro-German *Drang nach Osten* ("Urge toward the east"), the economic and diplomatic rivalries of the great powers over the future of "the sick man of Europe," all these virtually stamped the Balkan Peninsula as the region where the powder of war would eventually be ignited.

There was also another side to this question of nationalism. The exaggeration, no less than the violation, of the principle of nationality was a serious danger to peace. By 1914 being a "patriot" had often come to mean exalting one's own land above all others, looking down upon foreign cultures, extolling one's own customs and traditions as being those of a new Chosen People, and adopting a boastful, if not bullying, attitude towards one's neighbors. Although men like Heinrich von Treitschke, Houston Stewart Chamberlain, and Friedrich von Bernhardi added special color to German *Vaterlandsliebe,* the Germans merely revealed in more pronounced fashion a spirit prevalent also among the French, or the British, or the Japanese. Pan-Slavism was no less fiery than Pan-Germanism, though perhaps not so well organized. Just as General von Bernhardi, retired cavalry officer, in his *Germany and the Next War,* praised war as leading to the survival of the fittest and prophesied the millennium when *Kultur* should have been spread throughout the world, so Homer Lea, in his *Day of the Saxon,* maintained that this task of civilization had been reserved to the Anglo-Saxon peoples. Such national attitudes engendered ill-will, made diplomatic negotiations difficult, and led to international friction. Every country seemed to have its "war cult," and everywhere these cults stirred up hostilities. The newspapers often served as vehicles of their propaganda.

The second underlying cause of the war was the vogue of militarism and the system of military alliances. A militaristic state is one in which the military power is able to overawe the civil power. By 1914 Europe was thoroughly militaristic: France only less than Germany, Austria as much as Russia. Now, a militaristic state, particularly one in close contact with enemies or rivals, naturally seeks military alliances. And so it happened that Otto von Bismarck, who regarded militarism as the foundation of the strong German Empire which he had created, and who knew that France could not soon forget her humiliation, initiated the system of alliances which finally divided Europe into two hostile armed camps. Once Germany had allies, France perforce had to make similar arrangements.

For geographic and strategic reasons, and because of their concordant forms of government, Germany originally chose Russia and Austria-Hungary as her allies. In 1872 the basis was laid for the creation of a Three Emperors' League and in the following year written agreements bound the respective rulers to coöperate in the preservation of peace. In case a threat of war should arise, they engaged "to come to a preliminary understanding among themselves" in order to agree "on a common line of conduct." Austria and Russia, however, had conflicting interests in the Balkans and, when, at the Congress of Berlin (1878), Bismarck showed preference for Austria, the league virtually came to an end. Although revived, in modified form, from 1881 to 1887, the league really was superseded in 1879 by a Dual Alliance between Germany and Austria-Hungary in which these countries promised to assist one another in case of attack by Russia. Then, in 1887, Bismarck negotiated a separate Reinsurance Treaty with Russia in which were recognized the latter's predominating interests in the eastern Balkans.

Meanwhile Italy, anxiously seeking recognition as a great power, found herself at odds with France over Tunisia and over tariff policies. Italy therefore looked about for help. Remembering that Bismarck had made Austria cede Venice (Venezia) to them in 1866, the Italians once again approached the same friend. Thus it happened that in 1882 Italy was admitted into the Austro-German alliance system and the Dual Alliance was converted into a Triple Alliance. The latter was renewed four times and was in force when the First World War broke out.

The alliance was defensive in character and provided that "if one, or two, of the High Contracting Parties, without direct provocation on their part, should chance to be attacked and to be en-

gaged in a war with two or more Great Powers non-signatory
the present treaty, the *casus fœderis* will arise simultaneously f
all the High Contracting Parties." Further, Italy promised to ai
Germany in case of attack by France, and both Germany and
Austria agreed to support Italy if she were attacked by France.
Austria and Italy, finally, agreed on "reciprocal compensations"
in the Balkans: that is, if either power made any territorial advances in the region, the other was to be compensated with gains
of equivalent value, there or elsewhere. It was specifically stated
by Italy, in a supplementary declaration, that the alliance was not
directed against Great Britain—since Italy's long and exposed
coast line would make such action foolhardy. The reciprocal
Austro-German obligations entered upon in the Dual Alliance
remained in force. In this manner there was formed a solid central-
European bloc, with only isolated states to the east and west.[1]

The weakness of the Triple Alliance lay in the conflicting attitudes and interests of Austria and Italy. There was, first, the traditional hatred between the two powers, engendered in the long
period of Austrian domination in the Italian Peninsula. Secondly,
Austria still held some of "Unredeemed Italy." Lastly, the two
nations were rivals for control of the Adriatic. A definite indication of the frailty of the bond was the signing of a secret treaty
between Italy and France in 1902 wherein each promised to remain neutral in case the other were attacked by a third power, or
if, "as the result of a direct provocation," the other "should find
itself compelled in defense of its honor or security to take the
initiative of a declaration of war." [2]

After the formation of the Triple Alliance in 1882, Great
Britain, France, and Russia found themselves in highly disadvantageous positions. In the event of a crisis they would have to
act individually, whereas central Europe could act in concert. The
significance of this situation was quickly realized and, when Wil-

---

[1] In 1883 Romania joined this bloc. The latest renewal of a special Quadruple
Agreement among the four states was signed in 1913 to last until 1920. From 1881
to 1895 there was also in force an Austro-Serbian treaty whereby Austria promised
to recognize the prince of Serbia as king and to permit the southward extension of
Serbia's frontiers, while Serbia promised to prevent anti-Austrian intrigues on her
territory and agreed not to negotiate political treaties with third parties "without a
previous understanding with Austria-Hungary." Serbia was ready to promise these
things while temporarily angry over Russia's support of certain Bulgarian territorial
claims in 1878.

[2] Bismarck was under no illusion as to the loyalty of Italy to the alliance. As early
as 1880, when there had been talk of a treaty with Italy, he had said: "Her promise
will have no value if it is not in her interest to keep it."

liam II dropped the Reinsurance Treaty with Russia in 1890, the way was clear to a Franco-Russian *rapprochement*. A friendship was inaugurated by the investment of French capital in Russian railway and military enterprises; [1] it was consummated by the Franco-Russian Entente of 1891 and the Franco-Russian Alliance of 1894. The alliance, which was to have "the same duration as the Triple Alliance," was a defensive agreement providing that Russia would aid France if the latter were "attacked by Germany, or by Italy supported by Germany," and that France would aid Russia if the latter were "attacked by Germany, or by Austria supported by Germany."

Great Britain alone now remained isolated. To her statesmen this condition soon appeared to lose much of its reputed splendor. The danger of aloofness became all the more pronounced after William II expressed his conviction that Germany's future lay on the seas. Moreover, the introduction of the dreadnought type of warship, rendering older war vessels obsolete, greatly reduced the margin of naval power that Great Britain had over other countries.[2] Since all Britishers knew that their country was dependent upon imported raw materials and foodstuffs, they believed that she must have undisputed control of the seas. In Germany, on the other hand, there was a widespread feeling that Great Britain's desire for so overpowering a navy was actuated by a wish to ensure commercial supremacy. Something was to be said for each point of view, but the important thing is that Great Britain began to fear Germany as a menace. To make matters worse, both Russia and France were unfriendly towards Great Britain before 1900. With Russia there were disputes over Persia, Afghanistan, Tibet, and the Straits. With France there was disagreement over the Sudan and other colonial regions. Continued isolation, therefore, appeared increasingly unsafe.[3]

The entry (1898) into the French Foreign Office of the anti-German Théophile Delcassé and the succession (1901) to the British throne of Edward VII altered matters considerably. These two men succeeded in paving the way for the Entente Cordiale of 1904 in which France and Great Britain settled their outstanding

---

[1] In 1914 French long-term investments in Russia amounted to 11,300,000,000 francs. "The total French investment in Russia made up a quarter of all French ownership abroad." Feis, H. *Europe: The World's Banker, 1870–1914,* 1930, p. 52.

[2] The first dreadnought was completed in Great Britain in 1906. By 1908 Great Britain had authorized the laying down of 12 dreadnoughts and Germany of 9. Previously the ratio of British to German warships had been 7 to 3.

[3] In 1902 Great Britain signed an alliance treaty with Japan. See p. 20.

colonial differences and became diplomatic partners. After that, it merely remained for France to effect a reconciliation between her two friends, Great Britain and Russia. In 1907, to the delight of the French, an Anglo-Russian Entente was reached. No binding alliance was formulated, but the bothersome differences in Asia were settled and good feeling replaced enmity in the diplomatic relationship.

From 1907 on, therefore, Europe was split into two potentially hostile armed groups: the Triple Alliance and the Triple Entente, each with a number of satellites. Both sides were strong. Both were anxious to win diplomatic victories. Each was ready to resort to sword-rattling in order to intimidate the other. Should either group call the other's bluff, war would seem inevitable. The immediate effect of this alignment was a series of international crises beginning with the Moroccan incident of 1905 and ending with the assassination of Francis Ferdinand in 1914. These crises must be briefly considered.

Fearful lest Germany's interests in northern Africa be jeopardized by the agreement of 1904 between Great Britain and France, and doubtless also to test the strength of the entente, the German Foreign Office insisted that William II, against his wish, visit Tangier in Morocco (1905). There the emperor made a speech emphasizing the independent status of the native ruler and the determination of Germany to protect her interests in northern Africa. The German press further cautioned the sultan against accepting certain reforms proposed by the French, without the prior approval of an international conference of all powers claiming an interest in Morocco. Delcassé resented this German "interference" and preferred to go to war rather than attend a conference. However, in view of Russia's internal troubles and recent losses in the war with Japan, little help could be expected from that quarter. The French Ministry accordingly consented to the conference and Delcassé resigned. So far, Germany had won. But at the assemblage at Algeciras (1906) Germany's only consistent friend was Austria-Hungary. France was supported by Great Britain, Russia, the United States, and Italy. The affair greatly increased the ill-feeling and suspicion between Germany and France.

After two years of comparative calm following the Algeciras Conference, there occurred the Balkan Crisis of 1908. Austria-Hungary took advantage of the disturbances of the Young-Turk Revolution to annex the provinces of Bosnia and Hercegovina which she had occupied in 1878. This annexation was in accordance with an agreement reached at Buchlau in Moravia on September 15, 1908, between the Austrian Foreign Minister, Alois von Ährenthal, and the Russian Foreign Minister, Alexander Izvolski. The "Buchlau Bargain" sanctioned Austrian annexation of these territories without objection from Russia, in return for Austria's willingness to allow the opening of the Straits to the warships of the tsar. No specific time was set for carrying out the agreement and Izvolski, who proceeded on a leisurely tour to get the consent of the other European powers to the opening of the Straits, professed surprise and chagrin when he heard that Ährenthal had fulfilled his part of the scheme by October 7, 1908. Izvolski further was embarrassed when it appeared that Great Britain was willing to have the Straits opened to the warships of all countries, but not to those of Russia alone.

The Russian Minister tried to save face by insisting on a conference to sanction Austria's step. When Ährenthal rejected this proposition, war seemed imminent. But Russia was in no condition to fight and France showed little eagerness to do battle over a Balkan question. Germany, on the contrary, was ready to support Austria. Izvolski felt humiliated and angered over what was plainly an Austro-German diplomatic triumph. He now encouraged the Serbs to consider Bosnia-Hercegovina as their particular "Alsace-Lorraine" and began to agitate strenuously against the central-European empires. Serbia, heartened by Russia's open friendship, became more importunate than ever.

The year 1911 witnessed the next great international crisis. Dissatisfied with the execution of a compromise reached with France over Morocco in 1909, the Germans in 1911 sent the gunboat *Panther* to the port of Agadir, ostensibly for the protection of German property. For a time it seemed that Great Britain and France might take similar action. When Germany insisted that the matter was one for settlement between herself and France alone, David Lloyd George, British Chancellor of the Exchequer, took a strong stand. "If," he declared, "Great Britain be treated, where her interests are vitally affected, as if she were of no account in the Cabinet of Nations, then I say emphatically that peace at that price would be a humiliation intolerable for a great country like ours to endure." Fortunately, proper explanations were made, and in 1912 another compromise was ratified. Germany recognized the paramount interests of France in Morocco and France ceded to Germany one hundred thousand square miles of jungle land in equatorial Africa. Neither the German nor the French people were satisfied with the arrangement and in each country the press condemned the authorities for permitting themselves to be out-maneuvered.

Meanwhile the nerves of the statesmen were further frayed by the strain of the Turco-Italian War. Basing her actions on a variety of claims, Italy in 1911 tried to establish a protectorate over Tripolitania, which was under Turkish suzerainty. The resulting war, to the discomfiture of Berlin, really was a conflict between two members of the central-European alliance system, for Turkey was friendly to Germany at the time. The war involved a possible alteration of the *status quo* in the Balkans, particularly when Italy attacked Turkey in the Dardanelles. Hence the great powers were terrified lest Turkey be partitioned and a general European war be precipitated in a quarrel over the spoils. The Tripolitan War, in fact, led directly to the next crisis—the Balkan Wars of 1912 and 1913. And these, in turn, were little more than a prelude to the First World War.

The preoccupation of the Young Turks with domestic affairs and with the Italian quarrel encouraged several of the leading Balkan statesmen to organize (1912) a Balkan League among Greece, Serbia, Montenegro, and Bulgaria. This league success-fully fought Turkey in 1912, but then broke up in a dispute over the rewards. The resulting Second Balkan War upset the delicate balance in the peninsula and produced an "excessive nervosity" among European statesmen. The Balkan Wars, moreover, weak-ened Germany's friend, Turkey, and doubled the size of Austria's enemy, Serbia.

Russia and Serbia were jubilant over this outcome, but Ger-many was worried. In 1913 the legislature in Berlin passed an army bill calling out more men to active duty. The French, about the same time, increased the term of military service from two to three years. Russia expedited earlier plans for reorganizing her army and increasing the annual number of recruits. In 1914 the standing armies and navies of the six largest European countries included four and a quarter million men, and there were addi-tional millions of trained reserves.[1] In 1914, too, it was evident that another crisis such as those recently passed could hardly be

[1] In the forty-five years from 1868 to 1913 the annual armament expenditures of the world had increased from $460,000,000 to $2,531,000,000. Be it said here that United States dollar equivalents for items before 1933 are always given in terms of the gold content antedating the Roosevelt devaluation policy.

weathered peacefully. There was a general fear lest the next imbroglio mean war. It did. The Sarajevo crisis precipitated the conflict.

Economic rivalry and imperialism served as a third fundamental cause of the war. They were, in truth, at the bottom of most of the crises that have just been described. World history during the late nineteenth and early twentieth centuries was characterized by a struggle for markets, for sources of raw materials, for areas in which to invest surplus capital and to which to send surplus populations, and for sources of food supply. These factors eventually led to the partitioning of Africa and the penetration of the Near East and Asia, and were responsible for much international competition and ill-will. The commercial rivalry between Great Britain and Germany, the conflicting interests of Austria-Hungary and Russia, and even the dislike between the Dual Monarchy and Italy, all were traceable, in large part, to the rise of modern economic imperialism.[1]

The story is too long to be repeated here, but it should be pointed out that, with each passing year after 1880, the apprehension in Great Britain increased lest Germany outdistance her in the race for world commerce and trade. Business rivalry was responsible for the utterance of many unguarded statements in Great Britain between 1900 and 1914, and worried industrialists proved themselves willing to support and sustain commercial and naval propaganda. The British suffered from a veritable "Made in Germany" complex that boded ill for the continued quiet of Europe.[2] And economic rivalry in the Balkans similarly tended to stir the fires of hate among the subjects of Francis Joseph, Nicholas, and Victor Emmanuel.

The fourth underlying cause of the war was the lack of any machinery to control international relations. One of the worst phases of this international anarchy was the prevalence of an extraordinary secret diplomacy. Sometimes not even all members of a ministry knew of the agreements that existed between their own and other governments. Legislative chambers, in particular, were kept in ignorance of written or verbal diplomatic and military commitments. Thus it was possible for Sir Edward Grey, on August 3, 1914, publicly to deny that there was any restriction on

[1] The story of the Berlin-Baghdad Railway affords an excellent example of the imperialistic rivalry among the great powers. Cf. Earle, E. M. *Turkey, the Great Powers, and the Bagdad Railway*, 1923.

[2] Cf. Hoffman, R. J. *Great Britain and the German Trade Rivalry, 1875–1914*, 1933 and Williams, E. E. *Made in Germany*, 5 ed., 1897.

the freedom of action of the House of Commons, when actually there were commitments of the utmost importance to France.[1] International anarchy and secret diplomacy also were responsible for the circumstance that, as Arthur Ponsonby, M.P., told the House of Commons in 1927, "forgery, theft, lying, bribery, and corruption exist in every Foreign Office and every Chancellory throughout the world." [2] Such conditions lent uncertainty and uneasiness to all relations among countries. Issues and responsibilities were beclouded; confusion and hysteria ruled at the expense of sobriety and sincerity.

There was in existence a code of "international law and morality," but machinery for enforcement was lacking. The resolutions adopted at the Hague conferences in 1899 and 1907 proved to be merely so many pious hopes. Every land, with its exalted sense of sovereignty, felt accountable only to itself. Hence it was not considered incongruous for a member of one alliance secretly to make a bargain with an enemy of its allies. Italy, for example, had friendly agreements both with France (1902) and Russia (1909) simultaneously with her membership in the Triple Alliance. And Romania's king could be an ally of William II, while the Romanian people and parliament would seemingly have preferred friendship with Russia.

With this background of the European situation in mind, it is easy to comprehend the words uttered in 1914 by Wilhelm von Schoen, German Ambassador to Paris: "Peace remains at the mercy of an accident." On June 28 that accident occurred.

THE IMMEDIATE CAUSE OF WAR

The immediate occasion for the First World War was the enmity between Austria-Hungary and Serbia. This factor alone did not cause the war—it merely determined the time of its outbreak. The Serbs felt that they had a number of grievances against the Dual Monarchy. There was, first, the desire to include the Southslavic parts of Austria-Hungary in a Greater Serbia. Secondly, Austria-Hungary (and Italy) several times had blocked Serbian attempts to get a seaport on the Adriatic. As it was, Austria-Hungary virtually controlled Serbian exports, for the latter had to be shipped across her soil to an outlet. On more than one occasion, when Serbia had displeased the Dual Monarchy, the latter had

[1] See p. 19.
[2] *Parliamentary Debates, Commons, 1927,* v. 206, p. 2258.

checked the further import of Serbian goods—chiefly pigs. The practice adopted by Austria-Hungary of quarantining pigs whenever Serbia misbehaved was termed *Schweinepolitik* or "pig politics." In 1906 the quarrel reached the dimensions of a serious customs dispute called the "Pig War."

Eventually a group of Southslavs formed a secret society to terrorize Austria-Hungary into acceding to the wishes of the Pan-Slavists and Serbian nationalists. Among other things, the "Black Hand" or "Union or Death" society planned to assassinate General Oskar Potiorek, governor of Bosnia.[1] However, when it was learned that Archduke Francis Ferdinand was coming to Bosnia in 1914, it was decided to kill him instead of Potiorek. Meanwhile, members of the Serbian War Department, particularly Colonel Dragutin Dimitrijevich, head of the espionage section of the general staff, and Major Voya Tankosich, provided weapons, munitions, and instructors so that a group of young, exiled, Bosnian revolutionaries, who had volunteered to do the deed, might become expert in pistol-shooting and bomb-throwing.[2]

Archduke Francis Ferdinand was not popular at the court of the emperor-king. He was disliked by the German leaders in Austria and by the Magyar leaders in Hungary because he favored the establishment of a Triple (Austro-Hungarian-Slavic) Monarchy in place of the Dual (Austro-Hungarian) Monarchy. He also was unpopular with the older men at the court because he insisted upon reforms in the administration and the army. In 1906 he had brought about the appointment as chief of staff of Franz Conrad von Hötzendorf, whom the emperor did not like, to succeed the aged Friedrich von Beck. Partly because of his dislike for Conrad's methods and schemes for a "preventive" war upon Serbia, Francis Joseph gave up his custom of reviewing the major army exercises. Thus it happened that Francis Ferdinand went to Bosnia in 1914 to observe the June maneuvers.

According to the official plans, the archduke and his wife were to pay a formal visit to Sarajevo, the principal city of Bosnia, on June 28, 1914. This day, St. Vitus' Day, happens to be the Serbian day of mourning, commemorating the Battle of Kossovo (1389) in which the Serbs lost their independence to the Turks. While the official party was en route to the town hall in the early fore-

---

[1] The seal of the society showed a skull and crossbones, a dagger, a bomb, and a bottle of poison.

[2] In the summer of 1917 Dimitrijevich was shot on charges of conspiracy against the government of Serbia.

noon, one of a group of three Bosnian students, who had been assisted across the Serbian border into Bosnia by Serbian officials,
threw a bomb at the archduke's automobile. The bomb either
bounced or was thrown out of the open car and exploded on the
roadway to the rear. The following automobile was partially
wrecked and an officer and several bystanders were hurt. The
would-be assassin was captured and the party continued to the
town hall.

After the mayor had read the address of welcome (!) the party,
at the archduke's orders, proceeded according to schedule to visit
the city museum. As fate would have it, the archducal car turned
down a wrong street and the chauffeur had to back it up. This
difficulty provided a delay just long enough to enable Gavrilo
Princip, another member of the murderous trio, to step forward
from a group of onlookers and fire two shots point blank into the
automobile. One bullet entered the archduke's neck. The other,
possibly meant for Potiorek, killed Duchess Sophie.

THE LAST DAYS OF PEACE

The Austro-Hungarian authorities in 1914 were unaware of
the precise extent to which Serbian officials were involved in the
assassination. They did not know at the time that the Serbian
Prime Minister, Nicola Pashich, had learned of the plot several
weeks before it was carried out; that orders had been given to prevent the students' reëntry into Bosnia, but that the frontier guards,
themselves members of the Black Hand, had disregarded this order
and then declared that it had arrived too late; and that the Serbian
Government apparently had helped one of the leading conspirators to disappear after the assassination. Despite the lack of definite information, Vienna suspected Serbia of gross neglect, if not
of connivance. A troubled month therefore followed the shooting.

Europe expected Austria-Hungary to seek satisfaction, but it
was hoped that her demands would be reasonable. As week after
week passed without further incident, people began to breathe
more easily. Apparently the delay in drawing up a bill of complaint was caused by Vienna's desire to think the matter over
calmly. Unfortunately this was not the real reason for the pro-
traction. It was owing to a serious difference of opinion among the
members of the Austro-Hungarian Government.

Foreign Minister Leopold von Berchtold felt that the time had
come to crush forever the Russo-Serbian intrigues which were a

constant threat to the integrity of the Dual Monarchy. He believed that, unless Vienna demanded severe retribution, Serbia would continue her subversive machinations. He knew that Russia supported Serbia, but he hoped that the St. Petersburg Government eventually would yield as it had done in the crisis of 1908. He wanted to frame an unacceptable ultimatum and then, before any other power could intervene, have the Austro-Hungarian army crush Serbia. Thus all danger would quickly be past.

Berchtold wanted merely a "local" war and he hoped that fear of Germany would keep Russia neutral. From his point of view such a procedure would have been an act of self-defense and self-preservation. As a loyal subject of Francis Joseph he could see no other alternative. Chief of Staff Conrad was in full agreement with Berchtold, though he emphasized the need for definite assurances of German aid in case Russia entered the fray. Francis Joseph and the Hungarian Minister President, Stephen Tisza, on the other hand, opposed even a local war. The emperor desired peace and Tisza feared that the incorporation of parts of Serbia into the Dual Monarchy might lead to a triple monarchy and a decrease in the power of the dominant Magyars.

On July 5 and 6 Germany promised to support Austria-Hungary. No advice was given and no line of action outlined, beyond a suggestion to act quickly. This "blank check," combined with the "downright intolerable" utterances of Serbian officials and newspapers, finally converted Francis Joseph and Tisza to Berchtold's views. The foreign minister thereupon proceeded to frame an ultimatum. The only danger, he believed, lay in the possible circumstance that Russia might not be bluffing this time, but in that event Germany could be relied upon for aid. The Germans obviously would not sit by idly while their one loyal ally was being defeated.

On July 23 Serbia received a forty-eight-hour ultimatum. An outline of its terms had been made known to the German Foreign Office before the document was delivered to the Serbian Government, but after it was too late for Germany to bring about modification. Now Germany realized that she had put her neck into a noose and given Vienna the other end of the rope. Though William II was dismayed when he read the demands, he did not waver in his intention to lend the promised aid, if necessary.

The ultimatum reproached the Serbian Government with having failed to observe an agreement of 1909 "to live in future on good neighborly terms" with Austria-Hungary. It demanded the suppression of all anti-Austrian propaganda in Serbian papers, books, schools, and political circles; the arrest and trial of certain officers suspected of complicity in the assassination; the dissolution of the Union or Death society; and permission for Austro-Hungarian officials to "collaborate in Serbia" for the trial of the Sarajevo suspects and the suppression of the anti-Austrian movement.

On the day after Serbia received this ultimatum, the Russian Foreign Minister, Sergei Sazonov, notified the Serbian Ambassador at St. Petersburg that "Russia would in no circumstances permit Austrian aggression against Serbia." Thus encouraged, Serbia decided not to accept the ultimatum in full. Sending in her reply on July 25, just before the time limit expired, she agreed to a number of the terms but rejected as an infringement of her sovereign status the provision permitting foreign officials to function on Serbian soil. She also expressed her willingness to refer the whole matter to the Hague Tribunal or to a conference of the powers.

Most of Europe, including Germany, considered this reply reasonable. William II believed it removed "every reason for war." He and Chancellor Theobald von Bethmann Hollweg now urged Vienna to try mediation. But Berchtold was obdurate and declared the reply unsatisfactory. On July 28 Austria-Hungary declared war on Serbia. She did so in the belief that this was the only way to maintain her future security and in the hope that the war would remain local. The Serbian Government, when it declined to accept the ultimatum in full, knew that war would follow. Indeed, Serbia had ordered the general mobilization of her army more than two hours before submitting her reply.

Germany and Great Britain now strove to prevent the war from becoming general. During all the ensuing negotiations, however, the Germans had to keep this in mind: *if* the war became general, Germany's chief hope for success lay in the execution of the Schlieffen Plan, drawn up by the predecessor of Chief of Staff Helmuth J. L. von Moltke. This scheme, envisioning a simultaneous conflict with France and Russia, counted upon Russia's inability to mobilize rapidly to make up for Germany's inferiority in man power. In case of war, Germany was to concentrate her main strength in the west for a rapid drive against France, meanwhile keeping only a thin line in the east to hold back the Russians. Then, after France was defeated, a large body of troops was to be hurled against the Russians. The plan also contemplated the invasion of France via Luxembourg and Belgium in order to avoid the heavy fortifications and the Vosges Mountains in the eastern part of the republic. Accordingly, every day that elapsed, and that Russia could utilize for mobilizing, made the danger greater for Germany by decreasing the advantages accruing from her greater speed of mobilization and her better preparedness in war materials.

Since Germany was aware that France and Russia knew of the Schlieffen Plan,[1] she was suspicious of Russia's maneuvers, after July 28, to gain time and delay the spreading of the war. France, on the other hand, knew that Germany would be forced to declare war first in order to forestall Russian mobilization. The republic, therefore, could be certain that if she merely waited, Germany would have to become the aggressor and would invade Belgium. Thus the war would be offensive on the part of Germany and Italy would be released from all obligations under the Triple Alliance. Great Britain could be counted on to fight Germany as soon as the latter invaded Belgium.

While Berlin was trying to restrain Vienna after July 28, the Russians prepared in secrecy and haste. Tsarist military circles were greatly encouraged by the attitude of France. From July 20 to July 23 President Raymond Poincaré visited Russia. He promised French aid in any undertaking upon which Russia might embark to prevent Austria from humiliating Serbia. "Serbia has very warm friends in the Russian people," he said, "and Russia has an ally, France!" On the afternoon of July 30 Russia ordered general mobilization. Hereupon Germany sent an ultimatum to St. Petersburg demanding cessation of mobilization within twelve hours under threat of war. Russia failed to reply and, at five o'clock in the afternoon of August 1, Germany declared war. "It was primarily Russia's general mobilization, made when Germany was trying to bring Austria to a settlement, which precipitated the final catastrophe, causing Germany to mobilize and declare war." [2]

In Great Britain, Foreign Minister Grey, who had tried to maintain peace and substitute "direct conversations" for war, failed to seize either of the only likely opportunities for preventing a spread of the conflict. He *might* have prevented a general war either by telling Germany that Great Britain would help France and Russia or by warning these allies that Great Britain would remain neutral. In the former case, William II and Bethmann Hollweg might have exerted more pressure on Berchtold.

---

[1] The plan was discussed in French circles at least as early as 1904.

[2] Fay, S. B. *The Origins of the World War,* 2 v. in 1, 1930, v. 2, p. 555. Austria-Hungary declared war on Russia on August 6.

In the latter, Poincaré, Izvolski, Sazonov, and other French and Russian leaders might have been less unyielding. Yet Grey took neither step. He could not openly promise to help France and Russia because his cabinet was divided. He would not openly promise neutrality because of secret naval understandings (1912) which virtually obligated Great Britain to defend the northern and western coasts of France against German sea attacks. Nor did he care to risk a rupture with Russia, lest the St. Petersburg Government withdraw from the Anglo-Russian Entente of 1907. In answer to a parliamentary interpellation, Grey denied the existence of any secret understanding with France and avowed that the freedom of action of the House of Commons relative to the warring powers was in no way restricted by secret engagements.

Grey himself evidently believed that Great Britain's commercial and naval interests demanded adherence to the Triple Entente. He did not desire a general war, but, if such a situation should come about, he was ready to side with France and Russia. British public opinion, however, was opposed to war over a Balkan question. There was little sympathy in Great Britain with the Serbs, who, on the whole, were considered responsible for the crisis. Yet before long Germany herself converted the British people to another view. On August 4 German troops invaded Belgium. This action followed Germany's declaration of war on France on August 3, after France had answered an ultimatum demanding a declaration of neutrality by stating that she would "act in accordance with her interests." Belgium was asked to allow German troops to pass through her territory to France, with guarantees of integrity and indemnity. King Albert, considering this a violation of his country's neutrality as guaranteed by an international treaty of 1839, appealed to Great Britain for support. When, therefore, German troops entered Belgium on August 4, Great Britain forthwith declared war on Germany.

The First World War was on! And in every belligerent capital the people seemed relieved that the strain of the armed peace was at last broken.

CHAPTER II

A World War

THE SPREAD OF THE CONFLAGRATION, 1914–1917

Before the end of 1914, three more countries entered the war. Montenegro joined Serbia on August 7. Eight days later Germany received an ultimatum from Japan. She was "advised" to withdraw all German warships from Chinese and Japanese waters, and to surrender to Japan, "with a view to the eventual restoration of the same to China," the Kiaochow territory, leased in 1898 for ninety-nine years. Japan had several motives for this maneuver. In a treaty of 1902, as renewed and revised in 1905 and 1911, Japan and Great Britain had promised to aid one another in the event that either was attacked in her Far Eastern possessions by an enemy power. Now, since Germany was preparing to use Kiaochow on the Shantung Peninsula as a base from which to act against British commerce and shipping in the Far East, Great Britain called upon Japan to fulfill her alliance obligations. This request, together with a hope of falling heir to Germany's interests in China and a desire to gain revenge for Germany's unfriendly attitude of 1895 after the Sino-Japanese War, caused Japan to send the ultimatum. Upon Germany's failure to reply within the indicated eight-day limit, Japan declared war (August 23).[1]

Meanwhile Germany's hopes were raised by the advent of Turkey into the war on her side. On August 2, 1914, at the height of the diplomatic crisis, Germany and Turkey had signed a secret treaty to become effective in the event of war between Germany and Russia—a condition which already existed. Under the terms of the agreement Turkey was to help Germany in return for a

---

[1] By November 7 the Japanese had captured Tsingtao, the chief German stronghold in Shantung. Thereafter Japan confined her military activities to coöperating with the British in patrolling the Pacific Ocean; furnishing supplies and munitions to the Entente Powers, especially Russia; and contributing war vessels to help convoy ships through submarine zones in the Mediterranean Sea and eastern waters.

guarantee of territorial integrity. With the help of German officers and money, extensive military preparations now were made, for Turkey considered the time ripe to thwart Russia's designs on the Straits, to strike a blow at Pan-Slavism, and to end British dominance in Egypt and Cyprus. Since the Allies [1] were ignorant of this treaty, they continued to bargain with Turkey for her neutrality. The Sublime Porte, not yet ready to enter the fight, apparently enjoyed these negotiations, and the more the Allies offered, the more the Turks demanded.

In August 1914 two German cruisers, the *Göben* and the *Breslau,* eluded Allied war vessels and slipped into the port of Constantinople. The Germans failed to leave the port within the twenty-four-hour limit set by international law, but the Turks declined to intern them. To the protests of the Allies, the Turkish Government replied by "purchasing" the ships and forming a Turco-German squadron commanded by the German Admiral Wilhelm Souchon. On October 29, without a declaration of war, this fleet bombarded several Russian Black-Sea ports, and on November 3 Russia declared war on Turkey. Two days later Great Britain and France did likewise.

Turkey's step appeared tremendously important to Germany and for a time seriously worried the Allies. Communications between Russia and her partners via the Straits were now cut off, in consequence of which the Allies found it difficult to get Russian grain and to supply the tsar's forces with munitions and other war materials. Moreover it was generally expected that the declaration of a Holy War by the sultan would cause the Mohammedans in the French and British possessions in Africa and Asia to revolt. As it happened, the appeal of a Holy War was slight, and such British agents as Colonel Thomas E. Lawrence and Gertrude Bell actually were able to induce many Moslem Arabs to revolt against the sultan.

Unable to win Turkey as an ally, the Entente Powers consoled themselves by partitioning the Ottoman Empire—on paper. A secret agreement of March 1915 virtually wiped out European Turkey. Constantinople and the Straits were assigned to Russia. A small area around Adrianople and Kirk-Kilissa was left intact, apparently as a bait with which to entice Bulgaria. Asiatic Turkey was reserved to France and Great Britain, to be disposed of by these powers in a later agreement. In the same treaty, Russia per-

---

[1] Soon after the outbreak of war the Entente Powers came to be known popularly as "the Allies," while the German system was called "the Central Powers."

mitted Great Britain to extend her influence over most of the
central or neutral zone that had been established in Persia by the
Anglo-Russian understanding of 1907. Not until 1917, when the
Bolsheviks published the secret treaties found in the Russian
archives, did this pact become generally known.[1]

Italy, on August 3, 1914, had declared her neutrality on the
ground that the war was offensive on the part of the Central
Powers and that the terms of the Triple Alliance therefore were
not operative in so far as she was concerned. The chief immediate
advantage of Italy's stand accrued to France, since the latter could
now use most of her forces to stem the tide of the German invasion. Moreover, as a neutral, Italy would refrain from interfering with the transportation of troops from northern Africa to
France and from hampering British lines of communication in the
Mediterranean. On the other hand, neither Germany nor Austria-
Hungary had really expected Italy to render assistance in a general
war and they were content to have their "ally" remain neutral.
When Italy, however, withdrew her troops some distance from the
French frontier and concentrated her fleet in the Adriatic, Austria-
Hungary began to worry.

A flood of offers from both sides placed Italy in a position of
vantage. She could afford to sit back and await bids, entering the
fray only when she considered such action most profitable. Although a strong group in Italy favored joining the Allies, there
were many who felt that much could be obtained without going to
war. A third faction held that Italy had little cause for quarrel
with Germany and that, on the contrary, powerful economic,
spiritual, and political ties existed between the two countries.

Matters were brought to a head when Italy announced that,
under the Triple-Alliance convention, she was entitled to compensation for any Austro-Hungarian gains in the Balkans. In December 1914, therefore, after Austria-Hungary had occupied
Serbian territory, Italy extended her control over the Albanian
city of Valona (Avlona), at the mouth of the Adriatic. Rome
then demanded from Francis Joseph a part of *Italia Irredenta*

[1] The chief supplementary secret treaties dealing with the Near East were the
Sazonov-Paléologue Agreement of April 1916, in which France agreed that Russia
should get about sixty thousand square miles of Turkish Armenia; the Sykes-Picot
Agreement of May 1916, which assigned Syria and an extensive hinterland to France
and most of Arabia south of the French zone to Great Britain; the Treaty of London
(April 1915), whereby Great Britain, France, and Russia promised Italy an interest
in Anatolia; and the agreement of St. Jean de Maurienne (April 1917), in which
France and Great Britain agreed to let Italy have approximately the southern third
of Anatolia plus a sphere of influence north of Smyrna.

as additional compensation for Austro-Hungarian territorial gains. When the Italian Government discovered that Berlin was urging Vienna to compensate Italy even to the extent of ceding the Trentino, it demanded still more.

On February 21, 1915, Italy "refused her consent in the future to any military action by Austria-Hungary in the Balkans, unless an agreement . . . should have been previously reached on the subject of compensation, an agreement which it would be idle to hope to reach otherwise than upon the basis of the cession of ter-ritories at present in the possession of Austria-Hungary." Before long Vienna, frightened by Russian advances in Galicia, signified her willingness to negotiate with Italy on this principle. After much telegraphing back and forth, Italy finally presented (April 8) Austria-Hungary with a draft treaty of eleven articles as her price for neutrality. The demands far exceeded the Austrian maximum concessions.

During these months the Allies had not been idle. They had carried on negotiations to discover the bait that would bring Italy into the contest on their side. In the competitive bidding the Entente Powers had the advantage. Austria-Hungary, after all, did not care to cede her territories to one of her "friends." The Allies, on the other hand, were hampered by no such considerations. They could let Italy have most of what she wanted in Austria and along the Adriatic. Hence Italy, while still negotiating with Austria-Hungary, on April 26, 1915, signed a secret treaty at London with France, Russia, and Great Britain.

Under the terms of this document Italy agreed to join the Allies within a month in return for (1) the Trentino, Trieste, and the South Tirol with its German-speaking population of approximately 250,000; (2) Gorizia, Gradisca, Istria, and the islands of the Gulf of Quarnero, in all which Italians formed about one-third of the population; (3) northern Dalmatia, of whose inhabitants about 3 per cent were Italians; (4) a protectorate over Valona and its hinterland, that is, over part of Albania; (5) outright ownership of the Greek Dodecanese Islands in the Aegean, occupied since 1912 in consequence of the Turco-Italian War; (6) a sphere of influence in Asiatic Turkey; (7) an extension of her colonial possessions in Africa if France and Great Britain secured the German African colonies; (8) a special war loan and part of the war indemnity; and (9) a promise that the papacy would not be supported in any diplomatic action taken contrary to the wishes of the Italian Government. Thus the Adriatic was to be made an Italian lake; Austria was to be cut off from the sea; unredeemed Italians were to be freed; about half a million Austrians, Southslavs, and Greeks were to be subjected to Italian control; and the flag of Italy was to fly over larger African possessions.

One week later (May 3) Italy, claiming that Austria-Hungary had violated both the letter and spirit of the Triple Alliance, renounced that covenant and resumed "complete liberty of action." On May 23 the government of Victor Emmanuel issued a declaration of war against Austria-Hungary, to take effect the following morning. Not until fifteen months later (August 27, 1916) were hostilities declared against Germany.

In September 1915 Italy adhered to the Pact of London, an agreement reached in the previous September by Great Britain, France, and Russia. This bond, to which Japan later also became a party, converted the Triple Entente into a wartime alliance and stipulated that none of the Allies should entertain peace proposals or cease fighting without the previous concurrence of the other signatories. Meanwhile, in June 1915, the republic of San Marino, hidden away in the Apennine Mountains and with a population of 12,000, had "drawn its sword on the side of Italy" and sent a few hundred volunteers to fight against Austria.

A treaty of 1661, renewed on several occasions, obligated Portugal to lend military aid to Great Britain whenever the latter so requested. Hence, on November 23, 1914, Lisbon resolved to intervene as an ally of Great Britain immediately upon receipt of such demand. An actual grant of military support was voted in May 1915 and troops were despatched to fight in Africa. In February 1916, after German submarines had done considerable damage to Allied shipping and when about forty German and Austrian merchant vessels were resting in Portuguese harbors, the British Government asked Portugal to seize these ships. The request was obeyed and Germany retaliated by declaring war on March 9, 1916.

Both warring factions, meanwhile, were carrying on negotiations in the Balkans. In the competition for Bulgarian help, Germany had the advantage. The Bulgarians had not forgotten their humiliation in the Balkan War of 1913, for which they placed chief blame on Serbia, and they frankly awaited a chance to strike back at the hated enemy. There was no hurry, however, and Bulgaria carefully watched the course of military events. When, in 1915, the Allied campaign at Gallipoli failed and the Russians were retreating from Galicia and Poland, Bulgaria decided to join the Central Powers. Her policy and choice were dictated by a desire to achieve her "national ideals," that is, to incorporate in her possessions most of Serbian and part of Greek Macedonia. Through German influence Turkey was induced to agree to a rectification of her borders in Bulgaria's favor and thereupon the latter signed a convention of alliance with Austria-Hungary. Then, on October 14, 1915, with her troops already across the Serbian border, Bulgaria declared war on her neighbor.

Bulgaria's aid was of immediate advantage to the Central Powers, for it made possible the crushing of Serbia and Montenegro. Strategically this resulted in giving Germany control over a direct line of communication and transportation from Berlin to Constantinople, and even to Baghdad. The successful bid for Bulgarian help was the last diplomatic victory of the Central Powers. The remaining fifteen countries that entered as belligerents joined the Allies.

In Romania, the Hohenzollern King Carol I wanted to join the Central Powers in accordance with his treaty obligations. The cabinet preferred neutrality, particularly since it was undecided whether it was more anxious to get territory from Austria-Hungary or Russia. To make things worse for the Allies, Russia insisted on reserving for Serbia some of the Austro-Hungarian land that Romania wanted. However, the succession (October 1914) of Carol's nephew, Ferdinand, to the throne was favorable to the Allies, since the new ruler more nearly reflected the pro-Allied feeling of the people. The Austro-German military victories in 1914 and 1915 made the Romanians hesitate to take sides, but when, in 1916, the Central Powers met reverses on the French, Italian, Russian, and Near Eastern fronts, the government of Ferdinand decided to enter on the winning side—provided a price sufficiently high could be established.

As in the case of Italy and other late entrants, bids were entertained from both sides. Again the Dual Monarchy hesitated to promise a number of her provinces to a prospective friend, and the Allies had the upper hand in the bidding. A secret treaty was signed on August 17, 1916, among Romania, Great Britain, Russia, France, and Italy, whereby Romania was to enter the war at once in return for (1) Transylvania, which comprised about one-half of Hungary and was populated by an approximately equal number of Magyars and Romanians; (2) the large Austrian duchy of Bukovina, about one-third of whose inhabitants were Romanians; and (3) the Banat of Temesvár, also with a population only one-third Romanian. On August 27 Romania declared war on Austria-Hungary. Like Italy, she explained her defection from her former alliance obligations on the ground that altered circumstances had restored her liberty of action.

Greece remained as the only important neutral in the Balkans. King Constantine, related to William II and fearful of a Bulgarian invasion, favored neutrality, if not actual alliance with Germany. But Eleutherios Venizelos, prime minister since 1910, thought that by joining the Allies Greece would at last be able to complete her unification. He therefore urged that Greece fulfill the obligations of a prewar treaty with Serbia in which the signatories had promised to aid one another in case of attack by Bulgaria. Furthermore, France and Great Britain held out parts of Albania and Turkey as bait to the Greeks, even though some of these regions had already been promised to Italy. The king was obdurate. With the aid of the German-officered general staff he ousted the premier in 1914 and again in 1915. In the elections of December 1915 the Venizelists refused to vote and the remaining electorate endorsed the government's policy of neutrality.

By this time the Allies had become impatient. They wanted a base of operations at Salonika and wished to help Serbia from the south. Late in 1915 the French General Maurice Sarrail forcibly took over control of Salonika and set up an Allied headquarters. An Allied base also was established on the neutralized Greek island of Corfu. When Constantine protested these violations of Greek neutrality and compared them to Germany's violation of Belgium, the Allies rejoined that Greek neutrality had not been guaranteed by treaty. Then they established a blockade, demanded the demobilization of the Greek army, and recognized a Venizelist Government at Salonika which declared war on Germany in November 1916. In the summer of 1917 the Allies demanded the dethronement of the king and the abdication of his eldest son. An Allied army marched on Athens and on June 12, 1917, Constantine finally abdicated in favor of his second son, Alexander. Thereupon Venizelos was called to head a new government and on July 2, 1917, Greece officially became one of the Allied Powers.

THE ENTRY OF THE UNITED STATES

a. Neutrality in Thought and Deed

Most Americans, accustomed to basking in the sun of geographical isolation, received the news of the outbreak of war with amazement. At a time when people were still talking about the Hague conferences; when Secretary of State William J. Bryan was negotiating arbitration treaties with the more important countries of the world; when pacifists, economists, and diplomats were deprecating war as a means of settling international disputes; when the establishment of peace foundations had become almost a vogue; and when the Nobel Peace Prize, founded by the inventor of dynamite, was a coveted international award—at such a time it was incomprehensible to Americans that war could be precipitated. Hence, in the early days of the conflict, there was a widespread feeling that the United States could hardly become a party to the struggle. She might act as mediator, but active participation appeared remote, since it was foreign to her traditions.

In accord with this spirit, President Woodrow Wilson, on August 4, 1914, declared the neutrality of the United States. Five days later he appealed to his "Fellow Countrymen," urging "very earnestly upon them the sort of speech and conduct which would best safeguard the Nation against distress and disaster." He asked them to "act and speak in the true spirit of neutrality, which is the spirit of impartiality and fairness and friendliness to all concerned." He reminded them that "the people of the United States are drawn from many nations, and chiefly from the nations now at war," and warned that it would be "easy to excite passion and difficult to allay it." The United States, therefore, "must be neutral in fact as well as in name," and the people "must be impartial in thought as well as in action."

This appeal achieved a transient popularity. Even Theodore Roosevelt and the Anglophil ambassador to Great Britain, Walter Hines Page, concurred at first. But neutrality in thought as well as in action was well-nigh impossible. In the words of one magazine editor, "only persons mentally unsexed or paralyzed" could remain without a decided preference for one side or the other; and as Page later said, "a government can be neutral, but no man can be."

The reasons are clear why absolute neutrality could not be upheld. First, the United States, as a land of immigrants, contained many inhabitants of foreign birth or the children of foreigners. Most of these persons had come from countries engaged in the conflict, and traditional prejudices readily came to the surface, often to the indignation of "real" Americans. Some of these, such as Roosevelt, advocated the deportation of all "hyphenates" who openly expressed sentimental preferences for either group of belligerents. Secondly, as the neutral best able to supply war materials, the United States was bound to become closely associated with the warring powers, particularly since both sides were actuated by a double object with respect to her. They aimed at securing as much of American foodstuffs and supplies as possible, while simultaneously preventing the enemy's getting anything. Thirdly, as the strongest neutral the United States soon came to be regarded as the champion of neutral rights for the world. Finally, the activities of foreign propagandists in the United States made continued neutrality more and more difficult. The Allied agents, on the whole, understood American psychology; the Germans were tactless and inclined to methods of violence.

b. Problems of International Law

In the fall of 1914 the United States, Germany, and Great Britain were in a position reminiscent of that occupied by the United States, France, and Great Britain during the Napoleonic period. Germany realized that to defeat Great Britain it was necessary to cut off her overseas supplies. Great Britain likewise felt that Germany could be beaten only if her people were starved and her munition supply curtailed. The immediate economic victims of the policies embarked upon by the belligerents to accomplish their respective aims were American merchants, shippers, manufacturers, and laborers.

The first offenders of neutral rights were the British. Through Orders in Council they arbitrarily enlarged the list of contraband goods, on the ground that the changed conditions of modern warfare made obsolete even such agreements as the Declaration of London (1909).[1] Eventually the British seized as contraband nearly everything that was sent to Germany or to her neutral neighbors. An amusing instance of this British interference with trade among neutrals was reported in March 1916 when a case of ladies' silk hosiery, shipped on a Swedish boat by a New York department store to Sweden, was seized by the British on suspicion that the goods might be forwarded to the Germans. The shippers angrily protested that ladies' stockings ought not to be classed as war materials. The British also seized and opened mail addressed from the United States to Germany on the charge that pro-Germans in

---

[1] In August 1914 neither Great Britain nor Germany had ratified this declaration, which listed the war materials subject to confiscation as contraband if found on their way to an enemy country. When the United States now asked both sides to accept the declaration, Germany agreed, but Great Britain temporized.

America were sending copper and other contraband to Germany by post.

The quicker to starve out her enemy, Great Britain declared a blockade of Germany. According to international usage, only "effective" blockades were legal. In other words, a patrolling fleet of sufficient size had to be kept before the blockaded ports to prevent any ships from entering or leaving these ports. Yet, since the advent of the submarine and improved coast defenses made it impracticable for Great Britain to blockade German shores, her ships were stationed in the English Channel and at the entrance to the North Sea from Scotland to Norway, hundreds of miles from the German ports. Thus not only Germany but the neutral Netherlands and Scandinavian states were "blockaded." Moreover, the British gave up the customary practice of searching neutral vessels on the high seas and instead forced the ships into British ports, there to be searched, and, incidentally, often delayed for weeks. The United States protested against these illegalities and made it clear that damages would be claimed. To this threat the British raised no serious objections.

British ships adopted the practice of flying American flags as a *ruse de guerre* and as protection against German submarines. Again the United States protested, but to no avail. In July 1916 Great Britain published a "Black List" of about eighty American firms that were considered German-owned or friendly to the German cause. British subjects were ordered not to trade with these firms and British shippers were told not to handle their products. Neutral shippers, too, were warned not to carry the goods of the proscribed companies under penalty of losing coaling rights at British ports. Inclusion in the Black List, incidentally, made it difficult for the concerns in question to obtain loans from banks. This act of the British aroused serious protests in the United States and was partly responsible for the enactment of a huge naval-appropriation bill in August 1916.

Perhaps one explanation for the continued British violation of American neutrality rights, despite frequent protests from Washington, is to be found in some remarks of Grey to Ambassador Page. In 1916 Grey told Page: "America must remember that we are fighting her fight as well as ours. You dare not press us too far." The implication was that Germany had become as dangerous a commercial rival of the United States as of Great Britain, and that a defeat of the Teutonic power would materially benefit both English-speaking peoples. When President Wilson heard of Grey's remark he is reputed to have said: "(Grey) was right. War with England would mean a Germany victory. I will not embarrass England."

Among the American people the actions of the British created strong anti-Allied feelings. Anti-British protests poured in on Wilson from all parts of the country. Many Southerners protested against the blockade and the listing of cotton as a contraband. The packers of Chicago and the farmers of the Northwest urged Wilson to "open the way to hungry markets for their goods." In the East, the commission merchants of New York complained that their business should have to be carried on "by leave of England." Eventually several bills were placed before Congress for embargoes on munition shipments to Great Britain. In the spring of 1915 Colonel Edward M. House, on a mission to Europe as observer for the President, told the British that their course would have grave results. Touching, as it did, "the pocketbooks and the sensibilities of many Americans," the British quarrel could be forgotten only if eclipsed by a dispute with Germany.

With things at such a pass, the Germans provided the eclipse. On February 4, 1915, the German Government announced that

the waters surrounding Great Britain and Ireland, including the whole English Channel, are hereby declared to be war zone. On and after the eighteenth of February, 1915, every enemy merchant ship found in this said war zone will be destroyed without its being always possible to avert the dangers threatening the crews and passengers on that account. Even neutral ships are exposed to danger in the war zone, as, in view of the misuse of neutral flags ordered on January 31 by the British Government and of the accidents of naval war, it cannot always be avoided to strike even neutral ships in attacks that are directed against enemy ships.

This course, the Germans felt, was justified by Great Britain's illegal blockade. It was a desperate attempt to win the war, but it was a tactical blunder. The American Government at once threatened to "hold the Imperial German Government to strict accountability" if the submarine campaign led to the loss of American lives.

Germany's resort to unrestricted submarine warfare was the *direct cause* for the entry of the United States into the war. International law forbade the sinking of merchant vessels without warning and without provision for the safety of crews and pas-

sengers. Submarines, however, could not fulfill these requirements. The early submarines were small, frail craft which could
be destroyed by ramming or by one well-aimed shot at the peri-
scope. They were effective only when they could attack unseen.
If a submarine did warn a vessel prior to firing a torpedo, the
unfortunate crew and passengers could not possibly be taken
aboard the "U-boat," for lack of room. The submarine had not
been far enough developed before 1914 to gain recognition in
international law. The Germans, therefore, had a choice of obey-
ing international law and discarding a new and effective weapon
with which they alone were adequately equipped, or of violating
the law and risking the enmity of the neutral powers.

On February 20, 1915, the United States attempted to bring
about a *modus vivendi* by asking the belligerents to agree not to
sow floating mines, not to use submarines except according to the
rules of war, and not to use neutral flags for the purpose of dis-
guise. Great Britain was asked to allow the shipment of foodstuffs
to Germany, where American agents would see that they were
used only to feed civilians. Both belligerents found objections to
this scheme and nothing came of it.

In the midst of the discussions over the right and wrong of the
various measures resorted to by the belligerents, came news of the
sinking (March 28, 1915) of the British steamer, *Falaba,* with the
loss of one American life. The American tanker, *Gulflight,* was
torpedoed on May 1 with loss of two members of her crew. Before
the Washington authorities had found time to take definite action
on either of these cases, the Cunard liner, *Lusitania,* was sunk, on
May 7, 1915. She was torpedoed without warning, seven miles off
the southeastern coast of Ireland. Almost twelve hundred lives
were lost, including those of more than one hundred Americans.
Some Americans now clamored for an immediate declaration of
hostilities, but President Wilson felt that the nation was not yet
ready for war. He took a week to gather data and then forwarded
a protest to Germany.

In his note, the President reviewed the entire submarine controversy, called the sinkings a crime against humanity, insisted on
the punishment of the commander of the U-boat that had torpedoed the *Lusitania,* demanded an official disavowal of the act,
and asked for a promise that such activities would not be condoned in future. Before the reply arrived at Washington, the
German Ambassador, Johann von Bernstorff, explained that Germany had no intention of sinking neutral vessels if they did not

resist search and seizure. This assurance, however, did not protect neutral passengers on belligerent ships and therefore would not apply in cases similar to that of the *Lusitania*.

The reply of the German Government to Wilson's note stated that he had not taken cognizance of all facts in the case. The Germans claimed that the *Lusitania* was a British auxiliary cruiser, carried munitions, had concealed guns, and came under the category of transport, since she also carried Canadian soldiers. In these circumstances, it was said, the sinking was a justifiable act of self-defense. This answer was considered unsatisfactory and notes were exchanged over a period of more than three months. All the points of difference in the "facts" of the case as represented by Germany and the United States have not yet been settled, but on September 1, 1915, Germany agreed in future not to sink liners without warning and without saving the lives of noncombatants, provided that the liners did not try to escape or offer resistance. Wilson thereupon received warm applause for having won so signal a diplomatic victory by pacific means.[1]

c. From Peace to War

The *Lusitania* crisis introduced a period of neutrality during which America was "too proud to fight." In a speech of May 10, 1915, President Wilson declared: "The example of America must

---

[1] During the controversy Secretary of State Bryan resigned. He could not agree with Wilson that American citizens had the right to jeopardize the peace of their country by insisting on the prerogative of travel on belligerent merchant vessels.

It has not yet been absolutely proved or disproved whether the *Lusitania* was armed or whether she carried Canadian soldiers. It is known that she was a British auxiliary cruiser, that is, a liner so constructed as to be readily convertible into fighting form, and that she carried several million rounds of ammunition as well as tons of shrapnel shells. All this, however, did not justify the unwarned sinking of the ship, any more than did the issuance on May 1, 1915, of a special German notice warning Americans that they risked their lives if they sailed through the war zone on British or other Allied vessels.

It is also known that Captain William T. Turner of the *Lusitania*, despite special warnings from the British Admiralty regarding the presence of German submarines in the waters near the British Isles, failed to follow the official "advice" regarding precautionary measures. He failed to zigzag, he stuck to the usual trade route instead of varying the course, and he proceeded at about three-quarter speed. The vessel, though she was known to be in danger, was permitted to cross the ocean without escort and with not even the usual patrol to convoy her through the war zone. Perhaps the British felt that the presence of several hundred neutrals aboard was sufficient protection for the much-needed ammunition. They may have thought that Germany would never commit so serious a blunder as to risk drowning or blowing up hundreds of Americans and other neutrals. But the Germans did torpedo the vessel, and the effect on world sentiment towards Germany was perhaps more useful to the Allied cause than the cartridges would have been. Cf. Bailey, T. A. "The Sinking of the *Lusitania*," *The American Historical Review*, October 1935.

be a special example. The example of America must be the example not merely of peace because it will not fight, but of peace because peace is the healing and elevating influence of the world, and strife is not. There is such a thing as a man being too proud to fight. There is such a thing as a nation being so right that it does not need to convince others by force that it is right." Privately, if the testimony of his secretary, Joseph P. Tumulty, can be relied upon, Wilson hesitated to go to war chiefly because he was "not sure whether the present emotionalism of the country would last long enough to sustain any action (he) would suggest to Congress, and thus in case of failure (the government) should be left without that fine backing and support so necessary to maintain a great cause."

Several forces, however, were at work which gradually won over the public to the point of view of intervention. In May 1915 a group of New Yorkers sent a telegram to the President expressing their "conviction that national interest and honor imperatively required adequate measures both to secure reparation for past violations by Germany of American rights, and secure guarantees against future violations." Later in the same month this body, considerably augmented, decided that the best way in which its members, as loyal Americans, could put their patriotism into practice was to attend a summer camp for military training. General Leonard Wood, then in command of the Department of the East, favored the scheme and so the first military training camp for patriotic business and professional men was opened at Plattsburgh Barracks in the summer of 1915.

The enterprise attracted nation-wide attention and similar camps soon were established in other parts of the country. Since the number of men who were ready to display their patriotic feelings by attending camps was limited by the considerable expense involved, Congress, on June 3, 1916, authorized the secretary of war to furnish uniforms, pay, transportation costs, and rations to all who were willing to serve. The military ardor of the country was heightened in proportion to the increasing popularity of the camps, which attracted thousands of young men.

The spirit of preparedness engendered by the camps and the speeches of prominent men was further stimulated by the activities of European agents. The Allied emissaries carried on a skillful campaign, consisting chiefly of newspaper subsidies and the circulation of atrocity stories. The German and Austrian agents resorted to the blunter methods of conspiracy, fraud, and even violence. The Austrian Ambassador, Dr. Konstantin Dumba, and the German military and naval attachés, Captains Franz von Papen and Karl Boy-Ed, were accused of implication in conspiracies to blow up munition factories and transport ships, to foment strikes and sabotage in munition plants, to forge passports for German officers and reservists, and to prevent the manufacture of war materials in iron and steel works. Popular resentment soon flared high and in 1915 Washington requested the recall of all three men.

In the autumn of 1916, when the Allied fortunes of war were at ebb tide, Henry P. Davison, of the firm of J. P. Morgan, visited Europe. Upon his return he reported that the situation of the Allies was precarious. This news caused concern to an important group of American financiers, for it happened that in 1915 and 1916 Anglo-French loans of $1,500,000,000 had been floated in America, largely through the house of Morgan. Germany, on the other hand, had borrowed little. Obviously, "to those who sponsored and participated in these loans, whose financial reputation and whose principal and interest depended upon the continued solvency of the debtor nations, it was not a matter of indifference which side won the war."

Meanwhile President Wilson, apparently realizing the inevitability of some form of intervention, but still convinced that he "could not move faster than the mass of . . . people would permit," had toured the country in January and February 1916, making speeches on preparedness. Point was given to his warnings when Germany, on February 9, announced that her submarine commanders would be ordered to sink all armed enemy merchant vessels without warning. Since, by this time, every large British merchant vessel was armed, it was felt in many parts of the United States that American citizens should be forbidden to sail on such ships lest war with Germany result. Senator Thomas P. Gore of Oklahoma and Representative Jeff McLemore of Texas immediately introduced congressional resolutions designed to prohibit Americans from traveling on armed merchantmen. The President, however, used his influence to have the resolutions tabled. At this juncture a so-called House Memorandum or House-Grey Agreement was drawn up in London.

Colonel House had gone to Europe once more, in 1916, to see if it were possible to bring about peace, particularly a peace favorable to the Allies. On February 22 he agreed with Grey that Wilson should propose a conference to end the fighting. Should the Allies accept the proposal, it was understood, and should Germany refuse it, the United States would probably enter the war against Germany. "Colonel House expressed the conviction," wrote Grey, "that if such a conference met, it would secure peace on terms not unfavorable to the Allies, and if it failed to secure peace, the United States would leave the conference as a belligerent on the side of the Allies, if Germany was unreasonable." Nothing came of this memorandum, probably because the Allies expected the United States to fight Germany over the submarine issue.

It seemed as though the wishes of the Allies might be fulfilled when, in March 1916, the unarmed Channel steamer, *Sussex,* was attacked without warning and several Americans were injured. A note from the United States was soon forthcoming, which concluded with the following ultimatum: "Unless the Imperial Government should now immediately declare and effect an abandonment of its present methods of submarine warfare against passenger and freight-carrying vessels, the Government of the United States can have no choice but to sever diplomatic relations with the German Empire altogether."

To this the Germans replied in May by saying that they would do their "utmost to confine the operations of war for the rest of its duration to the fighting forces of the belligerents" and that their naval forces had been ordered not to sink merchant vessels "without warning and without saving human lives, unless these ships attempted to escape or offered resistance." However, this statement of policy was made contingent upon the United States requiring Great Britain to observe the rules of international law. This condition was not accepted by the state department, which warned Germany that she would be held to a "scrupulous execution" of the new policy regardless of the conduct of any other government. The outcome of the *Sussex* affair was regarded in many quarters as another diplomatic triumph for Wilson, who in June 1916 was renominated by acclamation to be the Democratic candidate for president.

A few days before Wilson's renomination, Congress had passed a National Defense Act (June 3, 1916). This provided for a substantial increase in the regular army, for a national guard of half a million men, and for the establishment of an officers' reserve corps. In the same spirit of preparedness Congress, less than three months later, passed the naval-appropriation bill, which carried the largest sum (more than $500,000,000) that had ever been voted at one time for national defense and which provided for the building of a navy approximately equal to that of Great Britain. The government also created a Council of National Defense, consisting of six cabinet members and seven civilian experts, to draft plans of defense in case of war, and a United States Shipping Board, to develop a sizable mercantile marine.

In the election of 1916 Wilson's campaign managers emphasized the energetic measures taken by the government in defense of national security and pointed with pride to "the splendid diplomatic victories of our great President who has preserved the vital interests of our government and kept us out of war." This idea—"he kept us out of war"—made an excellent slogan and gained many votes, particularly among the enfranchised women of the West and among German-American groups. The Republican candidate, Charles E. Hughes, promised to uphold America's neutral rights "without fear or favor." He avoided committing himself strongly on any side. The election was remarkably close and the result remained in doubt for several days. Then the victory was conceded to Wilson.

Five weeks after the election, on December 12, 1916, the Central Powers, victorious on every front, offered to discuss peace terms at a general conference but stated no specific bases on which they would be willing to negotiate. The Allies rejected this proposal as being less "an offer of peace than . . . a maneuver of war" and as designed to cause dissension among the Entente Powers. On December 18 President Wilson offered the mediation of the United States and requested both sides specifically to state their war aims in the hope that a comparison thereof might lead to an understanding. In the following month, while Germany still spoke in generalities, the Allies issued a statement of their peace conditions. Desiring, as they said, "to ensure a peace upon the principles of liberty and justice," they demanded the restoration with indemnity of Belgium, Serbia, and Montenegro; the evacuation "with just reparation" of France, Russia, and Romania; "restitution of provinces or territories wrested in the past from the Allies by force"; liberation of the Italians, Slavs, Romanians, Czechs, and Slovaks under foreign domination and of the peoples "subject to the bloody tyranny of the Turks"; expulsion of the Turks from Europe; and a "stable" reorganization of the continent.

The basis of these aims was the set of "Secret Treaties." The Central Powers did not take the demands seriously and even Wilson apparently regarded them as a bluff. On January 22, 1917, therefore, the President addressed the Senate on the subject of peace. He argued that the only durable peace was a "peace between equals," a "peace without victory," a negotiated, not an imposed, peace. He was ready, in the name of the United States, to guarantee any just peace that might be arrived at by an "international concert" and which would be based upon the acknowledgment of the equality of all nations and the recognition of the principle "that governments derive all their just powers from the consent of the governed."

Had they been wise, the diplomats of the Central Powers would immediately have issued a statement of their war aims. Instead, they refrained from such a procedure until January 29—two days before the world was notified that Germany would again resort to unrestricted submarine warfare. Then, though the German terms, in view of the military situation, were not altogether unreasonable, it was too late for negotiation.

On February 3, 1917, the United States replied to the submarine announcement by severing relations with the German Empire. On February 26, after several American vessels had been torpedoed without warning, the President asked Congress for authority to arm American merchantmen against submarines. A Senate filibuster, by what Wilson called "a little group of wilful men," held off a vote on the authorizing measure until the congressional session expired (March 4). Then the attorney-general discovered an old statute which conferred the desired power upon the President, and Wilson carried out his intention. In consequence there ensued a period of "armed neutrality" that could only be a prelude to armed participation.

Two additional events now occurred that tended to make the American people sympathetic to a war policy: the sending of the Zimmermann Note by Germany and the March Revolution in Russia. At the time that Congress was discussing the measure to arm merchantmen, the administration released for publication a copy of an intercepted German dispatch handed to Ambassador Page by the British Foreign Secretary, Arthur James Balfour. This dispatch was a note of January 19, 1917, from the German Foreign Secretary, Alfred Zimmermann, to the German Minister in Mexico, explaining that unrestricted submarine warfare would be renewed in the near future, but that endeavors would be made "in spite of this . . . to keep neutral the United States of America." In the event of this not succeeding, continued the message, Germany was ready to propose to Mexico an alliance providing for a joint war against the United States. As her reward, Mexico would be permitted to regain some of the lands lost in the Mexican War of the previous century. Japan was to be invited to adhere to the alliance. The government of Mexico, however, was not to be informed of any of this until "it is certain there will be an outbreak of war with the United States."

Considered objectively, there was nothing illegal about this so-called Zimmermann Plot. Germany violated no law by seeking additional allies in case of war with the United States. But in the words of Senator Henry Cabot Lodge, the note seemed to be "of almost unlimited use in forcing the situation." It greatly strengthened the war spirit, particularly in the hitherto lukewarm Southwest.

There now remained only one big obstacle to America's entry into the conflict—autocratic Russia. If, as Wilson had pointed out in his speech on January 22 and as the Allies now kept repeating, a just peace could only be arrived at through a recognition of the principle that all governments derived their powers from the consent of the governed, then it would be awkward for the United States to fight on the same side with tsarist Russia. In the middle of March 1917, however, Nicholas II abdicated and a liberal provisional government came into control. Thus there was removed, as Secretary of State Robert Lansing said, the last obstacle to regarding the war as one for democracy and against autocracy. The new situation was all the more important in view of the alarming frequency with which American ships now were being sunk by German submarines. Wilson summoned Congress to meet in special session "to receive a communication concerning grave matters of national policy," and devoted thirteen days to formulating a war message.

Gravely and amid solemn surroundings the President, on the evening of April 2, 1917, urged Congress to "declare the recent course of the Imperial German Government to be in fact nothing less than war against the government and people of the United States." He reviewed the long controversy with "this natural foe to liberty" and explained that the conflict had narrowed down to a life-and-death struggle between the forces of democracy and autocracy. The world had to be "made safe for democracy" and it was America's duty to dedicate her blood and might to the task. "God helping her, she can do no other."

A resolution declaring that a state of war existed between Ger-

many and the United States was passed in the Senate on April 4
by a vote of 82 to 6. A similar resolution was passed in the House
of Representatives on April 6 by 373 votes to 50. On the same day
Wilson proclaimed the war.[1]

· The Allies were overjoyed at America's entrance into the war.
The morale of their people and soldiers went up tremendously.
In Germany there was no great manifestation of feeling. Many
Germans felt that, in one way or another, the United States had
been helping the Allied cause, and so far as the matter of troops
went, it would be at least a year before any effective American
force could be injected into the struggle.

d. Twenty-three to Four

Cuba and Panama declared war on Germany one day later than
did the United States. Greece, Siam (Thailand), Liberia, China,
and Brazil entered the conflict later in the same year. In 1918
Guatemala, Nicaragua, Costa Rica, Haiti, and Honduras did
likewise. Altogether the count stood twenty-three nations against
four. Truly, the war had become a world war.

[1] On December 7, 1917, war was declared against Austria-Hungary. The United
States did not declare war on Bulgaria or Turkey.

CHAPTER III

The Altar of Mars

ADVANTAGES OF THE BELLIGERENTS

Few people realized, when the First World War broke out, how different this conflict would be from previous ones. The years from 1914 to 1918 witnessed the evolution of a new historical concept, the idea of a "nation at war." It was futile any longer to regard the nation merely as a "reservoir to pour its reënforcements into the army." Rather, each nation had to be considered as a "mighty river in which were merged many tributary forces of which the army was but one." The warring governments soon became aware that the outcome would depend not so much on the better professional army and the more daring leaders as on the availability of material resources. Every combatant, therefore, mobilized not alone its fighting men and leaders but its scientists, engineers, organizers, financiers, manual laborers, propagandists, inventors, artists, teachers, farmers, manufacturers, women, and production and transportation facilities.

For waging war each side had certain advantages. In physical equipment, Germany was the best prepared of any power. The German railway system was superbly coördinated for military maneuvering, the routes having been laid out under the supervision of the German General Staff. In 1914 there were thirteen double lines to the western frontier and it was possible to send 550 trains a day across the Rhine bridges. During the first two weeks of the war, a train carrying soldiers or military equipment passed approximately every ten minutes over the railway bridge at Cologne.[1]

The German army was the best-trained and disciplined fighting machine on the continent. Even the reserve forces were so thoroughly trained that the high command did not hesitate to

[1] Liddell Hart, B. H. *The Real War, 1914–1918,* 1930, p. 54.

throw them into the front lines at the outset of hostilities. At the apex of the German military pyramid was the general staff, a body which "by rigor of selection and training was unmatched for professional knowledge and skill, if subject to the mental 'grooves' which characterize all professions." There was, further, a corps of excellent officers. Though often conceited and harsh, these leaders were well versed in tactics and eager to maintain a tradition of victory. Complementing the commissioned-officer personnel was an efficient group of regular noncommissioned officers, men bred to the service and unexcelled in technical lore and ability to handle soldiers. The armies of Germany's allies were inferior to her own, but this circumstance eventually enabled the Germans to dominate the coalition.

In military equipment, the Germans before the war had developed and adapted to a greater degree than the other powers the howitzer, the machine gun, and the submarine. The effectiveness of the German heavy guns before which the massive walls of Liége in Belgium crumbled, the deadly and demoralizing effect of German machine-gun fire, and the ravages on shipping of the submarines soon made the Allies realize that they were not fighting "just another war." On the "home front," too, Germany, because of her highly industrialized state, was better able than any of the Allies except Great Britain to keep sending the necessary war materials to the fighting lines. Great stores of raw materials and of gold reserves were on hand in Germany, and commercial factories were converted with great rapidity into manufactories of munitions, shells, hospital supplies, military machines, and other wartime necessities. The process of transformation was efficient, but the resultant dislocation of the national economy was so great as to cause much misery after the return of peace.

The Central Powers enjoyed a temporary geographic advantage. After Bulgaria's entry into the war and the Serbian collapse, Germany and her allies formed a solid geographical unit from the North Sea to Arabia. Troops, supplies, orders could be sent from one part of the area, or from one front, to another with expedition and with relatively little danger of Allied interference. Whole armies could readily be shifted from France to Galicia, or from Galicia to the Italian front, or even from Prussia to the Near East. With the Allies the situation was otherwise. Russia was separated from her friends by enemy- or ice-bound seas. She could neither readily import those manufactured products which her industrial backwardness did not allow her to make at home nor supply Great

Britain and France with the grain of which, for a time, she had a surplus.

Certain advantages were possessed by the Allies. They had a far greater reserve of man power than had the Central Powers; Russia alone had a population about as great as that of all the enemy countries combined. A similar situation prevailed with regard to economic and industrial resources. Germany's resources were capable of quicker and more efficient mobilization, but the Allies had much larger reservoirs upon which to draw. The Entente Powers knew that the longer the war lasted the greater would the disparity between the respective human and economic means become, and the more enhanced would be the Allied chances of victory.

As long as the British navy, the largest and strongest in the world, could maintain control of the seas, the Allies would be able to secure supplies from the neutral world and prevent Germany from doing likewise. The successful blockade of Germany eventually proved to be one of the deciding factors in the conflict and that feat was the contribution of British sea power. Financially, too, the Allies enjoyed the brighter prospects. With few exceptions, notably Great Britain, the European countries had stored up gold reserves to meet the needs of a possible future struggle. In addition, the Allies could readily float loans in neutral states. The funds realized through these flotations often remained in the lending countries, being spent immediately for war supplies.

During the First World War, as on no previous occasion, national psychology played a prominent part. In the warring countries the governments resorted to all known means to keep up the morale and spirit of troops and people. The task became increasingly difficult as the war dragged on, but the slogan-coiners became correspondingly more ingenious. Even more important than domestic propaganda was the need for "proper" presentation of the respective cases in neutral countries. Here the Allies had the advantage. Their propagandists were more skilled than the Germans, and they understood the psychology of the neutrals, particularly the Americans, better than did their enemies.

MILITARY OPERATIONS, 1914–1915

The German armies in August 1914 were under the supreme command of General Helmuth von Moltke. The German plan of

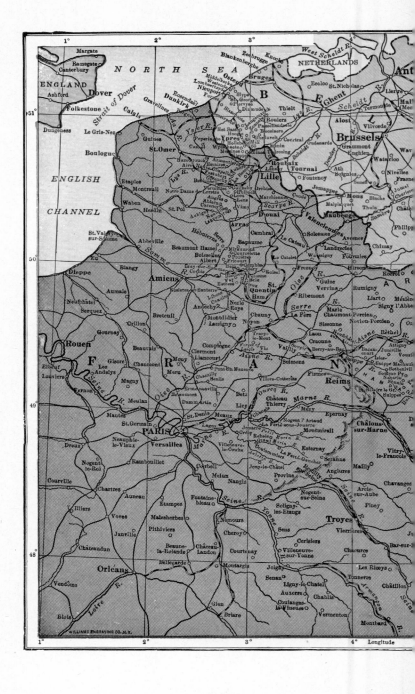

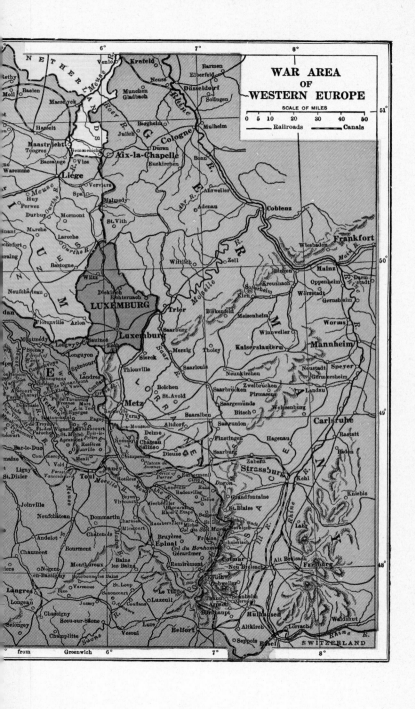

WAR AREA
OF
WESTERN EUROPE

SCALE OF MILES

0 5 10   20   30   40   50

———— Railroads   ———— Canals

campaign was Moltke's revision of one that had been drawn up by General Alfred von Schlieffen, chief of the general staff from 1891 to 1906. Schlieffen anticipated a war on two fronts and aimed at capitalizing Germany's superiority over Russia in speed of mobilization. Provision was therefore made for a relatively thin line of troops on the eastern frontier to hold up the presumedly slow-moving Russians, and for the immediate employment of a large force against France. But whereas Schlieffen had proposed that the German left wing pivot on the fortified area about Metz (where the chief French attack was expected) and that a powerful right wing circumvent the eastern French fortresses by sweeping through Belgium and a corner of the Netherlands into northern France, eventually to pass Paris on the west and fall on the main French army (that was expected to have entered Alsace-Lorraine) from the rear, Moltke strengthened the left wing at the expense of the right. Meanwhile Paris was to be prevented from aiding the French army by a besieging force of second-line troops. The official timetable allotted six weeks for this campaign. Thereafter, such soldiers as might be spared from the west were to be shipped eastward to subdue Russia.

In pursuance of this plan a German force advanced into Belgium early in August 1914, but before much progress could be made it was necessary to clear a path past well-fortified Liége. Here the Germans were held up for several days, but thanks to the skill of a staff officer soon to become famous as General Erich Ludendorff and the damaging effects of the sixteen-inch siege howitzers eventually brought up by the invaders, the passage was at last cleared. Thereafter, to the accompaniment of bloody fighting, the Germans continued through southeastern Belgium and reached the French border according to schedule. Meanwhile, believing that only offensive action was "in tune with French character and tradition," the French, under their Plan XVII, had poured across the border into Lorraine—only to be driven back in disorder. Instead of allowing the French to push back the German left wing, as Schlieffen had intended, so that the German right might swing into France all the faster, the Germans now launched an immediate counteroffensive in Lorraine. This succeeded only in driving the French to the fortified shelters of their own strongholds at Verdun, Toul, Epinal, and Belfort and the rough territory of the Vosges Mountains.

Despite the arrival of a British expeditionary unit and of French reënforcements, the Germans pushed steadily forward in Belgium, occupying Charleroi, Mons, Namur, Louvain, and Brussels as they went. By the end of August they had crossed into France and stormed Lille. They progressed through Picardy and Champagne in advance of the official timetable and forced the British-French-Belgian troops back on the whole line extending from Mons to Verdun. At the beginning of September the French retreated beyond the Marne River, the Germans were within fifteen miles of Paris, and the French Government fled to Bordeaux.

Marshall Joseph Joffre, the French commander-in-chief, influenced by General Joseph Galliéni, eventually decided to "resume the offensive" at the Marne. For five days, then, from September 6 to 10, there was fought a series of engagements called the First Battle of the Marne. The French were reënforced by troops released from duty on the southern frontier following Italy's declaration of neutrality and by a few thousand soldiers who were sent from Paris to the front in commandeered taxicabs. The Germans, on the other hand, were weakened by the dispatch of troops from the Marne to East Prussia, which was being overrun by the Russians. And it was the right wing—precisely that part of the line where Schlieffen had insisted on the greatest strength and where the brunt of the French attack now was aimed—which was called upon to release men for the emergency in the east. In the end, the Germans retreated in orderly fashion to the line of the Aisne River. Here they proceeded to "dig in" and organize behind a network of intricate trench and barbed-wire defenses—an innovation of modern warfare. At the end of the scheduled six weeks, therefore, the Germans, although in a dominant position, had failed to reach their goal.

After the Marne, both sides became aware of a large "gap" reaching approximately from an Arras-Antwerp line westward to the coast. Immediately there began a "race to the sea," a series of attempts by the Germans and the Allies to outflank each other and occupy the Channel ports. Had the Germans achieved this objective, they would have controlled all Belgium and been able to interfere seriously with British aid to France. For a time the Germans again seemed to be invincible, capturing Ghent, Bruges, Ostend, Zeebrugge, and Antwerp before the first fortnight of October had passed. But in Flanders, a little corner in southwestern Belgium and northwestern France, they were stopped at the First Battle of Ypres (termed "Wipers" by the British soldiers). Thereafter the Allies continued to hold a strip of Belgium and to control the cities of Calais, Dunkirk, and Boulogne for the duration of the war. These were important assets from both the strategic and the psychological points of view.

During the winter of 1914–1915 the enemies consolidated their positions along the entire six-hundred-mile front from southwestern Belgium to the Alps. Occasional, indecisive trench engagements only served to bring out more clearly the state of deadlock that had been reached. The actual advantage was unquestionably with the invaders. They were in control of most of Belgium with its industrialized regions and of northern France with its coal and iron mines and steel works. The military rule of the occupied areas was harsh.

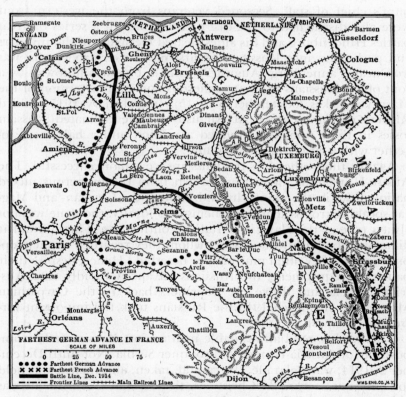

FARTHEST GERMAN ADVANCE IN FRANCE
SCALE OF MILES
0   25   50   75
●●●● Farthest German Advance
✕✕✕✕ Farthest French Advance
Battle Line, Dec. 1914
—·—·— Frontier Lines +++++ Main Railroad Lines

In the meantime the Russians had mobilized more rapidly than either their foes or their allies had anticipated and had sent two large forces against Germany and Austria-Hungary. Generals Paul von Rennenkampf and Alexei Samsonov advanced westward and northward into East Prussia while General Alexei Brussilov and others pushed westward and southward into Austrian Galicia.

So swift was the progress of the tsar's troops that enthusiasts in the Russian capital, the name of which was patriotically changed from St. Petersburg to its Russian equivalent of Petrograd, raised a prize of $100,000 for the first Russian soldier to set foot in Berlin. In alarm the German Government called upon General Paul von Hindenburg to stop the invader.

Hindenburg had been retired because of old age in 1912 (he was born in 1847), but he was regarded as the leading authority on the strategy and military geography of East Prussia and he responded at once to his country's call. General Erich Ludendorff, a younger man and an able strategist, was appointed Hindenburg's chief of staff. Seasoned veterans from the western front were also dispatched to the east at this time. In a series of great battles Hindenburg and his aides cleared Germany of the invaders and pushed on into Russia. The first major German victory was won near Tannenberg (August 26 to 31). This was followed by a rout of the Russians in the treacherous and swampy region of the Masurian Lakes (September 5 to 15). In February 1915 a third Russian defeat occurred, at Augustovo. The estimated Russian losses in these campaigns totaled a million and a half men, together with a large number of guns.

Against their other foes the Russians were more successful. The Austro-Hungarian forces were drawn from the numerous mixed nationalities in the monarchy and, though the German- and Magyar-speaking troops acquitted themselves loyally, the same was not always true of the Slavic and Italian contingents. These found it difficult to be faithful to leaders whom they regarded as their oppressors and they often mutinied or deserted.[1] Hence, despite their paucity of equipment, the Russians advanced rapidly into Austrian Galicia and drove the defenders back to the Carpathian Mountains. In March 1915 the Russians took the important fortress of Przemysl.

The need to send all available men against Russia made it impossible for Austria-Hungary to conquer Serbia. Not until December 2, 1914, was Belgrade, the capital, taken, and then it was held for only two weeks. By Christmas, the Serbian Government was able to return to Belgrade and before the year was up the invaders were pushed back across the border. The Serbs, however, were unable to fulfill their desire to penetrate into the provinces of Bosnia and Hercegovina.

---

[1] It was estimated that one hundred thousand Czechs and Slovaks were fighting in Allied ranks by 1916.

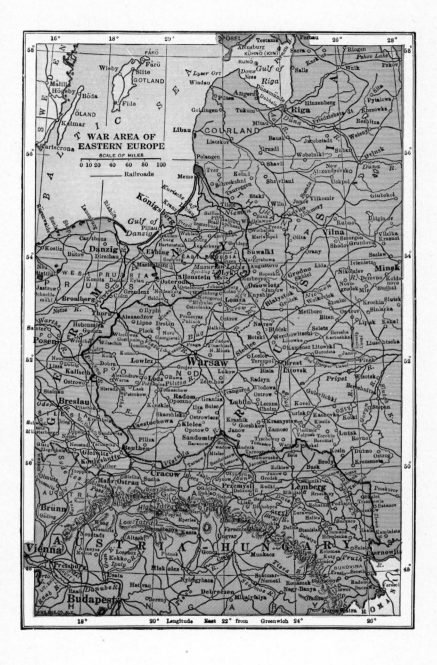

In the spring of 1915 the campaigns on the nine-hundred-mile eastern front were vigorously renewed by the Central Powers. As soon as the weather permitted, Hindenburg pushed further eastward. At the same time the German General August von Mackensen, who had been given command over a combined Austro-German force, planned the expulsion of the Russians from Galicia. From May 15 to 17 Mackensen's men were victorious in the Battle of the San, and in the course of a few weeks the Russians were made to give up the conquests of the previous nine months. By September the tsar's troops were cleared out of all but the eastern tip of Galicia, had been driven from Russian Poland, and had been ousted from Courland and most of Lithuania along the Baltic. Their casualties were enormous and their supplies were ebbing quickly. Only one rifle was available for every three recruits in training behind the lines and the ammunition supplies were nearing exhaustion. Russia required almost a year to recover from the blows of 1915.

Matters became still worse for the Allies when Bulgaria joined the Central Powers in October 1915 and coöperated with Mackensen and his Austro-Germans in a combined drive on Serbia. Within two months the kingdom was conquered. The same fate soon befell Montenegro and in the spring of 1916 the war was carried down into (neutral) northern Albania.

The acute shortage of materials in Russia led, in 1915, to the conception of an Allied attack on the Gallipoli Peninsula and the Dardanelles in order to open a direct path of communications among the various Entente Powers. Such a venture might simultaneously divert some of the Turkish troops who were harassing Russia from the south, make easier the Allied campaigns in Mesopotamia, and, if successful, isolate Turkey from her friends and encourage some of the still neutral Balkan states to throw in their lot with the Allied group.

A powerful Franco-British fleet was sent to the region and on February 19, 1915, the defenses at the entrance to the Dardanelles were subjected to a heavy bombardment. The forts soon were demolished and the ships sailed into the Narrows. Here, however, the vessels met disaster because of floating mines and the efficient fire of Krupp guns concealed behind massive, German-planned fortifications. After the loss of several ships and several thousand men the Allied fleet withdrew. There followed an attack by land, under the leadership of Sir Ian Hamilton. The attacking force consisted chiefly of French and British colonial troops and of the

"Anzacs" (Australian and New Zealand Army Corps). The men fought bravely and readily gained control of the plain on the peninsula, but they found it impossible to capture the fortified hills which commanded the plain. In the end, the Turks, well led though poorly supplied, were victorious. The attacking forces withdrew (December 1915–January 1916) and left the sultan in full control of the Straits. In April 1916 the Allies received the further disheartening news that the Turks had bottled up and captured General Charles Townshend with a few thousand men at Kut-el-Amara in Mesopotamia. It was only small consolation to the French and British that in the meantime they had occupied Salonika in neutral Greece.

While these things were going on in the east, there was relative quiet on the western front. Some attempts were made by both sides to break the deadlock in Flanders, but none of these assumed outstanding proportions. The Allies made some gains at Neuve Chapelle in March 1915, but the Germans counterattacked in the next month and precipitated the Second Battle of Ypres. Here, on April 22, the Germans made the first large-scale use of poison gas. The greenish chlorine clouds wreaked havoc among the unprotected British soldiers and a wide gap in the Allied lines was quickly created. The absence of any appreciable results on the few previous occasions when less poisonous vapors had been used had made the Germans skeptical of the value of the new gas and they were unprepared to take advantage of the hole in the Allied front. The lack of German reserves enabled the Allies to bring up sufficient British and Indian reënforcements to hold the contested ground. Further attempts of the Allies to push the enemy back in this region, in June and September, did little more than increase the toll of lives. The Germans, anxious to conserve man power for the big eastern drives, were content merely to hold their trenches. The entrance of Italy into the war, therefore, was the one high light in the Allied chronicles for 1915, though Italian aid did not assume formidable proportions for another twelve-month.

MILITARY OPERATIONS, 1916

As the year 1915 had witnessed a series of powerful offensives in the east, so 1916 was destined to be marked by big drives in the west. Each side launched one tremendous offensive, the Germans at Verdun, from February to July; the Allies at the Somme, from

June to November. The Germans had several reasons for attacking Verdun. The nominal German commander here was Crown Prince Frederick William. A big victory by his forces would do much to check any decline in Hohenzollern prestige in the fatherland. Moreover, Verdun was the greatest remaining French stronghold, the "heart of France." Its fall would probably mean an easy further German advance into French territory. In addition, if the French lost Verdun, the moral effect on both sides would be enormous. If, on the other hand, its capture could not be effected, France, thought the Germans, would at least be bled white and her people be ready to quit the war. Finally, French control of the Verdun region threatened both the German railway communications and the Lorraine iron fields, and this peril had to be removed.

On February 21, after weeks of secret preparation, the Germans opened their campaign with a terrific bombardment. More than one million shells, it is said, were hurled against the French from thousands of cannon within the first twelve hours of battle. Then, behind a protective "curtain of fire," the infantry advanced. At first progress was easy, for the shells had done their damage. But Verdun was a naturally fortified area, situated high and requiring attack from below. It was surrounded by a ring of auxiliary fortresses, all powerful and well designed. The French commanders several times wavered and contemplated withdrawal, but they permitted none of the men to discover their thoughts. Instead, the soldiers were urged to fight to the death, imbued with a spirit expressed in the words: "They shall not pass!"

In June the Germans were four miles from Verdun. As previously in the case of Paris, however, they were not *in* the city. They now found it necessary, moreover, to curtail further supplies of men and munitions in order to meet the Allied counteroffensive on the Somme. Hence, though they gained more than one hundred square miles of territory, the drive was a failure. Verdun was the second major check to the German advance as the Marne had been the first. This time the price in men was well over half a million on each side.

Costly and fierce as was the Verdun campaign, it was surpassed in number of men engaged, quantity of munitions used, casualties, and tactical difficulties by that of the Somme. Partly in order to relieve the pressure against Verdun and partly to make the most of simultaneous drives undertaken by the Russians and Italians, the British and French carefully prepared this offensive, whose strategic objectives were Bapaume and Péronne on either side of the Somme. During the first half of 1916 the British army had been strengthened through the introduction of conscription in Great Britain (January), and large stores of ammunition had been accumulated. In the last week of June the British began a bombardment of the German lines, utilizing more munitions "each day than the total amount manufactured in Great Britain during the first eleven months of the war."

In addition, the British in September brought into the fight a new weapon, the "tank." Lest the secret escape that a new weapon was being made in certain factories, the British War Office had let it be known that the government had ordered the manufacture of some tanks. In consequence, this inept name has continued in use as a designation for the armored cars which, running on caterpillar chains rather than wheels, are capable of passing over trenches and barbed wire, crossing muddy fields, and brushing aside shrubbery and trees with little danger of getting stuck or upsetting. Had the British refrained from using the tanks until large numbers thereof were available, the war might well have come to a quicker end, for the Germans at first were horrified by the strange steel monsters. As it was, the Germans themselves soon built a few tanks and devised effective antitank guns and land mines.

The Battle of the Somme netted the Allies more than one hundred square miles of land but failed to give them Bapaume and Péronne. On the other hand, the Germans were driven back several miles, were forced to ease the pressure on Verdun, and were prevented from sending any of the western troops to meet the advancing Russians in the east. The total loss of lives in this "titanic grapple," as Ludendorff called it, was estimated at more than one and a quarter million. Well over half the casualties were suffered by the Allies, but the latter were far better able than the Germans to afford great losses in man power. Indeed, the terrible cost in killed and wounded convinced a number of German officers that any undue prolongation of the conflict would make German defeat inevitable.

The year of the two great drives on the western front also witnessed the first great campaign on the Austro-Italian front. Here the terrain provided enormous difficulties. The Austrian province of Trentino was a salient protruding into Italy, but the territory was so mountainous that the fighting there soon resolved itself into a "series of machine-gun duels above the clouds for the possession of strategic hilltops," a veritable "combat in three dimensions amid the eternal snows." Sometimes, indeed, cannon had to be dragged thousands of feet up rough mountainsides by sheer man power. To the east of this mountainous region was the Italian province of Venice, extending northward as far as the Carnic Alps. South of Venice were the Gulf of Venice and the Adriatic Sea, while on its east lay the Isonzo plain and the Julian Alps, rugged mountains from which heavy artillery could command the approaches from all sides.

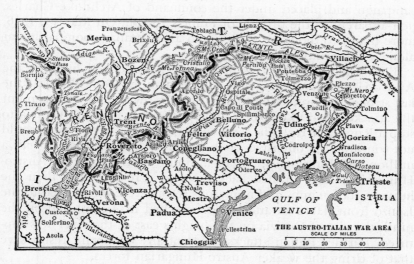

THE AUSTRO-ITALIAN WAR AREA
SCALE OF MILES
0 5 10   20   30   40   50

While the Austro-Hungarians, for the sake of conserving men, temporarily remained on the defensive, the Italian commander, General Luigi Cadorna, drew up a plan of campaign for an attack along the Isonzo River. It seemed to him better to launch the first movement eastward than to head into the inhospitable mountains of the Trentino. Because of Italy's poor state of preparation and the bad weather, the campaign did not start until some weeks after the country's entry into the war. Then, in June and July 1915, the First Battle of the Isonzo was fought. Despite large losses, the Italians gained little by their attack. A second campaign was launched in October and carried on until December. The defenders had better artillery than the Italians, but the latter outnumbered the former two to one. Again the Italians had virtually nothing to show for their sacrifices. Trench warfare now set in and continued until the following May.

Late in 1915 the Austrians had suggested to the German High

Command a combined attack on Italy. This idea had been spurned by the Germans and was again objected to when revived by the Austrians in 1916. Now, however, the latter determined to proceed with attack plans on their own account. They decided to launch a campaign from the Trentino salient and penetrate into the Venetian plain through which ran two railway lines. If the attack succeeded, the Italian flank would be broken and the railways, which brought men and supplies to the Isonzo front, would be captured. Four hundred thousand men were gathered for the campaign and placed under the command of Archduke Charles, heir-apparent to the thrones of Francis Joseph. On May 14, 1916, more than two thousand guns began a preliminary bombardment along a thirty-mile front.

The Italians fell back as had been expected and by June the Austro-Hungarians were only eighteen miles from Vicenza, the last stronghold protecting the northern railway line. At this point the attackers had to dispatch some of their divisions to Galicia to stop a Russian drive. The weakened remainder of the force could not continue the offensive. Soon Cadorna, having received half a million reënforcements, began a counteroffensive. The Austro-Hungarians were pushed back into the Trentino and then the heaviest Italian guns and numerous troops were transferred to the Isonzo front. Here an attack was launched in August and on the ninth the city of Gorizia on the heights east of the river was captured. Further Italian attacks failed of any important result save that of tiring the weaker Austro-Hungarian forces.

The emergency in Galicia that had necessitated the withdrawal of Austrian troops from Italy was the Brussilov campaign, opened on June 4, 1916. This offensive—the last great effort of Russia in the war—was originally planned for July. The Russian command felt that a smashing victory could be won if the country had until then to recover from the earlier defeats. But the French asked for a Russian offensive to relieve the German pressure on Verdun and the Italians pleaded for a Russian attack to force Austria to release her grip on Venice. It was in answer to these requests that Brussilov undertook his campaign prematurely.

The Austro-Hungarians were the victims of complete surprise. Many of their heavy guns and several divisions had recently been shifted to the Italian sector. Consequently the Russians were able to advance with relatively little opposition. They once more conquered eastern Galicia, occupied Bukovina, and headed toward Lemberg. Before the attack was spent, more than three hundred thousand men and four hundred guns were captured. The Russians themselves were astonished by the speed of their progress and they had not enough reserves at hand to follow up the victories. Their reserves were far away to the north and the north-south railway communications were inadequate. On the other hand, the Austrians soon rushed back some of their troops and guns from Italy. German reënforcements also arrived and command was

Scale of miles

0   25   50   75   100   125   150

Farthest Russian advance, 1915
Farthest German advance, 1915, 1917
Result of Brussilov's Drive, 1916

THE EASTERN FRONT, 1914–1917

taken over by the German Generals von Mackensen and Erich von Falkenhayn.

The Russian advance hence was quickly checked, but the hopes of the Allies were renewed when Romania espoused their cause in August. Again the optimistic outlook was destined to be short-lived. Romania was included in a vigorous Teutonic counter-offensive and, while Mackensen attacked with a Bulgarian force from the south, Falkenhayn hammered away at the new enemy from the west and north. Within less than four months the Romanian capital fell and, when the new year (1917) dawned, only a small northeastern corner of the kingdom remained unconquered. This triumph was all the more important to the Central Powers since they now were able to avail themselves of the large Romanian wheat crop and oil resources.

MILITARY OPERATIONS, 1917

Early in 1917 the position of Germany appeared fairly strong. In the previous August, Hindenburg, now a field marshal, had been given supreme command over all forces of the Central Powers. Ludendorff, as quartermaster general, was his chief of staff and the directing genius. Serbia, Montenegro, Romania, Poland, most of Belgium, northern France, all were in German hands. Russia was beaten down and the Italians were barely holding their ground. In April, however, the Allies had cause to rejoice —when the United States entered on their side. For about a year the United States rendered aid chiefly in the form of money, supplies, war and merchant vessels, and heightened morale. But after the following April American soldiers were in the thick of the fight.

Activities on the western front in 1917 commenced with a strategic German retreat, involving the voluntary relinquishment of about one thousand square miles of territory. The purpose of the retreat was to straighten and strengthen the battle line and to effect economies in men. This last was an important consideration with the Germans, since they had only 2,500,000 men in France with whom to oppose the Allies' 3,900,000. During their retreat the Germans destroyed everything that lay between their old position and the new line. The latter, a marvel of defensive strength, followed the direction Lens-St. Quentin-Reims. To the Germans it was known as the "Siegfried Line." The Allies called it the "Hindenburg Line."

All the offensive movements in the west in 1917 were undertaken by the Allies. In April the British launched an attack near Arras and the French one near Laon. Despite certain initial successes—the British took Vimy Ridge and the French both ends of the Chemin des Dames—the net results hardly justified the tremendous losses, particularly those of the French. The latter were led by General Robert Nivelle, who had achieved prominence at Verdun and had succeeded Joffre as commander-in-chief in December 1916. Joffre had been replaced because some groups in France had wearied of his cautious tactics which contemplated defeating Germany by a slow process of attrition of men and materials. Nivelle favored entirely different methods. He envisaged broader objectives, advocated the end of trench fighting, and promised speedy victory. He was vigorously supported by the new prime minister of Great Britain, David Lloyd George, and by Senator Georges Clemenceau of France, men themselves active and aggressive.[1]

Unfortunately for Nivelle, a number of factors militated against his success. The Germans everywhere occupied the commanding positions. They were aware of some of his plans through the capture of prisoners with documents. The morale of the French troops was poor, for numerous abuses had crept into the French military system and the soldiers regarded Nivelle's tactics as unnecessarily wasteful of human life. In May sixteen corps were affected by mutinies, though this intelligence was kept from the people by censorship. Nivelle soon was replaced by General Henri Philippe Pétain who was more expert in the art of handling men. Under the new leader trench duty was more nearly equalized, rest camps were established, more extensive leaves of absence were granted (some of the soldiers had been without leave for two years), the discipline was made less harsh, with the aid of the American Red Cross the wounded were better cared for, and Pétain himself went on visiting tours to the officers and men. Only twenty-three of the mutineers were executed and upwards of one hundred were deported to the colonies. For the remainder of the year 1917 French efforts were confined to minor attacks along the Meuse and Aisne rivers and to the recapturing of small areas around Verdun and Soissons.

The British were somewhat more active. From July to November they fought the Third Battle of Ypres, eventually taking Passchendaele Ridge, a highly prized observation post. Then,

---

[1] In November 1917 Clemenceau became premier and war minister of France.

later in November, without a preliminary bombardment, they launched a powerful drive at Cambrai, utilizing a fleet of nearly four hundred tanks. Rapid headway was made, but a German counterattack soon recovered most of the lost ground. Thus ended the campaigns of 1917 in the west. Few tactical or geographical gains were made by either side.

Even more discouraging to the Allied cause than the French mutinies and the costliness of the few small successes was the collapse of Russia. Conditions in the Russian army, always bad, became shocking after the defeats of 1916. Discipline was broken down and the men were suspicious of their officers, often considering them to be responsible for the continuation of the war. The peasant soldiers wanted to return home to their fields, many of which by this time stood greatly in need of cultivation. Other soldiers were anxious to return to their families, who were suffering want and needed providers. Simultaneously, the people behind the lines, especially the middle and working classes, became indignant over the short-sightedness, corruption, and repression that characterized official action.

The moderates among the discontented elements were strong enough to bring about the abdication of Tsar Nicholas II in March 1917 and the establishment of a liberal provisional government under Prince George Lvov. But military defeats continued, there was agitation for further changes, and the extreme radicals, known as Bolsheviks, organized councils or "soviets" of soldiers, workmen, and peasants, which demanded recognition as representatives of the people. In the summer Lvov fell from power and the more radical Alexander Kerensky reorganized the government.

It was Kerensky's hope to reform Russia and at the same time carry on the war against the Central Powers. He realized that the Russian people would not consent to make further sacrifices unless convinced that they were being asked to fight for an ideal rather than for imperialist aggrandizement. Therefore he sought to bring about an Allied conference for the formulation of war aims which would envisage a peace "without annexations and without indemnities." His frantic appeals unheeded by the Allies, Kerensky determined to launch one last, desperate offensive. Brussilov was replaced as commander-in-chief by General Lavr Kornilov, a shadow of discipline was restored among the troops, and a new drive was planned for July 1917.

The offensive was doomed to failure. Enemy agents had fomented a spirit of mutiny in and behind the lines. Bolshevik representatives had been equally diligent in spreading the contagion of desertion and disobedience. The soldiers sometimes organized debate meetings on whether or not to carry out their orders. The plan of campaign apparently was betrayed to the enemies. Consequently the Austro-Hungarians soon repelled those Russians who remained loyal and drove them out of Galicia and Bukovina before the end of August. The Germans similarly drove back the enemy and in September captured the city of Riga and pushed into Estonia. Meanwhile the Bolsheviks made further capital of the new military reverses and rallied great numbers to their cause by shouting the slogans "Peace! Land! Bread!" and "All power to the soviets!" In November the Kerensky Government was overthrown and the Bolsheviks, led by N. Lenin and Leon Trotsky, came into power.[1]

A few days later the Bolsheviks suggested to the Allies the conclusion of a general armistice and the termination of the war by a treaty embodying the principles of "no annexations and no indemnities" and "self-determination" for *all* subject peoples. The Allies, confident that the Russian people would repudiate the November Revolution, paid no attention to this proposal and, in fact, refused to recognize the Bolshevik Government. The latter then agreed to a separate armistice with the Central Powers on December 15. One week later a peace conference assembled at Brest-Litovsk, attended by delegates from Germany, Austria-Hungary, Bulgaria, Turkey, and Russia. The peace arrived at was a dictated one, but the Bolsheviks faced the alternatives of accepting the harsh German terms or suffering further invasion of Russia. Signatures were affixed on March 3, 1918.

Under the provisions of the Treaty of Brest-Litovsk the Russians agreed (1) to refrain from spreading propaganda in the lands owned or occupied by the Central Powers; (2) to evacuate the Armenian provinces of Kars, Ardahan, and Batum, which were to be reorganized "in agreement with the neighboring states, especially with Turkey"; (3) to evacuate Estonia, Livonia, Finland, and the Åland Islands; (4) to give up Poland, Courland, and Lithuania, their future status to be determined by the Central Powers "in agreement with their populations"; and (5) to clear the Ukraine of Russian troops, recognize and make peace with the newly established Ukrainian People's Republic, and recognize a peace treaty made between this republic and the Central Powers.

[1] For a detailed discussion of these events, see Chapter XIX.

By supplementary treaties of August 1918 Russia was obliged to pay an indemnity of $1,500,000,000, accord Germany most-favored-nation commercial treatment, and refrain from prohibiting or taxing the export of rough or hewn timber. Altogether, the Russians agreed to give up about five hundred thousand square miles of territory and sixty-six million people.[1]

With Russia out of the war, the cause of Romania was hopeless. Consequently, in May 1918, she accepted the Treaty of Bucharest. The Dobruja and the Carpathian foothills and passes were surrendered. Important oil concessions were granted to the Central Powers and Romania agreed to revise her tariff schedules in their favor. Mohammedans and Jews were to be accorded equal rights with Christians in the kingdom. Romania was given permission to extend her control over the fertile Russian province of Bessarabia and to have free acess to the Black Sea over a designated route through the Dobruja.

The year of Russia's defection was notable also for the near-collapse of another Allied power, Italy. There the troops in the line, the workers in the munition factories, and the civilians were all dissatisfied with the progress of the war. They were tired of the constant sacrifices which led to no appreciable military gain and, besides, they had no particular grievance against Germany. The example set by the Russians created a strong impression and agents of the Central Powers effectively spread germs of sedition. The Germans were well aware of the "defeatist" spirit in Italy and decided to turn it to their direct advantage through a surprise offensive at one of the most difficult and least expected points along the front.

Under the command of the German General Otto von Below, and "stiffened" by the reënforcement of six German divisions, the Austro-Hungarians began a terrific gas and shell bombardment on the Julian front on October 24, 1917. A breach was effected at Caporetto and within four days Cividale and Gorizia had been taken, Udine was threatened, one hundred thousand men and seven hundred guns had been captured, and the Italians were hastening back toward the Piave River in unparalleled confusion

[1] The Germans rapidly established their control over the northern areas given up by Russia. The throne of Finland was offered to Prince Charles of Hesse, brother-in-law of the German Emperor; William II himself became king of Estonia; and Lithuania was presented to Prince William of Urach. A pro-German government was set up in the Ukraine which, by the so-called Bread Peace, surrendered forty-two thousand wagonloads of grain to the Central Powers. After the war, all these states became republics.

and rout. By November 11, after the loss of another one hundred and fifty thousand prisoners and eleven hundred guns, the Italian army was forced south of the river.

There, however, the retreat came to an end. French and British

AFTER BREST-LITOVSK, 1918

Surrendered by
Russia in treaty
of Brest-Litovsk

Atlantic
Ocean

NORWAY

SWEDEN

DENMARK

Gulf of Bothnia

ALAND IS.
(FIN.)

FINLAND

G. of Finland

ESTONIA

LIVONIA

COURLAND

LITHUANIA

Baltic Sea

GERMANY

POLAND

SWITZERLAND

ITALY

AUSTRIA-
HUNGARY

ROMANIA

RUSSIA

UKRAINE

Black Sea

From *War Atlas,* Headline Book No. 23,
Foreign Policy Association, New York, 1940.

troops were hurriedly dispatched to Italy to bolster the resistance of the defenders; Cadorna was replaced by Armando Diaz, who better understood the psychology of the soldiers; and the line was strengthened by the injection of enthusiastic boys of seventeen and eighteen. The sudden danger to the country created, behind the lines, a patriotic feeling of unity which rapidly displaced the earlier spirit of defeatism. The Austro-Germans, on the other hand, had outrun their food and supply transport and were weary with the burden of rapid and sustained offense. Despite the loss of more than six hundred thousand effectives in the "Caporetto Disaster," the Italians now were able to regain some of the lost ground. Before much could be accomplished, the snowfall put an end to the fighting for the year.

Only in the Near East could the Allies boast of success in 1917, for there the earlier defeat of General Townshend was amply avenged. In March, General F. Stanley Maude took Baghdad. In December, General Edmund Allenby entered Jerusalem. Through skillful propagandist activities and vague promises of political advantage the British had succeeded in weaning a number of chieftains in Mesopotamia, Syria, Palestine, and Hejaz from their loyalty to the Turkish Sultan, their temporal and spiritual overlord. Prominent in this diplomatic aspect of the war was Colonel Lawrence, a young Oxford graduate who had learned several Arabic dialects while at work on archaeological excavations in Syria and Mesopotamia.

COLONIAL, NAVAL, AND AERIAL OPERATIONS

The war in the German colonies, except in the case of German East Africa, was of short duration. Kiaochow in China, as has been indicated, was captured by the Japanese in 1914. In the same year British ships, with aid from Japan, Australia, and New Zealand, seized all German islands in the Pacific. Togoland, in Africa, was taken by British and French colonial forces in 1914, and the Cameroons in 1916. German South West Africa was conquered in 1915 by General Jan C. Smuts, who first had to help put down a rebellion of Boers under Christian De Wet in the Union of South Africa. German East Africa, under Paul von Lettow-Vorbeck, held out against forces drawn from South Africa, the Belgian Congo, British East Africa, Rhodesia, India, and Portuguese East Africa until November 14, 1918—three days after the signing of the armistice.

The German navy was not nearly so well prepared for conflict when the war broke out as was the army. The extensive construction programs outlined in the navy laws of 1898 and 1900 had not yet been completed and the superiority of British sea power was an unquestioned fact. Similarly, the French navy was larger than that of Austria-Hungary. The German Admiralty therefore withdrew its high-seas fleet into protected homeland waters, under the guns of the forts at Kiel and on Helgoland. It was planned to wait in port until the opportunity should arise for a successful, concentrated attack on a section of the British fleet.

In the meantime the British blockade was established against Germany. The German merchant marine was swept off the seas and the vessels were either captured or interned. The same fate overtook the German naval vessels that happened to be located at outlying points when hostilities began. Thus, a squadron of cruisers under Admiral Maximilian von Spee, while attempting to return home from the Pacific, met and defeated a British squadron near Coronel off the coast of Chile (November 1, 1914), only to be itself destroyed a few weeks later off the Falkland Islands by a British fleet under Admiral Frederick Sturdee.

In the early months of the war the Germans attempted some raids against British coastal towns. In November 1914 a battlecruiser squadron attacked the British coast off Norfolk and in December another bombarded the Yorkshire coast. Both fleets returned home safely after doing considerable damage. A third raiding squadron got into a fight with a British fleet off Dogger Bank in January 1915 and was forced to return with some losses. Slightly more successful than these activities were the exploits of isolated commerce raiders, generally fast, light cruisers. Distinction in this class was won by the *Möwe* which, in fifteen months, sank or captured thirty-eight ships, and by the *Emden*, which operated in the Indian Ocean.

These feats, spectacular though they were, could hardly starve out the British. Great Britain's blockading policy, on the other hand, was fairly successful in cutting off Germany's imports. Hence the Germans, at the insistence of Grand Admiral Alfred von Tirpitz, tried to accomplish their end by means of the U-boat. The international difficulties with neutrals into which Germany was plunged as a result of the activities of this type of craft have already been discussed. Of the efficacy of the submarine as a weapon, at least temporarily, there could be no doubt. In April 1917, the banner month for submarines, one ship of every four that left the British Isles was torpedoed. Altogether, German undersea boats sank more than five thousand Allied and neutral merchant and fishing vessels. Surface craft and mines accounted for about seven hundred more, so that the total of destroyed tonnage approached the fifteen-million mark. About two hundred German submarines were destroyed.

Before the struggle ended, the Allies had devised several successful counterweapons against the submarines. Hydrophones were developed which betrayed the presence of the undersea craft while it was still miles away. Effective depth bombs were invented and heavy mine barrages laid. Wire netting was stretched across the English Channel. Merchant vessels were escorted by powerful convoys, especially after the services of the United States Navy became available. The American "Mystery" or "Q-ships" lured unwary U-boats to their destruction. The art of camouflage was perfected so that even large vessels became almost indistinguishable at short distances. The Germans, incidentally, had a limited number of trained submarine crews and the strenuous duties quickly exhausted the men.

The only large naval engagement of the war was the Battle of Jutland, or, as the Germans call it, Skagerrak (May 31 to June 1, 1916). The German High Seas Fleet at this time was commanded by Admiral Reinhard Scheer, a believer in aggressive action. Under his orders, Vice-Admiral Franz von Hipper sailed off in the morning of May 31, 1916, with a scouting squadron to attract part of the British Grand Fleet by a demonstration off the southwest coast of Norway. The British vessels were then to be attacked and annihilated by the main German fleet under Scheer, who followed Hipper at a distance of about fifty miles. It happened that the British were aware of the German plan to emerge from the base, though they were unfamiliar with the purpose of the maneuver. Accordingly a concentration of the British fleet in the North Sea had been ordered on May 30.

On the afternoon of the thirty-first, Hipper's scouting fleet came in accidental contact with a British scouting squadron under Vice-Admiral David Beatty. Hipper maneuvered to fall back toward the main fleet and Beatty simultaneously turned so as to draw the Germans toward the large British fleet under Admiral John Jellicoe. The latter came up with his ships late in the afternoon and succeeded in taking a position between the German fleet and its home base.

The resulting battle was the biggest in history up to that time from the point of view of tonnage and armament. The British had 151 ships, including 37 capital ships. Their opponents had 101 vessels, including 27 capital ships. Scheer, realizing the overwhelming strength of the British, determined merely to slip away from the enemy and make for the home port. During the night of May 31–June 1, accordingly, the Germans, aided by fog, eluded the British fleet. Altogether, the Germans lost 11 ships, with death to 2545 officers and men. The British lost 14 vessels, with death to 6097 officers and men. Great Britain, however, continued to exercise control of the seas.

The German fleet, despite its heavier armor and more accurate marksmanship, remained virtually inactive for the remainder of the war. Scheer made another sortie in August 1916 but returned when his Zeppelin scouts notified him that the British fleet stood ready to meet him. The last wartime sally of the German fleet was made in April 1918 in the direction of Norway. Again nothing was accomplished and the ships returned to port, this time because of an accident to the propeller of the battle cruiser *Moltke*.

Important among the many new weapons introduced during the war were the airships and airplanes. The Germans were first to make earnest use of airships against the enemy. Early in 1915 they began sending over to Great Britain large dirigible balloons or Zeppelins (named after their inventor, Ferdinand von Zeppelin) which dropped bombs over the coast towns. The late summer of 1916 witnessed an especially intensive Zeppelin campaign, but thereafter a rapid decline in the use of these raiders set in. They were large and offered easy targets to the antiaircraft guns that were developed. The invention of the explosive bullet, moreover, made impracticable the further employment of craft which depended for buoyancy on huge bags filled with gas.

The Zeppelins soon were replaced by the smaller, cheaper, and faster heavier-than-air craft or airplanes. These machines began making raids over England, particularly over London, from early in 1917 onward. Both sides quickly came to regard them as the "eyes" of their armies, reconnoitering the enemy lines, directing shellfire, warning of attack preparations, taking photographs of enemy positions, and scattering propaganda leaflets over enemy trenches and cities. Antiaircraft weapons were quickly developed and camouflage against air observations was practiced, but the craft remained useful.

Originally the aviators were equipped merely with pistols or rifles, but soon light machine guns were mounted in the planes. In May 1915 the twenty-five-year-old Netherlander, Anthony Fokker, invented an interrupter gear which made it possible for plane pilots to fire machine guns to the front without danger of having the bullets strike the propeller blades. For a time this de·

vice gave the Germans considerable air superiority over the Allies. In the beginning, air combats generally were single engagements in which individual pilots fought one another to the death. A chivalrous air code was developed and air "aces" became national heroes. Among the most distinguished of these aces were the Frenchmen, René Fonck and Charles Guynemer; Manfred von Richthofen, "the Red Knight of Germany"; and the American, Eddie Rickenbacker.

Single combat eventually gave way to organized squadron maneuvers, and regular battles occurred between enemy squadrons or "circuses" of from ten to fifty planes each. Every combat squadron was led by a squadron leader who picked his own pilots and who himself set an example of skill and daring. Such squadrons were also useful in harassing retreating columns of the enemy and impeding the advance of reserves.

POISON GAS AND PROPAGANDA

Though first successfully used by the Germans, poison gases soon became popular as weapons with both sides. Altogether, the belligerents experimented in the field with about three score gases or mixtures of gases. The effects in each case were either lethal or lacrimatory; the means of projection were hand- or rifle-grenades, toxic-smoke candles, artillery shells, minenwerfer, trench mortars, and aerial bombs or cylinders. Poison gases may be of the nonpersistent type, mingling with the air upon dispersion and quickly losing their effectiveness; or of the persistent type, lingering, upon dispersion, for hours or even days with continued strength and effectiveness. In the first class, used chiefly in the earlier days of the war, are found such sensory-irritant gases as lacrimators, sternutators, and vomiting gases, and such lung-irritant gases as chloropicrin, phosgene, and chlorine. Mustard gas (dichlorethylsulphide) is typical of the second class.

It is difficult to estimate the precise number of war casualties brought on by gas, since so many men were disabled by several agents. Besides, many of the men who were discharged from hospitals and died within a few years of their release probably did so as a direct or indirect result of their having been gassed. This inability to know exactly how many men were killed or badly affected by gas led the protagonists of chemical warfare to advertise gas as the most humane of weapons. Yet General A. A. Fries, head of the American Chemical Warfare Service in France, wrote:

Unquestionably many of those who died on the battlefield from other causes suffered also from gas. No other single element of war, unless you call powder a basic element, accounted for so many casualties among the American troops. Indeed, it is believed that a greater number of casualties was not inflicted by any other arm of the Service, unless possibly the infantry, and even in that case it would be necessary to account for all injured by bullets, machine-guns, and hand-grenades. This is true, in spite of the fact that the German was so nearly completely out of gas when the Americans began their offensive at St. Mihiel and the Argonne, that practically no gas casualties occurred during the St. Mihiel offensive, and only a very few until after a week of the Argonne fighting.[1]

The development of effective gas masks lagged somewhat behind the preparation of new gases and the masks offered only a fair amount of protection. Gases were developed which so irritated sensitive organs that the men in frenzy were forced to take off the masks and then the lethal gases were able to take quick effect. The Germans in 1917, for example, developed diphenylchloroarsine, which is atomized into fine particles upon explosion and which, in a concentration of as little as one part in ten million, causes sneezing cramps and burning sensations in nose, lungs, and throat. In stronger concentrations it causes severe vomiting. Considerable time was required before the masks used by the Allied troops were readjusted to secure immunity against this gas, which was projected in the notorious Blue Cross Shells.[2]

It has long been a commonplace that, "when war is declared, truth is the first casualty." Propaganda was not a new weapon during the war. It had been used for centuries as a means of converting people to desired viewpoints. As early as 1808 the Austrian Chancellor, Clemens von Metternich, had maintained that half a dozen of Napoleon's paid pamphleteers were worth as much to the French Emperor as an army of three hundred thousand men. On no previous occasion, however, had propaganda work been carried on in so widespread and scientific a manner as during the First World War. Every government gathered its propaganda experts into organized and supervised groups to work hard in order that

[1] Fries, A. A. and West, C. J. *Chemical Warfare,* 1921, p. 386. Reprinted by permission of the McGraw-Hill Book Company, Inc.

[2] In November 1932 Stanley Baldwin declared before the House of Commons: "There are some instruments so terrible that mankind has resolved not to use them. I myself happen to know of at least three inventions, deliberately proposed for use in the last war, that were never used—potent to a degree and inhuman." *Parliamentary Debates, Commons, 1931–1932,* v. 270, p. 638.

the country might be "educated and aroused as to the reason, justice, and necessity of the war." In each country an official propaganda bureau was erected: in Germany it was the *Kriegspresseamt;* Great Britain had her Crewe House, directed by Lord Northcliffe; in France it was *La Maison de la Presse,* supplemented by *Le Comité Catholique;* and in the United States George Creel supervised the activities of the Committee on Public Information. Toward the end of the war there was created an inter-Allied board, under the able direction of Northcliffe, to supervise the scientific propaganda system.

Atrocity tales were eagerly read by the people in all countries. Just as men and women in the Allied countries repeated the stories of how the Germans cut off babies' hands and attacked women, so the people in central Europe were anxious to hear about the latest French, Serbian, or Russian "atrocity," about the cigars filled with gunpowder which the Belgians were accused of offering to German soldiers, or the coffee and strychnine alleged to have been given by a French priest to a German sergeant. Faked photographs, with the caption "the camera cannot lie," were circulated throughout the world, and "in Vienna an enterprising firm supplied atrocity photographs with blanks for the headings so that they might be used for propaganda purposes by either side." The cinema also scored a great success as a vehicle of propaganda.

The following, from Arthur Ponsonby's *Falsehood in War-Time,* offers one of the most interesting examples of the "manufacture of news":

THE FALL OF ANTWERP

November 1914

When the fall of Antwerp got known, the church bells were rung (meaning in Germany).   *Kölnische Zeitung.*

According to the *Kölnische Zeitung,* the clergy of Antwerp were compelled to ring the church bells when the fortress was taken.
Le Matin (Paris).

According to what *Le Matin* has heard from Cologne, the Belgian priests who refused to ring the church bells when Antwerp was taken have been driven away from their places.   *The Times* (London).

According to what *The Times* has heard from Cologne via Paris, the unfortunate Belgian priests who refused to ring the church bells when Antwerp was taken have been sentenced to hard labor.
Corriere della Sera (Milan).

According to information to the *Corriere della Sera* from Cologne via London, it is confirmed that the barbaric conquerors of Antwerp punished the unfortunate Belgian priests for their heroic refusal to ring the church bells by hanging them as living clappers to the bells with their heads down.   *Le Matin*.[1]

Not only did the propaganda excite the necessary spirit of sacrifice among the various peoples but it led to much persecution. Arrests of and attacks on "enemy suspects" were frequent and brutal, and many an innocent person who happened to be cursed with a name of "enemy origin" found it expedient to change that name to something more "native." In the United States, grave suspicion attached to the housewife who absentmindedly attempted to purchase *sauerkraut* in the neighborhood delicatessen store, having forgotten that from the time of the entry of the land into the war that article of diet had become "liberty cabbage." German measles was rechristened "liberty measles." Truly, the "germs of hate" were widely and successfully spread.

PEACE MOVES AND WAR AIMS

Long before the armistice of November 1918 put an end to armed hostilities, a number of peace offers had been advanced by each side. The earliest important proffer of peace came from the Central Powers in December 1916. Thereafter, as defeatism and war-weariness among the peoples became progressively more marked, suggestions for ending the war followed one another in rapid succession. For a time, indeed, peace rather than victory was the cry of all who feared for the future of mankind.

The peace proposal of the Central Powers, made at a time (December 12, 1916) when they were generally victorious, and President Wilson's attempt, some days later, to secure a definition of war aims, have already been discussed.[2] The Allies, in reply, were content to stigmatize the German move as calculated more to sow dissension within their ranks than to end the war, and to publish in turn (January 1917) a series of peace demands based largely upon the Secret Treaties. Although the positions taken by the opposing diplomats were incompatible, Wilson made these moves the occasion for an optimistic speech to the Senate (January 1917) wherein he advocated a "peace without victory" and

[1] Reprinted by permission of E. P. Dutton & Co. and Geo. Allen & Unwin, Ltd.
[2] See pp. 36–37.

pledged the help of the United States in guaranteeing a just and lasting settlement.

About five months after Wilson's pronouncement, and two months after the entry of the United States into the war, there began to arrive in Stockholm, Sweden, delegates from the socialist parties and workers' organizations in Russia, Germany, Austria-Hungary, Bulgaria, and several neutral states, in order to discuss means whereby labor might help bring the conflict to a close. The corresponding bodies in the Allied countries (except Russia) were inclined at first to regard this move as a subtle phase of German propaganda, but when their suspicions were removed they selected delegates to represent Great Britain, France, Italy, and the United States. The governments of these four countries refused to issue the necessary passports to the delegates and in September 1917 the Stockholm conference broke up in failure.

On August 1, 1917, Pope Benedict XV issued a plea for a "just and durable" peace. He proposed the substitution in international affairs of the "moral force of right" for the "material force of arms," the restoration of all occupied territories, reciprocal forfeiture of indemnity claims, a guarantee of freedom of the seas, provision for the future settlement of international disputes by arbitration, a decrease in armaments, and a conciliatory settlement, involving plebiscites if necessary, of the rival territorial claims in such regions as Alsace-Lorraine, Poland, and the Trentino. Wilson, as spokesman for the Allies, replied to this plea by saying that the negotiation of peace on any condition with the Imperial German Government was out of question. Only when the German people repudiated their "irresponsible" government would the Allies consent to discuss peace. The Central Powers regarded with favor the general terms of the papal plan, but were silent on restorations and indemnities.

The Bolsheviks in Russia made an unsuccessful attempt to bring about immediate peace in 1917 by publishing the texts of the Secret Treaties to which Russia had been a party. In the same year came two important moves for peace from Austria-Hungary. Relations between the two leading Central Powers were no longer so cordial as they had been earlier in the war. Friction had developed between Austrian and German officers over such matters as the disposition of troops, the planning of campaigns, and the allotment of war materials. Upon the death of Francis Joseph in 1916, there came to the thrones of Austria-Hungary the young and inexperienced Charles, who viewed with alarm the increasing discontent and disloyalty of his subject nationalities. Some Austrians, fearing the preponderance of a victorious Germany, had come to add to 'the German plea, *Gott strafe England,* another—*Und schütze uns vor Deutschland!* It was not surprising, therefore, that Charles in the spring of 1917 should have attempted to achieve an immediate peace, even if that meant a separate peace. Charles asked his brother-in-law, Prince Sixtus of Bourbon-Parma, who had served with the Belgian army, to convey to President Poincaré the emperor-king's readiness to recognize the "just claims" of France to Alsace-Lorraine and to agree to the complete restoration of Belgium and Serbia. However, nothing came of this incident. Similarly devoid of results was a general restatement of Austrian war aims in December, by Foreign Minister Ottokar Czernin.

On January 5, 1918, while the memories of Russia's defection and Italy's disaster were still fresh, Lloyd George explained his latest conception of the Allied war aims in a speech to British trade-union delegates. Although his stand now was more moderate than it had been on any previous occasion, the premier's demands still entailed great sacrifices on the part of the Central Powers and only gains for the Allies. The best known statement of war aims came from President Wilson on January 8, 1918. In an address to Congress, the President summarized his program in "Fourteen Points" as follows:

1. "Open covenants of peace, openly arrived at," and the abolition of secret diplomacy.

2. "Absolute freedom of navigation upon the seas, outside territorial waters, alike in peace and in war" except by international action.

3. "The removal, so far as possible, of all economic barriers [tariffs] and the establishment of an equality of trade conditions. . . ."

4. "Adequate guarantees . . . that national armaments will be reduced to the lowest point consistent with domestic safety."

5. "A free, open-minded, and absolutely impartial adjustment of all colonial claims" with proper consideration of the "interests of the populations concerned."

6. "The evacuation of all Russian territory and such a settlement of all questions affecting Russia as will secure the best and freest coöperation of the other nations of the world in obtaining for her an unhampered and unembarrassed opportunity for the independent determination of her own political development and national policy. . . ."

7. The evacuation and restoration of Belgium.

8. The evacuation and restoration of France and the return of Alsace-Lorraine.

9. "A readjustment of the frontiers of Italy should be effected along clearly recognizable lines of nationality."

10. The "freest opportunity of autonomous development" for the peoples of Austria-Hungary.

11. Evacuation and restoration of Romania, Serbia, and Montenegro; free access to the sea for Serbia; determination by friendly counsel of "the relations of the several Balkan states to one another"; and international guarantees of the economic and territorial integrity of the Balkan states.

12. Autonomous development for the non-Turkish possessions of the sultan and internationalization of the Dardanelles.

13. Resurrection of an independent Poland with access to the sea.

14. Formation of "a general association of nations . . . under specific covenants for the purpose of affording mutual guarantees of political independence and territorial integrity to great and small states alike." [1]

Several times throughout 1918 Wilson reiterated in one form or another the main views expressed in this program in an effort to convince the people both in the Allied and enemy countries that the Fourteen Points really were the aims for which the war was being continued. Thousands of copies of the points were scattered over German trenches and towns by Allied airplanes to shake the power of the Hohenzollern Government. The authorities in Great Britain, France, and Italy, however, never officially accepted all the points, though they did not protest against them during the conflict. Consequently a protracted quarrel between Wilson and the Allied statesmen was made inevitable at the forthcoming peace conference.

THE END OF MILITARY OPERATIONS, 1918

Early in 1918 Generals von Hindenburg and Ludendorff decided on a plan of campaign which, they hoped, would bring the war to a close within the year. Preparations, therefore, were immediately begun for the supreme German effort of the war. Veteran divisions were rushed to the western front from Russia and for the first time since the early days of the contest the Allied superiority in numbers was overcome. Indeed, the four hundred

[1] Wilson may have been influenced in the formulation of these points by Jeremy Bentham's *Plan for an Universal and Perpetual Peace*, 1786 (?).

thousand British casualties of 1917 had not yet been replaced and American troops were arriving at the rate of only twenty-five thousand monthly. The Germans accordingly hoped to end the struggle within four months—before the effect of American man power could make itself felt.

The first drive opened on March 21, 1918, along the fifty-mile sector Arras-St. Quentin-La Fère. The Germans planned to drive a wedge between the independently commanded British and French forces and to crowd the former back to the sea. Within a few days the British actually were driven back thirty-five miles, forced to relinquish fifteen hundred square miles of ground, and made to suffer three hundred thousand losses, including one hundred thousand prisoners. For a time it appeared as though the desired gap might be created, but the British line rallied and retreated without breaking. The dismay of the Allies over this setback was heightened when the Germans brought into action a four-hundred-thousand-pound gun that projected shells into Paris from a distance of seventy-five miles. This "Big Bertha," however, did more psychological than material damage.

One reason for the success of the German drive was the failure of General Pétain to hurry French reënforcements to the support of the British. The Allied leaders took the lesson to heart and were constrained at last to set up a unified command. It is true that in the previous November, after the Caporetto retreat, the British, French, and Italian premiers, gathered at Rapallo, had established a Supreme War Council to give unity to Allied efforts. But this was valuable more from the point of view of economic and financial coöperation than from that of military coördination. Consequently, on March 26, 1918, General Foch, who had achieved some successes and was known for his determination, was placed in command of all Allied forces in France. A few weeks later he was appointed commander-in-chief of the Allied armies. Thereafter one master strategist was supreme, although the various national commanders retained direct control over their individual forces.

Unified command greatly strengthened the Allied military machine. Additional support came from the action of the British in passing a stricter conscription law and sending across the Channel 355,000 men in one month. Conscription, or the draft, had also been introduced into the United States by the Selective Service Act of May 1917, and in 1918 men were called and prepared for duty at an amazingly rapid rate. In response to urgent appeals by the French, 675,000 men were sent to Europe between April and July 1918. On April 28, 1918, an American division for the first time was assigned to an active fighting sector, in Picardy. The American commander-in-chief, John J. Pershing, resolutely refused to permit the use of his troops as fillers for casualty gaps in British or French units. He insisted that the Americans be assigned to fight as distinct and unbroken units even if that necessitated longer periods of battle acclimatization along quiet sectors. For this stand Pershing was accused by his Allied colleagues of having a noncoöperative temperament and of seeking personal glory, but in the United States his course was approved.

Meanwhile, on April 9, Ludendorff had launched a second drive against the British—this time west of Lille, between La Bassée and Armentières—the objective again being the Channel ports. The defenders, under Sir Douglas Haig, lost Armentières and Passchendaele and were driven back fifteen miles. The Béthune and Ypres salients, however, were held, and thus the ports were saved.

Their partial successes fired the Germans on to still greater efforts. With men discharged from hospitals and boys from the class of 1920, Ludendorff soon replaced almost three-fourths of his recent losses and was able to strike a third sledge-hammer blow, on May 27. On this occasion the brunt of the attack fell on the French, between Soissons and Reims. In two days Soissons fell. Soon thereafter the Marne was reached, but not crossed. Château-Thierry was captured. Paris was only forty-four miles away. Then the advance was checked. Reims held out, and the thousands of Americans hastily thrown into the line by Foch stopped the foe. In the region of Belleau Wood, the Americans regained some lost ground. A renewed German onslaught between June 9 and 15 netted only a six-mile gain between Montdidier and Noyon.[1]

With the courage of despair the Germans launched a fourth, and, as it happened, last drive in the middle of July. Reims was the first objective, and from July 15 to 18 the battle for the city raged. Between Château-Thierry and Epernay the Americans fought with a stubbornness that amazed the Germans, and at the point of their farthest advance the latter gained only six miles. Then their strength was spent. On July 18 the last German drive of the war merged into a great Allied counteroffensive. This was

---

[1] On May 28 the first offensive undertaken by an American unit resulted in the recapture of the strategic position of Cantigny.

followed by a series of relentless assaults that came to an end only with the signing of an armistice in November.

When Foch issued his orders for the counteroffensive in July, there were about 1,000,000 Americans in France. During the next few months additional troops arrived at an average rate of 10,000 per day. In November, therefore, the American soldiers in France numbered 2,085,000. War materials also were sent over in enormous quantities, and, thanks to the vigilance of the Anglo-American sea patrol, transport casualties and losses were few. Accordingly, Foch had no need to worry about conserving man power. He could press assault after assault without letup and without allowing the Germans to rest.

The initial encounter of the new offensive was the Second Battle of the Marne, which raged from July 18 to August 7 and in which 85,000 Americans participated. At its conclusion, Château-Thierry and Soissons were once more in Allied hands and the Germans had been forced to retire behind the Aisne-Vesle River. August 8, according to Ludendorff "the black day of the German army," saw the launching of another powerful attack along the Somme in Picardy and the Germans were driven back ten miles along the whole line. Before the end of the month, Montdidier, Bapaume, and Noyon had been retaken and 130,000 prisoners captured. Péronne fell on the first of September, Lens on the fourth. Two weeks later a force of more than 500,000 Americans wiped out the St. Mihiel salient near Verdun.

As September drew to a close the cause of Germany seemed hopeless. The Hindenburg Line was cracking. The morale of the troops was breaking. Supplies of munitions and food were rapidly dwindling. Revolutionary tremors were felt behind the lines. The submarine campaign was an obvious failure. Ludendorff's confidence was shaken and on September 29, following the receipt of news of impending collapse in Bulgaria, he had a nervous attack. On that day he informed the emperor at a Spa conference that the war was lost. Two days later Hindenburg insisted that Germany make a peace offer, and on October 3 the liberal-minded Prince Max of Baden was appointed chancellor. The prince took two socialists into his cabinet—the first such instance in the history of the empire. He then entered into negotiations with President Wilson for peace terms, expressing his satisfaction with the principles laid down in the Fourteen Points and stressing the circumstance that Germany was in process of being transformed into a democratic monarchy. Wilson, however, continued the exchange of notes for another month, intimating that Germany must drop the Hohenzollerns.

While the diplomats negotiated, the Allied soldiers continued their advance. St. Quentin, Cambrai, Lille, Laon were invested in rapid order and by the end of October few Germans were left in France. Some of the hardest fighting had occurred in the difficult terrain of the Meuse-Argonne region, where 1,200,000 Americans had helped cut the main line of German communications at Sedan. One-fifth of the entire battle line was at this time manned by Americans.

THE WESTERN FRONT, 1914 AND 1918

Bad as was the situation of Germany, the plight of her allies was worse. In June the Austro-Hungarians started a last desperate offensive in the hope of putting Italy out of the war. Unfortunately for the attackers, General Diaz gained knowledge of the plans and was prepared to meet the shock. At first the Austrians were able to advance a few miles. Then the Piave River suddenly overflowed and the torrents of water swept away ten of the fourteen bridges, causing panic among the invaders. Diaz now brought into action huge reserve forces and the Austrians soon were made to retrace their steps. On October 24 an Italian offensive was launched against the Trentino. At Vittorio Veneto the Austro-Hungarian army was split and routed, and by November 3 the Italians were in possession of Trieste. They had taken three hundred thousand prisoners.

In the meantime, on September 30, Bulgaria had surrendered unconditionally and signed an armistice at Salonika. The withdrawal of German forces to France and of Austrians to Italy had so weakened the Bulgarians that they feared a Franco-Serbo-Greek invasion from the south. To avoid such a contingency they announced their willingness to quit the fray. In the armistice the Allies were accorded permission to use Bulgarian territory as a military base. Bulgaria's withdrawal served to isolate Turkey from the Central Powers and made the Ottoman Government panicky. Not only was there danger of an attack from the west on Adrianople and Constantinople, but in the east Damascus, Beirut, and Aleppo, all had fallen, and the enemy was fast marching on Mosul. Hence the sultan expressed a readiness to surrender. On October 31 the Armistice of Mudros was signed and Turkey, too, became available as a base for Allied operations.

These disasters to its eastern friends naturally had a fatal reaction on the Dual Monarchy, which was itself in process of disintegration because of the separatist activities of the subject nationalities. As early as July 20, 1917, some Southslavic political leaders in Austria-Hungary had signed a Pact of Corfu with the Serbs, agreeing to unite with the latter in a new Slavic state. In the autumn of 1918 the Hungarians, Czechs, Slovaks, and Poles declared their independence. These difficulties made it almost impossible for Emperor Charles to offer further resistance to the advancing Italians. On November 3, at Villa Giusti, his representatives agreed with General Diaz to an armistice, based upon unconditional surrender and effective the next day. Thereafter Germany was left to continue the struggle alone.[1]

Two days after Austria's surrender, President Wilson notified Prince Max that he might apply to Marshal Foch for armistice terms. The Allies were willing to end the fighting, not only to stop the carnage but because even Foch thought it might take "four or five months" before the Germans could be driven east of the Rhine. Doubtless the retreating troops, though not particularly anxious to get killed for the sake of prolonging the occupation of Belgium, would fight much harder when it was a question of de-

[1] For the details of the Austro-Hungarian collapse see Chapter XVII.

fending the fatherland against invasion. Foch, accordingly, proceeded to draw up armistice terms that would make it impossible for Germany to renew the war if she accepted the truce. It was made clear that the peace which presumably was to follow the armistice would be based upon an *amended* form of the Fourteen Points. The amendments (1) reserved to the Allies "complete freedom" at the expected peace conference on the subject of freedom of the seas; (2) so defined the "restoration" of invaded territories as to include damages done to the civilian populations and property by the Germans; and (3) converted the demand for autonomy for the subject peoples of Austria-Hungary into one for independence. On the eighth of November the terms were handed to Germany's delegates. Three days were allowed for unconditional acceptance.

The armistice terms included thirty-five clauses. Within fourteen days Germany was to evacuate France, Belgium, Alsace-Lorraine, and Luxembourg; and within a month all the territory west of the Rhine. Allied troops were to occupy the evacuated territory in Germany together with the Rhenish bridgeheads at Cologne, Coblenz, and Mainz to a depth of thirty kilometers east of the Rhine. The treaties of Brest-Litovsk and Bucharest were to be renounced, and all German troops withdrawn from Russia, Romania, Turkey, and Austria-Hungary. A specified number of warships and all submarines were to be surrendered, and within two weeks the Allies were to receive, in good order, 5000 locomotives, 150,000 railway cars, and 5000 motor lorries. All Allied prisoners of war were to be repatriated at once, without reciprocity, and the blockade against Germany was to remain in force. Large quantities of artillery and war materials were to be surrendered.

The days preceding the signing of the armistice were turbulent in Germany. Ludendorff was forced to resign on October 26. The navy mutinied. A separatist movement broke out in Bavaria. The emperor and crown prince fled to the Netherlands. Prince Max was forced out of the chancellorship and a group of socialists led by Friedrich Ebert took over the government of a new German Republic (November 9).[1] Since the socialists had no desire to continue or subsequently renew the war, they accepted the armistice terms as presented. At five o'clock in the morning of November 11, 1918, in a railway car in the dark Compiègne Forest, the appointed delegates signed the papers that were to end the First

[1] For details of the German Revolution see Chapter XVI.

World War. At eleven o'clock the slaughter officially ceased. Millions throughout the world again became almost hysterical with joy.

THE PRICE OF WAR

The First World War, which lasted 1565 days, was the bloodiest and costliest war that had yet been fought. During the conflict about 65,000,000 men were mobilized and forced to participate, for a longer or shorter time, in the economically unproductive activity of organized destruction. Of these men about 13,000,000— one in five—died in action or of wounds. Approximately 22,000,- 000—one in three—were wounded, and of these, 7,000,000 were permanently disabled. A number of the wounded died within a few years after the war as a consequence of their disabilities, while many shell-shocked or gassed veterans continued to lead tortured existences.

More than twice as many men were killed in battle during the First World War as in all the major wars from 1790 to 1913 together, including the Napoleonic Wars, the Crimean War, the Danish War of 1864, the Austro-Prussian War, the American War between the States, the Franco-Prussian War, the Boer War, the Russo-Japanese War, and the Balkan Wars. Two-thirds of the men mobilized and two-thirds of those killed were on the Allied side. The estimated number of civilian deaths owing to the war was even greater than the number of soldier deaths. The noncombatants fell victim to such disasters as starvation, disease, massacres, epidemics, and raids. In addition, the various national birth rates suffered serious decline.

Equally staggering were the monetary costs of the combat and the destruction of property on land and sea. The average *daily* cost to all belligerents of the war in the first three years was $123,- 000,000. In 1918 the average daily cost was $244,000,000, that is, more than $10,000,000 per hour. The total net direct cost of conducting the war thus was $186,000,000,000, the Allies expending $126,000,000,000, and the Central Powers, $60,000,000,000. To this sum must be added property damage on land to the extent of almost $30,000,000,000; damage on sea aggregating $7,000,000,- 000; production losses of about $45,000,000,000; and war relief and losses to neutrals of more than $2,000,000,000. The total real economic cost amounted to $270,000,000,000.

If to this figure be added the $67,000,000,000 generally estimated as the capitalized value of the human lives lost as a direct consequence of the war, a total of $337,000,000,000 is reached. This sum does not take into account the additional economic loss caused by the wholesale crippling and devitalization of soldiers and civilians, the billions of dollars of interest due on the debts contracted by the fighting powers, or the vast sums which will continue to be appropriated for generations to come as pension money. And yet it represents five and a half times as many dollars as the number of seconds which have elapsed since the birth of Christ! Verily, the men who met to consider the terms of peace after the First World War faced a grave responsibility—the responsibility of so settling conditions that the ghastly loss in lives and goods should not have been entirely in vain.

CHAPTER IV

The Peace Conference of Paris

THE CONFERENCE LEADERS

Long before the armistice celebrations subsided, Paris, having been chosen as the site for the conclusion of peace, made ready for this new festival. At first it had been thought that the peace might be negotiated in neutral Switzerland, at Lausanne or Geneva, but the French would not hear of this. In Paris the Germans had humbled them forty-eight years previously, and in Paris they would now humble the Germans. The French capital therefore prepared to receive some of the most distinguished statesmen, jurists, and scholars of the Allied world, who would coöperate in the drafting of a peace settlement. There were not to be any Germans, Austrians, Hungarians, Turks, or Bulgarians at the conference. These would be called in later—to affix their signatures to completed documents.

In December 1918 Woodrow Wilson embarked for Europe. Against the advice of judicious friends the President had determined to attend the conference in person. His arrival in Europe was eagerly anticipated, not so much by the statesmen as by the people. A general feeling seemed to prevail that he was the one person who could "rise above the tumult of passion" that surged through the world. Everywhere the President's reception was commensurate with the glamour attached to his name. In England, Londoners crowded into the streets to get a glimpse of the great Wilson. Frenchmen, it is said, burst into tears in his presence. Not since the days of the ancient empire had Rome witnessed such a triumphal march as that accorded the President of the United States. Even in Germany he was considered a savior. Small wonder that he should have thought himself in control of matters in Paris.

But the glamour was deceptive. Actually Wilson did not have the support of his own countrymen. Though he announced that it was with the "greatest enthusiasm and pleasure" that he accepted the "mandate" of the American people to draw up a treaty of the type which he contemplated, his own party had been defeated in the congressional elections of 1918. The defeat might not have been so thorough if the President had not specifically asked the American people to elect a Democratic Congress so that he might be effectively supported during the critical months to come. Since the Republicans in Congress frequently had endorsed the President's war measures more warmly than had his own "followers," his attitude caused resentment among fair-minded citizens. The Republicans captured a majority in both houses and hence the new Senate—the one which would decide on the acceptance or rejection of the treaty to be drawn up in Paris—was hostile to the administration. To make matters worse, the President went to Europe without taking along any really influential member of the Republican Party.[1]

With the President went Secretary of State Lansing and Henry White. The last was a retired, wealthy, Republican career diplomat who spoke French fluently, dressed well, and had been ambassador to France, but who had little influence among Europeans or in the affairs of his party. The remaining two members of the delegation already were in Europe: General Tasker Bliss, a scholar as well as a soldier, and a man whose abilities were not always recognized at the time; and Colonel House, who had preceded Wilson to make the necessary preparations. So far as American politics was concerned, the peace would be Democratic, and some of the Republican senators would vote against it as a mere matter of party loyalty. Shrewd politics, it would seem, demanded the inclusion among the delegates of a man such as ex-President William H. Taft or Henry Cabot Lodge, chairman of the Senate Foreign Relations Committee.

Wilson's tactical mistakes were, in some measure, the result of his character and personality. His idealism frequently was above the heads of the people and he found it difficult to make himself understood. Apparently he was willing to sacrifice much, even friendships, for the sake of his ideals. Though his knowledge of European problems and affairs was limited, he sometimes failed or was unable to give adequate attention to the reports drawn up after months of investigation and research by the technical ex-

---

[1] Wilson further increased his unpopularity at home by ordering Postmaster-General Albert Burleson to assume control over all transatlantic cable lines in order that news to and from Europe might be censored.

perts whom he had taken to Europe to advise him on matters within their respective fields of knowledge. In diplomacy, Wilson was no match for his foreign colleagues at Paris.

The leading delegate from Great Britain was David Lloyd George, head of the Liberal Party and prime minister since 1916. Feeling that his government ought to receive a vote of confidence from the British people before he went to the conference, "Little Davey" called for elections in December 1918. His party's chief slogans during the ensuing "khaki campaign" were: "Make Germany Pay," "Hang the Kaiser," and "Shilling for Shilling and Ton for Ton." The London *Daily Mail,* owned by Lord Northcliffe and managed by his brother, Lord Rothermere, aided Lloyd George with the cry: "They will cheat you yet—those Huns!" The premier won an overwhelming victory, his coalition securing a majority of more than 250 seats.

Lloyd George was one of the most interesting personalities at the Paris Peace Conference. With his shock of gray hair, his boundless energy and restlessness, his alert mind and lightninglike decisions which often were unmade as quickly as they were made, with his dislike for matters of detail, his humor and wit, his emotionalism and cleverness, his indifference to any mistakes he might make, and his wisdom in relying upon the advice of a staff of expert assistants, the Welsh attorney would have occupied a position of prominence at the gathering even if he had represented a less important country than Great Britain. Lloyd George was rarely at a loss to find the most appealing argument to the "vanity, weakness, or self-interest" of his immediate listener. Consistently and unerringly he was able to find "the weak joints in an adversary's harness."

The British Premier and his contingent were much better informed on the day-to-day growth of the treaty than were the American or French delegates. The reason for this was no mystery. The treaty terms were drafted by numerous committees, each in charge of a certain section, and meeting in different hotels. The British committeemen were required every evening to send a report of the day's proceedings to a central office under Lord Hardinge at the Hotel Majestic, where mimeographed reports of all the minutes were made. By means of high-powered cars these were distributed, on the same evening, to all British representatives. This arrangement gave the British committeemen a great advantage over their colleagues.

The French deputation was led by Georges Clemenceau, vari-

ously nicknamed "Tiger" and *Père la Victoire*. Clemenceau, it
has been said, had one illusion—France, and one disillusion—
mankind, including Frenchmen. The "Tiger" was old. He had
been a newspaper correspondent in the United States during the
War between the States, almost sixty years before the meeting of
the peace conference. He had seen much and experienced much,
and he had become thoroughly skeptical and cynical. Until he
himself came into power, Clemenceau had been violently opposed
to governmental oppression and censorship and had been instrumental in bringing about the overthrow of almost a score of cabinets at various times in his career. Yet, when he became premier
and minister of war, from 1917 to 1920, he devised an efficient
"gagging-machine" of his own.

Clemenceau probably was the best diplomat at the conference,
far surpassing his colleagues in knowledge of world affairs and
human nature. More than anyone else did he enjoy little jokes at
his colleagues' expense. Though usually selecting for his targets
the representatives from the smaller countries, he reputedly exclaimed, on one occasion: "Even God was satisfied with Ten Commandments, but Wilson insists on Fourteen!" And on another he
is said to have remarked: "Lloyd George believes himself to be
Napoleon, but President Wilson believes himself to be Jesus
Christ." Despite this attitude, he was prudent and diplomatic
enough to pay lip service to American ideals and British hopes.
Clemenceau never lost sight of the goals which he had set for himself at the conference: to exalt and secure France and to weaken
Germany.

Premier Vittorio Orlando and Sidney Sonnino headed the Italian delegation. Orlando was a learned, eloquent, and artful diplomat, a Sicilian, and an ex-professor of law. However, he had no
command of English and hence exerted relatively little influence
in the general proceedings. Besides, he irritated Wilson by insisting on the fulfillment of the Secret Treaties which had been the
price of Italy's participation in the war. Sonnino, though usually
considered the dominant delegate, was too stubborn to be a good
diplomat. Signori Francesco Nitti and Tommaso Tittoni, who
later replaced these men as Italy's representatives, were little more
successful in pleading their country's cause.

The less important delegates at Paris also constituted an interesting group of personalities. Clemenceau's colleagues, well in the
background, were Stephen Pichon, André Tardieu, and Jules
Cambon. Since Clemenceau "was by nature and experience not

likely to share his power with any one," his aides rarely attempted to challenge his supremacy. President Poincaré and Marshal Foch, however, though not official delegates to the conference, had considerable influence. Both men had set their hearts upon crushing Germany and they were ready to go even further in achieving this aim than was Clemenceau. Indeed, Poincaré's policy of opposition to Wilson's ideas was so annoying to the American President that the latter long hesitated to accept a dinner invitation tendered by the French Executive during the last week of Wilson's stay in France.

Lloyd George was accompanied by Balfour, Andrew Bonar Law, and George N. Barnes, minister of pensions. From Greece came Eleutherios Venizelos, the "Ulysses of the Conference." Poland sent as her chief delegate Roman Dmowski, but when he failed to convince the conference of the justice of his demands the Poles sent the great pianist, Ignace Jan Paderewski, to see whether he could harmonize the conflicting interests of his countrymen with those of their neighbors. Paderewski soon discovered, to his sorrow, that he was no match for the international politicians gathered at Paris. The representatives of Japan, lead by Kimmochi Saionji and Nobuaki Makino, played a shrewd game at the conference. They had little to say on European questions, not wishing to make enemies, but when the discussions concerned the Far East they were all the more vocal. In general, they voted with the United States and Great Britain.

The long-suffering and persecuted Armenians sent as their chief spokesman Boghos Nubar Pasha, who demanded a stretch of territory extending from the Caspian to the Black and Mediterranean seas. He reënforced his pleas with a thrilling summary of Armenian massacres through the ages. From Belgium came Foreign Minister Paul Hymans; from new-born Czechoslovakia, Premier Karel Kramář and Foreign Minister Eduard Beneš; from Yugoslavia,[1] Pashich and Dr. Ante Trumbich. Romania was represented by her premier, Jon Bratianu, while from South Africa came Generals Smuts and Louis Botha, able statesmen both. The case of the Zionist Jews was placed in the hands of Dr. Chaim Weizmann of London. The Portuguese and Siamese, the Estonians and Livonians, the Lebanese and Georgians, all were represented, and even the far-off Koreans selected two delegates. These last, however, were able to accomplish little, for they arrived as the conference was about to wind up its affairs.

[1] For the sake of brevity, "Yugoslavia" will be used to designate the region known officially, until 1929, as "the Kingdom of Serbs, Croats, and Slovenes."

THE ORGANIZATION OF THE CONFERENCE

The leading belligerent governments, long before the armistice, had appointed experts to collect data on all subjects that might come within the sphere of discussion at the expected peace conference. Since the Allies made no attempt to coördinate their efforts in this direction, and since much of the work was done by subordinates or by people who had no connection with either the war or foreign-affairs departments in their respective countries, some of the labor was wasted. A large portion of it, however, was invaluable, and frequently "ideas appeared at the conference which could be traced back to laborious pens working at a time when the Germans seemed almost invincible."

In the United States, a group of experts was gathered by Colonel House, with headquarters in the New York offices of the American Geographical Society, to study the linguistic, economic, and ethnographic factors in central and eastern European history. The activities of this group provided the background for the Fourteen Points and furnished President Wilson with a tentative scheme for territorial settlements. Similar preparations were made in other countries and such national groups as the Poles and Czechs had well-functioning propaganda committees which did considerable work of a like nature. As a result, every delegation that came to Paris brought with it a clutter of statistics and memoranda.

The first plenary session of the peace conference was held on January 18, 1919. Most of the nations of the world were represented, there being seventy delegates and plenipotentiaries, and numerous substitutes. Accompanying each delegation was a large staff of secretaries, advisers, journalists, and representatives of varied interests. Fifty or sixty nationals came from even the smaller countries and each nation wanted at least one hotel as its own special headquarters. The British had five such hotels. Many of the accompanying "experts," incidentally, were that in name only. Thus, "at the opening of the conference, not one of the British experts on one country had ever been in that country."

So large and unwieldy a group could not possibly do business efficiently and only six plenary sessions were held. For all practical purposes, the conference consisted of the Supreme Peace Council, or Council of Ten, made up of the two chief delegates from the United States, Great Britain, France, Italy, and Japan. While this "Big Ten" assumed the right to decide what should or should not be taken up at the larger conference meetings, the five Principal Allied and Associated Powers also insisted on membership on every committee or commission that was appointed. Supported, as Clemenceau pointed out, by twelve million soldiers, the great powers found little difficulty in convincing the smaller ones of their paramount interests.

It soon was felt that even a body of ten was too large for expedition and secrecy, and in March 1919 it was announced that henceforth the brunt of the work would be borne by the Council of Four, consisting of the chiefs from the United States, Great Britain, France, and Italy. The "Big Four" held 145 sessions. Japan voiced no objection to this arrangement, since the Japanese delegates rarely had attended meetings anyway. In April, Orlando left Paris in a huff because Wilson addressed an appeal to the Italian people over his head, and thereafter the "Big Three" conducted their meetings in strictest secrecy. Clemenceau's knowledge of English made it possible to dispense with the services of even the official interpreter.

The routine and investigation work of the conference was accomplished in the sixteen hundred meetings held by the fifty-eight commissions and committees that were appointed. The Commission on the League of Nations, the Commission on Reparation for Damages, and the Commission on Territorial Problems were among the more important of these bodies. Because the final treaty was basically a summation of the work of the many committees, its terms probably were more severe than they would otherwise have been. Each committee went ahead with its assignment, frequently oblivious of what the other committees were doing. In the end, paradoxical as it may seem, the whole appeared greater than the sum of its parts. But by that time it was late and the delegates were impatient to go home.

Before discussing the general problems facing the conference it may be interesting to note some of the multifarious and tiresome engagements that the leading delegates were forced to keep. President Wilson's schedule on the fairly busy day of April 17, 1919, included the following appointments:

11:00 A.M.   Dr. Wellington Koo, to present the Chinese Delegation to the Peace Conference.

11:10 A.M.   Marquis de Vogué and a delegation of seven others, representing the *Congrès Français,* to present their view as to the disposition of the left bank of the Rhine.

11:30 A.M.   Assyrian and Chaldean Delegation, with a message from the Assyrian-Chaldean nation.

11:45 A.M.   Dalmatian Delegation, to present to the President the result of the plebiscite of that part of Dalmatia occupied by Italians.

Noon   M. Bucquet, Chargé d'Affaires of San Marino, to convey the action of the Grand Council of San Marino, conferring on the President Honorary Citizenship in the Republic of San Marino.

12:10 P.M.   M. Calonder, Swiss Minister of Foreign Affairs.

12:20 P.M.   Miss Rose Schneiderman and Miss Mary Anderson, delegates of the National Women's Trade-Union League of the United States.

12:30 P.M.   The Patriarch of Constantinople, the head of the Orthodox Eastern Church.

12:45 P.M.   Essad Pasha, delegate of Albania, to present the claims of Albania.

1:00 P.M.   M. M. L. Coromilas, Greek Minister at Rome, to pay his respects.

Luncheon   Mr. Newton D. Baker, Secretary of War.

4:00 P.M.   Mr. Herbert Hoover.

4:15 P.M.   M. Bratianu, of the Romanian Delegation.

4:30 P.M.   Dr. Alfonso Costa, former Portuguese Minister, Portuguese Delegate to the Peace Conference.

4:45 P.M.   M. Boghos Nubar Pasha, president of the Armenian National Delegation, accompanied by M. A. Aharonian and Professor A. Der Hagopian, of Robert College.

5:15 P.M.   M. Pashich, of the Serbian Delegation.

5:30 P.M.   Mr. Frank Walsh, of the Irish-American Delegation.[1]

The leaders at Paris also received thousands of written reports and requests. These concerned every variety of topic from Corsican demands for autonomy to Siamese demands for indemnities and Arabian chieftains' demands for higher pensions. Although the ranking delegates did not read all the petitions, many of these had to be given special consideration lest friendly feelings be hurt. In the circumstances, it seems remarkable that the peacemakers retained their sanity. And these circumstances also help explain the abandon exhibited in many of the social activities.[2]

[1] *The Daily Mail*, Paris Edition, April 18, 1919, Quoted in Dillon, E. J. *The Inside Story of the Peace Conference*, 1920, p. 111 n.

[2] The dance craze which affected so many people at the conference, from prime ministers to hotel chambermaids, reputedly led Clemenceau to remark: *"Je n'ai jamais vu les figures si tristes ni les derrières si gais!"*

THE PROBLEMS FACING THE DELEGATES

The number of knotty problems that faced the conference was legion. Not only did the Paris assemblage have to draw up peace terms which would satisfy at least the more important of the twenty-three Allied countries, and agree on a covenant for a league of nations that would be acceptable to forty or fifty not particularly friendly nations, but it had to feed the starving millions in central and eastern Europe,[1] control the restless victorious armies, satisfy hysterical public opinions at home, and make peace among the dozen nations that fought their own little wars after the First World War came to an end. In the days immediately following the war, Europe more nearly resembled a seething cauldron than at any previous time. Poles and Ukrainians, Romanians and Hungarians, Greeks and Turks, Serbs and Montenegrins, Czechs and Germans, Russians and Armenians, Italians and Yugoslavs, all were engaged in combat. The great powers themselves were so much at odds over policies and viewpoints that the Versailles Treaty in its final form might never have been signed had Germany possessed a second Bismarck or a Charles de Talleyrand to look after her interests. In retrospect it seems miraculous that any treaty was drawn up in the pandemonium that was Europe in 1919.

The question of publicity was among the first of the major problems requiring solution. Wilson's stand on the matter of "open covenants openly arrived at" seemed to imply that there should be no secrecy. Actually, most of the important meetings were held behind closed doors. Precisely what went on during the meetings of the Big Three may never be known, since few minutes were kept. Newspapermen were admitted to the plenary sessions and general meetings and were given releases for their papers, but the doors of the other council chambers were opened only occasionally, and then usually for photographers. All reports from France to the United States and from the United States to France were censored, lest Americans hear of the dissensions in Europe or Europeans discover the weakening support accorded Wilson by his countrymen. The secrecy was often justifiable. The war hys-

[1] Herbert Hoover served as director-general of Allied relief in Paris. Incidentally, the Allied blockade of Germany was rigidly enforced until March 14, 1919, when the Brussels Agreement was reached permitting Germany to buy foodstuffs from the outside world. This post-armistice enforcement was bitterly resented by the Germans.

teria, far from dying out with the signing of the armistice, seemed to become greater as the conference days dragged on, and the acrimonious haggling following each leakage of proposed territorial or other adjustments increased the tension.

In the plenary sessions, to which newspapermen had access, the bedlam of languages made it difficult to get accurate news. Everything that was said had to be interpreted for someone, and not infrequently the interpreter varied the style, increased the bombast, or added to the errors of the speaker. Paul Mantoux, the ablest of the interpreters, saved the dignity of many a speaker by translating freely but sensibly.

The question of which language to designate as official was another problem to bother the diplomats. Clemenceau demanded that the French version of the prospective treaty be regarded as final. The British and Americans insisted on equality for the English version, whereupon the Italians asked for a similarly authoritative Italian text. In the end it was agreed that the French and English texts of the treaty with Germany should be considered "both authentic," the claim of the Italians being disregarded when Orlando left the conference. The lesser treaties were drafted in all three languages, but in case of dispute the French copy was designated as authoritative.

Perhaps the greatest difficulty confronting the delegates was that of reconciling the dispositions agreed upon in the Secret Treaties with the idealistic principles laid down by Wilson in his Fourteen Points and accepted by Germany, in modified form, as the basis for the peace discussions. These treaties were incompatible with the idea of peace without victory. In defending the final Versailles Treaty before a group of United States Senators in the autumn of 1919, Wilson stated that he had known nothing about the Secret Treaties when he made his speech embodying the Fourteen Points (January 1918) and that he first saw the documents when he arrived in Europe for the conference. It is hard to reconcile this statement with available evidence.

During his mission to America in April 1917, Balfour discussed at least the London Treaty with both Colonel House and President Wilson, and in January 1918 he wrote directly to the President about "his thoughts on the Italian territorial claims under the Treaty of London concluded in 1915." In March 1918 he stated in the House of Commons that Wilson was being kept fully informed by the Allies, and in May he told the same body: "I have no secrets from President Wilson. Every thought I have in the way of diplomacy connected with the war is absolutely open to President Wilson." Furthermore, after their successful revolution of November 1917, the Bolsheviks gave out for publication the texts of all Secret Treaties found in the Russian archives. The texts were printed in the *Manchester Guardian* and a few weeks later in the *New York Evening Post,* thus becoming "public property" long before the armistice. As early as July 21, 1917, moreover, Wilson had written House to the effect that American economic power would be such that the Allies must perforce yield to American pressure and accept the American peace program. Great Britain and France, he wrote, "have not the same views with regard to peace that we have by any means. When the War is over we can force them to our way of thinking."

Here, then, appears to have been the crux of the matter. Wilson seems to have thought that he could force the Allies into his way of thinking and therefore did not trouble to remember the Secret Treaties. They were unimportant to him and hence were easily forgotten. When he was confronted with them again, in 1919, as an obstacle to his scheme of peace, their existence may well have been a shock to him. Consequently it is possible, as Colonel House pointed out nine years later, that, in the confusion and turmoil and under the suspicious cross-examination of inquisitorial senators, Wilson, in denying any foreknowledge of the documents, might have spoken "from conviction," not being able to remember "on the spur of the moment . . . when he first heard of this or that."

Be that as it may, Wilson's idealism certainly came into sharp conflict with materialism at the conference—and in most cases materialism triumphed. Sometimes Wilson was firm. Thus, during an impasse over the Saar question he threatened to go home unless he had his way. Again, he showed such firmness in refusing to give Fiume to Italy that Orlando and Sonnino went home, ill-humored and piqued. These instances, however, were rare and some of them doubtless hastened rather than arrested the decline of the President's prestige.

Last among the general obstacles to progress at the conference was the temporary return to their respective countries, in February and March 1919, of Wilson and Lloyd George. President Wilson returned to consider the bills that Congress had passed during his absence and to explain to the Senate the tentative draft of the League Covenant. Lloyd George returned to Great Britain to console the increasing number of unemployed with promises for a bright future. During this interim, too, Clemenceau was shot and it was found advisable to leave the bullet in his body. His attacker, one Emile Cottin, was convicted of "murder" and sentenced to death, but at Clemenceau's request the sentence was commuted to a term in prison.[1]

DRAFTING THE VERSAILLES TREATY

The greatest difficulty in the actual drawing up of the treaty terms was experienced in connection with the following points: (1) the wording of a league of nations' covenant; (2) the question of French security and the fate of the left bank of the Rhine; (3) the Italian and Polish claims; (4) the disposition of the erstwhile German colonies and the former possessions of the Turkish Empire; and (5) the reparation for damages that was to be exacted from Germany.

A serious difference of opinion arose over the advisability of incorporating the projected covenant in the general peace agreement. Wilson insisted on having it included in the treaty, lest the nations, in their preoccupation with other matters, shelve the covenant indefinitely. He had his way,[2] and the second plenary session, on January 25, 1919, appointed him chairman of a committee to draft the covenant. His leading colleagues on the commission, which represented fourteen states, were Robert Cecil, Léon Bourgeois, Orlando, Makino, and Smuts.

The basis for the commission's work was provided by a number of draft covenants and prior statements and outlines, such as the Smuts draft, the draft convention of Lord Phillimore, and the speeches of President Wilson. On February 14 Wilson presented a completed report to another plenary session of the conference. It met with considerable criticism, and, in all, twenty-six changes were made before the covenant was finally adopted (April 28). Against the wishes of France, a new article, 21, was added, giving recognition for the first time in a diplomatic document to the Monroe Doctrine: "Nothing in this Covenant shall be deemed to affect the validity of international engagements, such as treaties of arbitration or regional understandings like the Monroe Doctrine,

---

[1] The armistice with Germany, which had been renewed in December 1918 and January 1919, was again extended in February 1919.

[2] Wilson probably was correct in his reasoning, but the fact that the covenant formed an integral part of the peace treaties later proved to be a weakening factor in the life of the League.

for securing the maintenance of peace." The Japanese attempted to have inserted into the covenant an amendment confirming the principle of the equality of nations and the just treatment of their nationals. This was rejected, owing chiefly to the wishes of Great Britain and Australia, lest it lead to a movement for unrestricted oriental immigration.

Simultaneously with the problem of wording a covenant, arose the question of providing France with the security for which she longed. Reminiscences of what had happened along the Rhine frontier during the past century and the fear that Germany might seek revenge made the French delegates panicky in their attempts to forestall future invasions. The only means of achieving this security, it seemed to them, was so to cripple Germany—politically, militarily, territorially, economically, and commercially—that she never again could threaten France. Poincaré and Foch, in particular, were imbued with this idea, and during the course of the proceedings the marshal said: "Recourse must be had in the first place to all the means provided by Nature, and Nature has placed but one barrier across the line of invasion: the Rhine."

In accordance with this view, Foch and his followers demanded that Germany's western frontier be fixed at the Rhine and that the ten thousand square miles of territory between the Rhine on the east and the Netherlands, Belgium, and France on the west be erected into an autonomous, neutral state, more or less under French protection. Actually, in anticipation of a favorable opportunity, France and Russia in 1917 had signed an agreement providing for precisely this type of buffer state. The arrangement, however, had never met with the approval of Great Britain, and at the conference both the British and American delegations strenuously opposed the creation of "another Alsace-Lorraine."

After prolonged bargaining Clemenceau agreed to a compromise. The area in question was to be occupied by Allied troops for a stated period of years after the signing of the treaty. The northern sector, including the bridgehead at Cologne, was to be occupied for five years; the central zone, with the bridgehead at Coblenz, for ten years; and the southern sector, including the bridgehead at Mainz, for fifteen years. All the time limits, however, were made contingent upon Germany's prompt fulfillment of the other parts of the treaty; otherwise the occupation might continue indefinitely. In addition, a zone extending fifty kilometers (a little over thirty-one miles) east of the Rhine was to be "demilitarized." In other words, no fortifications might be built and no armed forces assembled in the district. *Die Wacht am Rhein* was to be termin̈ated.

Still further to reassure the French, Woodrow Wilson and Lloyd George promised to sign special treaties which should guarantee that the United States and Great Britain, respectively, would come to the aid of France in case of "invasion" by Germany. Upon Clemenceau's insistence the word "invasion" was changed to "aggression," and the "Tiger" at last was satisfied. On June 28, 1919, therefore, when the Versailles Treaty was signed, two supplementary Guarantee Treaties, one Franco-British and the other Franco-American, were also signed. These documents specifically guaranteed the eastern boundary of France against German aggression.[1]

Meanwhile another problem, related to that of French security, had arisen: the disposition of the Saar Basin. This Rhenish territory, lying east of Lorraine and belonging, at the time, partly to Prussia and partly to Bavaria, was known to be one of the world's greatest coal-producing sections. With an area of 723 square miles and a population of 660,000 (1919), it was a valuable stretch of territory.[2] In 1913 its coal output was 17,000,000 tons —equal to 40 per cent of the entire French production. In that same year it also produced 2,000,000 tons of steel, as well as large quantities of glass and pottery. The estimated coal reserves of the Saar Basin in 1913 were 17,000,000,000 tons, that is, more than those in all France and equal to more than a fifth of Germany's prewar reserves. Now, since the Germans had destroyed many of the coal mines in northern France, it was felt by the Allies that compensation in kind should be paid to the victims. Clemenceau demanded the cession of the basin.

From the viewpoints of history and ethnology, the claims of the French to the region were almost nil. Nearly all the inhabitants were German in stock and sympathy. From the point of view of reparation, France had better claims, particularly since Saar coal appeared essential to the proper development of the Lorraine iron fields. The two regions had formed a solid economic unit before the war.

The problem facing the conference, therefore, was how to give France the coal without giving her the land and people. A committee of British, French, and American experts was delegated to solve the riddle. The arrangement proposed by this group carried

[1] For the ultimate fate of the Guarantee Treaties see first page of Chap. VIII.
[2] In 1934 the population was estimated at 825,000.

out the intentions of the peace conference as nearly as seemed possible and hence was accepted as a solution. France was given
ownership of all the coal mines and mining accessories. The entire district was included in the French customs boundary and
French money was to circulate there freely. France was given permission to set up schools for the children of the miners and to
prescribe instruction in French. The value of the coal removed
was to be credited to Germany's reparation account.

While certain important rights were reserved to France, the
territory was to be governed by a commission of the League of
Nations. At the end of fifteen years the inhabitants should vote
"by communes or districts" as to "the sovereignty under which
they desire to be placed." This "sovereignty" might be an autonomous state under League control, or it might be France, or Germany. All men and women "more than twenty years old at the
date of voting," who lived in the Saar at the time of the signing of
the treaty, were declared eligible to participate in the plebiscite.
After the balloting the League of Nations should decide the
sovereignty, "taking into account the wishes of the inhabitants as
expressed by voting." If the Saar went back to Germany, the latter
should repurchase control of the mines from France at a price
determined by three experts, a Frenchman, a German, and an
appointee of the League.

The single item that took up more of the time of the conference
leaders than any other was that arising from the conflict of the
Italian demands with those of the newly formed Serbo-Croat-
Slovene state. In addition to insisting on the fulfillment of the
terms of the Treaty of London—under which she had been promised territory extending from the Brenner Pass in the Tirol to the
port of Valona in Albania, plus the Dodecanese Islands and some
land in Africa and Asia—Italy now also demanded the port of
Fiume and an extra part of the Dalmatian coast, both of which
had belonged to Austria-Hungary. That the Tirol contained 250,-
000 German-speaking Austrians; that the Italian acquisitions in
the northeast, including Gorizia, Gradisca, and Istria, contained
about 300,000 Southslavs; and that the Dodecanese Islands were
almost wholly Greek in population, did not deter Italy from
seeking, in addition, to annex more Dalmatian territory in which
the Slavs several times outnumbered the Italian residents.

Italy wanted Fiume not only for commercial reasons but to
prevent the appearance of a new, strong rival in the Adriatic. One
of the reasons for the prewar enmity between Italy and Austria-

Hungary had been the struggle for the control of the Adriatic, and now that the Austro-Hungarian peril was removed Italy did not propose to allow another rival to come upon the stage. Rome knew that without Fiume Yugoslavia could not readily achieve maritime greatness.

Orlando and Sonnino advanced several claims to the extra territory which they desired. They maintained, according to Henry White, that Italy had "saved" the Allies five times during the war and hence deserved special consideration. They pointed out that Russia's defection had made the conflict last longer than Italy had expected, thus entailing greater sacrifices than she had bargained for. Lastly, strategic and geographic reasons were advanced to establish Italy's claim to Fiume, it being demonstrated that the port was directly *connected* with Italy by sea, but *separated* from Yugoslavia by mountains!

The Slavic delegates were not backward in presenting their view of the case. They showed that of all their country's railways the only good ones led to Fiume. They cited the principle of national self-determination and quoted figures to show that the Slavs far outnumbered the Italians in Dalmatia, while in Fiume itself, if the suburb of Sušak were included, the two nationalities were at least equally represented. The fact that the Italians opposed a plebiscite in the region added to the plausibility of this claim. Finally, it could not be gainsaid that the new kingdom needed a seaport; and the only available good port was Fiume. The Serbs could see no reason, therefore, why Italy should further add to her already large Slavic minority.

After the Council of Four had listened to all arguments, a Dalmatian line was drawn, giving Italy somewhat less than the Treaty of London had promised. Orlando and Sonnino, knowing that its acceptance would result in the overthrow of their government, unhesitatingly rejected this "Wilson" or "American Line." When Wilson thereupon (April 23) appealed to the Italian people over the heads of the two delegates, the latter angrily quitted Paris. Though they returned after some days, cheered by a 10-to-1 vote of confidence in the Chamber of Deputies, their ministry did fall on June 19. Signori Nitti and Tittoni, who replaced Orlando and Sonnino, were equally unsuccessful in achieving a satisfactory settlement and so the Fiume-Adriatic controversy raged on after the conference terminated. It finally was settled by direct negotiation between Italy and Yugoslavia.[1]

[1] See beginning of Chapter XIV.

The Polish question, though perplexing enough, was not so disconcerting as that of Fiume. Since the Allies had promised to restore a united and independent Poland, with access to the sea, it merely remained for the committee in charge to delimit the proper boundaries. Few people took seriously the exaggerated demands advanced by the Polish delegates, but a snag was struck when it was suggested that in order to give Poland her outlet to the sea East Prussia might have to be severed from Germany. A corridor, including the city of Danzig with its German population of 300,000, might have to be created, it was explained, and placed under Polish control. In the case of Danzig, at least, this would be a violation of the principle of self-determination, but it was considered better to sacrifice German nationality than Polish commercial potentialities. Accordingly, there were assigned to Poland large sections of West Prussia and Posen, in which Germans and Poles were well intermingled because the German governments had fostered colonization in this originally Polish territory.

This arrangement, incidentally, fitted in well with the twofold plan of France to weaken Germany and to create a strong eastern ally to take the place which Russia had occupied in the prewar system of alliances. In the words of Pichon, France wanted a Poland *"grande et forte, très forte."* Owing chiefly to the opposition of Lloyd George, who had no interest in a strong Poland and who feared a German-Polish war, the Marienwerder district east of the Vistula River was not to be given to Poland without a plebiscite. Danzig, moreover, was made a free city, economically subservient to Poland but administered by the League of Nations.

The allocation of Germany's former colonies and of the erstwhile possessions of the crumbling Ottoman Empire was another troublesome issue. Some of the Allied statesmen favored outright partition and annexation, but others objected to this solution as being too obviously imperialistic and contrary to the expressed Allied war aims. Yet, since restoring the possessions to their former owners would be unwise from a business viewpoint as well as supposedly unjust to millions of mistreated natives, some other formula had to be evolved. A way out of the dilemma was suggested in a pamphlet entitled *The League of Nations*, published in December 1918 by General Smuts.

In this brochure Smuts discussed a scheme that had been mentioned by several persons at the conference and which has since come to be known as the "mandate system." The plan was to dispose of the territories that were to be taken from Russia,

Austria-Hungary, and Turkey by assigning them to the League. The last was then to "delegate its authority" to some other state which it might appoint "as its agent and mandatory," subject to certain supervisory restrictions. Wilson took this design and applied it to Syria, Mesopotamia, and Palestine and to all German possessions except Kiaochow.[1]

Approximately 1,250,000 square miles of land with a population of about 19,000,000 and an annual trade of $166,000,000 were given to the League of Nations which, in turn, was to allot them to various mandatory powers. These were to act as stewards for the League in the protection of the relatively backward peoples who as yet were unable to stand alone in the complex world. The actual mandatory distributions followed closely the terms of the Secret Treaties. All League members were promised equal commercial and trading opportunities in the mandates and the mandatories were required to report annually to a League of Nations Mandates Commission.[2]

The disposition of the Kiaochow leasehold caused great difficulties because China, one of the Allies, demanded its return to her, while Japan, another Ally, refused to give it up. Wilson favored the Chinese claims but, when Japan threatened to remain outside the League unless her occupation were recognized, Wilson wavered. Lloyd George and Clemenceau also explained to Wilson that in order to secure the assistance of the Japanese fleet against enemy submarines in 1917 they had promised to let Japan keep Kiaochow. Eventually, therefore, it was agreed to give Germany's former rights in the Shantung Peninsula to Japan. At the same time, however, Tokyo promised to restore the area to China, retaining only certain important economic privileges. The Chinese delegation opposed this decision and refused to sign the Versailles Treaty. Hence China did not become a member of the League until the ratification of the Treaty of St. Germain with Austria. It was some time before Japan kept her promise to give Kiaochow back to China.

One of the last items to be settled, though it had been among the first to be mentioned, was that of reparation. On the presumption that Germany was principally responsible for the war, the

[1] France also reincorporated in French Equatorial Africa the 100,000 square miles of land ceded to Germany in 1912 (see p. 10), while Portugal regained the "Kionga Triangle" (400 square miles) taken by Germany in the late nineteenth century from Portuguese East Africa or Mozambique.

[2] For the distribution of the mandates see pp. 144–145.

Allied pre-armistice note of November 5, 1918, had stipulated that the Germans would be expected to pay for "all damage done to the civilian population of the Allies and to their property by the aggression of Germany, by land, by sea, and from the air." Now, when the commission on reparation of the conference met, the British and French delegates insisted that Germany be held liable for all costs of the war and for pensions as well as for actual damages. The Americans denied the justice of this plea, in view of the pre-armistice negotiations, and appeal was made to the Council of Four. Here Wilson was able to arrange an agreement that, except in the case of Belgium, the war costs were not to be added to the damages. In consequence of a memorandum on the subject by General Smuts, however, pensions were reckoned as damages rather than as war costs. Ten categories of "damages" were listed and it remained only to set the figure that Germany must pay.

The American members of the commission, Thomas W. Lamont, Bernard Baruch, Norman Davis, and Vance McCormick, wanted to set a fixed sum, with definite time and methods of payment. They believed that the factor of certainty would be helpful to both sides, since the one would know on how much aid it could rely for rebuilding purposes and the other could make definite plans for paying off its obligations. The remaining commissioners, however, refused to give any definite statements of their damage estimates. They thought that any sum, no matter how large, would be unsatisfactory to their constituencies at home and might result in the overthrow of the existing ministries. Furthermore, they wanted Germany to pay to the limit of her capacity and they were afraid of setting too low a sum. It soon became evident, moreover, that even those who favored fixing a sum could not agree on a satisfactory figure, the demands varying from $15,000,000,000 to $200,000,000,000.

The best quick solution, obviously, was to shelve the matter for future settlement, making only a temporary arrangement for immediate payments on account. Accordingly it was stated that Germany should pay by May 1921, in gold or its equivalent, a total of 20,000,000,000 marks (almost $5,000,000,000). A special reparation commission, meanwhile, was to set a fixed total and regulate the method of future payments.

Now, with the chief stumbling blocks removed, the treaty was at last given definite form and the Germans were ordered to call for the document.

THE SIGNING OF THE TREATY

About three weeks before the presentation of the peace terms to the Germans, Henry White had written to Senator Lodge: "Marshal Foch has stated distinctly in the presence of General Bliss that nothing would give him more satisfaction than the refusal of the Germans to sign the treaty, as in that case he would be able to enter Germany at the head of an Allied army, to overrun the country completely, to take possession of the financial centers, and to squeeze out every bit of money available throughout the land." This attitude was reflected in the manner in which the treaty was handed to the representatives of the defeated power.

Upon receipt of the order to send delegates for the terms, Germany announced its intention to send subordinate officials to bring the document to Berlin for consideration by the authorities. The Allies interpreted this as insulting and warned Germany to send a full-fledged diplomatic delegation at once. The warning was heeded and on April 29 a German delegation of six, led by Ulrich von Brockdorff-Rantzau, former Imperial German Minister to Denmark and now foreign minister of the republic, arrived at Versailles. The movements of the delegates were carefully restricted: they were guarded by Allied officers, were kept in their hotel behind barbed wire, and were forbidden to communicate with any of the Allied deputies.

On May 7, the fourth anniversary of the sinking of the *Lusitania,* the peace terms were formally presented by Clemenceau in the small Trianon Palace near Versailles. As the Allied and American delegations arrived, they were saluted by a guard of honor. This guard was withdrawn when the Germans were called. Then Clemenceau, addressing the representatives of the German Republic as *"Messieurs les délégués de l'Empire allemand,"* said: "You have before you the accredited plenipotentiaries of all the small and great powers united to fight together in the war that has been so cruelly imposed upon them. The time has come when we must settle our accounts. You have asked for peace. We are ready to give you peace."

Brockdorff-Rantzau, possibly because of excessive emotion and oncoming illness, tactlessly replied to Clemenceau without rising. He admitted that his countrymen "were under no illusion as to the extent of their defeat and the degree of their helplessness," but he denied that Germany was solely responsible for the war and announced that Germany, though friendless, still had right and justice on her side. This attitude was widely interpreted as additional proof of Germany's inability to understand any language other than force.

Clemenceau notified the German delegation that three weeks would be allowed in which to consider the terms, that no oral discussion would be permitted, and that all complaints would have to be submitted in writing. Under this injunction an average of one German note a day reached the Allies and whatever discussion there was took place in the columns of the newspaper press. As was to be expected, the announcement of the terms in Germany resulted in an unrestrained outburst. Radicals, moderates, and reactionaries, alike, denounced Allied "treachery" and "deceit." Popular sentiment was well expressed by Chancellor Philipp Scheidemann (Social Democrat) when he said: "What hand would not wither that sought to lay itself and us in those chains?" [1] After a brief extension of the time limit, the German delegation, on May 29, submitted a detailed memorandum to the Allies. It contained an elaborate commentary on the treaty, denied that Germany alone was responsible for the contest, and emphasized the impossibility of fulfilling all the terms. The treaty itself covered 230 large printed pages; the German reply occupied 443 pages.

Ten committees were set to work on the German memorandum and on June 16 the results of their deliberations were incorporated into an Allied reply. Only a few modifications were made, and these chiefly owing to Lloyd George, whose intransigeance was lessening. The main alteration concerned the withholding of Upper Silesia from Poland until a plebiscite should have indicated the wishes of the inhabitants. The Germans were given five days, and then two more, in which to accept the revised treaty. Failure to do so, they were told, would mean invasion.

Although many Germans appeared ready to renew the struggle rather than sign the document, Hindenburg, on June 20, announced that further resistance on the western front, at least, was impossible. That same day the Scheidemann Government, including Brockdorff-Rantzau, resigned. There was no time for sentiment, however, and on June 21 Gustav Bauer, another Social Democrat, became chancellor. On the following day, a Sunday,

[1] Special criticism was aimed at the section of the treaty which demanded that hungry Germany hand over to France and Belgium 140,000 milch cows and 120,000 sheep within three months after the signing of the document. This demand, in Part VIII, Annex IV, of the treaty, was not published in the official summary of the terms as released to the Allied press. See also note on p. 107.

the German assembly at Weimar voted a conditional acceptance, objecting only to the articles saddling Germany with sole war guilt, accusing her of violating the code of war, and demanding the surrender, for trial before Allied courts, of certain "war criminals."

The Allies now repeated their demand for unconditional acceptance and refused any further extension of the time limit: seven o'clock in the evening of Monday, June 23, would bring acquiescence or invasion. At a little after five, therefore, Edgar von Haniel, the new German representative, announced Germany's acceptance. His country, he said, was yielding to "overwhelming force, but without on that account abandoning her views in regard to the unheard-of injustice of the conditions of peace."

It still remained for Germany to find someone willing to go to Versailles to sign the treaty. Eventually, Foreign Minister Hermann Müller and Colonial Minister Johannes Bell agreed to act as emissaries. Once again the German delegates, having arrived in Paris, were restricted in their actions and guarded like prisoners. It was decided to have the final ceremony in the Hall of Mirrors, where almost fifty years before the king of Prussia had become German Emperor. As the Germans left Paris for Versailles, mobs showered them with stones and vocal abuse.

At three o'clock in the afternoon of June 28, the fifth anniversary of the assassination of Archduke Francis Ferdinand, the Germans were admitted to the Hall of Mirrors. "Müller was pale and nervous. Bell held himself erect and calm." They signed first, and the Allied delegates followed in the alphabetical order of their countries' names in French. The United States was listed as *Amérique du Nord* and so Wilson's signature came first.[1]

On June 29, the day after the signing of the treaty, Colonel House left Paris for London to hasten the practical development of the League of Nations. On that day he wrote in his diary: "I should have preferred a different peace."[2]

---

[1] Ratifications between the Allies and Germany were finally exchanged in Paris on January 10, 1920. Four other treaties also were drawn up by the peace conference, with Austria, Hungary, Bulgaria, and Turkey. Collectively the five treaties, described in the next chapter, are known as the Peace of Paris.

[2] Seymour, C., ed. *The Intimate Papers of Colonel House*, 4 v., 1926–1928, v. 4, p. 489. Mr. House added that he doubted whether a different peace could have been made, since "the ingredients for such a peace as (he) would have had were lacking at Paris."

CHAPTER V

The Treaties of Peace

VERSAILLES, WITH GERMANY

The purpose of the Treaty of Versailles, according to its preamble, was to replace the state of war "by a firm, just and durable peace." The document comprised 15 parts, including 440 articles and almost a score of annexes.[1]

Alsace and Lorraine were returned to France. Belgium, after a "plebiscite" conducted by the Belgian authorities, received the strategically important regions of Eupen, Malmédy, and Moresnet, with a combined population of 70,000. As the result of another plebiscite, Denmark received northern Schleswig, taken from her by Prussia and Austria in 1864, while southern Schleswig voted to remain with Germany. Czechoslovakia was awarded a small section of Upper Silesia. To independent Poland, Germany ceded most of Posen and West Prussia—a stretch of territory 260 miles long and ranging up to 80 miles in width, with a population (excluding Danzig) about two-thirds Polish. After plebiscites favoring the Germans, the East-Prussian districts of Marienwerder and Allenstein were permitted to remain with Prussia.

In industrial Upper Silesia a plebiscite was ordered to be held under the supervision of an Allied commission and a Franco-Italian military force. The ballot returns showed more than 700,-000 votes for Germany and 480,000 for Poland; of the communes, 754 voted for adherence to Germany, while 699 preferred incorporation in Poland. The Poles thereupon claimed all the areas with Polish majorities, while Germany maintained that the entire region was an indivisible economic unit and belonged of right

[1] For Part I, the Covenant of the League, see next chapter. The text of the most important articles of the treaties with Germany and Austria may be found in Langsam, W. C. *Documents and Readings in the History of Europe Since 1918,* 1939, pp. 12–38.

to her. Strife ensued, particularly when France and Great Britain disagreed over a solution, and the matter was referred to the League Council. The latter accepted the recommendations of a special committee, partitioning Silesia so as to leave Germany more than half of the people and land area, but giving Poland

From *War Atlas*, Headline Book No. 23,
Foreign Policy Association, New York, 1940.

more of the economic resources. Thus, Poland acquired 53 of the 67 coal mines, 9 of the 14 steel and rolling mills, all the zinc and lead foundries, about three-fourths of the coal-production area, and 11 of the 16 zinc and lead mines.

Danzig, with a population almost wholly German, was made a free city under League control, but Poland was accorded special diplomatic and economic rights therein. The Memel district, at the northeastern tip of Germany and controlling the mouth of the Niemen River, was ceded to the Allies.[1]

Germany renounced "in favor of the Principal Allied and Associated Powers all her rights and titles over her oversea possessions," these being later apportioned among Great Britain,

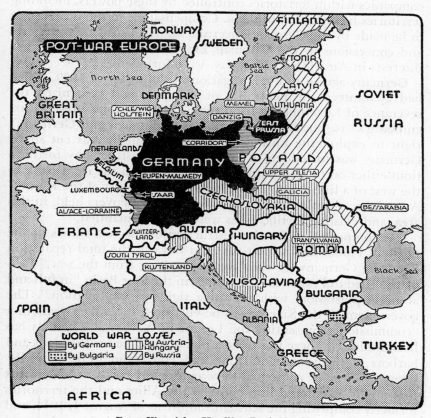

From *War Atlas*, Headline Book No. 23,
Foreign Policy Association, New York, 1940.

France, Belgium, Japan, the Union of South Africa, Australia, and New Zealand as mandates of the League. The German control

[1] In January 1923 a Lithuanian force seized Memel (eleven hundred square miles) from the French garrison which had been holding it. The League Council took the matter under advisement and in 1924 a convention was signed among Lithuania, France, Great Britain, Italy, and Japan providing for the transfer of Memel to Lithuania as an autonomous territory. The port was to be administered by a harbor board consisting of a Lithuanian, a Pole, and a citizen of Memel. The Lithuanians called the area Klaipéda.

of Kiaochow was renounced in favor of Japan. All Germany's special rights and privileges in China, Siam (Thailand), Liberia, Morocco, and Egypt were given up. The Allied and Associated Powers reserved "the right to retain and liquidate all property, rights and interest" belonging to private German nationals or companies within territories controlled by these powers, including territories newly ceded to them. Compensation to the owners was to be made by the German Government.[1] All Germany's property and concessions in the Ottoman Empire and Bulgaria, and her interests in Austria and Hungary, were forfeited.

Germany agreed to the abrogation of the treaty of 1839, which had guaranteed the neutrality of Belgium, and recognized the severance of Luxembourg from the German customs union. Luxembourg's "régime of neutrality" was terminated and Germany's right to exploit the railways of the grand duchy was cut short. Germany was forbidden to "maintain or construct any fortifications either on the left bank of the Rhine or on the right bank to the west of a line drawn fifty kilometers to the east of the Rhine." Armed forces could not be assembled, nor maneuvers held, in this area, and existing fortifications were to be dismantled.

"As compensation for the destruction of the coal mines in the north of France and as part payment towards the total reparation due from Germany for the damage resulting from the war," Germany ceded to France the coal mines in the Saar Basin "in full and absolute possession, with exclusive rights of exploitation." The government of the Saar was to be entrusted for fifteen years to a "commission representing the League of Nations." Then, as has been indicated, there was to be a plebiscite. The fortifications and harbors of the islands of Dune and Helgoland were to be destroyed. Germany consented to recognize any treaty arrangements that might be entered into between the Allies and the territories formerly comprising the Russian Empire as of August 1, 1914, and she acknowledged and promised to respect the independence of Austria.

Part V of the treaty contained the military, naval, and aviation clauses. The German General Staff was abolished. The army was limited to 100,000 men, including a maximum of 4000 officers. These forces were to be "devoted exclusively to the maintenance of order within the territory and to the control of the frontiers." Lest Germany resort to subterfuge, it was ordained that the num-

[1] Some of this property, notably in the United States, was later returned to the German owners.

ber of customs officers, forest guards, and coast guards must not exceed the number employed in 1913. The strength of the gendarmerie and police forces could be increased only in proportion to the population increase since 1913.

The manufacture of armaments, munitions, and war materials was limited and such materials could be stored only "at points to be notified to the Governments" of the Allies. No war materials were to be imported or exported, and poison gases, armored cars, and tanks were neither to be made nor purchased. Compulsory military service was abolished and only voluntary enlistments, of twelve consecutive years for privates and noncommissioned men and of twenty-five consecutive years for officers, were permitted. It was forbidden to discharge more than 5 per cent of the total effectives in men or officers in any one year. Finally, "educational establishments, the universities, societies of discharged soldiers, shooting or touring clubs and, generally speaking, associations of every description, whatever be the age of their members, must not occupy themselves with any military matters."

The naval provisions were equally drastic. Germany was permitted to retain only six battleships, six light cruisers, twelve destroyers, and twelve torpedo boats. No submarines were allowed her and no new warships might be built except for purposes of replacement. The naval personnel was limited to 15,000 men, including a maximum of 1500 officers. The periods of enlistment were similar to those stipulated for the army. No one in the merchant marine was to receive naval training. All war vessels in excess of the stated quota were either to be dismantled and converted into merchant ships or turned over to the Allies.[1] Germany was forbidden to have any military or naval air forces and all aeronautical war material had to be surrendered.

The Allies reserved the right to, and later did, appoint commissions of control to supervise the execution of the disarmament clauses. The commissions, whose expenses Germany had to bear, were given extensive powers of investigation. By 1927, however, they had all been abolished. Although the military, naval, and aerial restrictions were designed to last as long as the treaty itself, many of the clauses soon were modified in practice. Numerous changes were made with the assent of the Conference of

---

[1] On June 21, 1919, the crews of the surrendered German warships, which had been ordered to Scapa Flow in the Orkneys, opened the sea cocks and sent to the bottom 53 vessels. Germany thereupon was ordered to build additional merchantmen for the Allies.

Ambassadors.[1] The treaty indicated, moreover, that the restrictions upon Germany's fighting establishments were not merely calculated to render it impossible for her "to resume military aggression," but were the first steps toward a general reduction of armaments throughout the world. It was declared to be one of the first duties of the League to promote disarmament.[2]

"William II of Hohenzollern, formerly German Emperor," was publicly arraigned in the treaty "for a supreme offense against international morality and the sanctity of treaties." A special Allied tribunal was to be appointed to try him, "thereby assuring him the guarantees essential to the right of defense." However, the Allies were spared much embarrassment when the Netherlands refused to extradite William. Germany was also required to surrender for trial before Allied courts any designated "persons accused of having committed acts in violation of the laws and customs of war." Eventually the Allies permitted the trials to be held in Leipzig, where the court procedure was perfunctory. Only about a dozen of the less important "war criminals" were tried and they received light sentences.

The legal justification for demanding reparation from Germany was put into the so-called guilt clause of the treaty, Article 231:

The Allied and Associated Governments affirm and Germany accepts the responsibility of Germany and her allies for causing all the loss and damage to which the Allied and Associated Governments and their nationals have been subjected as a consequence of the war imposed upon them by the aggression of Germany and her allies.

In Article 232 it was recognized that the resources of Germany were not adequate "to make complete reparation for all such loss and damage" and Germany was required only "to make compensation for all damage done to the civilian population of the Allied and Associated Powers and to their property . . . by land, by sea, and from the air, and in general all damage as defined in Annex I. . . ." This annex listed ten loss-and-damage categories, including military pensions and the allowances paid by the Allied governments to the families of persons mobilized or serving at the fronts. In addition, Germany was to reimburse Belgium

[1] See p. 110 n.

[2] The opening sentence of Part V of the Versailles Treaty reads: "In order to render possible the initiation of a general limitation of the armaments of all nations, Germany undertakes strictly to observe the military, naval and air clauses which follow."

with interest at 5 per cent for all the money the latter had borrowed from the Allied governments during the war years.

A reparation commission was to be appointed by the Allies to determine the total amount of reparation and to "draw up a schedule of payments prescribing the time and manner for securing and discharging the entire obligation within a period of thirty years from May 1, 1921." Meanwhile, up to May 1, 1921, Germany was to pay, in gold, ships, securities, or commodities, the equivalent of nearly $5,000,000,000. Out of this advance sum the cost of the army of occupation was first to be met, and the balance applied to reparation.

Since full reparation could not be paid in cash, it was stipulated that Germany might pay part in the form of specified commodities. The right of the Allies was recognized "to the replacement, ton for ton and class for class, of all merchant-marine ships and fishing boats lost or damaged owing to the war." Germany therefore was made to surrender all her merchant vessels of sixteen hundred or more tons gross; one-half of her ships, by tonnage, of one thousand to sixteen hundred tons gross; and one-fourth, by tonnage, of her steam trawlers and fishing boats. If the Reparation Commission so demanded, Germany was also to build ships for the Allies up to a maximum of two hundred thousand tons a year for five years.

The economic resources of Germany were to be devoted "directly to the physical restoration of the invaded areas." The Allies consequently were permitted to file with the Reparation Commission lists showing:

(*a*) Animals, machinery, equipment, tools and like articles of a commercial character, which have been seized, consumed or destroyed by Germany or destroyed in direct consequence of military operations, and which such Governments, for the purpose of meeting immediate and urgent needs, desire to have replaced by animals and articles of the same nature which are in being in German territory at the date of the coming into force of the present Treaty.

(*b*) Reconstruction materials (stones, bricks, refractory bricks, tiles, wood, window-glass, steel, lime, cement, etc.), machinery, heating apparatus, furniture and like articles of a commercial character which the said Governments desire to have produced and manufactured in Germany and delivered to them to permit of the restoration of the invaded areas.[1]

[1] As an immediate advance on account of animals to be delivered, Germany was required to surrender within three months: "(1) To the French Government: 500

Germany next agreed to make annual coal deliveries for ten years as follows: 7,000,000 tons to France, 8,000,000 to Belgium, an average of 7,700,000 to Italy, and, "if directed by the Reparation Commission," a smaller amount to Luxembourg. In addition, France was to receive "annually for a period not exceeding ten years an amount of coal equal to the difference between the annual production before the war of the coal mines of the Nord and Pas de Calais, destroyed as a result of the war, and the production of the mines of the same areas during the years in question: such delivery not to exceed 20,000,000 tons in any one year of the first five years, and 8,000,000 tons in any one year of the succeeding five years." Likewise, for each of the three years following the coming into force of the treaty, France was to receive 35,000 tons of benzol, 50,000 of coal-tar, and 30,000 of ammonium sulphate. The Reparation Commission was given an option on the delivery of dyestuffs and chemicals up to 50 per cent "of the total stock of each and every kind of dyestuff and chemical drug in Germany or under German control."

Special provisions of the treaty required Germany to return the trophies, flags, and works of art taken from France in the war of 1870; to give to the University of Louvain documents and manuscripts equivalent in "number and value" to those destroyed during the war; to "restore to His Majesty the King of the Hedjaz the original Koran of the Caliph Othman, which was removed from Medina by the Turkish authorities and is stated to have been presented to the ex-Emperor William II"; and to "hand over to His Britannic Majesty's Government the skull of the Sultan Mkwawa, which was removed from the Protectorate of German East Africa and taken to Germany." [1]

The Reparation Commission was empowered to recommend action in case of any German default. It was stipulated that "the

---

stallions (3 to 7 years); 30,000 fillies and mares (18 months to 7 years), type: Ardennais, Boulonnais or Belgian; 2000 bulls (18 months to 3 years); 90,000 milch cows (2 to 6 years); 1000 rams; 100,000 sheep; 10,000 goats. (2) To the Belgian Government: 200 stallions (3 to 7 years), large Belgian type; 5000 mares (3 to 7 years), large Belgian type; 5000 fillies (18 months to 3 years), large Belgian type; 2000 bulls (18 months to 3 years); 50,000 milch cows (2 to 6 years); 40,000 heifers; 200 rams; 20,000 sheep; 15,000 sows. The animals delivered shall be of average health and condition. To the extent that animals so delivered cannot be identified as animals taken or seized, the value of such animals shall be credited against the reparation obligations of Germany."

[1] The skull was not surrendered, Germany pleading ignorance of its whereabouts. A group of officers and students in Berlin prevented the return to France of the flags captured in battle in 1870-1871 by burning them before the statue of Frederick the Great.

measures which the Allied and Associated Powers shall have the right to take, in case of voluntary default by Germany, and which Germany agrees not to regard as acts of war, may include economic and financial prohibitions and reprisals and in general such other measures as the respective Governments may determine to be necessary in the circumstances."

The remainder of the treaty disposed of such technical questions as international financial matters disturbed by the war, commercial relations, treaties, debts, property rights, contracts and judgments, industrial property, aerial navigation, the Kiel Canal, ports, waterways, and railways. By Article 264, the products of Allied manufacture were accorded most-favored-nation treatment in Germany.[1] The Elbe, Oder, Niemen, and Danube rivers were "declared international." Together with the Rhine they were placed under the control of international commissions in order that free access to the sea might be provided for the landlocked states of central Europe.

In the ports of Hamburg and Stettin, Germany was made to lease free zones to Czechoslovakia for ninety-nine years. Allied goods were to receive "the most favorable treatment" that was extended to internal traffic on German railways. The Kiel Canal and its approaches were made "free and open" on equal terms to the merchant and war vessels of all countries at peace with Germany. An International Labor Organization was created to help bring about an era of "social justice" as the basis of a universal peace.[2] Finally, Germany recognized in advance any treaties or dispositions that might be made between the Allies and Germany's former friends.

The guarantees for the execution of the treaty were written into Part XIV: "The German territory situated to the west of the Rhine, together with the bridgeheads, will be occupied by Allied and Associated troops for a period of fifteen years from the coming into force of the present Treaty." Depending on the faithfulness with which Germany carried out the terms of the treaty, the occupation was to be successively restricted, so that the bridgehead at Cologne might be evacuated after five years, that at Coblenz after ten years, and that at Mainz after fifteen. On the other hand, the occupation might be prolonged indefinitely, or any evacuated part reoccupied, if Germany misbehaved.

Actually, the last of the occupying troops were withdrawn in

[1] The tariff restrictions on Germany lapsed in 1925.
[2] See pp. 130 ff.

1930, after the adoption of the Young Plan for reparation. The American and British troops in the occupied zone got along fairly well with the German inhabitants. But the French aroused considerable hatred. They spread propaganda to alienate the people from Germany, used colored troops, and imposed severe penalties for slight offenses committed by the natives.

The Versailles Treaty, in summary, reduced the European area of Germany by one-eighth and her population by 6,500,000. It deprived her of all colonies and of virtually all investments and holdings abroad. She lost 15.5 per cent of her arable land, 12 per cent of her livestock, and almost 10 per cent of her manufacturing establishments. Her merchant marine was reduced from 5,700,000 tons to fewer than 500,000 tons. Her navy, formerly second only to Great Britain's, was virtually wiped out, and her army remained not much larger than Belgium's. By her European cessions Germany lost potash, iron, coal, zinc, lead, and food. She surrendered about two-fifths of her coal reserves, nearly two-thirds of her iron ore, about seven-tenths of her zinc, and more than half of her lead. The surrender of the colonies entailed the loss of large rubber, oil, and fiber supplies. The new territorial alignments "broke down the prewar organization of industry and commerce, so that for a long time even the industrial plant which Germany retained was incapable of working at its former level of efficiency." Finally, Germany signed a blank reparation check.

SAINT GERMAIN-EN-LAYE, WITH AUSTRIA

The Council of Four at Paris did not confine its treaty-making activities to the German situation. Before Wilson and Lloyd George left Paris, late in June 1919, the Big Four had sketched a preliminary draft treaty with Austria, had decided on the boundaries of Hungary, and had considered the cases of Bulgaria and Turkey. But the final form of the treaties with Germany's allies was the work largely of a special Council of Five. This new supreme council consisted of Chairman Clemenceau and one representative each from the United States, Great Britain, France, and Italy. It functioned until January 21, 1920, when, upon Clemenceau's resignation, it ceased to exist.[1] All the minor treaties bore considerable resemblance to that of Versailles.

---

[1] The execution of the treaties thereafter was left to the Council, or Conference, of Ambassadors made up of the ambassadors to Paris from the United States, Great Britain, Italy, and Japan, and of a French representative.

The Austrian peace delegation was presented with a draft peace treaty on June 2, 1919. Protests had to be submitted in writing. An interesting controversy developed when the Austrians insisted that the republic known as "German-Austria" (*Deutschösterreich*), which came into being on November 12, 1918, and with which the Allies were now dealing, was a newborn state that had never been at war with the Allies—at least no more so than Czechoslovakia or Poland or any other of the states that were created, in whole or in part, out of the former Austria-Hungary. Hence, it was argued, German-Austria could not be held responsible for the actions of the old Dual Monarchy. The Allies shelved this legal nicety and wrote into the preamble of the final treaty (signed September 10, 1919) that "the former Austro-Hungarian Monarchy has now ceased to exist, and has been replaced in Austria by a republican government." In Article 177, moreover, "Austria" was made to accept responsibility for causing loss and damage to the Allies "as a consequence of the war imposed upon them by the aggression of Austria-Hungary and her allies."

Despite, or perhaps because of, the fact that the new governments of both Germany and Austria favored an *Anschluss* or union, Article 88 of the Treaty of St. Germain forbade the amalgamation of Germany and Austria and imposed upon the latter the obligation to "abstain from any act which might directly or indirectly or by any means whatever compromise her independence." The Austrians were compelled, in fact, to change the name of their state from German-Austria to "Republic of Austria." The purpose of the Allies was, among other things, to prevent the strengthening of Germany by the addition of several million Austrians and to protect Czechoslovakia against a German encirclement.

It was no easy task to decide on the territorial redistribution of the former Habsburg domains. Not only did Austria and Hungary have to be dealt with, but all the heirs of the old monarchy—Czechoslovakia, Yugoslavia, Poland, Italy, and Romania—had to be at least partly satisfied. There were no clear-cut ethnic, national, or even economic border lines, and a dozen new and old national groups clamored for recognition. It was, indeed, easier to take the land from Austria and Hungary than to divide it among the "victors." Weary hours were spent in deciding the fate of particular railway terminals, canals, and strategic salients, and, in the end, no one was entirely happy.

To Italy, Austria ceded the South Tirol, the Trentino, Trieste,

Istria, and some islands off Dalmatia. The South Tirol, though inhabited by a quarter-million German-speaking people, was demanded by Italy on the strength of the Secret Treaties and on the ground that, since the Alps were "her natural defenses," she needed the strategic Brenner Pass for military and protective reasons. The section of Czechoslovakia made up from former Austrian territory included Bohemia, Moravia, part of Lower Austria, and nearly all Austrian Silesia, these areas containing about three million *Sudetendeutsche,* named after the Sudetes range. Poland received Austrian Galicia. The highly industrialized Teschen district, claimed by both Poland and Czechoslovakia, eventually was divided between the two by the Council of Ambassadors. Romania was awarded Bukovina. Bosnia, Hercegovina, and the Dalmatian coast and islands went to Yugoslavia. Altogether, the Austrian half of the Dual Monarchy was reduced in area and population by three-fourths.

The remainder of the 381 articles comprising the Treaty of St. Germain were, in general, adapted from the Versailles clauses. The articles of the League Covenant and the International Labor Organization were copies from the German treaty. Austria agreed to all terms arrived at between the Allies and her former friends; gave up all rights, privileges, and concessions in non-European areas; assented to a blank reparation check; accepted special regulations governing navigation on the Danube and concerning the transfer of railway lines and stocks; acknowledged the right of the Allies to try Austrian "war criminals"; and granted to Czechoslovakia the right to send her own trains over specified Austrian routes toward the Adriatic. Austria herself was guaranteed free access to the Adriatic via the territories formerly comprising the Austrian Empire. The prewar debt of the Dual Monarchy was to be divided proportionally among all former Habsburg domains. Austria surrendered her entire naval force, retaining only three police boats on the Danube. Her army was limited to thirty thousand volunteers, with restrictions on enlistment and discharge similar to those placed on the German forces.

NEUILLY, WITH BULGARIA

Bulgaria, to forestall punishment, sent a long memorandum to the peace conference some time before her peace terms had been decided upon. In the document it was explained (1) that Bulgaria's entry into the war was the fault largely of ex-King Ferdinand, who had abdicated on October 4, 1918; (2) that the kingdom in consequence was not deserving of penalty; and (3) that, for ethnological and historical reasons, Bulgaria had a right to considerable extensions of territory, especially in Macedonia and the Dobruja. The Allies curtly refused to accept these views and reminded Bulgaria that, after all, she was a defeated power. Bulgaria had no choice other than to sign the Treaty of Neuilly (November 27, 1919).

For strategic, military, and railway reasons, the treaty assigned to Yugoslavia four small regions in western Bulgaria. One of the ceded areas was the Strumitsa salient, which had proved bothersome to the Allies during the war, and all four cessions contained Bulgarian majorities. Greece was awarded western Thrace and a slight improvement in the Greco-Bulgarian boundary, with the consequent loss to Bulgaria of her Aegean coast line. The Allies, however, promised "to ensure the economic outlets of Bulgaria to the Aegean Sea."

Bulgaria's army was limited to 20,000 men and her other armed officials to 13,000—"so that the total number of rifles in use . . . shall not exceed 33,000." Her navy was abolished, though for "police and fishery duties" she was allowed to retain "four torpedo boats and six motor boats, all without torpedoes and torpedo apparatus." The economic, political, and international arrangements were similar to those made for Austria. In addition to the immediate surrender of some livestock to Greece, the former Serbia, and Romania, Bulgaria also had to accept reparation obligations. These eventually were fixed at $450,000,000, payable in thirty-seven years from January 1, 1921. Bulgaria's total losses in land and population were relatively small, but combined with her virtually landlocked position they helped to make her one of the weakest of the Balkan powers.

TRIANON, WITH HUNGARY

Not until June 4, 1920, was the peace treaty with Hungary signed, in the large Trianon Palace at Versailles. The delay was the fault mainly of the unsettled affairs in Hungary, where the downfall of the Habsburgs resulted in a fierce struggle for control among monarchists, republicans, socialists, and communists.[1] The turmoil was increased by frequent and violent anti-Allied outbursts which, occurring while the treaty was being drafted, influenced the Allies only to the extent that they made one important

[1] See Chapter XVII.

concession: they allowed the new state to take the name of "Hungary" rather than "Hungarian Republic." But the Magyars were warned that a Habsburg restoration would be "neither recognized nor tolerated."

All the states surrounding Hungary were allotted slices of the old Magyar kingdom. Romania received Transylvania, some of the plain west of Transylvania, and two-thirds of the Banat of Temesvár, including a total of approximately one and a half million Magyars. To Yugoslavia went Croatia-Slavonia and the western third of Temesvár, along with half a million Magyars. Slovakia became part of the new republic of Czechoslovakia, which also acquired some territory to the south and east of the Carpathian Mountains. Almost a million Magyars and half a million Ruthenians were thus incorporated into Czechoslovakia. Austria got Burgenland or West Hungary. The other treaty terms were similar to those with Austria and Bulgaria. Hungary's army was cut to thirty-five thousand men and her navy reduced to a few patrol boats. She too was made liable for reparation through a "guilt clause."

SÈVRES, WITH TURKEY

In 1920 Lloyd George told the House of Commons that the arrangements contemplated by the forthcoming treaty with the sultan would at last release "all non-Turkish populations from Turkish sway." In reality, the treaty contemplated a reversal of the situation by subjecting the Turks to the sway of Europeans. The principles underlying the treaty with Turkey were largely those embodied in the Secret Treaties, although a few modifications were made necessary by the Bolshevik Revolution and Russia's consequent temporary withdrawal from the imperialist scene, by President Wilson's stand on self-determination, and by the conflicting interests of Italy and Greece.

In the Treaty of Sèvres (August 10, 1920), Turkey acknowledged the loss of all her rights in Egypt, the Sudan, Cyprus, Tripolitania, Morocco, and Tunisia. She likewise renounced all rights over Arabia, Palestine, Mesopotamia, and Syria. Smyrna and southwestern Asia Minor were to be temporarily administered by Greece, which power also received some former Turkish islands in the Aegean and part of eastern Thrace. Italy was confirmed in the possession of Rhodes and the Dodecanese Islands, though she promised eventually to cede the latter to Greece.

The zone of the Straits was demilitarized and internationalized. It had originally been hoped by some that the United States might assume a mandate over Constantinople, but the unfavorable reaction of the American people to the peace treaties in general made it plain that President Wilson would not be upheld in the assumption of mandatory obligations. The city, therefore, remained under Turkish sovereignty, as did also a small part of the European mainland up to the limits of the town of Chatalja.

Turkey agreed to recognize Armenia as a "free and independent state" with boundaries to be drawn by Wilson in the area of the vilayets of Erzurum, Trebizond, Van, and Bitlis. Kurdistan was to receive autonomy, but her boundary might be rectified in favor of Persia (Iran). Nothing was left to Turkey save mountainous Anatolia (Asia Minor) and a corner of Europe. Moreover, on the same day on which the treaty was signed, a tripartite agreement was reached by the British, French, and Italian delegates, whereby spheres of influence in Anatolia were outlined for France and Italy. The French sphere was to the north of Syria; the Italian, south and east of Smyrna.

Though the treaty was signed by the representatives of Mohammed VI, and though the sultan, overawed by the Allied ships and forces at Constantinople, was willing to have the document ratified, an energetic group of Turkish Nationalists, led by Mustapha Kemal, determined to prevent its going into effect. The story of their success is told in another chapter.[1]

THE PROTECTION OF MINORITIES

The boundary adjustments of the treaties created an acute problem of national minorities. National spirit was fanned by the war and the peace conference, and national jealousies were aroused. Vengeful reprisals were to be expected. In the words of President Wilson, nothing was "more likely to disturb the peace of the world than the treatment which might in certain circumstances be meted out to minorities." To prevent trouble, safeguards for the minorities had to be set up. It appeared essential to guarantee at least a modicum of racial, religious, social, linguistic, and economic equality for the numerous national minorities.

In the cases of Austria, Hungary, Bulgaria, and Turkey the guarantees were included in the peace treaties. Then, despite considerable opposition on their part, Poland, Romania, Greece,

[1] See Chapter XXI.

Yugoslavia, and Czechoslovakia were required to sign special treaties embodying similar guarantees. Most of the countries concerned objected to the treaties as an infringement of their several sovereignties and as an encouragement to separatist tendencies. But the great powers were insistent and the obligations were assumed. In each instance the supervision over the minorities was left to the League and only with the consent of a majority of the Council might these guarantees be altered or modified. Eventually, Lithuania, Latvia, Estonia, Finland, and Albania entered into parallel agreements with the League.

The treaties followed a somewhat uniform pattern, any differences being the result of particular local problems. They included guarantees of life and liberty to all subjects regardless of race, nationality, or religion; they permitted the private and public worship of any creed or belief not inimical to public morals; and they protected the use of the minority languages, under certain conditions, in business and in the schools.

THE NEW WORLD: FUTURE IMPERFECT

Such, in brief, were the provisions of the treaties arising from the "war to end wars." They were one-sided. They were replete with unstable compromises. They reflected materialism tinged only here and there with idealism. They contained the seeds of future conflict. Yet, in appraising the work of the treaty-makers of 1919 and 1920, the enormous difficulties—material and psychological—under which they labored, must be remembered. Some of their mistakes were obvious at the time they were made, but many stood out more clearly only after the passing of several years. There was much hatred and vengeance, blindness and force, but all these factors were part of the "human nature" and the "civilization" of the day. The four years of blood and mire had not increased reasonableness nor sweetened tempers.

And now, before the story of the post-1918 world is taken up, a few of the outstanding changes effected by the First World War and the Paris Peace Settlement may be summarized:

(1) Four imperial governments were swept away, those in Germany, Austria-Hungary, Russia, and Turkey.

(2) A wave of republicanism swept over Europe. In 1914 France, Switzerland, Portugal, San Marino, and Andorra were the

only republics on the continent. Eighteen years later there were sixteen continental republics.

(3) Almost simultaneously with the extension of the republican form of government there appeared a distrust of democracy, owing, partly, to the inability of the new governments to solve the complex postwar problems. Consequently there arose a number of dictators who proposed, through despotism, to save their people from destruction.

(4) Three great politico-economic experiments were inaugurated: Bolshevism, Fascism, and Nazism.

(5) There was a decided change in the relative importance of nations in Europe. With the disruption of Austria-Hungary and the territorial changes in Germany and Russia there appeared a number of new states, such as Poland, Czechoslovakia, and Yugoslavia, which began to play an important role in international affairs. Before the war six great powers determined international relations in Europe. The temporary eclipse of Germany, Russia, and Austria-Hungary and the emergence of a number of states of the second rank increased the number of actors on the international stage and complicated the solution of international problems. The surrounding of Germany by many small states eventually played into the hands of the aggressive Nazis.

(6) The great emphasis on nationality during the war and the diffusion of the idea of national self-determination made political and economic international relations after the war more difficult than ever. Diplomatic intrigues, economic rivalries, jealous quarrels, and new oppressions fanned the flames of old hatreds and overwhelmed Europe with another dangerous hysteria.

(7) The spreading of the principles of nationality and self-determination stimulated unrest in nearly all the overseas possessions of the Allied Powers, in Egypt, India, Chosen, East Africa, and elsewhere.

(8) Despite the hopes of many that there would be no more war, the peace treaties created new wounds in the process of healing old ones. The suspicion and fear which for so long had overclouded diplomacy were not dispelled. New military alliances were formed, Europe was divided anew into hostile camps, the number of men under arms permanently exceeded the number in 1913, and the world's military and naval budgets continued to make increasingly heavy demands on the purses of harassed taxpayers.

(9) Instrumentalities for international coöperation and for the peaceful settlement of international disputes were provided by the establishment of the League of Nations and the World Court, but these were not always given the support they needed.

(10) In many countries democratic reforms were introduced, particularly in the direction of suffrage extension. Partly because of a new spirit and partly because of the services they had rendered during the war, women were widely enfranchised.

(11) Temporarily, at least, labor assumed a new importance in the world order. This was owing, apparently, to the transient shortage of skilled labor, to a realization that the man on the fighting line would have been helpless without the support of the man at the factory, and to a radical propaganda which throve during the periods of economic distress that followed the war. In eastern Europe, the hitherto downtrodden agrarians gained temporary control of a number of governments.

(12) There was a general, if temporary, religious revival. It was inevitable that many of the young men who were so constantly surrounded by death should seek refuge in religion and comfort in the belief in another and perhaps better world. Mysticism and spiritualism also enjoyed popularity in the early postwar years.

(13) Education suffered greatly during the war and in the lean years following it, but there was a general feeling that in the proper education of the young lay the best guarantee against a repetition of the catastrophe. Wherever money was available, increased attention was paid to the training of children and of adults.

(14) Youth movements became popular, especially in China, Germany, Italy, and the Soviet Union. The younger men and women of the world were made serious- and political-minded by the diplomatic and economic crises which grew out of the war and they eagerly anticipated a wholesale regeneration of their respective peoples. Generally the training to which they were subjected was, in the first instance, military.

(15) The war taught the nations lessons in coöperation and "teamwork," and all the value of these was not lost upon the return of peace. Often in attempts to solve outstanding international economic and social problems, use was made of the wartime experience in coöperation. World conferences became frequent, if not always successful, occurrences.

(16) The United States, occupying a position as debtor nation in 1914, emerged from the war as the world's greatest creditor.

Her new importance was the cause of much ill will and jealousy.

(17) Through their participation in the war, their membership in the League of Nations, and their increasing importance as markets, the Latin-American states came to have a new and more prominent standing in world affairs.

(18) The war served as a stimulus to scientific and commercial advances as well as to the development of more efficient machines of destruction. Advances were made in the field of medicine, there was progress in the art of shipbuilding, and great strides were made in aviation. New industries were stimulated, particularly where wartime conditions deprived a country of products which formerly had been available only through import.

(19) Temporary impetus was given to a movement for general disarmament, but progress in this direction was halting.

(20) A complete and world-wide economic rehabilitation was necessitated, for the war dislocated the economic machinery of all participants and even of the neutrals. In direct consequence of the war and its aftermath, a depression made its appearance toward the end of 1929 which, becoming universal, boosted the world unemployment figure to thirty million, bankrupted nations, and gave rise to unprecedented world unrest. By 1939 final proof was given that the preceding score of years had in reality been only a twenty years' armistice.

PART II

Twenty Years' Armistice,
1919–1939

CHAPTER VI

The League of Nations

ORIGIN, MEMBERSHIP, AND ORGANIZATION

The pertinence of the observation regarding the absence of anything new under the sun is strikingly illustrated in the history of plans for an association of the nations. Collected in book form, the texts of the most important schemes for international arbitration and organization from ancient times to the twentieth century cover about one thousand pages.[1] Most of the costly wars in history have produced new plans to preserve peace and settle international disputes by arbitration rather than armed conflict.

The outbreak of the First World War for a time made people lose faith in the value of peace work. Before long, however, the catastrophic nature of the struggle imbued idealists with new strength to agitate for the establishment of an instrument which would replace armed conflict as a means of settling international difficulties. During the first two years of the war there were formed in the United States an American League to Limit Armaments, an American Union against Militarism, a Women's Peace Party, and a League to Enforce Peace. This last counted among its sponsors some of the leading statesmen in the United States and Great Britain. In 1916 it prepared drafts for a covenant of an international league to prevent war and arbitrate disputes. President Wilson publicly endorsed the suggestions of the League to Enforce Peace and finally incorporated the idea of a "general association of nations" as the fourteenth of his famous points. Meanwhile a group of British lawyers, led by Lord Phillimore, had also drafted a league charter and by the time of America's entry into the war it was generally understood that the forthcoming peace conference would have to give the matter its earnest consideration.[2]

[1] Darby, W. E. *International Arbitration. International Tribunals*, 4 ed., 1904.

[2] The idea of a society of nations was also discussed during the war days by some German thinkers, notably Matthias Erzberger.

In an earlier chapter there was told the story of the drafting of the Covenant at Paris. Not only was this document made an integral part of each of the peace treaties, but the League of Nations which it created was given supervision over the fulfillment of many of the treaty clauses. The League, indeed, was entrusted with the task of "liquidating the war and implementing the peace"— an assignment which was made the more difficult by the refusal of the United States to become a member. Unfortunately, also, many people, particularly those in the defeated countries, were from the beginning prejudiced against the League *because* it was tied so closely to the peace settlement.

No better explanation of the purpose of the League can be given than to quote the preamble to the Covenant:

The High Contracting Parties,
In order to promote international coöperation and to achieve international peace and security

by the acceptance of obligations not to resort to war,
by the prescription of open, just and honourable relations between nations,
by the firm establishment of the understandings of international law as the actual rule of conduct among Governments,
and by the maintenance of justice and a scrupulous respect for all treaty obligations in the dealings of organised peoples with one another,

Agree to this Covenant of the League of Nations.

The original members of the League were the signatories named in an annex to the Covenant and such of a group of invited states as acceded without reservation to the document within two months of its coming into force. By a two-thirds vote of the Assembly, membership might further be extended to any fully self-governing state, dominion, or colony provided it could give effective guarantees of its desire to observe its international obligations and its willingness to accept such regulations as might be prescribed by the League with regard to its armaments.

Any member state which had fulfilled its obligations under the Covenant might withdraw from the League after two years' notice. By the close of 1932, only two states—Brazil and Costa Rica—had availed themselves of this privilege, but after 1933 many states forwarded to the League the required two years' notice of their intended withdrawal. In September 1934 Ecuador became the sixtieth member of the League, but by the time of the outbreak of the Second World War, five years later, only forty-six states had neither resigned nor served notice of intention to withdraw. The Covenant might be amended by the unanimous vote of the Council and a majority vote of the Assembly. A number of amendments, relating chiefly to procedure, were adopted.

The League budget, including the costs of the World Court and the International Labor Organization, never exceeded $10,000,000 in any one year. The expenses were allocated among the members according to a scale. The total cost eventually was divided into 1012½ units and a certain number of these units was charged to each member. The British Empire, exclusive of the dominions members of the League, was required to pay most—105 units. Such small countries as Albania and Liberia were asked to contribute one unit each.

The League functioned through an Assembly, a Council, and a permanent Secretariat. The Assembly consisted of representatives of all the members, each state being entitled to a maximum of three delegates, but only one vote. These representatives, as well as all officials of the League, enjoyed diplomatic immunity. Sessions were held annually at Geneva, in September. Special sessions might be held in times of emergency. The first Assembly was called by President Wilson and convened on November 15, 1920. The latest or twentieth ordinary session adjourned on December 14, 1939.[1]

Each new session of the Assembly was presided over by the president of the Council until such time as the permanent president and six vice-presidents were elected. Then these seven, together with the chairmen of six standing committees, constituted a General Committee which was responsible for the conduct of business. The standing committees, on which each state was represented by one delegate, were concerned with: (1) legal and constitutional questions; (2) the work of the technical organizations; (3) reduction of armaments; (4) budget and internal administration; (5) social problems; and (6) political questions. In addition to these groups there were numerous auxiliary and special committees.

At its meetings the Assembly might consider "any matter within the sphere of action of the League or affecting the peace of the world." From the start, "the Assembly established itself as a platform from which the representatives of the Governments as-

[1] Between 1920 and 1939 there also were five special sessions, making twenty-five in all.

sociated in the League could annually give expression to their general views, their grievances, their criticisms, and their aspirations." Specifically, the tasks of the body were to select the nonpermanent members of the Council, control the budget, admit new members, elect concurrently with the Council the judges of the World Court, and, if it saw fit, advise the reconsideration of treaties that might have become inapplicable.

The League Council, composed of one delegate from each of the states entitled to representation, corresponded somewhat to the executive branch in a national government. Originally, the Covenant provided for five permanent and four nonpermanent Council seats, the former to go to the United States, Great Britain, France, Italy, and Japan. Because of the refusal of the United States to join the League, there were until 1922 only eight members in the Council. In that year the Assembly increased the number of nonpermanent seats to six, thus giving the smaller states a majority. The terms of the nonpermanent members (increased to nine in 1926, ten in 1933, and eleven in 1936) were fixed at three years and staggered so that each year several states retired. In general, retiring members were not immediately reëlected. For the period of their membership in the League, Germany and the Soviet Union had permanent Council seats.[1]

After 1929 the Council normally held three meetings a year—in January, May, and September—usually at Geneva, but there were frequent special meetings. The presidency of the body was rotated in successive sessions among the delegates in the alphabetical order of the names of the member states in French. Except in matters of procedure, decisions of the Council had to be unanimous. Whenever a subject was under discussion concerning a nonmember of the Council, that state was entitled to temporary representation thereon. Like the Assembly, the Council might consider any question affecting world peace or threatening the harmony of international relations. Since this body was smaller than the Assembly and could be more quickly gathered, it was called upon to handle most of the emergency situations. The first Council meeting was summoned by President Wilson for January 16, 1920, at Paris. The latest or one hundred and seventh meeting closed on December 14, 1939.

The specific duties assigned to the Council by the Covenant in-

---

[1] The Council in 1940 was made up of France and Great Britain as permanent members and the following nonpermanent members: Belgium, Bolivia, China, Dominican Republic, Egypt, Finland, Greece, Iran, Peru, South Africa, and Yugoslavia.

cluded the formulation of plans for the reduction of national armaments, the study of the annual reports submitted by the mandatories, and the devising of means for the protection of the territorial integrity of member states against external aggression. It was to inquire into any international disputes which might be submitted to it and it might refer these disputes to the Assembly. Finally, the Council was supposed to recommend to the member states what effectives each should contribute in the event that "the covenants of the League" required protection.

The third agency of the League was the permanent Secretariat, or "civil service," established at Geneva. It consisted of a secretary-general (who also acted in that capacity at Council and Assembly meetings) and a staff selected by him with the approval of the Council. The first secretary-general, Sir James Eric Drummond, was named in the annex to the Covenant. With Allied approval he began to assemble his assistants and establish temporary quarters in London immediately after the adoption of the text of the Covenant on April 28, 1919—two months before the signing of the Versailles Treaty. Drummond soon proved himself an officer of remarkable ability, combining tactfulness, hard work, fairness, and efficiency. Future secretaries-general were to be appointed by the Council with the approval of the Assembly. In 1933 Drummond relinquished his post and was succeeded by his former deputy, Joseph Avenol of France. The latter resigned in 1940 and was succeeded by Seán Lester of Ireland as acting secretary-general.

The secretary-general came to be assisted by a staff of almost seven hundred employees drawn from more than fifty nations.[1] Staff members were employed and paid by the League; theoretically at least, they did not represent the interests of their respective countries. The Secretariat was divided into eleven sections which were concerned with such matters as mandates, disarmament, health, minorities, and economic and financial questions. The secretary-general was responsible for the registration and publication of all treaties entered into among the League members or voluntarily submitted to him by nonmembers. The number of documents so registered through August 1941 was 4733. The texts of the treaties were published in their original language as well as in French and English.

To lighten the work of these three main bodies the League

[1] In the spring of 1943 Mr. Lester was still in Geneva, assisted by a skeleton staff of about seventy-five.

created several auxiliary organs known as "technical organizations" and "advisory committees." In the former group were the Economic and Financial Organization, the Organization on Communications and Transit, and the Health Organization. Among the advisory committees were those on mandates, traffic in opium, and intellectual coöperation. There were, in addition, some temporary groups, such as was the Preparatory Commission for the Disarmament Conference. A number of international bureaus which originated independently of the League, such as the International Hydrographic Bureau at Monaco, also were placed under the auspices of the association.

THE PERMANENT COURT AND THE I.L.O.

Two other major agencies technically formed part of the machinery of the League: the Permanent Court of International Justice, or World Court, and the International Labor Organization. According to Article 14 of the League Covenant:

The Council shall formulate and submit to the Members of the League for adoption plans for the establishment of a Permanent Court of International Justice. The Court shall be competent to hear and determine any dispute of an international character which the parties thereto submit to it. The Court may also give an advisory opinion upon any dispute or question referred to it by the Council or by the Assembly. •

In execution of this mandate the Council, at its second session (February 1920), appointed a committee of jurists to draw up a statute for such a court. The committee met at The Hague and in less than six weeks agreed unanimously upon a detailed draft covering the organization, procedure, and jurisdiction of the proposed tribunal. The plan was forthwith delivered to the Council which, after making a few amendments, passed it on to the first Assembly. The latter added some more amendments and in December 1920 unanimously adopted it as the statute of the court.

The Council then prepared a protocol of ratification which included the statute as an annex and submitted the document to the League members. The court was to come into existence as soon as a majority of the League members should have ratified the protocol. By September 1921 the necessary minimum of ratifications was secured and the Council and Assembly concurrently but separately elected the first group of judges.[1] The Hague was picked as the seat of the court. Its expenses, about $500,000 annually, were financed through the League budget.

The World Court was originally composed of eleven judges and four deputy-judges, all chosen for nine-year terms by absolute majorities in the Council and Assembly. In order to emphasize the permanent character of the tribunal, a committee of jurists, appointed by the Council, recommended (1929) that the number of judges be increased to fifteen and that, except for fixed vacations, the court remain in session throughout the year. By the institution of rotation among the judges the burden on the individual jurists would remain within reasonable limits. A protocol embodying these recommendations was placed before the states members of the court and early in 1931 it became effective. The president and vice-president were elected by the judges themselves and held office for three years.

The jurisdiction of the court was of two kinds, voluntary and compulsory. When two or more states having a dispute referred it to the court for settlement, the tribunal's voluntary jurisdiction was being invoked. A certain number of states, however, signed an "Optional Clause" which was attached to the protocol of the court. This clause bound its ratifiers to accept the jurisdiction of the Permanent Court "as compulsory, *ipso facto* and without special convention" in all legal disputes concerning the interpretation of a treaty, any question of international law, a breach of an international obligation, or the nature and extent of reparation to be made for any such breach. For signatories of this clause the jurisdiction of the court was compulsory. In September 1939, thirty-nine states were bound by its terms. Reference of disputes to the court also was made compulsory by the terms of many of the bilateral treaties of conciliation and arbitration that were signed after the First World War.

The procedure of the court was like that of any regular tribunal. Briefs had to be filed, arguments heard, evidence examined, and decisions rendered by a majority vote of the judges after private deliberation. Only states might bring suit before the court and judgments might be given in default when a country failed to an-

[1] By September 1939 there were fifty ratifications. By this date, also, four Americans had served on the court. John Bassett Moore was among the original selections, but he resigned in 1928. Charles Evans Hughes was elected in the same year as his successor, but resigned in 1930. Frank B. Kellogg, chosen to fill the vacancy, served until 1935. Manley O. Hudson became the fourth American judge. For the attitude of the United States towards the court see Chapter XXIII.

swer a plaintiff's summons for trial. The court also was empowered to give advisory opinions to the Council and Assembly. The Council, especially, availed itself of this opportunity to get advice on legal points. The opinions, which were rendered after the usual court procedure, were binding on no one, but they were generally accepted as valid.

The Permanent Court did not entirely replace the old Hague Tribunal which was set up in 1899. The latter was a panel or list of 132 eminent jurists from which a court might be selected to arbitrate any dispute between signatories of the Hague Convention. The World Court did not arbitrate quarrels; it interpreted international law and decided on treaty violations. By the time the judges dispersed after the invasion of the Netherlands in May 1940, thirty-one decisions and twenty-seven advisory opinions had been handed down.

The International Labor Organization, although entirely autonomous and responsible only to itself and public opinion, also was an organ of the League. It was brought into being in the interests of labor through Part XIII of the Versailles Treaty. Since, under Article 23 of the Covenant, the League was pledged "to secure and maintain fair and humane conditions of labour for men, women, and children" in all countries, the Council and Assembly agreed to supply the I.L.O. with funds and make membership in it automatic with League membership. Germany, however, was represented in the labor association for some years before her entry into the League and Brazil remained a member of the I.L.O. even after her withdrawal from the League. On August 20, 1934, the United States became a member of the body, without assuming "any obligations under the Covenant of the League of Nations."

The structure of the I.L.O., which had its seat at Geneva, was similar to that of the League itself. There was a General Conference which corresponded to the Assembly, a Governing Body which was analogous to the Council, and an International Labor Office that was similar to the Secretariat. The General Conference, which met at least once a year, consisted of four delegates from each member state, one chosen by labor, one by the employers, and two by the government. The method of voting was by head.[1]

[1] Article 422 of the Versailles Treaty reads as follows: "Amendments to this Part of the present Treaty [Part XIII, the constitution of the I.L.O.] which are adopted by the Conference by a majority of two-thirds of the votes cast by the Delegates present shall take effect when ratified by the States whose representatives compose the Council of the League of Nations and by three-fourths of the members."

The General Conference had no legislative powers, but it could readily focus world attention upon certain evils and point the way to an improvement in labor conditions. By two-thirds votes, it might pass either recommendations or draft conventions. The former usually consisted of broad principles enunciated in order to guide the various states in their own labor legislation. The conventions were detailed legal proposals which, it was hoped, might be adopted by the states members. Both the recommendations and the conventions were transmitted to the various governments by the secretary-general of the League and each state was bound to submit the proposals to its legislative authority for consideration.

The Governing Body, which met at least once every three months, came to be made up of thirty-two persons, eight representing the workers, eight the employers, and sixteen the governments. In order that the states of greatest industrial importance might have a permanent voice in the activities of the I.L.O., it was provided that eight delegates among the government representatives in the Governing Body be always chosen by the "members which are of the chief industrial importance." In 1922 the eight states thus designated were Belgium, Canada, France, Germany, Great Britain, India, Italy, and Japan. After the United States and the Soviet Union joined the I.L.O., the Governing Body, in January 1935, decided to drop Belgium and Canada from this list of permanently represented states in order to make room for the newcomers. The remaining government representatives were chosen by the government delegates in the General Conference, excluding the delegates from the eight countries mentioned. The deputies of the workers and employers in the General Conference chose the respective representatives for the Governing Body. Members of the latter held office for three years. Their chief function was the election and control of a director of the International Labor Office.

This office had its headquarters in a separate building at Geneva and was served by a personnel of more than three hundred men and women. Its functions were to collect information on all phases of industrial life and labor, prepare the agenda for the annual General-Conference meetings, and maintain contact with the various volunteer labor societies throughout the world. It also published an *Official Bulletin,* an *International Labour Review,* and numerous studies, documents, and reports. In 1940 a temporary working center was set up at Montreal.

Most of the sixty-seven conventions proposed through 1940 by the I.L.O. dealt with the general improvement of working conditions. They related to the length of working hours, unemployment, workmen's compensation, sickness insurance, the labor of women and children, medical examinations, night work, sanitary conditions, the right of combination among agricultural workers, and the like. By January 1941 more than 50 states had registered with the League 879 ratifications of these conventions, 46 of which had come into force. Thus was marked the fair progress "of a uniform movement for social reform throughout the world." [1]

THE PACIFIC SETTLEMENT OF DISPUTES

Each member of the League of Nations entered into thirty-four specific engagements under the Covenant. Nineteen of these dealt directly or indirectly with the preservation of peace. To begin, the members undertook "to respect and preserve as against external aggression the territorial integrity and existing political independence of all Members of the League" (Article 10). In case of such aggression, it became the duty of the Council to "advise upon the means by which this obligation shall be fulfilled." To have force, any decision to which the Council might come in this regard had to be arrived at unanimously. Hence no power with representation in that body could be made to go to war against its will in order to meet its responsibilities under the tenth article.

Further, "any war or threat of war, whether immediately affecting any of the Members of the League or not," was declared to be a matter of concern to the whole League, and each member had the "friendly right" to bring to the attention of the "Assembly or of the Council any circumstance whatever affecting international relations which threatens to disturb international peace or the good understanding between nations upon which peace depends" (Article 11). All parties to the Covenant agreed to submit to arbitration or judicial settlement any disputes which, arising among them, were suited to such forms of settlement, or else to lay their difficulties before the Council.

As an added inducement to this course of action, the members promised not to go to war against any state which accepted the arbitral award, judicial decision, or Council report (provided the

---

[1] There was a meeting of the General Conference at Columbia University in New York in the fall of 1941. The main themes were means of strengthening "democratic resistance to the Axis powers and facilitating the work of reconstruction after the war."

latter was unanimous). If the Council failed to reach a report, the members reserved the privilege "to take such action as they shall consider necessary for the maintenance of right and justice" (Articles 13, 15). In no case, however, was resort to be had to war until three months after the award or report was made (Article 12).

Whenever the Council was asked to settle a quarrel, it might refer the dispute to the Assembly. Here a decision, to be conclusive, had to be concurred in by the representatives of all states having seats in the Council and by a majority of the remaining members of the League. If the Council found that a dispute arose "out of a matter which by international law is solely within the domestic jurisdiction" of one of the contending parties, then no recommendation of settlement whatever might be made (Article 15).

The Covenant also provided penalties for the infraction of its pledges. Whenever a nation resorted to armed hostilities in violation of its agreements, "it shall *ipso facto* be deemed to have committed an act of war against" the entire League. In such case the culprit was to be subjected to an immediate "severance of all trade or financial relations" both with the members of the League and with nonaffiliated countries. This "economic weapon" might be applied to the private affairs of the nationals of the guilty state as well as to its government (Article 16).

In order to minimize the loss and inconvenience which might result to the boycotting states from such procedure, the League members promised mutually to support one another in the financial and economic measures which might be taken against a covenant-breaking power. If the economic sanction proved of no avail in dealing with a recalcitrant state, the Council might go so far as to *recommend* to the governments concerned "what effective military, naval or air force the Members of the League shall severally contribute to the armed forces to be used to protect the covenants of the League" (Article 16).

The protective sanctions of Article 16 were equally valid in the event of an attack by a nonmember of the League on a member (Article 17). Whenever two nonmembers were involved, the Council might also "take such measures and make such recommendations as will prevent hostilities and will result in the settlement of the dispute."

In twenty years the League was called upon to examine about forty political disputes, most of them, in one way or another, legacies of the First World War. As a rule the cases were handled by the Council, but a few were referred to the Assembly, the Council of Ambassadors, or the Permanent Court. Some of the earlier quarrels, such as that of 1923 between Italy and Greece over the murder of several Italians on Greek soil, were really serious threats to world peace. Others, such as that of 1921-1922 between Finland and Soviet Russia over the treatment of the inhabitants of eastern Karelia, were of lesser importance. A number, including the Polish-Lithuanian controversy over Vilnius and the Hungaro-Romanian "optants" difficulty, the League was unable to settle. On the whole, the League was able to assert its political mission more strongly where small nations were involved. The larger nations were more likely to regard League investigations as infringing their sovereign rights. They were also better able to bring pressure to bear in their favor. From 1931 on, indeed, the great powers showed repeatedly that they were not prepared to uphold the ideal of collective resistance to aggression. The Covenant was violated with increasing frequency, and the League members simply refused to meet the challenge of the violations. Thus the powers failed the League, not the League peace.

One of the first disputes[1] brought to the attention of the Council concerned the Åland Islands which lie between Sweden and Finland and command the entrance to the Gulf of Bothnia. Both Finland and the islands, whose population in 1920 was 27,000, had once belonged to Sweden, but in 1809 they were acquired by Russia, which governed them as a single administrative unit until 1917. Then, when Finland declared her independence, she also extended her sovereignty over the archipelago. In January 1918 Sweden recognized the independent status of Finland, making no reservations regarding the Åland Islands, though the inhabitants of the latter were chiefly of Swedish stock and spoke Swedish.

Before many months had passed, the Ålanders, demanding the right of self-determination, began to agitate for union with Sweden. Two unofficial plebiscites showed a large majority in favor of the transfer of allegiance. The government of Sweden gave the separatist movement no support, but the Swedish people displayed considerable interest in the matter, particularly when open revolt seemed imminent. The Finns eventually dispatched troops to the islands and arrested the leading agitators. Thereupon the Swedes demanded action of their authorities and for a

---

[1] A number of disputes other than those here discussed, which were referred to the League for settlement, are considered in connection with the histories of the countries concerned. Consult index under "League of Nations, settlements of disputes."

time it looked like war. In June 1920, however, at which time Finland had not yet been admitted to League membership, Great Britain exercised her "friendly right" under the Covenant to direct the attention of Secretary-General Drummond to the case.

In July the Council was convened in London and it called on each of the disputants to present its side of the clash. Finland's representative held that the affair was of a purely domestic nature, that Sweden had interposed no reservations anent the islands at the time she recognized Finland, and that consequently danger of war was nonexistent. The Swedish delegate pointed out that the Ålanders obviously desired union with Sweden, that the latter country had in no way abetted the separatist movement, and that the Council had every right to consider the case since it clearly threatened a rupture of peace. By way of solution he advocated the holding of a plebiscite. The situation was further complicated by the doubt existing whether or not the provisions of an annex to the Treaty of Paris (1856), whereby the islands had been demilitarized, were still in force.

The Council, before proceeding with the investigation, assigned to a committee of jurists the task of answering two questions: (1) Did the matter really lie within the sole and domestic jurisdiction of Finland? (2) Were the international obligations regarding demilitarization still in effect? In September 1920 the committee reported, replying to the query of domestic jurisdiction in the negative and to that regarding demilitarization in the affirmative. Its legal competence to deal with the dispute thus established, the Council appointed another committee to visit Sweden, Finland, and the islands and to gather evidence upon which a fair decision might be based.

Four days after the evidence was placed before the Council, that body made public (June 24, 1921) its decision as follows: (1) Finland was to have sovereignty over the islands; (2) the Ålanders were to be guaranteed autonomy and the protection of their political rights; (3) the rights of private property and the use of Swedish in the schools were to be preserved; and (4) the archipelago should be neutralized and unfortified. On April 6, 1922, there went into force a new international convention which guaranteed the neutrality of the islands and afforded them requisite international protection. Thus was ended a dispute that might well have brought on another armed struggle in the wake of the First World War.

Another interesting dispute settled by the League was the

Turco-Iraqi or Mosul boundary controversy. According to the Treaty of Lausanne (1923), which made peace between Turkey and the Allies, the frontier separating the former from Great Britain's mandate-kingdom Iraq was to be drawn "in friendly arrangement" between Turkey and Great Britain. If no agreement could be reached within nine months by this method, the matter should be referred to the League Council.

In due time representatives of the two powers met at Constantinople but they failed to agree on a mutually acceptable boundary line. The difficulty centered in the disposition of the Mosul vilayet which, rich in oil, was claimed by both parties. At the time of the Armistice of Mudros (October 1918) the British had been in occupation merely of the southern third of the vilayet, but in the succeeding months, without military provocation by the Turks, they had advanced about ninety-five miles farther north. To all this occupied area, plus part of the vilayet of Hakkari, north of Mosul, the British now laid claim. On August 6, 1924, they lodged an appeal with the League.

In pleading her case before the Council, Great Britain maintained that Iraq needed the disputed region to provide a natural frontier and to furnish an unrestricted grain supply. The Turks, who had been given representation on the Council for the duration of the investigation, pointed out that the land had never been conquered during the war and that the Mosul population, on the whole, favored Turkish control. Neither side mentioned oil.

While the hearings were in progress the litigants agreed to uphold the *status quo* along the border. Unfortunately, the two powers variously interpreted the *status quo,* with the result that there occurred a number of frontier incidents. The emergency brought on a special Council meeting at Brussels, where a provisional boundary line was drawn, pending final judgment. Turkey was to maintain order north of this Brussels Line and Great Britain to the south of it. The provisional boundary coincided with the line of farthest British post-armistice military occupation. Meanwhile a neutral commission of inquiry went to London to hear the British story and then to Ankara to get the Turkish viewpoint; early in 1925 it arrived on the scene of the dispute. To the accompaniment of several exciting incidents a thorough investigation was conducted and in September 1925 the commission's report was laid before the Council.

The document established Turkey's sovereignty over the vilayet and explained that neither Great Britain nor Iraq had a right to claim it by conquest. If the Council, however, proposed to base its decisions on the best interests of the natives rather than upon sovereign rights, the vilayet should be assigned to Iraq, *provided* British control over that kingdom were extended for about twenty-five years. Unless British supervision were continued, Iraq would experience disorder and then the Mosul population would be better off under Turkish domination. The report opposed a plebiscite because of the backwardness of the people. If the Council, moreover, should decide in favor of Iraq, then it was morally bound to give the latter easily defensible boundaries, that is, to give it either the entire region claimed by the British, or at least all the land south of the Brussels Line.

While the representatives of Spain, Sweden, and Uruguay in the Council were asked to study these suggestions, the Permanent Court was asked for advisory opinions on two points that had been raised by the Turks: (1) Was the Council's decision to be regarded as an arbitral award, a recommendation, or a mediation? (2) Would a mere majority vote of the Council give validity to the final judgment or was unanimity required, and were the representatives of the disputants entitled to votes? The court expressed the opinions that the Lausanne Treaty made the Council's decision binding on both parties and that the final decision had to be unanimous, not counting the votes of the contending powers. Close upon this announcement came rumors of fresh disorders in Mosul, and a special Council investigator, an Estonian general, was sent to the scene. On December 10, 1925, he rendered a report unfavorable to the Turks.

Six days later the Council disposed of the quarrel. The Turkish representative refused to attend, explaining by note that he was not authorized to participate in proceedings based on the theory that Turkey could not veto any proposed solution. This attitude, combined with the investigator's adverse report, injured Turkey's cause, and a judgment was voted which incorporated those counsels of the commission of inquiry which favored Iraq. It was stipulated that the Brussels Line become the permanent Turco-Iraqi boundary, that Great Britain take steps to secure the extension of her control over Iraq for a further twenty-five years unless the kingdom should earlier become a member of the League, and that the Kurdish minority in Mosul be guaranteed the appointment of Kurdish local officials and the use of the Kurdish language in its schools.

Great Britain and Iraq accepted the award but Turkey was

angry. She became suspicious of the League and drew closer to the Soviet Union. The British, however, strove to effect a reconciliation, and in June 1926 an Anglo-Turkish treaty was negotiated whereby a small section of the vilayet was re-ceded to Turkey, the revised boundary was recognized as definitive, and some royalties from the Mosul oil fields were confirmed to Turkey.[1]

Less successful were the efforts of the Council to settle a Latin-American controversy. On December 8, 1928, the press announced that an armed clash had taken place in the Chaco district, a wilderness region long in dispute between Bolivia and Paraguay and reputed to be rich in oil. Further dispatches describing the progress of hostilities appeared at frequent intervals and war seemed inevitable, especially after the Bolivian Republic, which considered itself the victim of unjust aggression, rejected the mediation of Argentina.

Fortunately, a League Council meeting was scheduled for December 10 and, though neither disputant had referred the case to the League, the Chaco dispute was at once taken under advisement. A telegram was quickly dispatched by the Council expressing its "full conviction that the two States which, by signing the Covenant, had solemnly pledged themselves to seek by pacific means the solution of disputes arising between them would have recourse to such methods as would be in conformity with their international obligations and would appear in the present circumstances to be most likely to secure the maintenance of peace and the settlement of the dispute."

Both powers replied that they had no intention of violating their obligations under the Covenant. Instead, they agreed to accept the good offices of the Pan-American Conference on Arbitration and Conciliation which happened to be in session at Washington. The gathering appointed a committee that soon resolved the immediate quarrel, but the underlying cause of the dispute remained untouched and renewed disorders broke out in May 1929. After a vigorous interchange of telegrams between the two republics and Geneva, the former reiterated their peaceful inclinations and agreed to smooth out their fundamental differences at a conference table. In due time representatives of Bolivia and Paraguay met at Washington to conclude a pact of nonaggression, but this effort, too, involved a suspension rather than a cessation of hostilities.

In 1932 the quarrel was renewed and once more the League, the

[1] On later Anglo-Iraqi relations see p. 145 n. 2.

United States, and several South American countries acted to prevent war. The confusion resulting from these well-intentioned but uncoördinated efforts at mediation apparently "made it easy for both sides to evade responsibility" for what soon developed into a bloody conflict. Then, after the casualties had mounted into the tens of thousands, the chief obstacle to peace seemed to be "the aroused . . . nationalism of both countries, which made it difficult for either side to yield an inch."

In 1934, after investigating on the spot, a League Commission of Inquiry characterized the struggle as "inhuman and criminal" and outlined a peace treaty intended to be fair to both parties. The contestants, however, felt otherwise and the treaty was not adopted. The chairman of the commission thereupon suggested an embargo on arms shipments to the warring countries. A number of powers, led by the United States, acted upon the proposal. In the meantime the League appointed still another conciliation body to find a basis for ending the war.

The beginning of the rainy season in the autumn of 1934 found the Paraguayan troops in possession of most of the disputed territory. Consequently Paraguay rejected a comprehensive peace plan formulated in November by the League Assembly. While the League hesitated to invoke the full economic sanctions of the Covenant, it recommended that the arms embargo be lifted in favor of Bolivia. About a score of countries followed this suggestion but the rest refused to discriminate against Paraguay. The latter, indeed, responded by serving notice (February 1935) of her intention to resign from the League. (In 1937 her resignation became effective.)

In March 1935, after some military rallies by Bolivia, the League washed its hands of the affair, leaving it to the American nations to settle the dispute among themselves. Thereupon Argentina, Brazil, Chile, Peru, the United States, and Uruguay offered their friendly services as conciliators, with the result that, in June 1935, the foreign ministers of Bolivia and Paraguay signed a protocol at Buenos Aires outlining machinery for the negotiation of peace. Thereafter it took three years, until July 1938, before a peace treaty was signed. The document requested the presidents of the mediating states to fix a definitive boundary, a task which was accomplished, on a compromise basis, by the following October. Both Bolivia and Paraguay accepted the award and in January 1939 the peace conference declared its functions at an end.

LEAGUE ADMINISTRATION OF TERRITORY: THE SAAR

The Versailles Treaty placed upon the League responsibility for the government of the Saar Basin and the free city of Danzig. Early in 1920, therefore, the Council set up the necessary machinery for the rule of these areas. Regarding the basin, the peace treaty stipulated that a governing commission be appointed, to consist of five members: one a Frenchman by birth and citizenship, one a native of the territory, and three citizens of three countries other than France or Germany. All appointments were to be for one year, renewable at their expiration. The Council at its second session named such a commission and on February 25, 1920, the latter entered upon its duties.

France was represented on the commission by Chairman Victor Rault, ex-prefect of Lyon and a staunch patriot. The member for the Saar was Alfred von Boch, an able local official, while the remaining commissioners were a Belgian, a Dane who had been living in Paris for twenty years, and a Canadian. Boch was so irritated by the pro-French attitude taken on most questions by his colleagues that he soon resigned. His successor was more willing to coöperate with the French chairman.

In its first proclamation to the inhabitants, the commission stressed its determination "to carry out strictly the clauses of the Treaty of Versailles, and to enforce respect on the part of all for these clauses, both in letter and in spirit." The people were warned as follows: "Being firmly resolved to impose respect for its authority, (the commission) will fearlessly suppress all attempts, from whatever source, to disturb or mislead the population. It will tolerate neither open violence, intrigue, nor passive resistance. The treaty of peace does not leave it without the necessary authority, and the powers conferred will permit the commission to devote itself to its task without being troubled with useless and criminal opposition." In conclusion, however, the natives were consoled with the promise that the officials, in the exercise of their authority, would be "inspired by the principles which directed the establishment of the League of Nations."

Among the privileges which the peace treaty conceded to France in the district were the right to substitute French for German money in connection with the working of the mines that had been turned over to her, the option of establishing schools for the French mine employees' children in which the instruction should be in the French language, and the permission to incorporate the basin entirely within the French customs regime. The natives, on the other hand, were given certain protective guarantees. They had the right to lodge complaints against the administration with the League Council. None of the laws in force at the time of the armistice might be modified by the commission without the consent of elected representatives of the inhabitants. The maintenance of order was to be entrusted to a local gendarmerie established for that purpose.

Many Saarlanders were not only annoyed by France's exercise of her legal powers, they had a number of specific grievances against the commission. The election of representatives, for example, was deferred until March 1922; and, after their election, the people's deputies, organized as an advisory council, were not consulted by the commission on some of its most important measures. All sorts of privileges were extended to German children who could be induced to attend the French schools. Whenever the natives drew up a complaint, it had to be transmitted to the League Council through the commission, which minimized the objections. When the French Government protested to Rault against the heavy coal taxes in the basin, the tax rate was reduced. Finally, despite the treaty stipulation regarding the formation of a local gendarmerie to maintain order, a French army, varying in size from five thousand to eight thousand men, was stationed in the area.

In 1923, when the German miners went on strike out of sympathy for their fellow workmen in the Ruhr district which had been placed under occupation by French troops, the commission inaugurated repressive measures. Picketing was forbidden, it was made a penal offense to speak against the League, and the press was muzzled. Since the commission was responsible only to the League and not to the inhabitants, and since Rault was present at every Council session at which the Saar was a subject of discussion, the people ordinarily had little chance to secure an impartial hearing. On this occasion, however, the protests were so serious that London requested the League to conduct an investigation.

The Council had always seemed anxious to endorse the moves of the commission and the same spirit was evinced in the manner in which the investigation of 1923 was approached. Care was taken to prevent the appearance of an inquiry. The entire commission was invited to attend a Council session on the Saar and the commissioners were politely questioned by the Council delegates. During the proceedings Rault admitted that the commission had a branch office in Paris, that the French troops received both their pay and their orders from France, and that, as the representative of France on the governing body, he felt in duty bound to further the interests of his country.

The Council expressed no criticism of Rault's activities and merely suggested that the army might better be replaced by a local force of gendarmes. Despite this whitewashing of the affair, the prestige of the commission as an impartial group of international officials was undermined and gradually its membership was revised. In 1926 Rault resigned, being succeeded as chairman by George W. Stephens of Canada, who in turn was replaced by the Britishers, Sir Ernest Wilton (1927) and Geoffrey G. Knox (1932). These changes reduced the antagonism not only of the natives, but of the Germans in the Reich as well, for the latter sympathized with their vexed countrymen.

In 1927 the question once more arose of the French troops in the Saar, for the League recommendation of 1923 had resulted in only a partial withdrawal of the force. Since Germany now was a member of the League, there took place some vigorous discussions of the matter. In the end it was agreed that the troops should be recalled and replaced by an emergency Railway Defense Force of eight hundred men, recruited from the British, French, and Belgian armies of occupation in the Rhineland. Thus was the "Saar garrison" eliminated and a check placed on the number of men France might in future send to the region.

According to the peace treaty the permanent status of the Saar was to be decided in 1935 by a plebiscite of all inhabitants over twenty who were "resident in the territory" at the time the land was severed from Germany. For this purpose a records commissioner was ordered in 1922 to collect the necessary voting statistics and deposit them with the League. In 1934 the Council appointed a neutral committee to work out the details for the plebiscite. The committee's suggestions were adopted and the plebiscite date was set for January 13, 1935. The preparations for the plebiscite were to be supervised by a commission whose members were drawn from Sweden, Switzerland, and the Netherlands and which was to be assisted by a technical expert from the United States. Voting disputes were to be arbitrated by a special plebiscite tribunal.

Both France and Germany agreed not to exert official pressure to influence the voting and promised to prevent reprisals against persons because of their attitude during the plebiscite. Nazi Germany also promised, if the Saar were returned to her, not to hinder any individuals who might wish to leave the basin and not to apply the "Aryan legislation" for at least a year. Yet, as the date for the balloting neared, friction developed in the Saar. The trouble arose out of the excesses of Nazi sympathizers and the fears of German refugees who had fled to the Saar when Hitler came to power. Commissioner Knox therefore asked the Council for a guard and in December 1934 a League army of more than three thousand British, Italian, Swedish, and Netherlands soldiers was assembled in the Saar to help maintain order before and during the plebiscite.

It was also necessary, before the plebiscite, to settle a question regarding the Saar coal mines. If the voting favored Germany, the treaty provided that the Reich was to repurchase the mines from France at a price to be determined by three experts. Now, however, direct negotiations were carried on between Berlin and Paris in consultation with the chairman of the League's plebiscite commission. In December 1934 it was agreed that, if the plebiscite favored Germany, the latter would pay France 900,000,000 francs in settlement of all Saar claims. The payment was to be made partly in cash and partly in coal deliveries during the next five years.

As the day for the balloting approached, many Saarlanders who had lived in the valley at the time the treaty was signed, but who had since emigrated to Germany or France or even to North or South America, returned to cast their votes. The Nazis in Germany were confident of overwhelming victory, while their opponents hoped that the Catholic, liberal, and left-wing votes might carry the decision for the *status quo*. There was little belief, even in France, that a majority would favor incorporation into the Third Republic.

In a tense atmosphere, but without serious outbreaks, the plebiscite was held according to schedule. Approximately 98 per cent of those who had registered actually went to the polls. More than 525,000 votes were cast, and of these about 90 per cent were in favor of returning the Saar to Germany. Only 46,500 wanted continuation of League rule and 2100 asked for annexation to France. In no voting district was there a majority against reunion with the Reich. A few days after the plebiscite the Council awarded the entire basin to Germany and on March 1, 1935, the formal transfer took place. Thus was ended one of the most difficult tasks imposed on the League of Nations by the Paris Peace Settlement.

THE PROTECTION OF MANDATES AND MINORITIES

Under Article 22 of the Covenant, the League was made responsible for the well-being and development of the peoples inhabiting the late German overseas possessions (except Kiaochow) and the former lands of the Ottoman Empire in the Arabian Peninsula. Certain of the more advanced nations were to be delegated by the League as mandatory powers to exercise on its behalf a tutelage over these relatively backward areas. The mandatory powers would be obliged to render annual reports of their administration to the Council and there was to be constituted a Permanent Mandates Commission to examine the reports and in general advise the Council on all matters relating to the observance of the mandates.

The mandates were divided into three categories according to their political development, geographical situation, and economic conditions. First came the Class A mandates, which included the communities formerly attached to the Turkish Empire. The members of this group were regarded as having "reached a stage of development where their existence as independent nations can be provisionally recognized subject to the rendering of administrative advice and assistance by a Mandatory until such time as they are able to stand alone." The Class B mandates included the former German possessions in central Africa. These were held to need definite governmental supervision and their prospects for self-government were remote. In the Class C group were placed German South West Africa and the Pacific islands which had once belonged to Germany. These, "owing to the sparseness of their population, or their small size, or their remoteness from the centers of civilization, or their geographical contiguity to the territory of the Mandatory, and other circumstances," were thought to be "best administered under the laws of the Mandatory as integral portions of its territory," subject to certain safeguards in the interests of the indigenous population.

Since the Covenant made no mention of the mandatory powers nor of the manner in which the areas were to be distributed, these details had to be settled by special agreement. The C and B mandates were assigned in 1919 by the Big Four of the peace conference. In the C group, German South West Africa was assigned to the Union of South Africa; German Samoa, to New Zealand; the island of Nauru, to the British Empire; [1] all other German islands south of the equator, to Australia, and those north of the equator, to Japan. The Class B mandates were distributed so that Great Britain got one-sixth of the Cameroons, one-third of Togoland, and most of German East Africa (Tanganyika); France secured the remaining five-sixths of the Cameroons and two-thirds of Togoland; and Belgium received the northwestern corner of East Africa, Ruanda-Urundi. A conference at San Remo in April 1920 allotted the Class A mandates in such fashion that Iraq, Palestine, and Trans-Jordan went to Great Britain, and Syria and Lebanon to France. All these apportionments were later approved by the League Council. [2]

Late in 1920 there was created the Permanent Mandates Commission whose function would be to scan the mandatories' reports and present facts and recommendations to the Council. Eventually the commission came to consist of eleven members. A representative of the I.L.O. might be present in an advisory capacity at all meetings. The members were selected for indefinite terms on the basis of their personal qualifications. While no member might simultaneously be an officeholder in his country, an exception was made in the case of professors of state universities. The powers of the commission were purely advisory, but it kept the Council informed as to whether or not the various mandates were being administered in the interests of the natives and in accordance with the principles laid down in the Covenant. Unfortunately for its effectiveness, the commission could not hear petitioners nor visit the mandated territories.

The actual administration of some of the mandates is discussed in the chapters dealing with the various mandatory powers. Be it said at this point, however, that the mandate system proved of considerable value in focusing public opinion on the "sacred trust" of proper colonial administration and in substituting the idea of

[1] Nauru was administered for the British Empire by the United Kingdom, Australia, and New Zealand. Although its area is only 8.4 square miles, it has enormous phosphate reserves.

[2] In Iraq the hostility to British control was so great that the mandatory relationship did not go into effect. Instead, the proposed mandate was replaced by alliance treaties of 1922, 1926, and 1930 which, embodying the supervisory principles of the mandate system, converted Iraq into a British protectorate under its own king, Feisal I. In October 1932 Iraq was admitted to the League as a sovereign state. Under another treaty with Great Britain, however, the Arabian kingdom accorded London special financial and military rights. King Feisal I died in 1933 and was succeeded by his son, Ghazi. The latter was killed in an automobile accident in 1939 and was succeeded by his three-year-old son, Feisal II.

a trusteeship of backward peoples for the prewar concept of imperialist exploitation. The theory of League mandates opened the way to a somewhat more responsible "spirit of world politics."

In addition to the peoples in the mandated areas, there were placed under League guardianship about thirty million members of national minorities in central and eastern Europe. This protection was provided through special minorities treaties and conventions signed at, or soon after, the Paris Peace Conference.[1] Most of the minorities agreements provided that infractions of the accepted obligations towards minorities might be called to the attention of the Council by any member of that body. The responsibilities of the League in respect of the minorities were heavy, especially since they might so easily take on a political guise. The Council had to shield the minorities against mistreatment and yet had to be careful not to infringe the sovereign rights or hurt the national pride of the majorities. This phase of the League's activities was frequently subjected to hostile criticism.

In an attempt to remedy some of the evils the Council in 1929 slightly revised its procedure of dealing with minority disputes. A Minorities Committee was established, to consist of the president of the Council and two delegates chosen by him. To this organ was assigned the duty of deciding whether or not questions regarding minority rights should be laid before the Council. All communications between the committee and the governments concerned were to be carried on through the Minorities Section of the Secretariat, the latter also being responsible for the collection of pertinent data and information on the entire subject of minorities. It became the practice of the Council not to impose its decisions in minority disputes, but rather to point out the path of conciliation and compromise.[2]

THE WORTH OF THE LEAGUE

The Covenant imposed upon the League of Nations a multitude of tasks in addition to those mentioned. Valuable financial assist-

[1] See pp. 115–116.

[2] The Fourteenth Assembly in 1933 expressed the feeling that the states not bound by minorities treaties ought to show "at least as high a standard of justice" in the treatment of their minorities as was required of other states by the treaties. At the next Assembly, on the other hand, in September 1934, Poland declared that, until a new general system of protecting minorities should be developed, she would refuse to coöperate. Nationalists sometimes attacked the minorities treaties as tending to perpetuate undesirable internal differences.

ance was rendered by the League to needy states in central Europe and the Balkans. It played a prominent role in the search for national security and in the (unsuccessful) movement for a reduction of armaments. Highly important, if less spectacular, work was accomplished through its agencies in such fields as preventive medicine, epidemiology, the codification of international law, the suppression of the traffic in women, children, and opium, and the struggle against slavery and forced labor. Much was done under its auspices to promote international intellectual coöperation, to facilitate international transit and communications, and to coördinate the activities of various health and scientific organizations throughout the world. Systematization, continuity, and efficiency were brought into numerous spheres of human activity.

Perhaps the greatest general contribution of the League was its influence in spreading the idea of international coöperation. More than any other agency, the League helped to make people aware of the existence of world conditions and world problems and to dispel ideas concerning purely national and isolated difficulties. It appeared to be a decided advance merely to have a periodic assemblage of representatives from all over the world at one conference table, so that these delegates might come to know their respective worths and outlooks. The concept of an association of nations was old; the actuality of the League of Nations was new. And the League of Nations failed in the end to preserve peace because it could only be what the nations made of it—nothing less and nothing more.

CHAPTER VII

Reparation, Debts, Depression

THE FIRST FOUR YEARS, 1919–1923

In the Peace of Paris, as we have seen, the Allies demanded that the Central Powers, Germany in particular, because of their presumed responsibility for the war, make complete financial restitution for the property damage done to Allied civilians and assume the burden of the pension and separation allowances added to the Allied budgets in consequence of the conflict. War responsibility and reparation thus were expressly linked together.

To evaluate the amount of the damages and formulate a method of payment were tasks assigned by the peace treaty to a special Reparation Commission. This agency was to consist of one representative each from the United States, Great Britain, France, Italy, and the remaining Allied powers. Since the United States did not ratify the treaty, no American member was appointed. A Belgian was selected to represent the lesser states. In a brief struggle between Great Britain and France to dominate the commission, the French emerged triumphant. The commissioners had until May 1921 to hear and pass on Allied claims for damages and to set a total reparation figure. Meanwhile Germany was to pay on account, in gold or its equivalent, 20,000,000,000 gold marks or about $5,000,000,000.

While the commission deliberated, the Allied statesmen held conferences to decide on a scale of distribution of the reparation receipts and to attempt, independently of the official committee, to arrive at a total indemnity figure and a method of payment. At a Spa Conference in 1920 distribution percentages were agreed upon, France being allotted 52 per cent of the total receipts, the British Empire 22 per cent, Italy 10 per cent, Belgium 8 per cent, and all other claimants the remaining 8 per cent. At a later conference it was decided to present Germany with a bill for $56,000,-

000,000, but this high figure startled even Allied experts and its acceptance was not pressed.

Meanwhile, early in 1921, Germany announced that she had completed payment, in the form of coal, rolling-stock, and so forth, of the 20,000,000,000 marks demanded on account, and that further payments would be withheld until a final reparation total was established. The Reparation Commission quickly looked into the matter and declared the German claim to be false and based upon the fixing of an unduly high price level for the goods delivered. According to the commissioners, Germany's payments were still 60 per cent short of the twenty-billion goal. In the absence of any neutral arbitral body to reconcile these differences, a fruitless exchange of notes ensued, after which the commission declared Germany in voluntary default on her obligations. Thereupon the Allied zone of occupation immediately was extended across the east bank of the Rhine to include the industrial centers of Düsseldorf, Duisburg, and Ruhrort (March 8). The occupied area was surrounded with a customs wall against German products and special taxes were levied on German imports into Allied countries.

Seven weeks later (April 28, 1921) the Reparation Commission announced that the total German indemnity should be 132,000,-000,000 gold marks, or about $32,000,000,000 (plus interest). This was the lowest sum that had yet been given official sanction, but it was three times as high as the figure recommended by the economic experts at the peace conference. According to a "London Schedule" which was drawn up later, Germany was to pay this sum through fixed annuities of $500,000,000 plus variable annuities corresponding to a tax of 26 per cent on her exports. Following threats of an Allied occupation of the Ruhr district, the schedule was accepted on May 11 by the government of Chancellor Joseph Wirth.

In order to meet the annual outlay of hundreds of millions of dollars without return, Germany needed a favorable trade balance. Instead, for some time after the war, she had an unfavorable trade balance. Huge quantities of raw materials had to be purchased from abroad to replenish the stocks that had been used up or lost during the conflict. Since these imports could not be paid for in full by an immediate reëxport of manufactures, they made necessary the export of a large percentage of the none-too-plentiful gold. The resulting shortage of capital was made still more acute by the activities of some men who, like Hugo Stinnes, hastily invested their surplus funds in foreign securities lest the government place on their shoulders the chief burden of taxes for reparation purposes. German credit fell so low that foreign loans were unobtainable and high prices had to be paid for foreign exchange. The budget was balanced only through recourse to inflation and every time the government bought foreign currency to make reparation payments the value of the mark experienced a further decline.

Despite these difficulties, Germany, in the opinion of some authorities, might have been able to fulfill her obligations had she really been anxious to do so. There was evident in Germany a lack of will to pay—attributable in part to the circumstance that the stipulated annuities did not even cover the interest charges on the total reparation debt. In other words, the indebtedness would increase every year no matter how faithfully the payments were made. And the Allies for their part in no way tried to improve Germany's international credit standing or help her trade. Even so, the first instalment of $250,000,000 was promptly met, though at the price of another decline in the value of the mark and a further acceleration in the printing of paper money. A moratorium therefore was asked for the 1922 payments and then for two years and a half—until the end of 1924.

This suit, as did many later ones, precipitated a double quarrel: one between Germany and the Allies, and another between Great Britain and France. The British, bearing in mind that Germany had been one of their best customers in prewar days, had gradually come to realize that economic ruination of the republic could only lead to increased British economic distress. Hence Lloyd George, anxious to reopen the great German market to British goods at the earliest possible moment, was ready to grant the moratorium. The French, on the other hand, were indignant. They felt bad enough not to have been awarded full damages in the first place, and now, in addition, they were being asked to wait two years without receiving a sou. They estimated that in the past two years France had expended $5700 a minute on reconstruction and pensions, whereas Germany had been contributing only $381 per minute. Consequently Poincaré would agree to the moratorium only on condition that Germany furnished "productive guarantees," that is, transferred to French control the mines and dyestuff factories in the Rhineland. Inasmuch as Lloyd George was of no mind to allow a further disruption of German economic life, the remaining months of 1922 were spent in an exchange of notes among London, Paris, and Berlin. Finally Poincaré determined to apply the "big stick," for he was convinced that Germany could pay, if only she would.

Under the terms of the Versailles Treaty the Allies might undertake reprisals whenever Germany voluntarily defaulted on her obligations. Poincaré therefore scanned the record in search of defaults. He soon found them, in timber: Germany had defaulted on the delivery of telegraph poles. Later he also discovered shortages in coal and cattle deliveries. The Reparation Commission was notified and the culprit was called to account. The republic maintained that the default was temporary and involuntary, resulting from the necessity to draw up new contracts with the timber companies because of the declining currency. Over the protests of the British member, who, it is said, called the procedure the greatest timber scandal since the Wooden Horse of Troy, the commission declared Germany in default on the poles. Shortly thereafter she was declared in general default.

In January 1923 French, Belgian, and Italian troops occupied the Ruhr district as far east as Dortmund. Some of the French troops were colored. The administration of the region was entrusted to an international mission of control known from its initials in French as the MICUM. The British law officers of the Crown gave it as their opinion that the occupation was illegal and Great Britain refused to participate in the venture.

The Ruhr was the very heart of German industry, producing 80 per cent of the country's coal, iron, and steel, and being responsible for 70 per cent of its commercial railway traffic. By the occupation, therefore, the French in effect crushed the breath out of the German economic body, while yet demanding a continuation of reparation payments. Naturally the Germans were embittered by the turn of events. They could not fight, but they inaugurated a policy of passive resistance in which representatives of all classes of the population participated. The situation led a prominent German to remark: "Two men have united the German people—Bismarck in 1871 and Poincaré in 1923."

Despite harsh treatment by the occupying troops, the inhabitants of the Ruhr refused to carry out orders given by the invaders. The telephone, telegraph, and railway services came to a standstill. The mines and factories were deserted. Newspapers refused to publish French and Belgian decrees. Local officials disregarded foreign commands. Jail terms were accepted with patience. Promises of reward from the aliens for services were spurned. Most of the German mayors in the district eventually were imprisoned. In less than a year 147,000 natives either were deported or voluntarily left their homes in the Ruhr and migrated to other parts of Germany.

The Berlin Government now stopped all reparation payments, forbade the Ruhr inhabitants to have dealings with the intruders, and subsidized the striking miners and workmen with food and clothing as well as with plenty of freshly printed paper money. As a consequence the French were compelled to utilize their troops to work the mines and run the trains—with little success. The men found it difficult to operate the German machines and numerous accidents occurred. During the occupation, indeed, France secured only one-fourth as much Ruhr coal as she had received during equal time-periods prior to 1923. In anger the invaders declared a state of siege, prohibited the export of Ruhr products to Germany, and seized private as well as public funds and property. Blood was shed. About 100 persons were killed and 150 badly wounded. The mark, meanwhile, continued to decline, being quoted in August 1923 at five million to the dollar.

In the winter of 1923–1924 the French and Belgians tried to set up a separatist state in the Rhineland, called "Revolver Republic" by the loyal inhabitants. Discontented laborers and radicals, as well as released convicts and rowdies, from all over Germany were imported into the Rhineland and encouraged to proclaim the region independent. Here again strenuous opposition was encountered from the British, to say nothing of the angry natives, and the French withdrew their support from the movement in February 1924. Those separatists who were not fortunate enough to escape quickly under French protection were roughly handled by the patriots.

In unoccupied Germany conditions during 1923 became almost equally bad. Bankruptcy loomed on the economic horizon and the government was forced to choose between complete surrender and total disintegration. In September 1923 Berlin announced the immediate and unconditional cessation of passive resistance. Poincaré apparently had triumphed, but the price of victory was high. Friendship with Great Britain was strained to the breaking point; neutral opinion everywhere was alienated by what were considered France's bullying tactics; and the total suspension of German reparation payments, together with foreign distrust of French methods, caused an alarming drop in the value of the franc. It was therefore deemed advisable to resume negotiations and a proposal was adopted for the appointment of an impartial, international committee of experts to study the problem of Germany's capacity to pay and to render a report on the whole subject of reparation. The commissioners were to be economic experts rather than politicians and the report was to be based on fact, not sentiment.

THE DAWES AND YOUNG PLANS, 1924–1931

The selection of a group of economic experts to deal with reparation was entrusted to the Reparation Commission. In November 1923 that body appointed two committees: the first, consisting of two representatives each from the United States, Great Britain, France, Italy, and Belgium, was to study and report on ways and means for balancing the German budget and stabilizing the mark; the second, consisting of one delegate from each of the same five countries, should estimate the amount of German capital that had been exported and suggest means of bringing the funds back into the land.

The committees began work in January 1924 and reported to the commission on April 9. The smaller committee, headed by Reginald McKenna of Great Britain, reported that German capital to the extent of $1,687,500,000 was invested abroad at the end of 1923, while Germany held about $300,000,000 of foreign currency. For the rest, this committee merely endorsed the recommendations of the larger group which, under the chairmanship of the American financier, General Charles G. Dawes, submitted a comprehensive plan.

The committeemen who drew up this Dawes or Experts' Plan approached their task as "business men anxious to obtain effective results." They viewed the reparation question in the light of recovery of debt rather than imposition of penalties and they believed that "since, as a result of the war, the creditors of Germany are paying taxes . . . to the limit of their capacity, so also must Germany pay taxes . . . to the limit of her capacity." Though charged merely with the task of discovering means to balance Germany's budget and stabilize her currency, the experts had to stipulate the amount of reparation money that was to be included in her annual budgetary calculations. After its study of the situation, the committee came to the optimistic conclusion that the republic was "well equipped with resources and the means to exploit them" and that, provided her credit shortage were overcome, she would readily "be able to resume a favored position in world competition."

In summary, the Experts' Plan made the following recommendations: (1) full economic and fiscal sovereignty should be restored to Germany, that is, the Ruhr should be evacuated; (2) there should be established, as a depository for reparation payments, a central bank of issue (*Reichsbank*) having a fifty-year monopoly for the issue of paper money, and supervised by a board of seven Germans and seven foreigners under the chairmanship of one of the latter; (3) reparation payments should start at 1,000,000,000 gold marks for the first year and gradually rise over a period of four years to a "standard" annuity of 2,500,000,000 marks; (4) this standard might in future be raised or lowered in accord with the fluctuations of an "index of prosperity" to be calculated upon the base period 1927–1929; (5) an immediate foreign loan of 800,000,-000 gold marks should be concluded; (6) the sources for the reparation money should be a transport tax, railway bonds, industrial debentures, and pledged budgetary revenues from alcohol, tobacco, beer, sugar, and customs; (7) to watch over the execution of the plan in Germany there should be appointed a foreign Agent General for Reparation Payments, assisted by a number of foreign commissioners.

The Reparation Commission accepted the report as a basis for solving the reparation problem and notified Germany of its decision. The republic endorsed the plan and then Great Britain, Italy, and Belgium all quickly registered their acquiescence. France alone held out until, as a result of the May 1924 elections, Poincaré was toppled from power and the more conciliatory Edouard Herriot became premier. Thereupon a conference was held in London to draft a protocol for putting the scheme into effect at the earliest possible moment.

The course of the conference was not smooth. There was bitter wrangling before the British and Americans could make the French see the inadvisability of permitting any nation in future to apply military sanctions on its own account. Eventually it was decided that henceforth sanctions might be applied solely in case of a flagrant violation by Germany of her obligations and then only by the concerted action of all Allies following a specially called conference. Germany could be declared in default only by a unanimous vote of the Reparation Commission. On August 30, 1924, the protocol was signed and on the next day the plan became effective. Evacuation of the Ruhr began at once.

Under the supervision of Agent General Seymour Parker Gilbert, an American in his early thirties, the plan gave promise of working well. German business picked up, reparation payments were made promptly, and a general confidence in Germany's future was restored. There seemed little doubt that Germany eventually would be able to meet with relative ease even the large "standard" annuities. For the first time since the signing of the Versailles Treaty, the diplomatic tension in Europe was lessened.

Nevertheless, the Dawes Plan had some weaknesses. Because it had not been empowered to do so, the Dawes Committee had not fixed a total reparation bill. Technically, therefore, the total of $32,000,000,000 set by the Reparation Commission in May 1921 was still in force. Yet it was obvious (1) that so high a sum could not be the definitive total and (2) that Germany would not long continue making huge annual payments with no knowledge as to how many years the process would have to go on. Moreover the elaborate system of international economic control for which the plan provided was distasteful to both sides. These defects were pointed out by Agent General Gilbert in 1927 when he said: "As time goes on, and practical experience accumulates, it becomes always clearer that neither the reparation problem, nor the other problems depending upon it, will be finally solved until Germany has been given a definite task to perform on her own responsibility, without foreign supervision . . ." An additional German grievance, linked to the subject of reparation, was the continued Rhineland occupation which, presumably, would last until 1935.

In 1928 the air was rife with talk about the desirability of more satisfactory reparation and Rhineland settlements. While the Ninth Assembly of the League was in session at Geneva, representatives from Germany, Great Britain, France, Italy, Belgium, and Japan met and agreed that a new committee of experts should be appointed to work out a "complete and final settlement of the reparation problem." Later it was decided to invite the United States to membership on the committee and in due time a group of leading bankers was chosen to wrestle with one of the world's most difficult problems.

The new committee, soon to be known as "the Young Committee," after its American chairman, Owen D. Young, held its first meeting in Paris on February 11, 1929. It faced a difficult task, inasmuch as a compromise would have to be formulated among many differing demands. Germany wanted a considerable reduction in the annuities, below the level of the Dawes "standard." France favored an immediate liquidation of reparation through the flotation of a tremendous German bond issue and a division of the receipts among the Allies according to the Spa percentages. Great Britain hoped for an abolition of the deliveries in kind since these hurt her manufacturing industries. Germany and the bankers urged a termination of the political control of reparation.

After more than seventeen weeks of hard work, the committee's report was handed to the governments concerned and to the Reparation Commission. In presenting its findings and recommendations, the committee averred that its members had carried on in the spirit of the Dawes Committee and had tried to frame a fair and acceptable scheme "by determining the number and amount of annuities, and by providing for the conversion of the reparation debt from a political to a commercial obligation."

The Young Plan contemplated a new indemnity bill of 34,000,-000,000 marks, or $8,032,500,000, to be paid over a period of fifty-eight and a half years.[1] Significantly, the number of annuities coincided exactly with the number of inter-Allied war-debt payments still outstanding. In devising its schedule for these annuity payments the Young Committee had borne in mind three important principles: (1) the desirability of dividing the payments into an unconditional and a postponable part; (2) the need for a continuance of deliveries in kind, at least for a few more years; and (3) the advisability of formulating a specific procedure to be followed when economic stress made it necessary to postpone the conditional payments.

The average annuities to all creditors for the first thirty-seven payment years were set at $511,000,000; the remaining twenty-two annuities were to average $390,000,000 and were to correspond to the simultaneous "outpayments" of the creditor powers.[2] Thus the plan a second time linked reparation and war debts, for the reference to outpayments concerned the remaining instalments due on the inter-Allied debts. The unconditional or unpostponable part of each annuity was set at $162,000,000, of which three-fourths was assigned to France. In order to provide for a transitional period and avoid a sudden shock to German economy, it was advocated that some deliveries in kind be continued for a period of ten years, in annually decreasing amounts.

The railway and industrial bonds issued at the suggestion of the

---

[1] The actual payments, including interest at 5½ per cent, to be turned over to the Allies from September 1, 1929, to March 1, 1988, were to total $26,350,000,000.

[2] These figures are taken from the report of the committee and converted at the rate of 23.82 cents per mark. France was to get more than half of each annuity, while the British Empire was to receive about one-fifth. The United States was to get $16,500,000 per year to cover the cost of the army of occupation.

Dawes Committee were to be canceled and the Reparation Commission, along with most of the other foreign control boards, abolished. It was the firm belief of the committee "that the basis of security for the payment of annuities is the solemn undertaking of the German Government, to which no further guarantee can add anything whatsoever." To protect German currency against possible disorganization because of difficulty in meeting the conditional obligations, the plan provided that "the German Government by giving at least ninety days' previous notice shall have the right to suspend for a moratorium period of two years from its due date all or part of the transfer of that part of the annuity described as postponable."

It remained only to remove the shadow of politics from the reparation problem and to provide for some intermediary agency to handle the technical details arising between the original payment of the annuities by Germany in marks and the final receipt of these payments in their own currency by the individual creditor powers. To achieve these ends the committee recommended the establishment of a Bank for International Settlements.

In connection with the annuity payments this bank was to act as trustee for the creditor countries. It was to perform "the entire work of external administration of this plan, . . . act as the agency for the receipt and distribution of funds, and . . . supervise and assist in the commercialization and mobilization of certain portions of the annuities." Furthermore, the bank was "to provide additional facilities for the international movement of funds, and to afford a ready instrument for promoting international financial relations." Thus it was in reality to be a bank for the several national central banks, with a capital stock of $100,-000,000, only one-fourth of which was to be paid up immediately. It was hoped that the sound use of credit through the B.I.S. would help "contribute to the stability of international finance and the growth of world trade."

The bank was to be endowed with broad powers, including the authority to deal with all questions relating to the postponable reparation items. It was to be managed by a board of directors consisting (1) of the governors of the central banks of the seven nations represented on the Young Committee, or by their nominees; (2) of one additional director appointed by each of these governors from among his countrymen; and (3) of not more than nine additional directors chosen by the first fourteen from lists submitted by the other governments interested in the reparation settlement. Sound banking, not politics, was to guide the board in its deliberations.

The advantages of the Young Plan over that of 1924 were clearly set forth by the Young Committee itself:

The proposed plan continues and completes the work begun by the Dawes Plan, which the position alike of Germany and of the other countries made it impossible to do more than indicate in outline in 1924. By the final reduction and fixation of the German debt, by the establishment of a progressive scale of annuities, and by the facilities which the new bank offers for lessening disturbance in the payment of annuities, it sets the seal on the inclusion of the German debt in the list of international settlements. If it involves appreciable reduction of payments to the creditor countries on what might have been antici-pated under the continued operation of the Dawes Plan, it at the same time eliminates the uncertainties [such as the index of prosperity] which were inherent in that Plan and were equally inimical to the interest of the debtor and to the creditors, by substituting a definite settlement under which the debtor knows the exact extent of his obligations.

The Young Plan was fairly well received in diplomatic circles and delegates were selected to meet in conference at The Hague on August 6, 1929, to draft a protocol for putting the new arrange-ment into effect. After much wrangling and a lengthy adjourn-ment, the conference at last signed a final act on January 20, 1930.[1] It provided for the going into force of the Young Plan as soon as (1) it was ratified by any four of the following creditors: France, Great Britain, Belgium, Italy, Japan; (2) the laws necessary for its operation were promulgated in Germany; and (3) the Bank for International Settlements was established. The act also substituted the new schedule of payments retroactively for the Dawes schedule as from September 1, 1929, and provided for the complete evacua-tion of the Rhineland by Allied troops "not later than the end of June 1930."[2] Finally, because the French were frightened by a renewal of nationalistic outbursts in Germany, the idea of sanc-tions was revived by a clause which restored to the Allied states "full liberty of action" whenever the World Court should declare Germany in wilful default.

Ratification of the final act occurred in the spring of 1930. Only in Germany did the government encounter much trouble in secur-ing popular approval for the plan. There Dr. Schacht, maintaining

[1] The conference increased Britain's share of the annuities by about 10 per cent.

[2] The provocative question of the Rhineland occupation was thus ended five years before the minimum time limit set by the Versailles Treaty.

that the payments could not be met, resigned as head of the Reichsbank in protest, while Dr. Alfred Hugenberg, a former Krupp director and now leader of the Nationalist Party, forced the holding of a plebiscite on the question. Since the vote was favorable to the authorities, the plan went into effect. Once more the nations were relieved, feeling, apparently, that a "complete and final settlement" had at last been reached. Yet, within less than two years, the Young annuities had to be suspended.[1]

DEPRESSION AND MORATORIUM, 1931–1932

In the German parliamentary elections of September 1930 the bitterest opponents of the Young Plan won astonishingly many votes. Foreign investors thereupon became uneasy and a heavy withdrawal of money from Germany resulted. Within a few weeks $200,000,000 was recalled and, although a loan from a New York syndicate temporarily stabilized conditions, it was clearly apparent that "German finances were . . . easily capable of being upset."

Conditions elsewhere in Europe were little better. The whole structure of western political economy seemed to be breaking under the strain of postwar readjustments. The entire world soon came into the grip of a prolonged depression. As to the causes of this depression, there was considerable speculation and argument. Some authorities traced the economic difficulties to a supposedly inadequate world gold supply. The resulting decline in commodity prices, they believed, had a disastrous effect on international trade. Others regarded an oversupply of silver and the consequent decline in the purchasing power of such silver-standard regions as China and India as the root of the trouble. It was also pointed out that the continuing technological advances (1) so multiplied the output of industrial and agricultural products that a huge, undistributed surplus was piled up and (2) so decreased the amount of needed man power that the world's unemployment figure was swelled to an unprecedented total and the purchasing power of

[1] New reparation arrangements were also concluded in 1930 with Austria, Hungary, and Bulgaria. Austria was relieved of all further reparation payments, but from 1944 until 1966 was to pay Italy an annual sum of about $200,000 for certain administrative and relief costs incurred at the end of the war. Hungary's contributions until 1943 were to be poured into a general fund to reimburse Hungarian nationals whose lands in Romania had been expropriated. From 1944 until 1966 Hungarian reparation was to total about $2,750,000 per year. Bulgaria was required to pay 5,000,000 gold francs on April 1, 1930, plus 415,243,808 gold francs in thirty-six annual instalments. Turkey was excused from all reparation payments by the Treaty of Lausanne (1923).

the working groups suffered a steady diminution. Emphasis also was placed upon the circumstances that the years since the war had witnessed the general levying of high tariffs, the imposition of import quotas, the passage of restrictive immigration laws, the development of highly organized "buy-home-products" movements, and the invention of ingenious forms of economic discrimination and retaliation. The general shrinkage of foreign trade, it was explained, made the situation especially trying for those states which had to make reparation payments or meet war-debt instalments, for these states obviously needed favorable balances of trade with which to cover their obligations.

Relief proposals were legion, but the only really important development in 1930 was a scheme for the creation of an economic federation of Europe, discussed before the League Assembly by Aristide Briand, the French Foreign Minister. Unfortunately, it appeared to some that the motive behind this idea was not so much to revive the economic life of the continent as to consolidate the hegemony of France and uphold the peace treaties. Hence the Austrian Foreign Minister, Dr. Johann Schober, advised the Assembly that the situation was far too acute to permit of long-drawn-out negotiations for a Pan-Europa, but that a beginning in the direction of federation should be made by the prompt conclusion of regional agreements. The suggestion was favorably received and throughout 1931 a series of economic and grain conferences was held in European capitals. Economic rivalry and national jealousy, however, prevented the reaching of any important understanding other than an Austro-German agreement to conclude a customs union.

In March 1931 Germany and Austria made public the text of this agreement to conclude a treaty which, while maintaining the independence of the signatories and paying due regard to their respective obligations to third states, would "mark the beginning of a new order of European economic conditions on lines of regional agreements." Barring a few exceptions during a transitional period, customs duties between Germany and Austria were to be entirely abolished. Goods from other countries were to be subject to identical duties in the two republics, the schedules to be arrived at by joint agreement. Wherever possible, the signatories were to negotiate similar though separate trade treaties with third powers. The respective customs administrations were to be independent of one another, but all receipts were "to be apportioned between the two countries according to a quota." The parties were ready "to enter into negotiation for a similar agreement with any other country expressing such desire."

The announcement of the contemplated customs union was well received in Great Britain, where financial circles favored any move that might help safeguard international credit, but it caused excited outbursts in France and among France's allies. Seeing in the proposed customs pact a veiled Anschluss or Austro-German union, France sought to prevent its consummation by strong diplomatic and financial pressure. Thus she suddenly adopted an uncompromising stand in the current Anglo-Franco-Italian naval parleys which until then had been progressing fairly satisfactorily, and made the granting of a much-needed loan to Austria contingent upon the latter's renunciation of the customs protocol.

Austria needed this money to save from collapse the *Kredit Anstalt,* a bank which had numerous foreign branches, controlled almost three-fourths of Austrian banking, and dominated two-thirds of Austria's industry through share holdings and credit advances. Despite the emergency Austria rejected the politically weighted French terms and appealed to Great Britain instead. The Bank of England advanced the money in the form of a short-term loan renewable at seven-day intervals. This development was generally regarded as a diplomatic defeat for France and the authorities at Paris were obviously angry with the British. But the most serious international outcome of the Austrian affair was the precipitation of another financial crisis in Germany, for "although the commitments of the German banks in Austria were an insignificant part of their total assets, the (difficulties) of the *Kredit Anstalt* shook confidence in the solvency of Central Europe." Panic had indeed for some time been latent in Germany's adverse trade balance, in the vulnerability of her financial structure, and in her growing budgetary deficit.[1]

Hampered by reactionaries and communists at home and by French diplomacy abroad, the German Government had energetically striven to avert economic ruin. Between July 1930 and July 1931 Chancellor Heinrich Brüning, backed by President von Hindenburg, issued dozens of emergency decrees increasing taxes, lowering salaries, pensions, and unemployment benefits, and effecting other economies, chiefly at the expense of education and social welfare. Well-to-do Germans, fearing national bankruptcy, now hast-

---

[1] Germany's unfavorable trade balance for 1924–1931 was 6,300,000,000 marks. The accumulated budgetary deficit from 1925 to 1930 was 1,280,000,000 marks. Unemployment figures in 1931 advanced to almost six million. In July 1931 the short-term credits of the republic totaled $3,000,000,000.

ily invested in foreign securities, while panicky Americans, Netherlanders, and Swiss withdrew their credits at a rapid rate. In the first three weeks of June 1931 the Reichsbank lost 41 per cent of its total gold holdings.

At this point President Hoover, in the interest of the "economic recovery of the world," proposed a one-year world moratorium from July 1, involving postponement "of all payments on intergovernmental debts, reparations and relief debts, both principal and interest . . . not including obligations of governments held by private parties." Before making his announcement the President had secured the approval of his cabinet, of experts in international finance, and of leading senators and representatives. He was careful, none the less, to make it plain that he did "not approve in any remote sense of the cancelation of the debts to" the United States. The scheme was agreeable to every important country except France, who objected that the Hoover proposal bore no relation to the Young Plan. Consequently more than two weeks were spent in harmonizing the Hoover scheme with the Young Plan, and, although the moratorium by common consent was allowed to go into effect on July 1, 1931, the final arrangements were not concluded until five days later.

The main points of the moratorium were as follows: (1) all intergovernmental debt payments, including conditional reparation dues, were to be postponed for the year July 1, 1931–June 30, 1932; (2) the unconditional reparation payments were to be continued by Germany, but the B.I.S. was to reinvest the entire sum in government-guaranteed German railways bonds, the railway immediately returning the funds to the government; (3) the postponed dues were to be paid in ten equal instalments commencing July 1, 1933; (4) assistance was to be given the smaller European states, whose finances might be seriously disturbed by the discontinuance of reparation receipts, by loans from the larger central banks acting through the B.I.S.; (5) in the matter of deliveries in kind a committee of experts was to "reconcile the material necessities with the spirit of President Hoover's proposal"; and (6) assurances were to be given that Germany would use the money freed by the moratorium "for exclusively economic purposes," not for military preparations.

When the plan went into effect optimism in the United States ran high and commercial stocks registered a considerable advance. But as far as Germany was concerned, the moratorium negotiations were little more than a general advertisement of her financial exhaustion and of the continued bitterness of Franco-German diplomatic relations. Throughout July 1931 the heavy German gold losses continued and on the thirteenth the great *Darmstädter und Nationalbank* failed. On the fourteenth all German banks were forced by governmental decree temporarily to close their doors.

To deal with the new crisis, "conversations" were held in Paris and London. The whip hand at these gatherings was held by France, who alone in Europe had large funds available but who was angered by the continued attempts of Germany, Austria, Great Britain, and the United States to reach vital settlements without her assistance.[1] The French had few German investments, but they regarded their reparation claims as a sort of first mortgage on Germany, the payment of which was far more important to them than the security of the speculative investments of the British, Americans, and others.

In accord with a decision reached during the London conversations, the B.I.S. convened a committee "to inquire into the further credit needs of Germany and to study the possibilities of converting a portion of the short-term credits into long-term credits." This committee recommended that the existing short-term credit be continued for a period of six months and pointed out the need for additional credits in the form of a long-term loan. In this latter connection, however, the committee made clear that "financial remedies alone will be powerless to restore the world's economic prosperity until there is a radical change" in the policy of obstruction whereby the nations had permitted "the development of an international financial system which involves the annual payment of large sums by debtor to creditor countries, while at the same time putting obstacles in the way of the free movement of goods." Until international commerce should be freed from artificial obstructions such as tariffs, therefore, it was impossible "to suggest definite plans for securing to Germany long-term credits."

The first recommendation of the committee was promptly adopted and a "Standstill Agreement" reached whereby all short-term credits to Germany were extended for six months. At the end of that time the standstill was prolonged for another year, while Chancellor Brüning announced that Germany also would have to stop the Young-Plan annuities.[2] It was no longer a question of the *will* to pay, he indicated, Germany *could* not pay. In the meantime

[1] On September 3 Germany and Austria renounced the proposed customs pact.
[2] The Standstill Agreement was then extended from year to year, with Germany gradually reducing the short-term debt.

British finance had also crashed [1] and this new crisis shook still more the confidence of the world in its financial structure. Hopefully, Great Britain, France, Germany, Italy, Belgium, and Japan agreed to hold another reparation conference in June 1932, this time at Lausanne. "The object of the conference," said a British communiqué, "will be to agree on . . . measures necessary to solve the . . . economic and financial difficulties which are responsible for and may prolong the present world crisis."

On June 16, 1932, then, the representatives of Germany, Belgium, France, Great Britain, Italy, and Japan met at Lausanne to consider measures for the improvement of the world economic situation. After three weeks of discussion an agreement was reached which set aside the German reparation debt and substituted therefore an obligation upon Germany to contribute a total of 3,000,000,000 marks or $714,600,000 for the general purpose of European reconstruction. To meet this debt the Berlin Government was to deliver to the B.I.S. 5 per cent bonds for the entire amount. The bonds were to be held by the bank as trustee for three years, after which they might be negotiated and placed in the open market. Germany might at any time redeem at par bonds not yet issued and after fifteen years all bonds which the bank had been unable to negotiate were to be canceled. Interest on the bonds was to be calculated from the date of their negotiation.

It was not philanthropy which induced the creditor delegates to forego more than 90 per cent of the Young reparation figure. They were motivated primarily by a desire to make possible the revival of world trade and to remove the fateful cloud of insecurity which hovered over the nations. The return of prosperity, they felt, was dependent upon commerce and security, and these should be restored through the virtual abolition of reparation.

When the agreement was made public, the newspapers everywhere hailed the beginning of a new epoch in postwar history. But there was another side to the story. It soon was revealed that the delegates of Great Britain, France, Italy, and Belgium had come to a separate "gentlemen's agreement" which provided that the Lausanne convention would have final effect only after ratification by the several powers—and such ratification would not follow "until a satisfactory settlement had been reached between them and their own creditors." In case no such settlement could be arranged, "the agreement with Germany will not be ratified" and

[1] See p. 252.

J. RAMSAY MACDONALD AND EDOUARD HERRIOT AT LAUSANNE, 1932

the legal position "will revert to that which existed before the Hoover Moratorium."

Now, the chief creditor of the signatories of the "gentlemen's agreement" was the United States, and the American Government had consistently maintained that there was no official relation between reparation and war debts. Hence the news of the "gentlemen's agreement" was received in Washington with vigorous assertions that cancelation of the war debts was unthinkable even if reparation obligations were entirely abolished. Many Americans resented what they regarded as an attempt by Europe to pass on responsibility for the world dilemma to the United States. The Lausanne Agreement therefore was dropped and the world depression continued, while the nationalists in Germany intensified their attacks against the "weak" government which could force no large concessions from the former Allies.

The total amount of reparation and other treaty obligations paid by Germany up to the time that the Lausanne Conference met was, according to Allied estimates, about $5,500,000,000.[1] Technically the Young-Plan schedule remained in effect after the Lausanne Agreement fell through, but no further reparation payments were forthcoming. The larger portion of these had been raised through foreign loans; hence when, owing chiefly to the spreading depression, further foreign credits became unobtainable, Germany seemed to regard her reparation obligation as ended. Thereupon the other debtor governments also began to default, following the expiry of the Hoover Moratorium on June 30, 1932. Finland alone continued to meet her obligations to the United States.

THE INTER-ALLIED WAR DEBTS

The debts which the former Allies were so eager to link with reparation arose out of the exigencies of the war. Prior to the entry of the United States into the conflict, France, Russia, Italy, and lesser Allied powers had borrowed several billion dollars from Great Britain. Eighteen days after the United States joined the belligerents, Congress passed an act which authorized the lending of $3,000,000,000 to the Allies at 5 per cent interest. Other loans followed during the remainder of the war and in the postarmistice months. Altogether, the advances to twenty nations totaled $10,-338,000,000. Of this sum $7,077,000,000 was loaned before the

---

[1] The German estimates were considerably higher.

armistice and $3,261,000,000, or about 31 per cent, after November 11, 1918. The actual distribution of the funds is shown in the accompanying table.

During the sessions of the peace conference in 1919 the British announced their willingness to cancel the war debts owed them by the other Allies if the United States adopted a similar stand. President Wilson rejected this proposal and the succeeding Washington administrations, Democratic and Republican alike, chose the course of collection.[1]

UNITED STATES WAR LOANS
(Figures in Millions)

	Prearmistice	Postarmistice	Total
Great Britain	$3696	$ 581	$4277
France	1970	1435	3405
Italy	1031	617	1648
Belgium	172	207	379
Russia	188	5	193
Poland	....	160	160
Czechoslovakia	....	92	92
Yugoslavia	10	42	52
Romania	....	38	38
Austria	....	24	24
Ten others	10	60	70[a]
Total	$7077	$3261	$10,338

[a] The names and total borrowings of the "ten others" were: Greece, $15,000,000; Estonia, $14,000,000; Armenia, $11,000,000; Cuba, $10,000,000; Finland, $8,000,000; Latvia, $5,000,000; Lithuania, $5,000,000; Hungary, $1,600,000; Nicaragua, $166,000; and Liberia, $26,000. The figures are from "To Revise or Not to Revise: The Debts Issue" by Charles Merz in the *New York Times*, November 20, 1932.

Early in 1922 Congress created a World War Foreign Debt Commission to arrange funding agreements with the debtors, most of whom had not yet paid any interest on the loans. Between 1923 and 1930 accords were reached with all parties concerned for a funded total, including back interest, of $11,565,000,000. The agreements provided for the full repayment of the advances over a period of sixty-two years. The interest charges varied according to the commission's estimate of the debtors' capacity to pay. Czecho-

[1] In the "Balfour Note" of August 1, 1922, Great Britain explained that she still was "prepared, if such a policy formed part of a satisfactory international settlement, to remit all the debts due to Great Britain by (her) allies in respect of loans, or by Germany in respect of reparation." Since, however, the United States saw the matter in a different light, Great Britain was "regretfully constrained" to request repayment of the loans. The reaction of the other debtors to this principle was, in general, that they could repay Great Britain and the United States only as much as they themselves received from Germany.

HOW THE WAR LOANS WERE—

MADE

The United States Loaned
(Before the Armistice $7,077,000,000;
After the Armistice $3,261,000,000)

$10,338,000,000

Great Britain $4,277,000,000
France 3,405,000,000
Italy 1,648,000,000
All Others 1,008,000,000

Great Britain 41%
France 33%
Italy 16%
All Others 10%

FUNDED

The Borrowers Agreed to Pay
(In Principal $11,565,000,000; In Interest $10,623,000,000)

$22,188,000,000

Great Britain $11,105,000,000
France 6,848,000,000
Italy 2,408,000,000
All Others 1,827,000,000

Great Britain 50%
France 31%
Italy 11%
All Others 8%

REPAID

The Borrowers Have Paid to Date*
(In Principal $726,000,000; In Interest 1,902,000,000)

$2,628,000,000

Great Britain $1,912,000,000
France 486,000,000
Italy 98,000,000
All Others 132,000,000

Great Britain 73%
France 18%
Italy 4%
All Others 5%

THE INTER-ALLIED WAR DEBTS
Courtesy of the *New York Times*

*November 1932. Later payments increased the repaid total to $2,735,000,000.

167

slovakia was charged the highest rate, 3.327 per cent; Great Britain was required to pay 3.306 per cent; France, 1.64 per cent; and Italy, 0.405 per cent. The average for all debts was 2.135 per cent. The total amount of principal and interest to be paid to the United States was $22,188,000,000. Obviously these arrangements involved the cancelation of a large proportion of the debts.

As long as Germany, aided by borrowing, met her reparation instalments, the Allies promptly remitted their obligations to the United States. All payments, however, were suspended by the Hoover Moratorium of 1931–1932. After the expiration of the moratorium, the failure of the Lausanne Conference, and the appearance of the depression, there occurred an increasing number of defaults. Meanwhile American public opinion had become divided on the subject of collection.

Among the arguments advanced by the advocates of collection were these: (1) collection was essential to uphold the sanctity of contracts as a fundamental principle of business ethics; (2) cancelation was unfair to American taxpayers because the war bonds had to be retired whether or not Europe paid; (3) payment was necessary to restore confidence in Europe's good faith, since some countries were not taxing themselves as heavily as they might and others were spending huge sums on armaments.

Those who favored cancelation or drastic reduction maintained that: (1) since the United States entered the war late, lost few men, and spent relatively little money, she might consider the debt money her contribution to the cause; (2) the United States became wealthy as a result of her wartime activities and should be content with her new business contacts and markets; (3) moral arguments, such as that regarding business ethics, could never satisfactorily settle broad questions of world controversy; (4) American manufacturers would suffer if the country were flooded with foreign commodities without the sale of which Europe could not pay the debts; (5) insistence upon collection was causing ill-will against the United States, whereas cancelation would increase international harmony.

A third group of opinion favored some form of conditional cancelation. The debts, it was said, might be canceled on condition that the respective beneficiaries guaranteed to use the money thus saved for educational or economic, but not military, purposes. Again, the Allied debts and German reparation might be reciprocally canceled; or, finally, the dismantling of existing armaments might be made a condition of cancelation. The government, however, refused cancelation and in 1934 adopted a law forbidding defaulting nations to float loans in the United States.

SINCE 1933: THE ECONOMIC CONFERENCE AND AFTER

Part V of the final act of the Lausanne Conference contained an invitation to the League of Nations to convoke a world conference on monetary and economic questions. In accord with this request, the League Council made preparations for the convening of such a gathering in London in 1933. The coöperation of the United States was secured, though at the cost of a promise to omit from the agenda the subjects of reparation, war debts, and tariffs.

A preparatory commission of experts drafted the agenda for the conference. "Before setting forth the problems which require solution," ran the introduction to this report, "we wish to call attention to the gravity of the situation with which the world is confronted." The following summary of the economic plight of the nations at the end of 1932 was then presented:

Unemployment has recently been estimated by the International Labour Office as involving at least thirty million workers. Even this huge total, which does not include the workers' families or other dependents, is probably an underestimate. The burden of suffering and demoralisation resulting from unemployment of such proportions is appalling.

Wholesale commodity prices—expressed in gold—have declined since October 1929 by roughly a third; raw material prices on the average by 50 to 60 per cent. In the middle of December [1932], at Winnipeg, the price of wheat fell to the lowest level recorded in any primary market for wheat during the past four centuries. Such price-declines have produced profound disturbances in the economic system. They have thrown completely out of adjustment prevailing costs of the various factors of production, have made business enterprise generally unremunerative and have seriously disorganised practically all the world markets.

World stocks of agricultural products and of other raw materials continue to accumulate. The index of world stocks for 1932 was double that for 1925. Huge accumulations thus overhang some of the principal markets and burden the processes of orderly price readjustment.

Industrial production has been drastically curtailed, particularly in those trades producing capital equipment. The depths which have been reached in some instances are illustrated by the position of the United States steel industry, which, at the close of 1932, was operating at only 10 per cent of capacity. [According to the League of Nations, *World Economic Survey, 1932–1933*, 1933, p. 82: "Independent estimates agreed that, in 1932, the level of industrial production in the world as a whole fell below that of 1913."]

The international flow of goods, hindered by currency disorders and restricted by a multiplicity of new governmental interventions, has been reduced to incredibly low levels. The total value of world trade in the third quarter of 1932 was only about one-third of that in the corresponding period of 1929. The fall during the three-year period was continuous.

Moreover, the quantum of goods in foreign trade appears to have fallen by at least 25 per cent; by far the largest fall on record.

As a result of price-declines and the fall in the volume of production and trade, national incomes in many countries have fallen, it is estimated, by more than 40 per cent. The revenues of Governments, as a consequence, have suffered sharp reductions, while expenditures have shown no corresponding decline. The inevitable result has been a series of budget deficits which, in some cases, have reached unprecedented proportions.

Only a handful of countries now retain free and uncontrolled gold-standard currency systems. Almost half the countries of the world are off the gold standard, and, in some forty countries, exchange restrictions have been imposed.

Currency disorganisation, price-declines, curtailment of trade have thrown into sharp relief the vast and difficult problems of indebtedness with which many, if not most, countries are confronted. As matters now stand, there are countries the total value of whose export trade has fallen below the sums required for external debt service alone.

The conference proper assembled on June 12, 1933, representing sixty-seven nations. The questions of world monetary policy and removal of international trade restrictions soon loomed as the chief stumbling blocks of the gathering and early threatened to wreck the proceedings. France, Italy, Switzerland, the Netherlands, Belgium, and other gold-standard states formed a "gold bloc" which insisted that all talk about reduction of tariffs and removal of trade barriers must *follow* a general stabilization of world currencies. The United States, having gone off the gold standard some weeks before, announced that she would refuse to coöperate in any move for stabilization at least until such time as a sufficient rise in prices had been achieved at home. In other words, President Roosevelt placed improvement in the domestic situation above international coöperation on a basis which would interfere with his recovery plans. Great Britain seemed to have no fixed policy, but sided now with one view and then with the other.

Early in July it appeared as though the conference would break up without having achieved a single good. Such a dénouement was forestalled by the senior American delegate, Secretary of State Cordell Hull. Devoted to the ideal of international coöperation, and opposed to the "extreme economic nationalism" which guided the actions of the powers, Hull induced the delegates to continue the session in the hope of reaching conclusions on at least some of the "safe" questions over which there would be less disagreement. Unfortunately, the remaining meetings until adjournment on July 27 were remarkable chiefly for their listlessness.

The concrete achievements of the conference may be easily summarized. They were: (1) a short international tariff truce distinguished for its many loopholes; (2) a four-year agreement among the eight leading silver-producing and silver-holding countries not to dump their stores on the world market, in the hope that this might raise the price of the metal; (3) a resolution declaring for closer coöperation among the various national banks and between these institutions and the B.I.S. at Basel; and (4) a resolution advocating direct negotiation between international debtors and creditors and the better organization of creditors within each country. The general view, however, was that the conference had failed —for lack of a properly coördinated plan.[1]

In the months following the adjournment of the monetary conference, economic conditions throughout the world experienced a slight improvement. Charles Rist, who had been the chief financial adviser to the French delegation at the conference, later wrote: "One of the many curious paradoxes of the Economic Conference was the fact that it had been called to find a remedy for the crisis, but met when the depression had long since passed the peak and

---

[1] Somewhat more encouraging was the work of a London Wheat Conference which, in August 1933, concluded a Wheat Pact. By its terms the wheat-exporting states, particularly Canada, the United States, Argentina, and Australia, agreed to accept restrictive export quotas for two years. The wheat importers, including Great Britain, France, Germany, and Italy, consented to encourage greater wheat consumption, raise their import quotas, discourage any attempts at increasing domestic production, and lower their tariffs on wheat when the price thereof should have risen a specified amount.

was giving way to something like convalescence." But this revival, except in Japan and Australia, was almost entirely *domestic* in character. International trade remained stagnant. The gains, moreover, seemed to be most pronounced in those states which adopted emergency measures of an intensely economic-nationalist nature. And such gains promised little for the permanent revival of world trade.

The means employed between 1933–1939 to bring about and maintain "recovery" nearly all tended in the direction of *autarkie*, the latest descriptive term for economic self-sufficiency. They included further currency devaluations, national regulations governing the production of raw materials, the launching of huge public-works programs, currency-exchange restrictions, the development of new industries to supply goods otherwise kept out by tariff schedules and import quotas, and the like. Almost nothing was done to break down the international trade barriers, stabilize exchange, solve the intergovernmental debt problems, or restore economic good feeling and friendship among the nations.[1] With Nazi Germany leading the way, the nations of the world, sometimes in self-defense, sometimes willfully, continued to place political obstacles in the way of international trade. In the end, this intensification of economic nationalism, with its resultant controlled national economies, helped bring on the Second World War. More and more people came to believe "that the difficulties of international economic relations could be alleviated only by recourse to force." [2]

[1] An exception to the general trend was the effort of Secretary of State Hull to arrange reciprocal tariff agreements, under an act passed by Congress in 1934, with other countries.

[2] The price indices, in gold dollars, of world trade for the period 1913–1938 were as follows: (1929 = 100)

1913	73.5	1931	67.7
1924	109.4	1935	42.4
1929	100.0	1938	45.5

The quotation and figures are from Clough, S. B. and Cole, C. W. *Economic History of Europe*, 1941, pp. 792, 798.

CHAPTER VIII

The Search for Security

THE REVIVAL OF ALLIANCES, 1920–1927

Long before the last echoes of the war had died down, France embarked upon a prolonged search for security against another German invasion. Twice within the memory of living men had the pounding of German military boots been heard on French soil and the citizens of the Third Republic were fearful of still another incursion. As long as Germany remained economically and militarily strong and as long as her population increased at a faster rate than that in France, it seemed necessary to Frenchmen to seek iron-clad guarantees of protection and help.

The leader in this hunt for security was Raymond Poincaré who, born in Lorraine, nourished from early youth a bitter hatred of Germany. The foreign policies of other French premiers, however, of the conservative Tardieu, of the optimistic Briand, and of the liberal Herriot, were all motivated by the same fear. Differ as they might on domestic policies, the statesmen of France invariably sought one goal in international affairs: security.

The first practical step in search of security was the signing, on June 28, 1919, of two identical treaties between France and Great Britain, and France and the United States. These Guarantee Treaties, it will be recalled, provided that Great Britain and the United States, respectively, should "come immediately to (France's) assistance in the event of any unprovoked movement of aggression against her being made by Germany." Whatever comfort France might have got from these agreements was short-lived. The United States Senate would have nothing to do with the American treaty and thereupon the one with Great Britain, although already ratified, automatically became void; its acceptance had been made "contingent upon the United States Government undertaking the same obligation."

France, looking upon this development as little short of betrayal, immediately sought other and more certain allies. Her relations with Great Britain gradually becoming less intimate, she turned to the smaller states that also had cause to fear any change in the political *status quo*. First (1920) came a military alliance with Belgium. This apparently provided that each signatory should come to the support of the other in case of attack by Germany. The League of Nations was notified of the existence of the military accord but the actual terms were kept secret. As the price for this alliance France agreed to the inclusion of Luxembourg in a customs union with Belgium, although the Luxembourgers had earlier voted for economic affiliation with France.

Next, France sought a substitute to take the place occupied in the prewar alliance scheme by Russia. The logical candidate was Poland, for the latter stood in as much fear of Germany and, incidentally, of Soviet Russia, as did France. The natural attachment between the two republics was increased when France, in 1920, lent Poland men, money, and munitions with which to fight the Bolsheviks, whom the French feared only less than the Germans. A Franco-Polish treaty therefore was signed in 1921 and ratified in 1922. It bound the two governments to consult on all matters of mutual interest and to act in concert for the maintenance of treaties to which they were or might become parties. The better to defend their territories and legitimate interests, they also undertook to lend one another military aid in the event of any unprovoked attack. In later years this treaty was supplemented by half a dozen conventions, including a military agreement of 1922. This was renewed in 1932 for a further period of ten years.

The pivot of two alliances, France also determined once more to approach Great Britain. The Entente Cordiale, it was felt, was still in existence; why not strengthen it? Late in 1921, accordingly, Paris advanced plans for a definite political alliance. The ensuing negotiations were not happy. The British would promise immediate assistance only in case of a direct German invasion of France. But France was more apprehensive lest Germany attack Poland, and in that event the Third Republic was bound to aid her ally. It was against such a contingency that Paris sought assurance of British military support for thirty years. But Premier Lloyd George refused anything more than a ten-year agreement to help France in the event of a direct German attack. Such an arrangement was tentatively concluded early in 1922.

Meanwhile other differences had arisen between France and

Great Britain. At the Washington Conference for the Limitation of Armaments (1921–1922),[1] an Anglo-American proposal to abolish submarines was laid aside largely because of the opposition of France. The breach between the two former allies was widened still more by their opposing views on the reparation question. In the summer of 1922, therefore, alliance negotiations lapsed. Early in 1923, when France, over the protests of Great Britain, sent troops into the Ruhr, the Entente Cordiale was, for all practical purposes, terminated.

Worried by the complications arising from the Ruhr occupation, France set out to find additional friends. At the beginning of 1924 a Franco-Czechoslovak pact was concluded whereby the signatories agreed to settle by pacific means any disputes that might arise between them; promised to consult with one another if Germany and Austria tried to unite, or if Germany or Hungary attempted a monarchist restoration; and undertook to "concert upon" common measures in dealing with matters relating to their security or the peace treaties. Two years later (1926), France concluded a security agreement with Romania. The two powers promised never to attack each other and to submit to arbitration all disputes that might arise between them. Subject to any League resolutions, they agreed to act together in forestalling attempts to change the political status of Europe as determined by the peace treaties. Finally, they undertook to consult with one another regarding prospective action if either were attacked without provocation. In 1927 France signed a similar treaty with Yugoslavia.

Meanwhile the several eastern allies of France had formed a partnership among themselves. In 1920 and 1921 a Little Entente was organized by Czechoslovakia, Yugoslavia, and Romania for purposes of keeping intact the Treaty of Trianon, preventing a restoration of the Habsburgs, and opposing a solid front to any Hungarian irredentist outbreak. The entente was effected by the signing of three dual alliances, between Czechoslovakia and Yugoslavia, Czechoslovakia and Romania, and Yugoslavia and Romania. In 1921, moreover, Romania signed a treaty of alliance with Poland. Each signatory agreed to give military aid to the other in case of unprovoked attack along their respective eastern frontiers. During 1922 opportunity was found for the establishment of cordial relations between the remaining members of the Little Entente and Poland. Finally, for the sake of adopting a unified policy and making possible economic as well as diplomatic co-

[1] See pp. 187–188.

operation, the foreign ministers of the entente states decided to hold periodic conferences to which Poland might on occasion be invited.[1]

The new French hegemony thus created in the name of security was founded upon an armed camp of the type that had proved so futile and so dangerous in 1914. It was one of the moving factors behind the conclusion of two other treaty systems, centering, respectively, in the Soviet Union and Fascist Italy.

It happened that in April 1922 the representatives of thirty-four nations, including Germany and Russia, met at Genoa to devise means for improving the European economic situation. Discussions on various loans and credits were well advanced, when news reached the gathering that on Easter Sunday (April 16) Walter Rathenau and George Chicherin, chiefs, respectively, of the German and Russian foreign offices, had signed a treaty at the Italian watering place of Rapallo.

It was understandable that these two powers should have been drawn together. Neither had as yet been restored to membership in good standing among the nations of Europe. Both were fearful of the possible designs of an unfriendly Allied or French-controlled coalition. And both were anxious to establish new trade contacts. To many Germans the pact seemed to clear the way to an alliance with Russia and to make possible defiance of the Allies and their treaty demands. To the Russian leaders it meant the restoration of diplomatic relations with a great power, the opportunity to secure credits, and lessened fear of the Franco-Polish alliance.

By the terms of the Treaty of Rapallo the Soviet Government was accorded recognition by Germany, reciprocal consular and trade relations were reëstablished, and all prewar debts and claims were mutually canceled. If Russia ever paid her other creditors, however, Germany was to receive equal consideration. The news of the treaty angered the Allied delegates and the conference broke up without settling any of the major issues confronting the powers.

Soon after the conclusion of the Rapallo Treaty, the Bolsheviks began to fear the formation of a European bloc against Russia. Hence it was determined at Moscow to negotiate a series of non-

---

[1] The ties that bound these satellites to France were not alone those of treaty obligations, but those of finance. Over a period of years French bankers lent the four states hundreds of millions of dollars and extended to them huge credits for munition purchases in France.

aggression pacts with neighboring countries. The first such achievement was the signing in 1925 of a treaty of friendship and neutrality with Turkey. The Turkish Republic shared the Soviet Union's distrust of the western states, particularly of the League, because the latter had just awarded the Mosul district to Iraq and because of a dispute over the expulsion of the Greek Patriarch from Constantinople. In the treaty each signatory agreed not to attack the other and to remain neutral if the other were attacked by a third power or group of powers. Each also undertook to remain aloof from any general political, financial, or economic move aimed at the other.

Four months later (April 24, 1926) a similar covenant was signed at Berlin with Germany. The Reich, as we shall see later, was indignant over the bickerings attending the vote on its admission to the League in that year and consequently the German Foreign Office looked with favor on closer relations with Moscow. The Berlin Treaty provided for mutual neutrality in the event of attack without provocation. Each signatory agreed not to participate in any financial or economic boycott directed against the other. Before the end of 1926 the Bolsheviks had concluded like agreements with Afghanistan and Lithuania and in 1927 a nonaggression treaty was negotiated with Persia (Iran).

It was not to be expected that Italy would remain isolated while the other continental states were engaged in so lively a search for security. Italy, in fact, had great ambitions and bitter enemies, and Italy therefore needed friends.

The postwar period saw the development of a serious struggle between Italy and France for control of the western Mediterranean. The result was a dangerous armament race and extensive military preparations were made on both sides of the Franco-Italian border. Several times naval parleys among the powers broke down because Rome insisted on parity with France, while Paris just as firmly contended that mathematical parity was not allowable. Besides, France had land in Europe and northern Africa which, according to some Italians, belonged of right to them. Italy, finally, placed chief blame upon France for her inability in 1919 to get more colonies.

Steps to protect Italy against the potentially dangerous French diplomatic maneuvers were undertaken shortly after Benito Mussolini's advent to power. Treaties of friendship and neutrality were signed in 1924 with Czechoslovakia and Yugoslavia. In 1926 similar agreements were reached with Romania and Spain. A political treaty of 1926 with Albania was strengthened in the following year by a twenty-year defensive alliance. Finally, an Italo-Hungarian treaty was negotiated in 1927.

Thus, in 1927, nine years after the armistice, Europe was again divided into armed camps. In place of the two big prewar alliances, each with a host of satellites, there were now three major groups. But, as in the previous case, a number of the countries simultaneously had ties with two opposing alliance nuclei, and, as before, finance played a part in determining the line-up. The outlook was hardly one to inspire confidence in the hearts of any European people. France, in particular, was virtually bound by her various treaties to defend the frontiers of five protegés, not one of which was a first-class power and each of which had numerous enemies.[1] On the other hand, the organization of the new alliances was paralleled by several efforts to guarantee security through more conciliatory means. Most of these attempts originated within the framework of the League.

THE ERA OF PACTS, 1923–1933

According to Article 8 of the Covenant, the members of the League recognized "that the maintenance of peace requires the reduction of national armaments to the lowest point consistent with national safety and the enforcement by common action of international obligations." The task of formulating specific plans for the reduction of armaments was entrusted to the Council, assisted by a permanent advisory commission. Even before the League started functioning, a beginning was made in compulsory disarmament by the arms clauses of the peace treaties with the defeated powers. Moreover, in a note to Germany of June 16, 1919, the Allies plainly stated that German disarmament was to be regarded as one of the "first steps" toward a general reduction of armaments throughout the world.

Early in 1921 the Council appointed a commission to draw up proposals for the reduction of armaments. While the commission was at work, the Second Assembly suggested that the proposals be embodied in a draft treaty and the Third Assembly requested that the document provide some definite form of mutual security in exchange for the limitation of armaments. The commission acted

[1] It was one of the strategic mistakes of the peace settlement of 1919–1920 that it left a vengeful Germany surrounded by a ring of small and sometimes unfriendly states. Aside from France, these were Denmark, the Netherlands, Belgium, Luxembourg, Switzerland, Austria, Czechoslovakia, Poland, and Lithuania.

on these views and formulated a draft Treaty of Mutual Assistance which was unanimously adopted by the Fourth Assembly in September 1923.

The document provided security by a pledge of the signatories to aid any one of their number who was the victim of attack. Signatories might enter into supplementary regional alliances, if these did not conflict with the general convention and were acceptable to the League. The determination of the aggressor in any conflict was left to the Council, which was to render a verdict within four days after the outbreak of hostilities. Regarding armaments, it was stipulated that the Council should devise a scale of reductions to "a point compatible with national security." No country should benefit by the mutual guarantee which did not limit its armaments according to the Council plan within two years after the publication thereof. When the draft treaty was circulated among the powers, it failed to secure a single acceptance. Most of the states protested against the absence of any adequate definition of "aggression," objected to the lack of an arbitration formula, and complained of the vagueness of the disarmament provision.

In the meantime the governments of Great Britain and France had come under the leadership, respectively, of MacDonald and Herriot. Both premiers seemed earnestly resolved to devise some formula whereby "arbitration, security, and disarmament" might become established as the foundation stones of all future international relationships. In September 1924 they introduced a joint resolution at the Fifth Assembly of the League, reopening the entire question of security and disarmament. As a result of this move the Assembly, early in the following month, unanimously approved "the most ambitious peace plan that governments had ever discussed"—a Protocol for the Pacific Settlement of International Disputes.

The Geneva Protocol, as it came to be known, stigmatized aggressive war as an international crime. To prevent such wars, it stipulated that the nations adhering to its terms must agree (1) not to go to war against other signatories who abided by their international obligations; (2) to refer all justiciable disputes to the World Court and all political quarrels to the League Council or to special arbitration committees; (3) not to mobilize armed forces while a dispute was being arbitrated; (4) to regard as "aggressor" any nation which refused to submit a difference to peaceful settlement or which rejected an arbitral decision and resorted to war; (5) to recognize the power of the League Council to declare an economic boycott against such an aggressor state; (6) that the costs of any war be "borne by the aggressor state up to the limit of its capacity," but that such indemnity include no cessions of territory; and (7) to participate in an international conference for the reduction of armaments. No part of the protocol was to go into effect until the efforts of this conference should have resulted in at least partial disarmament.

Although some of the smaller states displayed eagerness to ratify the Geneva Protocol, the great powers found objections to it and the document never came into force. In Great Britain, MacDonald fell from power on domestic issues soon after his return to London, and his Conservative successors were of no mind to endorse world-wide commitments and sanctions. Happily this rejection of the first important attempt to define the aggressor in future conflicts was soon followed by the acceptance of another scheme which aimed at identifying any future aggressor in one of the worst of Europe's many sore spots: the Rhineland.

In the hope of allaying the mutual suspicions with which the French and Germans regarded each other's every action, Berlin had several times (1922–1923) suggested to Paris the negotiation of frontier guarantees, antiwar pledges, and arbitration projects. Each time, however, France had been cold to the proposals. Undismayed by these setbacks and by the fate of the Geneva Protocol, Germany, through Foreign Minister Gustav Stresemann, in February 1925 once more broached the subject to France.

Stresemann suggested (1) a pact among Great Britain, Italy, France, and Germany for guaranteeing the existing Rhine frontiers and settling future international disputes by arbitration, and (2) a series of arbitration treaties among Germany and her neighbors east and west. This time Briand in France and Austen Chamberlain in Great Britain lent willing ears to the plan, but before definite negotiations could be inaugurated the French insisted (1) that Germany seek League membership; (2) that Belgium become a signer of the proposed pact; (3) that nothing in the contemplated document interfere with France's obligations to Poland or with the Allies' obligations under the League Covenant; and (4) that Czechoslovakia and Poland be invited to attend the parleys. Stresemann accepted the conditions, being anxious to get new foreign loans and replace by a feeling of security the air of uncertainty which enveloped Europe.

From October 5 to 16, 1925, delegates from Germany, France, Great Britain, Italy, Belgium, Poland. and Czechoslovakia met at

Locarno in Switzerland. For the first time since the war all powers met on equal footing. The proceedings were carried on informally in a manner quite different from that which had prevailed at

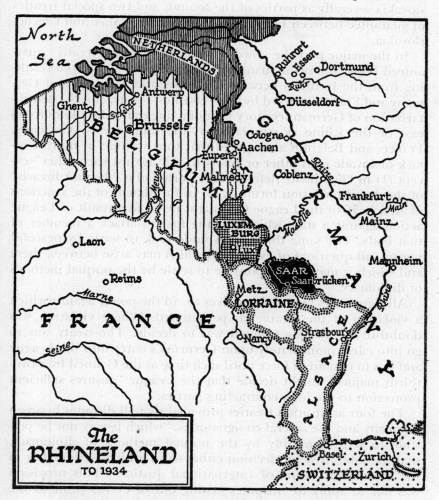

After Landman, J., *Outline History of the World Since 1914*, 1934
Courtesy of Barnes and Noble, Inc.

earlier gatherings. So different were the attitudes of the delegates on this occasion from the usual diplomatic poses that the phrase "spirit of Locarno" was coined to describe the changed atmosphere. In this spirit seven treaties were initialed, namely; a Treaty of Mutual Guarantee among Germany, France, Great Britain, Italy, and Belgium; four arbitration treaties between Germany as the party of the first, and Belgium, France, Poland, and Czechoslovakia severally as parties of the second; and two special treaties of guarantee between France and Poland, and France and Czechoslovakia.

In the major pact the powers "collectively and severally" guaranteed both "the maintenance of the territorial *status quo* resulting from the frontiers between Germany and Belgium and Germany and France" as fixed by the Versailles Treaty, and the demilitarization of German territory west of a line drawn fifty kilometers east of the Rhine as stipulated in the same treaty. Germany, France, and Belgium also agreed that they would "in no case attack or invade each other or resort to war against each other" except (1) in "legitimate defense"; (2) in case of a "flagrant breach" of the demilitarization formula; (3) in fulfillment of the sanctions of Article 16 of the League Covenant; or (4) as a result of League action against a state which was the first to attack a member of that body. The same three states undertook to settle by peaceful means "all questions of every kind which may arise between them and which it may not be possible to settle by the normal methods of diplomacy."

All signatories bound themselves to aid the power against which a violation of the treaty was perpetrated. Where violation was doubtful, the League Council was to decide. The treaty was to go into effect immediately upon Germany's entry into the League and was to remain in force until such time as the Council by a two-thirds majority might decide that the League "ensures sufficient protection to the high contracting parties."

The four arbitration treaties provided that all disputes between Germany and the several co-signatories, "which it may not be possible to settle amicably by the normal methods of diplomacy, shall be submitted for decision either to an arbitral tribunal or to the Permanent Court of International Justice." This provision was not to apply to "disputes arising out of events prior to the present convention and belonging to the past," and hence was not binding in the case of problems which, like that of the Polish Corridor, arose out of the peace settlement. The remaining treaties, those between France and her two allies, provided that if the respective signatories were made to suffer from a failure to observe the undertakings of Locarno, they would "lend each other immediate aid and assistance, if such a failure is accompanied by an un-provoked recourse to arms."

The Locarno achievements were widely hailed as precursors of a new era in world history. But neither the pacts nor the spirit of Locarno were actual guarantees of peace. True, the Rhine frontier apparently was safeguarded. Germany supposedly gave up all claims to Alsace-Lorraine and France all hopes of a Rhineland protectorate. Yet the problem of Germany's eastern frontiers remained unsolved and there was no real guarantee that it would be settled peaceably. The spirit of friendliness, moreover, was only sporadically evident in international affairs after 1925. It seemed to have been entirely forgotten in the very next year, while Germany's application for membership in the League was under consideration, but it experienced a gratifying revival in 1927.

In the spring of the latter year Foreign Minister Briand dispatched a note to Washington suggesting a Franco-American engagement "mutually outlawing war." After several months of correspondence the American Secretary of State, Frank B. Kellogg, proposed that France and the United States join in an effort to induce a number of the powers to sign a general antiwar pact. It was not difficult to interest the members of the League in such a scheme, for by signing the Covenant they had automatically promised to have recourse to war only as a means of last resort. Eventually, on August 27, 1928, delegates from fifteen nations subscribed to an antiwar agreement in Paris. The document soon came to be known as the Kellogg-Briand Pact or Pact of Paris.

In the first article the signers solemnly declared "in the names of their respective peoples that they condemn recourse to war for the solution of international controversies, and renounce it as an instrument of national policy in their relations with one another." In the second article the states agreed "that the settlement or solution of all disputes or conflicts of whatever nature or whatever origin they may be, which may arise among them, shall never be sought except by pacific means." The third and last article outlined the terms of ratification and adherence. According to the preamble "any signatory Power which shall hereafter seek to promote its national interests by resort to war should be denied the benefits furnished by this Treaty." If a signatory should break its pledge, therefore, the other parties would recover their freedom of action with respect to the trespasser. Copies of the document and invitations to adhere thereto were sent by Secretary Kellogg to

forty-eight other countries. Within four years sixty-two accept-
ances were recorded.[1]

Unfortunately the efficacy of this "outlawry of war" was considerably lessened by the qualifications and interpretations placed
upon the text by a number of the signatories. In effect, war was
outlawed except (1) when resorted to in self-defense; (2) in the
execution of obligations assumed under previous treaties; or (3)
in fulfillment of responsibilities incurred through the signing of
the League Covenant or the Locarno agreements. Great Britain,
moreover, made a special reservation with regard to "certain regions of the world the welfare and integrity of which constitute a
special and vital interest for our peace and safety." Fundamentally,
therefore, only wars of aggression were outlawed, and even in such
cases there was no provision for enforcement. The pact was
founded on the hope that public opinion might be strong and influential enough, even in time of emergency, to restrain any particular nation from violating what were simply moral obligations.
But such incidents as the Sino-Japanese controversy of 1931 and
after seemed to indicate that a warless future could be guaranteed
only if the Pact of Paris—or some substitute for this pact—were
provided with adequate "teeth" so that its violation would be regarded as something more serious than the perpetration of an un-
moral act.[2]

The suspicion and antagonism that characterized European relations during the early depression years and especially after Adolf
Hitler became chancellor of Germany, led to the formulation of
two additional peace agreements: the Pact of Rome and the London Agreements. To dispel the new war clouds, Mussolini suggested that the leading western powers act to guarantee peace at
least for a certain stated period. The result of his enterprise was
the signing (July 1933) of a ten-year pact at Rome by Great Britain, France, Germany, and Italy. The signatories agreed to consult on all important international political and economic questions, to work for the success of the disarmament proceedings at
Geneva, and to acknowledge once more the principle of treaty

[1] The Soviet Union was so anxious to have this document come into force that it
induced Estonia, Latvia, Poland, and Romania to adhere with it to the Litvinov
Protocol (February 1929) whereby the pact became effective at once, regardless of
the actions of other states. Later in the year Lithuania, Turkey, Persia, and Danzig
also adhered to the protocol.

[2] As it happened, one of the chief effects of the Paris Pact was the appearance of
the so-called undeclared war.

revision as stated in Article 19 of the League Covenant.[1] As first outlined by Mussolini the text of the pact was less general, particularly with regard to treaty revision and disarmament. But Poland and the Little Entente feared that the document in its original form would restore a hegemony of the larger states. France supported her allies and the pact therefore had to be revised.

The Soviet Union, far from regarding the pact as a guarantee of peace, looked upon it as another alliance against Bolshevism and seized the opportunity to propose a general nonaggression treaty to her neighbors. The idea quickly took hold and in July 1933, at the Soviet Embassy in London, the representatives of Afghanistan, Czechoslovakia, Estonia, Latvia, Lithuania, Persia, Poland, Romania, the Soviet Union, Turkey, and Yugoslavia signed three conventions which together were called the London Agreements. The signatories confirmed the inviolability of each other's territories, expressed the conviction that the Kellogg Pact, to which they were parties, forbade all aggression, and adopted a specific definition of the term "aggressor nation." An aggressor was defined as any signatory who declared war on another, invaded foreign lands without formal declaration of war, established a blockade, or supported on its soil armed bands organized to raid another state.[2]

DISARMAMENT AND REARMAMENT

The delegates who were gathered at Geneva in September 1925 for the Sixth Assembly of the League faced a grave responsibility. Five Assemblies had already met, and yet the problem of disarmament was hardly nearer solution than in 1920. True, there had been two League attempts—the Treaty of Mutual Assistance and the Geneva Protocol—to bring about a limitation of armaments, but both had been repudiated by the member states. Hence the time had come to take some definite action that would be accept-

---

[1] Article 19 of the Covenant reads: "The Assembly may from time to time advise the reconsideration by Members of the League of treaties which have become inapplicable and the consideration of international conditions whose continuance might endanger the peace of the world."

[2] Besides making clear who the aggressor would be in a future conflict in eastern Europe, the London Agreements achieved several other ends. Poland presumably no longer had to fear attack from two sides at once, from both the Soviet Union and Germany. The Soviet Union undertook not to use force to recover the province of Bessarabia which Romania had occupied in 1918. Czechoslovakia and Yugoslavia for the first time concluded an agreement with the Bolsheviks. And these last were freer to devote more attention to the situation in the Far East.

able to the governments of the world. In this spirit the Assembly requested the Council "to make a preparatory study with a view to a Conference for the Reduction and Limitation of Armaments in order that, as soon as satisfactory conditions [of security] have been assured . . . the said Conference may be convened and a general reduction and limitation of armaments may be realized."

The Council thereupon appointed a Preparatory Commission for the Disarmament Conference, to meet at Geneva in 1926. There were represented on the commission all the members of the Council, a number of other League members, Germany, and the United States. The Soviet Union was invited but refused to participate until 1927, after the settlement of a dispute with Switzerland arising from the assassination in 1923 of a Soviet diplomat on Swiss soil. The agenda of the commission consisted of a *Questionnaire* prepared by the Council. It was believed that the queries thus presented must receive constructive answer before a disarmament convention could be drafted.[1] The commission worked hard and by the middle of March 1927 had distributed replies to the *Questionnaire* to all member powers.

On the basis of these answers the British and French governments prepared draft conventions to serve as starting points for the talks at the next session of the Preparatory Commission. The two drafts conflicted on nearly every vital issue and there was little harmony in the conversations that were based upon them. The technical aspects of the disarmament problem were constantly pushed into the background by fear, jealousy, pride, and economics. In general, the United States, Germany, and Great Britain were to be found on one side in the voting, and France and her allies on the other.

Three problems proved to be especially thorny. Although it was agreed that limitation of land armaments necessarily involved limitation of effectives, there was a decided difference of opinion on how to estimate effectives. France and other conscriptionist countries objected to the inclusion of trained reserves in the category of effectives, while the states with volunteer armies maintained that a man who had just completed several years of service with the colors was as well prepared to fight as one who still drilled with his regiment. In the matter of naval limitation, Great Britain and the United States believed that there should be a total-tonnage restriction for each nation, plus a limit on the tonnage of each class of

[1] The questions may be found in Wheeler-Bennett, J. W. *Disarmament and Security since Locarno, 1925–1931*, 1932.

ship. France and Italy, however, while subscribing to the idea of a limited total tonnage, thought that each country should be free to build within its allotment whatever vessels it saw fit. On the question of international supervision, France and her *cortège habituel* were anxious to set up an elaborate system of international control, whereas the other states contended that the main reliance for the enforcement of any disarmament program must be placed on the good faith of the parties concerned.

The commission, unable to reach one final agreement, drew up (1927) a draft convention which embodied the points that had secured general assent and the alternative texts of all articles on which there had been dissension. This convention did not come up for a second reading until April 1929. In the meantime many things had happened in the spheres of security and disarmament.

To understand the story of the further disarmament proceedings, it is necessary first to refer back to the early postwar years. Inasmuch as the peace conference had ignored the question of the freedom of the seas, influential groups in the United States agitated soon after the war for the building of a navy, second to none, that would be able to enforce American rights in any future war. For a time it appeared as if the prewar Anglo-German naval rivalry would be replaced by an equally dangerous Anglo-American competition. By virtue of the Anglo-Japanese alliance, moreover, Japan might well be found on the side of Great Britain. To forestall any such catastrophe, President Warren G. Harding invited a group of powers to attend a conference at Washington in the winter of 1921–1922 to consider naval limitation as well as the entire question of Pacific and Far Eastern relations.

Seven treaties were signed by the conference. Of these, two five-power treaties dealt with naval limitation. In the one, which never came into force, the five powers (United States, Great Britain, Japan, France, and Italy) outlawed poison gas as a weapon and agreed that submarines should obey the same rules of naval warfare that applied to surface vessels. The other, effective from 1923, limited the total tonnage of aircraft carriers and restricted the number of capital ships to be allowed each of the signatories.[1] A ten-year "naval holiday" was declared during which no new capital ships were to be built, and no capital ship might be replaced until it was twenty years old. The eventual total capital-ship replacement tonnages were fixed at 525,000 for the United

---

[1] A capital ship was defined as one with a greater displacement than ten thousand tons and guns of larger than eight-inch caliber.

States; 525,000 for Great Britain; 315,000 for Japan; and 175,000 each for France and Italy. These figures established the ratio of 5:5:3:1.67:1.67. In order to achieve the Washington limit, most of the powers had to scrap ships that were already built or under construction.

Five years after the signing of these treaties, President Calvin Coolidge invited Great Britain, France, Italy, and Japan to attend with the United States a conference to consider the limitation of cruisers, destroyers, and submarines. He reminded the powers that the Washington Conference had imposed tonnage restrictions on capital ships and aircraft carriers, and suggested that the time had come to deal similarly with the remaining classes of war vessels. Only Great Britain and Japan accepted the invitation. The other two states declared that such a conference would serve merely to increase the difficulties of the Preparatory Commission. Hence it was a three-power conference that opened in June 1927 at Geneva. Hugh Gibson, the chief delegate from the United States, was elected president.

The Americans proposed a total-tonnage restriction in each of the ship categories under discussion and suggested the same ratio that had earlier been decided upon with regard to capital ships, namely, 5:5:3. Japan was, on the whole, inclined to side with the United States. Great Britain, ruled by a Conservative Ministry, held different views. She insisted that mathematical parity with the United States was by no means equivalent to practical parity and maintained that the need to protect 80,000 miles of trade and communication lines made it imperative that there be no restriction on her right to build small (7500-ton) cruisers. However, she was anxious to set a limit upon 10,000-ton cruisers, the type best suited to American needs because of America's paucity of naval bases and long coast line. After two months the conference broke up, with nothing accomplished toward the further limitation of naval armaments. Instead, there was a renewal of the suspicion between the United States and Great Britain that had temporarily subsided after the signing of the Washington treaties. Before long the suspicion in America changed to indignation and anger.

The *New York American* in September 1928 uncovered a secret military-naval compromise which earlier in the year had been reached by London and Paris. By its terms France promised to support Great Britain's stand on naval limitation at future disarmament meetings and Great Britain withdrew her objection to the exclusion of trained reserves from the category of military effectives. The publication of this arrangement was greeted with vigorous popular protests in both Great Britain and the United States. Although the two European powers protested that they had been motivated solely by a desire to speed disarmament, the American people were skeptical of London's sincerity. In 1929 Congress enacted a bill for the construction of a new aircraft carrier and fifteen cruisers of the very type that was most objectionable to the British Admiralty.[1]

While these events were taking place, the Preparatory Commission continued its deliberations. In the face of "international wrath and ridicule . . . the delegates wrestled with arguments about the effect of fog on war, split hairs about the allowances to be made for hogs in considering a nation's armament, and examined the history of international weather." In 1928 there was some excitement when the Soviet Union, represented by Maxim Litvinov, urged the abolition of all armed forces and war ministries, and the destruction of all heavy weapons, fortresses, and war-material factories. This task was to be carried out in either one or four years, and provision was to be made for the necessary national and maritime police forces to preserve domestic order and protect property.

The Soviet proposal was tabled after Lord Cushendun intimated that the real motive of the scheme was to enable the Bolsheviks the better to carry on their international propaganda. When Litvinov thereupon advanced a second plan, providing for gradual and proportional disarmament according to a fixed scale, Dr. John Loudon, president of the commission, requested the Soviet delegation to attend future meetings "in a constructive spirit and not with the idea of destroying the work . . . already done." Only Germany and Turkey supported the Soviet views, and it was rapidly becoming evident that Berlin was growing impatient with the delay of the former Allies in fulfilling their Versailles pledge to regard Germany's disarmament as "the initiation of a general limitation of the armaments of all nations."

During 1929, while the commission was reading for a second time the draft convention of 1927 and effecting compromises on several disputed points, there occurred a *rapprochement* between the United States and Great Britain. The ratification of the Kellogg Pact restored a measure of good feeling, and both President Hoover and Premier MacDonald expressed renewed hopes for a

---

[1] In 1930 France excluded William Randolph Hearst, owner of the *New York American*. He was classed as "an enemy of the Republic."

further reduction of naval armaments. The outcome of resulting conversations was the calling for 1930 of a London Naval Conference of the five great naval powers.

Almost exactly three months after the opening of the conference, the five powers signed (April 22) a London Naval Treaty. Because of their contest for control of the western Mediterranean, France and Italy withheld their signatures from the really vital part of the pact. The Italian delegation expressed a willingness to accept any naval figure, however low, provided it was not exceeded by that of any other continental power. The French argued that mathematical parity with Italy meant in fact inferiority in the Mediterranean since France had coast lines on three seas. Hence Paris and Rome could reach no agreement.[1]

In so far as the other three states were concerned, the treaty, which was to remain in force until the end of 1936, solved the problem of relative cruiser strengths by compromise. The United States was to have 18 cruisers of the 10,000-ton type and 143,500 tons of smaller cruisers (total 323,500 tons). Great Britain was to have 15 of the large cruisers (including 2 of 8400 tons each) and 192,200 tons of smaller ones (total 339,000 tons). Japan accepted a maximum of 12 battle cruisers (including 4 of 7100 tons each) and smaller craft to the extent of 100,450 tons (total 208,850 tons). The tonnage allotments for destroyers were set at 150,000 tons each for the United States and Great Britain and 105,500 for Japan. Each of the three powers was given a submarine tonnage of 52,700 and no new capital ships were to be laid down until 1936. The aircraft-carrier figures remained the same as in the Washington Treaty: 135,000 tons each for the United States and Great Britain and 81,000 for Japan.

Perhaps the most-discussed section of the treaty was Article 21, the so-called safeguarding or escalator clause. This permitted any signatory to increase its tonnage in any category if, in its opinion, its national security was endangered by new construction on the part of any nonsignatory. The only requirement in such case was prompt notification to the other treaty signers. The latter thereupon would become free to make proportionate increases in their own navies.

While the London Naval Conference was in progress, the Preparatory Commission had adjourned in the hope that the naval

[1] Actually, France left the gathering determined to maintain a fleet superior to any that Italy might build. Italy was equally determined to construct a fleet that would be on a par with the navy of France.

deadlock might be broken. The failure of France and Italy to sign the whole treaty, however, emphasized the need for reaching results. Discussions were resumed and in December 1930 a final draft convention for a general disarmament conference was adopted. After almost five years of effort the vote was still far from unanimous and disagreements persisted over virtually every important article.

The League Council now selected Geneva as the site of the world's first disarmament conference and fixed February 2, 1932, as the opening date of the meeting. Later the Council designated Arthur Henderson, then foreign secretary in Great Britain's second Labor Government, president of the conference. In August 1931 the Labor Government fell and Henderson became the leader of the Opposition, but when the gathering met he nevertheless attended as president. The Twelfth Assembly of the League, on a motion of the Italian Foreign Minister, Dino Grandi, requested (September 1931) the Council to urge all governments to help ensure the success of the forthcoming conference by agreeing for one year "to refrain from any measures involving an increase in their armaments." By January 1, 1932, such an arms truce had been accepted by fifty-four nations, including the United States and the Soviet Union. When the Geneva Disarmament Conference opened, there were present more than two hundred delegates representing about sixty states.

The draft convention that was placed before the conference was a general document which indicated the methods of limitation that might be adopted but which left to the conference the application of these methods and the decisions as to ratios and figures. It was a "skeleton lacking flesh and blood" and it offered blanks and dashes in place of figures. Among the specific recommendations were budgetary limitation of armaments; limitation of periods of military service; limitation of military, naval, and air effectives; acceptance of the form of naval restriction laid down in the London Naval Treaty; and the appointment of a permanent disarmament commission to sit at Geneva and advise the League Council on the progress of fulfillment of the projected disarmament treaty.

Perhaps even more ominous for the success of the conference than the flood of reservations to every one of these points was the clash of French demands for security and German demands for equality. The French representatives now steadfastly refused to vote for any general reduction of armaments unless adequate security were first guaranteed, preferably by the placing of a powerful military, naval, and air force under the control of the League of Nations. This means of achieving security, though endorsed by the allies of France, satisfied none of the other larger states. Deadlock therefore ensued.

The conference, unable to agree on any vital matter, wearily adjourned in July 1932. One of the most dangerous results of this failure of its first session was the reaction caused in Italy, the Soviet Union, and Germany. In the former two countries the authorities became more disdainful than ever of the impotence of the League. In the German Republic a fear of widespread military preparations and alliance formations, a resentment over the intransigeance of France, and a desire for the restoration of the fatherland to a plane of equality with the other great powers played directly into the hands of the restless nationalists. Through the mouth of Defense Minister General Kurt von Schleicher these nationalists now officially demanded that the world either disarm down to the level set for Germany in the Versailles Treaty or recognize the equality of the Germans and place no obstacle in the way of their arming up to the degree of their neighbors. Berlin also announced its intention to abstain from any further participation in the Geneva Disarmament Conference until its right to absolute equality among the nations should have been admitted.

Alarmed at the prospect that Germany might unilaterally abrogate the disarmament provisions of the Versailles Treaty, Premier Herriot of France announced a new compromise plan. On the basis of this offer, the powers issued a statement in December 1932 pledging that "one of the principles that should guide the Conference on Disarmament should be the grant to Germany and to the other disarmed powers of equality of rights in a system which would provide security for all nations. . . ." Germany now agreed to coöperate once more and in February 1933 the conference resumed the work it had begun just one year previously. In the meantime (January 30, 1933) Adolf Hitler, leader of the National Socialist Party, had become German Chancellor.

The new German Government displayed no mood for temporizing, and once more differences, chiefly Franco-German differences, threatened to disrupt the proceedings. To forestall disaster, Prime Minister MacDonald himself came to Geneva and eloquently presented a plan which tried to meet both the French desire for security and the German demand for equality. Unfortunately, nearly every power had objections to the plan and about 125 amendments were suggested. In June, therefore, the conference adjourned until October.

During the summer recess (1933) President Henderson toured the European capitals in the hope that personal contact with the premiers and ministers might lead to tangible gains. But though he was everywhere politely treated, he was nowhere greatly encouraged. It became evident that, whereas Germany was determined to rearm without further delay, France and her allies, alarmed by the nationalistic utterances of the Hitlerites, were unwilling to permit such rearming for some time to come. Meanwhile the armament expenditures of every large state continued to mount.[1] And into this atmosphere there burst the news, on October 14, that Germany was withdrawing from the disarmament conference which was scheduled to reconvene two days later. Simultaneously Germany served notice of her intended withdrawal from the League. Berlin maintained that there was clearly no prospect of the fulfillment of "Germany's recognized claim to equality," or of the "contractual obligations" of the other powers to disarm.

The resulting impasse seemed destined to continue indefinitely. The disarmament conference, after several further adjournments, finally did meet in May 1934. But after a few days of wrangling the delegates dispersed once more, never to meet again. During the remainder of 1934 France, Great Britain, and most of the other powers voted increasingly high appropriations for military, naval, and air defense measures, while Germany was more than ever determined to rearm.[2]

FROM REVISIONIST BLOC TO AXIS

Toward the end of the first postwar decade it became apparent that the three-cornered security system built up by France, the Soviet Union, and Italy was destined to undergo changes. As Ger-

[1] It was at this point that the Pact of Rome and the London Agreements were signed. See pp. 184–185.

[2] Total world armament expenditures, in round numbers and at similar price levels, rose as follows:

1913	$3,000,000,000
1928	3,500,000,000
1930	4,000,000,000
1935	5,000,000,000
1938	10,000,000,000

The world's expenditure for armaments in 1938 represented a sum large enough to run the League of Nations, the Permanent Court, and the International Labor Organization for twelve centuries (in terms of their budgets for that year).

many slowly regained strength and as the other defeated powers acquired more stability, there was a growing demand for broad revision of the peace settlement. Italy, moreover, because of her grievances against France and her general ambitions, gradually drew closer to her former enemies and began openely to side with them on matters pertaining to the peace treaties. By 1928 the fascist kingdom began to emerge as the leader of a "revisionist bloc" whose most insistent member, Hungary, clamored for the return of the many Magyars assigned to the neighboring states by the Treaty of Trianon.

In 1928 Italy concluded treaties of friendship and neutrality with Turkey and Greece, and in 1930 one with Austria. Owing largely to Italian influence, Turkey and Greece negotiated a similar convention in 1930, and a nonaggression pact in 1933. Italian friendship with Bulgaria was sealed in 1930 by the marriage of Princess Giovanna of Italy to King Boris. In 1933, Italy and the Soviet Union signed a pact of nonaggression. Thereafter Italy encouraged a resumption of diplomatic relations between the Soviet Union and Hungary, a condition which was completed in 1934.

In 1933 the rise to power of Adolf Hitler, who patterned some of his policies after those of Mussolini, seemed to foreshadow an Italo-German entente. The prospect for a time worried France, but Italy showed little sympathy with Germany's desire to absorb Austria into the Reich. For strategic and economic reasons Mussolini preferred to see Austria independent and closely tied to Italy. Hence Italy induced France and Great Britain to subscribe to a communiqué (February 1934) declaring that the three powers took "a common view regarding the necessity of maintaining Austria's independence in accordance with the relevant treaties." Exactly one month later the premiers of Italy, Austria, and Hungary signed the Rome Protocols. The signatories agreed to pursue "a corresponding policy directed to promote effective collaboration among the European states," and to conclude bilateral trade agreements to widen Austria's and Hungary's markets for manufactures and grain, respectively.

The new German nationalism, as voiced by the Hitlerites, and the continued activity of the revisionist bloc also affected the interrelations of the Little Entente, France, and the Soviet Union. Already in 1929, Czechoslovakia, Yugoslavia, and Romania had renewed the whole set of treaties that comprised the entente. Now it was found advisable still further to strengthen the ties of friendship, and in 1933 a "pact of organization" was signed which contemplated the transformation of the entente into a "higher international unity," directed by a permanent council composed of the respective foreign ministers and coöperating closely in economic and financial as well as political affairs.[1]

Further to protect themselves, the members of the Little Entente in 1933 signed the London Agreements with the Soviet Union and then also drew closer to Poland. The latter step was especially important inasmuch as all these smaller countries seemed to have wearied of being regarded as French satellites. On several occasions, notably at the disarmament conference, Poland and even the entente upheld views that were not entirely in harmony with those of France. As if to emphasize her new sentiments, Poland in January 1934 signed a ten-year nonaggression pact with Nazi Germany. Soon thereafter Poland also renewed a nonaggression treaty that had earlier been signed with the Soviet Union.

The Third Republic, too, figured in a changed diplomatic line-up. As early as 1931, France, for years the leading foe of the Soviet Union, had begun to shift her position. She had long wanted access to the Russian oil resources. The Soviet Union placed huge orders abroad and France saw no reason why these should nearly all fall to Germany, Great Britain, and Italy. In Germany the nationalists were becoming strong enough to frighten both the French and Bolsheviks: they threatened to repudiate the Versailles Treaty, vehemently denounced communism, and sometimes referred to Russia as a suitable field for eastward expansion. Hence Soviet-German relations cooled and France in 1932 signed a neutrality treaty with the Soviet Union.

After a time it appeared that Paris and Moscow wanted to conclude a general pact of nonaggression and mutual assistance with Poland, the Little Entente, and the Baltic states. Germany would be welcome to enter this system if she wished.[2] When nothing came of the proposal, France and the Soviet Union in May 1935 signed a five-year nonaggression pact of their own. They agreed to consult if aggression threatened and promised each other immediate aid in case of "unprovoked aggression." Once again membership was extended to Germany and the eastern states, but most

[1] Several meetings of the entente, chiefly economic, were held in 1933, and in 1934 an agreement was reached whereby Czechoslovakia promised greatly to increase her imports of Romanian and Yugoslav agricultural products. These states, in turn, offered to buy more Czechoslovak manufactures.

[2] Fearing that Germany might have designs in the Baltic area, the Soviet Union in 1934 suggested a treaty to Berlin guaranteeing the sovereignty of the Baltic states, but the Nazis rejected this offer as an unnecessary precaution.

of these appeared to have more confidence in bilateral treaties and hesitated to pledge mutual assistance in any and every conflict. Great Britain, it seemed, favored such an Eastern Locarno as a means of relieving German fears of a new "encirclement" and encouraging Berlin to coöperate in the restoration of general European stability. Meanwhile, in the summer of 1934 Great Britain had voted a huge program of aerial construction and Stanley Baldwin had announced that Britain's frontiers lay on the Rhine.[1]

Turkey took the lead in promoting a movement for Balkan coöperation. Bulgaria, Greece, Albania, Romania, and Yugoslavia were several times approached with suggestions for an inter-Balkan arrangement to foster political harmony and economic fellowship. In October 1931 the Turkish Government played host to a conference at which delegates from all Balkan states assembled to discuss the creation of a customs union and the negotiation of interlocking nonaggression pacts. The main accomplishments of the gathering were the establishment of an Inter-Balkan Chamber of Commerce and an Inter-Balkan Tobacco Bureau at Salonika.

During 1933 the foreign ministers of Turkey and Greece visited the Balkan capitals to sound out opinion on a program of collaboration based on the principles of "the Balkans for the Balkan peoples" and the maintenance of the territorial *status quo*. This latter point was objectionable to Bulgaria who wanted revision of her Greek and Yugoslav borders, and to Albania who, as an Italian protectorate,[2] upheld Bulgaria in her revisionist demands. Hence the Balkan Pact which was signed at Athens in 1934 bore the signatures of the representatives only of Turkey, Greece, Romania, and Yugoslavia. The four states (1) expressed their decision to assure "the maintenance of the territorial order at present established in the Balkans"; (2) mutually guaranteed the "security of all their Balkan frontiers"; (3) promised not to take any political action with respect to any Balkan nonsignatory "without previous mutual discussion"; and (4) agreed not to assume any political obligation towards another Balkan state without the prior consent of the remaining contracting parties. This agreement was welcomed by France but criticized by Italy. Without the adherence of Bulgaria and Albania, moreover, it failed to stabilize Balkan affairs.

Later in 1934 representatives of the United States, Great Britain, and Japan discussed the question of renewing the naval-limitation

[1] In 1934, also, Germany and Japan had ostentatiously exchanged expressions of good will.

[2] See section "Italy and Albania" in Chapter XIV.

THE FUTILE SEARCH FOR SECURITY, 1920–1935

The dates indicate the year of signing of the treaties. Supplementary agreements are listed only if exceptionally important.

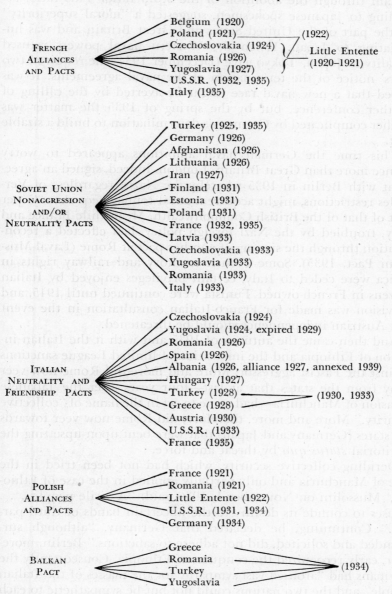

FRENCH ALLIANCES AND PACTS
- Belgium (1920)
- Poland (1921)
- Czechoslovakia (1924)
- Romania (1926)
- Yugoslavia (1927)
- U.S.S.R. (1932, 1935)
- Italy (1935)

(1922) Little Entente (1920–1921)

SOVIET UNION NONAGGRESSION AND/OR NEUTRALITY PACTS
- Turkey (1925, 1935)
- Germany (1926)
- Afghanistan (1926)
- Lithuania (1926)
- Iran (1927)
- Finland (1931)
- Estonia (1931)
- Poland (1931)
- France (1932, 1935)
- Latvia (1933)
- Czechoslovakia (1933)
- Yugoslavia (1933)
- Romania (1933)
- Italy (1933)

ITALIAN NEUTRALITY AND FRIENDSHIP PACTS
- Czechoslovakia (1924)
- Yugoslavia (1924, expired 1929)
- Romania (1926)
- Spain (1926)
- Albania (1926, alliance 1927, annexed 1939)
- Hungary (1927)
- Turkey (1928)
- Greece (1928)
- Austria (1930)
- U.S.S.R. (1933)
- France (1935)

(1930, 1933)

POLISH ALLIANCES AND PACTS
- France (1921)
- Romania (1921)
- Little Entente (1922)
- U.S.S.R. (1931, 1934)
- Germany (1934)

BALKAN PACT
- Greece
- Romania
- Turkey
- Yugoslavia

(1934)

197

treaties. Japan demanded parity with the United States and Great Britain through the abolition of the 5:5:3 ratio. This ratio, according to Japanese spokesmen, suggested a "moral superiority" on the part of the United States and Great Britain and was humiliating to Japan. When the Western naval powers refused equality to Japan, Tokyo gave (December 1934) the required two years' notice of the termination of the naval agreements. It was hoped that a new naval race might be averted by the calling of another conference, but by the spring of 1935 the matter was further complicated by Germany's determination to build a sizable fleet.

This time the German naval ambitions appeared to worry France more than Great Britain. London, indeed, signed an agreement with Berlin in 1935 whereby the Nazis, regardless of Versailles restrictions, might acquire a naval tonnage equal to 35 per cent of that of the British Commonwealth. Meanwhile France and Italy, troubled by the Nazi foreign policy, had effected a reconciliation through the signing of another pact at Rome (Laval-Mussolini Pact, 1935). Some French territory and railway rights in Africa were ceded to Italy, certain privileges enjoyed by Italian citizens in French-owned Tunisia were continued until 1945, and provision was made for Franco-Italian consultation in the event that Austrian independence should be threatened.

And then came the autumn of 1935 and with it the Italian invasion of Ethiopia and the imposition of limited League sanctions against the Fascist aggressor. More and more did Rome now veer away from the states that at last—four years after the Japanese invasion of Manchuria—had come to act in the name of "collective security." More and more, therefore, did Rome now veer towards the states (Germany and Japan) that were bent upon upsetting the territorial *status quo* by threat and force.

Deriding collective security, which had not been tried in the case of Manchuria and only partially applied in the case of Ethiopia,[1] Mussolini on November 1, 1936, said: "A virile people . . . refuses to confide its destiny to the uncertain hands of third parties." Continuing, he declared that Germany, "although surrounded and solicited, did not adhere to sanctions." Berlin, moreover, early recognized the conquest of Ethiopia. Consequently the Germans had "aroused vast sympathy for the masses of the Italian people" and the two nations could not but be sympathetic to each other's aims. This new friendship, thundered Il Duce, was bol-

[1] See Chapters XIV and XXII.

stered by common opposition to Bolshevism and was in reality "an axis around which all European states animated by the desire for peace might collaborate." Thus for the first time was the word "axis" used with the political connotation that it has since come to have. And thus also did Mussolini cede first place among the revisionists to the stronger Reich. Fascist Italy became content to follow where once she had led.

Soon after Mussolini made this speech, Germany and Japan were drawn closely together through the signing of an Anti-Comintern Pact (November 1936). The signatories agreed "to keep each other informed concerning the activities of the Third International, to consult upon the necessary defense measures, and to execute these measures in close coöperation with each other." One year later Italy also adhered to this agreement and the "Berlin-Rome-Tokyo axis" was an established fact. Referring to the ideological and practical differences of outlook of the axis and nonaxis states, Mussolini announced: "The struggle between two worlds can permit no compromise. Either we or they!" Thus was the challenge of battle hurled at the British Commonwealth, France, the Soviet Union, China, and the United States.[1]

[1] See also the opening pages of Chapter XXIV.

CHAPTER IX

Unrest in Africa and Asia

BLACK AND WHITE IN AFRICA

Shortly after the outbreak of the First World War, Germany, proposed to the Allies that the neutrality of the African colonies be maintained during the period of the conflict, on the ground that the preservation of Europe's ascendancy in Africa depended upon the solidarity of the white race on that continent. Perhaps the knowledge that she could not defend her overseas possessions against Allied attack stimulated Germany to advance this thesis. At any rate, the suggestion was disregarded and the war was carried into Africa. Then, after the war, the general disorganization following a long period of armed conflict combined with a number of other factors to produce great unrest from Morocco to the Cape of Good Hope. Among the most provocative of these factors must be counted, first, the reaction against a long period of subjection; secondly, the influence of some of the religious teaching; thirdly, the increasing competition for work between blacks and whites in such relatively well-developed regions as South Africa; and fourthly, the effect on the blacks of a certain amount of education.

When the Western peoples in the nineteenth century contemplated the partitioning of the Dark Continent, they were definitely aware of their moral obligations towards the Africans. As early as 1885, in the General Act of the Berlin Conference, the representatives of the leading countries of the Western world had agreed for the sake of humanity and civilization "to protect the natives in their moral and material well-being; to coöperate in the suppression of slavery and the slave trade; to further the education and civilization of the natives; to protect missionaries, scientists, and explorers"; and to preserve the freedom of religion. An attempt to persuade the conference to restrict the sale of liquor and firearms

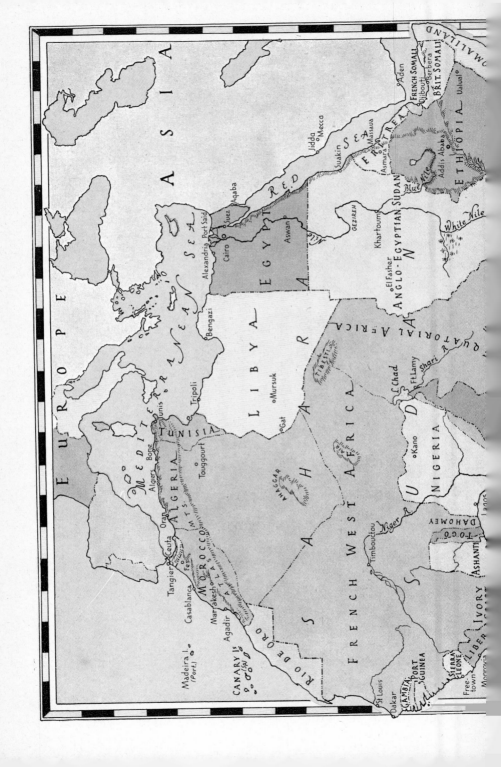

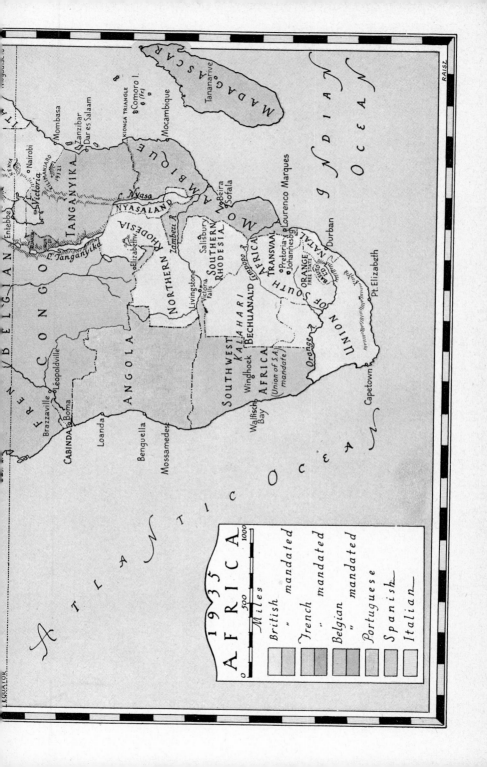

AFRICA
1935

Miles
0   500   1000

British
"   mandated
French
"   mandated
Belgian
"   mandated
Portuguese
Spanish
Italian

RAISZ

MADAGASCAR

Tananarive

INDIAN OCEAN

ATLANTIC OCEAN

FRENCH CONGO

BELGIAN CONGO

Brazzaville
Léopoldville
Boma
CABINDA

Loanda

Benguella

Mossamedes

ANGOLA

TANGANYIKA

KENYA
Nairobi
KILIMANJARO
1921
Mombasa
Zanzibar
Dar es Salaam

Entebbe
KAMPALA
L. Victoria

L. Tanganyika

Elisabethville

NORTHERN RHODESIA

Livingstone
Victoria Falls
Zambezi R.

KIONGA TRIANGLE
Comoro I. (fr)

Mocambique

MOZAMBIQUE

L. Nyasa

NYASALAND

Beira
Sofala

SOUTHERN RHODESIA
Salisbury
Limpopo R.

EAST AFRICA

TRANSVAL
Pretoria
Johannesburg
Lourenco Marques
Durban

ORANGE FREE STATE
NATAL

BASUTOLAND
SWAZILAND

SOUTHWEST AFRICA
(Union of S.A. mandate)
Windhoek
Walfisch Bay

KALAHARI

BECHUANALD

UNION OF SOUTH AFRICA

Orange R.

Capetown

Pt. Elizabeth

EQUATOR

had come to nothing more than the expression of a general wish in favor of the control of these traffics.

Neither the agreements nor the wishes of the conference were fully observed and for years there was carried on a thriving trade in whisky, arms, and slaves. While there was considerable talk about what soon came to be known as the "white-man's burden," relatively little was done before 1914 towards shouldering this · burden. Indeed, in order to earn sizable dividends on their investments, white concessionaires, from King Leopold II of Belgium to Barney Isaacs of London, frequently employed questionable tactics. The natural wealth of Africa and the physical powers of the inhabitants were often ruthlessly exploited until some natives were driven in despair to rebel against the "black-man's burden."

In Kenya, the former British East Africa, for example, the unrest reached a climax in 1921 when, as a result of a general economic depression, the white employers announced a reduction of wages for all black workers to two-thirds of their former level. The negroes at first were helpless, but eventually a native government clerk named Harry Thuku founded an East Africa Native Association and organized protest meetings. Thuku's speeches assumed an increasingly violent and anti-European tenor, and, in spite of his alleged criminal record, his meetings sometimes were attended by several thousand natives. In 1922 he was arrested for sedition and, when the crowds tried to interfere with the police at the jail where he was being held, the guards discharged their rifles, killing about twenty of the rioters. Thuku was deported to Jubaland and the now leaderless natives consoled themselves by forming a harmless sort of black trade union which they hoped would protect their common interests.

Although the religious doctrines disseminated by the missionaries in Africa frequently tended to make the natives satisfied with a position of inferiority relative to their white masters, some of the teachings had an opposite effect. The blacks were stirred by the recital of such incidents as David's victory over Goliath, by assurances that all human beings were God's children, and by the sentiments expressed in songs like "Onward, Christian soldiers, marching as to war!" In view of the apparent susceptibility of negroes to emotional movements of the revivalist-meeting type, it is not remarkable that there should have appeared in various parts of Africa performers of miracles and so-called prophets who attracted large native followings. Frequently such movements became violently anti-European.

The most threatening of these manifestations occurred in 1921 in the Belgian Congo. There the carpenter, Simon Kimbangu, who had become a Baptist, dreamed that he was divinely directed to go forth and heal the sick. He obeyed this injunction and possibly did effect some cures since his following increased tremendously. The "Kimbangists" established their own native chapels, churches, and schools, and eventually stopped working in the fields in order to be near Kimbangu the Prophet. The latter volubly quoted passages from the Bible and boasted that his enemies were powerless to harm him. Gradually the movement grew more radical and revolutionary, and the white inhabitants of the Congo became alarmed. Kimbangu was arrested, tried, and sentenced to death, though he had never advocated violent resistance to the whites. Later his sentence was commuted to life imprisonment. As a result of this and similar occurrences, a district commissioner forbade any native to teach or preach without a certificate from some Protestant or Catholic missionary organization.

In the Union of South Africa it was the increasing labor competition between the blacks and whites that led to unrest. Here the negroes, who outnumbered the whites three or four to one, gradually were becoming more and more skilled in the various occupations which previously had been monopolized by the latter. So serious did the challenge to white supremacy become that in 1918 the white trade unions threatened to call a strike unless the colored engineers were dismissed from a particular job.

Although the supreme court of South Africa took a hostile attitude towards regulations tending to discriminate between equally competent persons solely on the ground of color, the trade unions continued to agitate, together with the South African Labor Party, until the latter finally came into power. Then, in 1926, a "Color-Bar" Bill was passed definitely excluding blacks from certain occupations. Because whites were paid from five to ten times as much as were blacks for identical services, some employing groups preferred negro labor. The danger of a drastically lowered general standard of living, however, was serious enough to enable the more costly white labor to maintain its preëminence.

The modicum of education that had fallen to the Africans eventually led to the perception among a few leading natives that African conditions were badly in need of improvement and that a determined stand must be made for fairer treatment. In 1919 negro delegates from Africa and America met in Paris, under the auspices of a Pan-African Congress, and drew up a charter of liberties for the black man. Among the demands were those for political, economic, and educational equality; the restoration of confiscated native lands; the checking of industrial and concessionary exploitation; and the appointment by the League of Nations of direct representatives with powers of investigation in the mandated areas. Similar African conferences were later held in other large cities, generally biennially.

These meetings, though they failed to lead to any immediate improvement in conditions, laid the basis for a growing race consciousness and served notice that the blacks were cognizant of the economic value of "their" continent. Certainly, with its population of about 140,000,000 and with an area approximately equal to that of Europe and North America combined, Africa's value was destined to increase with the passing of years. Gold, diamonds, vegetable oils, cocoa, coffee, timber, copper, tin, rubber, sugar, cotton, all were found or could be raised in Africa in large quantities, to say nothing of ivory, cattle, meat, coal, fruits, and pepper. Intelligent natives naturally considered such a prize worth a struggle. An increasing number came to express the cry of "Africa for the Africans."

But it was not only the blacks in Africa who adopted a new attitude in the postwar years. The whites, too, changed their views on several aspects of the native situation. True, during the war the traditional policies had been reflected in the secret wartime dispositions made by the Allied powers of the German colonial possessions. At the Paris Peace Conference, however, as has been noted, President Wilson's idealism clashed with these imperialistic aspirations. A compromise was effected, and in the Covenant of the League the "well-being and development" of peoples "not yet able to stand by themselves under the strenuous conditions of the modern world" were designated as "a sacred trust of civilization." Hence, instead of becoming outright owners of the lands that were taken from Germany ostensibly on the ground of her mistreating the natives, the Allied countries became trustees or stewards of the League in the administration of affairs in these territories.

Although a cynical view of this arrangement was often taken, particularly since the assignment of the mandates followed almost exactly the lines of the secret agreements, the written reminder of trusteeship and the creation of a Permanent Mandates Commission continuously recalled to the white administrators their moral obligations to educate the colonials and develop the overseas areas for the benefit of the natives as well as the Europeans. This realization was responsible for the introduction of a number of colonial reforms, and on occasion the policies of the mandatory powers towards their nonmandatory possessions also seemed to be influenced by the spirit of trusteeship.

Eventually the whites came to realize that the continued abuse of native labor and the decimation of the population were entirely out of accord with their own economic interests. The concessionaires began to realize that rubber plantations were worthless without the necessary people to work them. The same condition held with respect to diamond and gold mines and fruit plantations. Thus the fear of economic loss was responsible for the better treatment of the natives in some sections.

From 1920 on, France made special efforts to stimulate the economic development of her overseas areas. She hoped to derive a larger proportion of her imports, particularly raw materials, from the colonies. Progress was slow, however, and after more than a decade of effort, which included an impressive colonial exposition in Paris (1931), most of France's colonial imports continued to come from other countries' possessions. The French authorities also began to pay more attention to the spread of vocational and professional education in their African territories. After the war, military conscription was introduced into all French African colonies. By way of encouraging the process of assimilation, French citizenship was offered to all natives who had served with distinction either in a civil capacity or in the armies during the war. The beneficent influences of education and economic improvement continued, on occasion, to be overshadowed by the harsh tactics of punitive expeditions.

A British Parliamentary Commission which visited East Africa in 1925 declared its conviction that "the status of trusteeship involves an ethical conception, that is to say, it imposes upon the trustee a moral duty and a moral attitude." Although the British authorities failed to abide wholly by the spirit of this report, the punishments for minor infractions of rules were made less severe in a number of the British-controlled areas. Educational opportunities for the negroes were increased and the government liberally assisted in the upkeep of native churches. Yet the whites usually were careful to retain the upper hand whenever the interests of the natives came into conflict with their own.

In other regions the doings of callous exploiters frequently reached the ears of groups that were able to force reform measures.

Thus, a report published by the American Professor Frank A. Ross upon the conditions which he witnessed during a trip through Portuguese Africa in 1925 was brought to the notice of the League and in 1926 the Portuguese Government was constrained to set up a committee of protection in each colonial district. Similar improvements took place elsewhere on the continent.

The problems of Africa, and of Europe in Africa, after the First World War, appeared, in short, to be these: given a certain amount of education and economic opportunity, the more intelligent natives generally came to desire at least autonomy, if not independence; kept in subjection, without education and without the opportunity to better themselves, the natives were considerably less useful in the development of the urgently needed natural resources. While renewed humanitarian and altruistic considerations served as stimuli to the extension of both spiritual and practical schooling, the limited amount of enlightenment actually spread was responsible for the appearance, here and there, of an unmistakable clamor for more equitable treatment. Obviously, the Western world soon would have to seek a workable solution for the African dilemma. Africa would continue to learn from Europe and it would be the white man's duty, for the sake of progress and civilization, to teach Africa in as friendly a way as possible.

THE "WESTERNIZATION" OF ASIA

One of the chief characteristics of the impact of West and East in Asia was the attempt to bring about an inordinately rapid industrialization of that continent. The huge, conservative Asiatic mass, containing one-half of the population of the world; tied to age-old cultures; weighed down by autocratic administrations, by caste systems, and by ancient traditions and methods; torn between a rising young nationalism and a greedy imperialism in some sections, but never yet visited by white men in other sections; with little linguistic unity, and full of conflicting and often fanatical religious beliefs—this Asia was profoundly stirred by its contact with the West, especially during the twentieth century. The very fact that Europeans and Americans, alien peoples, strove to impose a foreign culture upon the Asiatics drove many of these into a greater veneration for their own traditions and customs. They held to their accustomed ways with a fervent tenacity—often to their own woe. And into such an environment the Westerners tried posthaste to introduce steam railroads, electric current, factories, industrial machinery, and modern "efficiency methods."

Before Europe reached its pre-1914 state of civilization it passed through a Renaissance, a Protestant Revolt, a century of religious wars, a Commercial Revolution, a French revolutionary epoch, and an Industrial Revolution, but in Asia the aim was to remake a much vaster continent almost at one fell swoop. Asia was made to suffer all the pangs of a tenfold revolution at one and the same time.[1]

The attempted hasty industrialization of his continent was not the only bewildering phenomenon that the Asiatic was forced to witness. He was made to look out upon a confusing and terrifying series of contrasts. How startling it must have been to him on occasion to hear almost simultaneously the pacific words of a missionary and the sputtering of a machine gun; to be told of Wilson's Fourteen Points and self-determination, and at the same time to see foreign gunboats on Chinese rivers, foreign battle planes over Afghan villages, or foreign troops marching through Indian towns. He must have been amazed by the facility with which so many Westerners mixed lofty idealism with vulgar materialism, by the incongruity of charitable right hands and grasping left hands. He heard his autocratic systems of government denounced and he witnessed the setting up of even more autocratic regimes. Still more was he puzzled, after the war, to hear from some Europeans about the wonders of industrialism and the advantages of the capitalist order, and from others about the evils of capitalism and imperialism, and the supposed glories of an international brotherhood of man based upon a communist system. With his own condition, moreover, he was dissatisfied. What was he to do?

It was one of the unfortunate aspects of the situation that most of the people in Asia did not know exactly what they wanted. They were often discontented, poor, and oppressed. They groped in the dark and sometimes were hysterical when they were not phlegmatic. Their great stumbling block appeared to be the paucity of adequate leadership. Frequently such leaders as did arise were inexperienced, unpractical visionaries with grandiose

---

[1] One is reminded in this connection, of Rudyard Kipling's lines:

Now it is not good for the Christian's health to hustle the Aryan brown,
For the Christian riles and the Aryan smiles and he weareth the Christian down;
And the end of the fight is a tombstone white with the name of the late deceased,
And the epitaph drear: "A fool lies here who tried to hustle the East."

Reprinted from *The Naulahka* by permission of Mr. Kipling and Doubleday, Doran and Co.

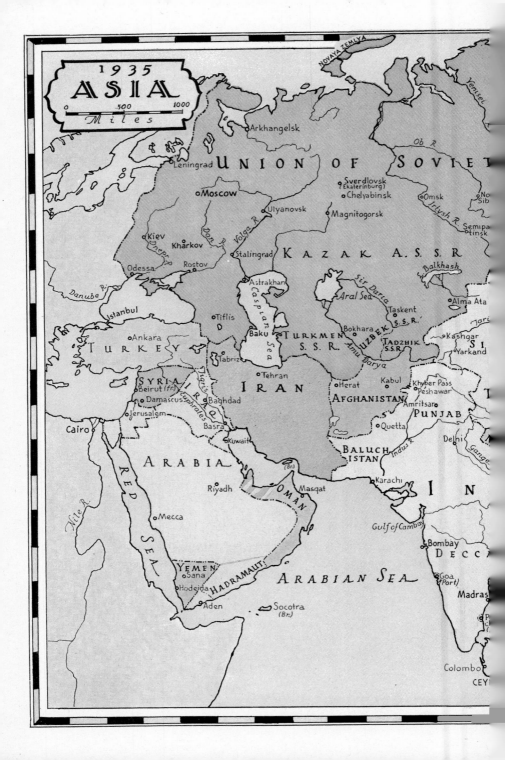

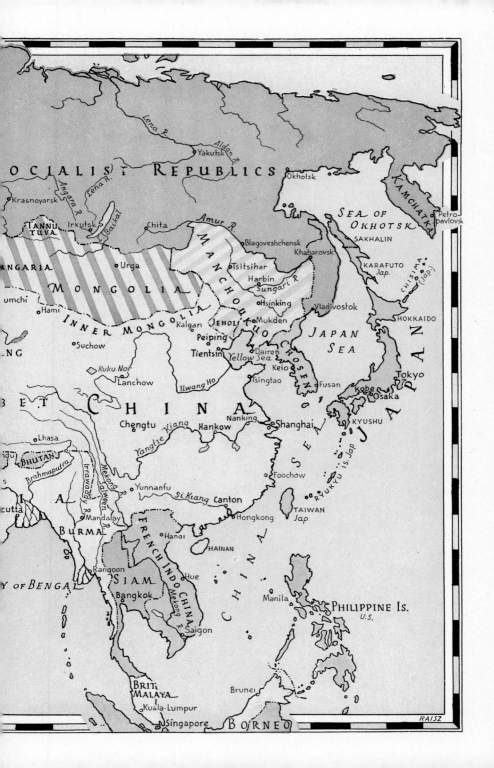

but mystical schemes and dreams. Interested groups generally found little difficulty in counteracting the influence of these leaders by holding them up to ridicule as adolescent schoolboys or else throwing them into prison. At best, it was oratory and curse against blast furnace and armored tank. To this rule, however, there were a few conspicuous exceptions, notably the "Chinese George Washington," Dr. Sun Yat-sen, and his successor, Chiang Kai-shek.

The hundreds of millions of people who comprise the mass population of Asia found their course of life little altered as a consequence of the military aspects of the First World War. Even India and China were only slightly affected by the actual fighting. In the case of India more than a million men fought on the side of the British, but upwards of three hundred million people remained at home, and of these many perhaps were unaware that a world struggle was in progress. In the case of China the official declaration of war resulted in little more than the confiscation of a number of German merchant vessels in Chinese harbors and the drafting of coolies to labor behind the lines.

More important were the economic and psychological effects produced in Asia by the war. Many of the moderate Indian leaders who hoped that a loyal India would be rewarded after the conflict with political autonomy became radical and bitter in their eventual disappointment. At the same time a few of these leaders added considerably to their experience and prestige by participating in the Paris Peace Conference and in some of the postwar British Imperial Conferences. During the war, moreover, India's iron and steel industries were stimulated and new commercial contacts were established with Japan. These economic developments, incidentally, reacted unfavorably on Great Britain's trade balance with India.

In China, the passing of Kiaochow from German to Japanese control caused a renewed flaring up of a young nationalism which strove to assert the right of the Chinese to their fatherland. Foreign interested groups, however, soon brought pressure to bear on the nationalists and, in addition, local chieftains apparently were encouraged to revolt and set themselves up as war lords in various parts of China. It thus appeared to many Chinese that, whereas nationalism was praised as the worship of the soul of nations in the West, this same spirit, when it appeared in so-called backward countries, was to be crushed under the heels of Western and especially Japanese imperialists.

In Persia, whose sovereignty had been seriously impaired by two Anglo-Russian agreements of 1907 and 1915 and on whose neutral soil Russians, Britishers, and Turks had fought some of their battles during the First World War, national resentment was strong enough in the postwar years to accomplish unexpected things. An Anglo-Persian treaty of 1919, that would have converted Persia into a British protectorate, was denounced because of an aroused nationalist opinion. The government which had consented to the treaty was overthrown early in 1921 by Riza Khan, an able soldier who, having risen from the ranks, became successively commander-in-chief of the army, minister of war, premier (1923), and, after the ousting of the weak ruler, hereditary shah (December 1925). The dynastic name chosen by the new sovereign was Riza Shah Pahlevi.

Under its nationalistic government Persia now made rapid political and economic headway. Foreign military and gendarmerie officers were dismissed, the army was converted into a well-drilled and efficient unit, and most of the hitherto autonomous desert tribes were brought under the central authority. Able foreign financial advisers, first an American and then a German, were employed to straighten out the monarchy's fiscal difficulties and to improve the conditions of health and education. Public works were undertaken, railroad construction was begun, the capitulatory rights of foreigners were abolished, women were placed on a social level more nearly that of men, and a small navy was created. Then the Persian Government forced the Anglo-Persian Oil Company, a majority of whose stock shares were owned by the British Government, to accept a revised lease-concession (1933) canceling an earlier document granted in 1901. The new agreement gave Persia far better financial terms than she had previously received and curtailed the company's sphere of interest. The outcome of this incident, which for a time threatened to precipitate a dangerous quarrel, constituted a triumph for a state which only a dozen years previously had generally been regarded as a legitimate field for aggressive exploitation. In 1935 the official name of Persia became Iran.[1]

Although the two main aspects of the Asiatic revolt—resentment at European domination and discontent over the suffering occasioned by the changes resulting from the "westernization" of

---

[1] Somewhat similar events occurred in neighboring Afghanistan whose able ruler, Amanullah Khan, secured British recognition of complete independence in 1922.

Asia—expressed themselves in a variety of ways, the most effective weapon which the natives for a time were able to use against western machinery and arms was the economic boycott. Uprisings could be crushed, bombs were more destructive than lances, tanks more deadly than fanaticism—but the only way to beat an oriental boycott was to make concessions. More than once Japan was forced to give way, when her demands on China were too unpopular, by the power of a Chinese boycott that threatened to cripple Japanese trade and commerce. Great Britain several times felt the force of Indian boycotts and, though she never actually surrendered, she much preferred not to have to deal with the unpleasant phenomenon. But here again the absence of effective native leadership precluded the unity necessary to support a successful demand for equitable treatment.

For a time after the First World War the universality of unrest in Asia gave rise to talk of a Pan-Asia movement. It was feared in some quarters that the Asiatics might attempt to set up a counterpoise to the League of Nations and thereby definitely divide East and West into two powerful, hostile combinations. Yet remote as a Pan-Europa seemed, a Pan-Asia appeared to be even more distant. It was said that the psychological differences between India and China, for example, were greater than the corresponding differences between western Europe and China. The groups so loosely termed "Asiatics" by the Europeans and Americans really were widely separated from one another by political, economic, social, and religious gaps that were far greater than those among the various European peoples.

Of more immediate importance were the relations of Asia with the League of Nations. Japan for a time was not only a member, but a leading member, with a permanent seat in the Council and an influential voice in affairs. China, too, became a member, and was elected to a temporary seat in the Council. Iran, India, Iraq, Afghanistan, and Siam (Thailand) were admitted to membership in their own right and soon took active part in the workings of the League. These relationships appeared the more remarkable when it was remembered that the League was conceived fundamentally as a preventive and remedy for antagonisms arising out of the developments of European, not Asiatic, life. But since much of Asia's future confidence in the League depended upon the latter's help to such struggling countries as China—countries that were striving to absorb the shock of the clash of West and East and to reach a working compromise between the two—it was unfortunate that the Geneva body failed to intervene more actively in the Sino-Japanese dispute of 1931 and after.

From a material standpoint much of Asia continued to require friendly assistance and needed to learn about Western advances. Millions of people needed to be educated, stable governments had to be set up, machines more generally utilized, agricultural methods modernized, certain religious rites modified, wider viewpoints introduced, and the economic systems brought into harmony with a general world economy. But this could not be achieved overnight nor by forceful imposition upon unwilling recipients. Asiatic traditions as such did not necessarily need to be discarded and replaced by European traditions. Instead, some Asiatic traditions required gradual modification to fit modern world conditions. First the new viewpoints and attitudes, then the new methods—that seemed to be the most effective approach in a region where custom played so important a role.[1]

[1] For specific discussions of India, Palestine, Syria, China, and Japan see Chapters XII, XIII, and XXII.

CHAPTER X

Changing Latin America[1]

PARTICIPATION IN THE FIRST WORLD WAR[2]

The Latin-American nations took little active part in the First World War, but the conflict worked significant changes in them all and they found in the war an opportunity for expansion of trade and industry. Indeed, Latin America's part in the struggle was primarily that of a supplier of materials. Her foodstuffs and minerals were of paramount importance to the belligerents. In supplying the demands, Latin America saw new industries arise, new commercial and industrial centers spring up or old ones revive, a shift in population to the industrialized and commercialized areas, a great expansion of wealth, a rapid increase of foreign investments, and a more active participation of the laboring and middle classes in politics. The postwar reaction in the form of economic depression (1920–1923), the subsequent prosperity to 1929, a second depression (1930–1933) with its attendant social upheavals, and the outbreak of the Second World War, all served to alter considerably the Latin-American scene.

GENERAL ECONOMIC DEVELOPMENT TO 1940

The economic growth so noticeable during and immediately after the First World War had its roots in the last quarter of the nineteenth century. Actually, except for a brief period or two, there was a greater acceleration in the amount of goods manufactured and consumed within the respective states themselves than in increased import-export commerce. Recovery after the

[1] This chapter was contributed by Professor Bailey W. Diffie of the College of the City of New York.

[2] Brazil, Costa Rica, Cuba, Guatemala, Haiti, Honduras, Nicaragua, and Panama joined the Allies. Bolivia, the Dominican Republic, Ecuador, Peru, and Uruguay severed diplomatic relations with Germany. Argentina, Chile, Colombia, Mexico, Paraguay, El Salvador, and Venezuela remained neutral.

depression of 1930–1933, moreover, gradually brought Latin America back to the level of export-import activity enjoyed in 1913, but not to the higher average of the years from 1916 to 1920.

At the outbreak of the First World War, Latin America suffered a temporary reduction in foreign trade because of the unsettled world conditions. From 1916 on, however, Europe's need for foods and minerals brought about a swift expansion. The total export-import trade more than doubled from 1913 to 1920. Then, after falling by more than a third in 1922, it rose again until 1929; in 1932 it dropped to one-fourth of the 1920 figure and then recovered gradually so that the trade in 1935 about equalled that of 1913 (c. $3,000,000,000). Following an exceptional spurt in 1937, it dropped again to an average of $3,000,000,000 a year for the period 1938–1940.[1]

In the years from 1913 to 1940 there were significant changes in the direction of Latin-American trade. Exports to the United States in 1939 totaled about as much as in 1913, comprising approximately one-third of all Latin-American foreign sales; but imports from the United States increased in the same period from one-fourth to one-third of all foreign purchases. During these years France, Italy, and Great Britain all *lost* trade in Latin America, while Japan and Germany made the greatest proportionate gains.

On the eve of the First World War, Germany supplied about 16 per cent of the Latin-American imports and took about 12 per cent of the exports. During that war and for some years thereafter her trade was small, but by 1938 she had rebuilt her Latin-American trade to approximately the 1913 position. The renewal of general warfare in 1939 once more sharply curtailed sales and purchases on both sides. Meanwhile a new merchant and customer had entered the Latin-American market, namely, Japan. For a long time her trade with Latin America had been negligible; even

[1] LATIN-AMERICAN FOREIGN COMMERCE

(In Thousands of Dollars)

Year	Imports	Exports	Total
1910	1,058,660	1,286,201	2,344,861
1913	1,321,861	1,552,751	2,874,612
1920	2,801,192	3,292,937	6,094,130
1922	1,625,845	2,252,627	3,878,472
1928	2,393,652	3,029,664	5,423,316
1932	610,448	1,030,393	1,640,841
1937	1,629,832	2,395,532	4,025,364
1940	1,332,962	1,763,997	3,096,959

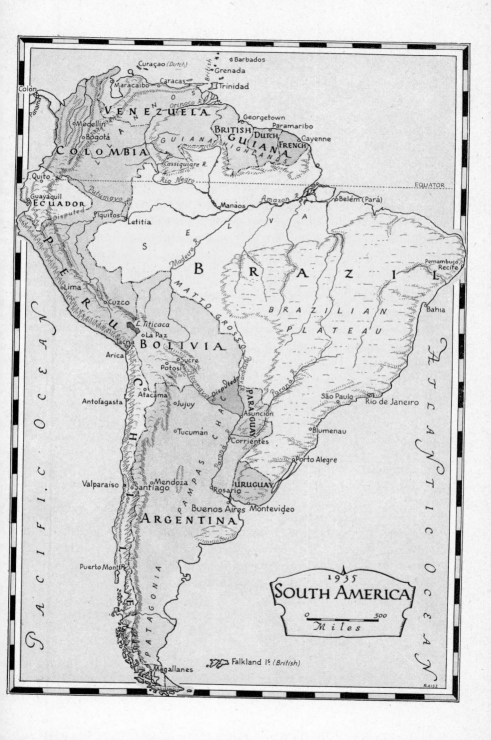

in 1932 it amounted to only $5,000,000. But by 1934 this had risen to $31,000,000, and by 1940 to more than $80,000,000. Then, after the attack on the United States in December 1941, it fell once again to negligible proportions.

Even a short list of the export products of Latin America in 1940 will make clear the importance of that region as a supplier of the materials of civilization. Mexico profited from her deposits of petroleum, silver, copper, and other minerals, and from such export crops as henequen—used for rope fiber and bags. Cuba became one of the world's leading sugar producers and also raised large amounts of tobacco. The Central-American states grew bananas and coffee, among a variety of tropical crops. Venezuela was one of the world's main sources of petroleum, while Peru exported oil, copper, sugar, and cotton in sizable quantities. Bolivia in 1939 produced one-fourth of the world's tin, while Chile had a virtual monopoly of natural nitrates and long ranked second in the world as a producer of copper. Argentina's production of cereals, meats, wool, linseed, and other agricultural products helped to make her the wealthiest nation per capita in Latin America. Uruguay became a great exporter of livestock, and Brazil excelled in coffee growing and cotton raising.

Latin-American economic development was greatly aided by foreign capital. Suffering from a collapse of her overseas markets after the First World War, Latin America was rescued from her worst difficulties by a rapid influx of foreign money. This was not a new phenomenon—European capital had flowed freely into Latin America during the nineteenth century—but the rate of capital imports increased rapidly. The United States supplied the bulk of the credits, partly displacing Great Britain, France, Germany, Belgium, and the Netherlands. United States direct investments in all Latin America were valued at $3,500,000,000 in 1929 and at $2,800,000,000 in 1940.[1]

Following the outbreak of the Second World War, Latin America was again, as in the previous conflict, cut off from some of her best markets. If anything, her position was more critical than on the earlier occasion since her foreign commercial ties now were much more numerous. The United States and Great Britain, however, took steps to lessen the economic stringency. Great Britain needed all the food and raw materials she could get. The

[1] "Direct" investments here means all United States holdings in Latin-American enterprises which were controlled or largely managed by a person or persons domiciled in the United States.

United States needed raw materials, was anxious to prevent purchases by the axis powers, and was ready to put into effect a policy of inter-American trade coöperation that had been carefully worked out by her economic experts. This policy included three instruments: loans, bilateral trade treaties, and commodity-purchasing agreements.

Owing to defaults on many loans during the depression of the early 'thirties, some Latin-American nations found it difficult to borrow when the time came for renewed expansion. To meet this situation and to promote inter-American commerce, Washington in 1934 organized an Export-Import Bank. According to an official estimate, this bank "created $560,000,000 worth of American trade" between 1934 and 1941. Further stimulus was provided by a number of reciprocal trade treaties whereby each signatory made special concessions regarding the importation of certain products of the other. Finally, the United States negotiated agreements to take all the exportable surpluses of specified products from a number of Latin-American states, notably Brazil, Mexico, Bolivia, and Peru.

Latin America had made little progress in manufacturing prior to the First World War. But eventually, and particularly after 1932, the high tariffs, the difficulty in getting certain finished goods from abroad, widespread currency depreciation, and the presence of a considerable amount of nationally owned capital stimulated industry. By raising their tariffs still higher and in other ways favoring native enterprise, the Latin-American countries forced many foreign firms to establish local branches. And while the value of raw materials in 1940 still was greater than that of manufactured products for Latin America as a whole, there had appeared a firmly established industry supplying consumer goods to the domestic markets. Argentina, for example, manufactured most of her own silk and woolen goods; Brazil manufactured virtually all her shoes and hats; Mexico had three times as many textile workers in 1940 as in 1910. The processing of ores for shipment abroad also made great strides, particularly in Chile, Bolivia, Peru, and Mexico. And even before 1940 some manufactured goods, especially chemicals, glasswares, and textiles, were shipped to overseas markets.

In many parts of Latin America the most important industries were those connected with raw materials partly processed in the areas of production. Oil, for example, was often refined at the fields, before shipment, and thus important local industries grew up. Many of the mining regions presented similar phenomena while in some agricultural areas, either because of processing or concentrated development, there developed considerable industrialization. This was true particularly of sugar production in the Caribbean area and of fruit raising in Colombia and Central America. Hence, in time of distress, the people faced the same problems of low wages and unemployment that were to be found in the more highly industrialized states.

Of particular significance in recent social and political developments was the fact that so much of Latin America became strongly urbanized. Although there was a distinct tendency, as far back as colonial times, to form cities at the administrative seats of the provinces and in the mining districts, the rapid recent growth of cities gave rise to the same problems of a mixed urban and rural society found in many other parts of the world. Latin America, contrary to widespread belief, some time ago ceased to be purely rural and nonindustrial. Buenos Aires, for example, came to hold about one-fifth of Argentina's population. Santiago contained one-sixth of the people of Chile and Montevideo boasted more than one-third of the total Uruguayan population. In many cases one large city dominated a vast rural area, with important social and economic results.

In the light of Latin America's industrial advances, the importance of communication and transportation facilities is obvious. The topography presents enormous international barriers and makes even internal communication difficult: the mountain passes of the Andes are from nine thousand to fifteen thousand feet above sea level. As late as 1940 there was a decided shortage of railway mileage and hard-surfaced roads. Shipping by way of the rivers and oceans offered only a partial solution, although the opening of the Panama Canal in 1914 shortened the trip from some of the west-coast ports to eastern United States and Europe by eight thousand miles. The introduction of regular air services proved to be of immeasurable commercial importance.

RISE OF THE MIDDLE AND LABORING CLASSES

Among the important results of the modern economic development in Latin America was the rise of the middle and laboring classes. True, a merchant class and unattached laborers had existed throughout colonial times, but even in the nineteenth century their political influence was much inferior to that of the landed aristocrats. A gradual change became evident in the last century when an increasing dependence of Latin America on world markets shifted farming little by little to a capitalistic basis and stimulated the growth of cities. In many of the countries the peasant thereupon became a hired laborer with no right to the soil. Or he migrated to the cities and mining districts to become, if fortunate, a member of the middle class, or, if less fortunate (and this was the rule), a proletarian worker. A distinction must be made, moreover, between the relatively small group of middle-class people owning great wealth and the relatively large number of petty merchants, professionals, and white-collar workers.

The upper middle class came to be composed largely of landed aristocrats who were forced by competition to manage their farms as capitalistic enterprises. Often they also invested in commerce, industry, and mining, and acquired new economic concepts to fit their new interests. In some of the countries, where no strong local middle class appeared, the influx of foreign capital created interests which affected political developments as much as, and often more than, local forces. As the traditional political policies of the landed group changed, the middle class, by virtue of its increasing numerical and financial strength, its congregation in the cities, and its educational advantages, came to wield great political power. The illiterate masses, on the other hand, until recently exerted little positive force on political happenings. In these circumstances the growth of a professional and white-collar group and a small-merchant class assumed special importance.

Argentina furnishes a good illustration of middle-class and labor growth in an agricultural and commercial country. The characteristic landholding unit in 1940 still was the large *estancia*, including from twenty-five thousand to five hundred thousand and even more acres. Before the First World War nearly a third of the province of Buenos Aires was owned by 93 proprietors, and the situation did not change materially in the next quarter-century. The large estates were worked by tenants and hired laborers, often immigrants from Europe. On the industrial side, meanwhile, the city of Buenos Aires in 1913 contained four hundred thousand workers, an increase of 240 per cent since 1895, but only half as many as in 1935.

Chile, on the eve of the Second World War, presented a similar picture. Not far from 50 per cent of the Chilean population was classed as urban. One-half of 1 per cent of the people owned about three-fifths of the land, and farms of five hundred acres or more took up 90 per cent of the land. In 1931, about five hundred large estates occupied half of the country's agricultural area. These estates were farmed as industrial enterprises, as in Argentina, and were worked by hired laborers and tenants "who were closely attached to the estate and could not leave it if they had any debts due to the owner."

Much the same picture was evident elsewhere in Latin America. In Uruguay, where the principal industry was stock raising, the great ranches were owned by a few individuals—but Montevideo contained a numerous proletariat. The great cattle- and sheep-raising sections of Argentina, southern Chile, Brazil, Mexico, Colombia, Paraguay, and Venezuela offered a similar view. The land was customarily held in enormous blocks and the packing plants were generally controlled by American or British packers. The coffee plantations of Brazil, Colombia, and Venezuela; the sugar estates in Peru, Brazil, Mexico, Cuba, and the Dominican Republic; the cotton fields of Mexico, Brazil, and Peru; and the banana groves of Venezuela, Colombia, Central America, and the Caribbean states were nearly all in large holdings. Some of the owners were local inhabitants, but many were foreign absentee owners. The wageworkers formed an Indian, negro, or white proletariat.

The industrialized areas of Latin America further illustrated the simultaneous rise of the middle and working classes in the decades before 1940. A numerous laboring class had existed even in pre-1914 days in the copper-mining regions of Chile and Peru, the tin-mining areas of Bolivia, and the silver- and lead-mining districts of Mexico. The mines were usually located in otherwise barren areas to which the produce necessary to sustain the miners had to be brought from hundreds of miles away. The mining populations generally were entirely dependent upon the mining activities for their livelihood. The agricultural regions, in turn, depended upon these industrial areas to furnish markets for their food products. The economic structure was further complicated by the fact that most of the mineral output had to be marketed abroad; and, if the foreign market failed, unemployment, depression, and social disturbances often followed. A parallel situation obtained in the petroleum-producing regions of Peru, Venezuela, Colombia, and Mexico.

Latin America between the two world wars thus offered a scene in which the comparatively recent rise of an upper middle class of industrialists, a lower middle class of white-collar workers, and a landless proletariat was a dynamic factor. About three-fourths of the Latin Americans lived under conditions characteristic of the Western economic structure. At the same time there still existed among the large Indian populations of Mexico, Guatemala, Ecuador, Peru, Bolivia, and Brazil, a semibarter economy.

The accumulation of local and foreign capital and the rise of the middle and laboring classes furnished the background for important political, educational, and social changes. The middle class demanded and received a greater voice in political affairs and brought about a revision of the educational system. Out of the universities, now attended by many students of middle-class origin, came new currents of thought and agitation for reform of the whole social structure. The laboring class was able to obtain partial recognition of its demands through political action or open revolution. A few examples may suffice to demonstrate the trend of these events.

The discontent aroused by the domination of the *estancieros* in Argentina led to the organization of the *Union Cívica Radical* late in the nineteenth century and the eventual passage (1912) of franchise reforms that made possible the election of this party's candidate, Hipólito Irigoyen (1916–1922), to the presidency. Since the election of Irigoyen was a triumph of the middle class in cooperation with the workers, the new executive faced the problem of satisfying both supporting groups. The Socialist Party and the Federation of Maritime Workers, in particular, voiced demands for sweeping reforms, and their strength was manifested in a strike of stevedores just after the First World War.

Although the strike was broken by force, the radicals still controlled sufficient followers to induce Irigoyen and his successor, Marcelino T. de Alvear (1922–1928), to enact a considerable body of social legislation. A Sunday rest law was passed, children were forbidden to work in factories, and a maximum work week of forty-eight hours was set for minors under sixteen. Seats were required for all women employees, a compulsory maternity-rest law was enacted, workers were insured against accidents, and pensions were granted to civil servants of thirty years' standing. No serious attempt was made, however, to bring about a broader division of the land, and Argentina's agriculture continued to be based on the *latifundia* system.

Irigoyen was again elected to the presidency in 1928, but a revolution headed by conservatives, anti-Irigoyen radicals, and army men unseated him in 1930. Thenceforth Argentina was governed by a conservative coalition which enjoyed army support. The international policies of this government seemed at times to favor the axis powers, especially under the administration of President Ramon S. Castillo, but the earlier social legislation was respected.

In Chile, where the upper middle class had shared power with the landed aristocracy since 1891, the post-1920 depression effected a change comparable to the election of Irigoyen in Argentina. A coalition of middle-class and labor votes brought the liberal-minded Arturo Alessandri into power in 1920. Characterized as "the first president of the Chilean *people*," Alessandri was responsible for the passage of a limited amount of ameliorative labor and social legislation and the adoption, in 1925, of a new and liberal constitution. This document increased the powers of the president, gave greater autonomy to the provinces, widened the suffrage, and separated state and church. Many reforms suggested by Alessandri were held up until General Carlos Ibáñez became dictator-president in 1927. Supported by the army, Ibáñez levied an income tax, published additional social-welfare laws, and reformed the educational system. At the same time he carried on a fight against his political enemies in a manner to win him the reputation of a tyrant.

When Chile began to feel the effects of the depression of 1930, Ibáñez tried to solve his problems by borrowing and by stringent economy measures, but this failed to stem a rising tide of opposition and his regime collapsed in 1931. Chile's economic position now was desperate and her politics were chaotic. Several ephemeral administrations held power before a new election in 1932 again brought the moderate Alessandri into the presidency for a six-year term. His administration saw the rise of a strong Communist Party, a further growth of the socialists, and a general shift to the left in politics. As a result of this, a coalition of left-wing parties, including communists, socialists, and Radicals, formed a Popular Front and elected Pedro Aguirre Cerda to the presidency in 1938. When the new executive died in 1941, after a prolonged illness, further elections placed Juan Antonio Ríos in the presidency.

The influence on social legislation of the middle and working classes was exceptionally strong in Uruguay. The executive power there came into the hands of the liberal Colorado Party in 1872 and was still there seventy years later. Traditionally progressive, this party was completely reorganized at the beginning of the twentieth century and became definitely an instrument of middle-class and workmen's interests. The chief opposition group, the Blanco Party, remained the representative of the large-estate owners and the Catholic Church. To retain the support of the laborers and to limit the growth of the socialists, who in recent years gained an increasing number of seats in the legislature, the Colorados consistently fathered social legislation and democratic governmental reform.

Among the more important of these reforms was the constitution of 1919 which gave broad powers to the lower house and lessened the prerogatives of the chief executive by creating an executive council with administrative functions independent of the president. The constitution also abolished noble titles, hereditary honors, primogeniture, and entails. The church was disestablished, the franchise was extended, and provision was made for the right of habeas corpus, equality before the law, trial by jury, freedom of speech and press, and liberty of religious belief. The government launched a serious study of the social needs of the populace, established a national labor office, and assumed ownership of a number of public services. Laws were passed instituting an eight-hour working day, old-age pensions, factory inspection, compensation for accidents, income and inheritance taxes, and a minimum wage in agriculture. A national mortgage bank was founded, the state acquired ownership of the electric-power industry, and a national refrigeration plant was built to handle shipments of frozen meat.

The depression precipitated a crisis in 1933 which Uruguay found it peculiarly difficult to meet because of the division of administrative powers. The framers of the constitution of 1919 had hoped to prevent dictatorship by creating an executive council with powers independent of the president, but the system was unwieldy. In 1933 President Gabriel Terra assumed dictatorial authority on the ground that the economic dilemma made strong action imperative. A new constitution in 1934 strengthened the hands of the president and put into the basic law many parts of the social legislation previously enacted as statutory law. Special prerogatives granted the minority were later to cause difficulty, since it was made possible for the minority to control at least one-third of the legislature regardless of the vote it had polled. When the Blanco or Nationalist Party under Senator Luis Alberto de Herrera prevented legislation which Terra's successor, President Alfredo Baldomir, deemed vital for national defense, the executive dissolved the congress early in 1942 and created a Council of State.

Colombia, too, made notable progress after the opening of the twentieth century in education, sanitation, penal reform, law codification, labor legislation, and political stability. After many years of Conservative rule, the Liberals elected Enrique Olaya Herrera president in 1928. Under him and his successors, Alfonso López (1934–1938), Eduardo Santos (1938–1942), and López again in 1942, Colombia achieved the reputation of one of the most liberal, progressive, and stable states in the Americas. Among the chief acts of the government, though one not widely publicized, was the land legislation. Under this, Colombia began the quiet but efficient redistribution of her agricultural wealth.

Peru wrote much social legislation into her constitution during the dictatorship of President Augusto B. Leguía (1919–1930), and continued this tendency under President Oscar R. Benavides (1933–1939). Much of Benavides' reform work coincided with what his political opponents advocated, but his dictatorial policies and harsh treatment of those who opposed him plus a somewhat proaxis leaning in international affairs turned many liberals against him. He was succeeded by Manuel Prado, who freed most of the political prisoners and adopted a policy of definite friendship with the United States.

Bolivia, Ecuador, the Central-American and Caribbean countries, and the other nations of Latin America also enacted extensive codes of social legislation. The Andean states outlined programs to improve the living conditions of the Indians who comprised large portions of their respective populations, but no marked success was achieved in this connection by 1940. Several Indian congresses were held under the auspices of the Pan-American Union, but, except in Mexico, the lot of the Indians remained backward. Throughout Latin America there was evident a tendency to include social-welfare measures in the national constitutions. But enforcement, on the whole, was lax, and the workers frequently were severely repressed when they showed an inclination to demand the full application of the existing codes.

EDUCATION, STUDENTS, POLITICS

During the colonial period and until recently, education was confined principally to a small upper class and the clergy. As late as the First World War, the curricula were usually based on classical studies and were ill suited to either the new scientific and social developments or the needs of the classes born of the industrialization and urbanization of Latin America. By 1940 notable progress had been made, but much remained to be done.

The task of setting up a modern educational structure was complicated by a variety of factors. The rural communities were hampered by bad transportation facilities. Governmental funds, never plentiful, tended to be spent on soldiers rather than school children. The leaders of Latin America were slow to adjust themselves to the idea of education for the "masses" rather than for the "classes." While the percentage of illiteracy in some regions remained distressingly high, others presented a creditable record in school work. Argentina, for example, had 14.4 per cent of her total population in school by 1940, compared with 17 per cent for the United States. Chile had 12.4 per cent of her people in school, Panama, 11.5 per cent, and Brazil, 7 per cent. Many Latin-American educators went to the United States or Europe for their training, and educators from foreign countries were invited to Latin America to aid in the reorganization of old, and the founding of new, systems of instruction. An increasing amount of attention was given to the formal education of girls.

In the universities, the progress after 1918 was characterized by broadening curricula, an improvement in the quality of instruction, a lessening of outside political influences, and the greater participation of students in the government of the schools through seats on the university councils. To the students themselves belonged much of the credit for these changes. A revolt against the antiquated system started at Córdoba, Argentina, in 1918, and thereafter the demand for university reform spread rapidly.[1]

The students soon discovered that reform in the government-controlled universities depended first upon certain general political changes. "Demands were made for the autonomous university, democratically self-governed, liberal and progressive. But these aspirations widened as the student forces grew. . . . Criticism was soon diverted from college officials to the governments whose servants they were. The students found that the shortcomings of their educational institutions reflected more virulent ills corroding the body politic." Accordingly the students of more and more states began to participate wholeheartedly in political upheavals against the old regimes. By way of example, a word may be said of the student agitation in Peru.

[1] In 1940 Latin America had sixty-seven universities, seventeen of them privately controlled.

In the midst of Peru's first postwar depression, President Leguía inaugurated a series of reforms that improved the material condition of the country. His eleven-year dictatorship, from 1919 to 1930, however, was marked by political corruption and persecution, and the students who sought educational changes beyond those which the government was willing to concede were among the chief sufferers. Under the leadership of Carlos Mariátegui and, after his death, under Victor Raúl Haya de la Torre, the students eventually founded the radical *Alianza Popular Revolucionaria Americana* (APRA), which became especially active after the downfall of Leguía. Within a few years it became one of the best organized parties in Peru, with a strongly nationalistic program that called for closer coöperation with the neighboring states, the division of the large landed holdings, liberal educational reforms, and a general reorganization of the national economy.

Because it was the local situations in all these countries which produced the issues that were taken up by the students, there was no one Latin-American-student policy or attitude. Allied with the workers in some states and with the middle class in others, the students on occasion furnished the intellectual leadership in radical labor movements, arrayed themselves against the landlords and the clericals, and fought against the continued domination of foreign economic groups. But, whether they were democrats, communists, or fascists, the students became an important influence in the life and development of Latin America.

BRAZIL

Brazil occupies a special place in Latin-American history. It was colonized by Portugal, not Spain, as were the other nations. The official language therefore is Portuguese. Brazil is about three times the size of the next largest Latin-American country, Argentina, and larger than the United States with an extra Texas. The population increased from 22,000,000 in 1914 to 44,000,000 in 1940. Railway mileage, largely owned by the federal and state governments, grew from about 13,000 in 1912 to 21,000 in 1937. The annual value of exports rose from an average of $293,000,000 for the years between 1911–1915 to $462,000,000 for the years 1925–1929; after a decided drop during the early 1930's, the annual average rose again to $300,000,000 for the period 1938–1941. Meanwhile all but 7 per cent of the inhabitants had become concentrated along the seaboard, the regions of greatest concentration and wealth production being the states of Bahía and Pernambuco in the north and Río de Janeiro, São Paulo, and Minas Geraes in the south.

Political developments in Brazil were strongly influenced by economic factors and the grouping of the people in a few areas. Prior to 1912, when rubber was a highly important Brazilian product, the northern states exercised some political power; but with the decline of the rubber industry (from exports valued at $78,-000,000 in 1912 to less than $1,000,000 in 1932) political influence became almost a monopoly of the coffee-growing and industrial southern states. The struggle for the control of the federal government came to be largely among São Paulo, Minas Geraes, and Río Grande do Sul—the chief producers of coffee and cattle and the centers of trade and manufacturing. The key to Brazilian politics, at least until very recently, could be found in the rivalries of these states and especially in the efforts of São Paulo to control the national government in order to protect her coffee interests. National political parties did not exist. There were, instead, separate state parties, such as the Minas Geraes Republican Party and the São Paulo Republican Party.

The scene was further complicated by the extensive autonomy of the individual states, their independence of the federal government being far greater than that of the commonwealths in the United States. They could levy tariffs and their police forces were in effect armies which on occasion opposed the federal government itself. The political machines in the states nominated the candidates for national office and then formed combinations in their support. Of the fourteen presidents chosen between the establishment of the republic in 1889 and 1940, ten were from the three southern states named above.

To speak of the political control exercised by these states meant, in reality, to speak of the influence of the great coffee and cattle raisers together with the middle class that had grown up in the industrial centers. The "people" of Brazil had very little voice in politics since three-fourths of them were illiterate and only the literate could vote. President Getulio Vargas stated in 1934 that of every 1000 Brazilians who should receive elementary education, 513 did not enter school and only 30 completed the work of the elementary grades. The situation thereafter improved somewhat, but not sufficiently to alter the political significance of illiteracy. The practical working of the state political-machine system may be seen in the events that transpired after 1930.

In 1930 Julio Prestes, then governor of São Paulo, was elected president in a manner which his opponent, Getulio Vargas, then governor of Río Grande do Sul, alleged to be fraudulent. Vargas was the candidate of the *Alliança Liberal,* a coalition composed of members of the old political machines and a variety of liberal and left-wing forces. His program promised wide social changes, including effective suffrage, constitutional reform, creation of a labor department, agrarian improvements, and guarantees that the states would not be interfered with by the central government nor the rights of the individual denied. When it became evident that Prestes would be credited with a majority of the votes cast, the *Alliança,* with the aid of part of the army, placed Vargas in power. He derived further support from the mere fact that Río Grande do Sul believed it was the turn of one of its own men to be president. Hence, when he came into office, Vargas was supported by a very heterogeneous group and Brazil was in the midst of a prolonged state of unrest.

Out of industrial growth had come labor unions on the one hand and capitalists on the other. Both had supported Vargas and both expected rewards. The army men wanted domestic order and respect for the military corps, an aristocracy all its own. Vargas moved slowly and skillfully through the conflicting political currents. When the state of São Paulo rose in revolt in 1932, using Vargas' earlier promise to grant a new constitution as a pretext, he was able to crush its forces. He kept his promise to the labor unions to appoint a minister of labor, but deprived them of their autonomy by placing them under federal control. He also broadened the system of social insurance, framed minimum wage laws, and enacted other decrees favorable to the workers; but the minimum wages were so low that the standard of living was only slightly affected.

In 1934 a new constitution was promulgated which incorporated many of the campaign promises, but the government in reality appeared to be moving in a rightist direction in both domestic and international affairs. The position of the president and the army as arbiters of a very delicate situation became clearly apparent. In 1935 Vargas' opponents again revolted, the rebels this time including elements of every political color, from communists to capitalists and disgruntled politicians. After the revolt was put down, Vargas ruled through martial law for almost two years. Then, by 1937, the political situation was again at the breaking point. Although many of the communists and left-wing leaders were in jail, their followings still were numerous. Since, under the constitution, new presidential elections were to be held in January 1938, opposing candidates were nominated and an intensive campaign was in full swing by midsummer of 1937.

In the meantime a new political factor, fascism, had entered the scene. In 1932 there was organized a fascist *Integralist Action* under the headship of Plinio Salgado and Gustavo Barroso. Taking the Guaraní Indian greeting "Anaue" as their equivalent of "Heil," the Greek letter sigma as their substitute for a swastika, and the color of the Brazilian flag, green, for their shirts, the Integralists grew rapidly and by 1937 claimed a membership of one million. No Brazilian village was too small to have an Integralist center. The Salgado program was frankly based on the Nazi-Fascist pattern. Adopting the motto "God, Country, and Family," the fascists boasted that through their "control of the teaching staffs of schools throughout the nation" they held in their "hands the future of Brazil."

Simultaneously, the German Nazis and Italian Fascists had formed strong organizations in Brazil. They owned a number of newspapers, carried on a vigorous propaganda, were directed and financed from abroad, and had the support of many Brazilians. They also maintained close contact with the Integralists and participated with them in parades and demonstrations. By the summer of 1937 the atmosphere was so tense that street fighting between the fascists and their opponents became a frequent occurrence. Salgado became a candidate for the presidency and on several occasions the Integralists held "practice mobilizations" in preparation, as they said, for the day when they would take over the country.

But President Vargas had other plans. Using the public disorders as an excuse for canceling the forthcoming elections, he staged another coup in November 1937 and issued a previously prepared constitution of a more authoritarian character than had been the one of 1934. Among other things, the new document extended the presidential term from four to six years and in the specific case of Vargas continued his incumbency until such time as a plebiscite might determine otherwise. No date was set for the holding of such a referendum. In 1938 all political parties were abolished. For some time thereafter Vargas assumed an attitude in international affairs that to many foreign observers seemed to be of a proaxis nature; but in 1942 he brought his country into the Second World War on the side of the United Nations.

RECENT MEXICAN DEVELOPMENTS

During the long dictatorship (1877–1911) of Porfirio Díaz, great economic progress came to Mexico. Foreign trade increased from $63,000,000 in 1885 to $239,000,000 in 1907. Internal peace was maintained. The credit of the country was reëstablished and foreign capital was attracted. The production of petroleum was developed and railway mileage increased from about 450 in 1867 to perhaps 16,000 in 1911. But some of these improvements occurred under conditions that were destined to cause trouble. The petroleum fields and the mines were largely foreign owned. The land was in the hands of relatively few people. Labor was meagerly paid and thousands of peons were "debt slaves," while the Indians in many cases had been driven from their lands. The governor of Chihuahua, Luis Terrazas, owned six million acres of land—a possession seven and a half times the size of Rhode Island. Almost 25 per cent of the privately owned land belonged to 114 proprietors.

In 1910–1911 a revolution, chiefly political in its aims, led to the overthrow and flight of Díaz. Then the demand for land by the rural workers and for better working conditions by the urban laborers gradually converted political revolution into social revolution. During the ten years to 1920 the fighting was almost continuous, but in 1917 a new constitution was adopted. In many features it resembled the old constitution of 1857, but it aimed especially at securing a "Mexico for the Mexicans." The document was strongly nationalistic, antiforeign, anticlerical, prolabor, and pro-Indian. It provided for a minimum wage, an eight-hour day, profit-sharing, the protection of women and children in industry, housing reform, social insurance, the right to strike, arbitration of labor disputes, agrarian reforms, nationalization of subsoil wealth, and the curbing of foreign land ownership. The realization of this constitutional program began during the administrations of Alvaro Obregón (1920–1924) and Plutarco E. Calles (1924–1928) and continued thereafter at a steady pace, despite the opposition of large landowners, clericals, and foreign investors.

The government, by the end of 1934, had reclaimed more than 34,000,000 acres of land from the control of private individuals. The redistribution of this land proceeded rapidly and by 1935 more than 700,000 heads of families (representing about 3,000,000 people), who had hitherto been landless, were settled on approximately 20,000,000 acres. Then, during the administration of General Lazaro Cárdenas (1934–1940), the amount of land redistributed (44,000,000 acres) was greater than the total distribution from 1911 to 1934. Nevertheless, Mexico still had many large landholdings.

Industrial working conditions were likewise bettered after 1910. Minimum-wage laws were put into effect, the government on occasion coöperated with strikers and aided them in securing the fulfillment of their demands, and the living conditions of millions were improved. The Mexican unemployment figure remained comparatively small. Much of this was accomplished through the efforts of the *Confederacion Regional Obrera Mexicana* (CROM), formed in 1918 after the constitution of 1917 had granted labor the right to organize. The CROM had more than two million members in 1927, but thereafter lost a large share of its following to newer labor organizations. The most important of these new unions was the *Confederacion de Trabajadores Mexicanos* (CTM), whose leader, Vicente Lombardo Toledano, played a prominent role in the Cárdenas Administration. The CTM leadership advocated socialization of Mexico and by 1940 had organized numerous coöperatives and was managing or participating in the management of the railroads, many street railways, petroleum companies, bus lines, sugar mills, and other enterprises.

Cárdenas was succeeded in 1940 by General Manuel Ávila Camacho, another member of the National Revolutionary Party. Generally regarded as more conservative than Cárdenas, Camacho transferred the railroads from CTM control to government management, made a compromise settlement of the petroleum controversy with the United States, and inaugurated a new land-ownership policy. The agrarian revolution of Mexico had long been based on a program of restoring the *Ejidos,* or communal village landholdings, characteristic of pre-Cortesian and colonial times; the tendency during the Camacho Administration was to substitute individual farm ownership.[1]

THE CHURCH IN LATIN AMERICA

In all stages of Latin-American history, the position occupied by the Catholic Church and its relations with the state were of paramount importance. During the colonial period and the first years of Latin-American independence, the Roman Catholic Church was everywhere the established church. Religious toleration did not

[1] Illiteracy in Mexico decreased from 70 per cent in 1910 to 60 per cent in 1930.

exist except in Argentina, the remaining nations having forbidden the public exercise of any but the Catholic religion. Education, charity, and hospitalization were monopolies of the church, whose wealth comprised half of the real estate of Latin America. The clergy, in general, seemed opposed to liberty of religion, press, speech, and assembly, and regarded itself as exempt from the operation of the laws of the land. The church claimed the right to maintain its own courts and to keep numerous *fueros* or privileges.

Gradually, however, the position of the church was weakened in many of the countries, sometimes, as in Ecuador, Colombia, and Mexico, to the accompaniment of civil war. A specific, though varying, state-church relationship existed in 1940 in Venezuela, Colombia, Peru, Bolivia, Paraguay, Argentina, Haiti, the Dominican Republic, Nicaragua, and Costa Rica. In Cuba and Panama the status of the church resembled that in the United States, while in Brazil the Catholic Church was accorded a preferred but not an established position. Uruguay completed the separation of church and state in 1917, as did Chile eight years later. In Mexico the conflict over religion was especially fierce.

Outstanding among many causes for religious strife in Mexico was the struggle for authority between the church and the state. The constitution of 1857 deprived the church of many privileges enjoyed in the first years of Mexico's republican existence. Díaz, however, had allowed it to regain most of the former rights, in practice if not in theory, by 1910. Hence the church actively opposed the revolt against Díaz and hence, in turn, the constitution of 1917 contained many anticlerical provisions.

Education was secularized and monastic orders were outlawed. Religious liberty was guaranteed and the church was forbidden to hold property. Article 130 denied the church juridicial personality, excluded foreign clergymen, limited the number of the clergy, and required all clergymen to register with the civil authorities. Up to 1925 the federal government made little effort to enforce these provisions and they were not seriously adhered to by the church. Then, however, several state legislatures moved to carry out the constitutional terms. In February 1926 an open conflict between the church and the civil authorities was precipitated by a clerical denunciation of the disputed articles.

President Calles answered this protest by urging the immediate enforcement of all hitherto unapplied constitutional articles. The church property was nationalized, foreign priests were deported, all schools, asylums, and convents where religious instruction was given were closed, and the state governors were advised to enforce the constitution. Private schools were required to register with the minister of public instruction. The teaching of religious subjects in primary schools was prohibited, clergymen of any creed and members of religious orders were forbidden to teach, and schools were warned against the use of holy pictures or other traditional means for the inculcation of religious ideas.

These measures encountered strong opposition.[1] A boycott was launched by faithful Catholics in July 1926 "to create in the nation a state of intense economic crisis." All priests were withdrawn from the churches and religious services were suspended. The civil authorities thereupon took over the churches and kept them open for worship. When it became apparent that the economic and religious boycott would fail, the National League for the Defense of Religious Liberty and other Catholic organizations and individuals "resorted to armed violence." Using the battle cry: *"Viva Cristo, Rey!"* ("Long live Christ, the King!"), the *Cristeros* or Church Party participated in serious disturbances that lasted from 1926 to 1929.

A truce was reached in June 1929 when the government agreed (1) to register only those priests who were duly appointed by their superiors; (2) that religion might be taught within church confines; and (3) that the church was entitled to the constitutional right of petition. Amid popular rejoicing, church services were resumed for the first time in three years. But the agreement satisfied neither side and the conflict was reopened in June 1931 when the state of Vera Cruz passed a law limiting the number of priests to one for each one hundred thousand of the population. Similar action soon was taken by Chiapas, Tabasco, and Yucatan, while some states entirely forbade any clergy to officiate. A federal law restricted the number of priests in Mexico, D.F., and in the territories, and in 1932 the papal legate was deported.

The struggle continued and became particularly bitter in 1934 and 1935 when the government proposed to make socialistic instruction compulsory in all schools and universities. It was the avowed aim of the controlling National Revolutionary Party to imbue the children with "a love for the exploited masses" and to analyze religions for them "in the light of reason and science." When faithful Catholics were ordered not to permit their children to attend school under pain of excommunication, the attorney-

---

[1] The Protestant clergy generally complied with the laws. Many religious organizations in the United States demanded intervention.

general of the republic was instructed to take action against all Catholic clerics who were "fomenting rebellion."

Fortunately, in 1936 state-church relations gradually improved as the Cárdenas regime permitted the Catholic Church to regain some of its lost privileges. Camacho continued this policy after 1940, thereby establishing another uneasy truce during which the church continued to press its claims. Meanwhile an Inter-American Seminar, meeting in the United States in the late summer of 1942 at the call of the National Catholic Welfare Conference, declared that "the crisis of our civilization that culminates now in the war is, before everything, a tragedy of morality." And that crisis, held the seminar, had "its ultimate origin in the disruption of Christian unity and [in] the pagan Renaissance."

PART III

National Developments, 1919–1939

CHAPTER XI

Great Britain

SIX DIFFICULT YEARS, 1918–1924

At the time of Great Britain's entry into the First World War, the Liberals, led by Herbert H. Asquith and supported by the Irish Nationalists and the Laborites, controlled the government. The ministry, however, soon became unpopular. There were clamors against the press censorship, the sluggishness of the munitions service, the activities of profiteers, the enlistment system, and the defeat at Gallipoli. In 1915, therefore, Asquith reorganized the cabinet. A new government was formed, supported by a coalition of Liberals, Conservatives, and Laborites. David Lloyd George was made head of the ministry of munitions.

The revised cabinet proved too phlegmatic to satisfy the dynamic Lloyd George. Within a year and a half he advanced himself into Asquith's place as premier, whereupon governmental proceedings rapidly assumed a new vigor. The life of the Parliament was extended for the duration of the war. An attempt was made to solve the long-standing Irish Question. Conditions in India were investigated with a view to the introduction of reforms in government. The electoral system was revised and women over thirty were enfranchised. Under the sponsorship of H. A. L. Fisher an education bill was passed which made elementary education compulsory for children and limited child labor, but funds to carry out the law were not immediately obtainable.

At the end of the war, Lloyd George, feeling that the electorate ought to express its sentiments by ballot once more, called for new elections in December 1918. In these "khaki elections" Lloyd George appealed to the people to support the wartime coalition on its record. He undertook, if endorsed, to advocate the trial of William II and the exaction of a huge indemnity from Germany. A pledge was given that measures would be passed to prevent the dumping of foreign goods and to protect the "essential industries." Finally, Lloyd George promised to care for the veterans, settle the Irish Question, and reform the House of Lords.

On this platform the coalition, which during the campaign was deserted by some Liberals and Conservatives and by all Laborites, captured two-thirds of the seats in the House of Commons. The Labor Party, with about sixty seats, became the official Opposition. The membership of the coalition was 70 per cent Conservative and hence, although the prime minister was a Liberal, the Conservatives predominated in the cabinet. Lloyd George at once went to Paris, but after the signing of the peace treaties his attention soon was absorbed by Great Britain's critical economic situation.

During the early postwar years British industry climbed to a peak of prosperity. The world, "bent on replenishing its depleted stocks, thought only of buying." Prices and wages rose steadily, the number of people employed increased rapidly, and there was a general tendency to shorten the work week. By the middle of 1920 there were three times as many registered companies in Great Britain as there had been in 1918. Unhappily, this state of affairs did not last. As 1920 drew to a close, conditions underwent a precipitate change. Numerous strikes broke out and unemployment increased so rapidly that a new Unemployment Insurance Act was passed to supersede that of 1911. By July 1921 2,000,000 persons, in a population of 42,000,000, were idle.[1]

The reasons for this decline were many. The war had impoverished several of Great Britain's best customers, including Germany, Russia, and the Danubian states. Then, while the British strove to reëstablish the pound sterling at its prewar value, most of the continental governments resorted to inflation. In the world market this meant that the price of British goods was high, for British manufacturing costs greatly exceeded those in countries where inflation resulted in cheap labor. The fact that Great Britain's factories remained intact during the conflict was not an unmixed blessing, for now, although the country still had plenty of machinery, much of this was antiquated and inefficient. Competition with the more modern methods and implements in use in the United States and Germany therefore became increasingly difficult.

During the war, the British had suffered a loss of markets, espe-

[1] In 1920 the value of exports from the United Kingdom was £1,577,000,000. The figure for 1921 was £810,000,000; and for 1922, £823,000,000.

cially to the United States and Japan. The former acquired much of Great Britain's trade in Latin America; Japan secured much of it in China and India. Between 1914 and 1919 thousands of British women had entered the labor field, taking jobs that formerly had been held by men. Not all the women relinquished their positions when the demobilized soldiers returned to look for work. The many tariff barriers erected by the newly created and strongly nationalistic continental states seriously curtailed Great Britain's export trade. Since both the population and the productive capacity of Great Britain were greater in 1922 than in 1913, the general reduction in the volume of her export trade caused grave concern.[1]

In addition to these factors there must be considered Great Britain's war losses, which were far greater than those of the rest of the British Empire combined. About 750,000 of her men had been killed and twice that number wounded. Her total war expenses surpassed £8,000,000,000, and her domestic- and foreign-debt burden at the end of the war was ten times that of 1914. About 2200 vessels, with a combined displacement of 8,000,000 tons, had been destroyed. This last factor might have acted as a stimulus to shipbuilding, but the forced surrender by Germany of most of her ships checked any such development. By 1921 almost a third of the men employed in the British shipbuilding industry were out of work. The unemployment problem was aggravated because the Britishers, unlike the French, could not fall back upon agriculture in time of industrial depression. Great Britain was primarily a manufacturing and exporting country. Only 7 per cent of her population lived on the soil and 60 per cent of her food supply had to be imported. Hence the only solution for the crisis lay in a revival of trade and industry.

The government that first had to cope with this situation was the coalition under Lloyd George. In the beginning resort was had to two temporary expedients. One was the readjustment of the unemployment-insurance scales so as to allot a "dole" of 15 shillings per week to involuntarily unemployed men and 12 shillings to women, for a maximum of fifteen weeks per year. This measure involved an annual outlay of millions of pounds and at best was of transitory value. It was not a cure for chronic unemployment. Secondly, the government encouraged the emigration of jobless workmen to other parts of the empire, especially Canada. Inasmuch as the laborers generally were not eager to migrate and

[1] The volume of British exports in 1922 was only 68.9 per cent of the 1913 volume.

the dominions set up severe qualifications for entrance, the scheme offered little relief.

In 1921, however, two specific attempts were made to get at the root of the trouble by reviving industry. First, Great Britain signed a trade agreement with Russia, based upon a mutual pledge that neither country would spread propaganda against the other. Then, with the reluctant acquiescence of Lloyd George, there was passed a Safeguarding of Industries Act. This measure, deviating from the traditional free-trade policy, levied a duty of 33⅓ per cent to protect certain "unstable key industries" which were considered "essential for war." The same act placed a tax on imports from countries with a depreciated currency.

Meanwhile the Conservatives had begun to weary of the dominance of Lloyd George. They disliked a treaty that had been signed with Ireland [1] and they favored closer coöperation with France. They complained about the troubles Great Britain was having in the Near and Middle East, and they charged the government with extravagance. In October 1922, therefore, the Conservatives decided to withdraw from the coalition. Thereupon Lloyd George resigned and the Conservative leader, Andrew Bonar Law, formed a ministry. Since the Conservatives controlled only a plurality of seats, new elections were set for November 15.

The Conservatives entered the campaign with a united front and with a platform promising "tranquillity and stability." The Liberals were disunited. Lloyd George, at the head of a group called the National Liberal Party, pointed once more to his war record, promised economy, and upheld the virtues of strong government. Asquith, still bitter over the Welshman's wartime tactics, had organized an Independent Liberal Party, favoring free trade and economy. Many of the electors who formerly had voted the Liberal ticket now appeared ready to turn for action to the Labor Party. The Laborites wished to bring about widespread social reform by parliamentary means, favored the nationalization of certain industries with compensation to owners, upheld the existing democratic monarchical form of government, advocated imperial development along lines of local autonomy, and opposed class warfare.

The contest ended in a triumph for the Conservatives, who secured well over half of the seats. The Labor Party, which in 1900 had captured only two seats, was now returned with 142. The Liberals formed a poor third. Bonar Law retained the pre-

[1] See p. 264.

miership, but illness soon forced him to resign and he was succeeded by the less experienced Stanley Baldwin. The new prime
minister was an ex-business man who had entered politics in 1906,
had occupied several financial offices between 1917 and 1923, and
had arranged the funding of the British war debt to the United
States.

Baldwin, who was said to be fond of repeating: "I am not a
clever man," was obliged to face an unemployment situation
which by this time had grown to be a "chronic malady." In his
perplexity he was converted to the view that protection and imperial preference (preferential tariff rates among the several parts
of the empire) were the only cures for the industrial depression.
Since, however, Bonar Law had pledged the party not to change
the tariff without a mandate from the people, Baldwin felt in
honor bound to dissolve Parliament and set new elections for
December 1923. Thus a safe majority was placed in danger on the
tariff issue.

This unexpected occasion stimulated the Liberals into renewed
action. Asquith and Lloyd George became reconciled, at least
outwardly, and vigorously campaigned for the continuance of free
trade. If they could not oust the Conservatives from power, the
Liberals hoped at least to recapture some of the seats previously
lost to the Laborites. The Conservatives pointed out that tariff
barriers against Great Britain were everywhere being erected and
that the kingdom was becoming a dumping ground for foreign
manufactures. They considered the empire self-sufficient and
maintained that an intraimperial system of preferential rates
would free its members from dependence upon foreign trade.
Though they desired to place high rates upon manufactured
articles, the Conservatives promised not to tax raw materials,
wheat, or meat, and agreed to reduce the rates on some items,
notably sugar. The Laborites favored free trade, proposed the nationalization of mines and railways, wanted the government to
subsidize housing and power developments, advocated a capital
levy on all fortunes exceeding £5000, and recommended revision
of the Versailles Treaty.

Although they polled nearly as many popular votes as in the
previous election and still comprised the largest party in the
House of Commons, the Conservatives now failed to command
the necessary majority to control that body. The Laborites, on the
other hand, increased their representation by more than a third
and the Liberals also registered a gain.

When Parliament met, in January 1924, the Liberals joined the Laborites in voting a lack of confidence in the Baldwin Government. The Lloyd George-Asquith group preferred to risk a coalition with the untried Laborites rather than encourage a continuance of Conservative rule. Hence J. Ramsay MacDonald, leader of the Labor Party, became prime minister and foreign secretary in Great Britain's first Labor Government.

MacDonald was born in 1866, the son of a laborer, in the Scottish fishing village of Lossiemouth. He acquired most of his education by attending evening classes and by avid reading. Eventually he chose the career of journalism and made frequent trips to various parts of the empire. In 1896 he married a girl who brought him valuable social contacts as well as considerable wealth. Meanwhile he had been active in bringing about a political fusion of the British intellectual socialists with the trade unionists, and he became one of the founders of the British Labor Party.[1] An effective orator, he was secretary of the party from 1900 to 1912 and its leader from 1911 to 1914. In the great crisis of 1914 he resigned his headship, feeling that he could not endorse the party's support of the war. As an avowed pacifist he was publicly denounced and defeated for Parliament in the "khaki elections" of 1918. Four years later he regained his seat in the House of Commons.

Among the premier's able assistants in the first Labor Cabinet were Philip Snowden and Arthur Henderson. Snowden, who became chancellor of the exchequer, was a former clerk, an ardent pacifist and free-trader, a financial genius, and a stubborn parliamentarian. Henderson, appointed home secretary, was an ex-iron worker who had become prominent as an aide to Lloyd George during the war. He was basically a "trade-union man."

The first Labor Government worked under serious difficulties. Despite MacDonald's insistence that the "labor movement had never had the least inclination to try short cuts to the millennium," there were persistent rumors that radical legislation would become the order of the day. Some investors became panicky and some American financiers began to withdraw their money from London. But aside from its avowed rejection of class warfare, the MacDonald Government had a very practical reason for refraining from revolutionary methods: it depended for its tenure of office on the support of the Liberal Party. This circumstance of necessity tempered its program.

[1] The British Labor Party grew out of the efforts of a Labor Representation Committee which, meeting for the first time in 1900, strove to secure adequate political representation for the workers. The name Labor Party was adopted in 1906.

The accomplishments of the Labor Government in the domestic sphere were not striking. The unemployment situation became worse rather than better during the nine months of Labor rule and unemployment relief had to be further extended. The idea of a capital levy was rejected. The Wheatley Bill was passed, providing for the construction, with governmental aid, of thousands of inexpensive houses. Some of the war duties were repealed and those on tea, coffee, and sugar were lowered.

More spectacular were the exploits in the foreign field. The government played a prominent role in the acceptance of the Dawes Plan. MacDonald urged the admission of Germany into the League and favored closer relations with that body. He supported the Geneva Protocol of 1924, which aimed at ensuring peace by defining the term "aggressor nation." The government voted to build several new cruisers, but simultaneously, as a gesture of disarmament, stopped the building of a naval base at Singapore. Relations with France, now led by Herriot, were improved. Finally, through general and commercial treaties, the Soviet Union was recognized and British goods were promised a more favorable reception in the Russian market.

Unfortunately for its continued existence, the Labor Government soon came under popular suspicion as being amenable to pressure from the Bolsheviks. The trade treaty was attacked and much excitement ensued when the government dropped the prosecution of an acting editor of the communistic *Workers' Weekly* who was accused of inciting British soldiers to mutiny. Opposing a parliamentary motion to appoint a committee of inquiry on this governmental policy, MacDonald was defeated through the defection of the Liberals. He dissolved Parliament and ordered new elections.

During the campaign (October 1924) the cause of the Labor Party was seriously injured by the publication of the so-called Zinoviev or Red Letter. This missive was supposed to have been written by a Bolshevik leader to British communists, urging the latter to prepare for revolution. Later it appeared that the letter was probably a forgery, but at the time it hurt the Laborites. Many voters seemed to feel uncomfortable in the thought that the Labor Ministry might have condoned unbridled freedom for communist propaganda and they preferred not to see it in office. The workers, moreover, grumbled because the Labor Government had done so little to improve the economic situation. That the distress was world-wide did not enter in their calculations.

The Conservatives garnered more than four hundred seats in the election, while the Laborites and Liberals together had fewer than two hundred. The Conservative Party secured this great majority of seats though it actually polled only a minority of the popular vote. This seeming paradox was traceable to the three-cornered elections and the absence of proportional representation. Naturally MacDonald resigned the premiership. Stanley Baldwin took the reins once more and Austen Chamberlain became foreign secretary.

FIVE YEARS OF CONSERVATIVE RULE, 1924–1929

Soon after his reëntry into office, Baldwin did something which *he* termed "safeguarding employment," but which his opponents, mindful of a campaign pledge of his not to introduce protectionist legislation, called a "back-door" step toward a high-tariff system. The government outlined a method of procedure whereby industries might obtain the aid of "safeguarding" duties. Any industry desiring such protection was to lay its case before one of several trade committees which was to make a study of the situation and report to Parliament. If the case for protection was upheld by the committee, Parliament was to authorize appropriate duties in the next finance bill.[1] This and other attempts to alleviate distress notwithstanding, the Conservative Government soon was faced by a serious labor crisis.

Among the hardest hit of British enterprises was the coal industry. Before the war Great Britain used millions of tons of coal annually in her own industries and sold additional millions abroad. But after the conflict, and especially after 1920, the importance of coal as a fuel began to decline. The rising popularity of oil as a fuel, the development of Diesel ship-engines, and the increasing use of hydroelectric power, all caused a drop in the demand for coal. Moreover, under the terms of the Versailles Treaty, Germany annually supplied huge quantities of coal to France, Italy, and other regions which formerly had depended on British coal. Russia, too, because of domestic difficulties, bought thirteen million tons less coal in 1925 than in an average prewar year. Simultaneously the general decline in British business lessened the domestic demand for coal.

[1] "Though this procedure was favourable to applicants for Protection, . . . only twenty safeguarding inquiries were held in the next four years, and only nine industries succeeded in satisfying the necessary conditions and obtaining a duty." Hirst, F. W. *The Consequences of the War to Great Britain*, 1934, p. 211.

Now, in 1924 the miners had forced the owners to sign a wage agreement that was to run until the summer of 1925. Before the contract term expired, conditions became so bad that many mines had to shut down. By June 1925 about one-fourth of the insured men in the coal industry were without work. When the miners nevertheless refused to accept a proposal to lengthen the working day from seven to eight hours and to take lower wages, the owners threatened to discontinue the system of wage agreements and to introduce a new time and wage scale. The workers disregarded this threat and were encouraged in their stand when the railwaymen agreed not to transport coal in the event of a lockout. The Baldwin Government, in order to prevent the closing of all mines, undertook temporarily to subsidize the industry so that the existing wage agreement might be continued pending investigation by a parliamentary commission. The total cost of this subsidy, which lasted for nine months, amounted to approximately one hundred million dollars.

The coal commission reported in March 1926. The members thought that the coal industry would have to be radically reorganized if it were to be kept alive. The report urged government ownership of the mines, with private management under lease from the authorities. In a number of instances it was recommended to close the mines because they were too deep to be worked profitably and in other cases amalgamation was advised. A continuance of the government subsidy was declared preposterous and a decrease in wages was considered inevitable.

This report satisfied neither party and, while the government tried to arrange further conferences, the operators gave notice that the wage agreement would be considered terminated on May 1, 1926. The workmen threatened to strike and the situation was made more ominous when the General Council of the Trades Union Congress, with which the Miners' Federation was affiliated, announced its intention to call a "general strike" unless the wishes of the miners were met by May 3. The owners remained adamant and the general strike began as scheduled. The following industries were affected: transport, printing, heavy chemicals, iron and steel, metals, and all building except hospitals and houses. Specific orders were issued against strikes in the electric, gas, sanitary, health, and food services, and against violence.

The strike actually involved less than half of the trade-union membership and less than one-sixth of the working population, but it frightened the government into declaring the existence of a state of emergency.[1] Thousands of volunteers tried to keep the trains, buses, and industries going, and a quarter-million special constables were commissioned to protect the volunteers. Troops and warships were stationed at strategic points. But there was little violence. Rather, a gay humor was discernible, possibly because of the novelty of the situation. Emergency bus and tram drivers vied with one another in displays of wit, and placards bearing inscriptions such as "Don't stop me! I can't start again!" were much in evidence.

After nine days the general strike came to an end. The Trades Union Congress called it off on the promise that further negotiations would be pushed by the government. Baldwin asked that there be no vindictiveness and that the men be taken back by their old employers. This caused new difficulties, for some employers found it hard to discharge their volunteer substitutes and the industrial disorganization following the strike temporarily decreased the amount of work to be done.

The coal strike continued for six more months, until November. For a time, indeed, coal had to be imported from the United States and Germany to keep the factories and railways running. Meanwhile the plight of the miners became desperate. Their resources dwindled, a cold winter was coming on, and the government appeared more friendly to the owners than to the workers. Gradually the cold and hungry men drifted back to work on the owners' terms and the strike had to be ended. The net result was the lengthening of the working hours, the lowering of the wages, and the disregarding of the coal commission's recommendations. Part of the blame for the waning of popular sympathy with the strikers must fall on the unwise tactics employed by "Emperor" Arthur J. Cook, secretary of the Miners' Federation and leader of the strike.[2]

Politically, the strike weakened both the Labor and the Liberal parties. In the former group, extremists pointed to the failure of the coal strike as proving the need for more direct action. MacDonald, however, succeeded in holding the party together. The Liberal Party was split asunder once more when Asquith and Lloyd George disagreed on the question of supporting the strikers. The Conservatives, on the other hand, were more solidly

[1] About 2,500,000 union members struck. The total union membership was 6,000,-000 and the total working population numbered about 16,000,000.

[2] His answer to the new working conditions proposed by the operators in April 1926 had been: "Not a penny off the pay, not a second on the day."

united than before and were determined to rid Great Britain by law of the possibility of a future general strike. Accordingly, in 1927, they put through Parliament the Trades Unions and Trades Disputes Act which made general strikes illegal, forbade picketing, and protected against any union "disability" or "disadvantage" union members who refused to join illegal strikes. The act also struck at the Labor Party by changing the old law which had permitted unions to collect assessments for political purposes from their members unless the latter formally protested. Now the political levy was forbidden unless the member gave his written consent in advance.

The Conservatives attempted to reap another advantage from the strike situation. They proposed to strengthen the House of Lords. By the Parliament Act of 1911 the power of the upper house had been severely curtailed. Money bills became law within thirty days after their passage by the House of Commons regardless of the attitude of the House of Lords, and the Speaker of the lower house was empowered to determine whether or not a measure was a money bill. In ordinary legislation the Lords were left with a suspensive veto. The Conservatives never had approved these arrangements and now they felt that the "socialist peril" warranted a strengthening of the upper chamber. Then, even though a temporary wave of public opinion might place a Labor Government in the saddle, the destinies of Great Britain would be safeguarded.

In 1927 Baldwin introduced a plan whereby, for the sake of efficiency, the number of seats in the House of Lords should be reduced from approximately 800 to about 350. This reduction would not involve a serious change since, under the existing system, the attendance in the upper house rarely exceeded 200. Some of the members should be appointed for life by the Crown and the others elected by the peers. The right of the Crown to create new peers in time of parliamentary deadlock should be surrendered and the legislative power of the House of Lords increased. But the whole scheme was so violently opposed in debate by the younger Conservatives as well as the Laborites and Liberals, that it never was formulated into a bill.

Among the more liberal reforms passed by the Baldwin Government were new provisions for widows', orphans', and old-age pensions, and the further extension of female suffrage. The electoral act of 1918 had limited the franchise to women over thirty, lest the women, who greatly outnumbered the men after the war, predominate in politics. This act, which simultaneously removed the few remaining property qualifications for male voters, had been passed in recognition of the services rendered by women during the war. It was in line with a general European tendency towards democracy immediately after the war. Not unnaturally, the women in Great Britain were dissatisfied with the age restriction and chose to consider the arrangement a slur on their maturity. A decade of active campaigning was crowned with success in 1928 when Parliament extended the vote to all women over twenty-one. With the addition of this "flapper vote," Great Britain's electorate numbered approximately 12,500,000 men and 14,500,000 women.

During the Conservative regime there occurred an interesting religious controversy. For many years the leaders of the established Anglican Church had been engaged in revising the old Book of Common Prayer. In 1927 an altered edition, in harmony with a new wave of Anglo-Catholicism, was presented to Parliament for its approval. The House of Lords accepted the revised form but the House of Commons rejected it. A few modifications then were made, but the lower house registered another adverse vote in 1928. The rejections came only after long and earnest debates both within and without Parliament, and the popular interest in the matter was attested to by the fact that for a time the book became a "best seller."

It was the professed fear of a restoration of "popery," more than anything else, that led to the final declination of the book, for the latter was more comprehensive and more Catholic than had been its predecessor. The Anglican bishops were grieved to find that their work failed of acceptance largely because of the votes cast by non-Anglican members of the legislature and so a stimulus was given to a movement for disestablishment. Such procedure would deprive the Anglican Church of prestige and revenue, but it would permit independence of action and perhaps instil more vigor into clerical activities.

In the matter of foreign policies the Conservatives did not play a heroic role. War-debt agreements with Italy and France were reached and the Locarno Pact, in part the outcome of MacDonald's activities at Geneva in 1924, was concluded. An equivocal part was acted during the negotiations for Germany's entrance into the League, and friendship with the United States was dangerously strained over the matter of naval disarmament. Most difficult were the dealings with the Soviet Union. Chamberlain unearthed a series of Soviet anti-British plots reaching from Great Britain to China, and in 1927 diplomatic relations with Moscow were severed. The foreign secretary, finally, was no more than lukewarm towards the Kellogg Pact.

The chronic industrial depression proved to be as much a thorn to the Conservatives as it had been to Labor. Higher tariff rates, the establishment of some new industries (such as the manufacture of airplanes) in southern England, the active support given by the government to foreign commercial advertising and propaganda, and the popularity of Great Britain with American tourists, all failed to revive industrial strength. On the other hand, irrational organization, antiquated methods, and emotional antipathy towards necessary amalgamation and coöperation persisted; only a few individuals pointed to developments in the United States and Germany as examples of the benefits to be derived from "rationalization" and concentration.

To make matters worse, report had it that there was no future for British industry and that capital would bring in a greater return if invested abroad rather than at home. As a consequence it was often difficult to raise sufficient funds for even urgently needed equipment. British exports in 1927, reduced to the price level of 1914, totaled only 79 per cent of those in 1913. From 1913 to 1927 British exports fell 21 per cent, although the total world's export trade rose in the same period by 18 per cent. In January 1927 Great Britain had 1,500,000 unemployed. By July 1928, 29.1 per cent of the man power in the coal industry was idle, as was 28.3 per cent of that in shipbuilding, 21.2 per cent in iron and steel, and about 15 per cent each in the cotton and woolen industries.[1]

THE SECOND LABOR GOVERNMENT, 1929–1931

Unemployment and industrial troubles loomed large in the regular parliamentary elections of May 1929. Baldwin, Lloyd George, and MacDonald made numerous speeches, and pains were taken to appeal to the newest voters, the five million "flappers" who, it was felt, would exercise a powerful influence in this, their first, opportunity to cast ballots.

The Conservatives adopted as their slogan "Safety First!" and pointed with pride to their firm stand during the general strike. They advocated permitting industry to "save itself" without gov-

[1] The figures are from Siegfried, A. *England's Crisis*, 1931, pp. 37–43.

ernmental interference, but also urged higher protective and anti-dumping measures as well as great imperial preference. They emphasized the increasing coöperation between employers and workmen that was in evidence and prophesied that this factor, combined with more vigorous rationalization, would soon restore prosperity. They opposed recognition of the Soviet Union without special guarantees as to propaganda and debts, stressed the need for sufficient imperial defense, and objected to any additional peace commitments beyond those embodied in the League Covenant, the Locarno Agreements, and the Paris Pact.

The Lloyd George Liberals once again thought they saw an opportunity to come out of oblivion. In a booklet called *We Can Conquer Unemployment* they recommended a stupendously large public-works program as the quickest solution for the difficulties. But on this score the other parties united in a campaign of anti-Liberal ridicule. In speech, press, and cartoon the Conservatives and Laborites attacked the Lloyd George program as little short of ludicrous, from the points of view both of expense and expediency. The Liberals also reaffirmed their reverence for free trade and advocated closer coöperation with the League and Germany. They favored friendship with the United States and the Soviet Union and urged immediate evacuation of the Rhineland.

The Laborites published a volume entitled *Labour and the Nation* and were particularly successful in their use of slogans and posters, many of which were especially designed to attract the younger voters. The Labor Party advocated nationalization of the leading industries, an extensive public-works program, longer compulsory education for children, the development of natural resources—particularly hydroelectric power—and the appointment of special economic committees to aid the government in formulating its policies. Promise was made of shorter working hours, higher direct taxes, additional social legislation, and the repeal of the Trades Unions Act of 1927. In foreign affairs the Laborites held about the same views as the Liberals. In some cases they were ready to be even more conciliatory, especially in their willingness to come to a naval agreement with the United States—this not only in the interest of peace, but in that of economy. They also stressed their determination to prevent future war.

More than 22,000,000 of the eligible 27,000,000 electors went to the polls. Labor captured 288 seats, the Conservatives 260, and the Liberals 59. Though no party had a majority and though the Conservatives actually secured 250,000 more popular votes than the Laborites, it seemed that the people had repudiated the Baldwin Government. In June 1929, therefore, MacDonald became prime minister for the second time. Again, however, he depended on the votes of the Liberals to remain in office. The poor showing of the Liberals, incidentally, gave rise to a feeling that the mission of the party had been fulfilled, or at least that the days of Lloyd George's leadership were numbered. Indeed, some Liberals now went over to the Labor side in the conviction that it alone was in a position to do the will of the people.

The cabinet appointments were much the same as those in 1924. Snowden again headed the exchequer and Arthur Henderson, "Uncle Arthur," became foreign secretary. James H. Thomas was appointed Lord Privy Seal. In this capacity his functions were nominal and he was expected to devote his time to coördinating plans for the relief of unemployment. For the first time in history a woman was appointed to a British cabinet: Margaret Bondfield, minister of labor.

The control of the Laborites became precarious when their Liberal supporters split into a left and a right wing. The former, led by Lloyd George, though not always in agreement with Labor's policies, still preferred Labor to any Conservative Government. The right wing, led by Sir John Simon, was ready to vote against the government at any time. The Labor Party itself suffered half a dozen defections when Sir Oswald Mosley and some friends became convinced that MacDonald was not striving sufficiently hard to remedy unemployment.[1]

The energies of the Labor Government soon were concentrated on urgent matters of foreign policy. Attempts were made to allay native disaffections in India, Arabia, and Egypt without prejudice to Great Britain's position. Diplomatic relations with the Soviet Union were restored and the promise of a wide Russian market secured. The Young Plan was accepted and Snowden won popular admiration for his fight on behalf of the financial rights of his country. MacDonald visited President Hoover in the United States and so prepared the way for the London Naval Conference of 1930. At the Imperial Conference of 1930 MacDonald refused to agree to the Canadian Premier's suggestion for a preferential-tariff arrangement under which foreign wheat would have been

[1] In 1932 Sir Oswald founded the British Union of Fascists whose slogan became: "Fascism is practical patriotism." This black-shirted group advocated a greater development of the home market, the establishment of a national council of industry and a general "social and moral rejuvenation." After 1934 the British Fascists several times clashed with the police. See also p. 257.

taxed, because this would have increased the price of bread in Great Britain and because the Labor Party was pledged to free trade. Throughout the spring and summer of 1931 Henderson was conspicuous in the movement for world disarmament. The Optional Clause of the World Court Protocol was signed and thus Great Britain was pledged to submit to judicial settlement any international dispute involving the interpretation of a treaty or a question of international law.

In the domestic field the Laborites again did nothing spectacular. The government contemplated a measure to keep children in school until the age of fifteen rather than fourteen as was the case; but when it became evident that many Catholic Labor members would join the Opposition in voting against such a bill because the Catholic schools had not the proper accommodations, the matter was dropped. An attempt to modify the Trades Unions Act of 1927 was abandoned after the government suffered a defeat in committee on one clause of its proposed bill. Agriculture was aided a little, the coal situation was slightly improved by the Coal Mines Act of 1930 which required a certain amount of collaboration in the marketing of the product, and numerous reforms were effected in the auto-vehicle-transport system. Snowden's budgets were fairly satisfactory to most groups of opinion, though his recommendations for higher income and land taxes aroused some hostility. On the question of supporting the land taxes, the right and left wings of the Liberal Party drifted still farther apart.

During this administration, finally, several important steps were taken in military matters. The government withdrew its grants for military training in the public schools, restored all civil and political rights of the conscientious objectors in the First World War, and abolished the death penalty for desertion or cowardice in the army.

The most important campaign pledge of the Laborites remained largely unfulfilled—that of unemployment relief. There was no dearth of attempts to restore trade, but they were of little avail. The Prince of Wales made good-will tours, notably to Latin America, in the hope that he might be an effective social sales manager. When he returned he delivered some frank addresses in which he urged British business men to wake up to modern methods and fashions and to go out and look for trade rather than remain at home and wait for customers at the door. A cabinet minister went to Canada in a vain effort to secure orders for British goods. Negotiations were undertaken to get the continental states to reduce their tariff schedules in the interest of a general trade revival, but again there was only failure to record. The total value of imports and exports fell by more than a third from 1929 to 1931.

Public works were inaugurated and the unemployment benefits were once more readjusted, with a view to caring for 1,000,000 persons at any time. The dole continued to eat away hundreds of millions of dollars per year. By the end of September 1931 the unemployed numbered 2,800,000. The people probably realized by this time that the situation was one of world-wide distress and was not peculiar to Great Britain, but the Labor Government had promised more than it could perform. Labor lost a number of seats in by-elections and MacDonald's position was not one to arouse envy in the hearts even of political opponents.

In the summer of 1931 the government noticed with alarm that the country's gold reserve was shrinking rapidly. The general effects of the depression, the decreasing tax receipts, the increasing dole appropriations, the falling confidence in Great Britain's financial stability and the consequent heavy foreign withdrawals, all combined to make the situation acute. Besides, there was a tense diplomatic situation on the continent, where Great Britain was trying to help Germany and Austria in their financial difficulties. To cap the misfortunes, a committee of financial experts, headed by Sir George May, reported that the deficit for the next fiscal year probably would reach $600,000,000. The May Committee therefore suggested slashes in government salaries, pensions, and unemployment benefits, and recommended slight tax increases. The premier and the chancellor of the exchequer favored these views, but a majority of the cabinet refused to endorse the proposals which, it was claimed, provided economy at the expense of the working people. On August 24, 1931, therefore, MacDonald tendered the king the resignation of the entire ministry. One day later he reassumed control with a new "National Ministry" composed of members drawn from all three parties.

Soon after this startling development became public, the Labor Party expelled MacDonald, Snowden, Thomas, and a few other leaders.[1] Arthur Henderson was elected to succeed MacDonald in the leadership of the party and the latter officially went into opposition.[2] These events were perhaps not so abrupt as they seemed.

[1] In 1931 Snowden entered the House of Lords as Viscount Snowden of Ickornshaw.

[2] After the elections of October 1931 George Lansbury became parliamentary leader of the Labor Party. He resigned in October 1935 when the party endorsed the use of sanctions against Italy in the Ethiopian dispute, and was succeeded by Major Clement R. Attlee. Henderson died in the same month.

While the rank and file of the party had been leaning more and more towards the left, MacDonald and his close associates had become middle-class liberals. Though still concerned with the welfare of the people, they appeared to be content with the social *status quo* of the land. It seemed to them that they were placing loyalty to national welfare above loyalty to party policies.

THE NATIONAL COALITION TO 1939

In September 1931 the National Cabinet pushed through Parliament a finance bill which embodied most of the proposals that had been suggested some weeks earlier. The government maintained that the new law exacted equal sacrifices from all citizens regardless of rank or station, but the Labor Party insisted that most of the savings were made at the expense of the working people. When the terms of the act were announced, Great Britain witnessed some astonishing events. Thousands of schoolteachers, postmen, and other government employees held protest meetings against the salary reductions. There were dozens of mass meetings of the unemployed and riots had to be put down in London, Liverpool, Salford, Glasgow, and other large cities. Most serious was a brief naval mutiny at Invergordon.

Such incidents shook foreign confidence in the stability of Great Britain. The kingdom's credit fell rapidly and at one time the foreign withdrawals from the Bank of England amounted to several million pounds daily. Some of these withdrawals might have had diplomatic motivation,[1] but, whatever the cause, the result was so great a depletion in the gold reserve that Parliament in September 1931 repealed that law of the realm which had required the government to issue and sell gold at par. In other words, Great Britain "went off the gold standard." Almost immediately the value of the pound fell from $4.86 to $3.49 and in the succeeding months fluctuated between $3.00 and $4.00. The chief consolations of this move were the belief that the cost of production would be considerably lowered, thus giving British goods a sales advantage in the world market, and a sizable diminution in the real value of the internal debt.

By this time it had generally become felt that the people should be given an opportunity to express their views on the policies of the National Government. Parliament therefore was dissolved

[1] See p. 163.

and new elections were held in October 1931. The candidates who supported the National Government ran as Conservatives-National Laborites, and National Liberals. The opposition candidates retained their names of Laborites and Liberals. As far as a platform was concerned, the Nationals were of necessity vague. They asked for a popular vote of confidence, advocated tariff protection, and requested a blank check to do what they considered best for the country. The Laborites had their customary platform, but lacking their old leaders they seemed to find it difficult to make their points clear to the voters. MacDonald and Snowden, indeed, joined the Conservatives in prophesying disaster if the Labor Party were victorious.

The result of the election astonished even the most experienced political sages. The government won a *majority* over its opponents of nearly 500 seats. The Conservatives alone had a majority of about 325 over all other groups and hence became the backbone of the next National Government. MacDonald, reëlected as a National Laborite, undertook to form another cabinet. It included four National Laborites, five National Liberals, and eleven Conservatives. Neville Chamberlain, a Conservative proponent of high tariffs, became chancellor of the exchequer. The Liberal Sir John Simon became foreign secretary. Not one of the outstanding Conservatives, such as Austen Chamberlain or Winston Churchill, obtained a ministerial post.

Though MacDonald retained the premiership for almost four years longer, his control was by leave of the Conservatives. In order to extend the life of the National Government and to maintain "national unity in the presence of the grave problems" that confronted "the whole world," the extraordinary step was taken of permitting individual members of the cabinet to express in Parliament "by speech and vote" views contrary to those held by the majority of the cabinet. Thus was broken a constitutional principle of 148 years' standing. In 1935, finally, MacDonald, because of illness, presented the king with his resignation and that of the cabinet. Thereupon (July) the Conservative leader, Stanley Baldwin, reconstructed the National Cabinet with himself as prime minister, Sir Samuel Hoare as foreign secretary, Neville Chamberlain as chancellor of the exchequer, and the youthful Anthony Eden as "Minister for League of Nations Affairs," a post especially created for him.

Before the year was out, Baldwin decided to appeal to the country for solid support of his stand in the Italo-Ethiopian dispute which was then raging.[1] As had been anticipated, the National Coalition triumphed with ease. Although some losses were sustained, the Baldwin Government was returned with a majority of about 250 seats. The Conservatives again formed the core of the coalition, having a sizable majority over all other groups combined. There was little change in the cabinet except that Eden soon succeeded Hoare as foreign secretary.

In January 1936 King George V died and was succeeded by his oldest son as King Edward VIII. The latter, the generally popular "Prince of Wales" of the war and postwar periods, before long became involved in a dispute with his ministers, particularly with Prime Minister Baldwin. The difference grew out of the king's desire to marry morganatically a woman of American birth, Mrs. Wallis Warfield Simpson, who was about to procure a second divorce. The government firmly resisted the king's wishes (a resistance stiffened because of the ruler's apparent readiness to participate in government affairs) and on December 10, 1936, Edward abdicated. He left immediately for the continent as Duke of Windsor and some months later married the woman of his choice in France. The dominion governments unitedly supported the British Ministry and the constitutional crisis was passed with relatively little outward disturbance. The Duke of York now became king as George VI and was crowned amid impressive ceremonies in May 1937. He and Queen Elizabeth seemed quickly to win the affection of their people and were wildly acclaimed on state visits in 1938–1939 to France, Canada, and the United States.

Meanwhile, soon after the coronation, Baldwin had retired from politics and become the Earl Baldwin of Bewdley.[2] He was succeeded as premier by his chancellor of the exchequer, Neville Chamberlain (May 1937). Aside from the perennial question of a budget, and that of rapid rearmament, itself a repercussion of the foreign situation, there was little in the way of domestic administration to which the new premier could devote his energies. The Mediterranean activities of Italy, the exigencies of the Spanish civil war, the territorial and military progress of Germany, the important relations with France—these demanded all Chamberlain's attention, particularly after the resignation in February

---

[1] See section on "Italian Foreign and African Relations" in Chapter XIV.

[2] In 1938–1939 he interested himself practically in the plight of refugees from Nazi-dominated central Europe. MacDonald, who retired from an honorary position in the cabinet at the same time as Baldwin, declined a peerage. He died in November 1937 while en route to South America.

1938 of Foreign Secretary Eden, who disagreed with his chief on the matter of further concessions to the totalitarian states. In explanation of his position, the premier addressed the lower house, outlining his views on the need for finding out "whether there was any common ground on which we might build up a general scheme of appeasement in Europe." This policy of appeasement he then steadfastly pursued throughout 1938 and into 1939 until the very outbreak of the Second World War.

From 1931 through 1938 the several National Governments resorted to a group of policies which, it was hoped, would revive prosperity. There was no definite program, but a series of measures was adopted with the aid of which Great Britain might be expected once more to "muddle through." While heavy dole payments continued, a minimum tariff of 10 per cent was imposed early in 1932 on all imports save raw cotton, wool, meat, fish, and wheat. A new "corn law" was passed which virtually guaranteed a minimum of $1.00 a bushel for a specified quantity of domestic wheat. Gradually many of the items in the tariff schedule were further raised and a tariff commission was empowered to increase any duty by as much as 100 per cent against countries that discriminated against British goods. The friends of protection were heartened when, soon after this legislation, several new industries sprang up in southern England and more raw materials were imported. A stimulus was given, moreover, to the movement for rationalization in industry.

In order to decrease government expenditures, the British war loan of $10,000,000,000 was converted and the interest rate reduced from 5 per cent to $3\frac{1}{2}$ per cent. Nevertheless, the interest on Great Britain's total national debt remained at more than $1,000,000,000 a year. The people were urged to help the government by paying income taxes in advance of the date required by law and to sell to the authorities their private gold possessions. Large quantities of gold were imported from India. To retain the foreign-trade advantages that presumably accompanied currency inflation, the government appropriated £350,000,000 for the maintenance of an Exchange Equalization Fund. The exact operations of this fund were secret, but its purpose obviously was so to "control" the inflationary process and "manage" the currency that a fairly stable relationship might be established between sterling and gold.

In foreign affairs, too, the policies were dictated chiefly by economic interests. An attempt was made at the Lausanne Reparation

Conference (1932) to draw more closely to the creditor, France, while yet remaining on good terms with the debtors, Germany and Austria. At an Imperial Economic Conference at Ottawa (1932) the representatives of Great Britain and the dominions sought to improve the economic situation within the empire by an exchange of trade concessions. A dozen bilateral trade treaties were signed, but they fell far short of accomplishing what had optimistically been hoped for from the conference. The sessions were characterized by a much greater willingness, especially on the part of the dominions, to demand sacrifices rather than to make them and gave evidence of the existence of serious intraimperial economic rivalries. But some concessions were granted, especially by the mother country, and the empire trade gave signs of improving. Incidentally, the agreements that Great Britain did make in the way of imperial preference eventually led to the resignation from the National Cabinet of the free-trade Liberal members and their replacement by Conservatives. Soon after the close of the Ottawa Conference, Great Britain also began to negotiate bilateral trade agreements with foreign countries, the first such pact being concluded with Argentina.

All these efforts, combined with a slight revival in other parts of the world, seemed to stimulate British economic life. Though wages remained low and taxes high, though strikes continued, the number of unemployed eventually declined from a peak of 3,100,000 in mid-1932 to 1,200,000 in mid-1939. The total turnover of British foreign trade for 1937 was the highest for any year since 1930, and it was estimated that in 1937 British money wages rose 4 per cent and real wages 10 per cent. Hundreds of large firms reported higher profits and savings banks generally listed increased deposits.

Many observers felt that permanent recovery could come for Great Britain, with its economic structure "geared to the world market," only through the return of a prosperous foreign trade. Yet business evidently was aided by a variety of immediate factors. These included a more vigorous trade with the dominions, the need to make replacements after years of "patching up," the coronation, an acceleration of official and private house construction and shipbuilding, and the enormous demands of the rearmament program.[1]

In 1938, moreover, there came to an end a six-year-old tariff

[1] In July 1938, for example, the House of Commons unanimously approved an appropriation of $1,500,000,000 as one year's arms outlay.

and trade war with Ireland [1] and there was signed with the United States a trade pact of the type which Secretary Hull had been negotiating over a period of years with a score of nations. The British granted concessions chiefly to American agricultural products, while Washington modified or bound its tariff schedules on British textiles, metals, and books. But with all that, the United Kingdom's national debt in 1938 for the first time rose above £8,000,000,000; in 1939 its per capita tax burden was double that of the United States.

The least hopeful economic problem in these years concerned certain "depressed" or "special" areas in northern Scotland and southern Wales. Here matters were so bad that commissioners were appointed to investigate and report to Parliament. Following their revelations some remedial measures were applied, but it was not possible to arouse much enthusiasm among industrialists for the establishment of new plants in the affected areas. High local taxes for relief purposes and the fear of labor trouble were often cited as reasons for this hesitancy. Under the new rearmament program some factories actually were set up where the unemployment was greatest. But the continued seriousness of the problem, plus a desire to tie the dominions more closely to the mother country for defense purposes, led to the appointment of an Oversea Settlement Board to find means for encouraging migration within the empire. The board's report, published in 1938, contained concrete recommendations for the "planned coöperation" of all agencies concerned, but little was done to put them into practice. A table in the report, incidentally, showed that for each year from 1931 through 1937 there had been a balance of empire migration *inward* to the United Kingdom.

The following, finally, were some interesting additional items of internal legislation in these years. In 1937 there became effective a Public Order Act which, aimed especially at Mosley's blackshirted British Union of Fascists, forbade the wearing of political uniforms and the formation of semimilitary organizations.[2] The same year saw the enactment of a new divorce law which recognized desertion, cruelty, and insanity as legal causes. And a Coal Act of 1938 provided for the transference of the coal-mine ownership of the kingdom to the state by July 1, 1942. Hoping to revive one of the country's most depressed industries, the government planned to buy the coal-mining royalties of more than four thou-

[1] See pp. 270–274 *passim*.
[2] During the Second World War Mosley was placed in confinement.

sand owners for a sum of £66,450,000—a figure computed by an arbitration commission whose findings the negotiators had agreed in advance to accept. A coal commission, made up of persons un-connected with either Parliament or the mining industry, was ap-pointed to assess the specific amounts to be paid each owner—among whom one of the greatest was the Church of England. The war emergency of 1939 delayed the process of valuation and pre-vented the completion of the task according to schedule.

GREAT BRITAIN AND THE DOMINIONS

The war and postwar periods witnessed some remarkable changes in the relationships among the component parts of the British Empire. Beginning with the year 1907, and interrupted only temporarily by the vicissitudes of war, numerous imperial conferences were held, attended by the premiers of Great Britain, Canada, Australia, New Zealand, the Union of South Africa, New-foundland,[1] and, for a time, the Irish Free State. At these gather-ings, which possessed no legal powers, the British and dominion delegates discussed problems that confronted the empire as a whole and that affected the relations of the members one to an-other. The method of the conferees was to seek agreement on gen-eral principles, embody the agreements in draft resolutions, and then work for the acceptance of the resolutions by the home gov-ernments.

The exigencies of the First World War, the dependence of Great Britain on the help furnished by the dominions, the in-dependent signature by the latter of the peace treaties, and the circumstance that the dominions became members of the League of Nations served greatly to alter the relations between the mother country and the colonies. Long before all the legal niceties in-volved in the new status of the dominions were worked out, the dominions proceeded with a number of actions that were usually regarded as falling within the category of sovereign powers.

Canada, for example, in 1923 signed with the United States a Halibut Fisheries Treaty which bore the signatures only of the American and Canadian representatives. This precedent was fol-lowed in a number of later treaties between Canada and the United States and Canada and European countries. Some of the dominions appointed their own diplomatic ministers abroad.

[1] In 1934, because of economic distress, Newfoundland temporarily surrendered its dominion status and accepted rule by a royal commission.

Australia, New Zealand, and South Africa administered mandates in their own names and on their own responsibilities. In 1930 the Australians successfully contended that their choice for the governor-generalship, who in this case happened to be a native, should be accepted. In 1931 an Irish Minister undertook directly to advise the king and the Irish Free State assumed a Great Seal of its own.

In principle, most of these actions had been affirmed by the Imperial Conference of 1926. In a document known as the Balfour Report this conference had declared: "They [Great Britain and the dominions] are autonomous communities within the British Empire, equal in status, in no way subordinate one to another in any aspect of their domestic or external affairs, though united by a common allegiance to the Crown, and freely associated as members of the British Commonwealth of Nations." It remained to have this principle enacted into imperial law, and in 1929 a committee representing Great Britain and the dominions was appointed to report on a method of bringing the old legal restrictions and the new constitutional practice into harmony. The report of the committee was accepted by the Imperial Conference of 1930 and steps were taken in each dominion and Great Britain to give it the force of law. This was finally accomplished in December 1931 with the passage by the British Parliament of the Statute of Westminster.

The statute recognized the equal status of the dominions with the mother country and thus virtually accorded them independence. It was provided that in future no law passed by a dominion parliament could be declared void "on the ground that it is repugnant to the law of England" or to the provisions of any existing or future act of the Parliament of Great Britain. The dominion parliaments were recognized as having full power to pass laws having extraterritorial operation, that is, laws applying to dominion citizens living abroad or traveling on the high seas. No law of the Parliament of Great Britain was to be applicable to any dominion unless the latter specifically requested and consented to the extension of such law to its domains. No longer might the king on advice of his ministers "disallow" an act of a dominion parliament, and henceforth no alteration in the laws concerning succession to the throne or the royal style and titles might be made without the assent of the parliaments of the dominions as well as that of Great Britain.

Thus there was created a "British Commonwealth of Independent Nations," a group of separate political entities avowing allegiance to one and the same symbol of unity: the Crown. The king, a feeling of commonwealth citizenship, and perhaps a certain pride in descent from common stock remained as the dominant ties between Great Britain and the dominions. It must not be overlooked, however, that the dominions, as long as they did not entirely break away from Britain, enjoyed the protection of a powerful navy which was paid for chiefly by the people of Great Britain.

The freedom accorded the dominions led some observers to believe that the British Empire, the "frailest of political structures" as they called it, was doomed. The answer to this view was well given by Sir Cecil Hurst in the words:

In truth, it is the full recognition of the right of each of the great self-governing communities of the Empire to be the master of its own destinies which renders it so unlikely that the connecting bonds of Empire will snap. What this full recognition of their autonomy has done is to eliminate from relations with the mother-country the elements that chafed and embittered the sentiments of the dominion peoples, and it is these elements that would have weakened and might ultimately have worn away the connecting bonds. . . . The British Empire will endure so long as it serves a useful purpose, so long as its constituent elements find it better to belong to it than to stand alone.[1]

Or as Field Marshal Smuts once phrased it:

The Empire is the greatest paradox of all time in that it derives its strength at the center from the weakness of its hold on the circumference.

[1] *Great Britain and the Dominions,* Harris Foundation Lectures for 1927, 1928. Reprinted by permission of the University of Chicago Press.

CHAPTER XII

Some British Problems of Empire

IRELAND

a. "England's Necessity Is Ireland's Opportunity"

In 1914 the British Parliament passed an Irish Home Rule Bill. This action, it was hoped, would end Irish agitation for autonomy, a movement dating from the time (1801) when Ireland became an integral part of the United Kingdom. In the nineteenth century Prime Minister William E. Gladstone had twice attempted to settle the difficulty by the grant of home rule, but his first bill had failed of passage in the House of Commons and the second had been vetoed by the House of Lords. In 1912 the lower house had passed a third Home Rule Bill and this time, though again opposed by the peers, the measure became law in 1914 after the lower house, in accordance with the Parliament Act of 1911, had passed it three successive times in an interval of two years.

If the provisions of the law had gone into force, Ireland probably would have been rent by civil war. The six "Ulster" counties in the northeast, being industrialized and largely Protestant, were resolved not to submit to the control of an Irish parliament, the majority of whose members would be elected by the Catholic farmers in the twenty-six southern counties. The people in the south were equally determined that one parliament should rule the entire island. Upon the passage of the bill both sides organized military forces in preparation for an armed conflict, but the outbreak of the First World War caused the British Government to suspend the operation of home rule. John Redmond, leader of a militant group of southern Irishmen who called themselves Irish Nationalists, assured London that his followers would remain loyal during the war. The fealty of the Ulsterites was a foregone conclusion.

The British authorities now pursued ill-advised tactics in Ireland. Although the Ulsterites were permitted to form a military division of their own for overseas service, the Irish Nationalists were denied a similar request and south-Irish recruits were encouraged to enter English regiments. With little apparent reason petty annoyances were multiplied until many people in the southern counties became indignant. In 1916 the discontent crystallized in an Easter Rebellion.

This uprising was the work of a group of radicals who had left the Irish Nationalist Party, which still officially supported the British, and formed an Irish Republican Brotherhood. Most of the "Brothers" also were affiliated with a society known as *Sinn Fein* ("We Ourselves"), which had originally been organized to bring about industrial betterment among the masses and to develop Irish national sentiment. In 1914 the association had entered the political field and during the war it became identified with the republican movement. The republicans, accordingly, were generally known as Sinn Feiners.

On Easter Monday, 1916, the Sinn Feiners seized some public buildings in Dublin and issued a proclamation in the name of the "Provisional Government of the Irish Republic." Germany had promised to aid the rebels by "land, sea, and air," but the tightness of the British blockade made such help impracticable. The British put down the rebellion within a week, shot a number of the leaders, and placed Ireland under martial law. Several thousand people were arrested and many were deported to Great Britain. These measures further swelled the ranks of Sinn-Fein sympathizers.

In 1917 Lloyd George attempted without success to solve the Irish question by a conference with representative leaders. The disorder increased and a crisis was reached in 1918 when Parliament applied a conscription act to Ireland. The opposition to this measure was so strong that the authorities saw little hope of enforcing it. Hence they offered to suspend its provisions on condition that a sufficiently large number of Irishmen volunteered for service. The volume of enlistments, however, was small and the outlook for the future ominous. The signing of the armistice occurred in time to prevent disaster.

The British parliamentary elections of December 1918, in which the Irish took part, assumed the form, in southern Ireland, of a contest between the Nationalists and the Sinn Feiners. The former stood for home rule, the latter for independence. In Ulster the

Unionist group, which preferred close ties with England, was supreme. Of the 105 seats to which Ireland was entitled in Parliament, the Unionists got 26, the Nationalists 6, and the Sinn Feiners 73. After election, the Sinn-Fein deputies refused to attend the Parliament at Westminster, preferring to consider their election as a mandate from the people to set up a separate Irish parliament. This they did, at Dublin, in January 1919. The deputies took the name of Irish Republican Party and called their parliament *Dáil Eireann.*

At the first meeting of this body twenty-nine men were present. The remaining forty-four were in prison, on their way to prison, or in hiding. Nothing daunted, the Dáil selected three delegates to attend the peace conference and plead the cause of Irish self-determination. The assemblage at Paris, however, refused to recognize these emissaries. At a subsequent meeting the Dáil appointed a ministry and elected Eamon de Valera president.

De Valera was born in New York in 1882 of a Spanish father and an Irish mother. While still in his infancy he was taken to Ireland. He grew up to be a professor of mathematics. A fervent orator and patriot, he had also been one of the leaders of the Easter Rebellion. On this occasion he had been captured and sentenced to death, but his sentence had been commuted to life imprisonment. In 1917 he benefited by a general amnesty but in 1918 was again imprisoned. This time he escaped to the United States, there receiving financial assistance for his plans. After the war he returned to Ireland and soon forged to the head of the republican camp.

The defiance of the Dáil led to an actual state of war between the "Irish Republic" and Great Britain. The British military and police forces were obliged to fight pitched battles with the Irish Republican Army led by the young and able Michael Collins. Cruelties were perpetrated on both sides and in December 1920 a large part of the city of Cork was burned. Especially hateful to the Irish were the "Auxiliaries" sent over from Great Britain to aid the police. These reënforcements soon were nicknamed "Black-and-Tans," because their uniform consisted of a khaki outfit with black bands on hat and arm.

To end the strife, Lloyd George secured the passage by Parliament of another Home Rule Act in December 1920. This law conceded more local autonomy to Ireland than had the earlier one, but it set up separate parliaments for northern and southern Ireland. The Ulsterites accepted the law and proceeded to put it into execution.[1] The other Irishmen balked. They no longer were satisfied with home rule and they objected to a division of the island. When London, despite this opposition, ordered elections held in the spring of 1921, the Sinn Feiners captured 124 of the 128 seats allotted to the "Parliament of Southern Ireland." At the opening session of this assembly, the four members from Trinity College, Dublin, were the only delegates present. The body at once adjourned, never to meet again.

Still hopeful, Lloyd George next invited de Valera to London to discuss an amicable settlement. A conference was arranged, but the proposals of Lloyd George were unacceptable to the Irish. Later a second conference was held so that means might be found whereby "the association of Ireland with the community of nations known as the British Empire could best be reconciled with Irish national aspirations." This time the Irish delegation was headed by Arthur Griffith, founder of Sinn Fein. Early in the morning of December 6, 1921, the British and Irish plenipotentiaries signed a treaty which, in effect, was the birth certificate of a new Irish Free State.

b. Free Staters versus Republicans

The treaty provided that "Ireland shall have the same constitutional status in the community of nations known as the British Empire, as the Dominion of Canada, the Commonwealth of Australia, the Dominion of New Zealand, and the Union of South Africa, with a Parliament having powers to make laws for the peace, order, and good government of Ireland and an Executive responsible to that Parliament, and shall be styled and known as the Irish Free State." Officials of the Irish Free State were to take an oath of allegiance to the king, but the office of lord-lieutenant was abolished. The Crown was to be represented, as in the case of Canada, by a governor-general. The coasts of Ireland were to be protected by the British fleet and Great Britain was to retain authority over a number of Irish ports as naval bases. The Irish Free State was to have its own military forces and revenue cutters, and

[1] On June 22, 1921, King George V formally opened the Parliament of Northern Ireland. It consisted of a House of Commons, elected by popular vote, and a Senate, composed of the mayors of Belfast and Londonderry and twenty-four other members elected by the lower house. Ministerial responsibility was provided for and the king was represented by a governor. Northern Ireland also retained the right to send thirteen delegates to the House of Commons at Westminster.

EAMON DE VALERA

eventually was to share in the burden of coast defenses. It was also to assume a portion of the British national debt, the amount to be determined later. Northern Ireland was given a choice of joining the Irish Free State or of continuing the relationship established with Great Britain by the act of 1920. Ulster chose the latter course, so that a suitable boundary line remained to be adjusted.

When news of the treaty reached Ireland, there was a break in Sinn-Fein ranks. De Valera denounced the document and resigned from the presidency when the Dáil accepted it by a close vote. Arthur Griffith and Michael Collins now led the movement for the organization of the Irish Free State and a committee was appointed to draft a constitution. De Valera and his followers thereupon withdrew from the Dáil, boasting, "We made it impossible for the British Government to rule Ireland, and we can also make it impossible for an Irish Government working under British authority to rule Ireland." For the next twelvemonth republican "Irregulars" terrorized the countryside. When, in June 1922, elections for a new provisional parliament were held, the chief issue was the acceptance or rejection of the treaty with Great Britain. The republicans interfered with the elections in an ingenious variety of ways, tearing up railway tracks, intimidating voters, and assassinating speakers. Nevertheless, the friends of the treaty were overwhelmingly victorious in the balloting.

The Irregulars were able for some time to continue their lawless activities with apparent immunity because many members of the provisional government were loath to deal harshly with the men who had been their comrades in the struggle against Great Britain. But in August 1922 the republicans killed Michael Collins from ambush. A few days earlier Arthur Griffith had died from overwork and worry. William Cosgrave and Kevin O'Higgins thereupon came to the head of the parliamentary forces and determined on a ruthless suppression of the disorder. The provisional parliament supported this stand and elected Cosgrave president. A struggle followed, fiercer and more brutal than that with the British in 1920 and 1921. Thousands were imprisoned and scores were assassinated or executed. Eventually the Free Staters triumphed and in the spring of 1923 de Valera ordered his followers to lay down their arms.

From 1923 to 1927 de Valera and his followers abstained from violence. Organized as the *Fianna Fáil*, or Republican Party, they put up candidates for election to parliament, but when elected these delegates automatically excluded themselves from office by refusing to take the oath of allegiance to the king as required by the constitution. For a time this actually was useful to Cosgrave, for it meant that there was no large opposition group in the legislature. In 1927, however, Kevin O'Higgins, Cosgrave's assistant, was assassinated. As minister of justice, O'Higgins had been active in repressing the Irregulars some years earlier, and he was generally regarded as the "strong man" of Ireland. Though de Valera and his aides denied complicity in the murder, the government determined to curtail the objectionable activities of the Fianna Fáil. A public-safety act empowered the authorities to deal vigorously with acts of lawlessness and the electoral law was amended so that no one might become a candidate for office without previously asserting his intention to fulfill all requirements of the constitution. In other words, all parliamentary candidates had to agree in advance to take the oath of allegiance if elected.

By this time popular opinion in southern Ireland was decidedly averse to the methods of de Valera. Moreover, a number of Irish-Americans who had been assisting de Valera financially were alienated by this latest murder outrage, which was generally regarded as an outcome of the Fianna-Fáil leader's tactics. De Valera therefore announced his intention to head a constitutional opposition in the national parliament and the political atmosphere became calmer. In the elections of 1927 de Valera's party, having forsworn violence, got 57 of the 153 seats in the Dáil. This success made it the second largest party in the parliament, with only four seats fewer than Cosgrave's Free-State Party, *Cumann na nGaedheal.*

c. The Cosgrave Administration, 1922–1932

The same provisional parliament which met in 1922 and elected Cosgrave president also adopted a constitution. The instrument was republican in character and was accepted by the British Parliament without change. On December 6, 1922, accordingly, King George V proclaimed the Irish Free State (*Saorstát Eireann*). Immediately thereafter the last British troops were withdrawn from the newest dominion.

Theoretically the executive power in the Irish Free State was made to rest with the governor-general; actually it was vested in a responsible Executive Council. A bicameral legislature called *Oireachtas* was set up. The upper house (*Seanad Eireann*) originally was to contain sixty members, each elected for twelve years, and was made renewable by one-fourth every three years. All citizens over thirty were permitted to vote for senators. By amendments of 1928, however, the senatorial term was reduced to nine years, the Seanad was made one-third renewable every three years, and the power of electing senators was transferred to the two legislative houses voting jointly on a panel nominated by them in equal parts. The Seanad was given no power to amend money bills and in general was accorded only a suspensive veto. The lower house or *Dáil Eireann* was to be elected for four years on a basis of proportional representation by all citizens over twenty-one. It was empowered to elect the president of the Executive Council, the chief administrative officer in the land. Religious freedom was guaranteed.

A thorny political question that remained to be settled grew out of Article 12 of the treaty of 1921. This article stipulated that, if Northern Ireland preferred not to join the Irish Free State, a commission of three should be appointed to determine the boundary between the two regions. One representative should be appointed by Great Britain, one by Ulster, and one by southern Ireland. When the British Government in 1924 tried to set up the boundary commission, the northern counties refused to send a delegate. The British therefore appointed one for them. The commission visited the border areas in 1925 and heard evidence for several months. The Irish Free State wanted to add the counties of Tyrone and Fermanagh, but the Ulstermen were determined to keep every inch of the six northeastern counties. The award of the commission was not published, but the Irish Free State delegate resigned on the ground that the two British delegates were moved more by political considerations than by the wishes of the inhabitants.

Before any overt action took place, an Irish Free State delegation was sent to London to negotiate directly with the British Government. The decisions of the commission were disregarded and a compromise was reached under which the boundary was to remain as fixed by the Home Rule Act of 1920. This was a complete victory for Ulster, but then the Irish Free State was relieved of responsibility for its share of the public debt of the United Kingdom as of 1921. This arrangement met with some opposition in the Dáil but was accepted late in 1925 by a fair-sized majority. The tension between the two parts of Ireland was eased and they agreed "mutually to aid one another in a spirit of neighborly comradeship."

It was to be expected that there would be a nationalistic reaction in the Irish Free State after the achievement of dominion status. The new country adopted its own flag of green, white, and gold and sent diplomatic representatives to the United States, France, Germany, Belgium, and to Geneva. In 1923 it was admitted to the League of Nations. Ireland now also secured representation at the British Imperial Conferences. There was a strong movement to make Gaelic the language of the people and many family and place names were Gaelicized. Thus, William Cosgrave became Liam McCosgair and the city of Queenstown became Cóbh. Irish coins and postage stamps were adopted and the mail boxes were painted green in place of the former royal red. In the spring of 1929 Gaelic was made compulsory for lawyers as it had previously been made for civil servants. The Irish delegate to the League Assembly delivered his speeches in Gaelic. But the language is difficult and English apparently remained more popular. The Irish Free State adopted a severe censorship system and many of the world's best known books, papers, and periodicals were proscribed on moral or political grounds.

The first elections under the constitution of 1922 were held in 1923. Cosgrave's party gained only a plurality in the lower house, but the absence of the de Valera Republicans enabled him to retain control of the Dáil. After the elections of 1927, when the Republicans took their seats, several attempts were made to oust Cosgrave. On one occasion it required the deciding ballot of the Speaker to thwart a vote of no confidence.

The Cosgrave regime, which lasted until 1932, could boast of laudable material achievements. Economies were effected by the consolidation of overlapping departments and the establishment of an efficient poor-relief method. The police and postal systems were reorganized, the standing army was reduced, and in 1929 the public-safety act was allowed to lapse. Land-purchase provisions were enacted and various forms of agriculture received subsidies. By 1929 the hydroelectric potentialities of the River Shannon had been developed. A modernized system of education was inaugurated, and for the first time in many years most of the three million inhabitants appeared to be reasonably prosperous and contented.[1]

Despite the general administrative success of President Cosgrave, there were signs, by 1930, that the days of his control were numbered. The economic depression and the vogue of economic nationalism strongly affected Erin and the antagonists of the govern-

[1] Large sums of foreign money were got by the legalization of sweepstakes for the benefit of Irish hospitals and charitable institutions. This device was opposed by both Cosgrave and de Valera, but it was popular with the citizenry.

ment made the most of the inevitable economic difficulties. Early in 1930, indeed, the Cosgrave Cabinet was defeated by two votes when it opposed an increase in old-age pensions. The president at once resigned, but was reëlected after a short interval. Other problems, however, soon arose to trouble the administration.

Many farmers were alienated by the strict enforcement of the laws against the exportation of low-grade agricultural products and the use of inferior bulls for breeding. Users of electric current expressed disappointment because the poor distribution facilities forced the state to exceed its promised rates for power from the Shannon plants. The refusal of the government to adopt a high tariff angered the manufacturers. Quiet citizens were offended by the violent tone which was adopted in debate by some of the ministry's ablest members. The reduction of salaries (1931–1932) in the army, the police force, and the civil service brought additional unpopularity.

When the discontent took the form of renewed disorders and secret military activities by the Irish Republican Army and other antigovernment societies, a new and more stringent public-safety measure was enacted (1931). It placed the stamp of illegality on a number of radical organizations and created military courts for the trial of persons accused of committing violence or engaging in armed drills, thus further arousing the ire of the malcontents. Finally, when Cosgrave declared that the Irish Free State could enjoy greater security within the British Commonwealth than outside it, he lost the chief appeal which attached to the traditional Irish hero, namely, that of being in opposition to the British. By contrast, de Valera now seemed much more heroic.

The approaching election in 1932 promised to be of unusual interest. The chief issue in the campaign was the acceptance or rejection of the platform announced by Fianna Fáil. This program, the keynote of which was political and economic self-sufficiency, included the following points: (1) abolition of the oath of "faithfulness" to the king which was required of all deputies by the treaty of 1921; (2) retention by the Irish treasury of certain land-purchase instalments (£5,000,000 annually) that were due British bondholders under financial agreements of 1921, 1923, and 1926; (3) suspension of the public-safety act of 1931; and (4) erection of a tariff wall.

Upon counting the ballots, it appeared that the new Dáil would include 72 supporters of de Valera, 65 followers of Cosgrave, 9 Independents, and 7 Laborites. When the house convened, the

Independents threw in their lot with Cosgrave and the representatives of labor joined de Valera. The latter therefore controlled the Dáil, by a narrow margin. In March 1932 he was elected president of the Executive Council.

d. The Rule of de Valera

President de Valera quickly became aware that it was easier to promise far-reaching changes than to inaugurate them. A majority of the senators still were pro-Cosgrave and the upper house had the constitutional right to hold up for eighteen months bills passed by the Dáil. The oath requirement was based on a clause in a bilateral treaty that had been registered with the League Secretariat. The annuity payments, though guaranteed by the British Government, were private debts. Retention of the money, therefore, though it would lighten the task of budget-making, would simultaneously violate financial conventions and moral obligations. A high tariff might be raised, but, since Ireland depended for her prosperity on exports, it was dangerous to invite retaliation. The suspension of the public-safety law was the only election pledge that could be carried out with relative ease and this was quickly done. Meanwhile the Labor members threatened to withdraw their support from the government unless prompt steps were taken to relieve unemployment.

London refused to countenance either the unilateral abrogation of the oath clause in the treaty or the repudiation of the annuities. In their public statements the British generally emphasized the illegality of the Irish contentions, but the underlying reason for their determined stand probably was strategic. In sheer self-defense Great Britain hesitated to tolerate the establishment of an Irish state which might at some time be used by a foreign power as a military or naval base. The threat of a high tariff caused the Britishers little worry since they could easily retaliate. Whereas Great Britain purchased nine-tenths of the exports of the Irish Free State, only one-twelfth of all British exports went to Ireland.

Throughout the spring and early summer of 1932 de Valera and J. H. Thomas, British Secretary for the Dominions, conferred, but with little success. Thomas warned that recourse would be had to a tariff war if the annuities were not paid. Many Irish farmers and small-business men were frightened at such a prospect, but de Valera remained firm. In fact, he added to his demands another: the unification of Northern Ireland and the Irish Free State. Meanwhile the Senate had delayed an attempt of the Dáil to remove the oath of allegiance from the constitution and the Irish Finance Minister had announced further extensive pay cuts and heavy tax increases. In June 1932 de Valera decided to withold from Great Britain some annuity money and expressed a willingness to have the Anglo-Irish dispute settled by arbitration. Thomas accepted the idea of arbitration, but refused de Valera's condition that some of the arbitrators be chosen from without the empire. The other dominions appeared to side with Great Britain in the quarrel.[1]

In July 1932 the long-expected tariff war was launched. Hoping to gain some compensatory economic advantages, the Irish Free State participated in the Imperial Economic Conference at Ottawa in July and August, but little benefit accrued to her from the agreements there reached since Great Britain granted her no concessions. Attempts were then made to negotiate trade treaties with Germany, Poland, and other countries, but again with little result. Meanwhile the British Parliament had empowered its government to place a duty up to 100 per cent on Irish products coming into Great Britain, in order that funds might be collected with which to meet the defaulted annuities. In the eight months from July 1932 to March 1933 the British collected about £2,123,000 in duties, while the total of suspended annuities by March 1933 was about £4,677,000. The Irish, moreover, heavily taxed the British imports and Anglo-Irish trade rapidly fell to a fraction of its former worth.[2]

During these months of diplomatic failure and economic difficulty, de Valera firmly retained his hold on the government. When he sensed a growing opposition in the Dáil, he dissolved that body and ordered new elections (January 1933). His party was returned with a majority of one, so that he no longer depended on the support of the Labor members. Since the suspension of the public-safety act, moreover, the Irish Republican Army had recommenced its drills and hinted that it was ready to back the government by force if necessary.

In pursuance of the campaign to sever all connections with Great Britain, the Dáil in 1933 once more passed the bill to abolish the oath of allegiance, and this time it became law. Then fol-

[1] No British or dominion flags were displayed at the Roman Catholic Eucharistic Congress which was held at Dublin in June 1932 and the governor-general was not invited to attend the official reception that was held on the occasion. Irish Free State ministers later also boycotted private affairs to which the representative of the king was invited.

[2] The costly customs war was continued until 1938. See pp. 273–274.

lowed legislation removing the need for the governor-general's assent to legalize acts. The Senate, moreover, agreed to a bill, previously adopted by the lower house, abolishing the right of appeal from Irish courts to the British Privy Council. Apparently it was chiefly the desire first to find some way of bringing about the union of all thirty-two Irish counties that delayed the immediate declaration of outright independence.

Opposition to the president's policies was not wanting. Many of the midland-county farmers and cattle raisers, who were hurt by the tariff war, had to be forced to continue making the annuity payments which now went into the Irish treasury instead of to Great Britain. The better to defend their interests, the farmers organized a Center Party under the leadership of Frank MacDermot. The unrestrained activities of the Irish Republican Army led a group of young men to form a counterorganization which, under the leadership of General Eoin O'Duffy, came to be known as the National Guard. The guardsmen adopted blue shirts and black berets as distinguishing marks and intimated that, in their opinion at least, parliamentary democracy had decided weaknesses as a form of government.

In 1933 MacDermot's Center Party, the National Guard, and the followers of Cosgrave combined to form the United Ireland Party (*Fine Gael*) under the presidency of General O'Duffy. The program of the new party included reconciliation with Ulster for a united Ireland and the ending of the tariff and annuity controversies with Great Britain. Throughout 1934 there were clashes between members of the Irish Republican Army on the one side and the O'Duffy Blue Shirts on the other. The public-safety act was once again invoked, though the Blue Shirts claimed that its prohibitions were applied only to them and not to de Valera's supporters. In 1934 a Blue-Shirt conference in Dublin pledged itself not to pay the annual land taxes until the Anglo-Irish trade war was terminated. This open defiance of the government by one wing of the United Ireland Party caused some dissension within the latter's ranks, whereupon O'Duffy resigned his leadership. Thereafter the party, under the leadership of Cosgrave, was content to oppose de Valera by constitutional means.

In 1935 and 1936 de Valera's position continued to be strong. The circumstance that the bigger farmers and the well-to-do business men opposed him made him the more popular with the masses, especially in the west of Ireland. His attempts to break up some of the larger estates, his plan to make the country self-sufficient by decreasing the emphasis on cattle raising and encouraging the sowing of grain, his negotiation of foreign-trade agreements, the fixing of certain prices by government boards, and the belief among many of the Irish that Great Britain and not de Valera was responsible for their economic difficulties, all won popular favor for the mathematician-president.[1]

The increasing trend away from Great Britain was reflected in a new Irish constitution which was enacted by vote of the people on July 1, 1937, and inaugurated in December.[2] The document declared the "national territory (consisting) of the whole of Ireland, its islands and the territorial seas" to be "a sovereign, independent, democratic state" henceforth to be known by its old Gaelic name of *Éire*, or, in English, Ireland. "Pending the reintegration of the national territory," that is, pending the union of northern and southern Ireland, only the Free State area was to be affected by the constitution. This last, which bore a strong Catholic impress, made no mention of king or commonwealth. In the six northern counties there was some excitement over this "paper annexation" but the British remained relatively calm, feeling that there was no practical change in the commonwealth relationship.

The new constitution provided for a directly elected president with a seven-year term and eligibility for reëlection. He was made dependent on the advice of a ministry, itself responsible to the lower house. A bicameral legislature was set up with a popularly chosen Dáil Eireann and a Seanad Eireann of sixty members selected largely on a vocational and indirect basis. In May 1938, Dr. Douglas Hyde, a Protestant professor of literature who had never taken part in politics, was chosen first president under the new instrument of government. Since he was an unopposed candidate, there was no actual popular election. De Valera was designated premier.

De Valera's domestic policies continued to aim at the goal of economic self-sufficiency and hence were dubbed, by some of the business men, "Dev's hair-shirt dream." The trade war with Great Britain, moreover, continued to have a disastrous effect on the Irish economic system. At last, in January 1938, British and Irish delegates met in London to negotiate a truce. The result of their

[1] In June 1936 the Senate of the Irish Free State was abolished.

[2] Meanwhile, as the result of an election held on the same day as the plebiscite on the constitution, de Valera had lost his majority in the Dáil. His followers numbered sixty-nine, exactly half the membership. But he was supported by the Laborites and reëlected chief minister.

deliberations was the signing (in April) of a political, a financial, and a trade agreement.

In the political agreement, Great Britain transferred to Ireland its admiralty property and rights at certain Irish coast towns— property and rights which had been reserved to Great Britain by the Anglo-Irish treaty of 1921. The financial arrangement provided for an Irish payment, before the end of November 1938, of a lump sum of $50,000,000 in "final settlement" of all financial claims, that is, in full settlement of the annuities that were due the British bondholders. Ireland also agreed to pay $1,250,000 per year until 1987 for damage done to property during the civil war in the early postwar years. Both countries undertook to abolish all special duties and charges that had been imposed since the outbreak of the trade war in 1932. The trade agreement provided for new customs arrangements that were more liberal than had been the case even before 1932.

All the agreements were ratified in May 1938 and thus a serious problem found at least temporary solution. Possibly in order to capitalize on the approval called forth by the agreements, de Valera requested a dissolution of the lower house and new elections. The balloting gave his party a majority in the new Dáil. Fianna Fáil captured 77 of the 138 seats. Now Premier de Valera could carry on his work without fear of parliamentary opposition.

In an effort to establish "social justice," de Valera, leaning heavily for justification on the encyclicals of Leo XIII and Pius XI, encouraged plans for a more equitable distribution of natural resources among the classes, fostered labor legislation, strove to decentralize industry while encouraging manufactures, and tried to bring more efficiency into agriculture. The opposition to such policies, to the enforced introduction of the Gaelic tongue to the exclusion of English, and to the continued separation of northern and southern Ireland led to numerous demonstrations and much violence. De Valera therefore declared the Irish Republican Army illegal (1936) and took strong measures to suppress outbursts that occurred at the time of the coronation of George VI. But in 1939 the I.R.A. renewed its activity, being charged with more than 130 bomb outrages throughout the United Kingdom in the first eight months of that year. The British Government replied in 1939 with an act which gave the police unprecedentedly wide powers to deal with terrorist suspects. These, despite their British status, might now be treated as undesirable aliens. De Valera himself denounced the terrorist campaign and ordered the Irish police to assist in checking the illegal activities of the I.R.A. But when the Second World War broke out, Ireland alone of the dominions or former dominions remained neutral.

EGYPT

When Turkey and Great Britain went to war in 1914, Egypt was placed in a unique position. Though occupied by the British since 1882, Egypt still was under the technical sovereignty of the Ottoman Sultan. In December 1914, however, Great Britain freed the people from the incubus of two loyalties by announcing that "the suzerainty of Turkey over Egypt is terminated." On the same occasion Great Britain extended a protectorate over the land of the Nile, deposed Khedive Abbas Hilmi II, who happened to be in Constantinople, and elevated Abbas' uncle, Hussein Kamel, to the throne as sultan of Egypt. Great Britain promised to take "upon herself the sole burden of the present war without calling on the Egyptian people for aid therein."

This pledge was soon modified and Egypt began to seethe with discontent. The British organized an Egyptian Labor and Camel Corps to provide transportation facilities for their armies in Palestine and Syria. Service in the corps at first was voluntary and good wages were paid, but as the war continued the treatment of the men became poor and in the end resort was had to forced recruiting. Because of the bad accommodations, many of the Egyptians froze to death during the cold Palestine winters, and some of the conscripts were made to fight. The British authorities, furthermore, requisitioned Egyptian livestock and grain at their own prices. Dubious methods were used to exact Red-Cross contributions from the peasants or *fellahin*. In addition to these material grievances, the Egyptians experienced the general hatred of patriots for foreign rule and the traditional dislike of Moslems for Christians. The desire for independence, too, was quickened by President Wilson's talk about self-determination. Yet open revolt did not occur during the war years, probably because British troops were quartered in the land.

After the armistice the Egyptians were amazed to find that, although a number of Indian rajahs and Arabian sheikhs had been invited to attend the peace conference, no such privilege was accorded them. The leader of the Nationalist Party (*Wafd*), Saad Zaghlul Pasha, resolutely placed himself at the head of a delegation which prepared to embark for Paris to present Egypt's case for independence. The British arrested the delegation and shipped it to Malta. This act precipitated an insurrection (1919). The rioting was so severe that an army under General Allenby was required to restore order. Eventually the imprisoned delegates were released and a mission of investigation under Lord Milner was dispatched to Egypt.

The mission investigated and then returned to London. Here Milner also interviewed Zaghlul, who had since gone to Great Britain. In its completed report the Milner Mission recommended that Egypt be given independence with a number of restrictions. When the proposals were incorporated in a treaty and offered to Egypt in 1921, the Nationalists unhesitatingly rejected them.

Rioting broke out anew, Zaghlul was again arrested and this time sent to Gibraltar, and Allenby once more utilized his troops. The general also suggested that Great Britain proclaim the treaty terms as a unilateral declaration. This was done, on February 28, 1922, and Egypt was proclaimed "an independent sovereign state." The following points, however, were "absolutely reserved to the discretion of His Majesty's Government": the defense of Suez, the defense of Egypt against foreign aggression, the protection of foreigners and their interests in Egypt, and the control of the Sudan —important as a source of cotton and as the area from which Egypt's water supply could be controlled. Coincident with the announcement of the "termination" of the British protectorate, Sultan Ahmed Fuad, who had succeeded Hussein in 1917, changed his title to that of king.

The "British Monroe Doctrine over Egypt" irked the Nationalists, but they were powerless to resist it. A constitution was promulgated for the new kingdom in 1923 and parliamentary elections were held. The *Wafdists* were overwhelmingly victorious at the polls and Zaghlul, who had returned home again, became premier (January 1924). He still hoped for complete independence and went to London to see Premier MacDonald, but his quest was in vain.

Another crisis occurred in November 1924 when Sir Lee Stack, governor-general of the Sudan and *sirdar* or commander-in-chief of the Egyptian army, was murdered in Cairo. Both Fuad and Zaghlul expressed their horror at the crime and promised swift prosecution of the assassins, but, inasmuch as this was merely the worst in a series of outrages, the British issued a severe ultimatum. They demanded an official apology, the punishment of the criminals, the suppression of political demonstrations, an indemnity of half a million pounds sterling, and the immediate withdrawal of all Egyptian soldiers from the Sudan. They further announced the indefinite extension for cotton cultivation of the Gezireh irrigation area in the Sudan, thus threatening Egypt's water supply.

Zaghlul accepted all terms save those relating to the Sudan. The British thereupon occupied the customs house at Alexandria and Zaghlul resigned in protest. He was succeeded by a more tractable premier, who agreed to the British demands. Subsequently Great Britain promised to use only the waters of the Blue Nile for the Sudanese irrigation projects and to leave the White Nile for Egypt, but the Egyptians continued to be alarmed by successive British dam projects. The parliament, controlled by Nationalists, appealed to the League of Nations for redress, but Great Britain maintained that the affair was not an international one and hence no member of the League brought it up for discussion.

The next few years witnessed a virtual stalemate in Egyptian politics. Several parliaments were convened and dismissed and the Nationalist majorities persistently voted down the measures of ministers who were friendly to Great Britain. In 1926 Zaghlul again would have become premier but for the objection of High Commissioner Lord Lloyd. Nevertheless, until his death in 1927, the Wafdist leader ruled the parliament. His last serious clashes with the British occurred over his proposal to increase the size of the Egyptian army and his opposition to a new treaty which would have prolonged indefinitely the stay of British troops in Egypt. Although the Nationalist Party remained intact after the death of Zaghlul, it was able to accomplish but little since the king and many of his aides, who owed their positions to the existing regime, displayed pro-British sympathies. Fuad, moreover, was not democratically inclined and he disliked the institution of parliamentary responsibility.

The return to power of a Labor Government in Great Britain in 1929 once more raised Egyptian hopes for independence. There was joy when Lord Lloyd was replaced as high commissioner by the more liberal Sir Percy Loraine and when Foreign Secretary Henderson announced the draft of a new treaty to be presented to the parliaments at London and Cairo. Although acceptance of this treaty would have been a further step in the direction of independence, it did not satisfy the new Wafdist leader, Mustapha Nahas Pasha. The agreement therefore was rejected by the Nationalist Government that had come into power after the elections of December 1929. The people became restless again and the parliament soon was suspended—the fourth such instance in five years. Ismail Sidky Pasha thereupon became dictator and in 1930 promulgated a new constitution.

This document, with its complicated, indirect electoral system, reflected a definite attempt to reduce the power of the Wafdists; but owing to careful governmental supervision the reactions of the people were less violent than might have been expected. In an endeavor to regain the constitution of 1923, however, and to oust Sidky from office, the Wafdists under Nahas now were joined by the Liberal Constitutional Party led by ex-Premier Mohammed Mahmoud Pasha. Prior to this union Mahmoud, who had accepted an honorary degree from Oxford, had been as obnoxious to the Wafdists as Sidky, but now common cause was made against the latter's newly organized People's Party (*Shaab*).

Nahas and Mahmoud, though claiming to control 90 per cent of the vote, threatened to boycott the election promised for 1931. Sidky's government thereupon forbade Wafdist meetings and prohibited the publication of boycott propaganda. In May 1931 the popular elections were held. The people were to select one voter in every fifty to act as parliamentary elector on June 1. Before the balloting, the opposition leaders were prevented from leaving Cairo lest they induce the people to abstain from voting. Many were reported killed and many more wounded in election riots. The secondary elections in June aroused less interest and disorder, and resulted in an overwhelming victory for the government. Because of the boycott, there were no Nationalists in the new parliament.

From 1931 through the summer of 1933 Sidky retained dictatorial control of the land. Parliament was convened and prorogued at his will and repressive measures were taken against overenthusiastic Wafdists and communists. Considerable economic distress was experienced in these years, largely because of the decline in the price of cotton. In June 1933, moreover, there began a series of anti-Christian outbursts, precipitated by the alleged attempt of a British schoolmistress at Port Said to coerce a Moslem girl into accepting Christianity. The latent anti-Christian sentiment in the country now grew into an organized campaign against missionaries and mission schools. The movement was guided by a Committee for the Defense of Islam and supported by the Moslem press, clergy, and populace. There was some violence and the government was petitioned to withdraw all subsidies from the missions, to tax missionary institutions, and to establish Moslem orphanages, schools, and clinics so that poor Egyptians might not be dependent upon Christians for education and medical attention. Only the last of these requests was acted upon, the government funds being supplemented by popular subscriptions. The violent outbursts eventually subsided, but the defense committee persisted in its campaign to uphold Islam against the "lure" of Christianity.

Apparently because of illness and the interference of the king in administrative affairs, Sidky resigned in September 1933. After fourteen troubled months, Mohammed Tewfik Nessim Pasha, a popular and patriotic man of independent political views, came to the helm. One of his first official acts was to persuade King Fuad to abolish the undemocratic constitution of 1930. The sovereign was to govern by decree until a new instrument could be promulgated. The Nationalists expected that the more democratic constitution of 1923 now would be restored, but a year passed without such action. It appeared, moreover, that the delay was owing at least in part to the attitude of the British Government, which hitherto had followed a policy of passive observation, allowing the Egyptians themselves to wrestle with their domestic difficulties. The whole situation became further complicated in the autumn of 1935 because of the Mediterranean crisis precipitated by Italy's Ethiopian venture.

When Great Britain took special military and naval precautions in the Egyptian zone, sensitive natives were hurt at the apparent disregard for the views of the Egyptian Government. Some natives feared lest they be drawn into an Anglo-Italian conflict while others regarded the time as opportune for exerting pressure on London. Nahas, the Wafdist leader, warned Great Britain to expect no help from Egypt except on a basis of "coöperation between equals." Britain thereupon promised that Cairo would be informed of every development that affected Egypt—but anti-British riots broke out in several cities. The violence increased when Foreign Secretary Hoare declared that the time was not ripe for renewing treaty negotiations, and late in 1935 all Egyptian political parties save one formed a United Front under ex-Premier Nahas.

Thereupon High Commissioner Miles W. Lampson, who had been appointed in 1933, announced Britain's readiness to negotiate as soon as Egypt had a government representing all parties. Nessim now prevailed upon the king to restore the constitution of 1923 and new elections were held in May 1936. The returns gave the Wafdists almost 80 per cent of the seats in the chamber and Nahas again became premier. Meanwhile King Fuad had died (1936) and been succeeded by his sixteen-year-old son, Farouk I. British and Egyptian delegates, moreover, already had begun work on a new treaty.

The negotiations lasted for months and several times appeared on the verge of breaking down. But Italy's aggressive tactics in eastern Africa had a sobering effect on both parties and made them more willing to coöperate lest a common enemy be the gainer. At last, in August 1936, an Anglo-Egyptian Treaty of Alliance was signed in London. Ratifications were exchanged just before Christmas and High Commissioner Lampson at once became Ambassador Lampson.

The treaty, of indefinite duration, provided that each signatory would aid the other in case of war. Great Britain was given the right, in the event of war, to utilize all Egyptian facilities and if necessary require the establishment of martial law. The British promised to support Egypt's candidacy for admission to the League of Nations, agreed to an exchange of ambassadors (with permanent precedence for the British Ambassador at Cairo), and undertook to confine their troops in Egypt to a zone at the northern end of the Suez Canal. These troops, in peacetime, were not to exceed ten thousand soldiers and four hundred pilots. Their removal to the restricted area was to occur over a period of not more than eight years, during which new barracks, roads, and improved means of communication were to be built. Joint rule over the Sudan was to be reëstablished with the right of unrestricted immigration for Egyptians. Great Britain also promised to use her influence to induce the twelve powers with extraterritorial rights in Egypt to surrender their privileged position and agree to the abolition of the mixed courts, leaving the full protection of the lives and property of foreigners to the Cairo Government.

In accordance with her promise, Great Britain helped arrange for a meeting of the capitulatory powers at Montreux in 1937. There the Montreux Convention was signed, providing for the complete abolition of extraterritoriality by 1949, with certain steps to be taken at once. Less than three weeks later Egypt became a member of the League, and in July Farouk was invested as the first king of independent Egypt. There was no full independence in the sense that Great Britain herself enjoyed this status, for London, with great foresight, maintained that the "facts of modern warfare" made essential some close relationship among technical equals.

The Nahas Government, which had negotiated the treaty of 1936, soon found itself at odds with the young king. There was trouble when Farouk, who combined "modern" tastes with proper respect for tradition, insisted upon a religious investiture ceremony. There was disagreement regarding the king's role under the constitution. There was a quarrel when Farouk demanded the disbanding of the Wafdist "Blue Shirts," young fascists who broke up the meetings of those not in sympathy with the Nahas program. Eventually, at the end of 1937, the king dismissed the cabinet and appointed the Liberal Mohammed Mahmoud to the premiership. When the latter dissolved the blue-shirt organization there were more riots and Great Britain dispatched additional troops to Egypt. Then, for a brief period, politics remained in the background while popular interest centered on the marriage of King Farouk to a beautiful girl of Egyptian birth and Circassian descent.

The spring of 1938 witnessed another exciting election campaign. Premier Mahmoud upheld the principles of liberal government and warned of the autocratic temper of the Wafdist leader, Nahas. The latter stood on his record of recent diplomatic achievements, but had to face a split within his own ranks. The leading dissident was Dr. Ahmed Maher, who demanded a return to the original Wafdist principles as enunciated by Saad Zaghlul and who organized a new Saadist Party that supported the government.

The poll represented an easy victory for the government coalition under Mahmoud. The reasons for this included Nahas' differences with the increasingly popular king, the control of the election machinery by the premier, and the split in Wafdist ranks. Mahmoud was therefore reappointed premier, continuing at the head of the Egyptian Government until August 1939. Then illness made him relinquish his post to Aly Maher, an Independent supported by the Saadists. Upon the outbreak of war in 1939, Aly Maher became military governor with wide powers.

During 1938 and 1939 Egypt—Mediterranean power and neighbor to Libya—felt the need to increase her armed strength. The king therefore urged relatively heavy arms expenditures upon his parliament. Legislation was introduced looking toward the creation of a small fleet and the gradual introduction of conscription to build up a small but well-trained standing army. The increasing gravity of the Palestinian situation also interested the Egyptians, who, in 1939, joined Iraq and Saudi Arabia in the expression of sympathy with the cause of the Arabs in that mandate.

INDIA

a. India and the War of 1914–1918

Within three months after the outbreak of the First World War, Indian troops were fighting on the western front, for India, like the other British colonies, remained loyal during the fight. Altogether, India supplied 1,300,000 soldiers and laborers who were utilized in Egypt, China, Africa, Arabia, and the Balkans, as well as in France. The government of India, moreover, presented Great Britain with a gift of $500,000,000. This was supplemented by a donation of $25,000,000 contributed by the several hundred princes of the quasi-independent Native Indian States. But the circumstance that she did not make it necessary for Great Britain to quell serious native revolts was India's greatest contribution to the Allied cause.

The political life of India had long been characterized by unrest. Conditions had been troubled under the regime of the British East India Company (1600–1857) and there had been only slight improvement under the administration of the British Government which, in 1857–1858, had relieved the company of its control. The Government of India Act (1858) and the Indian Councils Act (1909), both intended to better the political situation, had failed to satisfy the native leaders. A number of these, through their travels and studies in the West, had come to look upon representative government as an immediate goal. During the war, therefore, Indian leaders made it clear that they hoped to win concessions as a reward for their loyalty. Their hands were strengthened by the temporary *rapprochement* which the war brought about between the Moslems and Hindus in India.

The Mohammedans refused to heed the Ottoman Sultan's call for a Holy War against Great Britain and instead united with the Hindus in aiding the British and demanding political reform. In 1916 the Indian National Congress, organized in 1885, and the All-India Moslem League, founded in 1906, met together for the first time. Prominent at the gathering were the newspaper editor, Bāl Gangadhar Tilak, and a remarkably active Irishwoman, Mrs.

Annie Besant.[1] The fraternization of Moslems and Hindus resulted in the presentation to Great Britain (1916) of a reform plan known as the Congress-League Scheme.

With their attention centered upon the war, the British at first paid little heed to the scheme. Eventually, however, the growing unrest made some action imperative. In 1917 the secretary of state for India, Edwin Montagu, determined to investigate affairs with a view to the introduction of reforms leading ultimately to self-government. Careful to stress that the steps toward self-government would perforce be "gradual," Montagu went to India and, together with Viceroy Lord Chelmsford, held numerous interviews.

The consensus in British officialdom in India was that any diminution of British power would lead to disorder, repression, and caste warfare. This view was upheld by the European merchants in India and by some Moslems who feared the consequences of Brahmin rule. Nationalist spokesmen, on the other hand, heaped up charges of extravagance and waste against British rule. They complained of the laxity of famine control, of the cost of the army, and of the haughty attitude adopted by Britishers in their relations with the natives. They also demanded a protective tariff against certain British products.

Following these interviews, a Montagu-Chelmsford Report was published in July 1918. For several months thereafter, parliamentary committees were at work framing legislation based upon the principles enunciated in the document. Meanwhile an increasing discontent in India, manifested by strikes and agitation, led to the decreeing of the so-called Rowlatt Acts. These laws empowered the government to suppress revolutionary activities by the suspension of jury trial, the curtailment of the right of appeal, and the infliction of severe penalties. Later all public meetings were forbidden. In the spring of 1919 the conflict between the authorities and the natives reached a climax at Amritsar, in the Punjab.

Here the rioting had cost the lives of some British persons, including a woman missionary. Brigadier-General Reginald E. Dyer was called upon to restore order. On one occasion (April 13) the general discovered that a mass meeting was being illegally held in an enclosed public square. Dyer marched some troops to the meet-

[1] Mrs. Besant was president of the Theosophical Society and was so strenuous an advocate of Indian nationalism that she was several times imprisoned and deported. The slogan of her paper, *The New India*, was "Home Rule for India."

ing place and gave the command to fire into the crowd. About four hundred people were killed and three times as many wounded. Popular indignation was so great that Parliament appointed the Hunter Commission to investigate the "massacre." The report of this commission whitewashed the affair, though it did censure Dyer for shooting without notice and for continuing to fire after he had the situation in hand. The Indians were indignant over the report and their anger was hardly appeased when they found that Dyer, though recalled from India, lost neither rank nor pension.

The Indians, therefore, were in no happy mood when Parliament, late in 1919, passed the Government of India Act, based upon the Montagu-Chelmsford Report. This act, which applied only to the provinces comprising British India and not to the six hundred Indian States, increased the number of voters in *provincial* elections from 30,000 to 5,300,000, thus enfranchising 2.2 per cent of the population.[1] In central affairs the viceroy was to be assisted, as before, by a Council of State and a Legislative Assembly. The membership of the council was placed at 60. Thirty-four of the councilors were to be elected by a restricted body of voters numbering about 18,000; the remaining 26 were to be nominated by the viceroy. In the assembly provision was made for 144 seats, 103 of them elective. Fewer than 1,000,000 persons were entitled to vote for members of the lower house. Laws generally required the consent of the assembly, although in some instances the assent of the council was declared sufficient. In case of emergency the viceroy might issue decrees with the force of law and to him was left full control of the budget, defense, and foreign affairs. Further reforms, it was provided, would be considered after ten years.

The most remarkable feature of the law was that which created a dyarchy or double government in provincial matters. In each province such matters as police, law, and administration were "reserved" to the provincial governor and to the officials responsible to him. The governor was appointed by the viceroy, himself an appointee of the emperor of India. Affairs such as sanitation, education, agriculture, and health were "transferred" to the supervision of the provincial councils, a majority of whose members were elected. Officials carrying out transferred powers were made responsible to these councils.

[1] The census of 1941 gave British India 295,800,000 inhabitants and the Indian States 93,000,000, making an all-India total of 388,800,000.

The Indian Nationalists, now organized as a party, were not content with these reforms. They complained that the viceroy still would be supreme through his control of the purse strings; that the act, which in effect was India's constitution, ought to be subject to revision in less than the prescribed decade; that the franchise was too restricted; and that the provincial councils would not be able to appropriate sufficiently large sums for educational and agricultural projects. A movement to secure further concessions from the British was at once inaugurated, the leading agitator now being a fifty-year-old lawyer named Mohandas Karamchand Gandhi.

b. The "Great Soul"

Gandhi was born in 1869 of a politically prominent family. After a morbid and unhappy youth, which included a marriage at thirteen, he went to England to study law, under the threefold vow of celibacy, vegetarianism, and abstention from alcohol. "Shy, retiring, lonesome, awkward, uncouth in dress and speech, bewildered by strange manners, and nearly starving in a country where people took little pains to provide for vegetarians, he suffered pitiably. In time, however, he located a vegetarian restaurant; and with regular and ample meals his health improved." Following his admission to the bar, Gandhi returned to India to practice his profession. He was not particularly successful and was delighted when an opportunity offered itself in 1893 to handle a case in South Africa.

For the next twenty years Gandhi remained in South Africa, upholding the rights of immigrant Indian laborers. He rose to eminence as a pleader and the British Government usually supported his endeavors to establish the equality of Indians with other subjects of the empire. For this aid Gandhi was grateful and from 1914–1918 he was active in securing Indian military enlistments. After the return of peace, however, such measures as the Rowlatt Acts and the Amritsar incident converted him into an opponent of British policy.

Personally Gandhi seemed an enigma, having been labeled in turn a prophet, a madman, and a politician. A small, wizened ascetic, he spent much time fasting and praying and appeared little interested in riches or pleasure. His followers, over whose minds and actions he came to wield great power, called him *Mahatma,* the "Great Soul" or the "Holy One." Like many other Indians, he came to the conclusion that the "gigantic sordidness" of Western industrialism was incompatible with the soul-communing spirit of Orientalism.

Gandhi strove fervently to secure *swaraj* or home rule for India and was the leading advocate of the wearing of homespun cloth or *khaddar*. He abhorred violence and, when he saw that Great Britain hesitated to grant autonomy voluntarily, he began preaching a campaign of passive resistance. His followers were urged to adopt a policy of material and spiritual noncoöperation (*satyagraha*). Before long the Hindus effectively boycotted British schools, courts, receptions, and products; remained away from the polls; and disregarded the Rowlatt Laws. The natives hoped that by thus proving the British reforms a farce and by injuring British pocketbooks they would secure an early grant of *swaraj*. During 1920 and 1921 several incidents aided Gandhi's movement. Moslems flocked to his standard because of the manner in which the Allies treated Turkey in the peace negotiations at Sèvres. Additional recruits were gained when it was learned that the British Parliament had restricted the area in the African colony of Kenya in which Hindus might settle. The harshness of the police in dealing with Indian crowds and individuals also reacted to the Mahatma's advantage.

As it happened, the Indians displayed far more zeal in burning British cloth than in producing homespun. Gandhi attributed too much power to the spinning-wheel and he frequently talked over the heads of his listeners. Sometimes, after inflaming them with his eloquent speeches, he found it impossible to restrain them from rash action. A visit of the Prince of Wales to India in 1921 was made the occasion for serious strikes and riots, and in 1922 Gandhi was sentenced to six years' imprisonment for inciting the populace to violence.

With Gandhi in prison, the popular anti-British agitation subsided and the Moslems and Hindus fell to quarreling again. Noncoöperation had apparently proved a failure. Some of the Nationalists, led by Chitta Ramjan Das, now decided to abandon the boycott and run candidates for election to the Legislative Assembly. Here, as members of a newly formed Swarajist Party, they could at least air their views in public debate. From the end of 1922 to 1927 the home-rule agitation was confined chiefly to the legislative chambers. In these circumstances the government considered it safe to free Gandhi in 1924 after he had had an operation for appendicitis. Following his release, Gandhi remained in retirement for about five years.

c. The Continuance of Strife

Meanwhile abundant opportunity had been offered to observe the workings of dyarchy. In 1924 a committee of the assembly voted the dyarchic system a failure. Both the British and the Indian committee members were in agreement on this point. In 1925 Pandit Motilal Nehru, who had succeeded to the leadership of the Swarajists upon the death of Das, asked in the assembly for full responsible government in the provinces and responsible government in all national spheres save those of defense and foreign affairs. It soon became obvious, therefore, that the appointment of a commission to consider a revision of the Montagu reforms ought not to be deferred until 1929.

Accordingly a commission, representing all three British parties and headed by Sir John Simon, was appointed in 1927. There were no Indians on this body, but Simon issued an invitation to the leading native statesmen to work with the group "in joint conference." The Nationalists, however, resented their official exclusion and boycotted the delegation when it arrived in India. Although the commission's special train was heavily guarded, several attempts were made to dynamite it. The commission's investigations ended in 1929 and a two-volume report was published in June 1930.[1]

While the Simon Commission was at work, the tide of Indian nationalism rose once more. Gandhi emerged from retirement and was supported by an energetic group of leaders, among them the poetess, Mme. Sarojini Naidu, the well-liked Pandit Motilal Nehru, and the latter's fiery son, Pandit Jawaharlal Nehru. At an All-India National Congress of 1929, which represented Moslems as well as Hindus, a resolution was passed demanding immediate dominion status for India. There was a strong movement in favor of a resolution for absolute independence, but this was forestalled by Gandhi. The mahatma felt that dominion status was the only platform on which India could stand with a solid front. In March 1930 Gandhi issued an ultimatum to the viceroy for immediate dominion status.

When his demand was rejected, Gandhi once more launched a civil-disobedience campaign. Choosing as the main target for his passive resistance the government salt-monopoly, he determined to violate a law that forbade the natives to manufacture salt from sea water. For this purpose he and a band of volunteers marched 170

[1] The Simon Commission confined its investigation to British India. A Butler Commission simultaneously investigated conditions in the Native States.

miles to Dandi on the Gulf of Cambay to make salt. He first violated the law on April 6, 1930. This action was the signal for a general defiance of laws throughout India. Many Hindu officials resigned and the collection of taxes was resisted. In the cities, natives obstructed railway and street traffic by lying down on the tracks or in the path of vehicles. Gandhi again cautioned his followers to abstain from violence, but they were not all so gentle as he and much blood was shed. The authorities for a time refrained from arresting the Holy One lest he be regarded as a martyr, but eventually the situation became so bad that he and other prominent Nationalists were jailed.

The resulting anger of the people was heightened when the recommendations of the Simon Commission became known. The report aimed at increasing the powers of the secretary of state for India, of the governor-general, and of the provincial governors. It avoided even a reference to dominion status or independence and it hurt educated Indians by the curt manner in which it proposed making the provincial legislatures a school wherein the natives might secure "primary instruction and training in government." Now more and more members of the National Congress began to demand complete independence, but the incarceration of the leaders and the approach of the rainy season checked the outbursts as 1930 drew to a close. The bond of unity among the various groups had, as usual, been frail; and now, as in previous instances, the Moslems and Hindus, the high and low castes, found in union more strain than strength.

Meanwhile, Viceroy Lord Irwin (later Lord Halifax) had suggested, and the British Government had called, a Round-Table Conference in London as a possible means of arriving at some Indian compromise. It was understood that the recommendations of the Simon Commission would not be binding on His Majesty's Government and it was hoped that "Indians of all schools of thought" would be ready to participate in the deliberations. In November 1930 such a Round Table assembled. The gathering consisted of thirteen British members—Premier MacDonald and four members from each of the three political parties—and seventy-six Indians. The latter represented the Native States and virtually all political groups in British India save the Congress Nationalists, including Gandhi, who preferred to remain in jail rather than coöperate. The Indian delegation included both Moslems and Hindus as well as women deputies and even a pariah or member of the "untouchable" caste.

The Round Table sat for two months and achieved a number of results. The Native Princes announced their willingness to enter a federation with British India. It was agreed that the province of Burma should be separated from India without prejudice to its own constitutional development. The high-caste members signed a pledge approving political equality for the untouchables in the projected constitution. The greatest quandary that faced the conference was the Moslem-Hindu controversy. The Moslems feared for their treatment under an autonomous government since they formed only 22 per cent of the population. They insisted upon separate communal (religious) electorates and a share in the government services wherever sizable Moslem minorities existed. This problem was not settled by the conference, but it was hoped that the Moslems and Hindus together might work out a compromise solution for a second Round Table later in 1931. A draft constitution for an Indian federation also was considered, but the British delegates insisted that responsibility for defense, foreign affairs, and external financial matters must remain with the governor-general. Dominion status, accordingly, seemed out of the question.

When the Indian conferees returned from London to explain their accomplishments, the extremists at home, many of whom now were released from confinement, showed great dissatisfaction. They regarded the gains as no more than "a cup of milk for a hungry lion." Gandhi renewed his civil-disobedience campaign until March 1931 when a truce was reached, known as the Irwin-Gandhi Agreement or Delhi Pact. The Nationalists promised to refrain from civil disobedience, while the government granted some amnesties and consented to peaceful picketing and boycotting. Neither side fully observed the terms of the truce, and disorder was rife all through the summer. London therefore proposed a reassembling of the Round-Table Conference in September 1931. Gandhi, after much hesitation, accepted an invitation to attend.

The second Round-Table Conference was a disappointing affair. Not only were the proceedings made difficult by the conflicting views of the Indians and Britishers on the extent of self-government to be accorded India, but the delegates from the Native States and from British India could not agree on the kind of federation they wanted, the Moslems and Hindus found themselves farther apart than ever on the question of political safeguards for the former and for the other Indian minorities, and there were differences of opinion regarding the status to be assigned to the untouchables. Much to the annoyance of Gandhi, Premier MacDonald, now at the head of the National Cabinet, informed the Indians that the matter of a new constitution would have to wait until they themselves could reach a compromise on the question of communal electorates and minority safeguards. After several months had been spent in fruitless wrangling, the British Premier adjourned the conference, appointed three committees to work out various details, and promised to reconvene the Round Table when their reports were ready. Most of the Indian delegates went home feeling that the gathering had been a failure.

Throughout 1931 [1] the anti-British manifestations had repeatedly taken the form of attempts on the lives of officials. Now the unsuccessful conclusion of the Round Table spurred the natives to further violence. Conditions became so bad that Lord Willingdon, who had succeeded Lord Irwin, issued strict ordinances. Gandhi, upon his return from Great Britain, sought to induce the viceroy to rescind the decrees, but when his request was disregarded the civil-disobedience campaign was renewed. Thereupon the mahatma was once more jailed (January 1932). Soon thereafter President Mme. Naidu and four hundred other members of the National Congress were arrested when they defied a vice-regal injunction against meeting. The arrests for violation of special ordinances multiplied rapidly and each passing week saw an increase in the ranks of those who demanded independence.

Such incidents were hardly conducive to a settlement of the controversies laid bare at the Round-Table Conference. Not only did Anglo-Indian relations become bitterer than at any previous time, but the Moslem-Hindu rift widened rapidly. Bloody religious outbreaks occurred in Bombay, Calcutta, and other large cities. Eventually the All-India Moslem League repudiated the violence of the Hindu Nationalists and denounced the extreme demands of the All-India National Congress. The Moslems and Hindus apparently agreed on only one important point, and that for different reasons: they both decided to boycott the expected third Round Table.

The impasse sorely tried the patience of the British and in June 1932 Sir Samuel Hoare, secretary of state for India in the National Cabinet, announced that the British Government itself would devise a solution for the minorities question, would then recall the Round-Table Conference to draw up an Indian constitution, and

---

[1] In this year British exports to India were one-third less than they had been in 1930. The economic depression added greatly to unrest and turmoil in the land.

would finally submit all decisions, in the form of a bill, to Parliament. This news was greeted in India with more riots but London proceeded according to plan. A third Round Table met in London late in 1932, but Gandhi, whom the viceroy refused to release so long as the civil-disobedience campaign lasted, was not a mem-

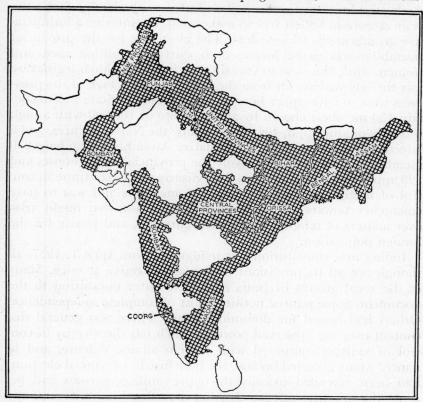

THE ELEVEN PROVINCES OF BRITISH INDIA

From Tschan, F. J., Grimm, H. J., and Squires, J. D., *Western Civilization*, 1942, courtesy of J. B. Lippincott Co.

ber. Before its adjournment, the conference drafted a definite constitution to replace the instrument of 1919.

The proposed new Indian constitution was published as a White Paper by the British Government in 1933. It was revised and favorably reported in 1934 by an India Joint Select Committee chosen from both houses of Parliament. After further amendment it became law as the Government of India Act on August 2, 1935, despite violent denunciation by British liberals and Indian

Nationalists. Four days later, Lord Linlithgow, chairman of the joint committee which had prepared the bill, was appointed viceroy.

The document provided for a central government and eleven provincial governments, the latter to carry the chief burden of domestic administration in British India. In the Native States the princes were to be left free to make whatever internal administrative arrangements they wished. The electorate for the provincial assemblies was to be increased to thirty-five million men and women, while the right to vote directly for the national legislature was entirely withdrawn from the Indian people. Five of the provinces were to have upper houses. The Council of State was to contain 150 members chosen by an electorate of 100,000 with a high property qualification, 104 appointed by the Native Princes, and 6 selected by the viceroy. The Legislative Assembly was to have 250 members chosen for five years by the provincial lower houses and 125 appointed by the princes. The viceroy was to continue in control of foreign relations and defense measures and was to have emergency powers to deal with domestic crises that might arise over matters of religion, minorities, currency, and justice for the foreign population.

India's new constitution was inaugurated on April 1, 1937, although not all its provisions were made effective at once. Many of the vocal groups in India expressed bitter opposition to the document. Some wanted nothing short of complete independence. Others had hoped for dominion status. There was general discontent over the "reserved powers" which left the viceroy in control of matters connected with foreign affairs, defense, and finance.[1] Many objected because the franchise in provincial elections had been extended to only thirty-five million persons and because the minority safeguards reacted to the disadvantage of the large Hindu majority.

The lead in opposition was taken by the Indian National Congress (largely Hindu) whose members now had a choice of two leaders. Gandhi still retained his influence with the moderate elements who, though dissatisfied, were ready to take every advantage offered by the law of 1935 in a campaign for further reform. The more impatient group followed the young Pandit Jawaharlal Nehru who believed in complete independence to be obtained through obstructionist tactics. Nehru, the president of the con-

[1] When the Legislative Assembly in 1936 voted one rupee to maintain the army, the viceroy was able to proclaim the government's original bill.

gress, had also come to be politically radical. In 1936 he informed his colleagues that he regarded socialism as the only solution for India's ills. This stand resulted in a further split among the Indians, for Nehru's attitude appealed to many among the masses, but alienated the sympathies of others—especially landlords and industrialists—who had actively supported Gandhi in his anti-British campaign.

In the voting of 1937 the National Congress Party gained control of six of the eleven provincial assemblies. This result seemed to astonish even the Nationalists and apparently induced Gandhi to take a more radical view. At any rate, he now endorsed the Delhi Resolution which Nehru pushed through the congress and which bound congress deputies not to accept ministerial posts in those provincial assemblies in which they had a majority unless the governors gave advance assurances that they would not use their special powers to set aside any legislative decisions. It was obviously illegal for the governors to make any such promises, a fact which the Nationalists eventually admitted when the Congress Working Committee authorized its deputies to accept ministerial office. The governors, for their part, with Viceroy Linlithgow's approval, agreed not to intervene "capriciously" or in "day to day" administration.

The first rupture over the interpretation of "day to day" administration came in 1938 when the ministries of Bihar and the United Provinces resigned because the respective governors had refused to permit the unqualified release of some political prisoners. A few days later the Indian Congress met and both Gandhi and Subhas C. Bose, the newly chosen president, threatened further resignations and a new campaign of civil disobedience. Lord Linlithgow now brought forward a compromise which was acceptable to the congress, and the protesting cabinets soon returned to office. It was agreed that the two governors in question would accept the advice of their ministries concerning the fate of these political prisoners, but only after an individual examination of each case.

In 1939 India witnessed increasing tension among three contending elements. The viceroy favored the gradual application of the law of 1935. Gandhi's followers advocated continued negotiation with the British—for the early achievement of dominion status. The adherents of Bose, who had been reëlected congress president, demanded more direct action for the immediate creation of a radical independent state. In April 1939 Gandhi recaptured his influence in the congress when Bose resigned, making way for the moderate Dr. Rajendra Prasad. The stalemate among the three groups, however, persisted through the summer. Following the outbreak of hostilities in Europe, Linlithgow announced that the final settlement of India's status must await the outcome of the war. Once again the provincial assemblies under congress control (now numbering eight) resigned (October 1939) and Gandhi threatened civil disobedience until an "acceptable" British declaration of war aims respecting India was forthcoming.

PALESTINE

In July 1922 the League approved the assignment of Palestine to Great Britain as a Class A mandate. At that time the Holy Land had a population of 757,000, including 600,000 Moslem Arabs, 83,000 Jews, and 73,000 Christian Arabs. The large Moslem majority was sorely disappointed to find that the terms of the mandate specifically confirmed the Balfour Declaration of 1917 whereby Great Britain had promised to establish in Palestine "a national home for the Jewish people." The Arabs found little consolation in the parallel promise that "nothing shall be done which may prejudice the civil and religious rights of existing non-Jewish communities." They failed to see how the arrangement fitted in with Great Britain's wartime promises of Arabian independence or with Wilson's theory of self-determination.

The first British High Commissioner, Sir Herbert Samuel, promulgated a constitution for Palestine in September 1922. It provided for a high commissioner, a commander-in-chief, and an appointive executive council. There was also to be a legislative council, consisting of the high commissioner and twenty-two deputies. Ten of these were to be appointed by the commissioner and the remaining twelve (eight Moslems, two Christians, and two Jews) were to be elected. The Moslems, however, refused to vote at elections for this council and Samuel was obliged to govern with the aid of an appointed advisory council. In 1940 the legislative process still consisted in the publication of draft ordinances which might be criticized by the several elements of the population; the government then promulgated the decrees with such amendments as it had decided to adopt.

The discontent of the Arabs with political, economic, and religious conditions crystallized in a violent anti-Jewish outbreak in 1929. Several Jewish communities were attacked and many

Jews were killed. The MacDonald Government rushed warships and airplanes to the scene and order was restored within a few weeks. A British commission of inquiry established as the cause for the rioting "the Arab feeling of animosity and hostility toward the Jews, consequent upon the disappointment of their political and national aspirations, and fear for their economic future." A report issued by the League Mandates Commission, however, claimed that the outburst was directed as much against Great Britain as against the Jews and blamed the British for failure to provide adequate military and police protection.

The Arabs did enumerate specific grievances against both the authorities and the Jews. They complained that the land legislation, by enabling the Jews to buy up large portions of the none-too-plentiful arable soil, was threatening the existence of thousands of Arabs. They objected to the government's favorable attitude towards Jewish immigration, for by 1930 the number of Jews had almost doubled. And they did not like the type of immigrant who entered Palestine. Most of the entering Jews came, or fled, from Poland, Russia, and Romania. They were usually poor and, so claimed the Arabs, frequently radical. It was certainly true that relatively few Jews of means attempted to settle in the Holy Land. The wealthy Jewry generally preferred to contribute financially to the upbuilding of the homeland and to foster Zionism by proxy.

A further Arabian-Jewish dispute involved the Wailing Wall in Jerusalem. At this wall, supposedly a relic of Solomon's Temple, the Jews had been accustomed to worship and to mourn. Since the wall adjoined a sacred Mohammedan shrine, the Mosque of Omar, there was great opportunity for strife whenever religiously excited Jews and Moslems appeared for worship simultaneously at the neighboring holy spots. So serious did this Wailing-Wall situation become that the British Government in 1930, with the approval of the League Council, appointed a commission, consisting of a Swede, a Swiss, and a Netherlander, to find a solution for the problem. In 1931 the commission reported that the wall and its adjoining pavement were Moslem property, but that, with certain restrictions, the Jews should be granted free access to the wall. These recommendations were at once put into effect by the high commissioner.

Meanwhile the British Government had come into sharp conflict with the World Zionist Organization and the Jewish Agency for Palestine. In May 1930 the authorities had indefinitely suspended immigration permits already issued to more than two thousand prospective Jewish immigrants. The ban was imposed pending a study of Palestinian economic conditions by a commission under Sir John Hope Simpson. The commission issued its report in October 1930 and simultaneously the British Colonial Office published a White Paper which announced a new official policy in the future administration of the mandate.

The White Paper maintained that too much haste had been shown in the upbuilding of the Jewish homeland and that, as a result, the future welfare of the Arabs had been jeopardized.

The condition of the Arab fellah [said the paper] leaves much to be desired, and a policy of land development is called for if an improvement in his conditions of life is to be effectd. The sole agencies which have pursued a consistent policy of land development have been the Jewish colonisation organisations, public and private. The Jewish settlers have had every advantage that capital, science and organisation could give them. To these and to the energy of the settlers themselves their remarkable progress is due. On the other hand, the Arab population, while lacking the advantages enjoyed by the Jewish settlers, has, by the excess of births over deaths, increased with great rapidity, while the land available for its sustenance has decreased by about 250,000 acres. This area has passed into Jewish hands. . . . It can now be definitely stated that at the present time and with the present methods of Arab cultivation there remains no margin of land available for agricultural settlement by new immigrants, with the exception of such undeveloped land as the various Jewish agencies hold in reserve.

Further, according to the White Paper:

It is only the closest coöperation between the government and the leaders of the Arab and Jewish communities that can prevent Palestine from drifting into a situation that would imperil, on the one hand, the devoted work of those who have sought to build up a Jewish National Home, and, on the other, the interests of the majority of the population who at present possess few resources of their own with which to sustain the struggle for existence.

Obviously, close coöperation between Arabs and Jews was impossible so long as the Arabs felt that Jewish immigration was depriving them of land, work, and political power. For, as the Simpson Report pointed out, the Jewish Foundation Fund, which leased land to Jewish colonies, had forbidden Arabian labor on its soil and the General Federation of Jewish Labor had adopted a policy of importing Jewish workmen rather than employing landless Arabs. In these circumstances Great Britain felt justified in continuing the suspension of immigrations.

The declaration of this new British policy was gratifying to the Arabs. But the Jews, both within and without Palestine, were angry. Dr. Chaim Weizmann resigned as president of the World Zionist Organization and the Jewish Agency. The British Government was accused of the "cruel and unfair betrayal" of a "harassed people." Even leaders of the Conservative and Liberal parties attacked the Labor Government for what they designated as a repudiation of the Balfour Declaration. The MacDonald Government, however, insisted that it was simply striving to carry out the threefold task of giving the Jews a national home in Palestine (not of making Palestine a Jewish national home), of dealing fairly with the large Moslem majority, and of preparing the land for eventual self-government.

In 1932 the government of Palestine eased its restrictions against further immigration and permitted free entry to any farmer, merchant, or business man who possessed a minimum capital of $2500. Each month, also, a quota of Jewish laborers was admitted, for the economic progress of the land was remarkable. Jewish capital to the extent of many million dollars flowed into the Holy Land and scientific methods were applied to agriculture and industry. Electrification proceeded rapidly through the efforts of the Palestine Electric Corporation. A large hydroelectric plant was constructed, utilizing the waters of the Jordan and Yarmuk rivers. A well-backed corporation was formed to extract the salts dissolved in the Dead Sea. A Hebrew University was opened in Jerusalem in 1925 and plans were laid for establishing a Moslem University in the same city. Harbor facilities were improved at Jaffa and Haifa. There was little unemployment and the Palestinian budget showed a substantial surplus. The total of land acquired by Jews in Palestine in the fifty-five years ending in 1937 was about 325,000 acres.[1] The rise to power of the National Socialists in Germany brought a new wave of Jewish migration to Palestine and additional worry to Arabian leaders. By 1937 the Jews numbered 400,000 out of a population of 1,400,000. Thus their proportion in the population rose from 11 per cent in 1922 to 28 per cent in 1937.

[1] About half of this was acquired before the British occupation in 1922. The area of cultivable land in Palestine has not yet been definitely determined; it is generally estimated to be about 2,000,000 acres. In the opinion of Zionists and of some British officials, Palestine, whose total area is 10,400 square miles, could support 3,000,000 people.

In 1936 the triple conflict among Arabian nationalism, Zionism, and British imperial interests once more became violent. The Arabian leaders late in 1935 had presented a list of demands asking for democratic government, the cessation of land sales to Jews, a law to protect small cultivators against loss of land through debts, complete suspension of Jewish immigration, and strict watch over illegal entry and residence. The refusal of the authorities to adopt this program led to renewed anti-Jewish riots and violent strikes in 1936. London thereupon appointed an investigating commission to ascertain the underlying causes of the disturbances, find out whether anyone had legitimate grievances against the way in which the mandate was functioning, and make any pertinent recommendations. In November 1936 the commission, headed by Earl Peel, began its sittings.

The Peel Commission conducted hearings for two months. All sides were listened to—Jews, Moslem Arabs, and Christian Arabs. At the conclusion of one particularly exciting session, Peel was said to have remarked that there was no such word as "compromise" in the East! The commission then returned to London to prepare its report on the basis of "a small mountain" of evidence plus the knowledge of Palestine's importance to Great Britain as an air and military base, as containing the terminus of an oil pipe line from Mosul, and as one of a number of strategic points from which to dispute Mussolini's claim to "our sea." The British had also to consider the effect of any decision upon the attitude of the Jews in the event of another war and upon the numerous Moslems scattered throughout the other portions of the British Empire.

The report was approved by the British Cabinet and made public in 1937. The commissioners declared that "the obligations Britain undertook towards the Arabs and the Jews some twenty years ago . . . have proved irreconcilable, and as far ahead as we can see, they must continue to conflict. . . . We cannot—in Palestine as it now is—both concede the Arab claim to self-government and secure the establishment of the Jewish National Home." Inasmuch as "neither race can fairly rule all Palestine, each race might justly rule part of it. . . . Partition offers a chance of ultimate peace. No other plan does."

It was therefore proposed to end the mandate and divide the country into three parts: (1) a new Jewish state occupying about one-fourth of the area of Palestine and extending southward from the Syrian border; (2) an Arabian section including most of the remainder of Palestine in union with Trans-Jordan; and (3) a neutral area, under British administration, of about five hundred square miles including Jerusalem, Bethlehem, and other holy places and extending westward as a corridor to the sea at Jaffa. Great Britain was also to remain responsible for Nazareth and the Sea of Galilee in the Jewish state because of their religious associations, and for the towns of Haifa, Acre, Safad, and Tiberias in the Jewish area because of their mixed populations. The Jewish and Arabian states were to be proposed for League membership but were to retain an alliance relationship with Great Britain similar to that of Egypt and Iraq. Each country was to control its own finances and the Arabian state was to receive subventions from both Great Britain and the Jews. Each state might frame its own immigration laws and an exchange of populations might be arranged.[1]

The plan aroused protests from all sides. The Jews once more raised the cry of betrayal. The Arabs claimed that "the richest zone is to be given to the Jews, the holiest to the British, and the most barren to the Arabs." Some Arabs again became violent, stimulated by Italian encouragement. It was reported that Italian radio sets were being distributed among the Arabs and certainly anti-British broadcasts emanated from the Italian sender at Bari.[2] Moderate Arabs who pointed to advantages in the Peel Plan were the victims of murderous attacks, while new strikes broke out, and a British district commissioner was assassinated. Scores of Arabian leaders, some of them non-Palestinians, were jailed or deported. Meanwhile the unrest had reacted to the disadvantage of economic life, with much attendant suffering for the mass of the population.

The British Government had declared its purpose to carry out the plan, but in the face of so much criticism the House of Commons hesitated. It ordered the submission of the whole matter to the League for further consideration and requested the government then to report back with a more definite scheme, not necessarily incorporating, but "taking into full account" the recommendations of the Peel Commission. The League Mandates Com-

---

[1] Viscount Samuel, former high commissioner, declared that "from the Jewish state as now proposed, one-third of the Jews of Palestine would be excluded, and within it would be included one-fourth of the Arabs."

[2] In 1938 the British Broadcasting Company inaugurated Arabic programs to counteract the Italian broadcasts. The British confined their broadcasts to news reports and music.

mission recommended another study of the entire Palestinian affair, a suggestion which was endorsed by the League Council and Assembly.

Early in 1938 another commission, headed by Sir John Woodhead, was directed to draw up a "more precise and detailed scheme" than the Peel Plan for solving the Palestine riddle. The Woodhead Commission was unanimously opposed to the earlier partition proposals, chiefly because it appeared impossible to recommend boundaries for the suggested areas that would afford a reasonable prospect of the eventual establishment of self-supporting Arab and Jewish states. The British Government thereupon decided once more that "the surest foundation for peace and progress in Palestine would be an understanding between the Arabs and Jews" and hence invited to a conference at London representatives of the Palestinian Arabs, the Arabs of neighboring states, and delegates from the Jewish Agency for Palestine.

This news came at a time when Great Britain had found it necessary to send many more soldiers to Palestine in an effort to restore order. For months Palestine had now been the scene of bomb outrages, attacks from ambush, and guerrilla warfare, and the British attempt at curbing native violence was costly in lives to both sides. Leader of the "rebel" Arabs, who demanded the end of Jewish immigration and the establishment of a Palestine-British treaty relationship similar to that enjoyed by Egypt and Iraq, was Haj Amin el-Husseini, Grand Mufti of Jerusalem and president of the Arab Higher Committee.[1] Although the mufti had fled to Syria, he obviously remained in contact with his followers. The latter, moreover, attacked moderate Arabs, who were willing to seek a compromise solution, as fiercely as they attacked Jews or British guards. During the period of the European crisis over Czechoslovakia the rebel campaign was intensified, the loss of lives continued, and the misery of the masses became worse. At last, in February 1939, the London conference on Palestine was opened by Premier Chamberlain. But because the Arab delegates refused to sit in the same room with the Jews, Chamberlain had to extend his official greetings in two sections!

The Arabs demanded the formation of an independent Arab state tied to Great Britain by treaty only, denunciation of the Balfour Declaration, prohibition of further Jewish immigration, and immediate stoppage of land sales to Jews. The Jews took an

[1] It was proposed that the Arabs and Jews have proportionate representation in the parliament of the new state.

opposite stand on each point. For a month the British, negotiating separately with the two groups, tried to find a compromise position, but to no avail. Then the meetings were suspended and soon the conference closed.

Meanwhile, to quiet certain Arab claims, London had published the so-called Hussein-McMahon correspondence. Sir Henry McMahon, said the Arabs, had in 1914–1916 promised Hussein, sherif of Mecca, that the Allies would establish a free Arabia in return for help against the Turks. The British maintained that Palestine had not been included in the promised state, but the Arabs held that there had been no such reservation. Unfortunately the publication of the letters did not settle the difference, there still being room for doubt as to whether or not Palestine came within the scope of the agreement. Apparently the two principals of the correspondence also differed in *their* interpretations.

In the spring of 1939 the British published a White Paper advancing another plan for Palestine. Both Arabs and Jews, however, opposed the plan and resorted to violence to lend emphasis to their protests. Rapidly losing patience, the British next announced the suspension of Jewish immigration for six months beginning October first. But any further progress in the direction of a final settlement was checked by the outbreak of the Second World War in September.

CHAPTER XIII

Unhappy France

POLITICS IN THE THIRD FRENCH REPUBLIC

The political structure of the Third Republic was somewhat different from that of other parliamentary systems. There were a few parties, particularly radical parties, that had definite organizations and party funds and held periodic conventions. In addition, there were numerous political groups which, though they had none of these characteristics, were listed under special names and were entitled to representation on parliamentary committees, provided they had a certain minimum number of adherents. The national legislature customarily contained from ten to fifteen such groups, with fewer groups in the upper than in the lower house.[1]

Since, in view of this situation, it was difficult for any one group to command a majority in the Chamber of Deputies, the government functioned through a system of coalitions or *blocs*. Frequently the make-up of a bloc was based upon a few major issues, and, when new issues arose, group realignments followed. Hence the average life of cabinets in France was short. By July 1940, when it came to an end, the Third Republic had had 110 ministries. Some degree of stability in governmental policies was nevertheless maintained by the presence of permanent undersecretaries and because the ministerial changes often involved merely a shuffling of portfolios.

During the war and until November 1919 France was governed by a bloc which assumed the name of "Sacred Union." After the elections of 1919 the union split into two other coalitions, the *Bloc National* and the *Cartel des Gauches*. The Bloc was made up of conservatives and moderates led by Clemenceau, Poincaré,

[1] The conservative groups in the legislature, as in most continental parliaments, were seated to the right of the Speaker, the moderates in front of him, and the radicals to his left. Hence the designations "Right," "Center," and "Left" indicated the general political stand of any group or party.

Alexandre Millerand, and Briand. It hoped to reduce Germany to economic bondage and make France secure, was opposed to socialism, and favored friendly relations with the papacy. The Cartel was led by Edouard Herriot. This group was anticlerical, favored higher income taxes and an extension of state social control, proposed to reduce the power of the Senate, and, while fully as anxious as the Bloc to give France security, advocated a liberal foreign policy, including friendship with Germany and Russia. Independent of these coalitions were the socialists and communists on the left and the *Camelots du roi* or royalists, led by Léon Daudet, on the right.

The powers of the French President were strictly limited in practice and he exercised far less control than the chief executive of the United States. "For all his ordinary prerogatives, the president was completely at the mercy of one minister or another." [1] Yet, if he happened to possess a dominating personality, the president might exert considerable influence on the course of politics. Poincaré, for example, was certainly more than a figurehead during his incumbency from 1913 to 1920.

When Poincaré's term expired, the National Assembly elected Paul Deschanel in his place. Clemenceau was a candidate in this election, but his popularity suffered in a general nationalistic dissatisfaction over the presumed moderation of the Versailles Treaty. Indeed, he soon heard himself called not *Père la Victoire,* but *Perd la Victoire!* In September 1920 Deschanel retired because of illness and was succeeded by the able and conservative Millerand.

Unfortunately for his tenure of office, Millerand tried to take a part in legislative as well as executive affairs. In 1922, for example, he virtually forced a Briand Government out of office and in 1924 he took the unusual step of having a presidential petition read before the Chamber of Deputies. During the parliamentary elections of 1924 he openly supported the Bloc National, one of whose founders he had been. When the Left came into power in 1924, therefore, Millerand was forced to resign. The next president was Gaston Doumergue—bachelor, lawyer, ex-magistrate, former president of the Senate, and a Protestant. Though himself a member of the Left, he was equally cordial to all parties and his charm and honesty won for him the confidence of most Frenchmen. In 1931, at the close of his seven-year term, the sexagenarian

---

[1] Under Article 8 of the Constitutional Law of July 16, 1875, however, the president was endowed with considerable treaty-making power.

Doumergue left the presidency to marry and retire to private life. Little could he realize, at the time, that he would be called upon within three years to accept the premiership in a grave national crisis.

In 1931 the National Assembly, dominated by the Right, chose Paul Doumer, president of the Senate, to succeed Doumergue as chief executive. Doumer's closest rival for the honor was Briand, but the latter lost many conservative votes because he was supported by the socialists and because his moderate foreign policy had aroused the ire of the nationalists. Like so many other French officials, Doumer had begun his career as a radical. Maturity, however, and a settled income tended to make him conservative in later life. He was well known in financial circles, had at one time been a colonial governor, and had twice been minister of finance in Briand cabinets.

To the sorrow of his countrymen, Doumer was assassinated in 1932 by a Russian émigré, Paul Gorgoulov, who in some mystic way hoped by the deed to help free Russia from Bolshevik control. Once more the Senate and the Chamber met together to select a president. This time the choice fell on Albert Lebrun, who earlier had succeeded Doumer as head of the upper house. The new president, whose parliamentary experience dated from 1900, had political sympathies similar to those of Poincaré. Reëlected in 1939, it was his lot to be in office when France collapsed in 1940.

THE FRANC AND ITS SAVIOR

In international affairs the attitudes of all postwar ministries in France were determined by a desire to make the republic secure against foreign aggression. French foreign policy, therefore, was an "integrated foreign policy of colonial empire, to guarantee tropical supplies and supplement a stationary domestic man power; of European alliances to hold the *status quo* and insure that if war came it would be fought on several fronts; and of support of the League to stay the crumbling of the Versailles Treaty, to provide that the alteration of existing public law be orderly and gradual, and to afford a forum in which world opinion might be won for the French case." [1] In carrying out this policy, some leaders, such as Poincaré and Tardieu, were generally unyielding; others, notably Briand and Herriot, were conciliatory. Nevertheless, since the same end always was kept in view, there

[1] Hill, H. *The Spirit of Modern France*, 1934, p. 22.

was a marked degree of unity in French foreign politics.[1] On domestic issues, however, and especially in economic and clerical matters, the various cabinets held divergent opinions.

When the war came to a close France was in domestic chaos. The northern tenth of the country had been reduced to wasteland. Farms, villages, mines, houses, factories, wells, public buildings, railway lines, roads, and private possessions had been laid in ruins. In their stead were barbed-wire entanglements, shell holes, débris, charred remains, trenches, ammunition dumps and duds, poisoned wells, and flooded mines. Almost 300,000 private houses and more than 6000 public buildings had been destroyed, and 435,000 houses together with 11,000 public structures were damaged. Two million persons had been forced to leave their homes. The number of wrecked factories totaled 20,000.

It must occasion little wonder, therefore, that in 1919 the army was restless, the laborers in the cities were clamoring for bread, and the middle class was afraid of the spread of communism. So great was the apprehension among conservative peasants and middle-class burghers of violence and disorder that the Bloc National was victorious in the elections of 1919 and moderate government thus was ensured at least until 1924.

Financial difficulties soon arose to plague the Bloc. Confidently expecting that Germany would be made to pay the total cost of reconstruction, the government, while refusing to raise the tax rate, spent billions on the restoration of devastated areas. The total value of expenditures assessed against a special reconstruction budget was estimated at $7,000,000,000, most of this money being raised through loans and the printing of paper money. Month after month went by, however, and the expected sums from Germany were not forthcoming. Indeed, late in 1921, as we have seen, Germany asked for a partial moratorium. The French conservatives, led by Poincaré and Tardieu, therefore agitated for the downfall of Premier Briand, who had come to the head of the government early in 1921. They succeeded in their endeavors (1922) and Poincaré soon assumed the chief ministerial post.

Raymond Poincaré was born in 1860 in Lorraine. He was an able lawyer and financier, was exceedingly energetic, and had a lucid and logical mind. Short and stocky, with a high voice and a cold manner, he won the respect of the French people through sheer ability and personal honesty. He gained a cabinet position for the first time in 1893, was many times premier, and from 1913

[1] See Chapter VIII.

to 1920 was president of the republic. Alternately showered with praise and abuse, he steadfastly pursued the goal of a powerful and secure France. "Nicknames were fastened upon him— Poincaré la Guerre, Poincaré la Ruhr—but without any parade he kept on his logical course."

The new premier floated foreign loans, introduced financial reforms, and raised the taxes, yet the inflated franc continued to decline in value and the budget remained unbalanced. Many of the *rentiers* who had been living on incomes from bond investments and who now found themselves facing starvation because of their shrinking real wealth lost all confidence in the government. Poincaré's tactics in the Ruhr, moreover, and his favorable attitude towards the papacy were also unpopular. The parties of the Left consequently hoped to overthrow him at the next election and promised the voters financial reform, greater reliance on direct taxation, closer coöperation with the League, and a more conciliatory foreign policy. In the balloting of 1924 the Left won control of the Chamber of Deputies and ex-Professor Herriot of Lyon, leader of the group called Radical Socialists, became premier. Despite their name, the Radical Socialists were liberals and not Marxists. They professed a firm faith in the republic and desired above all to ensure prosperity and security at home and abroad.

Herriot was the idol of Lyon, having been mayor of that city for a score of years. Even while prime minister he spent two nights a week on trains, commuting between Paris and Lyon in order that he might attend to both his national and municipal duties. He appeared sincere and honest but was inexperienced in national politics and for a time injured his reputation by his complete informality.[1]

In its foreign policies the Herriot Ministry was fairly successful. It accepted the Dawes Plan, established more cordial relations with Great Britain, the Soviet Union, and Germany, and took part in the framing of the Geneva Protocol. It was less fortunate in its domestic policies. Hence, when the Senate in 1925 refused to countenance further inflation, the ministry resigned. Some troublous months followed in which Paul Painlevé organized two ministries, Briand three, and Herriot another one. The franc continued to drop in value and by July 1926 was worth about 2 cents,

---

[1] "Think of the life of a man like Herriot who, simultaneously, has been President of the Council [premier], Minister of Foreign Affairs, Deputy, Mayor of the second largest city of France, President of the Radical-Socialist Party, and still finds the time to publish delightful literary works."

that is, one-tenth óf its prewar quotation. Government bonds sold below par and old loans matured faster than new ones could be floated. At this crisis group lines in the Chamber were effaced and a National Union Ministry was formed, headed by Poincaré and including six ex-premiers. The veteran prime minister now remained in office for three years, until July 1929. In these years he earned the title of "Savior of the Franc."

Poincaré speedily informed the legislature that financial salvation could be obtained only through increased taxation and stringent economy. Since the deputies had at last come to be in a reasonably receptive mood, new taxes were voted. The French people had to submit to one of the highest tax rates in the Western world, the imposts absorbing from 20 per cent to 22 per cent of the national income. The problems presented by the huge floating debt were solved by an Autonomous Fund Commission which paid off the short-term notes, consolidated and refunded other issues, and in some cases reduced the interest rate from 6 per cent to 3 per cent. Surplus local courts, prisons, and treasury offices were closed and the number of army officers was reduced.

In 1926 the budget was balanced—for the first time in thirteen years. There was, in fact, a small surplus. The franc consequently rose in value and by December 1926 was worth 4 cents. It was stabilized at this level in 1928. This action constituted a virtual repudiation of approximately four-fifths of the internal debt, for it reduced the value of prewar and war bonds to about 20 per cent of their original par rating. In the elections of 1928 the policies of Poincaré were upheld by vote of the people. Unfortunately for his successors, however, the power in the lower house was almost equally divided between Right and Left. Both groups, coöperating in the National Union, supported him, but when illness forced his retirement a year later (July 1929) they fell to quarreling.

SEVEN TRYING YEARS, 1929–1936

Following Poincaré's resignation several short-lived ministries struggled with the difficult financial and diplomatic problems. First came a government under Briand, but it fell on the questions of finance, the adoption of the Young Plan, and the evacuation of the Rhineland. Briand was succeeded by Tardieu, a journalist who had come into prominence as an assistant of Clemenceau and a follower of Poincaré. Since Briand entered this new cabinet as foreign minister, it appeared that the Tardieu Government might combine Poincaré's domestic firmness with a conciliatory foreign program. But the delicate balance in the parliament made matters difficult and Tardieu soon had to form another cabinet. Since this was recruited largely from the Right, the Left persistently voted adversely on whatever measures came up for action. In the summer of 1930 the premier ensured an extension of the life of his ministry by bringing about an adjournment of the Chamber.

Despite the handicap of an uncertain tenure of office, much was accomplished by the Tardieu ministries. Perhaps the outstanding domestic achievement was the final passage of an insurance law which went into effect on July 1, 1930. Frequent attempts had been made during the previous nine years to enact such a law and in 1928 one had actually been adopted. But certain technical difficulties stood in the way of enforcement and these were not removed until two years later. The act provided for the compulsory insurance against sickness, invalidism, old age, and death of all (about nine million) men and women between sixteen and sixty engaged in industry, commerce, agriculture, and domestic service, and earning less than a stipulated minimum. This minimum ranged from $600 to $1000, depending on the personal status and place of residence of the worker. The insurance system was to be maintained by contributions from employers and workmen (in each case equal to 3 per cent of the individual's wages) and by supplementary state contributions.

Under Tardieu, in addition, taxes were reduced, the term of military service was cut from three years to one, and the size of the army was diminished. The war budget, however, was considerably expanded so that new fortifications might be built and impressive maneuvers held on the Italian and German frontiers. Through the influence of Foreign Minister Briand the Young Plan was ratified, the evacuation of the Rhineland was completed, and the French scheme for a Pan-European federation was announced.

Now, in the German elections of September 1930 the nationalistic parties received an unexpectedly heavy vote. This occasioned a severe reaction in France because the German nationalists were the most determined opponents of the Versailles Treaty and the Young Plan. Many Frenchmen therefore became panicky over what they called Briand's weak foreign policy. Poincaré emerged once more to complain that, though it was pleasant to listen to "international hymns to the divinity of peace," France also needed "other things" to give her a "feeling of security." Hence, when the parliament met again, many of Premier Tardieu's conservative supporters turned against Briand. In December 1930 the government fell, on a senatorial interpellation as to its general policy. The occasion for the challenge was a bank scandal which appeared to involve several cabinet officers and undersecretaries.

Senator Théodore Steeg thereupon organized a government which proved to be perilously weak. Because it included Briand it failed to obtain the full support of the Right; it was opposed by the socialists for its attitude on financial and military matters. The situation was made still more complex for the premier by the world-wide depression which, beginning in 1929, had gradually come to make itself felt even in France—where the even balance between industry and agriculture had hitherto staved off the hardships attendant upon decreasing trade and increasing unemployment. Steeg gained a breathing spell by dismissing the legislature for the Christmas recess (1930) at his first parliamentary appearance, but when the chambers reconvened he was immediately ousted. He had been in office six weeks.

Another senator, Pierre Laval, next formed a cabinet (January 1931). An effective orator and clever politician, Laval, although only forty-seven years old, had already held the portfolios of public works, justice, and labor. His chief support came from the Right and he entrusted both Briand and Tardieu with ministerial posts. He remained premier for more than a year, but during this period he had to reconstitute his cabinet three times.

In domestic affairs the Laval cabinets faced a number of vexatious problems. Unemployment figures rose steadily, the volume of exports continued to decline, and there were faint prospects of a balanced budget. When serious financial losses threatened some of the most important business enterprises in the land, the government fought strenuously to win over the parliament to its view that the state was obligated to rescue such ventures from bankruptcy. In accord with this policy a credit was extended to the French Line (*Compagnie Générale Transatlantique*) and funds were advanced to the Bank of France so that it might withstand the losses incurred through the depreciation of its sterling holdings when Great Britain went off the gold standard. Important matters of international concern also arose to tax the patience of Premier Laval. It was during his incumbency that France interposed so strenuously against the projected Austro-German Customs Accord of 1931 and that she accepted, in modified form, President Hoover's plan for the temporary suspension of all inter-governmental-debt payments. Early in 1932 a delegation was sent to participate in the Geneva Disarmament Conference.

As time went on, Laval leaned more and more heavily on his conservative supporters. This circumstance became sharply evi-dent in January 1932 when Briand's place in the foreign office was taken by the premier himself, presumably because of the former's illness.[1] And soon thereafter Laval fell, in consequence of a senatorial interpellation on an electoral law which, had it been passed, would have reacted to the advantage of the Right in the forthcoming elections. Tardieu now became premier for the third time.

The elections of May 1932 betrayed a decided leftward swing of popular sympathies. The Radical Socialists, still led by Herriot, captured 160 of the available 614 deputies' seats and became the largest group in the Chamber of Deputies. The liberals and radi-cals had effectively pointed out during the campaign that the rule of the Right had bequeathed the country an empty treasury, a high unemployment figure, a heavy burden of military expendi-tures, and huge financial losses through state loans to bankrupt private firms and unstable foreign governments. Moreover, the voters apparently had not been in sympathy with Laval's and Tardieu's departures from the conciliatory principles of Briand's foreign policy.

Tardieu resigned after the election and was succeeded by Her-riot. As had been his lot in 1924 and for two days in 1926, Herriot once more came to power at a time of fiscal and economic distress. The value of French exports in the month of the elections had been lower than in any month since the war. The decline in the price of wheat made the farmers irritable. The number of civil employees on the national pay roll had increased enormously since 1914 and yet the government dared not dismiss any of its servants. Unemployment figures were rising to an unusual height for France, while income-tax receipts fell rapidly. In external affairs, the cabinet had to consider the Lausanne Reparation Conference and the Geneva disarmament parleys.

To meet the most urgent of these developments, the Herriot Government proposed and the parliament adopted a new budget which considerably reduced expenditures and increased taxes. Government bonds to the value of 85,000,000,000 francs and bear-

[1] Briand died on March 7, 1932.

ing from 5 per cent to 7 per cent interest were converted and the interest rate was lowered to 4½ per cent. Tax evaders, of whom there appeared to be many, were prosecuted, and, finally, a public-works program was undertaken.

It appeared in the autumn of 1932 that Premier Herriot might continue for some time to hold the confidence of a majority in the parliament. Yet he soon found it necessary to resign. The issue upon which the ministry fell was the war-debt question. Herriot urged that France meet the instalment of about $19,000,000 due the United States on December 15. But the deputies felt that France had renounced enough in the Lausanne Agreement [1] and that it was now up to the United States to make the next sacrifice. The government's motion to make the payment was defeated and the cabinet resigned (December 1932).

In the next thirteen months France had five ministries. Each of the premiers struggled to balance the budget while yet avoiding inflation and keeping France on the gold standard. The tariff was progressively raised, civil-service salaries and pensions were cut, and there occurred a limited amount of price-fixing. In December 1933 there came to light a municipal-pawnshop scandal in Bayonne, involving a notorious swindler named Alexandre Stavisky, who somehow had come to be director of the pawnshop. It soon appeared that a number of government officials were implicated in the scandal, which cost French investors millions of francs. Excited mobs in the larger cities demanded immediate action to find and punish the guilty. When the rumor spread that attempts were being made to cover up the crime, France was on the verge of revolution.

Certain other factors, however, besides the Stavisky scandal, had caused the French people to become restive. There had been a railway accident at Lagny in consequence of which about two hundred persons, many of them bound home for the Christmas holidays, had lost their lives. Popular opinion blamed the disaster on the negligence of the railway company and its failure to comply with the official safety regulations. Once again the investigation lagged and it appeared that the fixing of responsibility might be evaded.[2] Many persons, moreover, had become weary of the factiousness of the Chamber. It was felt that the deputies, blind to the urgent needs of the country, haggled and bargained and upset

[1] See pp. 164–165.
[2] The Lagny wreck and the Stavisky affair were only the worst of several commercial accidents and financial scandals.

ministries, instead of adopting constructive measures to cure the national ills. Consequently there had been a growing demand that the authority of the president and cabinet be strengthened and that the lower house be deprived of some of the powers given it by the constitutional laws of 1875.

During the third and fourth weeks of January 1934 there were violent demonstrations before the Palais Bourbon, where the deputies met. The participants were royalists, socialists, communists, civil employees protesting against pay cuts, a group of "Young Patriots," and a fascist war-veterans' association called *Croix de Feu*. On February 6 Premier Daladier attempted to protect the deputies from intimidation by placing troops and policemen around the Palais Bourbon and along its approaches. There was little excitement during the day, but at night the crowds became violent, property was destroyed, and a conflict ensued between the populace and the guards. On the following day the fighting spread to many other large French cities. In this crisis President Lebrun called upon ex-President Doumergue to leave his retirement and form a government that would place patriotism above politics and save the country from civil war.

Doumergue acted on this request and organized a cabinet which included leaders from all groups save the royalists, socialists, and communists. Among the members of the new government were Herriot, Laval, Tardieu, and Marshal Pétain of Verdun fame. There was a general belief that this ministry would restore order, strengthen the executive, and ensure security against foreign aggression. Hence there was a lull in the wave of demonstrations. The deputies, in chastened mood, awaited the government's proposals.

A budget for 1934 was adopted and the government was empowered to reduce expenses and change tariffs by decree. Commissions were appointed to investigate the various scandals and disasters and to report on the events of February 6. The number of civil servants was reduced by some tens of thousands and the salaries of the remainder were reduced by from 5 per cent to 10 per cent. Special military arrangements were made to compensate for the decline in the number of recruits occasioned by the lowered birth rate in the war years.

Despite these accomplishments the Doumergue Government faced criticism. In the parliament, the socialists, led by Léon Blum, voted against most of the cabinet's measures. Outside parliament, the Croix de Feu, led by Colonel François de la Rocque, and other so-called fascist groups threatened "action" if reforms in government were not soon forthcoming. Resentment was caused by the state's failure to fix responsibility for the Lagny incident, by the official whitewashing of the affair of February 6 in which eighteen persons had been killed, and by the failure to solve various riddles connected with the Stavisky swindle which continued to bring in its train suicides and possibly murders.[1]

In September 1934 the premier outlined his plans for constitutional reform. He proposed to give the cabinet exclusive right to initiate money bills, advocated a curb on the organization of civil servants, and wanted power delegated to the prime minister to dissolve the Chamber of Deputies without the consent of the Senate. This last suggestion was upheld on the ground that the deputies would be slower to upset ministries if there could be held over their heads the constant threat of a new election. To the Leftist groups in the parliament these reforms represented the setting up of a dictatorship. The cabinet, they said, must remain under the control of parliament, not parliament under the control of the cabinet.

The heated discussions aroused by Doumergue's plans, the increasingly bad economic situation and the high cost of living, the fears of socialists and communists that reactionaries were planning to seize the reins of government by force, the continued recurrence of political riots, the apprehension over the approaching plebiscite in the Saar, and then the assassination at Marseille of King Alexander of Yugoslavia and Foreign Minister Barthou,[2] all made the situation tense and the position of the ministry insecure. Another crisis was precipitated when Doumergue, withholding the proposed new budget from the Chamber of Deputies, requested that body to vote provisional credits for the first three months of 1935. Thereupon several members of the cabinet resigned and the Doumergue Ministry fell.

Another coalition cabinet soon was formed (November 1934), this time by Pierre-Etienne Flandin. Its political complexion was less Rightist than had been that of its predecessor, for it included neither Tardieu nor Pétain. Laval was entrusted with the task of carrying on the foreign policies of the deceased Barthou. Flandin, apparently more interested in tackling the economic problems of the country than in immediate political reform, concentrated his

---

[1] "In the summer of 1934 automobiles were still to be seen in Paris carrying on their windshields the inscription, 'Je ne suis pas député.' "

[2] Discussed later in connection with the Hungarian revisionist movement.

energies upon the delicate task of formulating a budget. In the spring of 1935 he appealed to the deputies for full power to do whatever he thought necessary to balance the budget and fight the depression. The answer was a vote of no confidence.

Pierre Laval then became premier on June 7, 1935. On the following day he was given extraordinary powers to take measures "in defense of the franc." He thereupon reduced governmental salaries and pensions, lowered the returns on national securities, raised the tax on incomes and on munition manufacturing, inaugurated new public works, lowered certain rents and the prices of some commodities, and appointed a committee to find ways for stimulating foreign trade.[1] These acts slightly relieved the financial strain but aroused much opposition. There was a growing demand for the devaluation of the franc as a means of stimulating foreign trade and there was an increasingly restless activity on the part of several antiparliamentary leagues, chief among which was the *Croix de Feu,* claiming a membership of one million. Laval dissolved several of the smaller leagues but was unable to retain his control. In January 1936 he was succeeded by Albert Sarraut (Radical Socialist), who formed a stopgap ministry which lasted through the elections of April–May 1936.[2]

The parties of the Left (chiefly Radical Socialists, Socialists, and Communists) combined to fight the election campaign as the Popular Front. They denounced fascism, urged the nationalization of munitions manufacture, and promised to "break the power of the two hundred families who control the economic life of the nation." They undertook to stimulate production, were opposed to devaluation in principle, were friendly to Great Britain and the League, and upheld a strong military program. The voters gave 381 seats (62 per cent of the total) to the Popular Front and the remaining 237 seats to the candidates of the Right and Center. The Socialist Party formed the largest single group in the chamber and its leader, Léon Blum (1872–   ), a well-to-do Parisian Jew of great legal and some literary renown who had first entered parliament in 1919, organized a government on

[1] The recruiting age was changed and the terms of military service for the period 1935–1938 were lengthened by laws of 1935 to compensate for the smaller number of available conscripts born in the First World War years.

[2] Two ballots, on successive Sundays, were generally required in the parliamentary elections. On the first ballot a candidate, to be successful, had to win a majority of the votes cast in his constituency. A plurality sufficed on the second ballot.

June 4, 1936.[1] The Communist Party, led by Maurice Thorez, refused representation in the cabinet but agreed to support Blum.
For the first time in French history, three women were taken into
the cabinet as undersecretaries.

THE POPULAR FRONT

During its year of office the Popular Front Government encountered many political storms. The first was an immediate epidemic of "sit-down strikes" in which about one million workers
"occupied" their places of employment (standing with folded arms
and later sitting and lying down) in newspaper plants, automobile,
aircraft, textile, and munition factories, department stores, butcher
shops, and so forth. Transport, lighting, and food services were, in
general, unaffected, so that the public was not seriously incon-
venienced. The real reasons for this demonstration are not clear,
but perhaps the proletariat wanted to make sure that the government would fulfill its election promises to labor. Certainly the
authorities were impressed by the evidences of discipline in the
strikes: the committees, the methods of provisioning, the military
efficiency.

Blum called representatives of both the employers and the
workers to a conference at the Hôtel Matignon (the new official
residence of the premier) and there managed to effect a temporary
settlement. Although both sides violated the agreement, the
government soon enacted its provisions into law. The new legislation provided generally for a forty-hour week without pay reduction, collective bargaining, the closed shop, paid vacations, wage
increases, and a form of compulsory arbitration in labor disputes.
These things brought some satisfaction to the workers but further
alienated many worried business men.

By the end of 1936 the Popular Front had also fulfilled the rest
of its campaign program. The Laval pay cuts were restored and
the pittance to soldiers was increased. The coal industry was reorganized and a national wheat office was created to control the
price of breadstuffs. Relief was provided for farm mortgagors and
small-business men who needed credit, and the public-works pro-

---

[1] Blum emerged as a popular figure when a group of royalists in February 1936
pulled him out of an automobile and severely beat him. President Lebrun had
thereupon decreed the dissolution of the two leading royalist societies, the *Camelots
du Roi* and the *Action Française*.

gram was expanded. The franc was devalued by approximately 30 per cent, probably because the new social legislation was believed to have increased the cost of production by about 35 per cent. The press (often corrupt) was required to publish its sources of revenue and the government was empowered to expropriate arms factories at prices to be fixed by arbitration. Finally, the Bank of France was reorganized so that the government secured more control while the so-called Regency Council, composed of the two hundred largest stockholders, was deprived of its direct powers.

In the matters of defense and foreign affairs, the Polish and Yugoslav alliances were renewed, the military and naval forces were strengthened, and the lead of the British was followed with respect to the Spanish situation. The sympathies of the voters who had elected the Popular Front were evidently with the Spanish "Loyalists." They could see no reason why the French Government should imitate the British and not permit the legal sale of arms to the legally constituted Madrid Government. It therefore required all Blum's oratorical skill to convince his supporters of the advisability of following Great Britain's example, particularly in a Europe so full of powerful dictatorships.

With the opening of the year 1937 it was apparent that the Popular Front Government, having achieved the aims which held its component parts together, must simply "coast along," hoping that no great issue would arise to disturb its equilibrium. In the spring unemployment figures were down to 380,000 and a large internal loan was successfully floated. Labor was, on the whole, temporarily satisfied and the conservative elements became less restive upon the promise of a legislative "pause." Blum now also agreed to place control of the Exchange Equalization Fund in conservative financial hands and refused the demand of Léon Jouhaux, leader of several million trade unionists (in the *Confédération Générale du Travail,* or C. G. T.), for a 10,000,000,000-franc public-works loan. The much-heralded and oft-postponed opening of the Paris Exposition occurred in 1937 and the exhibits attracted large crowds of natives and foreigners during the summer. The relative domestic quiet of the first half of 1937 was seriously disturbed only by a fight in the Parisian suburb of Clichy between some followers of de la Rocque and some local radicals.[1] The police intervened roughly against the leftists and Blum therefore had to rely

---

[1] The Blum Government had dissolved the *Croix de Feu* in June 1936, but Colonel de la Rocque then organized the *Parti Social Français* which claimed a membership of two million about the time of the Clichy incident.

once more on his persuasive oratory to calm his more radical supporters.

In the end, the financial situation proved to be the nemesis of Premier Blum as it had been that of so many of his predecessors. The interest charges on the public debt consumed more than one-third of the government's income when Blum took office, and during his incumbency the situation had not improved. In June 1937 Blum therefore requested broad powers to deal with the financial crisis. The Chamber of Deputies agreed but the Senate twice refused its assent. The premier therefore resigned and was succeeded by Camille Chautemps, a Radical Socialist. Blum entered the new cabinet as vice-premier.

THE LAST YEARS OF PEACE, 1937–1939

The Chautemps Government further devalued the franc, declared a moratorium on gold payments, temporarily closed the stock exchange, and announced the prolongation of the social-legislation "pause." The parliament thereupon voted to give Chautemps the extraordinary financial powers which it had denied to Blum, and the cabinet approved heavier direct and indirect taxes, increased import duties, higher telephone, telegraph, and postal rates, steeper tobacco prices, and an increase in passenger and freight rates to cut the annual railway deficit which had to be made up by the state.[1] Public works expenditures were curtailed and the franc was allowed to drop to the level which it sought for itself. In the fall of 1937 the authorities frustrated a plot on the part of an armed secret society, Les Cagoulards ("The Hooded Ones"), to overthrow the republic and reëstablish a monarchy. The forty-hour-week law was modified, with greater consideration for specific, particularly seasonal, industries. And at the close of the year a strike of public-utility employees in Paris was ended after one day, owing chiefly to the government's threat to call the strikers to the colors and order them, as soldiers, to carry on their jobs.

When 1938 opened, France appeared to enjoy relative domestic

[1] In the late summer of 1937 the entire French railway system was reorganized. Beginning January 1, 1938, all French railroads—whatever their previous status— were brought under the control of the Société Nationale des Chemins de Fer Français, over which the government exercised considerable supervision. It was thus hoped simultaneously to increase the efficiency of the service and reduce (eventually remove) the operating deficits.

calm, but Chautemps soon found it necessary to organize a new ministry, composed almost entirely of Radical Socialists. He would have nothing to do with the communists, while the socialists, having defeated a motion of Blum to participate in the cabinet, nevertheless promised their parliamentary support to the new, minority government. Chautemps now placed all activities of the war, marine, and air ministries under the supervision of a political leader, called "minister of national defense," and a military leader, called "chief of staff of national defense," the first such chief being General Marie Gustave Gamelin. Then Foreign Minister Yvon Delbos emphasized the need to coöperate with the League and Great Britain, hold fast to the alliances with the Soviet Union and the smaller states of central and Balkan Europe, and induce Italy to agree to a nonintervention program in respect of Spain. Though these policies were endorsed by the deputies, the Chautemps Ministry fell in March 1938 when the socialists and communists refused the premier's request for renewed emergency financial powers.

Since the overthrow was caused by the Left, President Lebrun asked Léon Blum to try to form another government. This Blum attempted to do, first, by asking all groups to coöperate in a national-union ministry, but when the Right and Center rejected his plea, he formed another Popular Front Ministry—without communist participants. The Radical Socialist, Daladier, became vice-premier and minister of national defense, while a journalist named Louis Oscar Frossard became France's first minister of propaganda. This time the Blum Cabinet lasted less than a month. The premier resigned when the Senate refused to follow the example of the lower house in voting him emergency financial powers similar to those which Chautemps had demanded one month earlier. Thus, again and again, the French Parliament, unable itself to cope with the country's financial difficulties, refused special powers to the premiers: the Chamber denying them to the rightists, the Senate, to leftists. And meanwhile Germany had absorbed Austria, and General Franco, with German and Italian aid, was extending fascist influence along the southern borders of France.

Blum now was succeeded (April 1938) by his former vice-premier, Daladier, who had risen above the popular ill will aroused during his premiership in 1934 when the Stavisky and other "affairs" threatened to bring on revolution. It had not been lost on Daladier that during the senatorial debate preceding

Blum's fall, the upper house had indicated its readiness to give emergency financial powers to *a* premier, but not to *Blum*. It had also become clear, by this time, that the Senate was veering further and further away from the principle of collective security in European international affairs and becoming reconciled to the idea of bilateral agreements with Hitler and Mussolini, in line with Chamberlain's policy of appeasement. Hence Daladier appointed a cabinet composed only of Radical Socialists and two centrists. There was not a socialist or communist in this "anti-Red" ministry, as it came to be called, and the portfolio of foreign affairs was entrusted to Georges Bonnet, known to be lukewarm towards the Soviet alliance. Now the parliament readily granted its government plenary powers and adjourned.

Thereupon appeared a lively succession of governmental decrees. All national taxes were immediately increased. The various state budgets were unified into one simpler and clearer whole. New credits were assigned to measures for national security and a defense loan was quickly oversubscribed by the public. A minimum was set to which the franc would be allowed to fall, and almost at once there was an appreciable return of capital to France. Easier credit facilities were made available to business and a sizable public-works program, including slum-clearance and housing projects, was outlined. Over the objection of the General Confederation of Labor, the forty-hour work week was modified, and, finally, the army was enlarged. In the face of an approaching foreign crisis, these measures appeared to win popular approval.

A pleasant interlude in political affairs was furnished by the visit to Paris of Great Britain's sovereigns in July 1938. But two months later the whole national life was caught in the web of events that accompanied the German demand for an immediate solution of the Sudetenland problem. This story of disaster which befell one of France's earliest postwar allies, Czechoslovakia, is dealt with in later pages. Be it said here, however, that the French people, in response to the orders of the government, faced the prospect of war and the actual preparations for an early armed conflict with a grim calmness and a fatalistic resignation that must have astonished as much as it delighted the authorities. When the crisis had passed, the Chamber overwhelmingly endorsed the conduct of the cabinet, though this, in effect, represented a virtual repudiation of France's whole postwar diplomacy.

This vote of confidence clearly indicated the breakup of the Popular Front, for the communists alone had voted against Daladier's conduct of diplomatic affairs. The split was widened when, in response to the premier's demand for further plenary powers, the request was granted through the votes of the Right, the Center, and the Radical Socialists. The socialists abstained and the communists voted "no." In November 1938, finally, the Radical Socialist Party specifically dissociated itself from the Popular Front. The latter henceforth ceased to be a moving factor in French politics.

The Radical Socialists' decision to quit the Popular Front reflected the rightist influence of Paul Reynaud who, in a reshuffling of the cabinet, had secured the portfolio of finance. His influence was further evident in a set of thirty-two cabinet decrees issued in November 1938 as the skeleton for a three-year plan and in a score or more of supplementary decrees.

The reasoned basis for the decrees was presented in a "General Report" submitted to the president of the republic by Messrs. Daladier and Reynaud. The decrees themselves, affecting labor, finance, and the national economic life in general, were acceptable to the conservatives but were denounced by Léon Jouhaux on behalf of the trade unionists and by the union of war veterans. The latter objected to the reduction in pension payments. The former feared the doom of the forty-hour-week system. Technically the principles of the earlier hour legislation remained in effect; but employers were permitted, in the interest of increased production, to extend the work week by a maximum of ten hours and to set the overtime pay at a figure only slightly higher than that for regular work. On the other hand, the government levied a tax of 10 per cent on the profits made by employers through this overtime labor.[1]

There now broke out a series of strikes during which the police and mobile guards engaged in violent clashes with the workmen. When the labor confederation threatened a general stoppage of work, Daladier called the strikes "political" and indicated that he would take proper measures to check them. Jouhaux and his assistants chose November 30, 1938, for a one-day general strike, whereupon the government mobilized the workers and civil servants and ordered them, as soldiers, to carry on with their jobs. This maneuver proved successful, especially in Paris and northern

---

[1] In 1937 a parliamentary Committee of Inquiry on Production investigated the causes of and suggested remedies for France's production lag. The committee reported in December 1937 and some of its recommendations were incorporated in later decrees on production and employment. For the report see Langsam, W. C. *Documents and Readings in the History of Europe Since 1918*, 1939, pp. 446–453.

France, and many men refused to obey the strike call. Although both sides, as often happens in such cases, claimed victory, the strike was not "general" and the government did fine or imprison a number of persons who had quit work despite the mobilization order. There was, however, little bloodshed, because Jouhaux enjoined his followers to avoid violence and because Daladier arranged to have the soldiers and guards placed in strategic but not obtrusive or challenging locations.

Meanwhile a fresh international complication had arisen: the demand loudly voiced in the Italian Chamber of Deputies on November 30 for the acquisition of French-controlled Tunisia and, indeed, even Corsica, Savoy, and Nice. Despite their advocacy of appeasement, Daladier and Bonnet seemed as firmly determined as any Frenchman to resist Italy's demands for French-controlled areas. The premier, in fact, took the occasion to make a triumphal tour of France's Mediterranean and North African possessions, being everywhere greeted with demonstrations of loyalty.

Although he endorsed the Chamberlain policy of appeasing the totalitarian regimes and although he had allowed his Foreign Minister Bonnet to sign a vague declaration of amity with Germany at Paris in December 1938, Daladier became convinced, after the absorption of Bohemia and Moravia by Nazi Germany in March 1939, of the need to build up the military strength of France. Almost immediately thereafter Daladier asked his parliament to pass a five-line bill granting his cabinet full power for eight months to rule by decree. The legislature quickly complied with his request, though he had refused to make any promises regarding what he might or might not do with his authority. The government at once proceeded to convert France into a "workshop of national defense."

Decree now followed decree, and the premier gradually came to be looked upon as a new "strong man" on the European political stage. The hours of labor in French industry were generally increased to fifty per week and might be raised to sixty or more if, in the opinion of the government, the national welfare so demanded. The press was placed under strict control. The army was further enlarged and General Gamelin was made commander-in-chief with unusually wide powers. The index of production went up, the national debt increased, prices rose, and unemployment virtually disappeared. The conservative Albert Lebrun, with Daladier's backing, was reëlected president. Finally, the life of the parliament was extended to 1942, and thus the regular quadren-

nial election which should have taken place in 1940 was eliminated.

The French people in general, it seemed, were content to have
the government take so firm a hold of affairs and put at least a
temporary stop to time-wasting debate and argument. Even Blum
endorsed Daladier's position, in principle, if not on every specific
point. Hence, when war came, in September 1939, France had
the outward appearance of a well-functioning economic and military machine.[1]

FRANCE AND THE PAPACY

Interesting among the cultural developments in postwar France
was the partial reconciliation of the government with the Catholic
Church. In 1901 and 1905 the French Government, controlled by
anticlericals, had greatly curtailed the number and activities of
the religious orders; had closed monasteries, convents, and some
of the church schools; and had nationalized the church property.
One of the effects of this policy had been a decrease in the number
of French missionaries who, going abroad, might have carried
overseas French culture along with Roman Catholicism. Besides,
trouble had been caused at home, for some of the faithful Catholics
joined the monarchists in agitating against the Third Republic.
Indeed, a monarchist-Catholic organization, *L'Action Française,*
had been formed to advocate the restoration of monarchy and the
reëstablishment of a state-supported Catholic Church.

After the war, in order to advance French interests abroad and
end quarrels at home, the French authorities gave evidence of a
willingness to resume cordial relations with the papacy. The
Vatican proved equally amenable to negotiations, for a *rapprochement* obviously would strengthen the position of the church not
only in France but wherever French culture was being implanted.
Moreover, L'Action Française now had come under the domination of a philosophical skeptic and an advocate of violence in
political life, Charles Maurras, many of whose works were placed
on the Catholic Index of Forbidden Books. Naturally the church
did not care to continue an alliance with Maurras.

The steps in the process of reconciliation were gradual. In 1919

---

[1] On September 26 the Daladier Government dissolved the Communist Party in
France and forbade communist propaganda. The basis for this action was the
signing of a petition by some communist leaders objecting to French military action
against the recently formed Nazi-Soviet "front."

Clemenceau nominated an Alsatian bishop. In the following year the French Government sent a representative to take part in the ceremonies attending the canonization of Joan of Arc. In 1921, after a lapse of seventeen years, diplomatic relations between France and the Vatican were restored and soon thereafter France permitted a number of religious orders to return. In 1927 the publications of L'Action Française were placed on the Index and some time later the archbishop of Paris issued an edict virtually excommunicating Catholics who remained affiliated with that monarchist group. The complete restoration by the state of the clerical property previously nationalized also received consideration, especially from the Right groups, but the anticlericals forestalled this final concession.

THE PROBLEM OF ALSACE-LORRAINE

When, eleven days after the conclusion of the armistice of 1918, French troops crossed the Vosges Mountains into Alsace-Lorraine, they were greeted with banners, triumphal arches, and kisses. Most of the people appeared to be happy that the "lost provinces" were freed from German control and reunited with a victorious France.[1] Troubles, however, soon followed. The newly recovered provinces and their motherland quickly found themselves at issue over questions of language, religion, political rights, and economic opportunities.

When France regained the provinces only about one-fourth of the natives habitually spoke French; the remaining three-fourths used any one of five German dialects. This situation had existed for centuries: under the rulers of the *ancien régime,* under Napoleon and his successors, and under the German emperors from 1871 to 1918. Yet, after the war, the French, feeling that only French-speaking people could be genuine patriots of the republic, tried to force their language on the provincials. German, therefore, was barred from all schools. The opposition to this attempt at Gallicizing the inhabitants was so great that a compromise soon had to be reached. Eventually it was agreed that children would have to learn French exclusively only during the first two school years. Thereafter they might receive three hours a week of German

[1] Between 1871 and 1914 several hundred thousand people migrated from Alsace-Lorraine to France, while many Germans came to settle in Alsace-Lorraine. There were further large movements of population in 1918–1919 and 1940.

instruction and German might also be used in the periods that were given over to religious teaching.

Meanwhile the provinces had been flooded with railroad officials and civic functionaries who spoke only French. This situation led to a Lorraine railway walkout in 1919, the strikers demanding the removal of all railway officials and foremen who could not speak German. Said one of the strike leaders: "It wasn't worth while to get rid of the Germans if the French come and take all the good jobs." The strikers won their point.

A further quarrel between France and the provinces arose out of religious differences. Alsace-Lorraine was inhabited mainly by a staunch Catholic population, and under German rule the region had been permitted to continue the relationship with the papacy that had been established under the Napoleonic Concordat of 1801. The local government had paid the salaries of the clergy and religious instruction had been given in the schools. The Bloc National acquiesced in this arrangement until 1924, but when the anticlericals came into power Premier Herriot decided that since France had scrapped the concordat, Alsace-Lorraine should be required to do likewise. He therefore proposed to disestablish the church and prohibit religious instruction in the classrooms.

The Catholic school children thereupon went on strike and refused to return to their classes until Herriot receded from his position. A compromise again was reached. All children, regardless of faith, were to attend the same "interconfessional" schools for academic instruction, while religious classes were to be held in separate Catholic, Protestant, and Jewish schools. The Catholic Church was not wholly content with this solution of the problem and complained that some of the religious education was being delegated to anticlerical teachers. Nevertheless the settlement was adhered to and it appeared to work in a fairly satisfactory manner.

Under German rule the natives had enjoyed local autonomy. They had had a separate parliament since 1911 and Strasbourg had been governed by its own municipal council. This situation was respected for a time by the French and a commissioner-general was appointed to govern the provinces from Strasbourg. In 1925, however, the office of commissioner-general was abolished, the local parliament and the municipal council were deprived of their powers, and the whole administration was centralized in Paris. Thus was created another grievance, for the Alsatians and Lorrainers were unaccustomed to, and much annoyed by, the centralized French system. They could not understand, for example, why a peasant who wanted to build a fence on his property along a public highway might first have to get the consent of the minister of the interior. In the prewar years life had been far less complicated. Even more painful to the natives was the official abolition of the geographical designations of Alsace and Lorraine and the redivision of the provinces into the three new departments of the Upper Rhine, the Lower Rhine, and the Moselle.

Finally, there were economic grievances. From the material standpoint many of the natives had been better off under German control than they now were under the postwar French regime. The coal, iron, textile, and potash industries all had prospered more before 1918 than thereafter.[1] Although this situation gradually changed with the passing of years, the natural trade outlets and business connections of the provinces still were with Germany, and Lorraine iron ore could best be worked with German coal from Westphalia. The normal development of renewed trade relationships between Germany and the freed region was greatly impeded by the constant political bickering between France and Germany.

Annoyed by such a combination of political, economic, religious, and social grievances, the natives often found it difficult to uphold an appearance of loyalty to France. In 1926 a *Heimatbund* or Home League was formed which, particularly strong in Alsace, demanded local autonomy and priority for German in the schools. In 1927 the French suppressed three German newspapers in Alsace on the ground that they were advocating reunion with Germany. The year 1928 saw fifteen Alsatians tried for conspiracy and disloyalty, four of them being convicted. An Alsatian butcher, moreover, attempted to assassinate the French state's attorney who had prosecuted the alleged conspirators. As a result of this incident a number of French parliamentary deputies left the chamber when a member from Alsace, some time later, rose to speak.

The situation became so critical that Poincaré, during a parliamentary debate in 1929, delivered a ten-hour speech on the question of Alsace-Lorraine. He reviewed the history of the conflict between France and the provinces and intimated that the autonomist movement was receiving moral and financial support from "east of the Rhine." He admitted that France had made some errors but promised better conditions in future. Upon the conclusion of his speech, the Chamber of Deputies overwhelmingly

[1] By its transference, however, Alsace-Lorraine was spared the horrors of the German inflation period.

voted its faith in the patriotic attachment of Alsace and Lorraine to France.

Despite this official vote of confidence in their fidelity, the people of Alsace and Lorraine continued to feel unhappy. While they were at first glad to be reunited with France, they soon became as restless as they had been under the German regime. The rise to power of the German Nazis further complicated the situation after 1933. Perhaps the basic difficulty lay partly in the character of the natives. To judge from an old local rhyme, the Alsatians have long regarded themselves as being habitually discontented:

> Hans, Hans of Schnokeloch
> Has all that he desires;
> But what he has, he doesn't want,
> And what he wants, he hasn't got.
> Hans, Hans of Schnokeloch
> Has all that he desires.[1]

THE SYRIAN MANDATE

The experiences of France in her Syrian mandate, an important silk-producing area, were even more troublous than those in Alsace-Lorraine. Difficulties began almost from the moment that French control was extended over the region.

For administrative purposes and perhaps to prevent the development of any strong national feeling, the land was divided into five (later four) administrative areas, each with a different name and law system, but all subordinate to one high commissioner. Martial law was declared, a censorship was established, and French became the language of the law courts. Much of the gold in Syria was drained away and a paper currency was introduced which fluctuated with the depreciated French paper francs. The Moslems, who comprised a majority of the population, believed that the French were favoring the Christian minority.

In 1924 High Commissioner General Maxim Weygand, a conservative Catholic, was removed at the insistence of the anticlericals in the Chamber of Deputies. He was replaced by General Sarrail, who antagonized the Christians as well as the Moslems and who crowned his administrative efforts in 1925 by inviting the leaders of some discontented Druse tribes to Damascus for a parley and then putting them in prison when they accepted the call.

[1] *Alsace-Lorraine: A Border Problem,* Foreign Policy Report, February 1930.

Thereupon the Druse tribesmen broke into open revolt. The French captured some of the rebels and, as a warning to other obstreperous natives, displayed in the public square of Damascus the corpses of twenty-four persons whom they had shot. When the city populace thereupon became enraged and attacked some French auxiliary troops, the latter were withdrawn from Damascus and the city was bombarded by artillery and bombed by airplanes. Many people were killed and the city was partially ruined. The Damascenes were required to pay a fine of $440,000 and to surrender three thousand rifles.

Sarrail was recalled and late in 1925 Senator Henri de Jouvenel was appointed to succeed him. Before de Jouvenel arrived in Syria the French subordinate officials had permitted the arming of Christians and thus paved the way for additional atrocities. The new governor tried to negotiate with the Druses but refused their demand for a "peace conference" since this would have implied recognition of their status as belligerents rather than insurgents. Early in 1926 hostilities were resumed. Damascus was again bombarded. The Permanent Mandates Commission thereupon issued a report criticizing French policy and condemning recourse in mandates to such expedients as air bombardments, incendiaries, destruction of villages, and collective fines except "in cases of absolute necessity." De Jouvenel now was replaced by Henri Ponsot who soon crushed all remaining armed outbreaks. But the discontent, particularly in the rural districts, and the demand for autonomy did not abate.

In 1928 Ponsot convened a Syrian Constituent Assembly to draw up an instrument of government for the mandate. When the nationalist delegates, who were in a majority, insisted on the establishment of an independent republic, the gathering was suspended *sine die*. In 1930 the commissioner himself issued a constitution, setting up a republic restricted only by the mandatory powers of France and by French control of its foreign affairs. The document also provided for a parliament and for a president who was always to be a Moslem and was to be chosen by the parliament for five years.[1]

The first elections under this constitution were held amid great disorder in 1932. Owing, it was asserted, to the interference of the French, the elected deputies included fifty-four members of the

---

[1] This constitution did not apply to Great Lebanon, an area which had earlier been given a republican charter of its own. The population of the entire mandate in 1939 was about 3,100,000 and the area 60,000 square miles.

Moderate Party and only fifteen representatives of the Nationalist
Party, the latter being opposed to the continuance of the mandate.
To the accompaniment of further violence, the parliament elected
the wealthy Ahmed Ali Bey el-Abed president of the republic.

Ponsot was succeeded as high commissioner in 1933 by Damien
de Martel. Late in the same year de Martel and the Syrian Premier
signed a treaty of friendship which provided that, after a four-year
transitional period, France would recommend Syrian membership
in the League of Nations. For a period of twenty-five years, however, France would continue to exercise supervision over Syrian
foreign, military, and financial matters. When it became clear that
the Syrian Parliament would not approve the document, the high
commissioner withdrew it and suspended the legislature. (The dis-
affection of the Syrians was not entirely owing to political reasons.
The economic situation of the mandate had become increasingly
bad during the depression years, as evinced by an alarming drop in
its foreign trade.)

In September 1936 France and Syria signed another treaty, this
one providing for the latter's independence after a probationary
period of three years. Exactly one month after the signing of the
document, Turkey requested that a politically autonomous regime
be set up in the new Syria for the sanjak (district) of Alexandretta,
including the city of Antioch and inhabited by a large proportion
of Turks. The matter was referred to the League Council and a
settlement was reached after some months. Alexandretta, it was
agreed, should remain under the sovereignty of Syria, with the
latter controlling its foreign relations and customs. The district
was, however, to enjoy internal autonomy, with its own legislature
and with Turkish as the principal official language. These principles were incorporated in a Statute and Fundamental Law and a
League commission was dispatched to Alexandretta to prepare for
elections in the spring of 1938.

The Turks objected to the commission's methods which, it was
claimed, would give them only a minority in the local assembly.
Rioting occurred and the League commission was eventually
forced to retire from the area. The critical situation in Europe in
the spring and summer of 1938 induced both Paris and Ankara to
seek an early settlement of the affair and in July a new Franco-
Turkish agreement was signed in the Turkish capital. The document dropped all reference to the League and provided that Alexandretta should become "an autonomous State under Franco-
Turkish administration, with French and Turkish troops as a joint

defense force." Thereupon Turkish soldiers equal in number to the French entered the sanjak, and new preparations were begun for the election of an assembly.

Elections were duly held and in September 1938 the first assembly convened. Its 40 members comprised 22 Turks and 18 Arabs, Armenians, and Greeks. On September 6 the assembly adopted for its constituency the name of Republic of Hatay.[1]

The new state was destined to have only a short life. As the European situation became more critical in 1939, both Great Britain and France became more interested in gaining assurances of Turkish friendship in the event of trouble in the eastern Mediterranean. The British negotiated an accord with Turkey providing for mutual assistance in case of attack. A similar treaty was signed by Turkey with France, but the latter had to pay a price. On the date of the treaty signature, June 23, 1939, France ceded to Turkey most of the republic of Hatay. A small section, inhabited largely by Armenians, was returned to Syria, and Turkey promised in future to remain aloof from Syrian questions. The Hatay Parliament accepted the transfer and voted itself out of existence.

Syria protested against the cession, claiming that France had no right to give away mandated territory. Germany and Italy joined in the protest (on the ground that the treaty violated the League Covenant!) and the Permanent Mandates Commission censured France. But Paris remained firm. The Franco-Syrian Treaty of 1936, moreover, was not ratified by the French Parliament, owing to France's desire to remain entrenched in the eastern Mediterranean area. When renewed rioting broke out in Syria, the mandate's constitution was suspended and the French High Commissioner assumed full control. Such was the situation when the Second World War began.

FRANCE AND THE FRENCH

France emerged from the First World War tired, but capable of a quick return to power. Enjoying a balance of industry and agriculture, and with half of her population engaged in farming, France was virtually self-sufficient in the matter of food supply. Moreover, there was a fairly even distribution of wealth in the land because the national inheritance laws provided for an equal

---

[1] Hatay is the Turkish name for the district and bears an obvious relation to Hittites, whom the Turks look upon as their ancestors. Hence Turkey's reluctance to allow the region to fall into the hands of a future independent Syria.

division of the father's estate among the children. The resulting large number of petty proprietorships furnished a strong undercurrent of popular stability, especially since the peasants were acutely aware of their importance to the state.

French industry made great strides after the war. The American and British wartime port installations were a permanent asset, as were the river, canal, and railway improvements. The French learned much from American experts and greatly bettered their methods and machines. Keen foreign competition eventually led even the individualistic French manufacturers to realize the value of trust combinations, especially in the chemical, textile, and metallurgical trades. Numerous technical schools were established throughout the country, with a consequent extension of technical and mechanical skill.

The French Government was noted for its intelligent and consistent business regulation. The state exercised considerable supervision over big business and the national commercial code required all corporations to divert specified portions of their earnings to reserves. The bankruptcy laws "were so severe that they made the bankrupt business man an actual outcast." At times of labor shortage foreign workers, usually from Poland, Italy, Spain, and Belgium, were invited—but nearly always under contracts which required them to return home when there was no more work for them. In this way unemployment was kept down to a minimum. Because of the official restrictions and the temperament of the people, there occurred no such overexpansion of industry as in postwar Germany. The French preferred, on the whole, to build their large industries "brick by brick out of earnings" rather than on credit.

The great depression affected France later than it did most other countries and found her in an enviable economic position. The unemployment figures, though large for France, were small when compared with those in other lands. The Bank of France had a gold reserve which was second only to that of the American Federal Reserve system. The sources of this wealth were the hoardings of the people; the savings entailed by the state through the repudiation of four-fifths of the domestic debt; the income from reparation payments, the tourist traffic, and shipping services; and the export of manufactures, chiefly luxuries. A sizable proportion of the wealth was manipulated in the traditionally skillful French manner to serve political as well as economic ends—to bind to France certain needy allies and to force political concessions from impoverished enemies. French foreign investments once more became noted for reaping diplomatic as well as financial dividends.[1]

No discussion of France could be complete without a word on the character of its people. To generalize about the French is difficult. George Meredith once spoke of them as "the most mixed of any European nation." Nevertheless, a few remarks may be risked.

The Frenchman, particularly the French peasant and the shopkeeper, was thrifty, prudent, realistic, and individualistic. Intellectual and economic self-sufficiency were his supreme desiderata; his dream was to have a little property and a little income from investments—not much, perhaps, but enough for comfort. To gain this end he would work unceasingly and deny himself pleasures and even necessities. He was suspicious, jealous, and "astonishingly void of sentiments when his interests were at stake." And "when at last he considered himself independent, with enough for his own wants, he ignored with beaming self-satisfaction everything that did not appertain to his own community, almost to his own person." The Frenchman's character was at one and the same time a fundamental reason for the power of his country and for its weakness. But it remained for the exigencies of the Second World War to lay bare this weakness.

[1] Most of the French investments abroad were in the form of short-term loans which could be recalled on demand and which, therefore, could be used as diplomatic levers.

CHAPTER XIV

Fascist Italy

THE REWARD OF VICTORY

Italy was the only major power among the victors to experience a complete change in its system of government soon after the First World War. This change, hastened by Italian disappointments at the peace conference, had its inception in the war years. There was, as we have seen, considerable disagreement among Italians in 1914 as to what course Italy should pursue in the struggle. The government issued a declaration of neutrality. The socialists, who had returned nearly eighty deputies to the Chamber of Deputies in the elections of 1913, endorsed this stand since they regarded the war as a capitalist enterprise. But there were many who, for material or emotional reasons, favored intervention. These groups, in the name of a "sacred egoism," finally brought about Italy's entry into the war in return for the offer of certain territories.

The Italians found the war more exacting than they had anticipated. About 5,500,000 men had to be mobilized and, of these, 700,000 were killed and 1,000,000 wounded. The net direct cost of the war to Italy was more than $12,000,000,000, while property damage amounted to an additional $3,000,000,000. Moreover, the rout at Caporetto in 1917 made the final victory of 1918 all the more emotionally exciting. In these circumstances, Victor Emmanuel's subjects were sorely disappointed not to achieve their desires in Dalmatia, Albania, the Near East, and Africa.

Reference has already been made to the problems encountered by the peace conference in dealing with the fate of Fiume on the east coast of the Adriatic. In order to encourage the Southslavs to break away from Austria in 1918 Italy, by the Pact of Rome, had made some general concessions to their ambitions in the Adriatic. But when it appeared, after the war, that one of the Slavic ambitions was the acquisition of Fiume, the Italians were enraged. Fiume came to have an emotional importance out of all proportion to its economic or strategic value. Histrionic effects were added to the situation when the poet, Gabriele d'Annunzio, led a band of black-shirted *Arditi* (shock troops during the war) to Fiume in a chartered boat and took the city by force—over the objections of the Supreme Peace Council and the inhabitants.

Giovanni Giolitti, who had become premier in 1920, deprecated such artificial nationalist stimulations and negotiated wth Yugoslavia the Treaty of Rapallo, whereby the independence of the free state of Fiume was recognized "in perpetuity." Soon thereafter Italian troops drove d'Annunzio's legionaries from their stronghold. The net result of the dramatic exploit was only further to infuriate the nationalists against the government.[1]

During the war, Austrians, Serbs, and Italians had fought on Albanian soil. Italian troops, moreover, continued to occupy the land for several months after the armistice. During this occupation the Italian delegates to the peace conference attempted to acquire Albania as an Italian mandate. By way of alternative, they were ready to agree to a partition of Albania among Italy, Greece, and Yugoslavia. The Italians were especially interested in the port of Valona, key to the forty-mile-wide Strait of Otranto. The Albanians, however, desired independence. Encouraged by Wilson's friendly attitude, they resorted to guerrilla warfare to drive out the foreigners. By the summer of 1920 Giolitti, preoccupied with domestic problems, signed a treaty withdrawing the Italian troops from all Albania save the island of Saseno. Italian nationalists bewailed this additional "inglorious page" in their country's history.

In the Near East, much of the territorial bait that had been held out to Italy either went to Greece or was retained by Turkey, the Italians receiving only some minor commercial concessions. In Africa, where Great Britain, France, and Belgium acquired the former German colonies, Italy got only small extensions to Libya and Somaliland. Despite the acquisition in Europe of about 8900 square miles of land and 1,600,000 people, therefore, the Italians accused their allies of "faithlessness." They were shocked and angry because "Italian achievements were being discounted and Italian imperialism denounced."

The nationalists flung uncomplimentary epithets at most of the diplomats at Paris. Then they turned against their own ministries,

[1] Neither the Italians nor the Slavs were satisfied with the arrangement and negotiations were resumed between 1922 and 1924. Eventually, by the Treaty of Rome (1924), Italy received the city of Fiume, while Yugoslavia received Port Baros and a fifty-year lease of part of the Fiume harbor.

accusing them of weakly consenting to the "mistreatment" of Italy. They blamed their older statesmen for the debacle whereby "the war had been won and the peace lost." Fiery young patriots referred to the "old men" as "parasites on the better blood of the nation" and vowed that they would re-create Italy in such fashion that the world would be "forced to sit up and take notice." Their new Italy would be "one of the nations without which it is impossible to conceive the future history of humanity."

Meanwhile the government faced a disheartening domestic situation. Millions of men had to be demobilized. It was impossible to find employment for many of the returned veterans because the nation's industry was demoralized, jobs had been filled by those who had remained at home, foreign markets were temporarily lost or closed, and foreign trade and tourist traffic were almost at a standstill. Even the "safety valve" of emigration was shut, owing to lack of funds at home and the restrictive legislation of foreign countries. The price of food rose quickly and there was the usual popular hatred of the war profiteers, called *pescicani* or "sharks." Budgetary deficits and currency inflation added to the general woes. To climax the particular troubles of the former soldiers, many of whom were economically and socially dislocated, military tribunals were set up to try as traitors those who had led the retreat at Caporetto.

In the elections of 1919 the socialists captured 156 parliamentary seats. These deputies consistently voted against government measures, thereby creating a parliamentary stalemate. The manifestations of discontent throughout the land soon took the form of violent strikes and riots. These were idly watched by the impotent authorities who apparently feared to call upon the army to restore order lest the soldiers fraternize with the people. Gradually Italy drifted toward radicalism. Socialism spread rapidly in city and country, owing in part to fantastic rumors regarding the marvelous changes being wrought by the proletarian rule in Russia and in part to the government's inaction. Shouts of "Down with the King!" and "Long live Lenin!" were frequently heard.

"Direct-action" schemes won increasing favor and many communes were seized by socialists. Peasant tenants refused to pay rent, large estates were broken up, ex-service men appropriated plots of ground, and numerous outrages, often economically unwise, were perpetrated. In some cities, when the employers announced their inability to continue in business unless wages were lowered and hours lengthened, the workmen themselves took over the factories. In the two years 1919 and 1920 a total of thirty-five million workdays was lost owing to strikes and disorders, and there was talk of the establishment of a dictatorship of the proletariat. Even the formation in 1919, by the Sicilian priest, Don Luigi Sturzo, of a new, moderately conservative, Catholic People's Party failed to stem the "Red tide."

But the period of factory and land "occupation" did not last long. The workers found it difficult to carry on without raw materials, without sufficient food, and without managerial experience. The peasants were illiterate and fundamentally conservative. The socialists split into right and left factions. The novelty of doing things as the Russians were supposed to be doing them soon wore off. A general feeling arose that a proletarian state might be no more able to cope with Italy's complex problems than was the existing weak regime. If neither the present parliamentary system nor a possible proletarian state could help Italy, then, wondered a large portion of the population, who should be entrusted with the government?

It so happened that the strife and violence of the war and postwar years had created bonds of sympathy among several important groups. Many landlords and property holders were much affected by the incidents of the brief reign of radicalism. They were determined that Italy should have a government strong enough to protect private property. Many university people, professionals, and young men were disgusted with the whole trend of events since 1914. They wanted to see a general governmental housecleaning and the emergence of a strong and patriotic administration. The nationalists and ex-soldiers were angered by the thought that the net result of their participation in the war might be an anarchic Italy. They, too, wanted to see new men at the governmental helm. At this critical moment Benito Mussolini came forward to seize control.

MUSSOLINI: FROM PRIVATE TO PREMIER

Benito Mussolini was born in Romagna in 1883. His father was a blacksmith, with socialistic leanings. His mother was a schoolteacher. Upon his mother's advice, Mussolini entered a normal school and eventually became a teacher. Dissatisfied with his lot and by nature rebellious and restless, he soon quit his position and went to Switzerland. There he did some studying, frequently finding it difficult to support himself. Eventually he obtained work on a socialist newspaper, but his activities in organizing labor and fomenting strikes led the Swiss Government to demand his departure. Returning to Italy for a time, Mussolini took up journalism, and then went to Austria. Once more his radical activities made it necessary for him to leave.

He came back to Italy, where he was kept under surveillance as a revolutionary. In 1911 he was arrested for agitating against the departure of troops for Tripolitania. In 1912, after some able speechmaking at a socialist congress, he became editor of *Avanti*, the official paper of the Italian Socialist Party. When the war broke out he favored Italian neutrality, but nationalism soon triumphed over socialism and he began to urge intervention. For this he was made to resign from *Avanti* and was expelled from the party. Thereupon he founded an interventionist paper in Milan, *Il Popolo d'Italia*, though he persisted for some years in calling himself a socialist.

When his class was called to the colors in 1915, Mussolini entered the army as a private. He served on the Isonzo front and rose to the rank of corporal. In 1917 he was sent to a hospital, wounded by the explosion of a trench mortar. Upon his recovery he was exempted from further military service so that he might return to the editorship of *Il Popolo d'Italia* and use its columns to combat the growing spirit of defeatism. Mussolini now displayed a dominating, magnetic personality. Though his voice was hard, he was an effective orator, adept in the use of short, crisp sentences. He had flashing black eyes, possessed both determination and imagination, and made the most of a supposed resemblance to Napoleon. He worked hard and paid much attention to matters of detail.

In 1919 Mussolini called a meeting of ex-service men and others who were interested in solving Italy's problems and anxious to defend her war record against the calumnies of a lot of "penitent Magdalenes." The meeting was attended by a colorful group of discontented agitators, many of whom had been affiliated some years earlier with societies known as *fasci d'azione*. These fasci had been organized as early as October 1914 by young "men of action" eager to have Italy join the Allies in the war. Within a few months more than one hundred fasci had been founded and vigorous methods of propaganda had been employed to win the country to the interventionist viewpoint. Mussolini had led the Milan fascio and his *Il Popolo d'Italia* had become the Fascist literary organ. Now, under Mussolini's guidance, these former

BENITO MUSSOLINI

interventionists reorganized themselves into *fasci di combattimento*.

The gathering adopted a revolutionary program which demanded proportional representation, a legal eight-hour day, a heavy capital levy and inheritance tax, confiscation of some church properties, abolition of the Senate, the calling of a national assembly to decide upon a new form of government, nationalization of the munition plants, the creation of economic councils with legislative powers, management of certain industries (such as railroads) by the workers, and outright annexation of Fiume and Dalmatia. The program was calculated to appeal especially to the returned soldiers, the "proletariat of the trenches." Said Mussolini: "During the war we all felt the incapacity of those who were governing us and we know that we won only by virtue of the Italian people, not by any intelligence or capacity on the part of the administration. Given the chance for a new regime, we must not be fainthearted. Therefore we are constituting the fasci, bodies capable of creative action and capable of going out in the squares and crying: 'It is we who have the right to succeed this government, for it was we who pushed the country into the war and led it to victory.'"

Despite the confidence of its leader, the cause of Fascism progressed slowly in 1919. In the elections of that year the two Fascist candidates for office in Milan, one of them Mussolini himself, polled fewer than five thousand votes. During the period of the communist factory occupation, the Fascist movement was dormant. With the end of the occupation, however, it took on a new life. Recruits came from among the property holders, the younger sons of business men and merchants, unemployed ex-soldiers who were grieved by the sneers at their wartime services, unoccupied ex-officers, and discontented professionals and students. The wealthier sympathizers seem to have made generous monetary contributions.

Filled with hatred for socialists and communists, the Fascists embarked upon a campaign of terrorization known as "squadrism." Castor oil, clubs, and guns were used to convert or dispatch the radicals. Upwards of a hundred "battles" were fought between the rivals from the summer of 1920 to that of 1921. The government watched the civil war with resignation, either because it was too weak to intervene or because it was glad to see communism destroyed.

Eventually the Fascists emerged triumphant. The "Reds" were divided among themselves, while the Fascists had gradually come under the domination of Mussolini's Milan group. The Fascists also conducted a vigorous propaganda campaign, using pamphlets, papers, books, and speeches in an attempt to convince patriots that they alone had saved the country from the horrors of Russian Bolshevism and that they alone could restore to Italy domestic security, prosperity, and international respect. In 1921 the Fascists, now with thirty-five deputies in parliament, constituted themselves the National Fascist Party. By this time, however, their program was much less radical than the one which had been adopted in 1919. During the fight against socialism the Fascists had given up their faith in the proletariat.

Following the lead of several other patriotic organizations, the Fascists now donned distinctive uniforms and adopted a ritual. Apparently because a large number of d'Annunzio's black-shirted followers had joined the Fascists, the latter decided to adopt the black shirt. They patterned their ceremonial after old Roman customs and chose the Roman salute. The *fasces* or bundle of rods enclosing a battle ax, as carried by the lictors in Roman days to symbolize strength and power, became the emblem of Fascism. A Turin student song, *Giovinezza* ("Youth"), popularized during the war, became the Fascist anthem.

Meanwhile the government was becoming so unstable that there was talk of forming a coalition ministry and of inviting Mussolini to accept a portfolio. But Mussolini refused, saying, according to report, "Fascism will not come into the government by the service entrance." Then, during the spring and summer of 1922, he several times hinted that the Fascists might overthrow the weak parliament and substitute a strong, nationalistic regime. In September 1922, at a patriotic celebration, he first raised the cry "On to Rome!"; but he also hastened to reaffirm his faith in the monarchical system of government, professing merely a desire to see the monarchy strengthened.

Not long thereafter Mussolini presented the Chamber of Deputies with a series of demands. He warned the parliament that failure to comply might lead to the use of force. The demands were for a dissolution of the lower house, electoral changes, new elections, financial reforms, a strong foreign policy, and five cabinet posts for Fascists. Although the recently organized Fascist Militia was gradually taking over control of the larger cities in the north, the deputies smiled at the ultimatum and seemingly regarded it as a joke. At a National Fascist Congress held at Naples in October 1922, Mussolini explicitly invoked force. Following the delivery of a threatening speech he entrained for Milan, while some thousands of armed Fascist militiamen began to concentrate on Rome.

Although it appears that the army could have been counted upon to meet this danger, King Victor Emmanuel III refused to sanction martial law. Instead, when the really insignificant Premier Luigi Facta resigned, the king on October 29 telephoned Mussolini, asking him to form a cabinet. Mussolini at once left Milan for Rome, announcing, "Tomorrow Italy will have not a ministry, but a government." On October 30 the new cabinet took office. Only four of the fifteen portfolios were placed in Fascist hands, but no socialists were appointed. The moderate composition of the government was owing to Mussolini's desire to follow a policy of compromise until he could be certain that popular opinion would support him in more venturesome steps.

MAKING ITALY FASCIST

The parliamentary opponents of Fascism, and there were many, hesitated to express an immediate lack of confidence in Mussolini. They hoped that his inexperience would lead him into some tactical blunder which might serve as an excuse for his ousting. But Mussolini was wary. With only slight difficulty he secured a grant of virtually dictatorial powers until the end of 1923. Then he assured himself of the loyalty of the administrative branch of the government by the appointment from Rome of Fascist prefects and subprefects to govern the various provinces into which the centralized Italian monarchy was divided. Control of the legislature was next assured by the passage of the Acerbo Election Law in 1923. In order to get parliament's consent to this law, Mussolini reminded the legislators that "the revolution has its rights" and that he was ready to use force.

The law stipulated that whichever party obtained the largest number of votes in a national election, provided also that it received no less than one-fourth of the total votes cast, was entitled to two-thirds of the seats in the Chamber of Deputies. The remaining seats were to be divided among the other parties in proportion to votes registered. Under this scheme the party that polled a plurality was sure of absolute control of the house, while at the same time there could be no single strong opposition group. In the first elections held under the new system (April 1924), the Fascists, not without recourse to violence, gained a sizable majority of the votes. With the aid of the law so skillfully drawn up by Signor Giacomo

Acerbo, Fascists occupied two-thirds of the seats in the new Chamber.

The chief opposition group in parliament was the Socialist Party, one of whose ablest leaders was a young deputy named Giacomo Matteotti. In an anonymously published book and in speeches he enumerated a series of Fascist outrages and threatened to expose as grafters and bribetakers certain members of Mussolini's new cabinet. Before he had a chance to present his evidence against these officials, Matteotti disappeared. His body was found in a wood some weeks later. This murder, which occurred in June 1924, aroused a storm of indignation, especially since it was only the most notorious of a number of excesses.[1]

Since it appeared that Matteotti's charges had been well founded and that high officials were implicated in the murder, Mussolini decided to bluff his way through the crisis and assumed full responsibility for the actions of his followers. As a sign of protest, most of the non-Fascist deputies now withdrew from parliament, vowing not to return to their seats so long as Fascism remained in power. The people, recalling the instances of Roman plebeian retirements to the Aventine Hill in order to force concessions from the patricians, soon referred to the schismatic deputies as the "Aventine Secession." Actually the secessionists made it easy for Mussolini by leaving him in absolute control of parliament; in 1926 he simply deprived them of their seats.

Meanwhile Mussolini had dismissed from office nearly every one who had been connected with the Matteotti incident. In addition, he had pledged law and order, appointed a commission for constitutional reform, reorganized the militia, and granted a number of minor political concessions. But not until almost two years later were the murder suspects brought to trial. They were defended by the secretary-general of the Fascist Party, Roberto Farinacci. Some of the accused were acquitted and the others given short jail terms. Thereafter Mussolini took a firmer stand against the violent "squadrists" who, led by local chieftains, still terrorized country districts. In 1927 he ordered the regular police to crush their illegal tactics.

Having weathered the crisis of 1924, Mussolini proceeded in earnest to make himself supreme in Italy. In 1925 and 1926 thousands of small municipalities and most towns and cities were deprived of their local political rights and placed under the control

[1] Soon after Matteotti's death, his book was published in Great Britain under the title *The Fascisti Exposed.*

of *podestàs* appointed from Rome. Rome itself was placed under a governor, and Naples and Milan were made subject to special commissioners, all selected by the national government. Parliament was deprived of the right to initiate legislation. The premier became solely responsible to the king and was empowered to issue decrees with the force of law. The press was censored and all opposition papers were bought up or suppressed. Nothing could be printed without the approval of the proper Fascist authority.

Mussolini became supreme commander of all military, naval, and air forces, and new members of the Fascist Party had to swear "to follow without question the orders of Il Duce and to serve the cause of the Fascist Revolution with all their might and if necessary with their blood." Secret societies, including the Masons, were abolished. Membership in the Socialist Party at first was made punishable with deportation and then, in 1926, all opposition parties were abolished. The Fascist Party remained as the only legal political organization. Thus was fulfilled a warning expressed by Mussolini some years earlier: "All parties must end, must fall. I want to see a panorama of ruins about me—the ruins of the other political forces—so that Fascism may stand alone, gigantic and dominant."

The membership of the Fascist Party in 1939 was about two million. At the apex of the hierarchical party organization was the Fascist Grand Council, headed by Mussolini as Il Duce, "the Leader." The council included most of the high party and government officials and had a membership of about twenty-five. By virtue of his power to add to its membership at any time, Mussolini entirely dominated the council, thus carrying out his maxim: "A hierarchy must culminate in a pin-point." By law, the Grand Council of the Fascist Party was recognized as the "supreme organ, coördinating all the activities of the regime." Its chief functions were to draft new legislation, fill its own vacancies, name the successors of both king and premier, deliberate on international treaties involving changes in Italian territory, and appoint the National Directory, the executive organ of Fascism. The members of the council occupied ministerial posts, and at one time Mussolini himself held eight portfolios simultaneously. The National Directory, consisting of the secretary-general of the party and nine council appointees, met monthly under the presidency of Il Duce.

The party base consisted of about ten thousand local fasci which in each province were federated and controlled by provincial councils and directories. The provincial secretaries appointed the secretaries of the local fasci. The entire organization exemplified well the theory of government stated in the constitution of the party: "The ordinances and hierarchies without which there can be no discipline of energies nor education of the people must be illuminated and guided from on top where there is a comprehensive view of powers, duties, functions, and merits."

Since the Fascist Grand Council, for all practical purposes, became the government of Italy, the roles of the Senate and Chamber of Deputies rapidly diminished in importance. Until the end of 1934 the consent of both houses was still needed for legislation, but Mussolini adopted the practice of taking action and then having it legalized by the "disciplined" parliament. Occasionally resistance was encountered in the Senate, whose membership consisted of the princes of the royal house and a group of men appointed for life by the king. But Mussolini might at any time request the king to make enough new appointments to outvote an opposition. As a consequence, the Senate in 1939 had about five hundred members, of whom all but a few were Fascists. The Chamber, as we shall see, voted itself out of existence in 1938.

While these changes in form of government went on, Mussolini saw to it that Italy was "purified." As part of the process of purification, anti-Fascist lawyers were disbarred, prominent opponents of the regime were imprisoned or exiled, the property of Italian emigrants who said anything adverse to Fascism in foreign countries was confiscated, and the universities were staffed with Fascist professors. "There is no room," declared Mussolini, "for the Opposition."

Work on a new penal code was completed in 1931. The death penalty, which had been abolished in 1888, was restored for those who attacked "the life or liberty of King, Queen, Crown Prince, or Prime Minister." Parents were forbidden to name their children after "socialists or other rebellious people." Divorce was restricted, the holding of masked balls prohibited, swearing made punishable with arrest, cabarets made to close at midnight, and the advocacy of birth control made a criminal offense. Emigration was curtailed and "the use of firearms" made "obligatory to prevent the unauthorized crossing of frontiers." An active secret-police force to repress whatever anti-Fascism still existed, the *Organizzazione Volontaria per la Repressione dell' Antifascismo* (OVRA), was organized and made directly responsible to Mussolini.

Believing that the country's future greatness lay in the hands of its young people, Mussolini decreed that Italian youth be well trained and disciplined. For this purpose there were organized several uniformed societies. Boys from six to eight became *Figli della Lupa,* or "Sons of the Wolf." The *Balilla*[1] was formed for boys from eight to fourteen. The *Avanguardia* (Advance Guard) claimed boys between fourteen and eighteen, and the *Giovani Fascisti* (Young Fascists) youths aged eighteen to twenty-one, as well as some who had been unable to join the other groups. The members of these organizations in 1939 numbered about five million. They were given military and physical training, as well as a thorough grounding in Fascist aims and achievements. After the beginning of 1927, except for a few months in 1933, membership in the Fascist Party was closed to all but graduates of the auxiliary groups.

A decree of 1934 subjected all males between the ages of eight and thirty-three to a definite schedule of military training. Drills and instruction in the traditions of Italian military history were prescribed for the Balilla. The Avanguardia received regular military instruction from officers of the army and of the Voluntary Militia for National Security.[2] Then followed three years in the militia and one year in the regular army. During the remaining years up to the age of thirty-three service was required in the reserve forces. Thus was military instruction made, in the words of Mussolini, "an integral part of the national education."

There was less emphasis upon the organization of women into Fascist groups, for Mussolini believed that women should remain attached to the household and at most engage in social-welfare work. But by 1939 there were about 500,000 members of *Fasci femminili* and there were four societies for girls, with a total membership of about 2,700,000.

THE FIRST CORPORATE STATE

A strong foothold had been gained among Italian workers before 1914 by a doctrine known as "syndicalism," which advocated the abolition of political government in favor of government by economic groups. During the war many of the syndicalists, led by Edmondo Rossoni, became imbued with nationalism and fought loyally to down the foreign enemy. In 1919 these nationalistic syn-

---

[1] Balilla was the nickname of a Genoese boy, Giovanni Battista Perasso, who in 1746 was the hero of a campaign against the Austrians.

[2] This organization in 1923 succeeded the Fascist Militia. The black-shirted *M.V.S.N.* took an oath of allegiance to Mussolini, whom it recognized as its supreme commander.

dicalists, who were firm believers in the right of private property, united with the nationalistic Fascists in the struggle against communism. After the victorious outcome of this conflict, Rossoni began organizing Fascist syndicates as a counterbalance to the socialist trade-union movement. He also hoped to reform the Italian governmental system so that representation would be based upon organized economic interests rather than upon geographic-political units. The Fascist syndicalists, unlike the followers of Georges Sorel, French founder of syndicalism, accepted "the capitalist class as socially productive," preferred "class collaboration" to class warfare, and were ready to accord producers' organizations a place in the governmental machine. Rossoni's movement made rapid headway and by 1925 the Italian Industrial Employers' Federation recognized the Fascist syndicates as labor's sole spokesmen. In 1926 the federated Fascist syndicates had a combined membership of 2,400,000. Mussolini therefore determined to control them.

By a law of 1926, thirteen confederated Fascist syndicates, six of employers, six of employees, and one of intellectuals, were given legal status.[1] Each confederation was to have provincial and local subdivisions. Additional associations might be organized upon the representation of 10 per cent of the workers or of the employers of 10 per cent of the workers in the industry concerned, but government officials were forbidden to participate in the formation. Only one syndicate was permitted in each field of production and its decisions were made binding upon all workmen and employers in the industry. The syndicates acquired the sole right to formulate collective contracts and were empowered to tax all persons engaged in their industry regardless of whether or not the taxpayer was a member of the association. The syndicates were forbidden to affiliate with any international organization and became subject to the direct control of a ministry of corporations. Mussolini was the first minister of corporations.

The same law prohibited strikes and lockouts, recognized the validity of collective labor contracts, and established sixteen labor courts from which there could be no appeal. Only persons acceptable politically to the Fascist authorities might become members of syndicates. Members were entitled to preference in employment over nonmembers. Some time after the law was passed a training school for syndicalist executives was opened at Genoa.

---

[1] One each for the employers and employees in Industry, Agriculture, Commerce, Maritime and Aerial Transportation, Land Transportation and Inland Navigation, and Banking, and one of Intellectuals, including professionals and artists.

The statute of 1926 contemplated the coördination of the activities of the syndicates by the creation of liaison organs known as "corporations." For several years technical difficulties stood in the way of the realization of this proposal. Then, to "adjust disputes among the various groups in the interest of national production," Mussolini in 1930 inaugurated a National Council of Corporations composed of representatives from the thirteen syndicates, from the government, and from such extrasyndical but coöperating institutions as *Dopolavoro*.[1]

The council was ordered to coördinate the existing organs, supervise the official employment bureaus, promote production, settle intersyndical disputes, and set up functioning corporations. For better administration, the council was divided into seven sections, corresponding roughly to the seven main syndicate divisions. By a decree of 1931 the seven sections of the council were transformed into corporations with tasks identical to those hitherto fulfilled by the sections. Thus the employers and employees in each of the seven chief branches of production were brought together into an organization which was at the same time an administrative agency of the state, controlled by the minister of corporations. The latter nominated and removed the corporation presidents.

It had been hoped that the establishment of national syndicates under governmental supervision would lead to an improvement in conditions of labor. Progress in this direction, however, was slower than had been anticipated. Rossoni therefore prevailed upon Mussolini to promulgate a "Charter of Labor." On April 21, 1927, the supposed anniversary of the founding of Rome, Mussolini proclaimed the charter, the final text of which he himself had drawn up. "The Italian nation," declared the document, "is an organism having aims, life, and means of action superior to those of the single or grouped individuals who compose it. It is a moral, political, and economic unity which is completely realized in the Fascist State." The object of all production was stated to be "the well-being of the producers and the development of national strength." Labor was defined as a "social duty" protected by the state.

For the rest, the charter dealt mainly with guarantees to the workers. Night work must receive higher pay than day work. Piece

[1] Dopolavoro ("After Work") was established in 1925 as an association to provide workers and their families with physical and cultural recreational facilities. The society promoted hygiene, education, and art, and its membership card entitled holders to reductions in fares and admission fees to theaters, museums, and exhibitions. In 1939 the society had 3,160,000 members.

work must be paid for fortnightly and be high enough to enable a normally industrious person to earn a basic wage. Sunday was made a legal holiday and an annual paid vacation for every workman was stipulated. Workers dismissed through no fault of their own must receive a discharge compensation. Labor contracts could not be broken because of military service, brief illnesses, or any change in the ownership of an enterprise. "Education and instruction, especially vocational instruction," were made "one of the principal duties of the syndicates." The state, finally, promised, and later did enact, a broad social-insurance program.

In 1928 a law was passed which made Italy the first Western state to have a national legislature representing economic divisions. The membership of the Chamber of Deputies was reduced from 560 to 400. These 400 deputies were to be elected by the entire kingdom, acting as a single electoral constituency. Candidates to the number of 800 were to be nominated by the executive councils of the 13 confederated syndicates, sitting at Rome. Each syndicate was given the right to nominate a definite number of candidates and in each field of production the employers and employees were to select the same number of nominees. Thus the agricultural employers' and the agricultural employees' confederations were each to nominate 96 men. Two hundred additional candidates were similarly to be nominated by a group of cultural and charitable institutions. From the list of 1000 candidates the Fascist Grand Council was to select 400.

The council might, if it chose, add names of its own or even reject the entire list and substitute a new one. When the council had decided upon a satisfactory "four hundred," the approved list was to be made public. On election day the voters would receive a ballot containing the single question: "Do you approve of the list of deputies designated by the Fascist Grand Council?" The answer had to be either "yes" or "no" for the entire list. No individual names might be rejected. If the majority of votes cast were "yes," the four hundred were to take their seats. If the majority were ever "no," new elections under a complicated system were ordained.

Universal suffrage was abolished by this electoral law. The franchise was restricted to those who paid a syndicate rate, or paid a certain minimum of direct taxes, or received pensions or salaries from the state or public institutions, or belonged to the clergy of a recognized cult. Women were excluded from the national franchise, while men, to vote, had to be twenty-one, or eighteen if they were married and had children. The male electorate thus was reduced by approximately three million. The employers, though less numerous than the workers, received equal representation with the latter. The entire electoral procedure was undemocratic, but the Fascists were proud of this very fact. They considered democracy to have been "a good method of government for the nineteenth century" but regarded it as inadequate for the twentieth.

Early in 1929 the executive councils of the syndicates and other institutions met to nominate their candidates for the first elections under the new law. Mussolini's name came first on nearly every list. The Fascist Grand Council then scanned the list of one thousand and selected four hundred men of suitable qualifications and "reliable Fascist faith." The list was published and the voters were permitted to accept or reject the entire list. During the interim between the publication of the list and election day, the Fascists carried on an energetic campaign. No opposition speeches were permitted. Approximately 90 per cent of the qualified voters went to the polls; the official list was endorsed by a proportion of more than 62 to 1. The second election under the law was held in 1934. Again the government's list of "deputies-designate" was accepted, this time by an even greater majority. But the new chamber soon was dubbed "Suicide Chamber" since it was expected, in view of certain new corporate developments, to vote its own dissolution.

In 1934 the Italian Government created twenty-two new corporations, each of which represented the state, capital, and labor. Falling into the three main divisions of agriculture, industry, and services, the corporations stood for the following branches of production: cereals, horticulture and fruit, wine, oils, sugar, stock raising and fishing, wood, textiles, metallurgy and machinery, chemicals, clothing, paper and printing, building and construction, public utilities (water, gas, and electricity), mining, glass and pottery, credit and insurance, arts and professions, sea and air transport, internal communications, the theater, and hospitality (restaurants, hotels, and travel). Each corporation included all the interests concerned with its particular branch of national economy —"from the farmer who grew the raw material or the miner who dug it . . . to the salesman who placed the finished product in the hands of the public." Three functions were assigned to the corporations: to advise the government, settle labor disputes, and regulate production, distribution, and prices. Under this system, said Mussolini, production remained in the hands of self-governing groups of employers and employees, while private initiative was transferred from the individual to the corporate sphere.

After several years of further study, the Fascist Grand Council in 1938 decreed the organization of a new legislative body to take the place of the Chamber of Deputies. Called "the Chamber of Fasces and Corporations," this house was to be composed of about seven hundred "national councillors" representing the state, the Fascist Party, and the twenty-two corporations; all members were to be appointed by the "Head of the Government" (Mussolini). This arrangement was promptly accepted by the "Suicide Chamber," which dutifully voted itself out of existence. The first meeting of the Chamber of Fasces and Corporations was opened by the king in March 1939. Thus were national elections abolished in Italy.

FASCIST DOMESTIC POLICIES

Financial conditions in the Italian Kingdom experienced an improvement during the first eight years (1922–1930) of the Fascist regime. The budget was balanced by 1926, after which year the treasury generally held a surplus until the time of the great depression. The smaller foreign war debts soon were paid off and the debts to the United States and Great Britain were funded. In 1927 the lira, which had stood at five to the dollar before the war, was stabilized at nineteen to the dollar.

In the years after 1930, however, the government found it necessary to reduce salaries, decrease the number of official positions, place restrictions on foreign-exchange transactions, and float and convert large internal loans. The number of unemployed fluctuated between 400,000 and 1,300,000 and every available force and propaganda method was mobilized to combat the crisis. In some localities the economic stress was lessened by the temporary forcing down of rents and food prices. Large producers were required to regulate output, sales, and prices, and restrictions were placed on the lowering of wages.

Beginning in 1932 the outlines of a planned economy became evident. A technical board was established, without whose consent no new factories could be opened and no old ones expanded. An institute was founded to advance long-term loans to deserving enterprises. New public works were launched and steps were taken to shorten hours of work, extend the system of labor rotation or shifts, abolish overtime work, and fix both wages and prices. Efforts were made to reduce the country's dependence upon foreign imports of wheat, cotton, and tobacco by producing more of these staples at home or in the African colonies. This would not only be an aid to self-sufficiency but would help lower the foreign-trade deficit. Most spectacular in this connection was the officially conducted "Battle of Wheat."

In order to increase domestic wheat production, national wheat-raising contests were inaugurated, the prizes being contributed by the government. The authorities also encouraged the formation of agricultural coöperatives. An agricultural-credit bank was established and educational facilities were provided to teach modern methods to the peasants. Traveling "movies," which demonstrated means whereby farm output might be increased, were sent to rural districts. Simultaneously there was a campaign to reduce the importance of spaghetti and macaroni as factors in Italian diet, since the large-scale manufacture of these products required huge quantities of wheat. Late in 1933 the further importation of wheat was greatly restricted through heavy customs duties. By this time, however, the slogan had been changed to "Battle of Agriculture" and energies were concentrated upon increasing the yield of rice, oats, and corn.

Energetic measures were taken to increase Italy's share of world shipping and the tourist traffic. Steamship companies received heavy subsidies and efforts were made to develop mercantile lines to the various Balkan ports, the Soviet Union, Turkey, Egypt, and India. In 1931 the three leading shipping firms were merged. For a time Italian shipyards were kept busy building war vessels for the Soviet Union, Turkey, Greece, and several South American states.

Many new cables were laid, the radio industry was encouraged, and a succession of tariff acts was passed. A law of 1930 doubled the duties on automobiles, thereby causing worry to American automobile manufacturers and giving the Italian Fiat Automobile Company a virtual monopoly of the Italian market. Henry Ford, however, established a branch factory at Milan. Trade pacts were signed with many countries. In an accord of 1931 with the Soviet Union the Italian Government guaranteed 75 per cent of the credit for Soviet purchases made in Italy. In 1929 Italy led Europe in completed hydroelectric-power developments and in the rayon and silk industries. These last, however, were greatly affected by the depression.

A survey of natural resources led to the discovery of new areas of mineral wealth. Reclamation projects, especially in the Campagna and Pontine Marshes, were set under way and much money and effort were expended upon reforestation schemes. The railway service was improved and the number of free passes, which according to some estimates averaged about a million a year before 1914, was reduced to a negligible quantity. Several air lines were subsidized and efforts were made to spread "air-mindedness" among the people. Despite these material advances, Italy remained dependent upon foreign capital and foreign coal, iron, oil, and phosphates.

These deficiencies became especially apparent during Italy's venture in Ethiopia in 1935–1936. Although the limited League sanctions against Italy [1] failed to prevent her successful completion of the war, they did place a severe strain upon her economic structure. The League "siege," as Mussolini called it, marked "the beginning of a new phase in Italian history," one during which the government tried to secure "in the shortest possible time, the maximum degree of economic independence."

Renewed energy was therefore put into the development of substitute products and the fullest exploitation of such resources (especially lignite, iron, aluminum, tin, manganese, lead, and zinc) as Italy did possess in some quantity.[2] To relieve the shortage in foreign exchange, the government required its subjects to surrender all their foreign holdings, even those deposited abroad, in return for Italian treasury bills. Restrictions were placed on the amount of money which Italian tourists might spend abroad, foreign tourists were offered transportation and accommodation concessions, the lira was devalued, and all lire transactions were placed under the control of a new government department. Patriotic citizens gave up wedding rings for iron bands, but the gold coverage for bank notes continued to fall and financial deficits had to be hidden away in "extraordinary" budgets.

In 1935, all foreign trade became, in Mussolini's words, "directly or indirectly a function of the state," while steps were taken to deprive the large-scale war industries of their "private character" and a law of 1936 virtually converted private commercial banks into state institutions. In 1937 shipbuilding became a government enterprise. Taxes rose from year to year. A sales tax was

---

[1] See pp. 366–367.

[2] Some Italians living abroad sent to Italy sheets of copper in ordinary envelopes. The occupation of Albania in 1939 increased Italy's lumber resources.

levied and a forced loan of 5 per cent was based on the capital value of real estate. In October 1937 there was a 10 per cent levy on the capital of stock companies. The rapid rise in prices and a drop in the standard of living led to decreed wage increases and a two-year prohibition on increased bread prices, rents, and transportation costs. In 1938 the trade balance continued unfavorable. Perhaps it was some consolation to Mussolini that the number of children born in that year was higher than for any twelvemonth since 1931.

Among the leading obstacles facing the Fascists was the illiteracy of the people. In 1911 almost 40 per cent of the Italians were illiterate, the proportion being much higher in the south than in the north. The Fascists attacked the problem by voting increasingly large educational budgets and by enforcing more strictly the laws for compulsory school attendance up to the age of fourteen. The number of children in elementary schools increased from 3,300,000 in 1921 to 5,200,000 in 1937. In order that the children might be reared "in a healthful spirit of Fascism," all textbooks were reëxamined and those not meeting Fascist standards were tabooed. Gradually a series of new Fascist texts was written. Since the schools provided one of the best fields for spreading propaganda, every teacher and professor had to swear to uphold the existing government and refrain from anti-Fascist activity. Several attempts were made to stimulate a new Fascist art in Italy, since Mussolini once said: "Without art there is no civilization." Progress in this direction was not striking.

A new cultural factor in Italian life under Fascism was national discipline. Mussolini provided the theme with his slogan: "Believe! Obey! Fight!" And the philosopher Giovanni Gentile wrote: "Fascism means to take life seriously. Life is toil, effort, sacrifice, hard work; a life in which we know very well that there is neither matter nor time for amusement. . . . We have no time to lose. Even in our sleep we must give account of the talents entrusted to us."

Perhaps it was as a result of some such nocturnal activity that a group of Italian university professors in 1938 published a report, prepared for the ministry of popular culture, which outlined the "scientific bases" for an "Aryan" Italian racial policy. The report contained ten propositions which became the platform for an Italian anti-Semitic campaign, although, according to figures released by the government itself, Italy contained only about seventy thousand Jews.

The propositions held that "a pure Italian race now exists" whose racial conception must be "essentially Italian and Aryan Nordic in trend." Jews, it was declared, do not belong to the Italian race; henceforth the "physical and psychological characteristics of Italians must not be altered in any way." Decrees and laws now followed in rapid order, barring foreign and native Jews from Italian schools, ordering all Jews (even citizens) who had entered Italy since the First World War to leave within six months, expelling Jews from the Fascist Party, prohibiting new trade licenses to Jewish business men, forbidding marriages between Italian "Aryans" and Jews or between Italian officials and *any* foreigners, and making it necessary for any private Italian to get official permission before marrying even an "Aryan" foreigner. Pope Pius XI vigorously opposed the new "racist" attitude in Italy, both because of its extreme nationalism and because of its effect on marriage, but his protests had little effect on the Rome Government.

ALTO-ADIGE, THE FORMER SOUTH TIROL

For strategic reasons the Paris Peace Conference assigned to Italy not only that part of the South Tirol which was inhabited by Italians and which was known as the Trentino, but also the portion which was inhabited almost exclusively by a quarter-million German-speaking Austrians. At the time of transfer, one of Italy's delegates to the conference, Tittoni, made a speech in the Italian Chamber of Deputies in which he assured the new subjects that "their language and cultural institutions would be respected, and their administrative officials enjoy all the privileges of our liberal and democratic legislation." When the Fascists came into power, this promise was disregarded. Fascist policy towards the German-speaking minority was summed up in Mussolini's words: "We shall make them Italians."

The process of Italianization was vigorous. The area was placed under a prefect appointed from Rome. Italian was made the official language of the courts and of all public services including railways, banks, and water, gas, and electric works. Only Italian-speaking citizens might serve on juries and all laws and decrees were published in Italian exclusively, even at a time when there still were many natives who neither read nor understood Italian. Most of the former officials were dismissed and replaced by non-German-speaking Italians. All inscriptions, signs, placards, catalogues, timetables, menus, and so forth had to be in Italian. Wherever villages, towns, rivers, mountains, or valleys had German names, these were Italianized. All maps, guidebooks, picture postcards, and advertisements were required to bear the new Italian designations. The old German names might not even appear in parentheses after the new ones.

The name "Tirol" was abolished and the area renamed Alto-Adige. The use of the words "Tirol" or "Tirolese" was made subject to severe penalties. All German newspapers were suppressed, except for one that was edited as a Fascist propaganda sheet. The numerous local touring and alpine clubs were abolished and their property was handed over to the single *Club Alpino Italiano*. The leading German bank was replaced by an Italian bank. The statues of such Tirolese idols as Walther von der Vogelweide and Andreas Hofer were torn down. Between 1923 and 1926 all German schools were closed. Early in 1928 German was forbidden even during the periods in religious instruction, but later in the year this prohibition was rescinded. The singing of songs in German, the giving of private instruction in German, and the expression of anti-Fascist views were forbidden. Although any Italian citizen throughout the remainder of the kingdom might learn German, the inhabitants of the German-speaking South Tirol were deprived of this right.

Most objectionable to the Tirolese was a decree of 1926 which ordered the "re-Italianization" of all family names that, in the opinion of the Fascist authorities, "had been translated into other languages or defaced by a foreign orthography or the addition of foreign terminations." Likewise, "names of topical origin, derived from places whose names have been translated into other languages, or disguised by a foreign orthography, will resume their Italian forms." All citizens were ordered to watch the *Official Gazette* to see what their names were henceforth to be. Adherence to German forms of officially Italianized names was made punishable by heavy fines.

Such measures led to repeated protests from both Austria and Germany. Mussolini eventually became aroused over these "interferences" and in 1928 made a belligerent speech, saying: "The next time I shall make acts do the speaking. . . . A self-respecting state does not tolerate such interference." He scoffed at the suggestion that the matter be referred to the League of Nations for settlement. Austria was worried by the tenor of Mussolini's speech and in 1930 signed a treaty of conciliation and arbitration. Thereafter Austria refrained from officially championing the cause of the Tirolese.

Germany, moreover, even after Hitler came to power, offered little in the way of concrete help to the "racial comrades" under Italian control. Instead, Hitler and Mussolini reached an agreement in 1939 whereby the Tirolese were given the choice of migrating to the Reich or else remaining and becoming loyal Italians. According to report, thousands of families took advantage of the opportunity to leave the land of their ancestors and settle in one or another of the regions which the Nazis were rapidly depopulating in pursuit of their wartime economic and social policies.

THE LATERAN ACCORD

In 1870 Napoleon III of France ordered the withdrawal from Rome, the sole remaining temporal domain of the pope, of the French troops that had been stationed there to protect the Holy See against Italian territorial encroachments. When the French were gone, an Italian army marched on the Eternal City. Pius IX made a show of resistance, but soon ordered the gates thrown open to the attackers. Thus Rome became the capital of Italy and thus was created the "Roman Question" which for fifty-nine years disturbed Italian national life.

The pope considered himself a victim of unjust force and denounced the government of Italy. In order to appease His Holiness, the Italian Parliament passed the Law of Papal Guarantees (1871). This act guaranteed to the pope and his successors perpetual possession of St. Peter's, the Vatican and Lateran palaces, and the Villa Castel Gandolfo. The pope was granted sovereign rights within these possessions, was recognized as personally inviolable and as having the right to send and receive ambassadors, was accorded free use of the Italian railway, telegraph, and postal systems, and was promised an annual pension of $645,000.

Pope Pius IX ignored this statute. He would not recognize any unilateral arrangement devised by the Italian Government for, if the *modus vivendi* between church and state were merely a law passed by a parliament, it might at any time be abrogated by a succeeding parliament. Moreover, if the status of the pope could be fixed by Italian law, he would become an Italian subject and would be deprived of the prestige accruing from his traditional position as the nonnational head of an international religion. The pope therefore retired to the Vatican, called himself "the prisoner of a usurping power," refused to recognize the Savoy dynasty, and directed Italian Catholics to abstain from participation in the political life of the kingdom. The successors of Pius IX continued this policy, with the result that Italians who aspired to be both loyal Catholics and patriotic citizens were confronted with a serious "conflict of conscience." The controversy deprived the monarchy of the services of many able Catholics and simultaneously curtailed the influence of Catholicism in the shaping of governmental policies.

As time went on, the crisis became somewhat less acute. Intelligent Italians "did their duty by the state, and still called themselves Catholics." The state tried in a number of ways to show that it regarded the popes not as Italian subjects but as foreign sovereigns. Pius X, in 1905, authorized Catholics to participate in parliamentary elections. Yet the "Roman Question" remained, in the words of Mussolini, "a thorn in the flesh of the nation."

When the Fascists came into control, they realized that so serious a conflict between church and state, between religious conviction and political duty, materially weakened the power of the nation. Religion, they felt, must be made to serve Fascism, not to combat it. And Catholicism, because of its personally disciplining aspects, had special appeal for the Fascists. The government therefore made some conciliatory moves. The crucifix was restored to classrooms. Religious instruction was made compulsory in the elementary schools. Chaplains were assigned to the army and the salaries of clergymen were raised.

At the same time Pope Pius XI, realizing that continued intransigeance would be unwise and convinced that no help could be expected from other countries, was equally prepared to end the quarrel. By 1926, therefore, "unofficial" negotiations were under way. The compulsory absorption of the Catholic Boy Scouts into the Balilla in 1928 threatened for a time to put an end to the conversations, but the church was mollified when it was stipulated that priests should give religious instruction to the Balilla units for one hour per week. The negotiations came to a successful conclusion on February 11, 1929. Three documents in all, collectively known as the Lateran Accord, were signed. They comprised a political treaty, a concordat, and a financial agreement.

The political treaty dealt with the international status of the papacy. In it the pope regarded the "Roman Question" as definitively and irrevocably" settled and recognized the kingdom of

Italy under the house of Savoy. Italy, in turn, through the establishment of Vatican City under the "complete ownership, exclusive and absolute power, and sovereign jurisdiction" of the Holy See, assured to the latter "absolute and visible independence" as well as "undisputed sovereignty in the field of international relations."

There was to be "no other authority" in Vatican City than that of the Holy See, except that Italian police might be stationed up to the foot of the steps leading to the basilica in St. Peter's Square, which alone remained open to the public. The person of the Supreme Pontiff was declared "sacred and inviolable" and his power was recognized to send and receive diplomatic representatives. "Italy guarantees always and in every case to allow free correspondence from all nations, including belligerents, to the Holy See and vice versa, and to permit free access of bishops from all parts of the world to the Apostolic See." The papacy declared its purpose to "remain extraneous to all temporal disputes among nations and to international congresses convoked for the settlement of such disputes unless the contending parties make a concordant appeal to its mission of peace." The territory of Vatican City was "in every case" to be considered neutral and inviolable.[1]

The concordat defined the future relations between the papacy and Italy. Roman Catholicism was established as "the sole religion of the state." The selection of archbishops and bishops was to rest with the Holy See, but before a candidate could be nominated his name must be communicated to the Italian Government "in order to be sure that the latter has no objection from a political standpoint against the nomination." Bishops, before taking office, were required to swear loyalty to the state, the king, and the government. The state agreed to pay the clerical salaries. The Catholic Church might freely exercise spiritual power and jurisdiction in ecclesiastical matters and the state granted "to ecclesiastics protection on the part of its authorities" whenever it should be necessary in the carrying out of their ministry. In other words, the state would assist in the enforcing, among Catholics, of the canon law. The state also agreed to revise those chapters of its civil law that conflicted with canon law in matters of faith and morals. This had reference chiefly to the institutions of marriage and education.

Marriage was recognized by the state as a sacrament and, provided certain formalities regarding banns and registration were observed, a religious ceremony was to be sufficient. A civil cere-

[1] The area of Vatican City is 108.7 acres; its population in 1941 was 1000.

mony was alike optional for Catholics and non-Catholics. The question of divorce among Catholics was left to the church. Religious instruction, formerly required only in elementary schools, was made compulsory in secondary schools as well. It was to be taught by state-paid instructors who were priests or other clerics "approved by ecclesiastical authority." The church was not to interfere with the normal curricula or the school administration. The Catholic Action and other popular religious societies were recognized by the state on condition that they refrained from political activity and confined their efforts to "the teaching and practice of Catholic principles." Finally, the Holy See took occasion "to renew its prohibitions to all the ecclesiastics and religious to enroll or take any part in any political party."

In the financial agreement Italy consented to pay immediately upon ratification of the accord the sum of $39,375,000, and, in addition, $52,500,000 in 5 per cent bonds. These moneys were accepted by the papacy "as a final settlement of its financial relations with Italy resulting from the events of 1870."

Thus was terminated a conflict that had lasted for two generations. Henceforth, according to Mussolini, "the citizen is a Catholic and the Catholic is a citizen." Or, as the pope remarked, "God has been restored to Italy and Italy has been restored to God." His Holiness soon emerged from the Vatican to bless the Italians, the royal family, and the world. In 1930 the Chamber of Deputies struck from the list of national holidays the anniversary of the taking of Rome in 1870 and substituted the date of the signing of the Lateran Accord.

Some differences of opinion regarding the respective spheres of influence of church and state caused a renewal of difficulties in 1931. On May 25 of that year, Pius XI issued an encyclical on labor. Proclaimed on the fortieth anniversary of the issuance by Pope Leo XIII of his encyclical on labor, *Rerum Novarum,* it was called *Quadragesimo Anno.* The encyclical deplored the fact that "the whole economic life has become hard, cruel, and relentless in a ghastly measure." The pope urged a "just" wage, advocated the attainment of some property by the workmen, and recommended that wage earners be made "sharers in some sort in the ownership or the management or profits" of capitalistic enterprise. Communism was declared "detestable" and socialism and Catholicism were called incompatible. Pius lamented the "dreadful scourge" of unemployment and blamed it, in part, on the "extreme freedom of competition."

Lest this plaint against unrestricted competition be considered an endorsement of the Fascist system, however, the pope added: "It is to be feared that the new syndical and corporative institution possesses excessive bureaucratic and political character, and that, notwithstanding (certain general advantages), it risks serving particular political aims rather than contributing to the initiation of a better social order." Pius also protested, and this could apply only to Italy and the Soviet Union, that the "destruction of a variety of prosperous institutions that were originally linked with one another has caused society to consist virtually of only individuals and the state."

Such ideas were displeasing to the Fascists. They maintained that the pope had no right to pass judgment on economic and social matters. Pius, on the other hand, held that the church could not surrender its right to exert influence over the economic and social welfare of the family. An open break between church and state threatened, for besides this difference of opinion there existed conflicting views regarding the education of Italian children and the activities of the Catholic societies. Before long, Fascist students started destroying church property, trampling the pope's portrait, and attacking priests. On the ground that they were engaging in political activity, Mussolini closed all clubs of the Catholic Action and dissolved all Catholic societies not directly connected with the Fascist Party.

Pius denied that the Catholic Action was dabbling in politics and accused the government of violating the Lateran Accord. In a letter he denounced Fascist claims regarding the education of youth, called "illicit" the Fascist oath which "even little boys and girls are obliged to take, about executing orders without discussion," and deplored the setting up of a "true and real pagan worship of the state." He also complained that Italian children were being diverted from attendance at church service in favor of participation in military and athletic events. The Fascists replied by reminding the pope that as sovereign of a foreign state he had no right to interfere in a purely domestic situation. Mussolini announced that "the child as soon as he is old enough to learn belongs to the state alone. No sharing is possible."

For a time it appeared as though the agreement of 1929 would be torn up, but eventually a compromise was effected. Mutual expressions of good will were exchanged and Enrico Rosa, a Jesuit and a militant anti-Fascist, was removed from the editorship of the leading Catholic review in Italy, while Major Giovanni Giuriati, the man who first accused the Catholic Action of spreading anti-Fascist propaganda, resigned the secretary-generalship of the Fascist Party. In addition, the pope placed control of the reopened Catholic Action clubs in the hands of the bishop of each diocese rather than in those of laymen, as had formerly been the case. The Fascists agreed that in future their military and athletic programs would be so arranged as not to interfere with Sunday church services for the children. In 1932 this new accord was "officially consecrated," but thereafter differences continued to flare up from time to time. The government was firm in its contention that, though Italy was Catholic, she was, above all, Fascist.

NATIONALISM AND POPULATION PRESSURE

The Fascists sounded warlike as well as nationalistic. They strove to revive the prestige of ancient Rome and many of them glorified war as a symbol of national virility. One of the leading publicists, Mario Carli, wrote: "The warlike spirit is the fundamental character of Italians; it is not a Fascist invention nor a post-bellum attitude. Find me a single moment of history in which we have not fought—for whom and for what little matters." Mussolini himself, in an article on Fascism in the *Enciclopedia Italiana* declared: "Only war carries human energies to the highest level and puts the seal of nobility upon peoples who have the courage to undertake it." A military atmosphere pervaded every phase of national and local activity. A nation which thus glorified combat, and which was desirous of expanding territorially as the old Roman Empire had expanded, naturally required a large population.

The population of Italy in 1927 was estimated at less than 41,000,000. In a speech of that year before parliament, Mussolini said: "If Italy wants to count for something, she must appear on the threshold of the second half of the century with a population of not less than 60,000,000 inhabitants. If we fall off, gentlemen, we cannot make an empire, we shall become a colony." In 1928 he wrote: "In disciplined, enriched, cultivated Italy there is room for 10,000,000 more men. Sixty million Italians would make their weight felt in the history of the world."

Acting on the theory that "without quantity there can be no quality," the Fascist Government prohibited the giving of contraceptive information, further restricted emigration, and placed a tax upon bachelors. On the other side, every conceivable form of propaganda was utilized to encourage early marriage and large families. The legal age for marriage was fixed at sixteen for boys and fourteen for girls, and newlyweds were offered trips to Rome on the state railways at a fare reduction of 80 per cent. In 1933 a fête was prepared in Rome for 93 Italian mothers who together had borne 1288 children. The first celebration of an Italian "Mothers' Day" took place on Christmas Eve of the same year. But by 1939 the estimated population had risen to only 44,000,000.

The combination of extreme nationalism and an increasing population pressure in a country with limited resources became a disturbing factor in international politics. With an area of only 120,000 square miles and a population density of 375 to the square mile, every addition to Italy's population increased the margin of economic insufficiency. The kingdom's African colonies offered few attractions to immigrants and even so large a reclaimed area as the Pontine Marshes between Rome and Naples accommodated only sixty thousand persons. Despite the variety of methods employed by the government to increase the country's food-supplying potentialities, the problem of feeding Italy became intensified. The only solution, in Fascist opinion, lay in territorial expansion. It was declared that "Italian nationals must work in Italian territories for the wealth and power of Italy" and that "demographic, economic, and political reasons justified Italy's desire for expansion."

Philosophically, too, the Fascists justified imperialism. To quote Mussolini again: "In the Fascist doctrine, empire is not only a territorial, a military, or a mercantile expression, but a spiritual or moral one. . . . Fascism regards the tendency to empire—that is to say, the expansion of nations—as a manifestation of vitality. . . ." This spirit made the conduct of Italian foreign affairs a dangerous matter.

ITALIAN FOREIGN AND AFRICAN RELATIONS

In the field of external relations the Fascist Government strove to make amends for the "weaknesses" displayed by the pre-Fascist ministries. Mussolini adopted a bellicose front and inspired Italy with confidence in her position as a world power. Simultaneously emphasis was placed upon the need for ever greater military, naval, and aerial armaments. The land, water, and air services of Italy were all placed under the direct control of Mussolini in 1933. To explain to the people the necessity for further military preparedness and to exercise stricter control over both domestic and foreign newspapers, a press and propaganda bureau was erected and placed (1934) under the supervision of Mussolini's son-in-law, Nobile Galeazzo Ciano.

Perhaps the most threatening of Italy's foreign relations in the early postwar years were those with France. Mussolini, during this period, did not like to see thousands of Italians flocking to France in search of employment. He was the more vexed when it appeared that France encouraged the immigrants to become naturalized. France also was too hospitable to émigrés who had left Italy through dislike for, or fear of, Fascism. Some Italians, moreover, maintained that Tunisia, Corsica, Savoy, and Nice, all in the possession of France, belonged of right to Italy. The Fascists placed chief blame on the French for the disregard of Italy's "legitimate" claims at the peace conference and the failure of the kingdom to acquire any mandated territory. The two countries were competing for control of the western Mediterranean and for superiority in naval armaments. On occasion, Franco-Italian relations became impaired because of quarrels between Italy and France's allies, especially Yugoslavia. Extensive military preparations were made on both sides of the Franco-Italian border but no "incident" occurred to precipitate armed strife.[1]

Meanwhile, soon after his rise to power, Mussolini had remarked: "On the west there are national states which have taken definite form and to which we can send nothing except our labor —though even our export of that may be prohibited or restricted any day." Hence strenuous efforts were made to consolidate Italian power in eastern Europe. In 1923 Rome was confirmed in the possession of the Dodecanese Islands. Fiume was definitely acquired in 1924. Treaties of friendship, neutrality, and commerce were signed with a number of the central- and eastern-European states.

In 1925 Italy signed the Nettuno Convention with Yugoslavia whereby the citizens of the latter gained some commercial rights in Italy, Italians were permitted to hold land in certain parts of Yugoslavia, and Italian firms in Yugoslavia were allowed to import Italian labor. There was so much opposition in Yugoslavia to this potential Italian "encroachment" that ratification of the treaty did not occur until 1928. Part of this opposition was owing

[1] France was not the only country which had territories coveted by Italy. Mussolini once referred to the British island of Malta as part of "Unredeemed Italy" and some Fascists clamored for the "restoration" of the Italian-speaking Swiss canton of Ticino.

to the development of a Southslavic irredentist movement whose goal was the acquisition of a large part of Dalmatia from Italy. The agitation was accompanied by violence, and relations between the two powers continued under high tension. The Italo-Yugoslav quarrel, which in essence was a struggle for the control of the Adriatic, was further intensified by the establishment of an Italian protectorate over Albania.[1]

After 1928 Italy attempted to consolidate her postwar orientation of friendships. While drawing further and further from France, Poland, and the Little Entente, she became increasingly friendly towards Germany, Austria, Hungary, Bulgaria, and Turkey. On the ninth anniversary of the March on Rome (1931) Mussolini, before a tremendous crowd, advocated (1) a final readjustment of reparation and inter-Allied war debts; (2) immediate progress toward disarmament; and (3) revision of the peace treaties in the interests of both the former Central Powers and Italy.

In 1932 Foreign Minister Grandi specifically proclaimed the urgency of a territorial redistribution in northern Africa. "If," he said, "at the close of the war, Italy's allies neglected her in the distribution of mandates, Italy must now labor all the harder to make known the real and beneficial forces that she can exert in the colonial field in the interests of civilization." Already in the spring of 1928 Great Britain, France, and Spain had invited Italy to share in the international government of the free city of Tangier on the west coast of Morocco. Then, in 1934, through the influence of Great Britain, the boundary between Egypt and Cyrenaica (in northeastern Libya) was readjusted in favor of Italy. Soon thereafter King Victor Emmanuel III reviewed the troops and inspected the military defenses of Italian Somaliland and other Italian African possessions.

Meanwhile, beginning in the summer of 1934, rumors were current that Rome was displeased with the efforts of the emperor of Ethiopia to modernize and enlarge his army. Emperor Haile Selassie I was equally worried over the strengthening of the defenses of Italian Somaliland and Eritrea, both of which bordered on Ethiopia. Late in 1934 several "incidents" occurred, involving clashes of armed patrols at Ualual (Walwal) and other points along the incompletely demarcated boundary. Ethiopia appealed to the League for arbitration while Italy dispatched troops to Africa.

[1] See p. 370. A five-year treaty of friendship and neutrality, signed in 1924 between Italy and Yugoslavia, was not renewed when it expired in 1929.

Before the League had time to study the Italo-Ethiopian dispute, France and Italy signed a pact at Rome in January 1935. Because of the recent political changes in Germany and the rising danger to Austrian independence, Mussolini, for a brief period, sought a *rapprochement* with Paris. France, afraid of Nazi Germany, welcomed the opportunity to improve relations with her

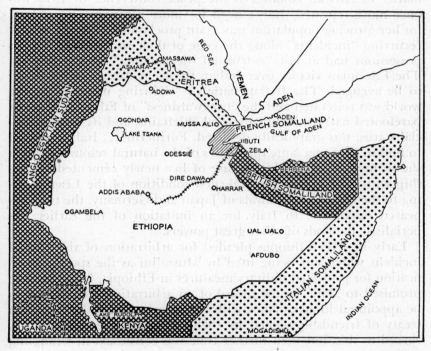

ETHIOPIA, 1935

From Townsend, M., *European Colonial Expansion since 1871*, 1941, courtesy of J. B. Lippincott Co.

neighbor to the southeast. The result of these changed outlooks was the Laval-Mussolini Pact wherein the countries settled some outstanding colonial differences and agreed to consult if Austrian independence were threatened. France ceded to Italy almost forty-five thousand square miles of territory adjoining Libya and a small piece of French Somaliland touching Eritrea. The Italians thus acquired an extra portion of the Sahara and an outlet on the Gulf of Aden. In addition, Italy was allotted a share in the French railway connecting Addis Ababa, the capital of Ethiopia, with

Jibuti, the administrative seat of French Somaliland. Special citizenship rights and school privileges were extended to the Italian residents of Tunisia. According to Mussolini, moreover, Laval secretly gave him a free hand to proceed as he wished in Ethiopia.

The Rome Government advanced many reasons to explain this particular colonial interest. The charge of unfair treatment in the matter of African colonies at the peace conference of 1919 was once more repeated. Italy's need for more room and more food for her growing population was again proclaimed. The constantly recurring "incidents" along the edge of their own and Ethiopia's possessions had at last "exhausted the patience" of the Fascists. The Ethiopian victory over Italian troops at Adowa in 1896 had to be avenged. The Italian nation's "civilizing mission" in the world was reiterated and the "backwardness" of Ethiopia, with its barefooted natives, its unruly local chieftains, and its retarded social status, was graphically depicted. Furthermore, Italy expected to find in Ethiopia large quantities of the natural resources which she so urgently needed.[1] Because of her newly cemented friendship with France and the weakened condition of the League owing to the recent withdrawals of Japan and Germany, the time appeared opportune to Italy for an imitation of the earlier imperialistic methods of other great powers.

Early in 1935 Ethiopia pleaded for arbitration of the Ualual incident which was being used by Mussolini as the specific justification for projected military measures in Ethiopia. Haile Selassie promised to abide by the award of an arbitration commission to be appointed in accordance with the terms of an Italo-Ethiopian treaty of friendship signed in 1928. Italy, after several months, agreed to this, but then further time was consumed in wrangling over the make-up and power of the proposed commission. Eventually the League Council ruled that the commission must fix responsibility for the clash of patrols without regard to the question of whether Ualual was in Ethiopian or Italian territory. On this basis the arbiters announced their unanimous decision in

[1] Ethiopia in 1934 had an area of about 350,000 square miles, a population of approximately 7,000,000, and a negligible foreign trade. There was reason to believe that the mineral and agricultural potentialities of the country were substantial, but reliable estimates did not exist. The well-educated Emperor Haile Selassie ("Power of the Trinity") made a serious attempt to unify the country, assert the power of the central government, and abolish slavery, but his task was rendered exceptionally difficult by the racial and religious differences among his subjects, the tradition of separatism and the ambitions of local chieftains, the prevailing ignorance and superstition, and the absence of proper communication facilities.

September that neither side was to blame since each believed itself to be fighting on its own soil. Meanwhile Ethiopia had made several appeals to the League under Articles 10, 11, and 15 of the Covenant[1] and Italy had mobilized men and supplies for an autumn campaign to begin as soon as the rainy season ended.

In the meantime, at the Council's suggestion, representatives of Great Britain, France, and Italy met at Paris (August) to seek a settlement of the whole Ethiopian problem. These three states, all with African possessions bordering on Ethiopia, were parties to more than a score of treaties, signed between 1888 and 1928, which alternately delimited the boundary of, upheld the political integrity of, and divided into spheres of influence the empire consolidated during the reign of Emperor Menelik II (1889–1913).

Now Great Britain and France agreed, subject to the consent of Haile Selassie, to give Italy extensive economic rights in Ethiopia. Mussolini, however, rejected this overture and announced his intention to annex the lowlands in eastern Ethiopia. The Rome Government had made such extensive war preparations and had so stirred up popular sentiment at home that it probably dared not forego the opportunity to create a "Fascist empire" through the "glory of Italian arms." The League therefore took up the matter once more and appointed a committee of conciliation representing France, Great Britain, Poland, Spain, and Turkey. Italy refused to curtail her mobilization activities while the committee deliberated and the League was cold to a request of Haile Selassie to dispatch neutral observers to the border regions.

The strongest anti-Italian stand at Geneva now was taken by Great Britain. The British feared that the successful conclusion of Italy's Ethiopian venture would (1) endanger British predominance along the Red Sea and in northeastern Africa; (2) lead to serious upheavals throughout British Africa; and (3) encourage the Fascists to contemplate further territorial expansion in the hope that they might eventually, like the ancient Romans, be able to refer to the Mediterranean Sea as *mare nostrum* (our sea).

France, on the other hand, was only mildly interested in the immediate Ethiopian controversy and was eager to preserve the friendship of both Great Britain and Italy in the event of trouble with Germany. To judge from their actions, the French would have preferred to uphold the prestige of the League and support the British (as the stronger potential ally) even to the extent of reënforcing British naval power in the Mediterranean—if only

[1] See pp. 132–133.

London had been ready to make a specific commitment of aid in case of a threat to French security on the continent. This, Foreign Secretary Hoare was not ready to pledge and so Premier and Foreign Minister Laval continued to search for a formula of conciliation that would satisfy both London and Rome.[1]

When the League's conciliation committee reported a plan for the international development of Ethiopia with a recognition of Italy's "special interests" therein, Haile Selassie accepted the scheme in principle but Mussolini rejected it. Thereupon the Council unanimously decided, in the absence of the Italian delegate, to sit as a committee of thirteen and prepare a report in accordance with paragraph 4 of Article 15 of the Covenant.[2] While the Council was at work, Italian troops advanced into Ethiopia from the north, east, and south (October 3, 1935). The pretext for beginning the invasion at this time was the Ethiopian withdrawal of its soldiers from the border. This "strategic move," according to Italy, "necessitated" an immediate advance in order to protect Eritrea and Italian Somaliland against further aggression! On October 7 the Council, except for Italy who was a party to the dispute, adopted a report which declared that "the Italian Government has resorted to war in disregard of its obligations under . . . the Covenant." Thus, for the first time since its establishment, the League designated the aggressor in an armed conflict. The Council's verdict was referred to the Assembly, where the representatives of fifty-one nations voted to invoke the sanctions of Article 16 against Italy.

Then the Assembly (minus Italy), sitting as a Committee for Coördination of Measures under Article 16, drafted five proposals. These imposed arms, credit, and raw-material embargoes, prohibited the importation by League members of any goods from Italy, and asked League members to replace imports from Italy by imports from such states as Romania and Yugoslavia which normally enjoyed a profitable Italian market. These proposals were

[1] In December 1935 Hoare and Laval agreed on a plan whereby Italy was to keep most of the extensive territory she had conquered by that date, while Ethiopia was to get "in exchange" a narrow corridor to the Red Sea through Eritrea. Laval published the plan before it was approved by the Chamberlain Cabinet, which then, in the face of unmistakable public condemnation, repudiated it. Hoare resigned and was succeeded by Anthony Eden.

[2] "If the dispute is not thus settled [through the mediation of the Council], the Council either unanimously or by a majority vote shall make and publish a report containing a statement of the facts of the dispute and the recommendations which are deemed just and proper in regard thereto."

accepted by most of the member states and it was decided to make the sanctions effective on November 18.[1]

The official opening of the economic fight was marked in Italy by the flying of flags. The "sanctionist" countries were warned that Italy would never forget their enmity and would use sanctions of her own in retaliation. Thus was begun the first "great experiment of the coercive powers" of the League. As it happened, the experiment was not complete. Sanctions were not imposed on oil—Italy's greatest foreign need. When Secretary Eden proposed oil sanctions in 1936, French Foreign Minister Flandin insisted that there first be another attempt at appeasement. Then, when Hitler remilitarized the Rhineland on March 7, all talk of an oil embargo was dropped.

While these events were occurring in Europe, the Italian military advance in Ethiopia continued at a moderate rate. The Ethiopians generally followed a policy of impeding the Italian advance without permitting themselves to be drawn into any large open engagement. At last, in May 1936, after seven months of warfare, the Italian troops entered Addis Ababa. On May 9, while Haile Selassie was on his way to Europe on a British warship, Italy formally annexed his country. King Victor Emmanuel took the title Emperor of Ethiopia.

Thus came to an official end the war which Mussolini had "perceived and willed for the prestige, the life, the greatness of the fascist motherland" and in which four hundred thousand soldiers and one hundred thousand workmen had participated.[2] Guerrilla warfare by recalcitrant natives and passive resistance, however, continued in serious proportion. Recognition of Italy's new empire by the other powers followed slowly, while relations between Rome and Geneva continued to be strained after the lifting of sanctions. It occasioned no astonishment when Italy submitted her resignation from the League in 1937. The League, indeed, gained no prestige in the Ethiopian dispute.

[1] Acting under the terms of a recent neutrality resolution, President Roosevelt issued two proclamations announcing that Italy and Ethiopia were in a state of war, placing an embargo on arms shipments to both belligerents, and warning American citizens against traveling on the ships of either warring country. Persons who traded with or traveled on the vessels of either Italy or Ethiopia did so "at their own risk."

[2] The quotation is from the decree by which the king-emperor conferred upon Mussolini the Grand Cross of the Military Order of Savoy. The figures are from Tosti, A. *The Greatest Colonial Enterprise in the World*, 1936, p. 10. There are no reliable figures on the financial cost of the war and the "pacification" measures.

A decree of 1936 united Ethiopia, Eritrea, and Italian Somaliland into Italian East Africa, and in 1937 Mussolini took the post of Minister for Italian Africa. A six-year plan was announced to develop Ethiopia and it was hoped to derive large quantities of cotton, coffee, meat, hides, wool, timber, and minerals from the new empire. It was still a matter of hopes when the Second World War began.[1]

After the Ethiopian War, Italy drew ever closer to Germany and became further estranged from Great Britain, France, and the Soviet Union. Germany had not participated in the sanctions against Italy and Berlin was quick to recognize the conquest of Ethiopia. Both the Nazis and the Fascists, moreover, supported General Francisco Franco in the Spanish Civil War that began in 1936. And so Italy and Germany finally reached a general understanding which Mussolini first called "an axis." Thereafter, despite some further efforts by Chamberlain to appease Italy in the Mediterranean, the Rome-Berlin axis began to capitalize its nuisance value in international politics.

In 1937 Mussolini expressed a lessened interest in the protection of Austria against Nazi advances, endorsed the German claim for colonies, and subscribed to the German-Japanese pact against communism. In 1938 he made the best of what was perhaps an unpleasant surprise and acquiesced in the sudden German absorption of Austria; soon thereafter he supported the Reich in the feverish negotiations over the Sudetenland. In 1939 he justified Germany's absorption of Bohemia and Moravia and annexation of Memelland. And in that year, also, he concluded a formal military alliance with Hitler.

For a time, Italy obviously was the lesser gainer from axis activities. Hence Mussolini in 1938–1939 made two efforts to swell the area of the "Italian Empire." Late in 1938, in the presence of a newly accredited French Ambassador and of Mussolini, a group of parliamentary deputies raised the cry of "Tunisia!", a cry which was rapidly taken up by the spectators and then by the crowds in the streets. According to French figures the number of French-

---

[1] The unsuccessful resistance of the Ethiopians against Italy's modern weapons brings to mind some lines from Samuel Johnson's *The History of Rasselas, Prince of Abissinia,* published in 1759. "The artist" replies to a query of Rasselas, saying: "If men were all virtuous, . . . I should, with great alacrity, teach them to fly. But what would be the security of the good, if the bad could, at pleasure, invade them from the sky? Against an army sailing through the clouds, neither walls, nor mountains, nor seas, could afford any security."

men and Italians in Tunisia was about equal, but Rome claimed that its nationals outnumbered the French residents by more than twenty thousand. Thus Italy began to plead the cause of an "oppressed nationality" in Tunisia much as the Germans had done in Czechoslovakia. In addition, Fascist voices were raised for Corsica, which France had bought from Genoa in 1768, and for Savoy and Nice, which had been ceded to France by treaty in 1860. Moreover, since the French Parliament had not yet ratified the Laval-Mussolini Pact of 1935, Mussolini renounced it at the close of 1938—but without returning any of the desert lands which Italy already had been allowed to occupy. On Tunisia, however, France remained firm, and so Mussolini next turned his aggressive attention to Albania. Let us, therefore, review Italo-Albanian relations since 1919.

ITALY AND ALBANIA

One of the results of the Balkan Wars of 1912 and 1913 was the emergence of a new state: Albania. A German prince, William of Wied, was selected to be *mpret* of Albania. William proved incapable of governing the mountainous state with its unruly inhabitants and, when the First World War broke out, he returned to Germany. During the war Albania was officially neutral, but the Austrians, Italians, and Serbs used it as a common battleground. At the peace conference the Italians sought an Albanian mandate, but Wilson objected and told the natives to form a government of their own.

In 1920 a shaky provisional government was established, which concentrated its efforts upon ousting the foreign soldiers who still occupied the country. At the end of the year Albania became a member of the League of Nations, but its final boundaries were not fixed until 1926. The area of Albania was 11,000 square miles and the estimated population 1,000,000.

The provisional government led a precarious existence, but out of the chaos emerged the conspicuous figure of a young Moslem chieftain, Ahmed Zogu. In 1922 Zogu became premier, retaining this position until 1924 when he was ousted by Bishop Fan S. Noli and forced to flee the country. Noli, who had studied at Harvard University and was head of the autocephalous Albanian Orthodox Church, was unable to achieve order and fell before the end of the year. Zogu returned and Noli fled to Italy. One month later (January 1925), Albania was declared a republic and Zogu was chosen president for seven years by an indirectly elected national assembly.

Zogu attempted to consolidate his power, but found himself obliged to turn to Italy for financial aid. In 1925 Italian initiative established the Albanian National Bank. Not long thereafter Italy lent the republic money, guaranteed by Albania's customs receipts. Other transactions followed and Italy soon stood in a fair way to dominate Albania and thus, incidentally, control the Strait of Otranto. Yugoslavia was vehemently opposed to any such scheme which would endanger her freedom of access to the Mediterranean Sea. Precisely such a factor, it will be remembered, had constituted one of the grievances of the old Serbia against the Dual Monarchy.

In the period 1926–1927 numerous internal improvements were prosecuted in Albania with Italian funds and under the supervision of an Italian development corporation, while Italian officers reorganized the Albanian army. Faced by another rebellion in 1926, Zogu once more turned to Italy for aid. This, Mussolini was ready to give—for a price. In November 1926 there was signed between the two countries the Treaty of Tirana. By its terms "Italy and Albania recognized that any disturbance directed against the political, juridical, and territorial *status quo* of Albania was opposed to their reciprocal political interest." To safeguard this interest the parties "undertook to give their mutual support and collaboration." They "likewise undertook not to conclude with other powers political or military agreements prejudicial to the interest of the other party." An accompanying letter gave Italy the right to intervene in the external or internal relations of Albania, but only whenever the latter so requested.

Thoroughly alarmed at this turn of events, Yugoslavia took advantage of a frontier incident to make certain military preparations. In 1927, after an employee of the Yugoslav Legation had been arrested at Durazzo for espionage, diplomatic relations with Albania were severed. Italy championed the cause of Albania and war seemed imminent. Upon the representations of several neutral powers the matter was adjusted without recourse to arms, but Yugoslavia now eagerly turned to France for an alliance. This was consummated in November. Thereupon Italy and Albania signed a twenty-year defensive military pact.

On September 1, 1928, Zogu had himself proclaimed king, as Zog I. In the following year an Italian company secured an oil concession from the king and in 1930 an arrangement was concluded whereby an Italian bank assumed supervision of Albania's coinage system. The Treaty of Tirana was renewed in 1931.

Thereafter, however, the Albanians displayed an increasingly anti-Italian feeling. Zog, late in 1932, rejected an Italian proposal for a customs union and in 1933 closed all private schools, most of which were controlled by Italian religious. During 1934 Zog tried, though with little success, to lessen the influence of Italian officers in his army and to check Italian immigration. Apparently as a warning against such tendencies, an Italian fleet now appeared in Durazzo harbor, near Tirana, without previous notice and without firing the customary salute. Though these omissions were officially explained as an oversight, it was widely believed that the demonstration had political implications. This belief was strengthened by a number of events in the next few years. In 1936 several new Italo-Albanian "commercial" agreements were announced. In 1938 Italy remitted a large sum of money owed by Albania as back interest and defaulted amortization payments on earlier loans. An Italian company acquired special fishing rights in Albanian waters and received permission to employ armed guards.

At last, on Good Friday of 1939, Italian soldiers landed on the Albanian coast and on the next day (April 8) entered Tirana. There was little resistance for the natives were poorly equipped. Zog fled the country with his queen (a lady of Hungarian-American origin) and their two-day-old son, and Albania was joined to Italy in a personal union. Victor Emmanuel III added to his titles of king of Italy and emperor of Ethiopia that of king of Albania. Germany appeared to know in advance of Mussolini's Albanian plan; the other powers accepted the *fait accompli*.

The new Italian possession received from the king a constitutional statute. Italy took over Albania's diplomatic services and the Albanian soldiers were absorbed into an Italian army. Legislation was to be the function of a native Superior Fascist Corporative Council, but no matter might come before this body without the authorization of the king. The latter also was endowed with final veto power. The natives did retain Albanian as their official language.

CHAPTER XV

Spain

HISTORICAL FACTORS

Maps show Spain as a united country from the time of the fall of Granada (1492), by which date there had been completed the reconquest, by local Christian kings, of the territories captured by the Moors between 711 and 718. Actually, the Spaniards, having little unity of language, thought, or traditions, were not a homogeneous people. The marriage in 1469 of Ferdinand of Aragon and Isabella of Castile, which foreshadowed the union of the two largest kingdoms in Spain, was opposed by some contemporary statesmen because of the great differences between the two peoples. A proud provincialism was the outgrowth of an unusually obstructive geography and centuries of isolated frontier existence occasioned by the struggles against the Moors. At times, foreign invasions, such as that of Napoleon, brought to the fore a militant embryonic nationalism, but ordinarily "the local legend (remained) the center and source of spiritual life." Patriotism in Spain seemed to be "a local thing that reflected the geographical division of the country."

The two most practical elements in the population of early modern Spain appeared to be the Jews and the Moriscos.[1] The former, who frequently served as the kings' tax collectors, were active in commerce and trading, and knew how to invest their capital in productive enterprises. The Moriscos, with the experience gained from their ancestors' African sojourn, were skilled in irrigation and reclamation, and did much to improve the livestock and extend the cultivation of cotton. The forcible expulsion of these peoples—the Jews in 1492 and the Moriscos in 1609—largely for religious reasons, left a population whose leaders, fond of adventure and display, were inclined to despise labor as dishonorable and undignified.

[1] The Moriscos were Moors who remained in Spain after the fall of Granada.

The very components of the population that in other countries became the middle class, in Spain often viewed labor as fit only for infidels and Jews. Those individuals who entered business despite this popular antipathy, were burdened with fiscal and social disabilities. Since monasteries and nobles were, ordinarily, exempt from taxation and since more and more land came into the possession of these privileged groups through royal favor or purchase, the levies on surviving trade and industry were necessarily heavy. Whereas rulers of other lands curried favor with the middle class, most Spanish sovereigns blocked its rise. The army and the church, both conservative, were considered sufficient pillars of the monarchy. Not until the regime of Charles III (1759–1788), and then only for a short interval, did the bourgeoisie come into prominence.

The same shortsightedness was apparent in the colonial field. A desire to exploit the mineral rather than the agricultural wealth of the land influenced the Spaniards in America as it had at home. Precious metals, not grain; mountains, not fertile valleys; monasteries, not trading posts, were their prime interests in the new world. The few colonials who did prefer farming and cattle raising were hampered by narrow mercantilist regulations.

Thus even during the years of her greatest apparent glory Spain contained within herself the causes of decline. Supported in the sixteenth century chiefly by the efforts of a few energetic rulers and by the influx of unearned silver and gold from the Americas, Spain's brilliance could not last in the succeeding centuries because the authorities failed to adapt their economic outlook to the changing economic conditions of the world. The flow of precious metals, instead of being turned into channels of permanent advantage, was dissipated in extravagant pageants and expensive foreign and religious policies.

The list of corroding influences upon Spanish development from 1500 to 1900 was long. Heavy military losses, the emigration of large numbers of colonial adventurers, the eagerness with which young men and women flocked to the monasteries and convents, the popular hostility towards foreign settlers even when these were officially encouraged to come to Spain (under Charles III), the relative poverty in mineral wealth, and the high percentage of illiteracy, all tended to weaken the monarchy economically and socially. During these centuries, also, the government discriminated against agriculture in favor of sheep raising. A powerful stock-raisers' corporation, the *Mesta*, organized in the medieval period, continued to exist until the middle of the nineteenth century. At its door must be laid much of the responsibility for a declining emphasis upon soil cultivation. The Mesta was granted the use of an extensive "royal sheepwalk," no part of which could be worked or enclosed by the people. In consequence, "starting from La Mancha and Extremadura in April, flocks of sheep annually ravaged Castile, returning in September to the places whence they had come."

Spain's economic life, then, for most of the period between the discovery of America and the Spanish-American War, was characterized by unrest, high prices, corruption, lack of financial equilibrium, gross inequalities in the tax system, governmental interference in trade, widespread particularism, and worn-out traditions of nobility. The military disaster suffered at the hands of the United States in 1898 was merely the unfortunate but logical outcome of an unhealthy past.

With this sketch of political, economic, and social difficulties in mind, it is understandable why the opening years of the twentieth century should have witnessed a sorry state of things in Spain. The decade and a half between the closing of the war of 1898 and the opening of the First World War saw the national stage almost continually occupied by mob attacks on churches, convents, and police forces; general strikes; martial law; colonial uprisings; attempts at political assassination; the suspension of constitutional guarantees; and innumerable military intrigues. Not until the outbreak of war in 1914 was there a temporary cessation of these symptoms of instability—and then the question of what course to pursue during the struggle served anew to arouse dissension among the people.

Although the choice of sympathies in 1914 was difficult for King Alfonso XIII (1886–1931), who had an Austrian mother and a British wife, the Spanish people readily fell into two opposing groups. Many intellectuals and, in general, persons who possessed liberal tendencies and antimonarchical and anticlerical views favored the Allied cause. The conservative elements, on the whole, sympathized with the Germans, as did some who were opposed to the French sway in Morocco and the French attitude towards the position of the church in the state. Those patriots, too, were anti-Allied, who resented Great Britain's hold on Gibraltar. In the circumstances, the safest decision for the country was to remain neutral and the *Cortes* (parliament) so voted. The wisdom of this policy soon became apparent when the belligerents began to send in orders for war materials. From 1915 to 1919 Spain, for the first time in many years, enjoyed a gratifying excess of exports over imports. After 1919, however, the adverse trade relationship was reëstablished.

Although it would seem that the increased industrial and shipping activities should have resulted in comparative prosperity and domestic quiet within Spain, such was not the case. No fewer than seven ministries held office during the period of the First World War and ten more rose and fell within the next five years. Liberal, Conservative, and coalition cabinets alike failed of stability. This unrest was traceable to four major developments: (1) the discontent and growing radicalism of the laboring classes; (2) the existence of strong regionalist and separatist movements, especially in Catalonia; (3) interference in governmental affairs by military juntas or councils; and (4) continued military disasters in rebellious Spanish Morocco. These factors must now be considered in detail.

DOMESTIC UNREST AND COLONIAL DEFEAT, 1917–1923

Although labor unrest was general throughout Spain, especially after 1916, it was most conspicuous in Catalonia. Here economic difficulties and regionalist dissatisfaction combined to make the opposition to the government exceptionally serious.[1] In 1917 Catalonia was the scene of costly strikes. In July of that year most of the Catalonian members of the national Cortes defied the government and met in a special assembly at Barcelona to demand reforms in administration and in the treatment of their section of the country. They charged that Barcelona's growing industries were burdened with crushing taxes and that the revenue was squandered in Madrid or spent on public improvements in other provinces.

The meeting of the Catalonian deputies was followed by a general strike in Barcelona and the authorities eventually used machine guns to restore order. Further attempts were made to allay the discontent by promising various constitutional reforms, but these concessions came too late. With the end of the war the unrest increased, and the wave of democracy which temporarily swept the continent encouraged the people to demand additional reforms. Critical events followed one another in rapid succession.

---

[1] Catalonia consisted of four provinces in northeastern Spain, including industrial Barcelona. The natives spoke Catalan.

In November 1918 a Catalonian parliamentary delegation issued a manifesto demanding the creation of "an autonomous Catalonian state" with its own cortes, a responsible executive, and its own judiciary. Catalan should become "the only official language" and the region should be united "with the other Spanish peoples in a federal union exclusively for foreign affairs, the army and navy, coinage, weights and measures, trade, customs, general communications, etc." The regionalists hoped to present this manifesto to President Wilson at the peace conference, but the fear of the government's military forces and the opposition of public opinion in the remainder of the kingdom prevented the taking of such a step.

Hardly had the excitement caused by the manifesto died down when, early in 1919, another general strike, provoked in part by radical propaganda, broke out in Barcelona. All constitutional guarantees were thereupon suspended and, to make matters worse, the civil and military authorities clashed over means to end the strike. Bloody street fighting occurred among the strikers, strike-breakers, police, and soldiery, and similar tragedies were enacted in other parts of the realm. At one time the Spanish Employers' Association threatened to institute a nation-wide lockout unless the government exercised moderation in its treatment of both employers and workmen. But the year 1920 brought with it a reign of terror and in 1921 the premier was assassinated.

The stability of the ministries, constantly endangered by the labor and regionalist crises, was further jeopardized by the activities of numerous military juntas. These councils, made up of army officers, criticized governmental policies, attempted to interfere with the civil administration, and pursued obstructionist tactics with regard to the Moroccan situation. So objectionable did they become that Premier Antonio Maura early in 1922 attempted to dissolve them by governmental decree. To this the king objected and so another ministry fell.[1]

During these years, also, the army was fighting a losing war against the rebellious Riffian tribes in Spanish Morocco. The more the troops were beaten, the heavier were the taxes imposed upon the people at home and the more oppressive became the weight of military service, censorship, and personal restrictions. A dramatic climax in the situation was reached in July 1921 when a force of Riffians under Abd-el-Krim routed a larger Spanish army, killing about twelve thousand men including the commander,

[1] In November 1922 the juntas were disbanded.

General Fernandez Silvestre.[1] The indignation in Spain now became so great that a parliamentary committee was appointed to investigate the government's conduct of empire.

While the army slowly continued the campaign against the rebels, the committee held sessions and examined evidence in both Spain and Morocco. A report was completed in the summer of 1922 and submitted to the council of ministers, but its contents were immediately suppressed. Though the exact charges and recommendations were not revealed, the report was believed to censure a large group of the highest officials and even the king himself. When it became evident that the report was not only being withheld from the public, but that its recommendations might be disregarded, protest meetings were held throughout the kingdom. The Cortes and the newspapers demanded the immediate and full disclosure of all accusations. In fear of a *coup d'état* the government hastily dissolved the parliament and ordered new elections. The temper of the next national legislature, however, was quite the same as that of the old.

To add to the troubles of the authorities, there came another series of strikes and radical outbreaks. Regionalist agitation increased and the news of the successful Fascist coup in Italy added to the general excitement. It occasioned little surprise, therefore, when, on September 13, 1923, Captain General Miguel Primo de Rivera, military governor of Barcelona, overthrew the national ministry, suspended the constitution, and set himself up as military dictator of Spain. To assist him in his dictatorship he appointed a directorate containing, besides himself, eight generals and an admiral. Though it was evident that the coup was directed against the archaic political system of the land rather than against the monarchy, it was not known until some years later that the plan had been carried out with the consent of King Alfonso. The latter had prudently extended a visit to France so as to arrive in Madrid shortly after the overturn and then had asked the general to place himself at the head of a military directorate and introduce the necessary reforms.

DICTATORSHIP, 1923–1930

Primo de Rivera, the Marquess de Estella, was born at Cadiz in 1870. During the Spanish-American War he served in Cuba and the Philippines, and later in Morocco. In the period 1915–1923

[1] There were rumors that Silvestre committed suicide.

he was military governor, successively, of Cadiz, Madrid, and Barcelona. During his career he had several times come into conflict with higher authorities because of protests against what he considered the needless "butchery" of soldiers in Morocco. Upon assuming dictatorial control Rivera ordered the dissolution of the newly convened Cortes, seized the important documents dealing with the Moroccan scandal, established a censorship of press and speech, abolished trial by jury, put an end to some of the remaining vestiges of local self-government, borrowed money through the issue of treasury bonds, and adopted the slogan "Country, Monarchy, Religion!" His solicitude for religion earned for him the friendship of the Catholic Church.

The marquess soon discovered how difficult it was to set up a government which was at the same time strong and satisfactory to a discontented people. Popular hostility to the dictatorship and, indeed, to the monarchy was increased by such incidents as the dismissal of provincial legislatures, the unending Moroccan troubles, the levying of heavy fines for slight misdeeds, and the exile of several popular republicans. The extreme censorship antagonized the leading intellectuals, many of whom began to devote their literary abilities to fighting the regime. Early in 1925, for example, thousands of copies of an antimonarchical pamphlet by the novelist, Vicente Blasco Ibáñez, were dropped over Spanish towns from airplanes.

Beginning in 1925, however, Primo de Rivera inaugurated policies calculated to win for the dictatorship the support of public opinion. Martial law was abolished. Generous subsidies were granted to the shipping and shipbuilding industries. The military directorate was replaced by a civil cabinet, all the members of which belonged to the *Unión Patriótica,* a nationalistic party that had been founded under the dictator's auspices. The good will of the business interests was sought through the creation of a national committee on industrial production which alone could sanction the establishment of new, or the extension or transformation of old, industries; the injunction upon Spanish coal consumers to obtain from 40 per cent to 60 per cent of their fuel needs from the domestic supply; the passage of measures to aid commercial aviation; and the formation of a state department of national economy.

Efforts also were made to settle labor disputes by arbitration, to break up some of the large landed estates, and to expand the educational facilities. To please the Catalonians a protective tariff was raised. The support of a section of the working class was gained by the appointment to public-service positions of some leaders of the National Labor Confederation. As a concession to constitutionalism there was convoked a National Advisory Assembly (September 1927) to sit in place of the Cortes that had been dissolved four years earlier. The assembly, whose four hundred members were all nominated, directly or indirectly, by the government, was given only consultative powers, but in 1928 it was directed to draft a new constitution to replace the one of 1876 which, though suspended, was still valid.

The backing of nationalists was sought by a vigorous foreign policy. In 1926 Spain and Italy signed a treaty of friendship in which each promised to maintain a benevolent neutrality if the other were attacked by a third party (presumably France). Then Spain served notice of her intention to withdraw from the League of Nations because her demand for a permanent seat in the Council had been refused.[1] Finally, although this was owing chiefly to a blunder by Abd-el-Krim, the Moroccan situation was brought under control.

In order to make good his claim to the title of "Sultan of Morocco," and incidentally to repay the French for their interference with the free movement of his grain supply, Abd-el-Krim committed the mistake of attacking the French as well as the Spaniards. Reënforced by a Spanish army, the French soon brought the colonial conflict to a successful close. In May 1926 Abd-el-Krim surrendered and within another year Madrid could announce the complete "pacification" of Morocco.

Despite these accomplishments of the government, indications of popular discontent were not lacking. In 1926 there was a mutiny in the artillery corps because men were said to be promoted through influence rather than by seniority and merit. A plot, in the same year, to set up an independent Catalonia was frustrated mainly by the alertness of the French police, who arrested several Catalonian separatist leaders across the border. In 1928 a plot was unearthed in Barcelona to overthrow the dictator and 1929 witnessed another serious outbreak in the artillery corps. Then thousands of university students struck because of the censorship and the alleged bad treatment of the engineering classes at Madrid.

[1] Before the required two-year notice of withdrawal took effect, Spain notified the League of her decision to retain membership. She did resign in 1941.

Matters were only made worse by the closing of the university and the dismissal of a number of professors. Soon it was deemed necessary temporarily to shut the doors of all higher schools. During these years frequent attempts were made to assassinate both the king and the dictator. Through all the manifestations there ran an undercurrent of republicanism which slowly but steadily was gaining in intensity.

In January 1930, after more than six years of difficult rule, Primo de Rivera resigned his powers as suddenly as he had assumed them. Illness, disagreements with the king, constant disorders, a renewed uprising of university students, and the refusal of some recently appointed captains-general to express their further confidence in him had induced the marquess to give up his office. In a farewell communiqué he listed among his achievements the pacification of Morocco, the wiping out of terrorism and secessionism, the restoration of national prosperity and prestige, and the calling of a constituent assembly. His opponents emphasized the prolonged disregard of constitutionalism, the failure to end corruption in public life, the economic depression, and the poor repute into which Spain had fallen in the eyes of the world.[1]

Upon his retirement Primo de Rivera was succeeded by General Dámaso Berenguer. Faithful and loyal to the king but lacking in qualities of leadership, Berenguer headed an unfortunate administration. Though he inaugurated his regime by easing the censorship and adopting a conciliatory attitude towards the students, he was unable, in the face of the world depression, to introduce prosperity, provide employment for all laborers, and dispense bread to all who needed it. Even before he had time to outline his plans there were renewed student riots, violent strikes, and complaints against the activities or inactivities of several municipal and local administrations. Weary of the hardship and distress attendant upon Spanish rule, moreover, a group of Catalonians began to agitate more strenuously than ever for "Catalonianism, Liberalism, Democracy, and Republicanism!"

The king and his ministerial council tried desperately in 1930 to regain the confidence of the people. The National Advisory Assembly was dismissed, but new parliamentary elections were promised for 1931. To aid the farmers, a decree was issued suspending the further importation of wheat. Tariff rates on manufactured products were boosted. Alfonso avowed that future military promotions should be determined by seniority and merit

[1] The marquess died in Paris a few weeks after his resignation.

alone. Some of the fines "unlawfully" collected by the previous administration were returned. Concessions were made to the freedom of speech and meeting. The police, unless they could secure warrants, were forbidden to search homes.

But all this was in vain. The increased freedom of discussion only showed how widespread the idea of republicanism had become. The people no longer wanted royal favors; they demanded royalty's abdication. In September 1930 a mass meeting in the Madrid bull ring cheered wildly for a republic and a month later the students at the University of Barcelona publicly shouted "Down with the King!" December brought a mutiny in the aviation corps and a premature republican revolt led by Niceto Alcalá Zamora, the son of a poor southern landowner.

Perhaps a word should be said at this point of Alfonso XIII. Courageous, an all-round sportsman, clever in repartee, this descendant of Bourbons and Habsburgs proved to be a most imperious person. He apparently liked to exercise autocratic power. The "sterility of parliament and the littleness of politicians" were objects of scorn in his eyes. Above all, he professed to be a Spanish patriot, intimating that the all-important question was of Spain, not of monarchy or republic. He long stayed on as ruler under conditions which might well have induced a weaker man to abdicate.[1]

By 1930 the continued existence of the monarchy rested upon three factors of uncertain strength: the loyalty of the bulk of the army (there was a general for every three hundred men), the support of the great landowners and the Catholic Church, and the dissension within the ranks of the opposition (twenty-two republican parties had been organized). Opposed to the old regime were the regionalists and separatists, who disliked the centralization of control in Madrid; the socialists and "New Industrialists," who longed for a changed order corresponding to their interpretation of the needs of the twentieth century; the intellectuals, who preached against the influence of the church and the backwardness of Spain's spiritual life; and the republicans, who hated the military and the unconstitutional conduct of the royalists. The year 1931 was destined to witness a decisive conflict among the contrary-minded groups.

---

[1] The support given by Alfonso to the building of University City further angered republicans and anticlericals who saw in the construction of a new great Catholic institution of learning a blow at the centers that had been established by "liberal intellectuals." Later, the republic continued work on the design.

BIRTH AND PROBLEMS OF THE REPUBLIC

In February 1931 Premier Berenguer restored the constitution which his predecessor had suspended in 1923 and decreed the holding of parliamentary elections. Contrary to the general's expectations, the people greeted this news with anger. Nearly all the antigovernment groups announced that they would refuse to vote in any election save one for a constituent assembly. They had no desire to participate in a resurrection of the outworn document of 1876. Berenguer thereupon resigned, just one year after assuming power, and was succeeded by Admiral Juan Aznar, another loyal monarchist. Orders now were issued for municipal and provincial elections in April 1931, following which there was to be a national election for a constituent assembly that would draft a new, albeit a monarchical, constitution.

To the dismay of the authorities the municipal elections of April 12 resulted in a republican landslide. Admiral Aznar consequently resigned, and Zamora, on behalf of a republican junta, threatened armed revolution unless the king abdicated. On the fourteenth, Alfonso took ship at Cartagena and sailed to France. He did not formally abdicate, but merely "suspended the exercise of the royal power" and left the country in order to permit the people freely to decide whether they preferred a monarchy or a republic. Zamora, however, immediately (April 14) proclaimed a republic with himself as provisional president and with executive authority vested in a previously selected coalition cabinet of moderate republicans and socialists.[1]

The new government set the date for constituent elections and pledged itself to bring about land and church reforms, personal liberty, and a fair degree of local autonomy. Although most of the political groups decided to await the results of the election before taking any further major step, the provisional government was kept busy for the first ten weeks of its existence putting down antirepublican movements and communist riots, pleading with the Catalonian separatists not to impair the unity of the state, and passing urgent preliminary legislation. Many former royal officials were imprisoned, titles of nobility were abolished, and a red

[1] President Zamora earlier in his career had been a monarchist and three times had occupied ministerial posts in royal cabinets. During the dictatorship, however, he became converted to republicanism and in December 1930, as has been mentioned, he led a premature revolt against the king.

yellow-purple tricolor was adopted as the flag of the republic.[1]

Two other serious developments commanded the attention of the government prior to the elections. First, anticlerical riots were precipitated when several church officials appealed to faithful Catholics to vote only for deputies who would defend their religion. Churches, monasteries, and convents were burned and looted, clerical property was destroyed, and the lives of members of religious orders were endangered. The Zamora Government showed little sympathy with this direct action and eventually proclaimed martial law in an attempt to restore order.

Secondly, a group of Catalonians, chiefly radical workmen who feared that the prospective constituent assembly would be conservative or at best mildly liberal, and who regarded any Madrid regime as obnoxious, declared an autonomous Catalonian Generalidad, elected Colonel Francisco Maciá president, and drew up a Statute of Autonomy which provided for virtual independence. It was obvious from the outset, therefore, that Spain's "Irish Question" would arise to disturb the domestic harmony of the republic as it had that of the monarchy. The action of Catalonia, moreover, encouraged other regions, especially the Basque Provinces and Galicia, to demand home rule.

On June 28, 1931, the people flocked to the polls in the first national election since 1923. The candidates for the office of deputy represented twenty-five parties, including all shades of political opinion from monarchism to communism. The result of the balloting once more was an overwhelming defeat for monarchy and a triumph for moderate republicanism. The Socialist Party, with 117 seats, became the largest single group in the Constituent Cortes. The Radical Party, which favored consolidation of the republic and the achievement of liberal reforms, was second, with 93 deputies. The remainder of the 470 seats were divided among a dozen other groups. Although men only had been permitted to take part in the elections, two of the deputies were women. Most of the representatives were young men and only 14 of them had had any previous parliamentary experience.

The Cortes voted to keep in power the provisional ministry which Zamora had appointed and then proceeded to the consideration of a republican constitution. While the document was being pieced together, the cabinet devoted itself to the solution of the more immediate problems. Efforts were made to stabilize the

[1] Of the 4200 titles abolished, about 350 were those of grandees, who had enjoyed the privilege of appearing before the king without removing their hats.

peseta, effect administrative economies, and bring efficiency into the conduct of government. Half of the civil employees were dismissed, but the salaries of the remainder were increased by a fifth. It required all President Zamora's persuasiveness to induce the Catalonian deputies to remain in the Cortes and consent that an agreement should first be reached on the central governmental powers and only later on the regional ones, for a plebiscite in Catalonia had resulted in an overwhelming endorsement of the Statute of Autonomy. Even so, it was necessary to dispatch soldiers to Barcelona to quell a radical-regionalist uprising.

Negotiations also had to be carried on with the Vatican concerning both the property damage done in the early days of the revolution and the future policies of the republic. Inasmuch as the entire non-Catholic population of Spain was less than thirty thousand, the relationship between government and papacy was of unusual importance. When the Cortes adopted resolutions to abolish a state religion, expel the Jesuits and confiscate their property, and prohibit members of religious orders from teaching or engaging in business, President Zamora resigned. His action was in protest against what he regarded as unnecessarily harsh terms.

The chief executive post thereupon was entrusted to Manuel Azaña, a leader of the Republican Action Party and minister of war in the Zamora Cabinet. As head of the war office, Azaña was reputed to have republicanized the army and converted it from a political clique into a spirited fighting force. So confident was the assembly of his ability and integrity that he was invested with extraordinary powers for the suppression of disorder and violence. One of the most spectacular acts of the assembly was to declare Alfonso XIII guilty of high treason. All his property in Spain was confiscated and he was sentenced to "perpetual imprisonment" if ever again he set foot on Spanish soil. The royal parks were thrown open to the people and some of the palaces were converted into office or institutional buildings.

On December 9 the Cortes finally proclaimed the new constitution. Based on the German, Soviet, and Mexican models, it proved to be a very democratic instrument. Spain was declared to be "a democratic republic of workers of all classes." Its government was to consist of a unicameral legislature made up of representatives elected for four years by equal, direct, secret suffrage of all citizens over twenty-three years of age without distinction of sex. The president of the republic was to be elected for six years by an electoral college made up of the members of the Cortes and an equal number (about 470) of popularly chosen electors. Successive presidential terms were forbidden and no one might be a candidate for the highest office who was an active or reserve military officer, a clergyman, or a member of the reigning family of any · country. The powers of the president were considerable but none of his acts was valid unless countersigned by a cabinet minister. The cabinet, in which was vested extensive power, was made directly responsible to the parliament.

In social and cultural matters the break with tradition was wide. There was to be no state church; complete religious freedom was established; marriages might be dissolved by mutual consent or on petition of either party upon due cause; education was secularized; and civil liberties, except in time of national emergency, were guaranteed. War was "renounced as an instrument of national policy" and the president, to whom was given the power to declare armed hostilities, might not exercise this function "except subject to the conditions prescribed in the pact of the League of Nations" and after the failure of all other means of nonbelligerent defense.

With a view to making Spain a country of "social justice," all the wealth of the land was subordinated to the interests of national economy. The state might "participate in the development and coördination of industries and enterprises," nationalize public services, and socialize large estates. It was also permitted, upon making due compensation, to expropriate all types of property, regardless of ownership. Work was made a social obligation and the state was specifically enjoined to protect the laborer, the farmer, and the fisherman.

In the matter of local autonomy the constitution, to the disappointment of the home-rule advocates, merely recognized the compatibility of autonomous regions with the integral character of the state. Any area desiring autonomy had to submit to the national Cortes for its approval a regional charter, and the national parliament might delegate to the local authorities the power to administer certain national laws.

By a special "temporary disposition" attached to the document, the Cortes was empowered to elect the republic's first constitutional president. This provision was fulfilled through the choice of Niceto Zamora, who had earlier resigned the provisional presidency. Manuel Azaña became prime minister. Instead of dissolving itself now and ordaining parliamentary elections, the Constituent Cortes determined to continue sitting as a regular parliament. The deputies apparently feared that a general election might reflect a popular reaction to their policies and felt that the body which had drawn up the constitution should also be permitted to launch the legislative program that would convert its principles into practice.

In 1932, then, the Jesuit Order was dissolved. Its corporate property was confiscated and ordered distributed for social-welfare purposes. The individual Jesuits soon left the land. Later legislation nationalized all ecclesiastical property, though leaving it in the custody of the clergy, and deprived churchmen of all governmental financial support after a specified date. An act of 1933 forbade members of religious orders to engage in industry, commerce, or the teaching of anything but religion. Teaching by religious was to cease by the end of September 1933 in secondary schools and by the end of December 1933 in primary schools. The church schools were to be closed and all educational matters were placed under the minister of education.

After the flight of Alfonso, the pope had directed the clergy to accept the Spanish Republic but to oppose by constitutional means the enactment of anticlerical legislation. Hence the priests and the Catholic Action had participated actively in the political life of the land and had labored to prevent the passage or bring about the repeal of hostile laws.[1] The apparent failure of these efforts led Pope Pius XI to issue (1933) the encyclical *Delectissimi Nobis*, protesting against the separation of church and state. Once more loyal Catholics were urged to obey the civil authority, but only in matters which did not infringe the rights of the Catholic Church. The members of the government were informed that their actions brought upon them automatic excommunication under the canon law. This did not appear greatly to worry most of them.

The closing of the church schools and the prohibition of teaching by religious made worse the bad educational situation in Spain. The national illiteracy in 1931 was estimated at more than 45 per cent. Despite the shortage of funds, therefore, and the scarcity of lay teachers, 9600 new state schools were opened from 1931 to 1933. The salaries of most of the lay teachers were increased and the minister of education was directed to build a complete secular school system with the least possible delay.

[1] When the monarchy fell there were in Spain about 60,000 nuns, 20,000 monks, and 30,000 priests.

Land reform proceeded slowly, but in September 1932 the Cortes adopted a bill providing for the distribution of about fifty-two million acres formerly held in large estates. There was to be no compensation to the nobles for these lands except where investments on improvements had not yet been realized or where it could be proved that the former owners possessed no other property. As was to be expected, the actual distribution of these lands involved considerable difficulty. The process was far too slow to satisfy the peasants and much too fast for the landlords.

In an attempt to aid domestic industry, the tariff, already the highest in western Europe, was raised still further. Numerous commercial treaties were negotiated. A large public-works program was initiated. Emphasis was placed on improved housing facilities in Madrid and other large cities. Because of its continuing deficits the *Còmpañia Transatlantica* was dissolved and the Spanish transoceanic steamship service was suspended. Plans were inaugurated for the economic development of Spanish Morocco. Economic prosperity, however, was not yet introduced to the Spanish people. The unemployed numbered perhaps 1,000,000 in an estimated population of 23,000,000 and there was considerable criticism of the fact that, despite the hard times, the annual appropriation for the president's salary and expenses totaled $200,000.

It was not to be expected that the various autonomist groups would be satisfied with the home-rule concessions granted in the constitution. In April 1932 a meeting of Catalonians demanded the immediate recognition by Madrid of the Statute of Autonomy. Like the Sinn Feiners, the Catalonians also founded a society called "We Ourselves" (*Nosaltres Sols*) and suffered no lull in the turbulence of their demonstrations. All summer long the Cortes debated home-rule measures, finally recognizing the Catalonian Statute of Autonomy. This was proclaimed in Barcelona (September 25) by Premier Azaña amid the thunderous acclamation of the assembled Catalonians.

The statute gave Catalonia the right to use its own language, anthem, and flag; permission to establish a state government with president and parliament; the right to communicate officially with the rest of Spain in Catalan; and the privileges of raising taxes, creating a school system, and enforcing national laws in Catalonia. In December 1932 a Catalonian parliament met—the first such instance since 1705. The Basque Provinces, Galicia, and other non-Castilian regions now became the more insistent in *their* demands for similar grants of autonomy. To many Spaniards it seemed desirable that the republic should eventually become a federation of Spanish states.

All the reforms just considered were the work of the constituent assembly which had been elected in June 1931 and which sat until October 1933. During most of this period the premiership was in the hands of Manuel Azaña, leader of the moderate radicals. Inevitably there appeared forces of opposition to the continued dominance of this government. To the right were the royalists, who favored restoration of the monarchy; the clericals, who abhorred the anti-Catholic legislation; and the landlords, who preferred to keep their large estates. To the left were the communists, who desired a reconstitution of Spanish life on the Soviet model; the syndicalists, who advocated "the erection of a society based on trade unions alone"; and the anarchists, who favored the entire abolition of government. The most radical elements were especially strong in Catalonia, so that at times the quarrel between Barcelona and Madrid looked more like a contest between radicalism and conservatism than between autonomy and centralization.

The first serious revolt against the Azaña Government occurred in August 1932. Led by General José Sanjurjo, a group of royalists seized Seville and a few small towns. A loyal army quickly crushed the movement and the general was captured. The highest court pronounced the death sentence upon Sanjurjo but this was commuted to life imprisonment. A number of the other rebel leaders, who represented some of Spain's most aristocratic families, were deprived of their honors and exiled to the west coast of Africa. Their property was confiscated.[1] In January 1933 a syndicalist-anarchist revolt broke out at Barcelona. It spread rapidly to other cities, but once more loyal republican troops were able, within a few days, to overcome the revolutionaries.

Less violent than these manifestations but perhaps equally indicative of the growing dissatisfaction were the results of two elections in the spring and summer of 1933. First, the municipal elections throughout the country showed a definite trend to the right. Then, the government's candidates for the Tribunal of Constitutional Guarantees, a body created to decide on the constitutionality of laws and protect the rights of individuals, were defeated. The Azaña Ministry thereupon resigned. In the succeeding weeks several parliamentary coalitions were attempted, with little success.

[1] Later some of these persons were retried and freed. On Sanjurjo see also p. 393.

It was therefore decided to hold the first national election under the republican constitution.

About 12,500,000 voters, more than half of them women, cast ballots in November 1933. Because a score of parties had nominated candidates and because the electoral law required that the successful party get at least 40 per cent of the total votes cast in any one district, it was necessary to hold a second election in December. The final result confirmed the general trend towards conservatism. The parties of the Right won 44 per cent of the seats in the Cortes, the Center got 35 per cent, and the Left 21 per cent.

The new Cortes met a few days after the election and Alejandro Lerroux, leader of the Radical Party (actually a party of the Right Center), formed a moderate, coalition ministry. Lerroux' program envisaged the payment of pensions to the impoverished members of the clergy, an amnesty for political offenders, reform of the electoral law, and a halt on the further closing of religious schools until sufficient lay teachers were available to meet the needs of the school population. The opening of the new parliament occurred almost simultaneously with the outbreak of a syndicalist-anarchist insurrection at Barcelona. It was fortunate for the authorities that the socialists refused to participate in the uprising and after several days of bitter fighting relative order was restored.

Throughout the spring of 1934 the country was torn by strikes and disorders. The "Reds" of various shades rioted because the laws against the church and the landholders were not enforced quickly enough, because religious processions were tolerated during Easter Week for the first time since 1931, and because of the growing strength of conservative agrarian and youth movements. Despite the proclamation of a national "state of alarm" the violence continued and became worse. Finally, Lerroux resigned, to be succeeded for the next five months (May–October 1934) by the moderate Ricardo Samper.

The new premier faced the same difficulties that had confronted his predecessor, with several additional ones. Early in 1934 the Catalonian parliament, impatient with the dilatoriness of the legislature at Madrid, had passed some land laws hastening the process of converting the farm laborers and tenants into owners. These laws were declared unconstitutional by the Tribunal of Constitutional Guarantees on the ground that such legislation could be adopted only by the central government. The authorities at Madrid acclaimed this decision, but Catalonia proceeded to put the laws into effect. At the same time the cabinet had to cope with bloody separatist outbreaks and an independence movement in the Basque Provinces. Samper resigned the premiership at the beginning of October and Lerroux once more shouldered the chief ministerial responsibilities. Within a day he was forced to deal with the worst rebellion that had yet threatened a government under the republic.

It appears that the immediate cause of the rebellion was the conservative composition of the Lerroux Cabinet. The radicals, both within parliament and among the people, objected especially to the inclusion in the ministry of several members of the Agrarian People's Party. This group was organized early in 1933 by José Maria Gil Robles, a lawyer and assistant editor of the leading clerical paper. Gil Robles advocated a kind of Catholic Fascism. He was opposed to most of the republic's land reforms, its concessions to labor, the expensive public works, and the extension of local autonomy. Intensely nationalistic and conservative, the party was pledged to the preservation of landed property, the defense of Catholicism, and the eradication of separatism. It drew its main support from the landed classes, industrialists, merchants, small-business men, and devout Catholic peasants and housewives. It had more than one hundred deputies in the Cortes.

When Lerroux offered several cabinet posts to these "fascists," all radical groups coöperated in a general strike which soon became violent and merged with a desperate attempt by the Catalonian radicals to break away from Spain. "President" Luis Companys actually declared the independence of Catalonia.[1] The Basque Provinces also renewed the fight for separation. Again the Madrid Government triumphed, with the aid of the army and navy, and at a high cost in blood and money.

Meanwhile Lerroux, strongly backed by the Cortes (many of the radical members of which either were under arrest or refused to sit while martial law was in force), entrenched the position of the Right. The Catalonian Statute of Autonomy was suspended for purposes of revision. Madrid assumed responsibility for the policing of Barcelona and other centers of disturbance. A Basque autonomy statute that had earlier been submitted to Madrid for consideration was laid aside. The regular municipal elections were postponed. In the spring of 1935 Lerroux had to reconstitute his cabinet twice and on the second occasion Gil Robles was made minister of war.

---

[1] President Maciá of Catalonia had died in December 1933.

CIVIL WAR, 1936–1939

The instability of the centrist ministries during 1935 led President Zamora to dissolve parliament in 1936 and call for new elections. The voters on February 16 had to choose between a leftist and a rightist coalition. The left parties (Republican Union, Left Republican, Socialist, Communist, and Syndicalist) organized a Popular Front and promised to further the republican political and social programs. The center and right parties combined in an effort to preserve the country from what they feared might be a proletarian regime.

The Popular Front received only a plurality of the popular votes but, because of their distribution, got 258 seats in the new cortes; the Center and Right secured the remaining 215 seats. Manuel Azaña, leader of the front, now became premier at the head of a cabinet composed entirely of republicans. It contained not a single socialist, communist, or syndicalist. Azaña quickly proclaimed an amnesty for political prisoners and ordered the reinstatement of all workers who had been discharged for revolutionary sympathies; the employers were to pay compensation for the lost time. While groups of unruly leftists burned churches and convents and attacked monarchist headquarters, the government took steps to restore Catalan autonomy and distribute large areas of land among the peasantry. Seventy thousand peasants had received land by the end of March 1936; but other thousands, determined to wait no longer for the grants which had first been promised them five years before, rose up and occupied many large estates—including two that belonged to the president.

In April 1936 President Zamora was removed from office, mainly because he supported the centrist viewpoint. Azaña was chosen president in May and Santiago Casares Quiroga, also a Left Republican, became head of a new cabinet which still contained only republican members. The public disorders meanwhile grew worse, there were widespread strikes, and numerous acts of violence were attributed to the partisans of both Left and Right. The authorities imprisoned many fascists and ordered the dissolution of the Spanish Phalanx, the most aggressive of the antigovernment groups.

The ministry was especially fearful of the attitude of restive army men. A decree therefore pensioned all military officers who had participated in politics. Politically minded officers who already were on the retired list lost their pensions and a general shake-up occurred in the high command. Suspected officers were dismissed or transferred to distant parts. General Francisco Franco, once commander of the Spanish Foreign Legion in Morocco, was "exiled" to the Canary Islands. Many officers of the Foreign Legion also were removed. Clearly the controlling group of general officers was in danger of being rendered impotent. Quick action was necessary if the traditional power of the army was to be upheld.

It was evident, by this time, that the Spanish Republic was approaching the decisive moment in its career. It had succeeded the monarchy in 1931 because the impoverished population was no longer willing to tolerate the rule of a small aristocratic minority composed of army officers, estate owners, clerics, and a few big industrialists. The reforms of the republic were intended to break the power and wealth of this minority. But they were put into effect at a pace which seemed far too slow for the impatient laborers and peasants. While the tension between Right and Left therefore became ever greater, the government tried to continue along a middle course. In the end, the extremists of each side came to regard force as the surest means of reaching their objectives. It remained only for an "incident" more serious than the rest to precipitate actual civil war.

About the middle of June 1936, José Calvo Sotelo, a fiery monarchist, launched bitter verbal attacks against the Quiroga Government. He uttered warnings of the army's growing impatience with the inability of the authorities to check popular excesses. There were frequent rumors regarding impending coups of both monarchists and communists. Each group, it was said, was working feverishly to forestall the plans of the other. Madrid, toward the end of June, was "a nervous city."

On July 12 José del Castillo, a police lieutenant in Madrid, was murdered, supposedly by fascists. Several of his comrades, early the next morning, appeared at the home of Calvo Sotelo and took him away in a police van. Shortly thereafter the monarchist's dead body was left with the porter of a Madrid cemetery. More blood was spilled at Sotelo's burial and on July 16 Gil Robles placed responsibility for his death at the government's door. On the next day, July 17, several regiments in Spanish Morocco revolted and civil war began.

General Franco left the Canary Islands and flew to Morocco to head the rebellious forces. With the support of most of the regular army, the Foreign Legion, and some Moorish contingents he quickly made himself master of Spanish Morocco. Simultaneously garrisons in all parts of Spain followed their generals in mutiny and General José Sanjurjo, leader of the unsuccessful monarchist coup in 1932 and apparently once again the choice of the anti-republicans, attempted to fly to Spain from his exile in Portugal. The plane, however, crashed near Lisbon and the general was killed; Franco therefore emerged as the leader of the new move-ment.[1]

It appeared that most of the military and naval officers, a majority of the soldiers, a goodly portion of the Civil Guards (constabulary), Moorish troops, and Foreign Legion, and numerous civilians of conservative, fascist, monarchist, and clerical sympathies rallied around Franco's standard.[2] These were reënforced by thousands of well-trained "volunteers" from Italy and Germany and, for a time, from the Irish Free State. The established government could count on only a small part of the organized armed forces, including the military air force and a part of the navy. It had to seek additional aid from the radical labor and peasant groups. This popular militia included many women. The Basques, though strongly Catholic and conservative in sympathies, also generally gave their help to the established authorities, because Franco brought his Moors to fight in Spain. Thousands of foreign sympathizers, especially from the Soviet Union, France, and the United States, fought for the Madrid Government in such units as the International Brigade, the Debs Column, and the Abraham Lincoln Battalion. Finally, there was a sizable contingent of antifascist Germans, Italians, and Poles.

Circumstantial evidence made it appear that the rebels envisaged rapid victory in three steps: seizure of Spanish Morocco, capture of the provincial capitals, and overthrow of the government in Madrid. The first step was successful but the others were blocked by the rapid arming and determined resistance of the "masses." Nevertheless, by November 1936 the rebels reached the outskirts of Madrid and the established government transferred its seat to Valencia. Germany and Italy thereupon recognized the

[1] On August 5, 1936, the *Manchester Guardian* reported that, before the outbreak of the revolt, Sanjurjo and Antonio Primo de Rivera, son of the former dictator, had spent several weeks in Berlin.
[2] The followers of Franco soon were called "Rebels," "Fascists," "Nationalists," and "Insurgents." The supporters of the Madrid Government came to be labeled "Loyalists," "Marxists," and "Reds." The only noncommittal terms from the point of view of international law seemed to be "rebels" and "established government."

Franco Government which had been set up at Burgos. Its leader came to be known as *El Caudillo,* "the Chief."

In the meantime several "loyalist" premiers had risen and fallen, until Francisco Largo Caballero assumed the chief portfolio on September 4. He unified the military command and converted the several proletarian units into a disciplined army. Being himself a socialist, he appointed several other socialists and two communists to his cabinet. Thus it was not until seven weeks after the civil war began that even socialists were included in the cabinet. The government's increasing dependence upon left-wing support as the fighting was prolonged made necessary the admission of decided leftists into the ministry. Once this process had started it was hard to go back. Indeed, after two months, Caballero, anxious to obtain the fullest support of Catalonia, assigned several cabinet portfolios to syndicalists. The established government now really *was* a "Red" government; it had not been so when the rebels first attempted to seize control.

Following a revolt of anarchists in Barcelona, the Caballero Ministry resigned (1937). It was succeeded by a more moderate one under Juan Negrín, a right-wing socialist and former finance minister. Thereafter the government followed a more conservative pattern, even the communists agreeing that social revolution should be subordinated to the successful termination of the war. The autonomous Barcelona regime was deprived of its control over Catalonia and the cabinet moved to Barcelona (October 1937).

The defense of the established government stiffened materially once the rebels reached the limits of Madrid. Thus far the Burgos Government had been the chief beneficiary of military supplies, especially planes and tanks, sent to Spain from Italy and Germany. Now, however, the "loyalists" also received considerable aid of a similar type, from the Soviet Union. The Madrid forces, commanded by General José Miaja, repulsed the rebel attack and during 1937 pushed the "nationalists" back to a safer distance. The Italian troops with Franco were badly defeated at Brihuega, on the Guadalajara front.[1]

The year 1938 was definitely more favorable, from both the military and diplomatic viewpoints, to the "insurgents" than the "loyalists." The air superiority and tank equipment which Franco

---

[1] The Madrid Government published and presented to the League of Nations a Spanish White Book entitled: *The Italian Invasion of Spain. Official Documents and Papers Seized from Italian Units in Action at Guadalajara,* 1937.

owed to the Italians and Germans, and the food shortage that affected chiefly the Barcelona Government areas, began to tell more and more decisively. Just before Christmas 1938 Franco prepared what was to prove the major offensive of the war. Having as its objective the city of Barcelona itself, the campaign was bitterly fought for a month. Then the "loyalist" capital fell.

The end of February 1939 saw the resignation of President Azaña and the recognition of the Franco regime by Great Britain and France. In March Premier Negrín flew to France, while in Madrid General Miaja was chosen by his colleagues to head a new defense council. Miaja had to fight not merely the "insurgents" but was forced to put down a communist uprising in Madrid itself. Franco meanwhile rejected all peace overtures short of unconditional surrender, and on March 28 his soldiers at last entered Madrid on his terms. Within twenty-four hours all remaining "loyalist" strongholds capitulated. Franco had won, after more than thirty-two months of bitter fighting.

Besides the long-term task of reconstructing war-torn, impoverished Spain, Franco faced certain vital immediate problems. These included feeding the starving populace; getting rid of the thousands of Italians, Germans, and Portuguese who had helped him to victory; demobilization; establishing a provisional government; negotiating with France over the future status of about 300,000 refugees who had gone or been driven northward across the Pyrenees; "settling accounts" with "loyalist" sympathizers and soldiers; and rebuilding as quickly as possible roads, railroads, bridges, public buildings, and factories that had been destroyed during the period of hostilities.

The foreign soldiers gradually departed, following the holding of a great "victory parade" in Madrid.[1] Man power for public works was procured through the imposition of labor service upon all males between eighteen and fifty and the use of concentration-camp inmates. Much-needed funds were raised through domestic loans and contributions. The Grand Council of the Spanish Phalanx met under Franco's presidency and drafted plans for the creation of a political and economic structure based on the Italian Fascist model. The repatriation of refugees was begun and arrangements were made with France for the return of money and

---

[1] In June 1939 the official journal of the Italian armed forces carried an article on Italy's military assistance to Franco. According to this report Italy sent 100,000 men to Spain. The activity of the Italian navy involved 149 vessels engaged on 870 missions. In February 1941 Mussolini sent Franco a "bill" for $275,000,000!

art objects earlier shipped northward by the "loyalists." Wholesale arrests were instituted against the "enemies" of the civil-war days. There were executions and there were jail sentences—the latter often with the opportunity to achieve "redemption through the penalty of labor" on public projects. Shortly after the Second World War broke out, Madrid once more became the sole capital of Spain.

THE "LITTLE WORLD WAR"

The "we or they" attitude in international politics had become sufficiently crystallized by the summer of 1936 so that the outbreak of civil war between conservatives and radicals in Spain threatened to precipitate another general war. The fascist states, including Portugal under President Antonio Oscar de Fragosa Carmona and Premier Antonio de Oliveira Salazar, professed to fear the rise of another "Bolshevik" state in Europe and hence determined to help Franco. Strategic and economic reasons were equally present with ideological ones. Italy and Germany felt that a fascist Spain would strengthen their own influence, while a radical Spain would be of advantage to France and the Soviet Union. It was hoped, presumably, that the rebels, if victorious, would be generous in the granting of concessions to develop Spain's coal, copper, iron, and other mineral resources. Finally, the triumph of a fascist government friendly to Italy might strengthen the latter's pretensions to control in the western Mediterranean.

To forestall the eventualities contemplated by Mussolini and Hitler, the Soviet Union decided to assist the established authorities. France and Great Britain, for their part, attempted, at least in the beginning, to steer a middle course. They were willing, for the sake of general peace, to forego their legal right to permit the sale of arms to the established government, but they also refused to accord rights of belligerency to the rebels. In Great Britain many persons were less opposed to the rebel than the "loyalist" economic views, while others, seeing Franco extend his control over those parts of Spain where British investments were heaviest, feared for personal reasons to alienate the rebel leader.[1] The British Labor Party and the trade unions, on the other hand, sympathized with the established government. Official Great Britain preferred to avoid any unnecessary entanglements at least until its

---

[1] Britishers were financially interested in the Rio Tinto copper and iron mines and the Jerez sherry trade in the south, and in the Bilbao iron regions in the north.

rearmament program should have been completed. The French Government sided emotionally with the "loyalists," but Premier Blum undertook to follow the lead of London, being convinced that only a policy of nonintervention would prevent Italy and Germany from taking the dangerous step of openly interfering on behalf of the rebels. In August 1936, accordingly, France proposed a European agreement to ship neither arms nor ammunition to either party in the civil war.

Eventually, twenty-seven European states, including all the great powers, agreed to set up in London an "International Committee for the Application of the Agreement Regarding Nonintervention in Spain." The committee held frequent meetings and was kept busy examining charges by the Soviet Union against Portugal, Italy, and Germany, and reciprocal charges by these powers against the Moscow Government, all alleging violations of the nonintervention agreement. Since the committee did little more than examine these charges, a steady flow of supplies entered Spain. When it became apparent that not merely supplies but soldiers and pilots were being sent to Spain, France and Great Britain suggested the extension of the nonintervention agreement to cover foreign "volunteers" as well as foreign weapons. In February 1937 such a ban became (theoretically) effective.

The promises of the powers were not fulfilled. Hence the nonintervention committee eventually decided to place a cordon of British, French, Italian, and German ships around Spain, with special inspectors stationed along the French and Portuguese land frontiers. After many delays, the patrol ships and officers took up their duties—only to be withdrawn after a couple of months.

The nonintervention committee meanwhile took up the question of withdrawal of "volunteers" already in Spain. While the discussions were in progress there occurred a series of submarine attacks on neutral merchant vessels carrying cargoes for the Barcelona Government through the Mediterranean. Suspicion centered on Italy, and Moscow openly accused Italian submarines of having torpedoed two Soviet freighters. This new form of piracy led Great Britain and France to call a conference of Mediterranean and Black Sea powers and Germany to meet at Nyon near Geneva. Germany and Italy refused to attend because the Soviet Union did attend, but on September 14, 1937, a Nyon Agreement was signed by nine states. An international patrol was established and patrol zones were assigned to the several signatories, with Great Britain and France undertaking to do most of the supervising. After London and Paris publicly recognized Italy as a "great Mediterranean power," Rome also joined the "piracy patrol." The submarine attacks now quickly ceased.

During the entire year 1938 the nonintervention committee tried to find a satisfactory formula for the withdrawal of the foreign "volunteers," but the last German and Italian fighters did not quit Spain until several weeks after the civil war was ended. Just before their departure, and coincident with Italy's occupation of Albania, Spain signed (April 1939) the Anti-Comintern Pact originally negotiated by Germany and Japan. Thus did the "little World War" end in victory for the axis.

CHAPTER XVI

Germany

FROM EMPIRE TO REPUBLIC

When the Imperial German Government in the autumn of 1914 appealed to the Reichstag for war credits, all parties, including the Social Democrats, voted favorably. This support in the face of a national crisis, however, was not meant as an endorsement of the general peacetime policies of the government. There was considerable opposition in the empire to a number of arrangements. The chancellor was responsible to the emperor rather than to the lower house. The members of the upper house were appointed by and responsible to the rulers, not the people, of the federated states. As king of Prussia, the emperor virtually controlled the upper house which, moreover, had greater powers than the Reichstag. Criticism was leveled at the undemocratic system of voting in Prussia, where the wealthier citizens had more voting power than the poorer ones. Social legislation and labor reform had not kept pace with the needs of the twentieth century. It was despite these grievances that most Germans in 1914 rallied to the support of the fatherland against what they considered wanton foes.

As the war continued and the weeks became months and the months years, an increasing number of socialists began to regard the struggle as an imperialistic venture rather than a defensive necessity. A definite split in the ranks of the Social Democratic Party was evident by the spring of 1915. The majority, headed by Friedrich Ebert and Philipp Scheidemann, believed in continuing support of the war; the minority, led by Hugo Haase, opposed the granting of further war credits. Early in 1916 Haase announced in the Reichstag that he and his followers were opposed to any further prolongation of the conflict, and a year later these men organized the Independent Social Democratic Party, favoring immediate peace without annexations.

Some radicals regarded even Haase's group as too conservative. Under the leadership of Karl Liebknecht and Rosa Luxemburg, these communists denounced the war and advocated the forceful establishment of a proletarian dictatorship. In 1916 Liebknecht had begun to publish denunciatory letters over the signature "Spartacus" and hence his followers came to be known as Spartacists. The eventual imprisonment of the Spartacist leaders failed to lessen the agitation, particularly since the inability of the army to win an early victory gradually alienated the affections of even the Majority Socialists and the Catholic Center Party under Matthias Erzberger.

Chancellor von Bethmann Hollweg, who had been in office since 1909, resigned in July 1917. His immediate successors were no more able than he had been to report victory or improve bad harvests. Finally, the liberal Prince Max of Baden organized (October 1918) a moderate coalition. Two Majority Socialists, Scheidemann and Gustav Bauer, were included in the cabinet. Prince Max was determined to grant widespread reforms in order to save the tottering throne of the Hohenzollerns, for by the time of his appointment the discontent had become ominous.

The Allied blockade worked havoc with the German food supply. The situation was made worse by bad harvests, particularly during the "turnip year" 1916–1917. The masses starved and froze, and only the rich were able to keep warm and satisfy their hunger. Profiteering reached unprecedented heights. The Russian revolutions of 1917 set a tempting example to some people, and Russian agents spread subversive propaganda. Already in 1916 there had been a munitions strike. Though sternly suppressed by the authorities, it was followed by a second strike in 1917 and a third in January 1918. Half a million persons in Berlin and Essen quit work on this last occasion for more than a week. The strikers committed no violence, but the government dealt harshly with the leaders and many of the men who had hitherto been exempt from military service because of occupation in the essential industries were sent to the front. Here they helped spread the idea of revolt among the soldiers.

The German navy, too, had become restless. It had been cooped up in the harbors with little for the sailors to do but discuss revolutionary doctrine and acquire a dislike for the officers. The latter themselves chafed under the prolonged inactivity and many of them vainly petitioned the emperor for commissions in the army. Meanwhile it had become evident to many that Great Britain would not be starved out by the submarine campaign and that the exaggerated expansionist hopes of the Fatherland Party recently organized by Admiral von Tirpitz could not be achieved. The participation of the United States in the war, moreover, had at last assumed gigantic proportions.

When Ludendorff's great drives of 1918 collapsed, the fall of the Hohenzollerns was foreshadowed. The army appeared ready to quit fighting and go home. With much courage Prince Max now rushed through a number of reforms which converted Germany into a constitutional monarchy. The emperor was made a figurehead, a mere symbol of unity. Ministerial responsibility was introduced and the Reichstag given control over war and peace. Freedom of speech, press, and assembly was granted and an amnesty was declared for political prisoners. Electoral reforms were promised in Prussia. Finally, Max began to negotiate with Wilson for an armistice. He emphasized that the new German administration was a government "of the people, in whose hands rested both actually and constitutionally the authority to make decisions."

Toward the end of October 1918 voice was frequently given to the idea that the emperor should abdicate. Since Wilson insisted that as long as the imperial government was in power he would discuss only surrender and not peace negotiation   Germans came to regard William as an obstacle to   ber 23 Haase demanded before the Reichstag On the following day, Gustav No made a similar plea. The news and on the evening of the of the Majority Socialists abdication. That night headquarters at Spa,

Meanwhile a disa base of Kiel. Whe tions would prob the Allies, the event. They pected—and But the eigh in this man dicated the British att refused to sulted, atte

Soon the spirit of revolt spread to the workers at Kiel, where revolutionary councils were formed which demanded the abdication of the Hohenzollerns, amnesty for the leaders of earlier mutinies, and equal suffrage rights. Other cities followed the example of Kiel and soon the demand for a republic was general along the north-German coast.

The government hoped in vain to keep the remainder of the country ignorant of these developments. At a demonstration held in Munich on November 7, an Independent-Socialist editor, Kurt Eisner, demanded the overthrow of the Bavarian dynasty. The Wittelsbach family made haste to flee and some of the people organized soldiers', workers', and peasants' councils. On the eighth, a "democratic and social republic" was set up in Bavaria with Eisner as its head. Similar councils were established and republican proclamations issued in Berlin and the chief industrial centers of the land. Indeed, the movement was so widespread as to be accompanied by relatively little disorder. The leaders of the Majority Socialists, fearing the loss of followers to the more radical Independents, now warned Max that, unless the emperor abdicated by the morning of November 9, they would resign from the government, demand William's deposition, and declare a general strike. M_____ing to save the monarchy for the Hohenzollern family_____iam II, labored to secure the latter's abdica-_____son of the crown prince.

_____listen to the chancellor's entreaties. _____in retaining the imperial crown. _____taff convinced him that the _____fight the German people. _____en Hindenburg agreed _____as Ebert and Scheide-_____ounce the expiration _____from Spa that the _____When, therefore, _____tuent assembly, _____nto his hands. _____fled to the _____e. Not until _____dication in _____er German _____to a federa-_____Council of _____e Majority

ns, many
peace. On Octobe
that the emperor abdicate.
ske of the Majority Socialists
papers quickly took up the cry
wenty-ninth Scheidemann, as leader
, requested Prince Max to get William's
the emperor went from Berlin to the army
stensibly to escape the influenza danger.

ster had occurred (October 28) at the naval
n the rumor spread that the armistice negotia-
ably result in a surrender of the German fleet to
German officers determined to forestall such an
preferred to seek an honorable death in an unex-
possibly successful—attack upon the British fleet.
ty thousand sailors who would have been involved
euver had no desire to become dead heroes. They in-
ir willingness to defend the German coasts against
cks, but with armistice negotiations under way they
participate in a wholesale suicidal venture. Mutiny re-
nded by arrests, shootings, and the raising of red flags.

ax, hop...

...y if not for Willi...

tion in favor of the infant...

William, at Spa, refused to...
He expected the army to aid him...
Eventually, however, the general s...
army could not be depended upon to...
At a Spa Conference of November 9 eve...
that abdication appeared the wisest step. Just...
mann called at the chancellor's palace to ann...
of the socialists' ultimatum, Max was informed...
formula of abdication was being considered...
Ebert promised to maintain order and call a consti...
Max felt justified in surrendering the government i...

Early in the morning of November 10 William...
Netherlands, soon to be followed by the crown prin...
November 28, however, did William send in a full a...
his name and that of the family. By that time all the oth...
princes had fled and the empire had been converted int...
tion of republican states, provisionally governed by a...
People's Commissars. The council was composed of thre...

and three Independent Socialists under the joint chairmanship of Ebert and Haase. The numerous subordinate officials of the former imperial service continued to serve the new government, but the Spartacists refused to coöperate. The commissars besought the people to maintain order, regard human life as sacred, and protect private property.

The Spartacists were as much opposed to the establishment of a social-democratic republic as they had been to the empire. Through their newspaper, *Die Rote Fahne* (*The Red Flag*), and by acts of terrorism, they strove to prevent the calling of a national constituent assembly at least until such time as their tactics should have cowed a sufficiently large number of citizens into accepting the ideal of a communist regime.

It would seem that in the presence of such an enemy the Majority and Independent Socialists, who had split chiefly over the question of ending the war, might have become reunited. But during the period of estrangement the Independents had become more radical. They now favored the rapid nationalization of industry and the postponement of constituent elections until the socialistic rule should have become entrenched beyond possibility of upset. The Majority favored slower nationalization, urged compensation for property owners, and desired an early expression of popular sentiment through the ballot.

The question of an election date finally was settled by a national congress of councils. In imitation of the organizations formed by the soldiers and workers of Munich and Berlin, local councils had appeared all over Germany. Frequently, too, they had assumed governmental powers. In December 1918 a national gathering of these councils was held. The congress, to the delight of the Majority Socialists, excluded communists and decided upon an early date (January 19, 1919) for the constituent elections. The angry communists, professing to see in these actions the germs of a counterrevolution, stirred up the sailors and marines in Berlin to revolt. When force was used to subdue the rebels, the Independent Socialists withdrew from all national and state posts. This circumstance enabled the Majority Socialists to fill the vacancies—even those in the council of commissars—with loyal supporters.

While awaiting election day, the commissars had to complete the demobilization of the returned troops, stave off further starvation despite the continuing Allied blockade, institute some immediate economic and social reforms, and hold in check the extremists of both the Right and Left. The ingrained desire of many Germans for law and order, their patriotism, and their willingness to accept any government which gave promise of being able to function smoothly rendered the problem of internal control less difficult than might have been expected. Yet, in anticipation of trouble from the Spartacist camp, the commissars held in readiness a well-equipped force of about three thousand, commanded by ex-imperial officers.

The Spartacists, meanwhile, had formed armed bands which roamed the streets of the larger cities, ready for violence at any moment. The "voice" of these extremists was "Spartacus" Liebknecht himself. Nothing short of outright communism would satisfy him. The "brain" of the movement was the crippled Rosa Luxemburg. The communists chose the week of January 5, 1919, for a supreme effort to oust the government.

A climax in the struggle for control was reached on Monday, January 6, when a vast crowd of armed workmen of Spartacist and Independent-Socialist sympathies assembled in the center of Berlin. Had these men been resolutely led, the government might have fallen without resistance. The commissars, themselves recruited largely from the laboring classes, dreaded to use troops against their kind. One after another they refused the responsibility of dealing with the situation, until finally Gustav Noske accepted the task. "All right," he was reported as saying, "someone must be the bloodhound. I do not shirk the responsibility." An experienced strike organizer, Noske was not afraid to deal with workers, but he had only a few thousand men with whom to face the mob. Fortunately for the government, the radical leaders failed their disciples at the crucial moment. They spent the day deliberating, until the crowds, cold and hungry, went home. Thereafter skirmishes between communist bands and the police or military continued daily until January 15, when both Liebknecht and Luxemburg were arrested and killed on the way to prison. "Spartacus Week" had failed of its objective and the Spartacist movement collapsed. On January 19 the elections for the national assembly took place in an atmosphere of relative quiet.

THE WEIMAR ASSEMBLY

More than thirty million of the eligible thirty-five million men and women over nineteen voted, on a basis of proportional representation. By the time of the elections the old political parties had all been reorganized and, in some cases, rechristened. The former Conservatives had been reconstructed on a monarchist platform as the German National People's Party (Nationalists). The right wing of the former National Liberals, chiefly business men, had been re-formed under Gustav Stresemann as the German People's Party. Though preferring a monarchy, this group was ready to support the republic in the interests of internal peace and unity.

The Centrists, under Matthias Erzberger, temporarily changed their party name to that of Christian Democrats, but soon reverted to the original form. They favored a democratic republic, a bill of rights, and social legislation. The former left-wing National Liberals and the Progressives united to form a new Democratic Party led, among others, by the banker, Hjalmar Schacht. The Democrats favored a bourgeois republic, were opposed to a return of the military bureaucracy, promised legal guarantees for workmen, and advocated the prosecution of the war profiteers. The Majority Socialists readopted the name of Social Democrats and continued to urge the gradual socialization of industry and property, while the Independent Socialists urged a more rapid nationalization process. The Spartacists, who meanwhile had taken the name of German Communist Party, refused to take part in the elections.

When the returns were counted, it appeared that the Social Democrats, with 163 out of the available 421 seats, would be the largest single group in the assembly. The Centrists received 88 seats, the Democrats 75, the Nationalists 42, the Independent Socialists 22, and the People's Party 21. The remaining ten seats went to four minor parties. Thirty-six women were elected. To protect the gathering against mob violence, Ebert convoked the assembly for February 6 in the peaceful city of Weimar.

The assembly met on the appointed day and adopted a previously drafted provisional constitution as its basis for government. Thereupon the commissars surrendered their powers and a "Weimar Coalition" of Social Democrats, Centrists, and Democrats became the official government. On February 11 the assembly elected Friedrich Ebert president of the republic (*Reich*). Ebert was an ex-saddler from Heidelberg who had come into prominence as coleader with Scheidemann of the moderate socialists. Upon his assumption of office he declared that he would regard himself as "the authorized representative of the entire German people, not as leader of a single party." Scheidemann became chancellor and Brockdorff-Rantzau, who was not affiliated with any political party, became foreign minister.

The assembly faced the threefold task of putting down internal opposition, concluding peace with the Allies, and giving the republic a permanent constitution. Noske, as minister of home defense, attended to the first of these duties. There were violent mining and railway strikes and there was much fighting. In Munich a communist government was established after a nationalist had murdered Kurt Eisner. Noske decided once and for all to "settle accounts with the lunatics" and with the aid of some former army officers crushed the radical movement by the summer of 1919.

The conclusion of peace proved to be more difficult. The various factions in the assembly spent precious time in accusing one another of having lost the war and no group was prepared to accept the treaty as it was presented on May 7 by the Allies. Scheidemann, indeed, resigned the chancellorship rather than agree to the document. But in view of the severity of the punishment threatened by the Allies if the assembly rejected the terms, a majority of the delegates on June 23, just before the expiration of the time limit, agreed to the treaty.

The final task of the assembly was completed in July 1919 with the adoption of a constitution. The document was based upon a draft made by Professor Hugo Preuss, a Democrat in politics and an opponent of states' rights. In the final balloting the Social Democrats, Centrists, and Democrats voted for the constitution, while the Independent Socialists, the People's Party, and the Nationalists opposed it.

The constitution vested supreme power in the people and defined the Reich as a federation of republican states called *Länder*.[1] The national government was given the usual powers of a central authority and in addition was accorded the paramount right to legislate upon railway and water traffic, the care of the poor, the protection of mothers, widows, and orphans, the protection of the flora and fauna, the use of natural resources, insurance, education, the protection of workmen, and the cinema. The central administration might also instruct the several states upon the best means of enforcing the national laws. There was a bill of rights, and the suffrage was accorded to all men and women over twenty on a basis of proportional representation. Provision was made for a

---

[1] In 1920 there were eighteen such Länder, but in 1929 Prussia annexed Waldeck and there remained seventeen.

president to be elected by popular vote for a term of seven years, without restriction as to reëlection. He might be removed from office by a popular referendum following impeachment by a two-thirds vote in the lower house. There was no provision for a vice-president.

The assembly's distaste for autocracy was reflected in the restrictions placed upon the *actual* powers of the chief executive, for in theory these powers were, as in France and Great Britain, fairly extensive. No action of his was valid unless countersigned by the chancellor or appropriate minister. He might dismiss the Reichstag, although any particular pretext for such action was not to be used more than once and new elections had to be held within sixty days. In time of emergency the president, acting with the chancellor, might suspend certain constitutional guarantees and issue decrees with the force of law (Article 48).[1]

The chancellor was empowered to formulate governmental policy and select the cabinet. The ministers did not need to be members of parliament, but they were made directly responsible to the Reichstag. Resignation of the cabinet had to follow only upon a specific vote of lack of confidence. Cabinet decisions were to be made by majority vote, the chancellor having the power to break a tie. A supreme court, sitting at Leipzig, was endowed, as had been its imperial predecessor, with only a limited original jurisdiction. It was set up chiefly as a tribunal of appeals to ensure uniform interpretation of the laws. Ordinary questions of justice were left to the individual states.

The chief legislative body, according to the constitution, was to be the Reichstag, with members elected for four years. After 1920 elections were held under the Baden system of proportional representation whereby each party secured one deputy for every sixty thousand votes that it polled. Since the number of voters fluctuated, the number of deputies changed with each election. This plan safeguarded the rights of minorities but it had important defects. The delegates were elected in the order in which their names appeared on the party lists and the top names had the best chance of victory. There was little contact between candidates and electors, since the latter had to vote for a party list rather than a personality. The political machines thus were able to keep their

[1] Legally the Reichstag could demand the repeal of any such measures, but in practice this was rarely done. In its effort to fight the economic depression, the Berlin Government eventually issued several hundred emergency decrees. Indeed, from 1930 to 1933 Germany was ruled under a "constitutional dictatorship," for in that period presidential emergency decrees virtually replaced parliamentary legislation.

favorites in office. Finally, the system resulted in the appearance of more than a score of parties in the lower house and the consequent inability of any one of them, at least until the advent of the National Socialists in 1933, to get a majority. The resultant inefficiency in the matter of legislation was grist to the mill of the Nazi propagandists.

The upper house, representing the states, was labeled the *Reichsrat*. It might hold up, but it could not veto, general laws passed by the Reichstag. Its consent, however, was necessary for the passage of any measure affecting the states as such. Each state was entitled to at least one delegate in the Reichsrat and the larger states had one for every seven hundred thousand of their population. Yet, lest Prussia secure a preponderating influence, it was provided that no state might have more than two-fifths of the total representation. The delegates to the Reichsrat were members of the various state cabinets and were paid by the state governments. In contrast to the Reichstag, the upper house did not die, although its composition changed frequently. In 1932 its membership was sixty-eight.

There was to be no state-supported church in the Reich and religious freedom was guaranteed. Education was placed under the supervision of the state and teachers became public officials. School attendance was made compulsory until the age of eighteen. Private schools were tolerated only in exceptional cases and for religious instruction. The constitution demanded the giving of instruction in art and in the latest scientific advances.

The influence of the Social Democrats and the Centrists was evident in the economic clauses of the constitution. All private property was to be used to "serve the public good." Expropriation of landed property became permissible where "necessary to satisfy the demand for housing, to promote settlement and reclamation, or to improve agriculture." Private business enterprises adapted for socialization might be transferred to public ownership upon payment of proper compensation. Provision was made for state insurance systems against sickness, accident, old age, and unemployment.

With the adoption of the constitution, the work for which the assembly had been called was completed. Instead of dissolving itself, however, that body moved to the Reichstag building in Berlin and proclaimed itself the official legislative organ of the republic. President Ebert's term of office was extended and eventually continued by a regularly elected Reichstag until 1925.

THE DEFENSE OF THE REPUBLIC, 1919–1923

For some time after the adoption of the constitution, the republic in Germany was in danger. While the government had concentrated its energies upon suppressing the communists, opportunity had been taken by ex-army officers, Junkers, and other die-hards to form such strong monarchist organizations as the League of the Upright and the *Stahlhelm* (Steel Helmet). The monarchists had formulated a long list of grievances against the republicans and the Weimar Assembly. It was rumored that cowardly republicans had made defeat inevitable by undermining the military power of the empire during the last months of the war. The assembly was attacked for accepting the "Versailles Dictate" and for permitting the country to be overrun by Allied commissions. Some individuals feared that the authorities might surrender certain "war criminals" to the Allies for trial. Finally, there was a widespread feeling that the assembly had refused to call regular presidential and parliamentary elections lest Hindenburg be elected to the highest office and the way thus paved for a monarchist restoration.

Reactionary activities reached a climax in March 1920 in an attempted *Putsch* or coup planned by Dr. Wolfgang Kapp. The latter, a New Yorker by birth and founder of a successful Prussian bank, had gained some notoriety during the war for a fierce attack upon Bethmann Hollweg's policies and for assisting Tirpitz in the organization of the Fatherland Party. He was inconspicuous during the revolution but remained in communication throughout 1919 and 1920 with such men as Ludendorff and Tirpitz. General Walther von Lüttwitz, commandant of Berlin, and a Major Waldemar Pabst fell in with Kapp's scheme for a forceful restoration of monarchy. The three men placed themselves at the head of about eight thousand soldiers and early one morning marched the dozen miles from the military barracks to Berlin. Noske had a force of only two thousand men with which to oppose the plotters and the government fled to Dresden and then to Stuttgart.

Kapp failed to make the most of his opportunities. Instead of playing the strong man he tried to conciliate his opponents. Confusion and hesitancy prevailed where quick action and audacity were needed. The chief factor in the overthrow of his regime of a week, however, was the attitude of the laborers. Upon the issuance of a stirring manifesto by Ebert, the workmen throughout the land went on a general strike. The water, gas, electricity, and tramway services were tied up and even the railways were operated only where it was necessary to do so lest the people be made to suffer undue hardship. Kapp's own followers now left him and he fled to Sweden, leaving behind a grandiose manifesto of his accomplishments. He soon returned, however, and surrendered to the authorities, only to die in prison while awaiting trial (1922). Lüttwitz and Pabst found refuge abroad. The immediate danger of overthrow was past.

Although the government had won a temporary triumph over the reactionaries, it once again found itself faced with attacks from the Left. The Independent Socialists urged the workers to continue the general strike until the hated Noske (who had organized the armed forces against the workmen) resigned, until the government's army was disbanded,[1] and until regular elections for a Reichstag were called. Under such pressure the government accepted the resignation of Noske and set a date in June 1920 for parliamentary elections.

In these elections the strength of the three republican groups which had formed the Weimar Coalition fell by more than one hundred seats. The Nationalists, People's Party, and Independent Socialists, all gained seats, while the Communist Party elected two delegates. In the first regularly elected republican Reichstag, accordingly, a coalition government was organized representing the People's Party, Centrists, and Democrats. Konstantin Fehrenbach, a Centrist who had been president of the Weimar Assembly, became chancellor.

The Kapp affair did not end the attempts of reactionaries to avenge the "betrayal" of the fatherland. They instituted a reign of terror against persons connected with the signing of the peace treaty, persons who in any way gave aid to the Allied commissions that were camped in Germany, and individuals prominently identified with socialism. Jews and Catholics were attacked and attempts were made upon the lives of Ebert and Scheidemann. The Centrist leader, Erzberger, who in 1917 had urged peace without annexations, was killed in 1921. In 1922 Walter Rathenau, successful industrialist, political philosopher, and efficient cabinet officer, was assassinated. The government replied to these acts by suspending the constitutional guarantees and passing a

[1] The Leftists held that the conservative army was much harsher in its suppression of radical than of reactionary movements.

Law for the Protection of the Republic, but the agitation continued.

In November 1923 another coup, the Ludendorff-Hitler *Putsch*, was attempted from Munich. General Ludendorff and Adolf Hitler, of whom more later, devised a plan to seize the government. Their scheme conflicted with the aims of a second group of Bavarian conspirators led by Gustav von Kahr, with the result that the plotters began to fight among themselves. A number of the leaders of this "beer-hall rebellion" were jailed and the harassed authorities once more turned to the numerous other problems that confronted the state. These were, to mention only the more perplexing ones, reparation, the Franco-Belgian invasion of the Ruhr, separatist movements in the Rhineland and Bavaria, the drop in value of the mark, closing factories, increasing unemployment, and a hungry populace. Economic ties and national patriotism acted as strong cohesive forces, else Germany might have crumbled into bits.[1]

FINANCES, LOW AND HIGH

The Imperial German Government had been so confident of an early and successful conclusion of the war that little attention had been paid to increased taxation as a means of meeting the war expenditures. Instead, the authorities had relied upon the people to buy war bonds, and upon the printing press. The Reichsbank, in fact, had been empowered to accept treasury bonds and bills as coverage for additional paper currency. Eventually the tax rates were raised and emergency sources of income created, but Germany financed only about 5 per cent of her war costs by direct levy, whereas Great Britain, for example, provided in that manner for more than 20 per cent of the extraordinary expenditures. At the end of the war there were almost five times as many marks in circulation as in 1913. Yet, because the world was ignorant of the precise facts and because there was for a time strong belief in the ability of Germany to recover quickly, the mark, at the close of 1918, still was quoted at half of its par value—at 12 instead of 23.82 cents.

This situation could not last long. When the emergency laws that had established maximum commodity-price limits during the war lapsed, prices began to soar in proportion to the abundance

---

[1] In 1922 the Social Democrats and Independent Socialists reunited and pledged themselves to preserve the republic.

of currency in circulation. The shortage of gold, much of which had been sent to neutral countries for war supplies, now became apparent with the discovery that Germany's wartime adverse trade balance had amounted to $12,000,000,000. The raw-material reserves were at a low point and the economic structure of the land was dislocated, for nearly every industry and factory had been reorganized to serve the military exigency. In the face of curtailed credits, unfavorable trade balances, and reparation payments, the Germans, in order to get essential foodstuffs and raw products, resorted to paper money.

Even in this critical situation the government hesitated to tax more heavily the war profiteers and the big capitalists, while realty and income-tax assessments continued to be based upon the inflated and fluctuating paper mark instead of upon a gold basis. Thus tax payments, when they fell due, had a lower real value than had been anticipated at the time of assessment. The circle of mounting deficits and further inflation became increasingly vicious with each passing month. By November 1922 a dollar, normally worth 4.2 marks, would purchase 7000 marks.

The crisis was heightened during the foreign occupation of the Ruhr. The seizure by the French of billions of Reichsbank notes and the attempt of the German Government to subsidize (with the aid of the printing press) the patriotically idle workers of the occupied region completely destroyed the value of the currency. Only a miracle could have stopped the "toboggan slide" of the mark, and no miracle occurred. A belated attempt to restrict the purchase by Germans of foreign currency failed of any definite result and the mark, standing at 160,000 to the dollar early in July 1923, fell by the end of the month to more than 1,000,000 to the dollar. The printers soon found it difficult to meet the demand for paper notes, especially since about 90 per cent of the government's revenue in the summer of 1923 was acquired by the simple process of assigning money value to scraps of paper. Late in 1923 the government owed the Reichsbank about 190 quintillion (190,-000,000,000,000,000,000) marks.

When the paper-money fever was at its height the Reichsbank employed 2000 persons as overseers of its paper, printing, and transportation establishments, while 30 paper factories, 133 printing offices, and 1783 printing presses were kept busy to meet the demand for notes. The middle of November 1923 saw the mark quoted at 2.5 trillion to the dollar in Berlin and at 4 trillion in Cologne. Milk sold for 250 billion marks a quart and was scarce at that price. Even private firms and individuals printed "emergency money." Eventually it became difficult to assign high enough values to the notes to cover the cost of paper and printing, particularly since the notes were adorned with artistic designs.[1]

The economic results of this debacle were terrible. It became almost impossible to negotiate loans or make contracts. The middle class suffered most, since its debtors seized the opportunity to retire bonds, lift mortgages, and pay notes. Hitherto comfortable incomes from investments and savings became worthless and many persons who had expected to live on their incomes now found themselves obliged to seek employment in an overcrowded labor market. Trade unions were unable to fulfill their ordinary functions because their funds were worthless. Many of the industrialists, on the other hand, benefited by the cheap labor and cheap cost of materials and invested *their* financial surpluses in comparatively safe foreign securities. On the strength of the cheap money supply, numerous "fly-by-night" businesses were set up, only to crash as quickly as they had been established. People hoarded goods and sought to exchange their marks for commodities having a more stable value, thus causing a veritable *"Flucht aus der Mark in die Ware."*

In the autumn of 1923 the German people virtually repudiated the mark and conditions became worse than at any time during the war. Peasants refused to take their products to the cities; merchants closed their shops; there was no standard of wages and, as was to be expected, the rise in wages lagged far behind the increase in prices; thousands of war cripples and persons who had expected to live on fixed incomes faced starvation. Hunger riots became common and the chaos was made worse by the activities of foreign troops in the Ruhr, by separatist movements in the Rhineland and Bavaria, and by the rise to power of communists in Saxony and elsewhere. National cabinets rose and fell with monotonous frequency and the country appeared on the verge of collapse. Finally, the government declared a state of siege.

Lest Germany fall into complete dissolution, the authorities decided (October 1923) to launch one last, desperate program whereby the people were to lift themselves out of the mire "by the hair of the head like Munchausen." A new currency and new bank of issue were to be created, the budget was to be balanced, and a partial restoration of industry brought about. The men who

---

[1] At its peak, the note circulation of marks exceeded 400 quintillion. The equivalent of this stupendous figure in dollars was only 60 million.

were asked to perform these deeds were Finance Minister Dr. Hans Luther and Dr. Hjalmar Schacht. Equipped with emergency powers, these men succeeded in stabilizing the mark—though again at a disastrous cost to many Germans and to foreign speculators.

The printing of any more paper currency was halted. A special *Rentenbank* was opened and empowered to issue a new, temporary currency called the *Rentenmark,* with an assigned par value equal to that of the prewar gold mark. Coverage was provided by a virtual blanket mortgage on the agricultural and industrial wealth of Germany. Altogether, 3,200,000,000 of these marks were issued, this sum being slightly more than half of the amount of Germany's prewar currency circulation. The Rentenmark was circulated along with the paper marks at a ratio of 1 to 1 trillion. Thus "there was created out of nothing . . . a currency which was kept stable by the confidence of the people."

The budget was balanced by ruthless measures. War claims were rejected and thousands of public employees, many of whom had received lifetime appointments, were dismissed with little or no compensation.[1] Salaries were cut and a temporary moratorium was declared on public loans. The government raised the tax rates, calculated tax payments on a gold basis, and instituted a better system of collection. The regular realty tax was supplemented by a new "house-rent tax" on rented houses, factories, and agricultural buildings.

Many of these acts had to be repealed or modified later, but not until they had served their immediate purpose—until the budget had been balanced and inflation stopped. General conditions also became easier when (1) the Dawes Plan went into effect in September 1924; (2) Germany got a foreign loan of 800,000,000 gold marks; and (3) the Ruhr was evacuated. A new Reichsbank then was created to take the place of the Rentenbank and a *Reichsmark* was substituted for the Rentenmark. Until mid-1925 paper marks were redeemable at the rate of one trillion to one Reichsmark.

The distress was not yet over. The low exchange-value placed upon paper marks wiped out many small fortunes. The lack of liquid capital for a time forced the interest rate up to more than 40 per cent. Unemployment became worse because of the bankruptcy of many firms and because goods were no longer in demand

[1] The Reich dismissed about 330,000 persons in all services, including the railway and postal systems; the states and municipalities dismissed 400,000 more. Many of these people later became Nazis.

for hoarding. But in the end a measure of stability and confidence was restored and the path to economic recovery was made less thorny.

DISAPPOINTMENT AND HOPE

In the years immediately following the war a wave of pessimism swept over the German people. In their defeat it seemed to them that the world was crumbling, that civilization was coming to an end. All was gloomy, and many a thinker could find refuge and solace only in metaphysical speculation and mysticism. As if by predestination there were available to the spiritual pessimists a number of relevant philosophical treatises.

One of these works was the two-volume *Travel Diary of a Philosopher* by Hermann von Keyserling. Although the first volume was in the hands of the printer in 1914 and the second was merely revised during the war years, the completed work did not appear until 1919. Unable further to sustain a lively interest in Europe and eager to "let fresh influences play upon" him, Keyserling had undertaken a leisurely journey around the world. His observations on the trip confirmed him in his belief of the supremacy of the soul and the preëminent virtue of spiritual perfection. "The shortest way to oneself is a voyage around the world." The diary praised the contemplative, unhurried life of Asia while indicting the bustling West which "recognized nothing to be unchangeable" and which "expressed its values in quantitative terms."

The philosopher, however, was enough Westerner to see good in individualism, and the "new man" whom he wished to see arise was to be an idealistic individualist, a man who would "blend the inwardness of Asia with the vigor of Christian Europe." Wisdom, not knowledge, Keyserling thought, was necessary to save Western civilization. So great was the popular response to these ideas, at least for a time, that the volumes sold in tens of thousands and a School of Wisdom was founded and endowed at Darmstadt for the training of sages. Oriental mysticism and the striving for wisdom seemed to many Germans the only consolation in a hopeless world.

Of even greater importance than the *Diary* to those who were pessimistic of the future was Oswald Spengler's massive *The Decline of the West*. Although this work, too, was conceived before the outbreak of the war and completed late in 1917 while German armies still were winning victories, it suited very well the disillusioned, despairing Germany of 1919 and after. Displaying erudition in philosophy, literature, history, mathematics, and art, the book had for its theme the cyclic character of the historic process. History was regarded as a succession of complete civilization cycles each with its birth in a spring and its death in a winter. The end of each cycle was as inexorable as its beginning. Three such periods had already come and gone: the Indian (beginning about 1800 B.C.), the Antique (from about 900 B.C.), and the Arabian (ushered in with the Christian and Moslem eras). The Western, dating from perhaps 900 A.D., now was in its winter and was doomed to die ere many more centuries passed. Then "there will be no more Western culture, no more German, English, or French." Though the author insisted that his book was not meant to be a pessimistic forecast, *The Decline of the West* came to be regarded in some circles as a well-founded prophecy of the downfall of Western supremacy. As such it achieved a considerable vogue, for in it the gloomy found confirmation of their fears, and the disillusioned, proof of the futility of things.

Books of pessimism and fatalism were not alone popular in postwar Germany. Volumes on the causes of the war, on how it might have been prevented, and on how it might have been won sold by the hundreds of thousands. There was a flood of memoirs, especially from officials who felt it necessary to justify their past actions and from persons who in one way or another had been connected with the imperial household. Although Wilson was a much-discussed personality, no full-length German biography of him appeared until more than a decade after the signing of the peace treaty.

Descriptions of the war and of life at the front appeared in great quantities and many of them rapidly went through numerous editions. Erich Maria Remarque's *Im Westen nichts Neues* (1929), translated as *All Quiet on the Western Front,* and then his more mature *The Road Back* (1931) took the country by storm. Psychological novels and psychoanalytical studies dealing with every sort of neurosis and mental illness led the lists of best sellers; and plays, in order to be successful, generally had to be tragic and horrible. In art, too, this spirit was reflected, and "expressionism" or "direct action in art" was carried further in Germany than elsewhere. Somber geometrical and bizarre representations of machinery, death, fate, and mental disorders, were all the fashion. Truly it was a gloomy period in the history of the German mind. "Night falls over Europe," said Walter Rathenau, shortly before his assassination in the streets of Berlin.

The despair which was so characteristic of the middle-aged and older people in Germany—those whose dreams of a happy and settled future had been blasted by the god of war—was not common among the younger persons. Their plans had not been upset, nor their calculations destroyed. They merely reflected upon the hunger, the privations, the regulations and restraints of the war period, and they regarded peace as a cause for optimism. This group believed that its elders had brought on the war by a blind stupidity, a fatalistic groping in the dark, the result of ignorance, conventions, and old-fashioned ideas. But the younger people were made of different stuff. They would not be led blindfold along the path of destruction. They would benefit by the experience of the earlier victims and they would know how to handle themselves in a future crisis.

As after the humiliation of Prussia by Napoleon in 1806, German youth now felt that regeneration depended upon a higher mental and physical development of the nation. The free, simple life of the ancient Germans, *that* was the cure for despondency and national lethargy. Gymnastics, forest air, sunshine, song, these were needed to revive faith and hope. Accordingly, an organized *Jugendbewegung* or Youth Movement, which had already made some progress before 1914, aroused renewed interest and attracted millions of recruits. The *Wandervögel,* or Birds of Passage, founded by Karl Fischer in 1904, became a great national society and German woodlands and mountains reverberated with the sound of cheerful voices. Moreover, just as the ancestral Germans loved their contests of strength and agility, so modern youth chose athletics as the favorite outlet for its restless energies. In every field the Germans strove to achieve superiority over the athletes of other nations.

The movement had its weaknesses. Sometimes freedom was confused with license. There was a tendency among some of the younger set to flout authority and to sneer at age and gray hair. Many of the youth organizations became identified with political, religious, or class groups, and often bitterness and strife ensued where brotherliness should have prevailed. The bad economic situation and the increasing ill will manifested among nations after 1929 led more and more of the growing young men and women to wonder if, after all, their optimism was justified. Eventually, many of them turned willing ears to the blandishments of the new prophets in brown shirts—of the followers of Adolf Hitler.

PARTIES AND POLITICS, 1924–1932

In 1924 the Reichstag that had been elected in 1920 was dissolved. During its session, four chancellors had striven to restore order and give stability to the republic. In the elections of 1924, however, the moderate parties with which these men were affiliated lost heavily, while the extremists, right and left, made sizable gains. Chancellor Wilhelm Marx (Centrist) therefore resigned and President Ebert asked the leaders of the Nationalist Party to create a new government. The reactionary temper of the Nationalists, some of whom suggested Tirpitz for the chancellorship, soon induced Ebert to recall Marx, who eventually effected another moderate coalition.

The majority which this group controlled was small. Hence, when, in order to pass certain railway legislation required by the Dawes Plan, it became necessary to secure a two-thirds majority, the government appealed to the Nationalists for support in return for the promise of some cabinet positions. The Nationalist Party, though officially opposed to the Dawes Plan, responded by permitting its members to vote on the pending legislation at their own discretion. Thereupon enough Nationalists voted affirmatively to make possible the desired enactments. When an attempt was made to fulfill the pledge regarding Nationalist additions to the government, however, the other parties protested so strenuously that the Reichstag was dissolved and a second election was ordered for 1924.

In this election the middle parties gained a number of seats at the expense of both monarchists and communists, but the Nationalists elected enough delegates to make difficult the formation of a government. Marx resigned rather than admit Nationalists into his cabinet and eventually a Centrist-People's-Nationalist coalition was formed under Dr. Luther. The continuance of a conciliatory foreign policy was assured when the portfolio of foreign affairs was left in the hands of Dr. Stresemann. The latter, indeed, remained in continuous control of the foreign office under every government from November 1923 until his death in October 1929.

A few weeks after the organization of the Luther Cabinet, President Ebert died (February 1925) and it became necessary to hold Germany's first popular presidential election. According to German electoral law the president had to be elected on a national ticket, the candidate who received a majority of all votes cast being the victor. In the event that no candidate got such a majority, a second election would have to be held. There was no elimination of candidates for the second election, though any party might nominate a new standard-bearer. The second election was to go to the nominee who received the largest number of votes.

Two elections had to be held in 1925, for in the first balloting no candidate was successful. Before the second election took place, two party coalitions were effected. The Centrists, Democrats, and Social Democrats, who together had polled almost 50 per cent of the votes, now jointly nominated the Centrist leader, Marx. The Right parties, which had got about 43 per cent of the votes, also combined, but instead of renominating one of the previous candidates they chose the aged and popular Field Marshal von Hindenburg. The Communist Party refused to unite with any other group and renominated Ernst Thälmann.

A spirited campaign ensued, each group striving to draw to the polls some of the millions of people who had neglected to vote in the first contest. The balloting took place on April 26. Almost 3,500,000 more votes were cast than in the first election and most of this increase, apparently, went to swell Hindenburg's total. The final returns credited the seventy-seven-year-old marshal with 14,655,766 votes. Marx got 13,751,615 and Thälmann secured 1,931,151. By refusing to join the coalition of middle parties, the Communist Party in a sense made possible the election of the candidate of the Right, for Marx and Thälmann together had more votes than the victor.

Hindenburg's election was widely regarded as a blow at the republic. The marshal, however, took the oath to support the republican constitution without reservation, and his policy of moderation soon won general confidence at home and abroad. By adopting a German rather than a partisan policy he was able to reconcile many factions in Germany and bring together a host of former opponents.

In December 1925, after eleven months in office, the Luther Ministry resigned. It had fallen into disfavor with the Nationalists because of its sanction of the Locarno Pact and had lost the support of other groups on domestic issues. Six weeks' time and a threat of presidential dictatorship were required before another cabinet was formed, again by Luther. Soon this government, too, fell (May 1926), over a question regarding the national flag.

The succeeding Marx Ministry experienced a lively battle on the subject of confiscating for state use the property of the former ruling houses. Various court opinions had already been rendered on this issue and the claims of the princes had usually been upheld. In June 1926 the matter was submitted to a referendum. More than fourteen million votes were cast for confiscation and only half a million against it. Since, however, a referendum was successful only in the event that a majority of the entire qualified voting body registered assent, the result was five million votes short of the number needed for confiscation.

Chancellor Marx found it necessary to reorganize his ministry in 1927 and to admit some Nationalists into the cabinet. Before the Centrists would agree to this, the Nationalists had to promise to uphold the republic, endorse Stresemann's policy of conciliation, and consent to coöperation with the League. The arrangement was not satisfactory and in 1928 the Reichstag was dissolved.

In the elections of May 1928 the Nationalists lost heavily, while the Social Democrats considerably increased their parliamentary membership. The Marx coalition of Center and Right elements therefore resigned and the Social Democrat, Hermann Müller, who nine years earlier had signed the Versailles Treaty, organized a temporary "Ministry of Personalities." He was the first socialist chancellor since 1920. The provisional ministry was only to function until a more stable one could be formed, preferably by a coalition of the Social Democratic, Democratic, Centrist, People's, and Bavarian People's parties. The wrangling among the groups was so prolonged that a final union was not cemented until ten months later. Then, with Müller still as chancellor, each of the five parties was represented in the new cabinet in proportion to its strength in the lower house.

Müller's regime was not happy. Budgetary difficulties were immense. The acceptance of the Young Plan aroused nationalistic opposition. There was bitter debating over a special levy and revised income taxes. The unemployment situation became critical and there was disagreement over what should constitute a feasible unemployment-insurance scheme. In March 1930 the Müller Ministry resigned. Dr. Heinrich Brüning, leader of the Centrist Party, formed a new moderate coalition.

The new ministry desired to continue the moderate policies of its predecessor, namely, to meet all international obligations, provide agricultural relief while yet practicing the strictest economy, and chart a foreign course based on the principles of Stresemann. Since the latter had died, in October 1929, the foreign portfolio was assigned to one of his close friends, Julius Curtius. The gov-

PÁUL VON HINDENBURG

ernment's tenure was disquietingly shaky and several times the cabinet was saved from falling merely because the opposition was divided among itself or because Hindenburg threatened to dissolve the Reichstag and rule as dictator in conformity with Article 48 of the constitution if the bickering did not cease. In July 1930, after the Reichstag had definitely rejected a government budget bill, the president carried out his threat. The legislature was dissolved and new elections were ordered for September. Meanwhile, in an attempt to check the rapidly mounting national deficit, several emergency budgetary decrees were put into effect.

The outstanding feature of the election of September 1930, for which twenty-seven parties nominated candidates, was the gain made by two extremist groups, the Communist Party and the National Socialists (*Nationalsozialistische Deutsche Arbeiterpartei*). Of the 35,000,000 votes cast, the Communist Party obtained 4,587,-000, or nearly 40 per cent more than it had polled in 1928. Simultaneously it increased its membership in the Reichstag from 54 to 77 seats. Even more striking were the gains of the National Socialists who raised their Reichstag contingent from 12 to 107 and their popular vote from 809,000 (1928) to more than 6,400,000. They now formed the second largest group in the lower house, being led only by the Social Democrats with 143 seats. Before analyzing the reasons for this success of the National Socialists, who were also called Hitlerites or Nazis, it is necessary to consider the earlier history of the party and the activities of its leader, Adolf Hitler.

The future chief of the National Socialists was born on April 20, 1889, in Upper Austria, the son of a minor customs official. Against the wishes of his father, who wanted him to enter the civil service, Adolf Hitler indulged his talent for drawing and painting, eventually going to Vienna to study architecture. Failing to gain admission to the imperial art academy, he eked out an existence as house-painter.

His free time was spent in avid reading on the racial, moral, social, economic, and political problems confronting the German-speaking people in Austria and Germany. At work and after work he meditated upon these subjects, and with the passing of time the spirit of German nationality grew stronger in him and the hatred of international socialism increased. He frequently argued with his fellow-workmen, particularly over questions of politics and economics, and he steadfastly refused to join the Austrian Social Democratic Party. On several occasions he found it advisable to flee before his irate fellow-laborers. In the end he came to attribute his inability to get and hold a job to the machinations of the socialists. Moreover, since he associated immorality and radicalism with Judaism, regarding the socialist movement as an attempt of international Jewry to control the workers, Hitler also became an anti-Semite.

In 1912 Hitler went to Munich to live and when the war broke out he requested permission from the Bavarian authorities to fight in the Bavarian army. Apparently he preferred not to join the Austro-Hungarian forces because he objected to the fact that the Dual Monarchy was a state composed of several nationalities rather than a national state. He acquitted himself well in action on the western front, was wounded and gassed, and received the Iron Cross.

The events of the German revolution of 1918 filled Hitler with bitterness. He remained in comparative obscurity until 1923, but then, with Ludendorff and others, participated in an unsuccessful attempt to overthrow the government. For his part in the movement Hitler was sentenced to five years' imprisonment in a fortress, but he was released after having served only a few months. Through his enlistment in the Bavarian army Hitler had lost his citizenship in Austria and because of his attempted coup and subsequent imprisonment he was for a long time unable to acquire citizenship in Germany. It thus happened that the leader of one of the most nationalistic groups in the world was for years (until 1932) a man without a country.

Upon his release from prison Hitler put new life into the National Socialist German Workers' Party, a political organization which he had joined in 1919 and which had suffered a decline during his enforced inactivity. A party program of "Twenty-five Points" had been drawn up for the group in 1920 by an engineer named Gottfried Feder, one of the half-dozen original colleagues of Hitler and later economic adviser to the Nazis. Eventually this outline of party policy was expanded by Hitler in a book of memoirs entitled *Mein Kampf.*

According to the *original* pronouncements the ultimate goal of the Hitlerites was a "Third Reich," [1] a Greater Germany wherein should be united in one national comradeship *all* those of "German blood without reference to confession," including the "Germans" in Austria, the Netherlands, Poland, Czechoslovakia, and Alsace. Jews were regarded as having alien blood.[2] The achieve-

[1] The first Reich was the Holy Roman Empire; the second was from 1871 to 1918.
[2] Hitler himself was Catholic.

ment of this "program for the ages" envisaged the abrogation of the treaties of Versailles and St. Germain; the refutation of war guilt; the drastic revision of reparation; the reacquisition of colonies; the expulsion of all persons not of German blood and of all non-German immigrants who had entered the country after August 1914; governmental assurance of employment and decent living conditions for the citizens; the abolition of unearned income and high interest, and the confiscation of war profits; the nationalization of trusts and department stores; agrarian reform and the abolition of speculation in land values; adequate state care for the aged and for the physical and mental development of the citizenry; religious toleration for all sects not dangerous to the welfare or morality of the nation; and parity with the other great powers in armaments. German supremacy on the continent was to be assured through alliances with Great Britain and Italy and through eventual wars with France and the Soviet Union. Several aspects of the program were modified in later pronouncements by Hitler, but the catchwords of the movement remained anti-Semitism and anti-Bolshevism.

A party organization was developed and the *Hakenkreuz* (hooked cross), better known by its Sanskrit equivalent of swastika (卐), became the Nazi emblem. As with the Italian Fascists, there were worked out an elaborate ritual and a military ceremonial. Ordinary party members, who in 1932 numbered more than seven hundred thousand, were asked to pay monthly dues and were expected to be faithful attendants at meetings, to which there was generally an admission charge. Above this rank and file were the *Sturmabteilungen* (S.A.), or "storm troops," assigned to such duties as the protection of Nazi meetings and the breaking-up of radical gatherings. In April 1932 the national government disbanded these storm troops because of their frequent resort to violence, but eventually they were permitted to re-form. Both the regular members and the storm troops wore the party uniform of a brown shirt with a black swastika mounted upon a red-and-white armband. There was also a smaller group of "Elite Guards," the *Schutzstaffeln* (S.S.), who were assigned to act as bodyguards for the Nazi leaders and to carry out especially difficult missions. They wore a black shirt decorated with a white skull.[1]

For purposes of agitation and organization the Reich was divided into districts and "cells," each "covered" by trained speakers.

[1] The members of the S.A. and the S.S. soon came to be called, respectively, "Brown Shirts" and "Black Shirts."

Hitler proved himself a highly successful orator, able to sway large audiences, but it appeared to be his manner of speaking more than the content of his speeches that produced the electric result. He became popular with German womanhood and the nationalist youth which latter, incidentally, was organized in a Hitler Youth Society. The party headquarters was the "Brown House" in Munich.

One of the chief pillars of the early Hitlerite movement was the white-collar section of the middle class. When judged by income and standard of living many of the three and a half million individuals in this category actually fell into proletarian ranks. Yet, unlike the workers, they did not look to the socialists for economic relief. Class pride made them seek aid elsewhere and Hitlerism promised help. Equally badly off, equally unwilling to acknowledge a common interest with the proletariat, and equally ready to try Nazi remedies, were thousands of former army officers, soldiers' widows, and retired tradesmen.

There were numerous other Nazi enthusiasts. The anti-Semitic stand of the Hitlerites appealed to many professionals who resented the competition of Jewry in law, medicine, banking, and trade. Retail shopkeepers, their livelihood endangered by the activities of the trusts and chain stores, favored the National-Socialist plan of governmental protection for small dealers. Much support also came from the peasants, particularly in southern Germany. In June 1931 the estimated total debt of the farmers was $3,000,000,-000, and, since these people had no sympathy with the Marxist attitude towards private property, they tended to rally around the Nazi standards.

University students and graduates formed another source of Nazi strength. The number of university students in the Reich increased by 60 per cent between 1914 and 1930, and thousands of unemployed educated persons had come to despair of any improvement in their lot under the existing system. Any program of overturn seemed promising to them, and in addition they generally favored the ending of reparation payments, reacquisition of colonies, and a large army. Finally, a number of industrialists, such as Fritz Thyssen, who feared communism more than National Socialism, supported Hitlerism. Feder was careful to point out that the proposed socialization of trusts was not aimed "at the real creators of our heavy industry—the Krupps, Kirdorffs, Thyssens, Mannesmanns, and Siemens."

Labor and some of the stronger Catholic districts gave only scant

ADOLF HITLER

support to Hitler. Less than 15 per cent of his following in 1932 came from the ranks of labor, and even of this group a sizable proportion probably was attracted more by the promise of jobs through Nazi influence than by political conviction.

As the election of September 1930 approached, the Nazis did all in their power to profit by the difficulties confronting the government. "Germany Awaken" and "Work and Bread" were adopted as slogans and in the fortnight preceding the balloting more than thirty thousand meetings were held. The Nazi speakers constantly reminded their listeners of Germany's "enslavement" and of the government's "subserviency" to the Allies. The "war-guilt lie" was furiously attacked and reparation was denounced. Hitler's election manifesto urged the voters to "send the betrayers of their future to the devil."

In protest against the existing conditions and against the apparent inability of the groups in control to remedy them, the voters, as has been indicated, cast their ballots in unprecedented numbers for both the Nazis and the communists. Yet Chancellor Brüning was able to muster sufficient moderate support in the Reichstag to remain in office until May 1932.

Early in 1932 Brüning suggested to the various party leaders that President von Hindenburg's term be extended by the Reichstag and the country thus spared the expense and trouble of an election. Hitler opposed this suggestion and March 13 was set as the election date. Hindenburg and Hitler both were candidates, the latter becoming (February) a citizen by accepting an appointment as attaché of the Brunswick Legation at Berlin. Ernst Thälmann again was the candidate of the Communist Party and the extreme nationalists nominated Theodor Düsterberg.

Hindenburg received 18,651,497 votes, one-half of 1 per cent less than the required majority for election, and 7,300,000 votes more than Hitler. Thälmann was third with 4,983,341 ballots. A second election had to be held and the people went to the polls again in April. This time the president was reëlected by a plurality of almost 6,000,000 votes in a total of about 36,500,000. Hindenburg, hailed even in Paris as the "safest" of all the candidates, began his second seven-year term in his eighty-fifth year.

Two weeks after the presidential contest, the Hitlerites made sizable gains in a number of state elections, particularly in Prussia. These advances were owing in part to measures taken by Brüning's Centrist-Socialist Government against the Nazis. The storm troops were dissolved and the wearing of the brown-shirt uniforms was forbidden. On the other hand, many Germans began to feel that the chancellor's system of government by emergency decree had accomplished but little. Unemployment figures rose to more than six million and the budgetary deficit soared. Brüning's conciliatory foreign policy had brought Germany little relief. Nationalists in Germany therefore clamored for more effective action and in May 1932, after two years and two months in office, the Brüning Cabinet resigned.

The president selected as the new chancellor, Lieutenant-Colonel Franz von Papen, the same who had perpetrated illegal activities in the United States during the period of American neutrality. Papen chose for his colleagues a group of conservatives who soon were dubbed the "Almanach de Gotha Cabinet." It was evident that the new government could not command a majority in the Reichstag and the latter was immediately dissolved. New elections were ordered, and the Nazis were permitted once more to don their brown shirts and revive their military organization. Defense Minister General Kurt von Schleicher, as well as other leaders of the government, publicly began to insist on equal treatment for Germany in the matter of armaments.

The Reichstag elections (July 1932) gave the Hitlerites 230 seats, an increase of 123 since 1930. They now had exactly as many deputies as the Social Democrats and Centrists combined. The Reichstag was convened in August and Captain Hermann Wilhelm Göring, one of Hitler's lieutenants, was elected speaker. After some further organization business, the house adjourned until September. When it reassembled, the chancellor immediately dissolved it and ordered still another election. Papen had the full support of President von Hindenburg, but was denounced by the Nazis and communists as a dictator and an unconstitutional premier.

In the election of November 6, 1932, the vote of the Nazis fell off by about two million while the Communist Party gained seven hundred thousand votes. No party or group of parties gained control of the Reichstag and the Papen Cabinet therefore resigned. Hindenburg now invited Hitler, as the head of the largest party in the chamber, to form a government, but when the Nazi leader demanded dictatorial powers, the president turned to Schleicher. The membership of the new government was similar to that of its predecessor and it lacked the backing in the Reichstag necessary to ensure longevity. Eight weeks later (January 1933) Schleicher resigned and Adolf Hitler became chancellor.

ECONOMIC RECOVERY AND DECLINE, 1924–1932

The German Empire of pre-1914 days was a closely knit economic organism deriving wealth and power from a fertile soil, an abundance of raw materials, an intelligent industrial leadership, a skilled and hard-working laboring class, a well-developed and coördinated network of rail- and waterways, overseas possessions, a thriving shipping business, profitable foreign investments, rich markets, and an excellent international credit standing. The First World War completely dislocated this intricate mechanism and made necessary widespread readjustments.

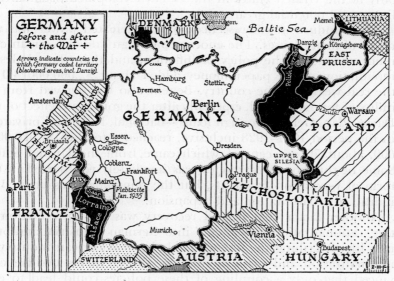

From Landman, J., *Outline History of the World since 1914*, 1934
Courtesy of Barnes and Noble, Inc.

Not only did the war cause enormous material damage, and death or permanent incapacity to millions of citizens, but the peace treaty deprived Germany of one-tenth of her population and one-eighth of her European land area. The defeated power lost about two-fifths of her coal supply, two-thirds of her iron-ore reserves, seven-tenths of her zinc, one-tenth of her manufacturing establishments, one-seventh of her agricultural production, all her colonies and foreign investments, most of her merchant marine, and nearly all her foreign-trade contracts. In addition the young republic had to face a hostile Europe and to suffer a temporary occupation of her chief industrial region, the Ruhr. In one respect Germany was fortunate: there was no need to reconstruct war-torn areas, since most of the fighting had been done on foreign soil.

During the years immediately following the war Germany sank lower and lower in the economic scale until nadir was reached with the collapse of 1923. Just as dissolution seemed imminent, government and people united in a determined effort to save the fatherland and rebuild its economic structure. Thereafter an upward trend set in which continued for six years, until the middle of 1929. In this year, the volume of industrial output reached a point in excess of that of 1913. Germany now seemed to be second only to the United States in industrial development, standard of living, and potential greatness.

This "industrial efflorescence" of the defeated power was the result of many causes. The enormous foreign sale of German currency and notes, the policy of inflation, and then the wholesale repudiation of the paper money added about $2,000,000,000 to the real wealth of the country. Benefit also was derived from an influx of foreign capital, especially after the going into effect of the Dawes Plan. German foreign loans—national, local, and private—in the period 1924–1928 inclusive, reached a total of $1,620,000,-000, about 70 per cent of which came from the United States. Some of this borrowed money was imediately reëxported in the form of reparation payments, but the remainder was utilized in industrial rehabilitation and expansion.

Another factor that helped recovery was the introduction of the "rationalization movement" into German industrial and business life. Ascribing the phenomenal rise of American industry to rationalization and mass production, the Germans became convinced that only a coupling of these policies could lead to economic regeneration. Frederick W. Taylor and Henry Ford, "fathers," respectively, of scientific industrial management and mass production, became heroes in the eyes of the Germans, and experts were delegated to investigate American methods.

As early as 1921 there had been established a National Efficiency Board (*Reichskuratorium für Wirtschaftlichkeit*) which studied and tried to solve the numerous problems that confronted German industry. Other boards, official and private, concerned themselves with promoting efficiency in the fields of agriculture and construction work. Specifically, the rationalization movement aimed at standardizing products and materials, introducing scientific management and planning, spreading vocational guidance and training, promoting the formation of trusts and combines to prevent duplication and ruinous competition, and coördinating the entire national production process.

Astounding savings were effected by rationalization. The average output per man, in the industries concerned, was 20 per cent higher in 1930 than in 1913. In the coal industry, 562,000 persons in 1925 produced 133,000,000 tons of coal; in 1928, after rationalization, 556,000 persons produced 151,000,000 tons. The number of employees in the automobile industry was reduced from 87,000 in 1925 to 83,000 in 1927, yet the value of the finished product rose during the same period from 771,000,000 to 908,000,000 marks. A large bank which in 1914 employed 334 persons to take care of 9080 accounts, required only 284 persons to handle 18,916 accounts in 1927. Similar results were obtained in agriculture and other departments.

That rationalization also had its drawbacks, no one could deny. The movement was sometimes carried to extremes and the Germans themselves came to speak of the need for "rationalizing rationalization." Because certain methods produced gratifying results in the United States was no guarantee that they would be equally useful under European conditions. The almost boundless hope placed in the value of rationalization encouraged extravagant borrowing and investments which later proved difficult to repay. Readjustment to smaller scale production when the supply ran ahead of the demand became difficult. The system threw an increasing number of men out of employment. Despite these disadvantages, the rationalization movement was a prime factor in Germany's economic renaissance.

Germany's industrial rise was owing, in addition, to the three "c's"—coal, chemists, and cartels. Despite her coal losses, the republic had little cause to worry about power supply, and the demands of the iron and steel industries were met without difficulty. Extensive reorganization and mechanization of the mines, along with the achievement of a generally higher mining technique, brought production up to a level comparable to that of prewar years. The coal areas within the postwar boundaries of Germany produced 140,800,000 tons of the mineral in 1913, but in 1927 they produced 153,600,000 tons. To compensate for the loss of some of the black-coal reserves, the production of the less valuable but readily available brown coal or lignite was greatly increased. It rose from 87,000,000 tons in 1913 to 151,000,000 in 1927. Since lignite was only one-fifth as expensive as coal, much of the product was converted at the source into electricity and transported cheaply, efficiently, and directly as power.

The traditional renown of German chemists was well upheld during and after the war, and Germany soon became the world's largest exporter of chemicals. Great advances were made in the development of dyes, drugs,[1] fertilizers, and photographic materials, and remarkable success was attained in the field of synthetics. There soon appeared on the market synthetic quinine, camphor, indigo, wood alcohol (methanol), nitrates, rubber, and gasoline, and artificial silk, resin, and leather. The production of synthetic nitrates, involving the use of liquefied air, became the largest single branch of the chemical industry. The domestic output of nitrates increased from 12,000 tons in 1913 to 800,000 tons in 1928. The imports of Chilean nitrates decreased in similar proportion. Thus Germany rapidly minimized her dependence upon the outside world for the raw materials of industry.

Realizing the value of trust combinations for greater efficiency in production, the Germans perfected the "vertical" trust system, "uniting all stages and parts of an industrial process, such as coal mines, iron mines, steel mills, and shipyards." This form of industrial organization was more highly developed in Germany than in most other countries and the government supported rather than opposed the process of combination. Perhaps the greatest trust-builder was Hugo Stinnes, who was responsible for the gigantic Siemens-Rhein-Elbe-Schuckert Union. At the time of his death (1924) Stinnes was said to have had an interest in almost fourteen hundred business undertakings and to have controlled almost a fifth of Germany's total production. He owned lands, forests, hotels, paper mills, summer resorts, oil fields, newspapers, electrical establishments, banks, coal and iron mines, copper mines, aluminum works, and scores of other properties.

The trust was not the only form of combine popular in Germany. As early as 1873 there had appeared a type of organization known as the cartel, which "may be loosely defined as any association of independent enterprises formed to regulate for the common benefit either prices, production, markets, or the conditions of purchase or sale, or for two or more of these purposes." It represented a form of voluntary "economic planning."

[1] Among the drugs discovered was Bayer 205, a powder for the cure of African sleeping sickness. The discoverers of this drug "refused to disclose its secret but . . . offered to make it a public formula if Germany were given back one of her African colonies." Luehr, E. *The New German Republic*, 1929, p. 348.

On the eve of the First World War there were in existence several hundred such cartels, but during the struggle they were not especially useful since the enormity of war needs virtually eliminated competition. After the war, and especially during the heyday of inflation, they enjoyed a mushroom growth. In 1923 there were about fifteen hundred cartels. These so abused their ability to control purchases, sales, and prices that a Cartel Law was passed (1923), providing for publicity and for governmental supervision of their activities. Thenceforth the influence of cartels in the domestic economic system suffered a decline, but compensatory progress was made in the formation of international cartels, particularly in the steel, rail, and potash industries. The largest of these international production- and price-controlling organisms was the Continental Steel Cartel representing Germany, France, Belgium, the Saar, Luxembourg, Czechoslovakia, Austria, and Hungary. But it was hard to make the members of international cartels abide by their limited production quotas and harder still to make them pay fines for overproducing.

Governmental aid was not confined to industry. Shipping and other essential lines of endeavor received support as well. The rebuilding of a merchant marine was undertaken with zest. The government advanced 700,000,000 marks at low interest to encourage shippers, and supplementary loans were made to shipyards to enable them to build cheaply and quickly. In 1913 the German merchant marine had ranked second only to that of Great Britain. In 1920 it occupied twelfth place among the world's commercial fleets, following Spain and Denmark. By 1930 it had risen again to third place, behind Great Britain and the United States, with a tonnage well over the four-million mark. Although this still was equivalent to only four-fifths of Germany's prewar tonnage, the ships were new and up to date in construction.

In lighter-than-air craft Germany similarly rose to a position of preëminence. The dirigible *Graf Zeppelin,* in August 1929, circumnavigated the globe in less than twelve days of flying time. Forbidden to manufacture war planes, the Germans developed commercial planes which achieved enviable records for safety and speed. Among the greatest accomplishments in the scientific field was the *Deutsches Museum* in Munich, one of the finest technological museums in the world.

Much good accrued to Germany, finally, from the establishment therein of branches of United States firms such as General Motors, Ford, Chrysler, Eastman Kodak, Otis Elevator, Mergenthaler Linotype, and National Cash Register. These enterprises not only brought foreign capital into the land, but gave employment to German labor and utilized German raw materials. The Germans imitated the methods of these companies and readily adopted such ideas as chain stores, "five-and-tens," and ready-to-wear suits. Berlin, with its "movie palaces," its motor cars, its machinery, and its skyscrapers, appeared to become the most "Americanized" of all continental cities.

But Germany's economic recovery was not destined to be of long duration. Even while prosperity rode high, factors appeared which forecast approaching decline. The adverse developments included an increasing difficulty in securing foreign loans; continual reparation quarrels; inability to recapture completely the former Russian market and those of other important prewar customers; the lessened demand on the part of the government for military and naval supplies; foreign tariff walls; the tendency of Germans to cut down on the consumption of rye and potatoes in favor of wheat and vegetables, thus dooming many farmers to surplus crops and to debt; and the decreased requirements of man power owing to the progress of rationalization.

There was a gradual but steady increase in the number of unemployed university graduates and workers of both the overall and white-collar types. During the world-depression years following 1930 the situation became acute and by 1932 it was estimated that Germany, with her population of 64,000,000, had an army of unemployed numbering 6,500,000. Unemployment-insurance schemes and doles seemed utterly inadequate to meet the problem and thus useful campaign material was provided for both Nazis and communists.

The government of Chancellor Brüning (1930–1932), supported by President von Hindenburg, strove to deal with the crisis, but the international situation precluded any domestic solution of the difficulties. Despite its heavy reparation obligations the German Government had appropriated money prodigally for various laudable but perhaps nonessential welfare projects and simultaneously had kept the per capita tax burden lower than that in either Great Britain or France. This procedure had been justified as the only means of forestalling revolution and securing loyal national support, but, whatever its motivating force, the policy was dangerous since it necessitated undue reliance upon foreign loans and credits. A crash was destined to come as soon as external conditions made further loans impracticable.

When Germany and Austria, in 1931, announced plans for a customs accord, the power of French finance and diplomacy was mobilized, as we have seen, to frustrate this move. French funds invested in the German-speaking countries were withdrawn and further loans made contingent upon unacceptable political terms. Apparently in order to prevent Great Britain from aiding the borrowers, the French drew heavily on the gold reserve of the Bank of England. The latter therefore found it impossible to continue making short-term loans to the Reich. Slight assistance was received from the Federal Reserve Bank in the United States, but so close to bankruptcy was Germany that only concerted international action could be of avail.

In June 1931, it will be recalled, President Hoover proposed an international one-year moratorium on war debts and the postponable reparation items. Such an arrangement was effected, to run until June 30, 1932. Early in the latter year, Brüning announced that Germany would not be able to resume reparation payments when the moratorium expired. The annual exportation of reparation moneys required consistently favorable balances of trade and Germany could not accumulate such balances under existing tariff and trade-restricting conditions. The Lausanne Reparation Conference of 1932 did little to solve the dilemma and Chancellors von Papen and von Schleicher soon reiterated Brüning's declaration. Germany, they said, could not make further reparation while her economic life was stagnant.

FOREIGN RELATIONS, 1919–1932

From 1919 to 1932 it was the chief aim of German diplomacy to regain for the fatherland admission into the family of nations as a member in good standing. This goal was not only urgent as a protective measure for the weakened state, it was vitally necessary to the revival of the trade and commerce upon which German economic recovery depended. German statesmen, however, were divided on the question of whether the new orientation should look eastward or westward, towards Soviet Russia or the Allies. The group which preferred to look eastward advocated alliance with the Bolsheviks and eventual defiance of the oppressive treaty restrictions. Those who looked westward proposed the fulfillment of treaty obligations and reconciliation with the former enemies.

At first it appeared that the pro-Russian viewpoint might triumph. In 1922, as we have seen, the German and Russian delegates to the Genoa Economic Conference concluded a recognition pact and trade treaty at Rapallo. Four years later the principles of the Rapallo agreement were reaffirmed in a treaty of friendship and neutrality negotiated in Berlin. Then the eastward trend of German policy was temporarily halted by the diplomats who advocated "a policy of fulfillment and reconciliation." These men were led by Dr. Stresemann.

Born in 1878, in Berlin, the son of a beer merchant, Stresemann studied at Berlin and Leipzig, specializing in philosophy, political science, and economics. He was a skillful organizer and when only twenty-three years old became secretary of the Union of Saxon Chocolate Manufacturers. Two years later he was one of the moving spirits in the founding of the League of Saxon Manufacturers, a body formed to reorganize the decadent local industries. In 1907 Stresemann was elected to the Reichstag as a National Liberal and ten years later he became the head of his party—which was the party of big business. During the war he advocated the vigorous prosecution of hostilities and after the revolution he reorganized his followers into the German People's Party, which favored a monarchy but was willing to support the republic in the interests of peace, internal unity, and business revival. As a member of the Weimar Assembly in 1919 he voted against acceptance of the Versailles Treaty.

In August 1923 Stresemann became chancellor, but the great internal disorder, particularly in southern Germany, and the foreign occupation of the Ruhr led to his downfall within a few months. Appointed foreign minister by his successor, Chancellor Wirth, he continued to occupy this post until his death in October 1929. The cardinal points of Stresemann's foreign policy, the peace treaty having been signed, were reconciliation with France and Germany's reëntry into the community of nations as an equal and respected partner. A gifted orator, honest and tactful, he soon acquired general trust and respect, though he did have numerous enemies both at home and abroad. In 1926 he, Briand, and Austen Chamberlain were awarded the Nobel Peace Prize for their contributions (at Locarno) to the cause of world peace. Stresemann was seriously ill most of his life and the duties of office became increasingly strenuous and difficult as the years passed. On October 2, 1929, he saved the Müller Government from downfall over an unemployment-insurance law by a brilliant and forceful, but tiring, speech. On the following day he died.

As foreign minister he had been responsible for the discontinuance of the policy of passive resistance in the Ruhr. He had eloquently urged the adoption of the Dawes Plan, thus preparing the way for the evacuation of the Ruhr, the restoration of foreign confidence in Germany, and the negotiation of advantageous commercial treaties. His greatest work was connected with the negotiation of the Locarno treaties (1925) and the admission of Germany into the League (1926).

The story of Locarno, as has been indicated, dated back to the years immediately following the war. It was apparent to competent observers even then that permament peace in Europe was improbable as long as France and Germany continued to be suspicious of each other's actions—as long as France was haunted by the specter of German recovery and revenge and Germany feared French designs on the Rhineland and on her economic strength. Stresemann several times suggested to France the signing of a guaranty pact and in 1925 his proposal met with favor. The result was the Locarno Pact.

After the initialing of the Locarno treaties, Stresemann asked the Reichstag for ratification of his actions. This he was granted over the bitter opposition of the Nationalists, who were not reconciled to the loss of Alsace-Lorraine. The foreign minister was supported by Hindenburg, by the Social Democrats, and by a group of industrialists who felt that more cordial diplomatic relations with France might lead to improved business relations. On December 1, 1925, the treaties were signed in London and on the same day, as a token of the new confidence, Allied military evacuation of the Cologne area was begun. Since the Locarno Pact was to go into force immediately upon Germany's admission to the League, the republic applied for membership. A special session of the Assembly was called for March 1926.[1]

Germany requested a permanent seat in the Council as one condition of her application for membership. To her astonishment, this procedure was followed by similar demands from Spain, Brazil, Poland, China, Czechoslovakia, and Iran. Immediately a complicated situation arose. Stresemann insisted that Germany's admission be free of any international bargaining. Yet, since Spain

[1] Accompanying Germany's request for admission was a statement, agreed to by the powers at Locarno, to the effect that Article 16 of the Covenant (see p. 133) bound a member only "to an extent which is compatible with its military situation and takes its geographical position into account." This was insisted upon by Germany since the republic had no desire to become a battle ground in case of League action against a continental state, or to permit the passage of French troops across her territory in case of a war between Poland and the Soviet Union.

and Brazil occupied nonpermanent seats in the Council, their votes were needed to give Germany a permanent seat. To make matters worse, it soon developed that Chamberlain was supporting the Spanish position while Briand was upholding the case of Poland. Stresemann finally exclaimed that he would never have signed the Locarno treaties had he known of the intrigue apparently connected with their negotiation. The Swedish delegate to the Council, Dr. Östen Unden, next announced that he would not vote to give Poland a permanent seat since all the circumstances involved were contrary to the spirit of the Covenant. Sweden did not waver from this position despite the threat of one foreign power to cancel a large order that had been placed for Swedish telephones and of another to renounce a commercial treaty already negotiated with Sweden.[1]

Neither Council nor Assembly could reconcile the differences and the League adjourned until September without having acted on Germany's application. A committee was appointed to work out a compromise solution and the delegates scattered, some angry, some disappointed. So great was the reaction in Germany that the policy of eastward orientation once more appeared attractive. It was at this time that the Treaty of Berlin already referred to was concluded with the Soviet Union.

When the Assembly met again in September 1926, Germany was unanimously elected to membership and was given the only additional permanent seat in the Council. By another resolution, however, the number of nonpermanent Council members was increased from six to nine and three-year terms for these seats were established. It was expected that Spain, Brazil, and Poland would be elected to such seats, but the former two powers at once gave notice of their intention to withdraw from the League.

German membership in the League soon led to further developments. In 1927 the last remaining Allied commissions in Germany were withdrawn. In the same year a German, Ludwig Kastl, was appointed to the Permanent Mandates Commission. In 1928 Germany, again owing largely to the efforts of Stresemann, adhered to the Kellogg Pact for the renunciation of war as an instrument of national policy. At the meeting of the League Assembly in 1928 the way was opened for a renewal of reparation parleys, which finally ended in the adoption of the Young Plan (1929) and the complete evacuation of the Rhine territory (1930).

After Stresemann's death, his foreign policies were continued

[1] Bassett, J. S. *The League of Nations*, 1928, p. 314.

for a time by his friend and successor, Dr. Curtius, but the latter resigned in 1931 after the unsuccessful attempt at economic cooperation with Austria. Thereafter the conduct of foreign relations became increasingly difficult, largely because of the activities of the various nationalistic groups and the diplomatic intransigeance of France. In 1932 Papen and Schleicher took a firmer stand on the questions of equality in armaments and relief from the reparation burden, but Europe made few concessions.

Although many of the postwar grievances that had irritated the Germans were removed by the close of 1932, there remained as disturbing factors the questions of Germany's eastern frontiers, union with Austria, reacquisition of the colonies, repudiation of war guilt, equality with the other great powers in armaments, and further revision of the reparation schedule. Early in 1933 these problems were passed on to a wholly new German Government— a National-Socialist Government.

DER FÜHRER

On January 28, 1933, after an incumbency of only eight weeks, Chancellor von Schleicher resigned because of the president's refusal to allow the dissolution of a hostile Reichstag. Two days later the chief ministerial post went to Adolf Hitler, whose party, in consequence of the elections of the previous November, held 196 of the 584 seats in the chamber. Associated with Hitler in the cabinet was a group of nationalistic conservatives, headed by Franz von Papen as vice-chancellor, Dr. Alfred Hugenberg, leader of the National People's Party, as minister of commerce and agriculture, and Konstantin von Neurath, nonparty nationalist, as minister of foreign affairs. The inclusion of these conservatives, who might act to check any "dangerous" Nazi experiment, apparently was made a condition of Hitler's appointment to the chancellorship by Hindenburg.

Since the Nazis were in a minority, both in the cabinet and in the Reichstag, Hitler demanded the dissolution of the latter and called for new elections on March 5. During the preëlection weeks the government instituted severe repressive measures against its political rivals, especially the Communist, Social Democratic, and Center parties. Papen, moreover, was appointed Reich Commissioner for Prussia, a post equivalent to that of Prussian Premier. The new commissioner at once brought about the dismissal of the Prussian Diet and ordered new elections to be held simultaneously with those for the national legislature. Thus the Nazis, confident of victory, also hoped to gain control of a body which hitherto had been a stronghold of their socialist opponents.

A few days before the voting the Reichstag building in Berlin was nearly destroyed by a fire of apparently incendiary origin. The followers of Hitler placed the onus for the deed upon the Communist Party; the latter, pointing out that a subterranean corridor led from the residence of Reichstag President Göring to the basement of the Reichstag building, accused the Hitlerites of plotting the affair as a means of discrediting communism in the eyes of the voters. Further restrictions now were put on the electioneering rights of the antigovernment parties and Hindenburg authorized the ministry to assume the executive power in any German state which neglected to provide "for the restoration of law and order." [1]

In an atmosphere tense with excitement, more than 39,000,000 citizens cast their ballots on the fifth of March. More than 17,000,-000 of them voted for National-Socialist candidates and an additional 3,000,000 supported the allies of the Nazis, the candidates of the German National People's Party. The Nazis captured 288 of the 647 seats in the new Reichstag and the Nationalists 52. The Nazi-Nationalist coalition thus received approximately 52 per cent of the popular vote and a majority in the Reichstag. The Social Democrats polled about 7,000,000 votes, the two Catholic parties (Center and Bavarian People's), 5,500,000, and the Communist Party, about 4,750,000. The results in the separate Prussian election were similar. One week after the election Hindenburg decreed that all public buildings must in future display the old imperial black-white-red standard and the swastika flag in place of the republican black-red-gold ensign.

On March 23, 1933, the new Reichstag, by a vote of 441 to 94, passed an enabling act, officially called the Law to Combat the Misery of People and Reich, whose five articles in effect suspended the constitution of 1919 and endowed the Hitler Government with dictatorial power for four years.[2] Henceforth the Hitler

[1] In December 1933 the Supreme Court found Marinus van der Lubbe, a young Netherlands communist, guilty of setting fire to the Reichstag building. A German and three Bulgarian communists who were held with van der Lubbe were acquitted. The Netherlander, who had seemed to be in a stupor during most of the trial but who had doggedly maintained that he had done the deed without accomplices, was executed in January 1934.

[2] The negative votes were all cast by the socialists who attended the session. Most of the remaining 26 socialist deputies and all 81 communists were either abroad, in

Cabinet alone was to have the right to enact laws for the Reich. The dictatorial powers, greater than any that Bismarck ever possessed, were assigned specifically to the "present national cabinet." To explain to the people and the world this startling development and any novel policies that the authorities might in future undertake became the function of a specially created "Ministry of Propaganda and Enlightenment" headed by Dr. Paul Joseph Goebbels.

It may be convenient, at this point, to recall some of the factors which underlay the rise to power of the Nazis. The war and the peace settlement left Germany disillusioned and crushed, spiritually and materially. The Germans could not easily forget the humiliation of defeat and of the "dictate of Versailles." The continuing hostile attitude of France; the quarrels over the Ruhr, the Rhineland occupation, the Saar, and reparation; the ceaseless wrangling over security and disarmament, all these fed the indignation and anger of many Germans. In such circumstances, the republic's acceptance of unfair disabilities, its policy of reconciliation and fulfillment, and its apparent inability to assert itself more strongly in international affairs rankled in the hearts of many patriots, especially the younger war veterans and the youth which believed itself deprived of a glamorous and secure future by the "treachery" and "cowardice" of the complacent republican politicians. During the period of temporary economic revival from 1924 to 1929 these factors remained somewhat in the background. But they did exist, and it required only a few years of hard times and increasing unemployment to bring them out in full force.

Many of the Germans, too, were weary of the manner in which the democratic parliamentary system was functioning. Those Germans who could remember the days when order and discipline prevailed in the Reichstag and many of those who had merely heard or read about such days were impatient with the bickering and quarreling and time wasting that characterized the republican lower house. In place of decision and patriotic accomplishment, the politicians offered words, empty promises, and mocking prophecies of a brighter future. Increasingly many Germans became convinced of the need of a "strong man" who would restore Germany's prosperity and prestige.

Psychological factors also played an important role in the overturn. The republic seemed unable or unwilling to pay due atten-

---

hiding, or under arrest. The Reichsrat passed the enabling act on the same day as the Reichstag. The law was later extended until 1943.

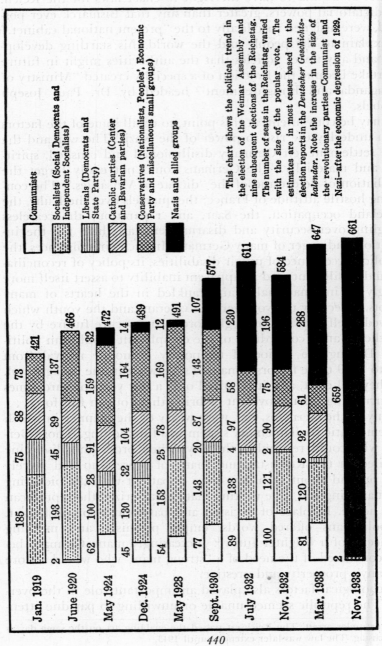

THE GERMAN ELECTIONS, 1919–1933

This chart shows the political trend in the election of the Weimar Assembly and nine subsequent elections of the Reichstag. The number of seats in the Reichstag varied with the size of the popular vote. The estimates are in most cases based on the election reports in the *Deutscher Geschichtskalendar*. Note the increase in the size of the revolutionary parties—Communist and Nazi—after the economic depression of 1929.

Communists

Socialists (Social Democrats and Independent Socialists)

Liberals (Democrats and State Party)

Catholic parties (Center and Bavarian parties)

Conservatives (Nationalists, Peoples', Economic Party and miscellaneous small groups)

Nazis and allied groups

Jan. 1919 — 185, 75, 88, 73, 421
June 1920 — 2, 193, 45, 89, 137, 466
May 1924 — 62, 100, 28, 91, 159, 32, 472
Dec. 1924 — 45, 130, 32, 104, 164, 14, 489
May 1928 — 54, 153, 25, 78, 169, 12, 491
Sept. 1930 — 77, 143, 20, 87, 143, 107, 577
July 1932 — 89, 133, 4, 97, 58, 230, 611
Nov. 1932 — 100, 121, 2, 90, 75, 196, 584
Mar. 1933 — 81, 120, 5, 92, 61, 288, 647
Nov. 1933 — 2, 659, 661

Reprinted with permission from Slosson, P. W., *Europe since 1870*, 1935. Published by Houghton Mifflin & Co.

tion to the inner feelings and desires of many of the citizens. The official toleration of attempts to drag down the ideals and heroes of imperial Germany; the readiness with which the old imperial flag was abandoned, and the old orders and colorful military uniforms were given up; and the friendship for the Soviet Union, all these alienated the sympathies of prominent elements of the population: the aristocrats, the young university people, the conservative peasants, the believers in *Kultur* and in Germany's mission, and the rank-and-file war veterans who hated the politicians. The Nazi leaders understood these grievances and with their remarkable propaganda methods capitalized them. Oratory, posters, banners, songs, uniforms, ceremonies, ritual, discipline, historic tradition, theories of race superiority, anti-Semitism, enthusiasm, the dynamic personality of Hitler, these things attracted millions of Germans at a time when the alternatives appeared to offer worse depression and continued foreign impasse.

Having surrendered its legislative powers, the Reichstag elected in March 1933 adjourned, while Chancellor Hitler proceeded to direct Germany's "national resurgence," that is, to "coördinate" under the Nazi aegis the entire political, economic, and cultural life of the nation (a process termed by the Nazis *Gleichschaltung*). The supreme and final authority in all matters was Hitler himself, later to be known officially as *Der Führer*. This principle of leadership (*Führerprinzip*) seemed to have as much appeal for the Germans as it did for some Italians under Mussolini. It was calculated to emphasize the complete unity of purpose of the whole nation.

ANTI-SEMITISM [1]

The most spectacular immediate consequence of the National-Socialist triumph was a reign of anti-Semitism, and most prominent among the active anti-Semites were Hermann Göring and Julius Streicher. Göring was a war ace and one of the most militant Nazis. He had participated in the Hitler-Ludendorff *Putsch* of 1923 and then had fled to Italy where he studied the fascist system. When the first Nazi Government was organized, Göring became deputy-minister of the interior for Prussia, federal commissioner of aviation, and Reich minister without portfolio. Streicher had been a schoolteacher in Nuremberg and was the editor of *Der Stürmer,* the most violently anti-Semitic (and often obscene) newspaper in Germany. Under their leadership, the Hitlerites

[1] According to the census of 1925, the full Jews in Germany numbered 560,000, that is, 0.9 per cent of the population.

launched wild attacks upon the Jewish population. The storm troops took the lead and the police made little effort to stop them. Göring explained the situation by saying: "We have been telling the people for years that they might settle accounts with the traitors. We stand by our word: accounts are being settled." After a time, and partly in response to foreign protests, physical violence against Jews lessened—only to reappear with greater fury, particularly, as we shall see, in 1938.

The first far-reaching anti-Semitic national legislation was contained in a civil-service law promulgated on April 7, 1933. This act ordered the dismissal of all officials who were "non-Aryan" or whose previous political activity did not offer surety that they would "at all times act unreservedly for the national state." The law applied, with certain reservations, to all officials and employees of the national, state, and municipal governments, to employees in semipublic enterprises and social services, to court officials and attendants, notaries, policemen, teachers, professors, and army officers. The exceptions were persons who had been appointed to office before August 1, 1914, or who had actually "participated with a fighting troop in a battle, a fight, a struggle for position, or a siege" in the First World War, or whose fathers or sons were killed in the war. Later legislation removed these exceptions.

A "non-Aryan" was defined as any person descended "from non-Aryan, particularly Jewish, parents or grandparents." It was sufficient if only one parent or grandparent had "professed the Jewish religion." Later it was decreed that a person with a Jewish great-grandfather or yet more remote Jewish ancestor, even if the latter had been baptized, might also be regarded as "non-Aryan" and ineligible for office. "Aryans" married to "non-Aryans" were placed under the same restrictions as the latter.

Through the law of April 1933 and its successors, the civil services and professions were ruthlessly "cleansed" not merely of Jews but of all elements objectionable to the Nazis. By the end of 1938 there were virtually no practicing Jewish or anti-Nazi "Aryan" doctors, dentists, nurses, professors, teachers, judges, lawyers, court clerks, notaries, and so on. Tens of thousands of these, moreover, had been placed under "protective arrest" in concentration camps. Additional legislation limited the proportion of Jewish registrants in any school to 1.5 per cent of the total, and from 1938 no Jews were admitted to German schools. Eventually the Jews were barred, in practice if not always in law, from any connection with the stage, musical performances, the cinema, and journalism.

Jewish artists could appear only before Jewish audiences; they were forbidden to present the works of "Aryan" composers or authors.

Inasmuch as the party program of the Nazis specifically excluded Jews from the fellowship of "German people," the authorities also modified the laws governing citizenship. In 1933 the government decided to withdraw German citizenship at its discretion from "undesirables" who had been naturalized by the liberal republic (November 9, 1918, to January 30, 1933) and from individuals who, having fled abroad, conducted anti-Nazi propaganda or refused to return on the demand of the Berlin authorities. The property of such persons and of any other "anti-state" elements was made subject to confiscation. In 1935 all Jews were deprived of German citizenship and classified merely as German subjects (*Staatsangehörige*).

The actions of the German Government were supplemented by the anti-Semitic activities of societies, associations, corporations, and individuals. Governing boards and boards of directors reconstituted themselves without Jewish members. Most firms eventually dismissed all Jewish employees. By order of the Association of German Booksellers and Publishers no books by Jews were to be published in the Reich. On May 10, 1933, bonfires were made in a number of cities and university towns of the works of about 150 writers whose works were regarded as Jewish, pacifistic, radical, liberal, immoral, or in any other way "un-German." Local boycotts of Jewish shops were continued. Jews were generally excluded from the public markets and fairs as well as from summer and winter resorts and playgrounds.

Throughout 1936 and 1937 there were put into effect the so-called Nuremberg or Ghetto Laws of September 1935. These forbade marital and extramarital relations between Jews and citizens of "German or kindred blood," deprived all Jews of German citizenship and political rights, and forbade any German female under forty-five to assist in a Jewish household. Then, in 1938, a decree of April 29 required all Jews who possessed property worth more than 5000 marks to render an itemized report of their belongings to the state. Article 7 of the decree empowered the state to make use of the property thus reported in furtherance of a Four-Year Plan that had been inaugurated in 1936. Another order compelled every Jew who did not already have given names that were officially classed as Jewish to add "Israel" or "Sarah" to his or her name. Jewish children born in future might be given only such names as were to be found in a "permissible" list; and the names had to be "spelled in the Yiddish manner so as to stamp them as foreign and ridiculous in the eyes of the Germans." And then, in the fall of 1938, there was ushered in a period of utter tragedy, during which the Jews were finally eliminated from the economic life of the Third Reich.

Following a report that Poland would refuse to readmit within her boundaries any Polish Jews living abroad whose passports were not validated by the end of October 1938, the Nazi authorities, without warning, rounded up thousands of Polish Jews who had long been resident in various parts of the new Great Germany, herded them aboard railroad cars, shipped them to the Polish border, and there, at gun-point, forced them to walk across into Polish territory. The Polish authorities strove to resist this wholesale dumping of freezing and panic-stricken unfortunates and finally threatened, in retaliation, to treat similarly Germans who were living in Poland. Official negotiations followed, the whole affair was labeled a "misunderstanding," and the deportations ended—but not so tragedy.

One of the deported Polish Jews sent a postcard to his seventeen-year-old son in Paris, telling of his unhappy adventure. The boy, Herschel Grynszpan, brooded over the matter and then (November 7, 1938) went to the German Embassy, apparently determined to avenge his people by killing the German Ambassador. When he arrived at the embassy he shot Ernst vom Rath, the third secretary. Two days later the young diplomat died, whereupon, early in the morning of November 10, there broke loose in Germany a horrible attack on Jewish persons and property. Propaganda Minister Goebbels maintained that the attacks were the "spontaneous" result of the "justifiable and understandable anger of the German people over the cowardly Jewish murder of a German diplomat," but the terror obviously was organized and directed. The government, after a time, "requested" the population to cease demonstrating and promised to give a "final answer" to the assassination "by way of legislation and ordinance."

The promised decrees soon appeared. Holding German Jewry collectively responsible for the act of a brooding Polish adolescent in Paris, the Berlin Government eliminated it from the economic life of Germany. The authorities began by imposing a collective fine of 1,000,000,000 marks (about $400,000,000) on the Jews of Germany. The fine was assessed in the form of a capital levy of 20 per cent of the property of all Jews owning more than 5000 marks' worth of goods. Each Jew was required to pay his quota of the fine in a lump sum or in quarterly instalments beginning December 15, 1938.

Obviously the property reports submitted by the Jews in obedience to the decree of the previous April were now of considerable use to the government. Lest the market be unduly disturbed by the sudden disposal of stocks by Jews seeking cash, restrictions were placed on such transactions. Only agents of the commissariat of the Four-Year Plan were authorized to purchase, at their own price, personal properties which the Jews might have to sell. Jewish shopowners were required to repair at their own expense damages done during the attacks on November 10 and insurance companies were ordered to pay any insurance due Jewish owners to the state. Such sums were deducted from each Jew's quota of the "atonement" fine. Further decrees prepared the way for the elimination of Jews, in 1939, from the retail, mail-order, and handicraft trades, and for the "Aryanization," at bargain prices, of remaining Jewish businesses.

The relegation of Jews to full ghetto life was also accelerated. In the big cities certain districts were closed to Jewish dwellers and certain streets were barred to Jewish pedestrians. Jews were forbidden to drive automobiles. A decree of July 1939 required all Jews to join a Reich Union of Jews, supervised by the minister of the interior. The union was to absorb all existing Jewish organizations, speed up emigration, and assume the full burden of supporting Jewish schools and the Jewish poor. Lucky were those who had been able to flee beyond the borders of the Third Reich! [1]

POLITICAL TOTALITARIANISM

Two months after Hitler came to power, the first steps were taken to coördinate the provinces and create a totalitarian state. A decree of March 1933 dissolved all provincial legislatures, except the newly elected one in Prussia, and ordered their reconstitution in a way to ensure Nazi control. The life of all state and local diets was in future to be four years, subject to automatic termination in case of dissolution of the Reichstag before *its* term of four years expired. The several state cabinets were empowered to promulgate laws, even laws contrary to the state constitutions, without consulting their respective diets.

On the first anniversary of the Hitler regime (1934), the Reichs-

[1] On the problem of refugees, see pp. 462–464.

tag unanimously adopted a measure abolishing the "popular representation of the states" and transferring their sovereign rights to the Reich. The bill also authorized the Reich Government to "determine new constitutional law." The unanimous acceptance of this bill on the same day by the Reichsrat, the direct parliamentary representative of the states, automatically made that body superfluous. Its formal abolition soon was decreed. Municipal diets, moreover, were abolished on the second anniversary of the Hitler regime.

Meanwhile an edict of 1933 had placed over each state a Reich Regent, nominated by the chancellor. At first these regents enjoyed wide administrative powers, but in 1935 they were made subject to cabinet order and became, for practical purposes, well-paid "intermediary agents between the central and the local administrations." But in Prussia, where Hitler himself was regent, he appointed Göring as minister president. The latter therefore became *the* ruler of that largest German state, responsible only to the Führer himself. Perhaps because Göring objected to a diminution of his power in Prussia and because of the opposition of various local interests, a plan first announced in 1935 to obliterate the old state boundaries and redivide the Reich into new administrative units of approximately equal population-size was indefinitely postponed.

While the superiority of the national government over the provincial and local authorities was thus being established, the National Socialist Party was rapidly becoming identified with the state itself. As a beginning, all other parties were abolished. The communists went first and the Catholic Center Party held out longest. Freemasonry also was abolished and the trade unions were broken up, their leaders being arrested and their buildings and funds confiscated. Simultaneously there occurred the gradual absorption into Nazi ranks of such veterans' organizations as the Steel Helmet and such conservative political groups as the National People's Party. Eventually, a law of July 14, 1933, confirmed the fact that the Nazi party was "the only political party in Germany" and imposed severe penalties on anyone who might undertake to form a new political party. The example of Italy in this regard was followed to its end by another law of 1933, which declared that the National Socialist German Workers' Party had become "the carrier (*Trägerin*) of the government and was inseparably connected with the state." Thereupon Ernst Röhm, chief of staff of the storm troops, and Rudolf Hess, deputy-leader of the party, were made members of the Reich Cabinet. With the creation of another new office, that of *Jugendführer* or "Leader of the Youth," and the subordination to its incumbent (Baldur von Schirach) of all German youth organizations, the state became politically totalitarian.

ECONOMIC COÖRDINATION

On the economic side the original Nazi program had a many-sided appeal. The attack on department stores pleased small shop-keepers. The condemnation of high interest charges attracted debtors. The denunciation of Marxism and trade unions was not unwelcome to industrialists. Nazi peasants hoped for debt relief and the break-up of large estates. Obviously, the program could not at once be fulfilled. Indeed, at the start, indecision and conflicting theories marked the Nazi economic way, but gradually there was evolved a definite program of state supervision and planning.

At first the Hitlerites generally coördinated the largest industries by appointing temporary Nazi supervisors or directors. This was relatively easy since thorough organization had long been a characteristic of most phases of German business and professional life. The official commissars merely purged the existing business, professional, labor, and peasant organizations of "objectionable" members and reconstituted them in accordance with their own principles. In July 1933, however, the chancellor issued a warning to his followers against unauthorized interference in private business affairs and industry. Thereupon the supervisors, who often had been appointed because of their party service rather than executive ability, were gradually removed from control.

To provide immediate relief for the unemployed some novel schemes to "make" work were advanced and within a year unemployment figures were reduced from more than six million to fewer than four million. This was accomplished chiefly by requiring certain industries, for example the Ruhr mines, to take on more men than the production would normally warrant; replacing dismissed liberals, Marxians, and Jews by Nazis and not recording the names of the former on the relief rolls; campaigning against the employment of married women; generally reducing the hours of labor to a maximum of forty per week; and enlisting several hundred thousand young men in a "voluntary" labor corps. Members of the corps received food, shelter, and small wages in return for work on governmental projects, reclamation works, and large estates.

To replace the trade unions which were abolished in 1933 and the employers' associations which were dissolved in 1934, there was established the German Labor Front. Completely controlled by Dr. Robert Ley, this body was intended to coördinate all German intellectual and manual employers and workers.[1] Its prime function was to be the indoctrination of Nazi principles, but it was given some power to arbitrate in labor disputes. Associated with this Labor Front was an elaborate recreational organization called "Strength through Joy." The latter arranged cheap vacation trips for workers and their families.

Relations between capital and labor were regulated by laws that took effect in May 1933 and May 1934. This legislation, rejecting the idea of an inevitable capital-labor conflict, upheld the principles of leadership and "the common welfare before individual welfare." Strikes and lockouts were prohibited. Employers in enterprises with more than twenty workers were designated as "leaders," while their employees officially became "followers." Each such business was required to choose a "council of confidence" to advise on the running of the business, working conditions, and possible ways of increasing the general efficiency. The council members were to be nominated by the leader and elected by the followers. In case of dispute, the workers might appeal to the appropriate "trustee of labor."

Provision was made for thirteen such labor trustees to supervise thirteen geographical areas. Charged with the maintenance of industrial peace, these appointees of the Reich Government were empowered to supervise the councils of confidence, fix wage scales, check any wholesale dismissal of employees, act as referees in cases of dispute between leaders and councils, and even oust exceptionally inefficient or inconsiderate employers from their own businesses. Violators of the new social ethics were to be haled for punishment before Economic Courts of Honor. After the introduction of the Four-Year Plan in 1936, much of all this was disregarded.

In respect of foreign trade and commerce the Nazis put into practice all the principles of economic nationalism. Every means was employed to create a self-sufficient "balanced" economy, that is, to make Germany an autarchic state (*Autarkie*). Pressure was exerted to decrease imports and increase exports. Raw materials

[1] In 1939 the front had about thirty million members.

were rationed. Tariffs were raised and citizens were urged to "buy home products." No one could engage in a new business without governmental permission. Currency-exchange privileges were granted travelers on German ships and in Germany. Shipping lines were reorganized. Debt moratoria were decreed and debt-service charges reduced. German firms were directed to ship their products on national vessels. The development of synthetics or *Ersatzmittel* was feverishly pushed. The government controlled all currency movements. Coördination, unity, and economic independence were the keywords of all striving.[1]

The new developments in the sphere of agriculture were interesting. It seems not unlikely that the Junkers or noble landholders of East Prussia and Pomerania were mainly responsible for the downfall of the Brüning, Papen, and Schleicher governments in 1932–1933. All three chancellors had contemplated relieving the economic distress by breaking up some of the large and debt-burdened landed estates—and all three had failed. For a brief period after Hitler's rise to power it appeared as though another effort would be made in this direction. Eventually, however, it became clear that the Nazis would not thus repay the Junkers who had actually helped to pave the way for their advent to power. Besides, large estates could be worked more efficiently than small homesteads.

It was of great import for the German peasants when Richard W. Darré became minister of agriculture. Believing that Germany should in future depend for her leaders upon a hereditary, Aryan, landholding nobility, Darré was instrumental in the promulgation (October 1933) of a novel Hereditary Farms Law. In order to create a new "farmer aristocracy" which would eventually be the chief source of strength of the German people, it was ordained that every farm of less than 309 acres must pass undivided, upon the owner's death, to his legal heir. The new owner was made responsible for the educational and professional training of the immediate remaining heirs. Only the head of the homestead was to enjoy the *honorary title* of "farmer" (*Bauer*). Hereditary farms could not be sold, mortgaged, or attached for debt. Only those might be "farmers" who were able to prove their "Aryan" ancestry to 1800. Agriculture as a whole was to be controlled by the cabinet minister through an all-inclusive Food Estate (*Nährstand*), which

---

[1] A law of 1934 limited cash dividends on most stocks to 6 per cent. Any excess earnings had to go to the Gold Discount Bank for investment in government loans. Additional types of forced loans were resorted to in later years.

was empowered to regulate and plan agricultural production, sales, prices, and distribution.

Despite export difficulties owing to trade barriers and boycotts, and despite raw-material shortages with resultant high prices, economic conditions in general showed some improvement by 1935. The national income rose above that of 1932 and the official unemployment figure fell to 1,750,000. The national wealth seemed to be more equally distributed and the specter of starvation was banished. Some of this development was owing to the widespread official work-creation schemes and the establishment of labor camps for youths; some to intensive rearmament. This was true particularly after Hitler's repudiation (1935) of the restrictive military clauses of the Versailles Treaty. The conscription and equipment of a new large army were of considerable aid in the further reduction of unemployment figures.

And then, in 1936, Germany really moved on to a "war economy." The entire economic life of the Third Reich was subordinated to the demands of a Four-Year Plan announced before the annual National Socialist Party Congress at Nuremberg in September 1936. "In four years," said Hitler, "Germany must be entirely independent of foreign countries with respect to all those materials which can in any way be produced through German capability, through German chemistry, or by our machine and mining industries." The execution of the plan was entrusted to General Göring, although Dr. Schacht was minister of economics.

It became increasingly evident during 1937 that Schacht and Göring were in disagreement on economic and financial questions. The former, worried by the increase in the floating debt and the 500,000,000-mark service charges on the foreign debt, advocated greater economy, a slowing up of the Four-Year Plan, and greater emphasis on the export business. Göring's attitude was expressed in the sentiment "cannon before butter"; he interfered more and more in the affairs of private business in order to relieve the raw-material shortage, increase the grain deliveries of farmers, and speed up the huge rearmament and public-works programs. Schacht therefore resigned as minister of economics and later was relieved of the headship of the Reichsbank. Dr. Walther Funk, long a friend and economic adviser of Hitler, replaced Schacht in both capacities.

The chief emphasis in the raw-material campaign was placed (a) on the development of synthetic fuel and oil, rubber, and fabric threads, and (b) on an increased production of iron through the more intensive working of old mines, the salvaging of used iron, and the development of a commercially satisfactory method of utilizing low-grade iron ore. The cause was aided by legislation which, among other things, required the use of a certain proportion of rayon or artificial wool in all textiles and limited the use of rubber for toys and bathroom supplies. After the absorption of Austria into the Reich in March 1938 the Four-Year Plan was speedily introduced into that new province, under the personal supervision of Göring.

The devaluation of several foreign currencies naturally decreased the value of Germany's foreign-exchange holdings, but the government continued to impose drastic penalties, even death, for the failure of subjects to surrender their foreign currency. Efforts were made to encourage a greater consumption of indigenous foods, and dairy products were rationed. The rearmament and public-works (especially motor highways) programs provided much new employment (particularly after military service was made compulsory for two years instead of one). In May 1938 the number of unemployed was only 338,000, and of these, most were regarded as unemployable. Indeed, though labor productivity had been stepped up considerably since 1928, the country now actually suffered from a labor shortage.

The late spring of 1938 found the German Government concentrating on three main domestic items. First, to repeat, there was the Four-Year Plan. The successful completion of this scheme was all the more necessary because foreign countries were becoming less and less eager to trade with Germany on her own terms. Germany wanted raw materials but she would pay for them only in goods or in special marks that had little free utility, and often payment was deferred for a long time. Trade could not flourish in such circumstances.[1]

Secondly, there was the desire to weld Germany's potentially great military might into an efficient whole. The march into Austria had shown that the army, at least in its mechanized units, was not functioning so smoothly as had been hoped. The speed and competence of the Czechoslovak mobilization in May 1938, when a crisis seemed to have been reached over the Sudetenland issue, evidently convinced the Nazis that they had further preparations to make. Simultaneously fortification work was pushed at a fever-

---

[1] The Germans were especially fond of paying their debts with razor blades and mouth organs, and in at least one case with a hippopotamus. See D. Miller's *You Can't Do Business with Hitler*, 2 ed., 1942.

ish pace along the western frontier, where the German complement of the French Maginot Line was to be made impenetrable. For this work, many of the unemployed men in the new province of Austria were drafted.

Finally, there was the need to integrate Austria with the whole German economic system. This was a difficult task, especially since Austria, though rich in iron ore and hydroelectric power, did not produce enough food to satisfy the needs of her population. From the point of view of sufficiency in foodstuffs, the absorption of Austria made the German economic problem more, rather than less, serious.[1]

To combat the labor shortage, a decree of 1938 made all "state members" subject to conscription for short-term labor service "on nationally urgent tasks." Although the decree established a compensation for such conscript labor equal to that for similar private labor, the Reich Labor Trustees were empowered, a few days later, to establish maximum wages for all kinds of work. The labor decree applied to every male and female capable of working, with the necessary exemption of expectant mothers, mothers with young children, and so forth. Thus it was hoped to provide the necessary labor for the completion of the Four-Year Plan.

Funds for carrying out the program were derived from various sources. There were the regular taxes and public loans. There were expropriations of properties still held by Jews and by Catholic monastic orders and societies (especially in Austria). There were special levies such as that of July 1938, which deducted 35 per cent of the profits of large corporations before the distribution of dividends. This levy was fixed at 40 per cent for the two years following 1938. There were energetic campaigns for "voluntary" contributions in aid of Winter Relief Work and increased taxes on bachelors, spinsters, and childless couples. Finally, loans were floated at relatively frequent intervals. Generally these loans were heavily oversubscribed, partly because of popular approval of the purposes of the loans, partly because business men, forbidden to expand their operations except by special permit, found it desirable to invest their surpluses in government bonds, and partly because organizations such as insurance companies usually found it expedient to invest heavily in government enterprises.[2]

[1] Later, the annexation of the German-speaking portions of Czechoslovakia further aggravated this situation, for there again the new territories added to the manufacturing wealth of the Reich but increased the need for grain.

[2] As part of the general campaign the demand for the return of Germany's colonies also became more insistent.

Thus did the Nazis with their totalitarian economics prepare for the total war which they precipitated in 1939.

CULTURE, EDUCATION, LAW

The coördination of German culture (literature, the press, music, painting, sculpture, architecture, the theater, moving pictures, and the radio) was entrusted to a Reich Culture Chamber under the direction of Dr. Goebbels. Through this body the Reich intended to "determine the intellectual course" and cleanse the national spiritual life of all that was non-Nazi or "non-Aryan." An extreme censorship was established and cultural activities came to be largely political and propagandistic. "Anyone who dares to question the National-Socialist world outlook," said a Nazi official, "must be branded as a traitor."

The chief task of the schools came to be "the education of the youth for service . . . in the spirit of National Socialism." Objectivity in the teaching of history was discarded as "one of the numerous fallacies of liberalism." According to Dr. Ernst Krieck, chief apostle of the Nazi educational gospel,

the clue to German history is the growth of a nation from blood and soil. . . . Blood and soil, as fundamental forces of life, are the symbols of the national-political point of view and of the heroic style of life. . . . In blood is embodied the race. . . . The soil signifies for us the place in which our life passes and ends.[1]

To students in the secondary schools and universities it was made clear that "a good examination record will be valuable only if accompanied by a good S.A. record." In the curricula main emphasis was to be placed on (1) the inculcation of Nazi racial theories; (2) the description of "the great traditions, history, and culture" of the German people; (3) the cultivation of the ideal of the politician-soldier and of the "military spirit"; and (4) the development of strong physiques through athletics, sports, and compulsory labor on farms and in camps. The traditional list of German heroes, including Barbarossa, Frederick the Great, and Bismarck, was extended to include Adolf Hitler, Leo Schlageter (killed while resisting the French occupation of the Ruhr), and Horst Wessel (composer of the party song and victim in 1930 of a fatal brawl).

The Nazi view of German racial supremacy had as a corollary

[1] Quoted in Kandel, I. L. *The Making of Nazis*, 1935, p. 9.

the desire for the greatest possible increase of population through the addition of biologically sound, "Aryan" children. Every conceivable means of propaganda was used to encourage early marriages and large families, particularly among blond-haired, blue-eyed people. The bearing of "Aryan" children by unmarried girls was officially encouraged with almost equal ardor. The state frowned, however, on reproduction among individuals who had heritable diseases or who were chronically alcoholic or congenitally feeble-minded. On January 1, 1934, accordingly, there went into effect a sterilization law "for the prevention of inherited disease in posterity." The law in its scientific aspects met with the general approval of authorities on sterilization in foreign countries, but it might readily be perverted for political purposes.[1]

It could hardly be expected that the judicial system of Germany would remain unaltered. The legal system, based to a large extent upon Roman law (which supposedly "served the interests of the materialist system of the world"), was to be scrapped for a system resting upon German common law (*Volksrecht*). Thus justice would be brought in closer touch with "the German consciousness" and the strong forces of the nation would be protected against the weak and unworthy elements. Since "the individual is nothing, while the people is everything," justice must be based upon the popular feeling of right as much as on legal texts. The political complexion of the new justice was exemplified in a decree of 1934 which established revolutionary tribunals called "People's Courts." These courts were, in general, to be composed of two judges and three laymen, all appointed by Hitler. Their chief jurisdiction was over cases of high treason, a term which was so defined that it might include even the distribution of a banned newspaper. Choice of defense counsel before these tribunals was made subject to the approval of the court president and there was no provision for appeal. The extreme penalty for treason was decapitation by means of the ax.

ATTEMPTED RELIGIOUS COÖRDINATION

The process of coördination in the Third Reich encountered its most persistent opposition in the sphere of religion. Until 1933 German Protestantism comprised twenty-nine groups—an intolerable situation in the eyes of the National-Socialist leaders. To

[1] Nazi law also forbade the issuance of marriage permits where either applicant failed to satisfy the prescribed eugenic standards.

achieve unity and control, a group of Nazi "German Christians" moved to establish a single Protestant Church under a national bishop appointed by the Führer. To forestall such action, representatives of the various churches organized (April 1933) a German Evangelical Church Union, to be governed by a national synod and presided over by a Lutheran bishop (for the Lutherans formed the majority of German Protestants). The first man chosen for this post was Dr. Friedrich von Bodelschwingh. Since the latter was prominent chiefly for his social-welfare work and had not been actively identified with any political faction, it was hoped that the government would refrain from interference.

But the "German Christians" were not content. Particularly was this true of one Dr. Ludwig Müller, Nazi chaplain and friend of the chancellor. Perhaps because Müller himself wished to be national bishop, he and his followers refused to accept Bodelschwingh's election. General Göring, moreover, declared that the churches had no right to act without his approval. As Prussian Premier he claimed the spiritual as well as the political powers of the former king of Prussia. Accordingly he appointed a lawyer, Dr. August Jäger, to be Reich Church Commissioner for Prussia. When Jäger proceeded to dissolve all local church councils, appoint "German Christians" to the main clerical offices, and use storm troops to enforce his edicts, Bodelschwingh resigned (June 1933). Strenuous efforts were simultaneously made to convert all pastors and theological students to the "German-Christian" point of view.[1]

The growing strife led President von Hindenburg to write a letter pleading for the restoration of harmony within church ranks. Thereupon Jäger was dismissed and deputies of the Müller and Bodelschwingh factions met to draft a constitution and set a church-election date. The document, when completed, provided for a Lutheran Reich Bishop elected by a national synod and assisted by a spiritual cabinet composed of one representative from each of the three chief German Protestant divisions. July 23 was fixed as the date for a threefold vote by the Protestant church-membership: (1) a referendum on the constitution; (2) the election of local church boards; and (3) the election of delegates to the national synod.

Two candidates were nominated for nearly every office, one by the "German Christians" and one by the Bodelschwingh group.

---

[1] There were parallel developments in several other predominantly Protestant German states.

The government actively supported the former and hampered the latter. The press and the radio were made available only to the Müllerites. Hitler broadcast an appeal to the voters to elect only those candidates who were pledged to support the "new national policy." The "German Christians" won, gained control of the national synod, and elevated Müller to the office of *Reichsbischof*.

The strife was not yet ended. There was a division of opinion among Bishop Müller's own followers. The more moderate elements were content to leave matters as they now were. But some extremists wished to do away with the Old Testament, discard the crucifix, and revise the New Testament in such manner as to make of Jesus Christ a historical rather than a divine figure. This group also seemed bent upon ending the split between Protestantism and Catholicism and eventually uniting all "Aryan" Germans in one "coördinated" national church. Such aims were anathema to the Bodelschwingh faction and, led by a fiery wartime submarine commander, the Rev. Martin Niemöller, some thousands of anti-Müllerites now formed a Pastors' Emergency League.

In January 1934 Müller, uneasy over the steadfast opposition, the rapidly increasing membership of the Pastors' Emergency League, and the resignation of his own appointees to the spiritual cabinet, attempted by decree to make himself dictator. This only served to increase the ardor of the opposition and the decree soon was rescinded. Müller then appointed Jäger to the post of Law Steward of the German Evangelical Church so that he might unify the whole religious administration.

Dr. Jäger induced several of the regional churches, in Saxony and Brandenburg, for example, to surrender their traditional autonomy and accept the full authority of Bishop Müller. But the opposition in other areas continued to fight against Müller and his decrees. The Pastors' Emergency League was disbanded, but its work was carried on by a Confessional Synod headed by Niemöller and the Protestant bishops of Bavaria and Württemberg. Among other things, this synod refused to regard the Nazi revolution as a revelation of the Divine Will or to serve two masters: God and political leaders. The reply to all this was the arrest, suspension, transfer, or retirement of hundreds of pastors and the removal of the two south-German bishops. This last action led to the holding of protest meetings in many cities and Jäger was once more dropped from office.

Thus far, Hitler had taken relatively little public part in the church conflict. He ostensibly adopted the attitude that, as long as it remained loyal to the state, the church might settle its own difficulties. But eventually, in September 1935, he decreed the supremacy of the Nazi State over the Evangelical (Protestant) Church. The Reich Bishop was shorn of his authority and full control of nondoctrinal church affairs was placed in the hands of Hanns Kerrl, "Minister for Church Affairs." The new minister was placed in complete charge of the personnel, property, and finances of the Protestant churches and empowered to appoint an administrative directorate to assist him in his functions. Henceforth resistance to Nazi church policy would constitute lawbreaking.

In 1937 it was made a crime to collect or contribute money for the Confessional Synod or any other church group not approved by the minister for church affairs. State contributions to church funds were simultaneously limited or stopped. Only church news that had received the approval of Kerrl might be published. And he usually passed only information emanating from the "German Christian" movement, still led by Bishop Müller. Pastors who displeased the authorities were jailed without trials. Niemöller, incarcerated since 1937, was tried secretly in 1938, on charges of sedition. The court freed him on all major charges but the police at once rearrested him and, without publishing any new charge, placed him in a concentration camp.

In the spring of 1939 Kerrl made Dr. Frederick Werner chairman of the Supreme Council of the German Evangelical Church. Werner issued several decrees which in effect endowed the council with totalitarian powers in the matter of church administration and procedure. When the opposition pastors thereupon announced their refusal to consider Werner's orders as "legally binding," further ministerial arrests followed and several theological seminaries were closed. The conflict continued briskly throughout the summer of 1939, but in the second month of the new war, the clerics agreed to a truce. In view of the national emergency, the Confessional Synod agreed to accept temporarily the administrative and spiritual headship of Kerrl and Werner.

Meanwhile another religious conflict had been in progress, a struggle involving the Nazi State and the Catholic Church. Hitler was grieved that relations between the Vatican and German Catholics were regulated by three separate concordats—between the papacy on the one hand and Prussia, Bavaria, and Baden severally on the other. Accordingly the Catholic von Papen was sent to Vatican City to negotiate a single concordat for all Germany's

Catholics. The latter hoped that such a treaty would put an end to the unpleasant encounters between storm troops and Catholic organizations that were a frequent occurrence in the early days of Nazi control.

On July 20, 1933, a new concordat was signed. The Catholic clergy was forbidden to participate in Reich politics and all future diocesan appointments were to be made by the Holy See after consultation with the government. The latter, for its part, sanctioned the continued existence of the Catholic Action as a non-political society. Catholic schools, youth groups, and cultural organizations were not to be disturbed so long as they refrained from any political moves.

It was not long before friction developed over the interpretation of this instrument. Everywhere in the Reich, Nazi political leaders strove to restrict the freedom of the Catholic Action, the Catholic Youth Movement, and the Catholic press. Quarrels arose over the control of education and leading Catholic churchmen openly denounced the sterilization law and the attacks on the Old Testament and the crucifix. Perhaps the most outspoken clerical fighter was the archbishop of Munich, Michael Cardinal von Faulhaber. Apparently to forestall the arrest of this prelate, the pope in 1934 conferred upon him the rank of papal legate which brought with it diplomatic immunity.

In the ensuing years the struggle continued to be marked by police action, press suspensions, and secular violence. A number of monks and nuns were imprisoned on the charge of smuggling money out of Germany. Membership in the Hitler Youth was made compulsory for boys and girls, who thus were more effectively removed from clerical influence. Pressure was brought to bear on parents to register their children in public rather than confessional schools and in 1937 most of the Catholic schools in Bavaria were converted into state institutions. When the pope criticized Nazi interference in religious matters and accused the government of having violated the concordat, his protests drew intemperate replies from Nazi officials and precipitated a new series of trials of monks and lay brothers on charges of immorality and exchange-law violations. But even after the outbreak of the Second World War, leading Catholic clerics in Germany continued to denounce Nazi efforts to destroy the institutions of the church and the family.

Meanwhile, however, *Der Stürmer,* founded by Julius Streicher, printed more and more scurrilous references to Jesus Christ; and

Das Schwarze Korps, organ of the Elite Guards commanded by Heinrich Himmler,[1] decorated its pages with blasphemous articles and cartoons aimed at making Christianity seem ridiculous. In 1937 Hitler awarded the National Prize, Germany's substitute for the Nobel Prize, to Alfred Rosenberg: outstanding philosophical foe of Christianity and spiritual leader of the Neo-Pagans, who advocated a return to the old Teutonic rites.

POLITICS, 1933–1939

The Reichstag that had been elected on March 5, 1933, was dissolved by the government in October of the same year, coincident with Germany's withdrawal from the disarmament conference and announced intention to resign from the League.[2] New elections were called for November, at which time the people were to elect deputies and register their approbation or disapproval of Nazi diplomacy. About 96.2 per cent of the qualified electorate went to the polls. Of these, 93.4 per cent endorsed the government's policies. And 92.3 per cent of the ballots marked were in favor of the single (Nazi) list of candidates. Such an endorsement greatly strengthened the hands of the government at home and abroad.

Yet, early in 1934 it became evident that there was dissatisfaction within Nazi ranks. Particularly was this noticeable among the storm troops (S.A.), many of whom had once been communists. Apparently it was resented that the "socialistic" items in the party program were seemingly being forgotten. A sizeable proportion of the rank-and-file Nazis seemed to regard the labor laws as a betrayal of their interests. Some were angry because of the decline in real wages. Others were still awaiting the jobs they had been promised. And the personal extravagances of a number of Nazi leaders added to the ill will and restlessness.

The leadership of these discontented Brown Shirts, who apparently wanted a "second revolution," was assumed by Captain Röhm, their chief of staff. The latter seemed eager, furthermore, to incorporate a large number of storm troops in the regular army or *Reichswehr.* To this, both the Reichswehr generals and Hitler were opposed,[3] and in April 1934 it was announced that all S.A.

---

[1] This same Himmler also was the dread chief of the Nazi secret police, called *Geheime Staats-Polizei* or *Gestapo.*

[2] The state legislatures also were dissolved and no new ones elected.

[3] On July 13, 1934, Hitler told the Reichstag: "There is in the state only one bearer of arms: the army, and only one carrier of the political will: the National Socialist Party."

men would be required to go on vacation for the month of July. Early in June Röhm himself was given leave of absence "for reasons of health" and it was rumored that his troops might be greatly reduced in numbers since the Reichswehr had no faith in a large "people's army." Meanwhile Vice-Chancellor von Papen also had raised his voice in opposition, by denouncing the extreme censorship, the resort to terrorism, and the use of force in the settlement of religious disputes.

The apparent intent of the government to weaken the storm troops and the fact that nothing happened to Papen for his temerity seem to have induced the malcontents to attempt an early seizure of power. The resultant happenings, which culminated in the "Purge of June 30," were thus described by Hitler in a speech before the Reichstag on July 13, 1934:

Throughout the morning of June 29 I received such alarming messages of impending conspiratory action that I had to cut short at noon the inspection of the Westphalian labor camps in order to be ready for any emergency. About 1 A.M. [June 30] I got two urgent alarm notices to the effect that coups were scheduled to take place (at 5 P.M. in Berlin and 9 P.M. in Munich). . . . At 2 A.M. I flew to Munich. Meanwhile General Göring had been commissioned, in case a purge were carried out, to take immediate and analogous measures in Berlin and Prussia. He destroyed with iron fist the embryo attack on the National-Socialist State. The necessity for lightning-like action was responsible for the circumstance that, in this decisive hour, I had only a very few individuals at my disposal [chiefly the S.S.]. In the presence of Minister Goebbels and the newly appointed chief of staff [Viktor Lutze] the familiar purge was carried out and brought to conclusion in Munich. . . . If anyone reproach me for not having had recourse to the regular courts, I can only reply: In this hour I was responsible for the fate of the German nation and thereby the German people's supreme judge. . . . I gave the order to shoot the ringleaders of this treasonable plot. . . . I am fully prepared to assume before history the responsibility for the twenty-fours hours in which I came to the bitterest decisions of my life. . . .

It is not known how many persons were killed in this "blood purge." Most prominent among the victims were, besides Röhm (who was accused of sexual perversion as well as treason), ex-Chancellor von Schleicher and his wife, the leader of the Catholic Action, and three of Papen's assistants. Papen himself was arrested by Göring and for some time his fate was in doubt. It was generally believed that the intervention of Hindenburg saved him. A cabinet decree legalized the purge as having been "in self-defense of the state," and the Reichstag thanked the chancellor for his vigorous forestalling "of civil war and chaos."

Soon after the purge the government took steps to reduce the number of storm troops. The primary function of this semimilitary organization was accomplished after the "winning of the streets" from the opposition elements. The membership, however, had continued to grow, and Röhm at one time claimed to be in command of 2,500,000 men. Increase in size was accompanied by a decline of discipline and neither Hitler nor the Reichswehr favored so large a private army. Consequently the S.A. was reduced in size and largely disarmed. Even the more exclusive, better disciplined, black-shirted Nazi bodyguards or S.S. were placed under restrictions at the end of 1934. The Reichswehr therefore emerged in 1935 as the supreme military organ of the Third Reich, particularly after the reintroduction of conscription and a large standing army.[1]

Less than five weeks after his victory of June 30, 1934, Adolf Hitler rose to new political heights. On August 2 the aged President von Hindenburg died. On the preceding night the cabinet had adopted a decree providing for the union of the offices of president and chancellor from the moment of Hindenburg's death. From August 2, therefore, Hitler ruled alone. Declining the title of president, he asked to be called only Der Führer. So that the people might register approval of his latest action, he ordered a plebiscite to be held. (Meanwhile the Reichswehr was required to take an oath of allegiance to Adolf Hitler, "the supreme head of the army.") In the plebiscite, the people were asked to vote "yes" as a "proof of German unity to the outside world." About 88 per cent of the 43,500,000 ballots cast were in the affirmative. "In the next thousand years," Hitler was then reported as saying, "no more revolutions will take place in Germany."

In the period 1935 to 1938, certain prominent leaders of the high command and of the foreign office fell into disfavor with Hitler. It may be that this was so partly because these men, some of whom were not actual members of the Nazi Party, still were fundamentally Christian in sympathies, partly because they continued to represent the outlook of Prussian Junkerism, and partly

---

[1] In October 1935 the German General Staff, abolished by the Versailles Treaty, was publicly reëstablished. By a law of September 1935 the swastika flag replaced the black-white-red ensign of imperial days as the national flag of Germany.

because they opposed the radical Nazi policies in the Rhineland and Spain and the formation of the Berlin-Rome-Tokyo axis. At any rate, the Führer's displeasure was vigorously manifested early in 1938 when he reorganized both these branches of the national administration.

Using the marriage of War Minister Werner von Blomberg to a lady of much lower "station" as a convenient time determinant, Hitler dismissed not merely this officer but also Commander-in-Chief Werner von Fritsch, Foreign Minister Konstantin von Neurath, and others of similar sympathies. They were replaced by men who were more closely attuned to Hitler's methods and views, men such as the raucous-voiced, promise-breaking new Foreign Minister Joachim von Ribbentrop, and the political-minded General Wilhelm Keitel.

Another reorganization was effected in January 1939. On this occasion Hitler, by decree, placed virtually all able-bodied males over seventeen, who were not actually engaged in military service or were not members of the Elite Guards, under the direct "educational" control of the storm-troop organization headed by Viktor Lutze. The S.A. was thus made responsible for the continued physical fitness and military education of a vast military reserve force, that is, of nearly every German man before and after the completion of his required term of service in the army. Thus the ground was well prepared for the international aggressions of 1939.[1]

THE PROBLEM OF REFUGEES

One of the most tragic consequences of the Nazi domestic and foreign policies was the fate of the hundreds of thousands of persons who were driven from their homes and rendered "stateless." No word picture can give full understanding of the misery of these refugees—this human flotsam.[2] The problem of dealing with large numbers of stateless refugees already had been thrust upon the world as an aftermath of the Bolshevik Revolution in Russia.

[1] The foreign relations of the Hitler Government are described in detail in the appropriate sections of the chapters on "The Search for Security," "Fascist Italy," "Spain," "Two Heirs of the Habsburgs," "Two Slavic Republics," "The Soviet Union," and "The Return to War, 1939." Be it noted, in addition, that in 1936 Berlin denounced the international control set up over her rivers by the Versailles Treaty.

[2] There is a gripping story of the refugee problem by E. M. Remarque, entitled *Flotsam*, 1941. The official account is in J. H. Simpson, *The Refugee Problem; a Report of a Survey*, 1939.

To deal with the Russian and other early postwar refugees, there had been created, under League auspices, the Nansen International Office for Refugees. This was joined, after the advent of the Nazi Government in Germany, by a League-supervised Office of the High Commissioner for Refugees, established to deal with the specific question of refugees from the Third Reich. Both organizations were concerned mainly with the political and legal protection of their charges and both were scheduled to end their labors on December 31, 1938. The far-reaching political developments of 1938, however, made the closing of these bureaus untimely and hence the League Council approved a plan for combining them under a single High Commissioner of the League of Nations for Refugees with headquarters in London. Sir Herbert Emerson was then appointed the first such commissioner.

Meanwhile the treatment meted out to the Jews by Germany induced the United States Government to ask (March 1938) twenty American and nine European states whether they would coöperate in the creation of an international committee to facilitate the emigration of refugees from central Europe. Funds for the project, it was expected, would be forthcoming from private organizations and individuals. (And funds were necessary because the German Government, while declaring its anxiety to get rid of the Jews, yet made it very difficult—in many cases virtually impossible—for them to emigrate.) All invited powers except Italy responded to the call, as did three British Dominions, so that thirty-two nations were represented at the consequent meeting at Evian in France (July). Machinery was set up to consider ways and means of handling the problem, humanitarian sentiments were expressed, and, while all agreed that something should be done and done quickly, each wanted the others to do it. Caution had to be exercised not merely because of the internal politics and economic and racial problems of each state represented, but lest any false move act as an invitation to other countries to imitate the German example of "human dumping." In the end, an Intergovernmental Committee on Refugees was set up, under the chairmanship of George Rublee of the United States.

The committee was to assist refugees by undertaking "negotiations to improve the present conditions of exodus and to replace them with conditions of orderly emigration" and by approaching "the governments of refuge with a view to developing opportunities for permanent settlement." The crisis over Sudetenland postponed the activities of the committee and ended by increasing its burden. Finally, Mr. Rublee managed to inaugurate discussions with a German representative regarding a possible solution of the problem, though Berlin did not officially recognize the existence of the committee on refugees.

Early in 1939 Rublee brought to the committee in London a German "unilateral statement" on the subject of refugees. The German proposals envisaged the emigration of 150,000 youthful Jewish "pioneers" over a period of five years. When these had established new homes overseas, their dependents were to be permitted to follow them. The emigration was to be financed partly out of remaining Jewish property in Germany and partly by foreign contributions. Meanwhile limited opportunities to earn a living within Germany would be reopened to the Jews who were left behind.

Mr. Rublee resigned after having presented and argued in favor of the German statement and was succeeded as director by League Commissioner Sir Herbert Emerson. The committee then adjourned, merely "taking cognizance" of plans to set up a huge resettlement corporation to "serve as an agency for financing emigration from Germany and for maintaining such contacts with the German authorities as might be necessary for the purpose." There, in effect, the international effort to solve the problem rested when war broke out anew in September 1939.

CHAPTER XVII

Two Heirs of the Habsburgs

AUSTRIA

a. From Monarchy to Republic, 1918–1920

On November 21, 1916, the aged Emperor-King Francis Joseph died. His reign of sixty-eight years ended, as it had begun, in the midst of tumult and warfare. He was succeeded by his grand-nephew, Charles. The new ruler was good-natured and courageous, but inexperienced in statecraft. Though his intentions were good, his decisions often were belated and his actions undiplomatic. It was his misfortune to become emperor-king at one of the most critical times in the history of his dynasty.

The events of 1916 to 1918 broke down the morale of the Austro-Hungarian people. The news of the Russian revolutions, the entry of the United States into the war, and the dissemination of Allied propaganda behind the lines helped to undermine the faith of the people in their government, particularly since the latter failed to grant liberal concessions. To make matters worse, the Czechs worked against the monarchy, there was mutiny among the Slavic and Hungarian soldiers and the sailors in the Adriatic, and the people in many cities faced starvation. The last blows to Habsburg power came with the appearance in Vienna of mobs shouting: "All power to the soldiers' and workers' councils" and the adoption of a resolution by the German-speaking deputies in the parliament at Vienna proclaiming a separate German-Austrian state.

In a last effort to hold his crumbling domains together, Charles issued a manifesto (October 16, 1918) calling for the formation of a new Austrian federative state in which each people should form an autonomous community. But it was too late for federation. On November 11, eight days after the armistice was signed with Italy, Emperor Charles abdicated.[1] In order not to "set his person as a barrier to the free development of the people whom he loved," Charles renounced any participation in the further administration of the state. Immediately thereafter he left Vienna for his castle at Eckartsau and four months later he and his family went to Switzerland as exiles.

Even before Charles had quitted Vienna, the Social Democrats, Christian Socialists, and German Nationals had set up a provisional government in German-Austria by an almost bloodless revolution. On November 12 this provisional government issued a tentative constitution which declared German-Austria to be a republic and an integral part of the newly formed German Reich. The black-and-gold standard of the emperors was replaced by a red-white-red banner, and Vienna, the erstwhile Imperial City, became the capital of the republic. Meanwhile the non-German portions of the defunct Dual Monarchy had gone to form the new states of Czechoslovakia and Hungary or to increase the territories of Italy, Romania, Yugoslavia, and Poland. The general absence of violence attending the breakup of the monarchy was owing, in large measure, to the action of Charles in releasing his former officials from their oath of allegiance to him.

In the interim between the creation of German-Austria and the elections for a constituent assembly in February 1919, the provisional government watched over Austria's welfare. The presidency was rotated among the controlling party leaders, most of whom were Social Democrats or Christian Socialists. These men had no intention of permitting Austria to become a communist state, quickly suppressed a number of minor "Red" uprisings, and desired the establishment of law and order at the earliest possible moment. Certainly this was a fortunate circumstance in view of the difficulties and hardships that faced the Austrians immediately after the war.

At the conclusion of military hostilities thousands of armed Czech, Polish, and Hungarian soldiers marched home through Austria from the various fronts. More than a million Russian and Italian ex-prisoners of war returned home after their release and, though most of them probably were anxious to leave Austria quickly, many paused to snatch some compensation for their suffering in the prison camps. In Vienna itself, the returned and starving German-Austrian soldiers threatened violence unless food and shelter were provided.

[1] Two days later he abdicated as king of Hungary.

As a member of the Dual Monarchy, German-Austria had been the center of a relatively self-sufficient economic unit. It had received many of its raw materials and foodstuffs from Bohemia and Moravia, had secured grain from Galicia and Hungary, had had two excellent ports on the Adriatic, and had sold its manufactured products to the various parts of the empire as well as to foreign countries. All this suddenly was changed. The great iron, steel, automobile, railway, electrical, textile, paper, and banking industries were ruined because the raw materials now were located in foreign areas, because tariff walls were raised against Austrian products by nationalistic neighbors, and because Austria could raise only a fraction of the food supply that she needed for her population.

The unemployment problem soon became appalling. Nearly every important organization in Austria was overstaffed as a result of the territorial losses. The Austrian bureaucracy had been notorious for its numerous employees and now thousands of officials were without a livelihood. The same was true of thousands of postmen, railwaymen, bank clerks, and newspapermen. Doctors, professors, and merchants were starving to death, as were large numbers of former army and navy officers and the dispossessed aristocrats.

For four months after the close of armed warfare the Allies maintained their food blockade of the Central Powers. Austria suffered severely from this action and in 1919–1920 many thousand Austrian children were sent abroad, especially to the Scandinavian countries, to be fed and reared. For a time, many of the unemployed, starving, and freezing Viennese were sent into the Vienna Woods to chop down trees for firewood which the wealthier inhabitants purchased, not because they wanted it but because that seemed the most expedient way to keep the proletariat busy and relatively quiet. Conditions were somewhat improved when the American Relief Administration came to Austria.

The chaos and disruption that threatened the new Austria gave rise to a general desire for the early restoration of order and economic stability. Hence the assembly elections of February 1919, conducted on a basis of proportional representation and universal suffrage, resulted in a triumph for the moderate parties. The provisional government resigned and control was placed in the hands of a "Pink Coalition" consisting of the urban Social Democrats, who secured a plurality of the seats, and the agrarian Christian Socialists. Karl Seitz was elected president of the constituent assembly and Karl Renner became chancellor. Both men were Social Democrats.

The Constituent Assembly confirmed the declaration of the provisional government to the effect that German-Austria was a republic and an integral part of Germany. Then most of the Habsburg family was banished, its property was confiscated, and a foreign policy was charted that would suit Austria's position as a member of the German federation. No effort was made to negotiate for the maintenance of the economic arrangements that formerly had existed with the other parts of the Dual Monarchy. Hence it was a shock to the authorities at Vienna to learn from the French Foreign Office, just prior to the publication of the German peace treaty, that the contemplated union between Germany and Austria would not be permitted by the Allies.

The Treaty of St. Germain which Austria was compelled to accept in September 1919 confirmed this prohibition and stipulated that union might take place only with the consent of the League Council. Inasmuch as Council decisions, in general, had to be unanimous, the outlook for early union or Anschluss was doubtful. Even the name "German-Austria" had to be purged of the word "German" and changed to "Republic of Austria." The assembly now had no choice other than to proceed, under protest, with the making of a permanent constitution, for this matter had been suspended in order that the document might be made to fit in with the projected German constitution. On October 1, 1920, the assembly adopted an instrument that followed closely the outline of a draft presented by the Christian Socialists. The latter, fearing the dominance of the numerous and radical Viennese proletariat in any centralized state, had devised a federal system similar to that in Switzerland.

The constitution created a government consisting of a president and a bicameral legislature. The lower house (*Nationalrat*) was composed of members elected for four years by all citizens over twenty. It could not be prorogued or dissolved except by its own resolution or law. The upper house (*Bundesrat*) was to contain a minimum of three and a maximum of twelve representatives from each of the nine provinces or *Länder*. The representatives were to be elected by the provincial diets and their powers were to be chiefly advisory. The chancellor and cabinet were made responsible to the lower house. Together the two councils constituted the Federal Assembly which, until 1929, had the power to elect a president. In 1929 provision was made for popular presidential elections. Every act of the president had to be countersigned by the appropriate cabinet minister. The provincial diets retained considerable local autonomy and in numerous instances the enforcement of national laws was left in their hands. The supreme court was given extensive powers of review. In the matter of social, labor, and agrarian reforms, the constituent assembly contented itself with outlining an extensive program, the execution of which was left to the provinces.

In the first parliamentary elections held under the new constitution, the Social Democrats lost their plurality to the Christian Socialists, partly through quarrels within their own ranks, partly because of a general dissatisfaction with the peace treaty, and partly owing to a wave of anti-Semitism. Two days after the election the Christian Socialists combined with the Pan-German Party to form a new government. After the elections for the upper house had taken place, the Federal Assembly elected Dr. Michael Hainisch, a man of considerable scholastic repute, to be Austria's first president. In the same month Austria was admitted to membership in the League of Nations.

Almost fifteen months after the adoption of this constitution the boundaries of the new republic were finally delimited (December 1921). Austria then comprised nine provinces: Burgenland, Carinthia, Lower Austria, Upper Austria, Salzburg, Styria, Tirol, Vorarlberg, and Vienna. The Klagenfurt Basin in Carinthia was conceded to Austria rather than to Yugoslavia after a plebiscite had shown that an overwhelming majority of the inhabitants preferred this settlement. Austria's possession of Burgenland was disputed until late in 1921 by Hungary, who withdrew her soldiers from the area only upon the motion of the Council of Ambassadors. A plebiscite held in the city and environs of Ödenburg (Sopron) in Burgenland, under the supervision of an Italian general, resulted in the eventual award of that district to the Magyars. The area of Austria was 32,369 square miles and the estimated population, 6,800,000. The inhabitants of Vienna alone numbered 1,800,000.

b. Storm and Stress, 1921–1932

During 1921 economic conditions in Austria became worse and worse. The winter of 1920–1921 was particularly harsh and thousands starved to death. The government's recourse to inflation made matters more complicated and the Austrian crown, worth

20 cents at par, soon stood at nearly 3000 to the dollar. Early in 1921 the despairing authorities appealed to the League for funds with which to purchase food for the hungering populace. The reply of the League was to send a commission to investigate the Austrian problem. Meanwhile various international loans and charitable expenditures provided temporary relief.

The terrible economic situation gave added impetus to the movement for union with Germany. In February 1921 a bill for a plebiscite on the Anschluss was presented in the parliament. If the vote favored union, the government should petition the League for its consent. The Allied Powers, however, refused to permit the holding of the plebiscite and threatened to punish Austria if the bill were passed. The proposal was dropped, but a number of the provinces decided that, even if Austria were forbidden to unite with Germany, this prohibition could not apply to the individual provinces. A plebiscite in the Tirol endorsed union by a vote of 145,302 to 1805. Salzburg voted for union by a count of 103,000 to 800. When Styria and Upper Austria prepared to hold similar plebiscites, the Allies threatened intervention and the central government blocked the project.

In June 1921 Dr. Johann Schober, police president of Vienna and leader of the Pan-Germans, became premier of another coalition cabinet. He remained in control until May 1922, though he twice had to reconstruct his cabinet in the interval. The Schober governments puzzled over ameliorative financial measures and countermanded a number of the steps toward socialization which had been taken by the earlier and more radical ministries. The republic participated in the conference of Porto Rosa (1921) at which several of the Danubian states readjusted their tariff schedules in each other's favor. As a result of the Treaty of Lana (Lány), signed in 1921, Czechoslovakia extended a moderate credit to Austria for trade purposes, in return for a pledge of friendship. This *rapprochement* with Czechoslovakia and a budget crisis finally resulted in Schober's overthrow.

In May 1922 there came into power as chancellor Ignaz Seipel, a middle-aged Catholic priest who was leader of the Christian Socialist Party. Seipel conciliated the Pan-Germans so that they continued to vote with the Christian Socialists and then proceeded on a foreign tour to get financial aid for Austria. Premier Facta of Italy took the occasion to announce that Rome would consider any union between Austria and Germany, or Austria and the other Danubian states, a cause for war. After visiting several capitals,

Seipel finally (September 1922—at which time the crown stood at 77,000 to the dollar) addressed a special appeal to the League.

The League Council, after due deliberation, submitted to Austria a plan whereby Great Britain, France, Italy, Belgium, Czechoslovakia, Spain, and the Netherlands should guarantee a loan of $130,000,000 to run for twenty years. Such Austrian assets as the government tobacco monopoly should serve as security and Austria should pledge certain economic reforms. The League should appoint a commissioner-general and a committee of control made up of one member from each of the guarantor countries. Both of these authorities should reside at Vienna, but there should be no infringement of Austrian sovereignty. Austria must repeat her promise not to alienate her independence.

The Austrian Parliament accepted this arrangement (First Geneva Protocol, 1922) and authorized the ministry to do all things necessary for the carrying out of the financial agreement. Dr. Alfred R. Zimmerman of Rotterdam became the League Commissioner and in 1924 a new monetary unit, the schilling, replaced the crown. Financial progress was rapid and in 1925 Austria was able to show satisfactory closed accounts for the year. Hence the Council, in June 1926, decided that League control should come to an end with that month.

Similar advances could not be reported in other fields. The general unrest was alarming and in 1924 there followed in fairly rapid succession an attempt to assassinate Seipel, a strike of metal workers, and a serious railway strike. The weary chancellor resigned, to be succeeded in December 1924 by another Christian Socialist, Rudolf Ramek.[1]

The domestic difficulties continued during Ramek's incumbency and by the close of 1925 the number of unemployed had risen to three hundred thousand. The discontent and economic stagnation once more brought to the fore the idea of Anschluss; demonstrations in its favor became so popular that Italy and the Little Entente warned the government to prevent any overt action. When Ramek resigned, in October 1926, he was succeeded by Seipel who soon came into conflict with the Social Democrats over old-age and invalid pensions. After new elections in 1927, Seipel formed another government. In July the cabinet was faced with a situation closely approaching civil war. To understand this crisis it is necessary to consider the development of two powerful, rival, political organizations, the *Heimwehr* and the *Schutzbund*.

[1] At this time Dr. Hainisch was reëlected president for a second term.

From the earliest days of the republic there existed a bitter feeling between the industrial and the rural interests in Austria. The workers of Vienna, of the plain which extends southward from Vienna as far as Wiener-Neustadt, and of the Styrian mining districts formed an industrial proletariat with socialistic and anti-clerical leanings. These workers were the core of the Social Democratic Party. Most of the remaining Austrians were agrarian, conservative, and religious. They supported the Christian Socialist and Pan-German parties and hated Marxism.

After the war Vienna fell completely into the hands of the Social Democrats and municipal control was extended to many fields. Rents were forced down by law to so low a figure that apartment houses became a drug on the market. In addition, a high rent-tax was levied, the proceeds of which were used to build municipal houses for the workmen. The buildings were constructed so as to provide plenty of light and air for the tenants and usually enclosed an attractive courtyard decorated with the bust of some well-known socialist leader. The *Karl Marx Hof,* completed in 1930, was the largest dwelling house in Europe, being more than three-fifths of a mile long and containing almost fourteen hundred apartments. The municipality acquired control of bus and trolly lines and of subway, water, and lighting systems. It established a municipal brewery, a bakery, an ice-shop, and a crematorium—this last over the protests of the Catholic Church. Old parade grounds were converted into public swimming pools and playgrounds. A number of the former palaces were leased as office buildings and the remainder were made to serve the use of government bureaus.

Most of this was anathema to the conservative peasants, and the bitterness between Vienna and the rural hinterland expressed itself openly in the organization of two rival militant bodies: the agrarian Heimwehr and the socialist Schutzbund. The original program of the Heimwehr called for the overthrow of the socialists in Vienna and union with Germany. Under the leadership of Richard Steidle, Walter Pfriemer, and Ernst Rüdiger von Starhemberg, the Heimwehr, in the earlier years of its existence, associated itself with the Hitler movement in Germany. By 1931 the Heimwehr included approximately sixty thousand armed men of whom only 10 per cent were laborers.

The Schutzbund in 1931 counted a trained membership of about ninety thousand men, concentrated in the industrial regions. It seemed to possess considerable quantities of munitions, stored away in such hiding places as the office buildings of socialist newspapers; but the government from time to time raided these private arsenals. With annoying frequency the Heimwehr and the Schutzbund arranged for parades or demonstrations in approximately the same place on the same day, and then the government could with difficulty preserve order. Since, by the peace treaty, Austria's national army was limited to thirty thousand men, the government really had the smallest armed force in the country.

Now it happened that in July 1927 a jury acquitted three members of the Heimwehr who had been accused of the murder of two socialists in Burgenland. Proletarian sentiment throughout Austria stamped the accused as guilty and on the day following the verdict, without any preliminary warning, thousands of Viennese workmen went on strike, swarmed into the fashionable *Ringstrasse*, overpowered a small police force, and set fire to the beautiful Palace of Justice. Rioting continued for three days, during which scores of people were killed and hundreds wounded. The palace was partially destroyed, thousands of documents and records were burned, water-soaked, or scattered, and business temporarily came to a standstill.

Following this crisis, clashes between the two organized factions occurred in alarmingly rapid succession. Several times during 1929 and 1930 the Heimwehr threatened to march on Vienna, as the Italian Fascists had marched on Rome, and put an end to what they considered a weak parliamentary government. In September 1931 Pfriemer actually proclaimed himself dictator and ordered his followers to seize some public buildings in Styria. The Austrian army, however, quickly put down the attempted *Putsch* and some of the leaders were arrested. All the accused were acquitted by a jury in Graz. By 1932 it was clear that Austria could not enjoy domestic quiet so long as the Heimwehr and Schutzbund continued to exist as private militias.

c. The Anschluss Question and Foreign Relations to 1932

The objections of France, Italy, Czechoslovakia, and other countries to an Austro-German union were based on a variety of considerations: (1) Alone, the area of Germany was smaller than that of France; united with Austria, Germany's area would have exceeded that of France. (2) The combined populations of Germany and Austria were one and three-fourths times that of France. (3) Had Austria been annexed to Germany, then Czechoslovakia, herself containing three million German-speaking people, would have been surrounded by German territory. (4) Anschluss would have made Germany, rather than weak Austria, the immediate neighbor of Italy and might thereby have complicated the question of the South Tirol. (5) An Austro-German union, by placing a solid, powerful block across central Europe, would have weakened the Franco-Czechoslovak and Franco-Yugoslav alliances from a military point of view. In addition, Germany would have gained direct contact with the Balkans. (6) Though Austria had little coal, she had plenty of iron and timber and a superabundance of hydroelectric power. The combined economic strength of Germany and Austria was formidable.

The two countries immediately concerned might have experienced certain further advantages from union. Austria would have got a free market in Germany, might have been able to secure better commercial treaties with foreign areas, and could have made use of Germany's highly developed marketing system. Germany would have found her trade relations with southeastern Europe greatly facilitated, would have had the use of Austria's power resources, and would have had a sizable accretion to her military strength.

Not all the citizens of Germany and Austria favored Anschluss. Many German Protestants, for example, were not anxious to incorporate in the Reich more than six million Austrian Catholics. Some Germans felt that the Austrians, on the whole, were too easygoing and carefree to be desirable adjuncts to the population. On the other hand, many devout Austrian Catholics feared the loss of influence of the church in case of union with Protestant Germany. There was also a general dislike of Prussia. The Austrians, except for some of the more aggressive business men, disliked Prussian efficiency methods. Many Viennese feared that union with Germany might reduce Vienna to the status of a second-rate provincial city with a glorious past but an overshadowed present.[1]

[1] Briand, in a speech before the French Chamber on December 4, 1928, advanced the following theory of the rights of minorities under the principle of self-determination: "Permit me . . . to dispute a rather improper interpretation which has sometimes been placed upon the formula: the right of self-determination of peoples. It is a very noble formula and deserves to have been proclaimed with due solemnity. But it has never signified the right of peoples to commit suicide (Cries of: 'Very good! Very good!') and it would be a most unfortunate development to invoke it as a sanction for such a political maneuver as the Anschluss. For a people to attempt, under cover of this formula, to do nothing less than abolish itself entirely as a nation, is, I believe, an altogether unwarrantable extension of the right of self-determina-

At any rate, organizations were founded in both countries to agitate for Anschluss. In 1927 a German and an Austrian committee met to discuss means for giving the two states an identical criminal code. In the summer of 1928 two hundred thousand Germans visited Austria during a festival to commemorate the one hundredth anniversary of Franz Schubert's death. In 1929, when Chancellor Seipel resigned (owing to strife within the Christian-Socialist ranks and to illness), he was succeeded by Ernst Streeruwitz, who included several pro-Anschluss leaders in his cabinet.[1]

Streeruwitz' tenure was brief and stormy. Soon after he took office he had to answer a public charge of Briand that the various armed forces of Austria made her a menace to her neighbors. The Austrian Government naturally denied this, but the socialists claimed that the authorities were in collusion with the Heimwehr. Thereupon the Heimwehr demanded a revision of the constitution whereby the influence of the industrial proletariat would be further decreased. When Streeruwitz opposed the suggested changes, his ministry fell and Johann Schober came back into power (September 1929) with a cabinet which tried to steer a middle course between radicals and conservatives. Several constitutional amendments were now adopted which strengthened the powers of the president in time of crisis, substituted popular for parliamentary election of the president, and reduced the political power of the courts.

Having restored order, Schober attended the Hague Reparation Conference early in 1930 and secured for Austria a release from her reparation obligations until 1944. Then he visited several capitals to seek more favorable trade arrangements, extend feelers for a new loan, and promise that the menace of the private armies in Austria would be reduced. His efforts met with limited success, but the economic outlook for Austria remained bleak. At one point in 1930 the unemployment figures embraced one workman of every four in the land. The perennial question of Anschluss thereupon again assumed prominence, but Berlin and Vienna dared go no farther than to sign a protocol for a projected customs

---

tion. And if in the particular country concerned only one-tenth of the citizenry were anxious to safeguard the national independence, do you think that the right of self-determination of peoples may properly be set up in opposition to so legitimate a sentiment? I am not aware that anyone has ever been able to demonstrate this." *Journal Officiel de la République Française, Débats Parlementaires*, No. 85, Mercredi 5 Décembre 1928, p. 3225.

[1] Meanwhile, however, the Federal Assembly had chosen Wilhelm Miklas, an opponent of Anschluss, to succeed President Hainisch.

union (1931). This was immediately opposed by France, the Little Entente, and other powers, and financial pressure was brought to bear to make Germany and Austria renounce the document. This they did, two days before the World Court, by a vote of 8 to 7, rendered an advisory opinion that the contemplated pact would have violated Austria's pledge in the First Geneva Protocol (1922) not to jeopardize her independence.

Though the renunciation of the scheme eased the international tension in Europe, it left unsolved the economic difficulties into which Austria had been plunged. In 1932 the world witnessed in Austria a sovereign state literally begging the League for a credit extension of a few million dollars in order that the starving inhabitants might be fed. The republic strove frantically to secure favorable trade treaties with her neighbors, usually without avail. Chancellor after chancellor resorted to desperate methods in vain attempts to prevent further decrease in the country's diminutive gold supply. The leading banks crashed and eventually no funds were left with which to pay doles.

During the summer of 1932 money was offered Austria—under political conditions that were unacceptable to her patriots. At length, however, economic need overcame all other considerations and the parliament, by a vote of 82 to 80, ratified the Lausanne Protocol. This document, drawn up under League auspices, gave Austria a loan of $42,000,000 for twenty years in return for a promise that the republic would not enter into any political or economic union with Germany until 1952. The fight for acceptance of the protocol had been led by Chancellor Engelbert Dollfuss, a Christian Socialist. The opposition had been headed by Dr. Schober. In the midst of the debates on the protocol Schober had died. Four days later the document had been ratified. Austria's foreign debt at the end of 1932 had risen to $500,000,000.

d. *The Five-Year Fight Against Nazism, 1933–1938*

The elevation of Hitler to the German Chancellorship in January 1933 moved the whole question of Anschluss to a different plane. Some years previously a branch of the Nazi party had been established in Austria. The members wore the same type of uniform as their German colleagues and adhered to the same doctrines of anti-Marxism and anti-Semitism. They were recruited mainly from the lower bourgeoisie and the peasantry and they placed their chief hope in the consummation of political union with the

Third Reich. The movement grew slowly and not a single Nazi was elected to the parliament in 1930. In the provincial elections of 1932, however, the Hitlerites won a number of seats in several of the local diets. Upon the triumph of the Nazis in Germany, the Austrian Hitlerites, led by Dr. Alfred Frauenfeld, at once concentrated their energies in an effort to bring about Anschluss.

In this endeavor they had the support of Germany. Although Berlin realized the dangers of outright annexation of Austria, there appeared to be no serious obstacle to the accomplishment of this end by indirect means. Since the Austrian Nazis took their orders from Hitler, it was believed that a National-Socialist victory at the polls would, for all practical purposes, complete Austro-German union despite the objections of the former Allies. To force the apparently unwilling Austrian Government to hold new parliamentary elections and to ensure the winning of the elections, the German Nazis exported funds and agitators to all parts of the little republic. Slanders, assaults, the detonation of paper bombs in public places, and even shootings became frequent occurrences. These activities encountered the determined resistance of Chancellor Dollfuss, who until recently had himself favored Anschluss.

Dr. Engelbert Dollfuss was born on a small Lower-Austrian farm in 1892. After working his way through school he studied law at the University of Vienna and economics at Berlin. During the First World War he served for three years at the front, advancing from the rank of private to that of lieutenant. Then he entered politics, as a Christian Socialist. In due time he became a parliamentary deputy and gained recognition as an agricultural expert. He was appointed minister of agriculture in 1931 and in the following year was asked to form a cabinet of his own. His coalition of Christian Socialists, Heimwehr, and Agrarian League had a majority of one over the Social Democrats and Pan-Germans. Dollfuss' simplicity of manner and good nature, his religious fervor and *Gemütlichkeit*, charmed those who came in contact with him. Because of his short stature (he was less than five feet tall) and his resolute spirit he was popularly dubbed "the Millimetternich."

For some time after his accession to power, Dollfuss devoted his energies to financial and economic matters. He successfully fought for the acceptance of the loan under the Lausanne Protocol,[1] reformed the civil service and the railway administration, and bargained for currency and trade treaties. In 1933 the lower house of parliament adjourned itself indefinitely when the speaker

[1] The money was not received until almost a year later.

and both deputy-speakers resigned in the midst of an excited discussion. Since by law only one or another of these men could call a meeting, the parliament was unable legally to reconvene. President Miklas thereupon invested Dollfuss with emergency powers and the government soon issued hundreds of decrees.

Many of these decrees were aimed at the Nazis and at other political groups objectionable to the government. Restrictions were placed on the freedom of the press and of assembly. Nazi propaganda was barred from Austrian radio broadcasts. German agitators were expelled. It was forbidden to wear the Nazi uniform or display any banner or political emblem other than the Austrian flag. Berlin replied with a scheme to injure Austria economically. A visa charge of $400 was placed on German tourists who wished to visit Austria. The Dollfuss Government thereupon ordered the closing of all Nazi "brown houses." In June 1933, after bombs had been thrown at a detachment of auxiliary police, the National Socialist Party was outlawed. Meanwhile the authorities had also dissolved the socialist Schutzbund (April), abolished the Communist Party (May), appointed commissions of public safety to rule the provinces, and required a new oath of loyalty from all state employees.

The struggle continued through the summer and autumn of 1933. The Austrians expelled Theodor Habicht, Hitler's special "inspector for Austria," and the Germans sent home the Austrian press attaché in Berlin. German planes dropped propaganda leaflets over Austrian towns and violent anti-Dollfuss speeches were broadcast from Munich. An armed "Austrian Legion," consisting of Austrian Nazis who had fled to Germany, was organized in Bavaria. The Austrian Chancellor appealed to the world for moral and economic backing, and at the London Economic Conference pleaded eloquently (June 1933) for increased foreign trade and tourist traffic so that Austria might enjoy an economic revival and not be forced by necessity to submit to German domination.

Upon his return from London, and after conversations with Mussolini, Dollfuss turned from defense to attack. He wanted to build up a concrete alternative to Nazism—a Catholic, antisocialist, authoritarian, *Austrian* movement. He believed that the republic "could live alone" and he hoped to unify it on a basis of Austrian patriotism. To this end he created the Fatherland Front, an organization which was to be above all parties. Its chief support came from the Christian Socialists and the Heimwehr. The latter, still led by Starhemberg, had changed its views on the Anschluss because of the methods of the Nazis and now upheld the idea of an independent authoritarian Austria.

The better to carry out his policies, Dollfuss reorganized his cabinet and himself retained the portfolios of foreign affairs, war, public safety, and agriculture.[1] Aside from the ever more serious economic dilemma, Dollfuss had three urgent political problems to consider: the position of the Social Democrats, the drafting of a new constitution, and continued resistance to the Nazis.

The Social Democrats, still the largest organized political group in Austria, had thus far given the chancellor their support. They feared the rise of Hitlerism and they regarded Dollfuss as the best safeguard against a Nazi coup. He, on the other hand, was no friend of socialism, being as much opposed to the "Reds" as to the "Brown Shirts." Furthermore, the Heimwehr's hatred of the Social Democrats had increased with the passing of years, and its leaders apparently demanded the destruction of socialism as the price of their loyalty to the Fatherland Front. It may be, also, that Mussolini indicated a desire to see Austrian socialism liquidated. At any rate the authorities, on February 11, 1934, dissolved all political parties. This decision was followed on the next day by police and Heimwehr raids on Social-Democratic headquarters in several cities.

The socialist leaders, feeling that this might be their last chance to fight back, issued a call for a general strike. The government retaliated by declaring martial law, outlawing the Social Democratic Party, and ordering the court-martial and execution of any civilian caught with firearms. Civil war resulted.

While the Austrian Nazis remained more or less aloof, the government forces everywhere emerged triumphant. The city hall in Vienna was taken over almost immediately. The most serious fighting occurred in and about the Viennese municipal dwellings, especially the Karl Marx Hof. Here the workers held out for four days against machine-gun and light-artillery fire. On February 15, however, after a promise of amnesty to every one but certain leaders, the socialists capitulated. Some of the leaders escaped abroad, others were hanged, and still others, including Mayor Seitz of Vienna, were imprisoned. The opportunity was also taken to deprive Vienna of self-government. A new municipal constitution replaced the elective council with an advisory body wholly subor-

---

[1] About this time Dollfuss was slightly wounded in the arm by a young Nazi. A second bullet was deflected by a button of his vest. The incident only added to the chancellor's popularity.

dinate to the mayor, himself an appointee of the chancellor. Thus the organized Austrian Social Democratic Party came to an end—and many of the former socialists, bitter at the turn of events, became Nazis.[1]

The question of a new national constitution was next settled. Dollfuss called together the parliament which had been out of session for more than a year and submitted to it a completed instrument of government. With nearly half of its members, including all socialists, absent, the legislature approved the document and then went out of existence. The preamble of this constitution, as proclaimed on May 1, 1934, read: "In the name of God Almighty, from whom all law emanates, the Austrian people receives this Constitution for its Christian, German, Federal State on an estate basis (auf ständischer Grundlage)."[2]

Legislation was entrusted to a Federal Diet assisted by four appointed advisory councils representing, respectively, the state, the cultural institutions, the economic corporations or guilds, and the provinces. The diet, consisting of about sixty members chosen from the four councils, was empowered to enact into laws bills suggested by the government. The president, to be elected at a secret session of all Austrian mayors, was accorded fairly broad powers. Thus was the formerly democratic republic converted into an "authoritarian" state on a corporative basis.

Simultaneously with the proclamation of this constitution, President Miklas announced (May 1, 1934) the ratification of a concordat between Austria and the Holy See. Among other things this document provided (1) for state financial aid to church officials and to Catholic seminaries; (2) that the Catholic Church might give religious instruction to all Catholic children in the elementary and middle schools; and (3) that the Austrian Government would be given an advance opportunity to protest the appointment of any archbishop or bishop. If no agreement could be reached on such an appointment, the pope was to be free to fill the vacancy as he saw fit.

Meanwhile the activities of the Nazis had again become serious. According to an official announcement there had been 140 bomb outrages in the first week of 1934 alone. Acts of sabotage continued through the spring and summer. Foreign tourists were frightened

---

[1] In March 1934 all trade unions were abolished and the workers were urged to join a new government-controlled union.

[2] Vienna ceased to be a province and became a "directly federated city" ranking equally with the eight remaining provinces.

away, railroads were blocked, power houses were destroyed, and individuals were assaulted. Dollfuss, Starhemberg (who had become vice-chancellor), Dr. Kurt von Schuschnigg (minister of education and leader of his own *Sturmscharen* or "storm bands"), and the other cabinet officers fought back vigorously. The general reaction to the German "purge" of June 1934 encouraged Dollfuss to proceed even more energetically than heretofore. He ordered all persons, on pain of death, to turn over to the government within five days whatever supplies of explosives they might possess, and he arrested hundreds of suspected ex-socialists and Hitlerites.

The increasing vigor displayed by the government induced the Nazi leaders to attempt an early *Putsch,* lest they be made to suffer the fate of the Social Democrats. About one o'clock in the afternoon of July 25, 1934, a group of armed Nazis seized the government radio station in the heart of Vienna's business district and forced the announcer to broadcast a statement that the Dollfuss Ministry had resigned. Shortly thereafter another group of Nazis, numbering about 140 and wearing Heimwehr uniforms, entered the chancellory on the *Ballhausplatz,* cowed the lesser officials and clerks into quiet submission, and captured several members of the cabinet who had just been engaged in consultation. Among the Nazis who rushed upstairs was Otto Planetta, who shot Dollfuss twice.[1] The Nazis were so easily able to seize the chancellory because the government, warned of a plot, had asked for a Heimwehr guard—and when the disguised conspirators arrived they were looked upon as the requested protectors. The real Heimwehrmen and the police arrived almost immediately afterward and laid siege to the building.

While the loyal troops withheld their fire lest harm come to the captive officials, Dollfuss was slowly expiring. No physician was called and the dying man's prayers for a priest went unheeded. President Miklas deprived the imprisoned cabinet of its authority and announced that no agreement forced from its members would be valid. Eventually the conspirators in the chancellory, realizing that the whole enterprise had been a failure, began to negotiate for their own surrender.[2] With the aid of the German Minister to Austria they arranged for the freeing of their victims in return for a promise of safe-conduct to the German border. About seven o'clock in the evening the government forces entered the chancel-

---

[1] The Nazis wanted Dollfuss to make way for Dr. Anton Rintelen, Austrian Minister to Italy. After a trial, Rintelen was sentenced to life imprisonment.

[2] The radio station was recaptured by the government after a short battle.

lory. The Nazis, contrary to their expectations, were arrested—because the safe-conduct had been promised only if none of the captives was injured. Dollfuss' death had altered the situation.

The Heimwehr, loyal army, and police had to put down other Nazi uprisings throughout the state. The conspiracy was widespread and the Austrian Legion had been ready to pour into Austria as soon as the news of Nazi success in Vienna should have arrived. Starhemberg, who had been visiting in Italy, flew back to Vienna to become acting chancellor, while Mussolini rushed troops to the Austrian border. It was evident that Il Duce believed the German Nazis to have been implicated in the revolt and that he was ready to use force to uphold Austrian independence. He was, moreover, fond of Dollfuss, and the latter's shocking end, a few days before he was to have joined his family as guests of the Italian Premier, affected Mussolini deeply.[1]

The Hitler Government denied any complicity, removed the members of the Austrian Legion to central and northern Germany, recalled the German Minister who had acted as intermediary for the plotters, and appointed Papen as its new envoy to Vienna. No connection was established between the Austrian conspirators and the German Nazis at the trial of the former. Planetta and a few others who were executed for murder or treason shouted *"Heil Hitler!"* just before they died, but not one revealed the identity of the real leader of the attempted coup.

Before the end of July, Schuschnigg became chancellor. His difficult task was made somewhat easier by the reaction among Austrians to Dollfuss' murder. Relative quiet prevailed during the ensuing months while Schuschnigg in general followed a domestic and foreign course based upon the principles championed by his predecessor. Nazi activities diminished and better relations with Germany were restored. Later in 1934 the Austrian press was forbidden to publish information regarding German rearmament and odered to print only pro-German comments on the impending plebiscite in the Saar. France and Italy, moreover, in their accord of January 1935, agreed to consult in the event that Austrian independence should be threatened.

After 1934 there was an increasingly strong sentiment for a revival of the Habsburg monarchy in Austria. It was notable that the new constitution nowhere made mention of the word "republic" and that both Schuschnigg and Starhemberg had monarchist leanings. As the uncertainty and disorder and economic

[1] Yugoslavia also sent troops to its Austrian border.

crisis had become progressively worse, more and more of the Austrians—clericals, aristocrats, soldiers, business men, and other anti-
Nazis—had come to look upon a Habsburg restoration as the only
remedy for Austria's troubles. Indeed, a number of Habsburg
princes who returned to the country somewhat in the role of advance agents for Archduke Otto, eldest son of the former Emperor
Charles, were well received. In 1935 the Austrian Parliament repealed the laws of 1919 under which the leading Habsburgs had
been excluded from the country and thus the way was paved for a
restoration as soon as international circumstances should permit.

Meanwhile, in April 1936, the government introduced compulsory military service, thus repudiating a provision of the treaty of
St. Germain and thus also abolishing such private armies as the
Heimwehr. An "armistice" in the struggle with Germany was
sealed by an agreement of July 1936, whereby Germany promised
to respect the sovereignty of Austria and recognized that National
Socialism in Austria was entirely a problem of the Austrian Government. On the other hand, Mussolini, now an axis partner, was
beginning to show a lessened interest in the problem of Austrian
independence. Yet when, by the opening of 1938, the movement
for a Habsburg restoration in Austria obviously was becoming
popular, Chancellor Schuschnigg, who favored such a solution of
the Austrian problem, hesitated to take immediate action.

Economic and general internal conditions in the little republic
were bad. Dependent on imported foodstuffs, unable because of
tariff walls to sell enough of its manufactures abroad, treated in
unfriendly manner by Germany and indifferently by Italy, its citizens divided into Pan-German Nazis, Austrian Nazis, upholders of
the Catholic corporate state, advocates of a Habsburg restoration,
underground socialists and communists, and still other groups,
Austria's position was difficult. Schuschnigg strove to do his duty
as he saw it, and to follow in the footsteps of his predecessor and
friend, Dollfuss, but the German pressure combined with a certain
tactlessness and dilatoriness on his own part, eventually nullified
his plans.

In February 1938 Schuschnigg visited Hitler at Berchtesgaden
and there received an ultimatum which Mussolini reportedly advised him to accept. Thereupon he formed a new cabinet, assigning the portfolios of justice, foreign affairs, and the interior to
Nazis. After the Nazi minister of the interior, Dr. Arthur Seyss-
Inquart, visited Hitler in Berlin, the Fatherland Front was opened
to Nazis and a wide political amnesty was granted. The Nazis in

Austria, especially in their stronghold Graz, now paraded openly, in defiance of the laws and despite a renewed pledge of Schuschnigg to maintain Austrian independence.

Suddenly, on March 9, 1938, Schuschnigg announced that a plebiscite on Austrian independence would be held on the next Sunday, March 13. The rules of the plebiscite made it easier to vote "yes" than "no" and permitted the participation only of persons over twenty-four—perhaps because the main body of Nazi enthusiasts was to be found among boys and girls under that age. Two days before the plebiscite was to be held, Hitler threatened to act unless the poll was canceled. Schuschnigg thereupon "took leave of the Austrian people" over the radio and on March 12 Seyss-Inquart assumed power. He at once invited Hitler to send in the German army to "preserve order," and by the close of the day the occupation of Austria was completed. Hitler in great emotion visited his native Braunau.[1]

The time chosen by Hitler for the coup was propitious from an international point of view. In Great Britain, Anthony Eden had recently left the cabinet and the proappeasement group remained in control. In France there was a cabinet crisis and disorganization in the government. Italy, bound by ties of friendship and by the fact that many of her soldiers were in Ethiopia, Spain, and Libya, merely accepted the fact and received Hitler's promise of eternal gratitude. Now *Hitler* announced the holding of a plebiscite, on April 10, simultaneously with the elections for the first Reichstag of the Great Germany.

Before the plebiscite was held two laws legalized the "reunion" of Austria with the Reich and provided for the introduction of the Four-Year Plan into the new province. An economic advantage accrued to the Austrians when the temporary rate of exchange was set at 3 (instead of 4) schillings to 2 marks; but this increased the cost of Austrian goods to purchasers living elsewhere in the Reich. The anti-Semitic decrees were quickly put into force in Austria, there was horrible cruelty, and former leaders of the Fatherland Front and known monarchists were especially harshly dealt with. Otto von Habsburg was declared a traitor and threatened with summary action in the event of his appearing on German soil.[2]

[1] President Miklas resigned and Schuschnigg was placed in confinement. Seyss-Inquart for a time became governor of Austria, soon renamed Ostmark. It has been well said that Seyss-Inquart's "name might easily have become the synonym of fifth columnists in place of Quisling's had it not been so awkward."

[2] In August 1939 it was announced that ten thousand associations in Vienna, many of them religious in character, had been dissolved and their property turned over to Nazi organizations.

The plebiscite was held on April 10, 1938, in all Great Germany. The ballot listed the single question: "Do you agree to the re-union of Austria with the German Reich carried out on March 13 and do you vote for the [Reichstag] list of our Leader, Adolf Hitler?" Under Nazi auspices, more than 99 per cent of the votes cast were in the affirmative. Thus about seven million more German-speaking people were added to the population of the Reich. But many Austrians continued to have full faith in the age-old prophecy: *Austria erit in orbe ultima*—"Austria will endure on earth forever."

THE KINGDOM OF HUNGARY

a. The Failure of Liberalism, 1918–1919

The attitude of the ruling Magyars towards their subject na-tionalities did much to hasten the collapse of Hungary after the war. Even in the darkest war days, the Magyars disregarded the demands of their minorities for liberal political and social treat-ment. Indeed, when Charles issued his Austrian Federalization Manifesto in October 1918, the Magyar leaders, not caring to have a similar decree promulgated with respect to Hungary, declared the Compromise of 1867 void.[1] An independent Hungary was pro-claimed, joined with Austria only through the person of the sover-eign. To the dismay of the Hungarian Premier, this action inspired the parliamentary deputies of the subject Romanians and Slovaks to insist on similar rights of self-determination. Moreover, when Wilson recognized the independence of Czechoslovakia and Yugo-slavia, the respective minorities in Hungary demanded union with their fellow nationals. Dissolution appeared inevitable.

In Austria, the existence of a fairly large bourgeois group had been responsible for the maintenance of a semblance of order even when the disruptive crisis was at its height, but in Hungary, where landholding nobles and small peasants comprised perhaps three-fourths of the population, there was less temperance. A brief ini-tial period of restraint was owing to the influence of Michael Károlyi. The latter organized a National Council made up of his personal followers in parliament, plus compatible elements from the Social Democrats and non-Magyar groups outside parliament. This revolutionary coalition, backed by the Budapest garrison, secured Károlyi's appointment as premier on October 31, 1918. The man who thus came to power was a liberal republican.

[1] This document regulated Austro-Hungarian relations from 1867 to 1918.

Despite his titled ancestry and great wealth he had been conspicuous as an agitator for universal suffrage and the breaking up of large estates. During the war he was consistently opposed to the policies of Germany and professed to fear worse consequences from a German victory than an Austro-Hungarian defeat. He was relatively popular with the Allies and hoped to receive special treatment for his country by assuming control. One of his first acts as premier was to get a release for his subordinates from the oath of fealty to Charles. Then, after ordering the withdrawal from the fronts and the demobilization of all Hungarian troops, he proceeded to Belgrade in an attempt to obtain from General Louis Franchet d'Esperey, commander of the French *Armée de l'Orient,* better armistice terms than General Diaz had granted Austria-Hungary at Villa Giusti.

Franchet d'Esperey bluntly showed his contempt for the unpolished individuals who composed Károlyi's delegation and assigned even more Hungarian territory to Romania and Yugoslavia than had Diaz. Károlyi's disappointment was slightly assuaged, on the same day, when he received a rescript from King Charles announcing His Majesty's retirement from participation in the affairs of Hungary. Actually this "abdication" had no constitutional validity since the document was not countersigned by a parliamentary minister, but for the immediate future Károlyi's course was made easier.

On November 16, 1918, Hungary was declared a republic. The National Council dissolved the old legislature and ordered the election of a constituent assembly by universal suffrage. The Károlyi Ministry, meanwhile, drew up a platform promising liberal press laws, trial by jury, freedom of association, agrarian and educational reforms, proportional representation, separation of church and state, honest settlement of the nationalities problem, friendship with the neighboring states, and the conclusion of a separate peace with the Allies.

The unfavorable foreign and internal conditions made it virtually impossible to put this program into effect. The subject nationalities no longer were interested in "rights"; they desired complete separation from Hungary. The Allies, far from treating Hungary with any special consideration, tightened the blockade. Returning soldiers swelled the ranks of the unemployed and starving, and foreign ex-prisoners of war ravaged the countryside. The conservatives objected to the proposed breaking up of the large estates. Communistic ideas trickled in from Russia. The resignation (January 1919) of Oscar Jászi, minister of nationalities, deprived the cabinet of one of its strongest men. Soon the entire group of Social Democrats deserted Károlyi, who thereupon postponed the date for the election of the constituent assembly.

The National Council now tried to thrust Károlyi aside by electing him provisional president of the Hungarian People's Republic. He tried to regain effective control by fostering an agrarian reform measure. Under this law, private estates were not to exceed seven hundred acres in area and the peasants were to receive governmental aid in the purchase of small holdings. Again reform had come too late. Many of the peasants opposed the plan because they could get land on better terms directly from their landlords. The socialists objected to the law lest it hinder the process of complete nationalization. The conservatives regarded it as confiscatory.

The final blow to Károlyi came with the news that the peace conference had definitely awarded Transylvania to Romania. Since neither the National Council nor Károlyi would acquiesce in this disposition, the president resigned and went into exile (March 1919). Now, in anticipation of Károlyi's exit, plans had already been drawn up by Sigmund Kunfi, a socialist member of the government, and Béla Kun, an imprisoned communist leader, for a union of the Social Democrats and the recently formed workers' and soldiers' councils. The coalition took the name of International Revolutionary Hungarian Socialist Party and was prepared to take the reins at any time. When Károlyi departed, Kun was released from prison to become head of a new government and commissar for foreign affairs. An ex-bricklayer, Alexander Garbai, became president.

b. "Red" versus "White"

Béla Kun was a journalist and politician who served as an officer in the Austro-Hungarian army until taken prisoner (1915) by the Russians. In the prison camp he formed friendships with a number of Russian revolutionists and, in 1917, was released to become head of the propaganda bureau for Kerensky. By the time of the Bolshevik Revolution he had found opportunity to become well acquainted with Lenin and Trotsky. After the war, he reentered Hungary and edited a subversive newspaper. He came into frequent conflict with the police and on one occasion was wounded and imprisoned. It was while he rested in jail that Kun negotiated the coalition with the Social Democrats.

Once in power, the people's commissars, as Kun's cabinet officers called themselves, promulgated drastic decrees. Political opponents were removed by revolutionary tribunals. The sale of alcoholic liquors was forbidden. A well-disciplined "Red Army" was organized. As soon as possible the Social Democrats were ousted from the government and then church property, mines, banks, means of communication and transportation, commercial firms employing more than twenty-five persons, estates of more than one hundred acres, and all private property above a certain minimum allowance, were nationalized.

In June 1919 a formal constitution of the Hungarian Soviet Republic was adopted and preparations were made for spreading the "Red" gospel into the neighboring states. Much of the available specie money remaining from the former regime was sent to Italy for munitions and warstuffs, and a new currency was introduced for domestic use. While Kun led his "Red Legions" against Czechoslovakia and conquered Slovakia with relative ease, the opposition at home was put down by a ruffian named Tibor Szamuelly.

The communist regime was doomed to early failure. The refusal of the peasants to accept the new currency for their foodstuffs and the maintenance of the Allied blockade brought the cities to the verge of starvation. The trade unionists were angry because factories were shutting down for lack of raw materials. At the same time thousands of counterrevolutionists, or "Whites," led by Archduke Joseph, Stephen Bethlen, Károlyi's half-brother Julius, and Nicolas Horthy, vice-admiral in the former Austro-Hungarian navy, gathered at Szeged in an area occupied by French troops. Though a premature "White" uprising in Budapest was easily suppressed, the discontent soon became widespread. Withdrawing from Czechoslovakia lest the wrath of the Paris Conference be converted into military measures against him, Kun now led his legionaries against a Romanian army which was marching toward Budapest. This time Kun was defeated. In August 1919 he fled to Vienna—there to be placed in a mental hospital. Eventually he made his way to Russia.

For a few days after Kun's flight, a Social Democrat took charge of the government, but soon Archduke Joseph, who had been proclaimed regent by the returning counterrevolutionaries, appointed Stephen Friedrich premier. This return of Habsburg influence so frightened Hungary's neighbors that they insisted upon Joseph's withdrawal from the government. In the meantime, the turmoil exceeded anything the country had yet experienced. The Romanian army, in defiance of the Allied Supreme Council, occupied Budapest for three months, pillaging whatever could be sent or carried away by train, truck, or person. Two days after the Romanians finally left Budapest, Horthy, who had succeeded Joseph in command of the "White" forces, entered the capital (November 1919). He replaced Friedrich with Karl Huszar and ordered the calling of an assembly to decide on the future form of government and make peace with the Allies.

Elections were held early in 1920. No party received a majority, but most of the delegates had monarchist leanings. The assembly at its first meeting virtually restored the former monarchical constitution. Inasmuch as an Allied note precluded the return of a Habsburg to the throne, Horthy was designated regent. The next twelve months witnessed little more in the political sphere than ministerial crises, a wave of reactionary legislation, and a wholesale massacre of Jews. Not until Bethlen became premier, in April 1921, was order restored.

In the circumstances, Charles was encouraged to return to Hungary and reclaim the throne, on Easter Sunday of 1921. Horthy, however, refused to surrender his powers without the prior consent of the assembly. Besides, the Allies registered vigorous protests and Czechoslovakia threatened military action unless Charles left Hungary immediately. The disconsolate Habsburg returned to Switzerland. In October he set out for Hungary once more, this time by airplane. He landed at Ödenburg and led a hastily gathered force on Budapest. Horthy attempted unsuccessfully to dissuade Charles from his enterprise and, when Czechoslovakia and Yugoslavia began to mobilize, the regent sent troops under Captain (later General) Julius Gömbös to dispute the royal contingent's entry into the capital. Charles was captured and taken to a British war vessel in the Danube.[1] The Little Entente then forced the Hungarian Constituent Assembly to pass a dethronement act, deposing the Habsburgs and making the kingship elective. Hungary also promised to consult with the chief Allies before electing a ruler.

Early in 1922 the constituent assembly came to an end. Except for the ratification of the unsatisfactory Treaty of Trianon, the assembly's accomplishments during two years were practically nil. It did not settle the question of monarchy and it neglected to or-

[1] Charles and his family were exiled to the Madeira Islands. On April 1, 1922, in his thirty-fifth year, Charles succumbed to island fevers and pneumonia.

dain the method of election of its own successor. Horthy and Bethlen thereupon drew up an executive electoral decree which restricted the number of voters and substituted open for secret balloting in the country districts. A press censorship was instituted and a prohibition laid on the publication and circulation of the works of such authors as Karl Marx, Lenin, and Walt Whitman. Naturally, the delegates elected to the new assembly were overwhelmingly progovernment. A group of Legitimists, those who wanted to make Charles' son, Archduke Otto, king, received little encouragement from the voters. The Bethlen Ministry, consequently, was spared further immediate foreign complications.

The real head of the government and virtual dictator of the land from April 1921 to August 1931 was Premier Bethlen, the "Sphinx of Europe." He was born of a noble and wealthy family in Transylvania in 1874. Entering parliament for the first time in 1901, he soon evinced an uncanny ability to clinch the argument in a debate for one side or the other with a few clear-cut sentences. The First World War and the Treaty of Trianon left him impoverished and embittered, since, as one of the Hungarian "optants," he preferred losing his large estates in Transylvania to acquiring Romanian citizenship.[1]

Gradually Premier Bethlen consolidated his control. In 1925 the franchise was restricted still more and a new drive against communists was undertaken. In 1926 the unicameral assembly created an upper house to take the place of the defunct Table of Magnates. Most of the members of this body were to be chosen by such groups as the nobility, the clergy, the municipal councils, the chambers of commerce, and other business and professional institutions. Some were to be appointed for life by the government. A few dignitaries, such as the commander-in-chief of the army, became ex-officio members. This chamber was given only a suspensive veto and no power over the budget. In December 1926 the third postwar assembly was elected, the progovernment Union Party scoring an easy victory.

c. Finances and Economics

When the Bethlen Ministry came into office it was confronted with two urgent tasks: the freeing of Hungary from fear of interference by the Little Entente and the financial and economic reconstruction of the kingdom. The worry over the Little Entente

[1] See p. 600.

NICOLAS HORTHY

was reduced when Hungary became a member of the League of Nations in 1922. Although Hungary, by signing the Covenant, tacitly pledged herself not to attempt a forceful revision of her boundaries, her own sovereignty and integrity were simultaneously guaranteed and she could feel relatively secure against any precipitate intervention by her nervous neighbors. Her new status in the family of nations, moreover, entitled her to assistance in the settlement of her financial difficulties.

While the League was engaged in the financial reconstruction of Austria, Hungary appealed to the Reparation Commission for similar aid. The commission investigated and drew up a plan of relief which was adopted by the League Council in December 1923. The plan provided for the floating of an international loan under League auspices, the establishment of a new bank of issue, the payment of reparation in twenty moderate annual instalments, the assignment of the revenues from customs and state monopolies as security for the loan, and the appointment of a League Commissioner-General. Hungary accepted the terms, and Jeremiah Smith, Jr., a Boston financier, went to Budapest as agent of the League. Under his supervision the kingdom managed to balance its budget eighteen months sooner than had been stipulated under the reconstruction plan. In 1926, therefore, the League voted to end its control. Smith, whose good humor and sympathy had made him extraordinarily popular, resigned, donating his fee to Hungary's poor. The budget continued to show a surplus until 1930.

Economic reconstruction was more difficult to achieve than financial rehabilitation. The Hungary which was partitioned by the peace treaty had been a well-defined geographic unit and a political entity of many centuries' standing. The Treaty of Trianon detached from the old kingdom two-thirds of its land area and three-fifths of its population, leaving the new Hungary without a seacoast, with negligible timber and water-power resources, and with few railway terminals.[1] The country did retain an excellent network of railways, a will to substitute new industries for those which were lost, and a high tariff.

Attempts to foster a new industrial life were partially successful, but Hungary remained predominantly agricultural. Eighty-two per cent of the land surface was devoted to agricultural purposes and pasturage. Although more than half of the population continued to earn its livelihood directly from the soil, Hungary was

[1] The area of Trianon Hungary was 35,875 square miles and its population averaged about 8,500,000. More than 90 per cent of the inhabitants were Magyars.

still a land of large estates. In 1930 one-third of the agricultural area was concentrated in about 1500 large holdings, while approximately 750,000 small owners possessed less than half of the cultivable soil.[1] In the years after 1930 Hungary suffered heavy losses owing to the falling price of grain in the world market.

Because of its importance as an exporter of foodstuffs and an importer of manufactures, Hungary came to occupy a strategic position in any move to bring about a Danubian federation. Numerous conferences were held in the early years of the great depression among the Little Entente, Austria, and Hungary, at which the question of an economic league was the chief topic of discussion. Each time the same obstacles to union were encountered. The states displayed so much jealousy of their national sovereignty that concession and compromise were difficult. The question of precisely what form to give the projected union was another stumbling-block. And the great powers, fearing a loss of markets because of the privileged positions which the industries of Austria and Czechoslovakia would have in federation, were lukewarm toward any effective unification schemes. Several times the unsuccessful outcome of the conferences resulted in tariff wars among the conferees.

d. *Restoration and Revision*

Hungarian foreign relations after 1920 were shaped primarily by the questions of the kingship and the peace treaty. The lenient attitude of the Hungarian courts toward monarchist agitators combined with the royalist sympathies of Bethlen might have led to an early solution of the monarchical complication, but for a split among the royalists themselves. The Legitimists insisted upon the coronation of Archduke Otto. The latter was only a boy—he was born in 1912—but his cause was ably promoted by his mother, the beautiful Zita, who never wearied of planning to regain her husband's crown for her son. The "Awakened Magyars," on the other hand, rallied around the standard of Archduke Albrecht, popular and wealthy Hungarian Habsburg. Albrecht's cause, too, was fostered by an ambitious mother, a Belgian princess of considerable spiritual and material resource.

In 1926 the activities of all royalists received a temporary check. To finance their schemes, a group of reactionaries had undertaken

---

[1] A decree of July 1928 ordered the 50,000 gypsies in the land to give up their nomad life, settle on farms, speak Hungarian, and pay taxes.

the wholesale counterfeiting of French francs. When the plot was discovered in 1926, the Little Entente became panicky again and the government reluctantly prosecuted the offenders. A number of high officials were found to have been implicated and the culprits, pleading patriotism, were lightly dealt with. At worst, they received short prison sentences.

The peace of mind of Hungary's neighbors continued to be upset periodically. In 1929 various rumors reacted so disturbingly that Bethlen was led to declare that the existing governmental situation would doubtless remain unchanged as long as Horthy lived. Despite this assurance there was renewed nervousness in the Little Entente with the approach of November 20, 1930, the day on which Otto would reach majority and, according to Habsburg tradition, become head of the house. When the day arrived, the headship of Otto was acknowledged by all members of the family, including Albrecht who, having in the meantime married a commoner, was no longer a rival for the throne. The government was prepared to meet a coup, but nothing exciting transpired. After a bit of ceremony at a little town in Belgium where his mother lived, Otto returned to the University of Louvain to finish his collegiate studies. He disclaimed any desire to endanger the peace of Europe.

The agitation for boundary revision was more ominous than that for monarchical restoration. The peace treaty not only greatly reduced the size of Hungary but assigned almost three million Magyars to neighboring states. Romania received a million and a half Magyars, Czechoslovakia almost a million, and Yugoslavia, half a million. Upon its publication in Budapest the treaty was printed with black bands of mourning around it and an irredentist movement was precipitated which became intensified with each succeeding year. In churches, schoolrooms, homes, trolleys, restaurants, and dance halls, everywhere were displayed maps of the old Hungary, with the lost territories in black and the whole surrounded by a crown of thorns. On these maps was printed the question, *"Maradhat ez így?"* ("Can it remain thus?") and the answer, *"Nem! Nem! Soha!"* ("No! No! Never!"). These same three words, *"Nem! Nem! Soha!,"* appeared on stamps, gummed seals, envelopes, postcards, badges, posters, plates, buttons, and other objects.

The propaganda was not confined to Hungary. It was early launched on a world-wide scale and was especially successful in Great Britain and Italy. Various societies were active in obtaining foreign sympathy for the cause of revision. Hardly an opportunity was overlooked to present Hungary's case in foreign areas. In 1931 two Hungarian aviators gave wide publicity to the movement by flying from Newfoundland to a point near Budapest in a monoplane named *Justice for Hungary*.

A treaty of friendship was signed between Italy and Hungary in 1927. This was followed, late in the same year, by a shipment of arms from Verona, ostensibly to a little Czech town, but really to Hungary. The shipment, labeled "machine parts," attracted the suspicious attention of the Austrian customs officials at the frontier town of St. Gotthard and was subjected to an inspection. Since the Treaty of Trianon forbade the importation of war materials into Hungary, the Little Entente entered a protest with the League of Nations (January 1928). An investigation followed, but the possible implication of Italy prevented definite disclosures. Hungary received a mild rebuke and the affair was dropped, but the psychological reverberations lingered for some time. And thenceforth Mussolini often expressed himself in favor of revision of the Treaty of Trianon.

In 1931 and 1932 the agitation for revision and restoration suffered a temporary decline. The reason was the need of the Hungarian Government for French financial aid. In August 1931 Premier Bethlen resigned, though his Union Party and its allies had captured almost 200 of the available 245 seats in the lower house in the parliamentary elections of the previous June. Although the motive for his action was officially listed as illness, several other factors apparently entered into the decision. One was the economic difficulty of the country in the midst of the world depression. Another was the circumstance that France, when appealed to for help in the crisis, made a loan contingent upon the cessation of revisionist agitation. At any rate, a much-needed French loan was granted and Bethlen resigned.

The new premier was a friend of Bethlen's, Julius Károlyi. Though he managed to secure the adoption of a budget, Károlyi was beset by problems of financial rehabilitation and political unrest. Fascist disorders and communist riots became frequent sights and tariff wars with Czechoslovakia and Romania added to the difficulties. After a tenure of little more than a year, the Károlyi Cabinet resigned and in October 1932 was succeeded by one under Julius Gömbös.

Although it was unusual for a commoner to win such high office in Hungary, Gömbös had gained recognition as a shrewd and forceful leader. He had played an important role in Horthy's ele-

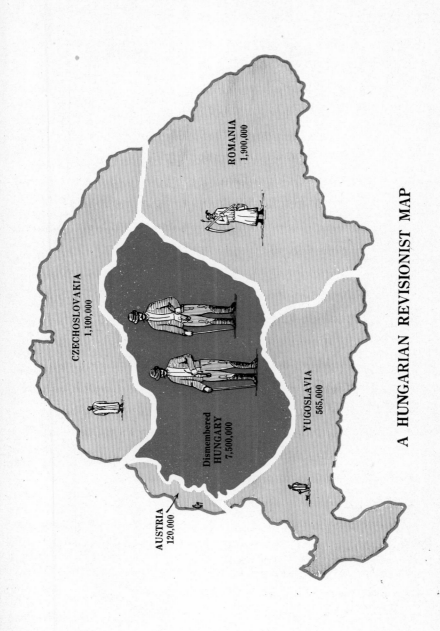

CZECHOSLOVAKIA
1,100,000

ROMANIA
1,900,000

AUSTRIA
120,000

Dismembered
HUNGARY
7,500,000

YUGOSLAVIA
565,000

A HUNGARIAN REVISIONIST MAP

vation to the regency and he had been conspicuous in preventing
Charles from regaining the throne in 1921. His appointment was
a blow to the Legitimists but was highly satisfactory to the ardent
revisionists and the Italophils. The Gömbös Government placed
the word "National" before the name of its chief supporting party,
the Union Party, and emphasized the need for agrarian reform, a
universal secret ballot, and continued agitation for revision. In
an unsuccessful attempt to balance the budget, the government
dismissed many civil servants, cut salaries and pensions, and raised
the tax rates. As nearly everywhere else, the volume of exports
continued low and unemployment increased.

The most spectacular developments of the Gömbös administration grew out of the question of treaty revision. The matter of a
monarchical restoration could, in Gömbös' opinion, easily be postponed, but the rectification of Hungary's boundaries was urgent.
Several times it appeared as if economic necessity might lead to a
rapprochement between Hungary and the Little Entente, but on
each occasion the negotiations failed because the entente first demanded a cessation of revisionist agitation and because Gömbös
refused to accept any such condition. Meanwhile, in 1933, a paper
in Vienna had announced its discovery of another Italian attempt
to send arms to Hungary. It was claimed that many carloads of
rifles and machine guns had been forwarded from Italy to the
Hirtenberg armaments factory in Austria for transshipment to
Hungary. The Little Entente threatened appeal to the League,
but later was satisfied to have the British and French governments
investigate the charges. As in the case of the arms incident of 1927,
not much could be done about the situation. Eventually Austria
promised to return to Italy whatever portions of the shipment
were still at Hirtenberg.

Throughout the remainder of 1933 and in 1934 Italo-Austro-
Hungarian relations became constantly closer. A personal friendship developed among the respective premiers, Mussolini, Dollfuss, and Gömbös. The culmination of a series of talks among
these men was the signing of the Rome Protocols in 1934, followed by the negotiation of several bilateral trade agreements.
Unfortunately these documents brought no appreciable upswing
in the economic life of any of the signatories.

In the spring of 1934, Hungary and Yugoslavia openly accused
each other of fomenting trouble along their mutual boundary.
The general bitterness of the Magyars further increased when it
was reported that new political and business restrictions were soon

to be imposed on the minorities in Romania. By this time, too, the Hungarians had begun to complain of the military provisions of the peace treaty which kept them in a state of virtual disarmament while permitting the neighboring countries (except Austria) to arm at will. The atmosphere in east-central Europe therefore was tense as the summer of 1934 drew to a close. And into this atmosphere there burst the news of the assassination (October 9) at Marseille of King Alexander I of Yugoslavia and Foreign Minister Barthou of France.

The king had just arrived in France for an official visit and was being driven through the streets of Marseille when a bystander rushed from the crowd, leaped on the running board, and fired into the car. Alexander died almost instantly, Barthou died within a few hours, and several other persons were slain or wounded. The assassin, Vlado Gheorghieff Chernozemsky, was trampled to death by the crowd. He was a Macedonian émigré in league with Croatian émigrés from Yugoslavia who had organized a terrorist society known as *Ustacha* with training camps in Italy and Hungary. The terrorists apparently expected that the death of the king would lead to a breakup of the Yugoslav State and the "freeing" of Croatians, Magyars, and Macedonians from Serbian control.[1]

The whole situation so closely resembled the events of June 1914 that Europe was gripped by a fear of war. But as it took several days for the police to identify the assassin, Yugoslav feelings had time to subside. After burial of the king, the foreign ministers of Yugoslavia, Czechoslovakia, Romania, Greece, and Turkey issued a joint communiqué. The document took note of the recent systematic attempts to overturn the peace treaties, demanded a coöperative effort to ascertain and punish the parties guilty of this latest outrage, and warned that "if the necessary international measures are not taken, . . . new and most serious disputes will necessarily follow." Yugoslavia then appealed to the League Council to fix responsibility for the deed. The appeal was couched in fairly general terms but the finger of blame was pointed at Hungary. Belgrade, moreover, ordered the immediate expulsion of

---

[1] The Croatian terrorist leader in Italy was Dr. Ante Pavelich, whom Italy refused to extradite to France after he had been implicated in the murder plot. In 1941, after the Nazi invasion of Yugoslavia, Pavelich became "head" of a new Croat state. The leading conspirator in Hungary was Gustav Perchetz. His followers, including Chernozemsky, had learned to shoot and throw bombs on a farm called Jánka Puszta, a few miles from the Yugoslav border. It was claimed that the instructors were Hungarian ex-army officers. In a note to the League of Nations dated April 26, 1934, Hungary had said that she had taken steps to evacuate this camp "some time ago."

large numbers of Hungarians who had been resident in Yugoslavia.

At the Council hearing (December 1934), the plaintiff was supported by France and by the other members of the Little Entente. Hungary had the sympathy of Italy. Great Britain and the Soviet Union appeared interested chiefly in maintaining peace. On December 10 the Council unanimously adopted a resolution which was accepted as a settlement of the controversy. "Certain Hungarian authorities" were declared responsible, "at any rate through negligence," for some of the "acts having connection with the preparation of the Marseille crime." The Budapest Government was therefore asked to seek out and punish these authorities. Thus Yugoslav sentiment was appeased, Hungary's dignity was upheld, and peace was preserved.

Throughout 1935 and 1936 Premier Gömbös continued to foster the friendship with Italy and Germany, to advocate peaceful treaty revision, and to contemplate the extension of secret suffrage to the rural areas. Following his death in October 1936 the cabinet was reconstituted by Kálmán Darányi, a wealthy landowner and experienced administrative official. Darányi, like Gömbös, received his chief support from the National Union Party which, composed of landowners, civil servants, clerics, and the more well-to-do peasants, had got a large majority of the seats in the lower house through the election of 1935. To this group the question of replacing the regent by a king seemed of no immediate importance. The chief opposition group was the Independent Agrarian Party which, led by Tibor Eckhardt, came to advocate a restoration of the Habsburgs as the greatest safeguard against the importation of Nazism.

An act of 1937, passed unanimously, extended the powers of the regent. He was authorized to return to parliament twice (instead of once) a bill of which he disapproved. If again upheld by the legislature, the law must be promulgated within fifteen days or else the lower house must be dissolved. The law of 1937 also dealt with the succession to the regency. It was provided that the two houses must meet jointly within eight days following the regent's demise and might not adjourn until a successor had been chosen. The regent might present a list of three nominees as his possible successors, but the parliament was not restricted in its choice to these names.

Hungary took a definite step toward repudiating the Treaty of Trianon in 1938 when Premier Darányi announced that rearmament would be one of the main features of a five-year plan of economic development. Darányi further outlined a scheme to place curbs on Jewish economic and professional activities in Hungary and a project to speed up land reform in favor of the peasant masses. There proposals were intended to "steal the thunder" of the various Nazi groups that had begun to spring up, but there was a feeling in parliament that more vigorous measures should have been taken in this connection.[1] Darányi consequently was overthrown and succeeded (1938) by Bela Imredy, a respected, conservative, Catholic financier of anti-Nazi but pro-German sympathies. (This seeming paradox applied to many members of the National Union Party. They sympathized with Germany in international affairs but had no desire to see their large estates broken up and the hold of the nobility on government posts shaken by a National-Socialist government. Following the union of Austria and Germany, the Budapest Government drew even closer to the latter, for the Third Reich now absorbed about 70 per cent of Hungary's agricultural exports—the main item by far in her foreign sales.)

Imredy at once turned attention to the Jewish question. The Jews numbered 5 per cent of the population but held about half of the positions in trade, banking, and the liberal professions. This was owing, in part at least, to the dislike of many Magyars for business as an occupation, but the figures were impressive. A decree therefore limited Jewish participation in any business, industry, or profession to 20 per cent. In February 1939, on the eve of his introducing new anti-Semitic legislation, Imredy resigned; upon investigation, he had found a remote Jewish strain in his own ancestry. His office and policy were taken over by Count Paul Teleki, a prominent geographer and Boy Scout leader.

The Teleki Government quickly secured the passage of a strict anti-Jewish law. The proportion of Jews in business and industry was limited to 12 per cent of all persons engaged in such callings; in the professions, the Jewish limit was placed at 6 per cent of the total. No Jew might hold public office nor occupy a leading position in journalism, the theater, or the cinema. The state was empowered to expropriate, with compensation, any Jewish farms of more than half an acre. Jews might vote in parliamentary elections, but only for Jewish candidates, and those elected might not exceed 6 per cent of the membership of the lower house.

[1] The most prominent Nazi group was organized in 1937 by Major Ferenc Szalasi. It continued to function in several disguises even when the government had ordered its dissolution. In 1938 Szalasi was sentenced to imprisonment but he was soon released and reorganized his followers and other Nazi groups into the Arrowcross Party.

The German annexation of the Sudeten areas in 1938 and the consequent weakening of the Czechoslovak state system led to a political crisis in Hungary, where the revisionist element demanded the immediate occupation of Slovakia and Carpatho-Ukraine. Imredy had resisted this pressure and had contented himself with the somewhat disappointing Vienna Award. But then, in March 1939, Carpatho-Ukraine was annexed and Hungary's population rose to about 11,000,000.[1]

As the year 1939 wore on, the pressure of the totalitarian bloc on Hungary became stronger. Hungary therefore recognized Manchoukuo, signed the Anti-Communist Pact, severed diplomatic relations with the Soviet Union, and announced her withdrawal from the League of Nations. During the electoral campaign of May 1939, however, Premier Teleki emphasized his government's intention to keep Hungary independent of foreign control or "protection." On this basis and that of social reform his supporters gained a majority in the new parliament.[2] The Nazi groups, however, registered sizable gains. (On this occasión, incidentally, Hungary for the first time since the First World War experienced an election in which the voting in all districts was secret.) Soon after the election, ex-Premier Bethlen announced his final retirement from political life. He expressed disgust with the politics of the day, saying: "Nowadays only those who breakfast on Jews, lunch on aristocrats, and after dinner deal out fortunes and properties not belonging to them are national heroes. . . . I do not see the strong will and the clear-sightedness that this country needs. This cannot come from without, but only from within."

[1] On the Vienna Award and Carpatho-Ukraine see pp. 515 and 517.
[2] The National Union Party had meanwhile become the Party of Hungarian Life.

CHAPTER XVIII

Two Slavic Republics

CZECHOSLOVAKIA

a. The Winning of Independence

The strongest state which emerged from the wreckage of the Dual Monarchy was Czechoslovakia, a republic consisting of the five districts of Bohemia, Moravia, Austrian Silesia, Slovakia, and Ruthenia, and comprising an area of 54,207 square miles.[1] Almost from the outset Czechoslovakia enjoyed an economic stability and a foreign respect unusual for one of the newer states of Europe. Credit for this achievement belonged not only to the high level of civilization attained by the Czechs before the war, but to the efforts of two former college professors: Thomas Garrigue Masaryk and Eduard Beneš.

Masaryk was born in Moravia in 1850, the son of a Slovak coachman. Despite the handicap of poverty, he managed to secure an excellent scholastic training and eventually became a professor of philosophy at Prague. He married an American girl, Charlotte Garrigue, and adopted her surname as his middle name. Through her family connections he acquired an extensive and useful acquaintance in the United States. In pre-1914 days he was conspicuous as a Czech nationalist, a philosophical liberal, and a lover of justice. He early succeeded in making himself unpopular with the Austrian authorities by his views on national and social rights for the subject Slavs, and when the war broke out he quickly made up his mind that "Austria must be opposed in grim earnest, to the death."

Feeling that he could be more useful to the cause of Czech lib-

---

[1] The first three of the districts named formerly belonged to Austria, the others to Hungary. The Slavic natives of Bohemia, Moravia, and Silesia are known as "Czechs," those of Slovakia as "Slovaks," and those of Ruthenia as "Ruthenians," "Carpatho-Russians," or "Ukrainians."

eration if he were free from the danger of arrest, Masaryk made his way into Italy in December 1914, and then spent the next four years disseminating propaganda and organizing opinion in the leading Allied states. In Russia he helped organize Czechoslovak legions; in the United States he raised funds; in France he set up

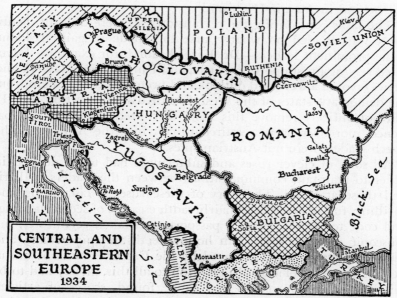

From Landman, J., *Outline History of the World since 1914*, 1934
Courtesy of Barnes and Noble, Inc.

propaganda headquarters; everywhere he labored to arouse sentiment for Czechoslovak independence. Contact with the "revolutionary movement" (as the struggle was called at home) was provided by means of an efficient "secret service" directed by Masaryk's student and friend, Eduard Beneš.

Beneš was born in 1884 near Pilsen (Plzeň). He studied at Prague, Berlin, Paris, and Dijon, specializing in law and philosophy. A prolific writer on social, economic, and political subjects, he was also a professor of philosophy and sociology at the Polytechnic School in Prague and an admirer of democracy. When he heard the news of the declaration of hostilities, Beneš felt that the Dual Monarchy either "would come to an end through losing the war, or it would come to an end in a social upheaval and revolution after the war." Consequently he was "determined to go to any length and to sacrifice everything, to carry out a revolution." Although at first remaining at home in order to keep Masaryk informed of what was happening there, Beneš, too, eventually found it necessary to flee. Arrived in Paris, his diplomatic ability and resourcefulness were of great aid in securing hearings for the cause and in keeping up communications with the revolutionary leaders left behind in Austria-Hungary.[1]

The tasks confronting the revolutionaries were difficult. Sentiment was divided on what course to pursue to gain freedom. Some prominent leaders—Dr. Karel Kramář, for example—advocated relying for support on Russia and Pan-Slavism. Masaryk and Beneš favored a westward outlook and preferred to seek help from the democratic states of the West. Even Russia's defection in 1917 did not entirely remove this bone of contention. Tact and patience, moreover, were required to convince the Allies that the Czech leaders were not Austrian spies.

All sorts of clever ruses and subterfuges had to be devised in order to maintain communications between the leaders in Paris and those at home. The story of these ruses is fascinating and thrilling, full of arrests and hairbreadth escapes, of secret meetings and code telegrams, falsified passports and faked certificates, microscopic messages carried in hollow teeth and pipe stems, and important state secrets betrayed by the Czech servants of unsuspecting Austrian officials. In addition to all this, money had to be raised, capable journalists had to be found, scores of articles, pamphlets, and manifestoes had to be got up, imprisoned leaders had to be replaced, and recognition had to be secured for the National Council of Czechoslovakia (sitting in Paris) as official spokesman for the Czechoslovak people.

With a dogged determination these problems were faced and solved. The first intimation of success came in January 1917 when the Allies listed as one of their war aims an autonomous Czechoslovak area. Then, when Allied victory seemed assured, Masaryk, with the approval of Beneš and Štefánik, issued a declaration of independence (October 18, 1918). Ten days later a Czech National Council at Prague, temporarily presided over by Antonín Švehla, reiterated the declaration of independence and took over the reins of administration from the imperial officers. On October 29 a Slovak National Council voted for union with the Czechs in a single state. The overturn was almost bloodless and on November

[1] Deserving to rank only below Masaryk and Beneš as a founder of the republic was the Slovak Milan Štefánik, who had become a general in the French Army.

THOMAS GARRIGUE MASARYK

14 a provisional assembly unanimously proclaimed the republic. Fittingly enough, Masaryk was elected president, Kramář became premier, Beneš was appointed foreign minister, and Štefánik took the post of minister of war. Kramář soon joined Beneš, who was still in Paris, to represent the new republic at the peace conference. Thus ended four centuries of Habsburg rule in the realms of "good King Wenceslas." [1]

b. Constitution and Land Reform

In February 1920 the provisional assembly adopted a constitution. The document was modeled after the constitutions of the United States and France, and provided for a democratic parliamentary regime with separation of powers. The preamble expressed the desire of the country "to join the League of Nations as an enlightened, peaceful, democratic, and progressive member."

The lower house was to consist of three hundred members who were elected for six years by the compulsory vote of all men and women over twenty-one. The Senate, only half as large, was to be elected for eight years by all voters over twenty-six. The ministry was made directly responsible to the lower chamber, whch was given the power to pass laws over the veto of the upper house. The houses were required to meet twice a year and might be called in extra session at any time. The question of the constitutionality of laws was left to the decision of a constitutional court. The president, who was given a suspensive veto, was to be elected for seven years by the two houses meeting together as the National Assembly. No one (except Masaryk) might serve more than two consecutive terms, although a second reëlection after the lapse of a term was permitted. Masaryk was elected president for his first full term in 1920 and reëlected in 1927 and 1934. Beneš succeeded the aged leader upon his resignation in 1935.

In Czechoslovakia there soon appeared numerous political parties. Thus, as a result of elections in 1929, fifteen parties were represented in the lower house. The political alignments were based in the first instance upon racial divisions and then subdivided according to economic and religious interests. Hence there grew up both Czechoslovak and German parties labeled Agrarian and So-

[1] The provisional assembly represented only Czechs and Slovaks. The several minorities held aloof, the German-speaking in the hope that it might achieve union with Germany or Austria, the Magyar in the belief that it might be permitted to remain with Hungary. Blood was shed when Czech troops occupied the "German" towns in Bohemia and Moravia, but Masaryk promised equality of treatment to all, and the disturbances gradually ceased.

cial Democratic. Similarly, there were organized Czechoslovak and Slovak People's Catholic parties, and German and Hungarian Christian Socialists. Communistic and independent groups also took root. The cabinets therefore came to be based upon coalition groupings.

Perhaps the most pressing domestic problem facing the new state was that of land reform. Previously the tendency had been to concentrate the land in a few large holdings. In 1918 about 2 per cent of the landlords in Bohemia owned more than one-fourth of the land. In Moravia nearly one-third of the land was controlled by less than 1 per cent of the landowners. In Slovakia half of the land was in possession of about one thousand persons. One-fourth of the farms in Bohemia and Moravia measured seven and a half acres or less. Most of the big landholders were German- or Magyar-speaking members of the former ruling classes.

In 1919, almost a year before the adoption of a constitution, the provisional assembly inaugurated a program of land reform which never reached completion. Laws were passed that provided for the expropriation of all estates exceeding in size 375 acres of arable land or 625 acres of mixed arable and nonarable land. Lands formerly belonging to the Crown or to the Habsburg family were to be expropriated without compensation, while in other cases compensation was fixed at a level below the real value of the property before 1914. The land thus acquired by the state was to be sold on easy terms to peasants, ex-service men, and, in general, any landless persons who were willing to till the soil. In no circumstance were more than 37.5 acres to be assigned to any one individual. Nonarable land was made available to scientific institutions, coöperative or public associations, and municipalities and parishes. Eventually hundreds of thousands of citizens became "middle-class farmers"—direct owners of sufficient land to provide a decent living.

The breakup of the large estates precipitated a quarrel between the government and the Roman Catholic Church. Many of the estates had been church property and the ecclesiastical authorities looked with disfavor upon the expropriation policy. Popular opinion, however, tended to support the government, for, although most of the population was nominally Catholic, the Czechs were lukewarm in their religious fealty. Countrymen of the heretic John Hus, who was burned at the stake in 1415, the Czechs had readily become Protestants during the sixteenth century—only to be reconverted to Catholicism through force in the seventeenth.

The Bohemians, as distinguished from the Slovaks, showed little sympathy with the land claims of the church.

Expropriation was not the only point of friction between church and state. Estrangement arose out of the circumstance that most of the high church offices in these Slavic provinces had been given, under the monarchy, to "Germans" and Magyars who were accused of using their clerical influence as much to foster the cause of the Habsburgs as that of Providence. The services had generally been conducted in German or Magyar, where Latin was not used, and the schools had been regarded as convenient monarchist-clerical propaganda agencies. The republic therefore set about secularizing education and abolished compulsory religious instruction in the schools. In Slovakia, where the clergy had an especially strong hold on education, hundreds of new state schools were opened.

The government insisted that the papacy redraw the diocesan boundaries so as to make them conform to the frontiers of the state, that natives be appointed to the higher clerical offices, and that the local tongue be substituted for German or Magyar wherever the parishes were predominantly Slavic. Some of the radicals and the nationalists in parliament demanded an absolute separation of church and state, and early in 1920, as part of an "Away-from-Rome" movement, there was established a Czechoslovak National Church which proclaimed its independence of the papacy and abolished the requirement of celibacy for the clergy. This church gained almost no Slovak adherents and relatively few Czech members.

The quarrels between the two authorities came to a head in 1925 when July 6, the anniversary of the day on which Hus was burned, was proclaimed a national holiday. The papal nuncio was withdrawn from the republic and the Czechoslovak Minister was recalled from the Holy See. After a deadlock of two years and a half, during which diplomatic relations were severed, both sides agreed to compromise. Harmony was restored by the signing of a *modus vivendi* in 1927. The diocesan boundaries were to be rearranged to coincide with the republic's borders, the state was to continue paying the salaries of the clergy but was to have a voice in the nomination of bishops, only Czechoslovak citizens were to be eligible for appointment as bishops, all church officials were to be required to take an oath of allegiance to the state, the native language was prescribed for certain services, and the papacy abandoned its opposition to Hus Day.

c. Economics and Foreign Affairs

From an economic point of view Czechoslovakia, whose territory was little touched by the ravages of the First World War, was one of the most fortunate states in Europe. A splendid system of railway lines and terminals was inherited from the Dual Monarchy, along with approximately 80 per cent of the industries of that defunct state. Though comprising only one-fifth of the area of the old Austria-Hungary and including only one-fourth of her population, Czechoslovakia became the possessor of four-fifths of the ex-monarchy's manufacturing equipment, three-fifths of its breweries, nine-tenths of its soft coal, and three-fifths of its iron ore.

On the agricultural side the situation was equally favorable, Czechoslovakia being virtually self-sufficient in the matter of food supply. Under the old regime Bohemia produced 90 per cent of the empire-kingdom's sugar beets, 80 per cent of the hops, and 75 per cent of the fruit. Forty-two per cent of the land in the republic was arable and Slovakia produced large quantities of flax, maize, and wine, as well as some tobacco. The soil was rich in graphite, copper, lead, and silver. During the period from 1919 to 1931 Czechoslovakia enjoyed a consistently favorable balance of trade. Her chief economic handicap was her landlocked position, but this disadvantage was mitigated by the provisions in the peace treaties which granted her access to the sea at Hamburg, Stettin, and Trieste, through foreign territory. She had eight hundred miles of navigable riverways within her own borders and was represented on the international commissions which supervised traffic on the Elbe and Oder rivers.

Since the country had an industrial equipment which originally was intended to take care of the needs of a large empire, the existing population could not absorb the entire manufactured output. Consequently Czechoslovakia depended for her economic prosperity upon cordial trade relationships with the outside world. Her best customers until 1933 were Germany, Austria, Great Britain, and Hungary in the order named, while her purchases were made chiefly in Germany, Austria, and Poland. With each of these countries and with many others Czechoslovakia early negotiated commercial treaties and established friendly business contacts.

Business was not the only incentive for Czechoslovakia's desire to have harmonious foreign relations. The republic was about 600 miles long and varied in width from 50 to 125 miles. Its access to the sea depended upon the upholding of the peace treaties. Five countries, most of them at one time or another hostile, completely surrounded the state: Germany, Poland, Romania, Hungary, and Austria. For about half of the length of her boundary she was surrounded by a pincers formed by the southern German and northern Austrian borders. Hence her eagerness to prevent the consummation of the Anschluss. Except for the region of the Carpathians and the Erzgebirge, her frontiers offered little natural protection.

Masaryk and Beneš, the latter of whom held the portfolio of foreign affairs without interruption from 1918 until 1935, both favored a policy of international peace and were guided in their decisions "first and foremost by (the republic's) geographical, economic, and political situation in Europe." Four main lines of policy were pursued: (1) support of the League as the protector of small states and the mainstay of peace and stability on the continent; (2) unswerving support of the peace treaties to which the republic owed its life; (3) endorsement in larger European affairs of the policies of Great Britain and France, especially the latter; and (4) united action with Yugoslavia and Romania in central-European matters, particularly where these related to Hungary. In pursuance of this last aim, Czechoslovakia joined Yugoslavia and Romania in the formation (1920–1921) of the Little Entente.

From 1921 to 1927 relations between the Little Entente and Austria were friendly. In 1921 Austria and Czechoslovakia signed a commercial convention at Lana and in 1926 they negotiated a treaty of friendship wherein (1) each promised to remain neutral in case the other were attacked by a third power; (2) each agreed to suppress within its borders any agitation directed against the other; (3) both pledged themselves to coöperate in preventing a restoration of the old regime; and (4) both agreed to submit all future disputes that might arise between them to peaceful arbitration. After 1923, when the Little Entente took a prominent part in the arranging of a League of Nations loan to Hungary, relations with the latter also experienced a temporary improvement.

Between 1923 and 1927 it appeared that the bonds of the entente might be loosed. But then a series of events reacted to give new life to the entente relationships: the revival of Anschluss agitation in Germany and Austria after 1926; the conclusion of a treaty of friendship between Italy and Hungary in 1927 followed by arms shipments from the former country to the latter in 1927 and 1933; the renewal of Magyar irredentist agitation; and the serious consideration during the depression years of a Balkan or Danubian federation to improve the economic standing of the countries concerned. In 1934 and 1935 the crisis resulting from the murder of King Alexander of Yugoslavia appeared to offer a successful test of the strength of the alliance bonds.[1] But then the problem of minorities helped bring ruin to all three members of the entente.

d. The Problem of Minorities

Czechoslovakia, according to the census of 1930, had almost 15,000,000 inhabitants, of whom two-thirds were Czechs or Slovaks. The remaining third was made up of approximately 3,300,000 "Germans," 700,000 Magyars, 550,000 Ruthenians, and some Poles and Jews. At the peace conference of 1919 Czechoslovakia was required to sign one of the minorities treaties for the protection of these nonnational subjects, and the constitution guaranteed equality before the law to all subjects without distinction as to race, language, or religion. In accord with these promises, schools were provided for the minorities, arrangements were made for the conduct of official business in a minority language where one-fifth of the population used that tongue, the printed matter on banknotes was repeated in three languages, and a voice in the government was assured to the minority groups through the adoption of proportional representation in parliament.

Despite these guarantees and concessions, considerable difficulty was experienced with the subject peoples. At first, relations with the Carpatho-Russians were particularly strained. Ruthenia was assigned to Czechoslovakia by the peace conference in order to provide the new state with a natural boundary in the Carpathian Mountains and to bring it in direct contact with Romania, thus forming a ring around Hungary. The republic was bound by treaty to extend local autonomy to Ruthenia, but since the Ruthenians as a group had been kept in a relatively backward state by the ruling Magyars, the Czechoslovaks for some time withheld autonomy lest—so they said—the better educated Magyars and Jews in the province obtain control. Moreover, since the Catholic Church and the Magyars still controlled the educational system of Ruthenia, the government made haste to establish state schools with instruction in the native Ruthenian or Ukrainian tongue, and to decree that, until such time as Ruthenians capable of hold-

[1] See pp. 496–497.

ing office might be developed, Czechoslovak officials should be put in charge of the important positions.

The processes of education and of substitution of Ruthenian for Czechoslovak officials were so protracted as to cause bitter complaint. In 1927 and 1928, however, laws were passed which reorganized the entire provincial administrative system of the land and granted Ruthenia not only an autonomous local administration but also an elective local diet. This allayed the discontent somewhat, but the Ruthenians still maintained that too many offices were reserved for persons who had the interests of Czechoslovakia rather than those of Ruthenia at heart.

The population question was further complicated by the antagonism of the Czechs and Slovaks themselves. The Czechs, who outnumbered the Slovaks almost two to one, were more Westernized than their compatriots and tended to dominate the governmental partnership. They had a higher percentage of literacy than the Slovaks, were more inclined towards political liberalism and religious skepticism, and were more interested in industry and commerce than agriculture.[1] The Slovaks, indeed, were among the most pious and conservative of continental peasant folk.

Disagreements and quarrels, sometimes to the accompaniment of bloodshed, soon arose. The Slovaks accused the Czechs of monopolizing the desirable offices and violating the Pittsburgh Pact of 1918 wherein Masaryk, in order to get the support of the American Slovaks for his Czech-Slovak unification project, had given a promise of Slovak autonomy. The Slovak People's Catholic Party was especially anxious to secure autonomy for the province, gain freedom from governmental interference with the school system, and ensure the continued influence of the clergy over the peasants. In 1924 there was inaugurated a Slovak movement to boycott everything of Czech origin, but between 1926 and 1929 several incidents occurred which lessened the dissension: in 1926 two Slovaks were taken into the cabinet; in 1927 the republic's quarrel with the papacy was terminated; and in 1929 the law which granted administrative autonomy to the provinces went into effect. But then another factor entered to revive the strife—Hungarian irredentism.

The Czechs accused the Magyars both in Slovakia and in Hungary of fomenting a separatist movement having for its ultimate

[1] Two-thirds of the people in Slovakia and Ruthenia depended directly on the soil for their subsistence, while fewer than half of the people in the west were dependent upon agriculture.

purpose the reunion of Slovakia with the Magyar kingdom. A crisis in this dispute was reached in 1928 when a Slovak deputy, Professor Voytech Tuka, was accused of being a Hungarian irredentist and was sentenced to fifteen years' imprisonment for espionage and high treason. During the trial, and while the case was being appealed, Slovakia seethed with unrest. The upholding of the verdict by the highest tribunal in 1930 lessened the agitation, but further trouble was caused by the circulation of reports that Tuka was being mistreated in jail. The Czech-Slovak controversy thus remained a potential danger to the unity of the state.

The most serious minority problem in the long run proved to be that of the millions of German-speaking people in Bohemia and Moravia. These had, on the whole, comprised the upper class in pre-1914 days and they now formed a powerful opposition unit. At first they boycotted the elections and cleverly put obstacles in the way of the administration, but gradually they came to realize that more might be gained by active participation in the political life of the state. Masaryk did all he could to encourage this attitude and in 1926 two "Germans" were appointed to the cabinet. In 1927 three-quarters of the "Germans" in the assembly voted to reëlect Masaryk president. Naturally there were irreconcilables on both sides, and in 1930 some Bohemian nationalists attempted to wreck theaters in which German films were being shown. The triumph of Hitlerism in the Reich in 1933 quickly gave the problem a dangerous international aspect.

The Czechoslovak Government took energetic measures to limit Nazi propaganda and in 1933 dissolved both the German National and the National German Socialist Labor parties. But their successor, the *Sudetendeutsche Partei* headed by Konrad Henlein, polled more votes than any other party in the parliamentary elections of May 1935. A coalition of the democratic parties succeeded in retaining control of the cabinet, but before the year was out the new president, Beneš, and the new premier, Milan Hodža, faced the worst situation in Czechoslovakia's history. And Germany took full advantage of the circumstances to conduct a vigorous diplomatic and press campaign against its neighbor to the south.

e. The Sudeten-German Crisis and Munich

The Czechoslovaks were accused by the Goebbels propaganda machine of harshly mistreating the "Germans" under their control and depriving them of economic and cultural opportunities.

They were also branded as being in league with the Soviet Union to spread the "Semitic communism" of the Third International. Beneš and Hodža replied to these attacks, defending their minorities policy, denying any intent to spread abroad doctrines of any kind, and explaining that strong measures were made necessary by the dangerous activities of Henlein's followers. Nevertheless, early in 1937 the Prague Government tried to conciliate its German-speaking subjects by promising them fuller cultural autonomy. Perhaps a third of the minority group (comprising three parties collectively known as "Activists" because they coöperated actively with the government) was satisfied with these concessions, but the Sudeten-German Party demanded political autonomy.

The great danger inherent in the situation was made plain in the international recriminations that followed the breaking up by Czechoslovak police of a demonstration arranged by Henlein's party at Teplice-Sanov (Teplitz-Schönau), near the German border, in October 1937. Thereupon the Prague Government forbade all political meetings and postponed some forthcoming municipal elections. When the elections finally were held, in May–June 1938, the Henleinists captured 90 per cent of the vote in the "German" districts, whereas in 1935 they had polled only 67 per cent thereof. This gain at the expense of the Activists was owing, apparently, to the fact of Germany's recent absorption of Austria.

It is impossible to give here a detailed account of the complicated happenings between March and October 1938 which led to the partial breakup of Czechoslovakia. Briefly, afer Neville Chamberlain made it clear in Parliament that he would not commit Great Britain to lend France military aid in the event of a war provoked by German action against Czechoslovakia, the Henleinists presented the Prague Government with an Eight-Point Program. The program demanded complete autonomy, ideologically as well as politically, and reparation for damages caused by "injustices inflicted since 1918." Despite pressure from London and Paris to make all possible concessions, Prague rejected the demands as being too vague and, when fighting broke out in the Sudeten areas and troop movements were observed in Germany, the Czechoslovak army was quickly mobilized.

The crisis thereupon subsided temporarily and the Czechoslovak Government agreed to accept unofficial British mediation in the minorities dispute. Thereupon Viscount Runciman went to the scene of the difficulties. He spent most of his time interviewing Nazis and did little in the way of bringing both sides together. In

August, Henlein turned down a compromise plan offered by Beneš and told the members of his party to resort to "self-defense" in case of attack. After some serious rioting, Prague proclaimed martial law.

On September 15, while Chamberlain was finding out from Hitler at Berchtesgaden what his demands really were, Henlein issued the first public statement demanding annexation of the affected area to Germany: "We wish to be home in the Reich!" [1] Meanwhile it had been made abundantly clear to Prague that in the event of armed resistance to German military action, she could not count on the support of any great power. The Soviet Union agreed to fight if France did, but France would not act without the prior commitment of Great Britain, and such a commitment was not forthcoming. A Czechoslovak note of September 21, therefore, announced acceptance of Franco-British proposals for the cession of territory to Germany. Now Poland and Hungary added their demands to Germany's, asking for the cession of territories in Teschen and Slovakia, respectively. Premier Hodža then was succeeded by General Jan Syrový.

Chamberlain, on September 22, flew to Godesberg in Germany to confer with Hitler and was disturbed by the increased severity of the demands now presented by the Germans. Nevertheless, he had a British diplomat transmit the demand to Prague without comment, Czechoslovakia having meanwhile ordered general mobilization. Beneš protested that the Godesberg demands went far beyond the scope of the Anglo-French proposals earlier accepted by his government, particularly in the insistence upon the immediate military occupation of certain specified areas. While Great Britain and France ordered preparations for war, and half-heartedly declared their determination to fight if Germany attacked Czechoslovakia, Hitler threatened the use of military force unless all his demands were accepted by October 1. President Roosevelt and Mussolini now appealed for further negotiations, and on September 28 Chamberlain sent a personal letter to Hitler, offering to come to Germany, together with representatives of France and Italy, in a last-minute effort to preserve peace.

Chamberlain, Daladier, Mussolini, and Hitler then met at Munich on September 29 and after a prolonged session signed the Munich Agreement of that date. The official text of the document reads as follows:

[1] The Sudeten areas had never belonged to Germany.

Germany, the United Kingdom, France and Italy, taking into consideration the agreement, which has been already reached in principle for the cession to Germany of the Sudeten German territory, have agreed on the following terms and conditions governing the said cession and the measures consequent thereon, and by this agreement they each hold themselves responsible for the steps necessary to secure its fulfillment:—

1. The evacuation will begin on the 1st October.

2. The United Kingdom, France and Italy agree that the evacuation of the territory shall be completed by the 10th October, without any existing installations having been destroyed and that the Czechoslovak Government will be held responsible for carrying out the evacuation without damage to the said installations.

3. The conditions governing the evacuation will be laid down in detail by an international commission composed of representatives of Germany, the United Kingdom, France, Italy and Czechoslovakia.

4. The occupation by stages of the predominantly German territory by German troops will begin on the 1st October. The four territories marked on the attached map will be occupied by German troops in the following order: the territory marked No. I on the 1st and 2nd of October, the territory marked No. II on the 2nd and 3rd of October, the territory marked No. III on the 3rd, 4th and 5th of October, the territory marked No. IV on the 6th and 7th of October. The remaining territory of preponderantly German character will be ascertained by the aforesaid international commission forthwith and be occupied by German troops by the 10th of October.

5. The international commission referred to in paragraph 3 will determine the territories in which a plebiscite is to be held. These territories will be occupied by international bodies until the plebiscite has been completed. The same commission will fix the conditions in which the plebiscite is to be held, taking as a basis the conditions of the Saar plebiscite. The commission will also fix a date, not later than the end of November, on which the plebiscite will be held.

6. The final determination of the frontiers will be carried out by the international commission. This commission will also be entitled to recommend to the four Powers, Germany, the United Kingdom, France and Italy, in certain exceptional cases minor modifications in the strictly ethnographical determination of the zones which are to be transferred without plebiscite.

7. There will be a right of option into and out of the transferred territories, the option to be exercised within six months from the date of

this agreement. A German-Czechoslovak commission shall determine the details of the option, consider ways of facilitating the transfer of population and settle questions of principle arising out of the said transfer.

8. The Czechoslovak Government will within a period of four weeks from the date of this agreement release from their military and police forces any Sudeten Germans who may wish to be released, and the Czechoslovak Government will within the same period release Sudeten German prisoners who are serving terms of imprisonment for political offences.[1]

Thus, without war, Germany achieved the goal which she had set for herself at Godesberg. The only deviations from that set of demands were minor ones, involving a somewhat longer time limit for evacuation by the Czechoslovaks and an added provision for exchange of populations. In an annex to the Munich Agreement, Great Britain and France agreed to "stand by" an earlier offer to "guarantee" the new boundaries of Czechoslovakia "against unprovoked aggression."

In accordance with the agreement, the Germans quickly occupied the first four districts, predominantly "German" in population, with all "installations" intact. Meanwhile, over strenuous Czechoslovak protests, the commission set up under Article 3 was delimiting the boundaries of the fifth zone on the basis of the Austro-Hungarian census of 1910. Finally, a protocol of November 20 transferred to Germany scattered additional small areas.[2] By the entire transaction, Germany gained about 11,500 square miles, rich in industry and electric power, and about 3,500,000 inhabitants, including several hundred thousand Czechs. With an area of approximately 226,000 square miles and a population of about 80,000,000, she was now easily the largest state in Europe, west of the Soviet Union.

f. The Collapse of "Czecho-Slovakia"

That same annex to the Munich Agreement which contained the promise of an Anglo-French guarantee of "the Czechoslovak

---

[1] Before Chamberlain returned home, he and Hitler signed another paper, confirming the "desire of (their) two peoples never to go to war with one another again."

[2] Germany and Czechoslovakia also signed agreements whereby the former got an extraterritorial corridor through the latter—for purposes of constructing a German-policed military highway to tie together the German pincers across Moravia

State's" new borders, also provided that "when the question of the Polish and Hungarian minorities in Czechoslovakia has been settled, Germany and Italy for their part will give a guarantee to Czechoslovakia." This stipulation regarding Polish and Hungarian minorities was necessary because, as the September 1938 crisis approached its height, the governments and people in both Poland and Hungary clamored for the equal treatment of their minorities living in Czechoslovakia with that accorded the "Germans." Poland wanted that part of the industrial Teschen district which had been awarded, in the immediate postwar period, to Czechoslovakia, plus some neighboring regions; Hungary demanded the return of Slovakia. Both Warsaw and Budapest appealed to Hitler and Mussolini for support of their claims.

When the Munich Agreement was announced, Warsaw sent an ultimatum to Prague requiring the immediate surrender of Teschen and the evacuation of the districts of Bohumin, Frystat, and Jablunkov over a period of ten days. On October 1, 1938, Prague yielded and Polish troops soon occupied an area of about 400 square miles with a population of 225,000. Of these, only about 80,000 were Poles, according to the census of 1930, and more than 120,000 were Czechs, but in this case, as in that of the Sudeten areas, the victorious negotiator insisted on the application of pre-1914 statistics.

Now Poland undertook to support the claims of Hungary, with whom she was anxious to form a common frontier. Italy appeared ready to back the Polish-Hungarian demands, but Germany, though willing to enlarge Hungary at Czechoslovak expense, evidently had no desire to see a relatively strong Polish-Magyar front established between herself and the east. When Hungary and Czechoslovakia requested Germany and Italy to arbitrate their dispute, the German and Italian foreign ministers met in Vienna and on November 2 announced their decision. The Vienna Award did not establish a common Polish-Magyar frontier but assigned to Hungary a part of Ruthenia and southern Slovakia (excluding the river port of Bratislava or Pressburg). The area of the cession was about 4600 square miles and the population 1,000,000.

Within Czecho-Slovakia, as the diminished republic now spelled

---

—and Czechoslovakia promised to assist Germany in the digging of an Oder-Danube Canal already under construction.

its name, great changes had meanwhile been taking place. On October 5, 1938, following announcement that the international boundary commission would base its decisions on the census of 1910, and feeling that German pressure might be somewhat relaxed if he left the scene, President Beneš resigned. The National Assembly thereupon chose as his successor, Dr. Emil Hácha, president since 1925 of the supreme court. On the same day the Syrový Cabinet was replaced by one under Dr. Rudolf Beran. One of the last acts of the Syrový Government had been to secure the passage of laws granting autonomy to the provinces of Slovakia and Ruthenia, the latter being reorganized under the name of Carpatho-Ukraine. Thereafter the Czecho-Slovak Cabinet was to contain representatives of all divisions of the republic: Czechia (Bohemia plus Moravia), Slovakia, and Carpatho-Ukraine.

Partly as a reaction to the "desertion" of her allies and partly because of German pressure and a practical desire at last to come to terms with her powerful neighbor, the republic completely reversed a number of her traditional policies. Most officials who had been strongly identified with the earlier regime were dismissed. Monuments to Masaryk and busts of Beneš were taken down. The Communist Party was suppressed and Masonic lodges were encouraged to dissolve themselves. Close economic relations were established with Germany, for Czecho-Slovakia had become a relatively poor agrarian state. Anti-Semitic outbreaks became frequent occurrences, especially in Slovakia where the Hlinka Guards, named after a nationalistic priest, pursued tactics similar to those of the German Brown Shirts. Upon Andrew Hlinka's death, moreover, his followers came under the leadership of another Catholic priest, the separatistically inclined Father Joseph Tiso. In October 1938 the latter became premier of autonomous Slovakia.

Prominent among the many immediate difficulties facing Czecho-Slovakia in 1938 and early 1939 was the problem of how to care for the numerous refugees who fled from the areas ceded to her neighbors, especially Germany. Many of these refugees were "Aryans" whose political outlook or national background differed markedly from that of the new masters. Many were Jews, whose lot was made the worse by the mounting anti-Semitic spirit manifested throughout central and southeastern Europe. To aid Czecho-Slovakia in handling this situation and to recompense her in part for her recent territorial and economic losses, Great Britain and France agreed to participate equally in a gift of $40,000,000 to the republic and to lend her an additional $40,000,000. With this total of $80,000,000 at her disposal, Czecho-Slovakia would, it was hoped, be able to provide necessary foreign exchange for some refugees, find means of settling others within her own borders, and in general rebuild her economic structure. Fate, however, had other things in store for the ill-fated republic.

In an effort to quell the mounting disturbances in Slovakia, Premier Beran of Czecho-Slovakia dismissed Tiso and several of his fellow ministers (March 1939) and appointed a more moderate cabinet under Karl Sidor. Tiso thereupon conferred with Hitler in Berlin and on March 15 German troops occupied what was left of Masaryk's republic. Czechia was declared (March 16) a German "protectorate" named Bohemia-Moravia under the nominal presidency of Hácha but the actual control of a "Reich Protector." Slovakia, too, became a "protectorate," and by a German-Slovak Treaty it was required to "conduct its policy in close coöperation with the German Government." Slovakia thus became a puppet state of the type represented in Asia by Manchoukuo. At Hitler's command, Father Tiso was installed as head of the new Slovak state, a situation which was not pleasing to the papacy. Meanwhile, finally, Hungarian soldiers had marched into Carpatho-Ukraine. On March 16 this remnant of the Czechoslovak state was incorporated in the Hungarian Kingdom, which thus gained a common frontier with Poland and brushed aside a major section of the Treaty of Trianon. Czechoslovakia, for the time being at least, was no more.

It was estimated that Germany, by virtue of her absorption of Bohemia and Moravia, had increased her steel-production capacity by about 10 per cent. According to report, too, the Nazis seized $80,000,000 in gold and foreign exchange in Prague, thus well supplementing the $90,000,000 which they had appropriated at the time of the Austrian union. German action in 1938–1939 with respect to Austria, the Sudeten areas, Czechia, Slovakia, and Memelland [1] added about 77,000 square miles and 20,000,000 people (including several hundred thousand more Jews) to the area and population of the Third Reich. Population pressure within Germany was thus increased rather than decreased and, what was even more serious, the areas in question (except Slovakia) "were actually more dependent upon foreign sources of food supplies and raw materials than was the German Reich."

---

[1] After 1933 there was considerable strife between Memel Nazis, supported by the Reich, and Lithuanian officials. On March 22, 1939, Lithuania acceded to German threats and surrendered Memelland to the Reich. On Memel see pp. 102–103 and n.

a. Pilsudski and Paderewski

Organized as a kingdom about the year 1000 by Boleslav the Mighty, Poland, during part of the Middle Ages, led a glorious existence. The period of glamor was followed by an era of gradually declining power and prestige. Internal dissensions and jealousies caused the Poles, on a number of occasions, to search among European nobles for a new "King of the Pollaks." Since the kingship was elective, the death of a ruler was frequently followed by civil war. The *liberum veto*, a privilege of every noble member of the diet, made it impossible to pass any law in the diet save by unanimous consent. The country, moreover, was lacking in natural, easily defensible frontiers. By the eighteenth century conditions were such as to invite dismemberment.

A crisis was reached in Poland's history when all her neighbors simultaneously came under the rule of powerful personalities: Prussia under Frederick II, Austria under Maria Theresa, and Russia under Catherine II. These monarchs inaugurated three partitions of Poland which, between 1772 and 1795, erased from the map of Europe the name of one of its proudest—and weakest—kingdoms. During the Napoleonic period, Poland was for a time in part restored as the grand duchy of Warsaw, but the Congress of Vienna once more partitioned the area.

Throughout the nineteenth century a Polish national spirit continued to grow under foreign domination, while Polish heroes participated in revolutions in western Europe, notably France. At last, in the twentieth century, many patriotic Poles thought they discerned in the First World War the long-sought-for opportunity to set up a Polish national state. Thanks to the friendship of the Allies and the efforts of Joseph Pilsudski and Ignace Jan Paderewski, this hope was realized.

Born in 1867, in Russian Poland, of a Lithuanian noble family, Pilsudski was reared in an atmosphere of revolt against tsarist autocracy. After visiting a number of universities and being expelled from each for revolutionary activities, he was sent to Siberia for several years. Upon his return he reëngaged in his former pursuits and helped found the Polish Socialist Party, whose basic creed was Polish liberty rather than Marxian theory. He was again arrested and, after he had feigned insanity, eventually sent to a combination asylum and prison in St. Petersburg. Here he remained under close watch for some months, though his friends occasionally managed to communicate with him. In 1901 he escaped, with the aid of a Polish physician who was sent to examine the supposed lunatic.

Pilsudski fled to Austrian Poland, then traveled in western Europe, and finally settled in the city of Cracow until the outbreak of the Russo-Japanese War. During this contest he returned to Russia to participate in the Revolution of 1905, but in 1907 he was back in Cracow. Here he organized and drilled a secret Polish military force. When the First World War broke out, he offered to lead the men against the Russians, considering them the worst oppressors of his people.

It was the hope of Pilsudski and his followers to use Austria "as the sword against Russia and the shield against Germany." They wished to take advantage of Austria's relatively liberal Polish policy to organize a Polish national army as the instrument of eventual independence. Not all Poles, however, shared this view. A considerable group, led by Roman Dmowski, preferred to fight on Russia's side in the belief that Polish unity depended on the defeat of the Central Powers. A third group wanted to achieve Polish independence unhampered by the restrictive aid of either Russia or Austria. This view was most popular among the Poles who lived abroad, particularly those in the United States. Their ablest representative was the pianist, Paderewski.

On August 16, 1914, a Supreme Polish National Committee was formed at Cracow to coördinate the activities and supervise the financial and political affairs of a number of Polish military units which had quickly been formed upon the model of Pilsudski's organization. Those Poles who preferred to look for Russian aid in their unification scheme organized a Polish National Committee in Warsaw. The Austrian authorities accorded limited recognition to the Cracow committee and organized two Polish Legions, commanded by Austrian generals of Polish extraction. Pilsudski's force became the first regiment of the first legion. In 1916 he was given command of a brigade.

Meanwhile the Central Powers and the Russians competed in the issuance of high-sounding manifestoes dealing with the future of Poland. The upshot was merely to convince the Poles that they could expect as little from one side as from the other, and that salvation lay in independent action. Encouraged by President Wilson's speech of January 1917, in which he held that "statesmen everywhere are agreed that there should be a united, independent, and autonomous Poland," and heartened by the Russian evacuation of Poland later in the same year, Pilsudski addressed his followers, saying: "Russia is beaten now; next we must fight Germany." Berlin replied by arresting Pilsudski, disbanding the Polish Legions, and dissolving the Supreme Polish National Committee.

At the close of the war, improvised local governments were set up throughout Poland. Pilsudski, recently released by the Germans, arrived in Warsaw. He took over command of the Polish armies and on November 14, 1918, became "Chief of State." Two days later he announced the existence of an independent Polish Republic. Meanwhile, under Dmowski's leadership, the Polish National Committee that had been set up in Warsaw in 1914 had moved its headquarters to Paris. Thus there were two bodies claiming to represent Poland.

The Allies, identifying Pilsudski's "socialism" with Russian Bolshevism, recognized the committee in Paris, as did most of the conservative Polish bourgeois and peasant groups. Pilsudski's Government, on the other hand, was supported by the laborers and the more radical peasants as well as by a rapidly growing army of war veterans. This contest for authority, combined with the hostility of Poland's neighbors, a number of local separatist movements, starvation, and the general disorganization following upon four years of warfare, seemed to forebode little good for the new state. Obviously compromise was essential if Poland's newly gained independence was to be preserved.

Eventually the major political differences were reconciled by Paderewski, who not only was held in esteem by his own country but had won the confidence of the western nations. Paderewski was in the United States when the war ended, but he quickly sailed for Paris and then went on a triumphal tour of Poland. In January 1919 Paderewski became premier and foreign minister, while Pilsudski continued as chief of state. Since the cabinet included leaders from all important political and geographical groups in the country, the compromise was complete. Then, while Pilsudski set out to establish wide frontiers for Poland by force of arms, Paderewski went to the Paris Peace Conference to render the same service around the diplomats' table.

Filled with ambition and a desire for natural frontiers, the Polish leaders sought to incorporate in the reborn state Lithuania, the Ukraine, Galicia, part of the new Czechoslovakia, and as much more of Germany and Russia as they could claim on ethnological, linguistic, historical, or sentimental grounds. Poland now actually engaged in war with Lithuania, the Ukraine, and Russia; threatened war on Czechoslovakia; disregarded the admonitions of the Allied Supreme Council; and ended by accepting frontiers which gave her an area of about 150,000 square miles rather than the 282,000 square miles that her spokesmen had demanded.

b. Internal Political Affairs, 1919–1939

We've a war, and a debt, and a flag, and if this
Ain't to be independent, what on earth is?

So wrote James Russell Lowell concerning Texas in the 1840's, and Poland in 1919 and 1920 presented much the same spectacle. Paderewski resigned as premier in December 1919, largely because of popular dissatisfaction with his accomplishments at the peace conference. Pilsudski, now a marshal, remained as chief of state until after the adoption of a constitution and the election of a president. The Polish constitution was drafted by a constitutent assembly elected in January 1919 by universal suffrage. Although its work was completed in March 1921, the assembly postponed parliamentary elections and retained control of the government until November 1922.

The constitution, based upon the French model, provided for an upper house called the Senate and a lower house called the *Seym*. Any bill passed by the Seym and vetoed by the Senate was to become law if repassed in the lower house by a majority of eleven-twentieths. The constitution established universal suffrage, with a voting age of twenty-one for the Seym and thirty for the Senate, and with proportional representation. The president, whose every act required countersignature by a member of the cabinet, was to be elected for seven years by the Senate and Seym sitting together as the National Assembly. Owing to the large number of parties, government soon began to be carried on through the medium of the bloc system.

The first parliament elected under the constitution met as a National Assembly in December 1922 and elected Gabriel Narutowicz president. He was assassinated two days after taking office and then was succeeded by Stanislas Wojciechowski. In consequence of these elections Pilsudski gave up his position as chief of state and instead became chief of staff.

During the next few years political conditions in Poland were reminiscent of the days of the decadent kingdom. Conservatives and radicals in the parliament were deadlocked, land reform lagged, the financial situation was critical, and corruption prevailed. To make matters worse, the president and the chief of staff, though at one time friends, became estranged. Pilsudski, in fact, went into temporary retirement, though he remained in close touch with both the army and the left groups in the Seym.

The marshal became more and more irritated at the dilatory tactics of the politicians, at the lack of legislative accomplishment, and at the perpetual parliamentary bickering. In May 1926, when one of his bitterest enemies, Vincent Witos, became premier, Pilsudski denounced the government for its weakness and corruption, for neglecting the army, and for withholding proper recognition from the Socialist Party. When it was hinted that the authorities would institute judicial proceedings against the "calumniator," Pilsudski rallied three regiments about him and began a March on Warsaw. After a three days' battle Pilsudski entered the capital while the president and premier resigned and fled (May 14). The marshal now refused to set up a formal dictatorship and declined the presidency. Instead, he urged the National Assembly to elect as president his friend and supporter, Professor Ignace Mościcki, a successful chemist. He himself was content to become minister of war in the new cabinet of Casimir Bartel.

In the next few months a bitter conflict developed between Pilsudski and the Seym. Although many deputies had come to dislike the forceful policies of Pilsudski, the latter, by controlling the army and attracting the support of public opinion, was able to force through the legislature several constitutional changes. These amendments gave the president greater control over the budget; permitted him, with the consent of the cabinet, to dissolve both houses of parliament; and empowered him to issue decrees with the force of law in certain economic and fiscal matters during the ninety-day interim which might elapse before the election of a new parliament. The powers of the cabinet were extended to include some legislative functions. When the Seym attempted to reassert its authority and defeated the ministry on two motions, Pilsudski requested the president to appoint him premier.

From October 1926 until June 1928 (with only a slight interruption because of illness) Pilsudski retained his post of premier. He was able to rule through parliamentary channels because the national legislature did not dare to oppose him. Hostility to this veiled dictatorship increased, however, and in June 1928 the marshal resigned on the grounds of illness and disgust with the corruption and inefficiency of the Seym. Bartel once again became premier and Pilsudski resumed the office of minister of war.

Parliamentary difficulties did not cease with the reorganization of the ministry. On the contrary, Pilsudski's own Socialist Party now joined the opposition. Thereupon Pilsudski in a violent press interview attacked the politicians in the Seym as unworthy intriguers who had "purposely framed the constitution so that the greatest shame which savage ignorant brains could devise would be placed on the nation's most popular men." He made it clear that although he had resigned as premier he was still "available for service in critical times," and that the control of Polish international affairs remained in his hands.

As minister of war, therefore, Pilsudski continued to dictate Polish policies and to urge a revision of the constitution so as greatly to increase the powers of the national executive. The draft of a new constitution, largely the work of Pilsudski's brother, was first published in 1929. Calculated to make the president very powerful, it passed its first reading in the lower house in 1931. But before the document was finally adopted, the parliament was persuaded (1932) to authorize the president for three years to issue decrees with the force of law.

During the years after 1928 Pilsudski showed his contempt for the parliament in a variety of ways. In January 1929 he refused to attend the official hearings on the budget or defend his requisitions, but, when the budget was announced, he criticized it severely. Two months later, when Finance Minister Gabriel Czechowicz was impeached for the unauthorized expenditure of a large sum in excess of the legal budgetary appropriations, Pilsudski assumed responsibility for the act and defied the Seym to try him. The case then was suspended, although both Czechowicz and Premier Bartel resigned. In October, Pilsudski was saluted in the lobby of the Seym building by a group of armed officers who refused the Speaker's bidding to leave. Frequently the convening of the parliament was postponed by presidential decree, while opposition voices were silenced by arbitrary actions of various sorts. Pilsudski once more announced "It is the deputies who endanger Poland most!" and just prior to the elections of November 1930 about ninety deputies and ex-deputies were arrested in accordance with an official scheme to "cleanse" the political life of the land.[1]

Eight different ministries, all controlled by Pilsudski, guided

[1] Witos, three times premier, and other opposition leaders were jailed after a sensational trial for conspiracy in January 1932.

the affairs of the republic from 1928 to 1935. The governments, because of their preponderantly military make-up, were popularly known as "Cabinets of Colonels." [1] Accustomed as he was to ruling the state in the face of hostile parliamentary majorities, it must have been a relief to Pilsudski when, as a result of the elections of November 1930, his followers, organized as a Non-Party Union, captured 249 of the 444 seats in the Seym and 75 of the 111 seats in the Senate. In 1933 the National Assembly reëlected Pilsudski's friend, President Mościcki, for another seven-year term.

In 1934 the government submitted to the Seym a new constitution that differed somewhat from the draft of 1929. The opposition leaders declared that the old constitution of 1921 could be supplanted only with the consent of two-thirds majorities in both houses. The ministry maintained that ordinary action by the lower house was sufficient. Thereupon the opposition withdrew from the hall and the government bloc rushed the measure through the required three readings in a single sitting. After some changes were made in deference to the wishes of the Senate, the new constitution was promulgated in 1935.

As supplemented by a later electoral law, the document put an end to parliamentary democracy in Poland. Henceforth there were to be only 208 deputies in the Seym, two for each of 104 electoral constituencies. The candidates were to be nominated by local councils, chambers of commerce, and other corporate bodies and approved by special electoral boards. The deputies were to be elected for five years by the vote of citizens over twenty-four. The Senate was to consist of ninety-six members, one-third appointed by the president and two-thirds elected by citizens over thirty who had been decorated for military or civil service or occupied high military, political, legal, trade, or educational posts. The Senate was given equal rights with the Seym except in the initiation of bills.

The president was made largely independent of parliament and was given a suspensive-veto power. He was empowered to appoint or dismiss ministers and summon or dismiss the Seym and Senate at his discretion. In future the president was to be chosen for seven-year terms as follows: the existing chief executive *might,* and an assembly of electors, largely designated by the parliament from its own membership, *must,* nominate a candidate. In the event that two individuals were thus selected, a popular vote would be re-

[1] Special favors were bestowed on the rank and file of the army and in 1931 Pilsudski exempted the soldiers from a general wage cut for government employees.

quired to choose between them. If the retiring president failed to nominate a candidate and order a general election, then the candidate of the assembly of electors was to be recognized as the new president.

Thus did Pilsudski arrange for a continuance of the "constitutional dictatorship" even after his own strong hand should have been withdrawn from the control of affairs. For by this time the marshal's health was rapidly failing and he had found it necessary to take frequent vacations in Egypt and other countries where the climate was more favorable to him than in Poland. On the ninth anniversary of his attack on Warsaw, Marshal Pilsudski died (1935).

Early in 1937 it appeared that Poland might join the group of totalitarian states. President Mościcki recognized Marshal Edward Śmigly-Rydz, friend and comrade-in-arms of Pilsudski, as "leader of the nation." About the same time Colonel Adam Koc reorganized the government party into a "Camp of National Unity." Ignace Paderewski thereupon issued a warning against the trend towards authoritarianism and in November 1937 several delegations from liberal and labor groups petitioned the president for a more liberal electoral law than that of 1935 and requested him to resist the menace of fascism.[1]

During 1938 President Mościcki, General Stanislas Skwarzyński, and other older friends of the late Marshal Pilsudski brought about the expulsion of certain fascist, anti-Semitic elements from the Camp of National Unity, including Colonel Koc himself. Believing that neither democracy nor totalitarianism would suit Poland's national genius, they hoped to lead her to a "lawful and disciplined democracy." Hence, in the parliamentary elections of 1938, the candidates—representing districts rather than parties— were nearly all government supporters. But before another year had passed, Poland had disappeared from the map as an independent state.

c. Financial and Economic Affairs

Poland, like so many of her neighbors, suffered in the postwar years from financial inflation and economic instability. The ravages of the war and of prolonged hostilities with Russia, a series of bad crops, an unsettled agrarian situation, and several knotty minorities problems constituted a grave threat to the republic. Even-

---

[1] Under the constitution of 1935 political parties as such could not be represented in the Polish Parliament, but they continued to exist outside parliament.

tually the crisis spurred the Seym to definite action and in 1923 a coalition cabinet of experts was appointed, headed by Premier and Finance Minister Ladislav Grabski. This government, which was entrusted with emergency powers to stabilize the finances, remained in office until late 1925.

Grabski energetically proceeded to check the continued depreciation of the Polish mark. He introduced economy into a number of government departments, reduced the state railway subsidies, advanced the tax rates, and imposed additional levies. Then he repudiated most of the national debt, set up a new Bank of Poland, and declared a temporary halt on the further issue of paper money. But to the disappointment of the finance minister, these reforms ended in failure. They seemed to be too drastic and bore too heavily on the people as a whole. The harvest of 1924 was so bad that large quantities of foodstuffs had to be imported and the cost of living rose. About the same time, in consequence of a minorities dispute, German purchases of Polish-Silesian coal came to a stop, while in 1925 a tariff war ensued with Germany after the failure of negotiations for a commercial treaty.[1] The funding of Poland's debts to the United States and Great Britain and the successful floating of another American loan offered only temporary relief. Premier Grabski resigned, but neither of his two immediate successors, Alexander Skrzynski and Witos, was able to create financial stability.

When the new currency unit, the zloty, fell to one-half of its par value, the Skrzynski Government invited Professor Edwin W. Kemmerer of Princeton University to study financial conditions in Poland and make recommendations for their improvement. This invitation was confirmed by the Pilsudski dictatorship which came into being in May 1926. The Kemmerer Commission made a number of sweeping recommendations, many of which were adopted in 1926 by the Polish Government.

The application of sounder monetary principles, the harvest of a good crop in 1926, and an increased foreign demand for Polish coal because of the British coal strike in the same year bade fair to inaugurate a period of economic prosperity. A foreign stabilization loan was obtained in 1927 and at the same time Charles S. Dewey, assistant secretary of the treasury of the United States, was engaged as financial adviser, with a seat on the board of directors of the Bank of Poland. During the next five years the Pilsudski

---

[1] The tariff war was concluded in 1934. Meanwhile German-Polish trade had dwindled from $300,000,000 in 1924 to $43,000,000 in 1933.

regime succeeded in keeping the zloty stable and in balancing the annual budgets. When Dewey resigned his office in 1930, Poland seemed well on the road to financial equilibrium.

The economic depression which affected the world after 1930 naturally made itself felt in Poland, particularly when the price of grain declined to a record low point for the twentieth century. By the strictest curtailment of expenditures the budget was balanced through the fiscal year 1931–1932 without recourse to inflation. The per capita wealth of Poland at this time was about one-third of the per capita wealth of France. But from the fiscal year 1932–1933 on, the official expenditures again exceeded the revenues, and by the end of 1934 the number of unemployed totaled 300,000.

Almost as pressing as the financial question in Poland was the agrarian situation. The socialists and the radical peasants, influenced by the example of Russia, favored the breaking up of all the large estates and the redistribution of the land on a wider basis. The peasants of Galicia and of former Russian Poland, in particular, clamored for more land to support their families. Furthermore, restrictive immigration acts in the United States and Germany added to the misery of the constantly increasing landless proletariat.

The conflicting interests of the estate owners and the agrarian radicals, and the fairly even influence of Right and Left in the parliament, held up for six years the application of remedial measures. An agrarian reform law of 1920 was never seriously put into effect, and in 1923 the presentation of another land measure led to the downfall of a cabinet. At last, in December 1925, an act was passed which provided for the gradual parceling of large estates at the rate of 200,000 hectares (494,200 acres) annually for ten years. It was provided that expropriation by the state should occur only as a last resort in the event that voluntary parceling fell behind the required minimum. Payment for the land should be made partly in cash and partly in bonds. Although neither extremist group was satisfied with the law, to which more than six hundred amendments were offered, it did prove to be a working compromise on the basis of which further legislation might eventually be enacted.

When the effects of the great depression made themselves felt in Poland, the government passed a number of agrarian relief measures. A law of 1932 lowered the interest rates on certain forms of land mortgages. In 1933 the short-term credits of farmers were extended to three years.[1] A presidential decree of 1934 enabled the peasants to convert their short-term indebtedness into fifty-year bonds bearing $4\frac{1}{2}$ per cent interest. Creditors were required to accept these conversions at par. Since more than 60 per cent of the population was directly dependent upon agriculture, these measures were of national importance.

In the course of years new railways were built and old ones improved, virtually all the arable land of the country was placed under cultivation, thousands of new houses were built, and production as a whole increased rapidly. Even so, the standard of living remained relatively low and 1936 witnessed clashes between government forces and some of the debt-burdened, land-poor peasants. The lack of markets proved to be one of the republic's chief handicaps. This difficulty was accentuated by the prevailing fashion of high tariffs and by the great depression. The strenuous efforts of the government to build up manufacturing industries were greatly hampered by the shortage of working capital. And the authorities dealt harshly with any radical labor movements, for Poland's geographic proximity to the Soviet Union made such developments seem doubly dangerous.

d. The Minorities

Since fewer than three-fourths of the inhabitants of Poland in 1919 were of Polish nationality, the Supreme Peace Council at Paris required the republic to sign a minorities treaty guaranteeing equality of civil and political rights to all citizens, whether or not they belonged to the majority group.[2] Minority nationals who lived within the borders of Poland were to be given the choice of becoming Polish citizens or leaving the country, and in no case might such persons be deprived of property or the free exercise of their religion. The right of minorities was guaranteed to establish schools and receive a fair share of state support for these schools wherever the minority formed a "considerable portion" of the population. There were to be no restrictions on the use of minority tongues in business, law courts, public meetings, and religious services. Appeal might be made to the League Council whenever any of these privileges was violated.

The largest minority group in Poland was the block of Ruthe-

[1] "Short term credits are [1932] granted for varying lengths of time, ranging from three months to a year. The interest is 12 per cent." Morgan, O. S., ed. *Agricultural Systems of Europe; A Symposium*, 1933, p. 269.

[2] The population of Poland in 1919 was 27,000,000; in 1937, about 34,000,000.

nians or Ukrainians in the east and south, who formed, according
to Polish figures, one-seventh of the total population. The Jews,
scattered throughout the land, came next with one-twelfth of the
total and the Germans were third with about one-twenty-fifth.
Between 1920 and 1924 the position of minorities was particularly
hazardous and there was considerable, albeit unsuccessful, agitation among nationalistic Poles to denounce the minorities treaty.

Although a law of 1922 granted a measure of local autonomy to
eastern Galicia, the Ruthenians complained bitterly of Poland's
governmental policies. "The lack of consistent administration,
. . . the endeavor to colonize the Polish soldiery on the expropriated lands in preference to the local peasantry, the flooding of
the region with new, inexperienced, and inefficient administrators," all seemed to bear witness to an attempt at the enforced
Polonization of the eastern provinces. In 1924 the situation became so bad that the Soviet Government protested to Warsaw and
brought the matter to the notice of the world. Moscow claimed a
direct interest in the treatment of these people because of the large
number of Ukrainians in the Soviet Union.

Though Poland replied defiantly to the Soviet notes, Premier
Grabski secured the passage of three laws concerning the use of
minority languages in administrative offices, courts, and schools.
Polish was confirmed as the state language, but the parallel use of
Ukrainian, Lithuanian, and White Russian was permitted in the
conduct of official and judicial business. Private schools giving instruction through the medium of any one of these languages were
to be tolerated, and, wherever the parents of forty children, in a
region containing a non-Polish minority of at least 25 per cent, so
requested, the state schools were to provide instruction in the
minority tongue. Instruction in the Polish language in history and
geography remained compulsory.

Political opposition for a time deferred the application of these
laws, but, even when they were enforced, relations among the several national groups remained inharmonious. The Ruthenians
continued to complain of mistreatment and some of them formed
a Ukrainian Military Organization to fight for the creation of an
independent Ukrainian state. The Polish Government accused
the association of sabotage and took severe repressive measures.
In 1930 the laments of the minority reached the ears of the League
Council, which remitted them to a committee for consideration.

While the committee investigated conflicting reports, the situation in Poland became aggravated. The Ukrainian peasants more

and more frequently engaged in such antistate activities as the nonpayment of taxes, and the government dispatched soldiers to arrest the leaders of the movement and compel obedience to the laws. In 1932 the authorities dissolved the Ukrainian Radical Party on the ground that it was communistic and anti-Polish. The persistent unrest caused the League Committee to request several extensions of time, but in the end it upheld the policy of the government.

Late in 1935 the government and the Ukrainian leaders arrived at a "gentlemen's agreement" wherein the minority was promised greater consideration for its demands, but before long a specially called Ukrainian Congress expressed dissatisfaction with the operation of the compromise. The authorities, on the other hand, placed responsibility for several political murders on Ukrainian nationalists. The matter threatened to become serious in 1938 when Germany, Hungary, and Poland expanded their possessions on the ground that Czechoslovakia had been unjustly ruling *its* minorities; but no overt act took place. And in 1939 the Soviet Union, as we shall see, occupied that part of Poland which had been inhabited by the Ukrainians.

Similarly disturbing had been the Jewish question in Poland. The Jews for some years after the war were subjected to bitter persecution. They were accused of being either pro-German or pro-Bolshevik, of lacking Polish patriotism, of refusing to conform their lives to the standards of the nation, and of valuing profits above the national welfare. They were the frequent victims of assault and murder, and they did not even derive benefit from the language laws of 1924. So serious were the rumors which spread abroad concerning the mistreatment of Jews that two foreign missions, one British and the other American, were sent to Poland to investigate. At length, in 1925, the Polish authorities and the Jews came to a conciliatory agreement known as the Declaration of Warsaw.

By the terms of this settlement the Jews, through their political representatives, promised to recognize their duties and obligations to the Polish State and confine any opposition tactics to the regular parliamentary and constitutional channels. In return, the authorities undertook to pay more attention to the educational and economic interests of the Jewry. Laws were enacted granting the Jews the same linguistic and religious rights as the other minorities, permitting them to keep their shops open on Sundays instead of Saturdays, and reducing certain special taxes on small business which had affected mainly Jewish storekeepers. It was also agreed that no elections should be held on Saturdays so that Orthodox Jews might not be deprived of their right of franchise.

These laws temporarily improved the situation of the Jews, but the effects of the great depression and the anti-Semitic excesses of the Nazis in Germany after 1933 led to a revival of the latent anti-Jewish attitudes. The number of violent attacks on Jews increased from year to year. In 1937 the country's Jewry engaged in a two-hour protest strike, but this only led to more rather than fewer assaults. The government strove to check the excesses, sent many of the most active agitators to concentration camps, and steadfastly refused to pass any new anti-Jewish laws. But by 1939 it was widely recommended in Poland that all Jews be settled in Palestine or in the French colonies.

The German minority problem involved two quarrels. There was, first, the question of the small tenant farmers who with the aid of the Hohenzollern Government had colonized Prussian Poland. After the war the Poles attempted to evict these colonists, who held the land under special contracts from the German Government, without compensation. Germany took up the case of her nationals and appealed to the League Council. Poland denied the competency of this body and the dispute was placed before the World Court. The latter upheld the jurisdiction of the Council and handed down an advisory opinion to the effect that Poland must respect the private rights of the German nationals. In consequence the Warsaw Government eventually agreed to compensate the evicted Germans.

The second difficulty concerned the status of the Germans in industrial Upper Silesia. Here the minority protested against Polish mistreatment and unfair discrimination, particularly in the matter of educational opportunities. A *Volksbund* was organized to agitate for better conditions and the sympathy of the Reich was solicited. It was alleged that, despite a German-Polish Agreement of 1922, the Poles exerted every form of pressure from censorship to terrorism to intimidate the German minority. Berlin several times brought the Silesian troubles to the attention of the League but got little satisfaction. In 1937 the German and Polish governments exchanged mutual guarantees of cultural and religious autonomy for their respective minorities, but the whole dispute really involved the broader problem of a general revision of Germany's eastern frontiers and as such was ever a threat to peace in Europe.

e. Danzig and the Polish Corridor

The Paris Peace Conference provided for the conversion of the German port of Danzig into a free city which should be under the economic authority of Poland and the general supervision of the League. Although nearly all the inhabitants of the city at the time were Germans, it was decided that such an arrangement would best solve the problem of giving Poland access to the sea and a means of establishing commercial contacts with western Europe. In accordance with these aims the League required the people of Danzig to draw up a constitution and reach an agreement with Poland regarding their future relationship with that republic. A Polish-Danzig Agreement was reached in November 1920 and the Danzig constitution received the final approval of the League Council in 1922.[1]

Under the terms of the agreement, the constitution, and a supplementary Polish-Danzig Treaty of 1921, Danzig was to be governed by a *Volkstag* (People's Diet) and a Senate, with executive power in the hands of a high commissioner appointed by the League. The high commissioner was to act as a court of the first instance in disputes between Danzig and Poland, both areas having the right of appeal to the League Council. Poland was made responsible for the foreign relations of the free city and was given supervision over its commercial customs. The port was never to be used as a military or naval base without the previous consent of the League. A customs union was established between the two areas and a harbor board, consisting of five Poles, five Danzigers, and a neutral president, was to administer the port and watch over the rights of both parties. In short, Poland would control the economic and diplomatic life of the free city, while the inhabitants would enjoy political autonomy.

It need hardly be pointed out that relations between Danzig and Poland were strained. During the first five years of the existence of the free city, the League Commissioner handed down almost fifty decisions. Until December 1927 "there was hardly any session of the [League] Council at which Danzig affairs did not appear on the agenda," and even the World Court was called upon to settle disputes. The difficulty of drawing a line between economic and political matters and the traditional hatred between the two peoples made the situation one of great danger. Moreover,

[1] The area of the free city was 754 square miles; its inhabitants, according to the census of 1929, numbered 400,000, of whom almost 96 per cent were German.

the Danzigers looked with fear upon the rival port-building project inaugurated by Poland at Gdynia.

In order to diminish the dependence of Polish merchants and shippers upon the harbor facilities at Danzig, the Warsaw authorities, with the aid of a French syndicate, pushed the development of Gdynia, a few miles west and north of Danzig. In 1920

Gdynia was a bleak region of sand dunes. A few fishermen's huts comprised its residential area. Today [1934] Gdynia is a city of more than 50,000 inhabitants. . . . In 1924, . . . 24 ships with a total weight of 14,000 tons entered the port. In 1930, 2200 ships weighing 2,000,000 tons loaded and unloaded cargoes which moved in and out of the new warehouses, the second largest refrigerating plant in the world which can accommodate a whole train of cars at a time, and along the miles of mostly cement docks. The coal transshipment equipment has a capacity of 450 tons per hour. In 1933, 7200 ships with a tonnage of 5,670,000 and representing 23 countries docked at this Polish port. Thirty-eight regular shipping lines now call at Gdynia.[1]

Naturally the Danzigers worried over this enterprise which deflected more and more of their chief business, shipping, to the neighboring city. Although Warsaw pointed out that Danzig's volume of trade consistently exceeded the prewar figures, the Danzigers with equal truth indicated that by 1933 Gdynia's trading volume had surpassed that of the free city.

The Germans in the Reich frequently expressed sympathy with the Danzigers, and the Hitlerites in particular declared their determination eventually to right what they called a glaring wrong of the Versailles Treaty. When the Nazis finally came to power in Germany, there was fear in Poland regarding future German official policy. This was increased when, as a result of the elections of May 1933, the Danzig Nazis gained control of the free city's Volkstag and Senate. The newly chosen Nazi president of the upper house, Dr. Hermann Rauschning, advocated a policy of conciliation with Poland and himself paid a visit to Warsaw. In August two agreements were signed wherein Poland promised Danzig more freight traffic and Danzig agreed to the establishment of special schools for the children of Polish residents. Later it was specifically provided that Danzig would get 45 per cent of Poland's seaborne foreign traffic while the remaining 55 per cent would pass

[1] Douglass, P. F. *The Economic Independence of Poland*, 1934, p. 7 n. Reprinted by permission of the author.

through the port of Gdynia. The task of enforcing the convention was placed in the hands of a mixed commission of Danzigers and Poles. During 1934 Polish-Danzig affairs continued to reflect a general improvement in Polish-German relations. Rauschning's retirement late in 1934, however, and his replacement by a more militant Nazi once more clouded the outlook.

West and south of Danzig was a stretch of territory 260 miles long and ranging in width up to 80 miles, which formerly comprised in part the provinces of West Prussia and Posen. Through it flowed the Vistula River, long one of the main arteries of commerce in east-central Europe. Under the terms of the Versailles Treaty this land was assigned to Poland, with a consequent division of Germany into two unconnected sections: Germany proper, extending eastward as far as Pomerania, and East Prussia. The transfer of territory was justified by the Allies on the ground that "the interests which Germans in East Prussia, who number fewer than two millions, have in establishing a land connection with Germany, are less vital than the interests of the whole Polish nation in securing direct access to the sea."

Through the creation of this "Polish Corridor" Poland became an economic unit. Germany was weakened from both the economic and military viewpoints and found it harder to exert her influence in the Baltic region. Particularly difficult was the fate of East Prussia, which no longer had a free market in the area of the corridor for its timber, cattle, and horses.[1] Eventually an agreement was reached between Berlin and Warsaw whereby Germany was granted freedom of transit for passengers and freight through the corridor to and from East Prussia. The arrangement, however, was not satisfactory. Germans who desired to cross the area without passports and without the bother of submitting their belongings to customs inspection had to travel in "sealed" cars. Often these cars were highly uncomfortable.

A further grievance of the Germans in the Reich was the belief that the Poles were mistreating the German minority in the corridor. The exact ratio of Germans to Poles in the region in 1918 was never determined, but the latter soon came to comprise a large majority of the inhabitants. The Warsaw Government induced many Germans to leave and encouraged the colonization of the land by Polish settlers. In 1934 the resident Germans numbered perhaps one hundred thousand.

[1] "The economic prosperity of Eastern Prussia is dependent chiefly on the Polish Hinterland. . . ." Smogorzewski, C. Poland, Germany, and the Corridor, 1930, p. 70.

The question of the Polish Corridor therefore was one of the prime factors in the mutual ill will manifested by Germany and Poland. A commercial treaty between the two powers was held up for nine years because of disputes over the corridor and the minority difficulties. In 1925, at Locarno, Germany refused to subscribe to a guarantee of her Polish frontiers. Thereafter official reference often was made to the urgent need for a revision of the eastern boundaries. Poland's claim, however, that her economic life depended upon the retention of the corridor, was consistently supported by France. A ten-year nonaggression pact signed by Germany and Poland in 1934 did much to ease the tension in this troubled area of the world, but conditions remained sufficiently upset so that H. G. Wells, writing in 1933, could prophesy that the next great war would begin over the Polish Corridor in 1940. He was wrong only in setting the date a few months late.[1]

f. Vilnius: Another Boundary Dispute

In medieval times Vilnius (Wilno) was the capital of the grand duchy of Lithuania. Later, when Lithuania and Poland became united, Vilnius gradually came under the cultural and economic domination of the Poles. After the first three partitions of Poland, the district remained under Russian control for about 125 years.

Following the Bolshevik Revolution of 1917, the Lithuanians declared their independence and attempted to set up a government at Vilnius. Fighting ensued and Bolshevik troops captured the city, only to be dislodged in turn by a Polish army. Meanwhile, since the Paris Conference had not drawn a Polish-Lithuanian boundary, the Allied Supreme Council laid down the so-called Curzon Line (1919) as a provisional frontier and assigned the city and most of the province of Vilnius to Lithuania. Poland, still engaged in her war with Russia, accepted this as a temporary disposition. By the Treaty of Moscow (1920), Russia definitely ceded Vilnius to Lithuania.

When the Russo-Polish War came to a close, the Poles claimed Vilnius on the ground of conquest and an armed clash with Lithuania resulted. The League Council dispatched a military commission to the scene to end the fighting and in October 1920 the two governments were induced to sign the Agreement of Suwalki whereby the Curzon Line, in slightly revised form, was again accepted as a provisional boundary and Vilnius was once more assigned to Lithuania.

[1] Wells, H. G. *The Shape of Things to Come*, 1933.

On October 9, the day before this agreement was to come into force, General Lucien Zeligowski, a Polish freebooter who led several thousand irregular troops, occupied the city. Although the Warsaw Government disclaimed responsibility for the act,[1] the general was hailed as a hero in Poland. Lithuania appealed to the League and that body for a time toyed with the idea of a plebiscite. Eventually, however, the Council recommended direct negotiations between the disputing powers. When these failed of result, the Conference of Ambassadors, in 1923, laid down another boundary—allotting Vilnius to Poland.

Lithuania refused to recognize this disposition of her historic capital and the technical "state of war" which had existed between her and Poland since October 1920 now continued until the end of 1927. In December 1927 the League Council was again forced to take note of the situation when Lithuania complained that her nationals in the Vilnius district were being mistreated, and Poland complained that the same was true of the Poles in Lithuania. Marshal Pilsudski and the Lithuanian Premier were requested to come to Geneva and there an agreement was reached whereby Lithuania consented to end the state of war and Poland promised to respect the complete independence and territorial integrity of Lithuania. The question of Vilnius, however, was not yet settled, so far as Lithuania was concerned. In May 1928 the Lithuanian Government promulgated a new constitution which designated Vilnius as the capital of the country, although the actual business of government was being carried on from Kaunas (Kovno). This action drew a rebuke from the League Council and the Vilnius controversy remained a disturbing factor in European politics until 1938. Then, during the international crisis accompanying the forceful German absorption of Austria, Poland was able to induce Lithuania to restore normal diplomatic relations and give up, at least temporarily, the campaign to reincorporate Vilnius. In October 1939, however, after the Nazi-Soviet partition of Poland, the U.S.S.R. once more ceded the ten thousand square miles of disputed territory to Lithuania.

g. Foreign Affairs

The external relations of Poland were shaped largely by her geographical propinquity to a number of unfriendly powers. To the east there was the Soviet Union; to the north, Lithuania and

[1] Cf. Machray, R. *Poland, 1914–1931*, p. 170: "Pilsudski disavowed its paternity at the time, but confessed to it later."

East Prussia; to the west, Germany. Poland, accordingly, placed her chief hopes for security upon military alliances and arbitration agreements. In 1921 alliances were formed with Romania and France and a treaty of neutrality was signed with Czechoslovakia. In 1922 friendly relations were established with the Little Entente. Three years later arbitration treaties were negotiated with Finland, Latvia, Estonia, Czechoslovakia, and Austria; the alliance with Romania was renewed; a pact of friendship was drawn up with Yugoslavia; the Locarno Agreements were accepted; and a concordat was signed with the Holy See. In 1929 Poland, the Soviet Union, Estonia, Latvia, and Romania agreed to the Litvinov Protocol whereby the Kellogg Pact became immediately effective among the signatories. In 1931 Poland reached a nonaggression accord with the Soviet Union and the alliances with France and Romania were renewed.

Several efforts were made under Polish auspices to create a Baltic Union, comprised of Poland, Latvia, Estonia, Finland, and possibly Lithuania. There were obvious political and economic advantages to such a confederation, but little actual progress was made in its direction. Moscow was opposed to any plan which might create a Polish hegemony in the Baltic; Lithuania harbored no friendship for Poland; and Finland leaned increasingly towards a Scandinavian rather than a Baltic orientation.

During 1933, however, it appeared that Poland was gradually drawing away from France and seeking closer relations with Germany and the Soviet Union. The Poles were no longer content to have their republic regarded as a satellite of France. For a time Warsaw seemed to hesitate between accepting the friendship of Berlin or of Moscow, but in the end amicable arrangements were made with both parties. A ten-year nonaggression pact was concluded with Berlin in January 1934, providing for the peaceful settlement of disputes and the creation of a "propaganda alliance" under which each government would seek to enlighten its people on the advantages of the *rapprochement*. The Bolsheviks looked upon this agreement with suspicion, but soon an earlier Polish-Soviet nonaggression accord was renewed until 1945. This new orientation of Polish foreign policy aroused considerable opposition in the Seym lest it lead to a loss of French protection and ultimate diplomatic isolation. But the foreign minister, Colonel Joseph Beck, discounted such fears.

For a time, indeed, it appeared as though Hitler and Beck would bring about a genuine improvement in German-Polish relations.

In October 1938 Poland, owing largely to Germany's aggressive actions, was enabled to enlarge her territory and population at the expense of Czechoslovakia. Warsaw's wish to achieve a common boundary with Hungary was fulfilled in March 1939, through the latter's annexation of Ruthenia. Meanwhile, in January 1939, during a visit to Warsaw by Nazi Foreign Minister Joachim von Ribbentrop, the spirit of the German-Polish agreement of 1934 had been called to mind through cordial speeches and friendly handclasps. But before the year was out, Nazi boots pounded on Polish soil in the opening stages of the Second World War.

CHAPTER XIX

The Soviet Union

THE OLD REGIME

Nicholas II, from 1894 to 1917 "Emperor and Autocrat of all the Russias," ruled over an empire that comprised almost one-sixth of the land surface of the globe. His lands, 8,764,000 square miles in all, stretched eastward from central Europe to the Pacific Ocean, and southward from the icy Arctic to the Black and Caspian seas, the Caucasus, Persia, and China. The inhabitants of this vast area numbered perhaps 180,000,000, slightly fewer than half of whom were Russians proper, or Great Russians. The remainder consisted of Little Russians or Ukrainians, White Russians, Poles, Finns, Letts, Turks, Mongols, Armenians, Jews, and many others. The cultures of these various peoples differed greatly, ranging from the advanced civilization of the European-Russian nobility and intelligentsia to the semibarbarous life of the Siberian aborigines.

Among every 1000 Russians subject to the rule of the emperor in 1914, there were 17 nobles, 125 merchants and townspeople, and more than 800 peasants. Until 1860 these last, with some exceptions, had been serfs, living under feudal restrictions on government or privately owned estates. Then Tsar Alexander II, by a series of decrees, abolished serfdom and prescribed a redistribution of the land. In accordance with his orders about half of the cultivated area of European Russia was assigned to the villages or *mirs,* each peasant being given the right to till, on his own account, a share of the soil belonging to the community. The government advanced the money to compensate the nobles for the resulting property losses, but the people were expected to reimburse the state over a term of years.

Aside from certain obvious benefits accruing from the grant of personal freedom, there remained many troubles to sadden the lot of the average Russian peasant. Often the freed serfs were unable to support themselves and their families on the farm allotments received from the mir. This difficulty became worse with the passing of years, for the increase in available allotment lands failed to keep pace with the rise in peasant population. An unduly large portion of each year's income was absorbed by remittances to the government for the land, by heavy direct taxes imposed by the village, the province, and the state, and by burdensome indirect levies. There was little incentive for the peasants to improve their holdings since the mirs, in a majority of cases, periodically redistributed the plots. The regulations of the village authorities were often strict, and peasants generally were not allowed to leave the village and migrate to the city without the approval of the mir.

These evils were somewhat mitigated by decrees issued after the revolutionary outbursts of 1905. The edicts, among other things, remitted the unpaid redemption dues of the peasants, reduced the power of the mirs over their members, and gave each villager the right to demand outright his share of land held by the community. As direct owner of the property, then, the peasant, as he saw fit, might use, lease, or sell his holding.

To some of the more enterprising countrymen these new opportunities had great appeal and they hastened to avail themselves of the right to become independent owners. Many of the peasants, who were "by taste and tradition petty cultivators, ready and eager to buy land, to rent it, sometimes even to rise up and seize it," soon began to crowd one another "for the opportunity to rent lands at a figure which did not leave them, in return for their labor, as much as they might have earned by working for wages on a neighboring estate." Some were unable "to maintain their holdings under the more individualistic system and sold them to their neighbors, becoming agricultural laborers themselves or going into the cities in search of work." Hence conditions failed to improve sufficiently to create a satisfied peasantry. The year 1914 still found millions of farming households living in poverty and greedy for additional land.

The plight of Russia's 2,500,000 industrial workers was similarly deplorable. They suffered from all the ills usually associated with the beginnings of industrial revolutions and were prevented by an unenlightened government from giving expression to their grievances. Some of their unions were broken up, strikes were suppressed, and there was relatively little social legislation. As a consequence, the industrial proletariat listened eagerly to apostles of reform, and, since the workers were herded together in factories and slums, it was easy to agitate among them and reach them with propaganda. During the Revolution of 1905 the workingmen had demonstrated their temper by strikes and riots in St. Petersburg, Moscow, and other cities, and by 1914 they seemed ready for another violent outbreak.

The percentage of illiteracy among the Russian peasants and workers was one of the highest in Europe, and the bane of the population was its thralldom to vodka, a strong alcoholic drink made from rye, or sometimes from barley or potatoes. The sale of the liquor had been made a state monopoly in order to raise revenue and lessen the evils attendant upon the private dispensation of spirits, but drunkenness remained a widespread curse. The masses, on the whole, were coarse, and they feared and hated the upper classes. The state-controlled Orthodox Church wielded considerable influence over the peasantry, but it was one of the most loyal supporters of the tsarist regime and did little to raise the people from their low cultural level.

Political conditions in the empire were unstable. The censorship was notorious and the police administration ruthless. Nicholas II was ill suited to the exercise of autocratic powers over a vast domain. Though well-intentioned and patriotic, he was timid and easily swayed by the arguments of whatever person happened to be with him at any particular moment. He was especially dominated by the Tsarina Alexandra, who herself was under the influence of a Siberian "monk" named Gregory Rasputin. The latter's origins and life are shrouded in legend and obscurity, but he appears to have had hypnotic powers. He acquired his control over the empress because he alone seemed able to soothe the hemophilic and cranky young Tsarevich Alexis. It was said that a word from Rasputin was sufficient to bring about the appointment or dismissal of a minister or general, and his authority apparently was not always wielded for the good of the nation. The whole situation was ominous, especially since the autocracy, in order to be maintained, required firm leadership. It could not endure under the guidance of a weak-willed imperial family and an illiterate adventurer.

As a result of the uprising of 1905, Nicholas had granted his people a parliament, or *Duma,* with limited powers. The electoral law rendered certain a conservative majority in this Duma and the government had little trouble in continuing its traditional policies. In 1914 the entire parliament, with the exception of five deputies, upheld the course of the administration in its decision to go to war.

The dissenting legislators, who were sent to Siberia, belonged to an organization which called itself the Bolshevik faction of the Social Democratic Party.[1]

Despite the achievement of some military victories in the first weeks of the war, it soon was evident that Russia would experience difficulty in any extended prosecution of the conflict. The country was ill prepared for war. There was a lack of factories and a consequent shortage of equipment; adequate transportation facilities were wanting; the generalship was poor and the empress and civil nobility interfered in military matters; corruption was rife in government departments; and there were rumors of treason in high ranks. Hence the German armies before long were able to inflict a series of disastrous defeats upon the Russians, which further weakened the morale and disorganized the industrial structure of the land.

In the first three years of the struggle the tsar called out fifteen million men—far more than could be suitably equipped and fed. Millions of hands thus were withdrawn from the fields, where they should have been engaged in planting and harvesting, and millions of men had to be fed at public expense. Since the soldiers' rations in many cases exceeded the average consumption of the individual peasants in peacetime, food was required in greater quantities than during normal periods. In addition, the government paid allowances to the families of soldiers.

The railway system was incapable of handling the wartime traffic. The empire in 1914 had only forty thousand miles of railway track—one-sixth as many as the United States, for an area almost three times as great. It was impossible expeditiously to forward supplies to the front, particularly where there was need for

[1] The "radical" groups in pre-1914 Russia were the Constitutional Democrats or Cadets, made up of middle-class intellectuals and business men who favored responsible government of the British type; the Social Revolutionaries, chiefly peasants, led by middle-class reformers, whose aim was the transfer of the land to the peasantry and who resorted to terrorism in their effort to bring about socialization and collectivization of agriculture; and the Social Democratic Party which found its main strength among the industrial workers and which advocated the abolition of private property and the control of production by the masses.

At a meeting of Social Democrats in London in 1903, opinion was divided on the questions of party discipline, organization, and coöperation with nonproletarian revolutionary factions. One group, led by Lenin, favored strict discipline, a centralized organization, and independence from bourgeois support. The other preferred a looser party organization and the admission of nonproletarian "sympathizers." A vote was taken on these two sets of views and the majority indicated a preference for the Leninist ideas. The partisans of the latter soon came to be known as *bolsheviki* from *bolshinstvo*, meaning "majority," while the others were called *mensheviki* from *menshinstvo*, meaning "minority."

north-south shipments. Rumors of terrible conditions among the fighting men and of the enormous casualties gradually leaked back from the lines, while woeful tales of hunger and misery at home filtered out to the trenches.

The pressure of wartime demands for goods and the success of many of the strikes which occurred in the cities made prices soar. Governmental expenditures were four times as high in 1916 as in an average prewar year, and, although much of the extra outlay was financed through Allied loans, taxes had to be boosted and resort was had to inflation, with the result that prices were stimulated to further rises. At the same time, in order to facilitate mobilization, the government instituted prohibition, thus depriving itself of income from vodka sales.

The bad conditions notwithstanding, little heed was paid by the authorities to the numerous demands for a more liberal policy and for ministerial responsibility. The officials strove to discourage voluntary popular movements, even where these were motivated by a desire to aid the cause of the war. The minister of the interior, Alexander Protopopov, once rejected the offer of a provincial council to provide certain comforts for the troops on the ground that "any form of voluntary coöperation by the Russian people tended towards revolution." Thus the groups in control simultaneously betrayed their fear of the lower classes and maintained an uncompromising attitude. Nicholas himself wavered and hesitated, undecided on any course of action, and glad to have things remain *in statu quo*. The assassination of Rasputin in December 1916 by a group of aristocratic conspirators did little to help the situation.

The first definite indication of the doom of the old regime in Russia was a general strike in Petrograd in February 1917. The walkout, though unorganized and unplanned, led to huge street demonstrations by the proletariat, which was weary of the war, the defeats, the privations, and the high prices. The city garrison, when ordered to disperse the crowds, refused to fire on the demonstrators and fraternized with the people. Had the tsar quickly called in troops from outside the city to suppress both the mobs and the Duma, which also was displaying a restive spirit, or had he agreed to the demands of the liberals for a new cabinet and responsible government, he might have averted, or at least postponed, the approaching crisis. Nicholas, however, could not act with decision. Unwilling to grant concessions, too irresolute to take swift action, he temporized and did nothing.

THE TWO REVOLUTIONS OF 1917

The vacillation of the ruler goaded liberal-minded men both within and outside the Duma into a revolutionary stand and supplied the more radical agitators with propaganda material. Early in March 1917 there were mob attacks in the larger cities and some peasant riots, while accusations of treachery were hurled against the government from the floor of parliament. The tsar ordered the members of the Duma to go home and the workingmen in Petrograd to cease striking and return to work. These imperial decrees precipitated the revolution.

The legislative chamber refused to disperse. Instead, it elected a committee to lead a revolution against the decadent autocracy. Simultaneously the radical elements outside the Duma organized a Petrograd Soviet (Council) of Workers' and Soldiers' Deputies which invited all factory and army units to send delegates to its deliberations. The Duma committee and the soviet agreed to cooperate, at least temporarily, and on March 14 a provisional government, headed by Prince Lvov, came into being. The cabinet included a majority of Constitutional Democrats. Its most radical member was the Social Revolutionary, Alexander Kerensky, spokesman of the soviet and vice-president of its executive committee.

On March 15 Tsar Nicholas recognized the new government and then abdicated in favor of his brother, Grand Duke Michael. The latter refused to accept the crown until an assembly, chosen by universal, direct, secret suffrage should have decided upon the future form of government for the realm. Six days later Nicholas and his immediate family became prisoners in the imperial palace near Petrograd. Thus the rule of the Romanovs, founded in 1613, came to an abrupt end.

The provisional government immediately issued decrees easing the press censorship, freeing political and religious prisoners, recognizing the right of workmen to unionize and strike, and humanizing the disciplinary codes in the army and the navy. Most of the civil and military officials in Russia agreed to serve under the new government, since the tsar himself had legalized its status. The Allied countries, following the example of the United States, accorded prompt recognition.

Despite these favorable omens the Lvov Cabinet, dependent upon a misalliance between the parliamentary revolutionaries and the Petrograd Soviet, was destined to have a short existence. The Duma had desired the overthrow of the tsar, for one reason, because he failed to prosecute the war with sufficient vigor, while the workingmen had been partially motivated by a wish to end the war. The soviet, moreover, wanted a thorough revision of the Russian property-holding system, a program with which most of the moderates in the Duma had little sympathy. Finally, whereas the government attempted to solve its difficult tasks by enunciating elaborate principles, without regard to the psychology or impatience of the masses, the soviet quickly perfected a central organization, sent agents to establish branch councils at strategic points throughout the land, spread seditious propaganda, and urged all labor, military, and naval units to send representatives to the parent soviet.

By a famous "Order Number One" of March 14, the Petrograd Soviet instructed the army and the navy to disregard any commands of the provisional government that conflicted with the soviet's regulations. Local revolutionary committees were set up by the soldiers and sailors, which assumed control over the auxiliary military weapons. Disposition of the latter was to be entrusted to the officers only when the respective local committees were certain that such action would not jeopardize the interests of the revolution. Army discipline thus was shattered, for the soldiers enjoyed their newly gained "responsibilities" and unceremoniously shot those officers who could not grasp the "significance" of the changed situation. There also resulted bitter quarreling among the men, for some desired to remain loyal to their officers and the old regime, while others refused to fight and started marching home.

In June 1917, at the initiative of the Petrograd Soviet, there met the first All-Russian Congress of Soviets. The thousand delegates included Social Revolutionaries, Mensheviks, and Bolsheviks, the last in a small minority. The gathering indulged in fervent speechmaking against imperialism and in favor of peace without annexations and without indemnities, while the chief practical accomplishment was the appointment of an All-Russian Central Executive Committee of the Soviets. This body, with a membership of three hundred, was to act as a sort of soviet parliament. It was placed under the leadership of a presidium of twenty, mainly Social Revolutionaries and Mensheviks.

As it gradually became apparent that the Lvov Ministry was unable to cope with the difficult situation, one after another of the moderate members resigned from the cabinet. By July only three of the original appointees, including Kerensky, remained. The latter had risen to be minister of war and head of the government, and he resorted to eloquence and skillful parliamentary procedure in an attempt to restore domestic order while continuing the contest against the Central Powers. By this time, however, even a Social-Revolutionary Government was unsatisfactory to the masses, who craved the return of peace and whose leaders demanded direct control over the national means of production. Kerensky's apparent anxiety to postpone elections for a national assembly weakened the confidence of many people in his ultimate motives.

In the fall of 1917 Russia was clearly at the threshold of another revolution. The soldiers were staging what was perhaps the greatest mutiny in military history. The peasants, when they felt certain of the downfall of the tsar and the landlords, rose and seized what lands they could, sometimes peacefully, ofttimes with bloodshed. The workers in the towns, many of whom originally had struck for higher pay and shorter hours, became more radical in their demands. Some of them now sought to take over control of factories and plants and to run them without private ownership. In order to give more force to their ideals, they formed local soviets and organized themselves into "Red Guards." The subject nationalities, notably the Ukrainians and Finns, took advantage of the general confusion to establish their independence, and the armies of Germany and Austria-Hungary were swarming over the western portions of the country. In the face of these conditions, Kerensky's grant of greater local autonomy to the provincial councils, the establishment of universal suffrage, and the promise of far-reaching social and economic reforms as soon as external conditions permitted, failed to satisfy any considerable portion of the people.

The Bolsheviks, although they had been overwhelmingly outnumbered in the soviet congress, continued to organize local soviets and to agitate against Kerensky. Everywhere they shouted the slogan "Peace! Land! Bread!" and promised freedom for the oppressed nationalities. The campaign was ably directed by Lenin, the "father of Bolshevism," who had been helped by the Germans to return to Russia from Switzerland. The Germans aided the revolutionaries not out of any sympathy for their ideals but in order the more quickly to undermine the Russian state system and end the war on the eastern front. The failure of the Allies to redefine their war aims, as Kerensky suggested, also reacted to the latter's disadvantage.

The cause of the Bolsheviks received a temporary setback in July when Kerensky successfully put down a premature uprising which had been strongly opposed by Lenin and reacted unfavorably upon the cause of all radical antigovernment groups. An equally futile reactionary coup under General Kornilov in September, however, not only enabled the Bolsheviks to recapture their lost ground but served to enhance their reputation.

Kornilov was an able strategist who had become popular among the soldiers for his energy and humaneness and his daring escape from an Austrian prison. He had been made commander-in-chief of the armed forces of the Kerensky Government, with almost no restrictions upon his military powers. For a time it appeared as though the general and Kerensky were jointly contemplating the establishment of a strong and moderate government that would cut short the internal disorder and continue the war against the Central Powers. However, when Kornilov started to march on Petrograd, Kerensky became frightened before the specter of a military dictatorship and hastily assembled some soldiers with whom to meet the general. Kornilov's men now refused to follow him any farther and the government was saved without striking a blow. In his anxiety Kerensky had called on the "Red Guards" for support; since they were mainly Bolsheviks, the prestige of these last was considerably enhanced among the people.

At last, at a party meeting of October 1917, at which were present delegates of soldiers, sailors, and workingmen, the Bolsheviks decided upon a *coup d'état*. On November 6 and 7 Petrograd was seized by force and the members of the government were arrested, only Kerensky managing to escape. The date for the event had been chosen so as to precede the meeting of the second All-Russian Congress of Soviets which had been called for the seventh. When this body assembled, therefore, it was faced with a *fait accompli*. Since the gathering contained a Boshevik majority, it received the announcement with glee and constituted itself the supreme authority in Russia.

The spirit of this second revolt soon spread and everywhere in Russia the local soviets seized power. The congress meanwhile appointed a new and Bolshevik-controlled central executive committee and an administrative board called "the soviet of people's commissars." The chairman of this cabinet was Lenin, while

Trotsky became commissar for foreign affairs, Alexei Rykov for the interior, and Joseph Stalin for nationalities.

The program which the commissars were expected to launch envisaged the following accomplishments: (1) the immediate conclusion of peace with the Central Powers; (2) the quelling of the numerous local revolts and combating of the separatist movements that had been in progress since the end of the old regime; (3) a complete revision of the economic, social, and political structure of the state, and the establishment of a dictatorship of the proletariat to last, supposedly, until such time as the entire population would be ready to participate in a communistic government; and (4) the spreading of the proletarian revolution throughout the world. Simultaneously, it would be necessary to care for the returning soldiers and provide food and shelter for the distressed multitudes in the cities.

As an earnest of the good intentions of the new government, the long-postponed elections for a constituent assembly were held on November 25, the date that had finally been set by Kerensky. To the chagrin of the Bolsheviks, this first Russian election in which the suffrage was universal, secret, and direct, resulted in an overwhelming victory for the Social Revolutionaries. The latter obtained about twice as many seats as the Bolsheviks. Had the government been of the responsible type, the Bolsheviks would now have resigned their authority into the hands of the majority party. Having no intention thus to jeopardize their future control, however, they postponed the meeting of the assembly until January 1918 and strove in the meantime to consolidate their strength and intimidate their opponents.

Despite these tactics the assembly, when it met, elected a Social Revolutionary president and voted down a Bolshevik proposal to disarm all classes of the population save the workmen. The Bolshevik delegates thereupon left the hall and on the following day the Bolsheviks dissolved the "reactionary" assembly by force, while accusing the Social Revolutionaries of "directing the fight of the bourgeoisie against the workingmen's revolution." Local soviets which betrayed anti-Bolshevik sympathies were likewise dissolved and many of their leaders imprisoned or exiled. A working-class dictatorship, to last, ostensibly, until the mass of the people could be made to comprehend and voluntarily accept the "benefits" of communism, replaced the short-lived democracy. It may be interesting, at this point, to survey the careers of the two most prominent commissars.

LENIN AND TROTSKY

Vladimir Ilyich Ulyanov, alias N. Lenin,[1] was born on April 22, 1870, at Simbirsk (Ulyanovsk) in the province of Kazan. The Ulyanov family, though it belonged to the lower nobility, was known for its radical tendencies, and Vladimir's brother, Alexander, was hanged in 1887 for complicity in a plot to kill the tsar. Another brother and two sisters were under police surveillance and Vladimir himself was expelled from the University of Kazan within a month of his matriculation for having participated in a student riot.

A few years later he was permitted to enter the university at St. Petersburg and in 1891 he got a degree in law. In the meantime he had become absorbed in the study of Karl Marx' *Capital* and had reached the conclusion that only socialism could "lead the Russian people to freedom." He joined a radical group and soon became one of its most active members, for which temerity he had to pay with an involuntary sojourn in Siberia. While in exile he married a fellow radical, Nadezhda Konstantinovna Krupskaya, who energetically aided him in his revolutionary activities throughout the remainder of his life.

In 1900 he went to Switzerland and, except for a brief visit during the Revolution of 1905, remained outside Russia until 1917. During these years he edited radical newspapers and traveled extensively in Germany, Austria-Hungary, France, and Great Britain, in each place making the acquaintance of outstanding agitators. In 1903, as has been indicated, he became the leader of the Bolshevik faction of the Social Democratic Party. Always the memory of his brother Alexander was his guide and comfort. The name of Lenin, indeed, had originally been the alias of the elder Ulyanov.

Lenin was unprepossessing in appearance: short, thickset, bald, and bearded. He never knew poverty, but he led a simple life, working hard and regularly taking physical exercise. He was full of confidence in his powers, conscious of his intellectual ability, and possessed of an iron will. He was uncompromising and unscrupulous in matters of policy. He disliked fruitless discussions and his calmness and skill in sizing up an opponent made him a dangerous adversary in debate. Capitalism appeared to him as evil

---

[1] Lenin seems not to have used the name "Nikolai," though he sometimes used the initial "N."

incarnate and world revolution as the highest goal. To achieve the destruction of the former and the attainment of the latter, he regarded all means fair.

In 1917 the Germans permitted Lenin to return to Russia in a sealed car in order that he might conduct subversive propaganda against the provisional government. He carefully planned the overthrow of the bourgeois regime and took note of the widespread peasant and worker movements which, after the first outbursts of violence, had assumed a new phase and now aimed at consolidating some of the social and economic results of the overturn. After several months of activity he decided that the time had come to strike and in October, as we have seen, he converted his followers to the same view.

One of Lenin's ablest lieutenants was Lev Davydovich Bronstein, alias Leon Trotsky. The latter was born in 1879 in the province of Kherson, the son of a fairly prosperous Jewish peasant. Trotsky enjoyed only eight years of formal schooling, but he was an avid reader and grew up to be a man of literary culture. The instances of human inequality and injustice which he saw about him in his childhood apparently made lasting impressions upon his sensitive mind, and while still young he came under the influence of radical thinkers. He was arrested for the first time a year after he left school, for having helped to organize a South Russian Workers' Union. Between 1898 and 1917 he spent four years in prison, was twice exiled to Siberia, and lived abroad for twelve years.

Like Lenin he traveled widely in Europe, lecturing and writing articles and pamphlets. When the break between the Bolsheviks and the Mensheviks occurred, he for a time led a middle group of Trotskyists and did not finally go over to Lenin's side until after the March Revolution (1917). During the war he was expelled from France and Spain and deported to the United States, living in New York for a time in 1917 and then attempting to return to Russia. On the way he was held in a concentration camp at Halifax, but upon representations from Kerensky he was allowed to proceed.

In appearance Trotsky was more striking than Lenin. His features were characterized by a prominent nose, black eyes, a high forehead topped with a mass of wavy hair, and heavy lips. Fond of theatrical display and susceptible to flattery, he none the less proved himself an indefatigable worker and an able organizer. A strong believer in discipline and system, he laid the foundations for the powerful and efficient "Red Army."

THE END OF FOREIGN AND CIVIL WAR

The conclusion of peace with the Central Powers was accomplished, it will be recalled, through the signing of the Treaty of Brest-Litovsk (March 3, 1918).[1] By the terms of this and some supplementary pacts Russia gave up five hundred thousand square miles of territory, with sixty-six million inhabitants, and agreed to pay a heavy indemnity. Harsh though these provisions were, nothing better could be achieved, for Russia was in no position to continue the struggle and Germany was in no mood to be merciful. The conclusion of this peace, bad as it was, permitted the Bolsheviks to concentrate upon domestic affairs.

Most urgent among these matters was the need to deal with the counterrevolutionary movements that were arising everywhere. For three years, from 1917 to 1920, the Bolsheviks were engaged in a life-and-death struggle with an opposition variously led by nobles, clergymen, moderate republicans, adventurers, ex-tsarist officers, and champions of local rights. For a time several groups of counterrevolutionaries, out of strategic considerations, were aided by the German invaders. Later the Allies sent men, money, and munitions to be used against the "Reds."

The Allies had several reasons for intervening in the affairs of Russia. They hoped by restoring bourgeois control to rebuild the eastern front against Germany. They wanted to keep from German or Bolshevik hands the stocks of war supplies at Murmansk and Archangel which they had earlier placed at the disposal of the Russians. They were angered by a Bolshevik declaration repudiating all Russian debts. The Allied blockade was therefore extended to Russia; Allied and American military contingents were sent to Murmansk, Archangel, and Vladivostok; and, when Turkey quit the war, the French bombarded and captured Odessa while the British attacked Baku.[2] Thousands of Czech and Slovak soldiers

[1] See pp. 57–59. Late in 1917 the Bolsheviks denounced and published the texts of the Secret Treaties to which Russia had been a party, but the negotiations with the Central Powers were undertaken only after the Allies had refused a proposal of Trotsky to consider a general peace based on the principles of self-determination for all subject peoples and "no annexations and no indemnities."

[2] The Japanese sent thousands of men to Siberia in the belief that the opportunity to acquire part of that area had at last arrived.

who previously had deserted to Russia from the Austro-Hungarian armies likewise turned against the Bolsheviks. Nationalistic groups in Estonia, Latvia, Lithuania, Finland, and the Transcaucasian states took advantage of the turmoil to declare the independence of these regions, and Romania stepped into the rich province of Bessarabia.

Wherever they were sent, the foreign troops coöperated with bands of anti-Bolshevik natives to set up counterrevolutionary or "White" governments. Around Murmansk and Archangel there was established a "North-Russian Provisional Government." At Omsk, in Siberia, Admiral Alexander Kolchak, former commander of the Imperial Black-Sea Fleet, with the aid of Allied and Czech soldiers, founded an "All-Russian Government." In the south of Russia there was a government under General Anton I. Denikin, and later, in the southern Ukraine and the Crimea, one under General Peter Wrangel. Nikolai Yudenich placed himself at the head of a "Northwest Government of Russia" with headquarters in the Baltic area, while General Baron Karl Gustav Mannerheim assumed control in eastern Finland and Karelia.

In the beginning it appeared that the Bolsheviks would be overwhelmed by all these foes. The few "Red Guards," capable though they were, could not cope with enemies who outnumbered them several times, and at one stage the followers of Lenin were in control only of Petrograd and Moscow and of a few provinces surrounding each of these cities.

Two factors, nevertheless, played into the hands of the radicals. First, the intervention of foreign soldiers, in what was definitely a matter for the Russians themselves to settle, induced a number of patriotic persons, especially young officers, to come to the aid of the "Reds" in repelling the outsiders. Secondly, many of the peasants, although they did not understand the economic theories of the Bolsheviks and did not like their grain-requisitioning policies, were even more opposed to the restorationist activities of the "Whites." Of the two evils, requisitions and landlordism, the peasants apparently preferred the former. The requisitions, they felt, would stop eventually; but landlordism, if reinstated, might remain a permanent bane. Consequently the Russian masses, by and large, obstructed the progress of the counterrevolutionaries as much as they dared.

While the "Red-White" conflict was at its height, it seemed dangerous to the Bolsheviks to keep the ex-imperial family confined near Petrograd, where it might become a rallying point for the reactionaries. Hence the Romanov prisoners were sent off into the country, eventually being lodged in the Ural town of Ekaterinburg (Sverdlovsk). It was planned at some future time to subject the former emperor to a public trial, with Trotsky as state prosecutor, but when, in the summer of 1918, the "Whites" under Kolchak fought their way to the neighborhood of Ekaterinburg, the local soviet officials became panicky and on July 16 ordered the shooting of Nicholas and Alexandra together with their son and four daughters.

As the months rolled by, the Bolsheviks gradually developed two powerful weapons with which to cut short domestic and foreign opposition. To crush the counterrevolutionaries there was created an "Extraordinary Commission to Combat Counter-Revolution, Speculation, and Sabotage," known from its initials in Russian as the Cheka. Trotsky believed that "terror, as the demonstration of the will and strength of the working class, was historically justified," and Felix Dzerzhinsky, who was placed at the head of the Cheka, agreed with the dictum. After an attempt to assassinate Lenin in August 1918, there was inaugurated a "mass terror." The Cheka was a powerful, secret, revolutionary tribunal which requisitioned, arrested, and executed at will, and then merely presented reports of its activities to the commissars and the central executive committee. There are no reliable statistics on the number of lives taken by this instrument of suppression, but it broke the backbone of the opposition and almost obliterated the influence of the bourgeoisie and intelligentsia.

The tsarist generals and foreign troops were dealt with by the "Red Army" which, by 1919, had become a well-drilled force of about 100,000 men, led, to a large extent, by ex-imperial officers loyal to Russia. As the Bolshevik army grew in strength, the Allies became less and less anxious to continue their armed interference. Besides, the vindictive actions of the "Whites" alienated the sympathies of Western Labor and of some of the Western diplomats, who eventually contented themselves with contributing supplies and a few officers to the cause of restoration. In the summer of 1920 Great Britain, the United States, and Italy began to raise the Russian blockade.

The "Red Army" required until late in 1920 to restore peace to Russia. Its first great successes came against Yudenich, who was driven back from the neighborhood of Petrograd to Estonia. The latter country soon repudiated the general and in February 1920 signed a treaty with Russia at Dorpat (Tartu). This same month saw the capture and shooting of Admiral Kolchak and the breakup of his government at Omsk. Supported by a strong force of Czechs, Kolchak had got control of the Trans-Siberian Railway and of most of the larger towns between Vladivostok and the Volga, but he was unable to penetrate very far into European Russia and lost his life in the attempt. Between July and October 1920 peace treaties were signed with Lithuania, Latvia, Finland, and Poland.

The war against the Poles, who wanted to extend their borders to the limits of 1772, was especially difficult, for they were led in part by French officers and equipped in part with French supplies. In May 1920 they occupied the city of Kiev, but then the Bolsheviks rallied and drove the invaders back to the gates of Warsaw. After several more months of war a preliminary peace was signed at Riga (October 12) and a compromise boundary was accepted by both parties. Meanwhile General Denikin in southern Russia was also being defeated. In order to continue his struggle he resorted to conscription among the populations under his control and even compelled "Red" prisoners to fight under his standards. In the spring of 1920 he resigned his command into the hands of General Wrangel and fled the country. The new commander was able to hold out in the Crimea until November; then he too went into exile. After six years of continuous warfare, Russia was at peace.

This "Russia" of 1920 comprised only a fraction, if a large one, of the territory which had formerly been the empire of the tsar. Poland, Finland, Latvia, Estonia, Lithuania, White Russia, the Ukraine, Transcaucasia, Bessarabia, and eastern Siberia, all were independent or under foreign occupation. There remained as Russia only an association of autonomous republics and regions known, since the spring of 1918, as the Russian Socialist Federated Soviet Republic (R.S.F.S.R.). The four Baltic states, Poland, and Bessarabia seemed permanently lost; but the other areas were all soon regained.

Between 1919 and 1921 the Bolsheviks overthrew the governments in the Ukraine and White Russia, and seized control in the Transcaucasian states of Azerbaijan, Armenia, and Georgia. Under Russian instigation these last three then combined to form the Transcaucasian Socialist Federated Soviet Republic, and in 1922, at Moscow, delegates from all the Bolshevik states, now four in number, signed a treaty of union. The treaty went into effect in July 1923 and the new federation was termed "the Union of Soviet Socialist Republics" (U.S.S.R.). The word "Russian" was omitted from the official title of the new state since it was hoped

REPUBLICS OF

From *Russia at War*, Headline Book N

that other countries, inhabited by non-Russians, might eventually seek to join the U.S.S.R.[1]

The members of the federation theoretically retained considerable autonomy and reserved "the right freely to leave the union." In 1924 two central-Asiatic republics, Uzbekistan and Turkmenistan, entered the union. A seventh member of the federation, Tadjikistan, formed out of those parts of Uzbekistan which were peopled by the Tadjiks, was admitted late in 1929. The constitution of 1936 recognized eleven republics by redividing Transcaucasia into Azerbaijan, Armenia, and Georgia, and by listing two new members: Kazak and Kirghiz.[2] Despite the supposed equality of the republics, the R.S.F.S.R., comprising the larger part of the area and population of the union, dominated the combination.

The constitutions of the several members of the U.S.S.R., and of the latter itself, were all patterned closely after that of the R.S.F.S.R. as adopted in 1918 and amplified on later occasions.

GOVERNMENT IN THE SOVIET UNION

The underlying theory of the constitution of the R.S.F.S.R. was communism, and many of its ideas were traceable to the *Communist Manifesto* published in 1848 by Karl Marx and Friedrich Engels. To the older Bolshevik leaders, communism was both a philosophy and a method. Philosophically it aimed at the building of a classless society through the abolition of private property and the common ownership of all means of production and distribution. Its method involved, first, a national, and then an international, social revolution under an organized dictatorship of the working people. These principles motivated the congresses of soviets which adopted or amended the fundamental law of the land.

The constitution of the R.S.F.S.R. proclaimed Russia a socialist republic of workers and peasants, with central and local authority vested in soviets of workers', peasants', Cossacks', and soldiers' deputies. All land, forests, mineral resources, livestock, factories, shops, banks, and means of production, communication, and transit were declared the property of the workers' and peasants'

[1] While under Allied occupation, that part of Siberia which lies east of Lake Baikal had been set up as an independent Far Eastern Republic. In November 1922, a month after the last Japanese soldiers were withdrawn, a constituent asssembly voted for immediate incorporation in the R.S.F.S.R.

[2] Soviet acquisitions in 1939–1940 increased the number of republics to sixteen.

state. To wipe out the so-called parasitic elements of society, labor was made the duty of every citizen. Special clauses guaranteed to workingmen the freedom of religious and atheistic opinion, and the enjoyment of education. Oppression of national minorities was forbidden and foreign workers who came to dwell in Russia were to have the same privileges and rights as native laborers.

Supreme authority in the R.S.F.S.R. was lodged with an All-Russian Congress of Soviets, and in the interim between its meetings in an All-Russian Central Executive Committee. The All-Russian Congress was to be composed of representatives of the city soviets on the basis of one deputy for every 25,000 *voters* and of representatives of the provincial soviets on the basis of one delegate for every 125,000 of the *population*.[1] Since the resulting body was too unwieldy for the efficient conduct of business, the congress soon empowered the central executive committee to act as "supreme legislative, administrative, and controlling organ of the R.S.F.S.R."

This committee, with a membership of about four hundred, was given power to issue decrees and decisions, to unify and coördinate the country's legislation and administration, and to appoint a cabinet known as the All-Russian Council of People's Commissars. The importance of the committee increased porportionally with the declining influence of the congress. The latter at first met frequently, then its gatherings became annual affairs, and eventually, at its biennial meetings, it appeared content to approve whatever the committee had ordained.

Since even the committee was regarded as too large for the efficient accomplishment of work, it soon came to meet only a few times a year, leaving the control of affairs and the supervision of the commissars to a presidium of about forty. Under the watchful eye of this body the council of commissars or *sovnarkom* carried on the actual work of governing the state. All decrees of the sovnarkom required eventual submission to the central executive committee for ratification or annulment.

Local authority was placed in the hands of local soviets, under the strict supervision of the central government. The cities were to be governed by urban soviets elected on a basis of one deputy for each one thousand of the population. Representation was based upon trade or vocation rather than geographical division and the people in the various occupations were to vote separately, the ironworkers in one group, the textile workers in another, and

[1] This arrangement was changed in 1936. See p. 560.

so on. In the case of housewives and individual workmen, resort was to be had to a special type of districting. In the villages and small towns the peasants, home workers, teachers, and doctors were to meet together to elect one deputy for each one hundred inhabitants. Voting was generally by show of hands.

Representation in the soviets above the city and village councils was made indirect. The village soviets were to send delegates to district congresses of soviets and these in turn to regional congresses. From these last had to be chosen the members of the All-Russian Congress. The town and factory soviets were permitted to elect their All-Russian Congress delegates directly, and also to send representatives to the district and regional congresses. The city workers, until 1935, were given more direct representation in the All-Russian Congress because they formed the core of the Communist Party.

The franchise was accorded to all men and women over eighteen who were productive workers, the housekeepers of such workers, soldiers, or sailors. This rule applied equally to native Russians and to foreigners living in Russia. The following groups, with occasional exceptions, were deprived both of the suffrage and the right to hold office: (1) persons who employed hired labor for profit or who lived on an income not derived from their own direct labor; (2) business men, traders, commercial agents, monks, and clergymen; (3) members of the former ruling dynasty and of the former police, gendarmerie, or secret service; and (4) individuals and the children of individuals who had registered opposition to the process of farm collectivization. The number of people disfranchised under these regulations varied from year to year. According to Soviet figures, only 2.5 per cent of the adult population was disfranchised for the elections held late in 1934. In that year citizenship and suffrage rights had been restored to those former landlords, members of the bourgeoisie and wealthier peasantry, priests, and "White" policeman and soldiers who had been engaged for at least five years in "socially useful work" or who had served faithfully in the Bolshevik army.

The constitutions of the remaining republics in the U.S.S.R., and of the union itself, were similar to the one just described. The supreme organ of authority in the Union was to be the All-Union Congress of Soviets elected, until 1936, by the city and regional soviets in each of the republics, again on a basis of one deputy each to every 25,000 urban electors and every 125,000 rural inhabitants. Since the congress in consequence of this arrangement contained more than 1500 delegates, it was to meet only biennially, for about a week, to approve the work of the Union Central Executive Committee and the Union Council of Commissars. Meetings of the All-Union Congress and Union Central Executive Committee were to be held in rotation at the several republican capitals.

Until 1936 the Union Central Executive Committee, endowed with supreme powers whenever the congress was not in session, consisted of two bodies, a Union Soviet and a Soviet of Nationalities. The Union Soviet was elected by the All-Union Congress and represented the republics in proportion to their population. The Soviet of Nationalities was elected by the local central executive committees in the various republics, subject to confirmation by the All-Union Congress. The creation of this council of nationalities was not only an official recognition of the fact that the Soviet Union included scores of distinct national groups, but an attempt to perpetuate the cultural and linguistic differences among these groups. The whole committee was to meet three times a year, its two branches sitting and voting separately. Between sessions, the committee's powers were delegated to a Union Presidium which supervised the work of the Union Council of Commissars, the "cabinet" of the U.S.S.R.[1]

Attached and subordinated to the Union Central Executive Committee there was a Union Supreme Court. The functions of this agency were (1) to provide the supreme courts of the republics with "guiding interpretations on questions of the general legislation of the union"; (2) to protest before the committee decisions of the republican supreme courts which might be in contradiction to union legislation or adverse to the interests of other members of the federation; (3) to decide legal conflicts among the republics; and (4) to examine cases against high officers accused of committing offenses in connection with their official duties.

Among the distinguishing characteristics of the Soviet governmental system, four features stood out most prominently. First, although the U.S.S.R. was a federal state, the central government had unusually broad powers. The member republics, despite their numerous councils and officials, might legislate freely only on affairs of definitely local importance. Secondly, since the Bolsheviks believed that the individual's attitude towards political questions was determined by his occupation, representation rested upon a

[1] See p. 560 for the changes made in these arrangements in 1936.

vocational rather than a geographical basis. Thirdly, the electoral system, at least until 1936, was highly indirect. The peasants were six steps removed from the Union Council of Commissars and the urban workers four steps. Thus many of the noncommunist deputies were weeded out in the successive elections and the su-

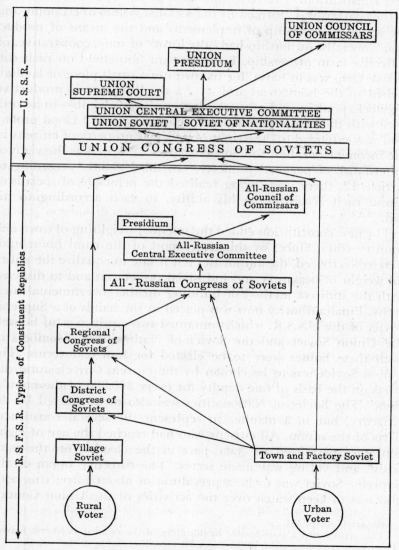

U. S. S. R.

UNION COUNCIL OF COMMISSARS

UNION PRESIDIUM

UNION SUPREME COURT

UNION CENTRAL EXECUTIVE COMMITTEE
UNION SOVIET | SOVIET OF NATIONALITIES

UNION CONGRESS OF SOVIETS

R. S. F. S. R. Typical of Constituent Republics

All-Russian Council of Commissars

Presidium

All-Russian Central Executive Committee

All - Russian Congress of Soviets

Regional Congress of Soviets

District Congress of Soviets

Village Soviet

Town and Factory Soviet

Rural Voter

Urban Voter

THE SOVIET POLITICAL STRUCTURE UNTIL 1936

preme authority was relatively free of popular control. Finally, there was no separation of powers in the Bolshevik arrangement. The Union Central Executive Committee had supreme legislative, administrative, and judicial control in the land.

In December 1936 the All-Union Congress of Soviets adopted a new constitution. The economic basis of the U.S.S.R., according to the charter, was "formed by the socialist system of economy and the socialist ownership of implements and the means of production." Socialist ownership had "the form" of state, coöperative, or collective-farm ownership. Every peasant household on each collective farm was to have "for its own use a small piece of land attached to the homestead and . . . a dwelling house, productive livestock, poultry, and minor agricultural implements—in accordance with the regulation of the agricultural artel." [1] Legal protection was extended to "the right of personal property of citizens in the income from their toil and savings . . . as well as the right of inheritance of personal property." In the U.S.S.R., according to Article 12, there was "being realized the principle of socialism: 'From each according to his ability, to each according to his toil.'" [2]

The new constitution ended the unequal weighting of town and country votes. Since, by this time, most of the rural households were collectivized, the authorities felt it safe to equalize the political weight of peasantry and industrial proletariat and to dispense with the indirect method of building up the governmental hierarchy. Final authority now was placed in the hands of a Supreme Soviet of the U.S.S.R. which contained two equipowerful houses: the Union Soviet and the Soviet of Nationalities. Members of both these houses were to be elected for four-year terms. The Union Soviet was to be chosen by the citizens "by electoral districts on the basis of one deputy for every 300,000 of the population." The Soviet of Nationalities was also to be elected by the citizenry, but in a manner to represent the several constituent parts of the union. All citizens who had reached the age of eighteen were permitted to "take part in the election on the same basis" and voting was made secret. The directive organ of the Supreme Soviet was to be a presidium of about forty; this body also was to keep watch over the activities of the Union Council

---

[1] On artels see p. 584.

[2] This represented a considerable modification of the original Bolshevik maxim: "From each according to his ability, to each according to his needs."

of People's Commissars. The first general election under the new constitution was held in 1937. The returns indicated a complete victory for the Stalinist candidates—there being no others.[1]

THE COMMUNIST PARTY

The All-Union Communist Party was at once the foundation stone of the soviet governmental structure and the source of its power. Without directions from the party "no important political or organizational problem was ever decided by the soviets." The roll of the party in 1939 included about 2,500,000 members and probationers.[2] In addition to the regular party, there were several junior communist societies, including the *Komsomol* or Alliance of Communist Youth. New members of the party came to be recruited chiefly from among the graduates of the Komsomol but not every graduate was admitted. From 1939 on a young applicant for membership had to be endorsed by three party members of three years' standing. It was impressed "on the mind of every candidate that there must be complete subordination of all personal feelings to the welfare of the party." Communists had to place themselves at the disposal of their superiors, obey orders implicitly, go without question wherever and whenever they might be sent, devote their spare time to preaching the gospel of communism, and be ready to defend the revolution with their lives.

Each year a control committee purged the party of some of its members. The percentage of expulsions varied from year to year, affecting 2 per cent of the membership in one year and 25 per cent in another (1934). The grounds for dismissal included drunkenness, immorality, slackness in propagandist zeal, tax evasion, nonpayment of dues, attendance at church services, the cultivation of bourgeois associations, or even tolerance shown to people of "heretical" views. Individuals who sought to utilize their party standing merely for the sake of advancing their careers were promptly expelled. Such persons were popularly known as *shkurniki*, or men who look after their own skins. Lenin is said to have

---

[1] The regular elections of 1941 were postponed because of war.

[2] Soon after the communists came into power those Bolsheviks who had been active revolutionaries in the days of tsardom organized themselves into a Society of Old Bolsheviks. Generally intelligent and well educated, these persons were for some time able to monopolize most of the important party and state offices. They imposed upon their younger followers a rigid code of discipline and morals. In 1935 the society was reported dissolved.

likened them to radishes, for they were "red" outside, but "white" at heart. Not all infractions of rules were punishable by expulsion. Delinquents often were reprimanded or demoted.

Until 1932 no communist was permitted to receive a wage or salary in excess of 225 rubles per month; then the maximum was raised considerably.[1] In 1934 the arrangement of a fixed maximum was abolished and a tax was placed on all communist incomes in excess of 500 rubles monthly. Officials were also entitled to traveling allowances and sometimes to living quarters and automobiles. Individuals who gave evidence of prowess with the pen frequently were rewarded for their literary propaganda activities by being permitted to share in the returns from sales of their productions. Other compensations of membership included eligibility for the important governmental as well as party offices and preferred treatment at times when food shortages might lead to the issuance of ration cards. At first, the children of communists were given prior claim over other children to the available scholastic instruction, but a decree of 1935 ordered an end to this form of discrimination.

The organization of the Communist Party was outlined in detail in a constitution adopted in 1925 and amended in 1934 and 1939. At the base of the pyramidlike party structure were thousands of local "primary party organs" or "cells." These cells elected representatives to a party congress which, being too large for efficient work, merely approved the decisions taken by its smaller committees.[2] Of these the most important were a central committee and a commission of party control. The latter, meeting every three months, was charged with consolidating the unity of the party and maintaining discipline and loyalty among the adherents.

The central committee—the actual directive agency of the party —was composed of about seventy members with almost as many alternates. Although it met frequently, its functions were really carried on through two small bureaus and a secretariat. An organization bureau (*Orgbureau*), consisting (1939) of nine regular members, was responsible for fixing the conditions of membership in the party, for promotions and demotions, and for supervising the

---

[1] At par a ruble was worth $0.51.

[2] Originally this congress met every two years, but gradually its gatherings became even less frequent. In addition to the local organs and the congress, the party hierarchy included county, provincial, city, and regional committees. There were no separate parties representing the federated republics in the union.

work of propaganda. It was subordinate to the political bureau (*Politbureau*) which, with nine members, determined the general policies of the party and, through it, of the state. The secretariat was responsible "for the current work of organization and execution." Since the personnel of these three bodies was closely interlocked, all power in the party was extremely centralized. Until his death in 1924 Lenin was chairman of the Politbureau.

The chief officer of the party was the secretary-general of the central committee. Joseph Stalin, as incumbent of this office and at once a member of the Politbureau, the Orgbureau, and the secretariat, was the most important factor in the determination of the party's policies. Inasmuch as the party was "the helm of the government," he became the dictator of the Soviet Union.[1]

To uphold its class dictatorship during the transitional period in which the U.S.S.R. was presumably to be prepared for thoroughgoing communism, the party resorted to a variety of means. It was the only organized political group in the land. Since the number of available party candidates was usually limited, the village soviets were sometimes made up largely of noncommunists. However, at least until 1936, the indirect process of selection for the higher offices invariably led to a gradual elimination of the nonparty deputies from the superior governmental agencies. The strict censorship, the communist propaganda, the open voting (until 1936), and the circumstance that the naturally hostile groups were deprived of the franchise were all great helps to the communist candidates in the cities. As has been indicated, the urban communistic strongholds were originally given a greater representation than the rural areas in both the republican and the union congresses. Most of the high state offices were reserved by the party for its own leaders.

In the earlier days of Bolshevik control, criticism of the party's policies was not entirely prohibited. Constructive suggestions, in line with communist policy, were accepted, though they had to come from within the party, not from organized opposition groups. Under Stalin, however, in accordance with the dictum that "the party is not a debating society," the repression became increasingly severe. The opposition was given no opportunity to speak, write, or print anti-Bolshevik views. The suppression was originally enforced by a Unified State Political Administration, known from its initials as the OGPU (sometimes called "Gay-Pay-

[1] In 1941 Stalin also became president of the council of people's commissars (premier).

Oo"). This branch of the government was in reality the heir of the Cheka, which was abolished in 1922. In July 1934 the dread tribunal, which had exercised the power to inflict summary death sentences, was replaced by a commissariat for internal affairs. The latter might inflict penalties, without public trial, up to exile at hard labor for five years. The first chief of the new commissariat was the former acting head of the OGPU. When one of Stalin's aides in the Politbureau, Sergei Kirov, was assassinated in December 1934, the government revived the OGPU methods.

AN ATTEMPT AT PURE COMMUNISM, 1917–1921

Sweeping as were the alterations effected by the Bolsheviks in the Russian political structure, the early innovations in the economic sphere were still more revolutionary. The Soviet Government, soon after coming into power, decreed the nationalization of the land, the natural resources, and the means of production and distribution. The immediate goal was to permit the peasants to use the land according to their needs, and to place the factories, mines, and transportation facilities under the control of the workers. The products of industry and agriculture were to be turned over to the state for distribution among the people, again on a basis of need. Thus, crops raised by the peasants in excess of their own wants were to be used in feeding the industrial proletariat, while the manufactured output of the latter was to be distributed among the peasantry. A Supreme Economic Council was charged with keeping the factories supplied with raw materials and fuel, providing food for the laborers, and making available to the peasants such manufactured goods as they might require.

While these projects were being formulated, the government, in order to feed the workers, found it necessary to issue food cards. For purposes of rationing, the people were divided into four classes according to the "social usefulness" or laboriousness of their jobs. Group I included the heavy-manual laborers, while Group IV was composed of the "parasitic elements" of society who performed no "useful" work. Since the unfortunates who were relegated to this lowest category received a food allowance one-fourth as large as that assigned to persons in Group I, many of the "parasites" died of hunger. The state depended on requisitions from the peasants to secure the food and in some cases farmers were permitted to keep only enough to feed themselves and to sow the next year's crop.

In order to ease the serious housing situation that developed in the larger cities after 1918, the local authorities were empowered to seize all apartment houses and dwellings and to quarter in them workers' families. Jewelry and other valuables above a small minimum were confiscated, as were surplus articles of dress and house furnishings. Private trading was listed as a counterrevolutionary activity, while foreign trade was made a state monopoly and all foreign and domestic debts were canceled. The substitution of barter for the money economy was encouraged.

The Orthodox Church was shorn of its power and wealth, and private schools were abolished. Marriage became a civil ceremony, wedlock and divorce were made easy, and the state undertook to care for unwanted children. Women were placed on a level of civil and economic equality with men, and there was an attempt to loosen family ties since family life was regarded as one of the pillars of the capitalistic system.

It had been planned to devise a schedule of nationalization and to confiscate at first only the large trusts, allowing the smaller businesses temporarily to carry on under the old forms. Actually, the process of nationalization, at least in its earliest stages, was haphazard, taking on the character of a punitive, rather than an economic, measure. The workers generally were impatient to oust their bosses and managers and to run the factories under the supervision of elected committees. In almost every instance the rate of pay was increased and the hours of labor were shortened, but since few of the men were trained in management there was little discipline and less efficiency.

To make matters worse, the railway system—demoralized during the closing months of the war—now threatened to break down completely. In the fall of 1919, according to Trotsky, 60 per cent of the locomotives were "diseased," and the state engineering experts gloomily predicted that, barring a miracle, the railway "epidemic" would result in "death" before the passing of another year. Hence it rapidly became almost impossible to transport the grain which had been requisitioned from the peasants or even the few manufactured products that were being turned out by the crippled factories. The resulting upward swing of prices was accelerated by the adoption of a lusty policy of inflation. The motive behind the continued issuance of paper money was probably as much to ruin the currency and force the general acceptance of an economy based on barter as to meet current governmental expenses.

For a while it seemed as if even the most radical transformations might be successful. As long as the counterrevolutionary exploits of the "Whites" and the intervention of the Allies continued, many of the changes were regarded by the workers and peasants as phases of a transient "War Communism" dictated by the military emergency. With the return of peace, however, the entire procedure began to appear impracticable and conducive more to chaos than to the increased welfare of the masses.

The greatest opposition to the communist regime came from the peasants. At first even these, in mortal fear lest the landlords come back, had offered relatively little resistance to the emissaries of the state who came to requisition their surplus crops. But when the danger was past, the peasants anticipated a new-found prosperity, for they interpreted the abolition of landlordism as the end of rents and taxes and the right to an extra strip of land. By 1920, indeed, they had succeeded in occupying more than 96 per cent of the arable soil in European Russia. They had neither the time nor the inclination to listen to theories concerning state ownership of land or the desirability of sharing their produce with the urban proletariat.

In return for their grain, the peasants wanted money or manufactured goods. Unfortunately neither of these desirables was available in quantity. There was little hard money in circulation and the peasants knew better than to accept the worthless paper. There was a dearth of manufactured goods because importation had almost ceased, the factories were short of raw materials, equipment had broken down, management was poor, and transportation facilities were almost nonexistent. In sheer disappointment the peasantry began to hoard its crops and plead poverty whenever the government requisitioners appeared.

In its attempt to enforce the policy of requisitions so that the urban workers might be fed, the state, as early as 1918, had organized the poorer peasants in each village into committees whose task it was to denounce the wealthier peasants and make them surrender their surpluses to the authorities. This measure added the bitterness of intravillage strife to the country's other difficulties and did little to increase the available grain supply for the cities. The war and devastation, moreover, and the fact that the counterrevolutionaries for a time controlled the southern parts of Russia added to the grain shortage. Despairingly the state now armed the workmen, enrolled them in a "Food Army," and sent them into the villages to force the peasants to disgorge their hoardings. Each district was assessed a certain quota on the basis of existing production statistics, but the searchers after food frequently disregarded the quotas and sometimes left the peasants without sufficient sustenance for their own families.[1]

It was now the turn of the peasants to despair. In self-defense they determined to resort to the only powerful weapon known to them—passive resistance. Since everything above their barest needs was to be taken from them, they would raise only enough to keep alive. As fate would have it, several other factors came to the aid of the peasants in their decision to cut down production. First, no fertilizers were being imported; secondly, the domestic manufacture of agricultural machinery was at a standstill; and thirdly, in the years 1920 and 1921 the country suffered from a severe drought. The grain harvest of 1921 consequently was only two-fifths as large as that of 1913. Famine resulted—one of the worst in the history of Russia. Forty million persons were affected by the food shortage in 1921 and 1922, and about five million starved to death. Conditions were frightful in city and country alike. Millions more might have perished but for the generosity of foreign, especially American, relief appropriations and contributions.

Meanwhile the industrial situation had well-nigh reached nadir. The Supreme Economic Council was altogether unable to carry out its functions, and, despite the issuance of official decrees lengthening working hours, reintroducing piece work, and establishing rewards for production above the required minimum, the total industrial output in 1920 was but 13 per cent of that of 1913. In the last year before the war, fifty times as much metal ore had been mined as in 1920, while the production of oil had been twice as great, that of raw cotton almost three times as great, and that of steel twenty-five times as great.

Cries of "Down with the Soviet Government!" became more and more frequent and vehement during 1920 at meetings of the workers and peasants, and the province of Tambov witnessed a military outbreak. In March 1921 the sailors at Kronstadt, once the very hotbed of Bolshevism, mutinied. Although most of the mutineers were recent recruits of peasant background, the uprising convinced the Soviet Government that a change in policy was urgent. Under the leadership of Lenin it was decided to effect a strategic retreat.

[1] The period 1918–1920 also witnessed some attempts to collectivize farming.

THE NEW ECONOMIC POLICY, 1921–1928

At the tenth party congress, in March 1921, the communists voted to adopt a "New Economic Policy" (NEP). They had come to realize that their enthusiasm had carried them too far, that they had pushed ahead with insufficient regard for the obstacles which an agrarian Russia offered to an industrial dictatorship, that the peasantry was far more interested in land and profits than in communist theory, and that, in order to keep intact the political changes that had been effected, it might be necessary to make some economic concessions. Such a course would involve retreat, but the withdrawal might be strategic; it need not be a rout. The communists might retain control of the government, the transport system, foreign trade, banking, and large-scale industry, while granting minor concessions with respect to such things as local trading and graduated wage scales. Lenin accordingly recommended that the party change its tactics from "assault to siege." Communism, he explained, must be upheld, but henceforth it would be a pragmatic communism—"as much communism as the exigencies of the situation would permit, and no more."

The essential features of the NEP were as follows: (1) The requisition of foodstuffs from the peasants was replaced by a fixed tax, at first in kind, but after 1924 in money, levied on all agricultural production; any produce raised above the amount of the tax might be disposed of in the open market. (2) Private retail trading was permitted under certain restrictions, but the state, in competition, set up retail stores of its own and encouraged consumers' coöperatives. (3) Small factories and shops employing fewer than twenty workers were denationalized and might be restored to private capitalists. (4) A money economy and an intricate state banking system were reintroduced. (5) To secure liquid capital, profit-sharing concessions for mining, manufacturing, transportation, and large-scale agricultural and engineering projects were offered to foreign capitalists on contracts which usually guaranteed the concessionaires' capital against nationalization and gave the state options on the purchase of the firms' products. (6) A graduated wage scale was introduced and the method of food rationing was modified; the quantity of essentials that could be bought at the government stores was still limited, but it became legal to buy additional goods in the open market. (7) State trusts were founded to control production and distribution in the large industries. (8) The compulsory membership of workers in the trade unions was abolished. (9) Plans were laid for the future coördination of all industry in a state-controlled system.

To the delight of the communists it appeared for a time as though the NEP would cure the major economic ills of the country. The area sown to grain by the peasants increased rapidly and by 1926 reached a figure almost equal to that of 1913. A majority of the peasants, although not yet satisfied with the notion that the land belonged to the state and not to them, seemed content to pay their taxes and dispose of their surpluses in the market. In 1925 the state retreated so far as to permit the renting of land for short periods and the employment of a limited number of farm laborers. Thereupon some of the more enterprising peasants leased their neighbors' lands and hired extra hands. As a result, the peasantry again fell into three classes: the poor, those who were fairly well off, and the well to do. In 1928 the authorities took cognizance of this by revising the tax schedules so as to exempt entirely the poorest 35 per cent of the peasantry, tax lightly the middle 53 per cent, and burden heavily the remaining 12 per cent, the more prosperous *kulaks,* or "fists."

The state had no intention of allowing the kulaks to develop into a strong class holding large stretches of land. They were tolerated for a time because their enterprise was needed to increase the production of grain, but they were given to understand that the days of their activities were numbered and that the government contemplated their eventual downfall. As one means of combating the kulaks and simultaneously increasing the grain output, the Bolsheviks elaborated an earlier program for the creation of state and collective farms. More than 12,000,000 acres were allocated for the establishment of 150 state farms and every effort was to be made to secure modern machinery and ambitious workers for the enterprise. Little progress, however, was made in this direction before 1928.[1]

In the industrial sphere the state continued its virtual monopoly of manufactures. Several hundred state trusts or syndicates were created and endowed with considerable autonomy. Each syndicate was placed under the direction of a committee of managers who were made responsible to the Supreme Economic Council. Wage rates were to be settled by direct bargaining between the

---

[1] To end the widespread illegal distillation of home-brew, the communists in 1925 repealed the prohibition on alcoholic drinks and reëstablished the government vodka monopoly. A law of 1929 forbade the sale of liquors on holidays.

trusts and the trade unions. About half of the profits went to the government, from one-tenth to one-seventh was expended for the welfare of the workers, and the remainder was used for expansion and reserves. In 1926 the state trusts produced about 77 per cent of the total industrial output of the Soviet Union, while coöperatives accounted for 5 per cent, foreign concessionaires for 3 per cent, and private enterprise for 15 per cent. By this year, too, the volume of industrial production approximated the prewar level, although quantity was achieved at the expense of quality.

For the first few years after the introduction of the NEP private trading flourished. In the fiscal year 1923–1924 three-fifths of the retail trade was handled by private merchants. Individuals who took advantage of the opportunity to gain profit in this manner, however, were generally unpopular and came to be known as "Nepmen." The government made every effort to fight the Nepmen, especially through the instrument of consumers' coöperatives. Admission to the latter was open to every one except priests and kulaks, and by the spring of 1927 there were about twenty-eight thousand consumers' coöperatives with fourteen million members. During the fiscal year 1926–1927 these societies handled almost half of the retail trade of the union, while the private traders controlled about one-third, and the state shops accounted for the remaining sixth. The state expected to turn the business of its own stores over to the coöperatives as rapidly as expedient.

The terms of the concessions offered by the Bolsheviks to foreigners were so attractive that contracts were concluded with more than one hundred companies, many from the United States. Frequently, however, the exploitation of the concessions was surrounded with difficulties and a number of the agreements eventually were canceled or forfeited.

Although the NEP did much to heal the ravages of the early communist experiments and gradually brought production figures back to the prewar level, considerable hardship was caused by the disparity between the prices of grain and of manufactured products. The state allowed grain to sell at the regular world market price, but manufactures could be bought only at figures arbitrarily charged by the state trusts. It thus happened that in 1928, while the cost of grain was only half again as great as it had been in 1913, the price of manufactured goods was three or four times as high.

While the NEP was in force state bureaus were established to gather statistical information on every phase of the union's economic life. The data thus accumulated were to be used in the projection of a five-year plan for the further increase of production and the acceleration of the process of industrialization. On October 1, 1928, this Five-Year Plan was inaugurated. Before considering its details, it is necessary to relate the story of a serious quarrel among the leaders of the Communist Party.

PARTY CONFLICTS AND THE SUPREMACY OF STALIN

Until the spring of 1922 Lenin, occupying the position of chairman of the Politbureau of the Communist Party, was dictator of the Soviet State. With his prestige and influence he was able not only to shape governmental policies but to prevent any outward appearance of disharmony among the lesser party leaders. The tremendous strain of the work gradually began to tell on Lenin's health. In 1922 he suffered a stroke and temporarily lost the use of his right arm and leg. Upon his recovery he once more applied himself to his work, but he soon found it necessary to entrust many of his administrative duties to friends and assistants—to Leo Kamenev, who had once studied law in France; to the enthusiastic Alexei Rykov, one of his earliest disciples; and to other devoted followers.

In 1923 he suffered a second stroke. This time, removed to a quiet village near Moscow, he lived in agony for months, buoyed up by the hope that his marvelous physique eventually would triumph over sickness. The end, when it did come, was unexpected. During an evening in January 1924 he fell into delirium and within one hour he was dead. To the rank and file of the communists his tomb in Moscow became a shrine; to the party leaders, sorrowful though they may have been, his passing signalized a struggle for control.[1]

Outstanding among the candidates for the leadership of the party and, through it, of the government, were two men: Leon Trotsky and Joseph Stalin. Firebrand, organizer of the "Red Army," prominent member of most of the important party organs, Trotsky was, after Lenin, the best known of the Bolsheviks to the non-Russian world. He had, however, many enemies within the party. Some communists were repelled by his aggressiveness and vanity. Others disliked him because he was so vitriolic in his attacks on persons for whom he had no use. His impatience to inaugurate the world upheaval regardless of the difficult domestic situa-

[1] Soon after Lenin's death the name of Petrograd was changed to Leningrad. Moscow became the capital in 1918.

tion in Russia and his disdain for the peasantry as being far too backward to be of any aid in the firm establishment of communism antagonized still others. The "Old Bolsheviks" had not yet forgiven him for his opposition to Lenin up to the very year of the successful revolution. Unfortunately for Trotsky's aspirations, finally, his opponents made effective capital of the trenchant epithets which he and Lenin had hurled at each other in the early days of their acquaintance and of his failure to attend Lenin's funeral.

The main opposition to Trotsky came from three men: Stalin, Kamenev, and Zinoviev.[1] The chief of this triumvirate was the Georgian peasant Stalin, really Joseph Vissarionovich Dzhugashvili, who was born in 1879 in the Caucasian town of Gori, the son of a shoemaker. Inspired by a decree of Alexander III which made it possible for poor men's sons to enter the priesthood, Joseph's parents decided to send the boy to a theological seminary. The burly youth, however, had little desire to become a priest and displayed greater acquaintance with Marx than with the Bible. He was soon expelled from the clerical institution to which he had been sent and became actively affiliated with the Social Democratic Party. Fearless, unscrupulous, and taciturn, Dzhugashvili proved adept in the execution of dangerous missions and achieved renown among radicals both in Russia and in exile. Of all the aliases which he found it expedient to assume, none seemed to fit him better than that of "Stalin," meaning "Steel." In 1903 he was one of the first to follow the lead of Lenin as a Bolshevik and thereafter he remained one of the master's most devoted disciples.

Stalin, despite his cunning and precautions, was six times arrested and exiled between 1902 and 1913. Five times, through sheer physical prowess, he managed to escape, but in 1913 he was sent to the Arctic Circle and remained a prisoner until released after the March Revolution. It appears that the tsarist police on no occasion recognized in him a previous offender, else one or another of his sentences might have been death instead of exile. In disregard of the danger, Stalin preferred to agitate from within Russia rather than from the safety of an office in Switzerland or Great Britain. He worked incessantly, writing articles and pamphlets, organizing revolutionary circles in the larger urban centers, forging bank notes, and "expropriating" money from the rich in order to finance the cause.

[1] Gregory E. Zinoviev was a cruel but able organizer, and director of the association charged with promoting the world revolution.

JOSEPH V. STALIN

More than six feet tall, with coal-black hair and an olive skin, Stalin looked every inch an Asiatic fighting man. After the November Revolution he won distinction as a military leader. His chief exploit was in connection with the successful defense of Tsaritsin on the lower Volga against the Cossacks. To commemorate his victory the name of the city was changed to Stalingrad, while upon him was conferred the Order of the Red Flag. When the government of the R.S.F.S.R. was organized, Stalin, already secretary-general of the party, was made commissar for nationalities (1917–1923), being instrumental, in this capacity, both in the unification of the Transcaucasian Republic and in the organization of the U.S.S.R. Himself a member of a national minority, he saw to it that the rights of the lesser national groups were protected.

The rival leaders, both of whom professed to be loyal "Leninists," in 1924 expressed antithetical views on several major points of doctrine. Stalin believed capitalism to be so firmly entrenched in the Western world as to render futile any efforts at bringing about its immediate overthrow. He therefore preferred to concentrate Bolshevik energies upon the economic advancement of the Soviet Union rather than upon uncertain attempts to dislodge the "enemy of the people" from its stronghold in the West. Trotsky, on the contrary, was intolerant of any letup in the world revolutionary movement.

Further, Stalin, the peasant, was aware that the welfare of the U.S.S.R. in the last analysis depended upon the coöperation of the country's food producers. Hence he strongly advocated the establishment of better relations between the government and the peasantry, even though this entail a prolongation of the compromise with petty capitalism. Trotsky, however, had no desire to wait until the peasants became reconciled to communism. Revolution in the capitalistic West appeared to him far more important than economic prosperity in the U.S.S.R. He would simply force the agrarians in all lands to bow to the rule of the "enlightened proletariat." Finally, whereas Stalin was convinced of the necessity of hiring foreign capital and technical assistance to hasten both the industrialization and the communization of the U.S.S.R., Trotsky looked upon any deal with Western financiers or experts as the equivalent of treason.

The duel for supremacy began immediately after Lenin's death and from the outset Stalin seemed to have the advantage. During his long tenure as secretary-general he had had ample opportunity to see that a majority of the important party posts, especially those in the central committee, were filled with his adherents. Elevated to succeed Lenin as chairman of the Politbureau, he quietly worked with Kamenev and Zinoviev to oust Trotsky from his positions as commissar for war and member of the council of labor and defense. Early in 1925 this feat was accomplished and soon thereafter many of Trotsky's followers were removed from the war and navy departments. Then the fallen leader himself was temporarily exiled to the Caucasus "for his health," and upon his return to Moscow he was entrusted with only a minor job.

With Trotsky out of the way, Stalin attempted to effect a number of compromises with the peasants and the foreign concession-hunters. So great was his apparent retreat from communism, that his erstwhile supporters, Kamenev and Zinoviev, now turned against him. Undaunted, Stalin skillfully got the approval of the party congress of 1925 for his actions and saw to it that his latest antagonists were demoted and ordered to cease their opposition. He also recruited a new circle of supporters headed by Rykov, chairman of the council of commissars; Dzerzhinsky, head of the OGPU; and Nikolai Bukharin, member of the Supreme Economic Council and editor of the official party newspaper, *Pravda* ("Truth").

Trotsky, seeing in the changed situation an opportunity to retrieve his position, joined forces with the disgruntled Kamenev and Zinoviev and made another effort to oust his enemy from control. Once more the party backed Stalin, for he had been careful to make his policies appear as a fulfillment of the wishes of the congress, whereas Trotsky persistently strove to bend the party to his will. The dissidents, or "deviationists," as they were called, received another admonition to cease their opposition tactics and submit to the party discipline. More demotions followed and Trotsky was retired from the Politbureau.

When the deviationists persisted in their anti-Stalinist agitations, the dictator ordered the OGPU on their trail. Every move of the dissenters was watched and they were given no chance to express their views either in speech or press. Driven to meet in secret, in suburbs and woods, the Trotskyists eventually were charged with the illegal organization of an opposition group. Late in 1927 Trotsky, Kamenev, and Zinoviev were expelled from the Communist Party and in 1928 the trio was sent to outlying parts of the union.

For a brief period Stalin's leadership seemed unchallenged. Kamenev and Zinoviev recanted and their plea for reinstatement in the party was granted. Trotsky, however, from his place of exile in central Asia, continued to agitate against the man whom he regarded as "the outstanding mediocrity of the party." Experienced revolutionary that he was, Trotsky readily managed to keep in touch with his following, which included a considerable number of dissatisfied workingmen who shared his distrust of Stalin and the peasants. When, in the winter of 1928–1929, his activities inspired several disturbances, the OGPU was ordered to stamp out the opposition. Wholesale arrests were made and early in 1929 Trotsky himself was accused of counterrevolutionary activity and of "preparing for an armed struggle against the Soviet power." He was promptly deported and assisted across the Turkish border. Settling down near Constantinople, he soon produced an autobiography, an account of the Bolshevik Revolution, and innumerable attacks on Stalinism.

All Stalin's actions against Trotskyism were duly upheld by later party conferences. During 1929 and 1930 he was equally successful in crushing a "rightist deviation" led by Rykov and Bukharin. The leaders were neither banished nor even expelled from the party, but their political importance was diminished. In 1932 Zinoviev was once more expelled from the party, only to be readmitted in 1933 following an abject recantation in which he admitted that his "sin against the party had been very great." Rykov and Bukharin, however, and Mikhail Tomsky, leader of the trade unions, were again denounced as "right deviationists" in 1934 and deprived of their posts on the central committee. At the same time Zinoviev was once more ousted from the party, for his "Trotskyist deviation," and early in 1935 he was sentenced to prison for ten years.

Slowly but surely, Stalin pushed ahead, determined to achieve his goal in his own way. Never openly forcing his views on anyone, carefully giving the impression of merely carrying out the mandates of the party, the "man of steel" appeared, in 1935, to be one of the most firmly entrenched of continental dictators. And then, in August 1936, a startled world was informed by the Soviet press that Zinoviev, Kamenev, and five others were accused of having formed terrorist groups to assassinate eight Soviet leaders, including Stalin, and of having carried out the "foul murder" of Stalin's aide, Sergei Kirov, in December 1934. Nine other men were simultaneously charged with "being members of the underground Trotskyite-Zinovievite organization" and as such of having participated in "the preparations to assassinate" the seven marked officials remaining after Kirov's death. All defendants were linked with Trotsky (who had since gone to Mexico) and with the Nazi secret police. They were charged with having planned a return to the capitalist system under some form of fascist dictatorship.

The public trial was held before the Military Collegium of the Union Supreme Court and, to the astonishment of the world, the accused vied with one another in their eagerness to confess guilt and to implicate others not yet on trial. All but two pleaded guilty to the whole charge and verbally castigated themselves for having betrayed Stalin. Within five days the defendants were declared guilty and sentenced to be shot. Twenty-four hours later the press reported that the executions had been carried out. Trotsky and his son, Lev Sedov, were also declared "convicted by the evidence" and made subject to "immediate arrest and trial" if ever discovered on Soviet soil.

Meanwhile the government had investigated other highly-placed personages and another sensational trial occurred in 1937.[1] The alleged Trotskyite conspirators now included Karl Radek, former editor of *Izvestia*, Grigori Sokolnikov, former ambassador to Great Britain, and Grigori Piatakov, former assistant commissar for heavy industry. They were charged with having established contact with representatives of Germany and Japan, agreed to support these powers in a joint war against the U.S.S.R., and, in the event of the defeat of the union, promised the two states "a large number of political and economic privileges and territorial concessions." All seventeen defendants pleaded guilty, though with less breast-beating than their predecessors, and thirteen were sentenced to be shot. Four, including Radek and Sokolnikov, were given prison terms of from eight to ten years on the ground that their crimes had been "political" rather than "terroristic."

A specific enumeration of undisputed facts in the Moscow trials yields meager results. Several prominent Old Bolsheviks were indicted for plotting against the Stalin regime. They were accused of conspiring to assassinate high officials, form alliances with potential enemies of the Soviet Union, wreck the industrial program of the government and ensure an industrial breakdown in the event of war, and substitute a fascist state for the existing setup. The defendants were brought to court, confessed guilt, and were condemned to punishment. Trotsky, in exile, was linked to all charges and denied connection with any of them. Nothing else is definitely

[1] Mikhail Tomsky, formerly leader of the trade unions and then director of the State Publishing House, committed suicide during the 1936 trial.

known, although the partisans of each side speculatively elaborated upon these facts.

Throughout 1937–1938 and into 1939 there were numerous additional purges and trials, and, apparently, hundreds of executions of civil, military, and church officials. Marshals, admirals, commissars, and vice-commissars were demoted, dismissed, imprisoned, or reported shot, and entire branches of the administration were reorganized. Inefficiency, sabotage, and conspiring with foreign agents were the usual charges. The need to replace so many officials in short order led to the appointment of numerous young and inexperienced executives under whose direction it was difficult to achieve efficiency and discipline. Hence a vigorous campaign was launched, in 1939, against lazy, tardy, and irregularly attending workers. And at the end of the year, Stalin again was undisputed head of the Soviet Union.

THE FIVE-YEAR PLANS

It was under the watchful eye of Stalin that the First Five-Year Plan, which supplanted the NEP, entered into operation (October 1928). The plan was nothing less than a complete forecast of the economic and cultural life of the Soviet Union for the quinquennium 1928–1933. It was formulated by a State Planning Commission or *Gosplan,* whose function it also was to inaugurate and direct the entire program. To ensure the proper balancing, according to schedule, of every phase of the country's production, distribution, and financing, it was stipulated that no major step in industry, agriculture, transportation, or finance might be undertaken without the prior consent of the Gosplan.

Under the plan it was hoped within half a decade to increase the industrial output of the U.S.S.R. by 136 per cent and the agricultural output by 55 per cent. The production of oil and coal was to be doubled; that of iron ore trebled. The power capacity was to be multiplied by three and the output more than quadrupled (thus reaching a figure eleven times that of 1913). Technical schools were to be established and foreign experts hired. The cost of production was to be lowered by a third and the productivity of labor doubled. Fifty-five million acres of cultivated land, representing one-fifth of the peasant holdings, were to be collectivized. Illiteracy was to be virtually wiped out; the number of books published greatly increased; and music and dramatic performances made available to every village.

To make possible the proper distribution of raw materials, food-stuffs, and the manufactured products that began to be turned out in relatively large quantities, the Russians strove to repair and improve their transportation facilities. Old lines were mended, new ones constructed, the wages of employees were raised, and the service was regularized. Progress was made in the development of motor-transport facilities, but the building of hard-surface roads proceeded slowly. The attempt was made, finally, to obtain the advice of foreign experts. "Technical-assistance agreements" were signed with foreign companies and individuals, and generous terms were offered to skilled foreign workmen who would agree to come to the U.S.S.R. Since the union's credit standing abroad was poor, it was necessary to raise at home the funds required for the execution of the plan. The three chief sources of income decided upon were the profits made by the state trusts, taxes, and domestic loans. Capital savings were effected by the introduction of greater economy in all branches of the government and by a ban on the importation of luxuries.

As soon as the plan was put into effect, every effort was made to secure the fullest coöperation of the citizenry. That the program would bring hardship to the people was no secret, particularly after the reintroduction in 1928 of a rationing system, which soon included nearly every food staple. By the unremitting use of oratory, press, radio, cinema, parades, ceremonies, and processions, the people were stirred to a fever of excitement. Everywhere "shock brigades" of young communists vied in the accomplishment of production tasks in order to spread the contagion of enthusiasm. The spirit of competition and rivalry was systematically exploited, prizes were awarded when production quotas were exceeded, and the completion of any exceptionally difficult job in advance of schedule was invariably made the occasion for a celebration.

To the amazement of observers, friendly and hostile alike, the plan in operation seemed actually to outstrip the plan on paper. The oil industry completed its five-year assignment in two years and a half. A few months later the 1933 quota output was reached in the manufacture of agricultural machinery, automobiles, and tractors. The five-year production goal in peat, sugar, coal, and electrical equipment was passed after three years, while the output of iron, steel, and textiles also ran ahead of schedule. The 1100-mile Turkestan-Siberian Railway was finished in 1930, more than a year ahead of time. A dam and 900,000-horsepower hydroelectric plant at Dnieprostroy were dedicated in the summer of 1932.

In agriculture the results for a time appeared equally gratifying. Although the plan envisioned a collectivization of only 20 per cent of the peasant homesteads by 1933, almost 60 per cent of all farm holdings were reported merged in collectives by 1931. Each collective farm or *kolkhoz* was managed by an elected board of directors. Since nearly all the board members were communists, the party and state virtually controlled the kolkhozi. Progress also was made in the development of the state farms, known as *sovkhozi*. The largest of these, the "Giant Farm," comprised more than a quarter-million acres. The enrolment in consumers' coöperatives, incidentally, had gone up to fifty-five million by 1932, and only 5.5 per cent of the retail trade remained in private hands. So encouraging were these results that the date for the ending of the plan was advanced to December 1, 1932.

Nevertheless, there were certain indications that the course of the first plan would not be entirely steady. In 1929 and 1930 it had been noticed that the plan lagged in two of its most important items: a lowered cost of production and an increase in the productivity of labor. It further was evident, often unpleasantly so, that quantity of output was being produced at the expense of quality. Then, in the spring of 1932, the automobile works at Nizhni-Novgorod (Gorki), which had been expected to turn out 144,000 cars per year, was closed—three months after its much-celebrated opening. This same spring witnessed an acute shortage of grain and livestock, and another serious agrarian crisis. Why?

So comprehensive a plan would have been difficult to fulfill in any country. It was especially hard in a region industrially as backward as the U.S.S.R. For a time, it is true, the projected schedule actually was exceeded. This was so particularly in construction work and in the setting up, with foreign help, of expensive and intricate foreign machinery. But once the factories were built and the machines installed, it soon became evident that the untrained native workmen were more likely to ruin than run the complex engines. There was a disastrous shortage of skilled, technical labor and the factories were staffed largely with inexperienced ex-peasants, many of whom were addicted to drink, a situation which was plainly reflected in the growing number of industrial accidents.

A further check to efficient production resulted from the vogue of "democracy" that prevailed in the management of the factories. The proper operation of the new plants was hampered by the reservation of numerous privileges to the workers. Whereas the successful direction of large-scale industry demanded a fairly rigid discipline and a certain minimum of regimentation, the system in the U.S.S.R. permitted an arrangement under which the workmen in a plant might refuse to carry out an order of the management until they had previously met to discuss its propriety. This "interference of democratic meetingism," as the communist leaders called it, was one of the most serious obstacles to the success of the plan.

To make matters worse, the Gosplan, in its original schedules, had failed to provide for an extension of transportation facilities adequate to meet the needs of expanding industry. In consequence freight piled up in the depots, perishable goods rotted at the terminals, and the factories ran short of raw materials. At one time the commissar for transport estimated that ten million tons of freight were assembled at various points, ready for shipment, but that they could not be dispatched for lack of trains and crews. The fact that some parts of the economic program could be completed far ahead of schedule while others could not was an additional weakness of the plan. It threw the entire scheme out of balance and made necessary complicated and often awkward readjustments.

In order to maintain for any length of time the feverish enthusiasm which the official propaganda created among the people and to enable the laborers to work at top speed over a period of years, a plentiful food supply was essential. Yet the Soviet Government, for various reasons, found it necessary to curtail the sustenance allowances of its workers. Since neither the U.S.S.R.'s credit nor her rubles enjoyed much standing abroad, and since she was in desperate need of foreign machines and goods, she had to export and sell at any price huge quantities of grain, timber, oil, and other domestic products. To obtain a surplus for export the state drastically reduced the rations, once more introduced a modified form of requisitions and grain collections, and used every method in its power to hasten the process of agricultural collectivization.

As a means of tempting individual farmers to pool their interests, the state extended special privileges, including tax reductions and easy credit facilities, to the members of collectives. Persistent nonjoiners, on the other hand, were subjected to a crushing tax, were ordered periodically to surrender to the authorities specified quantities of grain, and were deprived of their farms if they failed to meet the quotas. It was chiefly the kulaks who suffered under this arrangement, for they had little desire to merge their land, tools, and animals with those of their poorer neighbors, to get in return merely a share of the total profits proportionate to the amount and quality of labor which they would contribute in the fields.

One aspect of this attempt by the state to "liquidate the kulaks as a class" was the incitement of the poorer against the richer peasants. In each collective a liquidation committee was formed to select the victims for the local "drive" and from 1929 to 1931 the resulting bloodshed was reminiscent of the early days of the Bolshevik regime. The hounded kulaks banded themselves together for self-defense and reprisals, attacked the property of the collectives, and destroyed their own crops and livestock lest these fall into the hands of the hated opponents. Thousands were exiled to Siberia or the north to build roads and other public improvements. Some of the less courageous kulaks capitulated and entered the collectives. Before joining, however, they frequently slaughtered their animals, preferring to eat them rather than surrender them to the kolkhozi. Altogether more than a third of the country's livestock was killed, with the result that a meat shortage was experienced in 1931 and 1932. The rapid collectivization of the land by force or persuasion also resulted in the union's being short of the necessary agricultural machinery with which to work the large farms.

The net result at home of these stringencies and of the continued export of badly needed supplies was a lowering of the general standard of living beneath that which had prevailed in the later years of the NEP period. There was a parallel decline in the efficiency and enthusiasm of labor and in the progress of the Five-Year Plan.

The authorities, aware of these adverse influences, took steps to counteract them. In the industrial sphere, between 1930 and 1932, the workday was lengthened, discriminations against noncommunist skilled workers were lessened, and the control of factory managements over employees was increased while the power of the workers' committees was correspondingly reduced. Differential wage rates were instituted to reward the quick workers and to stimulate the slow ones. Piece work was introduced in new lines and more efficient methods of accounting and management were adopted in all branches of industry. A strenuous effort was made to end the rationing of certain staples and to increase the size of the remaining rations. This was all the more necessary since the high cost of foodstuffs made it hard, even with augmented wages, to buy extra-ration supplies. Simultaneously with these compromises, however, the war against private trading was continued with vigor. The state was determined to secure greater efficiency on the part of its citizens, but only within the framework of the socialist system.

In agriculture the concessions were equally sweeping. The process of collectivization was temporarily slackened. The abler members of the collectives, some of them former kulaks, were given managerial posts. Five per cent of the net income of each collective was set aside as a fund to reimburse members for the animals and machinery which they contributed to the association. Peasants and petty craftsmen were allowed to effect direct exchanges of food and manufactured goods.

These agrarian dispensations came too late to prevent a famine in 1932–1933. Unfavorable climatic conditions, heavy state exactions and requisitions, and the drive on the kulaks, all contributed to an agricultural crisis that was especially severe in the Ukraine, the northern Caucasus, and central Asia. Here the proportion of kulaks and of dissatisfied members of the collectives was larger than in other parts of the union and the government apparently determined to enforce complete submission by means of what has been called "organized famine." The requisitions were continued despite the patent shortage of grain and the censorship was tightened so that news of the resulting starvation might not escape. Foreign correspondents were refused permits to travel in the affected regions until the famine was over. In 1933 the people, weak and submissive but aided by favorable weather, worked hard and produced a bumper crop. They had, in the reported words of a Soviet official, "passed through a good, if ruthless, school."

The progress of the plan had important repercussions on the union's foreign relations. Because Russian goods were placed on the world market at prices which often were far below the cost of production, the cry was raised, particularly in the United States and France, that the Soviets were "dumping" their products in order to demoralize the economic system of the capitalist states and thus prepare the way for an immediate world revolution. The chief object of the Bolsheviks, however, was to secure, at any cost, certain urgently needed manufactures. Although willing to negotiate reciprocal trade agreements with any states that cared to solicit her business, the U.S.S.R., lacking credit and funds, was determined to dispose of her requisitioned surpluses under any conditions. Meanwhile the Gosplan compiled figures for a second five-year plan. Care was taken to avoid a repetition of the mistakes of the earlier program.

In 1933 the Gosplan announced that
the gigantic achievements of the first Five-Year Plan made it possible
to set, in the second Five-Year Plan [intended to run from January
1933 through December 1937], the task of finally abolishing the capitalist elements and of classes generally, and of transforming the whole
of the working population of the country into conscious and active
builders of classless socialist society; it has also permitted the raising
of the great question of completing the technical reconstruction of the
whole of the national economy of the Soviet Union, of bringing the
U.S.S.R. to the first place in Europe in regard to technical development, and of finally securing the technical and economic independence of the U.S.S.R.[1]

The new plan stipulated that the industrial output in 1937 was
to be 2.14 times as great as that of 1932, or 8 times the latest prewar figure. The agricultural output was to be doubled in the same
period and accompanied by the completion of collectivization and
the virtual completion of mechanization. The capacity of the steel
mills and the production of coal were to be doubled, while the
output of automobiles was to be multiplied by seven and that of
fertilizers by ten. Fifty per cent increases were called for in the
sugar and cotton-textile industries. The number of skilled special-
ists in all categories was to be increased by 46.5 per cent. Great
strides were planned in civil aviation. The kulaks, all remaining
"capitalist elements," and any still-existent "private property in
production" were to be wholly "liquidated." Illiteracy was to be
ended and compulsory polytechnical education for seven years for
all children was to be introduced into the villages as it already
existed in many cities.

Several general differences between the first and second plans
were readily evident. The second plan emphasized quality more
than had the first one and paid greater attention to transportation
facilities. More caution was exercised in the drawing up of the later
production schedules and the "giant mania" was less conspicuous.
The later program allocated the new industries in closer proximity
to the raw materials and definitely outlined an eastward trend in
the future establishment of manufacturing plants—this latter
being an important factor from the viewpoint of easier military
protection.[2] Finally, in an attempt to stimulate the growth of local

[1] State Planning Commission of the U.S.S.R. *Summary of the Fulfilment of the
First Five-Year Plan,* 1933, pp. 36–37.

[2] The wisdom of this step became especially apparent after the German invasion
of the U.S.S.R. in 1941.

industries, raise the standard of living, and increase the real wages, greater emphasis was now placed on the production of consumers' goods.

As had previously been the case, the estimates of the Second Five-Year Plan generally appeared on the road to fulfillment in the first two or three years of the functioning of the program. On the other hand, the advances in transportation once more lagged and neither the cost of production nor the price of goods fell so rapidly as had been anticipated. Hence the avowed goal to bring the U.S.S.R. "to the first place in Europe in regard to technical development" and to "overtake and outstrip America" was far from realization when the Second Five-Year Plan gave way to the Third Five-Year Plan on January 1, 1938. None the less, by the time of the outbreak of the Second World War in 1939, amazing industrial and agricultural progress had been made under the combined stimuli of the several five-year plans.

By the middle of 1939 about 93.5 per cent of all peasant households had become collectivized.[1] The collective farms, numbering approximately 245,000, accounted for 99.1 per cent of the area sown to grain, and the quantity of foodstuffs produced had increased at a steady rate. There was a vigorous "purge" of collectivized peasants in the spring of 1938 on the ground that many had become "wreckers." Because such an expelled "wrecker" and his family were doomed to starvation, officials were cautioned to refrain from being callous and arbitrary in their decisions.

Most of the collective farms were of the *artel* type. They combined communal features with the limited individual ownership of homesteads, minor implements, and livestock. These possessions were heritable. The work on the kolkhozi was done under a "brigade" system and each farm was required to deliver a specified quantity of grain to the state at fixed prices. No farm was permitted to own heavy machinery. Tractors and combines might be rented at a high (grain) fee from one of the government tractor stations. The peasants were permitted to sell any surplus directly to consumers but resale was forbidden. Under a law of 1935 each kolkhoz was given a boundary deed by the state and many of the farms benefited at the expense of neighboring model state farms.

There was a slow but steady trend toward urbanization in the union, the percentage having risen from 18 on the eve of the First

[1] About two million peasant households were still noncollectivized. The noncollectivized households had to deliver higher grain quotas and pay a higher agricultural tax than did their collectivized brethren.

World War to 25.5 in 1937. The number of industrial workers increased rapidly, as did the number of persons in the direct employ of the government, both as officials and as workers. The center of population, moreover, moved eastward, as Siberia and central Asia experienced an influx of settlers. Emphasis also began to be placed on small items of luxury and the government encouraged a spirit of domesticity in its subjects, but since there was a serious lag in the production of consumers' goods (especially in 1938), the standard of living rose only slowly. Savings-bank deposits increased from 1,600,000,000 rubles in early 1935 to 6,000,000,000 rubles in early 1939, but the accumulation doubtless reflected a shortage of purchasable goods as well as an increase in wages and thrift. The census of 1939 gave the Soviet Union a population of 170,500,000, an increase of almost 16 per cent over 1926.

EDUCATION AND RELIGION

Through its persecution of the intelligentsia and the professionals, and of the well-to-do people whose patronage supported these groups, the Soviet Government inflicted upon the state a serious cultural loss. It was the middle and upper classes which had supplied most of the empire's famed artists, actors, musicians, singers, dancers, scientists, educators, doctors, and writers; but with the death, exile, or suppression of so many of these talented individuals the country was left with a sort of cultural vacuum. Worse still, at the time of the communists' advent to power, almost two-thirds of the men and seven-eighths of the women in Russia were illiterate, for the war and revolutions had interfered with a program of the old parliament to establish compulsory, universal education by 1922.

The Bolsheviks, however, were determined "mercilessly to liquidate the bourgeois ideology" and build up a new culture. Every "toiler and toiler's child" was to be given the right to a schooling. This official resolution to educate the masses probably was based on a realization that wholesale illiteracy would hamper the material development of the state and make impossible the effective spreading of the gospel of socialism. Unless the people, especially the peasants, were literate and able to absorb instruction in the principles of Marxism, they would fail to understand or else misinterpret every policy that the authorities hoped to inaugurate. To new, communist-controlled schools, therefore, was assigned the threefold task of enlightening the adults, preparing a host of enthusiastic young communists to carry on the work of the revolution, and developing engineers and other technicians to fill the vacancies created by the ousting of the skilled masters of the old regime.

The control of education, which had formerly been in the hands of the imperial government, the Orthodox Church, or private individuals, was now placed to a considerable extent into those of the local authorities. As a consequence, the drive against illiteracy did not progress uniformly throughout the union. The larger cities boasted some of the most up-to-date schools in the world, while in the remote country districts there remained many one-room schoolhouses without blackboards, textbooks, or good teachers. Time, however, and readier funds seemed to be the chief requisites for an improvement of this condition.

Wherever it was found necessary to restrict the enrollment in the schools, discrimination was made, at least until the autumn of 1935, in favor of the children of members of the Communist Party. The offspring of noncommunist workers and peasants received secondary consideration, while the remaining children in any district could secure classroom instruction only if sufficient space was available. Special efforts were made to enroll the adults in factory schools or university extension divisions. As far as possible the schools were staffed with communists.

By 1926 the total school population of the U.S.S.R. was equal to that of the last prewar year in Imperial Russia. The fall of 1938 saw 33,000,000 children in elementary and secondary schools and more than a million persons in the higher institutions of learning. According to official figures, 81.2 per cent of the population was literate in 1939. A decree of 1933 made a minimum of seven years of school attendance compulsory for every child in the union, the ultimate goal being to introduce "universal obligatory technical education for all children up to the age of seventeen years." Forty Latinized alphabets had been created by 1935 for nationalities that hitherto had had no written languages.

In their efforts to shape a new ideology based on Leninism, the authorities placed reliance not merely upon schools and teachers but upon the stage, the cinema, art, literature, radio, and music. There was constant official direction of and curb on creative accomplishment, but the U.S.S.R. soon did produce some outstanding personalities in literature, science, and art. Boris Pilniak, author of *The Bare Year,* an impressionistic account of the famine and war years, and of *The Volga Flows to the Caspian Sea,* became perhaps the best known of the younger writers. Leonid Leonov, whose *Badgers* provides a vivid description of the peasant struggle against the communist ideal, and the poet Demian Bedny also acquired an international reading public. Vsevolod Meierhold achieved recognition as a stage director and the work of Sergei Eisenstein and Vsevolod Poduvkin in the production of films aroused admiration in Europe and the United States. Other prominent members of the new intelligentsia included the physicist, Abram Joffe, and the biophysicist, Petr Lazarev. Of the pre-revolutionary intellectuals who continued to serve Russia, perhaps the best known were the dramatist, Maxim Gorki, and the physiologist, Ivan Pavlov. In 1935 there was performed at the Metropolitan Opera House in New York a grim Soviet opera composed by the twenty-eight-year-old Dmitri Shostakovich and entitled *Lady Macbeth of Mtzensk.* His Seventh or Leningrad Symphony was widely acclaimed in the United States in 1942.

Radical as were the changes effected with regard to education, those inaugurated in respect of religion were even more startling. Since the followers of Lenin looked upon religion as "the opiate of the people," they resolved to banish the influence of the clergy. The Orthodox Church was disestablished, its properties were confiscated, and many of its edifices were torn down or converted into clubhouses and museums. The clergy was deprived of control over education, marriage, cemeteries, and the registration of births and deaths. At first religious instruction was forbidden, but eventually the teaching of religion to small groups was permitted outside school or church buildings. The state refused to have any relations with a church hierarchy but agreed to extend to congregations of twenty or more parishioners the use of some of the confiscated religious property.

Since the communists at first aimed their shafts specifically at the Orthodox Church and raised the ban on the free propagation of other faiths and of atheism, various religious groups, such as the Lutherans, Baptists, and Methodists, by dint of considerable social-welfare work, quickly won converts from Eastern Catholicism. This situation spurred into renewed activity the Orthodox Church, which had in reality continued to exercise a fair degree of influence over the minds and lives of the peasants. The state, quick to observe this turn of events, now limited the activities of all clerical bodies to preaching in churches. A constitutional amendment of 1929 forbade the general propagation of any and all spiritual doctrines except atheism. The fight against religion was made an aspect of the struggle against counterrevolution and "godless societies" soon sprouted in profusion.

Although attendance at church was not prohibited to the mass of citizens, it was forbidden to members of the Communist Party. Such anniversaries as Christmas and Easter continued to be observed, not as religious holidays, but as "traditional days of rest." An effort was made to substitute for them such revolutionary holidays as Lenin Day. Religion, clericals, and worshippers were held up to ridicule and scorn, and some of the most famous Russian churches and monasteries became antireligious exhibition halls.

THE U.S.S.R. IN INTERNATIONAL AFFAIRS

a. The Comintern

The ultimate mission of communism lay in four revolutionary steps: (1) the complete overthrow of the existing order of things; (2) the temporary establishment in all countries of a dictatorship of the proletariat; (3) the creation of a world federation of soviet republics; and (4) the achievement of a universal communist society. To carry out this program was the self-imposed task of an international gathering of communists at Moscow in March 1919. Assured of the support of the Bolshevik Government, the congress organized itself as the Third (First Communist) International or Comintern,[1] drew up a schedule of basic objectives and a plan of action, and elected Gregory Zinoviev as its first president.

At the Comintern headquarters in Moscow came to be represented most of the communist parties of the world. By virtue of its strength and backing, the Russian Communist Party dominated the proceedings. In its periodical congresses the International laid down iron-clad rules of discipline both for individual and national members, outlined a program of anticapitalistic activities, and encouraged the organization of new national branches. It sent out speakers and agitators, set up printing presses, raised funds and occasionally made contributions to needy communist groups, dispatched representatives to watch over the doings of the national

---

[1] The First (Socialist) International, really the International Working Men's Association, was organized in 1864 by Karl Marx and held annual sessions until 1876. The Second International, with which were affiliated most of the Socialist and Labor parties of the world, was established in 1889. Its activities were checked by the First World War but it came to life again in 1919. The Second and Third Internationals remained hostile to each other. The "Red" anthem is called the "Internationale." Its words were written in 1871 by Eugene Pottier.

members, determined the policies of all affiliates in both general and specific matters, and in every way tried to stir up the workers in the West and the peasants in the East against the existing social and economic order. The Communist International regarded itself as the "general staff of the world revolution."

The revolutionary efforts of the Comintern caused great annoyance to foreign governments. The authorities in Germany, Hungary, and the Baltic states bitterly resented the aid rendered by the body to the radicals who, in 1919, 1920, and later years, set up or tried to set up local Bolshevik councils. In the United States there was a "Red Scare" which eventually led to the deportation of hundreds of alien "suspects." In many parts of the United States, displaying a red flag—the communist emblem—was made punishable by imprisonment. Eventually, many Western governments extended to the communists freedom of speech, press, and assembly provided there was no violence and no incitement to direct action. In eastern and southern Europe, and in many of the colonial regions of Africa and Asia, agitators continued to be arrested upon identification as communists.

At the outset the Third International and the Soviet Government worked in close harmony. The latter contributed funds to the cause and encouraged every effort to foment disorder. Beginning with 1921 the coöperation was less pronounced. By this time many members of the Communist Party and the Moscow Government had come to the conclusion that the gains of the revolution must first be consolidated at home before any further major step could be taken. They realized that they were dependent upon the capitalist world for manufactures and technical advice, and they knew that these essentials would be available only if they could promise in return a cessation of Bolshevik propaganda. Consequently the supply of funds was curtailed and efforts were made to convince other countries of the independent status of the government and the International. Many high officials in the government, however, continued simultaneously to occupy ranking positions in the International.

For the sake of trade or other concessions the Soviet Government, over the objections of the International, occasionally ordered its representatives abroad to check Bolshevik propaganda. Sometimes the Comintern scolded the state for its domestic and foreign compromises with the bourgeois system, but these reprimands were lightly treated by the leaders who, like Stalin, claimed that the only worth-while communistic propaganda was the success of the Russian experiment. They regarded the fulfillment of successive five-year plans as more vital than world revolution. Gradually, especially after the rise of Nazism, the Comintern, while still working for world revolution, transformed itself largely "into an international body whose chief and immediate goal was the defense of the Soviet Union." In 1935 the Comintern permitted the various national communist parties to coöperate with the liberal-bourgeois elements in a fight against fascism, while simultaneously continuing to "bore from within" in order to "create a united proletarian front."

b. Conflict and Truce, 1918–1924

From 1918–1921 the policy of the Soviet Government in foreign affairs was to promote world revolution, use Russia as a base from which to launch the onslaught against capitalism, and aid Bolshevik uprisings wherever they might occur. Efforts were made to convert the masses of Asia to communism in the hope that they might then be united, under Russian leadership, in a gigantic "crusade against capitalism and imperialism."

To arouse sympathy for their cause among the Orientals, the Bolsheviks denounced the Anglo-Russian Entente of 1907 which had divided Persia into foreign spheres of influence, gave up most of the special privileges which the tsarist governments had acquired in China, surrendered all extraterritorial and financial rights in Turkey, and encouraged the Afghans to resist British control. In September 1920 they called together at Baku the First (and only) Congress of Peoples of the East. Almost nineteen hundred delegates, representing nearly forty nationalities, were present at the gathering, and numerous optimistic resolutions were passed. Since the deputies represented only certain elements in their respective countries and not the governments, little practical progress was made toward the formation of an oriental communist alliance. Neither Turkey, nor Persia, nor Afghanistan, nor China "went Red," and even in India the communists failed to gain control of the anti-British movement.

As 1921 drew on, capitalism in the West seemed more solidly entrenched than ever, while attempted pure communism had failed in Russia. Hence, coincident with the adoption of the New Economic Policy, the Soviets, convinced of the need to consolidate their power at home and improve the economic situation, were ready to enter into a truce with the bourgeois world. The latter, made confident by its successful resistance to radical propaganda and anxious to "do business" even with the Bolsheviks, was equally willing to negotiate.

The first fruit of the new attitudes was a provisional Anglo-Russian trade agreement of 1921. Pending the conclusion of a formal peace treaty between the two countries, this convention provided for the resumption of normal trade relations subject to the mutual renunciation of propagandist activities. Russia promised to desist from inciting Asiatics against the British, while Great Britain agreed to raise her blockade of Russian ports and help in the clearance of Russian waters from mines sown during the years of anti-Bolshevik intervention. Each government pledged itself not to requisition merchandise imported from the other's domains. Before the end of the year the Russians had completed similar trade pacts with eleven other states.

Although Russia had automatically been accorded *de facto* recognition [1] by the countries which thus signed conventions with her, she still was not a member in good standing of the family of nations. Full diplomatic relations were not yet restored and most of the treaty signatories merely exchanged with her semiofficial and commercial representatives. The flow of capital into Russia, moreover, remained inadequate to meet the needs of Russian economy. The chief reason for this continued Western aloofness was the fact that the Bolsheviks in 1918 had repudiated Russia's foreign debts, totaling about $8,000,000,000.

Still in 1921, therefore, George Chicherin, the commissar for foreign affairs, notified the powers that his government, though in no way feeling bound to honor the debts incurred by the former regime, was ready to discuss the matter at an international congress simultaneously with the questions of Russian recognition and the extension of foreign credit facilities. After some hesitation, and then chiefly through the efforts of Lloyd George, Russia was invited to attend a European economic conference at Genoa. Some of the Western statesmen apparently felt that the Chicherin note and the inauguration of the NEP, with its partial restoration of private trading, signalized a reversal of Soviet policy—the setting in of a "Russian Thermidor."

The conference opened in 1922 with all Russia's creditors officially represented except the United States. The lenders demanded (1) that the repudiated debts be recognized; (2) that due

---

[1] *De facto* recognition means recognition of a government as actually existing, with no implication as to whether or not its existence is legal. *De jure* recognition implies recognition of rightful and legal existence.

compensation be paid the foreigners whose private property in Russia had been nationalized; and (3) that a juridical system be set up to protect and enforce future contracts. The Russians held out for cancelation of Russia's war debt and the granting of large foreign credits. They promised to recognize all prewar foreign obligations provided the Allies accorded Russia an even larger sum for damages caused during the period of military intervention. Several weeks were spent in negotiation, but no agreement could be reached. Instead, to the dismay of the former Allies, the Russian and German delegates to the conference signed the Treaty of Rapallo. This document not only secured for the Moscow Government *de jure* recognition by a great power but provisionally freed Russia of her German debts, opened the way to eventual commercial agreements, and lessened Soviet dependence upon the good will of London and Paris.

By the end of 1923 Russia had got *de jure* recognition only from Germany and a few minor states. She therefore announced that henceforth prior unconditional recognition would be expected from any country that desired to discuss trade, concessions, or debts. As an inducement she offered a "prize" in the form of an especially favorable commercial treaty to that great power which first accorded recognition. Mussolini at once arranged for conversations with Bolshevik representatives. Although he promptly informed the Italian Parliament that he recognized the Soviet Union, he proposed to withhold a formal declaration to that effect until he could be sure of "a good trade treaty."

While the Italo-Soviet *pourparlers* were in progress, British elections resulted in the elevation to the premiership of MacDonald, leader of the Labor Party. In February 1924 the MacDonald Government extended to the U.S.S.R. unconditional *de jure* recognition. This news spurred the Italians to quicker action and the authorities at Rome formally recognized the Soviet Union a few days later. Negotiations for special commercial treaties were thereupon pushed with both Great Britain and Italy. Before the close of 1924 nine other countries recognized the Bolshevik Government. Diplomatic peace between the "proletarian" and "capitalistic" states at last appeared to have been effected.

c. Fifteen Difficult Years, 1924–1939

The good fortune that attended Soviet foreign endeavors in 1924 did not last into the following year. A proposed treaty with Great Britain in August 1924, respecting a debt settlement and credits, was thrown out by the Conservative Baldwin Government which succeeded the Labor Ministry. Efforts to negotiate a trade agreement with France came to naught, chiefly because the Bolsheviks frowned upon the importation of luxuries—the main item in French exports. Even the link with Germany seemed to be weakened when the latter signed the Locarno Pact, which was regarded in Moscow as a conspiracy against the U.S.S.R. Fearful lest a European bloc be formed against her, the Soviet Union now concluded nonaggression pacts with several near-by countries, including Turkey (1925) and Germany (1926).

These events annoyed the Conservatives in Great Britain and the Poincaré group in France. Anglo-Soviet friendship was further strained by the action of the Bolshevik trade unions in contributing funds to aid the participants in the British strike of 1926. In 1927 Chamberlain warned Moscow that diplomatic relations would once more be severed unless the anti-British propagandist activities in Europe and Asia ceased. Then, unexpectedly, the British police raided the private offices of Arcos, Ltd., the Soviet trading corporation in London. The reason for this action was the belief that the Bolsheviks were in possession of secret documents that had recently disappeared from the British War Office. Although the papers in question were not found, Downing Street declared that sufficient evidence of illegal activities had been uncovered to warrant the termination of diplomatic relations with the U.S.S.R. Parliament so voted. Not until 1929, when a second Labor Government was in power, was Anglo-Soviet diplomatic intercourse resumed.

The same year that witnessed the rupture in Soviet-British relations saw a crisis in Soviet-French affairs. The French, despite their official recognition policy, adopted an unfriendly attitude towards Moscow. They were vexed by Moscow's continued ban on the importation of luxuries and by their inability to redeem the Russian bonds that had been purchased prior to the summer of 1914. The Soviet-German *rapprochement* frightened them and they interpreted as an affront a remark of the Soviet Ambassador to Paris that he would regard it as his duty in case of a foreign war against the Soviets to encourage the soldiers and workers of the bourgeois states to join the "Red Army." In 1927 Poincaré rejected a Soviet offer regarding debts and credits and demanded the recall of the ambassador. In this year, also, the Chinese Nationalists raided the Soviet Embassy in Peking and the Soviet Ambassador to Poland was assassinated by an exiled "White."

Such incidents caused uneasiness in Moscow and further attempts were made to ensure security against united European action. Nonaggression treaties were negotiated with Persia and Latvia, the Kellogg Pact was signed, and a number of the U.S.S.R.'s neighbors were induced to adhere with her to the Litvinov Protocol (1929). Moscow also helped to bring about a reconciliation between Fascist Italy and Turkey, and made an arrangement (1931) with Germany whereby the Reich guaranteed to German industry a large Soviet credit.

It was now the turn of France to become worried. The Paris Government was alarmed at the growing Russian-German-Italian-Turkish friendship and disgruntled over France's inability to capture a profitable share of Soviet foreign trade. In 1930, therefore, Paris tried to build up a European federation against Moscow. She raised the cry that the Bolsheviks were "dumping" their goods upon foreign markets in order to break down the Western economic system, and she advocated the formation of a Pan-Europa minus the U.S.S.R. Soviet imports into France were placed under a licensing system which made it possible for the government virtually to abolish such imports. Soon thereafter Belgium inaugurated a similar measure. The cry of dumping was quickly taken up in other countries, notably the United States and Great Britain. In 1931 interested parties who objected either to Soviet sales competition or to the Soviet system agitated for embargoes on Soviet shipments, especially of wheat, timber, and cotton.

Then there came about another change in the attitudes of the U.S.S.R. and the European states towards each other. Moscow became suspicious of the anticommunist tactics of the Hitlerites in Germany, who pronounced a Soviet-German war inevitable. Germany suffered severely from the world depression and hence was growing less valuable as a Soviet customer. It was therefore felt that greater efforts might be made to gain the advantages of increased trade with both France and the United States. The states of western Europe, on the other hand, which quickly discovered the futility of having conferences at which the U.S.S.R. was not represented, now regarded prosperity as more important than prejudice.

The path to a reorientation of international policies seemed cleared at a Geneva conference of 1931 which deliberated upon the feasibility of a European union. At this gathering Maxim Litvinov, who had succeeded Chicherin as commissar for foreign affairs, created a favorable impression and he aroused some enthusiasm for a plan to negotiate an economic nonagression pact between capitalism and sovietism. Although this suggestion was not adopted by the conference, the door was opened for further individual developments. France, especially, seemed to reverse her former stand. She was anxious to destroy the solid front of those states—Germany, Italy, the U.S.S.R., and Hungary—which advocated a revision of the peace treaties. As a first sign of the new development, a Franco-Soviet treaty of neutrality and nonaggression was signed in 1932.[1]

As 1933 opened, the United States remained the only major power that refused to recognize the U.S.S.R. Washington wished to have no dealings with a government which neglected to fulfil its international obligations (Russia's American debt, including interest charges, amounted to about $800,000,000) and that attempted to subvert democracy in other lands. But when, in 1932, the value of American sales to the U.S.S.R. dropped to $13,000,-000—one-third as much as those of Great Britain and one-tenth as much as those of Germany—an important section of American business men came to favor closer relations with the Soviet Union. And the latter, meanwhile, had found new cause for worry in eastern Asia where Japanese and Soviet interests threatened to clash in Manchuria and Mongolia. In 1933, therefore, Moscow welcomed the invitation of President Franklin D. Roosevelt to send representatives to Washington to discuss the possible resumption of Russo-American diplomatic relations. Litvinov thereupon journeyed to Washington and diplomatic relations between the two states were formally reopened in November 1933, through an exchange of official letters.

In these notes each government agreed to respect the territorial integrity of the other and to prohibit "the formation or residence on its territory of any organization or group" which aimed at "the overthrow of, or bringing about by force of a change in, the political or social order" of the other.[2] The U.S.S.R. also assured to visiting Americans the right to worship in their own churches and

[1] In 1933, however, frightened by the rise to power of Hitler and by the conclusion of the Pact of Rome among Great Britain, France, Germany, and Italy, the Bolsheviks negotiated the London Agreements wherein the U.S.S.R. and ten of her small neighbors confirmed the integrity of each other's boundaries, reiterated the obligations of the Kellogg Pact, and adopted a clear definition of the term "aggressor nation." (See p. 185 and n. 2.)

[2] A strict interpretation of this provision would seemingly have required the Soviet Government to expel the Comintern unless the latter withdrew all support from the communist movement in the United States.

promised not to refuse entry into the country to American ecclesiastical functionaries because of their "having an ecclesiastical status." Both governments bound themselves, in the event of the arrest of nationals of the one in the other, to notify at once the appropriate consular agents. All American-Soviet financial questions were left to future settlement through the regular diplomatic channels. The U.S.S.R. waived her claims for damages arising out of American intervention in eastern Siberia from 1918 to 1920, while reserving the right to claim damages in connection with the American military activities at Murmansk and Archangel in northern Russia.[1] Those Americans who had expected recognition to lead to an immediate and enormous increase in trade with the U.S.S.R. were disappointed, for Soviet purchases in the United States remained at a low figure. Politically, however, the renewal of relations appeared to have some influence on the continued maintenance of peace in the Far East.

Fear of a possible Japanese imbroglio and of the ultimate aims of Nazi Germany not only induced the U.S.S.R. to welcome the opportunity for American recognition and for strengthening the ties of friendship with her smaller neighbors but led her to view the League of Nations with an almost kindly regard. At first the Soviets would have nothing to do with the League, considering it a superweapon of capitalism against communism. By 1927 they had been ready to participate in an economic conference held under League auspices, and in 1928 and 1929 they sent representatives to preparatory disarmament gatherings. In 1932 the U.S.S.R. took part in the Geneva Disarmament Conference and endorsed every important move to reduce armaments. Hence it caused little astonishment when, in 1934 (the year after Japan and Germany submitted their resignations), the Soviet Union was admitted to League membership with a permanent seat on the Council.

In 1935 the growing *rapprochement* with France, stimulated by mutual fear of German rearmament measures, led to the signing of a Franco-Soviet pact of mutual assistance which was in some ways reminiscent of the Franco-Russian Alliance of 1894. Then, while sympathizing actively with the established government during Spain's civil war and plainly showing displeasure over the Anti-Comintern Pact, the U.S.S.R. strove to keep strong its diplomatic connections with Paris and Prague. Understandably, how-

[1] The United States had made no attempt to appropriate territory in eastern Siberia; instead, she had exerted a restraining influence on Japan who had sent many thousands of soldiers into the area.

ever, it refused to come alone to the defense of Czechoslovakia against Germany in 1938. The Franco-British acquiescence in Germany's demands at Munich, indeed, marked another turning point in the relations of the Soviet Union with the great powers of Europe.

After the signing of the Munich Agreement, and especially after the Anglo-French acceptance of a German protectorate over Czechia and Slovakia early in 1939, Moscow obviously mistrusted the leadership of London and Paris. The first concrete evidence of a new Soviet orientation was the "resignation" (May 1939) of Foreign Commissar Litvinov, leading Bolshevik advocate of collective security in coöperation with Britain and France. He was succeeded by Viacheslav M. Molotov, close friend of Stalin and advocate of a Soviet foreign policy that might well have been termed nationalistic. Before long, Soviet policy once more appeared to reverse itself—through the signing of a neutrality pact with Nazi Germany shortly before the outbreak of the Second World War.[1]

[1] See Chapter XXIV. On Soviet relations in the Far East see Chapter XXII.

CHAPTER XX

Southeastern Europe

EUROPE'S "WITCHES' CAULDRON"

Long called "the sore spot of Europe," the region popularly known as "the Balkans" continued, in the period 1919–1939, to be characterized by restlessness and instability. To the turbulence, feuds, and corruption that were the heritage of centuries of Ottoman misrule, the more recent decades added the conflicting Near-Eastern policies of the great powers and the rivalries of half a dozen Balkan nationalisms. National lines were not clear-cut in Balkania, which for hundreds of years served as a convenient channel of entry from Asia into Europe for many and varied peoples. But the virus of nationalism was none the less strong. Each group, each racial mixture, had, or thought it had, proud traditions and heroic legends, and a mission to fulfill. Often these missions clashed.

The restive Balkan peoples, sharing in the general responsibility for the First World War, suffered severe hardship during the conflict and occasioned bitter tilts at the Paris Peace Conference. After 1918, moreover, the confusion and disorder abated little. Nationalist demands sometimes became more unreasonable, irredentisms grew fiercer, governments were overthrown at record rates, new chains of hostile alliances were formed, and intrigue and violence appeared to be little less common than they had been in the days before the war.

The story of one of the Balkan states, Albania, has already been considered. We turn now to the developments in Romania, Bulgaria, Greece, and Yugoslavia.

ROMANIA

Romania chose her side well in the war and was duly rewarded in the peace negotiations. When the boundary lines were finally adjusted, the kingdom comprised an area of 122,282 square miles —more than twice the prewar figure. Land was acquired from both the former ally, Russia, and the ex-enemy, Austria-Hungary. The latter gave up Transylvania, most of Bukovina, and part of the Banat of Temesvár. From Russia was taken Bessarabia, after a local council, said by the Bolsheviks to have been "packed," voted for union with Romania.

The Soviet Government refused to recognize this annexation and even Romania's friends were slow to acquiesce. In 1920 Great Britain, France, Italy, and Japan at last became parties to an agreement acknowledging Romanian sovereignty over the region, but the treaty was not to have legal force until ratified by three of the signatories. Moscow's opposition delayed the process of ratification, which did not occur until 1922 in Great Britain, 1924 in France, and 1927 in Italy. Meanwhile the uncertainty of ratification and the fear of a possible Soviet attack drove Romania into defensive alliances with Poland and France. Not until the two claimants signed a nonaggression pact at London in 1933 was the war danger in Bessarabia made remote rather than imminent.

The census of 1930 listed about 18,000,000 Romanian subjects, including more than 4,000,000 nonnationals. There were among the inhabitants 1,500,000 Transylvanian Magyars, 1,000,000 Bessarabian Ukrainians, 750,000 Germans, an equal number of Jews, and 250,000 Bulgarians. The problem of minorities consequently was serious, especially since the Romanians had a long record of discrimination against nonnational elements. In 1919 Romania agreed to sign a minorities treaty only after the Allies had presented as an alternative the surrender of some of her recent territorial gains. The treaty doubtless was of value in shielding the minorities against mistreatment, but complaints of injustice were frequent and loud, notably among the Magyars.

Particularly objectionable to the Hungarians was the land legislation. In 1914 about half of the arable land in Romania was held by a few thousand large proprietors. Some of the big estates comprised as many as forty thousand acres, while a million small farms measured less than twenty-five acres apiece. To remedy this situation and to appease a discontented peasantry, legislation was passed in 1917, 1918, and 1921 providing for the expropriation of five million acres from the large holdings, plus all the arable crown lands and the landed properties of absentee and foreign owners. Private estates of arable land in the "old kingdom" were to be cut down according to a scale, so that no farm of more than 1250 acres would remain. Compensation was provided through fifty-year national bonds carrying 5 per cent interest. The farming land thus acquired by the state was to be distributed among the peasants on easy terms and at 65 per cent of the expropriation price.

The maximum size of estates in the newly annexed territories was fixed at a level considerably lower than that for the "old kingdom." Thus, in Bessarabia private holdings were not to exceed 250 acres, in Bukovina 625 acres, and in Transylvania about 300 acres. The Magyars were the chief losers in the case of Transylvania, for here almost 80 per cent of the holdings in excess of 200 acres were in their hands. So rapidly were these laws put into effect that the largest Romanian farm in 1924 measured only 1235 acres and, by 1932, 90 per cent of the farm land was controlled by small peasant proprietors.

The lot of the peasants was bettered by the revised agrarian situation, particularly since progress was simultaneously made in the organization of coöperatives for the improvement of cultivation and the purchase of tools, seeds, and livestock. The use of primitive methods, however, continued widespread and the peasantry as a class remained poor. Some discontent arose from the practice of the government in sending people to settle on expropriated lands far from their native villages.

The application of the land reforms to Transylvania precipitated an international dispute which disturbed eastern-European relations for a decade. By the terms of the Treaty of Trianon, Magyars who lived in Transylvania and who wished to retain their Hungarian citizenship rather than become Romanian nationals were allowed to opt, that is, express a choice to that effect, within one year. Optants were given permission to keep their holdings in Transylvania. When, therefore Romania passed laws expropriating the estates of foreigners, the Magyars objected to the League of Nations that this action could not apply to their properties which were guaranteed by an international treaty. "The dispute turned upon the question of Romania's sovereignty over her territories as against rights of foreigners created by international sanction." The quarrel was made more serious by Magyar charges that the Romanian officials were unfair in their appraisals of Transylvanian estates and that compensation was being paid in depreciated bonds.

Hungary espoused the cause of its loyal optants and appealed to the League Council for intervention. The League tried from

1923 to 1928 to settle the dispute, but Romania refused to recognize the jurisdiction of either the League or the World Court in what she considered a purely domestic affair. In 1928 the League despairingly washed its hands of the matter and urged the disputants to negotiate directly. The quarrel dragged on until 1930, when it was settled at the conferences on reparations held at The Hague and Paris. An agreement was accepted whereby the leading Allies, Hungary, and some of the other central- and eastern-European states agreed to contribute directly or indirectly to a common fund for the reimbursement of the dispossessed optants.

Unfortunately the settling of the optants' dispute failed to pave the way for a genuine Romano-Hungarian *rapprochement*. Hungary's desire to recover Transylvania and bitter Magyar memories of the looting of Hungary by Romanian soldiers in 1919 still barred the way to the establishment of friendly relations. As a member of the Little Entente, moreover, Romania was pledged to help prevent the restoration of the Habsburgs regardless of the wishes of the Magyars and to uphold the provisions of Trianon.

Land reform in Romania was followed by political reform, and in 1923 a new constitution was adopted. Although patterned after its predecessor, it incorporated a few important changes in the direction of democracy and tolerance. The old three-class system of voting was abolished, universal suffrage was granted, Jews were made eligible for citizenship, and provision was made for parliamentary representation of minorities. The privilege of holding rural land was reserved to Romanian citizens, and subsoil resources and forests were declared the property of the nation. The Chamber of Deputies was to be elected for four years by the entire voting body, but the Senate was to contain life and ex-officio, as well as elected, members. The government was not to be of the "responsible" type, since the king might appoint and dismiss ministers without regard to the wishes of parliament. The monarch also was given a suspensive veto.

Before the war there had been two principal parties in Romania, the Liberal and the Conservative. The latter represented the wealthy, landed, pro-German aristocracy. The Liberal Party advanced the interests of the banking, commercial, and industrial groups, and was opposed to foreign economic control in any form.[1] Although pro-Allied from the beginning of the war, the

---

[1] In 1924 the Liberals secured the passage of a law which made it imperative for foreign mining and drilling companies to dispose of a controlling share of their stocks to Romanians. The act was aimed especially at the foreign oil companies. Such

Liberals, who happened to be in power, postponed Romania's entry into the conflict until Allied chances of victory seemed good and until a satisfactory bargain had been struck. Thanks to the ability of its leaders, Jon C. Bratianu and his sons, Jon and Vintila, and the support of the rulers Carol I (1866–1914) and Ferdinand (1914–1927), the Liberal Party ruled the country with few interruptions from 1866 to 1928.

After the war the Liberals for a time seemed exceptionally firmly entrenched. Not only had they led the country to eventual victory, but the rival Conservative Party had disappeared entirely, for the landed aristocrats had been discredited by their pro-German sentiments and crushed by the breakup of the large estates. Yet the continued reign of the Liberals was destined soon to be challenged by a new opposition group, since the assignment of property and the extension of suffrage to the peasants brought about a veritable political revolution.

The Bratianus antagonized many people by their extreme economic nationalism which deprived the country of necessary foreign capital, by their high-tariff policy which reacted injuriously on the agrarians, and by their indirect-taxation schemes which placed the heaviest burden on the poorer classes. Further opposition came from the people in the newly acquired territories. For the first eight years after the war the government was controlled by groups representing the "old kingdom," although the latter included less than half of the population of Greater Romania. This situation was owing largely to King Ferdinand's insistence upon appointing such ministers as he wished, without reference to the desires of the peasant, Transylvanian, and Bessarabian contingents in parliament. When the opposition showed signs of becoming too strong, an electoral law was passed (1926) which gave control of parliament to the party that polled 40 per cent of the votes and disbarred from the legislature any party which obtained fewer than 2 per cent of the ballots.

In order to protest more effectively against these acts, Dr. Julius Maniu, an able speaker who had had considerable experience in the Hungarian Parliament before the war, organized the dissident groups into a National Peasant Party, with a progressive foreign and domestic program. The party believed in continued adherence to the Little Entente, friendship with all neighbors, and close coöperation with the League. At home it advocated decen-

legislation made foreign investors wary and for a time the kingdom suffered from a lack of foreign capital.

tralization, responsible government, abolition of force and coercion in elections, state aid to farmers, enlightened labor laws, development of the natural resources, and a cordial reception to foreign capital.

The party's great opportunity came with the deaths of King Ferdinand and Jon Bratianu in 1927. Although Vintila Bratianu succeeded as the head of the ministry, he was not able to exert the same degree of control as had his brother, and antigovernment demonstrations were held throughout the kingdom. Eventually, Bratianu's inability to negotiate a foreign loan led to his resignation (1928). Maniu, now elevated to the premiership, immediately ordered elections. His party elected more than three hundred deputies, to thirteen for the Liberals and a few for the minor parties.

A new spirit was apparent in the type of legislation that now was passed, for Maniu made a definite attempt to place Romania, as he said, "on the constitutional basis which brought prosperity to the Western states." The censorship was lifted, the military law which still prevailed in some parts of the realm was abolished, anti-Semitism was suppressed, and foreign capital was invited. Railways and public works were built, educational opportunities were extended, a foreign loan was floated, and the currency was stabilized. But in 1931 the party, in spite of its favorable record, was forced out of power by King Carol II. To understand this move it is first necessary to go back to another story.

In December 1925 Romania was stirred by the actions of Crown Prince Carol in renouncing his right to the throne, deserting his second wife, Princess Helen of Greece, and going to Paris to live with his mistress, Magda Lupescu. Since Carol, who had early achieved notoriety for his instability, apparently was disliked both by his mother, Queen Marie, and by the Bratianus, his elopement was made the occasion for the passage of a new act of succession (1926). The law disbarred Carol from the throne, designated his five-year-old son Michael as crown prince, and provided for a council of regency in the event that Ferdinand should die before his grandson came of age.

Ferdinand died in 1927 and young Michael became king, with the queen-mother and the Bratianus dominating the regency council. Late in 1928, however, as has been indicated, Maniu and his National-Peasant following obtained control of the ministry. Since the Bratianu Liberals were unfriendly to Carol, the National Peasants were, on the whole, inclined to favor his return and accession to the throne—provided he became reconciled with Helen, who steadfastly refused to have the marriage annulled. The exiled prince, incidentally, was popular with the army.

It was not altogether astonishing, therefore, that Carol should have alighted in Bucharest in June 1930, after an airplane trip from Paris, and have been proclaimed king. In the National Assembly, Vintila Bratianu's was the only vote cast against his enthronement and recognition as king *de jure* since 1927. Michael was made crown prince and grand voyvod of Alba Julia. With the death of Vintila Bratianu late in 1930 it appeared as though the last remnant of official opposition to Carol II had vanished.

In October 1930 Maniu surrendered his leadership of the National Peasant Party and retired from politics. The ostensible reason was illness; the probable cause was disagreement with Carol over the latter's family difficulties. Each passing month made reconciliation between Carol and Helen seem more remote, until she finally was exiled. Mme. Lupescu, on the other hand, began to spend much of her time in the kingdom, usually not far from Carol. Although the army continued loyal to the king, the National Peasant Party was inclined to frown upon his actions. In April 1931, accordingly, the ministry was ousted and a new government organized under Carol's former tutor, Professor Nicolae Jorga. The latter, a prominent historian and a prolific writer, ordered new elections and placed himself at the head of a National-Union ticket. There was much violence during the campaign and the premier's group won nearly half of the votes that were cast. Thanks to the electoral law of 1926, the National Union secured three-fourths of the seats in the new chamber.

During the course of the next twelvemonth, Carol and Jorga ruled under a dictatorship thinly disguised behind the veil of a parliamentary majority. Both men seemed impulsive, fond of publicity, and strongly partisan. In spite of the energetic suppression of unrest and opposition, conditions rapidly went from bad to worse. The world economic depression added to the nation's woes and the government deficit increased at an alarming rate. A number of attempts to reach favorable economic agreements with neighboring states failed because of national jealousies displayed by one side or the other, and any hope of additional foreign loans was temporarily blasted by the publication in 1932 of a report on Romanian economic conditions by the French financial expert, Charles Rist. The report criticized the government for habitually exceeding its income, for recklessly launching expensive public

ALEXANDER OF YUGOSLAVIA AND CAROL II OF ROMANIA

works and assuming peasants' debts, and for overstaffing all government departments. On the day preceding the publication of the document, the Jorga Ministry had resigned. After several short-lived cabinets had risen and fallen, the ministerial leadership was entrusted (1933) to Jon G. Duca, the successor of Vintila Bratianu as head of the Liberal Party.

Duca ordered new elections and this time the Liberals received 54 per cent of the popular vote and 303 of the 387 deputies' seats. The premier followed a policy of moderation and attempted to curb the activities of a fascist, anti-Semitic organization called the "Iron Guards." Hundreds of "Guards" were arrested and their publications were suppressed. In retaliation, a student at Bucharest University assassinated Duca, and soon a fascist plot was disclosed which had for its object an attack on the king and cabinet and the establishment of a military dictatorship. The new Liberal Government of George Tatarescu, which had taken office in January 1934, met the threat with energetic countermeasures.

The Tatarescu Government then tried to concentrate on improving Romania's foreign trade, relieving her debt, and meeting the demands of her dissatisfied peasantry, but soon found itself concentrating instead on the rising tide of fascism. The anti-Semitic Romanian fascists, who received encouragement from German Nazis, were especially angered by the government's friendship with France, Czechoslovakia, and the Soviet Union. They denounced a plan of the government to build a railroad connecting the Soviet Union with Czechoslovakia via Romania, and in 1936 brought about the resignation of Foreign Minister Nicholas Titulescu. During 1937 the Tatarescu Ministry carried forward a considerable armament program, with aid from France and Czechoslovakia, but fascist agitation, particularly on the part of the Iron Guard, continued. An example of foreign encouragement came in February 1937 when the German and Italian ministers to Romania took part in an Iron Guard demonstration on the occasion of the funeral of two members who were killed while fighting for Franco in Spain. The ministers were recalled, while King Carol II upbraided the cabinet for its leniency toward fascist disturbers of the peace.

World-wide interest centered on the parliamentary elections which were held in December 1937. It was expected that a three-cornered fight would develop among the Carol-Tatarescu Liberals, the National Peasant Party under Maniu, and the All-for-Fatherland Party (Iron Guard) of Cornelius Z. Codreanu. Great was the general astonishment, therefore, when Maniu announced that his left-wing, pro-French peasant party would ally itself for electoral purposes with the anti-Semitic, right-wing, pro-German Iron Guard. Maniu explained that his purpose was merely to present a united front against the personal rule of Carol and that his move involved no compromise of principles.

When the returns were counted it appeared that the Tatarescu Government would not have a majority, wherefore it resigned. King Carol then asked Octavian Goga, anti-Semitic, pro-German leader of the National Christian Party, which had polled only 9 per cent of the popular vote, to form a cabinet. In February 1938, however, Carol dismissed Goga and proclaimed a new constitution. Thereupon traditional politicians were dropped, political parties and secret societies were banned, and the king indicated his determination to rule as he thought best for the country.

It appeared that Carol's actions were motivated by a fear that if he did not resolutely take hold and establish a firm government of the type he wanted, the fascist elements, with foreign backing, would take all power into their own hands. The absorption of Austria by Germany increased his suspicions and he proceeded with energy against all those who seemed a menace to his throne.

On April 19, 1938, Codreanu, youthful leader of the All-for-Fatherland group and advocate of mysticism and violence, was sentenced to six months' imprisonment for libeling ex-Premier Jorga. On the following day government officers raided fascist hide-outs and seized records which, it was said, showed that Codreanu and his followers were conspiring to seize the king and overthrow the regime. The fascist leader therefore was charged with treason, specifically with illegal possession of state documents relating to arms supplies and with having treasonable dealings with German agents. He was sentenced to ten years' imprisonment at hard labor.

The revolutionary movement now quieted down and the king issued numerous decrees. Prices were regulated, corruption was curtailed, the press was censored, a government propaganda organization was established, and efforts were made to increase foreign trade, particularly with Great Britain who was a good customer for oil, timber, and wheat. In order to improve relations with some of the neighboring states, especially Hungary, a nationalities statute was issued which placed all linguistic, religious, and racial minorities on a footing of equality with the Romanians. Only officials who understood the minority language might be assigned to areas inhabited by sizable minority groups, minority languages might be used in courts and in business, and the state agreed to subsidize schools for all groups in the country.

The autumn of 1938 saw a renewal of fascist outbreaks. Deeds of violence occurred in widely separated parts of the country. The police and guards took quick action to check the outbursts and on November 30 Codreanu and thirteen of his followers were shot by prison guards on the ground that they had tried to escape. Three more of his youthful followers were killed in similar circumstances three days later. There was no dangerous reaction to these incidents and, although further plots of Iron Guard sympathizers were uncovered throughout 1939, Carol seemed to have the situation under control. An election was held in June 1939, all candidates being members of a pro-Carol coalition called "the Party of National Regeneration." No meetings or posters were allowed, and the electorate comprised about one-tenth of the population. On the eve of the Second World War the Iron Guard once more became active. An attempt on Carol's life failed, but Premier Armand Calinescu was murdered.

BULGARIA AND MACEDONIA

South of Romania, and bordering also on Yugoslavia, Greece, and Turkey, was the state of Bulgaria. Under King (or Tsar) Ferdinand, Bulgaria entered the war on the side of the Central Powers and paid for the misstep in the Treaty of Neuilly. The latter deprived the country of considerable territory, limited its army to a small volunteer force, required it to make coal and livestock deliveries to the former enemies, and burdened it with a heavy reparation debt. Because of the poor economic condition of the kingdom, the indemnity was several times reduced until in 1930 a "final" settlement was evolved whereby Bulgaria contracted to pay about $84,000,000 in thirty-six annual instalments.

The population of Bulgaria in 1939 was estimated at 6,300,000; its area was 39,814 square miles. Approximately 85 per cent of the subjects were of Bulgarian origin, and in general they were a hardworking peasant class which neither wasted time complaining about defeat nor resorted to diplomatic legerdemain to obtain a reduction of its obligations. Possessing relatively poor land, dependent upon crude methods of farming, hampered by a system of community ownership of pasture and woodlands, and having little industrial life, the Bulgarians yet made every effort to fulfill the treaty requirements. In 1927 the last vestiges of inter-Allied control were removed.

Partial improvement in Bulgaria's economic status might conceivably have been forthcoming if the kingdom had been provided with a direct outlet to the sea. When the Allies deprived Bulgaria of her Aegean coast line in 1919, they promised to arrange for a satisfactory outlet through foreign territory, and at the Lausanne Conference of 1923 the possibility of making a Greek port available to Bulgarian producers and shippers was discussed. In 1924 a Greco-Bulgarian treaty was drawn up, assigning a narrow strip of Greek territory to Bulgaria under League supervision and authorizing the building of a port at Dedeagach on the Aegean for her use. Nothing definite came of this proposal since the Bulgarians insisted on complete ownership of the corridor, while the Greeks turned a deaf ear to any schemes involving territorial cessions. There the matter continued to rest.

In 1918 Ferdinand abdicated and was succeeded by Boris III. The new ruler was popular, being generally regarded as a pleasant young man more anxious to establish automobile speed records than to interfere with his ministers. Until 1934 Bulgaria continued to be governed under her constitution of 1879 as amended on several occasions. This provided for a unicameral assembly, or *Sobranye,* elected for four years by universal suffrage. No bill could become law without the king's consent. About four-fifths of the people belonged to the established Greek Orthodox Church, which was controlled by a synod of archbishops. In 1870, chiefly for nationalistic reasons, the Bulgarian Church was separated from the mother church at Constantinople. The patriarch in the latter city excommunicated the Bulgarian clergy for this defiance, but in 1929 the ban was lifted.

Perhaps the most remarkable postwar development in Bulgaria was the rise of the "Green" socialists, agrarians who favored state aid to farmers and social legislation, but opposed the confiscation of private property. Prominent among the leaders of the "Greens" was Alexander Stambulisky, a peasant by birth, and a man who had spent three years in prison for threatening King Ferdinand with personal violence if Bulgaria joined the Central Powers. Coming into power after the war, he signed the peace treaty for his country and then devoted himself to the introduction of political and economic reforms.

The program of the Agrarian Party, and of Stambulisky in particular, included the following points: (1) friendly relations with the neighboring countries; (2) punishment of the politicians who had plunged the kingdom into war; (3) fulfillment of treaty obligations in order to remove foreign control as quickly as possible; (4) state aid to farmers, and the expropriation, with compensation, of crown and church lands and large private estates, the soil thus acquired to be distributed chiefly among the refugees who were pouring into Bulgaria from the lost territories; (5) passage of laws limiting profits and taxing incomes and luxuries; and (6) compulsory, uncompensated labor of men and women on public works because of the national shortage in man power and money and the treaty restriction against conscription.[1]

Gratifying headway was made in the fulfillment of these policies between 1919 and 1923, but the methods employed by Stambulisky created numerous enemies. He was interested solely in the welfare of the peasant class and in order to carry out his plans he manipulated elections, arrested opposition leaders, closed universities, defied the church, and established a strict censorship. The opponents of the regime included leading representatives of the military, the bourgeoisie, and the intelligentsia, as well as some of the more moderate Agrarians. In 1923 Stambulisky was overthrown by a *coup d'état,* and a government of professors, lawyers, and generals, headed by Alexander Tsankov of the University of Sofia, came into power. The new cabinet was supported by a Democratic Entente which represented all the political parties save the Agrarians and the communists. Within a few days after his ousting, Stambulisky was assassinated, and for the next two years and a half the middle-class government, employing many of the same methods that had made the leader of the "Greens" unpopular, undid a large portion of his work.

Had the peasants rallied at once to the support of their champions, they might have regained control of the situation. As it was, they were taken by surprise, were slow to organize, and in the end resorted merely to reprisals and assassinations. The government

[1] A law of 1920, amended in 1921, empowered the state to demand of all able-bodied men a maximum of eight months' and of all able-bodied women a maximum of four months' service in any branch of economic activity and public-welfare work. The service might be required at any age between twenty and forty for men and sixteen and thirty for women. It was left to the government to decide in each case whether the work should be rendered on a single occasion or in instalments. Married women and soldiers were exempt from the provisions of the act. Eventually a growing number of exemptions was purchased by the payment of a tax calculated "according to the average wage and the economic position of the persons concerned." Cf. Lazard, M. *Compulsory Labour Service in Bulgaria,* 1922.

struck back with vigor and attempted to exterminate the opposition leaders. Worst among the numerous outrages that took place was the explosion of a bomb in the Cathedral of St. Nedelia in Sofia (1925) during the funeral services of a general who had been murdered by terrorists.

A new bourgeois ministry took office in 1926, headed by Andrei Liapchev, a Macedonian leader of the Democratic Entente. This cabinet, destined with a few changes to remain in power for more than five years, favored coöperation with the League, friendship with the neighboring states, financial and educational reforms, a balanced budget, reclamation, extensive public works, local autonomy, and conciliation with the opposition. Thousands of political prisoners were released, the censorship was lifted, and exiles were permitted to return. Although political murders and outrages ceased as a consequence of these policies, much discontent remained and the people were restless. The moderate Agrarians now adopted constitutional opposition tactics, being joined, shortly, by several other groups. Together they formed the National Bloc which, in the elections of 1931, defeated Liapchev and the Democratic Entente. By previous agreement the victors divided the spoils.

With occasional reorganization of his cabinet, Premier Nicolae Mushanov was able to retain control from October 1931 to May 1934. During his incumbency an amnesty was issued which permitted the return to public life of many of the agrarian leaders who had been proscribed at the time of Stambulisky's downfall. Among the peasants themselves, meanwhile, the hardship brought on by the deflation of agricultural prices and the high tariffs of the neighboring states had caused renewed unrest. The workers in the cities were equally discontented and readily listened to agitators. In the municipal elections of 1932 the comunnists captured more than half of the seats in the governing council of Sofia, the capital city. Thoroughly frightened, and spurred to activity by the demands of the League of Reserve Officers and other Rightist associations, the Sobranye in 1933 declared vacant the twenty-nine parliamentary seats held by communists.[1]

The conservative and army elements in the kingdom, dissatisfied with Mushanov's "lenient" policies, executed a bloodless *coup d'état* in May 1934. With the apparent hesitant consent of King Boris a military dictatorship was set up under Colonel Kimon

---

[1] The Bulgarian Communist Party was suppressed in 1925 but its former members reunited as the Labor Party.

Gheorghiev. When it began to appear that the new government was aiming at the complete abolition of royal political influence, Boris intervened and eventually (November 1935) set up a new civil government under George Kiosseivanov. Meanwhile (1934) all political parties had been abolished and the formation of new parties had been forbidden.

Boris and Kiosseivanov tried to steer their country along a middle course, striving to avoid the extremes of either Right or Left. Both fascists and radicals, however, grew in numbers, and in 1936 the authorities suppressed several fascist clubs. It was ex-Premier Tsankov who led the fascists in their demand that the lost portions of Macedonia be recovered from Yugoslavia and Greece, but the king preferred to pursue a policy of conciliation with all Bulgaria's neighbors.

In May 1938 a Bulgarian Parliament met for the first time in several years. The elections had been held on the king's orders and with a restricted suffrage. The candidates had had to base their campaigns chiefly on personal issues since they were forbidden to represent parties. And the assembly's powers by now had become mainly advisory. In 1939 an embryo Nazi movement was suppressed.

The course of Bulgaria's foreign relations was determined chiefly by the ramifications of the Macedonian question. Macedonia was a region of indeterminate boundaries including the fertile valleys of the Vardar and Struma rivers and situated partly in Greece, partly in Bulgaria, and partly in Yugoslavia. For centuries the area was under Turkish rule, but before 1914 it was claimed on historical and linguistic grounds by the three states mentioned. Each of these carried on a vigorous campaign in Macedonian churches and schools to convince the inhabitants that they really belonged to this or to that nation. The Bulgarians appeared to enjoy the greatest success in these efforts but as a result of the Balkan Wars of 1912 and 1913 they secured only a small northeastern corner of Macedonia. During the First World War they conquered some more of the area, but the Paris Peace Conference once more assigned most of it to Greece and Yugoslavia. Almost immediately thousands of Macedonian refugees began to pour into Bulgaria. The latter was regarded by them not merely as a likely place of refuge but as a base from which agitation for Macedonian independence might be carried on.

The unification and independence movement was directed by the Internal Macedonian Revolutionary Organization, a society founded in 1893 and long led by Ivan Mihailov. The members of the IMRO were grouped into armed bands of *comitadjis* whose methods were terrorism and guerrilla warfare along the international frontiers. The Bulgarian army was so small that the comitadjis could act with virtual impunity while keeping the government in constant dread of unpleasant border incidents. The problem of Greek Macedonia gradually became less pressing as the land vacated by the emigrating Macedonians was quickly taken up by the Greek refugees who were rendered homeless in consequence of the Greco-Turkish population exchange. But in Yugoslavia the situation remained fraught with danger, for there the IMRO was determined to block all attempts at "Serbifying" the Macedonians.

In 1922 Greece, Yugoslavia, and Romania united in sending a vigorous warning to Bulgaria to check the disorders along the Greco-Bulgarian and Yugoslav-Bulgarian frontiers. Two years later Athens complained of the mistreatment of some Greek nationals in the Bulgaro-Macedonian village of Voden. The protest apparently had the wrong effect, for soon thereafter the Greek mayor of the village was murdered. By way of reprisal a Greek army officer ordered the shooting of seventeen Bulgarians. A crisis in these border troubles was reached in October 1925 when a clash between frontier outposts resulted in the dispatch of a Greek army corps to Bulgaria. Within five days the invaders occupied about seventy square miles of territory. Sofia offered no military resistance and appealed to the League for protection.

The Council assembled immediately and ordered the Greeks to recall their troops from Bulgaria, under the supervision of a commission of British, French, and Italian officers. Then, having averted war, the Council sent a commission of inquiry to investigate the origin of the conflict and recommend action. This body reported that neither party to the dispute had appeared to act with premeditation, but that Greece had been hasty in ordering the invasion without prior investigation of the circumstances. The commissioners therefore suggested that Greece, instead of receiving the indemnity which she was demanding, be required to pay Bulgaria $220,000 for material and moral damages. The Council accepted these decisions, as did the disputants, and by March 1926 Greece had paid the last instalment of the fine. The peaceable outcome of the affair was not only a victory for the League but it paved the way for a better understanding between Bulgaria and Greece. The latter came to realize that the government of King Boris was not to blame for the border incidents, and in 1927 and 1929 Greco-

Bulgarian treaties of commerce and friendship were signed. Meanwhile, in 1926, some of the comitadjis had crossed from Bulgaria into Yugoslavia and there attacked a town. Once more Yugoslavia, Greece, and Romania jointly protested. Bulgaria expressed her regret, explained her physical inability to check the activities of the Macedonians, and invited her neighbors to co-operate in the better regulation of the frontiers. This offer was regarded favorably and friendly conversations were begun, but all harmony was dissipated when the comitadjis killed a Serbian general before the year was over. This time Yugoslavia determined to act, especially since she was further irked by the growing friendship between the Bulgarians and her Adriatic rival, Fascist Italy. For more than a year, consequently, the Bulgarian frontier was closed, while raids and assassinations continued apace.

The royal dictatorship which was established in Yugoslavia in 1929 regarded the boundary difficulties in a less serious light and reopened the frontier. This action opened a path for further negotiations and in 1930 the two countries adopted a protocol which regulated the control of the borders, settled some bothersome land disputes that were the heritage of the peace treaty, and provided for the settlement of future disagreements by peaceful arbitration.

The signing of the Bulgarian treaties with Greece and Yugoslavia somewhat lessened the danger of international war in this region, but the internal situation in Bulgaria was made worse when the Macedonians themselves split into two hostile groups. The Mihailovists and Protogerovists used such violent methods against each other, that in 1933 the government proclaimed a state of siege in Sofia and placed in concentration camps a large number of suspected Macedonian terrorists. The Gheorghiev Ministry of 1934 and its successors took even stronger measures. In those parts of the kingdom where the Mihailovists had exercised political control, new local officials were appointed by the central authorities. All Macedonians were ordered to surrender their arms and the IMRO leaders were imprisoned or removed to other parts of the land. In July 1934 the Protogerovist wing officially dissolved itself and two months later Mihailov fled to Turkey. The latter refused a Bulgarian request to extradite Mihailov on the ground that he was a political refugee, but in 1935 the leader of the IMRO was sentenced to death *in absentia*. Nevertheless, Bulgaria's difficulties were not yet ended, for Macedonian nationalist propaganda continued to be carried on both at home and in foreign countries.

The Sofia Government used the Macedonian situation as the

basis for a request to the League to permit the creation of a larger army than was stipulated in the Treaty of Neuilly. But success in this endeavor was not achieved until 1938. Then, Bulgaria and the Balkan Entente (Greece, Turkey, Yugoslavia, and Romania) signed a treaty at Salonika. In the document, Bulgaria's right to rearm was recognized by the entente and all signatories "assumed the obligation to abstain in their mutual relations from recourse to war." Soon thereafter Bulgaria got a loan for rearmament purposes from an Anglo-French banking group. The partition of Czechoslovakia reminded the Bulgarians of their own irredentist grievances with respect to their neighbors and on the nineteenth anniversary (1938) of the signing of the Treaty of Neuilly, the government found it necessary to proclaim martial law in order to prevent rash acts that might lead to international complications. Eventually the populace calmed down, but Bulgarian irredentism remained a disquieting factor in Balkan relations.

GREECE

In 1917 Premier Eleutherios Venizelos, with the aid of the Allies and against the wishes of King Constantine, had led Greece into the war. Then, at the peace conference, he had secured for his country numerous territorial awards, at least on paper. Not unnaturally, he expected a cordial reception upon his return home from Paris. Yet, for a variety of reasons, he had come to be generally disliked. It was common knowledge that his advent to power in 1917 had been based on forceful Allied support, and his action in compelling the king to abdicate in favor of the young Alexander had not been popular. Apparently some of the people also bore in mind that Venizelos' policies had already plunged them into three wars, in 1912, 1913, and 1917–1918, and they were not desirous of waging a fourth conflict in order to make good the claims acquired in Asia Minor by the Treaty of Sèvres. To make things still worse for Venizelos, King Alexander died in 1920 (from the bite of a pet monkey), whereupon his huge and genial father, Constantine, immediately announced his readiness to return from exile.

Hence it was not astonishing that the Venizelists should have been badly defeated in the elections of 1920 and that a plebiscite should have resulted in the recall of Constantine by an overwhelming vote. The premier discreetly left the country, passing on to the returned ruler a war against the Turks under Mustapha Kemal. Not only was Constantine forced by circumstances to continue this struggle, but his position was made precarious when the Allies refused to recognize his government and cut short the flow of supplies and ammunition which had been made available to Venizelos. Constantine therefore was blamed for a resulting Greek debacle at Smyrna, the threatened loss of Thrace, and the coldness of the Allies. When the military men now demanded that he quit, he abdicated a second time (1922). The throne went to his eldest son, George II.

Venizelos was recalled to salvage from the Turkish imbroglio what he could at the peace conference of Lausanne (1923). He had to give up Smyrna and eastern Thrace, and agreed to a compulsory exchange of populations with Turkey. Greece was thus left with an area of 50,257 square miles, about half of which had been added since 1912. As a result of the exchange of peoples, 1,000,000 refugees were dumped into the land from Turkey, bringing the total population up to 6,500,000. The lot of the refugees was miserable, since Greece found it almost impossible to provide the necessary food, clothing, and shelter for the incoming thousands. Some relief was afforded by the League of Nations Settlement Committee under the chairmanship of Henry Morgenthau, Sr., former American Ambassador to Turkey.

One of the hardest diplomatic problems arising from this enforced uprooting of so many people was the liquidation of the ensuing property disputes. This controversy between Greece and Turkey was not smoothed out until 1930, at which time a convention was signed whereby the two countries reciprocally renounced the claims of their exchangeable refugees against each other and agreed to permit the Turks in western Thrace and the Greeks in Constantinople to remain where they were. With these hindrances to cordial relations removed, the two peoples in 1930 concluded a treaty of friendship and naval parity. Three years later they signed a nonaggression pact.

Although only one-fifth of the land surface of Greece was arable, the chief occupation of the people was agriculture. Beginnings were made in the exploitation of the fairly rich mineral resources. As in the case of a number of other European states, extensive programs of reforestation were inaugurated, and a number of American companies were engaged to work on reclamation projects, particularly in the region of the Vardar River. The public works undertaken required large funds, but the international credit standing of Greece was good and little difficulty was encountered in contracting loans.

The early reign of George II was marked by confusion and unrest. An extreme censorship prevailed, there were frequent military executions, and the quarrels between the royalists and Venizelists, a majority of whom soon betrayed republican sympathies, became more and more vindictive. Finally, in 1923, after a Venizelist victory at the polls, the king and queen were requested to leave the country while parliament decided upon the future form of government. Admiral Paul Koundouriotis was appointed regent and in March 1924 the national legislature deposed the dynasty and declared a republic. This action was upheld in a plebiscite by a vote of more than 2 to 1, and the regent became provisional president.

Political life under the republic proved to be no less turbulent than under the monarchy. Koundouriotis was ousted from control after a short time by General Theodorus Pangalos, who in turn was driven from power by General George Kondylis. Then Koundouriotis asserted himself once more and maintained a precarious hold on the presidency until 1929. When he resigned, because of illness, he was succeeded by Alexander Zaimis who, at the time of his election, was president of the upper chamber and had been eight times prime minister. Since the new executive was duly chosen by the parliament, it appeared that the republic was on a tolerably firm footing. In 1934 Zaimis was reëlected by the parliament for another five-year term.

Meanwhile Venizelos, who had again left the mainland and retired to his native Crete, once more returned and in 1928 led the Liberal Party to victory in an election which was characterized by violence and the kidnaping of candidates. For the fifth time in his career the veteran became premier. He remained in power, with brief interruptions, for almost five years, until March 1933, and achieved a number of important reforms. A semblance of order was restored, public works were pushed, agriculture was aided, the educational system and public-health administration were improved, workmen's-insurance legislation was discussed, a debt settlement was effected with the United States and a new refugee loan obtained, and friendlier relations were established with the neighboring states and the former Allies. Venizelos appeared to be much in favor of a Balkan federation as a step toward the fulfillment of Briand's Pan-Europa scheme, but nationalist jealousies blocked progress in this direction.

Despite everything that the government could do, the economic prosperity of the republic after 1930 declined rapidly. Foreign trade decreased and unemployment increased until finally the premier decided upon a suspension of foreign-debt payments and the utilization of the money thus saved in the further construction of public works. Such measures were at best of temporary value and Venizelos retired once more to Crete without having solved the economic riddle. His successor was Panagiotis Tsaldaris, leader of the Popular Party which, though originally of royalist sympathies, now accepted the republic.

On March 1, 1935, just nine days before Premier Tsaldaris might have celebrated his second anniversary in office, there broke out a military and naval revolt which soon assumed the proportions of a civil war. The rebels apparently doubted the sincerity of Tsaldaris' devotion to the republic and desired to place the chief ministerial power back in the hands of Venizelos. They gained control of a portion of the Greek fleet and fought the loyal government troops in Athens, Crete, Thrace, Macedonia, and elsewhere. Not until March 11 was General Kondylis, the war minister, able to report final victory over the insurgents. Venizelos went into exile.

The victorious government arrested the leaders of the revolt, confiscated the property of the Venizelos family, dismissed Venizelist sympathizers from office, and abolished the Greek upper house which, ever since its revival under an article of the constitution of 1927, had been controlled by Venizelos' Liberal Party.[1] General Kondylis, who got the chief credit for crushing the revolt, was named a marshal and deputy-premier and reiterated his loyalty to the existing republican order.

In an election of June 1935 the Tsaldaris-Kondylis government party won 287 out of the 300 deputies' seats. Soon this parliament authorized a plebiscite in which the people should choose between parliamentary republicanism and constitutional monarchism. The popular vote was to be held in November. The premier and his deputy, meanwhile, had begun to differ on a fundamental matter of policy: whereas Tsaldaris was willing to countenance a restoration of the monarchy if the people expressed such a wish through an honest plebiscite, Kondylis, apparently disappointed that the republican forces generally did not accept him as their leader, suddenly announced his complete sympathy with royalism.

Irritated by Tsaldaris' determination to be strictly neutral in the approaching plebiscite and tired of the "uncertainty" of the situation, Kondylis engineered a *coup d'état* and forced the pre-

[1] The first meeting of a Greek upper house since 1862 occurred in 1929.

mier to resign. In rapid order the republic was declared abolished, the monarchial constitution of 1911 was restored, and Kondylis was made premier and regent pending the return of former King George. The idea of a plebiscite was retained, but the voters were merely to be given the opportunity to confirm Kondylis' action. George, who happened to be in London at this time, was informed of these events and expressed an eagerness to return to Greece; but he decided to await the result of the plebiscite. Meanwhile President Zaimis quietly passed into the political background, while Regent Kondylis ousted all leading republicans from office. The plebiscite was held according to schedule and resulted in an overwhelming endorsement of Kondylis' measures. The vote was 1,500,000 in favor of the restoration to 33,000 against it. King George II therefore returned to continue his interrupted reign (November 1935). But because the king and Kondylis found it difficult to coöperate, Professor Constantine Demerdjis became premier in the same month.

The first parliamentary elections following the restoration were held in January 1936. The issue was mainly one between the followers of Kondylis and the supporters of Venizelos, who was living in exile. The Venizelists captured two more seats than their chief opponents, but since no group had a majority, Premier Demerdjis continued in office with a nonpartisan cabinet including General John Metaxas as war minister. Within three months after the election, death removed Kondylis, Venizelos, Demerdjis, and ex-Premier Tsaldaris from the scene. Metaxas thereupon came to the head of the cabinet. He displayed impatience with the rise of radicalism owing to the bad economic conditions and induced the king on August 4, 1936, to dissolve parliament and suspend the constitution. On the next day he abolished all political parties, imposed a strict censorship, and announced that the country had been saved from communism. There were several movements during 1937 and 1938 to bring about the removal from control of Metaxas. In each case, however, he successfully forestalled the opposition. At the end of July 1938 there was a brief uprising on the island of Crete and on the day following its suppression Metaxas made himself premier for life.

The foreign relations of postwar Greece were troublous. The difficulties with Turkey over the terms of the peace treaties and with Bulgaria regarding the Macedonian situation have already been mentioned. Contacts with Italy and Yugoslavia were equally disturbing for a time. Italian control of the Dodecanese Islands in the Aegean since the close of the Turco-Italian War in 1912 gave rise to a Greek irredentist movement of sizable proportions, inasmuch as the islands were inhabited largely by Greeks. More serious was a rupture in the relations between the two countries in 1923 when some Italian army officers aided in the delimitation of a boundary between southern Albania and northern Greece.

It seemed to the Greeks that most of the disputed points were being decided in favor of Albania and there was much hatred of the Italian general who headed the boundary commission. In August 1923 the general, three other Italians, and an Albanian interpreter were killed on Greek soil. An ultimatum was immediately forthcoming from Rome. It demanded, among other things, an official apology, an indemnity of 50,000,000 lire to be paid within five days, and the granting of permission to the Italian military attaché to help in the apprehension of the assassins. The time limit for acceptance was twenty-four hours. Greece rejected a number of the demands as contravening her national sovereignty and appealed to the League for help.

Before this body could act, Italy bombarded and occupied the island of Corfu, inflicting casualties mainly upon some Armenian refugees who had been collected there. At the same time the Italians indicated their displeasure at the apparent intention of the League to interfere in the controversy. Hence the League adroitly turned the matter over to the Council of Ambassadors at Paris. These diplomats, in due time, decided that Greece had been at fault in the murders but that the ultimatum had been too harsh. It was recommended, therefore, that Greece apologize, seek out and punish the murderers, and pay the indemnity of 50,000,000 lire. Italy, it was understood, would evacuate Corfu. The suggestions of the ambassadors were accepted and relations between Italy and Greece gradually underwent an improvement. In a sense the outcome was a League victory, but it also seemed to show that that organization could not proceed so readily or so energetically against a large as against a small state.

The chief Greek quarrel with Yugoslavia arose out of a treaty of 1913 between Greece and Serbia wherein the former had promised the latter a free zone in the port of Salonika. The First World War forced the postponement of the final arrangements, but in 1923 a convention was signed whereby Yugoslavia was given a fifty-year hold on a Salonika free zone covering ninety-four thousand square meters. The area was to remain under Greek legal and police surveillance but to be under Yugoslav customs administration, and goods passing between the free zone and Yugoslavia were to be tax exempt. The accord went into effect in 1925, but it did not work well.

The Yugoslavs complained that the zone was too small for the proper handling of cattle shipments, that the forty-eight-mile section of railway between Salonika and the frontier town of Ghevgheli was under inefficient management, that the schedule of the trains was so slow as to result in damage to perishable goods, and that the freight rates were prohibitively high. Since Greece at this time was eager to secure an alliance with the neighbor kingdom comparable to the Greco-Serbian pact of prewar days, negotiations were reopened in 1926. An agreement was soon arrived at, but it was never ratified, for the Greek Government which negotiated it was overthrown almost immediately thereafter.

The ill will between the two peoples increased preceptibly until Venizelos returned to power in 1928. He visited Belgrade and was responsible for another renewal of negotiations in 1929. This time success attended the endeavors of the statesmen and a compromise was accepted under which (1) the free zone remained confined to its original size; (2) the railway was to remain entirely under Greek direction; (3) Greece was to remit 20,000,000 gold francs to Yugoslavia to liquidate all claims of the latter's nationals on the road; (4) the train service was to be regularized; (5) the freight rates were to be lowered; and (6) future disputes regarding either the zone or the railroad were to submitted for arbitration to a jointly appointed referee or to the League.

Thus Greece hurdled the last serious obstacle which stood in the way of relatively cordial foreign relations. Venizelos was quick to make the most of the favorable situation and concluded treaties of friendship with Italy, Yugoslavia, Bulgaria, and Turkey. The premiers who succeeded Venizelos generally continued this foreign policy and in 1934 Greece became a party to the Balkan Pact which was intended to assure "the maintenance of the territorial order at present established" in the Balkans. Under Metaxas trade agreements were signed with Germany and money was borrowed from the British; in 1939 Greece seemed at last to have achieved relative stability.

YUGOSLAVIA

In the summer of 1917 a group of leading Yugo- or Southslavs, representing Serbia and the Southslavic provinces of Austria-

Hungary, met at Corfu and signed a pact declaring their intention to form a new state, a "constitutional, democratic, parliamentary monarchy," to be known as the "Kingdom of Serbs, Croats, and Slovenes." These peoples had never before been united in one state and each group was anxious to reserve certain rights and privileges. It was agreed that the Serbian dynasty should rule the kingdom and that an appropriate national flag should be adopted, although the three old flags might still "be freely hoisted on all occasions." Moreover, since the Serbs were accustomed to the Cyrillic alphabet, while the Croats and Slovenes used the Latin, it was stipulated that both forms of writing should be retained. Again, since most of the Serbs were Greek Catholic, while the Croats and Slovenes were largely Roman Catholic and there were also 1,500,000 Mohammedans, the equality of all three religions was to be guaranteed. As soon as possible there was to be elected a constituent assembly by universal, secret, and direct suffrage. The pact was silent as to whether the future form of government should be unitary or federal, and this omission was destined to cause great difficulties.

The new state was formed according to these precepts in 1918–1919 under old King Peter I of Serbia. The actual ruler, however, was Peter's son, Alexander, who had been acting as regent since 1914 and who became sovereign in his own right in 1921. As finally constituted, the kingdom included the former Serbia, Montenegro, Bosnia, Hercegovina, Dalmatia, Croatia, and Slavonia, and parts of Carniola, Styria, Temesvár, and western Bulgaria, altogether comprising an area of 96,134 square miles. The population in 1939 numbered 15,700,000, of whom about half were Serbs and perhaps a third were Croats and Slovenes. There were several hundred thousand Romanians and half a million each of Germans and Magyars. The Croats were more westernized than either the Serbs or the Slovenes, and the leading Croatian city, Zagreb, was considerably more "modern" in appearance than the Serbian capital, Belgrade.

Almost from the beginning of the independent existence of the Serb-Croat-Slovene Kingdom, the people were split into two factions on the question of what sort of central government to establish. One group, which chose to regard the new state as a Greater Serbia, favored a strongly consolidated, unitary government, with all authority emanating from Belgrade. The leading advocate of this viewpoint was the aged but energetic Premier Nicola Pashich, the man who had been head of the Serbian Government when the war broke out. The chief opposition to centralized control came from the Croatian Peasant Party led by Stefan Radich, a short, stout, nervous, nearsighted man, a prodigious speaker, fiery, and ready to give up his life in the cause of Croatian autonomy.

Each side advanced certain arguments. Pashich remonstrated that the backward state of some of the regions acquired from Hungary made local autonomy preposterous. Moreover, he said, the Serbs, by sheer weight of numbers, would dominate the government anyway, and the fact might as well be given official recognition. Finally, the problem of reconstruction was so grave as to require the most patriotic and united action, directed from one central point, Belgrade. Radich turned a deaf ear to these pleas. He explained that the Croats had enjoyed a degree of autonomy under the Habsburgs and hence had every right to continue in control of their own affairs. He pointed out that the Croats as a group were more advanced than the Serbs and consequently should not be made subordinate to them. And he reminded Pashich that the union of the Croats with the Serbs had been entirely voluntary, wherefore they were entitled at least to make their own local laws.

For two years the question raged, while the king refused to call elections for a constituent assembly until the outstanding boundary disputes should have been adjusted. At last, late in 1920, the long-awaited call for elections was issued. Radich's Croatian Peasant Party elected 50 (out of 417) deputies, but, in compliance with his instructions, they refused to take their seats. The assembly therefore came to be dominated largely by the moderate Democratic Party and Pashich's Serbian Radicals. In 1921 the Radicals, who were the bitterest opponents of federation and who really favored *conservative* domestic policies, managed to secure the adoption of a document which fulfilled their fondest hopes. Many of the moderates abstained from the final vote.

The constitution provided for a centralized form of government. Old provincial frontiers were erased and local diets were abolished, to be replaced by a single national parliament, the unicameral *Skupshtina*. Universal suffrage was granted, but the people could elect only the members of parliament and a few local officials. The latter, moreover, were made responsible to the central authorities. In the opinion of Robert Seton-Watson, an experienced British observer who was instrumental in the establishment of the state, the constitution thus vested undue power in the hands of an "incompetent clique" in Belgrade.

After the adoption of the constitution, the most urgent domestic problem facing the Yugoslav people was that of "revision" of the document. Until 1924 the Croats refused to take any part in the political life of the state. They boycotted parliament and hampered the administration wherever possible. Radich himself spent much of the time either in jail or in exile. By 1924, however, he reached the conclusion that obstructionist tactics might be carried on more effectively from within parliament, and hence permitted the Croatian deputies to take their seats.

The Pashich Government, in consequence, was forced to resign (1924) and thereafter one short-lived ministry after another rose and fell, the monotony being enlivened by the vigorous epithets hurled by the deputies at each other across the floor of the legislative chamber. In despair, the king recalled Pashich, who energetically proceeded to crush the opposition by having Radich arrested on charges of high treason and conspiracy, and ordering new elections in 1925. The government resorted to the usual strong-arm methods known to Balkan politicians for securing victory, but the Croats elected 67 (out of 315) deputies, almost the same number as in the previous poll. The opposition accordingly remained strong enough to defeat most of the government's bills.

After a brief stay in prison, Radich once more decided to change his methods, this time letting it be known that he would recognize the constitution of 1921 and coöperate in parliamentary activity, provided his party were given representation in the government. The cabinet agreed to accept this offer and Radich was released to become minister of education. But meanwhile the personal element had entered the quarrel to such an extent that Radich seemed unable to refrain from making bitter verbal attacks on Pashich and other ministers. Before long, the partnership was dissolved. The death of Pashich in 1926 failed to end the controversy and merely deprived the proponents of centralization of their ablest leader.

Confusion soon was transformed into chaos both within parliament and among the people. On several occasions the police had to be called into the legislative halls to end fighting among the deputies, and riots and outrages became more and more common in the streets. A climax was reached in June 1928 when Radich got up in parliament and launched an especially bitter attack against the government because it proposed ratification of the Nettuno Convention with Italy.[1] He complained that the convention was an Italo-Serbian compromise drawn up at the expense of

[1] See p. 361.

the Croatian peasants. Angered by these denunciations, a progovernment deputy arose, drew his pistol, and fired directly into the group of Croatian deputies. Two of the latter died instantly and several, including Radich, were wounded. Radich succumbed to his injuries on August 8, and the dead leader became a saint and a legend.

The Croatian deputies withdrew in a body from the Skupshtina. They met again at Zagreb and there resolved to disregard any laws that might be passed by the "rump" parliament at Belgrade. Then the Croats, under their new chiefs, Svetozar Pribichevich and Dr. Vlatko Machek, and joined by some Dalmatian deputies, threatened to set up their own legislature and act independently of the central authorities. In December 1928 the Croatian people refused to participate in the celebration of the tenth anniversary of the kingdom, and an official call for the gathering of representative local councils went unheeded. Since the death of Radich, parliamentary government had broken down completely. The situation was perilous in view of the relative weakness of the kingdom and the circumstance that it was surrounded by a group of none-too-friendly states whose total populations were five times greater than its own.

Unable to foresee an end to the parliamentary deadlock and fearful of the growing separatist spirit, King Alexander, on January 6, 1929, dismissed parliament, abolished the constitution, set up a censorship, suppressed all parties and party activities, forbade the bearing of arms and the holding of political meetings, and established a royal dictatorship which was to function through a cabinet responsible solely to him and headed by the reputedly stern General Pera Zhivkovich. The ministry included men from Serbia, Croatia, Slavonia, Bosnia, and Dalmatia, and the king, now an absolute monarch, announced that the various restrictions would be removed as soon as domestic order had been reëstablished and friendly relations with the outside world restored.

Alexander, an energetic man and an able military officer, appealed to his subjects to forget their local prejudices and their Serbian, Croatian, or Slovene origin, and to remember only that they were all Yugoslavs. To give emphasis to this prayer, the official name of the country was altered by royal decree in October 1929 and became "Kingdom of Yugoslavia." The thirty-three former administrative divisions were wiped out and replaced by nine new districts, or banats, named after local rivers. In six of the banats the Serbs formed a majority.

In 1931 the king promulgated a new constitution. It restricted the formation of political parties,[1] recognized the equality of the three major languages, and set up a bicameral parliament, consisting of a *Senat* in addition to the Skupshtina. The senators were to hold office for six years, half of the membership being appointed by the king and the other half elected. The life of the lower house was to be four years, its members being elected by all men and women over twenty-one. The central government was endowed with broad powers and the banats were to be ruled by governors appointed by and responsible to the king. An electoral law stipulated that all voting should be oral and that the party securing a plurality of the ballots cast should receive two-thirds of the seats in the lower chamber. The remaining seats were to be divided proportionally among the other parties. For each party there was to be only one national electoral list.

The first elections under the new system were held in 1931 and concerned merely the lower house. The only voting list was that of Zhivkovich's Yugoslav National Party, formed through a combination of the chief former parties. The new deputies included 145 former Serbian Radicals, 57 former Democrats, and 28 from the old Croatian Peasant Party. Because of his unpopularity even with the loyal Serbs, Zhivkovich was able to retain the premiership only until April 1932. In the next two years and a half he was succeeded in turn by several other leaders of the Yugoslav National Party, including its chairman, Nicola Uzunovich. All these ministries, voluntarily assisted by a patriotic society called "Young Yugoslavia," repressed any separatist manifestations among the non-Serbian elements of the population.

The Croats steadily resisted the wholesale attempts at "Serbifying" the government and the people. Despite the strictest surveillance, their discontent was manifested on frequent occasions. Some of them, indeed, voiced resentment at the erection of a monument at Sarajevo to Gavrilo Princip, the murderer of Archduke Francis Ferdinand. A climax in the struggle was reached in October 1934 when, as has been discussed, King Alexander was assassinated at Marseille, apparently as the result of a Croatian-Macedonian conspiracy.[2] While the League Council busied itself with preventing the crisis from leading to war, since Yugoslavia accused Hungarian irredentists of connivance in the murder,

---

[1] New parties might be formed only if they were not based on regional, religious, or class divisions.

[2] See p. 496.

Alexander's eleven-year-old son was proclaimed King Peter II. In accordance with the testament of the deceased ruler, a council of regents was established, headed by Prince Paul, a cousin of Alexander.

The new ruling group was generally regarded as favoring a policy of conciliation and an amnesty was granted to Machek and other Croatian leaders who had been jailed under Alexander. In the parliamentary elections of 1935 the authorities permitted opposition candidates to stand for office but then adopted the customary methods for ensuring a government victory. Most of the opposition deputies who *were* elected were Croats and, following the advice of their leader, Machek, they refused to enter the new parliament. It appeared as a somewhat more hopeful sign when Dr. Milan Stoyadinovich, a Serb who had never approved of the dictatorship, became premier in June 1935.

Stoyadinovich attempted to win the good will of his country's minorities by including in his cabinet several Croats, Slovenes, and Bosnian Moslems in addition to the customary Serbs. He then organized the Yugoslav Radical Union which was pledged to maintain a strong central government but advocated the gradual transition from dictatorship to parliamentary democracy. Several of the Croats in the cabinet thereupon resigned and Machek insisted that Croatia favored federalism and would be satisfied only when she had acquired a status similar to that enjoyed by Hungary in the old Dual Monarchy.

Probably in order to win more loyal support from the Roman Catholic Croats and Slovenes, Stoyadinovich in 1937 presented to parliament for ratification a concordat negotiated with the pope in 1935 and granting the Roman Catholic Church a status equal to that of the Serbian Orthodox Church. The lower house agreed to ratification despite the bitter opposition of the Orthodox clergy and population, but when the Orthodox Church now excommunicated the cabinet and those members of the Skupshtina who had voted for ratification, Stoyadinovich capitulated and announced that he would not introduce the bill in the Senate. The Vatican protested this decision, but to no avail. The great ferment aroused by the incident encouraged the Serbian, Croatian, and Slovene opposition groups to unite in an Agrarian-Democratic coalition with the hope of overthrowing the dictatorship. In the parliamentary elections of December 1938 the government party union, while still victorious, suffered a loss of many votes to this coalition. Early in 1939, therefore, having been unable to effect a reconciliation with the Machek group and having aroused opposition among Serbs as well as Croats, Stoyadinovich resigned. Control over the "nation of three nations" passed to one of his former aides, Dragisha Cvetkovich.

During Cvetkovich's administration external danger succeeded in accomplishing what years of internal pressure had failed to do. Cvetkovich and Machek got together and began to discuss in earnest plans for a compromise Serbo-Croat agreement. The negotiations lasted several months, mainly because the council of regents and some of Cvetkovich's own followers thought he was going too far in his concessions to the Croats. But in August 1939 an agreement at last was signed by the premier, Machek, and Prince Paul.

The document set up a self-governing banat of Croatia with full autonomy in such matters as agriculture, manufacturing, forestry, health, and education, and partial fiscal autonomy. There was to be a local parliament elected by universal, secret suffrage. The king was to be represented by a governor, or *ban*. The banat comprised about 27 per cent of the kingdom's area and approximately 29 per cent of its population—about three-fourths of Croatia's inhabitants being Roman Catholic. Cvetkovich now resigned, feeling that the new government ought to rest on a broader base. He was immediately reappointed, with a cabinet that included eleven Serbs, six Croats (including Machek), one Slovene, and one Moslem Bosnian. Machek's brother-in-law was named the first ban of Croatia.

Nationalist difficulties were not the only problems confronting the Yugoslav state. The peasants, who formed more than 80 per cent of the population, were dissatisfied with the size of their holdings despite several efforts by the authorities to break up the large estates. The country lacked adequate outlets to the sea and suffered from a poor system of internal communications which made it hard to develop whatever mineral resources were available. The kingdom was heavily burdened with debts, it having been made to assume the pre- and postwar obligations of all its component parts.

The foreign relations of Yugoslavia have been considered in other connections. Mention has been made of her membership in the Little Entente, of her opposition to Habsburg restorations in Austria and Hungary, of her disputes with Bulgaria over the Macedonians and with Hungary over the Magyars and Croats, of her quarrels with Italy over Fiume and over the control of Albania and the Adriatic, and of her complications with Greece over a free zone in Salonika. In the circumstances, Yugoslavia clung tenaciously to the alliance of 1927 with France, her friend, protector, and creditor.

Premier Stoyadinovich in particular sought to establish friendship with Yugoslavia's neighbors and, while remaining loyal to the Little Entente, came to amicable agreements with Bulgaria and Italy (1937). The pact of 1927 with France was renewed for another five years (1937) and special trade agreements were reached with Germany in 1937 and 1938. In January 1939 a friendly treaty was signed with Hungary. The increasing *rapprochement* of Belgrade with Italy and Germany, especially after the Anschluss, was justified by the government as "making new friends while keeping old ones."[1]

[1] As a result of Yugoslavia's participation in the League sanctions against Italy in 1935–1936, her trade with the fascist kingdom dwindled rapidly. Thus her economic dependence on Germany was further increased. On June 1, 1939, Hitler declared that the German-Yugoslav borders were fixed "for all time."

CHAPTER XXI

Turkey for the Turks

FROM SÈVRES TO LAUSANNE

Had the Treaty of Sèvres, drawn up by the Allies and signed in 1920 by representatives of Sultan Mohammed VI, gone into effect, the once resplendent Ottoman Empire would have been reduced to an insignificant region of desert and mountains tucked away in Asia Minor, far from the orbit of Western civilization. But Fate, or Kismet, as devout Moslems called it, decreed otherwise, and on this occasion Fate acted through the person of a young army officer named Mustapha.

This Mustapha was born at Salonika in 1880, of good family. After earning a scholarship to the secondary school at Monastir he ran away from this institution to take up a soldier's life at the Staff School in Constantinople. Here, in recognition of his superiority as a student of mathematics, one of his professors bestowed upon him the name of *Kemal,* signifying "Perfection." Military life appealed to Kemal and he developed into an excellent soldier, but he also became an inspired reader of French-revolutionary literature and an ardent antagonist of the autocratic Turkish governmental system. Though Kemal's revolutionary tendencies doubtless were known to the agents of Sultan Abdul Hamid II, the police did not arrest him until his graduation. Then nothing more serious happened to him than a temporary banishment in the form of an assignment to a cavalry regiment in far-off Damascus. There the young officer found time to muse over the evils of misgovernment and to organize a secret political society called *Vatan* or "Fatherland."

During the Young-Turk Revolution of 1908 Kemal acted as chief of staff to Mahmoud Shevket, commander of the army that marched on Constantinople and forced Abdul Hamid to grant a constitution. The muddled tactics and political intrigues of the

629

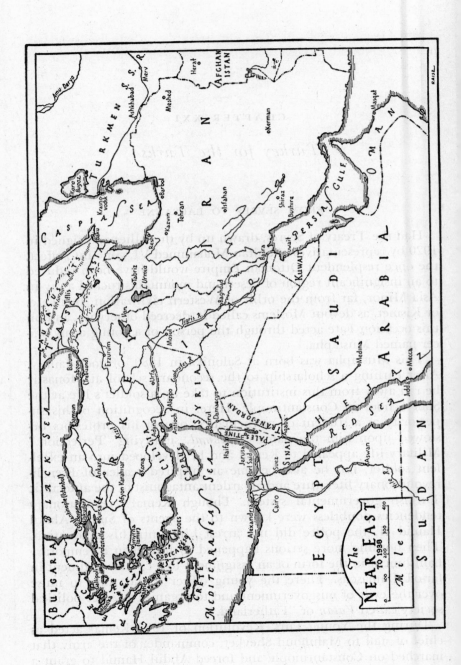

The Near East to 1936. Map showing the Near East region including Turkey, Iran, Arabia, Egypt, and surrounding areas.

Young-Turk ruling body, the Committee of Union and Progress, induced Kemal to devote his attention entirely to military affairs and reforms, and in 1910 he went to France to study the army maneuvers in Picardy. On his return, he stopped for a while in Paris and was deeply struck by the contrasts of West and East. He seemed to have been especially impressed by the relatively free position of women, the progressive civil and commercial life, and the general prevalence of literacy.

Kemal fought in Tripolitania during the Turco-Italian War of 1911–1912 and proved himself to be one of Turkey's best generals in the Balkan Wars of 1912 and 1913. Although he opposed as premature his country's entry into the First World War in 1914 and openly avowed misgivings as to Germany's eventual victory, Kemal's reputation as an able leader was definitely established when it became known that he had played a conspicuous part in the defeat of the Allies at Gallipoli in 1915.

In the circumstances it is not to be wondered at that Kemal was chagrined when the Allies successfully imposed on Turkey the Armistice of Mudros (October 1918). The terms of this document were so drastic that the Committee of Union and Progress, which was popularly held responsible for the disasters of the war, fled from the capital. Kemal in anger laid down his command in Palestine and hastened to Constantinople, only to be ordered into Anatolia by the sultan, as inspector-general in charge of the demobilization activities in an out-of-the-way area. He went, but used his commission to gather around him the nucleus of a new party, the Turkish Nationalist Party, and a makeshift nationalistic military force.

Meanwhile, in May 1919, following a decision of Great Britain and France to forestall Italian imperialist enterprises in Anatolia, Greece was encouraged to land troops at Smyrna. The pillaging of this port so aroused patriotic Turks that Kemal seized the opportunity to attempt to unite nationalists throughout the country. He called a Nationalist Congress to meet at Erzurum in July 1919 for a discussion of the future policy of the Nationalist Party. Two months later a second and more representative congress was convened at Sivas, which endorsed the resolutions of the Erzurum assemblage. At these meetings the basis was laid for the Turkish National Pact, a statement of principles adopted in January 1920 by a Constantinople Parliament which, elected late in 1919, contained a Nationalist majority.

The pact listed six conditions without which "the continued

existence of a stable Ottoman sultanate and society" was declared impossible. The first three articles dealt with the application of the principle of self-determination to all those areas of the old Ottoman Empire which still contained large numbers of Turks. The fourth article demanded the security of Constantinople but agreed to the opening of the Straits "to the commerce and traffic of the world." Article 5 "confirmed and assured" the rights of minorities in Turkey and the last article demanded the abolition of the foreign capitulations and all restrictions inimical to the country's "development in political, judicial, financial, and other matters." "It is a fundamental condition of (Turkey's) life and continued existence," read the document, "that she, like every country, should enjoy complete independence and liberty in the matter of assuring the means of her development."

The Nationalist members of the parliament were expecting too much if they thought that the Allies would permit them to proceed along the principles outlined in the pact. Within less than two months after the latter's adoption, an army commanded by the British General Sir Archibald Milne marched into Constantinople, proclaimed martial law, and deported about forty of the Nationalist deputies. Most of the Nationalist delegates who had escaped arrest hastened to Angora in north-central Anatolia, there to set up a "rump" parliament under the name of Grand National Assembly. When the sultan now convened another parliament at Constantinople, the country had two governing bodies: one, subordinate to the sultan and maintained by Allied troops; the other, supported by the national sentiment of the Turkish people and protected by the desert and mountains separating Angora from Constantinople and the Allied forces.

The Angora Assembly opened its first session in April 1920 and immediately elected Mustapha Kemal to be its president as well as commander-in-chief of the "Nationalist Army." Then, determined to "preside over the present and future destiny of Turkey, so long as her caliph-sultan and her Eternal City should remain under the dominion and occupation of foreigners," the body undertook to draw up a new instrument of government for the state. On January 20, 1921, such a document, called "Law of Fundamental Organization," was adopted. As amended and later written into the regular constitution, this law vested the sovereignty of Turkey in the people and in their representatives sitting as a Grand National Assembly at Angora. The deputies were to be elected for four years by the vote of all males over eighteen (changed in 1931 to twenty-one).[1] The executive powers were vested in the president and a responsible cabinet, and the judiciary was to be appointed by the assembly. The constitution also outlined an elaborate program of social reform.

While the assembly was engaged in lawmaking, Kemal, at the head of the Nationalist forces, launched a campaign to clear the country of foreign soldiers. In this undertaking he so covered himself with glory as to win the title of *Ghazi* or "Conqueror." In September 1920, after having come to a friendly agreement with Russia, Kemal invaded the recently established Armenian Republic of Erivan, routed the defenders, and soon reunited the provinces of Kars and Ardahan with Turkey.

Meanwhile three Greek armies, with British naval support, had driven the Nationalists out of Thrace and pushed eastward into Anatolia as far as Ushak. These victories, however, were soon counteracted by a number of unexpected diplomatic developments. The Greek Premier, Venizelos, who was chiefly responsible for these attempts on the part of Greece to take the territories assigned to her by the unratified Treaty of Sèvres, was defeated in the parliamentary elections of November 1920. British support was becoming less enthusiastic. The French began openly to favor the Turks out of dislike for the Greek King, quarrels with British policy, and discouragement over the defeat of French forces by Turkish Nationalists in Cilicia, northwest of Syria. Italy, finally, who herself coveted Smyrna, had never sympathized with the Greek venture. Accordingly an attempt was made at London in February 1921 to revise the Sèvres Treaty, chiefly at the expense of Greece. When it appeared that the demands of the Turks and Greeks could not be reconciled, the Athens Government, against the advice of the Allied Supreme Council, determined to enforce the original treaty on its own account. In May 1921 the Allies formally proclaimed their neutrality in the ensuing Greco-Turkish War.

The Greeks opened an offensive which in a few weeks brought them to the Sakharia River, about fifty miles from Angora. Then the drive was spent and they were unable to make any further advance. From August 24 until September 16 the ill-equipped but inspired Turks held in check an enemy who greatly outnumbered them. After the Battle of the Sakharia the Greeks began a general retreat. They retraced their steps gradually and remained in occupation of a large section of Asia Minor for a whole year, but in

[1] In 1934 the suffrage was extended to women.

September 1922 they were forced to evacuate even Smyrna. Physical exhaustion, poor leadership, uncertainty of the situation at home, and seditious propaganda so weakened the morale of the Greeks that they found it impossible to withstand the Turkish Nationalists who somehow managed to secure better equipment and whose enthusiasm increased as the campaign progressed.

When Kemal, in the flush of victory, proposed to cross the Straits and drive the Greeks out of eastern Thrace, he once more came into direct conflict with the British. At the time of the Allied proclamation of neutrality in May 1921 it had been stipulated that a specified area on each side of the Straits was to be considered as a neutral zone in which no fighting would be permitted. Now, fearing for the control of the Dardanelles, Lloyd George announced his determination to enforce this provision and prevent the Turks from fighting the Greeks in Thrace. Neither the French nor the Italians, however, cared to back the British Premier. France had come (1921) to an agreement with the Kemalists whereby she withdrew from Cilicia and permitted a rectification of the northern boundary of Syria in Turkey's favor, while Kemal promised to consider favorably the requests of certain French interests for financial and mining rights and a lease of part of the Baghdad Railway. Italy had likewise concluded (1922) an agreement with Angora, under which the Turks promised to give favorable consideration to some Italian applications for railways, mines, and public works in Asia Minor. Lloyd George therefore had to act alone and British reënforcements were sent to the Chanak region to prevent a Greco-Turkish clash in the zone of the Straits.

For a time war seemed imminent, but the British commander eventually induced Kemal to attempt a peaceful settlement of the controversy. On October 11, 1922, an armistice was signed at Mudania. The Greeks were ordered immediately to evacuate and restore to Turkey all Thrace as far as the Maritsa River, and invitations were issued to Great Britain, France, the United States, Italy, Romania, Yugoslavia, Russia, Japan, Greece, and Turkey to meet at Lausanne for the purpose of revising the Treaty of Sèvres to meet the new conditions. Less than three weeks before the first Lausanne Conference met, the Grand National Assembly deposed (November 1, 1922) Sultan Mohammed VI. But not until a year later, on October 29, 1923, did the legislature declare the nation to be a republic and unanimously elect Kemal as Turkey's first president.

At the Lausanne Conference the Turkish delegates, headed by Ismet Pasha, refused to sign any treaty which restricted the economic or judicial freedom of their country. In consequence, the gathering broke up in February 1923, but sessions were resumed in April. Ismet maintained his firm stand. Lord Curzon had been replaced by the more conciliatory Sir Horace Rumbold as Great Britain's chief delegate. The negotiations dragged on until July and then ended only because the Turks had been able to secure virtually everything that they had demanded in their National Pact of 1920. Only the question of Mosul, that is, of the boundary between Turkey and British-controlled Iraq, was shelved for later settlement.

Under the terms of the Lausanne Treaty, Turkey recovered eastern Thrace as far west as the Maritsa River, including the city of Adrianople (Edirne). In addition, she was permitted to recover the bridgehead and railway center on the west bank of the Maritsa, at Karagach, in satisfaction of reparation claims against Greece. Constantinople was restored as an integral part of the Turkish State, but the zone of the Straits was demilitarized and opened to the ships of all nations, no matter what their cargo, in time of peace and, when Turkey was a neutral, in time of war. In the event of Turkey's belligerency, enemy vessels might be kept out of the Straits, but not so neutral vessels.

In the Aegean Sea, Turkey retained Imbros, Tenedos, and the Rabbit Islands, while Dodecanesia, Rhodes, and Castellorizo were definitely ceded to Italy. Most of the remaining Aegean islands went to Greece. The Syrian boundary agreed upon with France in 1921 was confirmed. Sentiment dictated the granting in perpetuity to Great Britain, France, and Italy of a small "Anzac Area" on the Gallipoli Peninsula. Here the three powers might appoint custodians to watch over the graves of the soldiers who died in the campaign of 1915, but the region might never be built up or fortified.

Turkey gave up all claims to Libya, Egypt, the Sudan, Palestine, Iraq, Syria, and the Arabian kingdoms, and recognized Great Britain's annexation of Cyprus. In return for Turkey's promise to introduce judicial reforms and adhere to the same provisions regarding the rights of minorities as had the other eastern-European countries, the capitulations were recognized as abolished, all Allied claims for reparation arising out of the First World War were renounced, the foreign control of customs was lifted, and no restrictions were placed on Turkey's military, naval, and air forces. A supplementary Greco-Turkish convention provided for the compulsory exchange of Turkish subjects in Greece for Greek subjects in Turkey, and another stipulated the demilitarization of the Greco-Bulgarian-Turkish frontier in eastern Thrace. Turkey was left with an area of about 295,000 square miles, not quite the size of Texas and South Carolina combined, and with a population of 13,000,000 (18,000,000 by 1942). At peace with the world for the first time in many years, Turkey proceeded to set her house in order.

THE TURKS, THE GREEKS, AND THE KURDS

The Turkish Nationalists were eager to oust from the republic, especially from its Asiatic part, all peoples who were not "Turks." Since the largest group of nonnationals in 1923 consisted of Greeks, the Angora and Athens governments had agreed at Lausanne upon a wholesale exchange of populations on the basis, primarily, of religion. This proposal was commended as a solution of the Greco-Turkish minorities problem by Dr. Fridtjof Nansen, supervisor of Near East Relief for the League, and was carried out under the guidance of a mixed commission.

The actual process of exchange occasioned untold sufferings. It frequently was difficult to decide whether a family should be considered as Turkish or Greek, particularly where the original migration had taken place long ago. Besides, there were many Orthodox Christians in Anatolia who knew only Turkish and there were many Moslems residing in Greece who spoke no Turkish. Mismanagement, cruelty, and neglect were often in evidence, for the racial and religious antagonisms did not allow of humanitarian and just treatment in all cases. There was corruption, and official carelessness often resulted in the transplanting of mountaineers onto plains or the transference of plainsmen and farmers to the mountains.

Altogether about one million people were sent to Greece and four hundred thousand to Turkey. The misery of the Greeks was alleviated somewhat by the circumstances that the American Near East Relief concentrated particularly on Greek aid and that the Athens Government, because of Greece's membership in the League of Nations, was able to appeal for League assistance. The property disputes arising from the exchange continued to embitter Greco-Turkish relations until 1930. Then, as we have seen, a compromise agreement was reached, to be followed shortly by the signing of a treaty of friendship.[1] In the meantime the Turks had passed a law forbidding the immigration for purposes of settlement of any large group of foreigners.

After the ousting of the Greeks, the chief remaining obstacle to Turkish national homogeneity was the million or more Kurds inhabiting the former Armenian provinces and Kurdistan, in the eastern part of the republic. These tribesmen, speaking a language more akin to Iranian than Turkish, continued to be imbued with the spirit of clan allegiance rather than that of Turkish nationalism. The Kurds long were among the most unruly of the sultan's subjects and they continued to be restless under the new Turkey, especially since the Lausanne Treaty shattered hopes of autonomy which had been held out to them by the Treaty of Sèvres. In 1925, when the Turkish authorities arrested a few Kurds on the charge of sedition, the discontent crystallized into open revolt. The uprising was quickly put down and the rebel leader was executed.

The incident appeared to increase the solidarity of the state as a whole. Loyal Turks rallied to the support of the central government and the latter seized the opportunity to strengthen its military control in the country, to silence a critical Constantinople press, and to abolish the offices and distinctive costumes of the sheikhs, dervishes, and other religious or semireligious functionaries who still played a prominent role in Turkish life. Further Kurdish uprisings occurred in 1930 and 1937—to remind the Turks of their one remaining minority problem.

KEMAL, THE DICTATOR

As president of Turkey, Mustapha Kemal determined to abolish outworn institutions and methods and to raise his country to the level of Western civilization. In bringing about this transformation he adopted an admittedly dictatorial policy and a number of executions accompanied the march of reform. On the other hand, one of the chief reasons for Kemal's success was the fact that he customarily took just one big step in advance at a time. Reforms succeeded one another at moderate intervals and in this way the opposition rarely became so formidable as to crystallize into open resistance. Nevertheless, there were some plots to as-

---

[1] See p. 615. The labors of a conciliatory mixed commission did not end until 1934. Its work in the last four years was concerned chiefly with claims relating to nationality and property rights in Constantinople.

sassinate the dictator and overthrow the republic. The most serious of these were uncovered in the region of Smyrna, in 1926 and again in 1930, and each time the leading conspirators were executed. Eventually a majority of the people appeared to endorse the dictator-president's policies.

In Turkey, as in some of the western states, nationalism seemed to transcend the desire for liberty or democracy. So powerful was this spirit that there generally was only one political party, the Nationalists People's Party. Its first president-general was Kemal who, in 1927, was given the right to name all its electoral candidates for the assembly. In consequence of this arrangement foreigners came to speak of Turkish elections as "selections," particularly after Kemal had once remarked: "Unity is essential, and there can be no rival theories, and no rival parties."

In 1930 Kemal permitted Ali Fethi Bey, a prominent liberal politician, to organize a parliamentary opposition party. Fethi Bey thereupon formed the Liberal Republican Party which advocated a less pronouncedly nationalistic administration, a lessening of state interference in business, and greater freedom of speech and press. In October the Liberal Republicans in the assembly were able to muster only twelve votes on a motion of no confidence in the government, and Fethi Bey dissolved his party. His little band of followers, however, continued in association as "Independents."

Kemal was unanimously elected president four times, the last occasion being in 1935. But in 1938, after several months of illness, he died, aged fifty-eight. It was a tribute to the skill and success with which he had welded the Turkish Republic that, on the day after his death, the National Assembly unanimously and without any wrangling—and apparently with popular approval— chose as his successor, General Ismet Inönü. The new president had won fame as a general in the Turkish "wars of freedom," had proved his diplomatic ability in the negotiations at Lausanne in 1922 and 1923 and on later occasions, and had been premier during the major part of the republic's existence.

Inasmuch as Inönü had been chosen only to finish Atatürk's unexpired term, it was necessary to hold another presidential election in 1939. Inönü again was selected, partly, perhaps, because of his strong hold on the parliament, but also because his conduct of office had won general acclaim. Turkey's second president used his powers not merely to continue along the path that his predecessor had outlined, but to reconcile some of the ele-

MUSTAPHA KEMAL ATATÜRK

ments in the country that had been more or less disregarded by Kemal.[1] In domestic as in foreign affairs, the Turkish Government pursued one straightforward policy: a pro-Turkish policy. Thus it happened that by 1939 the once "sick man of Europe" was being courted by all the great powers that, a quarter century earlier, had been eagerly anticipating his early demise.

RELIGIOUS AND SOCIAL CHANGES

When the Grand National Assembly abolished the sultanate in 1922, it did not simultaneously abolish the caliphate, that is, the sultan's spiritual leadership of the Mohammedan world. Though Mohammed VI was deposed as sultan on November 1, 1922, he continued to be caliph until November 18, when, upon his flight from the country, the assembly elected his cousin, Abdul Mejid, to be caliph in his place. The new "Commander of the Faithful" had no direct political power, but, since he was a leading member of the Osman dynasty and since the assembly had declared the Turkish State to be "the emplacement on which the caliphate stands," it was virtually impossible for devout Moslems to dissociate his office from its traditional political implications. An Osman Caliph, therefore, was an incongruity in the new Turkey. Accordingly, in 1924, the assembly abolished the Turkish caliphate and exiled all members of the former ruling family.

The abolition of the caliphate had a wide significance in the Moslem world as a whole. By depriving themselves of a caliph, the Turks at the same time deprived most Mohammedans of a spiritual leader. It was true that even before the war many non-Ottoman Mohammedans, such as the schismatic Shiites in Persia, had ceased to recognize the caliphate; yet the office and its prerogatives were not shadows. Indeed, it was evident soon after the Turkish pronouncement that there was no lack of aspirants for the vacated honor. The king of Hejaz, the king of Egypt, the sultan of Morocco, and the aga khan of Bombay, all indicated their willingness to assume the title. But despite, or perhaps because of, this general scramble, the caliphate remained an unappropriated dignity.

In conformity with Kemal's policy of enacting only one major reform at a time, the constitution of 1924 and the revised document of 1925 still assigned to Mohammedanism the place of a state religion. Then, in 1928, the assembly unanimously deleted

---

[1] Inönü was again reëlected in 1943.

from the constitution the article which declared Islam to be the state religion. Thenceforth Mohammedanism was tolerated in Turkey in the same way that any other religion was tolerated. Officials, upon assuming office, no longer swore by Allah, but simply on their honor and by the republic. No special privileges were to be derived from confessing the Moslem faith, although the fact that most of the officials were Moslems did lend a certain prestige to that particular creed.

Minor changes in the religious ritual followed. It no longer was necessary to remove one's shoes prior to entering a mosque. Many of the mosques received pews and music was permitted at services. When it is recalled that only a few years earlier such things were capital offenses, it is evident how strong a hold Kemal had over the minds of his people and how ardently the Turks desired to become "modernized." It should be noted, however, that a serious religious outbreak occurred in the winter of 1930–1931 at Menemen, near Smyrna, where a group of dervishes unsuccessfully attempted to restore the caliphate.

Second in importance only to the changed attitude toward religion, and perhaps really but a phase of this modified outlook, was the altered status accorded Turkish women. Laws enacted in 1925 abolished legal polygamy, required the registration of marriages, and gave the president the power to grant divorces. Actually, except on farms, where most of the work was done by women, the economics of the situation had made polygamy much less general an institution in even the old Ottoman Empire than is usually imagined. But the practice is sanctioned in the Koran and was widely followed. Formerly, too, a Turk could divorce his wife by repeating three times the formula, "I divorce you," but now Turkish women were given marriage rights similar to those of women in most Western countries. Kemal almost immediately made use of his newly granted divorce power to dissolve his own marriage with Latifé Hanoum—a wealthy, cultivated, and European-educated feminist—to whom he had been married only three years. Apparently her tendency to mix in politics was largely responsible for the incompatibility that existed in the Kemal household during the time she was first lady of the land.

Civil marriages were made obligatory after September 1, 1926, though these might be supplemented by religious ceremonies. The minimum legal age for marriage was placed at seventeen for women and eighteen for men. The wearing of the veil was made optional and Western clothing was introduced, so that

Turkish ladies, unless they themselves so wished, no longer needed to resemble "coffin-shaped bundles of white linen." A demand arose for education for women and girls, and the foreign schools soon found it difficult to accommodate all the new seekers after knowledge. Women were permitted to engage in all the occupations that were open to their sisters in the West and women's clubs and societies became popular.

In 1929, following numerous petitions by the Union of Turkish Women, the right to vote in municipal elections and hold municipal office was extended to women. The following year witnessed the appointment of women as associate judges in some of the equity courts and in 1933 several women were made professors in the University of Istanbul. By a unanimous vote of the assembly in 1934 the constitution was amended so as to permit women to vote in national elections and become parliamentary delegates. In 1935 the government ordered the dissolution of the Union of Turkish Women on the ground that the purposes for which it had been organized, namely, the securing of an equal political status for women with men, had been achieved.

An outstanding example of the new Turkish woman was Halidé Edib, the first Turkish lady to receive a university degree, a distinguished writer and novelist, professor of Western literature at the University of Istanbul, aide-de-camp to Kemal in several military campaigns, and a Turkish Jane Addams in the matter of social work. Following some differences with Kemal over political policy, she left Turkey and became a popular lecturer in foreign countries. Her *Memoirs* and other written works are excellent records of Turkey's struggles during those trying years when the republic was in process of formation.

LEGAL AND EDUCATIONAL REFORM

The changed conditions of life in Turkey made imperative the scrapping of the old law codes, the *Sheriat* or Holy Law included. In 1926, therefore, the parliament adopted three new codes: civil, penal, and commercial, based, respectively, on those of Switzerland, Italy, and Germany. Three years later a new penal code, patterned more closely after the German, went into effect. The adoption of these Western legal systems was of international importance in view of the abolition of the capitulations when Turkey entered the war in 1914 and the confirmation of this action in the Lausanne Treaty.

One of the most difficult problems confronting the Turkish

Government was that of educating the people. School attendance was made compulsory for children from seven to sixteen, but the shortage of money, teachers, and school buildings prevented the full enforcement of the law. Nevertheless, by 1932 the national illiteracy was said to have fallen from 85 per cent to 42 per cent. The Gregorian calendar and the twenty-four-hour clock were adopted, and in 1928 a law was passed providing for the introduction of the Latin alphabet over a period of fifteen years. Newspapers were ordered to abandon the old Arabic type and the publication of books printed in Arabic characters was forbidden after January 1, 1929. An official dictionary was published in 1929, containing only words (to the number of about twenty-four thousand) that were definitely Turkish in origin, not Iranian or Arabic. The European numeral system came into general use from June 1929 and the employment of the metric system became compulsory in 1934.

Government officials and the heads of banks and business houses were ordered to attend special state schools for several hours a day, there to study from the new "abc" books. By the end of 1932 virtually all official correspondence and educational materials were in the Latin script. All Turks under forty years of age were made to take lessons in reading and writing, and after May 1931 certificates of literacy were in general required for the enjoyment of "the rights of citizenship." It was an unmistakable sign of the new Turkey that the government radio station was used to further these schemes.

Severe restrictions were placed on the teaching of religion in public and private elementary schools and in 1928 an American girls' school at Brusa was closed and three teachers were fined for disregarding the law prohibiting attempts at religious conversion. As a definite "symbol of intellectual liberation" the wearing of the fez or turban—the distinguishing mark of pious Moslems— was prohibited and a decree of 1934 forbade the wearing of clerical garb except during the performance of religious rites. During 1934, Turkish families generally were occupied with the task of providing themselves with family names, which had to be registered with the authorities by January 1, 1935. Mustapha Kemal accepted the surname suggested to him by the assembly, namely, "Atatürk" or "Father of the Turks." Such honorary titles as pasha, effendi, and hanoum were abolished and replaced by the old Turkish forms of bey and beyin for men and women, respectively.

"EFFICIENT TURKS FOR TURKEY"

In answer to a question regarding his opinion of the leaders of the Turkish Republic, a Bulgarian diplomat is reported to have said, "They are working as we never thought Turks could work." During the days of the sultans, relatively few Turks concerned themselves with trade, commerce, or industry. The masses, when not required to do military service, generally preferred to labor in the fields. Hence "business," as such, came to be almost a monopoly of the other racial groups in the empire, particularly the Greeks, Jews, and Armenians. But with the advent of the republic a new spirit became evident. The Nationalists wanted to have in Turkey nothing but Turkish labor, capital, ownership, and production. The obstacles to the fulfillment of such a program were enormous, but the pressure of economic circumstances soon led to the gradual rise of a commercial middle class whose nucleus was a group of the refugees from Greece, some of whom had there been engaged in trade. Since, however, the great majority of the people continued to be engaged in agriculture, the government also took pains to make efficient farmers of the Anatolian peasants.[1]

Commercial treaties were signed with many countries. Vast farm areas were settled with governmental aid in Anatolia. State departments were created to study agriculture, commerce, shipping, and industry. The government subsidized agriculture by the free grant of cattle, plows, and even houses to deserving families. Like Mussolini, Kemal had his own model farm on which he worked with rolled-up shirt sleeves, driving his own tractor. Agricultural production was further encouraged by such measures as the exemption from taxation of all grain used by the peasant families for their own needs. The good will of the peasantry was secured by the reduction of the term of compulsory military service to eighteen months.

In 1929 the National Assembly voted an appropriation for a consolidated public-works program to extend over twelve years and to include railway, port, irrigation, reclamation, and highway-construction projects. Swedish engineers were employed to supervise the completion of these works. Infant industries were

---

[1] From October 15 to October 20, 1927, Mustapha Kemal read to a congress of party delegates a speech of four hundred thousand words reviewing Turkish history and accomplishments since 1919. This source is available in English translation.

stimulated by means of a protective-tariff system—the leading industrial developments being textile factories, cotton gins, sugar refineries, and sawmills. A considerable amount of the machinery used in the factories and on those few farms where primitive methods of soil cultivation were no longer in use had to be imported. The leading Turkish exports were tobacco, fruit, cereals, and cotton, but the gradual development of transportation facilities made increasingly profitable the exploitation of enormous reserves of chrome ore, zinc, coal, copper, antimony, and petroleum.

There was a tendency in Turkey, in the interest of efficiency, to establish state control over a number of important industries. The government secured ownership of most of the railways and a large portion of the mercantile marine. It possessed tobacco, salt, gunpowder, and alcoholic-beverage monopolies, and established factories to supply the clothing needs of the army and navy. A batch of concessions was granted to foreigners, chiefly for the sake of getting additional capital and expert advice, but the authorities were careful in each case to safeguard Turkey's political and economic independence. In 1934 a five-year plan was adopted for the building of state and private factories, hydroelectric development, and the exploitation of mines. Six months later it was announced that only firms of Turkish registry might in future assist in the development of Turkey's natural wealth. In 1938 the Ankara Government became owner of all railways in the country, having recently purchased the last remaining private line, a French railroad extending from Istanbul to the Bulgarian border.

A number of Turkish cities rapidly increased in size. Angora, for example, whose name was officially changed in 1929 to Ankara, had a population of 5000 in 1918; in 1932 its population was 80,-000. Naturally the increase in this instance was stimulated largely by the new political importance which the city assumed. Kemal connected the capital with the sea by rail, undertook a campaign to annihilate the mosquitoes in the surrounding swamps, instituted reforms in sanitation, roads, police protection, and living conditions, and in general supervised the beautification of the city. Even statues, hitherto considered idolatrous, were erected—chiefly of Kemal. The building of movie houses and amusement palaces kept pace with the construction of trolley lines and sewer systems.

Despite these advances, Turkey by 1939 had not yet learned to know the meaning of prosperity. A succession of poor crops, the inertia of some of the people, and the hesitancy of the government to borrow from foreign bankers retarded material progress. When the harvests improved, the decline in the price of agricultural products in the world market had an equally unfortunate influence. From 1931 on, civil-service staffs and salaries were cut and drastic import quotas were fixed on foreign products. Attempts were made to mobilize the whole nation for a campaign of thrift and all citizens were urged to eschew as far as possible imported goods. Kemal himself set an example by wearing Turkish homespun clothes and drinking linden tea instead of coffee. A law that took effect in May 1934 ousted aliens from the professions, trades, and manual jobs. Thus thousands of foreigners were induced to seek naturalization.

TURKEY'S INTERNATIONAL RELATIONS

The harsh treatment meted out to Turkey after the First World War and the adverse decision of the League in the Turco-Iraqi boundary dispute of 1925 made the Turkish Nationalists highly suspicious of the West. This situation was in part responsible for the close relations that early developed between Turkey and the U.S.S.R., the latter being the only power with which Turkey had a treaty of friendship prior to 1928. But the communistic activities of the Russians eventually caused an unfavorable reaction in Turkey. In 1929 some Turks were sentenced to prison for having carried on communistic propaganda, and Kemal threatened "destruction" to all persons engaged in subversive enterprises.

The resulting estrangement with the U.S.S.R., combined with the friendly attitude now adopted by some of the Western powers who were eager to weaken Bolshevik influence in Turkey, gradually induced Ankara to look with increasing favor upon membership in the League. In 1927 the Permanent Court had rendered a favorable award to Turkey in a dispute with France over responsibility for the collision of the French steamer *Lotus* with a Turkish ship. In the following year a treaty of friendship was signed with Italy and in 1929 a new agreement with France was reached whereby the Turco-Syrian frontier was once more revised to the advantage of Turkey. Her suspicions at last removed by these and other incidents, the Turkish Republic, in 1932, accepted an invitation to join the League.

Under the terms of the Lausanne Treaty, the prewar debt of

the Ottoman Empire was to be distributed among the various areas that had been part of this empire in 1912 but that had been detached as a result of the Balkan Wars and the First World War. By an agreement of 1928 with its bondholders, the Turkish Republic offered to pay 62.25 per cent of the Ottoman debt as of October 1912 and 76.54 per cent of the debt incurred by the governments of the sultans after that date.

The relations between the United States and Turkey for some time after the war were peculiar. Although the two countries had never declared war upon each other, diplomatic and commercial relations had been severed and a new treaty arrangement had to be effected. A Turco-American Treaty of Amity and Commerce of 1923 was debated for several years in the American Senate and finally rejected. The opponents of ratification mustered a number of doubtful arguments, claiming that the treaty did not fulfill Wilson's award to Armenia (an arrangement which had been part of the defunct Treaty of Sèvres), that it failed to confirm the extraterritorial rights which had been granted to the United States by a treaty of the previous century (all other powers had recognized the abolition of the capitulations), and that it did not uphold the American nationality of certain naturalized ex-Turkish subjects (a stand which Turkey under international law was at liberty to take).

In the meantime, Turkey had placed an especially high tariff on imports from all countries with which she had no treaty agreements. Economic interests eventually outweighed diplomatic considerations and a Turco-American *modus vivendi,* providing for the restoration of diplomatic and consular relations, was concluded in 1927. Soon thereafter the high commissioner who had represented American interests in Turkey since 1919 was replaced by an ambassador. Commercial treaties, providing for "most-favored-nation" treatment, followed in due course.

Rumors were current, from 1934 on, that Turkey would seek permission to refortify the region of the Straits, demilitarized in accordance with the terms of the Lausanne Treaty. Finally, in 1936, Ankara did lay before the Lausanne signatories and the League a request for the revision of the appropriate treaty terms. Owing partly to the general feeling against Italy's Ethiopian venture and her apparent aims in the eastern Mediterranean and partly to gratification over the legal rather than unilateral method employed by Turkey to gain her ends, the powers readily agreed to consider her wishes. In July 1936 there was signed the Montreux Straits Convention permitting the refortification of the zone in question. In time of peace the Straits were to be open equally to all commercial ships and to a limited tonnage of war vessels. In war, Turkey might close the Straits to belligerents unless these were acting under League authority or in accordance with a pact to which Turkey was a party. The Ankara Government now lost no time in proceeding to refortify the strategic area connecting (and separating) the Black and Mediterranean seas.

Meanwhile Turkey had continued her policy of cementing diplomatic friendships with all her neighbors, north, south, east, and west. Especially interesting was an Eastern Pact signed in 1937 among Turkey, Iraq, Iran, and Afghanistan. The four states therein reaffirmed their obligations under the League Covenant and the Paris Pact, promised not to interfere in each other's internal affairs, undertook to prevent the formation within their respective borders of associations likely to disturb the peace among them, and agreed to consult on matters of common international concern. Henceforth, as a member of both the Balkan Entente [1] and the new Eastern League, Turkey occupied a strategic international position. This was further strengthened when, in 1939, she signed treaties with Great Britain and France providing for mutual assistance in case of attack. A few weeks later came the Second World War.

[1] See p. 196.

CHAPTER XXII

The Far East

THE COURSE OF REVOLUTION IN CHINA

About two years and a half before the outbreak of the First World War, the Western world received the startling news of a successful revolution in the largest and in many respects most conservative of Asiatic empires: China. The Manchu dynasty which had ruled China since 1644 was ousted from power and the empire was converted into a republic, bearing, at least outwardly, the earmarks of a European parliamentary system.

China had long been in a state of political, economic, and social "backwardness," while the West had been advancing toward world supremacy. China's government under the emperors had been corrupt and rotten; her social development, retarded. Education had been confined to the few and had been wholly out of tune with the requirements of a modern age. Famines, pestilence, and floods had wreaked havoc. Worse still, foreign "barbarians" had been able to exploit, chiefly for their own benefit, China's natural wealth and resources. Instead of guarding the land, many officials had pandered to the invaders, granting them concessions, tariff control, and leaseholds, and permitting them to set up their own laws and courts on Chinese soil.

Between 1898 and 1900 there had occurred two movements, both unsuccessful, to remedy the outstanding abuses of the Manchu regime and to curtail the activities of foreigners. In 1898 a group of patriotic intellectuals influenced the young Emperor Kwang Hsü to launch a sweeping reform program. But because of their very radicalness the reforms were foredoomed to failure. China was too backward to be modernized overnight by a bundle of edicts, and turmoil and reaction followed the sudden attempt at widespread reform. Then, during the period of reaction, the authorities, inspired by the Dowager Empress, Tsu Hsi, turned the popular dislike of "foreignism" into a concerted move to oust the "barbarians." The resulting Boxer Rebellion, however, brought on an international punitive expedition and the exaction of a heavy indemnity.

As the twentieth century wore on and the Chinese became aware of the remarkable transformation wrought by the Westernization of Japan, an increasing number of Chinese students went abroad to study. Especially was this true of many of the young people who lived in southern China, the region which had been last subdued by the Manchus and which had most frequently come in contact with the Westerners. At first, thousands of students went to Japan, which was relatively close and had a language similar to Chinese. But the Japanese schools often took advantage of the students and eventually many of the latter preferred to seek education elsewhere. Some of them came to the United States, particularly after Washington remitted part of the Boxer indemnity and the money was applied toward scholarship funds. The number of Chinese university students in the United States rose from 6 in 1898 to 650 in 1910 and 1500 in 1918.

Their foreign contacts and observations inspired these young people—some of them future leaders of China—with a fervent national spirit. The defeat at the hands of Japan in the war of 1894–1895 and the aggression of the foreigners helped to disseminate this spirit among the merchant and business classes and the professionals. The Manchus had never entirely lost their foreign aspect in the eyes of the Chinese intelligentsia, and a powerful secret agitation, dating from the late 1890's, had for its object the overthrow of the conquerors.

Sensing this widespread discontent and spurred by the example of Japan, who in 1904–1905 astonished the world by her stand against Russia, the Manchu Government inaugurated another reform program (1905). The literary examinations for governmental posts were abolished and replaced by tests in political science, economics, and history. A plan of constitutional reform was outlined and provision was made for the eventual calling of a national assembly. Before much progress in this direction was registered, the throne fell (1908) to Pu Yi, a boy not yet three years old. The regent was a conservative politician who attempted to halt the reform movement and who dismissed from the emperor's council Yuan Shih-kai, China's ablest military organizer.

The reformers now renewed their activities and a national assembly was convened at Peking in 1910. Although it was dismissed early in the following year, the assembly induced the government to issue a decree summoning a parliament in 1913. Meanwhile the year 1911 witnessed troop mutinies, movements for local autonomy, and violent reactions to the continued granting of concessions to foreigners. In despair, the regent recalled Yuan, but the latter, finding it impracticable to oppose the strong revolutionary groups in the south, advised the abdication of the Manchus. In February 1912 this suggestion was adopted and Manchu control came to an end after almost 270 years of rule. Pu Yi, however, whose reign-name was Hsuan Tung, was allowed to retain the title of emperor, and until 1924 he continued to reside in one of the imperial palaces.

Meanwhile, on January 1, 1912, a revolutionary assembly at Nanking had elected Dr. Sun Yat-sen president of a provisional republican government. Dr. Sun was a patriotic and capable scholar who, because of his radical ideas, had been forced to spend a considerable portion of his life in exile. As one of the founders and leaders of the *Kuomintang*, or Nationalist Party, he had spent most of the period since 1895 organizing Young China into an energetic association bent on achieving political and economic reform.

Sun believed that his country, which included one-fourth of the world's population and contained abundant mineral and agricultural resources, was destined to play a leading part in human affairs. He knew that the Chinese people would have to be aroused from the national lethargy into which they had fallen under Manchu control and that there must be no new oppression to take the place of the old. In 1924 he summed up his ideas regarding China's future in a series of lectures entitled *The Three Principles of the People (San Min Chu I)*. These principles, for which the new China was to strive, were Nationalism, Democracy, and Livelihood (economic equality). Sun pleaded for his people "the right to live" and "the right to a living."

At the time of his election to the provisional presidency, Sun agreed that, for the sake of unifying the country, he would soon retire in favor of Yuan Shih-kai, who had come into control of northern China. This arrangement was completed in February 1912, and Yuan thus became the first president of a united Chinese Republic. Friction soon developed between the northerners led by Yuan and the southerners under Sun. The former group favored the setting up of a strong executive and a weak parliament or no parliament at all. Sun and the Kuomintang preferred a democratic system with broad franchise privileges, a restricted executive, and a powerful parliament.

The Kuomintang deputies in the parliament (convened April 1913) persistently voted against Yuan and his policies. The mutual ill will increased steadily and in July—after the president had concluded an unpopular loan of £25,000,000 with a consortium of foreign bankers—an attempt was made to oust Yuan. This "second revolution" was easily crushed and Yuan expelled from parliament all members of the Kuomintang. Early in 1914 the whole parliament was dissolved and Yuan commenced a dictatorial rule which lasted, at least in the north, until 1916. Then, after an unsuccessful effort to found a new imperial dynasty in his own person, he died (June 1916).

Yuan was succeeded by Vice-President Li Yuan-hung, who supported the republic and reassembled the parliament, but who was unable to establish his dominance. The country was split over the questions of participation in the First World War and the further granting of foreign concessions. The central authorities found it virtually impossible to collect taxes and hence China's mineral and industrial resources were being given outright to foreigners in return for loans which were promptly squandered.

In mid-1917 the parliament was again dissolved and a group of monarchists attempted to restore the Manchus. Late in 1917, therefore, the Kuomintang and a majority of the dismissed parliamentarians set up at Canton a Southern Constitutionalist Government in opposition to the northern government at Peking. The confusion was increased by the activities of a dozen military governors (*tuchuns*) who did most of the local tax collecting and who used their armies to further private ambitions which ranged from brigandage to attempts at controlling all China. The Canton Government claimed to be the legitimate representative of the people, but Peking obtained both recognition and funds from the foreign powers who were seeking further privileges.

THE TWENTY-ONE DEMANDS

Japan, it will be recalled, declared war on Germany in August 1914 and soon thereafter captured the area about Kiaochow, which Germany in 1898 had leased from China. To carry out this project, Japan had landed troops on neutral territory more than one hundred miles from the German leasehold. Not only had China's neutrality thus been violated, but the Japanese soldiers had been billeted upon the native peasants and the latter were harshly treated. When, after the fall of the German strongholds, the Chinese asked the Japanese to retire, the latter replied, on January 18, 1915, by presenting to President Yuan a list of twenty-one demands. These demands, divided into five groups, were calculated to make of China a Japanese protectorate. The preoccupation of the great powers of Europe with the war afforded Japan, in the words of one of her publicists, "the opportunity of a thousand years" with respect to China.

The demands were handed to the Chinese President on Japanese War Office stationery, which was watermarked with machine guns and dreadnoughts. Yuan was warned to maintain secrecy regarding the transaction but its general import leaked out and soon was discussed in the Peking newspapers. Upon inquiries from abroad, the Tokyo Foreign Office issued a denial that any demands impairing China's sovereignty had been formulated and published an expurgated list which contained only an outline of eleven of the points. Thereupon the Chinese Government revealed a full list of the demands and Japan, driven into a corner, announced that the omitted demands had been only "wishes." No such explanation, however, "had been vouchsafed the Chinese Government."[1]

The United States and other powers protested that they would not recognize any Sino-Japanese arrangement that violated their own treaty rights, but in May 1915, after a threat of war by Japan, China finally signed two treaties. The documents embodied a modified version of the original demands, paid some respect to China's sovereignty, and contained clauses which provided for their going into force on the date of signature. Since the Chinese Parliament never ratified them, the treaties have consistently been regarded as invalid by the people of China. Japan was given special rights in southern Manchuria and eastern Inner Mongolia, options on all loans and on the construction of all railroads in these provinces, ninety-nine-year leases of the South Manchuria and Kirin-Changchun railways, the right to develop coal and iron projects, and a number of other economic concessions. The Kuomintang proclaimed its intention never to recognize the agreements.

---

[1] Hornbeck, S. K. *Contemporary Politics in the Far East,* 1916, p. 312. On pp. 307–311 of this volume may be found the parallel texts of the demands as originally handed to China and as furnished by Japan to foreign governments in expurgated form.

CHINA AND THE FIRST WORLD WAR

From the outset of the European conflict, China had feared that Japan would take advantage of the situation to establish her control in China. The Peking Government therefore had twice attempted (1914, 1915) to join the Allies, but each time the Japanese had been able to prevent such action. Japan had no desire to see China recruit an efficient army, mobilize her resources, or participate in a general peace conference. After the signature of the Sino-Japanese treaties of May 1915, Peking once more displayed anxiety to enter the war, but Tokyo successfully continued to object until 1917. Then Japan, for good reasons, reversed her policy.

The military position in 1917 of the Allied Powers was critical. Hence special efforts were made to secure additional help, not only from the United States, but from the Far East. The eastern countries had thus far done little to aid the Allies: China had remained neutral and Japan had confined her activities to the capture of the German leasehold and the sale of war materials. It was hoped that Japan might help convoy vessels through the Mediterranean and that China might turn over to the Allies the German ships that were interned in her harbors and supply coolies to labor behind the lines. A brisk exchange of notes therefore took place among the respective capitals.

In February 1917 a secret treaty was signed between Japan and Great Britain, whereby the former promised to dispatch some war vessels to the Mediterranean and the latter agreed to support the claim of Japan to Shantung and the German Pacific islands north of the equator at the peace conference. France undertook similar obligations with respect to the Japanese claims (March 1917) in return for Japan's promise to encourage China's participation in the war. A few days later Russia subscribed to an agreement of the same type and Italy announced that she "had no objections regarding the matter."

Upon the conclusion of these bargains, Japan urged China to break off relations with Germany. The United States, after her entry into the war in April, likewise suggested to China that relations with Germany be severed.[1] The Peking Government, more-

---

[1] On November 2, 1917, the United States and Japan concluded an interchange of notes known as the Lansing-Ishii Agreement. Renewed mutual assurances were given that the "Open Door" would be respected in China, that is, equal business

over, was annoyed at the renewal of unrestricted submarine warfare and the drowning of several hundred coolies through the sinking of a French ship which was transporting them to France to work in war-material factories. On August 14, 1917, the authorities at Peking declared war on both Germany and Austria-Hungary. Thereupon the Canton Government also issued a declaration of war.

China's participation in the war had little effect on the outcome of the struggle, though the interned German ships were seized and chartered to the Allies. After the war, however, China was entitled to representation at the Paris Conference, and President Hsu Shih-chang, elected in October 1918 by a group of northern military leaders, chose an able delegation drawn from southern as well as northern China. There was a fair degree of unanimity against foreigners among the Chinese plenipotentiaries at Paris.

Sino-Japanese difficulties developed at the conference as soon as Japan presented her claims to all former German rights and concessions in Shantung. To this the Chinese delegation offered strenuous objections. At one stage the Japanese declared that since the region had been conquered from Germany, it would be necessary to obtain the right of free disposal from that country before Shantung could be returned to China! President Wilson for a time upheld the Chinese view, but Lloyd George and Clemenceau insisted that they were bound by the secret treaties to back Japan. Besides, the Japanese delegates announced their intention to abstain from signing the peace treaty unless their wishes were met. Eventually the Japanese had their way, acquiring Shantung and mandatory rights over all former German colonies north of the equator. Thereupon China withheld *her* signature from the Versailles Treaty, later concluding a separate peace agreement with Germany. China became a member of the League of Nations by virtue of her adherence, against the wishes of Japan, to the Treaty of St. Germain with Austria.

THE WASHINGTON CONFERENCE

When the news of these events reached China, it was greeted with violent demonstrations. Student unions were formed in

opportunities would be upheld for the nationals of all countries. The United States recognized that Japan had "special interests in China, particularly in that part to which her possessions are contiguous." This agreement was canceled in April 1923 at the request of the United States.

north and south, protest parades were held, and Japanophil members of the government at Peking were attacked as national traitors. The merchants and bankers subscribed wholeheartedly to the agitation and resort was had to China's most powerful weapon—the economic boycott. The resulting decline in her foreign trade seriously worried Japan and, in accordance with a promise made at Paris to Wilson, she started negotiations for the return of Shantung to China. The latter rejected the offers that were made and appealed to the world for financial and diplomatic help. Foreign loans, however, seemed out of the question, for China's credit standing had entirely fallen away. At this point (1921) President Harding issued invitations to eight powers to attend a conference at Washington on the limitation of naval armaments and the settlement of outstanding international problems in the Pacific and Far East.

There were several motives for calling this gathering. The Department of State was anxious to check the race in naval armaments with Great Britain and to end the quarrel between China and Japan. In addition, the United States was aware that in 1921 there would come up the question of a renewal of the Anglo-Japanese Alliance that had been extended in 1911 for a decade. Washington had also noticed with inquietude that the Far Eastern policies of Great Britain and Japan were harmonious and that the British were tending to overlook the principles of the Open Door, principles that had been dear to American business men and diplomats since their formal enunciation in 1900 by John Hay. It was hoped that the conference might forestall any united Anglo-Japanese action injurious to the interests of the United States.

Invitations to the parley were extended to all states, except Russia, that had interests in the Far East: Belgium, China, France, Great Britain, Italy, Japan, the Netherlands, and Portugal. All governments but that at Tokyo willingly responded to the call. Japan agreed to participate only on condition that there be no discussion of matters that were "of sole concern to certain particular powers" or that might "be regarded as accomplished facts." The conference sat from November 1921 to February 1922 and concluded seven treaties. Two of these dealt with naval disarmament; the remaining five, with Pacific and Far Eastern questions.[1]

[1] The naval treaties (see p. 187) not only provided for a limitation of armaments but for restrictions on fortifications in the Pacific. The United States, Great Britain, and Japan agreed to a maintenance of the *status quo* in the defenses on a number of their insular possessions and naval bases. In some regions, such as the Aleutian Islands, fortifications were entirely banned.

Two additional treaties, one each dealing with Shantung and Yap, were signed outside the conference but by powers represented therein.

Two Four-Power treaties were signed among Great Britain, France, Japan, and the United States. In one, the states pledged themselves "to respect their rights in relation to their insular possessions and insular dominions in the region of the Pacific Ocean." If these rights should be threatened by the aggressive action of any other power, the contracting parties agreed "to communicate with one another fully and frankly in order to arrive at an understanding as to the most efficient methods to be taken, jointly or separately, to meet the exigencies of the particular situation." The treaty was to remain in force for ten years, subject to automatic renewal unless terminated by any signatory on twelve months' notice. The guarantees embodied in the document did not oblige the signatories to protect one another's holdings in the Far East, but they did bring about a lapse of the Anglo-Japanese Alliance. This fact, incidentally, pleased Canada, which had been more than a little concerned over Great Britain's exact obligations under the alliance in case of a war between Japan and the United States. The second Four-Power Treaty merely defined certain terms.

All the powers at the conference signed a Nine-Power Treaty which guaranteed the territorial integrity and independence of China and reiterated the principle of the Open Door. The signatories promised "not to support any agreements by their respective nationals with each other designed to create spheres of influence or to provide for the enjoyment of mutually exclusive opportunities in designated parts of Chinese territories." China pledged herself not to "exercise or permit unfair discrimination of any kind" on Chinese railways, particularly with respect to passenger or freight charges. The powers undertook to respect China's rights as a neutral in time of war. The treaty registered an advance in China's international status, but it applied only to the future and did not check the activities of established interests.

A second Nine-Power Treaty granted China greater control of her customs tariff than she had enjoyed in the past and a Six-Power Treaty allocated the cable lines in the Pacific which had formerly belonged to Germany among the United States, Great Britain, Japan, France, Italy, and China. The remaining documents signed at the conference were negotiated separately between China and Japan and the United States and Japan.

The Sino-Japanese agreement provided for the release of Shantung and all former German property rights therein to China in return for a monetary compensation reimbursing Japan for the railway and other improvements which she had fostered since 1914. In December 1923, twenty-two months after the signing of the treaty, the Shantung Peninsula was restored to Chinese control. Because of a series of unfortunate international "incidents," however, Japanese soldiers were again stationed in Shantung Province from 1927 to 1929.

The treaty between Japan and the United States concerned Yap, a former German possession which, over the protests of President Wilson, had been assigned as a mandate to Japan. Washington was anxious that the island be internationalized since the oceanic cables that converged at Yap formed one of the two American channels of communication with China and the only one with Netherland India. Especially vexing to the United States was the fact that the Japanese proceeded to move the Shanghai end of one of the cables to another island, Nawa. At the conference an agreement was reached which guaranteed the economic rights of American citizens in all the Japanese mandates and guaranteed Americans free access to Yap on an equal footing with Japanese "in all that relates to the landing and operation of the existing Yap-Guam cable, or of any cable which may hereafter be laid or operated by the United States or by its nationals connecting with the island of Yap."

It is difficult to evaluate the work of the Washington Conference. Regarding China it may be said that the principle of the Open Door was once more subscribed to by the great powers, that no new disabilities were imposed, and that a certain amount of lost autonomy was restored to the republic. Shantung was reacquired and China was given a breathing spell during which, if she had the capacity, she might rebuild her weak national structure. The signing of the Sino-Japanese conventions was followed by the adoption in Japan of a so-called friendship policy towards China which lasted until the spring of 1927. The moderate *Minsei-To* (Popular Government) Party under the leadership of Kijuro Shidehara attempted to harmonize the interests of China and Japan without force. However, when this group was replaced in power (April 1927) at Tokyo by the *Seiyu-Kai* (Political Fraternal) Party under Giichi Tanaka, recourse was once more had to a "positive policy" and to aggressive imperialistic methods. The naval and defense arrangements concluded at the conference temporarily eased the tension in the relations among the United States, Great Britain, and Japan. It was unfortunate that Russia had not been invited to the parleys, for the Soviet State was one of the most important Far-Eastern powers.

EDUCATION AND NATIONALISM IN CHINA, 1919–1931

The internal history of China from 1919 to 1927 was conspicuous chiefly for the administrative confusion which prevailed in every province of the land. Scores of generals ravaged country and town and laid waste much of the natural wealth of the republic. In addition there were catastrophic floods and famines, fanatical antiforeign outbursts, and political quarrels between republicans and communists. Out of the turmoil, however, there emerged two definite phenomena: a substantial progress in education and an organized nationalist movement.

Under the old regime, education in China had been reserved for a small minority. The written language contained thousands of ideographs and was difficult to learn. After the revolution of 1911, and especially after 1919, numerous efforts were made to increase literacy. At first a group of reformers attempted to introduce a phonetic alphabet of only thirty-nine symbols, but this, for various reasons, proved unworkable. Then Dr. Hu Shih, an American-trained scholar and philosopher, launched a movement to substitute in literature the colloquial language of the country for the ancient literary forms. In order the quicker to popularize the vernacular (*Pai Hua*) as a literary medium, Hu Shih and other leaders utilized it in the composition of poems, essays, novels, histories, and general works of high literary merit. In 1920 the ministry of education at Peking was induced to order the use of Pai Hua textbooks in the first two years of primary school. Later it was provided that all government documents be written in this popular form.

Another American-trained student, James Y. C. Yen, inaugurated (1922) a Mass Education Movement which aimed at familiarizing the masses with one thousand of the most commonly used Chinese ideographs. To teach these ideographs to the peasants and laborers, four easy readers were devised, and the lessons were so arranged that the information could be mastered by spending on them one hour a day for four months. The volumes cost only 5 cents a copy and by 1928 fourteen editions had been printed. Thanks to this project, millions of persons, who might otherwise have remained illiterate, learned to read. A further step in Chinese educational development was the increasing attention devoted to foreign works on history, politics, government, economics, philosophy, and literature. The Commercial Press of Shanghai, established at the close of the nineteenth century, published a library containing vernacular translations of 2000 of the world's masterpieces. The complete set was priced at the relatively moderate sum of $100. Despite the enthusiasm for education, the inadequacy of funds was responsible for a decided shortage of school facilities. Only gradually could this deficiency be remedied, but in the process the Chinese authorities extended their control over the foreign as well as the native schools.

The advances made in education were accompanied by the gradual emergence of the students as an important factor in the agitation for liberation from foreign restrictions and the shackles of tradition. In 1919 the most serious attacks on the Versailles Treaty and on the officials who proposed to endorse it were led by students. The same was true of many of the later patriotic demonstrations. Yet, although these activities heralded an awakening China, the Westernization of the land could hardly be brought about solely by the clamorings of an earnest but impatient Youth. The spirit displayed by the emancipated young people was encouraging, but it required mature leadership. Some direction was given to the students' movements by the Kuomintang or Nationalist Party, especially after the latter extended its control over the educational system of the republic.

Now, we have seen that in 1917 the Kuomintang and a group of nationalistic southerners had established at Canton a Southern Constitutionalist Government. This administration steadfastly opposed most of the moves undertaken by the northern government at Peking which continued to function under the guidance of interested foreigners. Led by Dr. Sun, the Nationalists devoted themselves for several years to the task of bringing the north under the sway of the Kuomintang and unifying the country, mainly through the use of force and propaganda. Considerable support for this endeavor was forthcoming from Soviet Russia, which meanwhile had surrendered most of the special privileges acquired in China in tsarist days. An able diplomat, Michael Borodin, was dispatched to China to win the confidence of Sun and his associates—a mission which he fulfilled with eminent success. Simultaneously Moscow had an ambassador at Peking.

In 1924 a Kuomintang Congress at Canton extended party

membership to all Chinese communists who were ready to accept the Kuomintang principles. Soon thereafter Peking signed an agreement with Moscow whereby the latter gave up its extraterritorial rights in China, remitted the unpaid balance of the Boxer indemnity, promised not to spread communist propaganda in Chinese territory, and pledged the restoration of Mongolia (occupied since the Boxer Rebellion) to the republic. Another treaty provided that the Chinese Eastern Railway in Manchuria, a Sino-Russian enterprise conceived in 1896, should remain under the joint control of the two states until such time as China could redeem the entire line "with Chinese capital." In 1924, also, Sun established the Whampoa Military Academy, along lines devised by Borodin. Soviet military officers were invited to train the Nationalist forces. The ablest of these soldiers was General Vassily Blücher, alias Galen.

With the approach of 1925 there became evident a rift in Kuomintang ranks. The right-wing members of the party were out of sympathy with the aims of the communist left wing and wanted to end the close relationship with the Soviet Union. Dr. Sun was able to hold the two camps together despite their opposing views, but after his death in March 1925 the breach rapidly widened. In 1927 Chiang Kai-shek, who had succeeded Sun as leader of the Nationalists, broke off relations with the Russian communists and discriminated against the communist members of the Kuomintang. Later in the year relations also were strained between the Moscow and Peking governments because of the propagandist activities of Bolshevik agents in China.

Just prior to the break with the U.S.S.R., the Nationalists had succeeded in extending their control over nearly all China. This achievement, though of only temporary duration, was accomplished in part through the military ability of Chiang, in part because of the aid rendered by the Russian advisers, and in part through a well-organized propaganda campaign aimed at the northerners and the foreign concessionaires. The fruits of the victory, however, were spoiled by the fierce struggle which had developed among the factions of the Kuomintang.

The communists tried to discredit Chiang and to force his hand by the commission of excesses, the most serious instance being the "Nanking Affair" of March 1927. After the capture of the city by the Nationalist forces, the left-wing elements attacked the persons and property of the foreign residents. The powers naturally demanded restitution and Japan landed several thousand soldiers

CHIANG KAI-SHEK

to protect her extensive interests. In the end, the doings of the communists reacted to the advantage of Chiang, whose support came increasingly from the commercial class and industrial leaders.

Chiang was born in 1888, the son of a merchant. He obtained a military education and attended the Tokyo Military College. During the crucial days of 1911 and 1912 he commanded a force of revolutionary soldiers and from 1913 to 1920 was secretary to Dr. Sun. After acquiring some financial experience in a stock exchange he went to Russia to study recent military developments. In 1924 he became director of the Whampoa Military Academy and soon thereafter succeeded Sun as leader of the Nationalists. As a result of his successes, Chiang was able in April 1928 to establish a Nationalist Government at Nanking. Two months later Kuomintang troops captured Peking and abolished the northern government. The name of the city was changed from Peking ("Northern Capital") to Peiping ("Northern Peace") and Nanking became the new national capital.

In October 1928 the central executive committee of the Kuomintang promulgated an Organic Law for the National Government of China. The law was to be executed under the supervision of the committee, which thus virtually became the government of the republic. The highest administrative unit in the land was to be a State Council, and the committee elected Chiang to be chairman of the first such council, an office equivalent to that of president of China. Having undertaken to satisfy the claims of the powers regarding the Nanking Affair, the Nationalist Government before the close of 1928 secured official recognition from most of the Western states and Japan.[1]

Chiang faced a difficult task as chief executive of China. He invited American and German experts to assist in the reorganization of the country and strove to weld the Chinese nation into a powerful state. However, the continuing need to lead his troops in battle interfered seriously with Chiang's plans. The constant scenes of disorder and the ravages of floods and famines had enabled the Chinese communists greatly to increase their numbers, and now they massed all their strength against the Nanking regime in an attempt to replace it by a soviet system. Chiang waged almost

---

[1] The organic law, revised as a provisional constitution in 1931 and again in 1932, was still in force in 1943. From 1931 on there was a regular "President of the National Government" who had little power; more important was the president of the Executive Yüan or cabinet, and this post went to Generalissimo Chiang Kai-shek.

uninterrupted warfare against the communists, who had established some control on a soviet basis south of the Yangtse River, and in addition had to deal with rival military leaders who hoped to turn the confusion to advantage and acquire control of one or more Chinese provinces.

Besides its domestic difficulties, the Nationalist Government in 1929 had a serious quarrel with the Soviet Union. The dispute grew out of Bolshevik propagandist activities in northern China and an attempt by the governor of Manchuria, Chang Hsueh-liang, to gain complete control of the Chinese Eastern Railway and to oust the subjects of the U.S.S.R. from the territory under his jurisdiction. In June and July 1929 Soviet consular offices in a number of Manchurian cities were raided and hundreds of Soviet officials and employees of the Chinese Eastern Railway were arrested. The U.S.S.R. retaliated by arresting many of the Chinese merchants who happened to be in the Soviet Union. Diplomatic relations were severed, troop movements were begun, and some minor battles occurred in which the Bolsheviks triumphed with ease. Moscow insisted that her rights under the treaty of 1924 as half-owner of the railroad be restored.

At the height of the crisis the United States and forty-one other co-signatories with the U.S.S.R. and China of the Kellogg Pact reminded the disputants of their obligation to settle the quarrel by peaceful means. This move apparently had little effect on the parties concerned, but actually they did find it practicable to reach a peaceful agreement. By the Khabarovsk Protocol of December 1929 the *status quo ante* was reëstablished and provision was made for the calling of a special conference to settle all causes of dispute. There the matter rested when a serious Sino-Japanese conflict occurred over Manchuria in September 1931.

ECONOMICS IN MANCHURIA AND IN JAPAN

China long was a tempting field for Western and Japanese financial investments and business enterprises. Billions of dollars were poured into the land through the purchase of government bonds, the construction of railways, and the erection of factories, plants, warehouses, and missionary establishments. It was estimated that of the total value ($3,500,000,000) of foreign monetary stakes in China at the end of 1930, Great Britain controlled 35.7 per cent; Japan, 35.7 per cent; the U.S.S.R., 7.8 per cent; the United States, 7.2 per cent; and France and Belgium together,

7.2 per cent. A lucrative foreign trade was developed, the average annual value of China's sales and purchases abroad from 1926 to 1930 totaling about $1,500,000,000.[1]

Among the most promising sections of China from the economic point of view was Manchuria. Situated in the northeastern part of the republic, this valuable region, with an area in 1931 of about 380,000 square miles and a population of perhaps 29,000,000, came to assume a tremendous importance in international affairs. The land grows numerous crops in abundance and the subsoil resources include large quantities of coal, iron, gold, silver, lead, copper, and asbestos. About 4000 miles of railways traversed the territory in 1931, making possible the expeditious shipment of products to the seacoast. In 1928 Manchuria alone was responsible for almost one-third of the commodity exports of China and about one-fifth of the imports. Chang Hsueh-liang, who became governor of Manchuria in 1928, was one of the richest men in China. Though virtually an autonomous administrator, he maintained a benevolent front towards the authorities at Nanking.

The Kuomintang Government regarded Manchuria in a special light. The region was looked upon as a vital outpost of Chinese culture. It was hoped that the steady migration of Chinese peasants into the area would emphasize this aspect. Between 1923 and 1929, more than four million Chinese were reported to have entered Manchuria, by rail, by boat, or on foot, to take advantage of the fertile land and the relative freedom from domestic turmoil. Many of these immigrants returned southward after they had accumulated modest savings, but perhaps half of them became permanent settlers. At the end of 1931 the Chinese inhabitants formed 90 per cent of the population. Nanking encouraged this latest of "people's wanderings" and at the same time was anxious to restrict the encroachments of foreigners in the area.

Most of the world's industrial powers, however, had interests of a financial or business nature in Manchuria. The U.S.S.R. and Japan felt that they had special rights. As we have seen, the Soviet Government was half-owner of the Chinese Eastern Railway, a line which, more than a thousand miles long, offered the most direct route from the west to the Siberian port of Vladivostok. The

---

[1] At the close of 1930, the United States had $155,000,000 invested in factories and plants in China and over $50,000,000 in missionary and other noncommercial establishments. Americans also held Chinese railway bonds with a par value of $41,000,-000, and had considerable interests in the oil and steel businesses of the country. American exports to China in 1929 amounted to $125,000,000 and imports from China to $165,000,000.

Bolsheviks, moreover, exercised considerable authority in Outer Mongolia, a wild region just west of Manchuria. The Japanese, too, had control of a railroad, the South Manchuria Railway. This line, seven hundred miles long, terminated at the Japanese-controlled port of Dairen through which passed more than half of the foreign trade of Manchuria. Not the least important item in the railway's business was the transportation of Chinese migrants to and from Manchuria. The foreign banking business of Manchuria was almost a monopoly of Japanese firms and early in 1932 Japanese investments in the area totaled $1,000,000,000. Large as were her financial holdings in Manchuria, Japan advanced even more important reasons for desiring recognition of her paramount interests in the territory. For an understanding of these motives it is necessary to survey the economic position of the empire.

At the middle of the nineteenth century Japan was a medieval country, cherishing feudal traditions and anxious to avoid all contact with the West. Before the close of the century, however, Japan had been "opened" by importunate Westerners seeking new trade outlets, and the Nipponese were imitating the intruders' methods and adopting their business views. With the coming of modern industry to the islands, there soon developed the same pressing needs which earlier had induced the Western powers to launch their campaigns for overseas expansion. Industrialized Japan began to seek sources of cheap raw materials for her factories, markets for her surplus manufactures, fields for the investment of her accumulated capital, food for her workers, and outlets for her surplus population.

During the First World War economic conditions in Japan took an unusually favorable turn. The Allies bought enormous quantities of war materials, new trade contacts were established in Asia, Africa, and the Americas, and Japanese ships were chartered to handle a considerable portion of the world's ocean commerce. Between 1913 and 1918 the aggregate horsepower employed in Japanese industry doubled and the number of factory workers was increased by half. In consequence of these activities Japan enjoyed a total favorable trade balance for the period from 1914 to 1918 of more than $2,000,000,000.

After the war there came a gradual slump. The former belligerents were able to reëngage in the manufacture of peacetime goods and compete once more in the struggle for foreign markets. Since foreign trade by this time had come to be the backbone of Japanese prosperity, normally accounting for one-third of the country's total commerce by value,[1] any appreciable decline in exports was sure to have a serious effect on the economic condition of the country.

For some years after the armistice, Japan's export figures remained at a relatively high level because the United States, in her new-found prosperity, became a heavy purchaser of silk. In an average postwar year silk yarn comprised 40 per cent of the value of Japanese exports, and more than 85 per cent of this was shipped to the United States. With the increasing popularity of rayon and other silk substitutes, however, and then the appearance of the world depression, there was a notable decline in the demand for silk and other products of Japanese manufacture. Compared with 1929, Japanese raw-silk exports in 1930 suffered a loss of 18 per cent in quantity and about 45 per cent in value. In an attempt to lower production costs, Japan abandoned the gold standard in 1931, but the results were disappointing in so far as they concerned any enlargement of foreign sales.

In 1930 the area of the Japanese Empire, including Korea (Chosen), was 265,000 square miles, or about that of Texas. Its population was estimated at 92,000,000. In Japan proper (area, 148,700 square miles; population, 65,000,000) more than 40 per cent of the people derived a meager existence directly from the soil, only one-sixth of which could be cultivated. The unemployed numbered about 1,000,000 and the national debt, having doubled in the decade since 1920, stood at $3,000,000,000. In the circumstances, Manchuria, with its plentiful resources, undeveloped opportunities, geographic nearness, and strategic location assumed a tempting aspect in the eyes of Japan. The work which was begun in 1915 with the presentation of the Twenty-one Demands, it seemed to her statesmen, must now be completed. The year 1931 appeared favorable for this undertaking.

CHINA, "MANCHOUKUO," JAPAN

Conditions in China in 1931 were turbulent. The right- and left-wing members of the Kuomintang exchanged accusations of self-interest and treachery, and sent military forces against each other. Famines and floods continued to deprive millions of food and shelter. Communist propaganda was rife and local chieftains revived their bandit activities. Foreign interference added to the confusion, particularly in Manchuria, where Chang Hsueh-liang

[1] In the United States the postwar ratio normally was about 1 to 10.

strove to resist further penetration by the U.S.S.R. and Japan.

Elsewhere in the world the governments were preoccupied with equally numerous, if less violent, problems. Unemployment, agrarian difficulties, tariff barriers, radical movements, taxes, debt moratoria, security, disarmament, elections, these were the matters which demanded the attention of the Westerners. Japan, therefore, pressed by many of the same problems, felt the moment ripe for the realization of her dreams in Manchuria. There seemed little likelihood that the Western powers would interpose forceful objections even if they did disapprove of Tokyo's plans. For a variety of reasons, the Japanese army now took the lead in the Manchurian venture.

In Japan the army and navy departments were virtually independent of the civil authorities. Their leaders might approach the emperor directly, without the regard for ordinary cabinet procedure which was mandatory upon other ministers. The defenders of the land enjoyed by tradition considerable influence over the ruler, who looked upon the empire as his personal domain. Suffering only a few casualties during the First World War, the Japanese army emerged after the armistice as one of the leading military units in the world.

The army had long been suspicious of the civil government and especially of the parliamentarians. It saw little good in the custom of ministerial responsibility which dated from 1918, or in the privilege of universal suffrage that had been proclaimed in 1925. The military men regarded many of the politicians as intriguing and selfish individuals who were interested solely in the welfare of certain business men, bankers, and bondholders. They, on the other hand, professed to be interested in the well-being of the farming and laboring classes from which came most of the recruits, and they believed that the country's difficulties might easily be alleviated by the conversion of Manchuria into a great agricultural colony and a busy industrial development. Actually the army worked hand in hand with another group of bankers and industrialists—those who had financial stakes in Manchuria. Indeed, the head of the South Manchuria Railway was a member of the Japanese military command. A successful military venture, incidentally, would shed additional glory upon the proud warrior class.

During the years from 1930 to 1932, the military succeeded in wresting the political control from the civil government. A section of "big business" feared possible Western economic retaliation against Japanese aggression, but millions of the people were induced by national pride and personal poverty to side with the army. Numerous societies of a fascist type were organized and there was a popular demand for the achievement of economic security and prosperity through the use of blunt force rather than by the negotiation of vague treaties.[1]

Unfortunately for China, there occurred in 1931 two incidents that provided the Japanese army with a pretext for removing the whole Manchurian question from the sphere of diplomacy to that of armed hostilities. First, the "honor" of the army was "violated" by the murder in Inner Mongolia of a Japanese captain, and then, on September 18, a short stretch of the South Manchuria Railway line was damaged by explosives. It has not been proved conclusively who was responsible for the explosion, but the Japanese troops who guarded the railway accused Chinese soldiers of the deed. Without prior notification to the Tokyo Foreign Office, the Japanese military machine was set in motion and a wide area of Manchuria was occupied.

The Chinese soldiers withdrew before the advancing Japanese forces and the Nanking Government appealed to the world for help. The diplomats at Tokyo quickly came to the support of the military by pointing out that the governor of Manchuria had violated a Sino-Japanese treaty of 1905 by building a railroad paralleling the South Manchuria Railway. Japan had said little or nothing about this while the line was being built, but now complaints were heard that the road constituted a military threat to Japanese interests and would deflect considerable Sino-Manchurian traffic from the South Manchuria Railway and the port of Dairen to the Chinese-controlled railway and ports.

While China appealed her case to the League and the United States, the Japanese troops, under the guise of efforts to end the disorders that were jeopardizing legitimate business, extended the area of occupation at a rapid rate. In September 1931 Japan had been in direct control of about fourteen hundred square miles of territory and eight hundred miles of railways in Manchuria. By January 1932 the area of control had been widened so as to include about two hundred thousand square miles of land and two

---

[1] Between February and May 1932 fanatical patriots in Japan assassinated a leading banker, an ex-finance minister, and a premier. The last was shot down in his home by a group of young cadets and army officers who later voluntarily surrendered to the police. They claimed to have committed the deed as a patriotic protest against the selfish and "traitorous" governmental policies inspired by certain commercial interests.

thousand miles of railways. Efforts were made to undermine the power of Governor Chang Hsueh-liang and to encourage local separatist movements. Loyal Chinese officials were replaced by friends of Japan.

On February 18, 1932, a small group of Manchurian leaders at Mukden (which was in Japanese hands) issued a formal declaration of independence of Manchuria and then constituted itself into a Northeastern Administrative Committee. One week later this committee issued an outline constitution for the new state which was given the name "Manchoukuo." Changchun, renamed Hsinking ("New Capital"), was designated as the seat of government. The world was officially notified of the establishment of the new state on March 1 and China was informed that Manchoukuo had severed all ties with the Chinese Government. Henry Pu Yi, the same who had been forced to abdicate the Chinese imperial throne, was inaugurated as "Chief Executive" of Manchoukuo. Virtually all governmental power was vested in his hands, but the government was patently under Japanese tutelage and protection.

Japan's activities, as was to be expected, exerted a unifying influence upon Chinese politics. In December 1931 a reconciliation was effected between the Nanking authorities and a rival government that had been set up at Canton by a group of left-wing members of the Kuomintang. Chiang Kai-shek resigned as head of the State Council in order to make the process of *rapprochement* somewhat easier, but he retained a dominant voice by becoming president of the Executive Yüan or cabinet. Anti-Japanese outbreaks again became frequent occurrences and Chinese residents in foreign lands sent home money to bolster the nation's defense against the invaders.

After the extension of the Japanese occupation to Mukden and other large Manchurian cities, the Chinese people once more resorted to their most powerful weapon, a nation-wide economic boycott. Since China normally was, after the United States, the best customer of Japan, taking one-fourth of the latter's exports, the boycott caused havoc to Japanese industry. Japanese sales to China in January 1932 were 68 per cent lower than those in January 1931. Most of the Japanese textile mills in northern China had to close their doors while Chinese managers and employees gave up their jobs in Japanese firms, and the Japanese shipping concerns, which had controlled more than a fourth of China's coastwise and river traffic, either suspended business or continued to

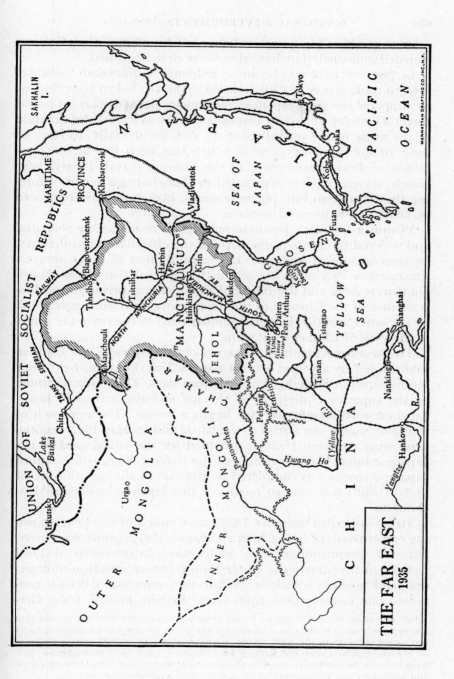

THE FAR EAST
1935

operate at a loss. The Japanese banks in China found their services spurned and small Japanese shopkeepers were ruined.

In January 1932 the Japanese residents of Shanghai, the chief foreign-trade center of China, called upon the Tokyo Government to suppress the anti-Japanese movement by a display of naval force. The navy welcomed this opportunity to follow the example of the army in the pursuit of glory and, incidentally, to retrieve some of the domestic prestige which had been lost at the time (1930) of Japan's adherence to the London Naval Treaty. War vessels, therefore, were dispatched to Shanghai as a means of forcing the Chinese to buy Japanese goods. Economic warfare was to be combated with naval warfare.

Within a few days Japanese marines were landed at Shanghai and ordered to occupy those parts of the city that were inhabited by large groups of Japanese. In the fulfillment of this command the marines inevitably clashed with the local Chinese garrison. Shots were fired and the Battle of Shanghai was precipitated. The resistance of the Chinese to the invaders was labeled "aggression" by the latter and the Tokyo diplomats tried to convince the world of the evils of China's militarism!

To the astonishment and chagrin of the Japanese, the Chinese soldiers, led by a young general named Tsai Ting-kai, held their ground around Shanghai for thirty-four days. Then, overwhelmed by the superior equipment of the foe and the arrival of heavy Japanese reënforcements, they began a retreat. The approach of the rainy season put a stop to the battle and in May 1932 negotiations were completed which provided for the withdrawal of the Japanese forces and the ending of the boycott. The withdrawal of Japanese troops was completed by the end of the month; one of the divisions was sent to reënforce the Japanese army in Manchoukuo.

Meanwhile, in December 1931, the Council of the League, acting on proposals of both China and Japan, had appointed an international commission of five, under the chairmanship of Lord Lytton, to investigate the whole Sino-Japanese situation and recommend possible solutions.[1] While the commission, which contained one member each from Great Britain, France, Italy, Ger-

[1] At one stage of the difficulties it was proposed among the Western powers that a general economic boycott be declared against Japan on the ground that the latter was acting contrary to the spirit of the Nine-Power Treaty of 1922 and in violation of her obligations under the Kellogg Pact. Nothing came of this suggestion, perhaps because the conflict resulted in the placing of large Japanese orders for cotton and munitions and Chinese orders for textiles in several Western countries.

many, and the United States, was at work, Secretary of State Henry L. Stimson announced that the United States henceforth would refuse to recognize the legality of any situation or treaty resulting from action taken in violation of the Kellogg Pact. This Stimson Doctrine, as it came to be known, failed to elicit any immediate coöperative endorsements from the European powers.

In September 1932, seventeen days before the report of the Lytton Commission was made public, Japan offered a veiled affront to the League by officially recognizing the "state of Manchoukuo." The motive behind this act presumably was to confront the League with a *fait accompli,* and the procedure called forth a sharp rebuke from the president of the League Council, who happened to be Eamon de Valera. Recognition was accorded through the instrument of a Japan-Manchoukuo Protocol wherein the former Chinese domain, in return for an endorsement of its "independent" status, promised Japan a long series of favors, including the right to station her troops at any desired point in Manchoukuo. Western reproaches were answered with defiant proclamations by the Japanese military commander in Manchoukuo, reëchoed by the Tokyo Foreign Office. The Japanese yen dropped during these months to less than half of its par value.

The Lytton Report proved to be a guarded document which carefully avoided hurting the sensibilities of any of the contending parties. In brief, it expressed grave doubts whether a government-inspired boycott was a "legitimate weapon of defense against military aggression by a stronger country"; recommended direct negotiation between China and Japan for the settlement of all outstanding difficulties; suggested that China set up in Manchuria an autonomous government which would acknowledge Chinese suzerainty; and proposed widespread internal Chinese reforms. The League Council referred the report for action to a special meeting of the Assembly. The latter then referred the matter to another committee, which was to recommend a solution of the dispute early in 1933.

During 1933, events moved rapidly forward. Japan continued to suffer diplomatic defeats at Geneva and to win military victories in northern China. From January through May the Japanese forces pushed on into the rich province of Jehol and into the regions south of the Great Wall. Jehol, rich in oil and potentially in opium poppies, was claimed as part of Manchuria and therefore of Manchoukuo. The penetration south of the Great Wall was justified as preventing further Chinese "raids" into Manchoukuo territory. Since Japan paid little heed to the pleas of the various committees of the League, China finally despaired of any practical help from Geneva and accepted an armistice at Tangku (May 31). Under this agreement the Japanese were to return north of the Great Wall and China consented to the creation of a demilitarized zone between the wall and a line drawn roughly from Tientsin to Peiping. This buffer area was to be administered by Chinese officials friendly to Japan. Thus did Manchuria go the way of other former Chinese provinces and thus was added another to the world's list of "unredeemed" territories.[1]

Meanwhile (March 1933) Japan had informed the League of her intention to withdraw from membership. In the official note it was explained that the Japanese Government had been led to realize "the existence of an irreconcilable divergence of views, dividing Japan and the League on policies of peace and especially as regards the fundamental principles to be followed in the establishment of a durable peace in the Far East." The difference of opinion arose chiefly because the League continued to advocate a settlement based upon the recommendations of the Lytton Report and involving at least the nominal restoration of Manchuria to China, whereas the Japanese maintained that the "independence" of Manchoukuo must be upheld. In March 1935, when Japan officially ceased to be a member of the League, Manchoukuo had been legally recognized only by her protector and El Salvador.[2] Undaunted by this foreign coldness, Chief Executive Pu Yi, on March 1, 1934, "in compliance with the will of Heaven" and with the consent of Japan, had taken the title of emperor under the reign-name of Kang Teh. The change in no way diminished Japanese influence in Manchoukuo, for behind every key political position stood a Japanese adviser.

In 1933 the U.S.S.R. offered to sell its half-interest in the Chinese Eastern Railway to Manchoukuo, which had already appropriated the half-interest of China. Negotiations among representatives of Moscow, Tokyo, and Hsinking were carried on for almost two years. Then a series of documents was signed (March

---

[1] Though its political efforts on behalf of China proved ineffective, the League tried also to render China technical aid. Beginning with the dispatch of a sanitary mission in 1929, help was rendered in the spheres of public health, finance, and education. In 1933 the League Council appointed a Special Committee on Technical Collaboration with China to assist the republic in an extensive program of economic reconstruction.

[2] Later Germany, Italy, Spain, Hungary, and Romania followed suit. Japan retained her mandates upon quitting the League but agreed to continue submitting the required reports of her stewardship.

1935) transferring all Russian rights to Manchoukuo in return for $52,000,000 payable over three years. Japan guaranteed the payments, "in view of the close relations existing between Japan and Manchoukuo." With the transfer of ownership, the name of the line was changed to the North Manchuria Railway; it was to be operated for the Manchoukuo Government by the Japanese-controlled South Manchuria Railway.

Renewed friction had meanwhile developed between Japan and several other states over the assignment of a Manchoukuo oil-sales monopoly to a firm under Japanese control. The United States, British, and Netherland governments protested this action as a violation of the Open-Door policy guaranteed in the Washington Nine-Power Treaty and confirmed by Kang Teh at the time of his elevation to the imperial throne. Tokyo replied by saying (1) that the monopoly in no way violated the principle of the Open Door; (2) that the emperor's promise could hardly be invoked since his government was not recognized by the complaining powers; and (3) that Japan could do nothing about the matter anyway since Manchoukuo was an independent state, capable of handling its own direct negotiations. This answer was regarded as unsatisfactory and, when the monopoly went into effect (1935), Washington and London declared, in substance, that they would hold Japan responsible for any resultant losses to their respective nationals. These last, however, made preparations to withdraw entirely from the oil business in Manchoukuo.

TOWARD A "NEW ORDER" IN EASTERN ASIA

Japan did not specifically enunciate the doctrine of a "new order" in eastern Asia until 1938, but the trend in this direction was foreshadowed in a declaration of 1934 made by Eiji Amau, spokesman of the Tokyo Foreign Office. Having, in a sense, broken with the West by her withdrawal from the League, having repeatedly declared herself to be "the principal protector" of stability in the Far East, and desirous of finding work and food for her rapidly increasing population, Nippon announced that she would continue to foster Sino-Japanese "friendship" while opposing "any attempt on the part of China to avail herself of the influence [even financial influence] of any other country in order to resist Japan." And then Tokyo proceeded to promote "friendship" with her neighbor by encouraging separatists in northern China to set up an autonomous Hopei-Chahar state under Japanese tutelage (1935) and by disarming the customs guards along the Great Wall so that Japanese goods might readily be smuggled into China (1936).

The increasing aggression of Japan on the Asiatic mainland for a time led to more serious difficulty with the Soviet Union than with any other third power. During the winter of 1935–1936 there was considerable friction between Moscow and Tokyo, occasioned by border incidents along the Soviet-Manchoukuo and the Manchoukuo-Outer Mongolian frontiers. Outer Mongolia, or the Mongolian People's Republic, declared its independence of China after the First World War and gradually came under the influence of the Soviet Union. The precise extent of this subserviency was not ascertainable, but it appeared that U.S.S.R. advisers had much influence in the Mongolian People's Republic (which itself had a soviet form of government), that nearly all Outer Mongolia's foreign trade was with the Soviet Union, and that Westerners wishing to visit Outer Mongolia had to have their passports visaed in Moscow. A mixed commission appointed in 1935 to demarcate a boundary between Manchoukuo and Outer Mongolia, and including both Russian and Japanese advisers, soon abandoned its efforts, and in 1936 the U.S.S.R. and Outer Mongolia signed a pact for mutual assistance in case of attack.

Meanwhile there were frequent rumors of clashes along the Manchoukuo-Siberian border. It was reported in the summer of 1937 that Japanese artillery had sunk two Soviet gunboats in the Amur River and one year later there was waged a prolonged Soviet-Japanese military and diplomatic battle over the border heights of Changkufeng. The incident had its origin in the occupation of the heights by Soviet soldiers who undertook the construction of defense works. When Tokyo heard of the affair it protested to Moscow that the area was in Manchoukuo territory. A map of 1886 appended to a Russo-Chinese frontier agreement of that year and now produced by the Soviets failed to shake the Nipponese in their official conviction, and a Japanese force attacked Changkufeng.

The dispute kept the two foreign offices busy, but in August 1938 an armistice was concluded. The two governments agreed to appoint a "bilateral commission, consisting on one side of two representatives of the U.S.S.R. and on the other of one representative of Japan and one representative of Manchoukuo," to demark the correct boundary. Japan had at first insisted on equal representation for the U.S.S.R., Manchoukuo, and herself, but this the Soviets successfully resisted. There was considerable delay in setting up the border commission, and in February 1939 renewed fighting broke out.

While the fighting continued, a new Soviet-Japanese dispute arose, this time concerning Japanese fishing rights in Soviet Pacific waters. After acrimonious exchanges, the two countries signed a one-year agreement, in April 1939, providing for Japanese participation, largely on Soviet terms, in the exploitation of Soviet fishing grounds. This problem temporarily settled, energies were once more concentrated on the fighting along the Mongolian-Manchoukuo border. There were frequent reports of land and air fighting on both sides of the disputed frontier, the Soviets backing Mongolia and the Japanese supporting Manchoukuo. The monotony of the accounts was relieved by Japanese charges that the empire's coal and oil concessionaires in the northern (Soviet) half of the island of Sakhalin were being subjected to unfair treatment. The Bolsheviks replied that the Japanese concessionaires were violating both their contracts and the laws. The signing of the Soviet-Nazi pact in August 1939, however, worried the Japanese, who seemed to fear that Moscow might now feel free to send large forces to the Far East. Hence another Soviet-Japanese armistice was concluded. But it was not until October 1941, some months after Moscow and Tokyo had signed a neutrality pact, that the Mongolian-Manchoukuo border was more clearly defined. The Siberian-Manchoukuo frontier, on the other hand, remained vague.

In China itself, meanwhile (1936), certain nationalistic leaders had warned the Nanking Government to resist further Japanese aggression lest there be a civil war. For in the summer of that year Generalissimo Chiang Kai-shek was the only outstanding military leader who still hesitated to adopt a strong anti-Japanese policy—probably because he felt that China must wait until she was more thoroughly unified and better prepared for war before risking an all-out conflict with Nippon. Chiang disregarded the warning, continued to order the suppression of anti-Japanese demonstrations, and in December 1936 proceeded to Shensi in the north. There General Chang Hsueh-liang, bitter foe of Japan who had been ousted from Manchuria in 1931, was supposedly acting under the orders of Nanking; but he was lukewarm in his campaign against the Chinese communists. The commander-in-chief wanted more energetic action against these "Reds."

Suddenly (December 12, 1936) Chiang Kai-shek was seized by

some of Chang Hsueh-liang's generals and held prisoner at Sian for two weeks. Not all aspects of this "kidnapping" are clear, but it seems that a growing number of northern soldiers had become reluctant to fight their own countrymen, even though these were "Reds," while the Japanese were penetrating farther and farther into China.[1] Chang Hsueh-liang apparently acted from patriotic motives and at first made his superior's release conditional upon the latter's promise to readmit the communists into the Kuomintang and thus make possible a united Chinese front in a war against Japan. Chiang refused to make any commitments until released and eventually he returned to Nanking with Chang Hsueh-liang in the role of voluntary prisoner. There was a trial of sorts and in January the offending general received a full pardon. Thereafter prolonged negotiations between the national and communist leaders took place. The latter apparently agreed to modify their social program and fight under Chiang Kai-shek's orders in return for a promise of democratic political reforms and a war of resistance against Japan.

Meanwhile, in Japan, following an electoral victory by the liberal party (Minsei-To), there occurred a military rebellion. Early in the morning of February 26, 1936, a group of young officers led about one thousand soldiers from their barracks to the center of Tokyo. While the troops seized a number of official buildings, designated officers murdered several of the nation's outstanding liberal statesmen. The rebels held their position for three days, disregarding even the emperor's command to surrender. When, finally, the men decided to yield, their officers were imprisoned. Eventually a number of these were condemned to death. The population remained relatively calm in the face of the army's seeming inability to control its younger officers—who were determined to abolish the constitutional regime and set up a dictatorship.

The conflict between the civil and military branches of the government was continuously manifested in the difficulties of the cabinet throughout 1936. It was aired in public when several parliamentary deputies bitterly attacked the army and its policies. The military, evidently unable to reply convincingly, precipitated additional cabinet crises until a new election was ordered for April 1937. The moderate elements won an overwhelming victory— which was promptly disregarded by the advocates of force. In July the advance into China was begun in earnest. The excuse

[1] The invaders had by this time entered Inner Mongolia.

was an exchange of shots between Chinese and Japanese troops at Lukouchiao (Marco Polo Bridge), west of Peiping.

The Nanking Government now announced its readiness to fight "to the death" and Tientsin and Peiping became the scenes of bitter warfare. The fighting spread to Shanghai and Japan declared a blockade of Chinese shipping along most of the Chinese coast. Thousands of civilans and refugees were killed by Japanese bombs in areas far removed from the fronts, while the Japanese army advanced slowly but steadily against the stubborn opposition of the Chinese soldiers. It was inevitable that the lives of neutrals should be endangered in this undeclared Far Eastern War, but the Japanese sometimes displayed great carelessness in their aim.[1] As thousands of Japanese fighters were sent to China and puppet governments were set up in the areas that were under their control, the Tokyo Premier, Prince Fumimaro Konoye, explained: "We have no territorial designs and no wish to make an enemy of the Chinese people. If we mete out direct punishment to the Chinese our final objective must be Sino-Japanese coöperation."

There were rays of hope for China in September 1937 when the communist armies in the north finally prepared to march against the Japanese invaders and when the League of Nations referred a Chinese appeal to its Far Eastern advisory committee. With regard to the first of these items, the "Soviet Republic of China" was dissolved and Chiang Kai-shek announced: "The Chinese Government and the communists have been fighting for the last ten years. This is the official conclusion of the war." With respect to the second item, the League's committee, on which the United States was represented, unanimously condemned Japan's policy and tactics and urged a meeting of the signatories of the nine-power treaties of 1922. Fifty League members endorsed the committee's findings, expressed moral support of China, and called a parley of the interested parties to meet at Brussels. The United States expressed its agreement with these conclusions.

The Brussels Conference sat for three weeks in November 1937 and then adjourned indefinitely. Nineteen countries were represented, including the United States, but not Japan. During its deliberations, the Japanese issued several defiant statements, while the chief Italian delegate ridiculed the whole proceeding. The United States, Great Britain, and France pleaded for satisfactory

[1] Shells several times fell on American and British fighting ships and the British Ambassador to China, Sir Hughe Knatchbull-Hugessen, was wounded when Japanese airplanes fired at the plainly marked automobile in which he was riding.

means of mediation, China and the Soviet Union urged direct action against the acknowledged aggressor, and Italy opposed any action. The only concrete achievements of the meeting were a resolution condemning Japan and an innocuous twelve-page report.

In the meantime the Chinese Government had moved its seat to the inland city of Chungking because of the Japanese advance on Nanking. As the highly mechanized Japanese forces pushed on, Chinese sympathizers in many of the Western countries organized boycotts against goods of Japanese manufacture. Except in so far as they expressed the widespread moral disapproval of Japan's methods these boycotts seemed not to have any immediate influence. The Tokyo Government successfully floated domestic loans and seemed not to fear any economic crisis in the near future. Chinese customs arrangements, moreover, were revised by the Japanese to suit themselves, despite repeated protests from the United States and Great Britain. And in December 1937 Japanese soldiers poured into Nanking, celebrating their victory with a reign of terror against the hapless population.

On the day preceding the fall of China's ex-capital, Japanese planes sank the United States gunboat *Panay* in the Yangtse Kiang about twenty-five miles above Nanking. At the same time three Standard Oil Company ships were sunk and all vessels were fired upon by Japanese machine gunners in a launch. Several Americans were killed and many more wounded, the survivors getting away to safety only under the greatest difficulty. The Japanese Government at once apologized, promised to punish those responsible for the crime, and gave a guarantee against future attacks. Washington was not satisfied with this note and Japan eventually presented a second apology. The attack was called "entirely unintentional," assurance was given of full indemnity, and it was pointed out that the responsible officers had been severely disciplined. The United States accepted this explanation and the incident was officially closed.[1]

In 1938 Japanese military victories in China continued, with occasional setbacks. Despite their defeats, despite air bombardments on their densely populated cities, despite the creation (March) at Nanking of a Japanese-controlled "Reformed Govern-

---

[1] It happened that an American newsreel photographer was able to take pictures of the sinking. The graphic recording was released in the cinema theaters of the United States and attracted large audiences. The newspapers reported that the spectators generally were tense but quiet.

ment of the Republic of China," and despite the loss of the services of the German General Alexander von Falkenhausen and his staff—recalled by Hitler presumably at the request of Tokyo—the Chinese continued to resist as best they could the invasion of the Japanese. Foreign sympathy China appeared to have in abundance, but little foreign aid. The League empowered every member state individually to appy the sanctions of Article 16 of the covenant against Japan, if it wished; Japan responded by threatening counter measures against any sanctionist state but there was little occasion to make good the threat. Supplies did reach the Chinese, chiefly from the Soviet Union and through Indo-China, but not in the desired quantities.

The domestic situation in Japan was not improved during 1938. There were frequent reorganizations of the cabinet, always in the interest of a more vigorous prosecution of the undeclared war, but though progress could often be reported, complete success could not. There were frequent clashes between the government and the parliament for many members of the latter, like the public at large, wanted to know the "ultimate purposes" of the costly campaigns in China. Various political-party headquarters were raided during the year and leftist movements were effectively suppressed. The entire electric industry of the empire was placed under state control and the government secured the passage of a National Mobilization Law which gave it complete power over every phase and detail of the national life in time of "emergency" or war. Although it was agreed that the powers granted by the law would not be used unless emergency absolutely commanded, decrees under its terms began to be issued in May. Restrictions were placed on the private use of cotton and pig iron and eventually all phases of raw-material economy were strictly regulated.

During the course of her advance in China, Japan frequently performed acts which aroused the protests of the Western powers. Considerable damage was done to foreign property, the Yangtse River was virtually closed to foreign shipping, foreign trading rights were ignored, and the provisions of the Nine-Power Treaty (1922) were violated. To all these charges the Japanese replied, at first evasively, then more plainly. By the end of 1938 Tokyo had explicitly declared her purpose to extend to all China the status "enjoyed" by Manchoukuo. The "ideas and principles of the past" were no longer applicable, she maintained, to the "new situation" in the Far East.

Throughout the year 1939 the Japanese continued the struggle in China, extending the area of their occupation, further impairing their own diplomatic relations with the Western powers, bombing more open cities, striving to set up under Wang Ching-wei a puppet government for China corresponding to that in Manchoukuo, and failing in their efforts to break down the morale and the resistance of the Chinese. While the Japanese stripped, insulted, and slapped British subjects in the presence of Chinese (to impress the latter with the new importance of Japan) and advanced challengingly close to Hong Kong, the British enlarged their credit advances to China and warned Tokyo of the future consequences of its acts. While United States property was being destroyed through Japanese air attacks in various parts of China, Washington gave the required six months' notice of its intention to terminate the American-Japanese Treaty of Amity and Commerce which had provided Japan with its much-needed United States market and United States supplies. And while in Japan itself prices rose steadily, consumers' goods began to run short, and casualty lists mounted, the military leaders ordered a further tightening of the people's belts and persisted in their conviction that the new order in Asia was close at hand.

CHAPTER XXIII

The United States

TROUBLOUS TIMES, 1918–1921

In the election of 1916 Woodrow Wilson defeated Charles E. Hughes for the presidency of the United States. The victorious candidate polled only 600,000 more votes than his rival. On the same occasion, the Democratic majority in the Senate was cut from 16 to 12 and in the House of Representatives the balance of power fell to a small group of independents. With the close of the war came a further decline in the popular appeal of the Democratic Party and its leader. There was a reaction, on the one hand, against the progressive policies fostered by the first Wilson Administration—policies expressed in such legislation as the Clayton Anti-Trust Law, the Federal Reserve Act, and the Underwood Tariff—and on the other, against the wide powers which the government had exercised during the war. Indeed, as a consequence of the congressional elections of 1918, the Republicans obtained control of both branches of Congress.

The blame for the high cost of living, popularly known as the "H.C.L.," that followed the war, was placed upon the Democratic Administration. The end of the conflict and the cancelation of government contracts running into billions of dollars partially disrupted the economic system of the country. Yet many of the manufacturers, who had become accustomed to reaping large profits, refused in the early postwar years to be satisfied with more moderate returns. "Profiteering" continued, and, for a time, became worse. Labor, skilled and unskilled, was equally insistent upon keeping wages up to and above the inflated war level. The consumer had to pay the piper, for the purchasing power of the dollar was 52 per cent lower in 1920 than it had been in 1913. The class that suffered most from these circumstances was the salaried group—the professionals and clerks whose pay was fixed for long periods in advance.

The truce under which the government had forced capital and labor to operate during the war now came to an end and the pent-up energies of the opposing groups broke loose with astonishing force. While certain branches of business once more were willing to let "the public be damned," the coal miners, for example, were ready to let it freeze. The year 1919 witnessed approximately three thousand major strikes, participated in by four million workers. At the same time Attorney-General A. Mitchell Palmer evoked so energetic a zeal in tracking down members of various radical organizations that even staid citizens were gripped by a "Red Scare."

Many Americans, in addition, were dissatisfied with the trend of affairs at the Paris Peace Conference. Some felt that the treatment accorded Germany was too severe. Others believed that Great Britain was reaping most of the benefits of the war. Irish sympathizers thought Wilson negligent of the aspirations of Erin, while friends of Italy and of Greece were dissatisfied with the gains of these states. There was some opposition to that portion of the treaty which dealt with the League of Nations, and a number of Republicans resented their exclusion from the Paris Conference. Hence, when Wilson placed the Versailles Treaty before the Senate (July 10, 1919) with a request for consent to ratification, the prospects for acquiescence were slight.

The Senate soon split into four main groups over the question of the treaty, in particular of the League. Wilson's Democratic followers favored ratification without amendments. Other Democrats, eventually led by Gilbert M. Hitchcock of Nebraska, proposed acceptance with mild reservations. The majority of the Republicans, led by Henry Cabot Lodge, chairman of the Senate Foreign Relations Committee and a personal opponent of the President, insisted upon more sweeping amendments. The "irreconcilable" Republicans, led by William E. Borah of Idaho, opposed America's entering a league in any form.

The main public attacks on the treaty were directed against the League Covenant, especially against the article that made possible League membership for Great Britain's dominions and against Article 10, which guaranteed the territorial integrity and political independence of the member states. The President tried to make clear that nothing could happen in the League Council without American assent since the vote had to be unanimous, and that all League obligations were "moral" rather than "legal." His antagonists, however, stigmatized Article 10 as an infringement on the right of Congress to declare war.

Harvey's Weekly, for example, declared: "If Article Ten be interpreted to mean anything, that meaning necessarily is that we engage to send our armed forces wherever and whenever a super-government of foreigners sitting in Switzerland orders us to send them." Senator Lawrence Y. Sherman of Illinois somehow arrived at the conclusion that the League would "embargo our commerce, close our exchanges, destroy our credits, leave our merchandise rotting on the piers, shut the Isthmian Canal, order Congress to declare war, levy taxes, appropriate money, raise and support armies and navies, and dispatch our men to any quarter of the globe to fight and die because an alien executive council has so willed." [1] In the circumstances, it was not surprising that the treaty, both with and without reservations, should have failed of acceptance when brought up for vote in November 1919 and again in March 1920.

Early in June 1920 the Republican National Convention met at Chicago. Four presidential "possibilities" held the spotlight: Herbert Hoover, famous as wartime food administrator; General Leonard Wood, an associate of Theodore Roosevelt; Senator Hiram Johnson of California, "irreconcilable" but progressive; and Governor Frank Lowden of Illinois, a friend of the farmers. When it was evident that the deadlock among these men could not be broken, a "dark horse" was selected—on the principle, it was said, that "any good Republican can be nominated . . . and can defeat any Democrat." The choice fell on Warren Gamaliel Harding of Ohio, a "genial standpatter" who had no national enemies. The platform censured the Wilson Administration and proposed the reaching of a world peace agreement "without the compromise of national independence."

The Democrats met at San Francisco on June 28. A three-cornered contest developed among former Secretary of the Treasury William G. McAdoo, who, as Wilson's son-in-law, was nicknamed the "crown prince"; Attorney-General Palmer, of "Red-Scare" fame; and Governor James M. Cox of Ohio, who eventually secured the nomination. The party platform advocated "the immediate ratification of the treaty without reservations which would impair its essential integrity." The Socialist Party for the fifth time nominated Eugene V. Debs, who then was serving a sentence in the Atlanta Penitentiary for pacifistic activities during the war. The outcome of the campaign of 1920 was influenced by all the

[1] United States Congress *Congressional Record,* 65 Congress, 3 Session, v. 57, pt. v, p. 4869, March 3, 1919.

political and economic factors that have already been mentioned, as well as by some additional important elements. The voting was affected, in one way or another, by (1) the return of the railways to private ownership under favorable conditions through the Esch-Cummins Act of 1920; (2) the fact that millions of dollars' worth of national property was visibly going to waste through the rotting, in the Hudson River and elsewhere, of hundreds of ships that had been built to meet war emergencies; (3) the ratification of the Eighteenth or Prohibition Amendment and the passage (1919), over Wilson's veto, of the Volstead Act, which defined as "intoxicating" any liquor containing more than one-half of 1 per cent of alcohol; and (4) the ratification of the Nineteenth or Woman-Suffrage Amendment.

Neither of the candidates was well known to the people. Cox was owner of the *Dayton Daily News* and had three times been elected governor of Ohio. Harding owned the *Marion Star*, had been lieutenant-governor of Ohio, and was a United States Senator. Harding had considerable popular appeal as a candidate. He was plain, kind-hearted, and religious. In his slogan, "A return to normalcy," he well expressed the sentiment of many people who were tired of reform crusades and who "wanted a rest from ideas that might develop into causes."

The League, it seems, played a relatively minor part in the campaign, being greatly overshadowed by a general discontent and the feeling that "our own yard is enough to worry about." Wilson earlier in the year had recommended that the election be made "a great and solemn referendum" on the League, but Harding straddled the issue, saying, in effect, that he opposed *the* League but favored *a* league, a "free association of nations." The Republican candidate won by a plurality of seven million votes. For the first time since the War between the States, a commonwealth that had seceded, Tennessee, "went Republican." Four months after the election Woodrow Wilson left the White House, tired, ill, repudiated.

HARDING AND THE "RETURN TO NORMALCY"

President Harding entrusted the affairs of the state department to the experienced Charles E. Hughes. One of the new secretary's first tasks was to bring to a close the technical state of war that still existed between the United States on the one side, and Germany, Austria, and Hungary on the other. President Wilson had vetoed a joint resolution that was meant to end hostilities without waiting for the formalities of a treaty agreement. In July 1921 Congress repassed and Harding signed this resolution, which declared the war "to be at an end" and reserved to the United States all the rights and privileges accruing to her under the unratified Peace of Paris. A few months later the treaties of Berlin, Vienna, and Budapest were signed and ratified, the United States in each case being guaranteed "all the rights and advantages stipulated" for her benefit in the German, Austrian, and Hungarian treaties with the Allies.

Once in office, Harding, realizing that the members of the League of Nations would hardly listen to any United States proposal to disband that organization and form a new one, dropped all talk of his "free association of nations." So completely did the administration try to forget the League that for almost six months no reply was sent to the communications which its secretary-general sent to Washington. The American Ambassador in London was "instructed to inform the League's authorities that as the United States had not joined the League she was not in a position to answer letters from it." Not until the situation was exposed in the *New York Times* did the state department send even formal acknowledgment of League notes.

Beginning in 1922, the attitude of the government towards the League changed sufficiently so that "unofficial observers" were sent to attend conferences "where matters of concern to the United States were under consideration." Such conferences were those on the opium traffic, on customs formalities, and on communications and transit. Despite his indifference to the League, President Harding urged membership in the World Court on condition that the United States be given an equal voice with other countries in the selection of judges. This proviso was necessary since the United States had no representation in the League bodies which elected the judges. The President died before the Senate acted on his suggestion.

Equally frigid during these years were Washington's relations with Russia. Secretary of Commerce Hoover insisted that under the Bolshevik economic system Russia could expect "no real return to production." Hence she would "have no considerable commodities to export and, consequently, no great ability to obtain imports." In these circumstances it was felt that there existed no motive for making diplomatic arrangements to facilitate the exchange of goods with Russia.

There were two spheres, however, in which the United States preferred not to remain aloof: naval construction and Pacific and Far Eastern relations. The naval rivalry between Great Britain and the United States, inaugurated by the American building program of 1916, seriously threatened harmonious relations between the two peoples. Neither could well afford the expense involved or the bitter spirit engendered. The matter was made more serious and broader in scope by the Anglo-Japanese Alliance which, it was feared, might become a menace to United States Pacific interests. The question of the status of all Far Eastern territories might therefore profitably be discussed. Accordingly a nine-power conference was held at Washington from November 1921 to February 1922 and, as we have seen, several agreements were reached on the limitation of naval armaments and on Pacific and Far Eastern problems.[1]

In domestic matters President Harding, by "a return to normalcy," understood a return to policies favoring business. In 1921 the secretary of the treasury recommended reducing the surtax on the largest incomes from 65 per cent to 32 per cent and then, within a year, to 25 per cent. Congress, however, merely repealed the excess-profits tax and fixed the surtax maximum at 50 per cent (1921), and then passed (1922) a Bonus Bill for the war veterans. Harding vetoed this measure on the grounds that it contained no provision for raising the necessary money; that the soldiers had never expected a bonus until the American Legion, founded in 1919, had proposed the idea; and that the government had been sufficiently liberal in the allotments and in the compensations made for disabilities. In the same session Congress passed the high Fordney-McCumber Tariff to supersede the moderate Underwood Act of 1913. The law authorized the President, after due investigations by a tariff commission, to increase or decrease the scheduled rates up to 50 per cent if the existing duties did not equalize the cost of production in the United States and the competing foreign countries.

In 1922 the road back to normalcy was partially blocked by the strikes of six hundred thousand coal miners and three hundred thousand railway shopmen. There was considerable violence in both instances and Attorney-General Harry M. Daugherty secured from a Chicago judge a sweeping injunction against the

---

[1] See pp. 187 and 655. The United States in 1921 made it plain to Great Britain and France that American oil companies were not to be excluded from a share in the oil concessions of the Near Eastern mandates.

railwaymen that virtually forbade all the activities of trade-union officials. Much of the disorder was charged to radicals and professional agitators and hence the public was not sympathetic to the cause of the workers.

Meanwhile Congress was becoming acutely aware of another problem, the economic plight of the farmers. During the war the process of farm industrialization had advanced at an unprecedented rate. The wartime food needs had made it profitable to devote every available acre of land to cultivation and the farmers consequently had borrowed heavily in order to buy more land and more machines. In 1919 the farm crop of the United States was valued at $16,000,000,000, as compared with $6,000,000,000 ten years earlier. After the war, however, the farmers found themselves saddled with a mortgage debt of more than $4,000,000,000.

Even in the heyday of war prosperity the average farmer had realized little more than 6 per cent on his total investment. Hence, when the prices of wheat, corn, cotton, and cattle experienced precipitate declines in the general business slump that followed 1919, the farmers were in a desperate situation. Though they had developed some fairly satisfactory marketing and purchasing cooperatives, they had no organization for regulating production or fighting price deflation. Wheat toppled from $2.14 a bushel in 1919 to $0.93 a bushel in 1923. The situation was similar with respect to other farm products. Freight rates, on the contrary, continued to be high and local tax rates remained at a level almost two and a half times that of 1912. And the interest payments had to be met or the mortgages would be foreclosed.

In their despair the farmers turned to the government for relief. A congressional Farm Bloc was created (1921) to represent the interests of the western farmers who cared little about the tax revision, shipping subsidies, or immigration bills which were the chief worry of the eastern legislators. Several farm-relief measures were passed between 1921 and 1923, designed chiefly to cut speculation in grain, make available additional agricultural-credit facilities, and tax agricultural imports. In the face of increasing competition from Canadian, Australian, and, eventually, Russian grain, these measures failed to solve the country's agricultural problem.

In June 1923 the Hardings started on an ill-fated tour across the country and a visit to Alaska. The President was not well when the trip began and he fell seriously ill in Alaska. He was returning home when death overtook him in San Francisco, on August 2. The exact cause of his death was not satisfactorily established, but there was reason to believe that his mind was troubled and his illness aggravated by certain deeds of official corruption in the years 1921 to 1923 which were reminiscent of the notorious happenings of the Grant administrations.

One of the first scandals to be uncovered grew out of the practices of Charles R. Forbes, director of the Veterans' Bureau. According to the report of a Senate Investigating Committee, the record of Forbes' activities in his official capacity was one of "almost unparalleled waste, recklessness, and misconduct," costing the government about $200,000,000. For his misdeeds Forbes was sentenced to a term in Leavenworth Prison. Another investigating committee, headed by Senator Burton K. Wheeler, discovered that Attorney-General Daugherty had surrounded himself in the department of justice with disreputable characters and had failed to prosecute grafters and leading bootleggers. When Daugherty denied the committee permission to search his department files for further evidence, President Coolidge dismissed him (March 1924).

The greatest scandal involved the leasing of some government oil reserves. It appeared that President Harding had signed an order permitting Secretary of the Navy Edwin Denby to transfer to Secretary of the Interior Albert B. Fall the administration of the petroleum reserves set aside at Elk Hills in California and Teapot Dome in Wyoming under Presidents Taft and Wilson for the use of the navy. Fall was prominent as an opponent of friendly relations with Mexico and as a man "who affected a cowboy pose and a fine contempt for reformers and conservationists." In 1922, Fall, without calling for competitive bids, leased the Teapot Dome reserves to Harry F. Sinclair and the Elk Hills reserves to Edward L. Doheny. In each case the government was to obtain a small royalty on the oil secured.

Soon the smell of oil was detected on official garments and Senator Thomas J. Walsh of Montana headed a committee of investigation which discovered an amazing trail of corruption. It developed that Sinclair had contributed heavily to Republican campaign expenses in 1920; that Doheny had "loaned" Fall $100,000 without security and without interest in 1921; that some time later Fall also had received a loan of $25,000 from Sinclair, and that he had accepted valuable gifts from other oilmen. Then he had resigned early in 1923 before the scandals were made public and had retired to a large ranch purchased with the "loans." In the following year Denby also resigned.

In 1924 the government instituted judicial proceedings against Fall, Doheny, and Sinclair. The authorities asked for the cancelation of the leases and the conviction of the defendants for bribery and conspiracy. The government won its first point in 1927 when the Supreme Court voided the leases and ordered the return of the reserves. Both Doheny and Sinclair were able to convince juries that they were not guilty of conspiracy or fraud, but that they had acted out of patriotic motives. They maintained that the oil was being drained away by people who had sunk wells near by, that the terms were favorable to the government, and that, after all, undeveloped oil reserves were not much good to the navy. Sinclair, however, blundered by hiring private detectives to shadow his jurors and by refusing to answer certain questions of the Senate committee. For this contempt he had to serve a three months' jail term in Washington. Fall, after several trial adjournments, was convicted in 1929 and sentenced to one year's imprisonment and a fine of $100,000. The jail term was served but the fine remained unpaid.

This "crime wave" in the years following the war was not confined to officialdom. Private crimes came to be everyday topics of conversation and the official misdeeds merely reflected on a large scale what happened privately on a smaller scale. In 1921 there was said to have been one major bank robbery per day throughout the country, while one automobile of every twenty-two in Chicago and every thirty in New York was stolen. "Burglary-insurance rates in American cities were from fifteen to twenty times as high as in England" and "the homicide rate of the United States was sixteen times that of England and Wales." Machine guns and sawed-off shotguns were among the weapons employed by postwar criminals. The custom of levying tribute under threat of violence was revived as a widespread source of illegal income under the name of "racketeering." Seemingly, the public, which for years had been reading daily accounts of the wholesale war killings, was but little shocked to see as familiar sights in the streets of the larger cities armored cars for conveying money and valuables.

COOLIDGE AND "SAFE AND SANE" POLITICS

Not much was known in the United States about the man who, on August 3, 1923, took the oath of office as Harding's successor. Calvin Coolidge was born in Vermont in 1872. A graduate of Amherst College, he studied law and then, having entered politics, gradually rose from one office to the next, finally becoming governor of Massachusetts. Quiet, thrifty, industrious, and staid, Coolidge never shocked anyone by advocating strange or radical things; nor did he ever hold back when he saw the majority moving in a definite direction.

He first attracted national attention when, as governor of Massachusetts, he had to cope with the Boston policemen's strike of 1919. He called out the state militia and informed the policemen that "there is no right to strike against the public safety by anybody, anywhere, anytime." Estimates differed widely as to the precise part that Coolidge played in the settling of the strike, but his friends hailed him as "the silent man of iron," and his party bestowed the vice-presidential nomination upon him in the following year. Though a favorite subject with cartoonists and jokesters, Coolidge maintained an unruffled calm in the face of both lavish praise and unvarnished abuse. He believed that "the business of America is business" and achieved a reputation for "saying much in little and often in silence." He "was dull and insistent as duty itself" and he "thoroughly approved of the Ten Commandments."

President Coolidge retained his predecessor's cabinet unchanged and in his first message to Congress made economy his keynote. In harmony with this stand he vetoed a second Bonus Bill which was passed by Congress in 1924 and which provided for a system of prepaid insurance policies with the principal going to the holder at the expiration of twenty years. This time the bill was passed over the President's veto. In the same year (1924) the income tax was further reduced and a highly restrictive immigration law, the Johnson Act, was adopted. This measure, which became fully effective in 1929, discriminated in favor of immigrants from the countries of northern Europe, limited the total number of annual entrants to about 150,000, and excluded entirely immigrants who were ineligible for citizenship, that is, Asiatics. The last provision gave rise to much foreign, particularly Japanese, ill will.[1]

Without having to fight any opposition, Coolidge secured the Republican nomination for the presidency in 1924. General Charles G. Dawes, of reparation fame and first director of the national budget bureau established in 1921, was selected as his running mate. The Democratic candidate was John W. Davis, a "dark-horse" conservative from West Virginia who had achieved success

[1] This immigration-quota or national-origins measure had been preceded by an emergency quota law in 1921 and was supplemented by another act of 1929.

as a corporation lawyer in New York. He received the nomination after 102 ballots had failed to break a deadlock between William G. McAdoo, "dry" and Protestant, and Governor Alfred E. Smith of New York, "wet" and Roman Catholic.

A third group, the Progressive Party, headed by Senator Robert M. ("Fighting Bob") La Follette of Wisconsin, also entered the lists in 1924. It attracted some "insurgent" Republicans and discontented progressives and intellectuals who wanted to register a vote of protest against the conservative stand of both the large parties. The Progressive Party, however, polled fewer than five million votes and died with the election. Aided by such popular slogans as "Keep Cool with Cal," "Coolidge or Chaos," and "Coolidge and Economy," the President swept the polls, receiving 54 per cent of the total vote and a plurality of more than seven million ballots.[1]

The second Coolidge Administration was marked by little startling domestic legislation. The national debt was reduced, the surtax was lowered to 20 per cent, and slight reductions were made in the tax on lower incomes. A few laws to aid agricultural production and marketing were passed and a large sum was voted for Mississippi flood control. In the matter of farm relief, the McNary-Haugen Bill, which, among other things, proposed a fixed domestic price for grain, was vetoed as being economically unsound. The enforcement of Prohibition continued to be one of the government's most difficult tasks. Much profit was derived from violations of the law by bootleggers and smugglers, and a leading racketeer boasted that in one year his organization had spent $30,000,-000 to check law-enforcement activities. Although such criminals operated in many fields, they were interested chiefly in the profits to be gained from the illegal manufacture and sale of intoxicating drinks.

In the summer of 1928 the customary presidential nominating conventions assembled. A flurry was caused in Republican ranks when Coolidge, whose name had again been mentioned despite the third-term tradition, handed to newspaper correspondents a slip of paper on which was written: "I do not choose to run for President in 1928." The statement occasioned some conjecture as

---

[1] The years from 1924 to 1926 witnessed a clearing of the political stage through the deaths of several of the older leaders. Theodore Roosevelt had died in 1919. Wilson, Lodge, and Samuel Gompers died in 1924. Death claimed La Follette and W. J. Bryan in 1925, and Eugene V. Debs and "Uncle Joe" Cannon, long the leading conservative in the House of Representatives, in 1926.

to its real meaning, but the President eventually made it clear that he was not to be considered a possible candidate.

With Coolidge eliminated, it soon was evident that Herbert Clark Hoover would be selected. A successful mining engineer, with experience and contacts in several continents, Hoover had also been head of the American Commission for Relief in Belgium, United States Food Administrator, secretary of commerce for two terms, and chairman of the Mississippi Flood Relief Commission in 1927. His public record was clear and commendable, and he had won respect abroad. He was nominated on the first ballot. Senator Charles Curtis of Kansas, Republican leader in the Senate, was chosen as vice-presidential candidate.

The platform promised strict enforcement of Prohibition, farm relief, friendly international relations, and railroad, mercantile, and flood-control legislation. The usual praise of the previous administration's accomplishments was included. "Economy," read one sentence, "has been raised to the dignity of a principle of government." Prosperity was held up as a shining light of Republican achievement.

When the Democratic nominators convened, they were reminded by the keynote orator that "the brilliant record of our eight years of power [under Wilson] is as a splotch of glorious sunshine against the smutty background of eight years of privilege and crime." The Democratic platform, accordingly, stressed the corruption under Harding, denounced the Republican taxation policy, and complained that in recent years the antitrust laws had been "thwarted, ignored, and violated." All this would be different under Democratic rule, it was stated, and in addition waterpower sites would be protected, labor receive fairer treatment, and a constructive foreign policy be adopted. In this convention, too, the nomination was decided on the first ballot. Alfred E. Smith, four times governor of New York and well known as an able politician, a progressive administrator, and a determined fighter, was the ready choice. Senator Joseph T. Robinson of Arkansas was selected for the vice-presidency.

The campaign was unusually exciting and attracted a surprisingly large vote. The extensive use of radio for speech-making and the presence of the religious and Prohibition issues roused millions from their normal political apathy. Hoover, a Quaker and a "dry" who considered Prohibition a "noble experiment," was backed by the Protestant and temperance organizations of the country. Such bodies as the Ku Klux Klan—which had come into renewed prominence after the war as an association for upholding the supremacy of white Protestants—aligned themselves against the Democratic candidate. The Catholic "Al" Smith's lack of higher education, his close connection with Tammany Hall, and his limited knowledge of foreign affairs militated against him. On the other hand, the Democratic candidate was supported by the many "wet" organizations in the land and by a large number of liberals.

Hoover was victorious by a plurality of more than 6,000,000 votes, although 15,000,000 ballots were cast for the man from "the sidewalks of New York." The Socialist candidate, Norman Thomas, a Princeton graduate and at the time of the campaign a minister, received 267,800 votes. Smith carried only six southern states, along with Massachusetts and Rhode Island. He lost his own state, New York, although the Democratic candidate for governor, Franklin D. Roosevelt, won easily.

HOOVER: "THE ENGINEER IN POLITICS"

The new President was known as a hard worker and a man with a high sense of duty. During his occupancy of the White House he gave ample evidence of his abilities as a planner and organizer, but he soon showed himself to be less apt as a leader. It was said of him that "he could run a department or set of departments with great skill; he could organize forces to meet an emergency; but he could not direct a party, lead a parliamentary group, or guide public opinion." Impatient of criticism, he placed his chief trust in the advice of expert commissions, appointing more such bodies than any of his predecessors. In politics he proved to be a conservative, and in economic theory a neo-mercantilist, favoring high tariffs and big business.

At the outset it appeared as though the Hoover Administration might be highly successful. Both houses of Congress contained substantial Republican majorities, the cabinet was able, the political appointments throughout the land were generally acceptable, and the country as a whole seemed to enjoy prosperity. Yet the President was immediately confronted with some problems of overwhelming magnitude and was induced to call Congress in special session without allowing himself sufficient time to formulate legislative recommendations of his own.

In his inaugural address Hoover had pointed out the need for "limited changes" in the tariff, early farm relief, and stricter enforcement of the laws. The first two of these problems were referred directly to Congress for action (April 1929). As a preliminary step in dealing with the question of law and order, the chief executive appointed a Law Enforcement Commission, under the chairmanship of former Attorney-General George W. Wickersham, to make a thorough survey of the crime situation.

By 1929 the "crime industry" had become so well organized that municipalities and even states confessed inability to cope with the dilemma. It was estimated (1931) that the annual cost of crime to the nation was at least $100 per capita, and probably more. A major portion of the crimes was connected, directly or indirectly, with the violation of the Volstead Act, but the racketeers, readily able to "buy protection," extended their activities to numberless other fields. Only a fraction of the criminals, many of whom were well known to the authorities, ever suffered arrest, and fewer still, conviction. Eventually the federal government itself found it easier to imprison racketeers for falsifications of their income-tax returns than for violations of the alcohol or homicide laws.

The "Wickersham Report," therefore, was eagerly awaited, but when it was published, early in 1931, the document displayed no sign of unanimity and was vague on some of its most important revelations. The net result of the labors of the commission was disappointing, although two definite gains were made: (1) it was clearly established that some sort of Prohibition reform was desirable; (2) upon the advice of the commission, Congress transferred the enforcement of the liquor laws from the department of the treasury to the department of justice.

In the matter of the tariff, Congress disregarded the President's advice concerning "limited changes" and quickly engaged in "logrolling." The Fordney-McCumber Act was replaced by the Hawley-Smoot Tariff which lowered the rates on 255 items, left them unchanged on 2170 items, and raised them on 890 items. Against the advice of more than 1000 economists and of numerous experts representing both political parties, Hoover signed the bill (1930), trusting to the tariff commission to uncover any injustices in the act. There was a storm of opposition to the President's decision and foreign countries generally resorted to one form or another of retaliation. The foreign-trade situation became worse instead of better.[1]

[1] The high rates on manufactures tended to raise the price of home-made products, especially those needed by the farmer. Simultaneously, in consequence of a succession of good crops, the farmer continued to receive low prices for his produce even though

The method adopted by the administration to provide farm relief was equally unsuccessful. In 1929 and 1930 Congress rejected several debenture plans whereby the farmers were to be aided by a kind of subsidy on agricultural staples. Instead, by an act of June 1929, there was created a Federal Farm Board of eight members, equipped with a revolving fund of $500,000,000. The board was to fight overproduction, encourage the formation of farmers' coöperatives, and form stabilization corporations for the several crops with power to buy and sell temporary surpluses in these crops. The measure, based on the hope that the grain surpluses would be temporary, was expensive and in reality tended to foster rather than discourage overproduction. A drought in 1930 resulted in a slight rise in the price of farm products, but in 1931 the prices fell to new lows.

Meanwhile, in October 1929, the stock market in Wall Street had crashed. On the 24th of that month uneasy speculators dumped almost thirteen million stock shares on the exchange market. The origins of the crash would seem to be traceable, at least in part, to the economic upheaval wrought by the First World War. During the period of hostilities there had been a great inflation of prices. Except for a brief depression soon after the war, the United States continued to prosper in the 1920's, chiefly because of the wartime depletion of goods and the readiness of Europe and Latin America to place orders here as long as credits were available and the American people were willing to invest in foreign bonds. In consequence there developed a speculative mania during which prices remained artificially inflated and "paper fortunes" were made. Prices rose, industry expanded, and production increased with little plan or precaution.

Yet, at the same time, tariff walls were raised still higher, nations everywhere placed obstacles in the way of world commerce, and the questions of reparation and war debts continued to embitter international relations. It was inevitable that postwar deflation should eventually set in, and a financial break was almost certain to come as soon as American investors should become uneasy about their holdings and foreign purchases should be checked. After the crash in the United States, disaster quickly attacked

---

the tariff also was designed to protect agriculture. Foreign countries retaliated by raising their import duties on American manufactures and cutting their purchases of American grain in favor of that from Argentina, Australia, Canada, or the U.S.S.R. The net result of the tariff appeared to be a loss of foreign markets and a decrease in domestic buying power. Cf. Jones, J. M. *Tariff Retaliation; Repercussions of the Hawley-Smoot Bill*, 1934.

Europe's weak financial structure. First, as has been shown, came collapse in Austria, then elsewhere, and finally the economic depression became world-wide.

The President's first public comment on the stock-market situation characterized the latter as being merely the result of a wave of uncontrolled speculation in securities. Hence the difficulty was temporary and recovery was close at hand. But when conditions became worse, and, indeed, affected the entire world, Hoover explained that the crisis was of global magnitude and was caused by factors obviously beyond the control of the United States. In order to speed the economic revival, the President proposed his international moratorium to be effective from July 1, 1931, to June 30, 1932. This action only emphasized the seriousness of the world's predicament and did little to restore confidence.

Energetic measures were taken to deal with the situation at home, for unemployment figures rose rapidly and by January 1932 were estimated at seven million.[1] Congress appropriated large sums for the construction of public buildings and highways. Unemployment-relief committees were appointed by cities, states, and the nation, and funds were collected from charitably inclined persons throughout the land. Employed citizens were encouraged to "share their work" with less fortunate neighbors and there was an increasing demand for the five-day week. Relatively little progress, however, was made in this last connection. National and local tax rates were raised but the national budgetary deficit at the end of 1932 passed $2,000,000,000.

To ease the financial stringency that resulted from foreign gold withdrawals and private hoarding, Congress, in 1932, passed a bill which amended the eligibility provision of the Federal Reserve Law so as to permit the use of certain government bonds as coverage for the issue of federal notes. Thus a portion of the banks' gold stock was released for business purposes. Groups of member banks, moreover, which had exhausted their collateral eligible for discount by Federal Reserve Banks and yet were in a solvent condition, were permitted to borrow from the Federal Reserve system on joint promissory notes.

Another act created a Reconstruction Finance Corporation with a capital of $500,000,000 subscribed by the United States Government and with power to issue obligations to three times that

---

[1] The wage bill of the nation dropped from $55,000,000,000 in 1929 to $33,000,000,-000 in 1931.

amount. The corporation was authorized to lend money to fiscal and other institutions for purposes of "financing agriculture, commerce, and industry, including facilitating the exportation of agricultural and other products." All loans were to be for three years and with the consent of the Interstate Commerce Commission money might be advanced to railroads. Later the resources of the corporation were increased to a total of $3,800,000,000. Its lending powers eventually were extended to include relief loans to states, for by this time financial breakdown threatened not only thousands of small companies but even municipalities, counties, and states. By August 1, 1932, after seven months of operation, the corporation had loaned $784,000,000 to 4324 banks and trust companies.

Among other incidents of the depression was a march on Washington (1932) by unemployed war veterans from all over the United States demanding that Congress provide for the immediate redemption in cash of the bonus certificates. Congress disregarded the plea on the ground that payment of a cash bonus would place an enormous strain on the already weakened financial system of the country. The Bonus Expeditionary Force (B.E.F.), as it came to be called, threatened to remain camped in Washington until its demands should have been met. The government eventually used troops to clear the city of the petitioners. Though the resulting casualties were slight, public opinion generally condemned the procedure.

In this atmosphere the country prepared for the election of 1932. The Republican National Convention met in Chicago and renominated President Hoover on the first ballot. Curtis was renominated for the vice-presidency. The Democrats also met in Chicago. After a contest between the supporters of Alfred E. Smith and Governor Roosevelt of New York, the latter secured the nomination. John N. Garner of Texas, Speaker of the House of Representatives (which had come under Democratic control in consequence of the elections of 1930), was selected for the vice-presidency.

The chief plank in each platform dealt with Prohibition. The Republicans favored what soon came to be known as a "wet-dry" plank that advocated a referendum on a proposed amendment providing for a limited form of state option, to be enforced with the coöperation of the federal authorities. The Democrats declared for outright repeal of the Eighteenth Amendment. The Socialist Party once more nominated Norman Thomas who, it was expected, would poll a sizable vote through the support of persons who were dissatisfied alike with Hoover's conservatism and Roosevelt's vagueness.

The Democratic candidate swept the polls, carrying 42 states and securing a plurality of more than 7,000,000 votes. About 880,-000 ballots were cast for the Socialist candidate, and William Z. Foster, the nominee of the Communist Party, which before the election expressed great confidence in its growing popularity, polled only 102,000 votes. Both branches of Congress also went to the Democrats, the House of Representatives by more than a two-thirds majority.

BROADENING PUBLIC INTERESTS

One of the most important phenomena in post-1919 United States was the growing popular interest in travel, made possible by the blessings of prosperity. Whereas in 1880 a total of 50,000 Americans visited foreign parts, the figure in 1930 was 500,000. The expenditures of United States tourists abroad in 1930 were estimated at $800,000,000. There was an even greater increase in the amount of traveling and sight-seeing within the United States, a circumstance for which improved railway service, the development of the automobile and good roads, and the organization of air traffic, all shared credit. In 1930 one person of every five in the land owned an automobile. "A dynamic history of the postwar period," wrote an observer in 1925, "might give a volume or two to the automobile and a foot-note to affairs of state."

The sales of radio sets in 1937 totaled 8,000,000; by the end of that year, there were 33,000,000 sets in United States homes, offices, and automobiles. The 3715 miles of airplane passenger routes in 1926 rose by 1936 to 60,451 miles. The number of airplane passengers rose from 6000 in 1926 to 1,500,000 in 1939. The United States led the world in number of business and private telephones and in the installation of most other types of modern conveniences. In many cases, however, families were enabled to purchase such objects only because of the "deferred-payment" system. Persons frequently were tempted to buy luxuries which they could ill afford, lured by attractive advertisements and skillful salesmen. The consumption-credit movement artificially stimulated production during the days of prosperity and left a large surplus of goods on the market when the depression curtailed the buying power of the public.

Horydczak

WASHINGTON, D. C.

There was an increasing interest in all fields of sport and millions of dollars were spent in the development of public and private playgrounds. "Spectators' sports," such as boxing and football, became amazingly popular. On occasion as many as one hundred thousand persons attended a single intercollegiate football contest and in 1927 the gate receipts in the second Tunney-Dempsey championship prize-fight were $2,650,000. American enthusiasm over the Olympic Games of 1932 in Los Angeles was unprecedented and the athletes of the United States again captured a larger share of individual and team honors than those of any other nation. During the depression years there was also an increasing amount of rank-and-file participation in sports, partly because that was cheaper than buying seats to watch others and partly because of the New-Deal policy of employing idle people by setting them to work building public parks, pools, playgrounds, and athletic fields.

Education came to occupy a more important place in United States life. The total expenditures of public elementary and secondary schools rose from $462,250,000 in 1910 to $2,316,800,000 in 1930. The college population grew rapidly after 1918 and in 1930 the total registration of students of all classes at Columbia University alone, the largest in the country from the standpoint of enrolment, was 33,144. By 1940, partly through the aid of a National Youth Administration (NYA) which helped needy students, one person of every five in the country was registered in a full-time day school of one kind or another. But while the registration in institutions of secondary and collegiate rank increased, the population in elementary schools declined, largely as the result of a falling birth rate. (There were fewer children under five in the United States in 1940 than there had been in 1920.) Meanwhile extension and home-study courses also had become popular.

While the influence of jazz made itself felt in many phases of public and private life, the people showed an increasingly discriminating interest in art, music, literature, and the theater. By 1939 there were in the country about sixteen thousand moving-picture houses with an estimated weekly attendance of ninety million. Technicolor films and mass animated cartoons produced by Walt Disney became especially popular. The number of legitimate theaters, however, suffered a corresponding decline, falling from about five thousand in 1890 to fewer than two hundred in 1939, not counting small "summer theaters." There were temporary crazes for cross-word puzzles, slot machines, and the old-fashioned lotto under the name of bingo; but there was a simultaneous growth in the number of civic music associations and book clubs. A wide market appeared for historical and biographical works, for lengthy adventure stories, for reprints of the classics, and for illustrated news magazines and "digests." Through the organization of "community chests" the citizens made private contributions up to $100,-000,000 a year to help their less fortunate fellows.

There developed, finally, a keen appreciation of scientific developments and discoveries. The newspapers found it profitable to carry science sections as well as supplements on art, music, theatricals, and sports. More and more frequently was the Nobel Prize for scientific achievements won by citizens of the United States. And a triumph of the American enterprisers', designers', and builders' art was the completion of the Empire State Building in New York in 1931. Rising 102 stories and measuring 1248 feet in height, this structure appeared a symbol of American confidence in the future.

FOREIGN INVESTMENTS AND AFFAIRS, 1923–1933

During the administration of President Harding, the foreign policies of the United States were concerned chiefly with a liquidation of the immediate political problems raised by the country's participation in the First World War and rejection of the Versailles Treaty. After 1923 the trend of foreign affairs was shaped by a realization among Americans of certain recent and vital changes in their national financial position in the world.

Up to 1914 Europe had been "the world's banker." The total foreign investments of Great Britain, Germany, and France on the eve of the war had amounted to $35,000,000,000, while those of the United States had totaled $2,600,000,000. As a consequence of the war and its aftermath, the situation underwent a striking transformation. In 1928 the total value of United States private loans in foreign countries was $13,000,000,000 and by 1930 the figure had climbed to $16,000,000,000, of which $5,000,000,000 was invested in Europe. At the same time, the European war debts to the Washington Government amounted to an additional $11,-000,000,000. In 1927 the interest payments to American citizens on private loans to foreign governments, municipalities, or companies reached $740,000,000.[1] It may be noted here, too, that America's foreign trade in the five-year period from 1924 to 1928 averaged $9,000,000,000 annually. The gross tonnage of the Ameri-

[1] At the end of 1940 total investments abroad aggregated $10,600,000,000.

can merchant fleet in 1928 was 14,540,000. The citizens naturally expected their government to protect these vast interests abroad, and Washington, in general, was ready to assume the obligation.[1]

In 1927, during the course of serious political disturbances in Nicaragua, several thousand sailors and marines and some airplanes were dispatched to the republic to protect American lives and property, and, it appeared, to prevent a group of Liberals from overthrowing the Conservative Party regime of President Adolfo Diaz. The sympathies of the state department were with the Conservatives, for these had been friendly to the United States ever since 1912, granting her a naval base, control of the Nicaraguan customs, bank, and railways, and the right to build a Nicaraguan canal. President Coolidge was criticized for his methods by liberal opinion throughout the United States and Latin America, and eventually he sent Colonel Henry L. Stimson to Nicaragua to strive for a peaceful settlement.

Stimson effected an agreement between one group of the Liberal Party and the Conservatives whereby the former were to cease fighting and surrender their arms at $10 apiece, and new elections were to be held in 1928 under American supervision. Another section of the Liberals, led by General Augusto Sandino, rejected this solution and continued to wage guerrilla warfare against the Conservatives and against United States property and lives. Sandino became particularly active in 1931, after an earthquake in Managua, the capital of Nicaragua, and successfully eluded capture by the United States marines and Nicaraguan National Guard. Finally, in January 1933, the last United States marines were withdrawn from Nicaragua in accordance with a recent announcement of the state department that it could not undertake the general protection of United States citizens in the troubled republic. Thereupon Sandino came to an agreement with the recently inaugurated Liberal President Juan Sacasa providing for the demobilization of all but one hundred of the "rebels," the remainder to be employed on farming and public-works projects.[2]

More serious than the intervention in Nicaragua was a Mexican

[1] The government looked with disfavor on three types of loans: those for such unproductive enterprises as armament expenditures, those to countries that had not funded their war debts, and those that might be used to develop foreign-owned raw-material monopolies to the disadvantage of American consumers.

[2] Later in 1933 conflicts arose between Sandino's men and the Nicaraguan National Guard. Apparently in order to end such disputes, Sandino visited Sacasa for a conference in February 1934. Following a dinner in his honor at the national palace, Sandino was seized at the palace gate by guardsmen and shot.

imbroglio which arose out of the interpretation and possible retro-active force of the Mexican land laws passed under authority of the constitution of 1917. This document vested the ownership of land and subsoil resources in the Mexican nation but permitted the latter to transfer its rights to private Mexican citizens or to foreigners if these agreed not to call on their governments for pro-tection in any dispute over such rights. In 1926 the president of Mexico issued regulations which, among other things, required all owners of land who had secured their titles prior to the pro-mulgation of the constitution of 1917 to exchange these titles for new fifty-year "concessions." A number of American oil companies, fearing for their interests, organized an Association for the Pro-tection of American Rights in Mexico to carry on propaganda against the land decrees. The passage of some Mexican anticlerical laws, which aimed at nationalizing the property of the Catholic Church, made the propaganda work easier.[1]

The state department denounced the regulations as infringe-ments of United States property rights, but the Senate, in January 1927, voted by 79 to 0 to arbitrate the questions in dispute. A few days earlier, however, Coolidge had maintained that American property rights required no arbitration, and Secretary of State Frank B. Kellogg, who had succeeded Hughes in 1925, had accused Mexico of spreading Bolshevik propaganda in the United States and Central America, and of aiding the Nicaraguan revolutionists. Fortunately no overt action was resorted to and the administration appointed the tactful Dwight W. Morrow to be ambassador to Mexico. Some time later Colonel Charles A. Lindbergh, hero of the first nonstop flight from New York to Paris (May 1927), and Will Rogers, Oklahoma cowboy-humorist, went to Mexico on suc-cessful "good-will tours."

Morrow tried to see the viewpoint of the Mexican officials and as a result was able to convince them that the United States had no desire to disrupt the amicable relations that had been estab-lished between the two governments after the settlement of the foreign-debt question in 1923. Both sides compromised. The American companies agreed to lay their cases before the Mexican Supreme Court and the latter declared unconstitutional (1927) some of the most obnoxious land and oil laws.[2]

In 1927 the Washington authorities also became worried over

[1] In 1925 the holdings of Americans in Mexico were estimated at $1,280,000,000.
[2] Beginning in 1931 there were revived demands in the United States for interven-tion because of Mexico's anticlerical policies. See pp. 229–231.

the safety of American lives and property in and around several cities in China. The activities of both the Chinese nationalists and the communists were a source of danger to foreigners, and the United States, following the example of other countries, dispatched a fleet and a detachment of marines to Nanking. (Socony Hill was the name of the place at which the foreign residents of Nanking had gathered for their defense.) When the nationalists appeared to have established their control and promised adequate protection, the United States forces were gradually withdrawn.

To complete this survey of American relations with non-European countries, mention must be made of the Pan-American conferences held at Santiago, Chile, in 1923 and at Havana in 1928. At the former conference the United States rejected the offer of the Latin-American states to assist in the interpretation and application of the Monroe Doctrine. At the latter, a resolution proposing that "no state has the right to intervene in the internal affairs of another" was withdrawn owing largely to the opposition of the United States. The Havana Conference provided for another gathering to be held at Washington for taking steps to adjust international disputes peaceably. The Washington assemblage, in January 1929, accepted two conventions for the arbitration and conciliation of all disputes except those "not controlled by international law."

In the relations between the United States and Europe, the question of the Allied war debts has already been discussed. Pending the final settlement of this problem, the United States was faced with the dilemma of whether or not to collaborate with Europe along general political lines. In December 1923 Coolidge, following the example of Harding, asked the Senate for its consent to ratification of the World Court Protocol. After considerable executive persuasion, the Senate, in 1926, agreed, but with five reservations. The most sweeping condition was the second part of the fifth reservation. The court shall not, it ran, "without the consent of the United States, entertain any request for an advisory opinion touching any dispute or question in which the United States has or claims an interest." The members of the court substantially accepted all reservations except this one, which would have given the United States a privileged position. The Senate disregarded the counterreservations which were offered by the court members and late in 1926 Coolidge announced that he would cease to urge adherence.

Here the matter rested for about two years, after which time the President announced his intention to resume negotiations in the matter of the court. Then, in 1929, the League Council charged a committee of jurists, which had been appointed to revise the court statute and of which Elihu Root was a member, simultaneously to consider the question of United States accession to the tribunal. Out of these beginnings there was evolved the so-called Root Plan which appeared acceptable both to the members of the court and to the state department.

The plan provided for the acceptance of the second part of the Senate's fifth reservation and stipulated that the United States might withdraw from the court "without any imputation of unfriendliness" if ever the court should persist in entertaining a request for an advisory opinion even though the United States was "not prepared to forego its objection" to such procedure. Upon this basis a protocol for American adherence was signed in 1929-1930 by fifty-four states, including the United States. Ratification, however, proceeded more slowly, and by the end of the Hoover Administration the necessary deposits of ratification were still lacking from nine countries, including the United States. In the Hoover-Roosevelt campaign of 1932 both main-party programs declared for adherence to the court.

In spheres other than that of the court, the United States, during the Coolidge and Hoover administrations, adopted a policy of increasing coöperation with the League of Nations. All the League's disarmament and economic conferences were attended by United States delegates. Usually American participation involved the sending of unofficial observers to take part in the discussions and make suggestions, but the United States never bound herself to accept any of the decisions reached. Hundreds of private United States citizens worked for the League as salaried officials, while many Americans headed boundary, railway, and river commissions, and some were chosen as judges of the World Court. Beginning in 1926, the United States voluntarily deposited with the League Secretariat copies of recently signed treaties.

The United States during these years also collaborated with Europe in efforts to establish world harmony on a firmer basis. In 1924 and 1929 United States financial experts played a leading, though unofficial, part in the formulation of new reparation arrangements. In 1927 the Geneva Conference on the limitation of naval armaments was held at the suggestion of President Coolidge. In 1928 Washington adhered to the Paris Pact for the renunciation of war as an instrument of national policy. In 1930 the United

States became a party to the London Naval Treaty. Efforts were made to aid disarmament at the Geneva Conference of 1932. Coöperation was effected in the Chaco boundary dispute. There was, finally, a steady exchange of notes with the League on the status of Manchuria, although the League failed to applaud Stimson's announcement that the United States would not recognize any territorial changes brought about in violation of the Kellogg Pact or other treaties.

ROOSEVELT AND "NIRA"

On March 4, 1933, when Franklin D. Roosevelt took the oath of office as President, the United States had for two years and a half been sinking lower and lower into economic depression. The unemployed numbered thirteen million, the national income had fallen to half of that of 1929, approximately 40 per cent of the farms were mortgaged, strikes and violence had become common occurrences, and virtually every state had found it necessary to place some restriction on banking operations. The new President, however, seemed optimistic. He prophesied that the nation would "revive and prosper," promised a "New Deal," and declared his intention of asking Congress for "broad executive powers to wage a war against the emergency."

The people rallied to the President's support. Roosevelt's cheerful informality, his cordial attitude towards the press, and his "heart-to-heart" talks with the citizenry over the radio won him much confidence. Congress, too, backed the executive, passing important bills in record time and making the President one of the most powerful rulers in the world. In fourteen weeks the Seventy-third Congress passed acts to aid the farmers, regulate industry, coördinate the railways, provide unemployment relief, and reduce that part of the national budget which could be classed as normal expenditure. On some occasions Congress did demur and show jealousy of the growing executive power, but the President so skillfully won over public opinion and withheld political patronage that he generally had his way. Since much of the "presidential planning" had been done in the months between Roosevelt's election and his inauguration, he could inform the people that the numerous proposals so quickly adopted were not a jumble of haphazard schemes, but the carefully thought-out parts of "a connected, logical whole."

On March 5, 1933, Roosevelt declared a nation-wide bank holiday and issued a call for a special session of Congress on the ninth. Then, on the very day of its meeting, Congress passed an act giving the President power to regulate currency and credit transactions, penalize the hoarding of gold, appoint conservators to assist the national banks whose assets were endangered, and issue Federal Reserve notes against government obligations. Later in the same month were passed (1) an Economy Bill which was expected greatly to reduce governmental expenditures; (2) a Beer Bill, modifying the Volstead Act so as to legalize the sale of beverages with an alcoholic content of 3.2 per cent by weight or 4 per cent by volume; [1] and (3) a bill establishing a Civilian Conservation Corps to provide employment for several hundred thousand young men on public works, especially in forests and national parks. Moreover, federal salaries were cut, the Federal Farm Bureau was abolished and all agricultural-credit matters were placed in the hands of a Farm Credit Administration, and most of the banks were reopened.

The drive of administrative action continued with equal vigor in April and May. One executive order reduced the pension and benefit payments to war veterans by $400,000,000 yearly. Another forbade the hoarding of gold or gold certificates. A third placed an embargo on the export of gold, thus taking the United States off the international gold standard.[2] The Agricultural Adjustment Act empowered the government to compensate with rental payments farmers who curtailed the production of certain crops, including wheat, cotton, and sugar; to tax the processing of basic farm products; to conclude marketing agreements with producers and processors as a means of discovering the most effective plan of acreage reduction and the wisest processing tax; and to embark upon a scheme of "controlled inflation." The inflation proposal authorized the President to expand Federal Reserve credits by as much as $3,000,000,000, issue treasury notes up to an additional $3,000,000,000, reduce the gold content of the dollar by as much as 50 per cent, and accept war-debt payments up to $200,000,000 in silver. There was considerable opposition to the inflation feature of the agricultural act, but the powers were only permissive

[1] This law was adopted pending state action on a proposed constitutional amendment, passed in February 1933, repealing the Eighteenth Amendment and forbidding the transportation or importation of intoxicating liquor only in those areas which retained dry laws of their own. Ratification proceeded swiftly and on December 5, 1933, the Twenty-First Amendment, repealing the Eighteenth, became effective.

[2] In June the gold clause in public and private contracts was abrogated and contracts and debts were made payable in legal tender.

and administration officials emphasized that inflation would be "kept under control."

The Wagner-Lewis Emergency Relief Act appropriated $500,-000,000 to be distributed for direct relief purposes. The Tennessee Valley Authority or Muscle Shoals Act gave the government full direction over the development of power and natural resources. This was advocated by Roosevelt not only to stimulate industry and relieve unemployment but to prevent the tremendous waste of resources resulting from continued lack of planning. The Securities Law, finally, gave the government regulatory powers over the sale of stocks and securities.

This sweep of legislative accomplishments was eclipsed by the lawmaking of June 1933. A Home Owners' Refinancing Act was passed by means of which, through federal credit extension, small-home owners would be saved from eviction by foreclosure. A banking bill (Glass-Steagall Act) was adopted which provided for the establishment of a Federal Deposit Insurance Corporation with capital subscribed by the United States Treasury, the Federal Reserve Banks, and the member banks.[1] A railway act placed railroad holding companies under the supervision of a federal railway coördinator and made provision for protecting workers against loss of employment as a result of coördination. On June 16 the President signed the National Industrial Recovery Act, soon to be known as NIRA.

The NIRA, in effect, empowered the President to set up machinery for "a great coöperative movement throughout all industry in order to obtain wide reëmployment, to shorten the work week, to pay a decent wage for the shorter work week, and to prevent unfair competition and disastrous overproduction." The act permitted the suspension of the antitrust laws, provided for the drawing up of codes of fair competition in the industries, contained protective clauses for labor, and outlined a public-works program involving an expenditure by a Public Works Administration (PWA) of $3,300,000,000, the money to be raised through taxes on the net worth, earnings, and dividends of corporations, and a higher impost on gasoline.

To integrate the recovery measures the President created an executive council composed of the cabinet and the heads of the agencies recently established by Congress, including Joseph B. Eastman, federal railroad coördinator, Robert Fechner, director of the

---

[1] Eventually most banks in the country insured deposits with the corporation. The insurance covered only accounts not exceeding $5000.

Civilian Conservation Corps, and General Hugh S. Johnson, administrator of the National Recovery Administration (NRA), the agency directly responsible for the preparation and enforcement of the codes. When it became evident that considerable time would elapse before approved codes could be drawn up for all industries, the administration provided a "blanket code" for shorter hours and minimum wages which business was asked to adopt pending the formulation of individual codes.

The blanket code was in the form of an agreement between the President and each employer. It did away with child labor under fourteen and established a working week of thirty-five hours for industrial laborers and forty hours for white-collar groups. The minimum wage for industry was $0.40 per hour; for white-collar workers it varied from $12 to $15 weekly depending on the size of the community. The blanket code was to remain in effect until the approval of a specific code for the particular industry. Employers who conformed to the code were permitted to display a "Blue Eagle" as proof of their coöperation with the government. It was estimated that within a few weeks about two million persons were thus returned to work while many others benefited by a shorter work week or increased pay.

The first code of fair competition to be approved and adopted related to the cotton-textile industry. It provided for the abandonment of child labor, a forty-hour week, and minimum wages of $12 weekly in the South and $13 in the North. Other codes followed in due time, but a number of criticisms of the NRA system soon were advanced. It was sometimes difficult to get the employers and workers to agree on the proper length of working hours. The American Federation of Labor took the opportunity to appear as a champion of labor, to increase its efforts to unionize all industry, and to fight the formation of company unions. Often the employers themselves in an industry found it almost impossible to agree, as in the soft-coal and oil businesses, and then the government had to act as arbitrator. Strikes continued and made the problem still more complex. Thus there was much opposition to the NRA from both capital and labor, but for the time being popular sentiment again backed the administration. Business, moreover, did seem to be experiencing an improvement.

The administration program was pushed with equal vigor during the second half of 1933. Public belief that the President would soon use his discretionary powers to invoke inflationary devices led, for a time, to a decline in the value of the dollar and a slight rise in commodity prices. To the London Economic Conference Roosevelt made it plain that, in his opinion, the immediate removal of trade barriers was far more urgent than any immediate stabilization of currencies (as proposed by France). In the presence of this fundamental difference of outlook, the conference had little choice but to adjourn. Meanwhile prices, especially on farm products, had once again begun to fall, with consequent farm strikes, accompanied by violence, in many parts of the West. There was a growing demand for inflation and the President finally authorized (October 1933) the Reconstruction Finance Corporation to purchase freshly mined domestic and foreign gold at prices to be fixed from time to time. Thus the dollar might be progressively cheapened and price levels "restored."

The RFC began buying gold until the value of the latter rose to $35 an ounce as against less than $21 under the old law. But the increase in commodity prices did not keep pace with the drop of the dollar. In December, therefore, Roosevelt ordered the treasury during the next four years to purchase all silver mined in the United States (about 24,000,000 ounces annually) at $64\frac{1}{2}$ cents an ounce, this being 50 per cent above the then market price.

In the meantime (November 1933) a Civil Works Administration had been organized with an appropriation of $400,000,000 from the PWA to finance public-works (and then "made-work") projects and thus remove names from the relief rolls. In some cases surplus food, clothing, and fuel were directly allotted as relief to distressed families—thus incidentally reducing some of the commodity surpluses that had forced down prices. Another PWA allotment went to an Emergency Housing Corporation, organized to purchase and clear slum sections in the larger cities of the country and erect on the sites modern, low-cost apartment buildings.

To ease the lot of some of the farmers living on submarginal lands and the industrial workers crowded in cities, a fund was set aside for the experimental establishment of several thousand "subsistence homesteads." The money was to be used as a revolving fund to aid such families in the acquisition in new communities of modest houses and farm plots at an average cost of $2500. "By raising crops for home consumption, engaging in various handicrafts, and working part time in factories, it was hoped that these communities would be largely self-sufficient." A number of such projects in several states were approved, but there was not enough money to allow the plan to advance beyond the experimental stage.

Another avalanche of New Deal legislation was started when Congress met in January 1934.[1] Government loans to farmers were facilitated. The production of additional crops was placed under official control. Time extensions were granted to bankrupt farmers during which they might retain possession of their land (Frazier-Lemke Farm Bankruptcy Act). State banks and trust companies unaffiliated with the Federal Reserve system were given borrowing privileges similar to those of the member banks. The reorganization of bankrupt corporations was made easier. Money was made available for home-repair loans and protection was offered to building and loan associations. A national board was created to mediate labor disputes growing out of the NIRA. Direct loans to industry were authorized, the maximum being $500,000 to any one organization. An additional sum was appropriated to continue the CWA projects, and the lending functions of the RFC were extended. The President was empowered, for three years, to negotiate foreign-trade agreements without the advice and consent of the Senate.

By a law of January 30, 1934, the President was authorized to call into the treasury all gold money, to revalue the dollar at some point between 50 per cent and 60 per cent of its existing gold content, and to use part of the resulting "profit" from the increase in the value of gold to set up a $2,000,000,000 "stabilization" fund. Almost immediately, Roosevelt fixed the value of the dollar at 59.06 cents in terms of its former gold value. It soon became evident that the Gold Reserve Act, as it was called, was a failure as a price-raising device. According to an official estimate, the whole-sale-price index of almost 800 commodities had risen 22 per cent between April 1933, when the United States "went off" gold, and May 1934, while the gold content of the dollar had been reduced more than 40 per cent. The inflation groups therefore demanded the "remonetization" of silver and in June 1934 Congress passed a Silver Purchase Act. This law aimed at maintaining silver as one-fourth of the monetary stock of the land, permitted the President to nationalize silver and to buy existing silver accumulations at not more than 50 cents per ounce, and placed a 50 per cent tax on

---

[1] The Twentieth Amendment, which went into effect on February 6, 1933, provided that "Congress shall assemble at least once in every year, and such meeting shall begin at noon on the third day of January, unless they shall by law appoint a different day." The terms of the President and Vice-President were made to end, in future, at noon of January 20 and those of senators and representatives at noon of January 3, "of the years in which such terms would have ended if this article had not been ratified."

silver-transaction profits. Since most of the country's "money," however, was in the form of bank credit rather than currency, this measure also fell short of its objective.

All this and more was done between January 3 and June 18, 1934, on which day Congress adjourned.[1] In the mid-term elections held later in the year, the Democrats gained seats not only in the congressional, but in most of the state elections. In the Seventy-fourth Congress, Roosevelt's party had a two-thirds majority in each house.

By the beginning of 1935 it was possible to estimate some of the effects of the New Deal legislation. Almost 550 codes, covering 95 per cent of the nation's industry, had been adopted. Industrial production had reached a level approximating 90 per cent of the average for the period from 1923 to 1925. About four million persons had been reëmployed. The banking system had been somewhat improved and unfair practices in business had been curtailed. The full effect on labor and on agriculture, however, it was not possible to gage. In the case of the former, there was brought to a head the conflict with the employers over the principles of the "closed shop" and collective bargaining. The dispute was marked by an increase in strikes, lockouts, picketing, court injunctions, and violence. In the matter of agriculture, a terrible drought in 1934 made it impossible to determine the effects of the official crop-reduction measures.

Certain results were definitely on the debit side. The number of unemployed was still about ten million. The balance between agricultural and industrial prices had not been successfully adjusted. The cost of living had gone up without a commensurate rise in wages. The net income of the chief railways for October 1934 was reported as less than half of that for October 1933 and less than one-third of that for October 1932, while the government found itself in possession of increasingly large blocks of railroad securities. The national debt had risen from $19,500,000,000 in June 1932 to $29,800,000,000 in March 1935. There was a widespread belief, on the one hand, that the system was favorable to the strengthening of the industrial monopolies, and, on the other, that an excess of government "meddling" was rapidly strangling business.

---

[1] Additional legislation included revision of the air-mail contracts; creation of a new federal commission to regulate interstate and foreign communication services by telegraph, telephone, cable, and radio; stricter crime control; and removal of all discrimination against women in the nationality laws.

Nothing daunted, President Roosevelt informed Congress of his conviction that "the fundamental purposes and principles of the (NIRA) were sound" and that their abandonment was "unthinkable." He then asked for a two-year extension (until June 1937) of the act in somewhat modified form and recommended the retention of its minimum-wage, maximum-hour, collective-bargaining, and child-labor features.

While this executive proposal was being discussed, Congress voted and Roosevelt signed (April 1935) a new work-relief bill which appropriated $4,880,000,000 to be spent by the President for recovery and "made-work" projects. Although there were specified restrictions on the executive's power to allot this money, he retained considerable freedom of action. Roosevelt dispensed the money in some cases to existing organs of administration and in others to newly created instruments, such as the Works Progress Administration (WPA). The most far-reaching new projects were concerned with the elimination of grade crossings, the electrification of rural areas, and rural rehabilitation or the transference of farming families from unprofitable marginal lands to more fertile regions. This last and most ambitious task was entrusted to the undersecretary of agriculture, Rexford G. Tugwell.

Three additional legislative efforts of 1935 must be given mention. In May Congress passed the Patman Bonus Bill, providing for the printing of $2,000,000,000 worth of greenbacks with which to cash immediately and at their 1945 face value the adjusted service certificates held by more than three million veterans. In this form the measure was supported by those who wanted the bonus as well as by those who favored inflation. Roosevelt vetoed the bill on the ground that it would set a dangerous precedent of legislation in favor of a particular class. Eventually, in January 1936, a slightly modified Soldiers' Bonus Bill was passed over another presidential veto. This law exchanged the certificates for bonds which were redeemable in cash on demand. By mid-1938 the redemptions totaled $1,500,000,000.

July 1935 saw the passage of the Wagner or National Labor Relations Act. This law required employers to bargain collectively with their workers and forbade them to engage in unfair labor practices or do anything which might interfere with the full realization of the objectives of trade unionism. A National Labor Relations Board (NLRB) was created to enforce the provisions of the act, "which was frankly class legislation, in that it spoke only of industry's duty to labor."

In August 1935, finally, there was adopted a Social Security Act. This provided federal participation in insurance measures covering old age, unemployment, needy dependent children, and the destitute blind; it also ordained federal aid, on a matching basis, to state public-welfare and vocational-rehabilitation services. The need for such legislation was emphasized by a study which showed that in 1935–1936 one-third of the families in the United States had an income averaging $471 for the year. The arrangements for unemployment and old-age retirement were not applied to public employees, domestic servants, farm laborers, marine workers, or the employees of religious, charitable, and educational institutions. But by mid-1938 about twenty-six million persons were insured against unemployment and about thirty-six million were assured old-age benefits.

Meanwhile some of the principles of the NIRA had been attacked not only by conservative business elements but by prominent Republican leaders and by district judges. In February 1935, however, the government was upheld by the Supreme Court on one of its most important actions: the virtual cancelation of the gold clause in financial contracts. Whereas this verdict caused satisfaction to the administration and was roundly denounced by the opposition, the Supreme Court in May shocked the government and delighted the opposition by declaring the unconstitutionality of the whole NIRA setup. The judges on this occasion handed down three unanimous decisions affecting the New Deal.

One decision declared that the President had acted illegally in removing an unsympathetic federal trade commissioner who had been reappointed in 1931 for a seven-year term by Hoover. Another held unconstitutional the Frazier-Lemke Farm Bankruptcy Act on the ground that it confiscated the private property of mortgagors.[1] And the third, growing out of an accusation of unfair trade practices by a wholesale poultry concern in Brooklyn, New York, declared that Congress had no right to delegate to the various code authorities the power to enact what in effect were laws for the regulation of their respective industries; that Congress could not delegate to the President the legislative power of prescribing or approving codes; and that the interstate-commerce clause of the Constitution, on which much of the new legislation was based, could not be construed "to reach all enterprises and transactions which could be said to have an indirect effect upon

[1] A second and modified Frazier-Lemke Act, passed in August 1935, was later upheld by the court.

interstate commerce," for then, "for all practical purposes, we should have a completely centralized government."

The President was angry and declared that the decisions took the country back to the "horse-and-buggy days of 1789," but leading opponents of the New Deal held that the Constitution and country, after narrow escapes, had at last been saved. While the administration busied itself with plans for continuing the best features of the NIRA without contravening the Constitution, spokesmen for capital and labor issued contradictory statements on nearly every phase of past and proposed recovery legislation. Indeed, neither the leading employers nor the labor leaders seemed agreed among themselves as to the actual benefits or dangers of NIRA. Hence it soon was evident that the electoral campaign of 1936 would be one of great excitement.

A SECOND TERM, AND A THIRD

The Republican Party, at its 1936 convention, shelved its older leaders and nominated Governor Alfred M. Landon of Kansas and newspaper publisher Frank Knox of Chicago for the country's two highest offices. Many of the better known party chiefs probably felt as did Coolidge, who had told an interviewer: "When I read of the new-fangled things that are now so popular, I realize that my time in public affairs is past. I wouldn't know how to handle them if I were called upon to do so." At any rate, Landon had no national enemies and was expected to attract a large Western vote. The platform accused the Democrats of waste and of prolonging the depression, but it was vague on substitute proposals for recovery. The Democrats unanimously renominated Roosevelt and Garner and pledged a continuance of New Deal policies.

The Socialist Party renominated Norman Thomas and the Communist Party named Earl Browder, while a new Union Party selected Congressman William O. Lemke of North Dakota. The Union Party made its appeal to all sorts of malcontents. These included the followers of Governor Huey Long of Louisiana, with his "Share-Our-Wealth-Society"; of Dr. Francis E. Townsend, who wanted the federal government to pay $200 monthly to all unemployed needy over sixty on condition only that they spend the money promptly; and of a Catholic priest, Charles E. Coughlin of Detroit, who built up his National Union for Social Justice through vigorous radio attacks on the administration and its advisers.

Much name-calling and bitterness characterized the campaign. The Roosevelt ticket was called "communistic," while the followers of Landon were labeled "economic royalists"—to mention only the mildest epithets that were current. An American Liberty League, founded by Republican industrialists but supported by ex-Democratic presidential candidates Smith and Davis, backed Landon, and a newly organized American Labor Party, functioning only in the state of New York, gave its support to Roosevelt. In the end, the Democratic leader captured the electoral votes of every state except Maine and Vermont. His popular vote was 27,-700,000 to 16,800,000 for Landon. The minor parties together were able to win only 3 per cent of all votes cast.

Following the election, Roosevelt determined to reap full advantage of his popular endorsement. He was now in position, it seemed to him, to demand that Congress consolidate the changes of the New Deal. For this purpose, further reform was needed in three fields: in the judicial (where the Supreme Court had nullified important New-Deal laws), in the administrative (where there was much waste, duplication, and inefficiency among government departments and bureaus), and in the legislative (where, in Congress, there were still too many antiadministration senators and congressmen to please the President).

Because it appeared to him that he was consistently opposed by five conservatives in the Supreme Court and supported only by four liberals, the President in 1937 asked Congress to make possible an increase in the number of judges to fifteen. Such action had been taken on previous occasions, notably during the administration of Ulysses S. Grant, but Roosevelt's request aroused a storm of opposition, both within and without Congress. The national legislature, indeed, backed by much liberal opinion as well as conservative, refused the President's bidding and instead merely permitted judges to retire at seventy at full pay. But though he was defeated in Congress, Roosevelt soon won a practical victory. One after another of the "nine old men" retired or died until, by 1941, the executive had been given opportunity to make seven new appointments. The judicial verdicts, meanwhile, had come to be much more frequently favorable to the viewpoint of the administration.

The President's proposals for the reorganization of government agencies were rejected by Congress in 1938, largely, it seems, because of personal animosity. Following the mid-term elections of that year, however, the President did receive authority to proceed with his reorganizational plans in somewhat modified form. During the elections, meanwhile, he had tried, through promise of further reform, to get the solid backing of labor, agriculture, the unemployed, and the more liberal section of the middle class. He specifically asked these voters to rid Congress of the "Bourbons" who opposed his policies; but this attempted purge of his political antagonists was almost a complete failure. Indeed, although the Democrats still controlled the national legislature, they lost a number of seats in both houses and had to surrender several governorships to the Republicans. The voting doubtless was affected by an economic "recession" that had begun in June 1937—perhaps because federal outlays were curtailed faster than private industry picked up—and by a growing feeling that the President was not wholeheartedly in favor of maintaining what many citizens regarded as basic property rights. As a result of the trend in the balloting, the country enjoyed a brief legislative pause.

During the Roosevelt administrations labor came to play an increasingly large part in national affairs. The membership of the American Federation of Labor, which had fallen from 4,000,000 in 1920 to 2,000,000 in 1933, rose once more to 3,500,000 by 1936. At this point, however, an internal dispute split American labor asunder. Under the headship of John L. Lewis, president of the United Mine Workers of America, a number of union leaders began to advocate the organization of *all* workers throughout the land in industrial or "vertical" unions to replace the "horizontal" or craft-union system which included only a limited number of *skilled* workers.

In the face of opposition from President William Green and the executive committee of the A.F. of L., Lewis in 1935 had gathered around him several prominent labor leaders and formed the Committee for Industrial Organization. This C.I.O. then sent out organizers into numerous fields which were as yet "only slightly touched by the trade union ideology." By the end of 1936 ten large unions belonged to the C.I.O.—and all ten were suspended by the A.F. of L. Since the latter had meanwhile launched a new organization campaign of its own, there were frequent clashes between the two labor groups.

One result of this intralabor strife was to bring the country twice as many strikes, involving twice as many workers, in 1937 as in 1936—to the great discomfiture of the employers and the obvious displeasure of the public. Another consequence was to keep busy the National Labor Relations Board, which led an exceedingly active existence settling strikes and supervising workers' elections to determine which of the two labor bargaining agencies was to be dominant in one or another of hundreds of plants throughout the land.

In 1938 the followers of Lewis quit the A.F. of L. and reconstituted themselves as the Congress of Industrial Organizations. Because the congress made widespread use of the sit-down strike, and because communists were able to rise to influential posts within its organization, public opinion gradually turned against the C.I.O. under Lewis' leadership. By the end of 1940, however, the C.I.O. and the A.F. of L. each claimed almost four million members. Organized labor in the United States thus had doubled its membership in the score of years since 1920. (In March 1943 the A.F. of L. claimed a membership of 6,190,000.) The C.I.O., incidentally, was particularly successful in the coal, steel, automobile, and textile fields.

It was to be expected that sooner or later the poorer farm tenants and laborers, especially those in the South, also would demand assistance from the federal authorities. To further their interests, a Southern Tenant Farmers' Union was founded in 1934, which came to include black as well as white members. Although conservative Southern sentiment was outraged by both the aims and methods of the union, Congress eventually acted on its pleas. In 1937 there was created the Farm Security Administration (FSA) to bring relief to sharecroppers and other tenant farmers. The agency was empowered to lend money to such individuals in order that they might acquire outright ownership of farms or move from bad land to good. In the first three years of its existence the FSA started thirteen thousand families on the road to land ownership, chiefly in the South. In addition, it made subsistence grants to thousands of families living in the Dust Bowl (embracing about one hundred counties in Kansas, Oklahoma, Colorado, Texas, and New Mexico) to keep them from becoming migratory workers; and it built camps in California to provide passable living conditions for thirty thousand families of "Okies" (from Oklahoma) who had gone west in search of work.[1]

Perhaps the most far-reaching domestic law of the second Roosevelt Administration was the Fair Labor Standards Act of 1938, which was intended by the President to put "a floor under wages and a ceiling over hours." The ultimate objective of the law was

[1] The plight of the Okies was called to popular attention by John Steinbeck in his novel *The Grapes of Wrath,* 1939.

the universal establishment of a forty-hour work week at a minimum pay of $0.40 per hour (with time-and-a-half for overtime) in businesses of an interstate nature. The products of firms employing children under sixteen were excluded from interstate commerce. Lest undue hardship be caused to small concerns, the provisions of the act were to be enforced gradually. Farm and marine workers, retail-store employees, and professionals were not covered by the law.

The political sphere also witnessed legislative changes in these years. Laws of 1938 and 1940 vastly extended the civil-service lists—an exceedingly important trend in view of the large amounts of money that relief administrators had available for spending. In 1939, moreover, the Hatch Act was passed, forbidding federal appointees below policy-making rank to use official favors to influence national elections, to solicit or accept contributions from recipients of relief payments, and to take an "active part" in election campaigns. A second Hatch Act (1940) extended these prohibitions to state and local employees whose remuneration was met wholly or partly out of federal funds. The law also limited the annual expenditures of any one political party to $3,000,000 and restricted individual contributions to a maximum of $5000.

All the government's efforts notwithstanding, the number of unemployed still was ten million in mid-1939. At that time, however, in view of the growing number of foreign and domestic armament orders, Congress provided for the gradual reduction of relief rolls. Simultaneously the name of the Works Progress Administration was changed to Work Projects Administration; but in initials the agency still remained the WPA. By August 1939, the eve of the Second World War, Congress had voted a total of $13,000,000,000 for relief, a sizable proportion of which was expended on defense measures.[1]

The volume of relief expenditures, the increasing cost of administration owing to the creation of so many new agencies, and the added outlays occasioned by the numerous new federal functions all combined to bring about a steady increase in the national deficit—and in taxes. The central government, moreover, had come to exert an increasingly direct influence over the lives of all people in the land. These circumstances plus the disturbing events

[1] The last PWA program was authorized in 1938 for continuance until June 30, 1942. The WPA was abolished in December 1942, with several months permitted for its final liquidation.

of the Second World War entered into that brisk contest which was the presidential election of 1940.

The Republican delegates in 1940 sidetracked the preconvention favorites and quickly nominated a "dark horse": Wendell L. Willkie of New York and Indiana. Willkie was a former Democrat who, as president of the Commonwealth and Southern Corporation, had become an outstanding foe of New Deal policies, particularly as these concerned rural electrification under the Tennessee Valley Authority (TVA). A corporation lawyer by profession, he had never held any elective or appointive public office. In foreign affairs he was an advocate of maximum aid to Great Britain. From the time the balloting for candidates began, the well-filled gallery chanted and shouted "We want Willkie" until, on the sixth ballot, they got him. To please the more orthodox Republicans and appeal to the farmers, the convention chose Senator Charles L. McNary of Oregon to be Willkie's running mate.

President Roosevelt studiously refrained from saying anything definite about a number of pre-Democratic convention moves to "draft" him for a third term. But when the delegates gathered, he won renomination on the first ballot—partly because of the well-oiled state of the New Deal machinery and partly out of a fear that no other candidate would be able to beat Willkie. Inasmuch as Vice-President Garner and Roosevelt were no longer on good terms, the convention nominated Secretary of Agriculture Henry A. Wallace, a former Republican, to complete the ticket.

The platforms of the two parties bore many resemblances. Both advocated keeping the United States out of the war and rendering all possible aid short of war to Great Britain. Both promised to build up America's defenses, to provide further economic relief, and to pass legislation favorable to agriculture and labor. The Republicans again condemned what they called the waste and extravagance of the New Deal, promised an administration friendlier to business, and expressed a determination to lessen rather than encourage "class hatred."

The campaign was a lively one. Both candidates were able, courageous, and popular. Each "put on a good show." The third-term issue engendered heated discussions. In view of the unhappy situation in Europe there was much talk about the advantage of keeping an experienced man in the White House and about the inadvisability of "swapping horses while crossing a stream." Party lines were widely crossed, so that there were Democrates-for-Willkie and Republicans-for-Roosevelt. Frequent and pointed reference was made to the evident upswing of business, though this was largely the result of additional arms contracts growing out of the war. John L. Lewis carried his personal animosity against the President to the point of threatening to resign his headship of the C.I.O. if Roosevelt were reëlected.[1]

In the end, Roosevelt won. He captured the electoral votes of 38 states to Willkie's 10; but in popular votes the count was 27,200,000 to 22,300,000. The Socialist and Communist candidates together polled 164,000 votes. Willkie congratulated the winner and readily coöperated with him in seeking solutions for some of the great problems facing the country. Having once more proved itself at home, American democracy soon found itself forced to fight for its existence against foreign enemies. We turn, therefore, to United States foreign relations since 1933.

FOREIGN RELATIONS UNDER ROOSEVELT

The pressure of domestic affairs for a time absorbed most of the government's energies, but foreign questions soon demanded their share of official attention. To supplement the domestic recovery efforts, Secretary Hull, by 1939, had negotiated reciprocal trade treaties with twenty-one foreign countries. In order to lighten the task of tariff bargaining, the President was authorized (1934, 1937, 1940) to lower or raise by not more than 50 per cent any existing duties on imports. The importance of both these items becomes apparent when it is realized that "by 1938 some 380 bilateral, special agreements were known to exist which excluded United States products." The secretary of state headed a delegation to the ill-fated World Economic Conference of 1933, and diplomatic relations with the Russians were reëstablished in the same year— partly for business reasons. To stimulate the lagging remissions of war-debt instalments, Roosevelt approved the Johnson Debt Default Act (1934) which declared "token payments" unsatisfactory

---

[1] After the election Lewis kept his promise, though he retained the presidency of the powerful miners' union. Under the leadership of its new chief, Philip Murray, the C.I.O. purged itself of some of its communistic influences and curbed its own readiness to strike. Public opinion therefore became friendlier to the organization than it had formerly been. In October 1942 the United Mine Workers of America, on Lewis' recommendation, voted to withdraw from the C.I.O. Lewis accused the C.I.O. leaders of villifying him and demanded the repayment of $1,685,000 which he claimed was loaned by the miners to the C.I.O. while he was president of the latter. The C.I.O. contended that the money had been a gift to help organization activities in various industries.

and forbade defaulting nations to float loans in the United States. On the next due date a payment arrived only from Finland.

Through action of the President and Senate in August 1934 the United States became a member of the International Labor Organization. Four years later Washington ratified its first international labor convention. Like his predecessor, moreover, Roosevelt once more brought up the question of adherence to the World Court under the Root Plan. The time seemed propitious since the Senate contained such a large Democratic majority. But after a heated debate the Senate in January 1935 refused its consent to ratification.

In the matter of armaments, the first Roosevelt Administration witnessed the collapse of the Geneva Disarmament Conference in 1934 and the expiration of the Washington and London naval-limitation agreements. The Japanese demand for naval parity with the United States and Great Britain was rejected by both of these powers and Tokyo exercised its right to renounce the restrictive treaties. The congressional appropriations for the war and navy departments rose rapidly with each passing year and additional sums for defense were forthcoming from work-relief funds. Simultaneously a committee headed by Senator Gerald P. Nye of North Dakota investigated (1934–1936) the munitions industry with a view to diminishing the possible influence of munition makers on international disharmony and on the defeat of armament-limitation proposals. The reports of this committee combined with the appearance of a large number of war novels of disillusionment and the stoppage of war-debt payments from the former allies all helped to spread a spirit of "isolationism" throughout the country. This made it hard for Roosevelt to get public opinion aroused over the dangers which he knew threatened the American way of life from the side of totalitarianism.

In March 1934 Roosevelt urged Congress to revive in amended form the Hawes-Cutting Act for Philippine independence. This measure earlier had become law over Hoover's veto but had been rejected by the Manila Legislature. It had provided as follows: (1) the islands were to become independent after a transitional period of twelve years during which they would be governed by their own legislature and executive; (2) the United States reserved the right to maintain military and naval stations in the islands; (3) Philippine exports to the United States were, in general, to remain duty-free only within fixed quotas and thereafter to be subject to the regular tariff rates; (4) Manila was required to service the public debt out of an excise tax on duty-free articles sent to the United States; (5) United States goods might enter the islands duty-free during the transitional period; and (6) Philippine immigrants to the United States were limited to fifty per year. Congress quickly acted upon Roosevelt's suggestion and passed the Tydings-Mc-Duffie Bill which merely eliminated the military and naval clauses of the previous law. The Philippine Legislature accepted it in May 1934.

The change in Latin-American policy which had appeared during the Hoover Administration was carried further under Roosevelt—a fortunate circumstance in view of the happenings on the European stage after 1933. In his first inaugural address Roosevelt declared that he "would dedicate this nation to the policy of the good neighbor." Later, affirming that "the definite policy of the United States from now on is opposed to armed intervention," he said:

The maintenance of constitutional government in other nations is not, after all, a sacred obligation devolving upon the United States alone. The maintenance of law and the orderly processes of government in this hemisphere is the concern of each individual nation within its borders first of all. It is only if and when the failure of orderly processes affects the other nations of the continent that it becomes their concern; and the point to stress is that in such an event it becomes the joint concern of the whole continent in which we are all neighbors.

Striking examples were soon furnished of the new official policy. The last American marines were withdrawn from Haiti in August 1934. A more liberal recognition policy as applied to Central America was inaugurated with the recognition (1934) of a *de facto* government in El Salvador. In 1934, also, came the abrogation of the Platt Amendment. It was by authority of this portion of the United States-Cuban treaty of 1903 that Washington had exercised certain controls over Cuban internal affairs for more than three decades. Now the treaty was virtually set aside except for the provision which allowed the United States to maintain a naval base at Guantanamo. In 1936 the United States relinquished the interventionist rights accorded her by a treaty of 1903 with Panama.

Friendly relations were maintained with Nicaragua and in 1938 a new accord was reached with Mexico. It was agreed that a joint commission would decide how much compensation was due

United States owners for agricultural lands taken from them since 1927. From 1939 on, Mexico paid the United States $1,000,000 per year on this account, while the troublesome oil claims remained to be settled. In 1940 Roosevelt ended the customs receivership which had been functioning in the Dominican Republic since 1905. Meanwhile every effort had been made to cooperate in a friendly manner in the settlement of the Chaco boundary dispute between Bolivia and Paraguay. And late in 1936, when Roosevelt visited Buenos Aires and Río de Janeiro, he had been received with tremendous ovations.

Out of these things grew closer general relations among all the American republics. In 1936 they signed at Buenos Aires an American Collective Security Convention which provided for the obligatory arbitration of disputes and consultation in the event of a threat to the peace of the Western Hemisphere. The Eighth Pan-American Conference at Lima in 1938 reaffirmed these principles in a Declaration of the Solidarity of America. Thus twenty-one nations, not the United States alone, became the interpreters and executors of the Monroe Doctrine. After 1939, when the United States and Great Britain needed Latin-American support against the axis powers, the wisdom of the good-neighbor policy was abundantly proved.

For some time after 1933 the international affairs of Europe filled Americans more with "distaste than alarm." Hence many citizens were confirmed in the isolationist views which they had built up on the foundations mentioned above. One result of this widespread feeling was an official change in the traditional neutrality policy of the United States, that is, in the historic contention that there must be freedom of the seas and no interference with neutral trade in noncontraband goods with warring countries. The change was expressed in joint resolutions of Congress in 1935, 1936, and 1937.

These Neutrality Acts required the President, whenever he found that a state of war existed between foreign states or that civil strife in any one foreign state might reach proportions dangerous to the peace of the United States, to proclaim such fact. Thereupon he also had to declare it unlawful to sell or transport war materials to any belligerent, purchase the securities of a belligerent, travel on belligerent ships, or arm American merchantmen. Then, at his discretion, he might forbid (1) the transportation on United States ships of *any* commodities to belligerents, (2) the shipment of goods until after they had been paid for and unless they were carried away in foreign bottoms (this cash-and-carry provision might be applied only until 1939), and (3) the use of United States ports to belligerent warships, submarines, and armed merchantmen. None of this applied to American republics if they were engaged in war with non-American states.

The President wanted the right to apply all these restrictions only against the belligerent whom he might regard as the aggressor, but this concession Congress refused to make. Thus it happened that during the Ethiopian War and the Spanish Civil War the various checks had to be applied to both sides, regardless of American sentiment in favor of one side or the other.[1] This circumstance obviously reacted to the advantage of Mussolini in the one case and to that of Franco in the second. In the Far East, on the other hand, where there had been no declaration of war, the President was able to give some help to the victim of aggression. He refrained from declaring the existence of a state of war and merely forbade government-owned ships to carry arms to either combatant while warning private shipowners that they transported war materials at their own risk. Thus it was possible to extend credits to China; but enormous quantities of scrap iron went to Japan.

Through this legislation Congress hoped to prevent a repetition of such incidents as the *Lusitania* sinking, which had helped to bring the United States into the First World War. But the exigencies of the Second World War, as we shall see, soon led to further revision of the neutrality laws. Meanwhile, as has been indicated, the war also played an important part in the presidential campaign of 1940. After the heated electoral contest was over, there followed a general and quiet acceptance of the results—but basic unity did not come to the nation until after the disaster at Pearl Harbor.

[1] For United States policy in the Ethiopian War see p. 367 n. 1.

PART IV

The Second World War

CHAPTER XXIV

The Return to War

The delegates of the Allied and Associated Powers who met at Paris in 1918–1919 to frame a peace settlement theoretically had, as we have seen, a choice among several alternatives. They might have made the treaty with Germany so crushing that an early and powerful comeback would have been out of the question. Or, had they possessed a superhuman detachment, they might have drafted a settlement so conciliatory as to provide little basis for the future growth in Germany of a movement aimed at violent treaty nullification. As it happened, the Allied leaders followed neither of these procedures. They adopted a middle course and drew up an instrument which was severe enough to make the Germans vengeful and moderate enough to enable the Reich to experience a great military revival within twenty years.

The Germans' ambition to nullify the provisions of the Versailles Treaty—on which they placed the blame for many difficulties that actually grew out of the First World War itself—was rendered the easier of fulfillment by the circumstance that France and Great Britain, both desirous of maintaining the *status quo* which they had helped to arrange, yet pursued the same end along different and divergent paths. As the former partners drifted farther and farther apart diplomatically, it became the easier and safer for Germany to revise the treaty terms unilaterally—especially since the peace settlement had largely surrounded her with small and relatively weak neighbors. Where, from the standpoint of practical politics, there should have been Anglo-French coöperation in the enforcement of most treaty terms and the legal revision of others, there actually was an individualistic pursuit of diverse foreign policies conditioned by the disparate internal needs and developments of the ex-allies. As a consequence, many of the worst postwar Franco-German quarrels quickly developed into Franco-British quarrels, to the obvious advantage of a Germany bent upon upsetting the arrangements of Paris.

The French, no matter whether the Right bloc was in power or the Left, sought with few exceptions to uphold the settlement of 1919. To the people of France, the Versailles Treaty became an object of high esteem; it represented to a harassed nation the only tangible guarantee of security; each concession from its terms was looked upon as weakening the whole structure; its general maintenance came to be regarded as the strongest protection against renewed evil from without—the more so since the Guarantee Treaties which had been signed in 1919 by the representatives of the United States and Great Britain never actually came into force. To prevent treaty revision, or at least to keep it to an unavoidable minimum, the French until 1935 gave active and directional support to the League of Nations and simultaneously sought military security according to a formula of their own making.

At League and disarmament-conference meetings, the French repeatedly proposed the creation of an international police force and regularly maintained that their existing state of armament was the minimum permissible vis-à-vis Germany's existing state of disarmament. Great Britain and several other large states did not agree with these views and so it happened that successive gatherings were devoted chiefly to quibbling. Paris therefore drew tight lines of alliance with Belgium, Poland, Czechoslovakia, Romania, and Yugoslavia. But in cementing friendships with these countries through political treaties and financial advances, France apparently did not realize that each of her allies also represented a strategic liability. Every one of these allies of France was relatively weak and surrounded by numerous past and potential enemies. And when the test at last came, when Czechoslovakia was in dire need of French help in 1938, France found it inadvisable to fulfill her alliance pledges. For by that time France had come to decide in favor of following the lead of Great Britain in appeasing Germany.

Great Britain, for her part, had steadfastly refused, from 1919 to 1935, to assume any universal commitments for the preservation of peace. Believing that imperial conditions and considerations imposed special obligations and duties on them, the British, at least up to the time of the Italian venture in Ethiopia, preferred to retain their freedom of action in matters of collective security. And without the full support of Great Britain such potentially effective plans of collective security as that outlined in the Geneva Protocol of 1924 had little chance of success.[1]

The British, feeling safe in the possession of a large fleet and content to rely on French armed might to shield them from the bare likelihood of a land attack, were interested chiefly in the revival of the world trade to which their economic system was geared. With the passing of years, more and more British business men came to realize that, whereas Germany had certainly been Great Britain's chief commercial and naval rival before 1914, she had also been one of Britain's best customers. Great Britain therefore came not only to tolerate but to welcome steps which might assist German economic recovery and which, it was hoped, would eventually help British business. Because the continuing international quarrels over reparation, war debts, Rhineland occupation, armaments, and boundaries were harmful to the free revival of trade and commerce, they were irritating to London. And so it came about that the British, feeling relatively secure and anxious mainly to foster world trade, and the French, feeling very much worried over the belligerent talk and warlike activities east of the Rhine and preferring to see Germany weak and internally disorganized rather than commercially prosperous, failed to see eye to eye in their foreign relations and, indeed, often acted at cross purposes.

The London authorities, generally speaking, felt free from any direct foreign threats until about 1935. It was only after the axis had definitely begun to demonstrate its nuisance value and after Italy had precipitated the Ethiopian crisis that Britishers in official circles seemed to wake up to the dangers inherent in Britannia's unprepared position. And now that Nazi Germany was vigorously and rapidly nullifying treaty terms, the British found that whether they wanted it or not, they dared not interpose what could only be inadequate armed resistance. Hence it may have seemed imperative to the Chamberlain Government to temporize and make concessions until such time as armament could be procured in sufficient quantity to implement injunctions with the necessary force. And the French, more fearful now than ever of the Nazi threat, unwilling to injure Italian *amour propre* in the absence of any outright British guarantee of help against German aggression, and torn by internal dissension occasioned by recent do-

[1] See pp. 179–180.

mestic legislation, followed where the British led. The Paris Government, retiring behind the imagined impregnability of the Maginot Line, appeared equally ready with the British to appease an aggressive Germany.

Meanwhile, in Germany, the Weimar Republic had at last lost its fight for existence. From the day of its birth to the day of its death, the German Republic had to meet the opposition, often armed, of extremists from both the Right and Left. Because it depended on the conservative army to do its fighting and because of its own nationalistic bent, the republic generally dealt more severely with radicals than with reactionaries. Because it was determined to uphold democratic forms, the republic extended all the advantages of legal protection to political extremists who themselves were not bothered by legal niceties. Because of its system of proportional representation in national elections, with the consequent presence of more than a score of wrangling parties in the Reichstag, the republic found it difficult to act with dispatch in times of emergency. The task of the republic was made the harder, finally, by its inability to achieve more substantial treaty revision than it did; thus it was unable to meet the challenge of the extreme nationalists who clamored for ever more international concessions. All these things and others paved the way for the onward march of Nazism, a march whose tempo was accelerated by the depression that came to Germany in 1930.

Once in power, the Nazis first concentrated on the coördination, according to their principles, of Germany's internal life and then embarked upon a foreign policy which was, to put it mildly, vigorous. Having made themselves supreme in Germany, the Nazis, motivated by their philosophy of the "master race," proceeded to spread their influence throughout Europe. A master race which wishes to live on a high level must have inferior races to work for it. And, in Nazi opinion, Europe was filled with aged, decrepit peoples who might and must be harnessed to serve the supposedly young and vigorous master race. For the sake of the nuisance value afforded by such a partnership, the Nazis flattered the Italians to the extent of admitting them temporarily into the company of master peoples.

At first the Nazis proceeded with relative caution, taking only one forceful step at a time and following each accomplishment with some form of pledge to make this achievement the last demand of its type. But as success followed success with little more than verbal interference from the presumed defenders of the *status quo,* the Nazis became bolder. They saw no point in stopping when it was so easy to go on. Only then, when the ultimate European aims of the Nazis became clear beyond a doubt, did the British and French, particularly the British, realize that danger threatened not merely the little states of central and eastern Europe, but that peril beckoned the entire British way of life.

Although it remained for Hitler to translate the challenge between the totalitarian and democratic ways of life into action so vigorous that the British and French at last were constrained to fight, it was Mussolini who first specifically formulated that challenge. "The struggle between two worlds," he exclaimed, "can permit no compromise. Either we or they!" Basically, the distinction between the two ideologies lay in their differing conceptions of the position of the individual in the state. Under the democratic conception, as it was generally understood in the Western democracies, the individual was regarded at once as the creator and the rightful beneficiary of all state activity; he might be interfered with only when his doings reacted to the harm of his fellow individuals. The totalitarian conception was wholly anti-individualistic.

The dominant powers of the two camps were divided along economic and territorial as well as spiritual lines. The nations which favored the maintenance of the political and territorial *status quo* were sometimes labeled the "Haves." They had no further immediate expansionist aims. The axis states were the "Have-nots." For reasons of economics, strategy, and prestige they demanded additional territory, old and new. In the cases of Germany and Japan, moreover, there were the additional incentives of political or religious philosophies which contemplated a world revolution culminating in the final hegemony of the respective "master race."

The groups that favored the democratic ideal generally placed an optimistic hope in the financial preëminence of the United States, Great Britain, and France, while those who advocated totalitarian control had confidence in the power of a disciplined will and a readiness to challenge opinion in the "spiritually weak" democracies. By the end of 1938, however, following wholesale German treaty repudiations, the democracies, if spiritually weak, had begun to show a determination to be militarily strong.

The British, for example, had outlined an arms' program to cost $1,500,000,000 per year, had replaced most of the members of the British Army Council with younger men, had completed the naval base at Singapore, and had drafted a plan of conscription to go into effect immediately upon the outbreak of war. The French had oversubscribed successive defense loans and taken various measures to strengthen the ties among the members of the French Empire. In the United States the administration's campaign for increased armament was so energetically fostered that it evoked shrill protests in the press of the totalitarian powers. As early as 1938, moreover, Washington tried, albeit unsuccessfully, to organize a joint American defense against external aggression.[1]

Meanwhile the major repudiation of an international agreement in these years of rearmament among the democracies had been the German denunciation (March 7, 1936) of the Locarno Pact of 1925. The Germans took the position that the Franco-Soviet Pact of 1935, which was presented to the French Parliament for ratification early in 1936, had deprived the Locarno agreement of its "inner meaning." [2] On the very day of Hitler's announcement, German soldiers reëntered the hitherto demilitarized Rhineland zone. The action was denounced in British, French, and other press organs, but no official effort was made to apply sanctions or take reprisals.

The Belgians thereupon showed worry over the self-confidence manifested in the new Germany and the disinclination of the London and Paris authorities to coöperate strongly in the face of German and Italian challenges to the *status quo*. In October 1936, therefore, the Brussels Government announced that henceforth Belgium would pursue an exclusively Belgian policy, would join no alliances, and, like Switzerland and the Netherlands, would remain neutral in any dispute among her neighbors. Eventually Britain and France endorsed this stand and bound themselves to preserve Belgium's integrity while releasing her from all obligations under the Locarno treaties.

The faith of the small states in the promises of their powerful allies was, however, severely shaken in 1938 and 1939 by the events accompanying Germany's absorption of Austria, the

---

[1] In 1936 the United States, Great Britain, and France had signed a new London Naval Treaty providing for the exchange of naval-building information, limiting the size of several categories of vessels, and forbidding the building of new heavy cruisers until 1943. The agreement was not to be binding if any signatory violated the pact or were threatened by war. The Soviet Union adhered to the treaty in 1937 but was not required to give information regarding her Far Eastern fleet. Germany also adhered in 1937 and Italy in 1938. Because of Japan's refusal to furnish information on *its* naval-construction plans, the original signatories modified the relevant treaty terms by a London Protocol of 1938.

[2] Ratifications of the Franco-Soviet Pact were exchanged on March 27, 1936.

Sudeten areas, Czechia, Slovakia, and Memelland, and Italy's occupation of Albania. It was only after all these things had happened that Great Britain and France officially discarded the policy of appeasement that they had for some years been following— partly through lack of military preparedness and partly because of a mistaken belief that a policy of concession would ensure "peace in our time."

In summary, then, the war of 1939 was caused, basically, by these circumstances: The disillusionment and humiliation following military defeat in the First World War filled many Germans with a desire for revenge. Then, the awkward tactics of the republic, an unhappy policy of alternating intransigeance and concession on the part of the former Allies, and the effects of the world depression brought to power in Germany a group whose impelling philosophy it was to establish its hegemony over the continent and eventually beyond the confines of Europe. Meanwhile the British and the French, both intent on maintaining conditions as they were, followed divergent international policies. They drifted apart diplomatically at a time when, from a realistic point of view, they should have coöperated to implement by force of arms the system which they had set up by force of arms. As time went on, there developed a great game of diplomatic bluff, with Germany and Italy playing as partners on one side and Great Britain and France playing as partners on the other. The Soviet Union sat by as an interested observer, leaning now to one side and then the other, determined not to become a pawn no matter how the game progressed. And when at last one side called the other's bluff, the consequence was war. Poland, as it happened, was the unhappy victim of the critical move in the ghastly game played in the spring and summer of 1939.

RENEWED RESORT TO FORCE, 1939

Success for years having followed success in the Nazi campaign for the unilateral revision of the Treaty of Versailles, the Germans late in March 1939 centered their attention on Danzig and the Polish Corridor. Resorting once again to psychological warfare, they now launched a press campaign against alleged anti-German excesses in Poland. This time the British were quick to grasp the Nazi strategy, that of stirring up minorities within neighboring states to the point of disorder and then intervening in the name of order. Hence, on March 31, Prime Minister Chamberlain announced that Great Britain and France would aid the Poles in the event of any threat to their independence. While military preparations were speeded on all sides, Hitler defied the British warning and threatened the Poles with dire consequences if they remained "obstinate."

On April 6 Poland accepted the Franco-British guarantee as a mutual obligation, and one week later Great Britain and France guaranteed the independence of Greece and Romania. Perhaps because Italy had meanwhile absorbed Albania, President Roosevelt on April 15 asked Mussolini as well as Hitler to help the cause of peace by giving a ten-year pledge of nonaggression against thirty-one enumerated states. Both dictators rejected the proposal and on April 28 Germany denounced both her naval agreement of 1935 with Great Britain and her nonaggression pact of 1934 with Poland. Simultaneously she demanded the return of Danzig and the right to maintain a rail and motor road across the Polish Corridor to East Prussia. Poland denied the German demands on May 5, shortly after Maxim Litvinov had left the Soviet Foreign Office and shortly before the conclusion of an Italo-German alliance.

The signing of the Italo-German alliance presented interesting material for reflection. Italy, as we have seen, had emerged in 1928 as the leader of a "revisionist bloc" which demanded a thorough modification of the *status quo* in a direction more acceptable to the dissatisfied signatories of the peace settlement of 1919–1920. The rise to power of Hitler had made it appear for a while that conflicting Italo-German views on Austria might estrange Rome from Berlin, but there were enough congruent elements in the Nazi and Fascist patterns and aims so that even the sudden liquidation of the Austrian problem in 1938 had little outward effect on German-Italian relations. Thereafter, indeed, Italy was content to cede first place among the revisionists to the stronger Reich, and to follow where once she had led. The resulting partnership seemed of considerably more benefit to Germany than to Italy, for, whereas the "nuisance value" of the Rome-Berlin axis brought territorial gains to both partners, Berlin's share greatly exceeded Rome's. At any rate, on May 22, 1939, Foreign Ministers von Ribbentrop and Ciano signed a ten-year alliance at Berlin which provided for diplomatic coöperation and consultation, collaboration in the "field of war economy," and immediate military aid in case either signatory became involved in hostilities. In the event of war, neither power would conclude a separate armistice or peace.

Then, while Great Britain and France came to agreements of mutual assistance with Turkey, Germany signed nonaggression pacts with Denmark, Estonia, and Latvia. In June Hitler began to speak of a new British plan to "encircle" Germany and in July Chamberlain indicated that any unilateral effort to reunite Danzig with the Reich would bring into operation the British guarantee of Polish independence. On July 8 Germany and Italy had agreed on a plan for the transfer to Germany of those Tirolese who preferred not to be Italianized, but in the case of the German minority in Poland, Hitler insisted on territorial cession.

In August, while military and naval conversations were held in Moscow among Soviet, British, and French officers, the German and Polish newspapers began to carry atrocity stories and there occurred a number of clashes involving death for both Germans and Poles. Hitler allowed himself to be driven to fury by the reports which were relayed to him concerning the alleged mistreatment of his "racial comrades" in Poland. Some of his advisers appeared confident that Great Britain and France would in no circumstance fight to save Poland and evidently they convinced the Führer of the soundness of their analysis.

On August 23, 1939, Germany and the Soviet Union, acting through Foreign Ministers von Ribbentrop and Molotov, signed a nonaggression pact. The agreement, effective at once and for ten years, provided that the two parties would in no case resort to war against each other, would not support any third power in the event that it attacked either signatory, would consult in future on all matters of common interest, and would each refrain from associating with any grouping of powers aimed at the other.

The announcement of the Nazi-Soviet Pact generally struck persons like the proverbial bolt from the blue. It was incredible, they said, that after all the Nazi attacks on Bolshevism and the Soviet charges against Nazism, Stalin and Hitler should have become diplomatic partners. And yet, viewed from the vantage point of hindsight, the signing of the treaty was not so astonishing. Germany doubtless wanted the pact to make sure that she would not have to worry about an immediate powerful eastern front in the event that Britain and France really came to Poland's support. Later, when the western states had been defeated, it would be easy to trump up charges of broken faith against Moscow—preferably after the invasion of the Soviet Union had begun. And the U.S.S.R., uncertain of the exact intentions of Britain and France, and herself weakened by recent military purges, needed all the extra time she could get to carry on with the military industrialization contemplated in the Third Five-Year Plan. At the time of its conclusion, the Nazi-Soviet Pact represented *Realpolitik* as much for one signatory as the other.

After the signing of the Nazi-Soviet Treaty, events moved swiftly to a violent conclusion. While military preparations were everywhere rushed, atrocity stories flourished, and neutral peace pleas filled the diplomatic atmosphere, Hitler became more and more demanding on Poland. The world waited breathlessly for the news that would mean peace or war, while tense conversations were held among Britishers, Germans, and Poles.

On August 29 Germany demanded from Great Britain, who held that direct discussions might yet lead to a peaceable solution of the Polish-German problem, that she arrange to have a Polish delegate with full powers to negotiate reach Berlin on the thirtieth. On the latter date the British explained that such a procedure was unreasonable and the time limit impracticable; London therefore urged that Germany follow the usual diplomatic procedure of transmitting her demands on Poland through the Polish Ambassador. When Ribbentrop received these advices from the British Ambassador at midnight, he replied by reading in German "at top speed" a sixteen-point proposal for the settlement of all German-Polish differences. But when Sir Nevile Henderson asked for a copy of the text of these proposals, Ribbentrop "asserted that it was now too late as (the) Polish representative had not arrived in Berlin by midnight."

On the next day, August 31, the German Government broadcast the sixteen points; but when the Polish Ambassador tried to communicate the terms officially to his foreign minister, he was unable to do so because Berlin had cut all communications between the two countries. The Nazis then managed to interpret as a rejection of their peace overtures the Polish Government's failure to send a plenipotentiary on twenty-four hours' notice to accept a quasi-ultimatum which had not yet been communicated to the Warsaw authorities. About five o'clock in the morning of September 1, therefore, Germany, without declaring war, sent its planes to rain bombs on Polish cities and its soldiers to invade the Polish countryside. And against such a background, Hitler announced: "No other means is left to me than to meet force with force." (!)

Fifty hours later, on September 3, after a German refusal to withdraw from the territory it already had occupied and attend an international conference of the great powers and Poland, Chamberlain informed the House of Commons that "this country is at war with Germany." The French Government adopted a similar view of the situation. Italy, as in 1914, declared her intention to remain neutral. And thus, twenty-five years and one month after the outbreak of the First World War, Europe entered the Second World War.

THE FIFTH PARTITION OF POLAND

In the war which thus broke out in 1939, the Polish army had little opportunity to prove its worth. Well-trained and well-led as it was thought to be, it was overwhelmed in less than a month by the mechanized might of Germany. Because Warsaw hesitated to order general mobilization until the last stage of political negotiations with Berlin, because Poland had few natural defenses on her western border, because Germany was kept fully informed by sympathizers of the day-by-day state of Polish preparations, because the Nazis disregarded the customary legal formalities preceding the opening of armed combat, and because the Germans had for some time been preparing for a drive on Poland, they were able, in a military sense, to "surprise" the Polish defenders and overwhelm them before the republic's armies were fully mobilized or properly concentrated.

The German forces, commanded by Colonel-General Walther von Brauchitsch, were equipped with heavy tanks, armored cars, motorcycle squadrons, heavy and light artillery, and efficient antitank and antiaircraft guns. Preceded and accompanied by hundreds of bombers and other war planes, the mechanized units and infantry entered Poland simultaneously from East Prussia, Pomerania, Silesia, and Slovakia. The suddenness of the onslaught made it possible for the invaders to destroy most of the Polish air force on the ground, and the German *Panzerdivisionen* or armored divisions traversed even the muddiest roads and cut-up fields of the Polish plain with relative ease. The loss of her air arm deprived Poland of her best means of reconnaissance, while the Germans, well aware of Poland's military dispositions, were able to disrupt communications behind the lines, prevent and break up formations, and terrorize the municipal populations and the refugees on the cluttered roads. On the first day of the fighting, moreover, the Nazi leader of Danzig, Albert Forster, proclaimed the reunion of the Free City with the Reich—an overture accepted with alacrity by Reichsführer Hitler.

Inasmuch as Great Britain and France, fifty hours after the invasion began, declared themselves to be at war with Germany, Poland hoped for aid from her allies. Such help might have taken two forms: aerial assistance and an attempt to divert German strength from Poland by a major attack on the Reich's western border. Actually, aid in neither form was forthcoming: German air superiority combined with the fact that Poland's air fields were destroyed made it little short of impossible to send French or British planes to Poland's support; and the French army, with its psychology of supposed security behind the Maginot Line and its apparent belief in the equal impregnability of the German West Wall, did not launch any large-scale attack.[1]

Meanwhile the Polish infantry and cavalry, heroic but only partially mobilized and unable properly to coöperate, retreated steadily before the advancing enemy. Within two weeks most of Poland's western provinces were occupied and Warsaw was virtually surrounded. Then, while the capital, under its gallant mayor, Stefan Starzynski, called "Stefan the Stubborn," defied bombings and bombardments for three weeks, several Polish armies withdrew to the south and east, hoping, apparently, to establish a new line along the Dniester River and there await direct Anglo-French aid through Romania. But then, on September 17, the soldiers of the Soviet Union poured into eastern Poland, ostensibly to protect the Ukrainian and White Russian minorities living there. President Mościcki, Foreign Minister Beck, and Marshal Śmigly-Rydz thereupon fled to Romania, where they were interned, and on September 27 battered Warsaw surrendered. Save for the brief further resistance of a few scattered Polish groups, the fighting now came to an end.

[1] On September 4, the day after Britain's entry into the war, the British steamship *Athenia,* en route from Liverpool to Canada and carrying several hundred citizens of the United States as well as about a thousand others, was sunk by torpedo without warning about 250 miles off the northwest coast of Ireland. "Unrestricted" submarine warfare thus got off to an early start in the Second World War. Eight days later, on September 12, an Anglo-French Supreme War Council, with Prime Minister Chamberlain as the chief British delegate and Premier Daladier as the leading French delegate, had its first meeting, on French soil.

On September 28, 1939, Foreign Ministers von Ribbentrop and Molotov signed another German-Soviet Treaty. This, according to its preamble, was supposed to "restore law and order" in the area affected by the "disintegration of the Polish State." Actually, it partitioned the defeated republic, with its area of 150,000 square miles and its 35,000,000 inhabitants, between its two powerful neighbors.

The German-Soviet boundary was made to run through the old Poland approximately in a line reaching from the southwestern tip of Lithuania to the northeastern edge of Hungary. The Soviet Union acquired slightly more than half the territory but only fourteen million of the people. Both conquerors gained large agricultural stretches. Germany, furthermore, secured much of the mineral and manufacturing wealth of the former Poland, while the Soviet Union established control over the bulk of its oil resources. In October 1939 the Moscow Government ceded to Lithuania the city and district of Vilnius, long a bone of contention between that Baltic state and Poland.[1]

President Mościcki, in Romania, resigned his office on September 30 and, as was his constitutional right, named Wladislaw Raczkiewicz as his successor. The latter then appointed a new cabinet, headed by General Wladislaw Sikorski. This Polish Government, having been accorded British and French recognition, set itself up at Angers in France where it received extraterritorial privileges and the right to receive foreign representatives. After the defeat of France, the government moved to Great Britain, where sizable Polish forces were reorganized to continue the fight against Germany. Thus was completed the fifth partition of Poland, following those of 1772, 1793, 1795, and 1815. Truly, "when in existence Poland constantly stands on the threshold of dismemberment, and yet when it is gone, there is constantly the promise of reincarnation."

And what of the fate of the inhabitants of partitioned Poland? In the provinces annexed by the Soviet Union, called "Western Ukraine" and "Western White Russia," a majority of the inhabitants were peasants, racially akin to their neighbors in the U.S.S.R. There were, however, large Polish and Jewish minorities, which formed the bulk of the manorial, professional, and commercial classes. The Moscow Government therefore advanced the claim that, by sending its soldiers into Poland, it had "liberated" millions of oppressed comrades. Then, with the Red Army look-

[1] See pp. 535–536.

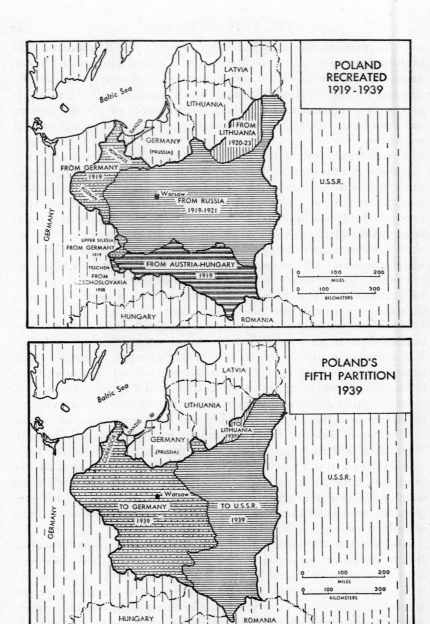

POLAND: RECREATED AND REPARTITIONED

From MacFadden, C. H., *An Atlas of World Review,* New York,
Thomas Y. Crowell Company, 1940. Reprinted by permission.

ing on, provincial assemblies were chosen which voted almost unanimously for union with the U.S.S.R. The Soviet Union agreed (November 1–2, 1939) to comply with the requests and the former Polish territories were incorporated in the Ukrainian and White Russian constituent republics of the U.S.S.R. The subsequent fate of the clergy, nonpeasant groups, and others whose political views were at variance with those of Stalin remained largely unknown.[1]

About 36,000 square miles of western Poland, which before 1919 had belonged to Prussia, Russia, and Austria, were directly incorporated by Germany in October 1939. The place names were then changed to German, so that Gdynia, for example, was renamed Gotenhafen, and Lodz, the center of the Polish textile industry, became Litzmannstadt. The small industrial Teschen area, which Poland had acquired during the partition of Czechoslovakia in 1938, was allotted to "independent" Slovakia. The remainder of western Poland, another region of about thirty-six thousand square miles, was converted into a "Gouvernement-Général" with its capital at Cracow and Dr. Hans Frank as its administrative head.

Eventual German intentions regarding this area were not made clear—perhaps because they were not clear in the minds of the Nazi leaders. But it appeared that the territory was to be used, at least temporarily, as a depository for Poles and Jews who had been or were to be removed from their original domiciles and herded into this one crowded area. The Polish and other lands vacated by their unfortunate inhabitants were to be converted into new homesteads for the 1,500,000 "Germans" still living in scattered parts of Europe, in the Tirol, for example, the Baltic states, and former eastern Poland. The task of organizing these transfers of population was placed in the hands of the much-feared head of the secret police (*Gestapo,* from *Geheime Staats-Polizei*), Heinrich Himmler. He apparently planned to exterminate the Jews and many Poles and force the remainder of the latter to act as servants for the supposed German master race.

The lot of those German-speaking people compulsorily transferred from places, such as the Tirol and the Baltic regions, where their families had lived for centuries, was bad; official sentiment towards them, however, was summarized by one Nazi paper in the

---

[1] After the Nazi invasion of the U.S.S.R., the Polish Government-in-Exile and the Soviet Government signed a treaty (July 30, 1941) in which the German-Soviet partition of Poland was declared null and void.

words: "Baltic Germans will not have the leisure to look backwards, but will be put straight into their new surroundings." But the lot of the non-Germanic victims of this policy was terrible. Western Poles, for example, were either forced into the Gouvernement-Général, where the cities rapidly became overcrowded, or were carried off by the thousands to work in German fields, or, at best, were ordered to raise on their own farms specified crops and then to surrender portions thereof to the conquerors.

By and large, the usage of Polish peasants was perhaps the least cruel of any; the harshest treatment was reserved for the clerical, professional, and commercial classes. The Germans regarded these as the leaders and the ones most likely to keep the flame of Polish nationalism alight, hence they marked them for annihilation. Polish participation in the trades and professions was everywhere reduced to a minimum, and intermarriage or even "comradeship" between Poles and Germans was forbidden. The cruelties perpetrated on the Jews were even greater. There was talk of the establishment of a Jewish Reserve in and around Lublin, and tens of thousands of Jews from all German-controlled territories in Europe were forced into one huge ghetto.

An interesting source of information on the executions, mass shootings, plundering, and destitution in Poland was a series of revelations made by the primate of Poland, Auguste Cardinal Hlond, who was an eyewitness of much that happened but who succeeded in escaping from the German-occupied area. Meanwhile the Nazi officials evidently found it necessary to steel even their own followers against some of the things that were going on. "You must remain hard," Dr. Robert Ley told one group, and, "a German can never live in the same condition as a Pole or a Jew," he informed a second. "We must inject a dose of iron into our spinal column," said another administrator, in demanding the "ruthless fulfillment of orders." The Poles, however, still seemed to have faith in a saying of the eighteenth century, that Poland can be swallowed, but never digested.

PRECAUTIONS OF THE SOVIET UNION, 1939–1940

The occupation of eastern Poland marked only the beginning of the Soviet Union's policy of erecting buffers between herself and Germany. On September 29, 1939, the day after Germany and the U.S.S.R. partitioned Poland, the Moscow Government signed a pact of mutual assistance with Estonia. Within less than two weeks similar pacts were signed with Latvia and Lithuania. In each case the Soviet Government had summoned the respective foreign minister to Moscow and there apparently convinced him of the desirability of acquiescence. The three treaties resembled each other closely. Always the contracting parties agreed to come to each other's aid in the event or menace of aggression by a third power. The U.S.S.R. promised to furnish arms and other military equipment "on favorable terms" to each of the other signatories. To ensure greater all-around safety, the Soviet Union acquired the right to maintain naval bases and aerodromes in each of the Baltic republics; the allotted sites were to remain the "territory" of the present sovereign, but they were to be defended by Soviet "land and air armed forces." Each signatory agreed not to enter any alliance or coalition aimed at a co-signatory.

Moscow promised, in the three pacts, that nothing would be done to impair the sovereignty or interfere with the political, economic, or social systems of the Baltic states. But the early dispatch of Soviet garrisons, in each case larger than the peacetime army of the republic concerned, boded ill for the independence of these former parts of the Tsarist Empire. The circumstance that the Nazi Government immediately began the repatriation of Baltic citizens of German descent lent color to the general belief that Berlin, willingly or unwillingly, had expressed prior approval of the Soviet Union's tactics.

Keeping pace with German victories and gains, the Soviet Union on June 14, 1940, the very day on which Nazi soldiers entered Paris by the Aubervilliers Gate, presented an ultimatum to the Lithuanian Government. The document complained of the kidnapping of some Red soldiers and the violation by Lithuania of the pact of mutual assistance. It demanded free passage for Soviet troops and the replacement of the government by one which would "enjoy the confidence" of Moscow. On the following day Soviet soldiers occupied Lithuania and on June 16 similar ultimata were sent to Latvia and Estonia. These two states also were accused of having violated the assistance pact, through mutual failure to cancel a previous military alliance, and were told to permit the free passage of Red soldiers and to change their governments. In all three cases the governments resigned at once and the territories were occupied by the Red Army. Soviet warships quickly appeared in the Baltic harbors.

While things appeared so easy of accomplishment and the international situation was favorable, Moscow also presented an ultimatum to Romania. On June 26, 1940, the Soviet Union, in the interest of "justice," demanded from the Balkan kingdom, already torn by internal dissension and foreign fears, the immediate "return" of the province of Bessarabia. The ultimatum pointed out that, in "robbing" Bessarabia in 1918, Romania had torn it from a century-old unity with the Ukraine. Hence the Bessarabians must now be restored to the fold of their Ukrainian racial brethren in the U.S.S.R. In addition, Romania was to give up northern Bukovina, whose inhabitants also were said to be "connected" with the Soviet Union through a "community of historic destinies" and through linguistic ties. This demand was called "all the more justified" since the surrender of Bukovina would represent "a compensation, if only an unimportant one," for the sufferings and losses of the Soviet Union and Bessarabia in the twenty-two years during which the latter was subject to Romania.

The government of King Carol II appealed to Berlin and Rome for advice—and apparently was told to meet the Soviet demands lest the war spread to the Balkans. Accordingly, on June 27, 1940, Soviet troops began the occupation of Bessarabia and northern Bukovina. This time the gain to the U.S.S.R. was twenty-one thousand square miles and four million people. Romania's loss, moreover, was destined to be even greater, for now Bulgaria and Hungary were encouraged to present additional demands; but this story must be left for later.[1] Meanwhile the Soviet Union had made further territorial gains in the north, but for these, made at the expense of Finland, she had had to fight.

The Soviet Government doubtless felt somewhat more at ease, strategically, after the acquisition in September–October 1939 of the right to establish naval and air bases in three of the four Baltic republics. But it simultaneously professed uneasines over the circumstance that the land and sea approaches to Leningrad (via Finland and the Gulf of Finland) were still largely in foreign hands. Moscow therefore adopted the same tactics vis-à-vis Finland that she was so successfully pursuing with Estonia, Latvia, and Lithuania. On October 5, 1939, the Soviet Government invited Helsinki to send a negotiator to the Kremlin.

It quickly became clear, however, that Finland would not remain so passive as did her sister republics. The government, indeed, advised the inhabitants in certain border cities to move into the interior of the country. By October 14 the Bolsheviks pre-

[1] See p. 797.

sented a specific set of demands. Pointing out that the industrial and commercial center of Leningrad, with its population of 3,200,000, was only twenty miles removed from the Finnish frontier, the Soviet Union demanded: (1) the cession of a number of islands in the Gulf of Finland; (2) the surrender of part of the Karelian Isthmus so as to put Leningrad outside effective artillery range from foreign-controlled soil; (3) the cession of some land in the extreme north, on the Rybachi Peninsula, so as to ensure Soviet dominance of the Finnish Arctic outlet at Petsamo; (4) the demilitarization of the Soviet-Finnish frontier; and (5) a thirty-year lease of the port of Hangö and adjacent land for the establishment of a Soviet naval base. In return, Moscow offered to give Finland 2134 square miles of Soviet territory on the east-central border of the republic.

Finland was prepared to acquiesce in most of the demands, but firmly refused, as incompatible with her neutrality, to lease, or, as the Soviets later proposed, sell the site for a foreign military base. The negotiations finally broke down in the middle of November. After an interval of about a week, the Red press began to heap abuse on the Helsinki authorities. Finland's "obstinacy" was berated and warnings were uttered of dire consequences. Soon Finnish soldiers were accused of having fired at a Soviet border patrol and then, after Helsinki refused to withdraw any troops from the frontier unless Moscow did likewise, the Bolsheviks denounced the Finnish nonaggression pact of 1932. Ignoring a proposal to renew negotiations, the Soviet Government on November 30, 1939, ordered its airplanes and soldiers to cross the frontier for war. And on the next day Moscow recognized a puppet "People's Government," set up near the Soviet border by Otto Kuusinen—who had been living as an exile, mostly in the U.S.S.R., for twenty years. While the regularly constituted government moved to defend Finland's borders and appealed to the League of Nations for help, the Kuusinen Cabinet granted the original Soviet demands.

The League acted with unwonted speed, probably because of the widespread indignation and because the U.S.S.R. responded to a note by claiming not to be at war with Finland. On December 14, 1939, the Soviet Union was declared the aggressor and expelled from the League as unworthy of membership. The Secretariat was authorized to coördinate whatever assistance the individual League members might feel disposed to lend Finland.

Thus left to their own devices, many League members sent

foodstuffs, medical supplies, and implements of war. Volunteers flocked to the Finnish colors and even Italy sent some airplanes. But any really effective accretion of fighting power was denied Finland by the stand of her neighbors, Norway and Sweden. Although Finland declared that she was fighting as an outpost of Western civilization, and although Norway and especially Sweden permitted almost unlimited private help, the two Scandinavian kingdoms firmly denied the right of passage to any of the thousands of soldiers whom France and Great Britain were willing to send to Finland's aid. At the beginning of March 1940 the two great powers apparently held one hundred thousand men in readiness for embarkation to Scandinavia, but Norway and Sweden, cowed by German threats, refused them free passage. Finland therefore never even made the official request for aid which London and Paris were awaiting; such action would only have caused embarrassment to her would-be helpers without being of any actual assistance. Thus Finland, with her population of 4,000,000, was left to fight it out with the Soviet Union and her 180,000,000.

Soviet strategy called for a five-fold invasion of Finland. In the north, one force was sent to capture Petsamo and another to take the railroad which connected Kemijärvi with Tornea on the Swedish border. A third army struck at Suomussalmi in an effort to cut through Finland at its "waist." Still another force moved along the northern shore of Lake Ladoga to carry out a flanking movement against the Mannerheim Line which, protecting the Karelian Isthmus, was itself the objective of a fifth Soviet army.

The defense of the Mannerheim Line, cleverly organized in depth on a plan similar to that of the French and German "walls," was entrusted to the experienced anti-Bolshevik fighter, General Baron Karl Gustav von Mannerheim. Here for weeks the Soviet troops exhausted themselves with little gain. Along the other fronts the Bolsheviks, though generally more successful, suffered high casualties. For the Finns, apparently less hampered than the invaders by the Arctic blasts and blizzards, fought stubbornly against great odds. The Soviet Command, moreover, made several mistakes. It launched its offensives with inadequately trained men. It neglected to provide proper transportation security for supplies. And it failed to ensure coördination among the armies.

Eventually the Reds decided to take firmer hold of the situation. Concentrating on the Mannerheim Line, they brought into the battle many more and better troops. The energetic General

Gregory Stern was placed in charge of operations. First-class artillery with a greater range than that of the Finnish guns was brought into action and, according to report, three hundred thou-

THE FINNISH-SOVIET WAR, 1939–1940

sand shells per day were dropped on the concrete fortifications. At last, through sheer weight of numbers and after many Finnish gun emplacements had been uprooted, the Bolsheviks, toward the end of January 1940, made a breach in the Line. Finnish cities meanwhile were being subjected to frequent bombings.

At the beginning of March 1940 the first Soviet soldiers entered the suburbs of Viipuri. Then, on March 12, while Great Britain and France dispatched a formal request to Norway and Sweden for the free passage of their men, Finnish representatives already were in Moscow receiving Stalin's peace terms. A few hours later the Treaty of Moscow brought a stilling of the guns. Helsinki later announced that sixteen thousand Finns had been killed in the war, and Moscow, forty-nine thousand Russians.

The terms of the treaty were far more exacting than had been the original demands of the U.S.S.R. Finland was made to cede (1) the entire Karelian Isthmus; (2) her second largest city, Viipuri, and the islands in its bay; (3) territory to the north and west of Lake Ladoga, so that this largest lake in Europe came to lie wholly within Soviet borders; (4) most of the islands in the Gulf of Finland; (5) a sizable triangle of land to the northeast, in the Salla region; and (6) enough of the Rybachi Peninsula to give the Soviet Union dominance over the Arctic port of Petsamo and the nearby nickel mines.

Finland also agreed to extend her northern railway eastward from Kemijärvi to meet a line which the Bolsheviks proposed to build westward from Kandalaksha on the Murmansk Railroad. Soviet citizens were given the right of free transit for themselves and, with limited restrictions, for their goods across the Petsamo region to and from Norway. No Finnish war vessels or military aircraft might be stationed in or adjacent to the republic's Arctic waters. The U.S.S.R. was permitted for thirty years to lease Hangö and some adjacent land and water; the area would be converted into a Soviet naval base. The two signatories agreed in future to refrain from acts of aggression against each other and to abstain from membership in coalitions aimed at each other. (Four months later, the Soviet Union demanded and got the right to use the Finnish railways for shipping men and supplies to the Hangö base; until then, contact had been by sea only.)

The Soviet Union organized the new territories into the Karelian-Finnish Socialist Federated Soviet Republic and thus added another to the constituent republics of the U.S.S.R. But most of the former inhabitants of this area, numbering more than

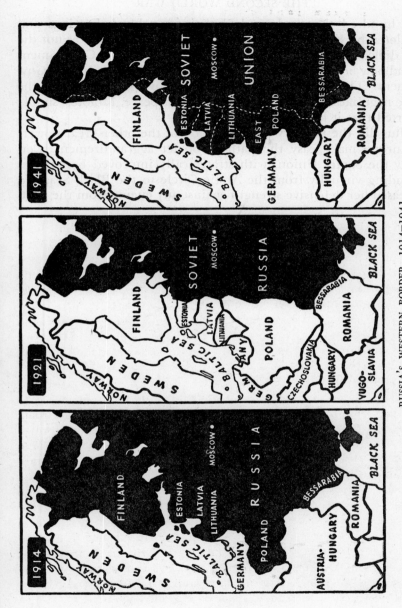

RUSSIA'S WESTERN BORDER, 1914–1941

From *Russia at War*, Headline Book No. 34, Foreign Policy Association, New York, 1942.

four hundred thousand, packed their movable belongings and wandered back across the new border into Finland. It was not the least difficult reconstruction problem of the Helsinki Government to find new homes for these loyal subjects. And the Kuusinen Government? That had been forgotten even by Moscow during the peace negotiations; after the conclusion of peace, Molotov simply reported that it had "dissolved itself."

Thus did the military preoccupation of the other great powers of Europe make easy the path of Soviet aggrandizement. Certainly the Soviet Union, with strategically improved boundaries extending virtually from the Arctic Circle to the Black Sea, had increased her defensive strength against any enemy from the west.

CHAPTER XXV

Sitzkrieg and Blitzkrieg in the West

THE WAR IN THE WEST, SEPTEMBER 1939–MARCH 1940

Following the close of the campaign in Poland, Hitler addressed the Reichstag saying: "Why should this war in the west be fought? For restoration of Poland? Poland of the Versailles Treaty will never rise again. This is guaranteed by two of the largest states in the world." Following the technique used in many of his earlier speeches, he then went on to point out that, with the "obsolescence" of the Versailles Treaty, Germany no longer had any "demands" to make save that "for the return of German colonies." If his peace offer were refused, he would have no further statement to make. "Then we shall fight."

As was to be expected, both France and Great Britain expressed a determination to carry on until more effective guarantees against aggression were forthcoming than Hitler's "unsupported word." Premier Daladier asked: "What people can ever feel that it has any protection against aggression if every six months, in spite of a pledged word, it has to look on at the annexation or partition of another people which has equal right to live a free and independent existence?" And Chamberlain rejected the German proposals as being simply based on a plea for recognition of Hitler's conquests "and his right to do what he pleases with the conquered." In any case, the Führer's "repeated disregard of his word" and "sudden reversals of policy" made it impracticable any longer "to rely upon the unsupported word of the present German Government." There was to be no further effort at appeasement. The war in the west had to be fought.

Benefiting by some costly lessons of the First World War, the Allies [1] in 1939 were quick to create unified military, naval, and

[1] All the British Dominions save Ireland quickly joined the mother country in the war. Australia and New Zealand entered at once, on September 3; the Union of

751

air commands. British officers were placed in charge of the Allied sea and air forces, and General Gamelin became commander of the Allied armies. In the first five weeks of the war, 158,000 British soldiers were transported to France.

For a time there was so little military activity on the western front that newspapers in the United States wrote of a "phony" war. Neither side, it appeared, cared to risk the disproportionate casualties that presumably would accompany an offensive against "impregnable" defenses. Certain French leaders, in particular, had become so steeped in a "Maginot psychology" and were so certain that the enemy could be worn down in a war of attrition, that they firmly refused to start "a new battle of Verdun." Hence, while the Germans were busy conquering Poland and consolidating their latest gains, the Allies contented themselves with capturing a few advance posts inside the western German border. Then, when thousands upon thousands of Germans, freed from duty in the east, were sent to the West Wall, the Allied soldiers were gradually withdrawn from German soil and put to work on improving the French defensive positions. Only occasional artillery duels and clashes of patrols gave evidence of the existing state of war.

The Germans, too, confined their land activities to bringing more troops up to the French border, and to those of Belgium and the Netherlands. In November 1939 and January 1940 there were "scares" in both monarchies lest the Germans invade them in an effort to outflank the Maginot Line; but the threat did not materialize until the spring. The frequent German warnings of the awful onslaughts to come apparently were not taken seriously by the French Command. And so it happened that the only *Blitz* or "lightning" of the winter of 1939–1940 was that provided by the weather—the severest in half a century.

The war in the air also was of casual nature during the first six months of hostilities. Neither side appeared willing to start the bombing of cities, the disruption of communication lines, or the destruction of manufacturing plants. Civilians were equipped with and instructed in the use of gas masks; some city children were evacuated to presumably safer country districts; nightly blackouts were imposed on coastal and industrial regions; and numerous air-raid shelters were constructed; but deadly combat was confined largely to clashing patrols.

South Africa on September 6, after a parliamentary defeat for Prime Minister James B. M. Hertzog, who favored neutrality, and his replacement by Jan C. Smuts; and Canada on September 10.

To many observers it appeared as a joke that British planes for months dropped only leaflets on Germany. But now, with the benefit of hindsight, it seems likely that many British pilots acquired on these apparently useless flights a thorough knowledge of German geography and the location of strategic and industrial sites. It may well be that much of the later success of British night flyers over Germany was owing to experience gained in these early reconnaissance trips. In December 1939, moreover, plans were completed for the training of British pilots in Australia, New Zealand, and Canada, far from the scene of combat and relatively safe from hostile interference. Eventually this circumstance was to prove of almost incalculable value to Great Britain in her great fight following the collapse of France.

The naval aspects of the war were spectacular even in 1939. The combined British and French fleets had a tonnage almost nine times that of the German—about 2,000,000 tons to 235,000—but there were tens of thousands of miles of sea lanes that had to be guarded against German raiders and submarines. It early became evident that the German naval commander, Grand Admiral Erich Raeder, intended to put into immediate practice the system of unrestricted submarine warfare advocated by his predecessor of German imperial days, Grand Admiral von Tirpitz. Once again it was to be British blockade versus German submarines, with the surface units of the German fleet generally remaining in the protected waters adjacent to the mainland. As in the First World War, also, Winston Churchill became Britain's First Lord of the Admiralty.

At the beginning of the war, the merchant marines of the British Empire and France had a tonnage of about 20,000,000. Of this total, 800,000 tons had been destroyed by the end of March 1940, that is, after seven months of fighting. In this same period, moreover, the British, through seizures of enemy ships, new construction, and transfers from neutral registries, recouped about five-sixths of their losses. To speed up their campaign, the Germans also torpedoed neutral ships and then resorted to the indiscriminate sowing of mines—some of them planted by airplanes and some so constructed as to function magnetically. Eventually, after some heavy losses, the British found that girding potential victims with metal cables considerably lessened the menace of these magnetic mines. Meanwhile the oceans had virtually been cleared of German merchant shipping.

One great naval battle there was in these early months of the war: the Battle of the (River) Plate. This involved, on the one side, the German pocket battleship *Admiral Graf Spee;* and on the other, the heavy cruiser *Exeter* and, after a while, the light cruisers *Ajax* and *Achilles.* The *Admiral Graf Spee* had been built with an eye to commerce raiding and was accompanied by a specially designed supply ship, the *Altmark,* which also, from time to time, took off the warship's prisoners. In striking power and gun range the German battleship was superior to the entire British squadron; but she lacked the speed of the smaller ships.

On December 13, 1939, the *Admiral Graf Spee,* cruising southward along the coast of Uruguay, sighted the French steamer *Formose,* escorted by the British cruiser *Exeter.* The Germans offered battle but after a time found themselves in less favored position when the light cruisers *Ajax* and *Achilles* appeared in response to a call from the *Exeter.* Although the battleship's eleven-inch guns had put out of action all but one of the *Exeter's* guns, the Germans tried to evade further battle with the small cruisers. But these, by making the best use of their superior speed and gunnery, laying down alternate smoke screens, and sending out an airplane to "spot" their fire, forced the fight and eventually, after a sixteen-hour battle, drove the battered *Admiral Graf Spee* into the harbor of Montevideo.

The Uruguayan authorities, after a wordy three-cornered diplomatic battle, ordered the warship to leave the harbor within four days. In this time it was not possible fully to repair the damage done to the vessel, which thus faced the prospect of heading out to sea for a renewal of the battle with the waiting British ships. (The *Cumberland,* meanwhile, had come up to replace the *Exeter.*) The Berlin Government, however, forestalled such action by ordering the scuttling of the ship. Shortly before the time limit expired, the captain took his ship about three miles offshore and scuttled it. Three days later, while his crew was being interned in Buenos Aires, he committed suicide.

A lively "epilogue" to the battle was provided in the later adventures of the *Altmark.* With about three hundred British seamen aboard as prisoners, she eluded British armed searchers for two months. Not until the middle of February 1940 was she found by British planes—and by that time she was heading south along the Norwegian coast, presumably safe in neutral waters. British warships soon appeared and demanded that Norway bring about the release of the prisoners unlawfully held on an armed belligerent ship in neutral territorial waters. During the parleys the *Altmark* slipped into the shelter of an ice-filled fjord, and when the Norwegian negotiations led nowhere, the British cruiser *Cossack,* on direct orders from the admiralty, went into the fjord after her. The *Altmark* now tried to ram the smaller ship but the latter was so skillfully handled as to avoid mishap. A boarding party leaped onto the decks of the German ship and after some hand-to-hand fighting the British sailors rescued their comrades. The *Altmark* remained aground in the fjord. Again there was a vigorous diplomatic correspondence among the three principals, but the matter naturally remained where it stood.

Leaving for later consideration the whole question of the relation of the United States to the war, we must here note three additional occurrences of these first seven months of the struggle. One was the signing, in October 1939, of a tripartite alliance among Great Britain, France, and Turkey. Long fearful of Italian ambitions in the eastern Mediterranean, and grateful to France for her part in making easier the Turkish acquisition during the previous June of the former Syrian district of Alexandretta,[1] the Ankara Government was ready to enter into diplomatic partnership with the Allies.

The treaty provided that France and Britain would aid Turkey in the event that she were attacked by a European power or became involved in war as a consequence of Mediterranean hostilities resulting from the aggression of any European power. In return, Turkey promised to help the Allies "in the event of an act of aggression by a European Power leading to war in the Mediterranean area in which France and the United Kingdom are involved." Turkey also agreed to aid the Allies if they became involved in hostilities while carrying out their guarantees to Romania and Greece. According to a protocol, however, Turkey's obligations were not to be effective vis-à-vis the U.S.S.R.

To avoid competitive bidding and to strengthen their economic position, Britain and France set up an Anglo-French Coördinating Committee. This agency was to organize the economic warfare, fix priorities, and in general supervise the activities of a number of intergovernmental committees established to coördinate the Allies' production and purchases of munitions, oil, aviation equipment, foodstuffs, shipping, coal, timber, and other commodities. Later an agreement was reached virtually making the British and French currencies interchangeable. There appears, in consequence, to have been effective and efficient collaboration in shipping, purchasing, and finance. There was talk, also, of eventual cultural,

---

[1] See pp. 328–329.

educational, and even parliamentary collaboration, but the events of spring 1940 put a very sudden stop to such plans.

The final item to be considered at this time was a change in the French Government. Daladier, reputed to be a "strong man" despite his weakness during the riots of 1934, seemed to enjoy general confidence in the fall of 1939. His strong measures against the communists in the early days of war—the suspension of communist municipal councilors and the unseating of most of the communist parliamentary deputies—were generally approved, even by the Socialists who, since the signing of the Nazi-Soviet Pact, seemed to have lost their faith in Moscow. But this popularity gradually waned as the public became increasingly dissatisfied with the leisurely prosecution of the war and especially with the failure to give more direct aid to Finland. The forced acceptance of an unfavorable peace by Finland was soon followed by the resignation of Daladier. He was succeeded (March 1940) by Paul Reynaud, until then minister of finance.

Reynaud generally had the confidence of French finance and was known to have been an opponent of appeasement. He was regarded as energetic and patriotic and a firm believer in democracy. But even he was not especially well received by the chamber. Some felt that his appointment of a "war cabinet" of nine members boded ill for the necessary efficiency in government direction. Others objected because he included three Socialists in the cabinet for the sake of national unity. Perhaps some Radical Socialists were jealous that their leader, Daladier, was now only war minister instead of prime minister. Unfortunately, it was not until after the middle of May that Reynaud had the fortitude to drop Daladier from the war ministry. Only thereafter (June) was he able to promote to a brigadier generalship and bring into the cabinet as undersecretary for war, Charles Joseph de Gaulle, leading, but hitherto unheeded, French advocate of mechanized warfare. Reynaud as a civilian had long shared de Gaulle's views as these were frequently expressed in writing; but the two men were not in position effectively to coöperate until it was too late. Too late, because the German mechanized advance was about to begin.

THREE MONTHS OF BLITZKRIEG, APRIL—JUNE 1940

Winston Churchill on one occasion tersely described what appeared as the chief obstacle to an effective blockade of Germany from the west. Speaking of the Norwegian territorial waters, he said:

The existence of this geographical and legal covered way has been the greatest disadvantage which we have suffered and the greatest advantage which Germany possessed in her efforts to frustrate the British and Allied blockade. Warships moved up and down it as they thought it convenient. U-boats used it as they thought it convenient. Stray German liners and merchant ships, trying to get back to Germany from the outer seas, followed this route, which is over 800 miles long, and can be entered or quitted at any convenient point.

There was ample evidence that these observations were accurate. Perhaps the most spectacular case of a "stray liner" reaching safety via this route was that of the *Bremen*. Having left New York shortly before the Nazi invasion of Poland, she succeeded first in reaching Murmansk, and then in making her home port by traveling down the long, much-indented Norwegian coast. But more important, in the long run, was Germany's ability to get shipload after shipload of high-grade Swedish iron ore by the same safe route. Swedish ore was carried westward from the mines by rail to the Norwegian port of Narvik, there loaded on freighters, and then taken down in territorial waters as far as the Skagerrak. From there onward the ships were fairly well protected by German minefields and other defenses.

During the First World War, in similar circumstances, the Allies eventually had been able to prevail upon Norway to strew mines in her own territorial waters; but in 1939–1940 Oslo refused to take such action. Indeed, the Norwegian navy now actually provided escorts for the iron-carrying freighters, on the ground that the kingdom was in duty bound to keep her waters "open to all legitimate traffic by ships belonging to belligerent countries." And yet, only two days before Norway gave this reason for permitting the German traffic, her foreign minister had deplored the illegal sinking, presumably by Germany, of numerous Norwegian merchant vessels, with considerable loss of lives. Obviously all the Scandinavian Governments, relying on Britain's reasonable observance of international law, were worried by the constant German threats of what would happen unless their actions conformed to Berlin's interpretation of "neutrality." Hoping against hope that they might again be as fortunate as they were in 1914–1918, they figuratively were treading on eggs. Unfortunately, despite their greatest care, the eggs were smashed—for them, not by them.

On the morning of April 8, 1940, the Allied Governments informed Oslo that they had "decided to prevent unhindered passage of vessels carrying contraband of war through Norwegian territorial waters." Hence they were giving notice that mines had been laid along three sections of the Norwegian coast, albeit in such a way as not to interfere with "the free access of Norwegian nationals or ships to their own ports or coastal hamlets." Patrol vessels, moreover, would be stationed nearby for forty-eight hours to guide neutral vessels past the danger zones. Oslo protested the act and demanded the removal of the mines, but before the dispute became bitter, a German action changed the entire setting. Early in the morning of April 9, German forces, acting in concert over a thousand-mile stretch, began the occupation of Denmark and Norway.

The occupation of small, poorly armed, and apparently unsuspecting Denmark was a simple matter.[1] Shortly before five o'clock in the morning of April 9, 1940, the Danish Government received a German note stating that Berlin had "indubitable evidence" of Allied plans to use the Scandinavian territories as a battleground. To forestall such action, Germany intended to "protect" these regions, for they obviously could not adequately defend themselves. Any and all resistance would be "crushed" by German military power. Actually, German troops and airplanes crossed the Danish frontier, and German war vessels entered Danish waters, before the Copenhagen Government had time to reply. King Christian X and Premier Thorvald Stauning therefore accepted the situation under protest and asked their people to "maintain a calm and controlled attitude." Only the Royal Guards in Copenhagen offered brief but futile resistance. Thus did Germany, within a few hours, assume a "protectorate" over another free country, one with an area of 16,500 square miles and a population of 3,800,000. Denmark, incidentally, was a great producer of bacon, butter, and eggs, about half the exports of which normally went to the United Kingdom.

In Norway the story developed differently. There, too, the presentation of a note demanding the surrender of the kingdom to German administration, in order to forestall supposed Allied de-

---

[1] On May 31, 1939, Denmark and Germany, at the latter's suggestion, had signed a nonaggression pact in which they agreed "in no circumstances [to] resort to war or to any other form of violence against each other."

signs, was accompanied by the landing of Nazi troops at half a
dozen ports, from Oslo in the southeast to Narvik on the northwest. King Haakon ·VII and Premier Johan Nygaardsvold, however, rejected the German offer and prepared to fight. Because the
Germans, despite the loss of some ships, readily succeeded in getting control of Oslo, the government had to flee; the king, indeed,

THE SCANDINAVIAN REGION, 1940

had to flee from place to place, everywhere hunted by German
airplanes.

The circumstance that the Germans met relatively little resistance in their simultaneous landings at six or more points was
owing, among other things, to three special weapons: to "Trojan
horse" tactics, fifth-column activities, and the giving of false orders. The first of these was well illustrated in the case of certain
Norwegian ports where, on the appointed day and at the appointed
hour, the hatches of supposedly empty German coal freighters
were opened and from them emerged fully equipped Nazi soldiers,

ready to land and take over the towns in question. The fact that such soldiers were available on April 9 in Narvik, situated a thousand miles from Germany by sea, made the original Nazi argument that the "protection" of Norway was necessary because of Britain's mining activities on the day before so transparent that the Germans themselves soon stopped using it. Obviously the freighters in question must have left Germany at least a week earlier.

Similarly helpful to the Germans were the activities of a so-called fifth column. This descriptive phrase is usually credited to General Emilio Mola, a supporter of Francisco Franco during the Spanish Civil War. He was reported to have said, on approaching Madrid, that, besides the four military columns then advancing on the "Loyalist" capital, a fifth column of "Nationalist" sympathizers already was inside the city ready to cut off the Republican retreat. At any rate, it was evident in Norway that natives were helping the Germans in their invasion attempt. Prominent among the fifth columnists was the military commander at Narvik, who failed to issue the necessary orders for the defense of that port. Most conspicuous, however, was Major Vidkun Quisling, head of the Norwegian Nazis (*Nasjonal Samling*) who, in the parliamentary elections of 1936, had failed to elect a single member. But as minister of war for a brief period in 1932–1933, Quisling apparently had appointed a number of the garrison commanders who now surrendered their charges to little bands of Nazi troops. And it was to him the Germans turned when they sought a native chief for a puppet government.

Vital as these factors were in making the task of the Nazis easier, it appears also that the simple Nazi ruse of transmitting false orders to loyal commanders of troops and ships was exceedingly effective. Thus, according to the testimony of Carl J. Hambro, a former Speaker of the Norwegian Parliament, the Germans easily entered the harbor at Kristiansand by issuing false orders to the local commander and by flying French flags. The "success" of the Nazis, then, was owing to a combination of factors: to careful preparation, disregard of international law, surprise, treason, espionage, and guile.

While the Germans were extending their control inland despite the resistance of isolated units of Norwegian fighters, the Allies promised "full aid" to the Scandinavian kingdom. A number of ships were sent and twelve thousand soldiers were landed, but, despite individual successes which sometimes were spectacular, the

Allied effort was a failure. The Germans, through their control of the best ports and with air superiority, were able to frustrate British plans for cutting the strategic rail communications between German-held Oslo and Trondheim. The British took and for a brief period held Narvik, but on June 9, 1940, with a German advance into France under way, they abandoned it, as they had earlier left Namsos and Andalsnes, and took King Haakon to London with them. The king at once issued a proclamation to his people to cease active resistance, and so another phase of the war ended in German victory. The conflict, moreover, had shown that, with air superiority and proper equipment, it was possible to conduct mechanized warfare even on such mountainous and snowy terrain as that of Norway.

The Germans now tried to win support for their cause in Norway by turning the civil administration over to the native Quisling and his followers. The major failed to convert his countrymen to the new doctrines and eventually was removed, at the instance of the German commissioner, Joseph Treboven, who did not like him. In September 1940, however, after a visit to Berlin, Quisling returned to head his Nasjonal Samling, the only party permitted by the Germans. To his discomfort and the Germans' irritation, the Norwegians continued to show great ingenuity in their resistance, both passive and active.

Through their Scandinavian venture the Nazis gained several advantages. They now had additional actual and potential air, naval, and submarine bases, some of them closer to northern Britain than any they had had before. They no longer had to worry about the possibility of attack through the northern countries. They acquired a large portion of the gold reserves of Denmark and Norway, and large stores of oil, foodstuffs, and munitions. They could divert from Britain and France and steer to themselves all the surplus dairy products, fish, minerals, metal ores, and timber output of the conquered areas. Even Swedish exports, chiefly iron and food, could now be counted almost wholly for the German side. True, Danish dairy production depended to a large extent on the importation of fodder, an item in which Germany herself was deficient; but the Nazis did not hesitate to lower the Danish standard of living and take for themselves whatever they needed.

The Allies, despite a loss of prestige, also made some gains. They got the use of about sixty Norwegian war vessels and most of the Norwegian merchant fleet, the fourth largest in the world.

These thousand ocean-going vessels helped keep Britain supplied with the oil and food without which she could not have continued the war. The merchant fleet's earnings, moreover, paid for the training and upkeep of Norway's exiled air force and the interest on her foreign loans. Presumably the people in the conquered regions would eventually become restive and hamper the German war effort. British and Canadian forces occupied the Faroe Islands, Iceland, and Greenland, all formerly tied to Denmark. And there was brought to a head in Great Britain a political crisis which culminated in the resignation of Chamberlain.

There had for some time been apparent a growing British dissatisfaction with the progress and conduct of the war. As the Finnish troubles finally led to the resignation of Daladier in France, so in Great Britain, in the words of a parliamentary leader, "the Norwegian campaign (was) the culmination of other discontents." It was plain that the people of Britain wanted vigor and imagination in their government, and Chamberlain possessed neither of these qualities. Hence, on May 10, 1940, a few hours after German soldiers had begun to swarm into Luxembourg, Belgium, and the Netherlands, Neville Chamberlain tendered his resignation to the king. On the following day Winston Churchill crowned a long and forceful political career by becoming prime minister. Fearless, energetic, and possessed of a vivid imagination, he gave promise of infusing a new spirit not only into the cabinet but into the whole conduct of Britain's greatest war.

The Churchill Cabinet still included Chamberlain, in a minor capacity, and a number of the latter's outstanding critics, such as Anthony Eden and Alfred Duff-Cooper. There were also several Laborite leaders, particularly Clement Atlee and Minister of Labor Ernest Bevin, who soon distinguished himself for his energy and organizing ability. Chamberlain at last retired in October 1940, dying shortly thereafter. And early in 1941, Viscount Halifax, who had long been one of Chamberlain's most consistent supporters and who had continued as foreign secretary under Churchill, was appointed British Ambassador to the United States, succeeding the late Lord Lothian. But now to return to what, in a favorite German phrase, were certain "unheard of" events of the spring of 1940.

At dawn on May 10, there began a German invasion of Luxembourg, Belgium, and the Netherlands. Twice before the Netherlands and Belgian governments, because of German military activities near their respective borders, had feared the imminence of invasion; yet when the blow actually fell, it came, in the words of the then Netherlands Foreign Minister, like a "bolt from the blue." It appears that late in the evening of May 9 the Netherlands Intelligence Service warned the government of impending attack in a five-word message: "Tomorrow at dawn; hold tight." The authorities took certain precautionary measures that had earlier been agreed upon, and then tensely awaited events. According to the testimony of Foreign Minister Eelco Nicolaas van Kleffens, "From a military point of view, there was little more that could be done. Every man was at his post, all precautions had been taken. Holland was ready to defend her neutrality to the utmost, her conscience clear."

But if the Netherlands Government was waiting, as it appeared to be, for even "a two-hour notice" of German intentions, it was to be sadly disappointed. For, about four o'clock in the morning of May 10, without notice of any sort, German soldiers poured into the Netherlands as German airplanes dropped bombs on sleeping cities and German parachutists took over Netherlands airports. Only then, after the "complete certainty of German aggression," did the Netherlands Government order its ministers abroad to ask Great Britain and France for help. Only then did its "policy of neutrality" cease. And therein lay one of the basic reason for later events. Throughout all the happenings of the past few years; throughout the opening months of the war; and even after the German occupation of Denmark and Norway, the Netherlands tried to remain strictly neutral. Relying partly on German promises and partly on its own strength, it hoped to keep its soil, untouched by war for a century, free of war in future.

Not until two hours after the attack began, did the German Minister to The Hague explain the grounds for Germany's action and demand the submission of the Netherlands. Once more Berlin claimed to have "irrefutable evidence of an immediately threatening invasion by British and French forces in Belgium, the Netherlands, and Luxembourg, prepared a long time beforehand with the knowledge of the Netherlands and Belgian governments." Once more, also, the victim was warned to submit quietly or face "annihilation." The Netherlands Government responded by accepting a state of war with Germany.

The Nazi airplanes, coming over in great numbers, soon destroyed the small Netherlands air fleet; then German land and sea transport planes easily brought over soldiers. Meanwhile other planes dropped parachutists, some armed with machine guns and others carrying radio sets, at strategic points throughout the country. Rotterdam, Amsterdam, and The Hague were subjected to terrible bombings, and mechanized forces, pushing back the Netherlands guard units, quickly seized strategic points everywhere. Again, however, the conquest of the country was speeded by the aid of helpers from the inside. Some of these fifth columnists were Netherlanders, followers of Anton Mussert and Rost van Tonningen. Others were Germans, who had earlier entered the Netherlands as "tourists," "salesmen," or "students." Some German soldiers, moreover, wore Netherlands uniforms, which had been smuggled across the border. (Queen Wilhelmina's Government had, in fact, several times been "disquieted" by the knowledge that not only military uniforms, but also those for policemen, postmen, and railway conductors were being smuggled into Germany.) It was doubtless at least in part the doing of such persons that a number of strategic bridges, waterworks, and canals remained in working order to make easy the passage of German soldiers.

The slaughter was so great that on May 14, after five days of fighting, General Henrik Winkelman ordered the Netherlands army to cease firing. The victorious Germans, however, were unable to achieve one major objective, namely, the capture of Queen Wilhelmina and the members of her family and government. These, after passing through many dangers, escaped to Great Britain on the day before the "war" in the Netherlands ended. They remained free to command the vast Netherlands colonial possessions and to continue the war as best they could on the side of the Allies. Meanwhile the kingdom itself, with its largest cities partially in ruins, was placed under the commissionership of Arthur Seyss-Inquart, the same who two years earlier had helped to hand his native Austria over to the Third Reich. He found his new task a difficult one, for the Netherlanders proved stubborn and unbending, and after years of Nazi overlordship they had not yet, according to their foreign administrators, come to understand "the true spirit of the new order." The staunch burghers were remarkably skillful in thinking up new forms of passive resistance.

The fall of the Netherlands rendered easier the conquest of Belgium.[1] Here again, the recent policies of the government had reacted to German advantage. In 1936 King Leopold III, it will be remembered, had declared that henceforth the kingdom must

[1] Luxembourg, with its population of 300,000, fell in a day, her Grand Duchess Charlotte managing to escape, first to France, and then to North America.

pursue a policy "exclusively and entirely Belgian," without any alliances. This virtual request for release from the obligations of the Locarno Agreements had been endorsed by Great Britain and France in April 1937. Six months later Berlin had promised to respect Belgium's "inviolability," unless she took part in a military action aimed at Germany. Thereafter, Belgium had stoutly resisted all efforts at close military coöperation, even with the Netherlands. It had preferred, unfortunately, to trust to the pledges of Germany and its own defenses.

Crossing into Belgium at the same time that they entered the Netherlands, the Germans again withheld an ultimatum until after the fighting had begun; then its terms were similar to those presented to The Hague. Bearing in mind the bitter days of 1914–1918, the Belgians decided to fight. With a larger and better equipped army than that of the Netherlands and in better geographic position to receive Allied aid, Belgium generally was expected to put up stiff resistance. But once again the Germans rushed ahead, taking bridges, canals, and forts; crossing rivers with "movable structures . . . built . . . to fit each place where they were needed"; investing cities and once more burning the library at Louvain; driving a wedge between the Belgians and their Allied reënforcements; and, as in Poland, breaking up the opposing armies and enveloping their sections one by one.

Within a week the Germans were in Brussels, and on May 18 Hitler reincorporated into the Reich the districts of Eupen, Malmédy, and Moresnet, lost to Belgium by the treaty of Versailles. Meanwhile, aware that the French had weakened the defensive system behind Sedan by moving soldiers from there to assist the Belgians, the Nazis on May 15 had struck in full force across the Meuse River. Because, for reasons still unknown, the bridges had not been destroyed, the Germans had been able to cross almost simultaneously at three points.

Unfortunately the Maginot Line was weak at this northern end, for the French had counted on a Belgian extension thereof to the Netherlands border. The Germans therefore were able, in effect, to break through where the Maginot Line was weak and thin and where it made no contact whatever with any Belgian line. Furthermore, the Germans struck before the French reserve troops, sent to take the place of their comrades who had been ordered northwestward into Belgium, had fully occupied their positions. Thus it was that the Nazis within four days created a sixty-mile gap in the French defenses and took possession of both St. Quentin and Rethel. A few more days, and the Germans had smashed their way westward from Rethel to Abbeville on the coast. The main French forces thus were driven south of the Somme River, and their comrades to the north, chiefly Britishers and Belgians, were reduced to dependence for supplies and help on the Channel ports alone.

From May 21 onward the Germans drove up along the French coast from Abbeville and simultaneously pounded away at the Belgian army to the northeast of Dunkirk. The situation was so serious that Generalissimo Maxim Weygand, recently appointed to Gamelin's place, flew to the headquarters of Leopold, who had taken personal command of the Belgian forces. The king warned Weygand that only "substantial new assistance" would enable the Belgians to continue the fight. When no such aid was forthcoming, Leopold, against the pleas of his entire government, asked the Germans for terms. The Nazis demanded unconditional surrender, and on May 28, 1940, the king complied; he ordered his soldiers to stop fighting, and himself was placed in "protective custody" in a palace near Brussels.

The Belgian Cabinet, some members of the Belgian Parliament, and many soldiers repudiated Leopold's action and fled to France and then Great Britain, there to continue the fight against the Germans. The king himself, in a letter to the pope, expressed the conviction that it was better to surrender than to fight another battle which "would have led to our annihilation without benefit to the allies," and better also to remain on Belgian soil and "stand by my people" than seek the safety of Allied territory. But whatever the verdict of history on Leopold's act, the end of Belgian resistance placed approximately four hundred thousand British and French soldiers, who had been sent to help Belgium, into a terrible predicament. Harried by the Germans on the south, and now with their northern flank exposed, they soon were pushed into a corner of Flanders, in the vicinity of Dunkirk, with only the sea at their back. Everywhere else were victory-flushed Nazis, whose Führer predicted the early "annihilation" of the enemy.

Yet, successful as they had thus far been, the Germans failed in their main efforts of May 29–June 4, 1940. On the latter day they did enter the ruins of Dunkirk, but in the preceding six days approximately 335,000 of the supposedly doomed Britishers and Frenchmen had been returned from there to England. Disaster had been averted and a "miracle" wrought through the aid of some determined but altogether natural instruments: through the gallant stands of a small Anglo-French force in the citadel of Calais to the south of Dunkirk and of a French tank unit under General René Prioux around Lille to the east of Dunkirk; through the tireless and effective work of the crews of about 220 Allied war vessels and perhaps 650 other craft of every size and description; through the ability of the Royal Air Force to achieve air superiority in the limited sphere above Dunkirk; and through foggy weather, which apparently helped the Allies as much as it hampered the Germans. The Allied naval losses were reported as 13 destroyers and 25 other vessels.

On the other hand, the Germans, after twenty-five days of fighting, were in occupation of Luxembourg, the Netherlands, Belgium, and France north of a line extending from Montmédy on the east to Abbeville on the west. Indeed, from Abbeville northward to the Arctic Circle, every mile of European coast now was under German domination. And the strategic basis for German victory in May again had been a combination of meticulous preparation, perfect coördination, surprise, the fullest use of mechanization, and the aid of persons behind the enemy lines.

In the actual fighting, the way was prepared by the dread dive bombers (*Stukas,* from *Sturzkampffliegzeug*). Then came enormous tanks, weighing between seventy and eighty tons, which made the breaches through which poured highly trained motorized units followed in turn by engineers and repair crews, armored troop carriers and supply cars, and the occupying infantry. The heavy tanks generally fanned out after making a breach and, accompanied by lighter armored cars, attacked areas to the rear. Thus was the defense disorganized while the airplanes disrupted communications and the heavy artillery "softened" objectives still to be stormed. The installation by the Germans of mobile telephones and the giving of false evacuation orders added to the welter of confusion in which the defenders tried unsuccessfully to reform their positions. The roads also were cluttered with refugees, who hampered the soldiers' movements and who were machine gunned from German airplanes. And now the Germans were to use similar tactics in their further assaults upon France.

While the fighting at Dunkirk was in progress, Generalissimo Weygand tried to create a new "line" south of the Somme and Aisne rivers, from Abbeville to Montmédy. The French worked feverishly, building defenses and making tank traps for even the heaviest of the motorized monsters. Then, on June 5, two days after the first air attack on Paris itself, the Germans launched a terrific attack along more than one hundred miles of this hastily constructed "Weygand Line." Again the Nazis chose 4 A.M. as the starting hour, this time for the Battle of France.

Eager to put France out of the war before the British could send another large expeditionary force across the Channel, the Germans used their full might in the new campaign. It was reported that, at the height of the battle, the Germans had one hundred divisions in action to forty for the Allies; and the Germans were far better equipped. They were, indeed, to quote Weygand, waging the war with a "hitherto unknown formula." Hence, although the French fought courageously and destroyed many German tanks, the Nazi drive could not be checked. Aside from man power, the greatest French deficiency was in planes and this deficiency the British could make up only in small part.

Reynaud now reorganized his cabinet, on this occasion making de Gaulle undersecretary for war, and Weygand wrote stirring orders to the soldiers; but such efforts could not hold back the steel and iron of the invaders. On June 9 the Germans took Rouen, crossed the Aisne at two points, and approached within thirty-five miles of Paris. On June 10 the French Government, taking Weygand's advice, left Paris.[1] And on this same day Italy entered the war.

Mussolini, "who had been becoming more and more bellicose with each advance of the Germans," told his people on June 10, 1940, that "the hour of irrevocable decision" had come. He informed a crowd in the Piazza Venezia that "a declaration of war already has been handed to the ambassadors of Great Britain and France." And he deemed it expedient to explain that Italy was taking the field "against the plutocratic and reactionary democracies who always have blocked the march and frequently plotted against the existence of the Italian people."

Unable now to get support or replacements from the soldiers stationed on the Italian border, the tired French fighters in the north continued to fall back. On June 11 the Germans crossed the Marne River and began an encirclement of the capital. Lest that city be made to suffer the fate of Warsaw and Rotterdam, the French Government decided to surrender it without a fight. Hence German soldiers were able to enter Paris on June 14, finding the French capital only slightly damaged, but with streets deserted and deathly still.

The fall of Paris doubtless had an adverse effect on the morale

[1] After four days at Tours, the government fled to Bordeaux.

of the French leaders, the more so since Weygand had informed a cabinet meeting on the twelfth that "all is lost." In this view he had been supported by the aged vice-premier, Marshal Pétain, the "hero of Verdun." Apparently a number of highly placed Frenchmen and Frenchwomen now urged Reynaud to ask for an armistice. Some of these advisers feared that continued fighting might end in a radical overturn similar to that of the Bolshevik Revolution in Russia. Others saw in the turn of events a chance to get rid of the Third Republic and restore a monarchy. Still others hoped to achieve high position in a new totalitarian world order. There also came to the fore a long-latent anti-British feeling and there were signs of bitter personal rivalries and jealousies.

Reynaud, however, for a time held out. He could not believe that France had collapsed and he did not want to desert his British allies. Supported by de Gaulle and by the energetic minister of the interior, Georges Mandel, he pleaded with Churchill and Roosevelt for quick and substantial aid. "Clouds of aeroplanes" were his most urgent demand. But these were not available. Roosevelt sent words of encouragement, and Churchill offered a constitutional "Franco-British Union" with common citizenship and joint ministries, but neither of these was of immediate help. On June 16, 1940, therefore, finding a majority of his cabinet and advisers in favor of "peace," Reynaud resigned. President Lebrun at once called on Pétain, then eighty-four years old, to form a new government.

Pétain quickly appointed a cabinet, the most conspicuous member of which was Pierre Laval, newspaper owner, former premier, long advocate of "collaboration" with Italy and Germany, leader of the "peace bloc," and bitter opponent of Reynaud. With equal speed the new premier requested Spain to act as intermediary in asking Germany for an armistice. He gave no satisfactory reply to the British officials who were sent to remind him that the British Government had informed Reynaud of its readiness to release France from her pledge not to conclude a separate peace only on condition that the "French fleet were dispatched to British ports and remained there while negotiations [between the French and Germans] were taking place."

The Germans, meanwhile, had easily continued their march through France. By June 16 they had outflanked and virtually surrounded the Maginot Line and were in occupation of about one-fourth of France. Hence Hitler was in no hurry to answer the French request. He held a meeting with Mussolini to talk over prospective terms and did not receive the French armistice delegation until June 21—in the same railway coach and in the same Compiègne Forest to which German delegates had been summoned on a similar mission twenty-two years earlier.[1] The Frenchmen accepted the armistice terms on the next day and then flew in a German plane to Rome, there to receive the Italian armistice demands. These were soon accepted, and firing ceased officially at 12:35 A.M. on June 25, 1940.[2] At this time the Germans were in occupation of more than half of France and claimed to have taken two million prisoners, with vast quantities of equipment. The Italians were in occupation of a narrow strip of French territory which they had conquered in an offensive begun on June 21, the day after France, on German prompting, had asked Italy for an armistice.

The Franco-German armistice, as published, contained twenty-four articles, calculated to prevent a French renewal of hostilities, enable the Reich advantageously to continue the war against Britain, and establish "preconditions" for an eventual peace arrangement. Germany was to occupy France to a line drawn roughly from the Swiss frontier near Geneva to a point about twelve miles east of Tours and thence southwestward to the Spanish border just below St. Jean Pied de Port. Occupied France—more than half of the republic—thus included most of the industrial regions, all the Atlantic ports, and Paris. After the close of hostilities with Britain, Germany would "reduce to a minimum" the occupation of the "western coast." Except for a small force necessary to maintain order, all French naval, military, and air effectives were to be demobilized. All land and coast defenses, fortifications, and war materials in the occupied area were to be handed over in good condition. Military supplies in unoccupied territory, apart from those authorized for use by the French, were to be stored for Germany and Italy. The manufacture of new war materials was to stop immediately.

The French fleet, except for ships needed to protect the colonial empire, was to be brought together in specified ports and disarmed under German-Italian control. Germany "solemnly declared" its intention not to use such naval units during the war, save for coast surveillance and mine sweeping. The French were to inform Ger-

[1] After the ceremonies of 1940 the coach was sent by the Germans to Berlin.

[2] According to the Franco-German armistice, hostilities were to cease six hours after the Italian Government had notified Berlin of the conclusion of the Franco-Italian armistice. This put the official moment of armistice at 12:35 A.M. on June 25, or 1:35 A.M. Italian summer time.

many of all mines they had sown and no French merchant shipping was to leave port. No Frenchman might serve against Germany in foreign units and no airplanes might leave from unoccupied France. All wireless transmitters were to be silenced and the transfer of merchandise between Germany and Italy was to be

THE INVASION OF FRANCE, 1940

facilitated through the unoccupied zone. France must pay the full costs of the occupying forces, repatriate the inhabitants of the occupied area, and release all German prisoners of war. French prisoners of war would remain confined until the conclusion of peace. France must hand over any German subjects whom Berlin might want but who had fled to the unoccupied region. Details of the application of all terms were to be entrusted to an armistice commission sitting at Wiesbaden. The armistice was to be effective until the conclusion of peace but might be denounced "at any moment" by Germany if France were delinquent in fulfilling her obligations.

The Franco-Italian armistice contained twenty-six published articles, many similar to the German ones. Italy, moreover, was to occupy that narrow strip of French territory which she had conquered. A thirty-one-mile stretch of French land beyond the line of occupation was to be demilitarized, as was a zone on the French side of the Libyan border. For as long as Anglo-Italian hostilities continued, France was to demilitarize her bases at Toulon, Bizerte (Tunisia), Ajaccio (Corsica), and Oran (Algeria). Finally, the coast of French Somaliland was to be demilitarized and Italy given use of the local port and railway facilities.

Marshal Pétain, in commenting on the acceptance of these terms, explained that they saved French honor and left the government "free." In the next section the policies of this "free" government will be surveyed, but a British action which largely nullified that provision of the armistice arrangement relating to the recall of French naval units should first be considered.

The British Government had reason to believe that the French navy, some of whose highest officers were strongly anti-British, would be surrendered to axis control. London also feared that, once the ships were in French ports, the Germans might either disregard their promise not to use them or else denounce the pledge on the ground that France had somehow violated the armistice agreement. Hence the British Cabinet unanimously decided to forestall any such eventualities. On July 3, 1940, without warning, British units were sent to take over all French war vessels then in British ports. This was accomplished with relative ease and virtually no bloodshed. The crews of the two battleships, two light cruisers, submarines, and several hundred smaller craft either entered the British navy, volunteered to fight as "Free French" units, or were returned to France. A second sizable portion of the French fleet, at Alexandria, was demobilized by mutual consent. But the major part of the French fleet, stationed at the base of Mers-el-Kebir near Oran in Algeria, was not so easily won over.

On that same July 3 the French commander at Mers-el-Kebir, Vice-Admiral Marcel B. Gensoul, received a note from British Vice-Admiral Sir James F. Somerville, offering him several alternative courses of action. He was asked either to sail with the British and continue the fight against the Germans and Italians; or to sail with reduced crews under British control to a British port, in which case the reduced crews would be promptly repatriated and the ships or their equivalent in compensation restored to France after the war; or to sail with reduced crews and under British control to the French West Indies where the ships might be demilitarized or "entrusted" to the United States until the end of the war; or to risk sinking of the ships after six hours. The French commander, using the intervening hours to prepare for action, decided to fight.

The British reluctantly opened fire in the late afternoon and put most of the assembled French ships out of commission. The French ships were cooped up in an unfavorable position, especially since British airplanes had dropped mines across the mouth of the harbor, but even so several of them were able to escape and eventually reach Toulon. A few days later the largest French battleship, the *Richelieu,* at anchor in Dakar, French West Africa, also was damaged beyond early repair after its commander had rejected any other alternative.[1] Meanwhile the Pétain Government had severed diplomatic relations with its former ally, which was valiantly continuing the fight against the axis powers. But before we turn to the Battle of Britain, let us examine the changes which occurred in France under its new administration.

FROM THIRD REPUBLIC TO VICHY FRANCE

The Third French Republic died during the second week of July 1940, when the National Assembly invested Pétain with "all power" to promulgate a new constitution. Its epitaph might well read, simply: "Born and died in military defeat, inflicted by German armies." But such an epitaph, while stating a fact, would hardly explain the demise of the republic in 1940. Even the scores of books and hundreds of articles that soon appeared on the tragedy, mystery, failure, betrayal, suicide, cancer, and purge of France failed to give a clear picture of the fundamental causes of the disaster. Many of the items listed as causes may, indeed, have been more in the nature of symptoms. This is true, also, of the explanation given by Pétain himself, when he complained that France had had "too few children, too few arms, too few allies." Nor was the issue made clearer by a tendency among some Frenchmen to accuse each other in a great hunt for scapegoats. In the circumstances, we may best leave it to the historian of the future to find the full answer to the riddle, contenting ourselves meanwhile with

[1] In February 1943 the *Richelieu* arrived in New York harbor for repairs.

a brief survey of what at present appear to have been contributory factors in the decline and fall of the Third Republic.

The collapse of France was not caused by the Nazi invasion alone. The very ease with which the Germans were able to advance offers circumstantial evidence that there must have been some internal weakness and dry decay. It seems equally plausible to say that this domestic decay was not necessarily the result of "democracy" nor a proof of "democracy's failure." The basic explanation would seem to go much deeper; hence it behooves us to see how close to the roots we may be able to dig.

The list of corroding influences would seem to include the following: the division of the country, ever since the Revolution, into two Frances, bitterly divided against each other; the fact that the constitutional laws of 1875, the legal frame of the republic's political system, originally were intended as temporary provisions, to be replaced by a permanent charter when the vexing question of kingship should have been settled; the fate which ordained that in France the parliamentary system should rest, not on a two-party system as in Great Britain and the United States, but on a multiplicity of "groups," thus making governments dependent on coalitions and, as in Weimar Germany, often making it difficult to achieve energetic action in time of crisis; the great effect on France in particular of the example of the Bolshevik Revolution in Russia; the development, in post-1919 days, of a "defense psychology"; and the complacency, lowering of moral values, and corruption that seem often to accompany prolonged national economic well-being. These influences may now be considered in turn.

An excellent description of the "two Frances" was given some years ago by a sympathetic observer in these words: [1]

The French Revolution irrevocably divided the internal politics of France; since that time there have been twin Frances, mortal enemies. The residual bitterness of the American Civil War is still a measurable political factor, yet in America the geographic solidarity of the two sides has been an incomparably softening influence. The French Revolution was a Civil War in which, over large areas, the lines were drawn on a social rather than a geographic basis; when it was over, no softening distance mitigated the bitterness of the ex-combatants. As the completeness of the democratic victory, with the passage of time and the coming of reaction, became less complete, two Frances emerged to confront each other—authoritarian France, founded on the ideo-

[1] Helen Hill [Miller] *The Spirit of Modern France,* Foreign Policy Association, New York, 1934, 14. Reprinted by permission.

logical trinity of monarchy, army and church, in later years particularly the church, and democratic France, founded on the ideological trinity of liberty, equality and fraternity between individual citizens. All through the nineteenth century these two were locked in an uncertain struggle for supremacy, with now one the victor, now the other. . . . The Third Republic has now lasted some sixty years, but its stability has more than once been highly doubtful. . . . Certain recurrent issues have never exhausted their dynamite. . . .

This national cleavage was responsible, at least in part, for the attitude taken in 1939–1940 by some of the French officers. They were royalist by tradition and in sympathy, and they found it difficult to put spirit into the fight for a system which they abhorred; which, they said, had made it possible for a Jewish socialist (Léon Blum) to become premier. They, and with them a sizable portion of the privileged class, were not pro-German and not necessarily pro-Fascist, but they were anti-Third Republic, anti-Red, and indifferent to, if not opposed to, the French form of democracy. To this group the speeches of Hitler and the blandishments of his well-chosen male and female agents sounded much more attractive than did, for example, the demands of French labor leaders for shorter hours and more pay.

Closely related to this attitude was that of many Frenchmen who had never forgiven the republic for its separation of the church and state in the early years of the twentieth century. It was Léon Gambetta, one of the founders of the Third Republic, who in 1877 had rallied republicans with the cry: "Clericalism! That is the enemy!" And as late as 1939, a leading native authority on French politics (later a Vichy official) held that "perhaps the surest criterion" of difference between the Right and Left was the matter of opinion on the position of the church in the state and relations with the Vatican.[1] There were, then, men and women in the France of 1940 who expected more freedom to set up the church-state relation which they desired through "collaboration" with Hitler than under the existing regime.

A second apparent weakness in the French political structure was the character of the constitutional laws of 1875. Under the terms of the Franco-German armistice of January 1871, the French people were to elect a national assembly which should decide on whether or not to continue the war of 1870. When the assembly met it contained about 650 deputies, including 200 republicans

[1] Barthélemy, J. *Le gouvernement de la France,* 3 ed., Paris, 1939, 44.

and 400 monarchists. This membership reflected the attitude of the voters towards the war rather than their domestic political wishes, for the monarchist candidates had promised peace and the republicans had advocated the renewal of hostilities. None the less, it would seem that a king should quickly have been chosen when the Bordeaux Assembly, as it was called, turned to the question of forming a permanent new government.

As it happened, the monarchists themselves were divided into two approximately equal groups favoring, respectively, a Bourbon or Legitimist and an Orleans candidate. Prolonged deadlock resulted, during which more and more liberals, tired of monarchist bickerings, veered to the republican side. Finally, in 1875, because it seemed futile to wait any longer for the monarchists to resolve their difficulty, three organic laws were passed which eventually came to be the French Constitution. The first law, which defined a method for electing future presidents, was adopted by a majority of one. And it was this one vote which, in effect, established the Third Republic. In the circumstances, it is not astonishing that the republican form of government should have collapsed after sixty-five years. The wonder, rather, is that a sketchy and presumably temporary political instrument, despised by unreconciled opponents, should have endured as long as did the laws of 1875.

Republican France, in the third place, had only few political parties with a definite organization, party funds, and periodic conventions. But it had numerous political "groups," each with its own name and each, provided it had a certain minimum number of adherents, with representation on parliamentary committees. Usually there were from ten to fifteen such groups in the lower house at one time; hence it was virtually impossible for any one of them to get a majority and government had to be by the bloc system. Sometimes the defection of one small group on a minor point brought the loss of a majority and the need for a reorganization of the government. This literal *ministerial* responsibility was largely to blame for the frequency of cabinet change in France. Unlike the experience of ministries in democracies operating under the two-party system, the average life of a French cabinet was little more than six months. Eventually, particularly in the hard years after 1930, this administrative fluctuability gave rise to a growing demand for a "disciplined," that is, authoritarian system.

A fourth contributory cause to the French overturn was, interestingly, the Bolshevik Revolution. When the Bolsheviks repudiated the foreign debts incurred by Russia under the tsarist regime, France was one of the heaviest losers. This circumstance, plus the Bolshevik attacks on private property and religion, aroused the implacable enmity of many influential Frenchmen. There was implanted in them a dread of communism and a readiness to do almost anything to avert a Bolshevik upheaval in France. While the Third Republic, until 1931, was officially among the most consistent opponents of the U.S.S.R., this feeling remained more or less in the background—though even then it was regularly fed by the many Russian émigrés who had found a refuge in France. But when, after the rise to power of the German Nazis in 1933, the Third Republic began to draw closer to the Soviet Union, the dissident classes in France were filled with yet greater aversion to the existing government.

The formation of a Franco-Soviet Alliance in 1935 and the joint sympathy of Moscow and the Blum Government for the Spanish "Loyalists" after 1936, seemingly turned the fear of these groups into terror. And in this emotional state they listened willingly to the honeyed words of such German agents as Otto Abetz, who convinced them that only a totalitarian French regime coöperating with Nazi Germany could save them from the loss of all they held dear. In the end, according to the testimony of the American observers, Edgar A. Mowrer and Colonel (later Brigadier General) William J. Donovan, many of the French army officers adopted the attitude: "If there is to be a war, then let it be against the Bolsheviki." With such a spirit, and bewildered by the new technique of the Blitzkrieg, these officers could hardly lead their fighting men to victory.

Mention was made, next, of a French psychology of defense. The people generally had fallen under the spell of the high command's preachments regarding the supposed safety of the country behind the Maginot Line. Whereas, in neighboring states, the people constantly were kept in a state of excitement and were being imbued with a spirit of aggressiveness, the French were told by their leaders, of whatever political complexion, that they needed only to remain behind their "impregnable" defenses to be safe. The French attitude well substantiated the view of the British historian, Arnold J. Toynbee, that nations tend to "idolize" a military technique which, revolutionary in its inception, helped them to win a previous war. Believing that during the First World War they had discovered in attrition a new way to beat Germany, the French regarded this "wearing down" process as being still the latest development in modern warfare. There were, to be sure, persons who realized the delusion of this view, particularly de Gaulle the soldier and Reynaud the civilian, but they were laughed at or disregarded by the "experts" until it was too late. Hence, when the Germans advanced with their "bewildering" new technique, the French had little more than bravery to offer in resistance.[1]

Finally, the French nation, for much of the period between 1919 and 1939, enjoyed a condition of relative complacency. Least affected of any great state by the depression, enriched by lavish tourist offerings, enjoying an almost even balance of agriculture and industry, France wanted only to be left alone in a world which, at Paris, she had helped to create. Out of the despair of the First World War and the ecstasy of glorious survival and revival, there grew up a generation which measured success by financial standards, looked on political and journalistic corruption as part of the normal national life, and took a cynical attitude towards things of the spirit. Against such a setting it was possible once more for mistresses to exert influence in national affairs and for personal animosities to affect critical cabinet decisions. Such a state of things was grist to the mill of Nazi sympathizers who spread propaganda calculated to ruin France through hypocritically singing of its rebirth in a new and totalitarian order. And thus French democracy, appearing to fail, gave way to another system.

The Pétain Government, having established itself at Vichy, in the north-central part of unoccupied France, and having concluded armistices with Germany and Italy, wished to change the republic's constitution. France, said Pétain, "at the cruelest moment of its history, . . . must understand and accept the necessity of a national revolution." On July 10, 1940, accordingly, the National Assembly, composed of both parliamentary houses, conferred on Pétain the power to draft a new constitution, which would have to be submitted to a plebiscite for approval. In no hurry to draw up such a document, the government contented itself with issuing numerous statutes and consecutively numbered "constitutional acts." Indeed, in August 1942 Pétain abolished the parliamentary bureaus, which then were the last vestiges of the National Assembly. Thus was the Third Republic converted into a Vichy Dictatorship.

By means of the first few constitutional acts Pétain made him-

[1] Some Frenchmen, on the other hand, had become so cowed by the repeated declarations of such leaders as Poincaré that France was helpless against Germany, that they could see no point in putting up any sort of defense.

self "Chief of the French State," gave himself "full governmental powers," and designated Pierre Laval as his successor in the event of his being "prevented from exercising the function of Chief of the State." The seventh act (January 1941) required all high officials in France to swear fidelity to Pétain's "person" and permitted the Chief of State to punish any dignitary who "betrayed his duties"; this punitive power, moreover, was made to cover officials who had held office at any time "within the past ten years." With a cabinet which gradually came to include only persons who were acceptable to the Germans, Pétain then issued law after law, all aimed at replacing the spirit of "Liberty, Equality, Fraternity" by the new one of "Labor, Family, Fatherland." [1] The government was watched and directed in its action by Ambassador Otto Abetz, the armistice commission at Wiesbaden, and other German agents. "I do not pretend," Pétain was reported to have said, "that this government is free. The Germans hold the rope and twist it whenever they consider that the [armistice] accord is not being carried out."

In December 1940 Pétain announced that Laval no longer formed "part of the government." There were rumors that the dismissed official, who advocated close collaboration with Germany, had arranged with the Nazis to execute a coup d'état on December 15, attendant upon ceremonies connected with the removal of the remains of Napoleon's son, the Duke of Reichstadt, from Vienna to Paris. (Napoleon's own remains were returned from St. Helena to Paris on December 15, 1840.) For a time Laval was placed in confinement but, upon German representations, he was released. In February 1941 a constitutional act designated the anti-British Admiral Jean François Darlan as successor to Pétain in the event of the latter's incapacity, and in August an attempt was made to assassinate Laval. He was merely wounded and recovered rapidly.

By April 1942 the Nazis were able to prevail upon the eighty-six-year-old Pétain to take the swarthy, proaxis politician back into the government. This time the ex-delivery-wagon driver who, after achieving financial success, displayed a special fondness for white ties, became "Chief of the Government," leaving to Pétain the now empty title of "Chief of the State." Collaboration with Germany thenceforth proceeded apace, and in October 1942 Laval obediently announced plans to draft French factory workers,

[1] This phrase appeared in the law of July 10, 1940, which empowered Pétain to frame a new constitution.

between the ages of eighteen and fifty, and ship them off to Germany. The Nazis promised to return one French prisoner of war for every three skilled workers received. Before this scheme could be put into effect, against the widespread opposition which it aroused, the Germans occupied all France following the United Nations' landings in French North Africa (November).

Meanwhile the Vichy Government had completely overhauled the country's legislative system. The new laws were anti-Semitic and suppressed secret societies. They made much more favorable the position of the Catholic Church, with respect both to education and to property rights. Unions and employers' associations were abolished, and strikes and lockouts were forbidden. The administrative divisions of the country were altered and the inheritance laws were revised so as to perpetuate the peasant basis of agriculture. Many persons were deprived of their acquired French citizenship and refugee Jews were forced back to Germany. A program of military youth training was instituted.

Measures were taken to regulate every phase of the nation's industry, commerce, labor, and agriculture. Homes were sought for the thousands of refugees who had been required by Germany to leave Lorraine and settle either in former Polish districts or in unoccupied France. The press agencies were taken over by the government. In short, unoccupied France rapidly approached totalitarianism, with Nazi legislation as its model. Simultaneously, by strict border supervision and by encouraging provincial separatisms and emphasizing local linguistic differences, the Germans were doing their best to make permanent the political, economic, and spiritual severance of industrial occupied France and agrarian unoccupied France.

So far did German influence go, that legal proceedings were instituted by Vichy against such former government leaders as Daladier, Blum, Gamelin, Reynaud, and Mandel. The Nazis wanted the accused pronounced guilty of having caused the new war, so that France actually would place upon herself the stigma of responsibility for the Second World War. But when the accused were at last brought to public trial at Riom early in 1942, they were charged by Vichy with having failed to *prepare* France properly for the approaching war. The defendants, especially Daladier and Blum, were brilliant in handling their own cases, despite obvious unfairness in the judicial procedure. Indeed, they came so close to proving things which neither Vichy nor Berlin wanted proved that the trials, after having been adjourned for the Easter recess, were indefinitely suspended. But the accused remained under arrest and in the spring of 1943 were transferred to German soil lest they be freed and assist in a United Nations' invasion attempt.

As might be expected, not all Frenchmen were in accord with the views and policies of the Pétain Government. General de Gaulle, who had gone to London after the collapse of the French army, called on all dissidents to rally behind him as leader of a "Free French Force" and thus continue the fight against Germany. In August 1940 a French military court tried de Gaulle *in absentia* and condemned him to death for treason and desertion, but a few days later the British Government made a formal military agreement with him. This regulated the conditions under which Free French resistance would continue, in coöperation with Britain, and excused the Frenchmen from ever having to take up arms against France itself.

When it appeared that some of the commanders in French West Africa and French Equatorial Africa were unwilling to follow the Vichy Government in its submission to Germany, de Gaulle decided to go to Africa. With a small force and accompanied by French and British war vessels, he appeared in September 1940 at the thriving Senegalese port of Dakar. It was unfortunate that he chose this point, for the local commissioner refused to allow the Free Frenchmen to land. Shots were exchanged and de Gaulle and the British withdrew when it became obvious that a major engagement would be required to take the port. Apparently de Gaulle had made a mistake or been misinformed about the temper of the local garrison, and the incident resulted mainly in an increase in bad feeling between Great Britain and France. De Gaulle's prestige, however, was restored when, in the succeeding weeks, he gained the adherence of French Equatorial Africa and some scattered island possessions of France. In 1941 and 1942 his followers, called "Fighting Frenchmen" since July 1942, fought with the British and Americans in Libya, the Near East, Madagascar, and Tunisia.

Immediately after the fall of Reynaud, it had appeared that French North Africa, Syria, and Indo-China might refuse allegiance to the Pétain Government and also continue the struggle. This would have been of great help to the British, particularly in the Mediterranean region, where it now was necessary to fight Italy. But through prompt action the Vichy Government was able to prevent this defection. A new governor was sent to Indo-China who observed the wishes of Pétain. Weygand flew to Syria and there persuaded the military commander to abide by the armistice conditions. In Morocco, the resident-general followed suit, and then Weygand himself arrived to assume supreme command over the French African forces. By 1941, however, Weygand had evidently become so disillusioned with the "new order" in France that he was recalled by Pétain, presumably as being "unsafe." Leaving for later consideration the further history of the French colonies, we come now to Britain's direct contest with Germany after the collapse of France.

DAUNTLESS BRITAIN, 1940

On the eve of what has come to be called "the Battle of Britain," Hitler advanced a second peace proposal. Toward the end of a speech to the Reichstag (July 1940) he said: "I can see no reason why this war must go on." Stating no terms, he merely indicated that if the war continued it could "end only with the complete annihilation of one or the other of the two adversaries." In such event, since he had now, as "victor," appealed to "common sense," he would have "relieved (his) conscience in regard to the things to come." Obviously the British could hardly stop fighting on such a flimsy basis without surrendering all they had claimed to be fighting for. Aside from a negative verbal reply by Lord Halifax, Britain's concrete response to the proposal was a new, all-time-high budget, based more on immediate taxation than on loans. The public welcomed its announcement.[1]

When the Germans turned their attention to Britain, after consolidating their earlier gains, they faced a new situation. Had Great Britain been another continental state, adjacent to France or one of the other areas under German control, the problem for the Nazis presumably would have been simple: one more application of Blitzkrieg technique. And this might well have been successful, for the Germans in June 1940 were far better equipped than the British. They had more planes, pilots, small arms, tanks, armored cars, and heavy mobile guns.[2] In addition, they had far more trained men under arms, and presumably had some sort of fifth column ready to aid the invaders. With their recent acquisi-

[1] The new tax law limited the annual net income of any one individual to about $25,000.

[2] In 1943 Churchill stated that Great Britain had only three hundred tanks left after Dunkirk.

tions, moreover, the Germans had acquired numerous airfields, and the conquered regions formed a geographic buffer of considerable extent between the enemy airports and the German industrial plants. Finally, Germany did have an ally in Italy, who at least made it necessary for the British to divide their strength.

GREAT BRITAIN VERSUS GERMANY, WINTER 1940–1941

These advantages were significant, but they lost some of their immediate utility because Great Britain, despite Hitler's earlier dictum that there were "no more islands," *was* an island. The English Channel, ranging in width from twenty miles upward, was a formidable barrier to mechanized land units. A second, was the British navy, much more powerful than those of Germany and

Italy combined. Not only would the main part of this fleet risk destruction to keep an invading army from the shores of Britain, but the sea arm once more effectively blockaded the German area from the west and south. Furthermore, it made possible the delivery to the embattled kingdom of vast quantities of foodstuffs and supplies from the rest of the world. German submarines, surface raiders, and airplanes did considerable damage to British shipping as the months went by, particularly since "neutral" Ireland refused to allow Britain to use her ports as bases, but many of the losses were replaced by building, seizures, and purchases.

The British advantages also included better planes than those of the Germans—who built theirs hurriedly—and better pilots, some of them carefully trained in the dominions. Since the Germans did not begin their really large-scale air attacks on Great Britain until the second week of August 1940, the British had more than two months' time in which to recover from the effects of Dunkirk, two months which were used to speed up military production, training, and defensive measures at an amazing rate. Finally, there was the astonishing spirit displayed by the Britons, from king through clerk to carter. The British citizen emerged as the outstanding hero in the first eighteen months of the war.

Since, in the circumstances, Germany could hope to invade Britain only after achieving air superiority, the Nazis at last began the long-expected Anglo-German air war. On June 18, 1940, German bombers inaugurated a system of daily air raids over Great Britain. The latter retaliated immediately, sending up fighting planes to disperse the German bombers, and Royal Air Force bombers to seek out targets on the continent. In the first few weeks neither side used many planes at a time and both tried to limit destruction to such military objectives as ammunition stores, oil depots, war-supply factories, and airfields. Simultaneously the pilots were becoming more accustomed to night flying (a technique in which the Royal Air Force excelled) and acquiring familiarity with foreign flying conditions and terrain.

With the coming of July 1940, and especially after Hitler's second peace "offer," the air warfare became more intense. The Germans, having been able better to organize the fields in the regions which they had conquered, now sent over larger squadrons, operating in the daytime as well as at night. In addition to their other objectives, they tried to establish a tighter "counter-blockade" by attacking shipping and wharves, and to "soften up" British resistance by lowering the morale of the people. The British, having to carry more fuel and therefore lighter bomb loads, similarly increased their activities, especially in night attacks on port installations, oil refineries, arms factories, and synthetics-producing plants. And to the evident astonishment of the Nazis, the British people did not become terror-stricken. The greater the danger, the more determined in its resistance democratic Britain seemed to become.

By August 8, 1940, which ushered in "mass" daylight raids involving hundreds of German bombers coming over in "waves," the British had succeeded in greatly improving their air defenses. Neither side had yet devised a really effective defense against air attack, but the British had built more and better antiaircraft guns, found new and effective ways of "spotting" enemy planes, and developed faster fighters which were relatively easy to handle and well designed to disperse enemy bombers and drive them back across the water. Large, vulnerable airfields were replaced by hundreds of small, camouflaged, hidden fields with only a few planes each. Balloon barrages were useful, too, at least in forcing invading planes to fly high and thus have less opportunity for good aim. These barrages were made up of huge balloons, rising thousands of feet into the air and connected by cables, from which hung long stretches of piano wire to catch low-flying planes.

The Germans also resorted to new weapons and techniques. In their effort to "erase" London before destroying lesser centers, they began to drop explosives indiscriminately and to use delayed-action or time bombs in an effort to shatter the nerves of the population. Then came incendiary bombs and attacks on midlands industrial towns and coastal ports. It was a tactical mistake when the Germans, having spread havoc in the London slums, also dropped bombs on Buckingham Palace, for now king and people were drawn even closer than before. In mid-November 1940 the city of Coventry was nearly ruined through attack by an estimated five hundred bombers, supposedly in retaliation for the recent bombing of Munich; but the survivors dug out and grimly prepared to continue the fight.

As the air raids continued, the British worked out a skillful system of civilian defense. An Air Raid Precautions department of the Home Office had been created in 1935 and parliamentary acts of 1937 and 1939 provided for the national organization of precautionary measures. By 1941 there was an efficiently operating system of Air Raid Precautions Services which included public and private shelters, lighting restrictions, air-raid signals, trained wardens (1200 to every 100,000 of the population), first aid posts, ambulance units, rescue and demolition parties, decontamination squads, and fire brigades. Many of the persons who took part in these activities were volunteers; others received pay; most performed their duties with courage and fortitude. Simultaneously a large conscript army was being whipped into shape and a home guard was trained in a variety of auxiliary functions. The year 1941 opened with four million Britons under arms, ready to meet any invader.

While the Germans continued their fierce raids in the months after August 1940, with only occasional letups, the Royal Air Force was equally busy watching for German invasion preparations, wrecking railway lines, destroying factories and plants, blasting French airfields and ports, ruining industrial works in the Rhineland region, raiding northern Italy, burning large sections of Hamburg and Bremen, dumping explosives on Norwegian and Danish ports, and breaking up barge concentrations. The coasts of Great Britain simultaneously were made as inhospitable as possible for invaders. Gun emplacements were provided, tracks were laid for heavy armored trains with special cannon, barbed-wire entanglements were stretched wherever feasible, land mines were planted, and a constant lookout was kept by pilots, soldiers, and civilian volunteers. Successive invasion rumors were not borne out; instead, the Germans continued raiding, alternating mass flights with expeditions of a few or even single bombers. These were harder to intercept and could cause damage over many areas in one night.

Precisely how much damage was done in the reciprocal bombardments it is not possible to say. Certainly the dropping of thousands of tons of high explosives over a period of many months must have caused serious hurt to both sides. Presumably production was slowed up, art treasures were ruined, shipping was destroyed, communications were disrupted, and in the case of Great Britain at least, many thousands were rendered homeless. Feeding, housing, and preventing disease among these was one of the most difficult of the innumerable tasks confronting the government. In the matter of fighting losses, the Air Ministry announced that the calendar year 1940 saw 1744 British planes destroyed in the air against 4974 enemy planes. If these figures were correct, they indicated a British superiority of almost three to one over the Germans. But German plane-production capacity still was generally assumed to be far in excess of British production. Such were the things Churchill must have had in mind when he told the Commons, in his first speech as prime minister (May 13, 1940): "I say to this House, as I said to the Ministers who have joined the Government, I have nothing to offer but blood and toil and tears and sweat."

AIR POWER AND THE WAR [1]

It may be convenient, at this point, to say a few general words about the "air arm" in the Second World War. Almost from the beginning of the struggle the airplane appeared as a dominant weapon. Airplanes blasted the way for the Nazi march across Europe and airplanes sank mighty battleships. Air power closed certain sea lanes and on the other hand made possible the rapid transportation of armies across mountains and waters. Air warfare tended to destroy the military value of buffer states, minimize the protection hitherto afforded by distance from the immediate fighting fronts, and make isolationism obsolete. Air power shattered long-standing traditions of attack and defense and made possible the capture of supposedly "impregnable" bases. Air warfare virtually erased the distinction between combatants and noncombatants.

In the fourth year of the Second World War the airplane still was used largely as an adjunct to land and sea fighting. Armies moved forward under canopies of planes. Ships ventured into enemy waters under the protection of "air umbrellas." Entrenched positions were "softened up" for assaulting mechanized and infantry units. Only in such missions as the destruction of cities, industrial plants, and railroad or shipping centers, and in such exceptional cases as the conquest of Crete did the airplane, as yet, function largely on its own.[2] Sometimes, moreover, planes that had helped win victory in certain circumstances, lost their effectiveness under changed conditions. Thus the Stukas, exceedingly effective in the Battle of France, were of far less value in the

---

[1] The quotations and much of the material in this section are, with the consent of the publishers, taken from or based on a volume in the "Air-Age Education Series" entitled *Education for the Air Age*, 1942, and written by N. L. Engelhardt, Jr.

[2] General Henry H. Arnold, Chief of the United States Air Forces, said of the Nazi conquest of Crete: "They came in gliders carrying from 12 to 30 soldiers. They were towed by lumbering old transports unsuited for aerial combat, but ideal for this new purpose, with as many as 10 or 11 gliders strung out behind each plane. In an incredibly short time the Germans, by air transport and gliders, landed 15,000 troops on the island, together with their rifles, light machine guns, heavy machine guns, and field pieces. They even brought medical supplies and radio equipment."

U.S.S.R. (where their limited cruising range in the face of vast distances and few airfields sometimes made it impossible for them to keep ahead of rapidly advancing mechanized spearheads) and in Tunisia (where the American and British veterans showed relatively little fear of them and, indeed, found in them moderately easy marks for their guns). In 1943 air power was handicapped in particular by the absence of any all-purpose military airplane and by the appearance of automatic gun-laying devices on antiaircraft weapons.

Eventually, however, in the opinion of experts, the airplane may become capable of fighting its own wars: "bombing enemies into submission, transporting armies, and maintaining supply lines, all without help from navies or land forces." Spurred on by the needs of the war, scientists probably will carry much further the progress made in aviation during the short period that elapsed between the close of the First and the opening of the Second World War. Within that score of years the airplane "changed from a small single-engined biplane to a seventy-ton monoplane with four engines. Commercial speeds rose from eighty miles per hour to more than two hundred miles per hour. The nonstop cruising range of transport planes jumped from a few hundred miles to more than five thousand miles. The technique of flying changed from 'contact' flying at low altitudes to instrument and over-weather flying. Automatic pilots, radio beams, blind-landing systems, and directional gyroscopes all became realities. . . ." [1]

In 1942 the world's record flying range was 7158 miles and the official maximum speed attained by land planes was 469 miles per hour; power-dive speeds of more than 600 miles per hour also had been recorded.[2] The importance of these figures becomes readily apparent when it is borne in mind that a "speed of 500 miles per hour can bring every point on the earth within twenty-four hours' distance of every other point." The advances in airplane speed and range were paralleled by advances in carrying capacity. Three large transport planes of 1942, operating as tankers, could carry the same amount of gasoline as a railroad tank car. The Martin Flying Boat *Mars* was equipped to carry 150 soldiers. "A fleet of 1000 air-age bombers could drop 20,000 tons of bombs

[1] Radio waves were utilized in a device patented in February 1941 by Joseph Lyman to detect approaching aircraft. Such a detector (radar) indicated the approach of Japanese planes to Pearl Harbor on December 7, 1941, when they were still 130 miles way. "It was not the fault of the apparatus that its indication was ignored." Cf. Stokley, J. *Science Remakes Our World*, 1942, p. 166.

[2] The speed of sound at sea level is 751 miles per hour.

or land more than 100,000 soldiers on an objective without any more warning than an air-raid signal."

These facts gave rise to numerous problems of national policy relating for each country to both its continued war effort and its postwar plans and ambitions. The chief immediate wartime problems were the speedy production of all possible planes of the best types and their utilization in the most effective manner; the continuous technical training of hundreds of thousands of soldiers and civilians as flight and ground crews; and the simultaneous development of air-defense measures ranging all the way from improved detectors and antiaircraft guns to more wholehearted coöperation by civilians in local protective plans. But even with the war still in progress, governments and commercial plane operators were considering some of the air problems that would face them upon the conclusion of hostilities.

The extension of airlines, particularly United States airlines, as a result of the exigencies of the war, created the problem of future use of foreign routes. In 1943 each nation still claimed sovereign rights over all air above its boundaries and all airfields and landing facilities within those boundaries. Only the air above the high seas remained theoretically free to the aircraft of all countries. Hence fields and facilities developed on foreign soil for war purposes would not necessarily be available to the developing companies after the close of hostilities. Other discriminatory restrictions also might be imposed against foreign planes, especially since the United States, and perhaps the Soviet Union, appeared to be the only great powers in position to continue manufacturing transport as well as fighting planes. In postwar military and commercial aviation, moreover, those powers would be favored which possessed plentiful sources of gasoline and controlled scattered bases for refuelling purposes. Planes that did not need to "tank up" for more than moderately long "hops" could carry heavier loads and operate more economically than planes that had to start out with sufficient fuel for long trips. These matters contained the seeds of future trouble unless they were made the subject of international agreement even before the end of the war.

A further postwar consideration was the need for effective air disarmament of the defeated states. The course of the Second World War seemed to prove that a nation without air power could be defeated no matter how effective its land and naval forces might be. Again, highly developed air transportation would probably put an end to actual, if not theoretical, isolation. Neither mountains nor seas would serve any longer as barriers or time-consuming obstacles. Hitherto almost inaccessible regions could be reached with relatively little difficulty and a comfortable margin of safety. The use of the great-circle routes would minimize the importance of land and water distances between cities on different continents and completely change the traditional geographic relations among nations.[1]

[1] The direct air route from New York to Bombay via Greenland and Moscow is six thousand miles shorter than the water route around Africa. In an "air-age" coastal cities might well lose their preferred positions in international dealings, for cargo planes could take off for distant parts directly from the sources of exportable commodities. As a consequence one might expect a movement of population away from ports whose chief commercial function has been the transshipment of goods.

CHAPTER XXVI

A Second World War

WAR IN AFRICA, THE BALKANS, AND THE NEAR EAST

The withdrawal of France from the war left the British in a precarious position in the Mediterranean and in eastern Africa. Italy, who had refrained from attacking France until after the latter had requested an armistice, now turned optimistically to the south, where the British suddenly were deprived of all support from French North Africa, Syria, and French Somaliland. Indeed, whereas formerly Italian East Africa and Libya had been hemmed in by Allied units on all sides, the British now found themselves with exposed flanks wherever they had relied on French support. Even so, there was a period of several weeks following Italy's entry into the war (June 10, 1940), during which Anglo-Italian hostilities were confined largely to air raids: the Italians attacking the British Mediterranean bases of Gibraltar, Malta, and Alexandria, and the British dropping bombs on Italian industrial centers and the island base of Rhodes.

Eventually, after entering French Somaliland and capturing some posts in the Anglo-Egyptian Sudan and Kenya, the Italians determined to seize British Somaliland. In August 1940 three Italian columns penetrated British territory. The numerically inferior defenders decided to withdraw, for the possession of British Somaliland would not greatly improve Italy's strategic position and would in no way better her economic status. For two weeks the British troops fought delaying actions, striving to inflict as much damage as possible on the invaders, and then they embarked on vessels under the protection of British naval guns. Italy rejoiced in this easy rounding out of her east-African empire, but in reality she had gained little. Italian East Africa was virtually cut off, except by air, from any contact with the mother country or her other possessions. In an effort to alter this situation, and to wrest from Great Britain control of the Mediterranean, the Fascists next turned their military attention to Egypt and the Suez Canal.

Before the outbreak of the war, Fascist leaders several times had proclaimed Italy's destiny to remove British influence from the Mediterranean. Contemplating their navy, their numerous submarines, their much-publicized bombers, and their naval and air bases on Sardinia, Sicily, the Dodecanese Islands, and Pantelleria,[1] the Fascists had expressed eagerness for a test of strength. But when the war at last came, the Italian navy avoided any major engagement with the British fleet. Whenever British and Italian squadrons sighted each other, the latter steamed full speed to the protection of the nearest shore batteries. Even the Italian airplanes and submarines did relatively little damage to the British fleet, which continued to patrol the entire sea and successfully convoyed merchant vessels carrying troops and much-needed supplies. From January 1941, however, German planes took off from Italian airfields. The Nazi aviators were less shy than their colleagues and did more damage to British ships, particularly through dive-bombing.

The task of approaching Suez by land was entrusted by Mussolini to Marshal Rodolfo Graziani, long experienced as a desert fighter. To reach Suez from Libya (Tripolitania plus Cyrenaica), it was necessary to march through the desert which was western Egypt, and this Graziani set out to do in September 1940. His opponent, who had far fewer men at his command, was General Sir Archibald P. Wavell. The latter's Army of the Nile was composed mainly of Australians, ably supported by a Polish contingent.

The position of Egypt in the ensuing struggle was interesting. Under the terms of an Anglo-Egyptian Treaty of Alliance (1936), Britain was permitted to use Egypt as a base in time of war and to call on her for military aid. Actually, the British were content to exercise only the first of these rights. Thus, while the British imperial forces fought from Egypt as a base, the Egyptians themselves were left free to produce foodstuffs and other essential supplies. (This later proved an important factor in enabling the British successfully to meet the Italian challenge.) Mussolini, on the other hand, refrained from declaring war on Egypt, presumably because he wanted to continue in his self-assumed role of "protector of Islam."

---

[1] Strategically situated near the narrowest crossing point between Sicily and Tunisia, Pantelleria is a 2500-foot rock which Italy acquired through the absorption of the Neapolitan Kingdom in 1860. Little attention was paid to the dependency until 1935, when the Italians decided to convert it into a naval base.

During the first days of the campaign, Graziani's men advanced rapidly. Before a week had passed, they were in control of Sidi Barrani, about sixty miles within the Egyptian border. There, however, the attack halted. The Italian commander presumably decided to consolidate his gains, accumulate fresh supplies, and develop security for his transportation lines. The British likewise built up their stores, received heavy reënforcements of men and supplies, and, from the air and the sea, bombed and shelled Italian camps, posts, roads, ports, forts, and supply trucks. At long

THE EAST-CENTRAL MEDITERRANEAN AREA, WINTER 1940–1941

last, in December 1940, Wavell's forces began a well-planned counterattack. Within five days the Italians were back in Libya. The British, now aided by Free French forays from French Equatorial Africa, pressed their offensive into 1941. Bengazi was captured on February 6 and the last remaining Italian outposts in Cyrenaica fell in March.

Graziani, in a report to Mussolini shortly before Christmas

1940, explained the defeat on the ground of British superiority in mechanized arms; but there appear to have been additional reasons. The victors had established full coöperation among land, air, and sea units. They employed skillful strategy and enjoyed a sufficiency of supplies—food, water, and military equipment. They displayed a fine fighting spirit and proved far superior in aerial combat. The Italians were less eager to do battle, suffered from a shortage of water and other supplies, and were demoralized by the constant bombing and shelling of their rear.

Meanwhile, in January 1941, the British, coöperating with Haile Selassie who had earlier flown from Britain to the Sudan, renewed operations in eastern Africa. Striking from both the Sudan and Kenya they readily penetrated Italian East Africa. Eritrea was conquered and Italian Somaliland, and finally Ethiopia. In May 1941, five years almost to the day since he had fled, Haile Selassie reentered his capital at Addis Ababa.[1] For the time being, Suez was safe from both west and south; but in the meantime new dangers threatened from the Balkans and the Near East.

Almost from the beginning of her unified existence, Italy displayed interest in the Balkan Peninsula as a field for the extension of her influence. This sentiment appeared in the terms of the Triple Alliance agreement into which she entered in 1882 with Germany and Austria-Hungary, in the provisions of the Secret Treaties which she signed with the other Allies during the First World War, in her difficult relations with Yugoslavia and Greece after that war, in many of Mussolini's speeches, and in the history of Italian relations with Albania from the little kingdom's creation in 1913 to its absorption by the Fascists on Good Friday of 1939. Hence it was not astonishing that Rome, dissatisfied to have gained control only of a few miles of France and French Somaliland, while Germany had extended her "protection" over most of northern and western Europe, should have cast longing eyes at Greece in the summer of 1940.

About the middle of August Italy began a diplomatic campaign to make Greece renounce the British guarantee of independence accepted in 1939. King George II and Premier Metaxas refused Italy's bidding. The Fascists thereupon accused Greece of being unneutral, charged her with surreptitiously aiding the British navy, and blamed her for terrorist activities on the Albanian frontier. Soon these threats were implemented by the seizure of Greek

[1] In October 1942 Ethiopia formally joined the United Nations.

merchant vessels, the bombing of Greek destroyers, and the massing of Italian troops on the Albano-Greek border.

The Athens Government protested these actions, strengthened its defenses, and sought aid on all sides. Metaxas, who had generally been regarded as axis-friendly, requested Berlin to restrain Rome, held consultations with Soviet officers, and carried on negotiations with Ankara and London. The situation became tense early in October 1940 when Hitler and Mussolini held a meeting and when German soldiers soon thereafter entered Romania. The crisis came when the Italian Minister presented a three-hour ultimatum to the Athens Government at three o'clock in the morning of October 28, 1940.

The document resembled those which Germany had presented to *her* victims in the previous spring. It reproached the Greeks with having been unneutral, complained of terrorist activities "against the Albanian nation," and charged Athens with having promised to put naval and air bases at the disposal of Great Britain. Therefore, in order to "avoid" hostilities between Italy and Greece, Rome demanded permission to occupy several strategic Greek areas for the "duration" of the war. Any resistance would be "broken" and the responsibility for the consequences would be that of the Greek Government. To the evident astonishment of Italy, Greece decided to resist. When Italian soldiers crossed the Greek frontier and Athens called on Britain for help, Churchill telegraphed a pledge of prompt assistance. Turkey offered aid "short of war."

The outbreak of the Italo-Greek war astonished few; its course amazed many. The Italians, after a brief advance, were not only halted by the Greeks but were thrown back across the border. Within a week the Greeks carried the fighting into Albania and for the next four months steadily pushed the Fascists back toward the Adriatic coast. By January 29, 1941, on which day Premier Metaxas died, the Greeks were driving toward Valona, chief port of entry for Italian supplies and reënforcements. The new prime minister, Alexander Korizis, former governor of the Bank of Greece, pledged himself to continue the struggle along the lines so ably laid down by his predecessor.

No satisfactory explanation has been given for the turn of events in the Italo-Greek war. It may be that the Italians expected little resistance and were unprepared to meet determined opposition. Apparently the invaders were not very successful in their attempts to use mechanized equipment in the rugged Pindus Mountains, where poor roads were made worse by rain, snow, and ice. The strategic ability of Metaxas and Marshal Alexander Papagos doubtless played its part in the Greek victories, while the Italian generals seemed unable to inspire their men with confidence or with the necessary determination to win. The British fleet and bombers, seconded by Greek planes and submarines, effectively hampered the shipment of Fascist supplies and men across the Adriatic, even though Italy controlled both sides of the narrow Strait of Otranto.

The entry of Greece into the war appeared of material help to Britain not only because it diverted some Italian energies, but because Britain now had several new bases, particularly on the island of Crete, from which to undertake operations against the Fascists. Naples and other southern Italian cities were frequently bombed, and on the night of November 11–12, 1940, the air arm of the British fleet inflicted a severe blow on the Italian navy. Appearing unexpectedly over the port of Taranto, inside the heel of the peninsula, the British airplanes, according to Churchill, put half of Italy's capital ships out of action, leaving her with only three "effective" battleships.

About three weeks later, Marshal Badoglio resigned as chief of the Italian General Staff, and on succeeding days a number of generals and admirals followed suit. No reason for these steps was published, and the mystery was heightened when a number of young Fascist officials, including Foreign Minister Ciano, reported to fighting units at the front. In January 1941 there were reports of riots in northern Italy over the presence of increasing numbers of German soldiers in the peninsula. It was admitted by Berlin that German planes and aviators had been dispatched to Italy and that these needed replacements, ground crews, and other auxiliaries in considerable number. Once more it was the northern axis partner who seemed to be winning the successes and making the gains, even in the Balkans. And so we come back to the misadventures of Romania.

The partitioning of this kingdom in 1940 was only a bitter climax to twenty years of misfortune and unrest. Emerging from the peace settlement of 1919–1920 as the largest and presumably strongest Balkan state, Romania was almost constantly torn by internal strife growing out of her minorities problems, her economic difficulties, the poverty of her peasants, and violent personal rivalries. The acquisition by the Soviet Union of Bessarabia and northern Bukovina in 1940 already has been discussed; [1] the next territorial beneficiaries were Bulgaria and Hungary.

In 1913, as a result of the Second Balkan War, Bulgaria had ceded to Romania the districts of Durostor and Caliacra in the southern part of Dobruja province. Now, in 1940, Bulgaria asked for the return of this "Quadrilateral," a majority of whose inhabitants were Bulgarians. Under axis pressure, Romania acquiesced in the demand and the neighboring kingdoms signed the Craiova Agreement (August 1940). This permitted Bulgarian civil and then military authorities to enter the southern Dobruja within a few weeks. An arrangement also was made for the partial exchange of populations and Bulgaria undertook to reimburse Romania for her permanent improvements in the ceded territory.

More difficult of settlement was the Hungarian demand for the return of Transylvania. This area, acquired by Romania in 1920, had ever since been among the most troublesome of Europe's sore spots. With the Magyar nationalists insisting on the return of the entire region, and the Romanian nationalists opposed to any cession, negotiations between the two countries quickly reached deadlock. After weeks of fruitless discussion, the Hungarian and Romanian diplomats were summoned to Vienna, where the German and Italian Foreign Ministers on August 30, 1940, simply handed down the Vienna Award. Romania thereby was forced to cede to Hungary the larger (northern) part of Transylvania, comprising 16,000 square miles with a population of 2,500,000. Those inhabitants—and they formed a majority—who were of Romanian origin, were permitted within six months to "opt" for Romanian nationality; if they chose this course, they must leave the ceded area within another year. Germany and Italy guaranteed the "integrity" of what was left of Romania.

The Vienna Award satisfied neither of the disputants, but whereas the Budapest Government at least could point to an extension of Hungary's frontier to the Carpathian Mountains, the Bucharest authorities once more had to admit territorial loss. The Fascist Iron Guards in particular were vehement in their renewed attacks on King Carol II who, in an effort to strengthen his position, appointed the nationalistic General Jon Antonescu as premier with full powers. Antonescu, only recently freed from prison where he had been sent for his political views, quickly prevailed upon the king to bow to the Iron Guard's clamor for his abdication. On September 6, 1940, Carol passed the crown on to his son,

[1] See p. 744.

who now for the second time became King Michael I; the ex-king fled the country with his friend, Magda Lupescu, whom the Iron Guards hated, and together they made their way first to Spain and eventually to Mexico. Antonescu then announced that Romania was entering the "political sphere" of the axis powers and appointed Horia Sima, Iron Guard leader, as vice-premier.

The import of this coördination of policies became evident

THE PARTITION OF ROMANIA, 1940

when large numbers of German soldiers began to pour through Hungary into Romania. The Hungarians expedited the transit of the Nazis, who in Romania garrisoned strategic zones, guarded the oil fields, and undertook the "training" of Romanian forces. Antonescu meanwhile brought Romania's internal life completely into harmony with Nazi principles. Finally, between November 20–24, 1940, Hungary, Romania, and the Nazi "protectorate" of Slovakia adhered to a German-Italian-Japanese alliance signed during the previous September.[1]

Two months later, in January 1941, Bucharest witnessed anti-Nazi and anti-Antonescu riots. The fighting was set off by the shooting of a German officer in the Romanian capital, allegedly by a Greek. But it soon appeared that the violence reflected a rift in Iron Guard ranks, with Antonescu heading one faction and

[1] See p. 806.

Sima another. The Antonescu group, which crushed the incipient revolt, was more pro-German in its outlook, while the Sima group was less pro-German, particularly since the recent partition of the kingdom. In February, Great Britain severed diplomatic relations with Romania.

On March 1, 1941, the premier of Bulgaria signed a document in Vienna whereby his country became the seventh member of the axis system. This action grew, at least in part, out of Bulgaria's desire to regain from Greece some land which she had had to cede to the Athens Government after the First World War. Within a few hours after the ceremony was completed, German forces were in occupation of the Bulgarian capital, Sofia. Since the distance from the Romanian border to Sofia is considerable, the Nazis must have entered Bulgaria several hours before the pact was signed. With German troops now massing on the Yugoslav, Greek, and Turkish borders, Great Britain also broke off relations with the kingdom of Boris III.

Following the occupation of Bulgaria, Nazi armies were poised all along the northern and eastern frontiers of Yugoslavia. On the northwest and southwest, moreover, Yugoslavia bordered on Italy and Italian-held Albania. This situation boded ill for the South-slavic state, whose economic life had come more and more under German domination. In the Greco-Italian War, Yugoslavia sympathized with her Balkan neighbor, but Belgrade carefully maintained official neutrality. This attitude was inspired both by a fear of Germany and by uncertainty regarding the loyalty of the Croats and Slovenes—long dissatisfied with Serbian predominance in the triune kingdom.

As early as February 1941 Berlin had demanded of Yugoslavia an alliance and permission for the passage of German soldiers to the Yugoslav-Greek border. The Regent Paul had secured a scaling down of the demands to a nonaggression pact and permission for the transit only of munitions and hospital trains. But when Paul recommended this compromise to his advisers, the Serbian leaders warned that its acceptance would mean the collapse of the government. Simultaneously Britain and the United States promised military supplies to help stiffen potential resistance to German pressure.

Paul, however, decided that the possibility of Italo-German invasion was more dangerous than that of civil war. On March 24, 1941, he went to Vienna to conclude his agreement with the Germans. But before the document could be ratified, a military coup of March 27 drove Paul into flight. King Peter II, though not yet eighteen, assumed full royal authority and chose as his premier General Dushan Simovich, popular chief of the air force and organizer of the "bloodless revolution." The Simovich Government offered continued friendship and economic coöperation with Germany, but refused to ratify the Vienna pact or demobilize the Yugoslav army. Lest this changed situation lead to effective Yugoslav defensive preparations and interfere with Hitler's plans to aid Italy in her Greek misadventure, the Nazis press now trumpeted forth the same atrocity stories that had earlier been used against the Czechs and Poles. And on April 6, 1941, Nazis soldiers entered Yugoslavia and Greece.

The outright war in Yugoslavia lasted only twelve days. Partly because Yugoslav mobilization had not been completed, partly because of the assistance extended to the invaders by discontented Croats and Slovenes, and partly because of the usual careful Nazi preparation, the fighting ended officially on April 18. Peter and his government fled eventually to London, while Yugoslavia was partitioned. Italy, Hungary, and Bulgaria all were rewarded territorially. The Germans themselves continued to occupy Belgrade and other Serbian places, and a new puppet state of Croatia-Slavonia was created. This supposedly "independent" region was placed under the control of the terrorist Pavelich [1] and then was given a king in the person of Aimone, Duke of Spoleto. The latter judiciously remained in Italy.

The official end of the war found large units of Serbian fighters in possession of their arms and imbued with a fierce desire to continue the struggle against the Germans. Eventually many thousands of these collected under the leadership of General Draja Mikhailovich who had for years studied the possibilities of organized mountain fighting. Now he and his *chetniks* carried on an amazingly successful mountain warfare that harassed the enemy without letup. In January 1942, when the Yugoslav Government-in-Exile was reorganized, Mikhailovich was appointed minister of war.

Meanwhile the fate of Greece also had been sealed. On April 21, three days after the collapse of Yugoslavia, the Athens Government gave up the struggle—to avoid the useless massacre of its people. Great Britain had tried to help by quickly sending veterans from the Libyan Front. But this move, undertaken more out of political than military considerations, proved futile. Indeed,

[1] See p. 496 n.

whereas the reënforcements were too weak to keep back the superior German land and air forces, their withdrawal from Africa paved the way for a new British retreat in Libya. By May 31 Crete, too, had fallen into German hands.[1] Henceforth, until the Nazi invasion of the Soviet Union, Britian was left to carry on the war without an ally or a foothold on the continent of Europe.

Thus far in the war the initiative on land had lain almost entirely with the Germans. From May to September 1941, however, the British acted swiftly in the Near and Middle East and forestalled German coups in Iraq, Vichy-controlled Syria, and Iran.[2] The first and last of these states were of vital importance to Great Britain because of their geographic relation to the Persian Gulf and India, their oil resources, and their potential value to Germany as bases from which to drive through Trans-Jordan and Palestine into Egypt. Syria in unfriendly hands obviously was a constant threat to Britain's whole position in the eastern Mediterranean area. Its control by the Nazis would more than compensate them for their evident hesitancy to attack Cyprus and march through Turkey en route to Suez and India.

Now it happened that in April 1941 a military coup in Baghdad had placed into power as premier of Iraq the pro-Nazi Rashid Ali Beg Gailani.[3] Axis propaganda and agents now flooded the country. Britain therefore exercised her right under a treaty of 1932 to send additional troops to certain strategic points in Iraq. Rashid Ali thereupon ordered resistance and appealed to Germany for help. Hostilities broke out on May 2 but were concluded on May 31. Germany was unable at the moment to do more than send a few planes via Syria and to induce the Vichy authorities in Syria to give Rashid Ali some war materials. None of the other Arabian states chose to intervene and Rashid Ali soon was driven to flight. The Regent Abdul Illah returned and Britain now was ready— not a day too soon—to act in neighboring Syria.[4]

There Nazi penetration was far advanced. The German armistice commission and German technicians had done efficient work,

[1] For a time the Nazis allowed the Italians to occupy conquered Greece; but when this led to trouble, the Germans themselves resumed control. King George II set up a government-in-exile in London. In 1942–1943 several thousand Greek refugees found new homes in the Belgian Congo. On the fall of Crete see also p. 787 n. 2.

[2] Historically the Near East includes, among others, all the Arabian states in western Asia. The Middle East comprises Iran, Afghanistan, Baluchistan, India, and Burma.

[3] The king was not yet six years old and the Regent Abdul Illah was forced to flee.

[4] Iraq declared war on the three chief axis powers in January 1943.

and the Vichy commissioner, General Henri Dentz, had been co-operative. The direct aid given by Dentz to Rashid Ali and to the Nazi planes sent to help the Iraqi dictator made British action urgent. On June 8, 1941, British and Free-French columns entered Syria from Iraq, Trans-Jordan, and Palestine. The invaders tried to keep casualties to a minimum despite Dentz' determination to fight, and so the campaign proceeded slowly. On July 12 hostilities were concluded. Those Frenchmen who preferred not to join the de Gaullists were repatriated, and Syria was safe, at least for the time being, from Nazi clutches.

Allied military attention soon thereafter was focused on Iran. With the German invaders of the U.S.S.R. approaching the Caucasus, it became essential for Great Britain to keep open feeder lines to the Russians via the Persian Gulf and Iran. There, however, Riza Shah [1] had for some time been receptive to German influences and had permited the influx of several thousand Nazi technicians and "tourists." London and Moscow therefore requested the expulsion of the German agents. When the shah evaded action on this demand, British and Russian soldiers entered Iran on August 25, 1941. They seized the chief oil centers and the one strategic railway line, encountering little more than "token" resistance. Within a few days the Teheran Government agreed to expel the Nazis and permit the transit of supplies across Iran to the Soviet Union.

Once again the shah adopted dilatory tactics; hence additional Allied soldiers were sent into the country. This encouraged many Iranians, particularly certain tribes in the southwest who had been harshly treated by Riza, to threaten revolt. The shah thereupon abdicated (September 16) in favor of his son, Mohammed Riza. With the new ruler's consent, Anglo-Russian control was consolidated and a regular transport service to carry British and American supplies to the Bolshevik forces was organized.

These Allied successes in the east occurred simultaneously with a renewal of the seesaw campaigns in northern Africa. After Wavell had driven the Italians out of Cyrenaica,[2] the Germans shipped large quantities of men and materials to Libya in preparation for another drive. The new commander of the axis forces was the experienced tank commander, General (later Field Marshal) Erwin Rommel. In March 1941, shortly before some British African units were sent to the aid of Greece, Rommel began his well-planned

[1] See p. 208.
[2] See p. 793.

push. Within less than a month the allies were ousted from Libya, except that the garrison in Tobruk, supplied by British ships, held out for more than seven months—until it was relieved late in November as the result of a British counteroffensive.[1] This was launched under the direction of General Sir Claude Auchinleck, successor to Wavell, who had been sent to command the British armies in India.

Auchinleck's offensive, aided by light American tanks, regained all Cyrenaica, but the retreating German *Afrika Korps* was not destroyed. Indeed, after getting additional reënforcements from the continent, Rommel struck back late in January 1942—at a time when several Australian divisions were withdrawn from Africa to the new theater of warfare in the Far East. Thrusts and counterthrusts by the opposing forces occupied most of the weeks until May, when Rommel embarked on a full-scale offensive. Although the two armies were fairly evenly matched in numbers and equipment, the German leader proved far more skillful than his immediate opponent, Lieutenant-General Neil M. Ritchie. The Nazis, too, were clever in avoiding direct tank clashes and on one occasion drew several hundred British tanks into a fatal ambush. Rommel also brought into use an 88-mm. gun which served both antiaircraft and antitank purposes and which fired a high-velocity, armor-piercing shell of amazing destructiveness.

After a temporary setback late in May, Rommel regained the initiative and drove ahead so furiously and with such skill that he now captured Tobruk with its garrison of twenty-five thousand men in a single day's assault (June 21). Auchinleck thereupon took personal charge of what was left of the British Eighth Army and retreated to El Alamein, about seventy miles west of Alexandria. Here he prepared to make a last stand in the Egyptian desert. The site was well chosen, for it was flanked on the north by the sea and forty miles to the south by the treacherous sands of the Qattara Depression. By this time, moreover, fresh Australian and other troops had arrived, as had large numbers of planes and much artillery and mechanized equipment, chiefly from the United States.

On July 1, 1942, Rommel assaulted El Alamein and made a breach in its defenses. But the British reserves closed the gap and Rommel was checked. By the narrowest of margins he had failed

---

[1] In the fight to keep the Mediterranean open to British ships and to hamper axis shipments to Africa, the British island base of Malta played an amazing rôle. It quickly became the world's most bombed area, experiencing an average of three air raids per day over many months.

to win the Battle of Egypt. For the next few months the British held against repeated assaults by Rommel, meanwhile building up strength for a smashing offensive that should drive the axis forces not merely out of Egypt but out of northern Africa.

THE WAR AND THE FAR EAST TO 1941

In existing world circumstances, it was inevitable that the war of 1939 should have had strong repercussions in the Far East. There the Japanese, as we have seen, some years earlier had embarked upon a policy designed to create a new order in eastern Asia, one which would satisfy Nippon's political, economic, and nationalistic desires. The continued resistance of the Chinese, however, spoiled the Japanese plans. Under Chiang Kai-shek the Chinese armies remained in the field, fighting well according to the tactics for which their limited equipment and the terrain best suited them. The Chinese people, moreover, were expert at passive resistance, and they helped the national cause with guerrilla warfare, boycotts, "scorching" of the earth, perseverance in the face of mass bombings, and untiring efforts in the hauling of supplies on their backs where trucks or trains were not available.

Presumably in the hope of causing a serious rift among the Chinese, Tokyo on March 30, 1940, recognized a puppet "Chinese National Government" set up at Nanking under the nominal headship of Wang Ching-wei, who recently had been expelled from the Chinese Nationalist Party as an advocate of appeasement. The results of this move, if such was its motivation, must have been disappointing to Japan. The nonaxis states continued to have relations only with the regularly constituted Chungking Government. Their own spirit and actions, supported by material aid from the Soviet Union, Great Britain, and the United States, thus enabled the Chinese to check the Japanese and force them to modify their plans for the immediate future.[1]

The Japanese Government lost "face" in its Chinese venture, with resultant unpleasantnesses on the home front. The mounting expenses and tension of prolonged war, the loss of overseas markets, exchange difficulties, the unsettlements of a warring world, the United States embargoes on essential commodities, and the increasingly authoritarian orientation of domestic policies, all ap-

[1] Hard-pressed Britain, in an effort to ease her relations with Japan, closed the Burma Road from July 18 to October 17, 1940, so that no military supplies could reach China via this important highway. Then the road was reopened.

peared to stimulate discontent. The conflicting reports emanating from Japan pointed to a confusion in the minds of the Japanese leaders and there seemed to be broad disagreement among several groups of advocates of positive action. In 1940, finally, Tokyo turned its attention southwestward to the area generally called "southeastern Asia."

After the withdrawal of France from the war, the Japanese be-

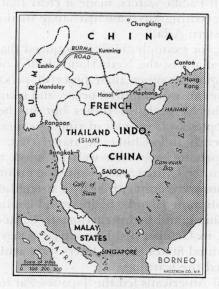

THE BURMA ROAD

gan to look with increasing concentration at the rubber, oil, tin, and rice of southeastern Asia—specifically, of the French, British, and Netherlands possessions in southeastern Asia. The longing for control over this richly endowed portion of the Far East was first officially expressed in the phrase "Greater East Asia," used in a statement issued on August 1, 1940, by the recently formed government of Prince Fumimaro Konoye. With France in collapse and Great Britain fighting Germany, the chief obstacles in the way of fulfillment of this ambition were, aside from China herself, the Soviet Union and the United States.

Japan, as events proved, was strong enough on the sea and in the air to overpower the defenses of French Indo-China, Singapore, and the Netherlands East Indies. But there also existed in Japan a traditional suspicion of Russia, especially since the Bolsheviks openly continued to lend material assistance to China in her fight against the new order. Hence, at least until after the Nazi invasion of the Soviet Union, some Japanese leaders seemed to fear lest a gathering of power in southeastern Asia sufficient to conquer that region would leave Japan unprotected in the event of a sudden attack by the U.S.S.R. Besides, the United States, through utterances of Secretary Hull and through a concentration of naval forces in Pacific waters, made it clear that she was vitally interested in preventing any violent change in the political relations of southeastern Asia.

In April 1940, for example, Hull announced that "intervention in the domestic affairs of the Netherlands Indies or any alteration of their *status quo* by other than peaceful processes would be prejudicial to the cause of stability, peace, and security not only in the region of the Netherlands Indies but in the entire Pacific area." And in September, apropos of rumors concerning Japanese demands on French Indo-China, he stated that, "should events prove these reports to have been well founded, the effect upon public opinion in the United States would be unfortunate." These official expressions were emphasized by a strengthening of the defenses in the Philippine Islands; by increased lending, in one form or another, to China; and by instructions to United States consuls in the Far East, in October 1940, to advise American citizens to return to the United States. Three liners were sent to bring home those who heeded the warning.

The exodus of Americans led the Japanese, at least in speeches, to be more considerate of United States feelings. But in practice Tokyo continued to increase her influence in southeastern Asia. Perhaps she was encouraged to do so because, on September 27, 1940, she had concluded an alliance with Germany and Italy, countries which, according to a rescript of Emperor Hirohito, "shared the views and aspirations" of the Japanese Empire.

As published, the pact contained six articles. Japan "recognized and respected the leadership of Germany and Italy in the establishment of a new order in Europe." Similarly, "Germany and Italy recognized and respected the leadership of Japan in the establishment of a new order in Greater East Asia." The three signatories agreed "to assist one another with all political, economic, and military means" whenever one of them might be "attacked by a power at present not involved in the European war or in the Sino-Japanese conflict." Joint technical commissions to implement the pact were to be appointed, and it was stated that the treaty in

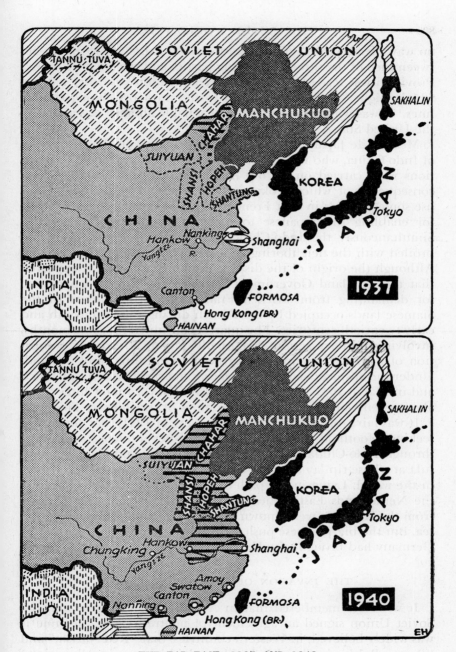

THE FAR EAST, 1937 AND 1940

From *War Atlas*, Headline Book No. 23,
Foreign Policy Association, New York, 1940.

no way affected the "political status which exists at present as between each of the three contracting parties and the Soviet Union." Provision was made for extending "coöperation" to other nations which might "be inclined to put forth endeavors" along similar lines.[1] It was widely held that the new triple alliance was aimed at the United States.

Meanwhile Japan had made specific demands on the authorities of Indo-China, who were loyal to the Vichy Government. Negotiations were carried on during August and September 1940, as a consequence of which Tokyo got the right to land soldiers and use some airfields in that French colony—presumably as a means for enabling the Japanese to strike at China from the south. Simultaneously the Indo-Chinese Government found itself embroiled with the neighboring state of Thailand, the former Siam. Although the origin of the dispute remained obscure, it appeared that the Thailand Government regarded the time as opportune for demanding from stricken France a return of some of the Siamese lands occupied by the French during the nineteenth and early twentieth centuries. The quarrel continued for some months, involving military action. Eventually Japan, already in occupation of a sizable portion of northern Indo-China, took a hand. Under the auspices of Japanese officers an armistice was concluded and in March 1941 peace was signed in Tokyo. Indo-China ceded about twenty-one thousand square miles of territory to Thailand.

It was fairly obvious, even in the spring of 1941, that Japan was seeking a foothold from which to extend her influence southward through Indo-China and Thailand to the long and narrow peninsula at whose tip lay Singapore, adjudged the strongest naval base in the world. Lying in the path of any Japanese campaign against the Netherlands East Indies or Australasia, Singapore's defenses from the land side were known to be weaker than those facing the sea. But the big Japanese push southward did not come until after Germany had brought the U.S.S.R. into the war.

THE INVASION OF THE SOVIET UNION

It will be remembered that in August 1939 Germany and the Soviet Union signed an agreement of neutrality.[2] At the time it was widely believed, in Western countries, that "Red Nazism" and "Brown Bolshevism" at last had been laid bare as equally poison-

---

[1] Thus it later was possible for several German satellites to join the alliance.
[2] See p. 735.

ous fruits of the same tree. Even former admirers of the Soviet system now turned against it, in sad disillusionment. Later events, however, cast a different light on the situation. With the advantage of hindsight, it appeared that Hitler had been motivated by a desire to ensure Soviet neutrality until he should have disposed, in battle, of France and Great Britain. Then, conqueror of the west, he would be free to enforce any demands upon the U.S.S.R. And Stalin, doubtful of the precise intentions of Paris and London, grasped at the opportunity to win time for the military industrialization which was the essence of the Third Five-Year Plan. Meanwhile, in 1939–1940, the shape of things enabled the Soviets to extend their western frontiers approximately to the line of 1914, and thus to place some additional mileage between the new German border and Moscow.

By the spring of 1941 there were unmistakable signs of growing tension between Moscow and Berlin. The eastward march of the Nazis, particularly the occupation of Bulgaria and Yugoslavia, led to outbursts in the controlled Soviet press. In April 1941 Moscow signed a neutrality pact with Tokyo, thus presumably leaving herself freer to act in the west. In May, Stalin himself assumed the premiership of the Soviet Union, thus for the first time taking the political leadership directly into his own hands.

Meanwhile the Nazi leaders appeared to have concluded that Britain could not be defeated while it was necessary to immobilize numerous German planes and soldiers in the east because of uncertainty regarding Moscow's course. Hence the U.S.S.R. must be defeated in another lightning land and air campaign and then full attention could be centered on Britain. In addition, direct access to the raw materials of the Soviet Union would be satisfactory compensation for the aid being rendered to Britain through growing American lend-lease activities. Finally, a German war on Bolshevism might lead to an ideological split in both Great Britain and the United States and thus weaken their determination to smash Hitlerism.[1]

At dawn on Sunday, June 22, 1941, Nazi soldiers without warning launched an attack across the Soviet frontier. The Germans

---

[1] It may be that this last objective also lay behind the airplane trip of Rudolf Hess, deputy-leader of the Nazi Party and successor-designate to Hitler and Göring, to Britain on May 10, 1941. Perhaps he was delegated to approach certain Britishers in the belief that they would respond favorably to an appeal for immediate peace with Germany and a joint crusade against Bolshevism. In any case, he was imprisoned by the British authorities, who withheld information concerning him and his projected activities.

again gained the advantages of surprise, but the Bolsheviks, though not fully mobilized, apparently had far more soldiers immediately available than the Nazis had anticipated. Later, indeed, Hitler in a speech accused the Soviets of being much better prepared than he or his advisers had expected! Churchill at once pledged full aid to the U.S.S.R. and Roosevelt two days later made a similar declaration of United States' help. On the other hand, Italy, Romania, Hungary, Slovakia, Bulgaria, and Finland all entered the war against the Soviet Union before the end of 1941. The Finns, evidently thinking only in terms of revenge, plunged into the war against the U.S.S.R. on June 25—and soon found themselves closely tied up with the axis powers in their global war against the United Nations. The Nazis also received the aid of several thousand anti-Bolshevik "volunteers" from France and Spain.

On July 12, 1941, London and Moscow signed a military pact of mutual aid, and later in the same month the Soviet Union reached agreements with the Czech and Polish governments-in-exile. These latter documents had little military but considerable political significance, since in them Moscow denounced the events of 1938–1939 which had culminated in the breakup of the two Slavic states. Before the close of the year, Great Britain declared war on Finland, Hungary, Romania, and Bulgaria, while Slovakia officially took up arms against the British. The type of resistance offered by the armies and the people of the Soviet Union soon won the admiration of even former opponents of the regime, so that any Nazi hopes of creating a major ideological rift in the English-speaking countries was doomed to disappointment. Indeed, there seemed to be widespread relief that the Bolsheviks had shattered the growing myth of German invincibility on land—a service akin to the one which the Russians performed in 1812 when they frustrated Napoleon's attempt to conquer their land.

Little can be gained by trying here to give a detailed description of the Nazi-Soviet campaigns. No accurate story can be told because of the censorship imposed by both sides and, more important, because "most of the vital information was prevented from ever reaching those channels over which censorship might be necessary." Secrecy surrounded every engagement and "whole provinces were conquered before the public knew they had even been attacked." The figures released from time to time by both sides in the titanic struggle obviously remained subject to major revisions. Hence it seems better to relate the events of the war only in broad outline.

By December 1941—after about six months of the fiercest kind of warfare—the invaders were in occupation of five hundred thousand square miles of Soviet territory, including all the regions annexed by Moscow in 1939–1940 and most of the rich Ukraine. But, by adopting a "scorched-earth" policy and guerrilla tactics, the Russian people greatly curtailed the economic value of the conquered area to the conquerors. The Germans, moreover, had failed in three prime objectives. They surrounded, but did not capture, Leningrad. They came within thirty-one miles of, but did not take, Moscow. And, most important, they did not "annihilate" the Russian armies.

The main reason for this last failure of the Nazis probably was that they left out of their calculations "General Space." Perhaps because they themselves had come to believe in their invincibility, the Nazis invaded the U.S.S.R. all along a two-thousand-mile front from the White Sea to the Black Sea. Instead of concentrating their power and striking at a few vital points, they overextended themselves. As a result, they encountered not merely the Russian armies and Russian spirit, but Russian spaces and distances. With sufficient man power and space for counterattacking, the Soviets often wiped out enemy motorized spearheads before the enemy infantry could come up to occupy the intervening terrain. No matter how far they were pushed back, the Russian armies still had room to maneuver; they could always retreat before they were destroyed; they skillfully offered a fluid resistance to fluid attack.

Other reasons there were, too, for the determined fight put up by the Reds in 1941 and after. Little Nazi propaganda was spread in the U.S.S.R. before the invasion began. In most countries which the Nazis overran with relative ease, they had first "softened up" the population by clever psychological warfare. This propaganda invariably stirred up internal quarrels, spread fear and terror, and created treacherous fifth columns. But in the Soviet Union the propaganda staff of Goebbels had little opportunity to spread subversive ideas, for there the censorship was as strict as in Germany itself. There could be few psychological preliminaries of the type that had helped bring about the collapse of France. And the Nazis, for their part, knew little about the true state of Soviet preparedness or about the readiness of the Russian people to fight any invader to the death. It seemed to puzzle German soldiers that "hopelessly surrounded" Russian units refused to surrender, as had troops elsewhere, but fought all the harder and often hacked their way out of encirclements.

The Bolsheviks, in addition, had long been preparing for a war against any Western enemy. The "liquidation" of many technicians in the early days of Bolshevik control made this process an awkward one at first, but in the successive five-year plans careful provision was made for the rapid increase of the country's military strength. More and more with each passing year did the Bolsheviks build their new plants to the eastward, first in the neighborhood of the ore-rich Ural Mountains and then in the raw-material-studded vastnesses of Siberia. A Western enemy might occupy most of European Russia and still the mechanized war could go on. Besides, the Russians showed great ingenuity in the eastward removal, piece by piece, of entire manufacturing plants, so as to keep them out of reach of the advancing Germans. Workers, too, were shifted, women and men alike, for in the Soviet Union women from the beginning of the war took a prominent part on the battlefields and in the factories.

Mechanized warfare was not novel to the Russians; they were pioneers in experimenting along such lines. They used such innovations as parachute troops, giant tanks, motorized units, tank-carrying airplanes, and the like long before the outbreak of war in 1939. Hence they knew what to expect and how to meet it. They also found in their Cossack cavalry units an effective weapon against parachute attacks. The horsemen were of little use against tanks and armored cars, but they were very effective against troops dropped from the sky. They could ride anywhere at any time, cut down the parachutists before they were free from their ropes, and dash off to the next place of danger. It would appear, furthermore, that the Bolsheviks had perfected some secret antiaircraft (and antitank) defenses which prevented the Germans from getting the air superiority they needed to keep up an unchecked advance.

The staff work and strategy of the Russians was good. The recently reported military "purges" had led many foreigners to believe that Stalin had "liquidated" his best officers and would be helpless against German attack. But the Red High Command appeared to make few mistakes, and such general officers as Klementy E. Voroshilov, Semyon Budenny, Semyon K. Timoshenko, and Gregory K. Zhukov, while they had to retreat, did so in a way to keep their main forces intact and full of fighting spirit. And when the time came they led them in well-directed counteroffensives.

With the coming of the cold winter of 1941–1942, the Soviets were better equipped to fight than were their enemies. The natives knew their winters and took the necessary precautions to keep their fuel fluid and their wheels turning despite the icy mud. The Germans, perhaps because they expected the war to be over before winter set in, were much more hampered by the prolonged subzero temperatures. The Bolsheviks therefore took the offensive and drove the Germans back in a number of places. But except for Rostov, the Reds were unable to recapture any great strongholds. At times they were able to drive around such defenses, as at Rzhev, but most of these bases held firmly and were used as springboards by the Nazis in their new campaign of 1942.

This time the Germans did not repeat the mistake of overextension. Without straining themselves to take either Leningrad or Moscow, they concentrated their efforts in the south. The goal was to conquer the remainder of the Ukraine and to drive forward to the Volga River and the Caspian Sea. Success in this endeavor would bring tremendous advantages. The Russian forces in the Caucasus—land of fertile steppes, of mountains, and of oil —would be cut off from the main Russian armies to the north. The Soviets, already deprived of much economic wealth and with at least a fourth of their population in German-occupied areas, would be deprived of additional industrial and food-producing areas, of raw materials, and of strategic railway lines. The Germans would be able to use the vast oil resources of Baku. They could check the further flow of American and British goods to Russia via Iran. They could by-pass Turkey, which would soon be encircled, and fan out into the Arabian Peninsula—heading on the one side for the Persian Gulf and a possible meeting with the Japanese allies in India, and on the other side for the Suez Canal. With these prizes beckoning, the Germans began a restricted offensive in May 1942 with a drive on the Crimean and Kerch peninsulas. When, after about two months of intensive fighting, these objectives were taken, the Nazis launched a full-scale drive toward the Volga River and the Caucasus.

The defensive task of the Bolsheviks—hampered by a lessened industrial war potential and loss of population—was twofold. The job was to preserve the main Russian armies while so prolonging the campaign as to leave the Nazis still short of their prime objectives at the beginning of the next winter. If, in the meantime, Great Britain and the United States could embark on major operations of their own, so much the better; but if not, then the

Soviets must hold out alone—aided by such supplies as the Western states could send through thousands of miles of submarine-infested oceans.

Relentlessly the Nazi machine rolled forward. By early September the axis forces had conquered the northwestern Caucasus, with its shores washed by the Sea of Azov and the Black Sea, and were in possession of the oil wells at Maikop. Early October saw them within fifty miles of the great Grozny oil fields. Russian resistance was stubborn, but relatively light, for the Bolshevik Command had withdrawn large forces from the Caucasus and the Ukraine in order to make a determined stand behind the great bend of the Don River near Stalingrad, itself on the Volga River. Simultaneously, smaller Russian drives had been launched against German position elsewhere in the Soviet Union, as diversionary measures, but the Germans met these thrusts without appreciably weakening their forces in the south. On August 22, 1942, the Nazis made the first direct attack on Stalingrad. On that day began an epic contest.

For three months a terrible struggle raged over one city. Stalingrad seemed almost to become a symbol in the clash of iron wills. No sacrifice of men or materials appeared too great for the Nazis in their effort to take the city; none seemed too great for the Soviets in their effort to hold fast. Eventually the capture, not of miles but of yards, not of suburbs but of individual buildings, became headline news. And late in November the Russians began a new winter offensive of their own. Attacking in force on the central and southern fronts, they gradually pushed the Germans back to the west of Moscow and in the Ukraine and the Caucasus. Although a large Nazi army remained encamped outside Stalingrad, the Bolsheviks encircled this force and drove on beyond it.[1] By January 1943 the Germans were in full flight along a front of many hundred miles, but it remained to be seen whether the Russians this time would be able to recapture large strongholds as well as the less-well-protected regions lying between these points. Meanwhile, with the attack of Japan on the United States, the war had assumed global proportions.

ENTRY OF THE UNITED STATES

The news of European war in 1939 was not nearly so startling to the American public as had been the similar news in 1914. During

[1] In February 1943 the last of the Stalingrad besiegers were killed or captured.

the intervening quarter-century, the people had come to know more about world affairs than at any previous time. Thousands of Americans had acquired familiarity with Europe through travel. Hundreds of thousands read the reports of newspaper correspondents who covered every scene on the European stage. Millions saw moving pictures of outstanding events or listened to broadcasts of "last-minute" bulletins from overseas. Clubs regularly invited speakers on international subjects, and courses in international relations were among the most popular in the schools and colleges. Most of the larger European states, finally, had established "libraries of information" which freely dispensed printed works for the enlightenment of the American public. If Americans were astonished in 1914 that war came, they were astonished in 1939 that the coming of war had been so long deferred.

Other contrasts there were, too, with the situation in 1914. In the early months of the First World War there appeared to be a general indifference in the United States as to who might win; and among those who *were* strongly partisan, there was no overwhelming majority on one side or the other. Probably only few envisaged the possibility of eventual American entry into the conflict. Such was not the case in 1939. In so far as it was possible to judge, it appeared that the American people were generally convinced that the war was the direct outcome of Nazi principles and technique. There was little disagreement over "war guilt" and the prevailing tendency was to recognize Germany as the aggressor. In like measure, there was a general sentiment of wishing the Allies well and hoping that they would now "finish" the job begun twenty-five years ago.[1]

The chief differences of opinion in 1939 came not over the question of where to place American sympathies—the totalitarian leaders had too often formulated the challenge between the two ways of life in the cry: "We or they!" Rather, disagreement arose over the specific form in which the general sympathy should be manifested. Should the United States try to "isolate" herself and be content to pray for an Allied victory, or should she render all aid "short of war" to the upholders of her own preferred way of life, or should outright military aid be given to the enemies of authoritarianism? The decision became all the more urgent after

[1] It was perhaps important, in the crystallization of opinion, that in the 1930's fewer immigrants had entered the United States than in any previous decade since the 1830's. In some of the more recent years, despite the influx of refugees, more people had left the United States than had come to live in it.

the collapse of France in 1940. To some, this catastrophe was a warning that full support must soon be forthcoming; to others it served as an argument for appeasement.

Meanwhile, on September 3, 1939, President Roosevelt had stated in a radio address that a proclamation of neutrality was being prepared. He expressed the hope and belief that "the United States will keep out of this war," but added: "I cannot ask that every American remain neutral in thought as well." Two days later, the actual proclamation, resembling those issued during previous international conflicts, was issued. Simultaneously, under the terms of the Neutrality Act of 1937, the President placed an embargo on the shipment of implements of war to the enumerated belligerents.

Having performed his duty under the law, the President then appealed to Congress to revise the neutrality legislation. In the light of public opinion, its operation appeared to him to be paradoxical. "These embargo provisions, as they exist today," he told the legislature, "prevent the sale to a belligerent by an American factory of any completed implements of war, but they allow the sale of many types of uncompleted implements of war, as well as all kinds of general material and supplies." Brass tubing, for example, might be sold in pipe form but not in shell form; and the American manufacturer and laborer were deprived of the profits attendant upon finishing goods. There was a widespread feeling, moreover, that the act in reality aided Germany. Since the British fleet in any case would make it impossible for Germany to buy American warstuffs, the embargo was hampering only the Allies. Hence its retention would be "very nearly equivalent to presenting Germany with an Atlantic fleet." The inevitable application of the act to Canada, when that dominion entered the war, became an especially potent argument for its repeal.

On November 4, 1939, Congress passed a new law called the Neutrality Act of 1939. Under its terms the President was required, in the event of international war, to enumerate the belligerent states. United States vessels and aircraft were forbidden to carry passengers or freight to any state so named. The exportation of goods to any belligerent was prohibited until title to such goods had passed to the purchasing state or one of its nationals. The President was further empowered to define specific "combat areas" and exclude from them all American citizens, vessels, or planes. United States citizens were forbidden to travel on belligerent vessels (to prevent a repetition of the *Lusitania* incident) and American merchantmen might not be armed. A prohibition was placed on loans or credits by any American to belligerent governments or their agents. Thus was instituted a cash-and-carry policy which, it was hoped, would enable the Allies to buy supplies without exposing the United States to the risk of having its public aroused to war fever by the acts of German submarines.

From time to time the President issued proclamations lengthening the list of belligerents and outlining new combat areas. The exclusion of American ships from these zones bade fair to cause hard times for shippers, but the problem was met, at least in part, by an expansion of coastal traffic and the sale of merchantmen to foreign purchasers. On occasion the administration made known its wish that manufacturers of war supplies coöperate in the placing of a "moral embargo" against countries which, like Japan, while not engaged in the European war, were bombing open cities. Meanwhile the Allies were beginning to receive appreciable shipments of airplanes and other war materials.

The entrance of Italy into the war, the rapid extension of German control, and the result of the election of 1940 led Washington to concentrate on three main defensive policies: the direct strengthening of the military might of the United States, coöperation in hemisphere defense with the other American countries, and the provision of all possible aid "short of war" to Great Britain while simultaneously pursuing economic warfare against the axis.

The process of building up defenses required the coöperation of President, Congress, and people. In 1940 alone, the government authorized the expenditure of $17,690,000,000 for mechanized equipment, a "two-ocean navy," planes, antiaircraft guns, arms, and camp constructions, thus raising the national debt to a new record figure. Fifth-column activities were searched out by the Federal Bureau of Investigation and by a House Committee on Un-American Activities under the chairmanship of Representative Martin Dies of Texas. The President in June 1940 took into his cabinet two Republican leaders who were energetic advocates of rapid rearmament and substantial aid to Britain: ex-Secretary of State Henry L. Stimson, who became secretary of war, and Colonel Frank Knox, publisher of *The Chicago Daily News,* who became secretary of the navy.

The job of organizing and coördinating the industrial resources of the nation was entrusted by Roosevelt in May 1940 to a National Defense Advisory Commission. Despite the ability of the commission's members, it soon was evident that national defense

was being impeded by a lag in production. It took time to negotiate the scores of contracts; many private manufacturers were reluctant to increase their facilities without some special provision
for meeting the cost of expansion; there was an insufficiency of
machine tools; the government hesitated to force priority for its
orders, with the result that the defense program was simply added
to the regular business load; capital and labor strove jealously to
maintain their respective rights; and the commission had neither
a coördinator nor the power to enforce its recommendations. To
meet some of these difficulties, the President in December 1940
created a new body, the Office of Production Management. This
OPM, authorized to "formulate and execute" all measures needed
to ensure efficient defense production, was headed by William S.
Knudsen, a Danish immigrant and former automobile executive,
and Sidney Hillman, a prominent labor leader; its other members
were the Messrs. Stimson and Knox.

To check a threatening skyrocketing of prices owing to increases
in wages, housing shortages in defense-manufacturing areas, and
declines in stocks of consumer goods, the President in April 1941
created the Office of Price Administration and Civilian Supply
(OPA) under Leon Henderson. In the following month there
came into being an Office of Civilian Defense (OCD), whose job
it was to establish and coördinate protective and morale-building
services throughout the country. Eventually, when the rapid
multiplication of agencies, some with overlapping authority, led
to a veritable scramble for priorities on goods, the President appointed (August 1941) a Supply Priorities and Allocation Board
(SPAB) under Donald M. Nelson. This was to function as a
kind of superagency to fix priorities and allocate supplies for all
defense and civilian purposes. Thereafter production of strictly
civilian products declined while the production of war materials
increased rapidly.[1]

Meanwhile, on September 16, 1940, the President had approved
the Burke-Wadsworth or Selective Training and Service Act of
1940. It was the first American law to prescribe compulsory military service in time of peace. Under its terms every male citizen
who was between the ages of twenty-one and thirty-six on the date
to be set aside for registration was made "liable for training and
service in the land or naval forces of the United States."[2] The

---

[1] In January 1942 Nelson became head of the War Production Board (WPB),
which virtually combined the functions of the OPM and the SPAB.

[2] The same applied to aliens who had filed their intention to become naturalized.

normal term of service was placed at one year, though this period might be extended by the President whenever Congress declared that the national interest was "imperiled." Upon expiration of his year's duty, each man was to enter a "reserve component" under regulations to be prescribed. Service by "selectees" in the land forces was restricted to the Western Hemisphere, except in the case of American territories and possessions, including the Philippine Islands.

The act set an upper limit of nine hundred thousand to the number of selectees who might be called to service at any one moment, and the President might induct only as many men as "Congress shall hereafter make specific appropriation for from time to time." The men were to be chosen by districts on a quota basis and the President was empowered to prescribe rules governing deferment for certain classes of registrants. The National Guard, moreover, might be called to federal service whenever the national security demanded a strengthening of the regular army, and manufacturing establishments were required to give government defense orders precedence over all other contracts. The provisions of the act were to expire on May 15, 1945.

The public appeared to favor the law, and on October 16, 1940, about 16,000,000 men registered for the "draft." The order of selection for service was determined by lot, the drawing of numbers taking place in Washington on October 29–30. President Roosevelt drew the first of the approximately 9000 numbers: 158. On November 18, 1940, the first groups of drafted men were inducted into the army. In August 1941, four months before the United States was at war, Congress increased the period of service for National Guardsmen and selectees to thirty months, but simultaneously provided for the early release or deferment of men over twenty-eight. After American entry into the war, the selective service act was amended to require the registration of all males between eighteen and sixty-four, inclusive, and making liable for military service all those between eighteen and forty-four, inclusive.[1]

In the matter of hemisphere, as distinct from strictly national, defense, the first outstanding development was a meeting of the foreign ministers of all American republics at Panama City in October 1939. Here the representatives of the twenty-one neutral

[1] Meanwhile the navy had begun a tremendous expansion program, in both ships and men, and, under the excellent supervision of a Civil Aeronautics Authority (CAA), there had been inaugurated a widespread plan of pilot training.

states adopted a "Declaration of Panama" which set up a supposedly neutral zone extending southward from Canada to the tip of South America and out to sea a distance ranging from three hundred to one thousand miles. No provision was made for the enforcement of this new doctrine and it soon came to be generally disregarded.

The gradual establishment of German control over European countries which had possessions in the Western Hemisphere brought sharply to the fore the need for clarifying Washington's stand on the Monroe Doctrine. On June 18, 1940, several days before the publication of the Franco-German armistice terms, Secretary Hull sent identical notes to Germany and Italy informing those powers that the United States "would not recognize any transfer and would not acquiesce in any attempt to transfer any geographic region of the Western Hemisphere from one non-American power to another non-American power."

The unsatisfactory reply which Germany sent to this note,[1] the abundant evidences of increasing Nazi fifth-column activities in several Latin-American states, the growing economic difficulties of many of the republics because of the British blockade of Europe, the fear that an axis victory might mean the imposition of a disadvantageous barter system on South America, and the desirability of closer economic and political ties between the United States and Latin America, all pointed to the need for one Pan-American policy on the vital issues of the day. Hence the foreign ministers of the twenty-one republics met once more, this time at Havana, in July 1940. On the thirtieth of that month the conference adopted a Final Act and a Convention on the Provisional Administration of European Colonies and Possessions in the Americas. The convention entered into force in February 1942, having then been ratified by the necessary fourteen states.

The act recommended certain measures, including exchange of information, to restrict fifth-column activities in this hemisphere. It proposed the organization of a permanent committee to help settle any disputes which might arise among the American states. It defined as aggression against all signatories any attempt on the part of a non-American state to infringe the territorial or political sovereignty of any one of the republics. Means were suggested for bringing about closer inter-American economic and financial co-

[1] Berlin called the American communication "pointless" on the ground that Germany had "given no cause for the belief that she intends to acquire" possessions in the Western Hemisphere. Italy sent no reply.

operation. And a method was outlined for preventing the transfer of a colony from one non-American state to another.

This "continentalization" of the Monroe Doctrine was accompanied by the setting up of a provisional coöperative administration for the governance of any foreign-owned possessions "in danger of becoming the subject of barter of territory or change of sovereignty." As soon as possible there was to be created, under the convention, an Inter-American Commission for Territorial Administration; but meanwhile there was to be appointed an emergency committee for the same purpose. In the event that action by even this emergency group could not be awaited, "any of the American Republics, individually or jointly with others, shall have the right to act in the manner which its own defense or that of the continent requires." Only then the committee would have to be notified immediately. Eventually, any colonies temporarily administered under American auspices might be returned to their previous status or organized as autonomous states—"whichever of these alternatives shall appear the more practicable and just."

Having thus arranged for coöperation with Latin America,[1] Washington turned to Canada. On August 18, 1940, President Roosevelt and Premier Mackenzie King agreed, at Ogdensburg, New York, to set up a Permanent Joint Board on Defense to "consider in the broad sense the defense of the north half of the Western Hemisphere." The board members were chosen within a few days, representing the public and the military services of each country. The six American members were headed by Mayor Fiorello H. LaGuardia of New York. Although the board appeared to be working energetically, little news was forthcoming of its recommendations. Meanwhile a defense "deal" was being negotiated between the United States and Great Britain. It was consummated on September 2, 1940, through an exchange of letters between Ambassador Lord Lothian and Secretary Hull. The President, on the next day, told Congress what he had done, appending to his message an opinion of the attorney-general supporting the chief executive's authority to make the arrangement.

"This Government," said the President, "has acquired the right to lease naval and air bases in Newfoundland, and in the islands of Bermuda, the Bahamas, Jamaica, St. Lucia, Trinidad, and Antigua, and in British Guiana. . . . The right to bases in New-

[1] In August 1940 the President created an Office for Coördination of Commercial and Cultural Relations between the American Republics, headed by Nelson A. Rockefeller. The agency, whose name later was changed to Office of the Coördinator of Inter-American Affairs, performed its functions well.

822 THE SECOND WORLD WAR

foundland and Bermuda are gifts—generously given and gladly received. The other bases mentioned have been acquired in exchange for fifty of our overage destroyers. . . . The value to the Western Hemisphere of these outposts of security is beyond calculation. . . ." The leases were for ninety-nine years, free of rent; and both countries were to appoint experts to determine the "exact location and bounds of the aforesaid bases." The chosen destroyers soon were handed over to Britain, and the United States prepared to fortify and garrison its new guardians of "the Panama Canal, Central America, the northern portion of South America, the Antilles, Canada, Mexico, and our own Eastern and Gulf Seaboards."

As a further step in hemisphere defense, Secretary Hull in April 1941, after German air activity had been noticed over Greenland, signed an agreement with the Danish Minister whereby that colony was placed under the temporary protection of the United States. The German-controlled Copenhagen Foreign Office declared the agreement void and recalled the minister, but Washington continued to recognize him "as the duly authorized Minister of Denmark." In July 1941, by which time the American freighter *Robin Moor* had been sunk in the Atlantic by a German submarine, United States forces began to replace the British garrison on Iceland.[1] The move was designed to forestall German occupation and to make easier the patrolling of the Atlantic. Throughout this period and afterward, incidentally, it was a great handicap to the maritime efforts of the United States and Great Britain that Ireland refused to allow them the use of certain ports as bases from which to fight the submarine menace. Thus, in the name of neutrality, Dublin rendered a considerable service to the Germans.[2]

The third aspect of Washington's policy in relation to the war concerned the provision of material aid to Britain and other immediate and potential opponents of totalitarian aggression. By January 1941, when Roosevelt entered his third term as President, the British in particular needed much more help than they were

[1] Following the German occupation of Denmark in 1940, Britain had sent men to both the Faroe Islands and Iceland, this last being an independent state with the same sovereign as Denmark.

[2] The ports had been surrendered to Irish control by London in 1938 (see p. 274). In September 1941, after several German attacks on American freighters and warships in the Atlantic, Roosevelt ordered the United States Navy to shoot first where Nazi attack seemed imminent. During October submarines damaged the destroyer *Kearny* and sank the destroyer *Reuben James*.

getting or than they could pay for. Hence, to make possible "all-out" assistance short of man power, an administration bill "to promote the defense of the United States" was introduced to Congress in January 1941. It bore the interesting lower house designation H.R. 1776 and was popularly called "the Lend-Lease Bill."

The bill proposed to permit the President, "notwithstanding the provisions of any other law," to manufacture for, exchange with, sell, lease, lend, or in any other way make available to "the government of any country whose defense the President deems vital to the defense of the United States" any "defense article." Information on defense articles might be communicated to or repairs of defense articles made for any such government. Payment might be in kind or property "or any other direct or indirect benefit which the President deems satisfactory." A foreign government so benefited would have to agree not to permit any such defense article or information to be transferred to any other government. The act would be financed through appropriations made, "from time to time, out of any money in the Treasury not otherwise appropriated." The President would be authorized to purchase or "otherwise acquire" any implements of war produced in a country benefited by the act whenever he regarded such acquisition as necessary for the national defense.

Congress at once plunged into lengthy debate on the bill. The public, too, hotly debated it. Opponents saw in it a ruse for getting Congress to resign all its powers into the hands of a would-be dictator who wanted war. Proponents regarded it as the only feasible way to meet and destroy the axis threat while this was still confined to continental Europe by the British fleet. The bill, with some modifications, became law on March 11, 1941. And the President immediately ordered the shipment of stores from the "arsenal of democracy" to the fighting bulwarks against totalitarianism.[1]

While American supplies in increasing quantity were dispatched to the peoples resisting axis pressure and while American relations with Germany were going from bad to worse, the disagreement between the United States and Japan over the Far Eastern situation was becoming ever more serious. The story of American-Japanese differences to the spring of 1941 has been discussed in earlier sections; it remains to list certain incidents of 1941 which

---

[1] The value of lend-lease aid to the close of 1942 totaled $8,253,000,000, of which the British Empire and the Soviet Union were the chief beneficiaries. Lend-lease was not a one-way affair since the allies provided American forces with supplies and services for which there was no direct payment.

marked the road to war between the United States and the axis powers.

On May 27, 1941, the President found it necessary to proclaim "an unlimited national emergency." In July, Japan got from Vichy France the right to land troops and set up naval and air bases in Indo-China, while Japanese assets in the United States were "frozen." Early in August the United States, British, and Netherlands governments announced that any Japanese action against Thailand would cause them great concern. On August 14 Roosevelt and Churchill issued a joint declaration of general aims soon to become famous as the Atlantic Charter.[1] Throughout September, although this was not revealed by the department of state until January 1943, Tokyo unsuccessfully tried to induce the President to meet Premier Konoye somewhere in the Pacific for an airing of the conflicting views of the two peoples.[2] About the middle of October Konoye resigned to make way for a prominent advocate of positive action, General Hideki Tojo. And on October 27, following the submarine attack on the *Kearny,* the President declared that "the shooting war has started."

On November 10 Churchill promised that "should the United States become involved in war with Japan a British declaration will follow within the hour," and on the next day Secretary Knox warned that danger beckoned not only in the Atlantic but that the United States was "likewise faced with grim possibilities on the other side of the world—on the far side of the Pacific." November 14 saw the arrival in the United States of "trouble-shooter" Saburo Kurusu who came ostensibly to help the Japanese Ambassador, Kichisaburo Nomura, iron out the differences with the American Government; actually, his mission was to cover up preparations for the imminent Nipponese attack on American possessions. The Neutrality Act of 1939 was amended on November 17 so as to permit American vessels to be armed and to carry cargoes into any belligerent port. One week later American troops landed in Surinam (Dutch Guiana), adjacent to Vichy-controlled French Guiana, to help the Netherlands authorities protect one of the world's largest sources of bauxite, from which is derived aluminum. Throughout November the United States tried to reach a peaceable understanding with Japan based on the principle that wanton aggression was unlawful, while Ambassador Joseph C. Grew

---

[1] See p. 826.

[2] In light of later events, it seems not improbable that the Japanese may have planned in this way to get Roosevelt into their power.

warned Washington to be vigilant against a sudden Japanese attack on areas not immediately involved in the Sino-Japanese conflict.

On December 6 President Roosevelt addressed a personal plea to Emperor Hirohito to help him maintain the peace, and on the following day Kurusu and Nomura requested a conference with Secretary Hull so that they might transmit the official reply to some American proposals of the previous month. While the Japanese delegates were proferring the document, on Sunday, December 7, 1941, word reached the President that Japanese planes, carrier-based and therefore of necessity en route for some days, had bombed the naval base at Pearl Harbor, Hawaii, where a large portion of the United States Navy was at anchor.

A few hours after the attack, Japan declared war "on the United States of America and the British Empire." On December 8 the state of war was recognized by a vote of 82 to 0 in the Senate and 388 to 1 in the House of Representatives. It is not known how closely the chief axis powers correlated their moves, but on December 11 Germany and Italy also declared war on the United States. Congress immediately and unanimously made a reciprocal declaration. Romania declared war on the United States on December 12, while Hungary and Bulgaria followed suit on the thirteenth; Washington responded with reciprocal declarations six months later, on June 5, 1942. The war had become global.[1]

GLOBAL WARFARE

The American military and naval commanders at Pearl Harbor were caught off guard despite recent and urgent warnings from Washington to remain continually on the alert for precisely the sort of thing that happened. Ironically, a detector's alarm of the approaching enemy aircraft was passed off by a junior officer as indicating the presence merely of friendly planes. The two commanders were quickly relieved of their posts, but it was not until a year after the event that the government felt free to publish a full account of the losses suffered at Pearl Harbor. These exceeded even the Japanese boasts in some respects and included several thousand casualties as well as destruction of or damage to 8 battleships, 10 other war vessels, a floating drydock, and about 250 planes.

Over a period of months, during which the Nipponese continued

[1] Thailand declared war on the United States and the United Kingdom on January 25, 1942.

to hold the military initiative, much of the damage was repaired; and in the meantime there had emerged two developments of great advantage to the allied cause. First, Tokyo's treachery and early victories brought the American people unity of spirit and a gradual realization that total effort would be needed to win the total war. Secondly, the antiaxis states were drawn more closely together in the conviction that only global coöperation could be effective in the fighting of a global war. Among the first manifestations of this understanding was a reaffirmation of the principles of the Atlantic Charter in a "Declaration by United Nations" signed by twenty-six powers on January 1–2, 1942.[1]

The charter, as announced on August 14, 1941, after a meeting of Roosevelt and Churchill aboard ship off the coast of Newfoundland, reads as follows:

Joint declaration of the President of the United States of America and the Prime Minister, Mr. Churchill, representing His Majesty's Government in the United Kingdom, being met together, deem it right to make known certain common principles in the national policies of their respective countries on which they base their hopes for a better future for the world.

First, their countries seek no aggrandizement, territorial or other;

Second, they desire to see no territorial changes that do not accord with the freely expressed wishes of the peoples concerned;

Third, they respect the right of all peoples to choose the form of government under which they will live; and they wish to see sovereign rights and self-government restored to those who have been forcibly deprived of them;

Fourth, they will endeavor, with due respect for their existing obligations, to further the enjoyment by all States, great or small, victor or vanquished, of access, on equal terms, to the trade and to the raw materials of the world which are needed for their economic prosperity;

Fifth, they desire to bring about the fullest collaboration between all nations in the economic field with the object of securing, for all, improved labor standards, economic advancement, and social security.

Sixth, after the final destruction of the Nazi tyranny, they hope to see established a peace which will afford to all nations the means of dwelling in safety within their own boundaries, and which will afford

---

[1] Meanwhile, on December 11, 1941, Germany, Italy, and Japan had reaffirmed their pact of 1940. Each signatory promised not to conclude a separate peace with the United States and Great Britain and all agreed to coöperate "after victory" in the establishment of a "new and just order."

assurance that all the men in all the lands may live out their lives in freedom from fear and want;

Seventh, such a peace should enable all men to traverse the high seas and oceans without hindrance;

Eighth, they believe that all of the nations of the world, for realistic as well as spiritual reasons, must come to the abandonment of the use of force. Since no future peace can be maintained if land, sea, or air armaments continue to be employed by nations which threaten, or may threaten, aggression outside of their frontiers, they believe, pending the establishment of a wider and permanent system of general security, that the disarmament of such nations is essential. They will likewise aid and encourage all other practicable measures which will lighten for peace-loving peoples the crushing burden of armaments.

The declaration signed by the United Nations on January 1–2, 1942, reads:

The Governments signatory hereto,

Having subscribed to a common program of purposes and principles embodied in the Joint Declaration of the President of the United States of America and the Prime Minister of the United Kingdom of Great Britain and Northern Ireland dated August 14, 1941, known as the Atlantic Charter,

Being convinced that complete victory over their enemies is essential to defend life, liberty, independence and religious freedom, and to preserve human rights and justice in their own lands as well as in other lands, and that they are now engaged in a common struggle against savage and brutal forces seeking to subjugate the world, *Declare*:

(1) Each Government pledges itself to employ its full resources, military or economic, against those members of the Tripartite Pact and its adherents with which such Government is at war.

(2) Each Government pledges itself to coöperate with the Governments signatory hereto and not to make a separate armistice or peace with the enemies.

The foregoing declaration may be adhered to by other nations which are, or which may be, rendering material assistance and contributions in the struggle for victory over Hitlerism.[1]

---

[1] The twenty-six original signatories of this declaration were the United States, Great Britain, the U.S.S.R., China, Australia, Belgium, Canada, Costa Rica, Cuba, Czechoslovakia, the Dominican Republic, El Salvador, Greece, Guatemala, Haiti, Honduras, India, Luxembourg, Netherlands, New Zealand, Nicaragua, Norway, Panama, Poland, the Union of South Africa, and Yugoslavia. By January 1943 these were joined, in chronological order, by Mexico, the Commonwealth of the Philip-

With the passing of time, inter-Allied coöperation increased steadily. In May 1942 Great Britain and the Soviet Union concluded a new and firmer alliance to supplement that of the previous year. In various theaters of the war inter-Allied armed units were placed under single commanders, chosen for their ability and knowledge of local fighting conditions rather than on a basis of nationality. Roosevelt and Churchill met three times in the first thirteen months following the attack on Pearl Harbor—twice in Washington and once (January 1943) at Casablanca in Morocco. An inter-Allied Pacific War Council, sitting in Washington, held its first meeting on April 1, 1942. The American and British general staffs coöperated as the Combined Chiefs of Staff, with Soviet and Chinese representatives present at their meetings. By the close of 1942 more than 1,500,000 American fighting men had been sent overseas, to coöperate in every part of the globe with their colleagues from others of the United Nations.[1]

There was also an increasing preoccupation, especially among the English-speaking peoples and the governments-in-exile, with the subject of postwar collaboration among the United Nations. Aside from official activity in this connection, there were hundreds of semipublic and private agencies and thousands of individuals in the United States and Great Britain who busied themselves with thoughts of peace aims. The discussion of postwar goals was made the more animated and the more complicated by a variety of factors: by the broad nature of the official statements on the subject; by a growing popular interest in the future of China, India, and the Netherlands East Indies; by Roosevelt's enunciation in February 1942 of the "four freedoms"—"freedom of speech, freedom of religion, freedom from want, and freedom from fear"; by the rapid march of social reform in wartime Britain; by the increasing weight of the American tax program with its combined intent of

pines, Brazil, Ethiopia, and Iraq. Bolivia declared a state of war against the axis in April 1943.

[1] Late in 1942 the War Manpower Commission, created in April under the chairmanship of Paul V. McNutt, reported that the American war effort for 1943 would require the services of 63,000,000 men and women, including 10,000,000 in the armed forces. In order to free as much personnel as possible for combat duty, the various services, following British example, recruited women for the numerous noncombat posts. These, in the order of their creation, were the Women's Army Auxiliary Corps (WAAC), the Women's Reserve in the Navy (WAVES, from "Women Appointed for Voluntary Emergency Service"), the Women's Auxiliary Reserve in the Coast Guard or SPARS (from the Coast Guard motto: "Semper Paratus, Always Prepared"), and the Women's Reserve of the United States Marine Corps.

raising revenue and more nearly equalizing the distribution of income; by uncertainty regarding the intentions and desires of the Soviet Union after the war; by the question of whether the governments-in-exile, after years of living abroad, still represented the feelings of the peoples in the occupied areas; by perplexity as to whether action should be taken after victory against all people in the axis states or only against the leaders, and so on and on and on.[1] Meanwhile the fighting spread rapidly.[2]

For some months after December 1941 Japan enjoyed a military success which, to most of her foes at least, was astonishing. Tokyo apparently had planned a clever campaign to gain control of the western Pacific area before the United States or Great Britain could bring any large forces to the scene of conflict. Time after time the Nipponese had superior numbers at the critical points, for "where Japan was hundreds of miles from its bases, the United States had to move its fighting forces thousands of miles." The Japanese Command regarded no sacrifice too great to achieve an objective, and over a period of years Tokyo had converted its scattered island possessions and mandates into a "fleet of anchored aircraft carriers."

The Japanese soldiers were hardened and tough, generally preferring death to surrender. Their leaders developed a skillful method of jungle fighting by dispersal and infiltration.[3] Their opponents at first were prone to underestimate their fighting qualities—partly out of a feeling of superiority to the "little yellow men" and partly out of the mistaken idea that Japan's inability to subdue China was owing to Nipponese weakness rather than

[1] The Nazi leaders deliberately identified the whole German people with their activities. This fitted in with their claim to "embody" the national will and tended to discourage the belief that a defeated Germany might get better treatment if the Nazi leadership were surrendered to allied justice. For this reason and in order to force collaboration from the peoples in the occupied zones, the Nazis also pursued a policy of terrorism against civilians. The wholesale execution of "hostages" reached a horrible climax after the assassination of "Hangman" Reinhard Heydrich who, as Himmler's chief assistant, had been sent to cow the people of Bohemia-Moravia into abject submission. His death was "avenged" by the Nazis through the massacre of unknown hundreds of innocents and the destruction of the village of Lidice. Charging that Heydrich's killers had found refuge there, the Nazis admittedly murdered every adult male inhabitant of Lidice and dispersed the women and children throughout central Europe (June 1942).

[2] In November 1942 Roosevelt appointed Governor Herbert H. Lehman of New York to be Director of Foreign Relief and Rehabilitation. In this capacity Lehman was to supervise the furnishing of "relief and other assistance to the victims of war in areas reoccupied by the forces of the United Nations."

[3] Realizing the difficulty of taking Singapore from the sea side, the Japanese penetrated the "impenetrable" jungles to the north of that base and again appeared at the critical fighting point with an overwhelming superiority of men and planes.

Chinese inner strength. Japan also was the beneficiary of treacherous aid and fifth-column activity, particularly in Vichy-controlled Indo-China, Thailand, and Burma. And by their successful advances, the Japanese soon deprived the Allies not only of most of the island bases they did have in the western Pacific, but of the precious tin, oil, and rubber which they had been deriving from the southeastern Asiatic mainland and the Netherlands East Indies.

Simultaneously with their attack on Pearl Harbor, the Japanese struck at the American island bases of Guam, Wake, and Midway. After truly amazing resistance, the first two fell, so that by Christmas 1941 Midway remained the only American stepping stone between battered Hawaii and the embattled Philippines. Meanwhile several British Pacific islands also were bombed and occupied, and on December 10 Japanese land-based planes sank the 35,000-ton *Prince of Wales* and the 32,000-ton *Repulse* off the eastern coast of Malaya. "Properly protected and properly employed, these two capital ships [which had arrived at Singapore only eight days earlier] could have done much to prevent Japanese landings on the coast of Malaya, in the southern Philippines and in the Netherlands Indies." Their loss, owing largely to an error in judgment by the courageous but inexperienced Vice-Admiral Sir Tom Phillips, left the immediate naval defense of the southwestern Pacific to "squadrons of cruisers and flotillas of destroyers and submarines" inadequately supported by aircraft.[1]

Thereafter the Japanese swept ahead, overcoming "insuperable" obstacles, slashing through "impassable" jungles, flying "inferior" planes with "worthless" gasoline, and braving heavy seas in small river boats. By June 1942 the Nipponese had taken Hong Kong,

---

[1] Cant, G. *The War at Sea*, 1942, p. 301. Cf. also Miller, E. H. *Strategy at Singapore*, 1942, p. 134: "In taking his fleet into enemy waters without air protection, Admiral Phillips had violated a cardinal tenet of modern naval strategy—the injudiciousness of risking capital ships in the vicinity of enemy air power unless such vessels are accompanied by an adequate air screen." On December 11 an American plane commanded by Captain Colin P. Kelly, Jr., sank the 29,330-ton Japanese *Haruna* off Luzon. Earlier in the year, in May 1941, the British themselves had demonstrated the effectiveness of coördination between the air arm and surface units of the fleet. In that month the German battleship *Bismarck*, estimated at more than 35,000 tons, sank the *Hood*, the world's largest warship. After being hit by the *Prince of Wales* and damaging her in return, the *Bismarck* tried to slip away from other British ships and eluded them during a squall. Although her speed had been reduced, the German ship was "lost" for thirty-one hours. Then she was sighted by a patrol bomber and her speed was further cut by hits from torpedo-planes sent out to harass her until the British ships could come up for the kill. On May 27 she was sunk, having been struck a number of times from small British vessels during the night and engaged by the powerful *Rodney* and *King George V* in the morning.

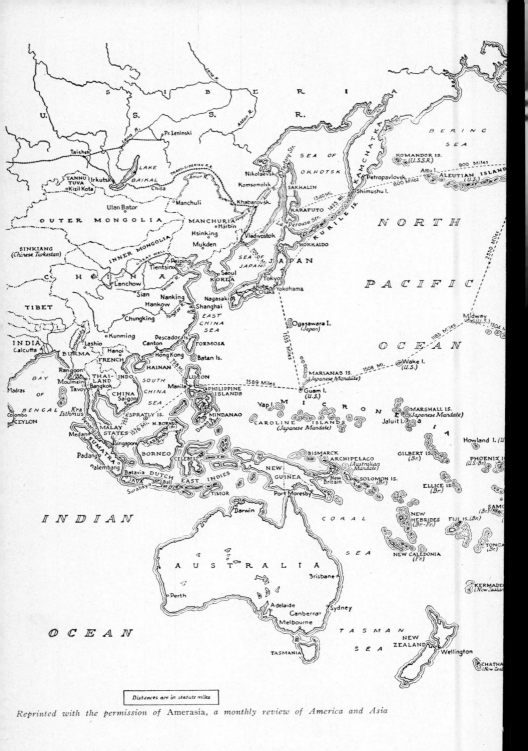

Reprinted with the permission of Amerasia, a monthly review of America and Asia

THE PACIFIC AREA
1941

Sarawak, Malaya, Singapore, Burma, the Philippines, the Netherlands East Indies, much of New Guinea, the Solomon Islands,
and even some of the Aleutian Islands off Alaska. After six
months of warfare Japan had control of the western Pacific area
"between India and Hawaii, and between Siberia and Australia."
In this period there did occur some episodes to bolster American
spirits—episodes such as the heroic stands on Bataan and at Cor-
regidor, the bombing of Tokyo in April 1942, the appointment of
General Douglas MacArthur of Bataan fame to supreme command
in the southwestern Pacific, and the naval victory over Japan in the
Battle of the Coral Sea in May—but the tide of Japanese advance
was not really checked until the summer of 1942.

The eventual call of "halt" to Japan came after long and arduous
preparation by the United Nations. While the damage sustained
at Pearl Harbor was being repaired and while Australian defenses
were being strengthened, American forces built up the bases at
Palmyra and Canton islands, on Samoa and New Caledonia, and in
the Fijis. American reënforcements also were sent to New Zealand,
Australia, the New Hebrides, and other Pacific regions, and American and British supplies were poured into the Far Eastern war
theater. The firm stand of the Soviet Union against Nazi armies
helped give the United Nations a much-needed breathing spell, as
did the continued resistance of China, another American naval
victory over Japan in the Battle of Midway Island (June), and the
British occupation of Vichy-controlled Madagascar between May
and September. This occupation not only forestalled a possible
Japanese-Vichy bargain similar to the one whereby French Indo-
China had become a Nipponese base of operations, but kept open
the vital sea route from the United States and Great Britain around
Africa to the Near, the Middle, and even the Far East.

Eventually, on August 7, 1942, the first step toward retrieving
lost territories was taken when American forces, operating from
New Caledonia, seized a number of small islands commanding
Tulagi harbor and a beachhead which included an almost-com-
pleted new Japanese airfield on Guadalcanal in the Solomon group.
During the winter of 1942–1943 these gains were consolidated
against energetic and reënforced opposition, and an Australian-
American counterattack was launched on New Guinea which gradually drove the Japanese invaders back to bare footholds in the
north. In the process Japan suffered further important naval
losses in a battle off the Solomon Islands during November 1942.
Thus was begun the process of Allied reconquest of bases which, it

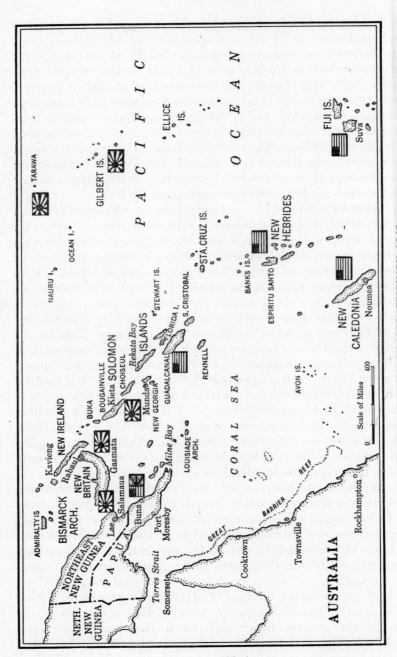

THE SOLOMON ISLANDS, FEBRUARY 1943

Courtesy of the *New York Times*.

was expected, would eventually become stepping stones on the route to Tokyo.[1]

The Japanese occupation of Burma, meanwhile, had given renewed importance to the long-standing problem of Anglo-Indian relations. There was widespread dissatisfaction in India that Great Britain was using the war as a reason for postponing indefinitely any further progress in the direction of Indian self-government. Eventually (March–April 1942), spurred by evidences of disloyalty to Britain and aid to Japan in Burma, London sent the liberal-minded Sir Stafford Cripps to India with a new set of proposals. It was suggested that, "immediately upon the cessation of hostilities," there be created a fully self-governing Indian Dominion with a constitution to be drafted by an Indian constituent assembly. Any province which preferred to remain outside the Indian union would be permitted to attain a dominion status of its own. During the war, however, the direction of India's defense and the organization of its resources would have to remain "the responsibility of the Government of India" as represented in the viceroy and his councils.

Most important Indian groups found reason to treat the proposals with more coolness than enthusiasm, and the Cripps Mission ended in failure. The largest single group, the Indian Nationalists or Congress Party, insisted on immediate self-government; when this was not forthcoming, Gandhi preached a new campaign of noncoöperation with Britain and nonresistance to Japan. The obstructionist tactics of the leaders—who advocated passive resistance against Britain's war effort and objected to the presence of American aviators and technical troops in India, while Gandhi made speeches which must have delighted Tokyo—led to a period of violence. In August 1942 Gandhi and other leaders at last were arrested and order was gradually restored. India continued to fight the axis with men and materials, far surpassing her contributions to the Allied cause in the First World War. The moderate natives appeared to find satisfaction in the belief that after victory the Indian demand for self-government would be supported by public opinion in all the United Nations. As the Indian situation gradu-

---

[1] It was fortunate for the Allies that Japan did little commerce raiding in the Pacific, for throughout 1942 and into 1943 the German U-boat menace in the Atlantic became ever more serious. The United Nations met the danger by building ships faster than the Germans could sink them, developing additional antisubmarine bases, setting up air-ferry routes, and improving the convoy system. Convoys plied the north Atlantic to the U.S.S.R., the middle Atlantic to Great Britain and Iceland, and the south Atlantic to and around Africa.

ally faded from the newspaper headlines in the West, northern Africa surged back into the limelight.

In the summer and early fall of 1942 there was a noticeable increase in the number and intensity of British and American air raids on the Nazi-occupied continent.[1] Lend-lease aid was stepped up to both China and the Soviet Union, the latter having received 4600 planes, 5800 tanks, and tens of thousands of trucks and other motor vehicles from the United States and Britain by January 1, 1943. Simultaneously the British were building up a really powerful army behind El Alamein in Egypt, an army strengthened by the support of numerous American bombers, tanks, and tank destroyers. These last were equipped with a new 105-mm. gun which soon proved to be far superior to the German 88-mm. gun. Meanwhile their augmented air strength in Egypt enabled the allies to check several projected eastward drives by Rommel and partially to close his supply routes from the continent and Libya.

Late in October 1942 the British Eighth Army, commanded by Lieutenant General (later General) Sir Bernard L. Montgomery, began a campaign to drive Rommel not only out of Egypt but out of Libya. On January 23, 1943, Montgomery's forces entered the city of Tripoli, having pushed westward a distance of more than 1300 miles in exactly three months. One week later a British vanguard followed the remnants of the Afrika Korps across the border into Tunisia. For the time being, at least, Italy's African empire was no more. Meanwhile it had become clear that Montgomery's offensive was intended to be only the eastern jaw of a vise whose western jaw was an American army driving through French North Africa, and whose closing would mean the complete expulsion of the axis from Africa.[2]

The American army in question had been landed at selected points in Vichy-controlled French North and West Africa early on November 8, 1942 (West African time). The plans for the operation were laid at a Roosevelt-Churchill conference in the previous June. The object of the occupation was to forestall similar German action, tighten the antiaxis blockade, make safer the south-Atlantic and Mediterranean routes, and set up a possible invasion base against southern Europe. The way was prepared for the landings during a daring preliminary trip to northern Africa by Major General (later Lieutenant General) Mark W. Clark and some other

[1] The first American raid on Germany proper came in January 1943.
[2] Axis agents, however, presumably would continue to function in Spanish Morocco.

EUROPE AND NORTH AFRICA
JANUARY 24, 1943

Axis, dominated areas & Finland
Allies   Nonbelligerents

Adapted from the New York Times

American officers, and by the work of Robert D. Murphy, a state-department official accredited to Vichy. The expeditionary force was transported in more than 500 vessels escorted by 350 warships and British and American air units. The losses en route were small, although troops came not only from Great Britain but directly from the United States. Some British military units participated in the landings but the entire expedition was under the command of the American Lieutenant General (later General) Dwight D. Eisenhower, hitherto chief of the American forces in Europe. It was anticipated that an American army would find less opposition in the French territories than would one composed largely of Britishers.

Although there was some fighting, especially at Casablanca and Oran, all Morocco and Algeria soon were brought under Allied control. Pétain ordered resistance and broke off diplomatic relations with the United States, but General Henri Honoré Giraud, who some months earlier had duplicated a feat accomplished by him during the First World War by escaping from a German prison fortress, promptly appeared in Algeria and urged coöperation with the Allies. Though Giraud apparently had been loyal to Pétain in the months since his escape, Eisenhower now placed him in command of the French North African forces, an appointment soon confirmed by Admiral Darlan.[1] The latter, who also had gone to Algeria, presumably on orders from Pétain, and who had been "captured" by the Americans, on November 11 "assumed authority over North Africa in the name of the Marshal" and ordered all French resistance to end. By these arrangements Eisenhower hoped to avoid the casualties that might result from a protracted Franco-American struggle and to concentrate on the conquest of Tunisia, where German and Italian troops, quickly flown over from Sicily and the Italian mainland, had begun to establish themselves. Meanwhile, also on November 11, Eisenhower appealed to the French fleet at Toulon—estimated at sixty vessels—to join the United Nations, and Hitler ordered his armies to march into hitherto unoccupied France, ostensibly "to repel an American and British landing." Italy assisted the German operation and occupied Corsica. Thus were the armistices of June 1940 scrapped.

The axis troops completed the occupation of France within a day, although, for the time being, they avoided Toulon. While Darlan now announced that he would speak for Pétain since the latter no longer was free to make his sentiments known, the Fight-

[1] On Darlan, see p. 779.

ing French proclaimed from London that they would participate
in the new campaign against the axis but would not accept any
political arrangement concluded between the Allies and the "Number Two traitor of France." On November 23 Darlan persuaded
French West Africa, with its powerful base of Dakar, to go over to
the antiaxis side, and four days later the larger part of the French
fleet at Toulon was scuttled. The wholesale sinkings, with death to
many gallant seamen, apparently were carried out according to
prearranged plan when Nazi soldiers entered Toulon and Nazi
planes appeared over the harbor at four o'clock in the morning of
November 27.

The difficult political situation took a turn on December 24,
1942, with the assassination of Darlan by a youth whose identity
and motive were not made public but who was reported executed
two days later. Thereupon Giraud assumed control and, with
Eisenhower's approval, eventually (February 1943) took the title
of "French Civil and Military Commander-in-Chief." The de
Gaullists, too, preferred Giraud to Darlan, although they were
disappointed when the new commissioner kept some former Vichy
officials in high position, only gradually released persons who in
previous months had been jailed for their pro-Ally sentiments,
and belatedly rescinded the Vichy decrees that had earlier been
promulgated.

Meanwhile, on November 15, American troops had crossed into
Tunisia, where a hard fight was in progress. The axis had the advantage of much shorter supply lines, a factor which became the
more important with the onset of really bad weather. The Allies,
moreover, still had to consolidate their gains and positions elsewhere in Africa. Hence, while Laval in France declared that German victory would save "civilization," the campaign in Tunisia
was marked chiefly by local engagements, air attacks, and supply-
ship sinkings in the Mediterranean. In January 1943 it became
clear that the Germans intended to withdraw what remained of
the Afrika Korps from Libya into Tunisia, there to join the fresher
forces recently arrived from Europe. Allied efforts to prevent a
union of the two groups were unsuccessful, but by April 1943 the
axis forces had been pushed into a corner of northeastern Tunisia.

While Tunisia became more and more important as a battleground, there occurred another Roosevelt-Churchill meeting, this
time at Casablanca (meaning "White House") in Morocco! Although it was widely guessed that a meeting was in progress, the
secret of the place was well guarded. For ten days, from January

HENRI H. GIRAUD, FRANKLIN D. ROOSEVELT, CHARLES DE GAULLE, AND
WINSTON S. CHURCHILL AT CASABLANCA, 1943

14–24, 1943, the two leaders met, each accompanied by the supreme fighting commanders of his country. Stalin and Chiang Kai-shek, though not present, were kept fully informed of all developments.[1] The conferees surveyed "the entire field of the war" and laid plans for "the campaigns of 1943 against Germany, Italy, and Japan."

At a press conference on January 24 Roosevelt declared that the United Nations would fight on until the axis was ready to cry "unconditional surrender." Then the President returned to Washington, stopping off on the way for a talk with President Vargas of Brazil. Churchill flew on to Turkey before going home, for apparently satisfactory discussions with President Inönü and other Ankara officials. Meanwhile, on January 30, 1943, Hitler allowed the tenth anniversary of his appointment as chancellor to pass without making a speech. Goebbels and Göring, however, spoke—to the accompaniment of blasts from bombs dropped by Royal Air Force planes in their first daylight raids on Berlin since the beginning of the war. By mid-April the air was rife with rumors of a forthcoming invasion of German-occupied Europe.

[1] Giraud and de Gaulle also attended the meeting and had an opportunity to agree "on the end to be achieved, which is the liberation of France and the triumph of human liberties by the total defeat of the enemy." Both recognized the need for full military coöperation "of all Frenchmen" on the side of the Allies, but neither was prepared to accept the leadership of the other in the interest of political unity.

Bibliography

Bibliography

Occasionally the titles of obviously mediocre works have been included, either because they are the recitals of participants or because they appear to be the only accounts in English of important occurrences. In the case of works published first in Great Britain, the date of publication generally is the British one; to cite the later American date might mislead one regarding the "up-to-dateness" of a volume. To satisfy the curious, be it noted here that I have not read every word of every book cited.

REFERENCE WORKS

ALLISON, W. H., FAY, S. B. *et al.*, eds. *A Guide to Historical Literature*, 1931.

BORTON, H., ELISSEEFF, S., and REISCHAUER, E. O., comps. *A Selected List of Books and Articles on Japan in English, French, and German*, 1941.

CHILDS, J. B., comp. *Government Document Bibliography in the United States and Elsewhere*, 3 ed., 1942.

COOKE, W. H. and STICKNEY, E. P., eds. *Readings in European International Relations since 1879*, 1931.

ELLINGER, W. B. and ROSINSKI, H., comps. *Sea Power in the Pacific 1936–1941. A Bibliography*, 1942.

HARLEY, J. E. *Documentary Textbook on International Relations. A Text and Reference Study Emphasizing Official Documents and Materials Relating to World Peace and International Co-operation*, 1934.

HAWGOOD, J. A. *Modern Constitutions since 1787*, 1938.

HUDSON, M. O., ed. *International Legislation; A Collection of the Texts of Multipartite International Instruments of General Interest Beginning with the Covenant of the League of Nations*, 1931–.

JONES, S. S. and MYERS, D. P. *Documents on American Foreign Relations, January 1938–June 1939*, 1939. Annually thereafter.

KELLER, H. R. *The Dictionary of Dates*, 2 v., 1934. Goes through 1930.

KERNER, R. J., comp. *Slavic Europe. A Selected Bibliography in the Western European Languages*, 1918.

KERNER, R. J., comp. *Northeastern Asia: A Selected Bibliography*, 2 v., 1939.

KUCZYNSKI, R. R. *Population Movements*, 1936.

LANGER, W. L., comp. *An Encyclopaedia of World History*, 1940.

LANGER, W. L. and ARMSTRONG, H. F., eds. *Foreign Affairs Bibliography; A Selected and Annotated List of Books on International Relations, 1919–1932*, 1933.

LANGSAM, W. C., ed. *Documents and Readings in the History of Europe since 1918*, 1939.

LASSWELL, H. D., CASEY, R. D., and SMITH, B. L., eds. *Propaganda and Promotional Activities; An Annotated Bibliography*, 1935.

MALLORY, W. H., ed. *Political Handbook of the World; Parliaments, Parties and Press as of January 1, 1928, etc.*, 1928–.

4 BIBLIOGRAPHY

MYERS, D. P., ed. *Manual of Collections of Treaties and of Collections Relating to Treaties*, 1922.

NAFZIGER, R. O. *Foreign News Sources and the Foreign Press: A Bibliography*, Minneapolis, Burgess, 1937. Multigraphed.

PRENTICE, E. P. *Hunger in History; The Influence of Hunger on Human History*, 1939.

RAGATZ, L. J., comp. *A Bibliography for the Study of European History 1815 to 1939*, 1942. Also *Supplement*, 1943.

SAUCERMAN, S. *International Transfers of Territory in Europe, with Names of the Affected Political Subdivisions as of 1910–1914 and the Present*, 1937.

SHANAHAN, W. O. "The Literature on War," in *The Review of Politics*, April and July 1942.

TOYNBEE, A. J. *Survey of International Affairs, 1920–1923*, etc., 1925–.

WANKLYN, H. G. *The Eastern Marchlands of Europe*, 1941. Finland to Yugoslavia.

WESLEY, E. B. *Reading Guide for Social Studies Teachers*, 1941.

WHEELER-BENNETT, J. W., ed. *Documents on International Affairs, 1928–*, 1929–.

WRIGHT, Q. *A Study of War*, 2 v., 1942. Facts and figures.

ZIMMERMANN, E. W. *World Resources and Industries; A Functional Appraisal of the Availability of Agricultural and Industrial Resources*, 1933.

PERIODICAL PUBLICATIONS

Amerasia. A Review of America and the Far East. Monthly.
American Journal of International Law.
American Year Book.
Annals of the American Academy of Political and Social Science.
Annual Register.
Bulletin of International News. Fortnightly summary by Royal Institute of International Affairs, London.
Current History. Monthly.
Facts on File: Person's Index of World Events, October 30, 1940–. Weekly summary.
Foreign Affairs. An informative quarterly review.
Foreign Policy (Association) *Reports.* Fortnightly research studies.
Geneva Research Center *Geneva Special Studies.*
Geographical Review.
Great Britain, British Overseas Trade Department *Reports.*
International Conciliation. Useful monthly published by Carnegie Endowment.
Journal of Modern History.
League of Nations publications, see under Chapter VI.
Life, weekly with good photographs.
New International Year Book.
Political Science Quarterly.
Statesman's Year-Book.
United States, Department of Commerce *Reports* and *Handbooks.*
Various national and regional year books.

CHAPTER I. THE COMING OF WAR

ANDERSON, E. N. *The First Moroccan Crisis, 1904–1906*, 1930.
ASQUITH, H. H. *The Genesis of the War*, 1923. By Britain's Premier in 1914.
BAERNREITHER, J. M. *Fragments of a Political Diary*, 1930. By Austrian politician.
BARNES, H. E. *The Genesis of the World War*, 1926. Criticizes France and Russia.

BERTIE, F. *The Diary of Lord Bertie of Thame, 1914–1918,* 2 v., 1924. By British Ambassador to France in 1914.

BETHMANN HOLLWEG, T. VON *Reflections on the World War,* 1920. By Germany's Chancellor in 1914.

BRANDENBURG, E. *From Bismarck to the World War,* 1927.

BRIDGE, W. C., transl. *How the War Began in 1914, Being the Diary of the Russian Foreign Office,* 1925.

BUCHANAN, G. *My Mission to Russia,* 2 v., 1923. By Britain's Ambassador to Russia in 1914.

BÜLOW, B. VON *Memoirs,* 4 v., 1931–1932. By German Chancellor, 1900–1908.

CARROLL, E. M. *French Public Opinion and Foreign Affairs, 1870–1914,* 1931.

CARROLL, E. M. *Germany and the Great Powers, 1866–1914. A Study in Public Opinion and Foreign Policy,* 1938.

CHANG, C. F. *The Anglo-Japanese Alliance,* 1931.

CHURCHILL, W. S. *The World Crisis, 1911–1928,* 4 v., 1923–1929. Abr. ed., 1931.

COOLIDGE, A. C. *The Origins of the Triple Alliance,* 2 ed., 1926.

DICKINSON, G. L. *The International Anarchy, 1904–1914,* 1926.

DUGDALE, E., ed. *German Diplomatic Documents, 1871–1914,* 4 v., 1928–1931.

DURHAM, M. E. *The Serajevo Crime,* 1925. Indicts the Serbs.

EARLE, E. M. *Turkey, the Great Powers, and the Bagdad Railway,* 1923.

EWART, J. S. *The Roots and Causes of the Wars, 1914–1918,* 2 v., 1925. Canadian.

FABRE-LUCE, A. *The Limitations of Victory,* 1926. French revisionist view.

FAY, S. B. *The Origins of the World War,* 2 v. in 1, rev. ed., 1930.

FEIS, H. *Europe: The World's Banker, 1870–1914,* 1930.

GLANVILLE, J. L. *Italy's Relations with England, 1896–1905,* 1934.

GOOCH, G. P. *Franco-German Relations, 1871–1914,* 1923.

GOOCH, G. P. *History of Modern Europe, 1878–1919,* 1923. Chiefly diplomatic.

GOOCH, G. P. *Recent Revelations of European Diplomacy,* 4 impr., 1930. Excellent appraisal of publications relating chiefly to 1888–1919.

GOOCH, G. P. and TEMPERLEY, H. W. V., eds. *British Documents on the Origins of the War, 1898–1914,* 1926–.

GREY, E. *Twenty-five Years, 1892–1916,* 2 v., 1925. British Foreign Secretary.

HALDANE, R. B. *Before the War,* 1920. By British diplomat.

HALDANE, R. B. *Richard Burdon Haldane; An Autobiography,* 1929.

HALE, O. J. *Germany and the Diplomatic Revolution; A Study in Diplomacy and the Press, 1904–1906,* 1931.

HALE, O. J. *Publicity and Diplomacy, with Special Reference to England and Germany, 1890–1914,* 1940.

HAMMANN, O. *The World Policy of Germany, 1890–1912,* 1927. Brief but good.

HOFFMAN, R. J. *Great Britain and the German Trade Rivalry, 1875–1914,* 1933.

HURD, A. and CASTLE, H. *German Sea Power; Its Rise, Progress and Economic Basis,* 1913.

KANTOROWICZ, H. U. *The Spirit of British Policy and the Myth of the Encirclement of Germany,* 1931. Sympathetic to Great Britain.

KNAPLUND, P., ed. *Speeches on Foreign Affairs, 1904–1914, by Sir Edward Grey,* 1932.

KREHBIEL, E. B. *Nationalism, War, and Society,* 1916.

LANGER, W. L. *The Franco-Russian Alliance, 1890–1894,* 1929.

LANGER, W. L. *European Alliances and Alignments, 1871–1890,* 1931.

LANGER, W. L. *The Diplomacy of Imperialism, 1890–1902,* 2 v., 1935.

LICHNOWSKY, K. M. *Heading for the Abyss,* 1928. By German Ambassador to London in 1914.

LUTZ, H. *Lord Grey and the World War,* 1928. German critique.

MARDER, A. J. *The Anatomy of British Sea Power. A History of British Naval Policy in the Pre-Dreadnought Era, 1880–1905,* 1940.

MICHON, G. *The Franco-Russian Alliance, 1891–1917,* 1929.

MONTGELAS, M. *The Case for the Central Powers,* 1925. Best German account.

MONTGELAS, M. *British Foreign Policy under Sir Edward Grey,* 1928.

MONTGELAS, M. and SCHÜCKING, W., eds. *Outbreak of the World War, German Documents Collected by Karl Kautsky,* 1924.

MOWAT, R. B. *The Concert of Europe,* 1930. Covers 1870–1914.

NICOLSON, H. *Portrait of a Diplomatist; Being the Life of Sir Arthur Nicolson, First Lord Carnock, and a Study of the Origins of the Great War,* 1930.

PALÉOLOGUE, G. M. *An Ambassador's Memoirs,* 3 v., 1923–1925. By French Ambassador to Russia in 1914.

POINCARÉ, R. *The Origins of the War,* 1922.

POINCARÉ, R. *The Memoirs of Raymond Poincaré,* 4 v., 1926–1930.

PORTER, C. W. *The Career of Théophile Delcassé,* 1936.

PŘIBRAM, A. F. *Austrian Foreign Policy, 1908–1918,* 1923. Brief.

PŘIBRAM, A. F. *England and the International Policy of the European Great Powers, 1871–1914,* 1931. British continental diplomacy.

PŘIBRAM, A. F., ed. *The Secret Treaties of Austria-Hungary, 1879–1914,* 2 v., 1920–1921. Evolution of Triple Alliance.

RENOUVIN, P. *The Immediate Origins of the War,* 1928. French account; covers June 28–August 4, 1914.

ROMBERG, G. VON *Falsifications of the Russian Orange Book,* 1923.

RUMBOLD, H. *The War Crisis in Berlin, July–August 1914,* 1940.

SAZONOV, S. *Fateful Years, 1909–1916,* 1928. Russian Foreign Minister's apologia.

SCHMITT, B. E. *England and Germany, 1740–1914,* 1916.

SCHMITT, B. E. *The Coming of the War: 1914,* 2 v., 1930. July 1914; scholarly.

SCHOEN, W. VON *The Memoirs of an Ambassador,* 1922. By German Ambassador to France in 1914.

SCHUMAN, F. L. *War and Diplomacy in the French Republic,* 1931.

SCHURMAN, J. G. *The Balkan Wars, 1912–1913,* 3 ed., 1916.

SCOTT, J. B., ed. *Diplomatic Documents Relating to the Outbreak of the European War,* 2 v., 1916. Translations of "rainbow books."

SCOTT, J. F. *Five Weeks,* 1927. European press in July 1914.

SETON-WATSON, R. W. *Sarajevo; A Study in the Origins of the Great War,* 1926.

SEYMOUR, C. *The Diplomatic Background of the War, 1870–1914,* 1916.

SEYMOUR, C., ed. *The Intimate Papers of Colonel House,* 4 v., 1926–1928.

SONTAG, R. J. *European Diplomatic History, 1871–1932,* 1933.

SONTAG, R. J. *Germany and England: Background of Conflict, 1848–1894,* 1938.

STIEVE, F. *Isvolsky and the World War,* 1926. German view.

WARD, A. W. and GOOCH, G. P., eds. *The Cambridge History of British Foreign Policy, 1783–1919,* 3 v., 1922–1923.

WEDEL, O. *Austro-German Diplomatic Relations, 1908–1914,* 1932.

WEGERER, A. VON *A Refutation of the Versailles War Guilt Thesis,* 1930.

WERTHEIMER, M. S. *The Pan-German League, 1890–1914,* 1924. Scholarly.

WILHELM II. *The Kaiser's Memoirs, 1888–1918,* 1922.

WILLIS, E. F. *Prince Lichnowsky, Ambassador of Peace. A Study of Prewar Diplomacy 1912–1914,* 1942.

WILSON, H. W. *The War Guilt,* 1928. British view.

WOLFF, T. *The Eve of 1914,* 1936. By German editor.

WOODWARD, E. L. *Great Britain and the German Navy,* 1935.

CHAPTER II. A WORLD WAR

ABBOTT, G. F. *Greece and the Allies, 1914–1922,* 1922. Critical of Venizelos.

ANDRASSY, J. *Diplomacy and the War,* 1921. By Austrian Foreign Minister.

ARNETT, A. M. *Claude Kitchin and the Wilson War Policies,* 1937.

BAILEY, T. A. "The Sinking of the *Lusitania,*" in *The American Historical Review,* October 1935. Documented.

BAKER, N. D. *Why We Went to War*, 1936. By American Secretary of War, 1916–1921.

BAKER, R. S. *Woodrow Wilson. Life and Letters.* Vols. v–viii (1935–1939) cover the period of the First World War.

BAKER, R. S. and DODD, W., eds. *The Public Papers of Woodrow Wilson*, 6 v., 1925–1927.

BEMIS, S. F., ed. *The American Secretaries of State and Their Diplomacy*, v. 10, 1929.

BERNSTORFF, J. H. VON *My Three Years in America*, 1920. By German Ambassador to United States.

CHURCHILL, W. S. *The World Crisis, 1911–1928*, 4 v., 1923–1929. Abr. ed., 1931.

CLAPP, E. J. *Economic Aspects of the War; Neutral Rights, Belligerent Claims and American Commerce in the Years 1914–1915*, 1915.

COCKS, F. S. *The Secret Treaties and Understandings*, 2 ed., 1918.

COSMETATOS, S. P. *The Tragedy of Greece*, 1928.   Indictment of Allies.

CZERNIN, O. *In the World War*, 1920. By Austrian Foreign Minister.

DJEMAL PASHA, A. *Memories of a Turkish Statesman, 1913–1919*, 1922.

DODD, W. E. *Woodrow Wilson and His Work*, rev. ed., 1932. Sympathetic.

DROSTE, C. L., comp. *The Lusitania Case*, 1915. Newspaper notices.

DUMBA, K. *Memoirs of a Diplomat*, 1932. By Austrian Ambassador to U. S.

DURHAM, M. E. *Twenty Years of Balkan Tangle*, 1920. Anti-Russian.

EARLE, E. M. *Turkey, the Great Powers, and the Bagdad Railway*, 1923.

FESS, S. D. *The Problems of Neutrality When the World Is at War*, U. S. Congress, 64 Congress, 2 Session, House Doc. 2111, 1917.

GARNER, J. W. *International Law and the World War*, 2 v., 1920.

GERARD, J. W. *My Four Years in Germany*, 1917. By American Ambassador to Germany.

GIOLITTI, G. *Memoirs of My Life*, 1923. By Italian Premier.

GOOCH, G. P. *Recent Revelations of European Diplomacy*, 4 impr., 1930.

GRATTAN, C. H. *Why We Fought*, 1929. Critical of American ideology.

GWYNN, S., ed. *The Letters and Friendships of Sir Cecil Spring-Rice*, 2 v., 1929. Papers of British Ambassador to United States.

HECKSCHER, E., BERGENDAL, K. *et al. Sweden, Norway, Denmark, and Iceland in the World War*, 1930.

HENDRICK, B. J. *The Life and Letters of Walter H. Page*, 3 v., 1922–1925. Papers of American Ambassador to Great Britain.

HIBBEN, P. *Constantine I and the Greek People*, 1920. Defense of Greek King.

HOUSTON, D. F. *Eight Years with Wilson's Cabinet, 1913–1920*, 2 v., 1926. By a secretary of the treasury and of agriculture.

HOWARD, H. N. *The Partition of Turkey; A Diplomatic History, 1913–1923*, 1931.

LANE, A. W. and WALL, L. H., eds. *The Letters of Franklin K. Lane*, 1922. Wartime correspondence of Wilson's secretary of the interior.

LANSING, R. *War Memoirs*, 1935. By American Secretary of State.

MARTIN, P. A. *Latin America and the War*, 1925.

McMASTER, J. B. *The United States in the World War*, 2 v., 1918–1920. Based largely on newspapers.

MILLIS, W. *Road to War; America 1914–1917*, 1935.

MILNE, A. B. *The Flight of the "Goeben" and the "Breslau,"* 1921.

MORRISEY, A. M. *The American Defense of Neutral Rights, 1914–1917*, 1939.

MOWAT, R. B. *A History of European Diplomacy, 1914–1925*, 1927.

NICHOLAS, Prince of Greece *Political Memoirs, 1914–1917; Pages from My Diary*, 1928. Allied policy towards Greece.

NOEL-BUXTON, E. and LEESE, C. *Balkan Problems and European Peace*, 1919.

PETERSON, H. C. *Propaganda for War. The Campaign Against American Neutrality, 1914–1917*, 1939. Good.

ROBINSON, E. and WEST, V. *The Foreign Policy of Woodrow Wilson, 1913–1917,* 1917.

SALANDRA, A. *Italy and the Great War; From Neutrality to Intervention,* 1932. By Italy's Premier in early war years.

SCOTT, J. B., ed. *Diplomatic Correspondence between the United States and Germany, 1914–1917,* 1918.

SCOTT, J. B., ed. *President Wilson's Foreign Policy,* 1918. Addresses and papers.

SELIGMAN, V. J. *The Victory of Venizelos; A Study of Greek Politics, 1910–1918,* 1920. Pro-Venizelist.

SETON-WATSON, R. W. *Roumania and the Great War,* 1915. Sympathetic.

SEYMOUR, C. *Woodrow Wilson and the World War,* 1921. Brief and good.

SEYMOUR, C. *American Diplomacy during the World War,* 1934. Authoritative.

SEYMOUR, C. *American Neutrality, 1914–1917,* 1935.

SEYMOUR, C., ed. *The Intimate Papers of Colonel House,* 4 v., 1926–1928.

SPINKS, C. N. "Japan's Entrance into the World War," in *The Pacific Historical Review,* December 1936.

SQUIRES, J. D. *British Propaganda at Home and in the United States from 1914 to 1917,* 1935.

TANSILL, C. C. *America Goes to War,* 1938. Exhaustive.

TUMULTY, J. P. *Woodrow Wilson as I Know Him,* 1921. President's secretary.

United States, Department of State *Papers Relating to the Foreign Relations of the United States,* annual.

United States, Department of State *Diplomatic Correspondence with Belligerent Governments Relating to Neutral Rights and Duties,* 4 v., 1915–1918.

United States, Department of State *Declarations of War. Severances of Diplomatic Relations, 1914–1918,* 1919.

WHITE, W. A. *Woodrow Wilson,* 1924.

CHAPTER III. THE ALTAR OF MARS

Military Operations

ADAMS, C. *Flight in Winter,* 1942. Serbian army's fight.

ARTHUR, G. C. A. *The Life of Lord Kitchener,* 3 v., 1920.

ARTHUR, G. C. A. *Lord Haig,* 1928. Brief.

ASPINALL-OGLANDER, C. F. *Military Operations, Gallipoli,* 2 v. in 4, 1929–1932. British Official History.

ASTON, G. G. *The Biography of the Late Marshal Foch,* 1929.

ASTON, G. G. *The Great War of 1914–1918,* 1930. Brief.

AYRES, L. P. *The War with Germany; A Statistical Summary,* rev. ed., 1919.

BALLARD, C. R. *Kitchener,* 1930.

BASSETT, J. S. *Our War with Germany,* 1919. American.

BOWMAN-MANIFOLD, M. G. E. *An Outline of the Egyptian and Palestine Campaigns, 1914 to 1918,* 1922.

BRUSSILOV, A. A. *A Soldier's Note-Book, 1914–1918,* 1930. Russian commander.

BUCHAN, J. *A History of the Great War,* 4 v., 1922.

BULLARD, R. L. *Personalities and Reminiscences of the War,* 1925. By an American general.

CALLWELL, C. *Field Marshal Sir Henry Wilson; His Life and Diaries,* 2 v., 1927.

CHAMBRUN, J. DE and MARENCHES, C. DE *The American Army in the European Conflict,* 1919.

CHARTERIS, J. *Field Marshal Earl Haig,* 1929.

CHURCHILL, W. S. *The World Crisis, 1911–1928,* 4 v., 1923–1929. Abr. ed., 1931.

CHURCHILL, W. S. *The Unknown War: The Eastern Front,* 1931.

CRUTTWELL, C. R. M. F. *A History of the Great War, 1914–1918,* 1934. Good.

CRUTTWELL, C. R. M. F. *The Role of British Strategy in the Great War*, 1936.
DANE, E. *British Campaigns in Africa and the Pacific, 1914–1918*, 1919.
DANE, E. *British Campaigns in the Nearer East, 1914–1918*, 2 v., 1919.
DEWAR, G. and BORASTON, J. H. *Sir Douglas Haig's Command*, 2 v., 1922.
EDMONDS, J. E., comp. *Military Operations, France and Belgium*, 1922–. British Official History.
ESSEN, L. VAN DER *The Invasion and the War in Belgium*, 1917.
FALKENHAYN, E. VON *General Headquarters, 1914–1916, and Its Critical Decisions*, 1919.
FALLS, C. *Military Operations, Macedonia*, 1933–. British Official History.
FOCH, F. *The Memoirs of Marshal Foch*, 1931.
FRENCH, G. *The Life of Field Marshal Sir John French, First Earl of Ypres*, 1931.
FRENCH, J. *1914*, 1919.
FROTHINGHAM, T. *A Guide to the Military History of the World War*, 1920. Maps.
FROTHINGHAM, T. *The American Reinforcement in the World War*, 1927.
GALET, E. J. *Albert, King of the Belgians, in the Great War*, 1931.
GOLOVINE, N. N. *The Russian Army in the World War*, 1931.
GOLOVINE, N. N. *The Russian Campaign of 1914. The Beginning of the War and Operations in East Prussia*, 1933.
GORDON-SMITH, G. *From Serbia to Jugoslavia; Serbia's Victories, Reverses and Final Triumph, 1914–1918*, 1920.
GORGES, E. H. *The Great War in West Africa*, 1930. Well illustrated.
GOUGH, H. *The Fifth Army*, 1931. Battle of March 1918 in France.
GRAVES, W. S. *America's Siberian Adventure, 1918–1920*, 1931. By American commander.
Great Britain, Committee of Imperial Defense *History of the Great War. Military Operations*, 1922–. British Official History.
Great Britain, War Office *Statistics of the Military Effort of the British Empire during the Great War, 1914–1920*, 1922.
HAMILTON, I. *Gallipoli Diary*, 2 v., 1920. By British commander.
HARBORD, J. G. *America in the World War*, 1933. By American general.
HARBORD, J. G. *The American Army in France*, 1936.
HAYES, C. J. H. *A Brief History of the Great War*, 1920.
HINDENBURG, P. VON *Out of My Life*, 2 v., 1921.
HOFFMANN, M. *The War of Lost Opportunities*, 1924. By German strategist.
HOFFMANN, M. *War Diaries and Other Papers*, 2 v., 1929.
HORDERN, C., comp. *Military Operations East Africa*, I, 1942. British Official History. Covers 1914–1916.
IRONSIDE, E. *Tannenberg; The First Thirty Days in East Prussia*, 1925.
JOFFRE, J. *The Personal Memoirs of Joffre*, 2 v., 1932.
JONES, J. *The Fall of Tsingtau*, 1915. Japanese attack on Shantung.
KANNENGIESSER, H. *The Campaign in Gallipoli*, 1927. German-Turkish view.
KLUCK, A. VON *The March on Paris and the Battle of the Marne, 1914*, 1920.
KNOX, A. *With the Russian Army, 1914–1917*, 2 v., 1921. By military attaché.
LAWRENCE, T. E. *Revolt in the Desert*, 1927. Excellent on Arabia.
LAWRENCE, T. E. *Seven Pillars of Wisdom*, 1935. Expansion of above.
LETTOW-VORBECK, P. VON *My Reminiscences of East Africa*, 1920. By German commander.
LIDDELL HART, B. H. *Reputations, Ten Years After*, 1928. Critical.
LIDDELL HART, B. H. *The Real War*, 1930. Good military account.
LIDDELL HART, B. H. *Foch, the Man of Orleans*, 1931.
LIDDELL HART, B. H. *"T. E. Lawrence"—In Arabia and After*, 1934.
LIDDELL HART, B. H. *A History of the World War, 1914–1918*, 1935.
LIDDELL HART, B. H. *The War in Outline, 1914–1918*, 1936.
LIGGETT, H. *Commanding an American Army; Recollections of the World War*, 1925.

10   BIBLIOGRAPHY

LIGGETT, H. A. E. F., 1928.
LIMAN VON SANDERS, O. Five Years in Turkey, 1927. For Turkish campaigns.
LLOYD GEORGE, D. War Memoirs, 6 v., 1933–1937.
LUCAS, C. P., ed. The Empire at War, 5 v., 1921–1926.
LUDENDORFF, E. Ludendorff's Own Story, August 1914–November 1918, 2 v., 1920.
LUDENDORFF, E. The General Staff and Its Problems, 2 v., 1920. Documents.
LUTZ, R. H., ed. The Causes of the German Collapse in 1918. Sections of the
    Officially Authorized Report of the Commission of the German Constituent As-
    sembly and of the'German Reichstag, 1919–1928, the Selection and the Transla-
    tion Officially Approved by the Commission, 1934.
MACMUNN, G. Military Operations, Egypt and Palestine, 2 v. in 3, 1928–1930.
    British Official History.
MADELIN, L. Foch, 1929. Read and annotated by Foch.
MARCH, P. C. The Nation at War, 1932. By American chief of staff.
MASSEY, W. T. How Jerusalem Was Won, 1919. By English correspondent.
MASSEY, W. T. Allenby's Final Triumph, 1920. Concludes above work.
MAURICE, F. The Last Four Months, 1919. Foch campaign of 1918.
MAYNARD, C. The Murmansk Venture, 1928. Intervention in Russia.
MCENTEE, G. Italy's Part in Winning the World War, 1934. Military study.
MCENTEE, G. Military History of the World War, 1937. Chronological study.
MCMASTER, J. B. The United States in the World War, 2 v., 1918–1920.
MOBERLY, F. J. The Campaign in Mesopotamia, 4 v., 1923–1927. British Official
    History.
NOGALES, R. DE Four Years beneath the Crescent, 1926. Turkish campaigns.
Official History of Australia in the War of 1914–1918, 1921–.
Official History of New Zealand's Effort in the Great War, 1921–.
O'NEILL, H. C. The War in Africa, 1914–1917, and in the Far East, 1914, 1919.
PAGE, T. N. Italy and the World War, 1920. By America's Ambassador to Italy.
PALMER, F. Our Greatest Battle, 1919. The Meuse-Argonne fight.
PALMER, F. Newton D. Baker—America at War, 2 v., 1931. About Wilson's
    secretary of war.
PERRIS, G. H. The Battle of the Marne, 1920. Detailed operations.
PERSHING, J. J. Final Report to the Secretary of War, 1919.
PERSHING, J. J. My Experiences in the World War, 2 v., 1931.
POLLARD, A. F. A Short History of the Great War, 3 ed., 1928. Good.
PULESTON, W. C. High Command in the World War, 1934.
RECOULY, R. Joffre, 1931.
ROBERTSON, W. Soldiers and Statesmen, 1914–1918, 2 v., 1926.
SHERSON, E. Townshend of Chitral and Kut, 1928.
SHOTWELL, J. T., ed. Economic and Social History of the World War, 150 v.,
    1921–1937. Many of the volumes are separately listed here.
SIMONDS, F. H. A History of the World War, 5 v., 1917–1920. Nontechnical.
SPEARS, E. L. Liaison, 1914, 1930. Anglo-French unity of action.
THOMAS, L. With Lawrence in Arabia, 1924.
THOMAS, S. The History of the A. E. F., 1920. Good.
TOWNSHEND, C. My Campaign in Mesopotamia, 1920.
TREVELYAN, G. M. Scenes from Italy's War, 1919. By chief of British Red Crc.
    in Italy.
TSCHUPPIK, K. Ludendorff; The Tragedy of a Military Mind, 1932.
TYNG, S. The Campaign of the Marne, 1914, 1935. Good.
VAN EVERY, D. The A. E. F. in Battle, 1928.
VILLARI, L. The Macedonian Campaign, 1922.
VILLARI, L. The War on the Italian Front, 1932.
WAVELL, A. P. The Palestine Campaign, 1928. Excellent.
WAVELL, A. P. Allenby: A Study in Greatness, 1941.
WILSON, A. Loyalties. Mesopotamia, 2 v., 1930–1931. Excellent for 1914–1920.

WISE, J. C., comp. *The Turn of the Tide, American Operations at Cantigny, Château Thierry, and the Second Battle of the Marne*, 1920.

Naval and Aerial Operations

ALEXANDER, R. *The Cruise of the Raider "Wolf,"* 1939. Thrilling.

ASHMORE, E. B. *Air Defence*, 1929. Air raids on London.

CAMPBELL, G. *My Mystery Ships*, 1928.

CARPENTER, A. F. B. *The Blocking of Zeebrugge*, 1922.

CARR, W. G. *By Guess and by God*, 1930. British submarine activities.

CHATTERTON, E. K. *Sea-Raiders*, 1931.

CORBETT, J. S. and NEWBOLT, H. *Naval Operations*, 5 v., 1920–1931. British Official History.

DANIELS, J. *Our Navy at War*, 1922. By Wilson's secretary of the navy.

DOMVILLE-FIFE, C. W. *Submarines and Sea-Power*, 1919.

DORLING, H. T. *Endless Story*, 1931. Work of British destroyers.

FAYLE, C. E. *Seaborne Trade*, 3 v., 1920–1924. British Official History.

FORSTNER, G. G. VON *The Journal of Submarine Commander von Forstner*, 1917.

FROST, H. H. *The Battle of Jutland*, 1936.

FROTHINGHAM, T. *The Naval History of the World War*, 3 v., 1924–1926.

GIBSON, L. and HARPER, J. *The Riddle of Jutland*, 1934.

GIBSON, R. and PRENDERGAST, M. *The German Submarine War, 1914–1918*, 1931.

Great Britain, Committee of Imperial Defense *History of the Great War. Naval Operations*, 11 v., 1920–1931. British Official History.

Great Britain, Committee of Imperial Defense *History of the Great War. The War in the Air*, 6 v., 1922–1937. British Official History.

GUICHARD, L. *The Naval Blockade, 1914–1918*, 1930.

HARPER, J. E. T. *The Truth about Jutland*, 1927. British account.

HASE, G. VON *Kiel and Jutland*, 1926. German account.

HASHAGEN, E. *The Log of a U-Boat Commander, or U-Boats Westward, 1914–1918*, 1931.

• HURD, A. *The Merchant Navy in the War*, 3 v., 1921–1929. British Official History.

JELLICOE, J. R. *The Crisis of the Naval War*, 1920. Antisubmarine campaign.

JELLICOE, J. R. *The Grand Fleet, 1914–1916*, 1919. By its commander.

LEHMANN, E. A. and MINGOS, H. *The Zeppelins*, 1927. Raids over England.

NEWBOLT, H. *A Naval History of the War, 1914–1918*, 1920.

POCHHAMMER, H. *Before Jutland; Admiral von Spee's Last Voyage*, 1931. Battles off Coronel and Falkland Islands.

PULESTON, W. D. *The Dardanelles Expedition*, 2 ed., 1927.

RALEIGH, W. and JONES, H. A. *The War in the Air*, 1922–. British Official History.

RAWLINSON, A. *The Defence of London, 1915–1918*, 2 ed., 1923.

REUTER, L. VON *Scapa Flow*, 1940.

SCHEER, R. *Germany's High Sea Fleet in the World War*, 1920.

SIMS, W. S. and HENDRICK, B. J. *The Victory at Sea*, 1920. By chief of American naval operations.

THOMAS, L. *Raiders of the Deep*, 1928. Story of submarines.

TIRPITZ, A. VON *My Memoirs*, 2 v., 1919.

TREUSCH VON BUTTLAR-BRANDENFELS, H. *Zeppelins over England*, 1931.

TURNER, C. *The Struggle in the Air, 1914–1918*, 1919. British activities.

WESTER-WEMYSS, R. E. *The Navy in the Dardanelles Campaign*, 1924.

Miscellaneous

ASTON, G. G. *Secret Service*, 1930. By a British officer.

BAILEY, T. A. *The Policy of the United States toward the Neutrals, 1917–18*, 1942.

BAKER, C. W. *Government Control and Operation of Industry in Great Britain and the United States during the World War*, 1921.

BARUCH, B. M.   *American Industry in the War*, 1941.   War of 1914.

BELL, G. L.   *Letters*, 2 v., 8 impr., 1928.   Near East.

BERNDORFF, H. R.   *Espionage!* 1930.

BEVERIDGE, W. H.   *British Food Control*, 1928.

BOGART, E. L.   *Direct and Indirect Costs of the Great World War*, rev. ed., 1920.

BRITTAIN, V.   *Testament of Youth*, 1933.   Effect of war on British family.

BRUN, A. H.   *Troublous Times*, 1931.   Austrian war prisoners in Asia.

BRUNTZ, G. G.   *Allied Propaganda and the Collapse of the German Empire in 1918*, 1938.

CALLWELL, C.   *Experiences of a Dug-Out, 1914–1918*, 1920.   By British general.

CHAMBERLIN, W., comp.   *Industrial Relations in Wartime Great Britain, 1914–1918*, 1940.   A bibliography.

CHAMBERS, F. P.   *The War Behind the War, 1914–1918. A History of the Political and Civilian Fronts*, 1939.   Convenient summary.

CLARK, J. M.   *The Costs of the World War to the American People*, 1931.

CLARKSON, G. B.   *Industrial America in the World War*, 1923.

COHEN-PORTHEIM, P.   *Time Stood Still; My Internment in England, 1914–1918*, 1931.   By an Austrian artist.

COOK, E.   *The Press in War-Time*, 1920.   In Great Britain.

CREEL, G.   *How We Advertised America*, 1920.   By chairman of American Committee on Public Information.

CROWELL, B. and WILSON, R. F., eds.   *How America Went to War*, 6 v., 1921.

CROZIER, J.   *In the Enemy's Country*, 1931.   French espionage account.

DAHLIN, E.   *French and German Public Opinion on Declared War Aims, 1914–1918*, 1933.

DAVISON, H. P.   *The American Red Cross in the Great War*, 1919.

DEWAR, G. A. B.   *The Great Munition Feat, 1914–1918*, 1921.   In Great Britain.

DE WEERD, H. H.   *Great Soldiers of the Two World Wars*, 1942.

Documents and Statements Relating to Peace Proposals and War Aims (December 1916–November 1918), 1919.   Introduction by G. L. DICKINSON.

DUMAS, S. and VEDEL-PETERSEN, K. O.   *Losses of Life Caused by War*, 1923.

EISENMENGER, A.   *Blockade; The Diary of an Austrian Middle-Class Woman, 1914–1918*, 1932.

EMIN, A.   *Turkey in the World War*, 1930.

FOLKS, H.   *The Human Costs of the War*, 1920.

FORSTER, K.   *The Failures of Peace. The Search for a Negotiated Peace during the First World War*, 1941.

FRADKIN, E.   *Chemical Warfare*, 1929.

FRIES, A. A. and WEST, C. J.   *Chemical Warfare*, 1921.   By an American general.

FULLER, J. F. C.   *Tanks in the Great War*, 1920.

GALLATIN, A. E.   *Art and the Great War*, 1919.

GIBSON, C. R.   *War Inventions and How They Were Invented*, 1917.

GILCHRIST, H. L.   *A Comparative Study of World War Casualties from Gas and Other Weapons*, 1928.

GLEAVES, A.   *A History of the Transport Service*, 1921.   U. S. convoys.

GORDON, H. L.   *The Jewish Legions in the British Army during the World War (1914–1918)*, 1940.

GRATZ, G. and SCHÜLLER, R.   *The Economic Policy of Austria-Hungary during the War in Its External Relations*, 1928.

GRAY, H. L.   *War Time Control of Industry*, 1918.   In Great Britain.

GREBLER, L. and WINKLER, W.   *The Cost of the World War to Germany and to Austria-Hungary*, 1940.

HARDIE, M. and SABIN, A. K., eds.   *War Posters Issued by Belligerent and Neutral Nations, 1914–1919*, 1920.

HAYS, A. G.   *Enemy Property in America*, 1923.   Technical.

HENNIKER, A. M., comp. *Transportation on the Western Front, 1914–1918*, 1937. British Official History.

HURLEY, E. N. *The Bridge to France*, 1927. The transport problem.

JOHNSON, H. *Vatican Diplomacy in the World War*, 1933.

KOHN, S. and MEYENDORFF, A. F. *The Cost of the War to Russia*, 1932.

LA FARGUE, T. E. *China and the World War*, 1937.

LASSWELL, H. *Propaganda Technique in the World War*, 2 ed., 1938.

LELAND, W. G. and MERENESS, N. D., comps. *Introduction to the American Official Sources for the Economic and Social History of the World War*, 1926.

LUTZ, R. H. "Studies of World War Propaganda, 1914–1933," in *Journal of Modern History*, December 1933.

LUTZ, R. H. "The World War in History: A Survey of Source Materials in the Hoover War Library," in *Journal of the Amer. Mil. Hist. Found.*, Spring 1937.

LUTZ, R. H. and BANE, S. L., eds. *The Blockade of Germany after the Armistice, 1918–1919*, 1943.

LYDDON, W. G. *British War Missions to the United States, 1914–1918*, 1938.

MANTEYER, G. DE, ed. *Austria's Peace Offer, 1916–1917*, 1921.

MARTIN, W. *Statesmen of the War in Retrospect, 1918–1928*, 1928. Swiss view.

MAURICE, F. *Lessons of Allied Cooperation: Naval, Military and Air, 1914–18*, 1942.

MILLARD, O. E. *Burgomaster Max. The Epic Story of the Occupation of Brussels*, 1936.

MILLARD, O. E. *Uncensored. The Story of "La Libre Belgique," 1914–1918*, 1937. The paper secretly circulated in occupied Belgium.

MILLER, H. W. *The Paris Gun*, 1930. Bombardment of Paris.

MOCK, J. R. *Censorship—1917*, 1941.

MOCK, J. R. and LARSON, C. *Words That Won the War*, 1939. Story of the American Committee on Public Information.

MOLONY, W. *Prisoners and Captives*, 1933. War Prisoners in Germany.

MULLENDORE, W. C. *History of the United States Food Administration 1917–1919*, 1941.

NEKLUDOFF, A. V. *Diplomatic Reminiscences before and during the World War, 1911–1917*, 1920. Useful for peace moves.

NICHOLSON, J. S. *War Finance*, 1918.

NICOLAI, W. *The German Secret Service*, 1924.

PAXSON, F. L. *America at War, 1917–1918*, 1939.

PLAYNE, C. E. *Society at War, 1914–1916*, 1931. British national psychology.

PLAYNE, C. E. *Britain Holds On, 1917, 1918*, 1933. Sequel to above.

PONSONBY, A. *Falsehood in War-Time*, 1928.

READ, J. M. *Atrocity Propaganda, 1914–1919*, 1941.

RITCHIE, H. *The "Navicert" System during the World War*, 1938.

SCOTT, J. B., ed. *Official Statements of War Aims and Peace Proposals, December 1916 to November 1918*, 1921.

SCOTT, J. B., ed. *Preliminary History of the Armistice*, 1924. Documents.

SHARTLE, S. G. *Spa, Versailles, Munich*, 1941. On Armistice Commission.

SLICE, A. VAN DER *International Labor, Diplomacy, and Peace 1914–1918*, 1941.

STAMP, J. *Taxation during the War*, 1932.

STOVALL, P. A. *Switzerland and the World War*, 1939. By the American Minister.

SURFACE, F. M. *The Grain Trade during the World War*, 1928.

THOMSON, B. *The Allied Secret Service in Greece*, 1931.

VIERECK, G. S. *Spreading Germs of Hate*, 1930. Propaganda in U. S.

WHEELER-BENNETT, J. W. *Forgotten Peace: Brest-Litovsk, March 1918*, 1938.

WHITLOCK, B. *Belgium; A Personal Narrative*, 2 v., 1919. By American Minister.

WILD, M. *Secret Service on the Russian Front*, 1932.

WILGUS, W. J. *Transporting the A. E. F. in Western Europe*, 1931.

WILLIS, I. C. *England's Holy War; A Study of English Liberal Idealism during the Great War*, 1928.

CHAPTER IV. THE PEACE CONFERENCE OF PARIS

ADAM, G. *The Tiger: Georges Clemenceau, 1841–1929,* 1930.

ALBRECHT-CARRIÉ, R. *Italy at the Paris Peace Conference,* 1938.

BAKER, R. S. *What Wilson Did at Paris, 1919.* Upholds Wilson.

BAKER, R. S. *Woodrow Wilson and World Settlement,* 3 v., 1922.

BARUCH, B. M. *The Making of the Reparation and Economic Sections of the Treaty,* 1920. By American economic adviser.

BEER, G. *African Questions at the Paris Peace Conference,* 1923.

BINKLEY, R. C. "Ten Years of Peace Conference History," in *Journal of Modern History,* December 1929.

BINKLEY, R. C. "New Light on the Paris Peace Conference," in *Political Science Quarterly,* September and December 1931.

BIRDSALL, P. "The Second Decade of Peace Conference History," in *Journal of Modern History,* September 1939.

BURNETT, P. M. *Reparation at the Paris Peace Conference from the Standpoint of the American Delegation,* 2 v., 1940. Documents.

CHURCHILL, W. S. *The Aftermath,* 1929.

CLEMENCEAU, G. *Grandeur and Misery of Victory,* 1930.

DEÁK, F. *Hungary at the Paris Peace Conference. The Diplomatic History of the Treaty of Trianon,* 1942.

DILLON, E. J. *The Inside Story of the Peace Conference,* 1920.

HARRIS, H. W. *The Peace in the Making,* 1919. Well informed.

HASKINS, C. H. and LORD, R. H. *Some Problems of the Peace Conference,* 1920.

HOUSE, E. M. and SEYMOUR, C., eds. *What Really Happened at Paris; The Story of the Peace Conference, 1918–1919, by American Delegates,* 1921.

LANSING, R. *The Big Four and Others of the Peace Conference,* 1921. By American Secretary of State.

LANSING, R. *The Peace Negotiations, A Personal Narrative,* 1921.

LANSING, R. *War Memoirs,* 1935. Valuable.

LLOYD GEORGE, D. *Memoirs of the Peace Conference,* 2 v., 1939.

LUCKAU, A. *The German Delegation at the Paris Peace Conference,* 1941. Documents.

MILLER, D. H. *My Diary at the Conference of Paris, with Documents,* 21 v., 1928. By American legal adviser. Forty sets were distributed to large libraries.

MILLER, D. H. *The Drafting of the Covenant,* 2 v., 1928. By one of the draftsmen.

NEVINS, A. *Henry White; Thirty Years of American Diplomacy,* 1930.

NICOLSON, H. *Peacemaking, 1919,* 1933.

NOBLE, G. B. *Policies and Opinions at Paris, 1919: Wilsonian Diplomacy, the Versailles Peace, and French Public Opinion,* 1935.

NOWAK, K. F. *Versailles,* 1928. German view.

ONCKEN, H. *The Historical Rhine Policy of the French,* 1923.

PALMER, F. *Bliss, Peacemaker. The Life and Letters of General Tasker Howard Bliss,* 1934. Good biography of American delegate.

POINCARÉ, R. *The Memoirs of Raymond Poincaré,* 4 v., 1926–1930.

RECOULY, R. *Foch; My Conversations with the Marshal,* 1929. On Rhine policy.

RIDDELL, G. *Lord Riddell's Intimate Diary of the Peace Conference and After, 1918–1923,* 1933.

SCHIFF, V. *The Germans at Versailles, 1919,* 1930.

SEYMOUR, C., ed. *The Intimate Papers of Colonel House,* 4 v., 1926–1928.

SHOTWELL, J. T. *At the Paris Peace Conference,* 1937. Valuable on the I. L. O.

SPENDER, H. *The Prime Minister; Life and Times of David Lloyd George,* 1920.

TARDIEU, A. *The Truth about the Treaty,* 1921. Defends Clemenceau.

TEMPERLEY, H. W. V., ed. *A History of the Peace Conference of Paris,* 6 v., 1920–1924. Documents.

THOMPSON, C. T.   *The Peace Conference Day by Day*, 1920.
United States, Department of State   *Foreign Relations of the United States, 1919*, 2 v., 1942.
WILSON, F.   *The Origins of the League Covenant*, 1928.
WOODHOUSE, E. J. and C. G.   *Italy and the Jugoslavs*, 1920.

CHAPTER V.   THE TREATIES OF PEACE

ALMOND, N. and LUTZ, R. H., eds.   *The Treaty of St. Germain*, 1935.   Documents.
BIRDSALL, P.   *Versailles Twenty Years After*, 1941.   Supports Wilson.
Carnegie End. for Int. Peace   *The Treaties of Peace, 1919–1923*, 2 v., 1924.   Texts.
CHAMBERLAIN, J.   *The Régime of the International Rivers: Danube and Rhine*, 1923.
COOKE, W. H. and STICKNEY, E. P., eds.   *Readings in European International Relations since 1879*, 1931.   Extracts from the treaties.
DICKINSON, T. H.   *The United States and the League*, 1923.
DONALD, R.   *The Tragedy of Trianon*, 1928.   Severe indictment.
EBRAY, A.   *A Frenchman Looks at the Peace*, 1927.   Indictment of Versailles.
EDMUNDS, S. E.   *International Law and the Treaty of Peace*, U. S. Congress, 66 Congress, 1 Session, Senate Doc. 156, 1919.
FLEMING, D. F.   *The United States and the League of Nations, 1918–1920*, 1932.
HOWARD, H. N.   *The Partition of Turkey; A Diplomatic History, 1913–1923*, 1931.
Hungarian Peace Delegation   *The Hungarian Peace Negotiations*, 4 v., 1920–1921.
KEYNES, J. M.   *The Economic Consequences of the Peace*, 1920.   Prophetic.
KEYNES, J. M.   *A Revision of the Treaty*, 1922.
LANGSAM, W. C.   "Maladjustments of the Peace Settlement," in *The Annals of the American Academy of Political and Social Science*, September 1934.
LANGSAM, W. C., ed.   *Documents and Readings in the History of Europe since 1918*, 1939.   Extracts from and divers comments on the treaties.
MAIR, L. P.   *The Protection of Minorities*, 1928.
MOLONY, W. O.   *Nationality and the Peace Treaties*, 1934.   By a League official.
MOWAT, R. B.   *A History of European Diplomacy, 1914–1925*, 1927.
MOWRER, P. S.   *Balkanized Europe*, 1921.
NITTI, F. S.   *The Wreck of Europe*, 1922.   Italian attack on peace settlement.
PICCIOTTO, C. M. and WORT, A. W., eds.   *The Treaty of Peace with Germany: Clauses Affecting Mercantile Law*, 1919.
PINK, G. P.   *The Conference of Ambassadors (Paris 1920–1931)*, 1942.
RIDDELL, G. et al.   *The Treaty of Versailles and After*, 1935.
SCOTT, A. P.   *An Introduction to the Peace Treaties*, 1920.   Analysis of Versailles.
SHOTWELL, J. T.   *What Germany Forgot*, 1940.   Shows that First World War, not Versailles, was to blame for many German troubles.
STEGEMAN, H.   *The Mirage of Versailles*, 1928.   Significance of the treaty.
STEPHENS, W. E.   *Revisions of the Treaty of Versailles*, 1939.
TEMPERLEY, H. W. V., ed.   *A History of the Peace Conference of Paris*, 6 v., 1920–1924.
TOYNBEE, A. J.   *The World after the Peace Conference*, 1925.
WAMBAUGH, S.   *Plebiscites since the World War*, 2 v., 1933.   Documents.

CHAPTER VI.   THE LEAGUE OF NATIONS

General

ALLEN, D.   *The Fight for Peace*, 1930.   American peace movement.
BAKER, P. J. N.   *The League of Nations at Work*, 1926.   Popular.

BASSETT, J. S. *The League of Nations*, 1928.

BEALES, A. C. F. *The History of Peace*, 1931.

BEER, M. *The League on Trial*, 1933.

BERDAHL, C. A. *The Policy of the United States with Respect to the League of Nations*, 1932.

BURTON, M. E. *The Assembly of the League of Nations*, 1941. Good.

CARROLL, M. J., comp. *Key to League of Nations Documents Placed on Public Sale, 1920–1929*, 1930. Annual supplements.

CECIL, R. *A Great Experiment. An Autobiography*, 1941.

CONWELL-EVANS, T. *The League Council in Action*, 1929. Study of 23 disputes.

CRUTTWELL, C. R. M. F. *A History of Peaceful Change in the Modern World*, 1937.

DARBY, W. *International Arbitration. International Tribunals*, 4 ed., 1904. Texts.

DAVIS, K. W. *The Soviets at Geneva; The U.S.S.R. and the League of Nations, 1919–1933*, 1934.

DE BREYCHA-VAUTHIER, A. C. *Sources of Information: A Handbook on the Publications of the League of Nations*, 1939.

DUNN, F. S. *The Practice and Procedure of International Conferences*, 1929.

EAGLETON, C. *International Government*, 1932.

ENGEL, S. *League Reform. An Analysis of Official Proposals and Discussions, 1936–1939*, 1940.

EPPSTEIN, J., comp. *Ten Years' Life of the League of Nations*, 1929. Illustrated.

FOLEY, H., comp. *Woodrow Wilson's Case for the League of Nations*, 1923.

GAVIT, J. P. *Opium*, 1927. League conferences on opium traffic.

GRAHAM, M. W. *The League of Nations and the Recognition of States*, 1933.

HARRIS, H. W. *What They Did at Geneva, an Account of the First Assembly*, 1920.

HEMLEBEN, S. J. *Plans for World Peace through Six Centuries*, 1943.

HILL, N. L. *The Public International Conference; Its Function, Organization and Procedure*, 1929.

HOWARD-ELLIS, C. *The Origin, Structure, and Working of the League of Nations*, 1928.

JACKSON, J. and KING-HALL, S., eds. *The League Year-Book*, 1932–.

JONES, R. and SHERMAN, S. S. *The League of Nations from Idea to Reality*, 1927.

JONES, S. S. *The Scandinavian States and the League of Nations*, 1939.

KELCHNER, W. H. *Latin American Relations with the League of Nations*, 1930.

KLUYVER, C. A., comp. *Documents on the League of Nations*, 1920.

KNUDSON, J. I. *A History of the League of Nations*, 1938.

League of Nations
—— *Armaments Year-Book.*
—— *Books on the Work of the League of Nations Catalogued in the Library of the Secretariat*, 1928.
—— *Committees of the League of Nations*, 1934.
—— *Communications and Transit*, 1924.
—— *Educational Survey.*
—— *International Intellectual Coöperation.* Annual.
—— *Monthly Bulletin of Statistics.* Trade.
—— *Monthly Summary of the League of Nations.*
—— *Official Journal.* Minutes of the Council.
—— *Quarterly Bulletin of Information on the Work of International Organizations.*
—— *Ratification of International Conventions Concluded under the Auspices of the League of Nations*, 1933.
—— *Records of the Assembly.*
—— *Report on the Work of the League*, 1942.
—— *Second Annual Report of the League Loans Committee*, 1934.
—— *Social and Humanitarian Work*, rev. ed., 1926.
—— *Statistical Year-Book of the League of Nations.*

—— *Ten Years of World Co-operation*, 1930. Excellent summary.
—— *The Health Organization of the League of Nations*, rev. ed., 1926.
—— *The League from Year to Year*, 1926–.
—— *The League of Nations and Intellectual Coöperation*, rev. ed., 1927.
—— *Treaty Series*, 1920–. All registered treaties.
LODGE, H. C. *The Senate and the League of Nations*, 1925. By opposition leader.
MANNING, C. *The Policies of the British Dominions in the League of Nations*, 1932.
MARBURG, T. *Development of the League of Nations Idea,* 2 v., 1932. Letters.
MATSUSHITA, M. *Japan in the League of Nations*, 1929.
McCLURE, W. *World Prosperity as Sought through the Economic Work of the League of Nations, 1933.*
MITRANY, D. *The Problem of International Sanctions*, 1925.
MORLEY, F. *The Society of Nations; Its Organization and Constitutional Development*, 1932.
MYERS, D. P. *Handbook of the League of Nations since 1920*, 1930.
PHILLIMORE, W. G. F. *Schemes for Maintaining General Peace*, 1920.
POTTER, P. *An Introduction to the Study of International Organization*, 3 ed., 1928.
QUIGLEY, H. S. *From Versailles to Locarno*, 1927. Brief.
RALSTON, J. *International Arbitration, from Athens to Locarno*, 1929.
RAM, V. and SHARMA, B. *India and the League of Nations*, 1932.
RAPPARD, W. *International Relations as Viewed from Geneva*, 1925.
RAPPARD, W. *Uniting Europe; The Trend of International Coöperation since the War*, 1930.
RAPPARD, W. *The Geneva Experiment*, 1932.
Royal Institute of International Affairs *International Sanctions*, 1938.
SWEETSER, A. *The League of Nations at Work*, 1920.
VINACKE, H. M. *International Organization*, 1934.
WEBSTER, C. K. and HERBERT, S. *The League of Nations in Theory and Practice*, 1933.
WENDELIN, E. C. *Subject Index to the Economic and Financial Documents of the League of Nations, 1927–1930*, 1932.
WILD, P. S., JR. *Sanctions and Treaty Enforcement*, 1934.
WILLIAMS, B. S. *State Security and the League of Nations*, 1927.
WILLOUGHBY, W. W. *Opium as an International Problem*, 1925.
WILSON, F. *The Origins of the League Covenant*, 1928.
WRIGHT, Q., ed. *Neutrality and Collective Security*, 1936.
YORK, E. *Leagues of Nations, Ancient, Medieval, Modern*, 1919.
ZIMMERN, A. *The League of Nations and the Rule of Law, 1918–1935*, rev. ed., 1939.

The World Court

BUSTAMENTE, A. S. DE *The World Court*, 1925.
FACHIRI, A. P. *The Permanent Court of International Justice, Its Constitution, Procedure, and Work*, 2 ed., 1932.
HUDSON, M. O. *The Permanent Court of International Justice, A Treatise*, 1934.
HUDSON, M. O. *The World Court 1921–1938*, 1938. Documents.
HUDSON, M. O., ed. *World Court Reports*, 3 v., 1934–1938.
JESSUP, P. C. *The United States and the World Court*, 1929. Documents.
KELLOR, F. A. and HATVANY, A. *The United States Senate and the International Court*, 1925.
League of Nations *Annual Report of the Permanent Court of International Justice*, 1925–.
LINDSEY, E. *The International Court*, 1931.

MARTIN, C. E. *The Permanent Court of International Justice and the Question of American Adhesion,* 1932.

Permanent Court of International Justice *Ten Years of International Jurisdiction, 1922–1932,* 1932. Short.

WHEELER-BENNETT, J. W. *Information on the Permanent Court of International Justice,* 1924. Documents.

WHEELER-BENNETT, J. W. and FANSHAWE, M. *Information on the World Court, 1918–1928,* 1929. Documents.

International Labor Organization

BARNES, G. N. *History of the International Labour Office,* 1926. Brief.

DILLON, C. H. *International Labor Conventions. Their Interpretation and Revision,* 1942. Legal.

Industry, Governments and Labor; Record of the International Labor Organization, 1919–1928, 1928.

International Labour Office *Monthly Summary of the International Labour Organization,* 1927–.

International Labour Office *Year-Book,* 1930–.

International Labour Office *The International Labour Code, 1939,* 1941. Conventions adopted 1919–1939.

International Labour Organisation *Constitution and Rules,* ed. of 1934.

JOHNSTON, G. A. *International Social Progress; The Work of the International Labor Organization of the League of Nations,* 1924.

MILLER, S., JR. *What the I. L. O. Means to America,* 1936.

National Industrial Conference Board *The Work of the International Labor Organization,* 1928.

OLIVER, E. M. *The World's Industrial Parliament,* 1925. Short but good.

PÉRIGORD, P. *The International Labor Organization,* 1926. Detailed.

SHOTWELL, J. T., ed. *The Origins of the International Labor Organization,* 2 v., 1934. History and documents.

SHOTWELL, J. T. *At the Paris Peace Conference,* 1937.

WILSON, F. G. *Labor in the League System; A Study of the International Labor Organization in Relation to International Administration,* 1934.

Mandates, Minorities, Plebiscites

BATSELL, W. R. *The United States and the System of Mandates,* 1925.

BENTWICH, N. *The Mandates System,* 1930. Emphasizes Class A Mandates.

CLYDE, P. H. *Japan's Pacific Mandate,* 1935.

DECKER, J. A. *Labor Problems in the Pacific Mandates,* 1940. British mandates.

GERIG, B. *The Open Door and the Mandates System; A Study of Economic Equality before and since the Establishment of the Mandates System,* 1930.

HOCKING, W. *The Spirit of World Politics,* 1932. Ethics of colonial control.

JUNGHANN, O. *National Minorities in Europe,* 1932.

League of Nations *The League of Nations and Minorities,* 1923.

League of Nations *The League of Nations and Mandates,* 1924.

MAANEN-HELMER, E. VAN *The Mandates System in Relation to Africa and the Pacific Islands,* 1929. Emphasizes B and C Mandates.

MACARTNEY, C. A. *Refugees; The Work of the League,* 1931. Greco-Bulgarian population exchange.

MACARTNEY, C. A. *National States and National Minorities,* 1934.

MAIR, L. *The Protection of Minorities,* 1928. Working of minorities treaties.

MARGALITH, A. *The International Mandates,* 1930. Question of sovereignty.

MATTERN, J. *The Employment of the Plebiscite in the Determination of Sovereignty,* 1920.

NOEL-BUXTON, E. and CONWELL-EVANS, T. P. *Oppressed Peoples and the League of Nations*, 1922. Criticisms and suggestions.
ROUČEK, J. S. *The Working of the Minorities System under the League of Nations*, 1929.
STEPHENS, J. S. *Danger Zones of Europe; A Study of National Minorities*, 1929.
STONE, J. *International Guarantees of Minority Rights*, 1932. Juridical study.
STONE, J. *Regional Guarantees of Minority Rights*, 1933.
STOYANOVSKY, J. *The Mandate for Palestine; A Contribution to the Theory and Practice of International Mandates*, 1928. Technical.
WAMBAUGH, S. *Plebiscites since the World War*, 2 v., 1933. Documents.
WHITE, F. *Mandates*, 1926. Popular.
WRIGHT, Q. *Mandates under the League of Nations*, 1930. Exhaustive.

Political and Territorial Questions

ACHÁ, J. A. *The Arbitration Zone in the Bolivian-Paraguayan Dispute*, 1929.
DONALD, R. *A Danger Spot in Europe and Its Government by the League of Nations*, 1925. Anti-French account of Saar question.
FLORINSKY, M. T. *The Saar Struggle*, 1934.
FOSTER, H. A. *The Making of Modern Iraq; A Product of World Forces*, 1935.
IRELAND, P. W. *Iraq. A Study in Political Development*, 1938.
League of Nations *Saar Basin and Free City of Danzig*, 1924.
League of Nations *Report of the Commission of the Iraq-Turco Frontier*, 1925.
League of Nations *Report of the Chaco Commission*, 1934.
LUKE, H. *Mosul, and Its Minorities*, 1925. First-hand account.
MAIN, E. *Iraq*, 1934. Excellent.
OSBORNE, S. *The Saar Question, A Disease Spot in Europe*, 1923. Factual.
REYNOLDS, B. T. *The Saar and the Franco-German Problem*, 1934.
ROOSEGAARDE-BISSCHOP, W. *The Saar Controversy*, 1924. Legal study.
RUSSELL, F. M. *The International Government of the Saar*, 1926.
SEDERHOLM, J. *The Åland Question from a Swedish Finlander's Point of View*, 1920.
STICKNEY, E. P. *Southern Albania or Northern Epirus in European International Affairs, 1912–1923*, 1926.
WAMBAUGH, S. *The Saar Plebiscite*, 1940. Authoritative.

CHAPTER VII. REPARATION, DEBTS, DEPRESSION

Reparation

ALLEN, H. T. *The Rhineland Occupation*, 1927. By American commander.
AULD, G. P. *The Dawes Plan and the New Economics*, 1927.
BASS, J. F. and MOULTON, H. G. *America and the Balance Sheet of Europe*, 1921.
BERGMANN, C. *The History of Reparations*, 1927. German view.
D'ABERNON, E. V. *The Diary of an Ambassador*, 3 v., 1929–1930. British Ambassador to Germany. Covers 1920–1926.
DAWES, C. G. *A Journal of Reparations*, 1939.
DAWES, R. C. *The Dawes Plan in the Making*, 1925. Best authority.
DULLES, E. L. *The Bank for International Settlements at Work*, 1932.
DULLES, E. L. "The Bank for International Settlements in Recent Years," in *American Economic Review*, June 1938.
EINZIG, P. *The Bank for International Settlements*, 3 ed., 1932.
GEDYE, G. E. R. *The Revolver Republic; France's Bid for the Rhine*, 1930.
GREER, G. *The Ruhr-Lorraine Industrial Problem*, 1925. Coal, iron, reparation.
KESSLER, H. *Germany and Europe*, 1923. German viewpoint.
KEYNES, J. M. *The Economic Consequences of the Peace*, 1920. Prophetic.

KEYNES, J. M.   *A Revision of the Treaty,* 1922.

LICHTENBERGER, H.   *The Ruhr Conflict,* 1923.   By a Frenchman.

LIPPMANN, W. and SCROGGS, W. O.   *The United States in World Affairs, 1931–1933,* 3 v., 1932–1934.

LLOYD GEORGE, D.   *The Truth about Reparations and War Debts,* 1932.   Critical.

LONG, R. E.   *The Mythology of Reparations,* 1928.   On Dawes Plan.

MACDONALD, W.   *Reconstruction in France,* 1922.

MCFADYEAN, A.   *Reparation Reviewed,* 1930.   Objective.

MOULTON, H. G.   *The Reparation Plan,* 1924.   Favorable to Dawes Plan.

MOULTON, H. G. and MCGUIRE, C. E.   *Germany's Capacity to Pay; A Study of the Reparations Problem,* 1923.   Thorough statistical study.

MYERS, D. P.   *The Reparation Settlement, 1930,* 1930.   Documents.

PHILIPS, A.   *Economic Aspects of Reparations and Interallied Debts,* 1930.

REINHOLD, P.   *The Economic, Financial, and Political State of Germany since the War,* 1928.   Lectures by German ex-Finance Minister.

SCHACHT, H.   *The End of Reparations,* 1931.   Arguments for cancellation.

SERING, M.   *Germany under the Dawes Plan,* 1929.

STEGEMANN, H.   *The Struggle for the Rhine,* 1927.

STREET, C. J. C.   *Rhineland and Ruhr,* 1923.   Anti-French.

TILLETT, B. *et al.*   *The Ruhr,* 1923.   View of British Labor Party.

WHEELER-BENNETT, J. W.   *The Wreck of Reparations, Being the Political Background of the Lausanne Agreement, 1932,* 1933.

WHEELER-BENNETT, J. W. and LATIMER, H.   *Information on the Reparation Settlement,* 1930.   History and documents of Young Plan.

War Debts

BATSELL, W. R.   *The Debt Settlements and the Future,* 1927.   Useful figures.

DEXTER, P. and SEDGWICK, J. H.   *The War Debts; An American View,* 1928.

FISK, H. E.   *The Inter-Ally Debts,* 1924.   Useful statistical tables.

FRASURE, C. M.   *British Policy on War Debts and Reparations,* 1940.

HOWLAND, C. P., ed.   *Survey of American Foreign Relations, 1928–1931,* 4 v., 1928–1931.

MOULTON, H. G. and PASVOLSKY, L.   *World War Debt Settlements,* 1926.

MOULTON, H. G. and PASVOLSKY, L.   *War Debts and World Prosperity,* 1932.

United States, Bureau of Accounts   *Memorandum Covering the World War Indebtedness of Foreign Governments to the United States (1917–1921) and Showing the Total Amounts Paid by Germany under the Dawes and Young Plans, Revised July 1, 1941,* 1941.

The Great Depression

ANGELL, J. W., comp.   *The Program for the World Economic Conference; The Experts' Agenda and Other Documents,* 1933.

BECKETT, G.   *The Reciprocal Trade Agreements Program,* 1941.

BONNELL, A. T.   *German Control over International Economic Relations, 1930–1940,* 1941.

BROWN, W. A., JR.   *The International Gold Standard Reinterpreted, 1914–1934,* 2 v., 1940.

CASSEL, G.   *Post-War Monetary Stabilization,* 1928.   Swedish authority.

CASSEL, G.   *The Crisis in the World's Monetary System,* 2 ed., 1932.

CASSEL, G.   *The Downfall of the Gold Standard,* 1936.

DALTON, H. *et al.*   *Unbalanced Budgets; A Study of the Financial Crisis in Fifteen Countries,* 1934.

DELAISI, F.   *Political Myths and Economic Realities,* 1927.

DELLE-DONNE, O.   *European Tariff Policies since the World War,* 1928.

DENBY, E.   *Europe Re-housed*, 1938.   Survey of six countries.

EINZIG, P.   *The World Economic Crisis, 1929–1932*, 1932.   Popular.

EINZIG, P.   *The Sterling-Dollar-Franc Tangle*, 1933.

EINZIG, P.   *World Finance, 1914–1935*, 1935.   Frequently thereafter.

ELLINGER, B.   *Credit and International Trade: How They Work in Practice*, 1934.

ELLIS, H. S.   *Exchange Control in Central Europe*, 1941.

FLORINSKY, M. T.   "France and the War Debts," in *Political Science Quarterly*, September 1934.

FRASER, H. F.   *Foreign Trade and World Politics*, 1926.

HARRIS, S. E.   *Exchange Depreciation*, 1936.

HAWTREY, R. G.   *The Gold Standard in Theory and Practice*, 3 ed., 1933.   Good.

HIRST, F. W.   *Safeguarding and Protection in Great Britain and the United States*, 1927.   Able criticism.

HODSON, H. V.   *Slump and Recovery, 1929–1937*, 1938.

HOLLAND, K.   *Youth in European Labor Camps*, 1939.

International Economic Relations; Report of the Commission of Inquiry into National Policy in International Economic Relations, 1934.   Survey by commission of Social Science Research Council.

JACK, D. T.   *The Restoration of European Currencies*, 1927.

JONES, J. M.   *Tariff Retaliation; Repercussions of the Hawley-Smoot Bill*, 1934.

KRANOLD, H.   *The International Distribution of Raw Materials*, 1939.

KUCZYNSKI, R. R.   *American Loans to Germany*, 1927.

LADAS, S. P.   *The International Protection of Industrial Property*, 1930.   Legal aspects of foreign trade.

LANGSAM, W. C.   "United States and British Press Opinion of the Proposed Austro-German Customs Union of 1931," in *Journal of Central European Affairs*, January 1943.

League of Nations   *World Production and Prices, 1925–1933*, 1934.

League of Nations   *Balances of Payments for 1933; Including an Analysis of Capital Movements up to September, 1934*, 1935.

League of Nations   *National Public Works*, 1935.

League of Nations   *World Economic Survey*.   Annual.

League of Nations   *Europe's Trade*, 1941.

League of Nations   *Commercial Policy in the Inter-War Period: International Proposals and National Policies*, 1942.

League of Nations, Institute of Intellectual Coöperation   *The State and Economic Life*, 2 v., 1932–1934.   Symposium.

MASON, D. M.   *Monetary Policy, 1914–1928*, 1928.   Brief.

National Industrial Conference Board   *A Picture of World Economic Conditions, 1928–*, 1928–.   Useful surveys.

PAISH, G.   *The Way to Recovery*, 1931.   Opposes trade barriers.

PATTERSON, E. M.   *The World's Economic Dilemma*, 1930.

PEEL, G.   *The Economic War*, 1930.   Emphasis on Great Britain.

PITT-RIVERS, G., ed.   *Problems of Population*, 1932.

PLUMMER, A.   *International Combines in Modern Industry*, 1934.

RAWLES, W. P.   *The Nationality of Commercial Control of World Minerals*, 1933.

ROBBINS, L.   *The Great Depression*, 1934.

ROGERS, L.   *Crisis Government*, 1934.   Upholds democracy.

SALTER, A.   *Recovery; The Second Effort*, 1932.

SALTER, A.   *World Trade and Its Future*, 1936.

SIMPSON, K.   *Introduction to World Economics*, 1934.

SOMARY, F.   *Changes in the Structure of World Economics since the War*, 1931.

STAMP, J. C.   *The Financial Aftermath of War*, 1932.   Nontechnical.

STERN, S.   *Fourteen Years of European Investments, 1914–1928*, 1929.

TILTMAN, H.   *Slump! A Study of Stricken Europe To-day*, 1932.

CHAPTER VIII. THE SEARCH FOR SECURITY

ALEXANDER, F. *From Paris to Locarno and After; The League of Nations and the Search for Security, 1919–1928*, 1928.

ARNOLD-FORSTER, W. *The Disarmament Conference*, 1931. Conference of 1927.

ARNOT, R. P. *Soviet Russia and Her Neighbors*, 1927.

BAKER, P. J. N. See Noel-Baker.

BALLA, V. DE *The New Balance of Power in Europe*, 1932.

BUELL, R. L. *The Washington Conference*, 1922.

BYWATER, H. *Navies and Nations; A Review of Naval Developments since the Great War*, 1927.

CAMERON, E. R. *Prologue to Appeasement*, 1942. French foreign policy.

CIPPICO, A. *Italy, the Central Problem of the Mediterranean*, 1926.

CORY, H. M. *Compulsory Arbitration of International Disputes*, 1932. Historical.

CRANE, J. O. *The Little Entente*, 1931. Upholds Czech viewpoint.

CRUTTWELL, C. R. M. F. *A History of Peaceful Change in the Modern World*, 1937.

EINZIG, P. *Behind the Scenes of International Finance*, 2 ed., 1932.

EINZIG, P. *The Economics of Rearmament*, 1934. Popular.

ENGELBRECHT, H. C. and HANIGHEN, F. C. *Merchants of Death; A Study of the International Armament Industry*, 1934.

ENGELY, G. *The Politics of Naval Disarmament*, 1932. Italian view.

FABRE-LUCE, A. *Locarno; The Reality*, 1928. French view.

FRADKIN, E. K. *The Air Menace and the Answer*, 1934.

GLASGOW, G. *From Dawes to Locarno, 1924–1925*, 1925. Documents.

GRAHAM, M. W. *The Soviet Security System*, 1929.

HABICHT, M., ed. *Post-War Treaties for the Pacific Settlement of International Disputes*, 1931.

HARRIS, H. W. *Naval Disarmament*, 1930. Various national policies.

HILL, N. L. *Post-War Treaties of Security and Mutual Guarantee*, 1928.

HINDMARSH, A. *Force in Peace; Force Short of War in International Relations*, 1933.

HUDSON, M. O. *International Regulation of the Trade in and Manufacture of Arms and Ammunitions*, U. S. Congress, 73 Congress, 2 Session, Senate Committee Print No. 1, 1935.

ICHIHASHI, Y. *The Washington Conference and After; A Historical Survey*, 1928.

Jane's All the World's Aircraft. Annual survey of military and civil air strengths.

Jane's Fighting Ships. Annual survey of world's navies.

KOROVINE, E. A. *The U. S. S. R. and Disarmament*, 1933.

LANGSAM, W. C., ed. *Documents and Readings in the History of Europe since 1918*, 1939.

League of Nations *Annotated Bibliography on Disarmament and Military Questions*, 1931.

League of Nations *Armaments Year-Book*, 1924–.

League of Nations *Documents of the Preparatory Commission for the Disarmament Conference Entrusted with the Preparation for the Conference for the Reduction and Limitation of Armaments*, 1925–1931.

League of Nations *Statistical Year-Book of the Trade in Arms and Ammunition*, 1924–.

LEFEBURE, V. *Scientific Disarmament*, 1931. By chemical-warfare expert.

LIDDELL HART, B. H. *Europe in Arms*, 1937.

LITVINOFF, M. *The Soviet's Fight for Disarmament*, 1932.

MACHRAY, R. *The Little Entente*, 1929.

MADARIAGA, S. DE *Disarmament*, 1929.

MILLER, D. H. *The Geneva Protocol*, 1925.

MILLER, D. H.   *The Peace Pact of Paris; A Study of the Briand-Kellogg Treaty,* 1928. Documents.

MILLIS, W.   *The Future of Sea Power in the Pacific,* 1935. Brief.

MILLS, J. S.   *The Genoa Conference,* 1922. Documents.

MITRANY, D.   *The Problem of International Sanctions,* 1925. Brief.

MYERS, D. P.   *Origin and Conclusion of the Paris Pact; The Renunciation of War as an Instrument of National Policy,* 1927.

MYERS, D. P.   *World Disarmament, Its Problems and Prospects,* 1932.

NOEL-BAKER, P.   *The Geneva Protocol for the Pacific Settlement of International Disputes,* 1925.

NOEL-BAKER, P.   *Disarmament,* 1926. Handbook.

NOEL-BAKER, P.   *The Private Manufacture of Armaments,* v. 1, 1937.

RAPPARD, W. E.   *The Quest for Peace since the World War,* 1940.

RICHMOND, H.   *Sea Power in the Modern World,* 1934. By British admiral.

SCHMIDT, R. and GRABOWSKY, A.   *The Problem of Disarmament,* 1933. German view.

SCHMIDT, R. and GRABOWSKY, A., eds.   *Disarmament and Equal Rights,* 1934.

SELSAM, J. P.   *The Attempts to Form an Anglo-French Alliance 1919–1924,* 1936.

SHOTWELL, J. T.   *War as an Instrument of National Policy and Its Renunciation in the Pact of Paris,* 1929.   Most complete account.

SLOUTZKI, M. N.   *The World Armaments Race, 1919–1939,* 1941.

The Soviet Union and Peace; The Most Important of the Documents Issued by the Government of the U. S. S. R. Concerning Peace and Disarmament from 1917 to 1929, 1929.

TOYNBEE, A. J.   *Survey of International Affairs, 1920–1923,* 1925–.

WHEELER-BENNETT, J. W.   *Information on the Reduction of Armaments,* 1925.

WHEELER-BENNETT, J. W.   *Information on the Renunciation of War, 1927–1928,* 1928.

WHEELER-BENNETT, J. W.   *Disarmament and Security since Locarno, 1925–1931,* 1932.

WHEELER-BENNETT, J. W.   *The Pipe Dream of Peace; The Story of the Collapse of Disarmament,* 1935. Covers 1932–1935.

WHEELER-BENNETT, J. W. and LANGERMANN, F. E.   *Information on the Problem of Security, 1917–1926,* 1927.

WILLIAMS, B. H.   *The United States and Disarmament,* 1931.

WILLIAMS, B. S.   *State Security and the League of Nations,* 1927.

WOLFERS, A.   *Britain and France between Two Wars: Conflicting Strategies of Peace since Versailles,* 1940. Indispensable for understanding the period.

CHAPTER IX.   UNREST IN AFRICA AND ASIA

ANTONIUS, G.   *The Arab Awakening. The Story of the Arab National Movement,* 1939.

BARNES, L.   *Caliban in Africa; An Impression of Colour Madness,* 1930. S. Africa.

BELL, H. J.   *Foreign Colonial Administration in the Far East,* 1928.   Indo-China and Java.

BOVERI, M.   *Minaret and Pipe-Line: Yesterday and Today in the Near East,* 1939.

BUELL, R. L.   *The Native Problem in Africa,* 2 v., 1928. Exhaustive. Documents.

BUXTON, C. R.   *The Race Problem in Africa,* 1931.

COOKSEY, J. J. and MCLEISH, A.   *Religion and Civilization in West Africa,* 1931.

DAVIS, S. C.   *Reservoirs of Men: A History of the Black Troops of French West Africa,* 1934.

DELAFOSSE, M.   *The Negroes of Africa,* 1931. By French ex-governor.

DENNERY, E.   *Asia's Teeming Millions: And Its Problems for the West,* 1931.

DU BOIS, W. E. B.   *Black Folk—Then and Now,* 1939. By a negro educator.

DU PLESSIS, J. *The Evangelisation of Pagan Africa*, 1930. Central Africa.

DUTCHER, G. M. *The Political Awakening of the East*, 1925.

ESSAD-BEY, M. *Reza Shah*, 1938.

EVANS, I. L. *Native Policy in Southern Africa*, 1934.

FARSON, N. *Behind God's Back*, 1941. Trip through Africa.

FITZGERALD, W. *Africa; A Social, Economic, and Political Geography of Its Major Regions*, 1934.

FORBES, R. *Conflict; Angora to Afghanistan*, 1931. Religious and social conflicts.

FORTES, M. and EVANS-PRITCHARD, E. E., eds. *African Political Systems*, 1940. Native institutions.

FOSTER, H. A. *The Making of Modern Iraq; A Product of World Forces*, 1935.

FRANKEL, S. H. *Capital Investment in Africa: Its Course and Effects*, 1938.

GARDNER, M. *The Menacing Sun*, 1939. Southeastern Asia.

GOWEN, H. H. *A Short History of Asia*, 1936.

HAILEY, LORD *An African Survey. A Study of Problems Arising in Africa South of the Sahara*, 1938. Encyclopedic.

HOCKING, W. E. *The Spirit of World Politics*, 1932. Plea for colonial ethics.

HUXLEY, J. *Africa View*, 1931. Observations in East Africa.

HYNDMAN, H. M. *The Awakening of Asia*, 1919.

IKBAL ALI SHAH *Afghanistan of the Afghans*, 1928.

IKBAL ALI SHAH *The Controlling Minds of Asia*, 1937. Leaders.

JONES, T. J., ed. *Education in Africa*, 1922.

JONES, T. J., ed. *Education in East Africa*, 1925.

KISCH, E. E. *Changing Asia*, 1935. A journalist in Soviet Central Asia.

KOHN, H. *A History of Nationalism in the East*, 1929.

KOHN, H. *Nationalism and Imperialism in the Hither East*, 1932.

LIPS, J. E. *The Savage Hits Back*, 1937. Interesting; illustrated.

MACMILLAN, W. M. *Africa Emergent: A Survey of Social, Political, and Economic Trends in British Africa*, 1938.

McMUNN, G. F. *Afghanistan, from Darius to Amanullah*, 1929.

MILLARD, T. F. *Conflicts of Policy in Asia*, 1924. Western rivalries.

MILLSPAUGH, A. C. *The American Task in Persia*, 1925. By financial adviser.

MOON, P. T. *Imperialism and World Politics*, 1926.

MOTT, J. R., ed. *The Moslem World of To-day*, 1925. Nonpolitical.

O'LEARY, D. E. *Islam at the Crossroads; A Brief Survey of the Present Position and Problems of the World of Islam*, 1923.

OLIVIER, S. *White Capital and Coloured Labour*, new ed., 1929.

ORDE BROWNE, G. *The African Labourer*, 1933.

ROSS, E. D. *The Persians*, 1931.

SAUNDERS, K. *The Heritage of Asia*, 1932.

SAUNDERS, K. *Whither Asia?*, 1933. Tendencies in India, China, Japan.

SMITH, E. W. *The Golden Stool of Ashanti*, 1928. Cultural conflict in Africa.

SMITH, E. W., comp. *Events in African History*, 1942. Chronology.

SOKOLSKY, G. E. *The Tinder Box of Asia*, rev. ed., 1933.

SPENDER, J. A. *The Changing East*, 1926. Chiefly India and Egypt.

STAMP, L. D. *Asia; An Economic and Regional Geography*, 1929.

SYKES, P. *A History of Afghanistan*, 2 v., 1941.

TINLEY, J. M. *The Native Labor Problem of South Africa*, 1942.

TOWNSEND, M. E. *European Colonial Expansion since 1871*, 1941.

VANDENBOSCH, A. *The Dutch East Indies*, 2 ed., 1941. Well documented.

WEINTHAL, L., ed. *The Story of the Cape to Cairo Railway and River Route from 1887–1922*, 3 v., 1923. Lavishly illustrated.

WORTHINGTON, E. B. *Science in Africa*, 1938.

YOUNG, E. H. et al. *Report of the Commission on Closer Union of the Dependencies of Eastern and Central Africa*, 1929. British official report.

See also bibliographies for Chapters XII and XXII.

CHAPTER X. CHANGING LATIN AMERICA

BAIN, H. F. and READ, T. T. *Ores and Industry in South America*, 1934.

BEMIS, S. F. *Diplomatic History of the United States*, new ed., 1942.

BOSQUES, G. *The National Revolutionary Party of Mexico and the Six-Year Plan*, 1937.

BRADERMAN, E. M. *A Study of Political Parties and Politics in Mexico since 1890*, 1938.

Bulletin of the Pan American Union, 1893–. Laws, treaties, etc.

CALOGERAS, J. P. *A History of Brazil*, 1939. By Brazilian authority.

Carnegie End. for Int. Peace *The International Conferences of American States, First Supplement, 1933–1940*, 1941.

CARR, K. *South American Primer*, 1939.

CHAPMAN, C. E. *A History of the Cuban Republic*, 1927.

CLARK, M. R. *Organized Labor in Mexico*, 1934.

DUGGAN, S. *The Two Americas; An Interpretation*, 1934. By American educator.

EZEKIEL, M. *Economic Relations between the Americas*, 1941.

GALDAMES, L. *A History of Chile*, 1942.

GRUENING, E. *Mexico and Its Heritage*, 1928. Excellent.

HANSON, E. P. *Chile*, 1941.

HARING, C. H. *South American Progress*, 1934. Good political treatment.

HERRING, H. *Good Neighbors*, 1941.

HERRING, H. and WEINSTOCK, H., eds. *Renascent Mexico*, 1935.

HOWLAND, C. P., ed. *A Survey of American Foreign Relations*, 4 v., 1928–1931.

INMAN, S. G. *Problems in Pan Americanism*, 1925.

IRELAND, G. *Boundaries, Possessions, and Conflicts in South America*, 1938.

JAMES, P. E. *Latin America*, 1942. Best human geography.

JONES, C. F. *South America*, 1930. Economic geography.

JONES, C. L. *Caribbean Backgrounds and Prospects*, 1931.

KIRKPATRICK, F. A. *A History of the Argentine Republic*, 1931.

KIRKPATRICK, F. A. *Latin America*, 1939.

LEVENE, R. *A History of Argentina*, 1937. By Argentinian authority.

LOEWENSTEIN, K. *Brazil under Vargas*, 1942. Sympathetic.

MACFARLAND, C. S. *Chaos in Mexico*, 1935. State against church.

MARTIN, P. A. *Latin America and the War*, 1925.

McBRIDE, G. M. *The Land Systems of Mexico*, 1923.

MECHAM, J. L. *Church and State in Latin America; A History of Politico-Ecclesiastical Relations*, 1934.

MUNRO, D. G. *The Latin American Republics*, 1942.

NASH, R. *Conquest of Brazil*, 1926.

NORMANO, J. F. *Economic Brazil*, 1935.

PERKINS, D. *Hands Off! A History of the Monroe Doctrine*, 1941.

RAUSHENBUSH, J. *Look at Latin America*, 1940. Social conditions.

RIPPY, J. F. *Latin America in World Politics*, 3 ed., 1938.

RIPPY, J. F. *Historical Evolution of Hispanic America*, 2 ed., 1938.

ROBERTSON, W. S. *History of the Latin-American Nations*, 2 rev. ed., 1932.

SIMPSON, E. N. *The Ejido: Mexico's Way Out*, 1937. The land system.

SMITH, H. L. and LITTELL, H. *Education in Latin America*, 1934.

STUART, G. H. *Latin America and the United States*, 1938.

TANNENBAUM, F. *The Mexican Agrarian Revolution*, 1929.

TANNENBAUM, F. *Whither Latin America?*, 1934. Economic and social problems.

TURLINGTON, E. W. *Mexico and Her Foreign Creditors*, 1930. Documented.

WHELESS, J. *Compendium of the Laws of Mexico*, 1939.

WHITAKER, A. P., ed. *Inter-American Affairs 1941–*, 1942–. Annual.

WHITAKER, J. T. *Americas to the South*, 1939.

WHITBECK, R. H. *Economic Geography of South America*, 2 ed., 1931.
WHITE, J. W. *Argentina: The Life Story of a Nation*, 1942. Good.
WILGUS, A. C. *Development of Hispanic America*, 1941.
WILGUS, A. C., ed. *Modern Hispanic America*, 1933. Symposium.
WILGUS, A. C., ed. *The Caribbean Area*, 1934. Symposium.
WILLIAMS, M. W. *The People and Politics of Latin America*, 1930.
WINKLER, M. *Investments of United States Capital in Latin America*, 1928.

CHAPTER XI. GREAT BRITAIN

ALLYN, E. *Lords versus Commons; A Century of Conflict and Compromise, 1830–1930*, 1931.
ANDRÉADÈS, A. M. *Philip Snowden; The Man and His Financial Policy*, 1930.
ASQUITH, H. H. *Fifty Years of British Parliament*, 2 v., 1926.
BEGBIE, H. *The Mirrors of Downing Street*, new ed., 1923. Biographical sketches.
BELL, T. *The British Communist Party: A Short History*, 1937.
BENHAM, F. *Great Britain under Protection*, 1941.
BERKELEY, R. *England's Opportunity*, 1931. Reply to Siegfried, listed below.
BERTRAM, A. *The Colonial Service*, 1930.
BRAND, C. F. *British Labour's Rise to Power*, 1941. Essays.
BRITTAIN, V. *Women's Work in Modern England*, 1928. Occupations.
CARR, E. H. *Great Britain: A Study of Foreign Policy from the Versailles Treaty to the Outbreak of War*, 1939.
CHANG, D. *British Methods of Industrial Peace*, 1936.
CHAPUT, R. A. *Disarmament in British Foreign Policy*, 1935.
CHENG, S. *Schemes for the Federation of the British Empire*, 1931.
CLAYTON, J. *The Rise and Decline of Socialism in Great Britain, 1884–1924*, 1926. As distinct from Labor Party policies.
COLE, G. D. H. *Labour in the Coal Mining Industry, 1914–1921*, 1923.
COLE, G. D. H. *A Short History of the British Working Class Movement, 1789–1927*, 3 v., 1925–1927.
DAVISON, R. C. *British Unemployment Policy: The Modern Phase Since 1930*, 1938.
DAWES, C. G. *Journal as Ambassador to Great Britain*, 1939.
DAWSON, R. M., ed. *The Development of Dominion Status, 1900–1936*, 1937.
DEARLE, N. B. *The Labour Cost of the World War to Great Britain, 1914–1922. A Statistical Analysis*, 1940.
DICKIE, J. P. *The Coal Problem, 1910–1936*, 1936.
EDWARDS, J. *David Lloyd George; The Man and the Statesman*, 2 v., 1929.
EDWARDS, K. *The Mutiny at Invergordon*, 1937.
EDWARDS, K. *The Grey Diplomatists*, 1938. British fleet in Mediterranean.
EDWARDS, W. *British Foreign Policy from 1815 to 1933*, 1934.
ELLIOTT, S. R. *The English Coöperatives*, 1937.
ELLIOTT, W. Y. *The New British Empire*, 1932.
Empire Opportunities: A Survey of the Possibilities of Overseas Settlement, 1938.
EVATT, H. V. *The King and His Dominion Governors*, 1936.
FAIRLIE, J. A. *British War Administration*, 1919.
FIDDES, G. *The Dominions and Colonial Offices*, 1926.
FLOURNOY, F. R. *Parliament and War*, 1927.
FRASER, H. F. *Great Britain and the Gold Standard*, 1933.
FYFE, H. *Behind the Scenes of the Great Strike*, 1926.
FYFE, H. *The British Liberal Party*, 1928.
GARRATT, G. T. *Gibraltar and the Mediterranean*, 1939.

GAUS, J. M. *Great Britain; A Study in Civic Loyalty,* 1929.

GLASGOW, G. *MacDonald as a Diplomatist; The Foreign Policy of the First Labour Government in Great Britain,* 1924. Eulogistic.

GOOCH, R. K. *The Government of England,* 1937.

GORE, J. *King George V,* 1941.

GRANT, A. T. K. *A Study of the Capital Market in Post-War Britain,* 1937.

Great Britain, Foreign Office *The Constitutions of All Countries, Vol. I: The British Empire,* 1938.

Great Britain and the Dominions, 1928. Harris Foundation Lectures, 1927.

GREENWOOD, G. A. *England Today; A Social Study of Our Time,* rev. ed., 1926.

GROSE, C. L. *A Select Bibliography of British History,* 1939.

GUEST, L. *The Labour Party and the Empire,* 1926. By a Laborite.

HALL, N. F. *The Exchange Equalisation Account,* 1935.

HALL, W. P. *Empire to Commonwealth; Thirty Years of British Imperial History,* 1928.

HAMILTON, M. A. *England's Labour Rulers,* 1924. Short biographies.

HAMILTON, M. A. *J. Ramsay MacDonald,* rev. ed., 1929.

HAMILTON, M. A. *Arthur Henderson: A Biography,* 1938.

HANCOCK, W. K. *Survey of British Commonwealth Affairs, Vol. I: Problems of Nationality, 1918–1936,* 1937; *Vol. II: Problems of Economic Policy, 1918– 1939,* 1942.

HARRIS, S. E. *Monetary Problems of the British Empire,* 1931.

HEATON, H. *The British Way to Recovery; Plans and Policies in Great Britain, Australia, and Canada,* 1934.

HICKS, V. K. *The Finance of British Government, 1920–1936,* 1938.

HILL, A. and LUBIN, I. *The British Attack on Unemployment,* 1934.

HIRST, F. W. *The Consequences of the War to Great Britain,* 1934.

HOHMAN, H. F. *The Development of Social Insurance and Minimum Wage Legislation in Great Britain; A Study of British Social Legislation in Relation to a Minimum Standard of Living,* 1933.

HUTT, A. *The Post-War History of the British Working Class,* 1938.

JENKINS, E. A. *From Foundry to Foreign Office,* 1933. On Arthur Henderson.

JENNINGS, W. I. *Cabinet Government,* 1936. Standard.

JENNINGS, W. I. *The British Constitution,* 1941.

JOHNSON, A. C. *Anthony Eden: A Biography,* 1939.

Journal of the Parliaments of the Empire, 1920–. Quarterly summary of British and Dominion parliamentary debates.

KEITH, A. B. *War Government of the British Dominions,* 1921.

KEITH, A. B. *Dominion Autonomy in Practice,* 2 ed., 1929.

KEITH, A. B., ed. *Speeches and Documents on the British Dominions, 1918–1931,* 1932.

KEITH, A. B. *The Constitutional Law of the British Dominions,* 1933.

KEITH, A. B. *The King and the Imperial Crown. The Powers and Duties of His Majesty,* 1936. Authoritative.

KEITH, A. B. *The British Cabinet System, 1930–1938,* 1939.

KRAUS, R. *Winston Churchill,* 1940.

KUCZYNSKI, J. *The Condition of the Workers in Great Britain, Germany, and the Soviet Union, 1932–1938,* 1939.

LOVEDAY, A. *Britain and World Trade,* 1931.

LOWELL, A. L. and HALL, H. D. *The British Commonwealth of Nations,* 1927.

LUBIN, I. and EVERETT, H. *The British Coal Dilemma,* 1927.

MACDONAGH, M. *The English King,* 1929. Popular.

MACDONALD, J. R. *The Foreign Policy of the Labour Party,* 1923.

MACKAY, R. A. *Changes in the Legal Structure of the British Commonwealth of Nations,* 1931.

MADDOX, W. P. *Foreign Relations in British Labour Politics: A Study of the Formation of Party Attitudes on Foreign Affairs, and the Application of Political Pressure Designed to Influence Government Policy, 1900–1924,* 1934.

MALLET, C. E. *Mr. Lloyd George; A Study,* 1930. Not sympathetic.

MASTERMAN, C. F. G. *England after War,* 1922. Social and cultural.

McENTEE, G. *The Social Catholic Movement in Great Britain,* 1927.

McHENRY, D. E. *His Majesty's Opposition: Structure and Problems of the British Labour Party, 1931–1938,* 1940.

MEDLICOTT, W. N. *British Foreign Policy since Versailles,* 1940.

MILNE-BAILEY, W., ed. *Trade Union Documents,* 1929.

MUIR, R. *How Britain Is Governed,* 3 ed., 1933.

MUIR, R. *The Record of the National Government,* 1936. Indictment of Baldwin.

NATHAN, M. *Empire Government,* 1929.

NEF, J. U. *The Rise of the British Coal Industry,* 2 v., 1932.

NICOLSON, H. *Curzon: The Last Phase, 1919–1925; A Study in Post-War Diplomacy,* 1934.

OGG, F. A. *English Government and Politics,* 1929.

PALMER, G., ed. *Consultation and Coöperation in the British Commonwealth: A Handbook on the Methods and Practices of Communication and Consultation between the Members of the British Commonwealth of Nations,* 1934.

PANKHURST, E. S. *The Suffragette Movement,* 1931.

PEEL, G. *The Economic War,* 1930. Great Britain and world trade.

PETRIE, C. *The Chamberlain Tradition,* 1938.

PIPKIN, C. W. *Social Politics and Modern Democracies,* 2 v., 1931. V. 1, England.

RAYMOND, E. T. (THOMPSON, E. R.) *A Life of Arthur James Balfour,* 1920.

RAYMOND, E. T. (THOMPSON, E. R.) *Mr. Lloyd George,* 1922.

Report on the British Press, London, 1938. Useful critique.

RICHARDSON, J. H. *British Economic Foreign Policy,* 1936.

RICHARDSON, J. H. *Industrial Relations in Great Britain,* 1938. Brief.

Royal Institute of International Affairs *Political and Strategic Interests of the United Kingdom,* 1939.

SCHUYLER, R. L. *Parliament and the British Empire; Some Constitutional Controversies Concerning Imperial Legislative Jurisdiction,* 1929.

SETON-WATSON, R. W. *Britain and the Dictators,* 1938. Foreign policy.

SIEGFRIED, A. *Post-War Britain,* 1924.

SIEGFRIED, A. *England's Crisis,* 1931. Useful economic summary.

SIPPLE, C. *British Foreign Policy since the World War,* 1932.

SLATER, G. *The Growth of Modern England,* 1932. Social and industrial history.

SNOWDEN, P. *An Autobiography,* 2 v., 1934. Labor Party history.

STEED, H. W. *The Real Stanley Baldwin,* 1930. An appreciation.

STEWART, R. B. *Treaty Relations of the British Commonwealth of Nations,* 1939.

TILLEY, J. and GASELEE, S. *The Foreign Office,* 1933. British.

TILTMAN, H. H. *J. Ramsay MacDonald; Labor's Man of Destiny,* 1929.

TOWNSEND, W. and L. *The Biography of H. R. H. The Prince of Wales,* 1929.

TOYNBEE, A. J. *The Conduct of British Empire Foreign Relations since the Peace Settlement,* 1928.

TRACEY, H., ed. *The Book of the Labour Party,* 3 v., 1925.

TROTTER, R. G. *The British Empire-Commonwealth,* 1932.

TRYON, G. C. *A Short History of Imperial Preference,* 1931.

TSIANG, T. F. *Labor and Empire,* 1923. Labor Party and imperialism.

WANG, C. K. *Dissolution of the British Parliament, 1832–1931,* 1934.

WERTHEIMER, E. *Portrait of the Labour Party,* 1929. German appraisal.

WHEARE, K. C. *The Statute of Westminster, 1931,* 1933.

WHITE, J. L. *The Abdication of Edward VIII,* 1936.

WILLERT, A. *Aspects of British Foreign Policy,* 1928. By British press officer.

CHAPTER XII. SOME BRITISH PROBLEMS OF EMPIRE

Ireland

BEASLAI, P. *Michael Collins, Soldier and Statesman*, 1938.

BEASLEY, P. *Michael Collins and the Making of a New Ireland*, 2 v., 1926.

BENNS, F. L. *The Irish Question, 1912–1914*, 1928.

BLÁCAM, A. DE *What Sinn Fein Stands For; The Irish Republican Movement; Its History, Aims and Ideals*, 1921.

BROMAGE, A. W. "Anglo-Irish Accord," in *Political Science Quarterly*, Dec. 1938.

BUTLER, H. D. *The Irish Free State; An Economic Survey*, 1928.

CLARKSON, J. D. *Labour and Nationalism in Ireland*, 1925. Scholarly.

COLLINS, M. *The Path to Freedom*, 1923. Anglo-Irish Treaty.

CURTIS, E. *A History of Ireland*, 3 ed., 1938.

DESMOND, S. *The Drama of Sinn Fein*, 1923.

FIGGIS, D. *Recollections of the Irish War*, 1927. Covers 1914–1921.

GWYNN, D. R. *The Irish Free State, 1922–1927*, 1928. Good.

GWYNN, D. R. *The Life and Death of Roger Casement*, 1930. Rebel of 1916.

GWYNN, D. R. *De Valera*, 1933.

GWYNN, S. *Ireland*, 1924.

HANNA, H. *The Statute Law of the Irish Free State, 1922 to 1928*, 1929.

HEALY, T. M. *Letters and Leaders of My Day*, 2 v., 1928. Sixty years of the Irish Question by former governor-general.

HENRY, R. M. *The Evolution of Sinn Fein*, 1920. Convenient summary.

HULL, E. *A History of Ireland and Her People*, 2 v., 1926–1931.

IRELAND, T. *Ireland, Past and Present*, 1941.

JONES, F. *History of the Sinn Fein Movement and the Irish Rebellion of 1916*, 1917.

KELLY, R. S. *Ireland's Bloodless Revolution, 1932–1936*, 1936. Economic struggle with Great Britain.

MACARDLE, D. *The Irish Republic. A Documented Chronicle of the Anglo-Irish Conflict and the Partitioning of Ireland, with a Detailed Account of the Period 1916–1923*, 1937.

MACNEILL, J. G. *Studies in the Constitution of the Irish Free State*, 1925.

MACNEILL, R. *Ulster's Stand for Union*, 1922. Good account.

MANSERGH, N. *The Irish Free State*, 1934. Government and politics.

MANSERGH, N. *The Government of Northern Ireland*, 1936.

MANSERGH, N. *Ireland in the Age of Reform and Revolution*, 1941. 1840–1921.

McCARTAN, P. *With De Valera in America*, 1932. Covers 1917–1920.

MOSS, W. *Political Parties in the Irish Free State*, 1933.

MURRAY, R. H. and LAW, H. *Ireland*, 1924. Good outline.

Ó BRIAIN, B. *The Irish Constitution*, 1929.

O'BRIEN, W. *The Irish Revolution and How It Came About*, 1923.

O'CONNER, F. *Death in Dublin: Michael Collins and the Irish Revolution*, 1937.

O'CONNOR, B. *With Michael Collins in the Fight for Irish Independence*, 1929.

Ó FAOLÁIN, S. *The Life Story of Eamon de Valera*, 1933. Brief.

O'SULLIVAN, D. *The Irish Free State and Its Senate*, 1940.

PAKENHAM, F. *Peace by Ordeal*, 1935. Treaty of 1921.

PAUL-DUBOIS, L. and GILL, T. P. *The Irish Struggle and Its Results*, 1934.

PHILLIPS, W. A. *The Revolution in Ireland, 1906–1923*, rev. ed., 1926. Good.

QUEKETT, A. S. *The Constitution of Northern Ireland*, 2 v., 1928–1933.

RYAN, D. *Unique Dictator: A Study of Eamon de Valera*, 1936.

SPINDLER, K. *Gun Running for Casement in the Easter Rebellion, 1916*, 1921.

TALBOT, H., ed. *Michael Collins' Own Story*, 1923.

WALLER, B. C.　*Ireland and the League of Nations*, 1925.
WELLS, W. B. and MARLOWE, N.　*A History of the Irish Rebellion of 1916*, 1916.

India

AIYER, P. S.　*Indian Constitutional Problems*, 1928.
ANDREWS, C. F.　*India and the Simon Report*, 1930.　Pro-Indian.
ANDREWS, C. F.　*Mahatma Gandhi's Ideas, Including Selections from His Writings*, 1930.　By friend of Gandhi.
ANDREWS, C. F., ed.　*Mahatma Gandhi, His Own Story*, 1930.
ANDREWS, C. F., ed.　*Mahatma Gandhi at Work; His Own Story Continued*, 1931.
ANDREWS, C. F. and MOOKERJEE, G.　*The Rise and the Growth of the Congress in India*, 1939.
ANSTEY, V.　*The Economic Development of India*, 2 ed., 1931.
APPADORAI, A.　*Dyarchy in Practice*, 1937.
BANERJEE, D. N.　*The Indian Constitution and Its Actual Working*, 1926.
BARNS, M.　*The Indian Press*, 1940.
BESANT, A.　*India: A Nation*, 4 ed., 1930.　Nationalist movement.
BESTERMAN, T.　*Mrs. Annie Besant; A Modern Prophet*, 1934.
BOSE, S. M.　*The Working Constitution in India*, 1940.　Act of 1935.
BRAILSFORD, H. N.　*Rebel India*, 1931.　Village and social conditions.
BROWN, J. C.　*India's Mineral Wealth*, 1936.　Scientific compendium.
BRUCE, C. E.　"The Indian Frontier Problem," in *Asiatic Review*, July 1939.
BUCHANAN, D. H.　*The Development of Capitalistic Enterprise in India*, 1934.
CATON, A. R., ed.　*The Key of Progress; A Survey of the Status and Conditions of Women in India*, 1930.
CHIROL, V.　*India*, 1926.　Well written.
CHUDGAR, P. L.　*Indian Princes under British Protection; A Study of Their Personal Rule, Their Constitutional Position, and Their Future*, 1929.
CUMMING, J., ed.　*Political India, 1832–1932; A Co-operative Survey of a Century*, 1932.　By British officials and scholars.
CURTIS, L.　*Papers Relating to the Application of the Principle of Dyarchy to the Government of India*, 1920.　Documents.
DODWELL, H. H., ed.　*The Cambridge Shorter History of India*, 1934.　To 1919.
DUNCAN, A.　*India in Crisis*, 1931.　Popular account since 1911.
EDDY, J. P. and LAWTON, F. H.　*India's New Constitution: A Survey of the Government of India Act, 1935*, 1935.
EDIB, H.　*Inside India*, 1938.　By a Turkish woman.
EMERSON, G.　*Voiceless India*, 1930.　Interesting on village life.
FULLER, J. F. C.　*India in Revolt*, 1931.　Causes of unrest.
GANDHI, M. K.　*Young India, 1919–1922*, 1923.　Noncoöperation.
GANDHI, M. K.　*Young India, 1924–1926*, 1927.
GANDHI, M. K.　*The Story of My Experiments with Truth*, 2 v., 1927–1929.
GANGULEE, N.　*The Indian Peasant and His Environment*, 1935.
GANGULEE, N.　*The Making of Federal India*, 1936.　On 1911–1935.
Government of India　*India in 1919*, etc., 1920–.　Annual.
HORNE, E. A.　*The Political System of British India; With Special Reference to the Recent Constitutional Changes*, 1922.
HORNIMAN, B. G.　*Amritsar and our Duty to India*, 1920.
HUBBARD, G. E.　*Eastern Industrialization and Its Effect on the West*, 1935.
HULL, W. I.　*India's Political Crisis*, 1930.　National Congress of 1928–1929.
India, Chamber of Princes　*The British Crown and the Indian States; An Outline Sketch Drawn Up on Behalf of the Standing Committee of the Chamber of Princes, by the Directorate of the Chamber's Special Organisation*, 1929.
Indian Year Book and Who's Who 1940–41, 1941.

Institute for Government Research (in U. S.)   *The Problem of Indian Administration*, 1928. Exhaustive.

International Labor Office   *Industrial Labour in India*, 1938.

JOSHI, G. N.   *Indian Administration*, 1937. Well organized.

JOSHI, G. N.   *The New Constitution of India*, 1937.

KARVE, D. J.   *Poverty and Population in India*, 1936.

KEITH, A. B.   *A Constitutional History of India, 1600–1935*, 1936.

KERALA PUTRA (PANIKKAR, K. M.)   *The Working of Dyarchy in India, 1919–1928*, 1928. By an Indian professor.

MADHAVA RAO, D.   *The Indian Round Table Conference and After*, 1932.

MANSHARDT, C.   *The Hindu-Moslem Problem in India*, 1936.

MELLO, F. M. DE   *The Indian National Congress*, 1934.

MISRA, K.   *Indian Provincial Finance, 1919–1939*, 1942.

MITCHELL, K. L.   *India without Fable. A 1942 Survey*, 1942.

MUKHTAR, A.   *Trade Unionism and Labour Disputes in India*, 1935.

MUZUMDAR, H. T.   *Gandhi versus the Empire*, 1932.

NEHRU, J.   *Toward Freedom: An Autobiography*, 1941.

PEARSE, A. S.   *The Cotton Industry of India*, 1930.

PUNNIAH, K. V.   *India as a Federation*, 1936.

RANGA IYER, C. S.   *India in the Crucible*, 1928. Moderate.

RAWLINSON, H. G.   *India: A Short Cultural History*, 1938. Balanced.

RAY, P.   *India's Foreign Trade since 1870*, 1934.

READ, M.   *The Indian Peasant Uprooted; A Study of the Human Machine*, 1931. Based on *Report of the Royal Commission on Labour in India*.

ROLLAND, R.   *Mahatma Gandhi*, 1924. Sympathetic.

SAMANT, D. R. and MULKY, M. A.   *Organisation and Finance of Industries in India*, 1937.

SCHIFF, L. M.   *The Present Condition of India*, 1939. Well informed.

SHRIDHARANI, K.   *War Without Violence: A Study of Gandhi's Method and Its Accomplishments*, 1939.

SIMON, J. A.   *India and the Simon Report*, 1930.

SLATER, G.   *Southern India*, 1936. Emphasis on social life.

SMITH, W. R.   *Nationalism and Reform in India, 1900–1937*, 1938.

THOMPSON, E.   *Reconstructing India*, 1930. Excellent general survey.

THOMPSON, E. and GARRATT, G. T.   *Rise and Fulfillment of British Rule in India*, 1934. Dispassionate.

VAKIL, C., BOSE, S., and DEOLALKAR, P.   *Growth of Trade and Industry in Modern India*, 1931.

VAKIL, C. and MUNSHI, M.   *Industrial Policy of India*, 1934.

VAN TYNE, C. H.   *India in Ferment*, 1923. American view.

VARADARAJAN, M. K.   *The Indian States and Federation*, 1938. Favorable.

WEBSTER, C. K.   *The Population Problem in India: A Census Study*, 1934.

WHITEHEAD, H.   *Indian Problems in Religion, Education, Politics*, 1924.

YOUNGHUSBAND, F. E.   *Dawn in India; British Purpose and Indian Aspiration*, 1930. Stresses spiritual factors.

Remainder of the Empire

ANDREWS, F. F.   *The Holy Land under Mandate*, 2 v., 1931.

ANTONIUS, G.   *The Arab Awakening*, 1939. By a Christian Arab nationalist.

ARMSTRONG, H. C.   *Lord of Arabia, Ibn Saud; An Intimate Study of a King*, 1934.

BARNES, L.   *Caliban in Africa; An Impression of Colour Madness*, 1930. S. Africa.

BARNOUW, A. J.   *Language and Race Problems in South Africa*, 1934.

BEAMAN, A.   *The Dethronement of the Khedive*, 1929. Criticism.

BENTWICH, N.   *England in Palestine*, 1932.

BENTWICH, N.   *Fulfilment in the Promised Land, 1917–1937*, 1938.

BROOKES, E. H. *The History of Native Policy in South Africa*, rev. ed., 1927.

BUELL, R. L. *The Native Problem in Africa*, 2 v., 1928.

BURSTEIN, M. *Self-Government of the Jews in Palestine since 1900*, 1934.

CHIROL, V. *The Egyptian Problem*, 1920. Thoughtful and well written.

CHRISTIAN, J. L. *Modern Burma*, 1942.

CLELAND, W. *The Population Problem in Egypt*, 1936. Not optimistic.

CONDLIFFE, J. B. *New Zealand in the Making; A Survey of Economic and Social Development*, 1930.

CROUCHLEY, A. E. *The Economic Development of Modern Egypt*, 1938. Scholarly.

CUMMING, H. H. *Franco-British Rivalry in the Post-War Near East*, 1938. To 1924.

DANDRIA, E. *The Malta Crisis*, 1930. Able, short criticism.

EDIDIN, B. *Rebuilding Palestine*, 1939.

ELGOOD, P. G. *Egypt and the Army*, 1924. Covers ably 1914–1919.

ERSKINE, B. *Palestine of the Arabs*, 1936.

FARAGO, L. *Palestine at the Cross-Roads*, 1937. Journalist's trip in 1936.

FAWCETT, C. B. *A Political Geography of the British Empire*, 1933.

FEINBERG, N. *Some Problems of the Palestine Mandate*, 1936. Legal study.

FEIWEL, T. R. *No Ease in Zion*, 1939. Among the best on Palestine.

FITZPATRICK, B. *The British Empire in Australia*, 1941. Economic.

FOSTER, H. A. *The Making of Modern Iraq; A Product of World Forces*, 1935.

GRANOVSKY, A. *Land Problems in Palestine*, 1926.

GRANOVSKY, A. *Land Settlement in Palestine*, 1930.

GRANOVSKY, A. *Land Policy in Palestine*, 1940.

GRATTAN, C. H. *Introducing Australia*, 1942. Interesting.

Great Britain *Correspondence between Sir Henry McMahon . . . and the Sherif Hussein of Mecca, July 1915–March 1916*, 1939.

Great Britain *Palestine Royal Commission Report*, 1937.

Great Britain, Colonial Office *Progress of Iraq during the Period 1920–1931*, 1931.

Great Britain, Colonial Office *Palestine and Trans-Jordan for the Year 1938*, 1939.

GRUNWALD, K. *The Industrialization of the Near East*, 1934.

HALL, W. P. *Empire to Commonwealth; Thirty Years of British Imperial History*, 1928.

HALLBERG, C. W. *The Suez Canal*, 1931.

HANCOCK, W. K. *Australia*, 1931.

HANNA, P. L. *British Policy in Palestine*, 1942.

HARRIS, M. *Egypt under the Egyptians*, 1925.

HAYTER, W. G. *Recent Constitutional Developments in Egypt*, 1924.

HIMADEH, S. B. *Economic Organization of Palestine*, 1938. Thorough.

HITTI, P. K. *History of the Arabs*, 1937.

HOFMEYER, J. H. *South Africa*, 1931.

HOROWITZ, D. and HINDEN, R. *Economic Survey of Palestine*, 1938.

HOWELL, J. M. *Egypt's Past, Present and Future*, 1929. American view.

JARVIS, C. S. *Three Deserts*, 1937.

JEFFRIES, C. J. *The Colonial Empire and Its Civil Service*, 1939.

JEFFRIES, J. M. N. *Palestine: The Reality*, 1939. Arab viewpoint.

KALLEN, H. M. *Zionism and World Politics; A Study in History and Social Psychology*, 1921.

KIEWIET, C. W. DE *A History of South Africa; Social and Economic*, 1941.

KOHN, H. *Nationalism and Imperialism in the Hither East*, 1932.

LLOYD, G. *Egypt since Cromer*, 2 v., 1933–1934. By a High Commissioner.

LODER, J. *The Truth about Mesopotamia, Palestine and Syria*, 1923. Effects of peace settlement.

LUKE, H. and KEITH-ROACH, E., eds. *Handbook of Palestine and Trans-Jordan*, 3 ed., 1934.

MACHOVER, J. M. *Jewish State or Ghetto: Danger of Palestine Partition*, 1937.

MAIN, E. *Iraq*, 1934. Interesting political and social account.

MAIN, E. *Palestine at the Crossroads,* 1937. Fair-minded.
MILLS, L. A. *British Rule in Eastern Asia. A Study of Contemporary Government and Economic Development in British Malaya and Hong Kong,* 1941.
PEARLMAN, M. *Collective Adventure,* 1938. Palestine.
PHILBY, H. *The Heart of Arabia,* 2 v., 1923. Fascinating travel record.
PHILBY, H. *Arabia of the Wahhabis,* 1928. Continuation of above.
PREISS, L. and ROHRBACH, P. *Palestine and Trans-Jordan,* 1926.
RAPPOPORT, A. S. *History of Palestine,* 1931.
REVUSKY, A. *Jews in Palestine,* 1935.
Royal Institute of International Affairs *The British Empire. A Report on Its Structure and Problems,* 1937.
Royal Inst. of Int. Affairs *Great Britain and Egypt, 1914–1936,* 1936.
Royal Inst. of Int. Affairs *Great Britain and Palestine, 1915–1936,* 1936.
SAMUEL, M. *On the Rim of the Wilderness,* 1931. Jewish-Arab problem.
SERENI, E. and ASHERY, R. E. *Jews and Arabs in Palestine,* 1936.
SHANN, E. *An Economic History of Australia,* 1930.
SIDEBOTHAM, H. *British Policy and the Palestine Mandate,* 1929.
SIDEBOTHAM, H. *Great Britain and Palestine,* 1937.
SMITH, A. N. *Thirty Years: The Commonwealth of Australia, 1901–1931,* 1933.
SOKOLOW, N. *History of Zionism, 1600–1918,* 2 v., 1919. Detailed.
STEIN, L. *Zionism,* 1925. Well informed.
STOYE, J. *The British Empire: Its Structure and Its Problems.* 1936.
SYMONS, M. T. *Britain and Egypt; The Rise of Egyptian Nationalism,* 1925.
The Times (London) *The Times Book of Egypt,* 1937.
WALKER, E. A. *A History of South Africa,* rev. ed., 1935. Excellent.
WALKER, E. R. *Australia in the World Depression,* 1933.
WILSON, A. T. *The Suez Canal; Its Past, Present, and Future,* 1933.
WINDETT, N. *Australia as Producer and Trader, 1920–1932,* 1933.
WISE, S. S. and DE HAAS, J. *The Great Betrayal,* 1930. On Palestine.
YOUNG, E. H. *et al.* *Report of the Commission on Closer Union of the Dependencies of Eastern and Central Africa,* 1929. Official report.
YOUNG, G. *Egypt,* 1927. Stresses period since 1914.

CHAPTER XIII. UNHAPPY FRANCE

ADAM, G. *The Tiger; Georges Clemenceau, 1841–1929,* 1930.
Alsace-Lorraine: A Border Problem, Foreign Policy Assoc. *Report,* Feb. 1930.
BAINVILLE, J. *The French Republic, 1870–1935,* 1936. Royalist view.
BELGION, M. *News of the French,* 1938. Good factual survey.
BROGAN, D. W. *France under the Republic: The Development of Modern France, 1870–1939,* 1940.
BUELL, R. L. *Contemporary French Politics,* 1920.
BUTHMAN, W. C. *The Rise of Integral Nationalism in France,* 1939.
CAHILL, R. *Economic Conditions in France,* 1934.
CLARK, F. I. *The Position of Women in Contemporary France,* 1937.
CLEMENCEAU, G. *In the Evening of My Thought,* 2 v., 1929.
CLOUGH, S. B. *France: A History of National Economics, 1789–1939,* 1939.
COHEN-PORTHEIM, P. *The Spirit of France,* 1933. By an Austrian artist.
DANIELS, H. G. *The Framework of France,* 1937. Impression of the people.
DAVIS, S. C. *The French War Machine,* 1937.
DULLES, E. *The French Franc, 1914–1928,* 1929.
EINZIG, P. *France's Crisis,* 1934.
FISK, H. E. *French Public Finance in the Great War and Today, with Chapters on Banking and Currency,* 1922.
FRANCK, L. *French Price Control,* 1942. Blum to Pétain.

FRASER, G. and NATANSON, T. *Léon Blum: Man and Statesman*, 1938.
GIDE, C., ed. *Effects of the War upon French Economic Life*, 1923. Technical.
GOOCH, R. K. *Regionalism in France*, 1931.
GOOCH, R. K. *The French Parliamentary Committee System*, 1935.
GRUNWALD, K. *The Industrialization of the Near East*, 1934. On Syria.
GWYNN, D. R. *The Catholic Reaction in France*, 1924.
HAIG, R. M. *The Public Finances of Post-War France*, 1929.
HAIGHT, F. A. *French Import Quotas: A New Instrument of Commercial Policy*, 1935.
HAIGHT, F. A. *A History of French Commercial Policies*, 1941.
HALE, R. W., JR. *Democratic France. The Third Republic from Sedan to Vichy*, 1941.
HAYES, C. J. H. *France: A Nation of Patriots*, 1930. Educational influences.
HILL, H. *The Spirit of Modern France*, 1934. Brief, excellent.
HUDDLESTON, S. *Poincaré; A Biographical Portrait*, 1924. Friendly.
HUDDLESTON, S. *Those Europeans*, 1924. Biographical sketches.
HUDDLESTON, S. *France*, 1927. Sympathetic.
HUNTER, N. *Peasantry and Crisis in France*, 1938.
KNIGHT, M. M. *Morocco as a French Economic Venture*, 1937.
LEEDS, S. B. *These Rule France. The Story of Edouard Daladier and the Men Around Him*, 1940.
MacCALLUM, E. P. *The Nationalist Crusade in Syria*, 1928.
MacDONALD, W. *Reconstruction in France*, 1922. On devastated areas.
MIDDLETON, W. L. *The French Political System*, 1933.
MOON, P. T. *The Labor Problem and the Social Catholic Movement in France; A Study in the History of Social Politics*, 1921.
MOORE, W. G. *France and Germany*, 1932.
MOULTON, H. G. and LEWIS, C. *The French Debt Problem*, 1925.
MURET, C. T. *French Royalist Doctrines since the Revolution*, 1933.
MYERS, M. G. *Paris as a Financial Center*, 1936.
OGBURN, W. F. and JAFFÉ, W. *The Economic Development of Post-War France*, 1929. Changes in agriculture and industry.
PEEL, G. *The Financial Crisis of France*, 1925.
PEEL, G. *The Economic Policy of France*, 1937.
PIPKIN, C. W. *Social Politics and Modern Democracies*, 2 v., 1931. V. 2, France.
PRIESTLEY, H. I. *France Overseas*, 1938. Complete colonial survey.
RENOUVIN, P. *The Forms of War Government in France*, 1927.
ROBERTS, S. *History of French Colonial Policy, 1870–1925*, 2 v., 1929. Excellent.
ROGERS, J. H. *The Process of Inflation in France, 1914–1927*, 1929.
SAIT, E. M. *Government and Politics of France*, 1920.
SAPOSS, D. J. *The Labor Movement in Post-War France*, 1931.
SCHUMAN, F. L. *War and Diplomacy in the French Republic*, 1931. Encyclopedic.
SHARP, W. R. *The French Civil Service: Bureaucracy in Transition*, 1931.
SHARP, W. R. *The Government of the French Republic*, 1939.
SIEBURG, F. *Who Are These French?*, 1932. Interesting, by a German journalist.
SIEGFRIED, A. *France; A Study in Nationality*, 1930. Brief and interesting.
SOLTAU, R. H. *French Parties and Politics, 1871–1930*, 1930.
SOUTHWORTH, C. *The French Colonial Adventure*, 1931.
SPENGLER, J. J. *France Faces Depopulation*, 1938.
STEIN, L. *Syria*, 1926. Racial and religious questions.
STOKES, R. L. *Léon Blum: Poet and Premier*, 1937.
THOMSON, V. *Briand, Man of Peace*, 1930. Uncritical.
VAUCHER, P. *Post-War France*, 1934. Political.
VINEBERG, P. F. *The French Franc and the Gold Standard*, 1939.
WERTH, A. *France in Ferment*, 1934. Background of 1934 disorders.
WERTH, A. *Which Way France?*, 1937. Excellent.

WERTH, A. *France and Munich: Before and After Surrender*, 1939.
WORSFOLD, W. B. *France in Tunis and Algeria*, 1930. Lively.

CHAPTER XIV. FASCIST ITALY

BADOGLIO, P. *The War in Abyssinia*, 1937.
BARNES, J. S. *Fascism*, 1931. Brief, sympathetic.
BERNHART, J. *The Vatican as a World Power*, 1939.
BINCHY, D. A. *Church and State in Fascist Italy*, 1942. Scholarly.
BONOMI, I. *From Socialism to Fascism*, 1924. By an ex-premier.
BOOTH, C. D. and I. B. *Italy's Ægean Possessions*, 1928. Dodecanesia.
BORGESE, G. A. *Goliath: The March of Fascism*, 1937. Critical of fascism.
BOVERI, M. *Mediterranean Cross-Currents*, 1938.
BROWNE-OLF, L. *Pius XI, Apostle of Peace*, 1938.
CARLEN, SISTER M. C. *A Guide to the Encyclicals of the Roman Pontiffs from Leo XIII to the Present Day (1878–1937)*, 1939. Bibliographical.
ČERMELJ, L. *Life-and-Death Struggle of a National Minority. (The Jugo-Slavs in Italy)* , 1936. Propaganda, but interesting.
CHEKREZI, C. A. *Albania, Past and Present*, 1919. Good account.
CIPPICO, A. *Italy, the Central Problem of the Mediterranean*, 1926. Pro-Fascist.
COTTA, F. *Agricultural Co-operation in Fascist Italy*, 1935. Brief.
CURREY, M. *Italian Foreign Policy, 1918–1932*, 1932. Friendly.
EBENSTEIN, W. *Fascist Italy*, 1939.
FARAGO, L. *Arabian Antic*, 1938. Italian activities in Red Sea area.
FERRERO, G. *Four Years of Fascism*, 1924. Hostile.
FIELD, G. L. *The Syndical and Corporative Institutions of Italian Fascism*, 1938.
FINER, H. *Mussolini's Italy*, 1935. Full treatment; hostile.
GLANVILLE, J. L. *Colonialism in the New Italy*, 1934. Useful pamphlet.
GOAD, H. E. *The Making of the Corporate State; A Study of Fascist Development*, 2 ed., 1934. Sympathetic.
GWYNN, D. *The Vatican and War in Europe*, 1941. Since 1914.
HAIDER, C. *Capital and Labor under Fascism*, 1930.
HALPERIN, S. W. *The Separation of Church and State in Italian Thought from Cavour to Mussolini*, 1937.
HENTZE, M. *Pre-Fascist Italy: The Rise and Fall of the Parliamentary Régime*, 1939.
HERFORD, C. H., ed. *The Case of German South Tyrol against Italy*, 1927.
HERRON, G. D. *The Revival of Italy*, 1922. Economic conditions.
HUGHES, P. *Pope Pius the Eleventh*, 1937.
HULLINGER, E. W. *The New Fascist State*, 1928. Sympathetic.
International Labor Office "The Settlement of Labor Disputes in Italy," in *International Labor Review*, October 1934.
Italy and the Jugoslav Minority within Her Borders, 1931. Yugoslav grievances.
JONES, S. *Benito Mussolini; An Introduction to the Study of Fascism*, 1927.
KEMECHY, L. *"Il Duce;" The Life and Work of Benito Mussolini*, 1930. By a Hungarian diplomat.
KING, B. *Fascism in Italy*, 1931. Critical.
LONGOBARDI, C. *Land Reclamation in Italy*, 1936.
MACARTNEY, M. H. H. and CREMONA, P. *Italy's Foreign and Colonial Policy, 1914–1937*, 1938. Good.
MACCALLUM, E. P. *Rivalries in Ethiopia*, 1935. Excellent background.
MACDONALD, J. N. *A Political Escapade; The Story of Fiume and D'Annunzio*, 1921.
MARRARO, H. *The New Education in Italy*, 1936.
MARRIOTT, J. *The Makers of Modern Italy; Napoleon—Mussolini*, 1931.

MARTELLI, G. *Italy Against the World,* 1937. Balanced British account of Italo-Ethiopian conflict.

MARTELLI, G. *Whose Sea? A Mediterranean Journey,* 1938.

MATTEOTTI, G. *The Fascisti Exposed,* 1924. By the deputy later killed.

MATTHEWS, H. L. *Two Wars and More to Come,* 1938. Ethiopia and Spain.

McCLELLAN, G. B. *Modern Italy,* 1933.

McGUIRE, C. E. *Italy's International Economic Position,* 1926.

MEGARO, G. *Mussolini in the Making,* 1938. Mussolini's views to 1922.

MILLER, H. S. *Price Control in Fascist Italy,* 1938.

MOORE, M. *Fourth Shore: Italy's Mass Colonization of Libya,* 1940.

MOORE, T. E. *Peter's City; An Account of the Origin, Development, and Solution of the Roman Question,* 1929.

MORI, C. *The Last Struggle with the Mafia,* 1933. By prefect who fought it.

MUNRO, I. S. *Through Fascism to World Power; A History of the Revolution in Italy,* 1933.

MURIELLO, R. *Mussolini, His Work and the New Syndical Law,* 3 ed., 1928.

MUSSOLINI, B. *My Diary, 1915–1917,* 1925.

MUSSOLINI, B. *My Autobiography,* 1928. Superficial.

MUSSOLINI, B. *Fascism: Doctrine and Institutions,* 1935. Speeches and laws.

MUSSOLINI, B. *The Corporate State,* 1936. Speeches and documents.

NENNI, P. *Ten Years of Tyranny in Italy,* 1932.

NITTI, F. F. *Escape,* 1930. Escape from a Fascist penal island.

NITTI, F. S. *Bolshevism, Fascism and Democracy,* 1927. By an ex-premier.

PARSONS, W. *The Pope and Italy,* 1929. Brief, Catholic view.

PENNACHIO, A. *The Corporative State,* 1927. Brief.

PETRIE, C. A. *Mussolini,* 1931. Short, popular.

PINI, G. *The Official Life of Benito Mussolini,* 1939.

PITIGLIANI, F. *The Italian Corporative State,* 1933. Detailed but clear.

POLSON NEWMAN, E. W. *The New Abyssinia,* 1938. Pro-Italian report.

POR, O. *Fascism,* 1923. Objective early account.

POTTER, P. B. *The Wal Wal Arbitration,* 1938. By one of the arbiters.

PREZZOLINI, G. *Fascism,* 1927. Moderate in tone.

REUT-NICOLUSSI, E. *Tyrol under the Axe of Italian Fascism,* 1930.

REY, C. F. *The Real Abyssinia,* 1935.

ROCCO, A. *The Political Doctrine of Fascism,* 1926.

ROSSI, A. *The Rise of Italian Fascism, 1918–1922,* 1938.

Royal Inst. of Int. Affairs *Abyssinia and Italy,* 1935.

Royal Inst. of Int. Affairs *The Economic and Financial Position of Italy,* 2 ed., 1935.

Royal Inst. of Int. Affairs *The Italian Colonial Empire,* 1940.

SALVEMINI, G. *The Fascist Dictatorship in Italy,* v. 1, 1927. Hostile.

SALVEMINI, G. *Under the Axe of Fascism,* 1936. Anti-Fascist.

SAN SEVERINO, B. DI, ed. *Mussolini as Revealed in His Political Speeches,* 1923.

SCHMIDT, C. T. *The Plough and the Sword. Labor, Land, and Property in Fascist Italy,* 1938. Critical.

SCHMIDT, C. T. *The Corporate State in Action,* 1939.

SCHNEIDER, H. W. *Making the Fascist State,* 1928. Excellent, philosophical.

SCHNEIDER, H. W. *The Fascist Government of Italy,* 1936.

SCHNEIDER, H. W. and CLOUGH, S. B. *Making Fascists,* 1929.

SILLANI, T., ed. *What Is Fascism and Why?,* 1931. By Fascist leaders.

SPENCER, H. R. *Government and Politics of Italy,* 1932.

STEER, G. L. *Caesar in Abyssinia,* 1937. Journalist's account.

STICKNEY, E. P. *Southern Albania or Northern Epirus in European International Affairs, 1912–1923,* 1926.

STEINER, H. A. *Government in Fascist Italy,* 1938. Excellent.

STURZO, L. *Italy and Fascismo,* 1926. By a Catholic cleric.

SWIRE, J. *Albania; The Rise of a Kingdom,* 1929. Extensive handbook.

SWIRE, J. *King Zog's Albania*, 1937.
TEELING, W. *Pope Pius XI and World Affairs*, 1937.
VARLEY, D. H., comp. *A Bibliography of Italian Colonisation in Africa with a Section on Abyssinia*, 1936.
VILLARI, L. *The Fascist Experiment*, 1926. Pro-Fascist.
VILLARI, L. *Italy*, 1929. Pro-Fascist.
VILLARI, L. *The Expansion of Italy*, 1930. A defense.
VOLPI DI MISURATA, G. *The Financial Reconstruction of Italy*, 1927. Statistics.
WALTER, K. *The Class Conflict in Italy*, 1938. Pro-Fascist.
WELK, W. G. *Fascist Economic Policy*, 1938.
WHEELER-BENNETT, J. W. and HEALD, S., eds. *Documents on International Affairs 1935*, v. 2. 1937. Deals with Italo-Ethiopian conflict.
WILLIAMSON, B. *The Treaty of the Lateran*, 1929. Documents.
WILLIAMSON, B. *The Story of Pope Pius XI*, 1931.
WOODHOUSE, E. J. and C. G. *Italy and the Jugoslavs*, 1920.
WORK, E. *Ethiopia; A Pawn in European Diplomacy*, 1935. Good.
ZAIMI, N. *Daughter of the Eagle. The Autobiography of an Albanian Girl*, 1937.

CHAPTER XV. SPAIN

ALTAMIRA, R. *A History of Spanish Civilization*, 1930. Excellent synthesis.
ALVAREZ DEL VAYO, J. *Freedom's Battle*, 1940. Loyalist foreign minister.
ATKINSON, W. C. *Spain; A Brief History*, 1934. Clear.
BERTRAND, L. and PETRIE, C. A. *The History of Spain, 711–1931*, 1934.
BLASCO IBÁÑEZ, V. *Alfonso XIII Unmasked; The Military Terror in Spain*, 1924.
BLÁSQUEZ, J. M. *I Helped to Build an Army*, 1939. Loyalist.
BORKENAU, F. *The Spanish Cockpit*, 1937. Sociological study of Loyalist Spain.
BRANDT, J. A. *Toward the New Spain*, 1933. Good discussion.
CASTILLEJO, J. *Wars of Ideas in Spain*, 1937. By a liberal.
COOPER, C. S. *Understanding Spain*, 1928. By an American traveler.
DEAKIN, F. B. *Spain To-Day*, 1924. Excellent critical survey.
ERSKINE, B. *Twenty-Nine Years; The Reign of King Alfonso XIII*, 1931.
GANNES, H. and REPARD, T. *Spain in Revolt*, 1937. Leftist.
GODDEN, G. M. *Conflict in Spain, 1920–1937: A Documented Record*, 1937.
GREENFIELD, E. V. *Spain Progresses; The Impressions and Experiences of a Student and Traveler in Spain*, 1932.
HARRIS, W. B. *France, Spain, and the Rif*, 1927.
HUME, M. *Modern Spain*, 3 ed., 1923. Standard, reaches 1918.
MADARIAGA, S. DE *Spain*, 1930. History and culture of Spain.
MANUEL, F. A. *The Politics of Modern Spain*, 1938. Readable.
MATTHEWS, H. L. *Two Wars and More to Come*, 1938. Italy in Ethiopia and Spain.
McCABE, J. *Spain in Revolt, 1814–1931*, 1931. Anti-clerical.
MENDIZABEL, A. *The Martyrdom of Spain*, 1938. Objective; 1923 to 1936.
ORTEGA Y GASSET, J. *Invertebrate Spain*, 1937. Thoughtful.
PADELFORD, N. J. *International Law and Diplomacy in the Spanish Civil War*, 1939.
PAUL, E. *Life and Death of a Spanish Town*, 1937. Fascinating story.
PEERS, E. A. *Catalonia Infelix*, 1938. Good history.
PEERS, E. A. *The Spanish Tragedy, 1930–1936*, 1937. Conservative British view.
PEERS, E. A. *The Church in Spain, 1737–1937*, 1938.
PILAR, PRINCESS and CHAPMAN-HUSTON, D. *Every Inch a King; Alfonso XIII; A Study of Monarchy*, 1932. By a relative of Alfonso.
ROGERS, F. T. *Spain: A Tragic Journey*, 1937.
SEDGWICK, H. D. *Spain; A Short History of Its Politics, Literature and Art*, 1925.
SENCOURT, R. *The Spanish Crown, 1808–1931*, 1932. Sympathetic.

SENDER, R. *Counter-Attack in Spain*, 1937. By Loyalist intellectual.
SMITH, R. M. *The Day of the Liberals in Spain*, 1939. Constitution of 1931.
Spanish White Book *The Italian Invasion of Spain. Official Documents and Papers Seized from Italian Units in Action at Guadalajara*, 1937.
STEER, G. L. *The Tree of Gernika*, 1938. The war in the Basque country.
STRONG, A. L. *Spain in Arms*, 1937. Leftist account.
VERDUIN, A. R., comp. *Manual of Spanish Constitutions, 1808–1931*, 1941.
VILAPLANA, R. *Burgos Justice*, 1938. Critical of Franco; by ex-Insurgent.
WEISSBERGER, J. A., ed. *They Still Draw Pictures*, 1938. Spanish children in the civil war; published for the American Quakers.
WHITE, E. *War in Spain*, 1937.
YOUNG, G. *The New Spain*, 1933. Post-revolutionary years.

CHAPTER XVI. GERMANY

The Weimar Republic

ALEXANDER, T. and PARKER, B. *The New Education in the German Republic*, 1929.
ANDERSON, B. M. *Germany and Russia*, 1922.
ANGELL, J. W. *The Recovery of Germany*, rev. ed., 1932. Economics.
BAUMONT, M. *The Fall of the Kaiser*, 1931. Story of abdication.
BEVAN, E. R. *German Social Democracy during the War*, 1918.
BLACHLY, F. F. and OATMAN, M. E. *The Government and Administration of Germany*, 1928.
BRACKMANN, A., ed. *Germany and Poland in Their Historical Relations*, 1934.
BRADY, R. A. *The Rationalization Movement in German Industry; A Study in the Evolution of Economic Planning*, 1933.
BRINCKMEYER, H. *Hugo Stinnes*, 1921.
BROOKS, S. *America and Germany, 1918–1925*, 2 ed., 1927.
BRUCK, W. F. *Social and Economic History of Germany from William II to Hitler, 1888–1938: A Comparative Study*, 1938. Difficult, but worthwhile.
BRUNET, R. *The New German Constitution*, 1922. Excellent commentary.
BRUNTZ, G. G. *Allied Propaganda and the Collapse of the German Empire in 1918*, 1938.
COAR, J. F. *The Old and New Germany*, 1924. Changes after 1917.
DANIELS, H. G. *The Rise of the German Republic*, 1928. Informative.
DANTON, G. H. *Germany Ten Years After*, 1928. Intellectual changes.
DAWSON, P. *Germany's Industrial Revival*, 1926. By a British expert.
DAWSON, W. H. *Germany under the Treaty*, 1933. Sympathetic.
DIESEL, E. *Germany and the Germans*, 1931.
DITTMAR, W. R. *The Government of the Free State of Bavaria*, 1934.
DOMERATZKY, L. *The International Cartel Movement*, 1928.
DOUGLASS, P. F. *The Economic Dilemma of Politics; A Study of the Consequences of the Strangulation of Germany*, 1932.
ELLIS, H. S. *German Monetary Theory, 1905–1933*, 1934. Scholarly criticism.
EMERSON, R. *State and Sovereignty in Modern Germany*, 1928. Political theory.
FISK, O. H. *Germany's Constitutions of 1871 and 1919*, 1924.
FLINK, S. *The German Reichsbank and Economic Germany*, 1930.
FRANCKE, K. *German After-War Problems*, 1927. Intellectual and cultural.
FRÖHLICH, P. *Rosa Luxemburg: Her Life and Work*, 1940.
GEDYE, G. E. R. *The Revolver Republic; France's Bid for the Rhine*, 1930.
GOOCH, G. P. *Germany*, 1925. Sympathetic.
GREER, G. *The Ruhr-Lorraine Industrial Problem*, 1925.
GUILLEBAUD, C. W. *The Works Council. A German Experiment in Industrial Democracy*, 1928.

GURADZE, H. "German Labor in Zenith and Eclipse," in *The American Scholar*, Spring 1939. The trade-union movement, 1918–1933.

HENEMAN, H. J. *The Growth of Executive Power in Germany; A Study of the German Presidency*, 1934.

HOETZSCH, O. *Germany's Domestic and Foreign Policies*, 1929. Lectures.

HOLT, J. B. *German Agricultural Policy, 1918–1934*, 1936.

KAUTSKY, K. *The Labour Revolution*, 1925. Socialization.

KESSLER, H. *Germany and Europe*, 1923. Interesting.

KESSLER, H. *Walther Rathenau, His Life and Work*, 1930.

KOCH-WESER, E. *Germany in the Post-War World*, 1930.

KOSOK, P. *Modern Germany; A Study of Conflicting Loyalties*, 1933. Good.

KRAUS, H. *Germany in Transition*, 1924. Political tendencies.

KRAUS, H. *The Crisis of German Democracy*, 1932.

KUCZYNSKI, R. R. *Postwar Labor Conditions in Germany*, 1925. Statistics.

KUCZYNSKI, R. R. *American Loans to Germany*, 1927.

KUCZYNSKI, R. R. *Bankers' Profits from German Loans*, 1932.

KÜHLMANN, R. VON *Thoughts on Germany*, 1932.

LEVY, H. *Industrial Germany; A Study of Its Monopoly Organizations and Their Control by the State*, 1935.

LICHTENBERGER, H. *Relations between France and Germany*, 1923. French view.

LUEHR, E. *The New German Republic*, 1929.

LUTZ, R. H. *The German Revolution, 1918–1919*, 1922. Excellent.

LUTZ, R. H. *Fall of the German Empire, 1914–1918*, 2 v., 1932. Documents.

LUTZ, R. H., ed. *The Causes of the German Collapse in 1918. Sections of the Officially Authorized Report of the Commission of the German Constituent Assembly and of the German Reichstag, 1919–1928, the Selection and the Translation Officially Approved by the Commission*, 1934.

LUXEMBURG, R. *Letters to Karl and Luise Kautsky from 1896 to 1918*, 1925. Early communist movement.

MANTHEY-ZORN, O. *Germany in Travail*, 1922.

MARTEL, R. *The Eastern Frontiers of Germany*, 1930.

MATTERN, J. *Bavaria and the Reich*, 1923. Legal aspects of federalism.

MAX, PRINCE *The Memoirs of Prince Max of Baden*, 2 v., 1928.

MENDELSSOHN-BARTHOLDY, A. *The War and German Society. The Testament of a Liberal*, 1937.

MICHELS, R. K. *Cartels, Combines, and Trusts in Post-War Germany*, 1928.

MOORE, W. G. *France and Germany*, 1932.

National Industrial Conference Board *Rationalization of German Industry*, 1931.

NORTHROP, M. B. *Control Policies of the Reichsbank, 1924–1933*, 1938.

OLDEN, R. *Stresemann*, 1930.

OPPENHEIMER, H. *The Constitution of the German Republic*, 1923.

OSBORNE, S. *The Upper Silesian Question and Germany's Coal Problem*, 2 ed., 1921.

PRICE, M. P. *Germany in Transition*, 1923. Social and economic changes.

PUCKETT, H. W. *Germany's Women Go Forward*, 1930.

QUIGLEY, H. and CLARK, R. *Republican Germany*, 1928. Good survey.

REICH, N. *Labour Relations in Republican Germany: An Experiment in Industrial Democracy, 1918–1933*, 1938.

REINHOLD, P. P. *The Economic, Financial, and Political State of Germany since the War*, 1928. Lectures.

RHEINBABEN, R. VON *Stresemann, the Man and the Statesman*, 1929.

RÖPKE, W. *German Commercial Policy*, 1934. History of tariff protection.

ROSENBERG, A. *The Birth of the German Republic, 1871–1918*, 1931. Outstanding.

ROSENBERG, A. *History of the German Republic*, 1936.

SCHACHT, H. *The Stabilization of the Mark*, 1927. By one of its stabilizers.

SCHEIDEMANN, P. *The Making of New Germany; The Memoirs of Philipp Scheidemann*, 2 v., 1929. Early years of the republic.

SCHMIDT, C. T. *German Business Cycles, 1924–1933*, 1934.

SCHNEE, H. *German Colonization, Past and Future,* 1926.

SCHULTZE-PFAELZER, G. *Hindenburg; Peace, War, Aftermath,* 1931.

SCHUMAN, F. L. *Germany since 1918,* 1937. Brief.

SERING, M. *Germany under the Dawes Plan,* 1929. Economic effects.

SHUSTER, G. N. *The Germans; An Inquiry and an Estimate,* 1932. Intellectual and moral conditions; by American observer.

STARLING, E. H. *Report on Food Conditions in Germany, with Memoranda on Agricultural Conditions by A. P. McDougall and on Agricultural Statistics by C. W. Guillebaud,* 1919.

STEGEMANN, H. *The Struggle for the Rhine,* 1927.

STERN, B. *Works Council Movement in Germany,* Bulletin of U. S. Bureau of Labor Statistics, Misc. Series, No. 383, 1925.

STOCKDER, A. H. *German Trade Associations: The Coal Kartells,* 1924.

STOLPER, G. *German Economy, 1870–1940,* 1940.

STREET, C. J. C. *Rhineland and Ruhr,* 1923. Anti-French.

STRESEMANN, G. *Essays and Speeches on Various Subjects,* 1930.

STRÖBEL, H. *Socialization in Theory and Practice,* 1922.

STRÖBEL, H. *The German Revolution and After,* 1923. Critical of events.

SUTTON, E., ed. *Gustav Stresemann. His Diaries, Letters, and Papers,* 3 v., 1935–1940.

TOWNSEND, M. *The Rise and Fall of Germany's Colonial Empire, 1884–1918,* 1930.

United States, Department of Commerce *German Dyestuffs Industry,* 1924.

VALLENTIN, A. *Stresemann,* 1931. By a friend.

WARRINER, D. *Combines and Rationalisation in Germany, 1924–1928,* 1931.

WATKINS, F. M. *The Failure of Constitutional Emergency Powers under the German Republic,* 1939.

WELLS, R. H. *German Cities,* 1932.

WELLS, R. H. "The Financial Relations of Church and State in Germany, 1919–1937," in *Political Science Quarterly,* March 1938.

WETERSTETTEN, R. and WATSON, A. *The Biography of President von Hindenburg,* 1930.

WHEELER-BENNETT, J. W. *Wooden Titan, Hindenburg in Twenty Years of German History, 1914–1934,* 1936. Good.

WUNDERLICH, F. *Labor under German Democracy: Arbitration, 1918–1933,* 1940.

YOUNG, G. *The New Germany,* 1920. Postarmistice conditions.

Nazi Germany

ABEL, T. *Why Hitler Came into Power. An Answer Based on the Original Life Stories of Six Hundred of His Followers,* 1938. Interesting.

BANSE, E. *Germany Prepares for War,* new ed., 1941. Military text.

BASCH, A. *The New Economic Warfare,* 1941. Nazi trade tricks.

BAYLES, W. D. *Caesars in Goose Step,* 1940. Sketches of Nazi leaders.

BAYNES, N. H., ed. *The Speeches of Adolf Hitler, April, 1922–August, 1939,* 2 v., 1943.

BENTWICH, N. *The Refugees from Germany: April 1933 to December 1935,* 1936.

BRADY, R. A. *The Spirit and Structure of German Fascism,* 1937.

BULLOCK, A. L. C., ed. *Germany's Colonial Demands,* 1939.

CHILDS, H. L., tr. The *Nazi Primer. Official Handbook for Schooling the Hitler Youth,* 1938. Interesting.

CLARK, R. T. *The Fall of the German Republic: A Political Study,* 1935. Good.

COLE, T. "The Evolution of the German Labor Front," in *Political Science Quarterly,* December 1937.

DODD, W. E., JR. and M., eds. *Ambassador Dodd's Diary, 1933–1938,* 1941.

DUNCAN-JONES, A. S. *The Struggle for Religious Freedom in Germany,* 1938. A chronological description by a British clergyman.

EBENSTEIN, W. *The Nazi State,* 1943. Excellent.

EINZIG, P. *Germany's Default: The Economics of Hitlerism,* 1934. Popular.

EMERSON, H. *International Assistance to Refugees. Report Submitted to the . . . League of Nations,* 1939.

ERMARTH, F. *The New Germany. National Socialist Government in Theory and Practice,* 1936.

FARAGO, L. and GITTLER, L. F., eds. *German Psychological Warfare: Survey and Bibliography,* 1941.

FEDER, G. *Hitler's Official Programme and Its Fundamental Ideas,* 1934. By the author of the Nazis' "25 Points."

FREY, A. *Cross and Swastika,* 1938. On Lutheran struggle.

GEDYE, G. E. R. *Betrayal in Central Europe,* 1939.

"GERMANICUS" *Germany, The Last Four Years,* 1937. Statistical; pessimistic.

GRZESINSKI, A. C. *Inside Germany,* 1939. By a pre-Nazi police official.

GUILLEBAUD, C. W. *The Economic Recovery of Germany, 1933–1938,* 1939.

GUMPERT, M. *Heil Hunger! Health under Hitler,* 1940.

GURIAN, W. *Hitler and the Christians,* 1936.

HARRIS, C. K. S. *Germany's Foreign Indebtedness,* 1935.

HARTSHORNE, E. Y. *German Universities and National Socialism,* 1937.

HAUSER, H. *Battle against Time. A Survey of the Germany of 1939 from the Inside,* 1939.

HEIDEN, K. *A History of National Socialism,* 1934. Valuable.

HEIDEN, K. *Hitler,* 1936. Able.

HEIDEN, K. *The New Inquisition,* 1939. Pogroms of 1938.

HITLER, A. *Mein Kampf,* in two English translations, 1939.

HOLT, J. B. *Under the Swastika,* 1936.

HOOVER, C. B. *Germany Enters the Third Reich,* 1933. Excellent for background.

JANOWSKY, O. I. *People at Bay: The Jewish Problem in East-Central Europe,* 1938.

JANOWSKY, O. I. and FAGEN, M. M. *International Aspects of German Racial Policies,* 1937. Documents.

JOHANNSEN, G. K. and KRAFT, H. H. *Germany's Colonial Problem,* 1937. German case for colonies.

KALIJARVI, T. V. *The Memel Statute,* 1937. Scholarly legal study.

KANDEL, I. L. *The Making of Nazis,* 1935. Education.

KIRKPATRICK, C. *Nazi Germany: Its Women and Family Life,* 1938. Good.

KNELLER, G. F. *The Educational Philosophy of National Socialism,* 1941.

KOLNAI, A. *The War against the West,* 1938. Nazi threat to Christian culture.

KRAUSS, H. *Work Relief in Germany,* 1934.

KUCZYNSKI, J. *The Condition of the Workers in Great Britain, Germany, and the Soviet Union, 1932–1938,* 1939.

LANGSAM, W. C., ed. *Documents and Readings in the History of Europe since 1918,* 1939. Translations of laws and proclamations.

LEISER, C. *Refugee,* 1940.

LEUTKENS, C. "Enrolments at German Universities since 1933," in *Sociological Review,* XXXI, no. 2, 1939.

LEWIS, W. *Hitler,* 1931. Brief.

LICHTENBERGER, H. *The Third Reich. Germany under National Socialism,* 1937.

LOEWENSTEIN, PRINCE H. *The Tragedy of a Nation; Germany 1918–1934,* 1934.

LOWENTHAL, M. *The Jews of Germany,* 1936.

LÜDECKE, K. G. W. *I Knew Hitler,* 1937. By a former friend of Hitler.

MACFARLAND, C. S. *The New Church and the New Germany: A Study of Church and State,* 1934. Dispassionate.

MARX, F. M. *Government in the Third Reich,* 2 ed., 1937.

McGOVERN, W. M. *From Luther to Hitler*, 1941. Doctrines.

MILLER, D. *You Can't Do Business with Hitler*, 1941. Indispensable.

MUHLEN, N. *Schacht: Hitler's Magician. The Life and Loans of Dr. Hjalmar Schacht*, 1939.

NEUBURGER, O., comp. *Official Publications of Present-Day Germany, with an Outline of the Governmental Structure of Germany*, 1942.

NEUMANN, F. L. *Behemoth: The Structure and Practice of National Socialism*, 1942.

NIEMÖLLER, M. *From U-Boat to Pulpit*, 1937. By chief Lutheran opponent of religious coördination.

"NORDICUS" (L. L. SNYDER) *Hitlerism: The Iron Fist in Germany*, 1932.

OLDEN, R. *Hitler*, 1936.

PELCOVITS, N. A. "The Social Honor Courts of Nazi Germany," in *Political Science Quarterly*, September 1938.

POLLOCK, J. K. *The Government of Greater Germany*, 1938.

POLLOCK, J. K. and BOERNER, A. V., JR. *The German Civil Service Act*, 1938.

POLLOCK, J. K. and HENEMAN, H. J., comps. *The Hitler Decrees*, 1934.

POOLE, K. E. *German Financial Policies, 1932–1939*, 1939.

POWER, M. *Religion in the Reich*, 1939. Based on direct observation.

RAUSCHNING, H. *The Revolution of Nihilism. Warning to the West*, 1939. Aims and methods of Nazism by former Nazi leader in Danzig.

RAUSCHNING, H. *The Voice of Destruction*, 1940. Conversations with Hitler.

REED, D. *The Burning of the Reichstag*, 1934. By London *Times* correspondent.

REIMANN, G. *The Vampire Economy: Doing Business under Fascism*, 1939.

ROBERTS, S. H. *The House That Hitler Built*, 1937. Good; Australian view.

ROUSSY DE SALES, R. DE, ed. *My New Order. By Adolf Hitler*, 1941. Speeches.

Royal Institute of International Affairs *Germany's Claim to Colonies*, 2 ed., 1939.

SACHAR, A. L. *Jew in the Contemporary World: Suffrance Is the Badge*, 1939.

SCHUMAN, F. L. *The Nazi Dictatorship; A Study in Social Pathology*, 2 ed., 1936.

SHIRER, W. L. *Berlin Diary. The Journal of a Foreign Correspondent 1934–1941*, 1941. Important.

SHUSTER, G. N. *Strong Man Rules: An Interpretation of Germany Today*, 1934.

SIMPSON, J. H. *The Refugee Problem: Report of a Survey*, 1939. Official.

SNYDER, L. L. *From Bismarck to Hitler; The Background of Modern German Nationalism*, 1935.

STEIN, L. *I Was in Hell with Niemoeller*, 1942.

STEPHENS, D. *The Problem of German Expansion*, 1938. German minorities.

STRASSER, O. *Hitler and I*, 1940. By a former associate.

SWEEZY, M. Y. *The Structure of the Nazi Economy*, 1941.

TAYLOR, K. *Address Unknown*, 1938. Interesting story of Nazi methods.

The German Reich and Americans of German Origin, 1938. Pan-German propaganda in the United States.

THYSSEN, F. *I Paid Hitler*, 1941. By German industrialist.

TOWNSEND, M. E. "The German Colonies and the Third Reich," in *Political Science Quarterly*, June 1938.

TRIVANOVITCH, V. *Economic Development of Germany under National Socialism*, 1937. Objective, but neglects agriculture.

VIERECK, P. *Metapolitics. From the Romantics to Hitler*, 1941.

WALN, N. *Reaching for the Stars*, 1938. Germany through Quaker eyes.

WARBURG, G. *Six Years of Hitler: The Jews under the Nazi Régime*, 1939.

WEINRYB, B. D. *Jewish Emancipation under Attack. Its Legal Recession until the Present War*, 1942.

WHEELER-BENNETT, J. W. and HEALD, S., eds. *Documents on International Affairs 1935*, v. 1, 1936. Devoted chiefly to German foreign relations.

ZIEMER, G. *Education for Death. The Making of the Nazi*, 1941. Reliable.

CHAPTER XVII. TWO HEIRS OF THE HABSBURGS

Austria

ALMOND, N. and LUTZ, R. H., eds. *The Treaty of St. Germain*, 1935. Documents.

BAGGER, E. *Francis Joseph*, 1927. Hungarian estimate.

BALL, M. M. *Post-War German-Austrian Relations. The Anschluss Movement, 1918–1936*, 1937. Excellent.

BASCH, A. and DVOŘÁČEK, J. *Austria and Its Economic Existence*, 1925.

BAUER, O. *The Austrian Revolution*, 1925. By a Social Democrat.

BITTERMAN, M. *Austria and the Customs Union*, 1931. A Czech view.

BULLOCK, M. *Austria, 1918–1938: A Study in Failure*, new ed., 1941.

BURIAN VON RAJECZ, S. *Austria in Dissolution*, 1925. By foreign minister.

DOTTRENS, R. *The New Education in Austria*, 1930.

FRISCHAUER, W. *Twilight in Vienna*, 1938. By pro-Schuschnigg journalist.

FUCHS, M. *Showdown in Vienna: The Death of Austria*, 1939. Good.

GEDYE, G. E. R. *Heirs to the Habsburgs*, 1932. Subjective.

GERMAINS, V. W. *Austria of To-Day, with a Special Chapter on the Austrian Police*, 1932.

GLAISE-HORSTENAU, E. VON *The Collapse of the Austro-Hungarian Empire*, 1930. By director of Austrian War Archives.

GREGORY, J. D. *Dollfuss and His Times*, 1935.

GULICK, C. A. "Vienna Taxes since 1918," in *Pol. Sci. Quart.*, Dec. 1938.

HAMILTON, C. *Modern Austria*, 1935.

HARDY, C. O. and KUCZYNSKI, R. R. *The Housing Program of the City of Vienna*, 1934.

HUDECZEK, K. *The Economic Resources of Austria*, 1922.

JÁSZI, O. *The Dissolution of the Habsburg Monarchy*, 1929. Thoughtful.

JÁSZI, O. "Some Recent Publications Concerning the Dissolution of the Habsburg Monarchy," in *Journal of Modern History*, March 1930.

KLEINWÄCHTER, F. F. G. *Self-Determination for Austria*, 1929.

LAYTON, W. T. and RIST, C. *The Economic Situation of Austria*, 1925.

League of Nations *The Financial Reconstruction of Austria*, 1926.

LENNHOFF, E. *The Last Five Hours of Austria*, 1938. Exciting.

MACARTNEY, C. A. *The Social Revolution in Austria*, 1926. Excellent.

MAHAN, J. A. *Vienna of Yesterday and To-Day*, 1928.

MARGUTTI, A. *The Emperor Francis Joseph and His Times*, 1921. Good for 1910–1917.

MORGAN, O. S., ed. *Agricultural Systems of Middle Europe; A Symposium*, 1933.

NOWAK, K. F. *The Collapse of Central Europe*, 1924. Well written.

PASVOLSKY, L. *Economic Nationalism of the Danubian States*, 1928. Excellent.

POLZER-HODITZ, A. VON *The Emperor Karl*, 1930. Good.

REDLICH, J. *Austrian War Government*, 1929.

REDLICH, J. *Emperor Francis Joseph of Austria*, 1929.

SCHUSCHNIGG, K. *My Austria*, 1938. Tragic story.

SLOSSON, P. W. *The Problem of Austro-German Union*, 1929.

STARHEMBERG, E. R. VON *Between Hitler and Mussolini*, 1942.

STRONG, D. F. *Austria, October 1918–March 1919: Transition from Empire to Republic*, 1939.

TSCHUPPIK, K. *Francis Joseph I; The Downfall of an Empire*, 1930.

WALRÉ DE BORDES, J. VAN *The Austrian Crown; Its Depreciation and Stabilization*, 1924.

WERKMANN VON HOHENSALZBURG, K. *The Tragedy of Charles of Habsburg*, 1924.

Hungary

APPONYI, A. *et al.* *Justice for Hungary,* 1928. Revisionist plea.
ASHMEAD-BARTLETT, E. *The Tragedy of Central Europe,* 1923. Sympathetic.
BAGGER, E. *Eminent Europeans,* 1922. For Károlyi and Horthy.
BANDHOLTZ, H. H. *An Undiplomatic Diary,* 1933. Member of Allied military mission to Hungary, 1919–1920.
BETHLEN, S. *The Treaty of Trianon and European Peace; Four Lectures Delivered in London, November 1933,* 1934.
BUDAY, K. *The International Position of Hungary and the Succession States,* 1931.
BUDAY, L. *Dismembered Hungary,* 1923. Statistics.
CSEKONICS, E. *Hungary New and Old,* 1926. Descriptive.
DEÁK, F. and UJVÁRY, D., eds. *Papers and Documents Relating to the Foreign Relations of Hungary, Volume I: 1919–1920,* 1939.
DONALD, R. *The Tragedy of Trianon,* 1928.
ECKHART, F. *A Short History of the Hungarian People,* 1931. Good.
GLAISE-HORSTENAU, E. VON *The Collapse of the Austro-Hungarian Empire,* 1930.
GOWER, R. *The Hungarian Minorities in the Succession States,* 1937.
GRAHAM, M. W. *New Governments of Central Europe,* 1924.
GRATZ, G., ed. *The Hungarian Economic Year Book,* 1939.
HORVÁTH, J. *Modern Hungary, 1660–1920,* 1922. With useful bibliography.
JÁSZI, O. *Revolution and Counterrevolution in Hungary,* 1924. By a Liberal.
KAAS, A. and LAZAROVICS, F. DE *Bolshevism in Hungary, the Béla Kun Period,* 1931. Documents.
KÁROLYI, M. *Fighting the World; The Struggle for Peace,* 1924.
KOSÁRY, D. G. *A History of Hungary,* 1941. Readable.
League of Nations *The Financial Reconstruction of Hungary,* 1926.
League of Nations *Proceedings of the International Conference on the Repression of Terrorism, November 1–16, 1937,* 1938.
MACARTNEY, C. A. *Hungary,* 1934. Good.
MACARTNEY, C. A. *Hungary and Her Successors: The Treaty of Trianon and Its Consequences,* 1937.
MACARTNEY, M. H. H. *Five Years of European Chaos,* 1923. Chapter on Bolshevism in Hungary.
MATOLOSY, M. and VARGA, S. *National Income of Hungary, 1934–35 to 1936–37,* 1938.
MORGAN, O. S., ed. *Agricultural Systems of Middle Europe; A Symposium,* 1933.
PASVOLSKY, L. *Economic Nationalism of the Danubian States,* 1928. Excellent.
RUBINEK, J. DE, ed. *The Economics of Hungary in Maps,* 4 ed., 1920.
SETON-WATSON, R. W. *Treaty Revision and the Hungarian Frontiers,* 1934.
STREET, C. J. C. *Hungary and Democracy,* 1923. On Magyar "imperialism."
SZÁSZ, Z. DE *The Minorities in Roumanian Transylvania,* 1927.
TELEKI, P. *The Evolution of Hungary,* 1923. Moderate tone; good maps.
TISSEYRE, C. *An Error in Diplomacy; Dismembered Hungary,* 1924.
TORMAY, C. *An Outlaw's Diary,* 2 v., 1923. Hungary in 1918–1919.

CHAPTER XVIII. TWO SLAVIC REPUBLICS

Czechoslovakia

BAERLEIN, H. *The March of the Seventy Thousand,* 1926. Czech legions in Siberia.
BAERLEIN, H. *In Czechoslovakia's Hinterland,* 1938.
BAGGER, E. *Eminent Europeans,* 1922. For Masaryk and Beneš.
BENEŠ, E. *My War Memoirs,* 1928.
BLOSS, E. *Labor Legislation in Czechoslovakia,* 1938. Scholarly.

BOROVIČKA, J. *Ten Years of Czechoslovak Politics*, 1929. Brief, useful.

BOYCE, G. C. and DAWSON, W. H. *The University of Prague: Modern Problems of the German University in Czechoslovakia*, 1937.

BROŽ, A. *The Rise of the Czechoslovak Republic*, 1919.

CAPEK, K., ed. *President Masaryk Tells His Story*, 1935.

CAPEK, K. et al. *At the Cross Roads of Europe. A Historical Outline of the Democratic Idea in Czechoslovakia*, 1938.

CAPEK, T. *Bohemian (Čech) Bibliography; A Finding List of Writings in English Relating to Bohemia and the Čechs*, 1918.

CAPEK, T. *Origins of the Czechoslovak State*, 1926.

CHMELAŘ, J. *Political Parties in Czechoslovakia*, 1926.

CHMELAŘ, J. *The German Problem in Czechoslovakia*, 1936. Moderate.

CHMELAŘ, J. *National Minorities in Central Europe*, 1937.

CÍSAŘ, J. and POKORNÝ, F., comps. *The Czechoslovak Republic*, 1922. Handbook.

Germany and Czechoslovakia, 2 v., Prague, 1937. Able Czech view.

GRAHAM, M. W. *New Governments of Central Europe*, 1924.

GRUBER, J., ed. *Czechoslovakia; A Survey of Economic and Social Conditions*, 1924.

HINDUS, M. G. *We Shall Live Again*, 1939. Fall of Czechoslovakia.

HITCHCOCK, E. B. *"I Built a Temple for Peace." The Life of Eduard Beneš*, 1940.

HOCH, C. *The Political Parties in Czechoslovakia*, 2 ed., 1936. Brief.

HOETZL, J. and JOACHIM, V., eds. *The Constitution of the Czechoslovak Republic*, 1920.

HOLLAND, C. *Czechoslovakia; The Land and Its People*, 1931.

KROFTA, K. *A Short History of Czechoslovakia*, 1934.

LOWRIE, D. A. *Masaryk: Nation Builder*, 1930. Eulogy.

LOWRIE, D. A. *Masaryk of Czechoslovakia*, 1938. Eulogy.

LÜTZOW, F. VON *Bohemia: An Historical Sketch*, 1939.

MACHRAY, R. *The Little Entente*, 1929.

MASARYK, T. G. *The Making of a State*, 1927. Especially for 1914–1918.

MORGAN, O. S., ed. *Agricultural Systems of Middle Europe; A Symposium*, 1933.

NOSEK, V. *Independent Bohemia; An Account of the Czecho-Slovak Struggle for Liberty*, 1918.

OPOČENSKÝ, J. *The Collapse of the Austro-Hungarian Monarchy and the Rise of the Czechoslovak State*, 1928.

PAPOUŠEK, J. *The Czechoslovak Nation's Struggle for Independence*, 1928.

PASVOLSKY, L. *Economic Nationalism of the Danubian States*, 1928. Excellent.

PERGLER, C. *America in the Struggle for Czechoslovak Independence*, 1926.

RAŠÍN, A. *Financial Policy of Czechoslovakia*, 1923. Reaches end of 1921.

SCHACHER, G. *Central Europe and the Western World*, 1936.

SETON-WATSON, R. W. *The New Slovakia*, 1924. Competent.

SETON-WATSON, R. W., ed. *Slovakia, Then and Now; A Political Survey*, 1931.

STREET, C. J. C. *President Masaryk*, 1930. Sympathetic.

TEXTOR, L. E. *Land Reform in Czechoslovakia*, 1923.

VONDRACEK, F. J. *The Foreign Policy of Czechoslovakia, 1918–1935*, 1937.

WELLEK, R. "Twenty Years of Czech Literature," in *The Slavonic Review*, Spring 1939.

WISKEMANN, E. *Czechs and Germans: A Study of the Struggle in the Historic Provinces of Bohemia and Moravia*, 1938. Excellent.

YOUNG, E. P. *Czechoslovakia: Keystone of Peace and Democracy*, 1938. Factual.

Poland

ASKENAZY, S. *Dantzig and Poland*, 1921. Polish case for union.

BONCZA, ST. J. *Joseph Pilsudski, Founder of Polish National Independence*, 1921.

BOYDEN, W. C. *My Impressions of New Poland*, 1920.

BUELL, R. L. *Poland: Key to Europe*, 1939. Excellent.

BUJAK, F. *The Jewish Question in Poland,* 1919.
BUJAK, F. *Poland's Economic Development,* 1926. Reliable.
DEVEREAUX, R. *Poland Reborn,* 1922. Survey of new problems.
DEWEY, C. S. *Combined Report of the Quarterly Reports of the Financial Adviser to the Polish Government,* 1930.
DONALD, R. *The Polish Corridor and the Consequences,* 1929. Hostile.
DOUGLASS, P. F. *The Economic Independence of Poland; A Study in Trade Adjustments to Political Objectives,* 1934.
DULLES, J. F., comp. *Poland, Plan of Financial Stabilization, 1927,* 1928.
DURAND, E. D. *Public Finance of Poland,* 1922.
DYBOSKI, R. *Poland,* 1933.
FELINSKI, M. *The Ukrainians in Poland,* 1931. Polish view.
FIRICH, C. T. *Polish Character of Upper Silesia According to Official Prussian Sources and the Results of the Plebiscite,* 1921.
FISHER, H. H. and BROOKS, S. *America and the New Poland,* 1928.
GOODHART, A. L. *Poland and the Minority Races,* 1920. Observer's diary.
GÓRECKI, R. *Poland and Her Economic Development,* 1935. Brief, optimistic.
GRAHAM, M. W. *New Governments of Eastern Europe,* 1927.
GROVE, W. R. *War's Aftermath,* 1940. Polish relief in 1919.
HUTCHISON, G. S. *Silesia Revisited, 1929; An Examination of the Problems Arising from the Plebiscite and the Partition, and the Relation between the British Coal Problem and Silesia,* 1929.
JANOWSKY, O. I. *The Jews and Minority Rights, 1898–1919,* 1933. Scholarly.
JANOWSKY, O. I. *People at Bay: The Jewish Problem in East-Central Europe,* 1938.
KALTENBACH, F. W. *Self-Determination, 1919: A Study in Frontier Making between Germany and Poland,* 1938.
KARSKI, S. *Poland, Past and Present,* new ed., 1933.
KEMMERER, E. W. *Reports Submitted by the Commission of the American Financial Experts to the Republic of Poland,* 1926.
KOROSTOWETZ, W. K. *The Re-Birth of Poland,* 1928. Unsympathetic.
LANDAU, R. *Pilsudski and Poland,* 1929. Journalistic.
LANDAU, R. *Ignace Paderewski, Musician and Statesman,* 1934.
LEONHARDT, H. L. *The Nazi Conquest of Danzig,* 1942. Covers 1928–1938.
Lithuanian Information Bureau *The Lithuanian-Polish Dispute,* 3 v., 1921–1923.
Lithuanian Information Bureau *The Vilna Problem,* 1922.
MACHRAY, R. *The Poland of Pilsudski, 1914–1936,* 1937. Sympathetic.
MARTEL, R. *The Eastern Frontiers of Germany,* 1930.
MORGAN, O. S., ed. *Agricultural Systems of Middle Europe; A Symposium,* 1933.
MORROW, I. F. D. *The Peace Settlement in the German-Polish Borderlands. A Study of Conditions Today in the Pre-War Prussian Provinces of East and West Prussia,* 1936. Objective, complete, documented.
MURRAY, K. M. *Wings over Poland,* 1932. The fight against the Bolsheviks.
OSBORNE, S., ed. *The Problem of Upper Silesia,* 1921.
PHILLIPS, C. *The New Poland,* 1923.
PHILLIPS, C. *Paderewski; The Story of a Modern Immortal,* 1933.
PILSUDSKI, J. *The Memories of a Polish Revolutionary and Soldier,* 1931.
REDDAWAY, W. F. *Marshal Pilsudski,* 1939. Good.
ROMER, E. *Economical Conditions of Upper Silesia and the Policy of the German State,* 1921.
ROSE, W. J. *The Drama of Upper Silesia,* 1937. Factual.
ROSE, W. J. "The Poles of Germany," in *The Slavonic Review,* July 1936.
SEGAL, S. *The New Poland and the Jews,* 1938. Post-war Poland generally.
SIMON, G. *Labour Legislation in the Polish Republic,* 1921.
SKRZYNSKI, A. *Poland and Peace,* 1923. By an ex-premier.
SLAWSKI, S. *Poland's Access to the Sea, and the Claims of East Prussia,* 1925.

SLOCOMBE, G. *History of Poland,* 1940.
SMOGORZEWSKI, C. *Poland, Germany and the Corridor,* 1930. Defends Poland.
The Cambridge History of Poland. From August II to Pilsudski (1697–1935), 1941.
WELLISZ, L. *Foreign Capital in Poland,* 1938.
WILDER, J. A. "The Danzig Problem from Within," in *Slavonic and East European Review,* January 1937.
WINTER, N. O. *The New Poland,* 1923. Popular.

CHAPTER XIX. THE SOVIET UNION

Biographies

ALEXANDER, GRAND DUKE *Once a Grand Duke,* 1932.
ALEXANDRA, EMPRESS CONSORT *Letters of the Tsaritsa to the Tsar, 1914–1916,* 1923.
BOTKIN, G. *The Real Romanovs, as Revealed by the Late Czar's Physician and His Son,* 1931.
BRYANT, L. *Mirrors of Moscow,* 1923. Sketches of leaders.
COATES, W. P. and Z. K. *Maxim Litvinov,* 1937.
EASTMAN, M. *Since Lenin Died,* 1925. Trotsky against Stalin.
FÜLÖP-MILLER, R. *Rasputin; The Holy Devil,* 1928.
GILLIARD, P. *Thirteen Years at the Russian Court,* 1921. By French tutor.
GRAHAM, S. *Stalin; An Impartial Study of the Life and Work of Joseph Stalin,* 1931.
HANBURY-WILLIAMS, J. *The Emperor Nicholas II as I knew Him,* 1922. Useful for 1914–1917, by chief of British military mission.
HUTCHINSON, L., ed. *Hidden Springs of the Russian Revolution; Personal Memoirs of Katerina Breshkovskaia,* 1931. Memoirs of a prominent woman leader.
KRUPSKAYA, N. K. *Memories of Lenin,* 1930. By his widow.
LENIN, V. (N.) *Collected Works of V. I. Lenin,* 1927–.
LEVINE, I. D. *The Man Lenin,* 1924. Good.
LEVINE, I. D. *Stalin,* 1931.
LYONS, E. *Stalin: Czar of All the Russias,* 1940.
MARCU, V. *Lenin,* 1928. Philosophical.
MARIE, GRAND DUCHESS *Education of a Princess,* 1931.
MIRSKY, D. S. *Lenin,* 1931.
NICHOLAS II *The Letters of the Tsar to the Tsaritsa, 1914–1917,* 1929.
PARES, B. *My Russian Memoirs,* 1931. Interesting on personalities.
RAPPOPORT, A. *Pioneers of the Russian Revolution,* 1918. Brief sketches.
RASPUTIN, MARIA *My Father,* 1934.
RODZIANKO, M. V. *The Reign of Rasputin: An Empire's Collapse,* 1927. By president of last Duma.
SOUVARINE, B. *Stalin: A Critical Survey of Bolshevism,* 1939. Thorough.
TCHERNAVIN, T. *Escape from the Soviets,* 1934. A thrilling account.
TCHERNAVIN, V. *I Speak for the Silent, Prisoners of the Soviets,* 1935.
TOBENKIN, E. *Stalin's Ladder; War and Peace in the Soviet Union,* 1933.
TROTSKY, L. *Lenin,* 1925. Chiefly on 1900–1903 and 1917–1918.
TROTSKY, L. *My Life,* 1930.
VARNECK, E. and FISHER, H. H., eds. *The Testimony of Kolchak and Other Siberian Materials,* 1935. Documents, 1918–1920.
VEALE, F. *The Man from the Volga; A Life of Lenin,* 1932. Personal.
VERNADSKY, G. V. *Lenin, Red Dictator,* 1931. Good though unsympathetic.
WERNER, R. M., ed. *Stalin's Kampf: Joseph Stalin's Credo Written by Himself,* 1940.
WHITE, W. C. *These Russians,* 1931. Popular sketches.
WILLIAMS, A. R. *Lenin; The Man and His Work,* 1919.
WILTON, R. *The Last Days of the Romanovs from 15th March, 1917,* 1920.

48   BIBLIOGRAPHY

WRANGEL, P. N.   *The Memoirs of General Wrangel, the Last Commander-in-Chief of the Russian National Army*, 1930.
YOUSOUPOFF, F. F.   *Rasputin*, 1927.   By one of his enemies.

Domestic Affairs

AGABEKOV, G.   *OGPU, the Russian Secret Terror*, 1931.   By an OGPU agent.
ALBERTSON, R.   *Fighting without a War*, 1920.   Allied intervention.
ALLEN, W. E. D.   *The Ukraine: A History*, 1941.
ARNOLD, A. Z.   *Banks, Credit, and Money in Soviet Russia*, 1937.   Reliable.
ASTROV, W., SLEPKOV, A., and THOMAS, J., eds.   *An Illustrated History of the Russian Revolution*, 2 v., 1928–1929.
ATHOLL, K.   *The Conscription of a People*, 1931.   Forced labor.
AVALISHVILI, Z.   *The Independence of Georgia in International Politics, 1918–1921*, 1940.
BADAYEV, A.   *The Bolsheviks in the Tsarist Duma*, 1932.
BASILY, N. DE   *Russia under Soviet Rule: Twenty Years of Bolshevik Experiment*, 1940.   By liberal ex-tsarist official.
BATSELL, W. R.   *Soviet Rule in Russia*, 1929.   Theory and practice of government.
BEST, H.   *The Soviet Experiment*, 1941.   By a sociologist.
BEAUCHAMP, J.   *Agriculture in Soviet Russia*, 1931.   Information on state farms.
BLANC, E. T.   *The Coöperative Movement in Russia*, 1924.   Thorough.
BORDERS, K.   *Village Life under the Soviets*, 1927.
BRAILSFORD, H. N.   *How the Soviets Work*, 1927.   Popular.
BRUNOVSKY, V. K.   *The Methods of the OGPU*, 1931.   By a victim.
BRUTSKUS, B.   *Economic Planning in the Soviet Union*, 1935.
BUKHARIN, N. and PREOBRAZHENSKY, E.   *The ABC of Communism. A Popular Explanation of the Program of the Communist Party of Russia*, 1922.
BUMGARDNER, E.   *Undaunted Exiles*, 1925.   Refugees in Constantinople.
BUNYAN, J. and FISHER, H., eds.   *The Bolshevik Revolution, 1917–1918*, 1934.   Documents.
BURRELL, G. A.   *An American Engineer Looks at Russia*, 1932.
BURY, H.   *Russia from Within*, 1927.   Religious aspects.
CEDERHOLM, B.   *In the Clutches of the Tcheka*, 1929.   By a victim.
CHAMBERLIN, W. H.   *The Soviet Planned Economic Order*, 1931.
CHAMBERLIN, W. H.   *Soviet Russia*, rev. ed., 1931.   Favorable.
CHAMBERLIN, W. H.   *Russia's Iron Age*, 1934.   Sequel to above, less favorable.
CHAMBERLIN, W. H.   *The Russian Revolution 1917–1921*, 2 v., 1935.   Excellent.
CHAMBERLIN, W. H.   *Collectivism; A False Utopia*, 1937.
CHASE, S., DUNN, R., and TUGWELL, R. G., eds.   *Soviet Russia in the Second Decade; A Joint Survey by the Technical Staff of the First American Trade Union Delegation*, 1928.
CLARK, C.   *A Critique of Russian Statistics*, 1939.
COATES, W. P. and Z. K.   *The Second Five-Year Plan*, 1934.
COLLARD, D.   *Soviet Justice and the Trial of Radek and Others*, 1937.
CONOLLY, V.   *Soviet Tempo*, 1937.   Amusing.
Communist Central Academy   *20 Years of Soviet Power*, 1937.   Useful.
COOKE, R. J.   *Religion in Russia under the Soviets*, 1924.   By an American bishop.
CURTISS, J. S.   *Church and State in Russia. The Last Years of the Empire, 1900–1917*, 1940.
DAVIS, J., ed.   *The New Russia between the First and Second Five-Year Plans*, 1933.   Articles by visitors.
DENIKIN, A.   *The Russian Turmoil*, 1922.   By a "White" leader.
DENIKIN, A.   *The White Army*, 1930.
DILLON, E. J.   *Russia Today and Yesterday*, 1929.   Cultural changes.

DOBB, M. H. and STEVENS, H. C. *Russian Economic Development since the Revolution*, 2 ed., 1929.

DOROSHENKO, D. *History of the Ukraine*, 1939.

DUNN, R. W. *Soviet Trade Unions*, 1928. Good.

DURANTY, W. *Duranty Reports Russia*, 1934. By able American correspondent.

ECKARDT, H. VON *Russia*, 1932. Well illustrated.

EMHARDT, W. C. *Religion in Soviet Russia*, 1929. By an Episcopal clergyman.

FARBMAN, M. S. *Bolshevism in Retreat*, 1923. Lenin and the NEP.

FARBMAN, M. S. *After Lenin; The New Phase in Russia*, 1924.

FARBMAN, M. S. *Piatiletka: Russia's Five-Year Plan*, 1931.

FEDOTOV, G. P. *The Russian Church since the Revolution*, 1928. Brief.

FEILER, A. *The Experiment of Bolshevism*, 1930. Discerning critique.

FIELD, A. W. *Protection of Women and Children in Soviet Russia*, 1932.

FISCHER, L. *Machines and Men in Russia*, 1932. With fine photographs.

FISHER, H. H. *The Famine in Soviet Russia, 1919–1923*, 1927. American relief.

FLORINSKY, M. T. *The End of the Russian Empire*, 1931.

FLORINSKY, M. T. *Toward an Understanding of the U.S.S.R.*, 1939.

FOSTER, W. Z. *Russian Workers and Workshops in 1926*, 1926.

FREEMAN, J. *The Soviet Worker*, 1932.

FREEMAN, J., KUNITZ, J., and LOZOWICK, L. *Voices of October; Art and Literature in Soviet Russia*, 1930.

FÜLÖP-MILLER, R. *The Mind and Face of Bolshevism; An Examination of Cultural Life in Soviet Russia*, 1927.

GIDE, A. *Return from the U.S.S.R.*, 1937. Disillusioned French leftist view.

GOLDER, F. A., ed. *Documents of Russian History, 1914–1917*, 1927.

GOLDER, F. A. and HUTCHINSON, L. *On the Trail of the Russian Famine*, 1927.

GORDON, M. *Workers before and after Lenin*, 1941. Thorough.

GOURKO, B. *War and Revolution in Russia, 1914–1917*, 1919.

GRINKO, G. F. *The Five Year Plan of the Soviet Union; A Political Interpretation by G. F. Grinko, Vice-Chairman, State Planning Commission of the U.S.S.R.*, 1930.

GRONSKY, P. P. and ASTROV, N. J. *The War and the Russian Government*, 1929.

GUBKIN, I. M. *The Natural Wealth of the Soviet Union and Its Exploitation*, 1932.

GURIAN, W. *Bolshevism: Theory and Practice*, 1932. Good.

GURKO, V. I. *Features and Figures of the Past. Government and Opinion in the Reign of Nicholas II*, 1938.

HAENSEL, P. *The Economic Policy of Soviet Russia*, 1930.

HALLE, F. W. *Woman in Soviet Russia*, 1933. Also situation before 1917.

HALLE, F. W. *Women in the Soviet East*, 1938. Soviet Asia.

HANS, N. and HESSEN, S. *Educational Policy in Soviet Russia*, 1930.

HARPER, S. N. *Civic Training in Soviet Russia*, 1929.

HARPER, S. N. *Making Bolsheviks*, 1931.

HARPER, S. N. *The Government of the Soviet Union*, 1938. Best brief survey.

HAZARD, J. N. *Soviet Housing Law*, 1939.

HECKER, J. F. *Religion under the Soviets*, 1927. Defense of Soviet policy.

HECKER, J. F. *Moscow Dialogues: Discussions on Red Philosophy*, 1933.

HECKER, J. F. *Religion and Communism*, 1935.

HEIFETZ, E. *The Slaughter of the Jews in the Ukraine in 1919*, 1921.

HINDUS, M. G. *The Russian Peasant and the Revolution*, 1920.

HINDUS, M. G. *Humanity Uprooted*, rev. ed., 1930. Interesting.

HINDUS, M. G. *Broken Earth*, 1931. Village life.

HINDUS, M. G. *Red Bread*, 1931.

HINDUS, M. G. *The Great Offensive*, 1933. The First Five-Year Plan.

HIRSCH, A. *Industrialized Russia*, 1934. By an American engineer.

History of the Communist Party of the Soviet Union (Bolsheviks), 1939. Edited by a commission of the central committee of the party.

HOOVER, C. B. *The Economic Life of Soviet Russia*, 1931. Objective.

HRUSHEVSKY, M. *A History of Ukraine*, 1941.

HUBBARD, L. E. *Soviet Money and Finance*, 1936.

HUBBARD, L. E. *The Economics of Soviet Agriculture*, 1939.

HUBBARD, L. E. *Soviet Labor and Industry*, 1943.

HUXLEY, J. *A Scientist among the Soviets*, 1932.

IAKOVLEV, I. A. *Red Villages*; *The Five-Year Plan in Soviet Agriculture*, 1931.

ILIN, M. *New Russia's Primer*, 1930. Translation of an elementary text.

International Labour Office *Industrial Life in Soviet Russia, 1917–1923*, 1924.

JUST, A. W. *The Red Army*, 1936.

KARLGREN, A. *Bolshevist Russia*, 1927. Valuable survey.

KATZENELLENBAUM, S. S. *Russian Currency and Banking, 1914–1924*, 1925.

KAYDEN, E. and ANTSIFEROV, A. *The Cooperative Movement in Russia during the War*, 1929.

KERENSKY, A. F. *The Prelude to Bolshevism; The Kornilov Rising*, 1919.

KERENSKY, A. F. *The Catastrophe*, 1927.

KERENSKY, A. F. *The Crucifixion of Liberty*, 1934.

KING, B. *Changing Man: The Soviet Education System of the U. S. S. R.*, 1937.

KIRBY, L. P. *The Russian Revolution*, 1940.

KOHN, H. *Nationalism in the Soviet Union*, 1933.

KOHN, S. and MEYENDORFF, A. F. *The Cost of the War to Russia. The Vital Statistics of European Russia during the World War, 1914–1917*, 1932.

KORFF, S. A. *Autocracy and Revolution in Russia*, 1923.

KORNILOV, A. *Modern Russian History*, 1924. Background of the revolutions.

KUCZYNSKI, J. *The Condition of the Workers in Great Britain, Germany, and the Soviet Union, 1932–1938*, 1939.

LANGSAM, W. C. "Trotsky versus Stalin," in *Events*, March 1937.

LAWTON, L. *The Russian Revolution, 1917–1926*, 1927.

LAWTON, L. *An Economic History of Soviet Russia*, 2 v., 1932. Good.

LENIN, N. *The Soviets at Work*, 5 ed., 1919.

LENIN, N. *The Revolution of 1917: From the March Revolution to the July Days*, 2 v., 1929. Volume 20 of *Collected Works*.

LENIN, N. *Toward the Seizure of Power. The Revolution of 1917: From the July Days to the October Revolution*, 2 v., 1933. Volume 21 of *Collected Works*.

LENIN, N. *et al.* *The New Policies of Soviet Russia*, 1922.

LEVIN, A. *The Second Duma. A Study of the Social-Democratic Party and the Russian Constitutional Experiment*, 1940.

LOBANOV-ROSTOVSKY, A. *Russia and Asia*, 1933.

LYONS, E. *Assignment in Utopia*, 1937. By disillusioned correspondent.

MAKEEV, N. and O'HARA, V. *Russia*, 1925. Difficult but valuable.

MALEVSKY-MALEVITCH, P., ed. *Russia-U.S.S.R., a Complete Handbook*, 1933.

MALEVSKY-MALEVITCH, P., ed. *The Soviet Union Today*, 1936. Statistics.

MARGOLIN, A. *The Jews of Eastern Europe*, 1926. Before and after 1917.

MARYE, G. T. *Nearing the End in Imperial Russia*, 1929. By American Ambassador to Russia, 1914–1916.

MASLOV, S. *Russia after Four Years of Revolution*, 1923.

MAVOR, J. *An Economic History of Russia*, 2 v., 2 ed., 1925.

MAVOR, J. *The Russian Revolution*, 1928. Excellent.

MAXWELL, B. W. *The Soviet State; A Study of Bolshevik Rule*, 1934.

MEHNERT, K. *Youth in Soviet Russia*, 1933.

MELGUNOV, S. *The Red Terror in Russia*, 1925. Documented.

MEYENDORFF, A. F. *The Background of the Russian Revolution*, 1929. By a vice-president of the Duma.

MICHELSON, A. *et al.* *Russian Public Finance during the War*, 1928.

MIKHAYLOV, N. *Soviet Geography: The New Industrial and Economic Distributions of the U.S.S.R.*, 1935.

MILIUKOV, P.   *Outlines of Russian Culture,* 3 pts., 1942.

MIRSKY, D. S.   *Russia, a Social History,* 1931.

MOLOTOV, V. M.   *The Communist Party of the Soviet Union,* 1929.

MOLOTOV, V. M.   *The Success of the Five-Year Plan,* 1931.

MONKHOUSE, A.   *Moscow, 1911–1933,* 1934.   By a British engineer.

NEWSHOLME, A. and KINGSBURY, J. A.   *Red Medicine: Socialized Health in Soviet Russia,* 1933.   Favorable.

OWEN, L. A.   *The Russian Peasant Movement, 1906–1917,* 1937.

PARES, B.   *A History of Russia,* rev. ed., 1928.

PARES, B.   *The Fall of the Russian Monarchy,* 1939.   Interesting.

PASVOLSKY, L.   *The Economics of Communism, with Special Reference to Russia's Experiment,* 1921.

PAVLOVSKY, G.   *Agricultural Russia on the Eve of the Revolution,* 1930.

PINKEVICH, A. P.   *The New Education in the Soviet Republic,* 1929.

POPOV, G. K.   *The Tcheka: The Red Inquisition,* 1925.

POPOV, N.   *Outline History of the Communist Party of the Soviet Union,* 2 v., 1934.

POSTGATE, R. W.   *The Bolshevik Theory,* 1920.   Competent.

PRICE, G. M.   *Labor Protection in Soviet Russia,* 1928.

PRITT, D. N.   *At the Moscow Trial,* 1937.   Brief, fair.

PROKOPOVICH, S.   *The Economic Condition of Soviet Russia,* 1924.   On NEP.

ROBERTS, C. E. B.   *In Denikin's Russia,* 1921.   The Caucasus in 1919–1920.

ROBINSON, G. T.   *Rural Russia under the Old Régime,* 1932.   Excellent.

ROSENBERG, A.   *A History of Bolshevism, from Marx to the First Five Years' Plan,* 1934.   Not confined to Russia.

ROSS, E. A.   *The Russian Bolshevik Revolution,* 1921.   By American sociologist.

ROSS, E. A.   *The Russian Soviet Republic,* 1923.

ROTHSTEIN, A., ed.   *The Soviet Constitution,* 1923.

RUKEYSER, W. A.   *Working for the Soviets; An American Engineer in Russia,* 1932.

SAROLEA, C.   *Impressions of Soviet Russia,* 2 ed., 1924.   Education and culture.

SCHEFFER, P.   *Seven Years in Soviet Russia,* 1931.   Penetrating observations.

SCOTT, J.   *Behind the Urals: An American Worker in Russia's City of Steel,* 1942.   Magnitogorsk.

SEIBERT, T.   *Red Russia,* 1932.   A severe indictment.

SEREBRENNIKOV, G. N.   *The Position of Women in the U.S.S.R.,* 1936.

SERGE, V.   *Russia Twenty Years After,* 1937.   Anti-Stalinist.

SHUMEYKO, S.   *Ukrainian Movement,* 1939.

SISSON, E.   *One Hundred Red Days, 25 November 1917–4 March 1918. A Personal Chronicle of the Bolshevik Revolution,* 1931.   By President Wilson's special representative in Russia.

SMITH, J.   *Woman in Soviet Russia,* 1928.   Sympathetic.

SMOLKA, H. P.   *40,000 against the Arctic: Russia's Polar Empire,* 1937.

SOKOLNIKOV, G. Y. et al.   *Soviet Policy in Public Finance, 1917–1928,* 1931.

SPARGO, J.   *The Psychology of Bolshevism,* 1919.

SPINKA, M.   *The Church and the Russian Revolution,* 1927.   From 1905.

STALIN, J.   *Leninism,* 2 v., 1933.   Pronouncements of Stalin.

STALIN, J.   *The October Revolution,* 1934.   Articles and speeches.

STALIN, J.   *Marxism and the National and Colonial Questions,* 1936.   Speeches.

STALIN, J. et al.   *From the First to the Second Five-Year Plan,* 1934.   Symposium.

STEWART, G.   *The White Armies of Russia; A Chronicle of Counter-Revolution and Allied Intervention,* 1933.   Objective.

STRONG, A. L.   *The Soviets Conquer Wheat,* 1931.   Pro-Bolshevik.

STRONG, A. L.   *The New Soviet Constitution: A Study in Socialist Democracy,* 1937.

The Soviet Union Looks Ahead, 2 ed., 1930.   Translation of First Five-Year Plan.

TIMBRES, H. and K.   *We Didn't Ask Utopia, A Quaker Family in Soviet Russia,* 1939.   Interesting.

TIMOSHENKO, V. P.   *Agricultural Russia and the Wheat Problem,* 1932.

TROTSKY, L.   *From October to Brest-Litovsk*, 1919.

TROTSKY, L.   *The Defense of Terrorism*, 1920.

TROTSKY, L.   *The Lessons of October, 1917*, 1925.

TROTSKY, L.   *The Real Situation in Russia*, 1928.   Opposed to Stalin.

TROTSKY, L.   *The History of the Russian Revolution*, 3 v., 1932.

TROTSKY, L.   *The Revolution Betrayed*, 1937.   Attack on Stalin.

U.S.S.R. People's Commissariat of Justice   *Anti-Soviet Centre Trial, Verbatim Report*, 1937.

U.S.S.R. State Planning Commission   *The Second Five-Year Plan*, 1937.

VERNADSKY, G.   *A History of Russia*, rev. ed., 1933.   Good, by an émigré.

VERNADSKY, G.   *The Russian Revolution, 1917–1931*, 1932.   Brief.

VULLIAMY, C. E., ed.   *The Red Archives; Russian State Papers and Other Documents Relating to the Years 1915–1918*, 1929.

WALSH, E. A.   *The Fall of the Russian Empire; The Story of the Last Romanovs and the Coming of the Bolsheviki*, 1928.   By American priest.

WEBB, S. and B.   *Soviet Communism: A New Civilization?*, 2 v., 1936.   Sympathetic.

WHITE, D. F.   *Survival through War and Revolution in Russia*, 1939.   Well told.

WICKSTEED, A.   *My Russian Neighbors*, 1934.   By a teacher in Moscow.

WILLIAMS, A. R.   *Through the Russian Revolution*, 1921.   Sympathetic.

WILLIAMS, A. R.   *The Russian Land*, 1927.   Pictures of village life.

WILLIAMS, A. R.   *The Soviets*, 1937.   Handbook of facts.

WOLLENBERG, E.   *The Red Army*, 1938.   Authoritative.

WOODY, T.   *New Minds: New Men?*, 1932.   Excellent on educational system.

YARMOLINSKY, A.   *The Jews and Other Minor Nationalities under the Soviets*, 1928.

ZAGORSKY, S. O.   *State Control of Industry in Russia during the War*, 1928.

ZIMAND, S. D.   *State Capitalism in Russia*, 1926.   Brief.

Foreign Relations

American Foundation, Committee on Russian-American Relations   *The United States and the Soviet Union*, 1933.

ARNOT, R. P.   *Soviet Russia and Her Neighbors*, 1927.   Brief, good.

BENN, E.   *About Russia*, 1930.   Baltic states and Russia.

BESEDOVSKY, G.   *Revelations of a Soviet Diplomat*, 1931.   Informative.

BORKENAU, F.   *The Communist International*, 1938.   Published in U. S. as *World Communism*.

BRON, S.   *Soviet Economic Development and American Business*, 1930.

BUCHANAN, G.   *My Mission to Russia*, 2 v., 1923.   By British Ambassador in 1917.

CLARK, C. U.   *Bessarabia; Russia and Roumania on the Black Sea*, 1927.

COATES, C. H.   *The Red Theology in the Far East*, 1927.   Propaganda in China.

COATES, W. P.   *Armed Intervention in Russia, 1918–1922*, 1935.

CONOLLY, V.   *Soviet Economic Policy in the East; Turkey, Persia, Afghanistan, Mongolia and Tana Tuva, Sin Kiang*, 1933.   Well documented.

CONOLLY, V.   *Soviet Trade from the Pacific to the Levant; With an Economic Study of the Soviet Far Eastern Region*, 1935.   Excellent.

CUDAHY, J.   *Archangel; The American War with Russia*, 1924.

CUMMING, C. K. and PETTIT, W. W., eds.   *Russian-American Relations, March, 1917–March, 1920*, 1920.

DAVIS, K. W.   *The Soviets at Geneva; The U.S.S.R. at the League of Nations, 1919–1933*, 1934.

DENNIS, A. L. P.   *The Foreign Policies of Soviet Russia*, 1924.   Thorough.

FISCHER, L.   *The Soviets in World Affairs*, 2 v., 1930.   Based on Soviet sources.

FLORINSKY, M. T.   *World Revolution and the U.S.S.R.*, 1933.   Excellent.

GANKIN, O. H. and FISHER, H. H., eds.   *The Bolsheviks and the World War. The Origin of the Third International*, 1940.

GRAVES, W. S.   *America's Siberian Adventure, 1918–1920*, 1931.

HARPER, S. N., ed. *The Soviet Union and World Problems,* 1935.
HOPPER, B. *Pan-Sovietism,* 1931.
HUBBARD, L. E. *Soviet Trade and Distribution,* 1938.
HUNTINGTON, W. C. *The Homesick Million, Russia-out-of-Russia,* 1933. Émigrés.
LASERSON, M. M., comp. *The Development of Soviet Foreign Policy in Europe, 1917–1942. A Selection of Documents,* 1943.
MAYNARD, C. *The Murmansk Venture,* 1928. By British commander.
NORTON, H. K. *The Far Eastern Republic of Siberia,* 1923. Journalistic.
PASVOLSKY, L. *Russia in the Far East,* 1922.
STRAKHOVSKY, L. I. *The Origins of American Intervention in North Russia, 1918,* 1937. Excellent.
TARACOUZIO, T. A. *Soviet Union and International Law,* 1935.
TARACOUZIO, T. A. *Soviets in the Arctic: An Historical, Economic, and Political Study of the Soviet Advance into the Arctic,* 1938.
TARACOUZIO, T. A. *War and Peace in Soviet Diplomacy,* 1940.
The Soviet Union and Peace; The Most Important of the Documents Issued by the Government of the U.S.S.R. Concerning Peace and Disarmament from 1917 to 1929, 1929.
The Soviet Union and the Cause of Peace, 1936.
TROTSKY, L. *The Third International after Lenin,* 1936.
WEIGH, K. S. *Russo-Chinese Diplomacy,* 1928.
WHEELER-BENNETT, J. W. *Forgotten Peace: Brest-Litovsk, March 1918,* 1938.
YAKHONTOFF, V. A. *Russia and the Soviet Union in the Far East,* 1931.
ZHIRMUNSKI, M. *Soviet Export,* 1937.

CHAPTER XX. SOUTHEASTERN EUROPE

General

ARMSTRONG, H. F. *The New Balkans,* 1926. Useful brief survey.
ARMSTRONG, H. F. *Where the East Begins,* 1929. Chief Balkan problems.
BAGGER, E. *Eminent Europeans,* 1922. Interesting brief portraits.
BELL, H. T. M., ed. *The Near East Year Book, 1931–32,* 1932.
CRANE, J. O. *The Little Entente,* 1931.
GESHKOFF, T. I. *Balkan Union,* 1940.
JONES, F. E. *Hitler's Drive to the East,* 1936. Anti-Nazi.
KERNER, R. J. and HOWARD, H. N. *The Balkan Conferences and the Balkan Entente, 1930–1935,* 1936. Excellent; documents; bibliography.
LADAS, S. P. *The Exchange of Minorities; Bulgaria, Greece, and Turkey,* 1932.
MACHRAY, R. *The Little Entente,* 1929.
MACHRAY, R. *The Struggle for the Danube, and the Little Entente, 1929–1938,* 1938.
MILLER, W. *The Ottoman Empire and Its Successors,* 3 ed., 1934.
MITRANY, D. *The Effect of the War in Southeastern Europe,* 1936.
MORGAN, O. S., ed. *Agricultural Systems of Middle Europe; A Symposium,* 1933.
PANARETOFF, S. *Near Eastern Affairs and Conditions,* 1922. Bulgarian view.
PASVOLSKY, L. *Economic Nationalism of the Danubian States,* 1928. Excellent.
ROUCEK, J. S. *The Politics of the Balkans,* 1939. Excellent review.
Royal Institute of International Affairs *The Balkan States I: Economic,* 1936.
Royal Institute of International Affairs *South-Eastern Europe. A Political and Economic Survey,* 1939.
TOYNBEE, A. J. *Survey of International Affairs, 1920–1923,* etc., 1925–.

Romania

ALVAREZ, A. *et al. Agrarian Reform in Roumania and the Case of the Hungarian Optants in Transylvania before the League of Nations,* 1927.

American Committee on the Rights of Religious Minorities *Roumania Ten Years After*, 1928. Advocates change of minorities policy.

BUCHAN, J., ed. *Bulgaria and Romania*, 1924.

CABOT, J. M. *The Racial Conflict in Transylvania*, 1926.

CLARK, C. U. *Greater Roumania*, 1922. Decidedly friendly.

CLARK, C. U. *Bessarabia; Russia and Roumania on the Black Sea*, 1927.

CLARK, C. U. *United Roumania*, 1932. Very friendly.

CLERK, J. *Politics and Political Parties in Roumania*, 1936.

COFFEY, D. *The Coöperative Movement in Jugoslavia, Rumania and North Italy during and after the World War*, 1922.

CORNISH, L. C., comp. *Transylvania in 1922*, 1923. School and church affairs.

CORNISH, L. C., comp. *The Religious Minorities in Transylvania*, 1925.

DEÁK, F. *The Hungarian-Roumanian Land Dispute*, 1928.

DRAGOMIR, S. *The Ethnical Minorities in Transylvania*, 1927. Pro-Romanian.

EVANS, I. L. *The Agrarian Revolution in Roumania*, 1924.

FORTER, N. L. and ROSTOVSKY, D. B. *The Roumanian Handbook*, 1931.

JORGA, N. *History of Roumania: Land, People, Civilization*, 1925.

MADGEARU, V. *Roumania's New Economic Policy*, 1930. Authoritative.

MITRANY, D. *The Land and the Peasant in Roumania; The War and Agrarian Reform, 1917–1921*, 1930.

PARKINSON, M. R. *Twenty Years in Roumania*, 1921. Interesting.

POPOVICI, A. *The Political Status of Bessarabia*, 1931. Romanian study.

RAKOVSKY, C. G. *Roumania and Bessarabia*, 1925. Soviet claims.

ROUČEK, J. S. *Contemporary Roumania and Her Problems*, 1932. Excellent.

SEBESS, D. *Landownership Policy of New Roumania in Transylvania*, 1921.

SETON-WATSON, R. W. *A History of the Roumanians, from Roman Times to the Completion of Unity*, 1934. Sympathetic.

SZÁSZ, Z. DE *The Minorities in Roumanian Transylvania*, 1927. Hungarian view.

Bulgaria and Macedonia

ANASTASOFF, C. *The Tragic Peninsula: A History of the Macedonian Movement for Independence Since 1878*, 1938. Hostile to Greece and Yugoslavia.

BUCHAN, J., ed. *Bulgaria and Romania*, 1924.

BUXTON, L. *The Black Sheep of the Balkans*, 1920. Criticism of Allied policy towards Bulgaria and Turkey.

CHRISTOWE, S. *Heroes and Assassins*, 1935. The Macedonian question.

LAZARD, M. *Compulsory Labour Service in Bulgaria*, 1922. An I.L.O. study.

LESLIE, H. (SCHÜTZE, G. H.) *Where East Is West; Life in Bulgaria*, 1933.

LOGIO, G. C. *Bulgaria: Problems and Politics*, 1919. Pro-Stambulisky.

LOGIO, G. C. *Bulgaria Past and Present*, 1936. Well balanced.

MISHEV, D. *The Truth about Macedonia*, 1917.

MOSELY, P. E. "The Post-War Historiography of Modern Bulgaria," in *Journal of Modern History*, September 1937.

PASVOLSKY, L. *Bulgaria's Economic Position, with Special Reference to the Reparation Problem and the Work of the League of Nations*, 1930.

SWIRE, J. *Bulgarian Conspiracy*, 1939. On IMRO.

Greece

ABBOTT, G. F. *Greece and the Allies, 1914–1922*, 1922. Critical of Venizelos.

ANDREW, PRINCE OF GREECE *Towards Disaster; The Greek Army in Asia Minor in 1921*, 1930.

CHESTER, S. B. *Life of Venizelos*, 1921. Sympathetic.

COSMETATOS, S. P. P. *The Tragedy of Greece*, 1928. Anti-Allied.

CUNLIFFE-OWEN, B. *Silhouettes of Republican Greece*, 1927. On refugee problem.

EDDY, C. B. *Greece and the Greek Refugees,* 1931. Authoritative.
GIBBONS, H. A. *Venizelos,* 2 ed., 1923. An appreciation.
HIBBEN, P. *Constantine I and the Greek People,* 1920. Friendly to the king.
LAVELL, C. F. *A Biography of the Greek People,* 1934.
League of Nations *The Greek Refugee Settlement,* 1926.
LOWELL, A. L. and HUDSON, M. O. *The Corfu Crisis,* 1923.
MACARTNEY, C. A. *Refugees; The Work of the League,* 1931. Greco-Bulgarian population exchange.
MAVROGORDATO, J. *Modern Greece: A Chronicle and a Survey, 1800–1931,* 1931.
MEARS, E. G. *Greece Today: The Aftermath of the Refugee Impact,* 1929.
MILLER, W. *Greece,* 1928. Authoritative.
MILLER, W. "A New Era in Greece," in *Foreign Affairs,* July 1936.
MORGENTHAU, H. and STROTHER, F. *I Was Sent to Athens,* 1929. On refugees.
NICHOLAS, PRINCE OF GREECE *My Fifty Years,* 1926.
PALLIS, A. A. *Greece's Anatolian Venture, and After,* 1937. On 1915–1922.
STICKNEY, E. P. *Southern Albania or Northern Epirus in European International Affairs, 1912–1923,* 1926. Scholarly.
TOYNBEE, A. J. *The Western Question in Greece and Turkey; A Study in the Contact of Civilizations,* 2 ed., 1923.

Yugoslavia

ADAMIC, L. *The Native's Return; An American Immigrant Visits Yugoslavia and Discovers His Old Country,* 1934. Well-written description.
BAERLEIN, H. P. B. *The Birth of Yugoslavia,* 2 v., 1922. Subjective.
BEARD, C. A. and RADIN, G. *The Balkan Pivot: Yugoslavia,* 1929. Politics.
BUCHAN, J., ed. *Yugoslavia,* 1923.
Central Press Bureau of the Presidency of the Ministerial Council of Yugoslavia *Kingdom of Yugoslavia, 1919–1929,* 1930.
COFFEY, D. *The Coöperative Movement in Jugoslavia, Rumania and North Italy during and after the World War,* 1922.
ELLISON, G. *Yugoslavia: A New Country and Its People,* 1935.
GRAHAM, M. W. *New Governments of Central Europe,* 1924.
GRAHAM, S. *Alexander of Yugoslavia, Strong Man of the Balkans,* 1938.
KERNER, R. J. *The Jugo-Slav Movement,* 1918.
LAFFAN, R. G. D. *Jugoslavia since 1918,* 1929. Good survey.
PATTON, K. S. *Kingdom of Serbs, Croats, and Slovenes: A Commercial and Industrial Handbook,* 1928.
SFORZA, C. *Fifty Years of War and Diplomacy in the Balkans. Pashich and the Union of the Yugoslavs,* 1940.
TOMAŠIĆ, D. "Constitutional Changes in Yugoslavia," in *Political Science Quarterly,* December 1940.
WARREN, W. *Montenegro; The Crime of the Peace Conference,* 1922.

CHAPTER XXI. TURKEY FOR THE TURKS

ALLEN, H. E. *The Turkish Transformation,* 1935. Sociological study.
ARMSTRONG, H. *Turkey in Travail,* 1925. Events of 1916–1923.
ARMSTRONG, H. *Turkey and Syria Reborn; A Record of Two Years of Travel,* 1930.
ARMSTRONG, H. C. *Gray Wolf, Mustafa Kemal,* 1933. Unfriendly.
ARNOLD, T. W. *The Caliphate,* 1924.
BARTON, J. L. *Story of Near East Relief (1915–1930),* 1930. Complete.
BURTT, J. *The People of Ararat,* 1926. Armenian troubles.
EDIB, H. *Memoirs of Halidé Edib,* 1926. By an able Turkish feminist.
EDIB, H. *The Turkish Ordeal,* 1928. Second volume of memoirs.

EDIB, H. *Turkey Faces West*, 1930. Lectures.

ELLISON, G. *Turkey Today*, 1928. Social conditions.

EMIN, A. *Turkey in the World War*, 1930. Highly informative.

FROEMBGEN, H. *Kemal Atatürk*, 1937.

GORDON, L. J. *American Relations with Turkey, 1830–1930*, 1932. Excellent.

HOWARD, H. N. *The Partition of Turkey; A Diplomatic History, 1913–1923*, 1931.

IKBAL ALI SHAH *Kamal: Maker of Modern Turkey*, 1934. Iranian view.

JOHNSON, C. R., ed. *Constantinople To-day*, 1922. Sociological studies.

KRÜGER, K. *Kemalist Turkey and the Middle East*, 1932. Foreign relations.

LADAS, S. P. *The Exchange of Minorities; Bulgaria, Greece, and Turkey*, 1932.

LAMMENS, H. *Islām: Beliefs and Institutions*, 1929.

LEVONIAN, L. *Moslem Mentality*, 1928. Interesting.

LEVONIAN, L. *The Turkish Press*, 1933. Selections from 1925–1932.

LINKE, L. *Allah Dethroned*, 1937.

MARRIOTT, J. *The Eastern Question*, 3 ed., 1930. Good.

MASSE, H. *Islam*, 1938. Valuable guide.

MEARS, E. G. *Modern Turkey; A Politico-Economic Interpretation, 1908–1923 Inclusive, with Selected Chapters by Representative Authorities*, 1923.

MIKUSCH, D. VON *Mustapha Kemal; Between Europe and Asia*, 1931. Good.

MOTT, J. R., ed. *The Moslem World of To-day*, 1925. Nonpolitical.

NANSEN, F. *Armenia and the Near East*, 1928. By League representative.

O'LEARY, DE L. *Islam at the Cross Roads*, 1923. Newer tendencies.

OSTOROG, L. *The Angora Reform*, 1923. Lectures.

PARKER, J. and SMITH, C. *Modern Turkey*, 1940.

SHERRILL, C. H. *A Year's Embassy to Mustafa Kemal*, 1934. Sympathetic, by American Ambassador, 1932–1933.

SHOTWELL, J. T. and DEÁK, F. *Turkey at the Straits*, 1940.

SOUSA, N. *The Capitulatory Régime of Turkey; Its History, Origin, and Nature*, 1933.

TOYNBEE, A. J. *The Western Question in Greece and Turkey; A Study in the Contact of Civilizations*, 2 ed., 1923.

TOYNBEE, A. J. *The Islamic World since the Peace Settlement*, v. 1 of *Survey of International Affairs, 1925*, 1927.

TOYNBEE, A. J. and KIRKWOOD, K. P. *Turkey*, 1927. Good; sympathetic.

WAUGH, T. *Turkey; Yesterday, Today, and Tomorrow*, 1920.

WEBSTER, D. E. *The Turkey of Atatürk*, 1939. Factual.

WHITE, W. W. *The Process of Change in the Ottoman Empire*, 1937.

WORTHAM, H. E. *Mustapha Kemal of Turkey*, 1931. Interesting sketch.

YOUNG, G. *Constantinople*, 1926.

YOUNG, H. B. *Moslem Editors Say—. A Selection of Excerpts from the Moslem Press of Iran, Syria, Palestine, Turkey, and Egypt*, 1937. Interesting.

CHAPTER XXII. THE FAR EAST

General

BAIN, H. F. *Ores and Industry in the Far East*, rev. ed., 1933.

BARNES, J., ed. *Empire in the East*, 1934. Competent essays.

BISSON, T. A. *Japan in China*, 1938. Since 1933; friendly to China.

BISSON, T. A. *American Policy in the Far East: 1931–1940*, 1940.

BLAKESLEE, G. H. *The Pacific Area; An International Survey*, 1929.

BLAKESLEE, G. H. *Conflicts of Policy in the Far East*, 1934. Admirable, brief.

BLAND, J. O. P. *China, Japan and Korea*, 1921. Well informed.

BLOCH, K. *German Interests and Policies in the Far East*, 1939.

BREBNER, J. B. "Canada, the Anglo-Japanese Alliance and the Washington Conference," in *Political Science Quarterly*, March 1935.

BUELL, R. L. *The Washington Conference,* 1922. Excellent.

BUSS, C. A. *War and Diplomacy in Eastern Asia,* 1941.

BYWATER, H. C. *The Great Pacific War,* 1932. Imaginary U. S.-Japanese war.

BYWATER, H. C. *Sea-Power in the Pacific; A Study of the American-Japanese Naval Problem,* new ed., 1934. Authoritative.

DENLINGER, S. and CARY, C. B. *War in the Pacific: A Survey of Navies, Peoples and Battle Problems,* 1936.

ELDRIDGE, F. *Trading with Asia,* 1921. Resources and commerce of eastern Asia.

FARLEY, M. S. *America's Stake in the Pacific,* 2 ed., 1937. Brief.

FELLNER, F. *Communication in the Far East,* 1934.

FIELD, F. V., ed. *Economic Handbook of the Pacific Area,* 1934.

FISCHER, L. *The Soviets in World Affairs,* 2 v., 1930. Uses Soviet sources.

GELDEREN, J. VAN *The Recent Development of Economic Foreign Policy in the Netherlands East Indies,* 1939.

GODSHALL, W. L. *Tsingtau under Three Flags,* 1929. Kiaochow under German, Japanese, and Chinese administration.

HORNBECK, S. K. *Contemporary Politics in the Far East,* 1916.

HSÜ, S. *How the Far Eastern War Was Begun,* 1938. Documented.

HUBBARD, G. E. *Eastern Industrialization and Its Effect on the West,* 1935.

HUDSON, G. F. *The Far East in World Politics,* 1937.

KAMESAKA, T., ed. *1940–1941 Who's Who in Japan, with Manchoukuo and China,* 1940.

KANE, A. E. *China, the Powers and the Washington Conference,* 1937.

KENT, P. B. H. *The Twentieth Century in the Far East: A Perspective of Events, Cultural Influence and Policies,* 1937.

KOHN, H. *A History of Nationalism in the East,* 1929.

LASKER, B. and ROMAN, A. *Propaganda from China and Japan,* 1938.

LIU, S. S. *Extraterritoriality: Its Rise and Its Decline,* 1925.

MACNAIR, H. F. *The Real Conflict between China and Japan: An Analysis of Opposing Ideologies,* 1938. Excellent.

MILLARD, T. F. *Conflict of Policies in Asia,* 1924.

MITCHELL, K. L. *Indutrialization of the Western Pacific,* 1942.

MORSE, H. B. and MACNAIR, H. F. *Far Eastern International Relations,* 1931.

PASVOLSKY, L. *Russia in the Far East,* 1922.

PEAKE, C. H. "Refugees in the Far East," in *Annals of the American Academy of Political and Social Science,* May 1939.

Problems of the Pacific 1925–, 1926–. Proceedings of biennial conferences of Institute of Pacific Relations.

QUIGLEY, H. S. *Far Eastern War 1937–1941,* 1942. Excellent.

QUIGLEY, H. S. and BLAKESLEE, G. H. *The Far East: An International Survey,* 1938. Elementary.

Royal Institute of International Affairs *China and Japan,* 1938. Pamphlet.

SHEPHERD, J. *Australia's Interests and Policies in the Far East,* 1939.

STEIN, G. *Far East in Ferment,* 1936. Well-balanced survey.

STIMSON, H. L. *The Far Eastern Crisis,* 1936. By American Secretary of State.

TAMAGNA, F. M. *Italy's Interest in the Far East,* 1941.

TSUCHIDA, K. *Contemporary Thought of Japan and China,* 1927.

WARE, E. E. *Business and Politics in the Far East,* 1932.

China

ABEND, H. and BILLINGHAM, A. J. *Can China Survive?,* 1936.

AYSCOUGH, F. *Chinese Women Yesterday and Today,* 1937.

BAKER, J. E. *Explaining China,* 1927. Enlightening.

BAU, M. J. *The Foreign Relations of China,* rev. ed., 1922. Documented.

BAU, M. J. *The Open Door Doctrine in Relation to China,* 1923. Documented.

BAU, M. J. *Modern Democracy in China*, 1924. Sympathetic.

BAU, M. J. *China and World Peace*, 1928.

BERKOV, R. *Strong Man of China: The Story of Chiang Kai-shek*, 1938. Readable.

BERTRAM, J. M. *First Act in China. The Story of the Sian Mutiny*, 1938.

BERTRAM, J. M. *Unconquered*, 1939. Tribute to people of northern China.

BONNARD, A. *In China, 1920–1921*, 1927. "Young China facing Old China."

BUCK, J. L. *Chinese Farm Economy*, 1930. Case studies.

BUCK, J. L. *Land Utilization in China*, 3 v., 1937. Monumental.

BUCK, P. *The Good Earth*, 1931. Novel of Chinese life, followed by *Sons* (1932), *A House Divided* (1935), *The Patriot* (1939), and *Dragon Seed* (1941).

BUXTON, L. H. D. *China, the Land and the People; A Human Geography*, 1929.

CARLSON, E. F. *The Chinese Army*, 1940. Nontechnical.

Carnegie Endowment for International Peace *The Sino-Japanese Negotiations of 1915; Japanese and Chinese Documents and Chinese Official Statement*, 1921.

CHAPMAN, H. O. *The Chinese Revolution, 1926–1927*, 1928. Communists at Hankow.

CHEN HAN-SENG *Landlord and Peasant in China*, 1936.

CHEN TSUNG-HSI et al. *General Chiang Kai-shek: The Builder of the New China*, 1929.

CHIANG KAI-SHEK and CHIANG MAY-LING *Sian: A Coup d'État*, 1937. The story of Chiang Kai-shek's "kidnapping."

CHIANG KAI-SHEK, MME. *This Is Our China*, 1940.

China, Annals of the American Acad. of Pol. and Soc. Science, Nov. 1930.

CLARK, G. *Economic Rivalries in China*, 1932. Useful data.

CLARK, G. *The Great Wall Crumbles*, 1935. Problems in historical setting.

CONDLIFFE, J. B. *China To-Day: Economic*, 1932.

CRESSEY, G. B. *China's Geographic Foundations*, 1934.

CROW, C. *Four Hundred Million Customers*, 1937. By American business man.

CROW, C. *The Chinese Are Like That*, 1939. Interesting observations.

DANTON, G. H. *The Chinese People*, 1938. Excellent interpretative study.

DJANG, FENG DJEN *Diplomatic Relations between China and Germany since 1898*, 1936.

FORSTER, L. *The New Culture in China*, 1937. Western cultural penetration.

FRIEDMAN, I. S. *British Relations with China, 1931–1939*, 1940.

Fundamental Laws of the Chinese Soviet Republic, 1934.

HEDIN, S. *Chiang Kai-Shek, Marshal of China*, 1940.

HOLCOMBE, A. N. *The Chinese Revolution*, 1930.

HOLCOMBE, A. N. *The Spirit of the Chinese Revolution*, 1930. Trends and leaders.

HOMMEL, R. P. *China at Work*, 1937. Well illustrated.

HORNBECK, S. K. *China Today: Political*, 1927.

HOWLAND, C. P., ed. *Survey of American Foreign Relations, 1929*, 1930.

HSIA CHING-LIN *The Status of Shanghai*, 1929. Documents.

HSU, L. S., ed. *Sun Yat-Sen, His Political and Social Ideals; A Source Book*, 1933.

HSU SHIH-CHANG *China after the War*, 1920. By a former president.

HUGHES, E. R. *The Invasion of China by the Western World*, 1938. Cultural.

HU SHIH and LIN YU-TANG *China's Own Critics*, 1931. Essays.

HUTCHINSON, P. *What and Why in China*, 1927. Brief survey.

Inst. of Pacific Rel. *Agrarian China*, 1940. Sources.

JOHNSTONE, W. C. *The Shanghai Problem*, 1937.

KEETON, G. W. *The Development of Extraterritoriality in China*, 2 v., 1928.

KING, L. M. *China in Turmoil, Studies in Personality*, 1927.

Kuomintang *Dr. Sun Yat Sen, His Life and Achievements*, 1925.

LA FARGUE, T. E. *China and the World War*, 1937. Excellent.

LATOURETTE, K. S. *The Development of China*, 4 rev. ed., 1929.

LATOURETTE, K. S. *A History of Christian Missions in China*, 1929.

LATOURETTE, K. S. *The Chinese, Their History and Culture*, 2 v., rev. ed., 1934.

LATTIMORE, O. *Inner Asian Frontiers of China*, 1940.
League of Nations *The Reorganization of Education in China*, 1932.
LEGENDRE, A. F. *Modern Chinese Civilization*, 1929. Good.
LINEBARGER, P. M. A. *Sun Yat Sen and the Chinese Republic*, 1925.
LINEBARGER, P. M. A. *Government in Republican China*, 1938.
LINEBARGER, P. M. A. *The China of Chiang K'ai-Shek. A Political Study*, 1941.
LIN YU-TANG *My Country and My People*, 1935.
LIN YU-TANG *A History of the Press and Public Opinion in China*, 1936.
LO, R. Y. *China's Revolution from the Inside*, 1930. The nonpolitical revival.
LYALL, L. A. *China*, 1934. Understanding.
MA, W. H. *American Policy toward China as Revealed in Debates of Congress*, 1934.
MACNAIR, H. F. *China's New Nationalism*, 1925.
MACNAIR, H. F. *China in Revolution; An Analysis of Politics and Militarism under the Republic*, 1931. Readable.
MALLORY, W. H. *China; Land of Famine*, 1926.
MILLARD, T. F. *The End of Exterritoriality in China*, 1931.
MONROE, P. *China; A Nation in Evolution*, 1928. By an American educator.
MORSE, H. B. *The International Relations of the Chinese Empire*, 3 v., 1910–1918.
MORSE, H. B. *The Trade and Administration of China*, 3 ed., 1921.
MOWRER, E. A. *The Dragon Wakes*, 1939.
NORTON, H. K. *China and the Powers*, 1927. Dispassionate.
OVERLACH, T. W. *Foreign Financial Control in China*, 1919.
PADOUX, G. "List of English and French Translations of Modern Chinese Laws and Regulations, 1907–1935," in *Chinese Social and Political Science Review*, January 1936.
PEAKE, C. H. *Nationalism and Education in Modern China*, 1932. Good.
PEFFER, N. *China: The Collapse of a Civilization*, 1930. Good.
POLLARD, R. T. *China's Foreign Relations, 1917–1931*, 1933.
PURCELL, V. *Problems of Chinese Education*, 1936.
QUIGLEY, H. S. *Chinese Politics and Foreign Powers*, 1927.
REMER, C. F. *The Foreign Trade of China*, 1926. Scholarly.
REMER, C. F. *Foreign Investments in China*, 1933. Authoritative.
REMER, C. F. and PALMER, W. B. *A Study of Chinese Boycotts, with Special Reference to Their Economic Effectiveness*, 1933.
RESTARICK, H. B. *Sun Yat Sen, Liberator of China*, 1931. Important.
RIASANOVSKY, V. A. *Chinese Civil Law*, 1938.
SHARMAN, L. *Sun Yat-Sen; His Life and Its Meaning*, 1934.
SMEDLEY, A. *China's Red Army Marches*, 1934. Vivid, procommunist.
SMEDLEY, A. *China Fights Back*, 1938. Communist guerrilla tactics.
SNOW, E. *Red Star over China*, 1938. On Red Armies.
SUN YAT-SEN *The International Development of China*, 2 ed., 1929.
SUN YAT-SEN *San Min Chu I; The Three Principles of the People*, 1927.
SZE, T. Y. *China and the Most-Favored-Nation Clause*, 1925.
T'ANG LEANG LI *The Foundations of Modern China*, 1928. Nationalism.
T'ANG LEANG LI, ed. *Suppressing Communist Banditry in China*, 1934.
TAYLOR, G. E. *The Struggle for North China*, 1941.
TONG, H. K. *Chiang Kai-shek: Soldier and Statesman*, 2 v., 1937–1938.
TYAU, M. T. Z., ed. *Two Years of Nationalist China*, 1930. Documents.
UTLEY, F. *China at War*, 1939.
VAN DORN, H. A. *Twenty Years of the Chinese Republic; Two Decades of Progress*, 1932. Nonpolitical.
VINACKE, H. M. *Modern Constitutional Development in China*, 1920. Documents.
VINACKE, H. M. *Problems of Industrial Development in China*, 1926.
WALES, N. *Inside Red China*, 1939. By wife of correspondent Edgar Snow.
WALES, N. *China Builds for Democracy: A Story of Cooperative Industry*, 1941.

WEIGH, K. S. *Russo-Chinese Diplomacy*, 1928.
WHEELER, W. R. *China and the World War*, 1919.
WHYTE, A. F. *China and the Foreign Powers,* rev. ed., 1928. Brief.
WILLIAM, M. *Sun Yat Sen versus Communism*, 1932.
WILLIAMS, E. T. *China Yesterday and Today*, 5 ed., 1932. Good, cultural.
WILLIAMS, E. T. *A Short History of China*, 1928. Good.
WILLOUGHBY, W. W. *China at the Conference; A Report*, 1922. Documents of Washington Conference.
WILLOUGHBY, W. W. *Foreign Rights and Interests in China*, 2 v., rev. ed., 1927.
WILLOUGHBY, W. W. *The Sino-Japanese Controversy and the League of Nations*, 1935. Authoritative. Documents.
WOO, T. *The Kuomintang and the Future of the Chinese Revolution*, 1928. Good.
WOOD, GE-ZAY *China, the United States and the Anglo-Japanese Alliance. The Chino-Japanese Treaties of May 25, 1915. The Twenty-One Demands*, 2 v., 1921. Three documentary studies.
WOOD, GE-ZAY *The Shantung Question; A Study in Diplomacy and World Politics*, 1922.
WU, C. C. *The Nationalist Program for China*, 1929. Lectures.
WU, C. K. *The International Aspect of the Missionary Movement in China*, 1930.
YAKHONTOFF, V. A. *The Chinese Soviets*, 1934.

Japan

ALLEN, G. C. *Modern Japan and Its Problems*, 1928. Social and economic.
ALLEN, G. C. *Japan: The Hungry Guest*, 1938. Excellent British account.
ALLEN, G. C. *Japanese Industry: Its Recent Development and Present Condition*, 1940.
ASAMI, N. *Japanese Colonial Administration*, 1924. Documented.
BALLARD, G. A. *The Influence of the Sea on the Political History of Japan*, 1921.
BORTON, H. *Japan since 1931*, 1941. Brief.
BROWN, A. J. *Japan in the World of Today*, 1928.
CAUSTON, E. E. N. *Militarism and Foreign Policy in Japan*, 1936.
CHAMBERLIN, W. H. *Japan Over Asia*, 1937.
CHANG, C. F. *The Anglo-Japanese Alliance*, 1931. Excellent.
CLYDE, P. H. *Japan's Pacific Mandate*, 1935.
COLEGROVE, K. W. *Militarism in Japan*, 1936.
COLEGROVE, K. W. "The Japanese Cabinet," in *American Political Science Review*, October 1936; "The Japanese Constitution," *loc. cit.*, December 1937.
CROCKER, W. R. *The Japanese Population Problem; The Coming Crisis*, 1931.
ETHERTON, P. T. and TILTMAN, H. H. *Japan: Mistress of the Pacific?*, 1933.
FAHS, C. B. *Government in Japan*, 1940.
FLEISHER, W. *Volcanic Isle*, 1941. Fascist Japan.
GRIFFIS, W. E. *The Mikado: Institution and Person*, 1915.
GRISWOLD, A. W. *The Far Eastern Policy of the United States*, 1938. Authoritative.
GUBBINS, J. H. *The Making of Modern Japan*, 1922.
HERSHEY, A. S. and S. W. *Modern Japan, Social—Industrial—Political*, 1919.
HINDMARSH, A. E. *The Basis of Japanese Foreign Policy*, 1936. Bibliography.
HOLTOM, D. C. *The National Faith of Japan*, 1938. Shinto.
International Labour Office *Industrial Labour in Japan*, 1933.
ISHII, R. *Population Pressure and Economic Life in Japan*, 1937.
KAWABÉ, K. *The Press and Politics in Japan*, 1921.
KAWAKAMI, K. K. *Japan's Pacific Policy*, 1922. Apologia.
KEENLEYSIDE, H. L. and THOMAS, A. F. *History of Japanese Education and Present Educational System*, 1937.
KENNEDY, M. D. *The Changing Fabric of Japan*, 1930. Press, religion, feminism.
KITAZAWA, N. *The Government of Japan*, 1929. Brief and reliable.

LATOURETTE, K. S. *The Development of Japan*, 3 ed., 1931. Useful summary.
LEDERER, E. and LEDERER-SEIDLER, E. *Japan in Transition*, 1938. Brief.
MATSUNAMI, N. *The Constitution of Japan*, 1930. Scholarly.
MEARS, H. *Year of the Wild Boar. An American Woman in Japan*, 1942.
MERRILL, F. T. *Japan and the Opium Menace*, 1942.
MOULTON, H. G. and KO, J. *Japan; An Economic and Financial Appraisal*, 1931.
NITOBÉ, I. *Japan; Some Phases of Her Problems and Development*, 1931.
NITOBÉ, I. et al. *Western Influences in Modern Japan*, 1931.
NORMAN, E. H. *Japan's Emergence as a Modern State*, 1940. Brief.
ODATE, G. *Japan's Financial Relations with the United States*, 1922.
ORCHARD, J. E. *Japan's Economic Position*, 1930.
PENROSE, E. F. *Food Supply and Raw Materials in Japan*, 1930.
PENROSE, E. F. *Population Theories and Their Application, with Special Reference to Japan*, 1934.
SAITO, H. *Japan's Policies and Purposes*, 1935.
SANSOM, G. B. *Japan; A Short Cultural History*, 1931.
SCHUMPETER, E. B. et al. *The Industrialization of Japan and Manchukuo, 1930–1940: Population, Raw Materials, and Industry*, 1940. Encyclopedic.
STEIN, G. *Made in Japan*, 2 ed., 1935.
TAKEUCHI, T. *War and Diplomacy in the Japanese Empire*, 1935.
TANIN, O. and YOHAN, E. *Militarism and Fascism in Japan*, 1934.
TANIN, O. and YOHAN, E. *When Japan Goes to War*, 1936.
TREAT, P. J. *Japan and the United States, 1853–1928*, 1928.
TUPPER, E. and McREYNOLDS, G. E. *Japan in American Public Opinion*, 1937.
UYEDA, T. *The Future of Japanese Population*, 1933.
UYEHARA, S. *The Industry and Trade of Japan*, 1926. Authoritative.
WILDES, H. E. *Social Currents in Japan*, 1927. Press and opinion.
WILDES, H. E. *Japan in Crisis*, 1934.
YAKHONTOFF, V. A. *Eyes on Japan*, 1936. Good on background.
YAMASAKI, K. and OGAWA, G. *The Effect of the World War upon the Commerce and Industry of Japan*, 1929.
YOUNG, A. M. *Japan in Recent Times, 1912–1926*, 1929.
YOUNG, A. M. *Imperial Japan, 1926–1938*, 1938. Religion and national policy.
YOUNG, A. M. *The Rise of a Pagan State: Japan's Religious Background*, 1939.

Manchuria (Manchoukuo)

ADACHI, K. *Manchuria; A Survey*, 1925. Pro-Japanese.
CLYDE, P. H. *International Rivalries in Manchuria, 1689–1922*, 2 ed., 1928.
ETHERTON, P. T. and TILTMAN, H. H. *Manchuria; The Cockpit of Asia*, 1932.
Geneva Research Center *Geneva Special Studies*: "The League and Manchuria"; "The League and Shanghai"; "The League and the Lytton Report"; "The League and 'Manchoukuo,'" 1931–1934.
KAWAKAMI, K. K. *Manchoukuo; Child of Conflict*, 1933. Japanese view.
KINNEY, H. W. *Manchuria Today*, 1930. Statistics.
LATTIMORE, O. *The Mongols of Manchuria*, 1934.
LATTIMORE, O. *Manchuria, Cradle of Conflict*, rev. ed., 1935.
League of Nations *Report of the [Lytton] Commission of Enquiry . . .* , 1932.
League of Nations *The Verdict of the League: China and Japan in Manchuria*, 1933.
PAN, S. C. Y. *American Diplomacy Concerning Manchuria*, 1939.
PARLETT, H. G. *A Brief Account of Diplomatic Events in Manchuria*, 1929.
PRICE, E. B. *The Russo-Japanese Treaties of 1907–1916 Concerning Manchuria and Mongolia*, 1933.
REA, G. B. *The Case for Manchoukuo*, 1935. By adviser to Manchoukuo.

STRASSER, R. *The Mongolian Horde*, 1930. Interesting, by a German artist.
WILLIAMS, E. T. "Japan and Jehol," in *American Journal of International Law*, v. 27, 1933.
YOUNG, C. W. *Japan's Jurisdiction and International Legal Position in Manchuria*, 3 v., 1931.

CHAPTER XXIII. THE UNITED STATES

Domestic Affairs

ADAMIC, L. *Dynamite; The Story of Class Violence in America*, rev. ed., 1934.
ADAMS, J. T. *Our Business Civilization; Some Aspects of American Culture*, 1929.
ALLEN, F. *Only Yesterday; An Informal History of the Nineteen Twenties*, 1931.
ALLEN, F. *Since Yesterday*, 1940.
ANDERSON, N. *The Right to Work*, 1938. Relief.
BEARD, C. A., ed. *America Faces the Future*, 1932.
BEARD, C. A. and M. *America in Mid-Passage*, 1939. The depression years.
BRISSENDEN, P. F. *The I.W.W.*, 2 ed., 1920.
Brookings Institution *The Recovery Problem in the United States*, 1938.
BURNS, A. R. *The Decline of Competition*, 1936.
BURNS, E. M. *Toward Social Security*, 1936.
CHAFEE, Z. *Freedom of Speech*, 1920. On censorship.
CHERRINGTON, E. H. *The Evolution of Prohibition in the United States*, 1920.
CLAIRE, G. S. *Administocracy; The Recovery Laws and Their Enforcement*, 1934.
CLARK, E. and GALLOWAY, G., eds. *The Internal Debts of the United States*, 1933.
COCHRAN, T. C. and MILLER, W. *The Age of Enterprise*, 1942. Business and industry.
COOLIDGE, C. *Autobiography*, 1929.
CORWIN, E. S. *The Twilight of the Supreme Court*, 1934.
CUNNINGHAM, W. J. *American Railroads: Government Control and Reconstruction Policies*, 1922.
DAUGHERTY, C. R. *Labor Problems in American Industry*, rev. ed., 1938.
DENISON, J. H. *Emotional Currents in American History*, 1932.
DODD, W. E. *Woodrow Wilson and His Work*, new ed., 1932.
DUFFIELD, M. *King Legion*, 1931. The American Legion.
EPSTEIN, R. and CLARK, F. *Industrial Profits in the United States*, 1934.
FIELDS, H. *The Refugee Problem in the United States*, 1938.
GARIS, R. L. *Immigration Restriction*, 1927. Substantial survey.
HACKER, L. M. *A Short History of the New Deal*, 1934.
HACKER, L. M. *American Problems of Today. A History of the United States Since the World War*, 1938. Excellent.
HALLGREN, M. A. *Seeds of Revolt; A Study of American Life and the Temper of the American People during the Depression*, 1933.
HARRISON, L. V. and LAINE, E. *After Repeal*, 1936.
HINES, W. D. *War History of American Railroads*, 1928.
HULEN, B. D. *Inside the Department of State*, 1939.
ICKES, H. L. *Back to Work; The Story of the PWA*, 1935. By its administrator.
International Labour Office *Social and Economic Reconstruction in the United States*, 1935. Objective view of NRA.
JOHNSON, G. G., JR. *The Treasury and Monetary Policy, 1933–1938*, 1939.
JOHNSON, H. S. *The Blue Eagle from Egg to Earth*, 1935. By NRA administrator.
KELSEY, R. W. *Farm Relief and Its Antecedents*, rev. ed., 1929.
KENT, F. R. *The Democratic Party*, 1928.
KNIGHT, E. *Education in the United States*, new ed., 1934.
LIPPMANN, W. *Men of Destiny*, 1927. Leading American personalities.

LOCKLIN, D. P.   *Railroad Regulation since 1920,* 1928.
LOCKLIN, D. P.   *Economics of Transportation,* 1936.
LYND, R. S. and H.   *Middletown; A Study in Contemporary American Culture,* 1929.
LYND, R. S. and H.   *Middletown in Transition,* 1937.
LYON, L. S. *et al.   The National Recovery Administration; An Analysis and Appraisal,* 1935.
MALIN, J. C.   *The United States after the World War,* 1930.
MAYERS, L., ed.   *A Handbook of NRA,* 2 ed., 1934.
MAZUR, P. M.   *American Prosperity,* 1928.   By a well-informed banker.
McKENZIE, R. D.   *Oriental Exclusion,* 1928.
MECKLIN, J. M.   *The Ku Klux Klan: A Study of the American Mind,* 1924.
MERZ, C.   *The Dry Decade,* 1931.
MYERS, W. S.   *The Republican Party,* rev. ed., 1931.
MYERS, W. S., ed.   *The State Papers and Other Public Writings of Herbert Hoover,* 2 v., 1934.
MYERS, W. S. and NEWTON, W. H.   *The Hoover Administration,* 1936.
NICOLSON, H.   *Dwight Morrow,* 1935.
NIXON, H. C.   *Forty Acres and Steel Mules,* 1938.
ODEGARD, P.   *Pressure Politics; The Story of the Anti-Saloon League,* 1928.
ODEGARD, P.   *The American Public Mind,* 1930.
OGBURN, W. F., ed.   *Social Change and the New Deal,* 1934.
OSTROLENK, B.   *The Surplus Farmer,* 1932.
OVERACKER, L.   *Money in Elections,* 1932.   Scholarly.
PARKER, R. A.   *The Incredible Messiah: The Deification of Father Divine,* 1937.
PEEL, R. V. and DONNELLY, T. C.   *The 1928 Campaign,* 1931.
PEEL, R. V. and DONNELLY, T. C.   *The 1932 Campaign,* 1935.
PRATT, F.   *The Navy: A History. The Story of a Service in Action,* 1938.
Report of the Committee on Recent Economic Changes of the President's Conference on Unemployment, 2 v., 1929.
Report of the President's Research Committee on Social Trends; Recent Social Trends in the United States, 1 v. ed., 1933.
RIPLEY, W. Z.   *Main Street and Wall Street,* 1927.
ROBEY, R. W.   *Roosevelt versus Recovery,* 1934.
ROBINSON, E. E.   *The Presidential Vote, 1896–1932,* 1934.
ROOSEVELT, F. D.   *On Our Way,* 1934.
ROOSEVELT, F. D.   *Public Papers and Addresses,* 9 v., 1938–1941.
SAPOSS, D. J.   *Left Wing Unionism,* 1926.
SELIGMAN, E. R. A.   *The Economics of Farm Relief,* 1929.
SIEGFRIED, A.   *America Comes of Age,* 1927.   By a sympathetic Frenchman.
SLOSSON, P. W.   *The Great Crusade and After, 1914–1928,* 1930.   Social history.
SMITH, A. E.   *Up to Now; An Autobiography,* 1929.
SOKOLSKY, G. E.   *Labor's Fight for Power,* 1934.
SPAULDING, O. L.   *The United States Army in War and Peace,* 1937.   To 1920.
STEPHENSON, G. M.   *A History of American Immigration, 1820–1924,* 1926.
STOLBERG, B.   *The Story of the C. I. O.,* 1939.
STOLBERG, B. and VINTON, W. J.   *The Economic Consequences of the New Deal,* 1935.
SULLIVAN, M.   *Our Times,* v. 5 and 6, 1933, 1935.
SWEET, W. W.   *The Story of Religions in America,* 1930.
THOMPSON, J. G.   *Urbanization; Its Effects on Government and Society,* 1927.
THOMPSON, W. S. and WHELPTON, P.   *Population Trends in the United States,* 1933.
TUGWELL, R. G.   *Industrial Discipline and the Governmental Arts,* 1933.
Twentieth Century Fund   *Big Business: Its Growth and Its Place,* 1937.
United States, Bureau of Labor Statistics   *P.W.A. and Industry, A Four-Year Study of Regenerative Employment,* 1938.
United States, Bureau of Labor Statistics   *Strikes in the United States, 1880–1936,* 1938.

WALLACE, H. A.   *New Frontiers*, 1934.
WALLACE, S. C.   *The New Deal in Action*, 1934.
WHARTON, D., ed.   *The Roosevelt Omnibus*, 1934.   Photographs and cartoons.
WILCOX, C., FRASER, H. F., and MALIN, P. M., eds.   *America's Recovery Program*, 1934.
WILLOUGHBY, W. F.   *Financial Condition and Operations of the National Government, 1921–1930*, 1931.
WITTE, E. E.   *The Government in Labor Disputes*, 1932.
WOLL, M.   *Labor, Industry, and Government*, 1935.
WOODDY, C. H.   *The Growth of the Federal Government, 1915–1932*, 1934.

Foreign Affairs, Trade, and Foreign Debts

ANGELL, J. W.   *Financial Foreign Policy of the United States*, 1933.
BAILEY, T. A.   *A Diplomatic History of the American People*, 1939.
BASSETT, J. S.   *The League of Nations*, 1928.   Good chapter on U. S.
BEARD, C. A. and SMITH, G. H. E.   *The Idea of National Interest; An Analytical Study in American Foreign Policy*, 1934.
BEARD, C. A. and SMITH, G. H. E.   *The Open Door at Home; A Trial Philosophy of National Interest*, 1934.   An argument for self-containment.
BECKETT, G.   *The Reciprocal Trade Agreements Program*, 1941.
BEMIS, S. F.   *Diplomatic History of the United States*, 2 ed., 1942.
BEMIS, S., ed.   *The American Secretaries of State and Their Diplomacy*, v. 10, 1929.
BLAKESLEE, G. H.   *The Recent Foreign Policy of the United States*, 1925.
BLAKESLEE, G. H.   *The Pacific Area; An International Survey*, 1929.
BUELL, R. L.   *The Washington Conference*, 1922.   Excellent.
BUELL, R. L. et al.   *Problems of the New Cuba*, 1935.   Report of a commission.
CALLAHAN, J. M.   *American Foreign Policy in Mexican Relations*, 1932.
COLE, T.   *The Recognition Policy of the United States since 1901*, 1928.
COOPER, R. M.   *American Consultation in World Affairs for the Preservation of Peace*, 1934.
COX, I. J.   *Nicaragua and the United States, 1909–1927*, 1927.
DENNY, H. N.   *Dollars for Bullets; The Story of American Rule in Nicaragua*, 1929.
DENNY, L.   *We Fight for Oil*, 1928.
DENNY, L.   *America Conquers Britain*, 1930.   Fight for raw materials.
DOWELL, A. A. and JESNESS, O. B.   *The American Farmer and the Export Market*, 1934.
DULLES, F. R.   *America in the Pacific; A Century of Expansion*, 1932.
DUNN, R. W.   *American Foreign Investments*, 1926.
EMENY, B.   *The Strategy of Raw Materials; A Study of America in Peace and War*, 1934.   Statistics and charts.
FARLEY, M. S.   *America's Stake in the Pacific*, 2 ed., 1937.   Brief.
FLEMING, D. F.   *The United States and the League of Nations, 1918–1920*, 1932.
FLEMING, D. F.   *The United States and World Organization, 1920–1933*, 1938.
GANTENBEIN, J. W.   *Financial Questions in United States Foreign Policy*, 1939.
GODSHALL, W. L.   *American Foreign Policy*, 1937.   Useful source book.
GRISWOLD, A. W.   *The Far Eastern Policy of the United States*, 1939.   Excellent.
GUGGENHEIM, H. F.   *The United States and Cuba*, 1934.
HACKETT, C. W.   *The Mexican Revolution and the United States, 1910–1926*, 1926.
HARING, C. H.   *South America Looks at the United States*, 1928.
HAYDEN, J. R.   *The Philippines. A Study in National Development*, 1942.
HILL, D. J.   *The Problem of a World Court*, 1927.
HOWLAND, C. P., ed.   *A Survey of American Foreign Relations*, 4 v., 1928–1931.
ISE, J.   *The United States Oil Policy*, 1927.
JESSUP, P. C.   *The United States and the World Court*, 1929.
JONES, C. L.   *The Caribbean since 1900*, 1934.

JONES, J. M. *Tariff Retaliation; Repercussions of the Hawley-Smoot Bill,* 1934.

JONES, S. S. and MYERS, D. P., eds. *Documents on American Foreign Relations, January 1938–June 1939,* 1939. Annually thereafter.

KEENLEYSIDE, H. L. *Canada and the United States,* 1929.

KIRK, G. L. *Philippine Independence,* 1936.

KLEIN, J. *Frontiers of Trade,* 1929. Interesting on American foreign trade.

LEWIS, C. *America's Stake in International Investments,* 1938.

LIPPMANN, W. and SCROGGS, W. O. *The United States in World Affairs, 1931, 1932, 1933,* 1932–1934. See Shepardson below.

MADDEN, J. T. *America's Experience as a Creditor Nation,* 1937.

MOULTON, H. G. and PASVOLSKY, L. *War Debts and World Prosperity,* 1932.

MOYER, G. S. *Attitude of the United States towards the Recognition of Soviet Russia,* 1926. Documented, opposed to recognition.

NOURSE, E. G. *American Agriculture and the European Market,* 1924.

NOYES, A. D. *The War Period of American Finance, 1908–1925,* 1926.

OFFUTT, M. *The Protection of Citizens Abroad by the Armed Forces of the United States,* 1928. Covers 1813–1927.

PAUL, R. W. *The Abrogation of the Gentlemen's Agreement,* 1936. Japanese immigration.

PHELAN, E. G. "The United States and the International Labor Organization," in *Political Science Quarterly,* March 1935.

REID, C. F. *Education in the Territories and Outlying Possessions of the United States,* 1941.

RIPPY, J. F. *The United States and Mexico,* rev. ed., 1931.

RIPPY, J. F. *America and the Strife of Europe,* 1938.

SCHMECKEBIER, L. F. *International Organizations in Which the United States Participates,* 1935.

SCHUMAN, F. L. *American Policy toward Russia since 1917,* 1928.

SCOTT, J. B., ed. *The International Conferences of American States, 1889–1928,* 1931.

SHEPARDSON, W. H. and SCROGGS, W. O. *The United States in World Affairs, 1934–1935,* 1935. Issued annually. For earlier volumes see Lippmann.

SIMONDS, F. H. *American Foreign Policy in the Post-War Years,* 1935.

SOUTHARD, F. A. *American Industry in Europe,* 1931. Valuable.

SPROUT, H. and M. *Toward a New Order of Sea Power. American Naval Policy and the World Scene, 1918–1922,* 1940.

STUART, G. H. *Latin America and the United States,* 2 ed., 1928.

TAUSSIG, F. W. *The Tariff History of the United States,* 8 ed., 1931.

TURLINGTON, E. *Mexico and Her Foreign Creditors,* 1930.

United States, Bureau of Foreign and Domestic Commerce *Oversea Travel and Travel Expenditures in the Balance of International Payments of the United States, 1919–38,* 1939.

United States, Department of State *Foreign Relations of the United States.* Annual.

WARE, E. E., ed. *The Study of International Relations in the United States,* 1934.

WERNER, M. R. *Privileged Characters,* 1935. Political scandals, 1920–1934.

WERTENBAKER, C. *A New Doctrine for the Americas,* 1941. Good-neighbor policy.

WILLIAMS, B. H. *Economic Foreign Policy of the United States,* 1929.

WILLIAMS, B. H. *American Diplomacy, Policies and Practice,* 1936.

WILLIAMS, B. H. *Foreign Loan Policy of the United States Since 1933,* 1939.

CHAPTERS XXIV–XXVI. THE SECOND WORLD WAR

AIKMAN, D. *The All-American Front,* 1940. Hemisphere defense.

ALSOP, J. and KINTNER, R. *American White Paper: The Story of American Diplomacy and the Second World War,* 1940. Well informed.

American Geographical Society *The European Possessions in the Caribbean Area,* 1941.

ANGELL, N. *Raw Materials, Population Pressure and War,* 1936.

ARMSTRONG, H. F. *"We or They" Two Worlds in Conflict,* 1936.

ARMSTRONG, H. F. *Chronology of Failure: The Last Days of the French Republic,* 1940.

ASHTON, E. B. *The Fascist: His State and His Mind,* 1937.

BARNOUW, A. J. *The Dutch: A Portrait Study of Holland,* 1940.

BARZUN, J. *Race: A Study in Modern Superstition,* 1938.

Belgian Amer. Educ. Foundation *The Belgian Campaign and the Surrender of the Belgian Army, May 10–28, 1940,* 1940. Defends Leopold.

Belgium, Ministry of Foreign Affairs *The Official Account of What Happened, 1939–40,* 1942.

BENEŠ, V. and GINSBURG, R. A. *Ten Million Prisoners,* 1940. Occupied Czechia.

BENSON, O. *Through the Diplomatic Looking-Glass: Immediate Origins of the War in Europe,* 1939.

BEVERIDGE, W. *Social Insurance and Allied Services,* 1942. In Britain.

BIDWELL, P. W. *Economic Defense of Latin America,* 1941.

BIRCHALL, F. T. *The Storm Breaks: A Panorama of Europe and the Forces That Have Wrecked Its Peace,* 1940. Able journalism.

BOWMAN, I. et al. *Limits of Land Settlement. A Report on Present-Day Possibilities,* 1937.

BRODIE, F. M. *Peace Aims and Post-War Planning,* 1942. Bibliography.

BRYAN, J. *Siege,* 1940. Photographs of Warsaw siege.

CANT, G. *The War at Sea,* 1942.

CHAMBERLAIN, N. *In Search of Peace,* 1939. Speeches of 1937–1939.

CHAMBRUN, R. DE *I Saw France Fall: Will She Rise Again?* 1940.

CHILDS, H. L., ed. *Propaganda and Dictatorship,* 1936.

CHURCHILL, W. S. *While England Slept: A Survey of World Affairs, 1932–1938,* 1938. Speeches.

CHURCHILL, W. S. *Blood, Sweat, and Tears,* 1941. Speeches.

CLARK, G. *The Balance Sheets of Imperialism. Facts and Figures on Colonies,* 1936.

CLARK, G. *A Place in the Sun,* 1936. Maintains colonies do not "pay."

CLARKE, R. W. B. *The Economic Effort of War,* 1940. In Britain.

COLBY, C. C., ed. *Geographic Aspects of International Relations,* 1938.

CONOVER, H. F., comp. *French Colonies in Africa. A List of References,* 1942.

CORBETT, P. E. *Post-War Worlds,* 1942. One of ablest discussions.

COWIE, D. *War for Britain. First Part: September 1939 to September 1940,* 1941. Empire contributions.

CURTIS, M., ed. *Norway and the War. September, 1939–December, 1940,* 1942. Documents.

Czechoslovakia *Two Years of German Oppression in Czechoslovakia,* 1941.

DALLIN, D. J. *Soviet Russia's Foreign Policy, 1939–1942,* 1942.

DAVIS, F. and LINDLEY, E. K. *How War Came. An American White Paper; From the Fall of France to Pearl Harbor,* 1942.

DE WEERD, H. H. *Great Soldiers of the Two World Wars,* 1942.

DIES, M. *The Trojan Horse in America,* 1940. Interesting.

DUPUY, R. E. *World in Arms,* 1939. Good survey.

ELIOT, G. F. *Bombs Bursting in Air: The Influence of Air Power on International Relations,* 1939.

ELLISTON, H. B. *Finland Fights,* 1940. Correspondent's report.

EMERSON, R. *Malaysia. A Study in Direct and Indirect Rule,* 1937.

Finland, Ministry for Foreign Affairs *The Finnish Blue Book. The Development of Finnish-Soviet Relations during the Autumn of 1939, Including the Official Documents and the Peace Treaty of March 12, 1940,* 1940.

FLORINSKY, M. T. *Fascism and National Socialism,* 1936. Thoughtful.

FOERTSCH, H. *The Art of Modern Warfare,* 1940.

France *The French Yellow Book. Diplomatic Documents (1938–1939),* 1940.

FRANCIS, E. V. *Britain's Economic Strategy,* 1939. Comprehensive.

FRIED, H. E. *The Guilt of the German Army,* 1942.

GALLOWAY, G. B. *Post-War Planning in the United States,* 1942. List of agencies.

GAULLE, C. DE *The Army of the Future,* 1941.

Germany *Documents on the Events Preceding the Outbreak of the War,* 1940.

GRAHAM, S. *From War to War, 1917–1940: A Datebook of the Years Between,* 1940.

GRANDIN, T. *The Political Use of the Radio,* 1939.

GRATTAN, C. H., ed. *The German White Paper. Full Text of the Polish Documents Issued by the Berlin Foreign Office,* 1940.

Great Britain *Documents Concerning German-Polish Relations and the Outbreak of Hostilities between Great Britain and Germany on September 3, 1939,* 1939.

Great Britain, Air Ministry *Bomber Command. The Air Ministry Account of the Bomber Command's Offensive against the Axis,* 1941. By H. A. Saunders.

Great Britain, Air Ministry *The Battle of Britain. An Air Ministry Record of the Great Days from August 8th to October 31st 1940,* 1941. By H. A. Saunders.

Greece *Italy's Aggression against Greece,* 1940. Documents.

Greece *The Greek White Book,* 1942.

GREW, J. C. *Report from Tokyo,* 1942. By last prewar U. S. Ambassador.

HEIDE, H. VAN DER *My Sister and I. Diary of a Dutch Boy Refugee,* 1941.

HENDERSON, N. *Failure of a Mission: Berlin 1937–1939,* 1940. By last prewar British Ambassador.

HLOND, A. *et al. The Persecution of the Catholic Church in German-Occupied Poland,* 1941.

HOOVER, C. B. *Dictators and Democracies,* 1937.

HOOVER, H. and GIBSON, H. *The Problems of Lasting Peace,* 1942.

HORNBECK, S. K. *The United States and the Far East: Certain Fundamentals of Policy,* 1942. Authoritative.

HUSAIN, M. *The Quest for Empire. An Introduction to the Study of [the] Contemporary Expansionist Policy of Japan, Italy and Germany,* 1937.

Institute of the Aeronautical Sciences, sponsor *Air-Age Education Series,* 1942–1943.

International Labor Office *Wartime Transference of Labour in Great Britain,* 1942.

International Studies Conference *Peaceful Change: Procedures, Population Pressure, the Colonial Question, Raw Materials and Markets,* 1938.

JACKSON, J. H. *Finland,* 1938. Brief, good.

JACKSON, J. H. *Estonia,* 1941.

JOHNSTONE, W. C. *The United States and Japan's New Order,* 1941.

JONES, S. S. and MYERS, D. P., eds. *Documents on American Foreign Relations January 1938–June 1939,* 1939. Annually thereafter.

JOSEPH-MAGINOT, M. *He Might Have Saved France,* 1940. By A. Maginot's sister.

KAHN, A. E. and SAYERS, M. *Sabotage: The Secret War against America,* 1942.

KEESING, F. M. *The South Seas in the Modern World,* 1941.

KENNEDY, J. F. *Why England Slept,* 1940. By son of U. S. Ambassador.

KENNEDY, R. *The Ageless Indies,* 1942. Life of the people.

KERNAN, T. *France on Berlin Time,* 1941. Occupation.

KLEFFENS, E. N. VAN *Juggernaut over Holland. The Dutch Foreign Minister's Personal Story of the Invasion of the Netherlands,* 1941.

KOHN, H. *World Order in Historical Perspective,* 1942.

KOHT, H. *Norway: Neutral and Invaded,* 1941. By foreign minister.

KRAUS, R. *The Men Around Churchill,* 1941.

KUCZYNSKI, R. R. *Colonial Population,* 1937. Statistics.

LANDON, K. P. *Siam in Transition,* 1939.

LANDON, K. P. *The Chinese in Thailand,* 1941.

LANGSAM, W. C. *In Quest of Empire: The Problem of Colonies,* 1939.

LAVINE, H. and WECHSLER, J. *War Propaganda and the United States,* 1940.

LEE, D. E. *Ten Years: The World on the Way to War, 1930–1940,* 1942.

LEFF, D. N. *Uncle Sam's Pacific Islets,* 1940. Interesting; brief.

LISSITZYN, O. J. *International Air Transport and National Policy,* 1942.

MACKENZIE, A. J. *Propaganda Boom,* 1938. Totalitarian techniques.

MACKINDER, H. J. *Democratic Ideals and Reality,* 1919, reissued 1942. Basis of geopolitics.

MACKINTOSH, J. *The Paths That Led to War, Europe: 1919–1939,* 1940.

MADDOX, W. P. *European Plans for World Order,* 1940. Useful pamphlet.

MATTERN, J. *Geopolitik. Doctrine of National Self-Sufficiency and Empire,* 1942.

MAUROIS, A. *Tragedy in France: An Eye-Witness Account,* 1940.

McINNIS, E. *The War: First Year,* 1940. Annually thereafter.

MENDERSHAUSEN, H. *The Economics of War,* 1940. Thorough.

MILLER, E. H. *Strategy at Singapore,* 1942.

MILLIS, W. *Why Europe Fights,* 1940.

MOËN, L. *Under the Iron Heel,* 1941. German-occupied Belgium.

MONROE, E. *The Mediterranean in Politics,* 1938. Interests and motives.

MURPHY, M. E. *The British War Economy, 1939–1943,* 1943.

Netherlands *Netherlands Orange Book,* 1940.

Netherlands Information Bureau *Ten Years of Japanese Burrowing in the Netherlands East Indies,* 1941.

NEUMANN, S. *Permanent Revolution. The Total State in a World at War,* 1942. Excellent.

POL, H. *Suicide of a Democracy,* 1940. Good; collapse of France.

Poland *Official Documents Concerning Polish-German and Polish-Soviet Relations, 1933–1939,* 1940.

QUIGLEY, H. S. *Far Eastern War 1937–1941,* 1942.

REDDAWAY, W. F. *Problems of the Baltic,* 1940.

ROMULO, C. P. *I Saw the Fall of the Philippines,* 1942. Authoritative.

ROSINSKI, H. *The German Army,* 1940.

Royal Inst. of Int. Aff. *Raw Materials and Colonies,* 1936.

Royal Inst. of Int. Aff. *The Colonial Problem,* 1937.

Royal Inst. of Int. Aff. *The Baltic States: A Survey of the Political and Economic Structure and the Foreign Relations of Estonia, Latvia, and Lithuania,* 1938.

Royal Inst. of Int. Aff. *International Sanctions,* 1938.

SCHMITT, B. E. *From Versailles to Munich, 1918–1938,* 1939. Brief.

SCHUMAN, F. L. *Night over Europe: The Diplomacy of Nemesis, 1939–1940,* 1941.

SFORZA, C. *Europe and Europeans. A Study in Historical Psychology and International Politics,* 1936.

SFORZA, C. *The Totalitarian War and After. Personal Recollections and Political Considerations,* 1941.

SNYDER, L. L. *Race: A History of Modern Ethnic Theories,* 1939.

STALEY, E. *Raw Materials in War and Peace,* 1937. Effects of unequal distribution.

STRAUSZ-HUPÉ, R. *Geopolitics. The Struggle for Space and Power,* 1942.

STREIT, C. K. *Union Now: A Proposal for a Federal Union of Democracies of the North Atlantic,* 1939.

STREIT, C. K. *Union Now with Britain,* 1941.

STURMTHAL, A. *The Tragedy of European Labor, 1918–1939,* 1943.

TAYLOR, E. *The Strategy of Terror,* 1940. Nazi propaganda technique.

The Atlantic Charter and Africa from an American Standpoint, 1942.

The Background of Our War, 1942. From lectures prepared by U. S. War Department.

The Black Book of Poland, 1942. German decrees and actions.

THOMPSON, V. *Postmortem on Malaya,* 1943.

TOBIN, H. J. and BIDWELL, P. W. *Mobilizing Civilian America,* 1940.

TOLISCHUS, O. *They Wanted War*, 1940. Nazi preparations.

United Nations Information Office *War and Peace Aims. Extracts from Statements of United Nations Leaders*, 1943.

United States, Department of State *Peace and War, United States Foreign Policy, 1931–1941*, 1943.

United States, War Department *The German Campaign in Poland, September 1 to October 5, 1939*, 1942. Brief.

VARWELL, J. H. *The War up to Date*, 1942. Brief, British account.

WALLER, W., ed. *War in the Twentieth Century*, 1940. Background of the war.

WELLER, G. *Singapore Is Silent*, 1943.

WERTH, A. *The Last Days of Paris*, 1940.

WERTH, A. *The Twilight of France*, 1942.

WILLKIE, W. L. *One World*, 1943. Account of trip around world.

WILLOUGHBY, W. W. *Japan's Case Examined: With Supplementary Chapters on the Far Eastern Policies of the United States, and the Significance to the World of the Conflict in the Far East*, 1940.

WISKEMANN, E. *Prologue to War*, 1940. Good on Nazi "infiltration."

WOLFERS, A. *Britain and France between Two Wars: Conflicting Strategies of Peace since Versailles*, 1940. Indispensable.

WOOD, B. *Peaceful Change and the Colonial Problem*, 1940.

WUORINEN, J. H. *Nationalism in Modern Finland*, 1931.

Index

INDEX

Names preceded by "de" or "von" are listed under the names themselves, e.g., under Valera and Hindenburg. The first names of persons may generally be found on the first page reference to those persons, except that full names of British peers are given in the index. The dates given for persons are those of birth and death, except for rulers and popes, whose dates are those of incumbency. Battles are listed under the cities or places after which they are named. All treaties, pacts, agreements, protocols, conventions, and concordats are listed under Treaties.

Abbas Hilmi II (1892–1914), 275.
Abbeville, 766, 767.
Abd-el-Krim, 376–377, 379.
Abdul Hamid II (1876–1909), 629.
Abdul Illah, 801 and n.3.
Abdul Mejid, 639.
Abetz, O., 777, 779.
Abraham Lincoln Battalion, 393.
Acerbo Election Law, 339–340.
Achilles, 754.
Action Française, 315n., 322–323.
Addis Ababa, 363, 367, 794.
Aden, Gulf of, 363.
Admiral Graf Spee, 754.
Adowa, 364.
Adrianople (Edirne), 635.
Adriatic Sea, 4, 7, 13, 22–24, 93–94, 112, 332–333, 362, 370, 627.
Advance Guard, 343.
Aegean Sea, 113, 608, 635.
Afghanistan, 8, 185, 208n., 209, 590, 647, 801n.2.
Africa, 9, 10–11, 12, 23, 60, 93, 96n.1, 144–145, 198, 200–205, 362–369, 589, 751n., 791–794, 801 and n.1, 802–804, 834–836.
Afrika Korps, 803, 834, 836.
Agadir Crisis, 10.
"Aggressor," 179–180, 185, 241, 366, 595n.1, 724, 745, 815.
Agrarian conditions, 118, 169; Austria, 472, 476; Bulgaria, 607–610; Czechoslovakia, 504, 506–508, 509 and n.; France, 329–330, 780; Germany, 413, 424, 432, 449–450; Great Britain, 237; Greece, 615; Hungary, 486, 487, 491–

492; Ireland, 269, 272–273; Italy, 334–335, 349; Japan, 665, 666; Latin America, 215–221, 224–225, 227–228; Palestine, 296ff.; Poland, 525–528; Romania, 599–602; Russia, 539–540, 552, 564–571, 579–584; Spain, 372–374, 380; Turkey, 643, 645; United States, 687, 691, 695, 705, 706, 709, 710, 711, 712, 717 and n.; Yugoslavia, 627.
Agricultural Adjustment Act, 706.
Ahmed Ali Bey el-Abed, 328.
Ahmed Fuad. (*See* Fuad.)
Ahmed Zogu. (*See* Zog I.)
Ährenthal, Count von, 10.
"Aid to Britain," 719, 815, 817, 822–823.
Aimone, Duke of Spoleto, 800.
Air-Age Education Series, 787n.1.
Airplanes, 63–64, 105, 394–395, 431, 698, 711n., 737, 738, 745, 752–753, 754, 761, 763, 767, 769, 783, 784–786, 787–790, 792, 796, 803 and n., 812, 819n., 830 and n., 834 and n.1, 837.
Air Raid Precautions Services, 785–786.
Aisne River, 44, 55, 73, 768.
Ajaccio, 772.
Ajax, 754.
Alamein, El, 803–804, 834.
Åland Islands, 57, 134–135.
Albania, 22–23, 26, 47, 86, 116, 125, 196, 333, 350n.2, 362, 369–371, 398, 619, 734, 794–795.
Albert I (1909–1934), 19.
Albrecht, Archduke, 492–493.
Aleppo, 75.
Alessandri, A., 219.
Aleutian Islands, 655n.1, 831.

Alexander I, of Greece (1917–1920), 26, 614.

Alexander II, of Russia (1855–1881), 539.

Alexander I, of Yugoslavia (1921–1934), 313, 496, 621, 622, 623, 624–626.

Alexandra, Tsarina, 541, 553.

Alexandretta, 328–329, 755.

Alexandria, 277, 772, 791.

Alexis, Tsarevich, 541.

Alfonso XIII (1886–1931), 374, 376, 377, 380, 381 and n., 382, 384.

Algeciras Conference, 9.

Algeria, 772, 835.

Ali Fethi Bey, 638.

Allenby, E., 60, 276.

Allenstein, 101.

Allied Supreme Council, 71, 84, 333, 489, 521, 528, 535, 633.

Allies, First World War, 136, 176, 470, 486, 489, 502, 518, 520, 534, 544, 546, 551–552, 608, 614–615, 632–633, 727; and neutrals, 21ff., 653; peace aims, 36–37, 56–57, 67–70; advantages, 42; military operations, 42–60, 70–76; naval, 60–63; colonial, 60, 200; losses, 77; peace settlement, 79–116 passim.; reparation, 148–158, 162, 164–165, 166n.; war debts, 165–169; Second World War, see United Nations.

All-India Moslem League, 282–283.

All Quiet on the Western Front, 416.

Alsace-Lorraine, 3–4, 43, 49, 68, 69, 70, 76, 91, 101, 183, 323–326, 435.

Altmark, 754–755.

Alto-Adige. (*See* South Tirol.)

Alvear, M. T. de, 218.

Amanullah Khan (1919–1929), 208n.

Amau Declaration, 673.

American Federation of Labor, 708, 716–717.

American Legion, 686.

American Liberty League, 715.

"American Line" (Dalmatia), 94.

American Relief Administrations, 467, 692, 829n.2.

Amritsar, 283–284, 285.

Amsterdam, 764.

Anatolia, 22n., 23, 114–115, 631; *see also* Turkey.

Andalsnes, 761.

Andorra, 116.

Angers, 739.

Anglican Church, 246, 258.

Anglo-Egyptian Sudan, 8, 114, 276–277, 280, 635, 791, 794.

Anglo-French Coördinating Committee, 755.

Anglo-French friction over German policy, 150–151, 163, 174–175, 727–728, 733.

Anglo-French Union, proposal, 769.

Anglo-Persian Oil Company, 208.

Angora (Ankara), 632, 644.

Annunzio, G. d', Prince of Monteneveso, 333, 338.

Anschluss, 111, 161, 175, 194, 368, 451, 466, 468, 470, 471, 473–485, 507.

Antigua, 821.

Antioch, 328.

Anti-Semitism. (*See* Jews.)

Antonescu, J., 797–799.

Antwerp, 44, 66–67.

Anzac Area, 635.

Anzacs, 48.

Appeasement, 255, 316, 319, 321, 368, 396–398, 484, 511–514, 597, 728, 729–731, 733, 804 and n.1.

APRA, 223.

Arab Higher Committee, 300.

Arabia (Arabs), 21, 22n., 114, 294–301, 801n.2; *see also* Saudi Arabia.

Archangel, 551, 552, 596.

Arcos Raid, 593.

Ardahan, 57, 633.

Arditi, 333, 338.

Argentina, 138, 139, 171n., 211n.2, 213, 215, 216–219, 222, 223, 229.

Argonne, 74.

Armaments expenditures, 11n., 193n.2; *see also* Disarmament.

Armenia (Armenians), 22n., 57, 83, 86, 115, 329, 554, 555, 619, 633, 637, 646.

Armentières, 72.

Armistice, Austria-Hungary (Villa Giusti), 75, 465, 486; Bulgaria (Salonika), 75; China (Tangku), 672; France (Compiègne), 770–772, 820, 835; Germany (Compiègne), 76–77, 90n.1; Hungary (Belgrade), 486; Russia (Brest-Litovsk), 57; Turkey (Mudros), 75, 136, 631, (Mudania), 634.

Armistice Commission, Franco-German, 771.

Arnold, H. H., 787n.2.

Arras, 55, 71.

"Arsenal of democracy," 823.

Artels, 560, 584.

"Aryan" legislation, Germany, 143, 442ff., 449, 454.

Asia, 93, 205–210, 589, 590, 591.

Asia Minor. (*See* Anatolia.)

Asquith, Earl of Oxford and (1852–1928), 235, 238, 239, 240, 244.
Association for the Protection of American Rights in Mexico, 702.
Atatürk, M. K. (1880–1938), 115, 614, 629–644 passim.
Athenia, 738n.
Athens, 26.
Atlantic Charter, 824, 826–827.
Atrocities in war, 66, 735, 736, 742, 800, 829n.1.
Attlee, C. R., 251n.2.
Attrition, war of, 55, 777.
Auchinleck, C., 803.
Augustovo, Battle of, 46.
Australia, 60, 91, 103, 145 and n.1, 171n., 172, 258–259, 751n., 753, 792, 803, 831.
Austria, 194, 198, 332, 353–354, 363, 431, 437, 452, 485, 492, 507, 684–685; peace settlement, 96, 100n.1, 104, 110–112, 114, 115, 468, 469; reparation, 112, 159n., 475; German customs accord, 160–161, 163n.1, 433, 475–476; economic conditions, 161, 466–467, 469–473, 474, 475–485; establishment of republic, 465–469; loans to, 470, 475, 476, 477 and n.; Nazis, 472, 476–485; authoritarianism, 478–484; attack on socialists, 479–480; unions, 480n.; *Putsch* of 1934, 481–482; Habsburg restoration, 482–483; named Ostmark, 484n.1; *see also* Anschluss.
Austria-Hungary, 101, 422, 519; First World War, 3–7, 9–10, 12–17, 22–25, 39n., 45–47, 50–54, 57–59, 61, 68–69, 70, 74–75, 654; peace settlement, 79, 93–94, 110–112; disintegration, 74–75, 465–466, 500–502.
Austrian Legion, 478, 482.
Autarkie, 172, 272–273, 350, 430, 448–453.
Automobiles, 349, 698.
Avanguardia, 343.
Avanti, 336.
Avenol, J., 127.
"Aventine Secession," 340.
Aviation. (*See* Airplanes.)
Avlona. (*See* Valona.)
Axis Powers, 132n., 198–199, 219, 368, 396–398, 462, 729, 731, 734–735, 751–837 passim., 794, 796, 825, 834n.2.
Azaña, M. (1880–   ), 384, 385, 387, 388, 391, 395.
Azerbaijan, 554, 555.
Aznar, J., 382.

Baden, 457; System, 407–408.
Badgers, 587.
Badoglio, Pietro, 796.
Baghdad, 25, 60, 801.
Bahama Islands, 821.
Bahía, 224.
Baker, N. D., 86.
Baku, 551, 590, 813.
Baldomir, A., 220–221.
Baldwin of Bewdley, Earl (1867–   ), 65n.2, 196, 239–240, 242ff., 245, 247, 253–254 and n.2, 593.
Balfour, Earl of (1848–1930), 37, 83, 88–89; Declaration, 294, 300; Note, 166n.; Report, 259.
Balilla, 343 and n.1, 355.
Balkan Crisis (1908), 9–10; Entente, 193, 614, 620, 647; Federation, 616; League, 11.
Balkans, 196, 361–362, 598–628; First World War, 5–7, 9–10, 11, 20–26, 46ff., 70; peace settlement, 112–116, 598; Second World War, 794–801.
Balkan Wars (1912–1913), 11, 24, 369, 611, 797.
Balloon barrages, 785.
Baltic area, 195 and n.2, 537, 744; Germans, 741–742, 743.
Baluchistan, 801n.2.
Banat. (*See* Temesvár.)
Bank for International Settlements, 157–158, 162–164, 171.
Bank of England, 161, 252, 433; France, 316, 330; Poland, 526.
Bapaume, 50, 73.
Barcelona, 375, 381, 387, 388, 389, 394, 395.
Bare Year, The, 586–587.
Bari, 299.
Barnes, G. N., 83.
Barroso, G., 226.
Bartel, C., 522, 523.
Barthélemy, J., 775n.
Barthou, (J.) L., 313, 496.
Baruch, B., 97.
Bases-destroyers deal, 820–821.
Basque Provinces, 383, 387, 390, 393.
Bataan, 831.
"Battle of Agriculture," 349.
Batum, 57.
Bauer, as honorary title, 449.
Bauer, G., 99, 400.
Bavaria, 76, 92, 402, 406, 411, 413, 457.
"Bayer 205," 430n.
Bayonne pawnshop scandal, 311.
Beatty, D., 62.

Beck, Count von, 14.
Beck, J., 537, 738.
Bedny, D., 587.
Beirut, 75.
Belfort, 43.
Belgian Congo, 60, 202, 801n.1.
Belgium, 126n., 131, 145, 148, 151–152, 431; First World War, 17–19, 36, 43–45, 69, 76; peace settlement, 83, 97, 101, 103, 104, 106–107, 108; since 1918, 174, 180–183, 213, 732; Second World War, 752, 762, 764–766, 767.
Belgrade, 46, 486, 621, 622, 624, 800.
Bell, G., 21.
Bell, J., 100.
Belleau Wood, 72.
Below, O. von, 58.
Benavides, O. R., 221.
Benedict XV (1914–1922), 68.
Beneš, E. (1884–   ), 83, 500–503, 507, 510, 511–512, 516.
Bengazi, 793.
Bentham, J., 70n.
Beran, R., 516, 517.
Berchtesgaden, 483, 512.
Berchtold, Count von, 15–16, 18.
Berenguer, D., 380, 382.
Berlin, 400, 402–404, 409, 412, 432, 460, 837; Baghdad Railway, 12n.1, 634; Conference (1885), 200–201; Congress (1878), 6.
Bermuda, 821–822.
Bernhardi, F. von, 5.
Bernstorff, Count von, 31.
Besant, A., 283n.
Bessarabia, 58, 552, 554, 599, 600, 744, 796.
Bethlehem, 299.
Behtlen, Count (1874–   ), 488, 489, 490, 492–493, 494, 499.
Bethmann Hollweg, T. von, 17, 18, 400, 409.
Bethune, 72.
Bevin, E. (1884–   ), 762.
"Big Bertha," 71.
"Big Five," 110; "Four," 85, 94, 110, 144; "Ten," 84–85; "Three," 85, 87.
Bihar, 293.
Bilbao, 396n.
Bismarck, Prince, 6, 7n.2, 87, 151, 453.
Bismarck, 830n.
Bitlis, 115.
Bizerte, 772.
"Black-and-Tans," 263.
"Black Hand," 14 and n.1, 15, 17.
Black List of American firms, 29.

Black Sea, 58, 397.
"Black Shirts." (See Arditi, British Union of Fascists, and Schutzstaffeln.)
"Blank Check," 16.
Bliss, T., 80, 98.
Blockade, during First World War, 29–30, 35, 42, 61, 76, 400, 551, 553; after armistice, 87n., 403, 467, 486, 488, 591; of China, 677, 679; during Second World War, 753, 784, 820, 823, 834.
Blomberg, W. von, 462.
Blood-and-soil concept, 453.
Blücher, V., 660.
"Blood purge," 460–461, 481.
Blue Cross Shells, 65.
"Blue Eagle," 708.
"Blue Shirts," Egyptian, 281; Irish, 272.
Blum, L. (1872–   ), 312, 314–319, 322, 397, 775, 780–781.
Boch, A. von, 140.
Bodelschwingh, F. von, 455–456.
Boer Revolt, 60.
Boghos Nubar Pasha, 83, 86.
Bohemia, 112, 500 and n., 504, 506, 510, 516, 517, 829n.1.
Bolivia, 126n., 138–139, 211n.2, 213, 214, 218, 221, 229, 723.
Bolshevism, 22, 57–58, 68, 89, 545–597 passim.; origin of name, 542n.; influence of, on France, 769, 774, 776–777.
Bombay, 790n.
Bonar Law, A. (1858–1923), 83, 238–239.
Bondfield, M., 249.
Bonnet, G., 319, 321.
Bonus Bills, 686, 690, 706, 712; Expeditionary Force, 697.
Book of Common Prayer, 246.
Borah, W. E. (1865–1940), 682.
Bordeaux, 44, 768n.
Boris III (1918–   ), 194, 608, 610–611.
Borodin, M., 659, 660.
Bose, S. C., 293–294.
Bosnia-Hercegovina, 4, 9–10, 14–15, 46, 112, 621.
Boston policemen's strike, 690.
Botha, L., 83.
Boulogne, 44.
Bourbon-Parma, S. de, 69.
Bourgeois, L., 90.
Boxer Indemnity, 660; Rebellion, 649.
Boycott. (See Economic boycott.)
Boy-Ed, K., 34.
Bratianu, J. (1864–1927), 83, 86, 602, 603.
Bratianu, J. C. (1821–1891), 602.
Bratianu, V., 602–604, 605.
Bratislava, 515.

Brauchitsch, W. von, 737.
Brazil, 39, 124, 130, 139, 211n.2, 213, 214, 217, 218, 222, 223–226, 229, 435–436, 837.
"Bread Peace" (1918), 58n.
Bremen, 757.
Brenner Pass, 93, 112.
Breslau, 21.
Brest-Litovsk, armistice and conference, 57.
Briand, A. (1862–1932), 160, 173, 180, 183, 303, 304, 305, 306, 308–310 and n., 434, 436, 474n., 475.
Brihuega, 394.
British Broadcasting Company, 299n.1.
British East Africa. (See Kenya.)
British East India Company, 282.
British Guiana, 821.
British Somaliland, 791.
British Union of Fascists, 249n., 257.
Brockdorff-Rantzau, Count von, 98–99, 406.
Bronstein, L. D. (See Trotsky, L. D.)
Browder, E., 714.
"Brown House," 424; "Shirts," see Sturmabteilungen.
Bruges, 44.
Brüning, H. (1885–   ), 161, 163, 420–421, 425–426, 432–433.
Brussels, 44, 765; Conference (1937), 677–678; Line, 136–137.
Brussilov, A., 45, 52–53.
Bryan, W. J., 27, 32n., 691n.
"Buchlau Bargain," 10.
Buckingham Palace, 785.
Budapest, 485, 488, 489.
Budenny, S., 812.
Buenos Aires, 139, 215, 216, 723.
Bukharin, N., 574, 575.
Bukovina, 25, 57, 112, 599, 600, 744, 797.
Bulgaria, 7n.1, 11, 194, 196; First World War, 21, 24–25, 26, 39n., 41, 47, 57, 73, 75; peace settlement, 100n.1, 104, 110, 112–113, 115, 607; reparation, 113, 159n., 607; and Greece, 113, 608, 612; and Yugoslavia, 113, 612, 613, 621; economic conditions, 607–608; compulsory labor, 609 and n.; fascism, 611; Macedonia, 611–614; Second World War, 797, 799, 810, 825.
Burgenland, 114, 469, 473.
Burgos, 394.
Burke-Wadsworth Act, 818 and n.2–819.
Burleson, A., 80n.
Burma, 289, 801n.2, 830, 831, 833; Road, 804n.

Business under fascism, 350, 448–452.
Butler Commission, 287n.

CAA, 819n.
Caballero, F. L., 394.
Cadorna, L., 51, 59.
Cagoulards, 317.
Cairo, 276, 278.
Calais, 44, 767.
Caliacra, 797.
Calinescu, A., 607.
Caliphate, 639.
Calles, P. E., 227, 229.
Camacho, M. A., 228, 231.
Cambon, J., 82.
Cambrai, 56, 74.
Camelots du roi, 303, 315n.
Cameroons, 60, 145.
Camouflage, 62, 64.
Campagna, 350.
Canada, 131, 171n., 237, 250, 254, 258–260, 656, 751n., 753, 816, 820, 821.
Canary Islands, 392.
Cannon, J., 691n.
"Cannon before butter," 450.
Cantigny, 72n.
Canton, 651, 652, 668.
Canton Island, 831.
Caporetto, 58–60, 71, 332, 334.
Cárdenas, L., 228, 231.
Caribbean area, 215, 217, 221, 821–822.
Carinthia, 469.
Carli, M., 359.
Carmona, A. O. de F., 396.
Carol I (Prince, 1866–1881; King, 1881–1914), 25, 602.
Carol II (1930–1940), 603–607, 744, 797–798.
Carpathian Mountains, 46, 58, 114, 507, 508, 797.
Carpatho-Ukraine, 499, 508–509, 516, 517; see also Ruthenia.
Cartels, 430–431.
Casablanca, 828, 835, 837.
"Cash-and-carry policy," 816–817.
Castellorizo, 635.
Castillo, J. del, 392.
Castillo, R. S., 219.
Casualties, 64–65, 77, 237, 332, 748.
Catalonia (Catalonians), 375–376, 379, 380, 382–385, 387–388, 389, 390, 394.
Catholic Action, Germany, 458; Italy, 357–359; Spain, 386.
Catholic Church, Austria, 474, 480, 484-n.2; Czechoslovakia, 504–505; France, 303, 304, 306, 322–323, 324, 775, 780;

Catholic Church—*Continued*
Germany, 424, 452, 457–458; Great Britain, 246, 250; Ireland, 273; Italy, 352, 354–359; Latin America, 228–231; Spain, 373, 378, 381, 383–386, 389, 390; Uruguay, 220; Yugoslavia, 626; and First World War, 23, 68.

Caucasus, 582, 813–814.

Cecil of Chelwood, Viscount, 90.

Central America, 213, 215, 217, 221, 701–702, 722–723.

Central Powers, 519, 551; name, 21n.; and neutrals, 20ff.; peace moves, 36–37, 67–69; advantages, 40–41; military operations, 42–60, 70–76, 546; friction, 68–69, 486; war losses 77; peace settlement, 79–116, 148.

Cerda, P. A., 219.

C. G. T., 316, 320–321.

Chaco dispute, 138–139, 723.

Chamberlain, (J.) A. (1863–1937), 180, 242, 246–247, 253, 434, 436, 593.

Chamberlain, H. S., 5.

Chamberlain, (A.) N. (1869–1940), 253, 254, 300, 366n.1, 368, 512–514 and n.1, 729, 735, 737, 738n., 751, 762.

Chamber of Fasces and Corporations, 348.

Champagne, 44.

Changchun, 652, 668.

Chang Hsueh-liang (Chang Hsiao-liang), 662, 663, 665, 668, 675–676.

Changkufeng, 674.

Charles I, of Austria, IV, of Hungary (1916–1918), 52, 68–69, 75, 465–466 and n., 485, 486, 489 and n., 495.

Charles, of Hesse, 58n.

Charles III, of Spain (1759–1788), 373.

Charlotte, of Luxembourg (1919–   ), 764n.

Charter of Labor, 345–346.

Chatalja, 115.

Château-Thierry, 72, 73.

Chautemps, C., 317–318.

Cheka, 553, 564; *see also* OGPU.

Chelmsford, Andrew Thesiger, Viscount, 283.

Chemin des Dames, 55.

Chernozemsky, V. G., 496 and n.

Chetniks, 800.

Chiang Kai-shek (1888–   ), 207, 660–662, 668, 675–676, 677, 804, 837.

Chiapas, 230.

Chicago, 689.

Chicherin, G., 176, 591, 594.

Child labor, United States, 708, 712, 718.

Chile, 61, 139, 211n.2, 213, 215, 216–217, 219, 222, 229.

China, 159; First World War, 20, 39, 207, 651, 653–654; peace settlement, 96, 104, 654; and Japan, 96, 209, 649, 651–658, 662–680, 804–808; League, 96, 126n., 435, 667–672, 677–678; Russia, 590, 593, 659, 662; United States, 649, 652–658, 662, 663n., 667, 670–671, 677–680, 702–703, 724; education, 649, 658–659; Kuomintang, 650–652, 659–661, 665, 676; foreign trade, 655, 662–663 and n.; boycotts, 655, 668–670 and n., 671; Sian mutiny, 675–676; Second World War, 804–808, 831.

Chinese Eastern Railway, 660, 662, 663, 672.

"Chinese National Government," 804.

Chosen, 83, 117, 665.

Christian X (1912–   ), 758.

Chungking, 678, 804.

Church conflicts, Czechoslovakia, 504–505; Egypt, 278–279; France, 303, 304, 306, 322–323, 324, 775; Germany, 452, 454–459, 484n.2; Great Britain, 246; Italy, 352, 354–359; Mexico, 229–231, 702 and n.2; Russia, 561, 565, 570, 587–588; Spain, 374, 383–386, 389, 390; Turkey, 640; United States, 692; Yugoslavia, 626.

Churchill, W. S. (1874–   ), 253, 753, 756–757, 762, 769, 782n.2, 795, 796, 810, 824, 826, 828, 834, 836–837.

Church of England, 246, 258.

Ciano di Cortellazzo, Count (N.) G. (1903–   ), 361, 734, 796.

Cilicia, 633, 634.

C. I. O., 716–717, 720 and n.

Cividale, 58.

Civil Aeronautics Authority, 819n.

Civilian Conservation Corps, 706, 708.

Civil Works Administration, 709, 710.

Clark, M. W., 834.

Clayton Anti-Trust Act, 681.

Clemenceau, G. (1841–1929), 55 and n., 81–83, 85, 86n., 88, 89, 91, 92, 96, 98–99, 110, 302–303, 654.

Coal Act, 257–258; Mines Act, 250; strike, British, 242–244.

Cóbh, 268.

Coblenz, 76, 91, 109.

Codes. (*See* Industrial codes.)

Codreanu, C. Z., 605–607.

Collective farms, 567n., 577, 579, 580–582, 584 and n.

Collins, M. (1890–1922), 263, 265.

Cologne, 40, 76, 91, 109, 412, 435.
Colombia, 211n.2, 215, 217, 221, 229.
Colonies, German claims, 424, 430n., 452-n.2, 731.
Color-Bar Bill, 202.
Columbia University, 132n., 699.
Comintern. (*See* Third International.)
Comitadjis, 612–613.
Comité Catholique, Le, 66.
Commercial Press of Shanghai, 659.
Commissions, Inter-Allied, 105, 409, 410, 436.
Committee for Industrial Organization, 716.
Committee for the Defense of Islam, 278.
Committee of Inquiry on Production, 320n.
Committee of Union and Progress, 631.
Committee on Public Information, 66.
Communism, 357; Austria, 466, 473, 478; Brazil, 225; Bulgaria, 609, 610 and n.; Chile, 219; China, 660, 661, 675–676, 677, 703; Czechoslovakia, 504, 516; France, 312, 314, 315, 318, 322n., 756, 777; Germany, 161, 400, 403–404, 405, 406, 409, 413, 419, 421, 424–426, 437–438, 459; Great Britain, 241; Greece, 618; Hungary, 486–488, 490; Italy, 334–335, 337; Russia, 542n., 544–597 passim.; Spain, 382, 388, 391, 394, 395; Turkey, 645; United States, 698, 714, 717, 720 and n.
Communist International. (*See* Third International.)
Communist Manifesto, 555.
Community Chest, 700.
Companys, L., 390.
Compiègne Forest, 76, 770.
Compromise of 1867, 485 and n.
Concordats. (*See* Treaties, Concordats.)
Confédération Générale du Travail, 316, 320–321.
Conference of Ambassadors, 105–106, 110n., 112, 134, 469, 536, 619.
Confessional Synod, 456–457.
Congress-League Scheme, 283.
Congress of Berlin (1878), 6; of Industrial Organizations, 717, 720 and n.; of the Peoples of the East, 590; of Vienna (1814–1815), 3, 518.
Conrad von Hötzendorf, Count, 14, 16.
Conscription, 11, 186, 188; Austria, 483; Egypt, 281; France, 204; Germany, 450, 452, 461; Great Britain, 50, 71, 732; Ireland, 262; United States, 71, 818 and n.2–819.

Constantine I (1913–1917, 1920–1922), 26, 614, 615.
Constantinople (Istanbul), 21, 115, 632, 635, 637n.
Constitutions, Albania, 371; Austria, 466, 468–469, 475, 480, 482; Brazil, 225; Bulgaria, 608; Chile, 219; China, 649, 661n.; Czechoslovakia, 503; Danzig, 532; France, 303n., 312, 313, 773, 774, 775–776, 778–779; Germany, 406–408, 438 and n.2; Greece, 617, 618; Hungary, 489–490; India, 282, 284, 290–293; Ireland, 266–267, 271, 273; Lithuania, 536; Mexico, 227, 229, 702; Palestine, 294; Poland, 521, 522, 523, 524, 525n.; Russia, 555–561, 562, 587; Spain, 379, 383, 384–385; Syria, 327; Turkey, 629, 632–633 and n., 639–640, 641; United States, 684, 697, 706n.1, 710n., 713–714; Uruguay, 220; Yugoslavia, 622–625.
Continental Steel Cartel, 431.
Contraband, 28 and n.
Convoys, 62, 833n.
Cook, A. J., 244 and n.2.
Coolidge, C. (1872–1933), 188, 688, 689–692, 701, 702, 703, 704, 714.
Copper sheets, sent to Germany, 29; Italy, 350n.2.
Coral Sea, Battle of the (1942), 831.
Corfu, 26, 75, 619, 621.
Cork, city, 263.
Coronation, British (1937), 254, 256, 274.
Coronel, Battle of (1914), 61.
Corporations, Italy, 345–348.
Corsica, 86, 321, 361, 369, 772, 835.
Cosgrave, W. (1880–), 265–270, 272.
Cossack, 755.
Cossacks, 812.
Costa Rica, 39, 124, 211n.2, 229.
Cottin, E., 90.
Coughlin, C. E., 714.
Council of Ambassadors. (*See* Conference of Ambassadors.)
Council of Five, 110; Four, 85, 94, 110, 144; Ten, 84–85; Three, 85, 87.
Council of National Defense, 36.
Councils of Confidence, 448.
Courland, 47, 57; *see also* Latvia.
Covenant of the League of Nations, 112, 127; drafting, 90–91, 123–124; preamble, 124; amendments, 124; maintenance of peace, 132–139; Article 8, 178; Article 10, 132, 365, 682–683; Article 11, 132, 365; Article 12, 133; Article 13, 133; Article 14, 128; Article 15, 133,

Covenant of the League of Nations—
Continued
365, 366 and n.2; Article 16, 133, 182,
366, 435n., 679; Article 17, 133; Article
19, 185 and n.1; Article 22, 144, 203;
Article 23, 130.
Coventry, 785.
Cox, J. M., 683–684.
Cracow, 519, 741.
Creditanstalt, 161.
Creel, G., 66.
Crete, 617, 618, 787 and n.2, 796, 801.
Crewe House, 66.
Crimea, 552, 554, 813.
Crime Wave, United States, 688–689, 691,
694.
Cripps Mission, 831.
Cristeros, 230.
Croatia-Slavonia (Croats), 114, 496 and
n., 621, 625–627, 799–800.
Croix de Feu, 312, 314.
CROM, 228.
Crown Prince, Germany, 49, 76, 402.
Cuba, 39, 211n.2, 213, 215, 217, 229, 722.
Cumberland, 754.
Curtis, C., 692, 697.
Curtius, J., 421, 437.
Curzon, George, Marquess of, 635; Line,
535.
Cushendun, Ronald McNeill, Baron, 189.
Cvetkovich, D., 627.
CWA, 709, 710.
Cyprus, 21, 114, 635, 801.
Cyrenaica, 793, 802–803; see also Libya.
Czechia, 516–517.
Czech National Council, 502.
Czechoslovakia, 431, 451, 452n.1, 488,
489, 521, 728; peace settlement, 83, 101,
109, 112, 114, 116; minorities, 112, 114,
116, 503n., 508–515; foreign policy,
175, 180, 185 and n.2, 435–436, 506–
507; Sudeten areas, 319, 499, 510–514;
Czech-Slovak controversy, 509; Nazism,
510–514; break-up, 514–517; govern-
ment-in-exile, 810.
Czechoslovak National Church, 505.
Czechowicz, G., 523.
Czechs, 46n., 75.
Czernin, Count von und zu Chudenitz,
69.

Daily Mail, 81, 86n.1.
Dairen, 664, 667.
Dakar, 773, 781, 836.
Daladier, E. (1884–   ), 312, 318–322,
512ff., 738n., 751, 756, 780–781.

Dalmatia, 23, 86, 93–94, 112, 337, 362,
621.
Damascus, 75, 326–327.
Dandi, 288.
Danube River, 109, 112.
Danubian federation, 492, 508.
Danzig, 95, 101, 102, 184n.1, 532–534,
733–734, 735, 738.
Darányi, K., 497–498.
Dardanelles, 11, 47, 70, 634; see also
Straits, at Constantinople.
Darlan, J. F., 779, 835, 836.
Darmstädter und Nationalbank, 163.
Darré, R. W., 449.
Das, C. R., 286, 287.
Daudet, A., 4.
Daudet, L., 303.
Daugherty, H. M., 686, 688.
Davis, J. W., 690–691, 715.
Davis, N., 97.
Davison, H. P., 34.
Dawes, C. G., 153, 690.
Dawes Plan, 153–155, 157, 158, 241, 306,
414, 418, 428.
Day of the Saxon, 5.
Dead Sea, 297.
Debs, E. V., 683, 691n.
Debs Column, 393.
Decline of the West, 415–416.
Delbos, Y., 318.
Delcassé, T., 8–9.
Delectissimi Nobis, 386.
Delhi Pact (1931), 289; Resolution (1937),
293.
Demerdjis, C., 618.
"Democratic meetingism," 580.
Dempsey, J., 699.
Denby, E., 688.
Denikin, A., 552, 554.
Denmark, 101, 758 and n., 761, 762, 822
and n.
Dentz, H., 802.
Depressed areas, British, 257.
Depression. (See Great Depression.)
Dernière Classe, La, 4.
Déroulède, P., 4.
Deschanel, P., 303.
Destroyers-bases deal, 821–822.
Dethronement Act, 489.
Deutsches Museum, 431.
De Wet, C., 60.
Dewey, C. S., 526–527.
Diaz, General A., 59, 74, 75, 486.
Diaz, President A., 701.
Díaz, P., 227, 229.
Dies, M., 817.

Dimitrijevich, D., 14 and n.2.
Disarmament, 69, 104–106 and n.2, 112, 113, 114, 127, 161, 177, 178ff., 184, 185–193, 241, 426, 686, 721, 728, 731–732 and n.1; Conference, Geneva (1932–1934), 191–193, 596, 705, 721.
Disney, W., 699.
Dive bombers, 767, 786–787, 792.
Divorce, Great Britain, 257; Italy, 342, 357; Spain, 385; Russia, 565; Turkey, 640.
Dmowski, R., 83, 519, 520.
Dnieprostroy, 578.
Dobruja, 58, 113, 797.
Dodecanese Islands, 23, 93, 114, 361, 618–619, 635, 792.
Dogger Bank, 61.
Doheny, E. L., 688–689.
Dollfuss, E. (1892–1934), 476, 477–482, 483, 495.
Dominican Republic, 126n., 211n.2, 217, 229, 723.
Dominions, British, 256, 258–260, 264, 271, 463, 751n.
Donovan, W. J., 777.
Don River, 814.
Dopolavoro, 345 and n.
Dortmund, 151.
Doumer, P. (1857–1932), 304.
Doumergue, G. (1863–), 303–304, 312–313.
Draft. (See Selective Service Act.)
Drang nach Osten, 5.
Dreadnought, 8 and n.2.
Drummond, (J.) E., 127.
Druse Revolt, 326–327.
Dublin, 262, 271n.1.
Duca, J., 605.
Duff-Cooper, A., 762.
Duisburg, 149.
Dumba, K., 34.
Dune, 104.
Dunkirk, 44, 766–767, 782n.2, 784.
Durazzo, 370, 371.
Durostor, 797.
Düsseldorf, 149.
Dust Bowl, 717.
Düsterberg, T., 425.
Dutch Guiana, 824.
Dyarchy, 284, 287.
Dyer, R. E., 283–284.
Dzerzhinsky, F., 553, 574.
Dzhugashvili, J. V. (See Stalin.)

East Africa Native Association, 201.
Eastern Locarno, 196.

Easter Rebellion, 262, 263.
Eastman, J. B., 707.
East Prussia, 44, 45–46, 95, 449, 534.
Ebert, F. (1871–1925), 76, 399, 402–403, 405, 408, 409, 410, 418.
Eckhardt, T., 497.
Economic boycotts, 209, 450, 655, 668–670 and n., 671, 678.
Ecuador, 124, 211n.2, 218, 221, 229.
Eden, (R.) A. (1897–), 253, 254, 255, 366n.1, 367, 484, 762.
Edib, H., 641.
Edirne, 635.
Education, Africa, 200, 202–203, 204; Alsace-Lorraine, 323–324; Brazil, 224; China, 649, 658–659; Czechoslovakia, 505, 508–509; Germany, 408, 424, 442, 453–454; Ireland, 268; Italy, 346, 351, 356–359; Latin America, 221–223, 228n., 229–230; Poland, 529; Russia, 541, 562; Spain, 386; Turkey, 641–642; United States, 222, 698–700.
Edward VII (1901–1910), 8.
Edward VIII (1936), 250, 254, 286.
Egypt, 21, 104, 114, 126n., 275–282, 635, 792–793, 801, 834.
Eighteenth Amendment. (See Prohibition.)
Eight-Point Program, 511.
Éire. (See Ireland.)
Eisenhower, D. D., 835.
Eisner, K., 402, 406.
Ekaterinburg (Sverdlovsk), 553.
Elections, method of, France, 314n.2.
Elite Guards. (See Schutzstaffeln.)
Elizabeth, Queen of England, 254.
Elk Hills, 688.
Emden, 61.
Emergency Housing Corporation, 709.
Emerson, H., 463, 464.
Emigration, from Alsace-Lorraine, 323n.; Finnish cessions, 748–749; Germany, 445, 462–464; Great Britain, 237–238, 257; Italy, 334, 342, 361; Poland, 527; Spain, 373.
Empire State Building, 700.
Engels, F., 555.
England, 247, 255; see also Great Britain.
English Channel, 29, 62, 766–767, 783.
Epernay, 72.
Epinal, 43.
Eritrea, 362, 363, 366, 368.
Erivan, 633.
Ersatzmittel, 430, 450–451.
Erzberger, M., 123n.2, 400, 405, 410.
Erzurum, 115, 631.

"Escalator clause," 190.
Esch-Cummins Act, 684.
Esperey. (See Franchet d'Esperey.)
Essen, 400.
Estonia, 57, 58n., 83, 116, 184n.1, 185, 553.
Ethiopia, 198, 251n.2, 350, 362–368, 794.
Eucharistic Congress (1932), 271n.1.
Eupen, 101, 765.
European federation, 160, 308.
Evian Conference, 463.
Exchange Equalization Fund, 255.
Exeter, 754.
Experts' Plan. (See Dawes and Young Plans.)
Export-Import Bank, 214.
Extraterritoriality, 280, 635, 641, 646, 660.

Facta, L., 339, 470.
Fair Labor Standards Act, 717–718.
Falaba, 31.
Falange. (See Phalanx.)
Falkenhausen, A. von, 679.
Falkenhayn, E. von, 54.
Falkland Islands, Battle of (1914), 61.
Fall, A. B., 688–689.
Falsehood in War-Time, 66.
Famine, Russia, 567, 582.
Far East, 83, 185n.2, 187, 551n.2, 555n.1, 648–680, 686, 724, 803, 804–808, 823–825, 829–833.
Far Eastern Republic, 555n.1.
Farinacci, R., 340.
Farm Bloc, 687; Credit Administration, 706; Security Administration, 717.
Faroe Islands, 762, 822n.1.
Farouk I (1936–   ), 280, 281.
Fasces, 338.
Fasci di combattimento, 337; femminili, 343.
Fascism, Austria, 478–484; Brazil, 226; Bulgaria, 611; Czechoslovakia, 510–514; Egypt, 281; France, 312–313, 314, 317; Germany, 417, 421–426, 437–464; Great Britain, 249n., 257 and n.2; Hungary, 494, 498–499; Ireland, 272; Italy, 336ff.; Japan, 667 and n., 676; Poland, 525; Romania, 605–607; Russia, 576; Spain, 390, 392–398.
Fascist Grand Council, 341–342, 346–348.
Fascisti Exposed, The, 340n.
Faulhaber, M. von, 458.
Fechner, R., 707.
Feder, G. (1883–1941), 422, 424.
Federal Bureau of Investigation, 817.

Federal Deposit Insurance Corporation, 707 and n.
Federal Farm Board, 695, 706.
Federalization Manifesto, 465, 485.
Federal Reserve Act, 681, 696; System, 696, 706, 707, 710.
Fehrenbach, K., 410.
Feisal I (1921–1933), 145n.2.
Feisal II (1939–   ), 145n.2, 801n.3.
Ferdinand I, of Bulgaria (Prince 1887–1908; King 1908–1918), 112–113, 607, 608.
Ferdinand I, of Romania (1914–1927), 25, 602, 603–604.
Fermanagh, 267.
Fethi Bey, Ali, 638.
Fifth-column activities, 760, 764, 817, 820, 830.
Fighting French. (See Free French.)
Figli della Lupa, 343.
Fiji Islands, 831.
Finland (Finns), 57, 58n., 116, 126n., 134–135, 552, 721, 744–750, 810.
Finland, Gulf of, 744, 745, 748.
Finnish-Russian Wars, 552, 744–750, 756, 810.
First International, 588n.
Fischer, K., 417.
Fisher Education Act, 235.
Fiume, 89, 93–94, 332–333 and n., 337.
Five-Year Plan, First (1928–1932), 571, 577–583; Second (1933–1937), 583–584; Third (1938–1942), 584–585, 736, 809, 811.
Flanders, 44, 48.
Flandin, P., 313, 367.
"Flapper vote," 246, 247.
Flucht aus der Mark in die Ware, 413.
Foch, Ferdinand (1851–1929), 71–73, 75–76, 83, 91, 98.
Fokker, A., 63.
Fonck, R., 64.
Forbes, C. R., 688.
Ford, H. (1863–   ), 349, 428, 431.
Fordney-McCumber Tariff, 686, 694.
Foreign Relief and Rehabilitation, 829-n.2.
Formose, 754.
Forster, A., 738.
Foster, W. Z., 698.
"Four Freedoms," 828.
Fourteen Points, 69–70, 73, 76, 84, 88, 123, 206.
Four-Year Plan, German (1936–1940), 443, 445, 448, 450ff., 484.

France, 126, 131, 212, 379, 431, 433, 435n., 494, 512–514, 516, 593–594, 633–634, 709; First World War, 3–4, 7–11, 17–19, 21–26, 36, 43–45, 47–50, 54–56, 61, 70, 71–76; and Italy, 6–7, 13, 22, 44, 177, 190 and n., 318, 321, 361, 362, 363–369, 396–398; peace settlement, 79–110 passim., 727–728; security and disarmament, 91–93, 173–199 passim., 308–309, 316, 321, 729, 731–732 and n.l; reparation, 93, 96–97, 99n., 104, 148–159, 162, 164–165, 305; mandates, 144–145, 326–329; reconstruction, 150, 305; economic conditions, 150, 305–321, 329–331; war debts, 165–169, 311; colonies, 204; politics, 302–304, 756, 774, 776; anti-clericalism, 303, 304, 306, 322–323; franc stabilized, 304–307; insurance law, 308; riots (1934), 312; Popular Front, 314–320; sit-down strikes, 315; railways, 317n.1; trend to Right, 318ff.; reversal of foreign policy, 319; papacy, 322–323; people, 331; Second World War, 728, 730–732, 734, 737, 738, 746, 748, 751–770 passim., 791, 830; influence of Bolshevism, 774, 776–777, 796; armistice, 770–772, 835; fleet, 769, 770, 772–773; severance of British relations, 773; reasons for collapse, 773–778; Vichy, 778–782, 801–802, 808, 835–836; collaboration, 779–780; Far East, 805, 808, 824.

Franchet d'Esperey, L., 486.

Francis Ferdinand, Archduke (1863–1914), 3, 9, 14–15, 100, 625.

Francis Joseph (1848–1916), 5, 14, 16, 68, 465.

Franco y Bahamonde, F. (1892–), 368, 392–398.

Frank, H., 741.

Frauenfeld, A., 477.

Frazier-Lemke Farm Acts, 710, 713 and n.

Frederick William, Crown Prince (1882–), 49, 76, 402.

Freedom of the seas, 69, 76, 187, 723–724, 816–817.

Free French, 781, 793, 802, 835–836.

Freemasonry, 341, 446, 516.

French Equatorial Africa, 10–11, 96n.1, 781, 793.

French Indo-China, 679, 781, 806–808, 824, 830.

French North Africa, 321, 781–782, 791, 834–836.

French Revolution (1789), 774–775.

French Somaliland, 363–364, 772, 791, 794.

French West Africa, 773, 781, 834–835, 836.

Friedrich, S., 488–489.

Fries, A. A., 64–65.

Fritsch, W. von, 462.

Frossard, L. O., 318.

FSA, 717.

Fuad I (Sultan, 1917–1922; King, 1922–1936), 276–277, 279, 280.

Führerprinzip, 441, 448.

Funk, W., 450.

Gailani, R. A. Beg, 801, 802.

Galen. (See Blücher.)

Galicia, Austrian (Polish), 45–46, 47, 52–53, 57, 112, 527, 529; Spanish, 383, 387.

Galliéni, J. S., 44.

Gallipoli Campaign, 24, 47–48, 235, 631, 635.

Gambetta, L., 775.

Gamelin, M. G., 318, 321, 752, 766, 780–781.

Gandhi, M. K. (1869–), 285–294, 833.

Garbai, A., 487.

Garner, J. N., 697, 719.

Gaulle, C. J. de (1890–), 756, 768, 769, 777, 781, 836, 837n.

"Gay-Pay-Oo." (See OGPU.)

Gdynia, 533–534, 741.

General Staff, German, 41, 104, 461n.

General strike, Austria, 479; France, 320–321; Germany, 410; Great Britain, 243–244, 245, 593; Russia, 543; Spain, 375, 376, 390.

Geneva, 125, 127n., 130, 190; Conference (1927), 188, 704; (1931), 594–595; (1932–1934), 191–193, 596, 705, 721.

Genoa Economic Conference, 176, 591–592.

Gensoul, M. B., 772–773.

Gentile, G., 351.

George V, of Great Britain (1910–1936), 254, 264n., 266.

George VI, of Great Britain (1936–), 254, 274.

George II, of Greece (1922–1924, 1935–), 615, 616, 618, 794, 801n.1.

Georgia (U.S.S.R.), 55, 83, 554.

"German Austria," 111, 466–468.

German Christians, 455–457.

German East Africa, 60, 145.

German Evangelical Church, 455–457.

German South West Africa. (*See* South West Africa.)

German West Hungary, 114.

Germany, 212–213, 226, 308, 323–326, 354, 466, 468, 476–485, 510–514, 576, 684–685; First World War, 3–4, 6–12, 16–19, 20ff., 28ff., 40–76, 200, 211n.2, 399–402, 551, 651–652, 653; and Japan, 20, 199, 368, 398; colonies, 60, 200, 424, 430n.; revolution (1918), 73, 76, 401–404, 422; naval mutiny, 76, 401–402; peace settlement, 79–100 passim., 100–110, 178n., 406, 427–428, 727, 729, 733; reparation, 93, 96–97, 99n., 104, 106–109, 110, 148–159, 162, 164–165, 166n., 305, 414, 418, 420, 433; security and disarmament, 104–106 and n.2, 173–199 passim., 426, 732n.1; and League, 126, 130, 177, 180, 182, 193, 435–436; economic conditions, 149–150, 152, 153, 161–164, 400, 411–414, 424–425, 427–433, 447–453, 517, *see also under* reparation; inflation, 150, 411–414, 428; Customs Accord (1931), 160–161, 163n.1, 433; unemployment, 161n., 420, 424, 426, 429, 432, 447, 451; foreign relations, 173–199 passim., 396–398, 433–437, 473–485, 510–517, 533–535, 628 and n., 730–742; anti-Semitism, 297, 410, 422, 424, 441–445, 454; Spanish Civil War, 393, 395, 396–398; defense of republic, 404, 406, 409–411, 730; states' rights, 406, 408; constitution, 406–408; emergency powers of president, 407 and n., 421; education, 408, 424, 442, 453–454; presidential elections, 408, 418–419, 425; intellectual changes, 415–417; politics, 418–426, 445–447, 454, 459–462; Nazi Party, organization, 422–425; swastika, 423, 438, 461n.; Hitler chancellor, 426; "rationalization," 428–429; reasons for rise of Nazism, 439–441; Four-Year Plan, 443, 445, 450ff.; Labor Corps, 447–448; capital-labor relations, 448; Food Estate, 449–450; labor shortage, 451, 452; religion, 452, 454–459; sterilization law, 454, 458; legal concepts, 454; purge (1934), 460–461, 481; refugees, 462–464; Second World War, 727–728, 730–742, 746, 752, 757–772, 774, 779–787, 792, 796, 798–804, 808–814, 820 and n., 825, 829n.1, 834n., 835.

Germany and the Next War, 5.

Gestapo, 459n.1, 741.

Gezireh, 277.

Ghazi, of Iraq (1933–1939), 145n.2; of Turkey, *see* Atatürk.

Ghent, 44.

Gheorghiev, K., 611, 613.

"Ghetto Laws," 443–444.

Giant Farm, 579; "Mania," 583.

Gibraltar, 374, 791.

Gibson, H., 188.

Gilbert, S. P., 154–155.

Gil Robles, J. M., 390, 392.

Giolitti, G. (1842–1928), 333.

Giovani Fascisti, 343.

Giovanna, Princess of Italy, 194.

Giovinezza, 338.

Giraud, H. H., 835, 836, 837n.

Giuriati, G., 358–359.

Glass-Steagall Act, 707.

Gleichschaltung, 441.

Gliders, 787n.2.

Göben, 21.

Godesberg, 512, 514.

Goebbels, P. J. (1897–   ), 439, 444, 453, 460, 510, 811, 837.

Goemboes, J. (*See* Gömbös.)

Goering, H. W. (*See* Göring.)

Goga, O., 606.

Gold Reserve Act, 710.

Gold standard, 170, 252, 309, 665, 706.

Gömbös, J., 489, 494–495, 497.

Gompers, S. (1850–1924), 691n.

Good-Neighbor Policy, 722–723.

Gore-McLemore Resolution, 34.

Gorgoulov, P., 304.

Göring, H. W. (1893–   ), 426, 438, 441–442, 446, 450–451, 455, 460, 837.

Gorizia, 23, 52, 58, 93.

Gorki, M., 587.

Gosplan, 577, 580, 582–583.

Gotenhafen, 741.

Gott strafe England, 69.

Government of India Act (1858), 282; (1909), 282; (1919), 284; (1935), 291–293.

GPU. (*See* OGPU.)

Grabski, L., 526, 529.

Gradisca, 23, 93.

Graf Zeppelin, 431.

Grandees, 383n.

Grandi, D., 191, 362.

Graz, 473, 484.

Graziani, R., 792–794.

Great Britain, 126, 131, 208, 212–213, 411, 493, 516, 632–634, 677n.–680; First World War, 7–10, 17–19, 43–60, 71–76; commitment to France, 13, 19, 21ff., 28ff.; peace settlement, 79–100 passim.;

Iraq, 136–138, 801–802; mandates, 136–138, 144–145; reparation, 148–159, 164–165, 166n., 255–256; economic conditions, 150, 164, 236–244, 247–250, 252, 255–258, 729; war debts, 165–169; security and disarmament, 173–199 passim., 250, 256 and n., 731–732 and n.1; woman suffrage, 235, 245–246; elections, (1918), 235–236, 240, 262, (1922), 238, (1923), 239, (1924), 241–242, (1929), 247–249, (1931), 253, (1935), 253–254; reform in Lords, 236, 245; unemployment, 236, 237, 239, 241, 247, 250, 251, 256; trade and tariffs, 236, 239, 241, 242 and n., 247, 249–251, 255ff., 270ff., 592; migration, 237–238, 257; national debt, 237, 255, 257, 265, 267; coal industry, 242–244, 526; general strike, 243–244, 245, 593; prayerbook, 246; National Coalition, 251–258; riots of 1931, 252; cabinet procedure, 253; position of king, 254; appeasement, 255, 368, 396–398, 484, 511–514, 597, 728, 729–731, 733, 804n.1; divorce, 257; bases in Ireland, 264, 274; Ethiopia, 365–367; Second World War, 728–730, 731–732, 734, 736–737, 738, 746, 748, 751–767 passim., 799, 800–801; and Norway, 757–758, 760–761; French fleet, 769, 772–773; Battle of Britain, 782–787; African campaigns, 791–794, 802–804, 836; Near and Middle East, 801–802; Far East, 804–808, 824.
Great Depression, 159–165, 169–172, 211–212, 219, 220, 251–258, 269, 290n., 309ff., 328, 330, 348ff., 426, 432–433, 476, 527–528, 604, 665, 666, 695–697, 699, 705ff.
"Greater East Asia," 805, 806.
Great Lebanon, 83, 145, 327n.
Great Wall, 671–672, 674.
Greco-Turkish population exchange, 615, 636–637 and n.; War (1921–1922), 614–615, 633–634.
Greece, 11; First World War, 24, 26, 39, 614; peace settlement, 83, 113, 114, 155, 333, 614; economic conditions, 615–617; revolt of 1935, 617; return of George II, 618; foreign relations, 126n., 196, 608, 612, 614–615, 618–620, 631, 633–637 and n.; Italy, 24, 134, 619, 794–796, 801n.1; Second World War, 734, 755, 794–796, 800–801 and n.1.
Greek Orthodox Church, Bulgaria, 608; Russia, 541, 561, 565, 570, 587–588; Yugoslavia, 626.
Green, W., 716.

Greenland, 762, 790n., 822.
"Green" socialists, 608–609.
Grew, J. C., 824–825.
Grey of Fallodon, Viscount (1862–1933), 12–13, 18–19, 29–30, 34–35.
Griffith, A. (1871–1922), 264, 265.
Grozny, 814.
Grynszpan, H., 444.
Guadalajara, 394 and n.
Guadalcanal, 831.
Guam, 830.
Guantanamo, 722.
Guatemala, 39, 211n.2, 218.
"Guilt clause," Austria, 111; Germany, 96–97, 100, 106, 148, 423, 425; Hungary, 114.
Gulflight, 31.
Gypsies, Hungarian, 492n.
Guynemer, C., 64.

Haakon VII (1905–   ), 759, 761.
Haase, H., 399–400, 401, 403.
Habicht, T., 478.
Habsburgs, 113, 114, 175, 468, 482–483, 489, 492–493, 497, 504, 505, 622.
Hácha, E., 516, 517.
Hague, The, 128–129, 764; Peace Conferences (1899, 1907), 13, 27; Reparation Conference (1929–1930), 158, 159n., 475, 601; Tribunal, 17, 130.
Haig of Bemersyde, Earl, 72.
Haile Selassie (Regent, 1916–1928; King, 1928–1930; Emperor, 1930–   ), 362–367, 794.
Hainisch, M., 469, 471n., 475n.
Haiti, 39, 211n.2, 229, 722.
Hakkari, 136.
Halidé Edib, 641.
Halifax, Edward F. L. Wood, Baron Irwin, Viscount, 288, 289, 290, 762, 782.
Hall of Mirrors, 100.
Hambro, C. J., 760.
Hamburg, 109.
Hamilton, I., 47.
Hangö, 745, 748.
"Hang the Kaiser," 81.
Haniel von Haimhausen, E. von, 100.
Harding, W. G. (1865–1923), 187, 655, 683–688, 700.
Hardinge, Charles, Baron, of Penshurst, 81.
Haruna, 830n.
Harvey's Weekly, 683.
Hatay, 329 and n.
Hatch Acts, 718.

Havana Conference (1928), 703; (1940), 820.
"Haves vs. Have-nots," 731.
Hawaii, 830, 831; see also Pearl Harbor.
Hawes-Cutting Act, 721–722.
Hawley-Smoot Tariff, 694 and n., 720.
Haya de la Torre, V. R., 223.
Hearst, W. R., 189n.
Heimatbund, 325.
Heimwehr, 471–473, 475, 478–479, 481–482, 483.
Hejaz, 60, 108.
"He kept us out of war," 36.
Helen, Princess, of Greece, 603, 604.
Helgoland, 60, 104.
Hemisphere defense, 819–822.
Henderson, A. (1863–1935), 191, 193, 240, 249, 250, 251 and n.2, 277.
Henderson, L., 818.
Henderson, N., 736.
Henlein, K., 510, 511–512.
Hercegovina. (See Bosnia-Hercegovina.)
Hereditary Farms Law, 449.
Herrera, E. O., 221.
Herrera, L. A. de, 220.
Herriot, E. (1872–), 154, 173, 179, 192, 241, 303, 304, 306, 310–311, 312, 324.
Hertzog, J. B. M., 751n.
Hess, R., 446–447, 809n.
Heydrich, R., 829n.1.
High Commissioner . . . for Refugees, 463.
Hillman, S., 818.
Himmler, H. (1900–), 459 and n.1, 741.
Hindenburg und Beneckendorff, P. von (1847–1934), 46, 47, 54, 70, 73, 99, 161, 402, 409, 419, 421, 425–426, 432, 435, 437, 438, 455, 461; Line, 54, 73.
Hipper, Ritter von, 62.
Hirohito (1926–), 806, 825.
Hirtenberg, 495.
History of Rasselas, Prince of Abissinia, The, 368n.
Hitchcock, G. M., 682.
Hitler, A. (1889–), 192, 194, 354, 367, 411, 417, 421–426, 437–462 passim., 476, 477, 483–485, 512ff., 514n.1, 515, 537, 628n., 679, 731, 734, 735, 736–737, 738, 751, 765, 769, 775, 782, 783, 784, 835, 837.
Hitler-Ludendorff Putsch, 411, 422.
Hitler Youth, 424, 447.
Hittites, 329n.
Hlinka Guards, 516.

Hlond, A., 742.
Hoare, S., 253, 254, 279, 290, 366 and n.1.
Hoare-Laval Proposal, 366n.1.
Hodža, M., 510, 511–512.
Hohenzollern property, referendum, 419–420.
Holland. (See Netherlands.)
Home Owners' Refinancing Act, 707.
Honduras, 39, 211n.2.
Hong Kong, 680, 830.
Hood, 830n.
"Hooded Ones," 317.
Hoover, H. (1874–), 86, 87n., 162ff., 189, 249, 433, 683, 685, 692–698, 713, 721, 722.
Hoover-Laval Moratorium, 162, 165, 168, 433, 696.
Horthy de Nagybánya, N. (1868–), 488, 489, 490, 493.
Hostages, execution of, 829n.1.
Hötzendorf. (See Conrad.)
House, E. M. (1858–1938), 30, 34–35, 80, 84, 88–89, 100 and n.2.
House Committee on Un-American Activities, 817.
House-Grey Agreement (House Memorandum), 34–35.
H. R. 1776 (1941), 823 and n.
Hsinking, 668.
Hsuan Tung. (See Pu Yi.)
Hsu Shih-chang, 654.
Hudson, M. O., 129n.
Hugenberg, A., 159, 437.
Hughes, C. E. (1862–), 36, 129n., 681, 684–685, 702.
Hull, C. (1871–), 171, 172n.1, 257, 720, 806, 820–822, 825.
Hungarian Soviet Republic, 488.
Hungary, 194, 431, 466n., 469, 512, 515, 517, 599ff., 625, 684–685; peace settlement, 100n.1, 104, 110, 113–114, 115; Habsburgs, 114, 175, 489–490, 492–493, 497; reparation, 114, 159n., 491; republic, 114, 485–487, 491; irredentism, 114, 493, 495–497, 509–510, 517, 797; revisionism, 194, 493–499; land question, 486, 488, 491–492; "Red" vs. "White," 487–490; optants, 234, 600–601; economic conditions, 486, 487, 491–492, 494–495, 497–498; League, 491, 494, 496n., 497, 499; gypsies, 492n.; counterfeiting, 492–493; Nazism, 494, 498–499; and Yugoslavia, 495–497; regency law, 497; Jews, 498; Second World War, 797, 810, 825.
Hunter Commission, 284.

Hurst, C., 260.
Hus, J., 504, 505.
Hu Shih, 658.
Husseini, H. A. el, 300.
Hussein Kamel (1914–1917), 275, 276.
Hussein-McMahon Correspondence, 301.
Huszar, K., 489.
Hyde, D., 273.
Hydroelectric power, 268, 269, 349, 474.
Hymans, P., 83.
"Hyphenates," 27.

Ibáñez, C., 219.
Ibáñez, V. B., 378.
Iceland, 762, 822 and n.1.
Imbros, 635.
Immigration, 91; Alsace-Lorraine, 323n.;
Belgian Congo, 801n.1; France, 330;
Great Britain, 257; Manchuria, 663;
Palestine, 295–297, 301; South Africa,
285; Sudan, 280; Turkey, 637; United
States, 690 and n., 815n.
Imperial Conferences, 249, 256, 258–259,
271.
Imperialism, 12 and n.1, 336, 360.
Imperial preference, 239, 256.
Imredy, B., 498, 499.
IMRO, 611–613.
India, 60, 131, 159, 207, 209, 255, 282–
294, 590, 801 and n.2, 833.
India Joint Select Committee, 291.
Indian Councils Act (1909), 282.
Indian National Congress, 282–294, 831.
Indian Ocean, 61.
Indians, in Latin America, 218, 221.
Indian States. (See Native States.)
Indo-China. (See French Indo-China.)
Industrial codes, 707–708, 711, 713.
Inheritance, France, 329–330; Germany,
449; Russia, 560.
Inönü, I., 635, 638–639 and n., 837.
Integralist Action, 226.
Inter-Allied Commission, 105, 409, 410,
436.
Inter-Allied Debts, 156, 165–169, 311,
348, 700, 720–721.
Inter-American Commission for Terri-
torial Administration, 821.
Intergovernmental Committee on Refu-
gees, 463–464.
Internal Macedonian Revolutionary Or-
ganization, 611–613.
International, First, 588n.; Second, 588n.;
Third, 588–590, 595n.2.
"International anarchy," 12–13.
International Brigade, 393.

International Committee for . . . Non-
Intervention in Spain, 397–398.
"Internationale," 588n.
International Labor Organization, 125,
145, 721; creation, 109, 112, 130 and n.;
General Conference, 130–131, 132n.;
Governing Body, 130–131; Office, 130–
131; and United States, 130, 721; conventions, 131, 132.
International Police force, 192, 728.
Interstate Commerce Commission, 697.
Invergordon, mutiny, 252.
Iran, 8, 22, 115, 126n., 184n.1, 185, 208,
209, 435, 590, 647, 801 and n.2, 802.
Iraq, 136–138, 145 and n.2, 209, 282, 635,
647, 801 and n.4, 802; see also Meso-
potamia.
Ireland, 258–259, 261ff., 393; Easter Re-
bellion, 262, 263; I.R.A., 263, 269, 271–
272, 274–275; creation of Free State,
264; Cosgrave administration, 266–
270; economic conditions, 268–269,
270–274; rule of de Valera, 270–275;
Second World War, 275, 751n., 822 and
n.2; see also Northern Ireland.
Irigoyen, H., 218.
Irish Home Rule Bills, 261, 263–264, 267.
Irish Republican Army, 263, 269, 271–
272, 274–275.
Iron Guards, 605–607, 797–798.
"Irreconcilables," 682, 683.
Irredentism, First World War, 4; Aus-
trian, 352–354; Bulgarian, 611–614;
Chinese, 672; German, 503n., 508, 510–
515; Greek, 618–619; Hungarian, 114,
493, 495–497, 509–510, 515, 517, 599,
625; Italian, 4, 361n., 368–369; Lithu-
anian, 535–536, 739; Southslavic, 362.
Irwin, Baron. (See Halifax.)
Isaacs, B. (Barnato, B.), 201.
Ismet Pasha. (See Inönü.)
Isolationism, British, 8; United States,
682–683, 685, 703–704, 721, 723–724,
815–816, 823.
Isonzo River, Battles of the, 51–52.
Istanbul, 21, 115, 632, 635, 637n.
Istria, 23, 93, 112.
Italia Irridenta, 4, 7, 22–23, 361n., 368–
369.
Italian East Africa, 368, 791.
Italian Somaliland, 333, 362, 366, 368,
794.
Italo-Greek War, 794–796.
Italy, 9, 13, 159n., 180, 196, 212, 226, 279,
280, 299, 482–484, 513, 592, 613, 618,
628n., 633–635, 746; First World War,

Italy—*Continued*
4, 6–7, 22 and n.–24, 26, 44, 48, 50–52, 58–60, 70, 74–75, 332; France, 6–7, 13, 22, 44, 177, 190 and n., 318, 321, 361, 362, 363–369, 396–398; papacy, 23, 352, 354–359; peace settlement, 82, 84–85, 88, 93–94, 108, 111–112, 114, 332–334; League, 126, 131, 134, 362–367; war debts, 166–168, 348, 362; economic conditions, 171n., 334–335, 337, 345–351, 362–368; security and disarmament, 177–178, 190 and n., 191–192, 194ff., 362, 732n.1; revisionism, 193–199, 362, 368, 493–496, 734; Ethiopia, 198, 350, 362–368, 794; war losses, 332; colonies, 333, 362–368; Fascist Party, 336–343; women, 343; corporate state, 343–348; Charter of Labor, 345–346; suffrage, 346–347; education and art, 346, 351, 356–359; resources, 350, 360, 368; government and business, 350; nationalism and population, 350, 359–360, 364; discipline, 351; racism, 351–352; South Tirol, 352–354; militarism, 359–360; Spanish Civil War, 393, 394 and n., 395 and n., 396–398; Second World War, 729, 734–735, 737, 770, 783, 806, 810, 820 and n., 825, 835; entry, 768; African campaigns, 791–794, 802–804; Greek campaigns, 794–796, 801n.1.
Izmir. (*See* Smyrna.)
Izvolski, A. (1865–1919), 10, 19.

Jäger, A., 455–456.
Jamaica, 821.
Japan, 9, 164, 196n.1, 207, 212–213, 237, 599; First World War, 20, 24, 38, 60, 651–652, 664; peace settlement, 83, 85, 96, 103, 104; and League, 91, 126, 131, 209, 667, 670–673, 677–679; China, 96, 209, 649, 651–658, 662–680, 804–808; mandates, 145; economic conditions, 172, 664–665, 666, 668–669, 679; disarmament, 187–188, 190, 196–197; Russia, 551n.2, 555n.1, 576, 596n., 672–673, 674–675; United States, 596n., 652, 653n., 655–658, 665, 667, 670–671, 677–680, 686, 690, 721, 724, 805–808, 823–825; army and navy, 666–667, 670, 676, 679; Manchuria, 666–675; Second World War, 804–808, 823–825; Japanese as fighters, 829 and n.–830.
Jászi, O., 487.
Jehol, 671.
Jellicoe, J., 62.
Jerez sherry, 396n.

Jerusalem, 60, 297.
Jesuits, Spain, 384, 386.
Jewish Agency, 295, 297, 300; National Home, 294–301.
Jews, Austria, 469, 484; Czechoslovakia, 516; France, 775, 780; Germany, 297, 410, 422, 424, 441–445, 462–464, 741–742; Hungary, 498; Italy, 351–352; Palestine, 294–301; Poland, 529, 531–532, 741–742; Romania, 58, 601, 603, 605–606; Spain, 372–373; Zionist, 83.
Jibuti (Djibouti), 364.
Joan of Arc, 323.
Joffe, A., 587.
Joffre, J. (1852–1931), 44, 55.
Johnson, H., 683.
Johnson, H. S., 708.
Johnson, S., 368n.
Johnson Debt Default Act, 169, 720–721.
Johnson Immigration Act, 690 and n.
Jordan River, 297.
Jorga, N., 604–605.
Joseph, Archduke, 488–489.
Jouhaux, L., 320–321.
Jouvenel, H. de, 327.
Julian Alps, 51, 58.
Junkers, 409ff., 449, 461.
Juntas, 376 and n.
Jutland, Battle of, 62–63.

Kahr, Ritter von, 411.
Kamenev, L., 571, 572, 574, 575.
Kamerun. (*See* Cameroons.)
Kandalaksha, 748.
Kang Teh. (*See* Pu Yi.)
Kapp-Lüttwitz *Putsch*, 409–410.
Karagach, 635.
Karelia, 134, 552, 745, 746, 748.
Karelian-Finnish Republic, 748.
Karl Marx Hof, 472, 479.
Károlyi, J., 488, 494.
Károlyi von Nagykároly, Count M., 485–487.
Kars, 57, 633.
Kastl, L., 436.
Kaunas, 536.
Kazak, 555.
Kearny, 822n.2, 824.
Keitel, W., 462.
Kellogg, F. B. (1856–1937), 129n., 183, 702.
Kellogg Pact. (*See* Treaties, Paris Pact.)
Kelly, C. P., Jr., 830n.
Kemal. (*See* Atatürk.)
Kemijärvi, 746, 748.
Kemmerer, E., 526.

Kenya, 60, 201, 204, 286, 791, 794.
Kerch, 813.
Kerensky, A. (1881–), 56–57, 487, 544, 546–547, 548, 550.
Kerrl, H., 457.
Keyserling, Count von, 415.
"Khaki campaign," 81, 235, 240.
Kiaochow, 20, 60, 96, 104, 207, 651–652, 653, 655, 657.
Kiel, 60, 401–402; Canal, 109.
Kiev, 554.
Kimbangu, S., 202.
King, (W. L.) M., 821.
Kingdom of Serbs, Croats, and Slovenes. (See Yugoslavia.)
King George V, 830n.
Kionga Triangle, 96n.1.
Kiosseivanovm G., 611.
Kirghiz, 555.
Kirk-Kilissa, 21.
Kirov, S., 564, 575.
Klagenfurt, 469.
Klaipėda, 103n.
Kleffens, E. N. van, 763.
Knatchbull-Hugessen, H., 677n.
Knox, C. G., 142–143.
Knox, (W.) F. (1874–), 714, 817, 818, 824.
Knudsen, W. S., 818.
Koc, A., 525.
Kolchak, A., 552, 553, 554.
Kolkhozi. (See Collective farms.)
Komsomol, 561.
Kondylis, G., 616, 617–618.
Konoye, Prince F., 677, 805, 824.
Koo, W., 85.
Korea, 83, 117, 665.
Korizis, A., 795.
Kornilov, L., 56, 547.
Koundouriotis, P., 616.
Kovno, 536.
Kramář, K., 502–503.
Kredit Anstalt, 161.
Krieck, E., 453.
Kriegspresseamt, 66.
Kristiansand, 760.
Kronstadt Mutiny, 567.
Krupskaya, N. K., 549.
Ku Klux Klan, 692.
Kulaks, 569, 570, 580–581, 583.
Kun, B. (1885–), 487–488.
Kunfi, S., 487.
Kurdistan (Kurds), 115, 137, 637.
Kurusu, S., 824–825.
Kut-el-Amara, 48.

Kuusinen, O., 745, 750.
Kwang Hsü (1875–1908), 648.

La Bassée, 72.
"Labor, Family, Fatherland," 799 and n.
Labor Front, Germany, 448.
Labor Representation Committee, 240n.
Labor Trustees, 448, 452.
Lady Macbeth of Mtzensk, 587.
La Fère, 71.
LaFollette, R., 691 and n.
Lagny accident, 311, 313.
LaGuardia, F. H. (1882–), 821.
Lake Ladoga, 746, 748.
Lamont, T. W., 97.
Lampson, M. W., 279–280.
Land-annuities dispute, 269ff., 274.
Länder, Austria, 468, 469; Germany, 406 and n.
Landon, A. M., 714–715.
Lansbury, G. 251n.2.
Lansing, R. (1864–1928), 38, 80.
Laon, 55, 74.
Latifé Hanoum, 640.
Latin America, 119, 237, 250, 701–703, 722–723; First World War, 211; economic development, 211–215; classes, 215–221; students, 221–223; fascism, 226; Catholic Church, 228–231; Second World War, 819–822.
Latvia, 116, 184n.1, 185; see also Livonia.
Lausanne Peace Conference, 608, 634–635; Reparation Conference, 164–165, 168, 255–256, 433.
Laval, P. (1883–), 309–310, 312, 313–314, 315, 363–364, 366 and n.1, 769, 779–780, 836.
Law, A. Bonar. (See Bonar Law.)
Law of Papal Guarantees, 354.
Lawrence, T. E. (1882–1935), 21, 60.
Law to Combat the Misery of People and Reich, 438–439.
Lazarev, P., 587.
Lea, H., 5.
"Leaders," German industry, 448.
League of Nations, The, 95–96.
League of Nations, 70, 100, 169, 174, 177, 193, 203, 209, 258, 268, 277, 280, 304, 353, 379 and n., 385, 435–436, 469, 476, 491, 494, 496n., 499, 532, 596, 600–601, 608, 615, 619, 645, 646, 682–684, 728, 745; drafting Covenant, 90–91, 123; administration of territory, 93, 95, 104, 140–143; mandates, 95–96, 144–146, 203–204, 294ff., 326–329; minorities, 116, 146, 328, 529–531; membership

League of Nations—*Continued*
and organization, 124–128; budget, 125, 193n.2; Russia, 126, 131, 134, 596, 745; settlements of disputes, 132–139, 363–367, 396–398, 496–497, 667–672, 677–679; sanctions, 133, 251n.2, 350, 366–367, 368, 679; financial aid, 147, 470, 471, 476, 491; worth, 147; disarmament, 178ff., 185–193; Asia, 209–210; Spain, 379 and n., 385, 396–398; refugees, 462–464, 615; United States, 90–91, 126, 131, 682–684, 685, 704–705.

League of Nations Assembly, 124–126, 132–134; (1920), 125; (1921), 178; (1922), 178; (1923), 179; (1924), 179; (1925), 185–186; (1926), 435–436; (1928), 155, 436; (1930), 160; (1931), 191; (1933), 146n.2; (1934), 146n.2; (1935), 366.

League of Nations Council, 125–127, 132–134, 169, 182, 435–436, 468, 471, 491, 497, 528, 535–536, 625, 682, 704; Silesia, 102; Memel, 103n.; Saar, 140–143; Åland Islands, 134–135; Mosul, 136–138; Chaco, 138–139; mandates, 144–146, 294–301 passim.; minorities, 116, 146, 529–531, 600–601; disarmament, 178ff., 185–193; Alexandretta, 328–329; Ethiopia, 364–367; refugees, 463; Hungaro-Yugoslav dispute, 496–497; Greco-Bulgarian dispute, 612; Sino-Japanese dispute, 670–673; Spanish Civil War, 396–398.

League of Nations Secretariat, 127, 146, 745.

League of the Upright, 409.

League to Enforce Peace, 123.

Lebanon, 83, 145, 327n.

Lebrun, A. (1871–), 304, 312, 315n., 318, 321, 769.

Leguía, A. B., 221, 223.

Lehman, H. L., 829n.2.

Leipzig, trials, 106.

Lemberg, 52.

Lemke, W. O., 714.

Lend-Lease Act, 822–823 and n., 834.

Lenin, Mme. (*See* Krupskaya.)

Lenin, N. (1870–1924), 57, 487, 490, 542n., 546, 547, 549–550, 553, 567–568, 571 and n., 572, 573, 587.

Leningrad, 571n., 744–745, 811, 813; Symphony, 587.

Lens, 54, 73.

Leo XIII (1878–1903), 274, 357.

Leonov, L., 587.

Leopold II (1865–1909), 201.

Leopold III (1934–), 764, 766.

Lester, S., 127 and n.

Lerroux, A., 389, 390.

Lettow-Vorbeck, P. von, 60.

Lewis, J. L., 716–717, 720 and n.

Ley, R., 448, 742.

Liapchev, A., 610.

Liberia, 39, 104, 125.

"Liberty, Equality, Fraternity," 779.

Libya (Tripolitania plus Cyrenaica), 11, 114, 333, 362, 363, 635, 791, 792–793, 801, 802–804, 834, 836.

Lidice, 829n.1.

Liebknecht, K., 400, 404.

Liége, 41, 43.

Lille, 44, 72, 74, 767.

Lima Conference (1938), 723.

Lindbergh, C. A., 702.

Linlithgow, Victor Hope, Marquess of, 292–294.

Lithuania, 47, 57, 58n., 103n., 116, 184n.1, 185, 517n., 520–521, 535–536, 739.

Little Entente, 175–176 and n., 185, 194–195 and n.1, 362, 471, 489, 490, 492, 493–495, 497, 507, 537, 601, 628.

"Little group of wilful men," 37.

"Little World War," 396–398.

Litvinov, M. (Meier Finkelstein, 1876–), 189, 594, 595, 597, 734.

Litzmannstadt, 741.

Livonia, 57, 83; *see also* Latvia.

Li Yuan-hung, 651.

Lloyd, George, Baron, 277.

Lloyd George, D. (1863–), 10, 55, 69, 81, 82, 83, 89, 92, 95, 96, 99, 110, 114, 150, 174, 235–240, 244, 247–248, 249, 262, 263–264, 591, 634, 654.

Lodge, H. C. (1850–1924), 38, 80, 682, 691n.

Lodz, 741.

London, 252; air raids, 63, 785; Economic Conference, 169–171, 478, 709; Naval Conference, 190, 249; Schedule, 149; Round Tables, 288–291.

Long, H., 714.

López, A., 221.

Loraine, P., 277.

Lothian, Philip Kerr, Marquess of, 762, 821.

Lotus, 645.

Loudon, J., 189.

Louvain, 44; University, 108, 765.

Lowden, F., 683.

Lowell, J. R., 521.

Lower Austria, 112, 469.

Lubbe, M. van der, 438n.1.

Lublin, 742.
Ludendorff, E. (1865–1937), 43, 46, 50, 54, 70, 72–73, 76, 401, 409, 411, 422.
Lukouchiao, 677.
Lupescu, M., 603, 604, 798.
Lusitania, 31–32 and n., 98, 724, 816.
Luther, H., 414, 418, 419.
Lüttwitz, Freiherr von, 409–410.
Lutze, V., 460, 462.
Luxembourg, 17, 76, 104, 174, 431, 762, 764n., 767.
Luxemburg, R., 400, 404.
Lvov, Prince, 56, 544, 545.
Lyman, J., 788n.1.
Lytton Report, 670–672.

MacArthur, D., 831.
MacDermot, F., 272.
MacDonald, J. R. (1866–1937), 179–180, 189, 192, 240–242, 244, 249, 251–253, 254n.2, 276, 288, 290, 295, 297, 592.
Macedonia, 5, 25, 113, 496, 611–614.
Machek, V., 624, 626–627.
Maciá, F., 383, 390n.
Mackensen, A. von, 47, 54.
Madagascar, 781, 831.
Made in Germany, 12n.2.
Madrid, 375, 388, 392–396.
Maginot Line, 738, 752, 765, 769, 777.
Magyars, 14, 16, 25, 75, 485, 490n.; in Czechoslovakia, 114, 493, 505, 508, 509–510; Romania, 114, 493, 599; Yugoslavia, 114, 493; see also Hungary.
Maher, Ahmed, 281.
Maher, Ali, 281.
Mahmoud, M., 278, 281.
Mahmoud Shevket, 629.
Maikop, 814.
Mainz, 76, 91, 109.
Maison de la Presse, La, 66.
Makino, Baron, 83, 90.
Malaya, 830, 831.
Malmédy, 101, 765.
Malta, 361n., 791, 803n.
Manchester Guardian, 89, 393n.1.
Manchoukuo. (*See* Manchuria.)
Manchu dynasty, 648–650.
Manchuria, 499, 652, 662–673, 674–675.
Mandates, 95–96, 103, 115, 136, 144–146, 203–204, 294–301, 326–329; see also Permanent Mandates Commission.
Mandel, G., 769, 780–781.
Maniu, J. (1873–), 602–604, 605–606.
Mannerheim, Baron von (1867–), 552, 746; Line, 746–748.
Mantoux, P., 88.

March on Rome, 339; on Warsaw, 522.
Marco Polo Bridge, 677.
Mariátegui, C., 223.
Marie, of Romania, 603.
Marienwerder, 95, 101.
Marine Corps, Women's Reserve, 828n.
Maritsa River, 634, 635.
Marne River, 768; First Battle of the, 44; Second Battle of the, 73.
Mars, 788.
Marseille assassinations, 496–497, 625.
Martel, D. de, 328.
Marx, K., 490, 549, 555, 572, 588n.
Marx, W., 418, 419–420.
Masaryk, T. G. (1850–1937), 500–503, 507, 509, 510, 516.
Master race. (*See* Racism.)
Masurian Lakes, Battle of, 46.
Matignon Agreement, 315.
Matteotti, G., 340 and n.
Maude, (F.) S., 60.
Maura, A., 376.
Maurras, C., 322.
Max, Prince, 73, 75–76, 400–402.
May Committee, 251.
McAdoo, W. G., 683, 691.
McCormick, V., 97.
McCosgair, L. (*See* Cosgrave, W.)
McKenna, R., 153.
McMahon-Hussein Correspondence, 301.
McNary, C. L., 719.
McNary-Haugen Bill, 691.
McNutt, P. V., 828n.
Mediterranean Sea, 177, 279, 361, 365, 396–398, 755, 791, 792; Patrol, 397–398.
Meierhold, V., 587.
Mein Kampf, 422.
Memel, 102–103 and n., 517 and n.
Menelik II (1889–1913), 365.
Mensheviks, name, 542n.
Meredith, G., 331.
Mers-el-Kebir, 772–773.
Mesopotamia, 47, 48, 60, 96, 114; see also Iraq.
Mesta, 373–374.
Metaxas, J., 618, 620, 794–796.
Metternich, Prince, 3, 65.
Metz, 43.
Meuse-Argonne offensive (1918), 74.
Meuse River, 55, 765.
Mexico, 37–38, 211n.2, 213, 214, 217, 218, 221, 227–228 and n., 229–231, 701–702, 722–723.
Miaja, J., 394, 395.
Michael, Grand Duke, 544.

Michael I, of Romania (1927–1930, 1940–   ), 603–604, 798.
MICUM, 151.
Middle East, 801 and n.2–802.
Midway Island, 830; Battle of (1942), 831.
Mihailov, I., 612–613.
Mikhailovich, D., 800.
Miklas, W., 475n., 478, 480, 481, 484n.1.
Milan, 336, 337, 339, 341, 349.
Militarism, First World War, 5–6.
Miller, D., 451n.
Miller, H. H., 774n.
Millerand, A., 303.
Milne, A., 632.
Milner Mission, 276.
Minas Geraes, 224.
Mines, 31, 61, 757, 758, 760; magnetic, 753.
Minorities, 115–116, 734; Czechoslovakia, 116, 493, 503n., 505, 508–515; Germany, see Jews; Hungary, 485, 493; India, 282–283, 286–290; Italy, 111–112, 352–354, 474, 735; League, 116, 146 and n.2; Palestine, 294ff.; Poland, 115, 528–531, 534, 535–536, 734, 738; Romania, 115, 493, 599ff., 744, 797; Russia, 556, 558, 573, 586; Turkey, 115, 328–329; Yugoslavia, 116, 493, 621–627; see also Population exchange.
Minorities Committee of the League Council, 146.
Minorities treaties, 115–116, 146 and n.2, 528, 599.
Mississippi flood control, 691, 692.
Mkwawa, skull of, 108 and n.
Mohammed VI (1918–1922), 115, 629, 634, 639.
Mohammed Riza (1941–   ), 802.
Mola, E., 760.
Molotov, V. M. (1890–   ), 597, 735, 739, 750.
Moltke, H. J. L. von, 17, 43.
Moltke, 63.
Mongolia, Inner, 652, 667, 676n.; Outer (Mongolian People's Republic), 660, 664, 674–675.
Monks' trials, Germany, 458.
Monroe Doctrine, 90–91, 703, 723, 820–821.
Mons, 44.
Montagu-Chelmsford Report, 283.
Montdider, 72, 73.
Montenegro, 11, 20, 25, 36, 70, 621.
Montevideo, 215, 754.
Montgomery, B. L., 834.
Montmédy, 767.

Moore, J. B., 129n.
Moors, 372, 393.
Moratorium, German requests for, 150, 305; Hoover-Laval, 162, 165, 168.
Moravia, 112, 500 and n., 504, 510, 516, 517, 829n.1.
Moresnet, 101, 765.
Morgan, J. P., and Company, 34.
Morgenthau, H., Sr., 615.
Moriscos, 372 and n.
Morocco, 9, 10–11, 104, 114, 782; French, 374, 834–836; Spanish, 376–377, 378, 379, 387, 392–393, 834n.2.
Morrow, D. W. (1873–1931), 702.
Mościcki, I. (1867–   ), 522, 524, 525, 738, 739.
Moscow, 571n., 588, 790n., 811, 813; Trials, 575–577.
Moslems, 21, 58, 278–279, 282–283, 286–290, 294–301, 326ff., 639–640, 642.
Mosley, O., 249 and n., 257 and n.2.
Mosul, 75, 136–138, 635.
Möwe, 61.
Mowrer, E. A., 777.
Mozambique, 60, 96n.1, 205.
Mudania, Armistice, 634.
Mudros, Armistice, 75, 136, 631.
Mufti, of Jerusalem, 300.
Mukden, 668.
Müller, H., 100, 420, 434.
Müller, L., 455–457.
Munich, 402, 403, 406, 411, 422, 460, 478, 785.
Murmansk, 551, 552, 596, 748.
Murphy, R. D., 835.
Murray, P., 720n.
Muscle Shoals Act, 707.
Mushanov, N., 610.
Mussert, A., 764.
Mussolini, B. (1883–   ), 177, 184–185, 198–199, 335–371 passim., 478, 479, 482, 483, 494, 495, 512ff., 515, 592, 731, 734, 768, 769, 792, 793, 795.
Mustapha Kemal. (See Atatürk.)
Mutiny, British navy, 252; Chinese army, 675–676; French army, 55; German navy, 76, 401–402; Japanese army, 676; Russian army, 57; navy, 567.
M. V. S. N., 343n.2.
"Mystery ships," 62.

Nahas, M., 277, 279–280, 281.
Naidu, S., 287, 290.
Namsos, 761.
Namur, 44.

Nanking, 661, 668, 678, 804; "Affair," 660–661, 703.
Nansen, F., 636; Office for Refugees, 463.
Naples, 338, 341, 796.
Napoleon I, 65, 323, 336, 372, 779.
Napoleon III, 354.
Narutowicz, G., 521.
Narvik, 757, 759, 760, 761.
National Council of Corporations, 345.
National Council of Czechoslovakia, 502.
National Defense Act, 35.
National Defense Advisory Commission, 817.
National Guard, United States, 35, 819.
National Industrial Recovery Act, 707–714.
Nationalism, First World War, 3–5, 13–14, 22ff.; economic, 12 and n.1, 171–172, 268–269, 448–453, 602, 645; see also Autarkie.
Nationalities Statute, 606–607.
National Labor Relations Act, 712; Board, 712, 716–717.
National Origins Act, 690 and n.
National Prize, German, 459.
National Recovery Administration, 708–714.
National Socialist German Workers' Party, founding, 422; program, 422–423; organization and supporters, 423–425; rise, 425–426, 439–441, 446; internal conflicts, 459–462.
National Youth Administration, 699.
Native States, 282, 284, 287n., 288–290, 292.
Naulahka, The, 206n.
Nauru, 145 and n.1.
Naval limitation and rivalry, 29, 35, 186–187, 189, 196–197, 655 and n., 732n.1; Anglo-American, 187–189, 655 and n., 686; Anglo-American-Japanese, 187–188, 196–197, 655 and n., 721, 733n.1; Anglo-German, 8 and n.2; Franco-Italian, 177, 190 and n.
Naval warfare, 8 and n.2, 60–63, 73, 738n., 753–755, 757–758, 767, 769, 770, 772–773, 781, 783–784, 792, 796, 806, 816–817, 833n., 835–836.
Nawa, 657.
Nazareth, 299.
Nazis. (See National Socialist German Workers' Party.)
Near East, 5, 20–22 and n., 60, 333, 686n., 801 and n.2–802; Relief, 635.
Negrín, J., 394–395.
Nehru, J., 287, 292–293.

Nehru, M., 287.
Nelson, D. M., 818 and n.1.
Neo-Paganism, 459.
NEP. (See New Economic Policy.)
"Nepmen," 570.
Nessim, M. T., 279.
Netherland India, 657, 805–808, 830, 831.
Netherlands, 29, 106, 213, 752, 762–764, 767, 824.
Neurath, Freiherr von, 437, 462.
Neutrality Acts (1935–1939), 367n.1, 723–724, 816–817, 824; Proclamations, 22, 27, 816; Zone, 820.
Neutral rights, 27–39, 61.
Neuve Chapelle, 48.
New Caledonia, 831.
New Deal, 705–720.
New Economic Policy, 568–571, 590, 591.
Newfoundland, 258 and n., 821–822.
New Guinea, 831.
New Hebrides, 831.
New York, 689, 700, 790n.
New York American, 188.
New York Evening Post, 89.
New York Times, 685.
New Zealand, 60, 103, 144, 145n.1, 258–259, 751n., 753, 831.
Nicaragua, 39, 211n.2, 229, 701, 702, 722.
Nice, 321, 361, 369.
Nicholas II (1894–1917), 38, 56, 539, 541, 543–544, 553.
Niemöller, M., 456–457.
Nile River, 277.
Nineteenth Amendment, 684.
NIRA, 707–714.
Nitrates, 430.
Nitti, F., 82, 94.
Nivelle, R., 55.
Nizhni-Novgorod (Gorki), 579.
NLRB, 712, 716–717.
Nobel Prize, 27, 434, 459, 700.
Noli, F. A., 369.
Nomura, K., 824–825.
Non-Intervention Committee, 397–398.
Norfolk, 61.
Northcliffe, Alfred Harmsworth, Viscount, 66, 81.
Northern Ireland, 261–264 and n., 265, 267, 270, 274.
North Manchuria Railway, 673.
North Sea, 29, 62.
Norway, 29, 63, 746, 748, 754–755, 757–762.
Nosaltres Sols, 387.
Noske, G., 401, 404, 406, 409, 410.
Noyon, 72, 73.

NRA, 708–714.
Nubar Pasha, 83, 86.
Nuremberg Laws, 443–444.
NYA, 699.
Nye, G. P., 721.
Nygaardsvold, J., 759.

Obregón, A., 227.
OCD, 818.
Ödenburg, 469, 489.
Oder-Danube Canal, 514n.2.
O'Duffy, E., 272.
Office of Civilian Defense, 818; Price Administration, 818; Production Management, 818 and n.1; the Coördinator of Inter-American Affairs, 821n.
Ogdensburg, 821.
OGPU, 563–564, 574–575.
O'Higgins, K., 265, 266.
Oil, 58, 136–138, 195, 214, 298, 367, 370, 577, 578, 601n., 671, 673, 675, 686n., 688–689, 702, 723, 739, 761, 801, 802, 805, 813–814, 830.
Okies, 717 and n.
Old Bolsheviks, 561n., 572, 576.
Omar, Mosque of, 295.
Omsk, 552, 554.
OPA, 818.
"Open Door," 653n., 655, 656, 657, 673.
Opium traffic, 147, 685.
OPM, 818 and n.1.
Optants, 134, 600–601.
Optional Clause, 129, 250.
Oran, 772, 835.
"Order Number One," 545.
Orgbureau, 562.
Orlando, V., 82, 85, 88, 89, 90, 94.
Orthodox Church. (See Greek Church.)
Oslo, 759, 761.
Ostend, 44.
Ostmark, 484n.1.
Otranto, Strait of, 333, 370, 796.
Ottawa Economic Conference, 256, 271.
Otto, Archduke (1912–), 483, 484, 490, 492–493.
Oversea Settlement Board, 257.
OVRA, 342.
Oxford, Lord. (See Asquith.)

Pabst, W., 409–410.
Pacific area, 654–658, 686, 806–808, 823–825, 828–833; War Council, 828.
Paderewski, I. J., 83, 518, 520, 521, 525.
Page, W. H., 27, 29, 37.
Pai Hua, 658.
Painlevé, P., 306.

Palestine, 60, 96, 114, 145, 275, 294–301, 635, 801, 802.
Palmer, A. M., 682, 683.
Palmyra Island, 831.
Pan-African Congress, 203.
Panama, 39, 211n.2, 215, 222, 229, 722; Declaration of, 820.
Pan-American Conference (1923), 703; (1928), 703; (1938), 723; on Arbitration, 138, 703; meetings of foreign ministers (1939), 819–820; (1940), 820.
Pan-American Union, 221.
Pan-Asia, 209.
Panay sinking, 678 and n.
Pan-Europa, 160, 308.
Pangalos, T., 616.
Pan-Germans, 5; see also Fascism, Germany.
Pan-Slavism, 5, 14, 21, 502.
Pantelleria, 792 and n.
Panther, 10.
Panzerdivisionen, 737.
Papacy. (See Catholic Church.)
Papagos, A., 796.
Papen, F. von (1879–), 34, 426, 433, 437, 457–458, 460–461, 482.
Paraguay, 138–139, 211n.2, 217, 229, 723.
Paris, 4, 43, 320, 767–768, 770.
Paris Peace Conference (1918–1920), 263, 332–334, 352, 361, 364, 520, 532, 611, 682; leaders, 79–83; structure, 84–86; problems, 87–90, 654; drafting of treaties, 90–97, 110–116, 203; signing, 98–100.
Parliament Act of 1911, 245, 261.
Party designations, continental, 302n.
Pashich, N. (1846–1926), 15, 83, 86, 621–623.
Passchendaele Ridge, 55, 72.
Pastors' Emergency League, 456.
Patman Bonus Bill, 712.
Paul, Prince, 626, 627, 799–800.
Pavelich, A., 496n., 800.
Pavlov, I., 587.
Peace aims, First World War, 36–37, 56–57, 67–70; Second World War, 751, 782, 784, 789, 826–827, 828–829.
"Peace! Land! Bread!", 57, 546.
"Peace without victory," 37, 67.
Pearl Harbor, 724, 788n.1, 825, 830, 831.
Peel Report, 298–299.
Peking (Peiping), 649, 651, 652, 661, 672, 677.
Perasso, G. B., 343n.1.
Permanent Court of International Justice, 125, 134, 158, 179, 182, 531, 532,

645; structure, 128–130; optional clause, 129, 250; United States, 129n., 685, 703–704, 721; advisory opinions, 130, 476, 703–704.

Permanent Joint Board on Defense, 821.

Permanent Mandates Commission, 96, 144, 145, 203, 295, 299–300, 327, 329, 436.

Pernambuco, 224.

Péronne, 50, 73.

Pershing, J. J., 72.

Persia. (*See* Iran.)

Persian Gulf, 801, 802, 813.

Peru, 126n., 139, 211n.2, 213, 214, 217, 218, 221, 223, 229.

Pétain, H. P. (1856–   ), 55, 71, 312, 313, 769, 772, 773, 778–782, 835.

Peter I, of Serbia (1903–1918), of Yugoslavia (1918–1921), 4, 621.

Peter II (1934–   ), 626, 800.

Petrograd, 46; Soviet, 544–545; *see also* Leningrad.

Petsamo, 745, 746, 748.

Pfriemer, W., 472–473.

Phalanx, Spanish, 391, 395.

Philippine Islands, 721–722, 806, 819, 830, 831.

Phillimore, Walter, Baron, 90, 123.

Phillips, T., 830 and n.

"Phony war," 752–756.

Piatakov, G., 576.

Piave River, 58, 74.

Picardy, 44, 71, 73.

Pichon, S., 82, 95.

"Pig War," 14.

Pilniak, B., 586.

Pilsudski, J. (1867–1935), 518–520, 521, 522–525, 536 and n.

Pindus Mountains, 796.

Pink Coalition, Austria, 467ff.

"Piracy," Mediterranean, 397–398.

Pius IX (1846–1878), 354–355.

Pius X (1903–1914), 355.

Pius XI (1922–1939), 274, 352, 355–359, 386.

Place de la Concorde, 4.

Plan XVII.

Planetta, O., 481, 482.

Plate, Battle of the River (1939), 753–754.

Platt Amendment (1901–1934), 722.

Plattsburgh Barracks, 33.

Plebiscites, 68, 93, 94, 95, 99, 101–102, 104, 137, 142–143, 159, 459, 461, 469, 470, 484–485, 616, 618, 778.

Poduvkin, V., 587.

Poincaré, R. (1860–1934), 18, 19, 69, 83, 91, 150–152, 154, 173, 302–307, 308, 325, 593, 778n.

Poison gas, 48, 64–65, 187.

Poland, 444, 508, 593, 751; First World War, 47, 57, 70, 75, 519–520; peace settlement, 83, 95, 101–102, 112, 115, 520–521; minorities, 95, 115, 146n.2, 528–532, 534, 535–536, 734; foreign relations, 174, 175–176, 180–183, 184n.1, 185, 195, 435 and n.–436, 512, 515, 536–538, 733–734, 736–737; partitions, 518, 739; independence, 520; politics, 521–525; economic conditions, 525–528; Danzig and Corridor, 532–535, 736; Vilnius, 535–536; Russian wars, 535, 554; Second World War, 733–742, 792.

Polish Corridor, 95, 534–535, 733–734.

Polish Legions, 519, 520.

Polish National Committees, 519, 520.

Politbureau, 563, 571, 574.

Ponsonby, Baron, 13, 66.

Ponsot, H., 327–328.

Pontine Marshes, 350, 360.

Popolo d'Italia, Il, 336.

Popular Front, France, 314–320; Spain, 391ff.

Population exchanges and shifts, 323n., 354, 615, 636–637 and n., 735, 741–742, 743, 750, 780.

Port Baros, 333n.

Porto Rosa, Conference of (1921), 470.

Portugal, 24, 83, 96n.1, 116, 205, 223, 395, 396–397.

Portuguese East Africa, 60, 96n.1, 205.

Posen (Poznań), 95, 101, 534.

Potiorek, O., 14–15.

Pottier, E., 588n.

Prado, M., 221.

Prasad, R., 294.

Pravda, 574.

Preparatory Commission for the Disarmament Conference, 186–187, 188, 189, 190–191.

"Preparedness movement," 33.

Press, 5, 9, 11, 66–67, 87–88, 141, 316, 325, 341, 353, 361, 377, 378, 401, 458, 482, 490, 637, 700, 780.

Pressburg (Bratislava), 515.

Prestes, J., 225.

Preuss, H., 406.

Pribichevich, S., 624.

Primo de Rivera, A., 393n.1.

Primo de Rivera, Marquess de Estalla (1870–1930), 377–380 and n.

Prince of Wales. (*See* Edward VIII.)

Prince of Wales, 830 and n.

Princip, G. (1894–1920), 3, 15, 625.
Prioux, R., 767.
Private property in Russia, 560, 564ff., 777.
Prohibition, Russia, 543, 569n.; United States, 684, 691, 692–694, 697, 706 and n.1.
Propaganda, in United States, 28, 33–34, 42, 66, 67, 702; general, 42, 57, 60, 65–67, 226, 299 and n.2, 338, 351, 359, 361, 439, 441, 453, 465, 477, 478, 487, 493–494, 550, 563, 578, 585ff., 588ff., 591, 593, 660, 662, 777, 778, 811.
Protogerovists, 613.
Protopopov, A., 543.
Prussia, 92, 101, 401, 406n., 408, 425, 437–438, 445, 446, 455, 457, 460, 474; East, 44, 45–46, 95, 449, 534; West, 95, 101, 534.
Przemysl, 46.
Public Order Act, 257.
Public Works Administration, 707, 709, 718n.
Purge, Germany, 460–461, 481; Russia, 576–577.
Pu Yi, H., 649–650, 668, 672, 673.
PWA, 707, 709, 718n.

Qattara Depression, 803.
"Q-ships," 62.
Quadragesimo Anno, 357.
"Quadrilateral," 797.
Quarnero, Gulf of, 23.
Queenstown. (See Cóbh.)
Quiroga, S. C., 391, 392.
Quisling, V. (1887–   ), 760–761.

Rabbit Islands, 635.
"Race to the sea," 44.
Racism, Germany, 422–423, 453–454, 730, 741–742, see also Jews; Italy, 351–352, 730; Japan, 731.
Racketeering, 689, 694.
Raczkiewicz, W., 739.
Radar, 788n.1, 825.
Radek, K., 576.
Radich, S. (1871–1928), 622–624.
Radio, 299 and n.2, 456, 478, 586, 698, 788n.1, 825.
Raeder, E., 753.
Railways, China, 652, 656, 660, 663; France, 317n.; Germany, 40; Italy, 337, 350; Romania, 605; Russia, 8, 542–543, 565, 578, 580; United States, 684, 698, 707, 711; Yugoslavia, 94.
Ramek, R., 471.
Rashid Ali Beg Gailani, 801, 802.

Rasputin, G. (1871–1916), 541, 543.
Rath, E. vom, 444.
Rathenau, W. (1867–1922), 176, 410, 416.
Rationalization, Germany, 428–429; Great Britain, 247; weaknesses, 429.
Rault, V., 140–142.
Rauschning, H., 533–534.
Recognition, diplomatic, 591n.
Reconstruction Finance Corporation, 696–697, 709, 710.
Red Cross, 55.
Red Flag, The, 403.
"Red Knight of Germany," 64.
"Red Letter," 241.
Redmond, J., 261.
"Red Scare," United States, 589, 682.
Red Sea, 365.
Refugees, 254n.2, 395–396, 462–464, 516–517, 615, 780, 801n.1.
Reich Regents, 446.
Reichsbank, 154, 162, 411–414.
Reichsrat, 408, 446.
Reichstadt, Duke of, 779.
Reichstag fire, 438 and n.1.
Reichswehr, 459–462.
Reich Union of Jews, 445.
Reims, 54, 72.
Religion, 118, 200, 201, 202, 228–231; see also Church conflicts.
Remarque, E. M., 416, 462n.2.
Rennenkampf, Edler von, 45.
Renner, K., 468.
Rentenmark, 414.
Rentiers, 306.
Reparation Commission, 97, 107–108, 148–156, 491; German, 93, 96–97, 99n., 104, 106–109, 110, 148–159, 162, 164–165, 166n., 305, 414, 418, 420, 433; non-German, 112, 113, 114, 159n., 475, 607.
Repulse, 830 and n.
Rerum Novarum, 357.
Rethel, 765.
"Return to Normalcy," 684–689.
Reuben James, 822n.2.
Revanche, 4.
Revisionism, 193–199, 362, 368, 493–499, 595, 614, 734.
"Revolver Republic," 152.
Reynaud, P. (1878–   ), 320, 756, 768–769, 777, 780–781.
RFC, 696–697, 709, 710.
Rheims. (See Reims.)
Rheza Khan. (See Riza.)
Rhineland, 104, 180–183; occupation, 91–92, 109–110, 149, 151–154, 155; separatism, 152, 411, 413; evacuation,

154, 158 and n.2, 436; remilitarization, 367.

Rhine River, 76, 91, 109, 196.

Rhodes, Island of, 114, 635, 791.

Rhodesia, 60.

Ribbentrop, J. von (1893–   ), 462, 538, 734, 735, 736, 739.

Richelieu, 773 and n.

Richthofen, Freiherr von, 64.

Rickenbacker, E. (1890–   ), 64.

Riff Tribes, 376–377.

Rintelen, A., 481n.1.

Río de Janeiro, 224, 723.

Río Grande do Sul, 224–225.

Riom Trials, 780–781.

Ríos, J. A., 219.

Río Tinto copper mines, 396n.

Rist, C., 171, 604.

Ritchie, N. M., 803.

Rivera. (*See* Primo de Rivera.)

Rivers, internationalized, 109, 462n.1, 506.

Riza Shah Pahlevi (1925–1941), 208, 802.

Road Back, The, 416.

Robin Moor, 822.

Robinson, J. T., 692.

Robles. (*See* Gil Robles.)

Rockefeller, N. A., 821n.

Rocque, F. de la, 312.

Rodney, 830n.

Rogers, W., 702.

Röhm, E., 446–447, 459–460, 461.

Romania, 7n.1, 13, 159n., 175, 184n.1, 185, 196, 366, 485, 488–489, 496, 552; First World War, 25–26, 36, 54, 58, 70; peace settlement, 58, 83, 112, 113, 114, 115, 598–599; minorities, 114, 115, 599ff., 744, 797; optants, 134, 600–601; land reform, 599–601; politics, 601–607; economic conditions, 600, 603, 604–605; fascism, 605–607; Second World War, 734–744, 755, 795, 796–799, 810, 825; partition, 744, 796–797.

Roman Question, 354–359.

Rome, 354–356; March on, 339.

Rommel, E., 802–804, 834.

Roosevelt, F. D. (1882–   ), 11n., 171, 367n.1, 512, 595, 693, 697–698, 705–724 passim., 734, 769, 810, 817–825, 826–828, 834, 836–837.

Roosevelt, T., 27, 683, 691n.

Root, E., 704.

Rosa, E., 358.

Rosenberg, A., 459.

Ross, F., 205.

Rossoni, E., 343–345.

Rothermere, Harold Harmsworth, Viscount, 81.

Rotterdam, 764.

Rouen, 768.

Round Tables, London, 288–291.

Rowlatt Acts, 283, 285, 286.

Ruanda-Urundi, 145.

Rublee, G., 463–464.

Ruhr, 141; occupation, 149, 151–154, 175, 306, 412, 435; evacuation, 159, 414.

Ruhrort, 149.

Rumania. (*See* Romania.)

Rumbold, H., 635.

Runciman, Walter Runciman, Viscount, 511.

Russia (R.S.F.S.R. and U.S.S.R.), 91, 114, 174, 335, 358, 435n., 462–463, 487, 499, 502, 519, 536; First World War, 5–10, 11, 16–19, 20–22, 23, 25, 36, 38, 41–42, 43, 44, 45–47, 52, 56–58, 68, 69, 70, 89, 542–543, 653; and Turkey, 20–22, 114, 138, 184n.1, 185, 590, 593, 645; Germany, 20–22, 176, 592, 593, 735–736, 808–814; March Revolution, 57, 544–545; November Revolution, 57, 546–548; League, 126, 131, 134, 596, 745; debts, 176, 551, 590, 591–592, 595, 776; foreign relations, 176–177, 184n.1, 185 and n.2, 195–196, 241, 246–247, 394, 395, 396–398, 433–434, 512, 529–530, 589–597, 599, 735–736, 808–814; Far East, 185n.2, 551n.2, 555n.1, 658–660, 662, 663, 672–673, 674–675, 678, 805–806; disarmament, 186–193, 732n.1; old regime, 539–543; economic conditions, 593–541, 542–543, 546, 564–571, 577–585; unions, 540, 569, 570, 576n.; education and religion, 541, 561, 562, 565, 585–588, 595–596; party conflicts, 542n., 571–577; Petrograd Soviet, 544–545; and United States, 544, 551, 567, 595–596, 685–686; Lvov Government, 544–545; Kerensky Government, 546–547; Congress of Soviets, 545, 547; counterrevolution, 548, 551–554, 567; becomes R.S.F.S.R. and U.S.S.R., 554–555; government, 555–561; franchise, 556, 557, 560; nationalities, 556, 558, 573, 586; Supreme Court, 558; inheritance, 560; party organization, 561–564; OGPU, 563–564, 574–575; attempted pure communism, 564–567; finances, 565, 566, 568, 578, 585, 590–592; famine, 567, 582; NEP, 568–571, 590, 591; private trading, 565, 568, 583; Five-Year Plans, 571, 577–

Russia (R.S.F.S.R. and U.S.S.R.)—Continued
585, 736, 809, 811; purges and trials, 575–577; urbanization, 584–585; Comintern, 588–590; Second World War, 583n.2, 738–750, 802, 805–806, 823n.; territorial additions (1939–1940), 739–741, 742–750; invasion, 808–814.
Russian Socialist Federated Soviet Republic, 554, 555–557, 573.
Ruthenia, 114, 500 and n., 508–509, 515, 528–530, 538; see also Carpatho-Ukraine and Ukraine.
Rybachi Peninsula, 745, 748.
Rykov, A., 548, 571, 574, 575.
Rzhev, 813.

S. A. (Sturmabteilungen.)
Saar, 89, 92–93, 104, 140–143, 431, 482.
Sacasa, J., 701 and n.2.
"Safeguarding clause," 190.
Safeguarding of Industries Act, 237.
Sahara, 363.
St. Gotthard, 494.
St. Jean Pied de Port, 770.
St. Lucia, 821.
St. Mihiel, 73.
St. Petersburg. (See Petrograd and Leningrad.)
St. Quentin, 54, 71, 74, 765–766.
Saionji, Prince, 83.
Sakharia River, Battle of the, 633.
Salazar, A. de O., 396.
Salgado, P., 226.
Salla, 748.
Salonika, 26, 48, 619–620; Armistice, 75.
Salvador, El, 211n.2, 672, 722.
Salzburg, 469, 470.
Samoa, 144, 831.
Samsonov, A., 45.
Samuel, H., 294, 299n.1.
San, Battle of the, 47.
Sanctions, League, 133, 251n.2, 350, 366–367, 368, 679.
Sandino, A., 701 and n.2.
Sanjurjo, J., 388, 393 and n.1.
San Marino, 24, 86, 116.
San Remo Conference, 145.
Santiago, 215, 703.
Santos, E., 221.
São Paulo, 224–225.
Sarajevo, 3, 12, 14–15.
Sarawak, 831.
Sardinia, 792.
Sarrail, M., 26, 326–327.
Sarraut, A., 314.

Saseno, 333.
Satyagraha, 286ff.
Saudi Arabia, 114, 282, 635.
Savoy, 321, 361, 369.
Saxony, 413, 456.
Sazonov, S., 17, 19.
Scapa Flow, 105n.
Schacht (Horace Greeley) H. (1877–   ), 158–159, 405, 414, 450.
Scheer, R., 62–63.
Scheidemann, P. (1865–1939), 99, 399–402, 405–406, 410.
Schirach, B. von, 447.
Schlageter, L., 453.
Schleicher, K. von, 192, 426, 433, 437, 460.
Schleswig, 101.
Schlieefen, Count von (1833–1913), 43, 44; Plan, 17, 18 and n.1, 43.
Schober, J. (1874–1932), 160, 470, 475, 476.
Schoen, Freiherr von, 13.
School of Wisdom, 415.
Schubert Festival (1928), 475.
Schuschnigg, K. von (1897–?), 481, 482–484 and n.1.
Schutzbund, 471–473, 478.
Schutzstaffeln, 423 and n., 459, 460–462.
Schwarze Korps, Das, 459.
Schweinepolitik, 14.
Scotland, 29, 257.
Second International, 588n.
Secret diplomacy, 7, 12–13, 19, 21ff., 69, 87.
"Secret Treaties," 21–22 and n., 36, 67–68, 96, 112, 114, 551n.1, 653, 794; Wilson and, 82, 88–89.
Securities Law, 707.
Security, search for, 173–199; see also Disarmament.
Sedan, 74, 765.
Seipel, I. (1876–1932), 470–471, 475.
Seitz, K., 467, 479.
Selective Service Acts, 71, 818 and n.2–819.
Self-determination, 57, 94, 95, 114, 117, 206, 275, 294ff., 485, 632; Briand on, 474n.; see also Plebiscites.
Self-sufficiency. (See Autarkie.)
Separatism, Alsace, 325; Bavaria, 76, 402, 406, 411, 413; China, 673ff., 678–680; France, 780; Rhineland, 152, 411, 413; Slovakia, 509; Spain, 372, 375–376, 377, 379, 380, 382–385, 387–388, 389, 390, 394.
Serbia (Serbs), 7n.1, 620, 621; First World

War, 3, 4, 10, 11, 13–17, 20, 22, 24–25, 26, 36, 41, 46, 47, 70, 75; *see also* Yugoslavia.
Seton-Watson, R., 622.
Seyss-Inquart, A., 484–485 and n.1, 764.
Shanghai, 670, 677.
Shannon River, 268, 269.
Shantung Peninsula, 20, 60, 96, 104, 207, 651–652, 653, 655, 657.
Sheriat, 641.
Sherman, L. Y., 683.
Shevket, M., 629.
Shidehahra, Baron, 657.
Shostakovich, D., 587.
Siam. (*See* Thailand.)
Sian Mutiny, 657–676.
Siberia, 551n.2, 555n.1, 585, 596n., 674–675.
Sicily, 792.
Sidi Barrani, 793.
Sidky, I., 278–279.
Sidor, K., 517.
Siegfried Line, 54, 73.
Sıkorski, W., 739.
Silesia, Austrian, 112, 500 and n.; Upper, 99, 101–102, 531.
Silver Purchase Act, 710–711.
Silvestre, F., 377 and n.
Sima, H., 798–799.
Simon, J. (1873–   ), 249, 253, 287; Commission, 287-288.
Simovich, D., 800.
Simpson, J. H., 296, 462n.2.
Simpson, Mrs. W. W., 254.
Sinclair, H. F., 688–689.
Singapore, 241, 808, 829n.3, 830, 831.
Sinn Fein, 262–265.
Sit-down strikes, 315, 717.
Sivas, 631.
Sixtus, Prince of Bourbon-Parma, 69.
Skagerrak, 62–63, 757.
Skrzynski, A., 526.
Skwarzyński, S., 525.
Slesvig, 101.
Slovakia (Slovaks), 46n., 75, 114, 485, 488, 499, 500 and n., 505, 506, 509–510, 515, 516–517, 741, 798, 810; *see also* Czechoslovakia.
Slovak National Council, 502.
Slovenes. (*See* Croatia-Slavonia.)
Śmigly-Rydz, E., 525, 738.
Smith, A. E. (1873–   ), 691, 692–693, 697, 715.
Smith, J., Jr., 491.
Smuts, J. C. (1870–   ), 60, 83, 90, 95–96, 97, 260, 751n.

Smyrna (Izmir), 22n., 114, 115, 615, 631, 633, 634, 638.
Snowden of Ickornshaw, Viscount (1864–1937), 240, 249, 250, 251 and n.1, 253.
Socialist Conference, Stockholm, 68.
Social Security Act, 713.
Socony Hill, 703.
Sofia, 610, 799.
Soissons, 55, 72, 73.
Sokolnikov, G., 576.
Soldiers' Bonus Bill, 712.
Solomon Islands, 831.
Solomon's Temple, 295.
Somerville, J. F., 772–773.
Somme River, 73; Battle of the, 49–50.
Sonnino, Baron, 82, 89, 94.
"Sons of the Wolf," 343.
Sophie, Duchess of Hohenberg, 3, 15.
Sopron, 469, 489.
Sotelo, J. C., 392.
Souchon, W., 21.
South Africa. (*See* Union of South Africa.)
Southern Constitutionalist Government, 651, 659.
Southern Tenant Farmers' Union, 717.
South Manchuria Railway, 652, 664, 667, 673.
Southslavs, 3, 4, 13–14, 24, 75, 93–94, 332–333, 362, 620ff.; *see also* Yugoslavia.
South Tirol, 23, 93, 111–112, 352–354, 474, 735, 741; *see also* Tirol.
South West Africa, 60, 144.
Sovkhozi, 579.
Spa Conference (1918), 73, 402; (1920), 148; Percentages, 148, 156.
SPAB, 818 and n.1.
Spain, 223, 316, 769; Morocco, 374, 376–377, 378, 379, 387, 392–393; and League, 379 and n., 435–436; historical background, 372–375; regionalism, 372, 375–376, 377, 379, 380, 382–385, 387–388, 389, 390, 394; economic conditions, 372–380, 387–388; Catholic Church, 373, 374, 378, 381, 383–386, 389, 390; First World War, 374–375; dictatorship, 377–381; republicanism, 380, 381, 382–390; syndicalism, 388, 389; education, 386; civil war, 391–398; reconstruction, 395–396; and "Little World War," 396–398.
Spanish White Book, 394n.
SPARS, 828n.
Spartacists, 400, 403–404, 405.
"Special areas," British, 257.

Spectators' sports, 699.
Spee, Count von, 61.
Spengler, O. (1880–1936), 415–416.
Squadrism, 337, 340.
S. S. (See Schutzstaffeln.)
Stabilization funds, 255, 710.
Stack, L., 276.
Stahlhelm, 409, 446.
Stalin, J. (1879–   ), 548, 563, 571–577, 589, 809, 837.
Stalingrad, 573, 814.
Stambulisky, A. (1879–1923), 608–609.
Standard Oil ships, China, 678.
Starhemberg, Prince (1899–   ), 472, 478, 481, 482.
Starzynski, S., 738.
State Planning Commission. (See Gosplan.)
Statute of Autonomy, Catalonia, 383–384, 387, 390.
Statute of Westminster, 254.
Stauning, T., 758.
Stavisky, A., 311, 313, 319.
Steeg, T., 309.
Steel Helmet, 409, 446.
Štefánik, M., 502 and n.
Steidle, R., 475.
Stephens, G. W., 142.
Sterilization Law, 454, 458.
Stern, G., 747.
Stettin, 109.
Stimson, H. L. (1867–   ), 671, 701, 817; Doctrine, 671, 705.
Stinnes, H. (1870–1924), 149, 430.
Stockholm Conference, 68.
Stokley, J., 788 n.1.
Storm Troops. (See Sturmabteilungen.)
Stoyadinovich, M., 626–628.
Straits, at Constantinople, 8, 10, 11, 21, 47–48, 115, 632, 634, 635, 646–647; at Otranto, 333, 370, 796.
Strasbourg, 4, 324.
Streeruwitz, E., 475.
Streicher, J., 441–442, 458.
"Strength through Joy," 448.
Stresemann, G. (1878–1929), 180, 405, 418, 420, 434–436.
Strumitsa, 113.
Stukas, 767, 787–788, 792.
Sturdee, F., 61.
Sturmabteilungen, 423 and n., 425–426, 453, 459–462.
Stürmer, Der, 441, 458.
Sturmscharen, 481.
Sturzo, L., 335.
Styria, 469, 470, 472, 473, 621.

Submarines, 29–39, 41, 61–62, 73, 175, 187–188, 397–398, 401, 738n., 753, 757, 761, 814, 822 and n.2, 830, 833n.
Sudan, 8, 114, 276–277, 280, 635, 791, 794.
"Sudetenland," 112, 319, 499, 510–514.
Suez Canal, 276, 280, 792–794, 813.
Suffrage extensions, 118, 235, 245–246, 284, 292, 406, 497, 499, 556–560, 633n., 641, 684.
"Suicide Chamber," 347, 348.
Sun Yat-sen (1867–1925), 207, 650, 659, 660.
Suomussalmi, 746.
Supply Priorities and Allocation Board, 818 and n.1.
Supreme Court, Germany, 407, 438n.1; Russia, 558, 576; Spain, 388, 389; United States, 689, 713–714, 715.
Supreme Peace Council, 84, 333, 489, 521, 528, 535, 633.
Supreme War Council, 71; Second World War, 738n.
Surinam, 824.
Sušak, 94.
Sussex, 35.
Švehla, A., 502.
Svetkovich. (See Cvetkovich.)
Swaraj, 286ff.
Swastika, 423, 438, 461n.
Sweden, 28, 134–135, 436, 746, 748, 757, 761.
Sweepstakes, Irish, 268n.
Switzerland, 116, 186.
Syndicalism, France, 344; Italy, 343–345; Spain, 388, 389.
Synthetic products, 430, 450–451.
Syria, 22n., 60, 96, 114, 145, 275, 326–329, 634, 635, 645, 781–782, 791, 801–802.
Syrový, J., 512, 516.
Szalasi, F., 498n.
Szamuelly, T., 488.

Tabasco, 230.
Tadjikistan, 555.
Taft, W. H., 80.
Tanaka, Baron, 657.
Tanganyika, 60, 145.
Tangier, 9, 362.
Tangku Armistice, 672.
Tankosich, V., 14.
Tanks, 50, 56, 737, 767, 782 and n.2, 803, 812.
Tannenberg, Battle of, 46.
Taranto, 796.

Tardieu, A., 82, 173, 304, 305, 307–310, 312, 313.
Tariff Retaliation, 694n.
Tariffs and trade, 6, 58, 69, 109 and n.1, 160, 163, 169–172, 211–215, 236–238, 239, 241, 242, 247, 249–251, 255ff., 269, 270ff., 273, 309, 310ff., 334, 349–350, 379, 380, 387, 448–453, 470, 476, 483, 492, 495, 506, 526 and n., 582, 591ff., 594, 595, 628, 643–644, 681, 686, 694 and n., 695, 720.
Tatarescu, G., 605–606.
Taylor, F. W. (1856–1915), 428.
Teapot Dome, 688.
Teleki, Count, 498–499.
Temesvár, 25, 114, 599, 621.
Tenedos, 635.
Tennessee, 684; Valley Authority, 707, 719.
Teplice-Sanov (Teplitz-Schönau), 511.
Terra, G., 220.
Terrazas, L., 227.
Teschen, 112, 515, 741.
Thailand, 39, 83, 86, 104, 209, 808, 824, 825n., 830.
Theaters, 699.
Thälmann, E., 419, 425.
"They shall not pass!" 49.
Third International, 588–590, 595n.2.
Third Reich, meaning, 422 and n.1.
Thomas, J. H., 249, 251, 270–271.
Thomas, N. (1884–   ), 693, 697–698, 714.
Thorez, M., 315.
Thrace, 113, 114, 615, 633–634, 635.
Three Emperors' League, 6.
Three Principles of the People, 650.
Thuku, H., 201.
Thyssen, F., 424.
Tibet, 8.
Ticino, 361n.
Tientsin, 672, 677.
Timoshenko, S. K., 812.
Tirol, 93, 469, 470; *see also* South Tirol.
Tirpitz, A. von (1849–1930), 61, 401, 409, 418, 753.
Tiso, J., 516–517.
Tisza, Count, 16.
Tittoni, T., 82, 94, 352.
Titulescu, N., 605.
Tobruk, 803.
Togoland, 60, 145.
Tojo, H., 824.
Tokyo, 676, 831, 833.
Toledano, V. L., 228.
Tomsky, M., 576n.

Tonningen, R. van, 764.
Torre. (*See* Haya de la Torre.)
Toul, 43.
Toulon, 772, 773, 835–836.
Tours, 768n., 770.
Tourists, American, 698.
Tounshend, C. V. F., 48, 60.
Townsend, F. E., 714.
Toynbee, A. J., 777.
Trade, world. (*See* Tariffs.)
Trades Union Congress, 243–244.
Trades Unions and Trades Disputes Act, 245, 248, 250.
Trade unions, Austria, 480n.; France. 316, 320–321, 780; Germany, 413, 448; Great Britain, 243–245; Russia, 540, 569, 570, 576n.; United States, 708, 716–717, 720 and n.
Transcaucasia, 554–555, 573.
Trans-Jordan, 145, 299, 801, 802.
Trans-Siberian Railway, 554.
Transylvania, 25, 114, 487, 599, 600, 797.
Travel Diary of a Philosopher, 415.
Treaties are listed in alphabetical order according to the cities in which they were signed or the adjectival forms of one or another of the signatories:
American-Austrian Treaty (1921), 685.
American-Canadian Treaty (1923), 258.
American Collective Security Convention (1936), 723.
American-French Treaty (1919), 92, 173, 728.
American-German Treaty (1921), 685.
American-Hungarian Treaty (1921), 685.
American-Japanese Agreements (1911), 680, (1917), 653n., (1922), 657.
Anglo-Egyptian Treaties (1921, 1922), 276, (1929), 277, (1936), 280, 792.
Anglo-French Commitment (1912), 13, 19.
Anglo-French Military-Naval Compromise (1928), 188.
Anglo-French Treaties (1904), 8–9, 174–175, (1919), 92, 173, 728.
Anglo-French-Turkish Alliance (1939), 755.
Anglo-French Union, proposal (1940), 769.
Anglo-German Naval Agreement (1935), 198, 734.
Anglo-German Peace Avowal (1938), 514n.1.
Anglo-Iraqi Treaties (1922, 1926, 1930, 1932), 137, 145n.2.

Treaties—*Continued*

Anglo-Irish Treaties (1921), 264–265, 267, (1938), 273–274.

Anglo-Japanese Alliance (1902, 1905, 1911), 8n.3, 20, 187, 655, 656, 686.

Anglo-Persian Treaty (1919), 208.

Anglo-Russian Alliances (1941), 810, (1942), 828.

Anglo-Russian Entente (1907), 9, 19, 22, 208.

Anglo-Russian Trade Agreement (1921), 237, 591.

Anglo-Turkish Treaties (1926), 138, (1939), 329, 735, 755.

Anti-Communist Pact (1936), 199, 368, 398, 499, 596.

Austro-Czechoslovak Treaties (1921), 470, 507, (1926), 507.

Austro-German Agreement (1936), 483.

Austro-German Alliance (1879), 6–7.

Austro-German Customs Accord (1931), 160–161, 163n.1, 433, 475–476.

Austro-Italian Treaty (1930), 194.

Austro-Serbian Treaty (1881), 7n.1.

Balkan Pact (1934), 196, 620, 647.

Belgian-French Alliance (1920), 174.

Berlin, Treaties of (1921), 685, (1926), 177, 434, 436.

"Bread Peace" (1918), 58n.

Brest-Litovsk, Treaty of (1918), 57–58, 76, 551.

Brussels Agreement (1919), 87n.

Bucharest, Treaty of (1918), 58, 76.

Budapest, Treaty of (1921), 685.

Bulgarian-Balkan Entente Treaty (1938), 614.

Bulgarian-Greek Treaties (1924), 608, (1929), 612–613.

Chinese Treaties. (*See under* Sino-.)

Concordats, Austria (1934), 480; Czechoslovakia (1927), 505; France (1801), 324; Germany (1933), 457–458; Italy (1929), 354–359; Poland (1925), 537; Yugoslavia (1935), 626.

Convention on . . . European Colonies . . . in the Americas (1940), 820–821.

Corfu, Pact of (1917), 75, 621.

Craiova Agreement (1940), 797.

Croat-Serb Agreement (1939), 627.

Czechoslovak-French Treaty (1924), 175.

Czechoslovak-Italian Treaty (1924), 177.

Czechoslovak-Romanian Treaty (1921), 175.

Czechoslovak-Russian Agreement (1941), 810.

Czechoslovak-Yugoslav Treaty (1920), 175.

Danish-German Pact (1939), 735, 758n.

Danzig-Polish Agreements (1920), 532, (1921), 532, (1933), 533–534.

Declaration by United Nations (1942), 826–827 and n.

Declaration of the Solidarity of America (1938), 723.

Declaration of Panama (1939), 820.

Delhi Pact (1931), 289.

Dorpat, Treaty of (1920), 553.

Dual Alliance (1879), 6–7, (1894), 8.

Eastern Pact (1937), 647.

Entente Cordiale (1904), 8–9, 174–175.

Estonian-German Pact (1939), 735.

Estonian-Russian Treaties (1920), 553, (1939), 742–743.

Ethiopian-Italian Treaties (1888–1928), 364.

Finnish-Russian Treaties (1920), 554, (1932), 745, (1940), 748.

First Geneva Protocol (1922), 471, 476.

Four-Power Treaties, Rome (1933), 184–185, 193n.1, 595n.1; Washington (1922), 656.

Franco-German Agreement (1938), 321.

Franco-Italian Treaties (1902), 7, 13, (1935), 198, 363–364, 482.

Franco-Polish Alliance (1921), 174.

Franco-Romanian Treaty (1926), 175.

Franco-Russian Entente (1891), 8.

Franco-Russian Treaties (1894), 8, (1932), 195, 595, (1935), 195, 318, 319, 596, 732 and n.

Franco-Syrian Treaties (1933), 328, (1936), 328, 329.

Franco-Turkish Treaties (1921), 634, (1938), 328–329, (1939), 329, 735.

Franco-Yugoslav Treaty (1927), 175, 370, 628.

Geneva Protocols, First (1922), 471, 476; Second (1924), 179, 241, 306, 729.

German-Italian Alliance (1939), 734–735.

German-Italian-Japanese Pact (1940), 798, 806–808 and n.1, 826n.

German-Japanese Pact (1936), 199, 368, 398, 499, 596.

German-Polish Treaties (1921), 534, (1922), 531, (1934), 195, 535, 537, 734, (1937), 531.

German-Russian Treaties (1887), 6, 8,

(1922), 176, 434, 592, (1926), 177, 434, 436, (August 1939), 675, 735–736, 808–809, (September 1939), 739.

German-Slovak Treaty (1939), 517.

German-Turkish Treaty (1914), 20–21.

Greco-Italian Treaty (1928), 194.

Greco-Serb Alliance (1913), 26, 619.

Greco-Turkish Treaties (1923), 615, 636, (1930), 194, 615, (1933), 194, 615.

Greco-Yugoslav Treaty (1929), 620.

Guarantee Treaties (1919), 92, 173, 728.

Halibut Fisheries Treaty (1923), 258.

Hussein-McMahon Correspondence (1914–1916), 301.

Irwin-Gandhi Agreement (1931), 289.

Italo-Albanian Treaties (1926), 178, 370, 371, (1927), 178, 370.

Italo-Hungarian Treaty (1927), 178, 494.

Italo-Papal Accord (1929), 354–359.

Italo-Romanian Treaty (1926), 177.

Italo-Russian Treaties (1909), 13, (1924), 592, (1931), 349, (1933), 194.

Italo-Spanish Treaty (1926), 177, 379.

Italo-Turkish Treaty (1928), 194.

Italo-Yugoslav Treaties (1920), 333 and n., (1924), 177, 362n., (1928), 361–362, 623–624.

Japanese-Manchoukuo Protocol (1932), 671.

Khabarovsk Protocol (1929), 662.

Lana, Treaty of (1921), 470, 507.

Lansing-Ishii Agreement (1917), 653n.

Lateran Accord (1929), 354–359.

Latvian-German Pact (1939), 735.

Latvian-Russian Treaties (1920), 554, (1939), 743.

Lausanne Protocol (Austria, 1932), 476, 477 and n.

Lausanne Reparation Agreement (1932), 164–165, 169.

Lausanne, Treaty of (1923), 136, 137, 615, 635–636, 637, 641, 646.

Laval-Mussolini Pact (1935), 198, 363–364, 482.

Lithuanian-Russian Treaties (1920), 554, (1926), 177, (1939), 743.

Litvinov Protocol (1929), 184n.1, 537, 594.

Locarno Agreements (1925), 181–183, 246, 419, 434, 435–436, 535, 593, 732, 765.

London Agreements (1933), 185 and n.2, 193n.1, 195, 595n.1.

London, Declaration of (1909), 28 and n.

London Naval Treaties (1930–1931), 190, 670, (1936), 732n.1.

London, Pact of (1914–1915), 24.

London Protocol (1938), 732n.

London Schedule (1921), 149.

London, Treaty of (1915), 22n., 23–24, 88, 93–94.

London Wheat Pact (1933), 171n.

Mongolian-Russian Pact (1936), 674.

Montreux Convention, Egypt (1937), 280.

Montreux Straits Convention (1936), 646–647.

Moscow, Treaties of (1920), 535, (1922), 554, (1940), 748.

Munich Agreement (1938), 512–515, 597.

Mutual Assistance, Treaty of (1923), 179.

Mutual Guarantee, Treaty of. (*See* Locarno Agreements.)

Nettuno Convention (1928), 361–362, 623–624.

Neuilly, Treaty of (1919), 112–113, 607, 614.

Nine-Power Treaties (1922), 656, 670n., 677, 679.

Nyon Agreement (1937), 397–398.

Panama, Declaration of (1939), 820.

Paris Agreement on Eastern Reparations (1930), 159n., 601.

Paris Pact (1928), 183–184 and n.1 and 2, 185, 189, 247, 436, 594, 662, 670n., 705.

Paris, Peace of (1856), 135.

Paris, Peace of (1919–1920), 100n.1, 101–119, 124, 178n., 685.

Pittsburgh Pact (1918), 509.

Polish-Romanian Treaty (1921), 175.

Polish-Russian Treaties (1920), 535, 554, (1931, 1934), 195, 537, (1941), 741n., 810.

Protocol for the Pacific Settlement of International Disputes (1924), 179, 241, 306, 729.

Quadruple Agreement (1913), 7n.1.

Rapallo, Treaties of (1920), 333 and n., (1922), 176, 434, 592.

Reinsurance Treaty (1887), 6, 8.

Riga, Treaty of (1920), 554.

Rome, Pacts of (1918), 332, (1933), 184–185, 193n.1, 595n.1, (1935), 198, 363–364.

Rome Protocols (1934), 194, 495.

Rome, Treaty of (1924), 333n.

Russo-Afghan Treaty (1926), 177.

Treaties—*Continued*

Russo-Iranian Treaty (1927), 177, 594.

Russo-Japanese Agreement (1939), 675.

Russo-Japanese Neutrality Pact (1941), 675, 809.

Russo-Turkish Treaty (1925), 177.

St. Germain-en-Laye, Treaty of (1919), 96, 110–112, 423, 468, 483, 654.

St. Jean de Maurienne Agreement (1917), 22n.

Sazonov-Paléologue Agreement (1916), 22n.

Second Geneva Protocol (1924), 179, 241, 306, 729.

"Secret Treaties" of First World War, 21–22 and n., 36, 67–68, 96, 112, 114, 551n.1, 653, 794; Wilson and, 82, 88–89.

Sèvres, Treaty of (1920), 114–115, 286, 629, 633, 637, 646.

Silver Pact (1933), 171.

Sino-Japanese Treaties (1905), 667, (1915), 652, 653, (1922), 657.

Six-Power Treaty (1922), 656.

Standstill Agreements (1931ff.), 163 and n.2.

Suwalki Agreement (1920), 535–536.

Sykes-Picot Agreement (1916), 22n.

Tartu, Treaty of (1920), 553.

Tirana, Treaty of (1926), 370, 371.

Tokyo, Treaty of (1941), 808.

Trianon, Treaty of (1920), 113–114, 175, 489, 491 and n., 493, 494, 496, 497, 600.

Tripartite Pact (1940), 798, 806–808 and n.1, 826n.

Triple Alliance (1882ff.), 6–9, 18, 22–24.

Triple Entente (1907), 9, 19, 24.

Turco-British-French Alliance (1939), 755.

Turco-British Treaties (1926), 138, (1939), 329, 735.

Vatican Accord (1929), 354–359.

Versailles, Treaty of (1919), 189, 192, 198, 303, 304, 406, 409, 410, 450, 654; drafting, 79–100; ratification, 100n.1; terms, 101–110, 130 and n., 140, 151, 427–428, 534; revisionism, 239, 423; United States and, 682–684; Second World War, 727–729, 733.

Vienna Awards (1938), 499, 515, (1940), 797.

Vienna, Treaty of (1921), 685.

Washington Treaties (1921–1922), 187–188, 654–658.

Wheat Pact (1933), 171n.

Yugoslav-Romanian Treaty (1921), 175.

Treaty registration, 127.

Trebizond, 115.

Treboven, J., 761.

Treitschke, H. von, 5.

Trentino, 23, 50–52, 75, 111, 352.

Trialism, 14, 16.

Trieste, 23, 75, 111.

Trinidad, 821.

Triple Monarchy, 14, 16.

Tripoli, 834.

Tripolitania. (*See* Libya.)

Tripolitan War (1911–1912), 11, 336.

"Trojan-Horse tactics," 759–760.

Trondheim, 761.

Trotsky, L. D. (1877–1940), 57, 487, 548, 550–551 and n.1, 553, 565, 571–576.

Trotsky, L. S., 576.

Trumbich, A., 83.

Trustees of Labor, 448, 452.

Tsai Ting-kai, 670.

Tsaldaris, P., 617.

Tsankov, A., 609, 611.

Tsingtao, 20n.

Tsu Hsi, 648.

Tugwell, R. G., 712.

Tuka, V., 510.

Tulagi, 831.

Tumulty, J. P., 33.

Tunisia, 6, 114, 198, 321, 361, 364, 368–369, 788, 834, 836.

Tunney, (J. J.) G., 699.

Turco-Iraqi boundary. (*See* Mosul.)

Turco-Italian War (1911–1912), 11.

Turkestan-Siberian Railway, 578.

Turkey, 11, 189, 496; First World War, 20–22 and n., 25, 26, 36, 39n., 47–48, 57, 70, 75, 275; and Russia, 20–22, 114, 138, 184n.1, 185, 590, 593, 633, 645; peace settlement, 95–96, 100n.1, 110, 114–115, 629, 631, 635–636; League, 136–138, 645; Mosul, 136–138, 635, 645; Kurds, 137, 167; reparation, 159n., foreign relations, 196, 328–329, 632–637 and n., 645–647; Greece, 614–615, 631, 633–637 and n.; republic established, 634; United States, 634, 646; Independents, 638; religion, women, education, 639–642; economic conditions, 640, 643–646; Straits refortified, 646–647; Second World War, 755, 795, 837.

Turkish National Pact, 631–632, 635.

Turkmenistan, 555.

Turner, W. T., 32n.

"Turnip year," 400.
TVA, 707, 719.
Twentieth Amendment, 710n.
Twenty-first Amendment, 706n.1.
Twenty-five Points, 422–423.
Twenty-one Demands, 652 and n.
Tydings-McDuffie Bill, 722.
Tyrone, 267.
Ualual, 362, 364.
U-boats. (*See* Submarines.)
Udine, 58.
Ukraine (Ukrainians), 57, 58n., 520–521, 528–530, 552, 554, 582, 738, 739–741, 744, 811, 813–814; *see also* Ruthenians.
Ukrainian People's Republic, 57, 58n.
Ulster. (*See* Northern Ireland.)
Ulyanov, A., 549.
Ulynaov, V. I. (*See* Lenin.)
Unden, Ö., 436.
Underwood Tariff, 681, 686.
Unemployment, 159, 169; Austria, 467, 475; France, 309, 310; Germany, 161n., 420, 424, 426, 429, 432, 447, 451; Great Britain, 236, 237, 239, 241, 247, 250, 251, 256; Hungary, 486; Italy, 334, 348; Spain, 387; United States, 696, 705, 706, 708, 709, 711, 713, 718.
Union of South Africa, 60, 83, 103, 126n., 144, 202, 258–259, 285, 751n.
Union of Soviet Socialist Republics. (*See* Russia.)
Union of Turkish Women, 641.
"Union or Death," 14 and n.1, 15, 17.
United Mine Workers of America, 716, 720n.
United Nations, 751–837 passim., coöperation, 751–752, 755–756, 810, 826–828, 834, 836–837; members, 827n.; post-war problems, 789–790, 828–829.
United Provinces, 293.
United States, 9, 11n.1, 118–119, 258, 263, 428, 431, 433, 463, 526; First World War, 26–39, 54, 62, 66, 67–70, 71–76; elections (1916), 35–36, 681, (1918), 80, 681, (1920), 683–684, (1924), 690–691, (1928), 691–692, (1930), 697, (1932), 697–698, 704, (1934), 711, (1936), 714–715, (1938), 715, (1940), 719–720; peace settlement, 79–100 passim., 104n., 115, 682–685; League, 90–91, 126, 131, 682–684, 685, 704–705; reparation and war debts, 97, 153, 155, 156 and n.2, 162, 165–169, 311, 348, 700, 703, 720–721; tariffs and trade, 169–172 and n.1, 257, 595–596, 663n., 665, 681, 686, 694 and n., 695, 700–701, 720; economic condi-

tions, 170–171, 681–682, 686–687, 691, 694–697, 705–720; disarmament, 186–193, 196–197, 654–658, 732; foreign investments, 213 and n., 700–701, 702n.1; education and culture, 222, 698–700; foreign relations, 228, 367n.1, 596n., 646, 652, 653 and n., 654–658, 662, 663n., 667, 670–671, 677–680, 686, 690, 701–705, 720–724, 804–808, 823–825; neutrality legislation, 367n.1, 723–724, 816–817, 824; "Red Scare," 589, 682; Russia, 544, 551, 567, 595–596, 685–686; Far East, 596n., 649, 652, 653 and n., 654–658, 662, 663n., 665, 667, 670–671, 677–680, 686, 690, 702–703, 721, 724, 804–808, 823–825; strikes, 682, 686–687, 690, 708, 716–717; Socialist Party, 683, 693, 687–698, 714, 720; Prohibition, 684, 691, 692–694, 697, 705–706 and n.1; "Return to Normalcy," 684–689; Bonus, 686, 690, 697, 706, 712; farm problems, 687, 691, 695, 705, 706, 709, 710–712, 717 and n.; scandals and crimes, 688–689, 691, 694; Supreme Court, 689, 713–714, 715; immigration, 690, 815n.; Progressive Party, 691; religion, 692–693; depression, 695–697, 699, 705ff., 716; gold measures, 696ff., 705–706 and n.2, 707, 709, 710; New Deal, 705–720; child labor, 708, 712, 718; national debt, 696, 711; rural rehabilitation, 709–710, 712, 717; Union Party, 714; Labor Party, 715; Congressional "purge," 716; civil-service extension, 718; Second World War, 803, 804–808, 814–825, 826–837 passim.; rearmament, 817–819; hemisphere defense, 819–822; aid to Britain, 719, 815, 817, 822–823; African campaigns, 834–836.
United States of Europe, 160, 308.
United States Shipping Board, 36.
University City, Spain, 381n.
"Unredeemed Italy," 4, 7, 22–23, 361n., 368–369.
Untouchables, 288, 290.
Upper Austria, 469, 470.
Upper Silesia, 99, 101–102, 531.
Ural Mountains, 811.
Urbanization, 215–218, 584–585.
Uruguay, 139, 211n.2, 213, 215, 217, 219–220, 229, 754.
Ustacha, 496.
Uzebkistan, 555.
Uzunovich, N., 625.

Valencia, 393.
Valera, E. de (1882–   ), 263, 264–266, 268 and n., 269–275, 671.
Valona (Avlona), 22–23, 93, 333, 795.
Van, 115.
Vargas, G., 224–226, 837.
Vatican City, 356 and n.
Venezuela, 211n.2, 213, 217, 229.
Venice (Venezia), 6, 50–52.
Venizelos, E. (1864–1936), 26, 83, 614–620, 633.
Vera Cruz, 230.
Verdun, 43, 48–49, 52, 55.
Veterans' Bureau, 688.
Viborg. (See Viipuri.)
Vicenza, 52.
Vichy Government, 778–782, 801–802, 808, 824, 830, 834–836.
Victor Emmanuel III (1900–   ), 339, 362, 367, 371.
Vienna, 465, 466, 467, 468, 469, 472–473, 474, 479–480 and n., 481; Award (1938), 499, 515, (1940), 797; Congress of (1814–1815), 3, 518.
Viipuri, 748.
Villa Giusti, Armistice, 75, 465, 486.
Vilnius (Wilno), 134, 535–536, 739.
Vimy Ridge, 55.
Vistula River, 534.
Vittorio Veneto, Battle of, 75.
Vladivostok, 551, 554, 663.
Voden, 612.
Volga River, 554, 813, 814.
Volga Flows to the Caspian Sea, The, 587.
Volstead Act, 684, 706.
"Volunteers," in Russia, 810; Spain, 393, 396–398.
Vorarlberg, 469.
Voroshilov, K. E., 812.
Vosges Mountains, 17, 43.

WAAC, 828n.
Wafd, 275–281 passim.
Wagner-Connery Labor Relations Act, 712.
Wagner-Lewis Emergency Relief Act, 707.
Wailing-Wall Dispute, 295.
Wake, 830.
Waldeck, 406n.
Wales, 257.
Wallace, H. A., 719.
Walsh, T. J., 688.
Walwal. (See Ualual.)
Wang Ching-wei, 680, 804.

War, renunciation of. (See Paris Pact.)
War aims, 36–37, 56–57, 67–70, 751, 782, 784, 789, 826–827, 828–829.
"War criminals," 100, 106, 112, 409.
War debts. (See Inter-Allied Debts.)
Warfield, Mrs. W., 254.
War Guilt. (See Guilt clause.)
War Manpower Commission, 828n.
War Production Board, 818n.1.
Warsaw, 554, 738; Declaration of, 530; March on, 522.
Washington, 703, 828; Conference, 175, 187, 196–197, 654.
Wavell, A. P. (1883–   ), 792–793, 803.
WAVES, 828n.
Weimar Assembly, 100, 404–408, 409; Coalition, 405–408.
Weizmann, C., 83, 297.
Wells, H. G., 535.
"We or They," 199, 396, 731, 815.
Werner, F., 457.
Wessel, H., 453.
Westminster, Statute of, 259.
West Prussia, 95, 101, 534.
West Wall, 452, 738, 752.
Wet, C. de, 60.
Weygand, M., 326, 766, 767–769, 782; Line, 767–768.
Whampoa Military Academy, 660, 661.
Wheatley Bill, 241.
Wheeler, B. K., 688.
White, H., 80, 94, 98.
White Russia, 554, 738, 739–741.
Whitman, W., 490.
Wickersham, G. W., 694.
Wiesbaden, 771.
Wilhelmina (1898–   ), 764.
William II, of Germany (1888–1918), 7–8, 9, 16–17, 18, 26, 58n., 73, 76, 106, 108, 235, 401–402.
William, of Urach, 58n.
William, of Wied and Albania, 369.
Willingdon, Freeman Freeman-Thomas, Earl of, 290.
Willkie, W. L. (1892–   ), 719–720.
Wilno. (See Vilnius.)
Wilson, (T.) W. (1856–1924), 166, 369, 376, 401, 416, 485, 519, 646, 657, 681–684, 691n.; First World War, 27–39, 73ff.; peace moves, 36–37, 67–70, 73–75; peace conference, 79–100 passim., 110, 114, 115, 333, 654; "Secret Treaties," 82, 88–89; mandates, 96, 203.
"Wilson Line" (Dalmatia), 94.
Wilton, E., 142.
Windsor, Duke of. (See Edward VIII.)

Winkelman, H., 764.
Winter Relief Work, 452.
Wirth, J., 149, 434.
Witos, V., 522, 523n., 526.
Wittelsbachs, 402.
Wojciechowski, S., 521, 522.
Woman suffrage. (*See* Suffrage extensions.)
Wood, L., 33, 683.
Woodhead Report, 300.
Workers' Weekly, 241.
Work Projects Administration, 718 and n.
Work Relief Bill, 712.
Works Progress Administration, 712, 718.
World Court. (*See* Permanent Court.)
World Monetary and Economic Conference, 169–171, 478, 709.
World War, First, 133, 207, 258, 261–262, 332, 374–375, 519, 542, 588n., 651, 653–654, 757; fundamental causes, 3–13; immediate causes, 13–15; spread, 20–39; entry of United States, 26–39; peace moves, 36–37, 56–57, 67–70; advantages of belligerents, 40–42; military operations, 43–60, 70–76, 369; naval, 60–63; colonial, 60, 200; air, 63–64; costs, 77–78; general results, 116–119; Latin America, 211, 212; India, 282.
World War, "Little," 316, 396–398.
World War, Second, 719; and Latin America, 213–214; fundamental causes, 727–733; immediate cause, 733–737; Polish invasion, 737–742; peace moves and aims, 751, 782, 784, 789, 826–827, 828–829; Norwegian invasion, 757–762; Danish occupation, 758; Netherlands invasion, 762–764; Belgian invasion, 762, 764–766; Battle of France, 767–769; entry of Italy, 768; armistices, 770–772; African campaigns, 791–794, 802–804, 834–836; Balkans, 794–801; Far East, 804–808, 825, 828–833; invasion of U.S.S.R., 808–814; entry of United States, 814–825; global war, 825–837.
World War Foreign Debt Commission, 166.
World Zionist Organization, 292, 297.
WPA, 712, 718 and n.
WPB, 818n.1.

Wrangel, P., 552, 554.
"Wreckers," in U.S.S.R., 584.
Yangtse River, 678, 679.
Yap, 657.
Yen, J.Y.C., 658.
Yorkshire, 61.
You Can't Do Business with Hitler, 451n.
Young, O. D. (1874–   ), 155.
Young China, 650.
Young Fascists, 343.
Young Plan, 110, 155–158, 163, 164, 165, 307, 420; advantages over Dawes Plan, 158.
Young Turks, 9, 10, 629.
Young Yugoslavia, 625.
Ypres, 72; Battles of, First, 44, Second, 48, Third, 55.
Yuan Shih-kai, 649, 650–651, 652.
Yucatan, 230.
Yudenich, N., 552, 553.
Yugoslavia, 83n., 126n., 175, 185 and n.2, 196, 482n., 489; peace settlement, 83, 93–94, 112, 113, 114, 116, 469; minorities, 113, 114, 116, 625–627, 799–800; Italy, 93–94, 332–333 and n., 361–362, 366, 370, 623–624; Hungary, 495–497, 625; Greece, 619–620; creation, 620–621; dictatorship, 624ff.; economic conditions, 627; Germany, 628 and n.; Second World War, 799–800; government-in-exile, 800.

Zaghlul, S., 275–277, 281.
Zagreb, 621.
Zaimis, A., 616, 618.
Zamora, N. A. (1877–   ), 381, 382 and n., 383–385, 391.
Zeebrugge, 44.
Zeligowski, L., 536.
Zeppelin, Count von, 63.
Zeppelins, 63, 431.
Zhivkovich, P., 624, 625.
Zhukov, G. K., 812.
Zimmerman, A. R., 471.
Zimmermann, A., 37; Note, 37–38.
Zinoviev, G. (1883–1936?), 572 and n., 574–575, 588; Letter, 241.
Zionism, 83, 294–301 passim.
Zita, of Austria, 492.
Zog I (1928–1939?), 369–371.